THE THIRD STATISTICAL ACCOUNT OF SCOTLAND

THE CITY OF EDINBURGH

"... by Statistical is meant ... an inquiry into the state of a country for the purpose of ascertaining the quantum of happiness enjoyed by its inhabitants and the means of its future improvement."

SIR JOHN SINCLAIR, BART,
1798

THE THIRD STATISTICAL ACCOUNT OF SCOTLAND

The 'Third Statistical Account of Scotland' is compiled and edited by the four Scottish Universities, each University being responsible for the county volumes in its own region. Tribute must be paid to the Scottish Council of Social Service under whose aegis the work is being published and to the Local Authorities throughout Scotland for contributing towards costs of publication.

The complete list of volumes is as follows:

1. The County of Ayr*
2. The County of Fife*
3. The County of East Lothian*
4. The City of Aberdeen*
5. The City of Glasgow*
6. The County of Dunbarton*
7. The County of Aberdeen*
8. The County of Lanark*
9. The County of Argyll*
10. The County of Banff*
11. The Counties of Renfrew and Bute*
12. The County of Dumfries*
13. The County of Ross and Cromarty
14. The Counties of Kirkcudbright and Wigtown*
15. The City of Edinburgh*
16. The County of Inverness
17. The Counties of Moray and Nairn*
18. The Counties of Stirling and Clackmannan*
19. The Counties of Caithness and Sutherland
20. The Counties of Orkney and Zetland
21. The County of West Lothian
22. The County of Midlothian
23. The County of Berwick
24. The Counties of Peebles and Selkirk*
25. The City of Dundee
26. The Counties of Kincardine and Angus
27. The Counties of Perth and Kinross
28. The County of Roxburgh

* *Already published*

High above the Old and the New Towns juts the castle on its throne of solid rock. Running across the centre of the picture is Princes Street and behind it the New Town. Beyond the buildings the city terminates at the southern shores of the Firth of Forth, with the hills of Fife beckoning to the north on the other side.

THE THIRD STATISTICAL ACCOUNT OF SCOTLAND

THE CITY OF
EDINBURGH

EDITED BY

David Keir

COLLINS
144 CATHEDRAL STREET, GLASGOW, C.4.
1966

FIRST PUBLISHED 1966

THE THIRD STATISTICAL ACCOUNT OF SCOTLAND

EDINBURGH UNIVERSITY REGION

*COUNTY OF EAST LOTHIAN, *Dr. Catherine P. Snodgrass*

*COUNTIES OF PEEBLES, *J. B. P. Bulloch*
and SELKIRK, *J. M. Urquhart*

CHAIRMAN OF COMMITTEE
JAMES WREFORD WATSON
Professor of Geography in the University of Edinburgh

SUBSEQUENT COUNTY VOLUMES: GENERAL EDITOR
JOHN MACPHERSON, D.F.C.
Deputy Secretary to the University of Edinburgh

COUNTY OF WEST LOTHIAN, *A. MacPherson*
COUNTY OF MIDLOTHIAN, *J. B. P. Bulloch*
COUNTY OF ROXBURGH, *A. Baxter*
COUNTY OF BERWICK

**Already published.*

PRINTED IN SCOTLAND BY
BLACKIE AND SON, LTD.

FOREWORD

The description of this book as "statistical" may seem at first forbidding. It is also a little misleading, for the book's aim is not to provide a mass of statistics, already available in official publications, but rather to give a true contemporary account of Edinburgh life in the early and middle 1960s.

As most Scottish readers (and many others) will know, the term "statistical" comes down from the 18th century when Sir John Sinclair persuaded Scottish ministers to write accounts of the general state of their parishes, and so provided—in the first *Statistical Account of Scotland* (1791-98)—an absorbing and, as many historians have since recognised, the first complete picture of any country's life as a whole. In the 19th century *The New Statistical Account* (1832-45) was sponsored by the General Assembly of the Church of Scotland; but though the parish ministers' help was again invoked, their efforts were this time less successful—for at least one obvious reason. Since the 1790s the Industrial Revolution had matured so quickly that in the growing towns and cities the old parish divisions no longer had the same significance, and the parish ministers were confronted with mass population problems not quite so easily described as those of their predecessors.

When *The Third Statistical Account of Scotland*, for our own century, was proposed towards the end of the last war, the Scottish Council of Social Service and the four ancient Scottish Universities—St. Andrews, Glasgow, Aberdeen and Edinburgh—accepted responsibility for its production; and happily thc parish ministers were again able to play a large part in the preparation of the county volumes. Publication for the series was ensured by the promise of financial assistance not only from local authorities but from generous private benefactors as well. So one by one the volumes began to appear; and here in its turn is *The City of Edinburgh*.

It is only too easy in writing or editing a book about Scotland's capital to let its stormy past overlay its present. But primarily this book, while glimpsing the past throughout, seeks to describe the contemporary scene. What are the city's problems and its successes? Can it boast a vigorous intellectual life, or is it lagging behind less ancient centres of thought? How also do the people of Edinburgh earn their living, get their food, house themselves and pass their leisure hours? Is the city still, as the old joke goes, East-windy and West-endy?

To all these, and a great number of similar queries, the book should give the answers—with a proviso. So many changes are taking place in Edinburgh during the middle '60s that there may be omissions in our record. As for the future, it is hoped that the book will give political, social and industrial historians in the centuries to come an accurate picture of what is both an ancient and a modern city.

It is, of course, this dual function as a museum of the past and as a modern financial and trading centre that gives the city its unusual diversities and at the same time its unity. Not only do Britain's major industries—engineering, shipbuilding, shipping, agriculture, building, contracting and coal-mining—play a considerable part in Edinburgh's industrial life, but the city can also claim an unusually wide array of trades and lighter industries. On the other side of the medallion, history and the arts speak for themselves through their many and distinguished storehouses in the city itself.

In a book of this kind, however, history poses certain editorial problems because of the book's main purpose. With a city such as Edinburgh there are many matters affecting civic progress which are often best interpreted by at least a hint of the historical trends and events behind them. Readers will therefore find that although nearly all the contributors have had to suffer some reduction of their contributions (or production costs would have been prohibitive), a certain amount of Edinburgh's history remains.

Although a private trust has made a generous and much-appreciated grant towards the cost of the illustrations, the volume's chief financial sponsor is the Edinburgh Corporation, and city officials have naturally played a considerable part in its preparation. But the final editorial responsibility rests with the University, many of whose Professors, Readers and Lecturers have also made illuminating contributions.

Much honoured by the University Court's request that I should act as editor and contributor, I have found the editorial problems lightened a little by our mutual agreement that as far as possible we should work in broad brush strokes rather than try to etch all the minutiae. But as the picture still had to be fairly detailed, a special debt of gratitude is due to the 200 contributors, who must surely compose one of the most distinguished lists associated with a volume of this kind, (though regrettably not all can be mentioned by name), and to the many individuals and organisations who generously gave their assistance and advice.

DAVID KEIR

OTHER ACKNOWLEDGMENTS

Apart from the contributors who brought this book into being, grateful acknowledgments for help in other ways are due to Professor J. Wreford Watson, M.A., PH.D., F.R.S.C., F.R.S.E., Chairman of the University Court's *Statistical Account* Committee; the University's Deputy Secretary Mr. John MacPherson, D.F.C., M.A., LL.B., who is also the *Statistical Account* Committee's Secretary; and the City Chamberlain, Mr. Ames L. Imrie, C.B.E., whose intimate knowledge of Edinburgh's public services was quite invaluable.

I am also much indebted to Sir David Milne, G.C.B., a noted authority on Scottish administration, and Mr. George Pottinger, C.V.O.; the Rev. Ronald Selby Wright, D.D., whose counsel on various aspects of the book went far beyond his own ecclesiastical contributions; the Hon. Lord Cameron, a Court of Session Judge with great knowledge of the city; Mr. William Beattie, M.A., LL.D., Librarian of the National Library of Scotland; Sir Norman Gwatkin, G.C.V.O., K.C.M.G., D.S.O., and Mr. David MacIntyre, V.C., C.B., for guidance on various State matters; Professor Alan Peacock, D.S.C., M.A.; Mr. James Kyd, C.B.E., F.F.A.; and Edinburgh's Chief Constable, Mr. John R. Inch, C.B.E., M.A., LL.B.

In the complex field of finance and industry my warm thanks are due to Mr. W. V. Stevens, O.B.E., J.P., B.COM., Secretary of the Edinburgh Chamber of Commerce, and his indefatigable lieutenant Mr. David Mowat, M.A., Sir William McEwan Younger, Bt., D.S.O., D.L., and Mr. Ian W. S. Wilson for their help in securing up-to-date information about various aspects of the city's trade and commerce; to Mr. James O. Blair Cunynghame, O.B.E., M.A., LL.D., and Mr. George Brodlie, M.A. for their advice on financial matters, and to Mr. George High for information about the Edinburgh Trades Council.

As the public services today are no less complicated I must also gratefully acknowledge the expert guidance of Mr. W. A. Nicholson, O.B.E., (Secretary of the Scottish Tourist Board); Mr. Frank Jones (late of British Railways, Scottish Region); Mr. John Mack (Traffic Manager, Scottish Omnibuses Ltd); Mr. Maurice Nockles (H.M. Customs and Excise); Miss Lorna Rhind (City Chambers); and the Automobile Association which arranged—through Mr. Cecil Orr, O.B.E. in London and its Area Secretary in Edinburgh, Mr. J. T. Russell—a special survey of the city's traffic problems.

Another debt of gratitude is due to the authors and publishers of books mentioned in the text for permission to use quotations from them, and also to the proprietors and the editor of *The Scotsman*, Mr. Alastair M. Dunnett, for permission to reproduce not only extracts but many illustrations. It should perhaps be added that there has been a congenial two-way traffic here since one or two expert articles originally written for this volume somehow first appeared in *The Scotsman*.

Among other pleasant debts are those due to a multitude of public and private bodies, not least the city's librarians and their staffs, to Messrs. John Bartholomew and Son, Ltd for the excellent map of Edinburgh at the end of the book, and to Miss Hilary Smith, B.A., for helping me, in her spare time, to read the proofs before publication.

There are two acknowledgments I should have wished to make in their presence. One is to the late H. J. L. Robbie, M.A., PH.D., who, when Headmaster of Daniel Stewart's College, edited the chapter on the fee-paying schools and offered most helpful assistance on other aspects of the city's educational life. The other is to the late Miss Marjorie Brown, M.A. of the University's School of Social Study, who not only carefully investigated the statutory welfare societies but provided other information on the city's social life. I am particularly grateful to Miss Emily Anderson, M.A., and Miss Mary Coverdale who later added valuable details to Miss Brown's contribution.

Finally, I must express my warm thanks to those who gave me their advice on many editorial problems. Among these were Mr. John Kerr, who acted for a time as Assistant Editor; Mr. Stewart Sanderson, M.A. (of the University of Leeds and formerly of the University of Edinburgh); Mr. Walter H. MacGregor, M.A.; Mr. Wilfred Taylor, M.A.; the Hon Mrs. Rosemary Russell; Professor David Abercrombie, B.A.; Mr. W. D. Barnetson, Managing Director of Provincial Newspapers Ltd; Mr. George B. Millar of the United News Service (Edinburgh) Ltd; Miss Marigold McLaren, B.A.; Mr. John Forgie and Miss A. M. Whitecross, M.A. for expert guidance on the book's illustrations; Mr.

George Baird of Portobello who put at my disposal the fruits of his own researches into Edinburgh's modern social history; Mrs. Dorothy Ogilvie, Mrs. F. C. Hutchins, Mrs. Iris Farrow and Mrs. Brenda Hall for their help in handling, in their spare time, a vast number of manuscripts, documents and correspondence; and, finally, Mr. W. Hope Collins, C.B.E., Mr. George Young and Mr. Ronald Mongredien of Messrs. William Collins who, as its publishers, bring this book before the public after a long and friendly cooperation with the editor.

D.K.

CONTENTS

Part Three

THE PUBLIC WEAL

Part Four

THE SOCIAL PATTERN

Part Seven

THE ARTS AND HUMANITIES

Part Eight

NATURE

LIST OF PHOTOGRAPHS

ACKNOWLEDGEMENTS

All photographs, except those listed below, have been kindly supplied by The Scotsman Publications Ltd., North Bridge, Edinburgh.

Page 401 George Outram & Sons Ltd., 496 (2) and 528 (2) John Mackay, 625 A. D. S. MacPherson, 656 (Science) Norward Inglis, 913 Photo Illustrations, Edinburgh.

Part One

THE PLACE AND THE PEOPLE

Chapter 1

EDINBURGH

Edinburgh is rich in dramatic contrasts. The visitor senses this as soon as he emerges from the railway station into Princes Street and lifts his eyes to the skyline. Traffic streams past his elbow; yet in springtime the heavy scent of wallflowers in the public gardens mingles in his nostrils with exhaust fumes. Beyond the flowerbeds and across a narrow valley he sees the humped ridge of the Old Town rising towards the Castle Rock, its tenements and steeples silhouetted jaggedly against the sky, while the Castle itself dominates the scene, riding high in the air like a castle in a fairy-tale. The whole effect is theatrical, unreal almost, as if some designer had painted an impressive and romantic backdrop against which the life of the modern city should be played out.

In such a setting, where past and present are forever meeting in contradiction or again in harmony, it is easy to be spellbound; and the spell is not easily broken. If you fall in love with Edinburgh when you are young, you are not likely ever to love any other place in quite the same way.

Many who have fallen under the city's spell have written about her. They have responded not only to the story of her embattled past but also to the present. Their emotions have been stirred by the beauty of light and shadow falling on trees and buildings, by the Canaletto skies of early autumn, by the crisp and invigorating winds that powder the roof-tops with the first snows of winter and by the dazzle of spring sunshine on rain-washed cobbled streets. And these cobble-stones have resounded to the clash of much of Scotland's history. Patriots, traitors, gentlemen and rogues; a red-haired queen and her lovers; men of letters, philosophers, statesmen, soldiers, harlots, footpads and physicians have all trodden these ancient streets: this too has continually touched the emotions and stirred imagination. It is not surprising that with Sir Walter Scott Edinburgh gave birth to one of the leading figures of the Romantic Movement which inspired Europe in the 19th century; nor is it surprising that the same literary mood should, like a subtle dye, stain the pages of those others from Robert Louis Stevenson to our own day who have written about the city. But this response is only one of the moods of the Scottish temperament: romance and fancy are counter-balanced by more sober and practical virtues.

If you stand on the Castle ramparts your eye ranges beyond the towering "lands" along the Royal Mile—those early skyscrapers of the 16th and 17th centuries—to one of the first experiments in town-planning. The orderly terraces and crescents of the New Town contain a city shaped with the calm logic of the 18th century, a monument to good sense, good taste and good form. The contrasts between the Old Town and the New, the way in which these opposites are held in equilibrium within the city's greater unity, are typical of both the Scottish character and of Scotland's capital.

The view of Edinburgh, however, does not end there. Further afield there are first the villa quarters and then the modern housing schemes on the city's perimeter, while beyond them again the eye travels over the industrial belt of central Scotland, the foothills of the Highlands, the old kingdom of Fife across the waters of the Forth, and eastwards and southwards to the rich corn land of the Lothians and the sheep farms of the Border hills and valleys. Edinburgh lies in its setting at the heart of Scotland, while at the heart of the city lies the accumulated history of the nation.

If many of the symbols of this history are obvious—the castle, the kirk, the courts, the banking and insurance offices that finance modern industry and trade—others are less easily observed. Yet Scotland's history permeates in some way every street in the capital city and the life of all the citizens, little though they may be conscious of it as they negotiate the traffic flowing past the West End or climb the narrow wynds to the High Street.

It is with these people that this book is concerned. The life they lead, the work they do, the administration of their civic affairs and the enthusiasms of their leisure hours are all portrayed here. The lineaments of the city are traced in each successive chapter; yet one wonders how recognisable the portrait may be to the bulk of the citizens themselves.

Does Edinburgh seem a romantic town, or perhaps a paradigm of civic rationalism, to the suburban tenants of the Town Council in mid-20th century? The majority of Edinburgh people have probably never thought it to be either, never given it much thought at all, though they have always felt strongly about it: one suspects that their basic attitudes have changed very little throughout the years. The cheering crowds at the Tynecastle football field support more than the local team—the very honour of the city is at stake when Heart of Midlothian play Glasgow Rangers or Celtic—yet their overt comments on Edinburgh are probably confined to grumbles about rents and rates and the length of the housing queue. Are they really then so very different from the citizens of other Scottish burghs? And if so, what is it that makes them different? Does life in Edinburgh offer some special quality of experience that marks them out as distinctively Edinburgh men and women? Such questions are bound to remain largely speculative, but they are none the less worth asking and worth trying to answer.

Fate sometimes offers an answer ready-made. A century ago, for instance, an old "land" in the High Street crashed to the ground bringing death and ruin to some 30 families: when the back wall of a condemned tenement also collapsed in 1959, making 22 families homeless, the voice of history echoed, for those who had ears to hear, across the intervening decades.

It may be true that the skilled tradesman in the electronics factory today is divided from the Hammermen of Edinburgh by more than the e of centuries and the development of modern technology. On the r hand, the old-age pensioner living in a "single-end" in the Canongate ld be acknowledged as a sister-soul by the lady of fashion who used same small room as her parlour 200 years ago. That there is some d of continuity, some special quality in the Edinburgh character, seems ond dispute: the best proof, perhaps, lies in the fact that non-Edinburgh ots recognise it. "East-Windy, West-Endy" runs the old gibe, playing t another variation on the theme of Edinburgh's contrasts. But how ould it be otherwise? Edinburgh is still a city of paradox, and paradox makes for dramatic surprises which her citizens have learnt through the centuries to take in their stride. This is why Edinburgh is a stimulating place to live in: it is also why strangers are often mystified by Edinburgh life, and why again the city makes such a fascinating subject of study in our time.

In Edinburgh more than most cities the romantic and the matter-of-fact exist side by side, with old things and new settling down in comfortable symbiosis. This can only happen in an ancient city with a vigorous tradition. To take but one example of the contrasts which combine to make the city unique—a capital without a Parliament is an almost unthinkable paradox: yet there is no question that Edinburgh is, and is felt to be, a capital city. It is the home of our national institutions, of our national church, our law, and our educational system. The administration of the country is centred in it. And also—as the final test of a capital city—it arouses in the hearts of those who live elsewhere in the country a baffling mixture of admiration and contempt. Yet two centuries and a half have gone by since the blackened beams of the Parliament Hall last rang to the clash of political debate, and now both Edinburgh's and Scotland's ultimate destinies are largely decided 400 miles away.

These paradoxes and contrasts appear at every turn when one tries to present an authentic picture of Edinburgh and her people. They run through the very fabric of the place and enrich the texture of every aspect of the city's life, whether one is dealing with objective things like demographic statistics or industrial output, or whether one is trying to write truly about less easily measured things such as human happiness and misery, the "statistical" condition of the nation which the originator of these *Accounts* first tried to elicit. Amongst Glaswegians, for instance, Edinburgh people are held to be aloof and cold in manner; but visitors from abroad find them friendly, hospitable and convivial. For every man who castigates them as staid and old-fashioned, complacent and self-righteous, another will be found to call them enterprising, receptive of new ideas, and tolerant. The simple truth is that Edinburgh people are all these things and more besides. The city has always made room for the whole gamut of personality, character and even eccentricity amongst her citizens of all classes and degrees. If Edinburgh lacks any common quality, it is that her *lumpen-proletariat* is even today intellectually so much less lumpish than in most other places that argument in an Edinburgh pub is as likely to turn on such subjects as bishops in the Kirk, or civic administration, as on football scores and pop-singers.

But then Edinburgh is a unique place. The word is often used unw ily; yet of all cities Edinburgh surely merits the description. More his has been made here, according to John Buchan, than in any place of size, save Athens, Rome and Jerusalem.

This may or may not be true. Yet events in Scotland during the 1 and 17th centuries in particular affected the future of the British Is and in some measure Europe and the Americas, and these events we decided largely in the little city clinging to the rib of rock between th Castle and Holyrood. From this centre ideas spread like waves aroun the world. The eyes of Protestant Europe were fixed on the Scottish Reformation and the subsequent bloody collision of ecclesiastical and political authority. In due course England stood divided and hesitant while the Scots broke Cromwellian republicanism and restored Charles II to his throne. In America clergymen admitted to the apostolic succession at the hands of Scottish bishops led the Episcopalian Church and ministers ordained by Scottish presbyteries formed the Presbyterian. A century later a united parliament in Westminster scotched the Jacobite risings and broke the old clan system; and in the decades of so-called pacification and the Highland clearances, as also in later decades of economic set-back, Scotsmen emigrated in their thousands to the New World and to the countries of the British Empire and the Commonwealth. At this time, too, Edinburgh began to exert a new influence as an arbiter of taste and a leader in the arts. As the New Town grew, the names of Adam, Playfair, Ramsay, Raeburn and Wilkie were synonymous with architecture and painting, while the renown of her historians, philosophers, physicians and lawyers spread far beyond the British Isles. The scholarship of such men as David Hume and Adam Smith (though we must cede him partly to Glasgow), and of Robertson, Ferguson and Blair led on to the great period when Sir Walter Scott dominated the literary world at home and abroad, and the reputations of more than English bards were made or blasted by Scotch reviewers.

These glories have departed, but not without leaving something behind them. Edinburgh is still a city of cosmopolitan vision.

Although the newspaper columns reflect each year the carpings of artists of minor talent and philistines of unshakable conviction, no other city in the United Kingdom has ever attempted anything on the scale of the annual Edinburgh International Festival, which has enjoyed a high reputation amongst both artists and amateurs of the arts in every country since the first Festival was held in the golden summer of 1947.

The city is a magnificent setting for such an event, with its old grey stones laced with green foliage and its ever-varying prospects of sky, sea and hills. At every turn of an Edinburgh street there is another dramatic view—now of the fringes of the Highlands, now of the Lowland hills, now of a serene classical mansion or the romantic profile of the Castle, now again of the wind-whipped waves of the Firth of Forth. If only a worthy opera-house were to dominate some corner, it is said, Edinburgh would be the perfect Festival city.

In its streets not only the eye is filled with delight. There are the smells of Edinburgh too—roasting coffee at a George Street corner, the hot buttery smell of baking shortbread, the drowsy warmth of flowers in the parks and the sharp muskiness of mayflower blossom in the gardens of the New Town. There are also more noisome smells to remind us of the other face of Edinburgh—fumes from a rubber factory, and the sour odour of decay in the city's slums, now rapidly diminishing.

For Edinburgh is not paradise, though it is fatally easy to idealise her. Squalor and vice are to be found here too; the faces of poverty, ignorance, cruelty, crime and violence grimace mockingly from the wings as the pageant of civic life is enacted amid scenes of beauty and grace. Again one returns to the extreme contrasts of which most citizens are aware in this unique capital.

How all-embracing they are! Within the city boundaries there are coal mines and a bird sanctuary, skyscraper blocks of flats and medieval houses, sheep-shearing in the Queen's Park and elegant hair-dressing salons. In winter time snow can pile up in drifts along the suburban streets and melt on the electrically-heated surface of the main road up the Mound, and, incidentally, on the " electric blanket "—the first of its kind—which protects the international rugby pitch at Murrayfield. For a city often accused of being behind the times, Edinburgh can boast of having introduced many such technical innovations long before other places of comparable size. They include municipal refuse-composting plants, parking meters and—in a city which retained horse and cable-cars when most had given them up—the abolition of electric trams in favour of buses. New techniques have been applied in other fields too, not least in education, where Edinburgh has given a lead in experimenting with modern methods of teaching arithmetic and French to tiny school-children.

But education has always been prized in Scotland. Edinburgh is naturally one of the chief scholastic centres in the United Kingdom, with its ancient University, its unusually wide range of types of school, and its training and technical colleges. The latest of these is symbolic of the city's marriage of past, present and future: its steel-framed glass and concrete buildings, where new generations of technologists will be trained, are centred on the ancient tower of Merchiston Castle, home of John Napier the inventor of logarithms. This is not, as might be supposed, a symptom of escape into antiquarianism. It is too easy, and false, to assume—as a leader-writer in *The Times* did recently—that Edinburgh is mostly concerned with the exhibition of splendours that have passed. The size of its industrial labour force and its annual financial and commercial turnover bely that: besides, no city of comparable size can afford today to live on past glories.

Technology and industry—themselves rich in contrasts—flourish in this city of professional men, ranging from a vast electronics factory, and another for manufacturing surgical sutures from man-made fibres, to the old pantiled building which houses the last working salt-pan in Scotland; and yet this industrial hotbed has engulfed in its growth a number of villages whose sense of identity and community is still strong. In one of these, less than ten minutes by car from the central bustle of Princes

Street, the only sounds to break into a silent room are the bleating of sheep on the flanks of Arthur's Seat and the creaking flight of swans circling at dawn and dusk before they settle on Duddingston Loch. Coveys of partridge and occasional pheasants feed on garden lawns; hungry foxes and deer have been seen prowling inside the city in severe winters; owls are heard at night and mallard seen by day in Princes Street Gardens; and there are peacocks at Prestonfield House. Sometimes too on a Sunday morning, a shepherd followed by his collie can be seen striding down Shandwick Place, having passed beneath the windows of the Princes Street clubs whose members fly regularly to London and back on business between breakfast and dinner. And also—to complete the tale of contrasts—at the West End of Princes Street St. Cuthbert's Presbyterian Kirk and St. John's Episcopal Church face each other in sturdy opposition.

There is continuity as well as change in Edinburgh. An occasional fishwife with her creel can still be met, while in every suburban grocer's shop the deep-freeze food counter is to be found. The children's street songs mingle old and new, commemorating the Queen's four Maries and the heroes of current television programmes. The traditional industries of the city—brewing, printing, publishing—continue along with new industries, and themselves are revitalised by catering for changing tastes and by adopting new methods. Seamen still come to the Port of Leith from distant parts; Italians and many other foreigners settle in the town; the ton-up boys and beatniks are descendants of earlier bands of rowdies; and if in some quarters the night is disturbed by the blare of transistor radios, the heart is still touched beyond tears when at sunset a lone piper on the Castle rampart sounds the Retreat.

If Sir John Sinclair, who inspired the *Statistical Accounts of Scotland*, were to return today to Edinburgh he would see much that was incomprehensible, and he might well feel that some of the city's glory had departed. In a century and a half its mere size and area have grown beyond recognition, while the presence of shops along Princes Street and George Street, the comparative emptiness after working hours of many parts of the Old Town, and the congested traffic in the broad streets of the New, would doubtless astonish and even sadden him. But he would also find much that was familiar in the landscape, in the faces of the people, in their accents and in their attitudes to life. These familiarities, along with the innovations and the changes, are mirrored in this volume of the *Third Statistical Account*. The mirror may sometimes distort an image, more often, one hopes, present it clearly. It is impossible to reflect every angle and facet within the confines of even a substantial volume; and besides no book about Edinburgh is ever good enough.

The story of the city is after all the roof and crown of the story of Scotland, and at the centre is set Edinburgh's High Street, Lawnmarket and Canongate—the Royal Mile which leads from the Castle past the High Kirk, St. Giles Cathedral, to the Palace of Holyroodhouse. This street has seen rich history—English invasion and William Wallace the liberator; the Flowers of the Forest on their way to be cut down at

Flodden; John Knox thundering against Queen Mary and the monstrous regiment of women; Montrose carried above the heads of the crowd on a hurdle after his defeat at Invercarron, his wounds " still green and smarting, his visage comely but wan and worn," carried to the gallows past the window where Argyll mocked him and Argyll's lady, loyal to her lord, spat in the drawn face. Down this street in the following century, to the cheers of the bystanders, one of Gordon's three lively daughters galloped merrily bareback on a pig; and later Johnson, having drunk deep with Boswell in a tavern, told his friend " I can smell you in the dark." Here Robert Fergusson, one of Edinburgh's own poets, lived out his short and mildly dissipated life; here Sheriff Scott limped across to the Parliament Hall with the fame of the Waverley Novels reverberating around him, and later the shock of his bankruptcy and the eventual salvation of his honour; here Robert Louis Stevenson was called to the Bar and dabbled his way into literature instead of legal briefs; here more than 140 years ago King George IV aroused the ridicule of the ladies and the satire of the cartoonists by clothing his portly person in too short a kilt; and here too, Elizabeth II of England—but the first Queen of that name in Scotland—drove from her Palace of Holyrood to a dedicatory service in St. Giles after her coronation, along the self-same street as her ancestor Mary Queen of Scots when she went to be harangued by Knox and finally put to death by her English cousin after the years at Fotheringay.

All this and more forms part of the heritage which lies about the inhabitants of Edinburgh as they grow up and live their lives in the city of their birth; and here where memories are long this heritage remains very real and compelling in people's minds. It is not easy for the stranger to take Edinburgh by storm: history shows that it never has been easy, literally or metaphorically, to conquer her hauteurs by frontal assault. But those who give themselves to Edinburgh, and are accepted, gain a rich and rewarding experience.

THE ANCIENT PAST

The landscape of Edinburgh is everywhere adorned with the traces of human life. Patterns of field and furrow were early imposed on it and may still be seen in the open spaces; but these patterns too have been largely overlaid by fresh patterns of streets and buildings, now following contour and valley, now marching boldly across them to point a contrast or impose the print of human dominance on the natural scene. Life came to this landscape far back in time, and still continues to work upon it in our own day.

Yet by virtue of its geographical position Edinburgh cannot make any claims to vast antiquity as an area of settlement by ancient man. The great glaciations of the last phase of geological time before the present, the Pleistocene Period, brought the permanent ice-sheet at its worst to a southern edge in the English Midlands: habitable Britain, then an extension of the Continental mass, was a small area indeed, sparsely populated by migrant hunting bands.

Even with the withdrawal of the ice in Late Glacial times, the more northerly regions of Britain were still cruelly inhospitable and, it seems, uninhabited. The extinct Giant Deer that roamed the grasslands of the Edinburgh suburb of Corstorphine in the comparatively warmer interval around 9,000 to 8,000 B.C. surveyed a landscape unsullied by man. But with increasingly mild climatic conditions human settlement, however tentative and precarious, was extending by 6,000 B.C. or so into the Forth estuary where small communities of hunters and fishers led their nasty, brutish and short lives, working in stone, flint, bone, antler and wood; feasting on stranded whales when such sea-treasures became available; and consuming vast quantities of shell-fish, of which the middens of shells on Inchkeith and at other places along the old shore of the Forth are a tangible reminder today.

Such communities were certainly living in the Edinburgh region about 5,000 B.C., and probably until a later date. But by 3,000 B.C., and possibly earlier, the first farmers were arriving in Scotland—stone-using agriculturalists who crossed the English Channel from the Continent and coasted up by both eastern and western sea-routes. Some of them settled east of Edinburgh along the coastal sand-dune country of Gullane and North Berwick, an area colonised by immigrants from the Netherlands bringing with them the knowledge of agriculture, and no doubt the seed-corn which would enable them to plant their first fields of barley on British soil, and thereby to establish the primitive and tentative foundations of the East Lothian farming tradition—to say nothing of Scotch.

With farming there soon followed the knowledge of metal working in copper, bronze and gold—a technological advance which also meant a social adjustment from the almost wholly self-sufficient stone-using communities to others dependent for essential commodities on trade which might of necessity be far-flung. Copper and gold from Ireland and from West Britain, tin from Cornwall, were brought by the first tinkers and traders who were on the move all over Britain, and indeed Europe. For by 1,500 B.C. we can see that the British Isles are part of a European pattern, sharing in trade and commerce which might on occasion stretch to the amber-bearing shores of Jutland, the Ore Mountains of Czechoslovakia, or the distant world of the earliest Greeks themselves.

The burials of such farmers and metal-workers within the Edinburgh area show the beginnings of what must have been an increasing concentration of population in this region. Of course, such a population would be incredibly small by any modern industrial standards, and we must think here in terms of settlements such as those of the North American Indians at the time of European contact, or of the Masai today. Nevertheless, it can hardly be chance that the area now occupied by Edinburgh has produced evidence for some concentration of peoples from before or around 1,500 B.C. The explanation is not to be sought in the accident of archaeological finds being more prolific where there is intense activity in digging the ground for building or for drains, since other Scottish towns have not produced any comparable mass of finds, despite much recent activity in disturbing the soil.

For the period c. 1,500 B.C. to c. 800 B.C. our evidence is almost wholly from graves by inhumation or cremation, often accompanied by a pot: the settlements unfortunately remain inferential. One other aspect of life is hinted at by the carved boulder from the Braid Hills, decorated with the cup and ring patterns of a ritual symbolism now lost but once potent in the earlier Bronze Age from Ireland to Northumberland and into southern Scotland. Similar patterns were also carved by contemporary peoples on the rocks of Galicia in North Spain, and it has been suggested that we have here some sort of metal-workers' magic.

From the eighth century B.C. the Continental contacts in the bronze-working trade are intensified; and from such familiar places inside the city as Arthur's Seat, Duddingston, Murrayfield and Grosvenor Crescent come scrap-metal hoards, carefully put aside and buried by anonymous metal-smiths with an intention to recover which was never in fact achieved. From the objects in these hoards, destined for the melting-crucible but, by the fortunate accident of their non-recovery by the original owners, now evidence for the archaeologists, we can see contacts with Central Europe, North Germany, Ireland, and the South of England. These hoards, and the stray finds of bronze tools and weapons for the period c. 800–500 B.C. in the Edinburgh area, suggest that there may have been something of a port, or even small trading station, somewhere on the Water of Leith, perhaps between Stockbridge and the Dean Village. In primitive conditions, the port of a river is as far up its course as the craft of the day can go, and such a settlement at the highest navigable point on the Water of Leith is inherently likely.

It is from this point onwards for some centuries, though, that the story of the settlement of what was to become Edinburgh becomes a blank. In the Pentlands not far away, as at Braidwood and at Castle Law (Glencorse) iron-using peoples speaking a Celtic dialect of the Old Brittonic type, allied to modern Welsh, were building little fortifications on hill-tops in some circumstances of temporary uneasiness, which may well have been those attendant on the movement of Roman troops into the area in the 1st century A.D. Forts were built at Inveresk and at Cramond, the former at least a supply base which could be maintained by sea traffic from the southern part of the Province, bringing stores (especially grain) to provision the military forces in a barbarous north still largely pastoral in economy.

The evidence of archaeology hardly gives us a glimpse of Edinburgh in the post-Roman Dark Ages, but here literary sources come to our aid, however obliquely and imperfectly. We are, as we have seen, in a Celtic world, the ancient kingdom of Strathclyde, with people speaking a language of the Old Brittonic group of which the modern representatives are Welsh, Cornish and Breton. The first mention of Edinburgh is as *Dineidin*, the fort of Eidin, in a narrative poem of the late 6th century A.D. known as the *Gododdin*. This fort must, by any reasonable analogy, have been on the Castle Rock—a site eminently suitable for the type of hill-fort which was being built at this time in Scotland, represented today by sites like Dunadd or Dundurn, or, nearer home, the fort of Dalmahoy Hill west of Edinburgh. Stirling, too, must have started its life as a fortification with such a prehistoric structure on the site of the medieval castle: indeed, there is some reason to believe that this was the *Urbs Guidi* mentioned by Bede.

But that must be debated elsewhere. Here in Edinburgh, as we enter the dim light of the earliest Scottish history, we also become involved in the thick mists of fairy-tale and romance. King Arthur is just round the corner: after all, " on the mountain of Eidyn he fought with dog-heads." From this glimpse of the valiant (if cynocephalous) citizens of Edinburgh defending themselves on Arthur's Seat or the Castle Rock, we move forward by way of the early chronicles into clearer historical facts, and can trace in bold outlines the way in which this small northern settlement grew into the capital of a proud and ancient nation.

TOWARDS THE PRESENT

From the 6th century onwards a string of Anglo-Saxon kingdoms stretched from the rich lands of Wessex to the equally rich southern shore of the Firth of Forth. The frontiers of these petty kingdoms changed and shifted as alliances were formed and broken; and bones were broken too. But in the end the powerful kingdom of Northumbria emerges on the scene unifying Deira (roughly speaking, modern Yorkshire) and Bernicia (Durham, Northumberland, Berwickshire and the Lothians). This was the kingdom of Edwin (617–633), whose name was a gift to amateur philologists, from Simeon of Durham in the 12th century to many Edinburgh citizens today, as they tried to settle the derivation of modern Scotland's capital city. But Eidin was probably the name of the district in which the Gododdin's Dineidin lay.

The Northumbrian kingdom was not fated to endure against the attacks of Scottish Gaeldom. According to the *Pictish Chronicle* the Anglian settlers in Dunedin were driven from their home by the Scots in the reign of King Indulph—a figure whose name is written still in the shadowy margin of history's page. But the Lothians certainly became a Gaelic province, and every Lowland Scot forever thereafter to some extent a Highlander, when Malcolm II set the seal on Gaeldom's supremacy in the south-east by his victory over the Northumbrians at Carham-on-Tweed in 1018, a mere half-century before Duke William and his Normans conquered England. Malcolm's victory meant that Edinburgh was no longer a frontier town: the Scottish border had moved south.

In the second half of this century a new chapter was written when Malcolm Canmore married an English wife. Niece of Edward the Confessor, Queen, Saint and refugee from the Norman conquest, Margaret took her king and his people to her pious Christian heart. The tiny chapel she built on the Castle Rock—the Castle of the Maidens as her son David's Norman-French court called it—is the oldest structure in

Edinburgh. Besides encouraging the Christian faith Queen Margaret brought other secular graces to the rude manners of the Scottish court and left her name to history at the Queensferry crossing—spanned by a new road bridge in 1964—where she habitually embarked when travelling between Edinburgh and the main royal palace at Dunfermline near the Fife shore of the River Forth. For Edinburgh was not yet the capital city nor the home of the Scottish court. But from charters of David I's reign we learn of the existence of a burgh under the walls of the Maidens' Castle; and when David founded the Abbey of Holyrood and conferred various rights upon it he wrote the first paragraph of the long history of the Canongate, then a separate burgh of barony, but now a part of Edinburgh.

So during the centuries Edinburgh grew from a mean huddle of huts and cottages around the walls of the fortress on the rock to a sizable royal burgh stretching down the spine of the Castle hill towards the Canongate and Holyrood and southwards by the Cowgate to Kirk o' Field. This growth reflected increasing prosperity. The Scottish burgh was essentially an incorporation of merchants and craftsmen, who were given the privileges of exercising their crafts or trading in certain commodities within the area of the burgh. The Canongate was from an early date closely linked to Edinburgh, for its burghers were allowed to trade in the Edinburgh market in bread, ale and cloth. Leith also became associated with Edinburgh as the main port for its trading outlet, but tolls had to be paid on all goods moving between Edinburgh and Leith.

As Edinburgh grew in size and wealth some familiar landmarks appeared. The church of St. Giles was one, burnt down in 1385 by Richard II and subsequently rebuilt. Despite the long tale of wars with England the city prospered. Increasingly King and Court were housed for periods in the Castle; and by the end of the 15th century there was no doubt that Edinburgh was the capital city of the kingdom. Around the court of James IV flourished poets and musicians; in the Firth the sails of Scotland's navy could be seen reefed against the boisterous north-easters; and in Edinburgh itself the rising merchant class was building slate-roofed houses of dressed stone to replace the thatched wattle-and-daub or half-timbering and clay panels of a more makeshift age.

But Scotland's story, and that of her capital city, were still chequered by the black disasters of war with England. In 1513 on Flodden Field the King lay dead with the flower of his nobles; and on the perimeter of Edinburgh old men and striplings toiled at the building of a new defensive wall—parts of which are still to be seen on the south of the Old Town—while young widows dried their tears and set about rearing the next generation of Edinburgh burghers.

They too, like their forefathers—and their descendants—prospered, and with prosperity adorned their city and their homes. But we are moving now into more modern times, whose history and developments, dealt with more fully elsewhere in this *Account*, needs here no more than a quick review.

Edinburgh continued to grow at an ever-increasing pace; but the memory of Flodden lingered and the new houses grew upwards to the sky rather than spreading out beyond the city walls. Edinburgh embarked on a pattern of building which was to last for two centuries and a half, in which successively the towering " lands " or tenements of the High Street saw Mary Queen of Scots arriving vibrant and young from France; her son James VI removing the court to his southern kingly inheritance; Catholics, Episcopalians and Presbyterians playing their impassioned parts in the struggles between Church and Crown and briefly the Protector; the Parliament of Scotland passing sentence of death on itself in 1707; Prince Charles Edward Stuart holding court in Holyroodhouse; and finally the Hanoverian peace clamped firmly on Highlands and Lowlands alike.

But by this time the gardens behind the High Street's lands were themselves covered by tenements, many of them 10 or more storeys high, where cobblers had flats in the same houses as countesses and my lady had perforce to swing up the hoop of her crinoline to squeeze past her grocer or his errand-boy on the common stair. The Old Town of Edinburgh was literally crammed to overflowing; and in the second half of the century overflow it did, partly southwards towards the Meadows and more significantly to the north of the Burgh Loch.

The story of the building of the New Town, whose broad streets, squares and crescents form both one of the earliest examples of town-planning and one of the glories of 18th century architecture, is told elsewhere. Here it is enough to say that the contrast between the huddled densely-packed life of the teeming Old Town and the spacious vistas of the New were to satisfy the citizens of Edinburgh for the span of a century. Then in the later years of Queen Victoria's reign the area of the city doubled as villas crept outward—to be followed in the 20th century by a yet greater spread of suburban bungalows and blocks of flats radiating towards all points of the compass, as the citizens of Edinburgh move further away, both geographically and historically, from their earliest ancestors in Dineidin.

The realm of transport reflects the many mid-century changes in the city. Here is Waverley Station not so long ago, with steam engines exuding smoke and steam. Today most of the engines are diesel operated.

The once familiar city trams have been replaced by buses. Their rails have been lifted and the cobbles removed in favour of a Scottish invention, tarmacadam. This picture shows Tollcross a few years ago, but being an area scheduled for re-development, new buildings have already changed the skyline.

The dignity of the Capital is well illustrated in this picture taken from Charlotte Square, looking over Princes Street and the gardens towards the skyline of the Castle, the Royal Mile and Arthur's Seat.

CHAPTER 2

THE FACE OF THE CITY

A CITY is both geography and history. Historically, it expresses what people have done with a place through time. Geographically, it springs from situation and site—more precisely from that choice of site which successfully exploits its situation. Nowhere is this truer than of Edinburgh; for Edinburgh found a rock and forged a realm. Here in the centre of the Scottish lowlands, close to the Borders and yet not far from the Highlands, a people discovered a centre where they could rally against their enemies, subdue dissension, and bring their many diversities into a fruitful unity. In this way it rose above other lowland burghs as the one pre-eminently fitted to be the nation's capital. Glasgow, Lanark and Dunbarton were, like Dunfermline, Perth and Dundee, too eccentrically placed to draw the various parts of the Lowlands together; Stirling and Linlithgow, though central enough, were too far from the Borders to afford them protection; Haddington, on the other hand, was too near the English for safety. Edinburgh could gather up the routes from Glasgow and the west, or from Perth and the north, guard the border entries from Berwick to Carlisle, and find in its own vicinity a wealth of agriculture, fuel, sites for power, and opportunities for trade that enabled it to attract and command.

Few capitals better mirror their country. In the Edinburgh scene are grouped all the elements, though on a reduced scale, which make up Scotland. Here are the stumps of old mountains lifted above the inroads of the sea, the smooth little plains busy with traffic between knubbly hills guiding the roads, ice-stripped land and land made over by ice, difficult and easy terrain, poor and rich soils, quarries and coal mines, rapids and havens, power sites and harbourage, the possibilities and problems of development; practically everything, indeed, to make it a cross-section of the country unique in Scotland. Moreover, this is all so concentrated that it is everywhere evident. Scotland rushes in upon Edinburgh at almost every turn. Thus the wider landscapes of mountain, lowland, and sea are not merely implicit in the local scene; they are *in* that scene, they are the backdrops to it. There is hardly a part of Edinburgh without a nearby viewpoint from which one can see either the long, broad, rolling summits of the Southern Uplands or the abrupt, serrated edge of the Highlands. At some vantage points, as for instance Arthur's Seat, both the Borders and the Highlands can be seen, together with the swell and sag of the Midland Valley in between. Thus the wider situation is always present in the local site either as part of an actual view or of a view remembered from a local spot. Edinburgh is Scotland at almost every road's end.

This helps to give a national flavour to its character. Nevertheless, its *main* lineaments are derived from the immediate region. The clean sweep of the seafront, the ridge on ridge rising behind it with their broad flats in between, the spectacular eminences dominating the skyline—the Castle Rock, Arthur's Seat, the Pentlands—and what man has made of them; the lay-out and silhouette of old town and new town, of the southern hilly suburbs and the northern stepped-down ones, of the ribbon-like extensions of the city to west and east along the Firth and its star-like development southwards between the hills; the pattern of what has been paved and built up and the shape of what still remains green and open; the castle battlements, the cathedral spires, the domes of the university, tenement chimneys, factory stacks, bare crags and tree-choked gorges—all this is part of the local geography.[1]

That geography is many-sided and at first confusing. However, it reflects a few basic physical elements which, when understood, give meaning to the whole. Edinburgh has grown up in a gap within a gap; i.e. in the gap between the Pentlands and the Firth of Forth, features which are themselves in the gap between the Highlands and the Southern Uplands. Just as the larger gap is very uneven, being, in spite of the name *The Scottish Lowlands*, a congeries of volcanic hills, fold ridges, and narrow basins, so is the smaller one, with its seven volcanic peaks, four-fold ridges, several distinct basins, as well as riverside terraces and old marine benches within its five mile compass. The gap has drawn main roads into it, and these have knotted themselves into a city among its volcanic hills.

The Edinburgh gap has brought together six or seven principal routes. There is first the main coast road from England via Berwick and Dunbar which joins the coast road coming down from Aberdeen and Dundee via the Broughty Ferry and Queensferry crossings of the Tay and Forth. A third road comes down the estuary from Stirling, where it has collected the routes in from Callander and Dunkeld, gateways out of the Highlands. The main road from the west, the Glasgow road, follows the north flank of the Pentlands in the long depression between those hills and the Campsie Fells. Another route from the west is that out of western England by Carlisle and Biggar, coming in on the southern flank of the Pentlands. An alternative to this route is the one by Moffat water, the upper Tweed and the Broughton gap, which again leads into Edinburgh in the depression between the Pentlands and the Moorfoots. The most direct route to England is that down the Gala water between the Moorfoots and Lammermuirs and so across the Cheviots either to Wooler or Hexham. Of all these routes the main ones are east to west and have confirmed the west-east axis the city developed originally down the High Street.

Without question this high concentration of roads on the Edinburgh gap has given it importance since early times. Also moving across this gap is a series of rivers and streams, fed by the Pentlands and shed into the Firth. These consist of the central Water of Leith and the flanking courses, the Almond and the Esk, one flowing from the northern, the

[1] The map at the end of this book might be consulted here.

other from the southern, side of the Pentlands. Lesser streams like the Braid and Niddrie burns are of local significance. It might be supposed that where the roads crossed these rivers and, in particular where they bridged the Water of Leith, they would have produced Edinburgh's main nuclei. Yet this is not the case. Edinburgh does not have its London Bridge. The fact is that the rivers are so short and steep, so youthful, so deeply entrenched and full of rapids that they have often been more of a nuisance than a help and the roads try to keep to the interfluves between them. The region where they have come together lies between the Water of Leith and the Esk, and here is the core area of the town.

This area is perhaps the most uneven and accidented of the whole gap. At its centre rise three closely grouped volcanic peaks, the massive and complicated structure of Arthur's Seat and Salisbury Crags, together with the more restricted but more abrupt features of Calton Hill and the Castle Rock. These three form a triangle with the Castle Rock at the apex. From this cliff-faced volcanic plug a long, gently sloping ridge runs down to the hollow between Calton Hill and Salisbury Crags. It is on this ridge that the original nucleus, grown up into the Old Town, lies, with the castle on the crag and the abbey and palace in the hollow.

Much attention has been paid to the crag-and-tail formation which dominates castle, town, and palace in old Edinburgh, and rightly so; it is the central geographical feature of the city, sited almost exactly between the Pentlands and the Firth of Forth, and between the Water of Leith and the Esk basins. Yet one must not forget the significance of the hollows that flank this ridge to north and south and terminate it on the east. These hollows, known as the Nor' Loch, the Cowgate, and Holyrood Loch respectively, long remained undrained and more or less forced the growing town to stay up on the High Street ridge. Had they not been as deep and wet they might have invited the downward spread of the city, relieved the tremendous pressure for space on the ridge between them, and thus allowed a very different kind of old town to emerge. (Only one of them, the Cowgate, was amenable to development, but until high-level bridges were built over it, this extraordinarily sharp-sided, deep little valley continued to offer difficulties.) Consequently, confined by these hollows, the old town grew up in the narrow limits between the castle and the palace: dense, tightly-packed, devious, varied and tall. There have been few urban areas in Britain as congested as this.

THE HIGH STREET

Edinburgh was for long a one street town, and, even though it expanded across the Cowgate to High School Yards or behind Holyrood to Abbeyhill, it was always dominated by the High Street. Having had to group houses, shops and workplaces along its front, together with administrative and business offices, churches and halls, it was forced to cut out all gardens, parks, and other open spaces (with the exception of a single cemetery), reduce side streets where possible to mere wynds, build gable-end on, and raise the height of buildings until many of them exceeded

10 storeys. Thus the old town came to develop a silhouette all of its own, dominated by tall, narrow buildings, tightly pressed together.

These buildings consist in the main of continuous, high tenements, rising right from the street pavements. In the High Street they have shops beneath them and are entered not from the front but from narrow closes that run down their sides, like rabbit-warrens. The closes usually open out into a back court from which winding, circular staircases, enclosed in towers jutting out from the tenements, take people to their small apartments. The closes run steeply down hill from the High Street to link up lower blocks of tenements. There are virtually no gardens or drying greens; women dry their clothes on little balconies built across the backs, or on poles sticking out from kitchen windows. The old gardens have mostly been taken up by the expansion backwards of the shops, warehouses, printeries or breweries that can find no more room on the front street. Their premises are generally entered from back roads, like the Cowgate. The tall, massive tenements all but dwarf the public buildings such as St. Giles' Cathedral, the Law Courts, and the City Chambers that lie in their centre about the widening in the High Street which was the old market place. Indeed, they are topped only by the high spires of the Canongate Tolbooth, the Tron Church, the Highland Tolbooth, New College, a few towers like that on Lady Stair's house, and by the occasional chimney of a mill.

Yet although this part of central Edinburgh must be one of the most thoroughly urbanized pieces of ground, it constantly offers vistas of green hills or hollows at the end of close or court. Arthur's Seat and Salisbury Crags lift their grassy slopes steeply upwards from the breweries and tenements of Canongate, Cowgate and the Pleasance; Calton Hill provides a more restricted yet still green space north of Canongate and Abbeyhill; while the old Nor' Loch, transformed into Princes Street Gardens, meets the view down any of the wynds of upper High Street. Thus an inner green belt all but surrounds the old town and sets it off from the newer and larger parts of the city.

The High Street ridge was unique among ridges in Edinburgh in that it began low enough to allow Palace and Abbey plenty of room for their gardens, then climbed slowly to a broad-shouldered back accessible to commerce, and finally reached a dominating height, from which the Castle could command the area. None of the other ridges offered these advantages, being lower and more gentle. On the other hand, at least one of these—that now followed by George Street—was nearer to the port of Leith, and also nearer to the roads coming in from the east via Musselburgh, from the north via Queensferry, and from the west via Linlithgow. As long as the main role of Edinburgh was to rally Scotland to defence or to keep the peace among its rival factions no doubt the High Street was ideal. But as urban requirements changed, as there grew up a need for trade and commerce, as people wanted more room to work and live in, then the High Street must have become frustrating. A time came for other more accessible, or more spacious, features within the Edinburgh gap to be used. What were these features?

First and foremost has been the ridge to the north, once followed by the Lang Dykes and now crowned by George Street, which parallels High Street, but is not so cut off. It slopes gently northward to the valley of the Water of Leith, and, beyond that, to a broad, flat terrace, once cut by the sea, that borders the Firth of Forth. Eastward it dips gently to the same bench that runs on behind Portobello and Joppa. On this ridge Edinburgh's new town was to rise.

South of High Street occur two other well-marked ridges, with their flanking hollows, which have also had some importance. These are, beyond the deep depression of the Cowgate and the Grassmarket, the ridge of Lauriston, flanked by the Meadows (formerly the Borough Loch), and the ridge of the Grange, dropping down to a hollow once partially filled by the Jordanville and Blackford lochs. This whole series of low and high strips of land, more or less parallel to the old town, has given rise to a number of well-known districts between Nicholson Square and Morningside.

Next, there occurs a wide outer arc of volcanic peaks or sills that have provided ideal sites for latterday suburban developments. This arc stretches from Craigmillar in the south-east through Blackford, Braid and Craiglockart hills in the south, to the hill of Corstorphine in the west. Between these abrupt, craggy masses are broad low saddles. At least two of these had large lochs in them. Between Craigmillar and Blackford hills lay an arm of Duddingston Loch. Between Craiglockart and Corstorphine hills stretched the much bigger Corstorphine Loch. These flat areas, now drained, have brought in railways, industries and working-class houses.

Finally, there are the slopes of the Pentlands themselves which have invited outer suburban settlement from Fairmilehead through Colinton to Currie. As these slopes steepen, however, and come to present what is virtually a mountain front they play a negative role. They effectively terminate settlement and force the city to expand northwestward or southeastward.

Each of these features has come to have a say in the growth and character of the city—those nearer to the Old Town of Edinburgh or to the port of Leith first coming into force, those farther away achieving their part later.

When in the middle 18th to early 19th centuries the Old Town could contain itself no more but had to branch out, it did so by developing the Lauriston and George Street ridges. Coaching roads crossed the Cowgate valley or climbed out of the Grassmarket and brought tentacles of houses up the slopes of Lauriston ridge as far as Bristo. George Heriot's school was built on one side, George Watson's college on the other. The High School, University, Surgeons' Hall and Infirmary grew up where the ridge died away into Kirk o'Field and the Pleasance. Building on wynds or around small courts was abandoned for the new fashion of the square, as in Argyll Square, and more notably, George Square. Families began to want to move out, and those who could afford it did so.

THE NEW TOWN

The year 1765 and the building of George Square by James Brown really marked the new departure. In the next year Craig's new town, a much more ambitious scheme, supported by the Town Council itself, was begun. Shortly thereafter high-level bridges were built across both the Nor' Loch and the Cowgate Valley to connect the old axial ridge of the High Street with the ridges beyond. North Bridge (1772) and the Mound (1830) came to link the High Street with the George Street ridge; the South Bridge (1788) and George IV Bridge (1836) connected it with the Lauriston ridge. The stimulus to the Old Town was immense. A much bigger business area developed, in the form of a great cross, consisting of the older shops and offices of the middle High Street and the newer, larger, more varied ones of the Bridges. The fashion shops especially—jewellers, hat shops, haberdasheries, and men's clothiers—sought the Bridges. Today, large drapery and household furnishing shops, often combined into modern departmental stores, still maintain the Bridges-Hill Street confluence as one of the city's main commercial areas.

The developments to north and south of the Old Town were not meant to threaten this commercial superiority, since they were planned as residential outlets. This intention profoundly affected the new townscape, which became one of formal, dignified, gracious and spacious lines and shapes. True, George Street was to have its shops, but shops of a kind that would not quarrel with the residential tone of the new town. As a result long, broad, open avenues have been left us, which in spite of having become commercialised, still carry an air of classical restraint and dignity about them.

In the event, shopping, banking and other types of business activity soon saw the opportunities offered by the new town and, pressing on beyond the North Bridge, invaded Princes Street, St. Andrew Square and George Street. Still more fashionable shops—jewellers, women's hair-dressers, women's hat shops and clothiers, umbrella stores, tobacconists, book stores, and coffee shops—moved rapidly into the new streets. Businesses followed suit, particularly the banks and insurance houses. A theatre, the Music Hall, and hotels came swiftly on behind, together with gentlemen's clubs and various social institutions. " The fine fields to the north of the Town," which had been slated for " people of fortune and of certain rank," came gradually to see the rise of a new commercial area. Financial houses virtually took over St. Andrew Square and spread along George Street; hotels, restaurants, clubs, fashionable shops and large departmental stores pre-empted the use of Princes Street. Thus a new business district was created which not merely challenged but largely superseded the old and is regarded today as the central business district of Edinburgh.

This was all but inevitable. The new district soon made much better contacts with the London road to the east and with the Stirling and Glasgow roads to the west. It drew new transportation terminals to it, housing the two main railway passenger stations and the regional bus station. Moreover, it became much more accessible than was the High Street to the western, northern, and eastern ends of the city, where the main shift of population and growth of industry occurred in the 19th century. Above all, when Leith and Edinburgh became united in 1920 the Princes Street–George Street nucleus served as the real focus of the city, in all but administrative matters.

A greater contrast between the geography of the Old and the New Town can scarcely be imagined. The one is crowded, crooked, and involved, offering great variety, and full of surprises; the other is quiet, dignified, and open, with geometric, expected vistas, having a flat restrained skyline pierced only by the occasional church dome or spire. It counts empty space as of equal value with built-up ground in the total urban appearance. It is redolent of discipline, balance and grace.

Edinburgh residents distinguish between an old New Town and a new New Town, and certainly the difference is there, in the respective townscapes. West of Charlotte Square, north of Queen Street Gardens, and east of Princes Street the strictly rectilinear lay-out of Craig's New Town gives way to one in which crescents, ovals and circles have been used, as well as long straight avenues and large squares. Thus the new New Town is more plastic, has altogether more flowing lines, and is thought by many to be more varied and interesting than its earlier counterpart. This was fortunate because the new New Town had to fit in to more variable contours altogether, going down from the straight side of the George Street ridge to the devious banks of the Water of Leith. The beautiful curves of Ainslie Place, Randolph Crescent and Lynedoch Place follow the no less lovely swings of the river through Dean Gorge. Further north the great circles of Moray Place and Royal Circus break up the regularity of that march down the hill of the stepped-streets of Heriot Row, Northumberland Street and Great King Street. In the west, Atholl Crescent and Coates Crescent suddenly open out from Shandwick Place to vary the straightness of the exit to the Haymarket and the Glasgow Road. Drummond Place likewise intrudes into the straightness of the northern descent from St. Andrew Square to Scotland Street. Finally, in the east end, Playfair has given us the incomparable Regent and Royal terraces which make the most of the lower slopes of Calton Hill.

These are amongst the most pleasing parts of Edinburgh. The quite extensive private gardens behind the houses, and the not infrequent enclosed gardens in the crescents and circles, mean that there is nearly as much green as grey. Indeed, the way in which open spaces vie with built-up ones gives a surprisingly bosky appearance to what is after all a mid-town area. The houses are all built in terraces, and have been planned to give a tasteful variety within a pleasing uniformity. On the whole the skyline is still lower than that of the first new town and much lower than that of the Old Town. This allows the few high spires, like those of St. Mary's Cathedral and St. George's Church West, to be thrown into all the stronger relief.

THE GROWTH OF THE SUBURBS

The spread of the city beyond the George Street and Lauriston ridges met with the obstacle of the gorge of the Water of Leith, to the north, and of the borough muir, to the south. With the erection of the Dean Bridge in 1832 the northern suburbs soon began to develop, first on the formal Georgian lines already adopted by Raeburn on his land, roughly between Raeburn Place and Ann Street, and then more freely. The circumvention of the lower part of the borough muir, called the Meadows, and the absorption of the remainder for building purposes, was a much slower affair and it was not until about forty years later that the southern suburbs forged ahead. By that time the Georgian movement had spent itself and new, though hardly less formal, styles of buildings were in vogue.

These mid- to late-19th century developments produced townscapes different again from the Old and the New Towns. For one thing, building was not so continuous; along with rows of apartments there were semi-detached villas and detached mansions. For the first time long vistas of tenement walls or terraced villas were broken up and gave way to interrupted fronts. Instead of being tempted to look *between* houses, as in the Old Town, at sudden snatches of green at the end of a wynd, or being directed to look *along* houses, as in the New Town, at carefully displayed parks and gardens, one was invited to look *at* the houses themselves, with their individual styles, and at gardens which were private idiosyncracies. Even where rows of houses were built in long stretches they were different. They were not the upper-class terraced villas, each with its own entrance, of the New Town; nor were they the lower-class tenements, entered from a back court, of the Old Town, but rather middle class flats, entered from a series of common doors which opened from the street into an interior stair well. These flats would have at least two high, spacious public rooms, looking to the front, together with a kitchen and two or three bedrooms at the back. They had their own laundry and toilet facilities, unlike the communal ones in so many of the Old Town tenements.

The growing variety of buildings and opening up of space are still striking as one surveys these later 19th century areas. North of the Water of Leith the terraced villas march from Dean Bridge and Stockbridge, in their stately " crescents " and " gardens " as far as Comely Bank; then they change, giving way to rather taller rows of middle-class flats; while beyond these again are the detached houses of Ravelston Dykes or of Inverleith set about with gardens behind dividing walls or hedges. Similarly, beyond Canonmills terraced villas march along Howard Place as far as the Royal Botanic Garden and then there is a mixture of detached houses continuing down to Granton Road and Trinity Road with blocks of tall flats at Goldenacre. At Ferry Road the northern advance of Edinburgh meets the western expansion of Leith, but the two movements are expressed in the same patterns. Leith moves west through the terraced houses, albeit not of the Georgian style, of Dudley Avenue, to continue into blocks of flats at Stanley Road and East Trinity, and to extend into the Laverock Bank area of large private houses.

One remarkable feature of the city's north side is the great amount of flat land, suited for industry and housing, which has been kept in open parks, playing fields or institutional grounds. This was partly due to the fact that expansion occurred at a time when room had to be found for new schools and hospitals. Heriot's, though fortunate in having plenty of space initially, could not find room in the Lauriston district for new playing fields; it secured them at Goldenacre. No doubt when Edinburgh Academy was founded, just on the edge of the New Town where the George Street ridge flattened out by the Water of Leith, there seemed to be sufficient room; but when playing fields were needed they had to be found north of the Water. Other schools, as we shall see later, were established to the north, and some of these, like John Watson's and St. George's, were set in spacious grounds. Daniel Stewart's College was also built in the north but, in spite of large grounds on Queensferry Road, had to acquire sports grounds still farther north on Ferry Road. Fettes College secured itself with most extensive grounds and fields. The further fixing of green land by the establishment of the Royal Botanic Garden, Inverleith Park, and the grounds of the Victoria and Western General hospitals has set a wide green belt between that part of Edinburgh moving down to Comely Bank and that part which incorporated the seafront expansion of Leith.

While this movement was going on in the north, a parallel one had started in the south. This had to climb down from the Lauriston ridge, circumvent the Meadows, and then climb up the long, slow incline of the next ridge, that of the Grange. Two coach roads had already been built across the western and eastern end of the Meadows, one from the Grassmarket by the West Port, the High Riggs and Tollcross to Bruntsfield, the other from the Grassmarket by Candlemakers' Row, Bristo Street and Causewayside to Liberton. The latter was parallelled by the route from the South Bridge out by the Newington Road to Liberton. These ways were followed by blocks of flats, often with shops underneath them, to just south of the Meadows; and thus the Tollcross, Surgeons' Hall and Newington districts became established. After 1875 there was a great extension of building from the Meadows to the Grange, when the flatted quarters of Sciennes, Marchmont, Bruntsfield and Viewforth sprang up. Relics of the old manor houses and estates that used to occupy much of this region are left in Bruntsfield House, now part of Gillespie's school, and Merchiston Castle, where fortunately there was room to build recently Napier technical college. Between these areas of middle-class flats there emerged the suburban districts of large detached villas such as occur in the Mayfield, Grange, Churchill, Merchiston and Morningside neighbourhoods. Thus we find once more long rows of tall continuous buildings, forming veritable grey-walled canyons, though with tiny gardens in front of them and large drying greens behind, alternating with streets of discontinuous, detached dwellings, set in spacious woody gardens enclosed by private walls.

THE GROWTH OF COMMERCE

Obviously such a large expansion, northwards to Inverleith and southward to the Grange, even though mainly residential, called for shopping and business services. The whole commercial life of Edinburgh was stirred. The population which by 1850 was about 150,000 had increased to over 300,000 by 1900. This was partly a response to business, yet it also promoted business. Shops and offices sprang up in four situations: along the front of the New Town; on the fringes of the Old Town; on the new arterial roads leading out from the town centre; and at suburban sub-centres.

The New Town secured the lion's share of this expansion. Most of Princes Street became commercialised by 1875; the coming of the horse-drawn trams and of the telephone made it increasingly easier in the 1880s for people to shop or do business in the centre no matter in which suburb they lived, and by the end of the century the process was largely completed in this area.

These changes in use gradually reflected themselves in changes in façade. After the firm of Renton's put in the first plate glass windows coming right down to the street, the front of Princes Street altered remarkably and became definitely commercial. In George Street the upper tiers remained residential in appearance but the street floor was turned into display windows or large office doorways. Families became anxious to sell out and move, and thus provided an opportunity for more firms to buy in and establish themselves.

The commercialisation is still going on. There are now only three or four of the original three-storey buildings in Princes Street, with the upper storey left as living quarters. Most of the dwelling houses have been completely replaced by six to eight storey buildings housing large departmental stores or hotels. In George Street on the other hand there are more upper storeys left as residential quarters, but here too most of the dwellings have been displaced by five storey office blocks built by insurance companies, and by building societies. Only the north side of St. Andrew Square *looks* residential;[1] the rest has been turned into tall buildings occupied by banks and insurance companies. Queen Street alone of the three main thoroughfares of the old New Town still has a residential appearance, and indeed some of the upper storeys continue to be lived in as flats. Most of the street-level storeys, however, are now offices, while here and there large office buildings interrupt the Georgian façade.

If the main commercial expansion of the late 19th century was in the New Town, some of it also occurred in the Old. Many shops invaded the Grassmarket and West Port; others moved into the new streets created by widening some of the old wynds, such as St. Mary's and Blackfriars Streets, or took advantage of thoroughfares built to connect the Old Town and the New, such as the Mound and Cockburn Street. Some of these like the head office of the Bank of Scotland on the Mound, were of

[1] Most of the residences have been converted into offices.

city-wide importance, but most of them were only of local significance, and did not compete with the New Town developments.

The building of long arterial roads to connect the city with wider regions invited a ribbon-like expansion of shops and businesses. These tended to start out from Princes Street and move along its main extensions northward, in Leith Street and Queensferry Street; west or east, in Shandwick Place–Haymarket and Waterloo Place; or southward, in Lothian Road and the Bridges. Long tentacles of shops, warehouses and showrooms thus reached out towards the suburbs. Some of these have continued to grow. The Leith Street expansion has produced what is probably the longest line of shops in Edinburgh, having merged in Leith Walk with the uphill commercial invasion from Leith. Another long string of shops continues almost unbrokenly along Newington Road as far as Salisbury Place.

Finally, there are the suburban shopping centres. Most of these grew out of little groups of shops in pre-existing villages later absorbed by the city. This was the case in Broughton and Pilrig to the northeast, Canonmills and Stockbridge to the north, Roseburn, Gorgie and Slateford to the west, and Bruntsfield in the south. As the city has continued to grow many more of these have sprung up. The village shopping clusters of Blackhall and Davidson's Mains in the west; of Craiglockhart, Colinton and Juniper Green in the southwest; of Liberton and Gilmerton in the southeast; and of Duddingston, Craigmillar and Niddrie in the east—all these have developed into smaller or larger suburban centres, with an interesting mixture of old village shops and modern branch stores.

The growing commercialisation of Edinburgh has been parallelled by a growing industrialisation. Actually the industrial sectors of the city were never conspicuous, except perhaps to the railway traveller from outside. It was always Edinburgh as a University town and a town of famous schools; Edinburgh as the head of Law, Church and Army; or Edinburgh as a banking and insurance centre that attracted and supported people, as it still does. Industry, now important, was for many years of lesser account. Today, however, the presence of water-power sites beside the Water of Leith, the nearby reserves of coal and of shale oil, the junction of national railways, and the services of a significant port, have given Edinburgh such a successful basis for both industry and trade that mills and factories have continued to increase, making use of riverside terraces, the raised beaches behind the seafront, and the low saddles between the hills, especially where these are floored with old glacial-lake deposits.

As the city expanded north and west it came upon small milling centres at Bonnington Mills, Canonmills, Stockbridge, Bells Mills, Saughton, Slateford, and Colinton. In the lower centres the town climbed down to low-level bridges, merged with the villages, and then transformed them. In doing so the town was itself transformed. As it descended it tended to deteriorate. The fine terraced villas of Royal Circus, Cumberland Street and Fettes Row passed to rows of tightly packed tenements going down to Stockbridge and Canonmills. At the upper river sites the mill settlements grew up in the bottoms of steep-sided, gorge-like valleys, and the town jumped over them on high-level bridges and flowed around them. Some of them, like Dean Village, are scarcely parts of the town to this day. A person may look across from one section of Georgian Edinburgh to another and see hardly any indication of a small milling village in between except for the tops of the mill chimneys. At Colinton the essentially residential nature of the city across the Water of Leith has scarcely been affected by the milling hamlet down in the Dell. Town houses of grey stone or white harling line the high terrace on the south side, give way to modern branch stores going down Bridge Street, look across a row of red-tiled cottages, a few village shops, and the large porage oats mill down by the river, and face town houses on the north terrace set in their large, long gardens.

The main industrial sections are much more evident. They lie behind Leith and Granton in the north; along the railway belt from Abbeyhill to Portobello in the east; and along both the Forth–Clyde canal and the railway belt from Haymarket to Sighthill in the west. In the Leith, Abbeyhill–Piershill, Haymarket–Gorgie, and Viewforth areas the industrial townscapes are much alike—large areas of railway sidings; extensive yards for storing coal, scrap and barrels; tall many-storied mills, usually of soot-blackened stone; streets of tall, grey-stone working-class tenements interrupted by railway overhead bridges or rising above smoking tunnels; rows of small shops with "co-op" branches here and there; numerous saloons and the not infrequent mission hall. The Hibernian football ground is in the eastern industrial sector, the Heart of Midlothian ground in the western, but otherwise there are few green spaces. In these crowded conditions buildings reach upward and the competition between them, as between mill and tenement, stack and spire, has led to a high, irregular skyline.

Very different are the two really modern industrial areas, that west of Granton at Crewe Toll, where the raised beaches are at their broadest, and the industrial estate at Sighthill, in the wide, low saddle between Craiglockhart and Corstorphine hills which carries railway and canal to Glasgow. Here the layout is much roomier; the factories are long and low, many of them only one-storied, and often surrounded by their own grass-covered grounds. They are separate from the working-class homes which have been built as distinct residential areas, as for example at Pilton and at Broomhouse. Recreation areas have been preserved and the long, low schools have extensive playing fields. The skyline is altogether lower and more regular.

These later industrial developments are really part of a final wave of urban expansion which, beginning in the 1920s, continues with us, and has carried the city to its present boundaries. This expansion has occurred mostly along the coastal terraces west of Granton and east of Piershill, in the north of the city; or up into the southern hilly flanks, from Craigmillar, through Liberton, Fairmilehead and Colinton, to Corstorphine. In this period a new townscape has emerged in Scotland—that of suburban bungalows and council housing estates. Although for all but 600 years—

from 1329 when King Robert I granted the city its charter to 1919 at the end of World War I—the vast bulk of the people of Edinburgh, as elsewhere in Scotland, had been content to live in tenements, terraced houses or flats, with only a very small minority housed in separate dwellings, suddenly in the 30 years since, everyone who has needed new accommodation has tried to get it at the city margins and, if possible, has sought a house and garden of his own. This still largely unappreciated and unchronicled change—a symptom, no doubt, of that assumption by one and all of what used to be the privilege of the few—constitutes a psychological revolution of great significance for the city. Coupled with the fashion for the flat factory and the flat school it is now the single greatest factor in that urban sprawl which is making the city more and more countrified, or is swallowing up the countryside in an increasingly urban way of life.

It is as though, all of a sudden, people had decided to have the best of both worlds. They are no longer willing to buy the blessings of urbanisation with the loss of country life by packing themselves together in crowded, dimly-lit, noisy and smell-ridden buildings; but, at the same time, they are no longer anxious to obtain the benefits of country life at the expense of city conveniences, by isolating themselves in remote and badly-equipped villages.

In any event, whatever the explanation, this tremendous outward drift, led by waves of bungalow builders and followed by the housing estate planners, is now well established. Since the inner ridges and depressions lying between the Pentlands and the sea were already occupied, the new developers had perforce to seek the farther seafront or the outer rim of hills. The earlier expansion, in the '20s and early '30s, occurred in the less restricted spaces behind Portobello, as for example, in Craigentinny and along Milton Road, or spread more widely between Davidson's Mains and Cramond. A similar swash of bungalows has run up the accessible slopes of Liberton, Greenbank, Fairmilehead, Craiglockhart, Colinton and Currie. Along with some of these developments has gone the building of large, detached modern houses, with big private gardens, especially in the Barnton, Colinton and Frogston Road districts.

HOUSING ESTATES

The most recent aspect of this flight to the city margin has been the development of council housing estates, begun in the '30s and now reaching its widest extent. This great movement grew out of the need to clear slums or otherwise relieve the excessively high density of the downtown population. Edinburgh must be unusual in having such a high proportion of residential space in the buildings within its central business area, where in the basement and attic tiers of shops and offices, or in crowded tenements facing narrow closes and confined courts, great numbers of people still continue to live. The rising standard of living makes such conditions untenable and has called for public housing on a fairly large scale. But obviously it has been difficult if not impossible to find the space for this in downtown or midtown areas. Some interesting attempts have been made to do so, largely to prevent the break up of social life at old historic centres. But in spite of new housing schemes which have replaced the slums *in situ* in the Canongate, the Pleasance, St. Leonard's, Piershill, and elsewhere, there simply is not the room for residential expansion where shops, businesses, light industries, new administrative and social institutions, and the University are all pressing for space. Consequently Edinburgh has, like similar cities, decided to develop suburban sites for council housing estates.

These have been planned mainly on or near arterial or ring roads where the people can get downtown for shopping, or go to industrial areas in town to work. They tend, therefore, to be in the north, on the flat seafront bench, or in some of the wider saddles between the southern hills. A number of them vie with the bungalow quarters and may, indeed, come up against them. A few, as at Barnton, even overlook areas of large private houses. Most of them, however, are developed as separate entities, rather than as rivals to established suburban districts. The larger estates lie well to east or west as at Newcraighall, Craigmillar, Bingham Road, and Lochend; or Pilton, West Pilton, and Muirhouse. Further south the estates have had to go out a greater distance to get beyond pre-existing suburbs, as for instance at Fernieside, Moredun, and Burdiehouse —beyond Liberton (which has itself expanded greatly); Colinton Mains—beyond Greenbank and Craiglockhart; and Broomhouse and Longstone—beyond Stenhouse. In these various developments there has been a return to crescents and circles and to the roomy layout of Georgian times, far different from the Victorian working-class areas. There are many short rows of double-storied flats and restricted blocks of three or four storey tenements, set in both front and back gardens, and enclosing ample play space for children: working-class homes have never before had such light and air and quiet about them.

Together with the bungalow and private-villa developments they form an outer residential rim which, full of gardens and with streets lined by trees, is barely urban in aspect but draws the country into the city, binding the one to the other. This outer rim is, indeed, quite different from anything else in the city, being much more varied than any of the other residential areas. Discontinued blocks of flats, streets of one-storied or one-and-a-half-storied bungalows, park-like belts of villas enisled by lawns; grey or light brown council-house exteriors, with slated or red tiled roofs, somewhat more colourful bungalows with at least differently painted doors and windows, and private villas with all colours of walls, roofs, woodwork and gates, and having very individual styles of architecture, provide a townscape of immense verve and variety. Here at least, perhaps one should say here at last, the all-pervasive greyness of Edinburgh —the grey of the stone tenements in the Old Town and industrial districts, the grey repeated by Georgian builders in their terraced houses, the grey of Victorian architects trying their hand at a dignified manner—this greyness breaks up. Though it is still present in the inter-war bungalows and council houses, especially the latter, it gives way in post-war building to an unashamed (though not unrestrained) joy in colour.

THE GREEN BELT

Beyond this outermost surge of houses there are still tracts of land within the city boundary, but they are taken up mainly with golf-courses, an airfield, riding stables, private estates, a number of farms and, above all, tracts of hill or dell held as public parks. The hill lands and the river declivities will probably never be built on; they are too steep for the purpose, especially round the flanks of the Pentlands, and have been protected by the Parks and Water Boards of the city. Thus Edinburgh terminates in a considerable green belt, except for the few strings of houses following the Queensferry, Glasgow, Lanark, Biggar and Dalkeith roads out to neighbouring communities.

To what extent this green belt will be preserved remains to be seen. Should urban sprawl continue, the green belt will be eaten into, or leapt over; and indeed this problem was becoming acute in the 1960s in many outlying areas. Recent trends have revived the tall housing unit, in the form of either modernised tenements or luxury flats, and in the early '60s these were going up in already built-up areas, as at Pilrig and Leith Fort. They were also rising in appropriate sites at the margin and thus slowing down the city's encroachment on the country, an encroachment that takes place, in the main, along strips of lowland where the region's best farming occurs. The struggle between suburban development and market gardening or dairy farming is intense, and marks the frontier of the city. Just as the outward invasion of shops from the centre of Edinburgh, leading to a flight of residences, has created a shattered, uneasy transition belt in the middle of the town, so the invasion of residences into the country has led to an outer transition zone in which city and country are vying with each other.

At every stage of advance—from the Old Town to the New, from Georgian to Victorian Edinburgh, from the commercially dominated core, through rising industrial sectors, to modern far flung suburban developments—geography has played its part. The use of local relief by the separate traditions of the times has created distinctive urban patterns and silhouettes which make Edinburgh a fascinating cross-section of Scottish life and landscape.

CHAPTER 3

THE OLD AND THE NEW TOWNS

THE long street climbing up from Holyrood to what an English newspaperman once called " the Wagnerian fantasy of the Castle " is the backbone of the city's history. In the Royal Mile, as it is called, a bustling present still preserves the ancient stones of a stormy past and recalls historic and famous figures, among them the association of Mary Queen of Scots and other monarchs with Holyroodhouse and the parish of Canongate. It is indeed here in the Canongate that we must start our survey of the city with a quick glance at its history; for the recent striking changes in the district and in the High Street and the Lawnmarket above it, have been largely dictated by the buildings and the habits of the past.

CANONGATE

Until 1856 the Canongate was a Burgh of its own. It lay outside the city wall, and grew round the Abbey of the Holy Rood, along the main way (the Canons' Gait) that led from the Abbey to the east gate (Netherbow) into the city of Edinburgh. It was at first largely occupied by members of the aristocracy and their servants, either through their connection at Court, or to give them spacious and peaceful residences outwith the more crowded and noisy city. Later it became almost a suburb of Edinburgh. Throughout its history, the Canongate has been the scene of constant change, and any account of it today of necessity describes a still-changing situation.

Holyrood Abbey—founded in 1128 " in honour of the Holy Rood, and of St. Mary the Virgin, and of all the Saints, "—was the home of monks of the Augustinian order, who were granted a charter by King David I to build a burgh under ecclesiastical jurisdiction between the Abbey and the walls of Edinburgh. At the Reformation this independent burgh of Canongate reverted to the Crown and was later granted by James VI to the Earls of Roxburghe. From the time of its foundation, Scottish kings made the Abbey their residence when they were in the district until James IV started to build a palace which was later expanded and rebuilt until we have largely today the Palace of Charles II. As a result of the presence of Royalty, the Canongate acquired a natural lustre and importance as the home of the Court and of foreign ambassadors who took up their residence there. But also the Canongate was then the main entrance to Edinburgh from the busy Port of Leith, the Water Yett being the Canongate's eastern entrance. With the comings and goings of nobility, their balls and entertaining, with the transport of merchandise to and from the city and with the crowd of idle and common beggars who loitered about in the hope of receiving alms from the wealthy inhabitants, the burgh must usually have presented a stirring and colourful scene.

As a Royal Burgh it had the right to have its own Council and duly elected burgesses. The Abbots of Holyrood who had the power of nominating " bailies " early in the town's history, resigned this right in favour of the people. There was a " superior "—normally one of the noble lords resident in the burgh until the City of Edinburgh acquired this position in 1640—who had the right of nominating a Baron-Bailie and holding Courts, both civil and criminal. There were also a town clerk; popularly elected magistrates, whose duty it was to keep strict order in the burgh; and by no means least the active, censorious, and often uncompromising vigilance of the Ministers and Kirk Session of the Parish Church.

The city fathers had their centre in the Tolbooth Council Chambers. There were also strong Trade Incorporations, a reminder of which exists in the name of "Shoemakers' Land." The Incorporations in the Canongate were Shoemakers, Wrights, Hammermen, Tailors, Weavers, Fleshers, Baxters (Bakers) and Barbers, of which the oldest was the Incorporation of Shoemakers whose records date back to the year 1554. Only freemen and burgesses were permitted to carry on trade in the burgh. But although the Canongate's corporate existence as a burgh was ended only in 1856 by the Edinburgh Municipal Extension Act, its heyday had already begun to wane after the Union of the Scottish and English crowns in 1603. When James VI went to London he was followed by a number of nobles who had previously been in residence in the Canongate. The burgh still flourished for some time after this, but the 1707 Act of Union further encouraged the southward drift, with "worse" to come. During the 18th century not only was a new road opened from the east into Edinburgh, thus decreasing the Canongate's importance as a main access to the capital, but the building of George Square to the south and the New Town to the north drained away so many of the professions and the merchants that the Canongate gradually became first a backwater and then a squalid slum.

Although in 1769 the street still numbered among its inhabitants 2 dukes, 16 earls, 2 countesses, 7 lords, 7 lords of Session, 13 baronets, 4 Commanders-in-Chief and many men of literary and professional eminence, Allan Ramsay had written a year or two earlier:

> O Canongate, puir eldrick hole,
> What loss, what crosses dost thou thole;
> London and death gars thee look droll
> And hang thy heid.
> Wow but thou hast e'en a cault coal
> To blaw indeed.

The street as a whole was obviously declining in intellectual, social and material importance.

This decline was typified in the history of most of the Canongate houses. In the late 17th and early 18th century many of the aristocracy were still building new town residences in the Canongate, beautiful houses standing in spacious courts and gardens, of which the most famous was the Moray House garden sloping down in four terraces to the Crags, in the summer house of which, still standing, the Treaty of Union of the Parliaments was signed. Moray House was erected in 1618 by the Countess of Home, and passing to her sister the Countess of Moray, remained in possession of her family for almost 200 years. By the beginning of the 19th century, it had passed to the Linen Company of Scotland (now the British Linen Bank), and thence it came into the hands of Alexander Cowan, a paper merchant. In 1847 it was acquired by the Free Church as a Training Institution, and is now part of the Moray House College of Education.

In like manner, Panmure House (built about 1691), the residence of the Earls of Panmure and Dalhousie and of Adam Smith (1778–1790), during which time it had a spacious courtyard and garden, degenerated from an iron-foundry into a ruin until restored in 1957; and Acheson House, erected in 1633, became a squalid slum housing 14 families until it was beautifully restored by the Marquis of Bute in 1937.

Not until the Industrial Revolution did the parish really begin to fall into the deplorable slum conditions in which it largely remained until recent times; for if the conditions before that were grim, they were no grimmer than the conditions prevailing in many other towns. But with the Industrial Revolution the larger houses were divided up to accommodate a new in-rush of people; and what had formerly been a room in a house became a house in itself. Overcrowding, bad sanitary conditions and poverty were rampant, and as many as 10 people might be housed in one room.

In 1850 Andrew Bonar, Minister of the Canongate and author of *The Church of Scotland's Duty to the Masses*, gave a long and rather sad description of the parish, with which he was very familiar. He invited his readers to go up one of the more dingy-looking tenements that fronted the street, where each flat, perhaps 50 years before, had been the commodious and well-furnished house of an opulent shopkeeper or substantial man of business. The inhabitants, he explained, were still respectable though different, being tradesmen and artisans' families who had succeeded to these dwellings. But cleanliness was generally " somewhat at a discount." Water, he wrote, was scarce and had to be carried from the nearest well up a long flight of stairs in which were " noisy urchins and little girls of astonishing strength of lungs and hair in much-admired disorder, whose hands and faces allowed you to draw an easy inference that they were much addicted to dabbling in the neighbours' gutters and romping, to the serious interruption of the chance explorer." Higher still there were dreadful hovels " as destitute of furniture as the habitations of a savage islander or an inmate of a wigwam." Unemployment, he added, was often caused through no fault of the workers themselves, and months might elapse before any work could be found. The few weekly shillings of the wages they received had not allowed them to have any savings; furniture, dress, and other things were sold until the barest dwellings remained.

One of the most interesting descriptions of the Canongate at the beginning of our present century came to light during the reconstruction of Bible Land in 1954 when there was discovered behind a wall a statement written by a certain Adam Prophet Profit. Profit requested in a footnote that this document should be reburied, but not before it had been carefully read and a copy of it made; and for this we are indebted to Mr. Hartmann, proprietor of the Royal Mile Boutique.

After describing the various items that would come today under the heading " Cost of Living," Profit gives an extremely grim picture of the parish. Drunkenness, he says, was very common, especially on Saturday, among both old and young; fighting went on far into the Sunday morning; and poverty was a constant " neighbour " with thousands through drink. The women, he felt, were not what the grandmothers of the period were (were they ever?). They were " sly drinkers, taking on debt, dressing by instalments, deceiving their husbands; and many of their offspring are rickety, ill-bred brats growing up to fill their mothers' places and act like them."

We do not yet know the background of Profit's life (or even his matrimonial life, if he had one) but he certainly had a poor view of Canongate women. He said that many men from his own knowledge had been killed by the conduct of their wives towards them, that hundreds of children were " murdered " slowly with neglect, and that many of the unmarried women belonged to " the oldest profession in the world." He had little time, too, for the Canongate youth at the beginning of this century: all they thought about seemed to be kicking a ball, " shows," games, drinking and idle company. As for the working men, these had sunk to a low ebb also and were largely in debt. Their conversation was all about " kick-ball " and where they could find free charity. Many were compelled to go to the poorhouse because of the way they were living, their children following in their footsteps, marrying young, and faring little better. He blamed the Church for its neglect, but also blamed nearly everything else.

A former Parish Sister of Canongate, who was still a member of the congregation in 1963, gives a rather different picture from Profit's dismal view of the teeming masses of the parish at the beginning of this century:

" It was a busy scene with barrows selling oranges, apples, pears, nuts, etc. on either side of the street, interspersed with women sitting beside creels, selling penny saucerfuls of boiled mussels, ' buckies ' in shells, or shrimps. Ovens with baked potatoes, or roasted chestnuts in season, gave a warm fragrance to the air. At the old fountain, ' Cocoa-nut Tam ' once had his stance with his well-known cry; ' Coky-nit, coky-nit, ha'penny the bit, bit, bit.' Then there were the ' soup kitchens.' Oh, how welcome they were on cold, raw days to the children or hungry ones having little to feed themselves with—1*d.* soup and bread, 2*d.* or 3*d.* sausages and potatoes. Second-hand clothes were also sold on barrows, while strains of music came from an old ' hurdy-gurdy ' resembling a large box supported on a stick, with a broad strap passing round the shoulder and back of the old man who usually turned the handle of this wheezy organ with ' Home Sweet Home ' or Scots or English airs. Little children congregated round, some dancing, some fascinated by the organ-grinder's monkey, sitting on the organ, dressed in a little red coat or dress, with a little red cap on its tiny head. There was also a ' balloon man ' from whose airy collection jelly jars, bottles and rags procured a balloon. Then there were the little shops selling ' gaudy,' ' gundyballs,' burnt sugar, locust beans, etc., in farthings or halfpennyworths, tea and sugar mixed in ' infusings ', penny or twopenny slices of bread and cooking butter, sandwiches or bread and cheese or cold meat—meals could be bought in these days. That, roughly, is the Canongate's exterior—but it was the people, the warmth of kindly spirit met, each life deeply interesting, each life carrying somewhere a trace of the Divine Father, that gripped and held one most."

Yet though times were slowly changing for the better there were still sordidness and overcrowding, poverty, drunkenness, much of which is still remembered and even a little of which still remains; and with it the kindness and courage that is still characteristic of all who face any common adversity. In any event, out of all this—it may be partly through a survival of the fittest—there have arisen in the Canongate men and women and children second to none in Scotland (as their parish minister thinks) for their hardiness, their courage, their honesty, their generosity and their kindness.

HOUSING

" When I knew Canongate first as Warden of the Boys' Club in 1927 " (Dr. Selby Wright continues) " many of the children still wore very ragged clothing and the number of heads of houses unemployed exceeded those employed; and when 10 years later I became Minister of the Canongate and stayed at the then manse at 3 St. John Street, a now departed relic of the more spacious days of this once ' exclusive ' street, there were as many as 159 people living at No. 1.

" As the years passed the property became more and more neglected and with the added neglect of the war years it was damp, drab, ill-lighted, and in a few cases crowded together; though since the Canongate was not originally bounded by a city wall, overcrowding of property on the land has never been so necessary as in the old walled city. Where condemned property had been evacuated and closed, it was in such a depressing state of disrepair as to be near ruin: for example Shoemakers' Close, Bible Land and Morocco Land, part of the last having collapsed in ruins in March 1947 after standing empty for 18 years.

" Although from an historical and architectural point of view there was still a feeling of romance, too many of the buildings were crumbling into ruins through lack of care, attention and restoration; and for the inhabitants of the still-tenanted closes and tenements, historical interest in no way compensated for lack of the basic necessities of making a comfortable home, though in the same type of house, different tenants made an unbelievable difference in comfort, cleanliness and homeliness. The people in the Canongate, as in most other places, were very mixed, containing as they did all grades from the housewife who takes a pride in her family and housekeeping, and makes the most of sometimes unpromising surroundings, to the ' feckless ' woman who would make little, without help and training, of any kind of house. The majority of the houses fell midway between these extremes."

The following housing statistics for 1946 are illuminating:

	No.	*Per cent of Canongate dwellings*
Dwellings of one room	205	27·74
Dwellings of two rooms	391	52·28
Dwellings of three rooms	63	8·52
Dwellings of four rooms	8	1·08
Dwellings of five rooms	3	0·40
Dwellings overcrowded	210	28·38

It will be seen from the above that the number of dwelling houses inhabited in the Canongate by this time was comparatively small. Depopulation had been going on for a number of years as new housing estates were built and slum property was condemned, and much of it closed. Soon long lists of uninhabitable houses in the Canongate and adjoining courts and closes with good old names were drawn up. By December 1947 almost the whole area was scheduled for restoration or rebuilding, so that when labour and material became available to tackle the work, the character of the street began to be changed for the better.

Till recent times, then, the majority of dwellings were obviously small, and overcrowding was one of the evils of the district. " Kitchen " is included in the term " room " so that in 27·74 per cent of the dwellings in the Canongate meals were prepared and eaten, families slept and carried on the whole business of living all in the same room. The 52·28 per cent of two-roomed houses were in little better state. One room was generally used as kitchen, dining-room and living-room, and usually contained a bed, while the second room was used as a bedroom by those of the family who didn't sleep in the first room. Where 80 per cent of the dwellings consisted of one or two rooms, family life was difficult, unless the family consisted of one or two old people or a young couple with at the most two children.

Statistics of the degree of overcrowding after the last war were not readily available, but by the standards laid down by the 1935 Housing (Scotland) Act, the amount of overcrowding was 30 per cent. The pressure was worst on families where there were a number of children; and when the effects of overcrowding on health, morality, and education are taken into account, it will be seen that the evil was very serious. In one family two parents with two sons aged 16 and 6 and three daughters aged 12, 11 and 3 lived in two rooms. In another family, where a mother, two sons and two daughters all over 17, occupied two rooms, the mother alone was able to sleep in the living-room as only one corner was free enough from damp to allow a bed to be placed; so the four children had to sleep in three beds in the small bedroom. In yet another family the father, mother and small son slept in one bed, while the daughter aged 16 and son aged 13 slept in another.

The rents at the time varied considerably, not only from close to close but also from house to house within the closes. The lowest recorded rent in 1947 was 1*s*. 3*d*. per week for what was said to be a very poor room in Whitehorse Close, the only one over 10*s*. being for a house in 60 Canongate. The rents then varied roughly from 3*s*. per week to 10*s*. per weeks, rents below 5*s*. being rather more numerous than rents above that figure. However, in no case was the rent a very heavy item in the family budget, and the largest part of the often small income was normally left for food, personal expenses, heating, lighting and entertainment, and not always, it should be added, rightly proportioned.

Most houses were in private hands, but only three were occupied by the owners, and no great amount of property was held by any one person. This multiplicity of ownership by private persons, many of whom had inherited the property and were unable to repair it, made development or restoration of the Canongate an expensive and complicated business for the Town Council, and one which often required lengthy legal adjustment.

As a contrast to these conditions, the all too few houses built by the Town Council between the wars consisted of four rooms and bathroom with basin and W.C. This was a big improvement on the old tenements, as W.C. accommodation and often the water supply was usually shared by all the houses on one flat, which meant that up to five households were sharing the same conveniences. The new houses also gave every incentive to neatness and cleanliness, as the housewife had space for storing her possessions—an amenity often lacking in the old houses—and she had a foundation on which to build a good home.

POPULATION AND EMPLOYMENT

Since housing is so closely linked with population it might be well at this point to look at Canongate's residents, though it was impossible in 1966 to estimate their numbers with precision since the population was fluctuating from month to month while some buildings were being demolished and others were being built or rebuilt. We might however put on record that in 1946—before the new drive of rebuilding and restoration began—the population figures were:

Class	*Number*	*Percentage of total population*
Adults (over 14)	1,738	75·5
Adults (15–64)	1,544	67·08
Adults (65+)	194	8·42
Children (0–14)	565	24·5
Children (0–5)	208	9·03
Children (5–14)	357	15·47

These figures are consistently below those at the beginning of the century, and there has been a further fall since 1946 in this once congested area. The 1961 Census showed that the decrease of population in the Holyrood ward, of which the Canongate was a most congested part, was 6,010 since 1951—a percentage decrease of 30·1 and one notable for being the highest recorded in the city.

Where employment could be found it was largely unskilled and seldom secure, the boys who left school at the age of 14 being content with casual work of uncertain duration. The 1946 statistics showed 51 persons in the Canongate (mainly heads of families) unemployed—considerably fewer than pre-war—and 682 (men, women and juveniles) in employment.

THE CANONGATE TODAY

It has been thought necessary to recount at length some of the Canongate's past because the present of such an ancient area is better understood, at a time of change, if we know what went before; and the change has been profound, in less than a generation.

Today the Canongate boasts nearly as many coffee houses as public houses, some of the latter being no more than drinking houses, others setting a standard as to what such places could be. Such drunkenness as there is seems to be largely, though no more commendably, confined to closing time on Friday and Saturday nights, though there is a regrettable tendency now for older teenagers to take fortifying drinks like vodka and rum with tomato juice or blackcurrant before dances.

In general the conditions of the people have changed from Bonar's or Profit's descriptions almost beyond belief. The people, and especially the younger generation, take far more pride in their appearance than they have ever done before and most of them have the right sort of ambition to make good and " get on." More of the boys and girls, for example, either attend secondary education up to the Edinburgh Certificate or " O " level, and some the Higher Leaving Certificate standard or " A " level, or else they seek apprenticeships as printers, mechanics, etc., and attend day classes and night schools—to such an extent, indeed, that it is not now possible to find one night a week when a full attendance at the Boys' Club or other youth organisations can be guaranteed. The effect of wireless and television too has been of far more good than harm. Nor does one require the evidence of the former Chief of the C.I.D. to show that Canongate is now one of the best-behaved and least troublesome quarters of the city. Juvenile delinquency—in its less harmful form happily no new phenomenon—is less than in most places where 60 per cent of it is confined to Sunday afternoons and evenings.

As the Industrial Revolution of the last century brought new hardships to the Canongate, so the gentler revolution of the Welfare State, sponsored by all political parties, has brought a new, and it is hoped lasting, prosperity. Unemployment is almost unknown and wages are comparatively high, even compared with the higher cost of living. The wages of the younger members of the community especially are very much greater than their fathers had, and in some cases than their fathers have now. To add to the household budget many wives work too, either part-time or all day, and often to the financial advantage of the house and detriment of the home. Yet with these increased incomes and better material conditions there is often too little sense of the old Scottish concept of thrift, less of values and less still of "giving." With the new feeling of emancipation, money is used often carelessly and wastefully. Too often the cheap and the shoddy are mistaken for the economical; much is tied up with hire purchase; entertainment claims a larger share than it should; the new betting-shops are well-patronised; and there is too often an understandably human demand for more and more money for less and less work. Also it remains sadly true that the "givers" are often those who have always given, and who now sometimes have less money than those who have never learned the new art to them of voluntary giving and, in the fullest and best sense of the word, Christian charity.

With the rebuilding of the Canongate rents are certainly different nowadays. In 1963 the rents of houses belonging to the Town Council varied:

	Old Houses		New Houses	
No. of Apartments	*Rent*	*Rateable Value*	*Rent*	*Rateable Value*
2	£7–£16	£10–£15	£38–£40	£24–£30
3	£13–£32	£15–£18	£45–£50	£35–£42
4	—	—	£55	£41–£49

The rents shown above include a sum of £3 where bicycle sheds have been provided. Yet despite the increased rents the new houses are not an economic proposition and are subsidised by the Edinburgh ratepayers. There are, however, some houses, for example the restored Whitehorse Close and Chessel's Court, where the rents vary from £300 to £450 a year. With the new houses have also come new shops. Some of these are notable for their good taste and products—woollen goods for instance—and because of this they attract people from far outside the parish. There is usually such a great desire for cleanliness that clean faces and clean windows, clean clothes and clean curtains fight a valiant battle with the belching smoke of chimneys and passing trains.

EDINBURGH CASTLE AND THE CANONGATE

If one were to take a tour of Canongate today one would, strictly speaking, have to start at Edinburgh Castle which, although another parish intervenes, has remained in the Canongate parish since King David I founded the Abbey of the Holy Rood. There is no need here to re-tell the story of the Castle and its connections with Canongate in any detail. But it is worth noting that the Governor of the Castle has not only a seat within the parish Church but a new Governor officially "takes his seat," and having been greeted by the Minister of Canongate is then introduced to the members of the Kirk Session. The full revival of this pleasant custom took place during the years of the Governorship of General Sir Neil Ritchie in 1945–7, and it was Sir Neil and the next three Governors after him who presented the flagpoles that stand outside the Canongate Kirk and fly each Sunday not only the official flag of the Canongate Kirk Session but also, when he is preaching, the official pennant of the Minister of Canongate.[1] And in 1955 the eight Governors from 1945 to 1965 presented a plaque to the Church telling its history, which was unveiled by H.M. the Queen and dedicated by Dr. Warr, Dean of the Chapel Royal.

The Governors of the Castle during the years have taken a very real interest in the work, as well as the worship, of Canongate and have attended quite a number of the functions that take place in the Church, including presentations of the Duke of Edinburgh's Award. It is worth mentioning also that in 1942 there was started, under the convenership of Lady Russell of Silverburn, the St. Margaret's Chapel Guild which is responsible for attending to the needs of St. Margaret's Chapel; for example, putting flowers each week in the sanctuary. This Chapel, beautifully restored by the late Sir David Russell of Silverburn, owes much to the Guild and to H.R.H. Princess Margaret for becoming its first and continuing Patron. The President of the Guild is the Minister of Canongate in his capacity as Minister of Edinburgh Castle, and the Vice-Presidents are the Governor of Edinburgh Castle and the Assistant Chaplain General, Scottish Command.

RECENT CANONGATE CHANGES

From the Castle we come back to the other end of the Royal Mile where within the parish of Canongate there towers, over all Edinburgh, Arthur's Seat and round it the Royal park, with the Palace of Holyroodhouse at its feet, and beside it the ruins of the Old Abbey Kirk, which was for so short a time the Chapel Royal in the 17th century. As we saw earlier, for long periods the Palace remained unused, but from the days of King Edward VII there have been frequent visits from the Royal Family, and this has naturally given new dignity and vitality to the Canongate especially in its present stirring period of transition.

At the gate of the Palace on the north side, the Ministry of Works has restored the Abbey Sanctuary, now largely used as their offices, and on the south side the Abbey Court. At the same time the buildings around the Sanctuary as far as what is commonly called Queen Mary's Bath House have recently been removed to make an open garden. Incidentally, the debate as to what the real purpose of the Bath House used to be still continues: most likely it was a rather less romantic gate-house at an entrance to the Palace. Then on the north-east border of the Palace stands Croft-an-Righ (perhaps Croft Angry) which once, it is said, was the home of the Regent Moray. It is now the home of the Palace gardener. At

[1] In 1959 the Lord Lyon King of Arms granted to the Minister of Canongate the distinction of a string gules of one tassel on each side purpure. The present minister adds his own Arms with string and tassel gules. In 1952 the Lord Lyon had already matriculated the Arms of the Kirk and of the Minister.

the Holyrood junction of Canongate and Abbeyhill a roundabout stands today where formerly an ugly underground lavatory existed; and going up the famous street to the right the distinguished Whitehorse Close, where formerly the coaches for London set out, has been rebuilt and restored. On the left, Queensberry House too has been renovated, and in spite of its rather stern exterior has taken on a kindlier appearance, greatly to the benefit of the Canongate but even more greatly to the benefit of the elderly patients who now live there. Its " House of Refuge " ceased to exist in 1959—an optimistic sign of the times. Whitefoord House on the other side of the street is now the Scottish Naval, Military and Air Force residence where more than 100 servicemen enjoy their years of retirement in excellently-kept surroundings. The buildings immediately beyond on either side of the street have recently been removed, and are soon to become modern houses; while on the right beyond them stands Reid's Court, once again the Manse of the Canongate after its restoration and dedication by the Very Rev. Dr. George Macleod in 1958. Built about 1690 it had been used as a manse until 1832, the last occupant being the Rev. Walter Buchanan, D.D., who did so much for the parish in his day, not least in education; and for a time, according to old maps, it had been a coach-house. It then became the home of the famous Kindergarten School and now at considerable expense—borne by the church itself and by friends who included the Russell, Ivory, Pilgrim and Baird Trusts—it has taken on a new life by returning to its old.

On the entry to Reid's Court on the right stands the early 18th century Russell House, owned by the Church and called after Sir David Russell whose Trust has done so much to help it. Immediately across stands Dirleton Land, completely rebuilt on the pattern of the old house, and beside it is Milton House School with the little that remains of the old house of Fletcher. On the opposite side and next to Reid's Court the old Lochend Close is transformed, and in 1966 fine new houses fronting it were being rebuilt by Sir Basil Spence, Glover and Partners; behind this there now stands the beautifully restored late 17th century house of the Earls of Panmure, now the headquarters of the Canongate Boys' Club. Overlooking the frontage of this is Cadell House, recently well-restored by the Town Council as dwelling-houses. West of Cadell House is Dunbar's Close, an outstanding example of the need for restoration or even for demolition; and opposite the entrance to Dunbar's Close is Wilson's Court, likewise greatly in need of attention. Then comes Acheson House, now the headquarters of the Scottish Craft Centre, with beside it Huntly House, the City Museum. Opposite stands the Canongate Kirk itself, restored within and without in recent years, with its beautifully-kept churchyard around it, where lie the bodies of Adam Smith, Sir William Fettes, " Clarinda " whom Burns made famous, Lord Provost Drummond, Robert Fergusson the poet, Handel's favourite bassoon player and so many more of the famous in Scotland's story. The Mercat Cross of Canongate stands where the old Burgh School and later Church Hall once stood, having been removed from the outer gate of the Church in 1953 where it stood in company with the Home Fountain, now also removed. Westward is the Canongate

Tolbooth (now an annexe to the Museum at Huntly House). The Legal Dispensary which met for so long in the Tolbooth has now been removed to Milton House School and meets each Thursday evening as still a valuable source of free legal advice to people in the district. To the west of the Tolbooth all the houses have been rebuilt and form not only a pleasing amenity to the Royal Mile, with pillared shops in certain parts and good houses above, but a memorial to the architectural taste of the late Robert Hurd who played an important part in the reconstruction. On the south side Moray House stands proud with its former story, but no less proud of its present usefulness as a training college for teachers; and in the lands in the entrance into St. John Street, that street of famous memory where the *Waverley Novels* were first read by Scott, and Burns used to visit Monboddo, and Smollett stayed with his aunt, there has been a complete renovation. The famous Canongate Lodge Kilwinning remains largely unaltered since the days when Burns was Poet Laureate. Farther west on the south side stand derelict buildings up to and beyond Playhouse Close, soon to be restored. The houses in the Chessel's Court area have now been restored or rebuilt with good taste, and at considerable expense, by the Town Council; so that now on the north side the newly-restored houses and shops, along with the good pre-war rebuilding, stretch the whole length from the Tolbooth to Jeffrey Street. The old Canongate proper finishes really on the east side of St. Mary's Street and Jeffrey Street, and the rest belongs to Edinburgh.

THE CHURCH

In this restoration of the parish the Canongate Kirk can claim to have taken a lead. For though the days succeeding the second World War saw many building difficulties the whole front of the Church was completely cleaned and repaired in 1946, including the painting in heraldic colours of the Coat of Arms of William of Orange, and a start was made to restore the interior when the Kirk Session appointed Mr. Ian G. Lindsay R.S.A. as architect. This ultimately included the opening up again of the apse, the removal of the side galleries, the restoration of the Royal and Castle pews, and the rebuilding of the Minister's and Choir Vestries. Early encouragement was given by the Royal Family and in particular H.M. Queen Elizabeth (now the Queen Mother). The interior reconstruction of the Church was nearly complete in 1952 when a visit was paid by H.M. the Queen, on the first day of her arrival in Edinburgh as Queen, and in the following year, after the final reconstruction of the interior, by Prince Philip, Duke of Edinburgh, who opened a door to commemorate the visit of Her Majesty the year before.

The Crown has of course a special interest in the Church since it is the Kirk of Holyroodhouse and a royal foundation. A small part of the Minister's stipend comes from the Crown, and as an example of the Royal Family's interest, King George VI presented to the Church new antlers to replace those on the apex of the building, and each year he sent a Christmas tree, a gracious and kindly custom which has been followed ever since by the Sovereign. In 1961 H.M. The Queen presented a silver Chalice to the Church on the occasion of the semi-jubilee of the Minister: this was handed over on her behalf by the Dean of the Chapel Royal. At the same time she appointed the Minister as a Chaplain to Her Majesty in Scotland.

The outer reconstruction of the Church, including its complete re-harling, was completed in 1956, and five years later the Church was fully treated for acoustics (a complaint since 1690) and completely redecorated under the direction of Mr. Esme Gordon, A.R.S.A., the architect.

The worship of the Church too,[1] since the coming of the present Minister in 1936, has been restored to conform with the Reformed Liturgy according to the Book of Common Order with monthly celebrations of Holy Communion; and also, to enhance the beauty and order and dignity of its worship, there is now a bright sanctuary of light grey-blue and white, with a scarlet-cassocked choir of boys.

An increasingly large number of younger men attend the parish Church and though there are few Roman Catholics in the parish these, as always, are faithful to their religious duties. Today without doubt more people attend services than in the middle of last century, or the beginning of this. In the Church on Sundays and throughout the week, especially in the summer months, there are usually a large number of visitors, many from overseas. The impact of the Church on the parish—though not always obvious—is considerable and the general attitude to it most friendly. Much of this friendliness is due to the long respected ministries of two great men who have, in Canongate if nowhere else, their memorial—Canon A. E. Lawrie, M.C., D.D., who came as Lay Reader to Old St. Paul's in 1885 and was Rector there from 1897 until his death in 1937, and the Rev. Thomas White who came to the Canongate in 1886 as Assistant and was Minister there from 1888 to 1936. The present Minister has an Assistant and Deaconess to help with the work of the parish, an enthusiastic body of Elders and Church workers in the Woman's Guild, Mothers' Club, and other organisations, and also Divinity students at Russell House.

INDUSTRY

The industries of Edinburgh are dealt with later in this book, but perhaps a fleeting reference should be made here to those carried on inside the boundaries of this historic parish. The main industry is still brewing, with the long-established firm of William Younger and Company Limited, (now Scottish and Newcastle Breweries Limited) as the largest and the one owning most property (including houses) within the parish. Other well-known breweries connected with Canongate are John Aitchison and Company Limited, J. and J. Morison Limited and, on the outskirts of the parish, Steel, Coulson and Company Limited at Croft-an-Righ, and Robert Younger Limited at St. Ann's Brewery. The old Canongate

[1] For a fuller history of the Church and its worship see *The Kirk in the Canongate* by Ronald Selby Wright, DD. (Oliver & Boyd 1956).

glassworks have gone, but there are certain small crafts—a firm of silversmiths for example—which still remain. Until 1965 Lady Haig's Poppy Factory at Canongate was employing chiefly disabled ex-servicemen. There are chemical works at Abbeyhill in Holyrood Road (formerly known as the South Back of Canongate) and in Calton Road (formerly known as the North Back of Canongate). And also within the parish, there are the Scottish Gas Board's Edinburgh District store yards; the headquarters, works and large garage of the Scottish Omnibuses Limited on a former football pitch; the British Railways goods station; branches of the Bank of Scotland and of the British Linen Bank beside the new shop centres, which include what is becoming a minor " industry," the "Fudge Shop "; a number of antique dealers who form no mean part of Canongate's industry, especially during the tourist season; three big newspaper garages and the Postal Telegraph branch of the General Post Office.

LEISURE

In their spare time most of the children are members of one or other of the many youth organisations—the Boys' Club, The Boys' Brigade and Lifeboys, the Scouts and Cubs and organisations such as the Girl Guides. Naturally in Canongate itself the Canongate Boys' Club takes a large share of the young people, though there too a number of the boys come from without the parish, most of them from families in new housing areas whose original roots are in the Canongate. The Club was founded in 1927 by the present Minister of the Canongate (who is still the Warden) nine years before he became Minister; and for its first nine years it was run under the auspices of St. Giles' Cathedral. It is divided into four sections—the Apprentices, from the age of 8 to 11, the Gytes from the age of 12 to 16, the Uppers from the age of 15 to 18, while the ex-members of 18 plus are known as Outers. The chief activities of the Club, which are varied and many, include table tennis, billiards, chess, draughts, physical fitness, library, dancing, training in hobbies, canteen, ambulance work—all indoors; and it was one of the first clubs to take part in the Duke of Edinburgh's Award Scheme. Among its outdoor activities are the usual interest in football—not least in rugby (two Scottish internationalists, N. G. Davidson and J. Pringle Fisher), cricket, basketball and among some, golf. One of the most important of the Club's activities is camping and the Club has an excellent permanent camp site with five huts near Dunbar, where camps are held over the New Year, at Easter, at holiday weekends, and most of all for several weeks in the summer. The Club has had many headquarters in the parish, Gullan's Close, Brown's Close, Old Playhouse among them, but acquired a new home through the generosity of Mr. Roy Thomson (as Lord Thomson of Fleet then was) at Panmure House. This, after complete reconstruction, was opened on 6th October, 1957 by H.R.H. The Princess Royal (whose death in 1965 was much lamented in Edinburgh), and dedicated by the Right Rev. Sir George F. MacLeod, Bt, the Moderator. In the following year (on 1st July) the Club was further honoured by the visit of H.R.H. Prince Philip, who unveiled its War Memorial and met all the members. The Duke of Hamilton is the Honorary President of the Club, an interest typical of that which he takes in the Church and Parish as Hereditary Keeper of the Palace of Holyroodhouse, and H. W. Richmond—a former head boy—has been Deputy Warden since 1952.

A successful Girls' Club is also run under the Leadership of the Church Deaconess with the Duchess of Sutherland as its Honorary President; and many of the women belong to some Club or meeting connected either with the Church or some outside body; and some to both. Many go out working during the day to earn extra money or to relieve boredom, and their chief occupation when not engaged in usually harmless gossip at the wash-house, the Bendix Laundry, the shop queue or the doorstep, is looking after the family. The craze for Bingo interests a number. Most have some Church connection and few, if any, would be happy if the baby had not been baptised, or as some of them put it, " done." It is also true that most parents want their children to have a better chance than they had and do their best to see that their hopes are fulfilled.

The chief leisure activity of the Canongate men is watching and discussing football. Most spend some money on football pools, and some on horse or greyhound racing, though few indeed could be called gamblers. Few now are heavy drinkers. They are, by and large, fairly uninterested in politics and many are Socialists of the old Radical–Liberal persuasion rather by habit than by thought, though all parties have their supporters. Most who are eligible are members of the Trade Union movement though a great many seldom attend Union meetings; and there are practically no Communists. To a large number their " temple of worship" is either a Masonic Lodge, Easter Road (headquarters of the Hibernian Football Club) or the Heart of Midlothian Football Club's ground at Tynecastle. But most are friendly disposed to the Church; some are regular attenders and many attend on special occasions such as the Christmas Eve Midnight Service, Remembrance Sunday, the " big " Communions, or Church services arranged specially for the British Legion, Old Army Comrades, or some sporting club like a Bowlers' Association; and also of course full use is made of the Church for weddings, funerals, baptisms, and not least as " a very present help in time of trouble." But this we could expect. Even in the midst of a strenuous new era like our own, the burgh's ancient traditions are such a source of pride and loyalty to the parish that one still hears Canongate folk talk about " going up to Edinburgh."

THE HIGH STREET AND THE LAWNMARKET

Beyond the site of the old Netherbow Port, where St. Mary's Street cuts across the road from the Canongate to the Castle, we reach first the aptly-named High Street of Edinburgh and then the Lawnmarket. The High Street stretches from the Netherbow to St. Giles, and the Lawnmarket (where " lawn merchants " once used to pitch their stalls and sell-linen and every sort of cloth) from St. Giles to Castle Hill.[1] On either side of this long straight thoroughfare tall tenement houses—six, seven and eight stories high—picket the slope shoulder to shoulder. Many date from the 17th and 18th centuries; some are in good repair, some in disrepair; a few have been done up by local authority and other bodies. There are also big commercial and municipal buildings of a much later date. An array of shops takes up the whole length of the street, and most of these are small (some indeed very small) and independently owned. They supply most local needs; prices in the High Street in 1965 were still among the lowest in the city and so its shops keep popular. Perhaps the High Street has never quite lost its market character. It has still a street-life of its own, and at least until a very few years ago people who lived in the Lawnmarket knew their neighbours and their neighbours' business.

From end to end the Royal Mile has been wrested from real slum conditions during the last 100 years. Like the Canongate, and for the same reasons, the scene in the High Street, Lawnmarket and adjoining West Bow in the last half of the 19th century was one not only of dirt, near-starvation and chronic poverty, but almost incredible overcrowding. Thus in 1865 there were 646 people to the acre in the Tron area of the High Street. " It is believed," stated the first Medical Officer of Health, Dr. Littlejohn, " that with the possible exception of some districts of Liverpool, in no part of the world does there exist greater over-crowding of population." This was due to the sub-division of once spacious apartments into flats of three rooms, two, or " single ends," and sometimes to the sub-division of these again. It is hardly surprising that the Tron district had the highest mortality rate in the city.

Dr. Littlejohn recommended among other things the regular inspection of cow byres in the city, a large number of which, inadequately paved and drained, were situated in courts, passages and closes. He suggested that " as in Paris " manure should be lifted weekly instead of fortnightly. As about a ton of general refuse was lifted from each court daily, he regarded the renovation of dilapidated paving to help scavenging as more important than the enforced introduction of water-closets into the houses of the poor. He also recommended that more public conveniences be put up in the courts, and that water and gas must be introduced, common stairs cleaned, and necessary repairs effected. He advised too that the number of persons in each apartment be limited, that houses be lowered in height (an idea since invalidated with the advent of the lift), and that tenements in a ruinous condition be removed.

As a consequence of Dr. Littlejohn's report sanitary inspectors were appointed who, along with the Medical Officer of Health, became instruments in the prevention and control of infectious diseases and the abatement of practices prejudicial to health.

A social step below those who lived in their own rooms or " single ends " were those who lived in furnished lodgings. Whole tenements were

[1] Some authorities assert that the Lawnmarket sold *land* produce (pronounced laun' in the old Scots way). It may be that the Lawnmarket sold both.

given over to this form of accommodation. Slum landlords could be past masters at extorting the weekly rent, and one good lady had the habit of instantly removing the bed-clothes when the four and sixpence or six shillings were not forthcoming. Many tenants were hard put to save even this, but in any case many rooms were no better than damp, draughty, leaky, stinking, disease-ridden hovels. Not all landlords were to blame for the conditions of the houses, for some did try to do their property up. But their tenants had come to regard it as proper to break up fittings and furnishings for firewood when necessary, so there was not much encouragement.

Common Lodging Houses, which are still with us today, were the third form of living quarters open to the poor. The pattern of the lodging house was simple: beyond the cash desk on the ground-floor was a kitchen where the lodgers cooked and ate round a common fire, talked and lounged. Here too they might carouse of an evening in a sad attempt to forget their miserable surroundings. Upstairs were bedrooms and dormitories for any number from two to 40 or more. There was no privacy when commonly two or three married couples and their children occupied one room. The lodging houses sheltered the unfortunate—tramps, beggars and even criminals.

Finally there were the homeless, who were to be found any night sleeping on stairs, in passages or in cellars. They were numbered in hundreds. They favoured particularly the upper stairs and passages, which in old Edinburgh tenements are usually made of wood and are therefore warmer than the stone flags below. Condemned dwellings were also a popular night resort.

A photograph of a Bread and Potato Store at this time shows a card in the window giving whisky prices. Drink was a common escape from sordid reality; and in those days it had a great hold over the poorer people, with ravaging effects. Methylated spirits, known as " Blue Biddy " or " Dynamite," was often drunk when dearer liquors could not be got or by those who had come to prefer it. The raising of the price of whisky during the 1914 war and the Methylated Spirits Act just after, by which all methylated spirits for public use had to be rendered unpalatable, helped to stem the flood of drinking in the area.

A NEW OUTLOOK

" Do you wonder Edinburgh is renowned for its medical schools? " was Patrick Geddes' caustic remark on this fearsome situation which was still the state of the High Street and Lawnmarket at the turn of this century and later still.

But changes were on the way, however slowly. The first real burst of interest in re-housing had come in the 1860s, and a second in the '90s, though it has been said of the houses then built in Edinburgh that many of the rich men's houses were built by bad architects and poor men's by no architects at all; and there was a tendency among those who were concerned with slum clearances in Edinburgh to have had good will without much vision. Patrick Geddes was an exception. A brilliant naturalist, and a pioneer in sociology and civic experiment, Geddes lived in Edinburgh at the turn of the century. As a young man he had not only been among the founders of the Edinburgh Social Union in the '80s but he and his wife had moved from Princes Street to James's Court off the Lawnmarket. It was not a tempting step at the time.

Starting with very little in the way of capital, he first renovated property in Mound Place where he founded a University Hall, and later did the same in Riddle's Court and Blackie House. There had been no official " digs " for students, all of whom had to fend for themselves, and the halls that Geddes founded were in their turn independent of the University. In nine years he took over and either reconditioned or built four University Halls, 85 apartments for working people, and a number of shops. Being a prophet in his own country he made some lasting enemies, but by the time the Town and Gown Association Limited was formed in 1896 to relieve him of the management of his house property—the total value came to over £66,000—" he had managed to improve a pretty extensive neighbourhood; he had tackled the work of a philanthropist with the skill and daring of a financial adventurer; he had fought the power of Mammon with some of its own weapons, and scored a significant victory." It is largely due to Patrick Geddes' work at this time that so many interesting buildings in the Lawnmarket have survived.

The gradual social change wrought in the area since those days and in other poor quarters in Edinburgh is a study in itself, as the footnote shows.[1] By contrast, in 1956 the Royal Mile and Lawnmarket Social and Welfare Clubs had to give up for lack of attendance; and as any resident of the Old Town will confirm, there is no comparison between the well-fed, well-clothed bairns of today and the barefoot hungry waifs of yesterday.

PRESENT DAY PROBLEMS

At present the population of the Lawnmarket, High Street and the adjoining West Bow numbers some 1,500 adults, and is decreasing. Between the wars some 5,000 people left central Edinburgh for housing schemes on the outskirts of the city, and the process continues. We saw earlier how between the Censuses of 1951 and 1961 the population of the Holyrood Ward of the city, which included the Canongate as its most populous area, had decreased by 6,010. But the decrease of 6,177 in the St. Giles Ward which has the High Street and the Lawnmarket as its

[1] It was in 1876 that a social club called " The Holly Tree " was founded beside Baxter's Close to give local boys a cheerful place to spend their evenings. Between 350 and 400 used to visit its five-roomed premises every day. Then there was the Carrubbers Close Mission and the Salvation Army which had its Edinburgh beginnings in the High Street. The Mechanics' Institute ran a well-stocked library in Baillie MacMorran's House before the City Library existed, and the Working Men's Club and Institute also had a reading-room. Elsie Inglis founded her hospice for midwifery in the High Street in 1904. The first Health Visitor volunteered in 1908; a Toddler's Playground was opened in the Pleasance in 1915 and others in various premises in the High Street afterwards; St. Anne's Roman Catholic School opened in 1917. The Housing Trust was founded by Mrs. Somervill; in the 1920s mothers could attend cooking lessons given by Miss Gilmore, using one pan and a biscuit barrel for oven; and in 1933 came a new Housing Act, and the appointment of the first Child Welfare Officer.

centre, was even greater. So the last chemist in the Lawnmarket has gone. A Lawnmarket pieman and grocer have also left to follow the shift in population. The only remaining Lawnmarket butcher in 1963 had been there for 32 years, and but for the fact that his old customers came back from the housing estates at weekends to buy their meat from him, the recent exodus would have seen him ruined. He is gone now, his place taken by yet another fancy tartan shop. Then again, before the 1939 war there were three bakers, one in Deacon Brodie's Close employing seven men. Today there are none the whole length of the Lawnmarket and High Street. There are still however some grocers.

The continuing policy of the Corporation has been to clear the centre of the city, originally to reduce the population density and now to make the centre a municipal, cultural, commercial and educational enclave. Much of the area is in fact in dry dock at the moment, awaiting refitting as administrative and commercial offices, community centres and museums.

In the '30s there was much outcry for the preservation of old houses in the High Street; and in the plans drawn up for the Royal Mile by the City Architect at the end of the last war he not only deprecated senseless demolition, but while advocating a long-term proposal to convert the building area for different use, stipulated that interesting buildings should be allowed to remain.

That interesting buildings should be allowed to remain is indeed important. Nonetheless, in the writer's view, it is hard to understand the enthusiasm for clearing out the population of a locality in order to put buildings which stand together all to similar uses, thus stratifying an area and in this case pickling the heart of the city. Let judges rub shoulders with bookies when taking a short cut through a close, and lawyers rescue little boys from communal court dustbins. There is no particular reason why the Sheriff Court should stand among other buildings of a mausoleum type, or why town councillors should be divorced from the sort of teeming crowd they represent.

On the face of it, then, the High Street and Lawnmarket is a becoming part of the town, and a great stravaiging place for visitors even in its slummiest days. Looking down from St. Giles to the green foreshore of the Firth of Forth, and often into a haar, one gets the impression that the houses are falling away down the hill with only the upstanding steeple of the Tron Kirk to hold them back. From either side some 50 closes lead through lime-washed pends. Some lead on to a stairway or two, others into courts overlooked by windows and overhung by washing dangling above endlessly playing children. Some are marvellous places, others are dark and dirty, and though all are playgrounds in most the paving is broken up. But many provide excellent short-cuts for the pedestrian, and all are quiet places where neighbours can meet and talk and children can play, safe from the traffic and sheltered from the Edinburgh winds.

In the Lawnmarket–High Street area there are six churches whose denominations range from the Church of Scotland and the Episcopal Church to the Free Kirk and the Roman Catholic Church. But the Tron

Parish has been transferred to Moredun, the kirk itself is shut up, and both steeple and 17th century kirk, in the middle 1960s, were in danger of being demolished. There are five libraries, the Court of Session, the City Chambers, the Sheriff Court, the Police Courts, a Further Education Centre and the Midlothian County Council Buildings. But unlike the Canongate with its breweries there are few local industries in this area. A small ice-cream factory in the West Bow (just off the Lawnmarket) employed five men in 1963; and, they said, " the bosses work too." There is a blacksmith's forge in James's Court, and Hewit's Tannery has been at work in the High Street for more than 160 years. Until 1959 Alexander Ferguson's famous Edinburgh Rock factory and shop occupied the building which forms the south-west corner between the Lawnmarket and George IV Bridge, having been there since 1836; but now they have left even the shop at the corner, known to generations as " Sweetie Ferguson's".

The Lawnmarket especially has always been self-contained. Two hundred years ago a large number of its inhabitants formed themselves into a club, and were described as being " a dram-drinking, news-mongering, facetious set of citizens". Whether or not this is a fair description, the fact of the matter is that Lawnmarket people are proud of being distinctive. To have been born and brought up in the Lawnmarket is quite a different thing from having been reared 200 yards further down the road. Overheard recently in a Lawnmarket shop was the remark of a Grassmarket " scaffie ":

> " Are ye gaun tae the Butcher's ball tonight, Dauvid? "
> " I beg your pardon? "
> " Och, ye and yer Lawnmarket ' beg your Pardon! ' "

Until the first World War Castle Hill and Lawnmarket were much populated by regimental families, some with perhaps as many as six sons in the same regiment; and as the military burying ground was in the Canongate churchyard, a soldier might begin and end his career in the Royal Mile, so often the scene of military junketings and regimental send-offs. But although this changed with the withdrawal of the full regiment when Redford Barracks were built, and later still when new headquarters were found for Scottish Command, some of the old connection remains.

As with the Canongate, the High Street–Lawnmarket stretch of the Royal Mile has reached a period of transition. It is perhaps a truism to say that to erect large car-parks, enormous commercial buildings and office blocks on the site of what has previously been residential housing or public gardens in the centre of a town is not conducive to the well-being and vitality of the town. Unfortunately this is a truth which few with authority in towns will care to face. We need to look west across the Atlantic to find cities where this policy of allowing commerce and motor transport to set the pattern has been brought to its ultimate desolate conclusion. Los Angeles, now a city twenty-five times the area of Edinburgh, would cover the whole of Central Scotland: two-thirds of its central area is asphalt and one third multi-story office blocks. But looking east to the continent, in Germany and Italy one may find towns in which the new building has not been carried out at the expense of the old, and old populations have not been ousted. Edinburgh certainly seems to have reached a point where it is faced with the choice, either to follow London and Los Angeles in creating a conurbation of commuters, or to start seriously on the more comprehending task of maintaining the city that is Edinburgh, while developing it wisely.

AT CLOSER QUARTERS

Starting down the Royal Mile from the Castle Esplanade one passes, on the left, Ramsay Gardens, that distinctive block of buildings built around Allan Ramsay's " goose-pie " house by Patrick Geddes. On the right stands Cannon-Ball House, so miscalled because of the lump of lead stuck in the wall by the German Engineer Peter Brusche, in 1609, to show the Corporation the height of the Pentland wells from which he hoped to bring water to a city reservoir on Castle Hill. To the left again is the reservoir which still helps to supply the city. Opposite, in Boswell's Court, lived the family of General Sir David Baird, hero of Seringapatam, who as a boy threw cabbage stalks at the chimney vents of the Grassmarket—a practice not entirely unknown today. Below Ramsay Lane stands the Outlook Tower with its Camera Obscura (described later) which was once the town residence of the Lairds of Cockpen. Then comes Semple's Close which is empty and barred-up and has a small deserted tenement at the back.

The Lawnmarket is dominated by Pugin's spire of Tolbooth St. John's, the largest spire in Scotland. On Festival evenings there is often a grand mêlée at this corner when the theatrical audience issues from the back exit of the Assembly Hall to mingle with the crowds coming from the Tattoo: troops, pipe bands, Spahis on Arab stallions perhaps, or Turkish soldiers, or French Cavalry silver-helmeted and red-plumed. Here once stood the palace of Mary of Guise, replaced in 1846 by New College.

Mylne's Court, built in 1690, was the first attempt to substitute an open square for the narrow closes. Its elegant front land is still inhabited and the ground floor houses tartan and antique shops. A northerly land dating from 1590 looms high over the Mound and is one of the most kenspeckle features of that approach. It has been empty for the last seven years and is in a bad state of repair; its windows have been smashed despite the barbed-wire entanglement surrounding, which makes the place look much like a prisoner-of-war camp. Strangely contrasting are the two elegant 17th century stairways, their iron banisters bowed to let ladies' crinolines pass.

In James's Court lived James Boswell, David Hume, and later Patrick Geddes. Two blocks of flats built by Geddes protrude into the court; they were designed for their confined site so as to let the light into all windows from east or west and give each family a sheltered balcony for children and for washing. Until recently Mylne's Court and James's Court between them have housed the majority of Lawnmarket folk. The north lands of James's Court house the Law Society's Offices and the Free Kirk Library, but in the residential part there are only three families left. The south lands are well-occupied; this is a pattern which repeats itself in most of the courts and closes down this side of the High Street. The Traverse Theatre is reached through the first entry to James's Court, and within the last year a Chinese Restaurant has opened between the theatre and the blacksmith's forge.

Nearby J. and R. Glen, bagpipe makers since early last century provide an example of the fascination to be had in a shop which has not changed. But Lady Stair's House, now a museum, is a sad example of how a beautiful old Scottish house could be restored in Victorian times with more energy than historical learning or taste. A few years ago the Duke of Hamilton bought Blackie House and modernised it to provide six flats for people with higher incomes. Its red-washed wall makes a cheerful splash of colour in Lady Stair's Close.

The broad stone gable-end at the corner of Bank Street is now spruce and smart, the property having recently been converted by the Corporation into 18 flats. Beside it are three blocks of flats built by Geddes. At this part of the Royal Mile two forestairs lead from street level to first floor. One of these is an entry to Gladstone's Land, a house built about 1631 by Thomas Gladstone, a merchant ancestor of the great Prime Minister, and now the headquarters of the Saltire Society.

Opposite, some numbered Lawnmarket houses, first renovated for housing by Geddes, have recently been modernised to make the Lothians and Peebles Police Headquarters; they turn two charming fronts, one of stone and one harled, to the street. A masonic lodge has its home in Brodie's Close, where the notorious Deacon himself once lived.

The building beyond the newly reconstructed Scottish Central Library has just been converted into nine modern flats, with entrance balconies to the south. " There was a rush to get these flats; for strange to say people like living in this part of the town," was a surprised Assessor's remark. But the weekly rent has naturally increased six-fold from that formerly paid by tenants.

Behind the renovated land is Riddle's Court, where James VI and his queen banqueted " with great solemnity and merriness." It served for the first few years of the Edinburgh Festival as theatre for the Oxford and Cambridge Players whose success was no doubt partly due to this unique setting. Many will remember the lively Shakespearian performances enacted on its small stage, and the cocoa served in the inner courtyard by candle and by starlight. *Vivendo Discimus* is the Geddesian motto carved over the courtyard arch (*By Living We Learn*); but subsequently it passed into the hands of the Department of Education and beyond a few exhibitions there was little life about the court for a long time. It has now been restored by the Corporation as an educational centre.

At the Upper Bow corner stood one of the finest specimens of wooden-fronted houses, dating from 1540. It was demolished in 1878, having been so massively built that it had to be blown up. Nelson's the publishers had their first premises here, and still use a picture of the house as their colophon; the Victorian housing which took its place is still residential.

THE WEST BOW

Once even more steep and twisted than it is today the West Bow, which joins the Grassmarket and Cowgate in the lower town with the Lawnmarket, was reconstructed in Victorian days. But it still retains at its foot a group of 16th century houses, partly empty, which form one of the best groups of old street architecture in Scotland. Once the West Bow was both an entry to the city for Royalty and the way out for criminals being taken to the Grassmarket. The shop of William Bell the cordage dealer is the one which provided the rope which hung Captain Porteous on the night he was lynched.

Most of the shops in the West Bow are old, and include a cord and moleskin shop, three scales merchants, two brushmakers, welders, tool-merchants and ironmongers where lamps, oils and other drysalteries may be sold, or not as the case may be: in some shops an independent line is taken, quite unaffected by modern ideas of salesmanship. For example: " And if ye can't make that work, well . . . I've misjudged ye." There is also a shop which still sells horn and woodware—commonplace utensils in every working class home less than a century ago and now something of a fashionable novelty.

When the West Bow was rebuilt the north side was arcaded. Along the Upper Bow Walk the buildings provide quarters for an imposing string of fraternities—the Freemason's Hall, the Scout Headquarters, and the Boys' Brigade Centre. The east corner block with its arcading and upper walk is a fine example of 19th century building and street planning: it is unfortunate to learn, as these words are written, that it may be demolished.

On the south side what was built as St. John's Established Church now houses a big firm of book-makers. Above this are the India Buildings, chiefly headquarters for municipal affairs and societies and one or two wholesale stores. On the other side of George IV Bridge stand the Midlothian County Council Buildings.

The new Sheriff Court on the island site was built in the 1930s, and took the place of many old tenements and closes; which meant of course the evacuation of a good proportion of the Lawnmarket population. People still talk of the places that vanished with them, and tell of the removal of tons of oyster shells embedded in a close where a popular oyster tavern had stood. Until a few years ago there lived an old lady in the Lawnmarket who remembered as a small girl of three being held up by her nurse as a treat to see the hanging of George Bryce the Ratho murderer, opposite the Sheriff Court. That was in 1864, and he was the last man to be publicly hanged in Edinburgh.

In Parliament Square, as we saw, are the Law Courts, including Parliament Hall, with its hammer beam ceiling, and the Signet Library built in the early 19th century by Stark, two long pillared halls of beautiful proportions. " A Paradise of bokes," wrote Dibden in his *Northern Tour*, " and if Edinburgh produce not a genuine breed of all that is good and gracious in boke-lore, the fault must not be laid at the doors of those to whome this magnificent and richly furnished library is entrusted." It was nearby in Creech's Land that in the 18th century Allan Ramsay founded the first circulating library in Scotland.

Beyond St. Giles stands the new Mercat Cross, from which public proclamations are read. The old Mercat Cross of 1617 used to stand in front of the present headquarters of the City Police, and saw many notable hangings and executions during that century. This part of the High Street below St. Giles was completely gutted in the great fire of 1824 and the present police court buildings were then constructed.

For many years before being moved to headquarters at Lauriston the Fire Brigade kept their primitive engine at the head of Old Fish Market Close; at the cry of " Fire! " ropes were seized and the cumbersome thing was dragged to the scene. Later on horses were introduced, and a sloping gangway gave them access to the High Street. Old Fish Market Close was also the home of the City Hangman, and hereabouts were the Penny Waxworks, and the premises of the Night Asylum and Strangers Friendly Society. The Close now boasts a " beat " coffee-bar.

The Cross Post Office has recently been moved to 136 High Street. Below are some decent buildings incorporating several restaurants: the corner shop, Hyam's, was the first Jewish establishment in Edinburgh to start in business. In Hunter Square, with its pleasant matching façades, the Royal Bank of Scotland occupies the old Merchants' Hall. Blair Street until recently afforded second class housing, but has been evacuated. However, one has recently become a men's boarding house, and presents a far less formidable aspect than some in the Grassmarket. No. 15, a forlorn building, is architecturally notable. Further down the hill are the premises of MacNiven and Cameron, long-established manufacturers of pen-nibs: " They come as a boon and a blessing to men, The Pickwick, the Owl and the Waverley Pen." The fate of the Tron Kirk, which has its original hammerbeam ceiling was still undecided in 1965.

Between the Tron Kirk and St. Giles four of the closes lead into Tron Square, which contains one of the earliest town-plan housing schemes in Britain. Built in 1897, it consists of four four-storey blocks of flats, one below the other on the hill and separated by three plateau-like playgrounds or washing areas. All around stand gaunt and crumbling backs of older houses, many in disrepair, and therefore a sad-looking place to live in, besides being what sociologists call a " problem area ": a murder took place here a few years ago. On the first court is the Toddlers' Playground, descendant of the one first founded in the Pleasance in 1915. Here very small children swing or see-saw or stalk unruffled pigeons.

In the prim Victorian St. Giles Street by the Sheriff Court are the premises of the Youth Employment Service, the Schools Museum Service, the City Education Department, and a firm of law publishers.

Advocate's Close got its name from the last Lord Advocate in office at the time of the Restoration, the Revolution and the Union. Though most of the Close has been demolished it still has a fine hexagonal stair tower and two old door-ways, one graved *Blisset Be God of Al His Giftis* on the lintel, and the other *Spes Altera Vitae* 1590 (Another Hope of Life). All around are parts of deserted empty 16th century houses.

The new City Chambers erected in the 1930s occupy a site once the centre of club and tavern life in old Edinburgh. Over the street was the Cross and there the literati and genius of Edinburgh assembled. In Craig's Close was the famous Isle of Man Tavern patronised by Robert Fergusson, Raeburn, Alexander Runciman and Deacon Brodie, and here *The Scotsman* once had its offices. The taverns then frequented were usually down closes, and the coming of the pub into the main street is a comparatively modern innovation, and one that needs a further word of explanation here.

Pubs in the High Street today—there are more than a dozen—are often so full they have been described as " drinking dens " by shocked English visitors. But this judgment is not entirely fair. They are warm and light places which many houses around them are not. Moreover, the pubs are patronised not only by local residents, but by people from the housing schemes on the city outskirts, where not many licences have been granted. These come in to foregather with friends, or stop for a drink on their way home from work, especially on pay nights. Another convivial sign, perhaps with the same cause, is the return of the eating house to the High Street.

But the tavern in the closes has gone, and not only the taverns. Altogether by the 1930s life in the closes had undergone a revolution, or as some veterans would have said an extinction. The City Chambers' extensions on either side of the stately Royal Exchange buildings wiped away half a dozen closes. Anchor Close, once the busiest in the city, is now an empty-like place, though the Anchor Ballroom and an R.A.F.A. Club are there. By Geddes Entry a well-established firm of pawn-brokers have had premises since 1824; the Entry itself is centuries older still, but is now barred by a dust-bin and much refuse.

In Old Stamp Office Close, where Flora MacDonald was once at boarding school, are the Polio Vaccination Centre, a Child Welfare Clinic, and a café. Off Flesh Market Close Henry Dundas, afterwards Lord Melville, had rooms when he first began to practise as an advocate; here too William Creech started business as a bookseller.

Cockburn Street, which cuts behind this part of the High Street, was completed in 1859. Solidly Victorian and prosperously commercial, Cockburn Street has a pleasant air of security about it. The houses show a great range of gothic imagination on the part of their architect, yet seem all of a piece in their street and there is something rather fine about it.

Climbing up again, we find one or two not very convincingly palazzo-like but prosperous commercial buildings. In Carrubbers Close beyond stands Old St. Paul's Episcopal Church, founded in 1689 after the expulsion of the congregation from St. Giles, and a stronghold of the Jacobite cause during the '15 and '45 risings. In an old building with a small gable facing the street is a tool shop, " Tommy a' thing," well-established since 1834. Below are two Victorian tenements and then Heave Awa' House, the little low elevation which took the place of the famous tenement which collapsed in 1861 and led to the Littlejohn reforms.

A very pleasant house is the one taken over by a sewing and knitting machine company. Then comes Moubray House and a well-known antique shop, and the popularly visited John Knox's House. Some however think it is more likely to have been the house of James Mossman, Mary Queen of Scots' jeweller. The Moray Knox Church and the Art Centre in its back premises were being demolished in 1966. The last two tenements on this side are Victorian and still residential, and here a launderette has recently been opened, a boon to people from up and down the High Street, though until it closed recently, the old-fashioned Public Wash-House farther up the street still drew a great throng.

Of the closes in this stretch of the street perhaps the pleasantest is Bailie Fyfe's, where an attractive early 18th century tenement with open stair windows looks north to the Calton Hill. Though many of the houses degenerated into unseemly slums some closes held out bravely. A few have kept their names for centuries, North Gray's Close taking its name from a burgess who lived there more than four and a half centuries ago.

At the foot of Niddry Street stands St. Cecilia's Hall, designed by Robert Mylne in 1763 as a concert hall for the Musical Society of Edinburgh. Its varied fortunes have even seen it used as a dance-hall, but recently it was purchased by the University for use partly as a museum for a collection of clavichords and harpsichords, and partly as the concert room it used to be.

Between Niddrie's Wynd and Black Friar's stand several fine 18th century lands, some as many as seven stories high. Though not irreparable they have been empty for some years and at the time of writing are being demolished.

In a block of Victorian housing, No. 13 in Blackfriar's Street, lived Margaret Sinclair, the Scots factory girl whose cause for beatification has gone forward to the Holy See in Rome. Born in 1900, her home was in this street for almost the whole of her life; she died in 1925. The house of the infamous Regent Morton still stands here; and though much altered it still has a round stair tower and an interesting entrance door. Also entered from Blackfriars Street is St. Anne's R.C. School, a fine old L-plan building. It was here that Dr. Guthrie founded his famous " ragged school " in 1847.

Beyond four Victorian tenements, another two empty unrenovated lands are in process of demolition, including shops and South Gray's or Public Wash-house Close. This last was a throughway to St. Patrick's R.C. Church, built as an Episcopal chapel in 1774 and bought by the Catholics in 1856.

Fountain Close, a dark place barred with an iron gate, presents a miserable aspect. Next to it is what was once the New Palace Cinema, until a few years ago the most old-fashioned cinema in Edinburgh. Now it is the Hong Kong Chinese Restaurant and its entrance is gaily painted.

There is a fine old tenement above Tweeddale Court. Every court and close in the Royal Mile differs in character, and somewhat in upkeep, but Tweeddale Court is in very good condition, for Oliver and Boyd the publishers have had their premises here since 1806. There is also in the Court an old tenement with flats which were renovated before the war and two other tenements in quite good condition and fully occupied. So the whole court is usefully inhabited.

Finally we come to World's End Close. It is a sad place and its paving is not in good order, and here again is the by now familiar sight of empty broken windows and wreathes of barbed wire: yet it is made gay with chirping sparrows nesting in the rhones, and the occasional bright face of a child.

THE CHILDREN AT PLAY

Before the war the children of the closes used to earn an honest penny by chanting the Old Town's history to the tourists . . . " Yon's the hoose whaur Baillie MacMorran wis murdered, mister." They no longer need to do this, some having enough pocket money to shock the local sweetie-shop keepers, who come of a cannier generation.

Diminutive shades of robust ghosts, the children still fight with swords (wooden), parrying, attacking, slashing, bleeding, retreating up the Grassmarket steps, or hurtling down them on tin trays. In winter good sport is to be had from the Castle esplanade by throwing snow-balls at the passers-by below. Until very recently it was the custom on 5th November and 25th May to build enormous bonfires in the courts and closes. These looked like revolution barricades made up of old tables, chairs and a thousand other cast-off things. But in 1961 the Corporation decided against such celebrations, and since then all bonfire material has been systematically taken away by municipal dustmen, if it can be found. Before that—in 1959—the children had set fire to the Castle Rock, where the grass at the time was as dry as tinder. It was a great success. The fire-brigade had to be called in, and while some firemen with hose-pipes squirted from below, others hung out of the castle windows hosing from above, while the children sat in a delighted row watching. Of course they did it again. But this time more drastic measures were taken; spiked iron railings were replaced along the bottom of the castle bank, though these have never been an insurmountable barrier to Lawnmarket and High Street bairns. What with courts and closes, Castle, Queen's Park, the slopes of Arthur's Seat and Salisbury Crags, the Vennel and Princes Street Gardens, central Edinburgh has superlative attractions for city children.

SOCIAL PROBLEMS

But the predominant picture in the Lawnmarket and High Street is now that of an ageing population; for the younger people with families go out to new houses on the outskirts, and this in itself creates a problem, since it means that many old people are left alone. However, at weekends the

High Street teems with children come to see their grand-parents, while their parents do the shopping and meet friends. But the fact remains that if an old person gets ill it is no longer a case of sending down to St. Mary's Wynd or up to St. Leonard's for one of the family, nor is it easy for a daughter living perhaps three miles away and not on a bus route to call in, cook, clean up and then rush home to get supper for her husband and children.

As young families leave the High Street their place is often taken by other young families, a floating population waiting to get into new houses themselves. But a community cannot be built out of passengers. Indeed, no-one would advise them to stay, considering the condition and size of some of the flats. But a basic social problem remains for both the housing estate dwellers and the folk so many of them have left behind in the Old Town.

With regard to the housing estates on the city outskirts, Community Centres and the activities of the Women's Institutes or the Citizen's Associations, no matter how laudable, are not in the end a good enough substitute for truly local shops, pubs, hospitals, churches and schools, for which not enough allowance has been made in the new housing schemes, though it is said that this is improving. There the shops are few and consequently expensive, as are the visiting vans; and economically it is often far more worth a housewife's while to take a bus into the High Street, which she knows, make her purchases, and travel back again. So clearly the problems of the new housing schemes have a direct bearing on the state of the centre of the city, and vice versa.

However, space unfortunately does not allow us to look into the many social consequences of separating families who have been neighbours or lived in the same locality for many years, sometimes generations. But it is certainly not true that everyone wants to get out of the centre of the city. When people are asked if they want to get out, the answer is usually "yes" because the new houses with the amenities they want are all on the outskirts. Once out and asked if they would like to return to the centre, they again answer "yes," because they long to get back to their old intimate life, and for many there are financial reasons as well.

THE COWGATE AND THE GRASSMARKET

Down a steep descent from the Royal Mile lie the Grassmarket and its neighbour the Cowgate. Both are peopled with ghosts from the centuries, and both are being utterly changed. Yet indefinably some of the spirit of the past is being preserved while the reconstruction of these ancient places goes on.

Here, after all, more so than in the most desolate section of the Royal Mile itself, were the homes of the ragged, despondent poor. Shunned by respectable citizens, the Cowgate and the Grassmarket were gathering places for the community's outcasts; places where evil prospered and the police patrolled in twos and threes. But that is an ugly dream of the past.

The dark, evil-smelling closes and pends, the grossly overcrowded, crumbling tenements and the noisy throngs are gone, and certainly the Cowgate has almost become an academic grove—but without as yet the erection of many new buildings to replace the old.

In 1963, in fact, the only example of new building in either street was the tall extension made in the Cowgate to the rear of the Heriot–Watt Engineering College. Elsewhere, wisely, the decision has been to demolish slums, leaving the vast spaces so created open to sunshine and air, and retaining only those buildings in reasonably sound condition. As the result of this few residents now remain in the Cowgate and Grassmarket, and their formerly congested pavements carry only the occasional pedestrian.

Many buildings of utility or historical importance remain of course. In the Cowgate there are the Magdalene Chapel (founded in 1547), which is certainly one of the most important of the city's historic buildings since it contains the only important pre-Reformation stained glass in Scotland, and beside it the premises of the Edinburgh Medical Missionary Society which were opened in 1848 as a dispensary commemorating David Livingstone. But Livingstone House has grown since then and is now the headquarters of two pioneering ventures that are arousing keen interest throughout the United Kingdom and overseas. These are the Family Doctor Centre, operated under the auspices of the Department of Health for Scotland, and the General Practice Unit of Edinburgh University.

In the Grassmarket a paradoxical symbol of the human regeneration effected there recently can be found in The Grassmarket Mission. This undenominational organisation was established in 1886 to work among the poor of the district, and has a notable record of public service. But the poor and the " down and outs " are now much fewer; for the Mission's adherent, on the whole, has moved up the social scale. It nevertheless continues to be part of the local tradition, and so an encouraging number of families now resident in distant housing schemes remain in membership, with the children attending the Sunday school classes and other gatherings that were patronised by their parents.

On the other side of this spacious thoroughfare, there stands the Mine Rescue Station of the Heriot–Watt College. Here teams of colliery workers from a wide area are trained in the techniques of rescue work. There is change too in the old Corn Exchange. This was once the scene of important political meetings, social gatherings, flower shows and charity fetes but has entered on a new career of usefulness as an extension of the Heriot–Watt *University* as the College now is.

But some of the old tradition remains. In an area where there were good eating houses in the 18th century—with oysters drawn from the Forth—there is the Beehive restaurant now. And yet another link with the life of former days is to be found in the Carriers' Quarters at the western end of the thoroughfare. Here are collected goods going out to the country districts. But the horsedrawn vehicles of former days have given way to high-powered motor transport; and, where over the years the traders pitched their stalls in the centre of the wide street, tall graceful trees now spread their branches as further symbols of changing times.

THE NEW TOWN

We have already seen how the revolutionary concept of the New Town replaced—for the well-to-do—the extraordinary pattern of the Old Town and provided instead long terraces of substantial town houses, each with a basement accommodating staff, kitchen and wine cellars, and a short back garden which housed the game cupboard. At the foot of the garden was either a small coach house or a stable, or both. On the ground floor of most of these houses, apart that is from the entrance hall, were the dining-room and pantry; the first floor usually consisted of a large L-shaped drawing room (in Heriot Row and Regent Terrace the two sides of the L may each be 30 feet long) and one retiring room; the second storey housed bedrooms, and the third storey bedrooms and nursery.

Sweeping changes, however, have taken place since the New Town was so symmetrically laid out. The splendid 18th century façades of the squares and crescents, and the long imposing terraced streets, are on the outside what they were; but the interior life of the great stone houses has changed profoundly in the last few decades.

As late as the end of last century a child of the leisured class in the New Town grew up in surroundings of solid security with furnishing to match and often lavish entertaining. One writer[1] remembers how " the interiors of all those imposing Georgian and Regency houses had a dreary similarity," and also how " the upper and middle classes were divided up into sets and cliques more sharply defined than anywhere else in the country and to an extent quite unknown today. Even the members of the Bar and of the Society of Writers to the Signet were portioned up into exclusive groups according to their social background. Everyone knew where they belonged."

Recollections of a similar way of life in the New Town, but regarded from a different point of view, come from an old lady of over 90,[2] who remembers how at the frequent dinner parties in her childhood home a glittering galaxy of glasses, pale green and deep ruby, would be laid out on the long damask tablecloth around the silver épergne piled high with grapes, tall crystal dishes of crystallised fruits, and specimen glasses each holding one spray of maidenhair fern and one bloom of scarlet geranium. The hostess would probably be dressed in black silk with a cap of white net and lace, adorned by a brooch of garnets and with a long gold chain attached to a watch set with pearls tucked into her belt; while the small daughter of the house would feel stiff and uncomfortable in a new black velvet frock with starchy frilling at the neck and wrists known as *mourning* frilling. There would be a great play with fans by the ladies, and the gentlemen wore lavender gloves.

Today there are still upper-middle class edifices in the New Town, delightful dinner and cocktail parties and considerable comfort. But the

[1] Dr. Charles L. Warr in *The Glimmering Landscape*, Hodder and Stoughton, 1960.

[2] Eleanor Sillar in *Edinburgh's Child*. Oliver and Boyd, 1961.

residential accommodation has diminished as many old-time residents have moved out to the suburbs and businesses or administrative offices have moved in, while many of the terraced houses have been converted into flats.

Thus today, apart from hotel and club accommodation and an occasional attic flat, there is virtually no residential accommodation in Princes Street, George Street and Queen Street, nor in the smaller streets between. None of the original domestic frontage of Princes Street remains, though in George Street the shop fronts are still held partly at bay by public buildings like the Royal Society of Edinburgh, St. Andrew's Church and the Assembly Rooms. Queen Street, apart from the few alterations made to its frontage 50 years ago, remains almost entirely as it was designed, but is given over to offices. There are no hotels; its windows face gardens but look north; no clubs have prospered there; and only a few shop fronts have crept round the corners of Hanover Street and Frederick Street. These last two retain between them some half dozen of the original front doors, which now seem out of place. Their continuations, Dundas Street and Howe Street, originally designed as terraces of flats, are still, above the ground floor shops, almost completely residential and architecturally unaltered. But the frontages of the shops have a great diversity of design.

St. Andrew Square, the richest square in Edinburgh and indeed one of the richest in Britain, exhibits an equal diversity of styles in building. On the east side the town house built by Sir William Chambers—now the Royal Bank of Scotland—and its flanking buildings remain; on the north side the shapes of six of the original domestic fronts can be seen, and these include the house in which Henry Brougham was born in 1778; but that is all. On the south-west corner, the house in which David Hume spent his last years happy with fame and his own cooking was replaced with a new office block not long ago.

Charlotte Square, on the other hand, has changed from domestic to commercial life without altering its architectural face. But the roadway has been cambered and canted like a race track so that the motorist may speed on his way to Queensferry Street (now virtually all shops) or by the unchanged frontages of Ainslie Place and Randolph Crescent, Melville Street and Crescent, to Coates or Atholl Crescents.

While frontages remain unchanged one can only estimate the extent to which the New Town remains residential. The following recent survey, although carried out by no more penetrating a method than laborious door-plate examination in some chosen streets gives a fair picture of the present position: *See top of page 61.*

Since frequently two or more houses have been joined to make one hotel, the above totals naturally will not be the same as the house postal numbers. Furthermore, as advocates sometimes have their professional chambers within their houses, and doctors and surgeons consulting rooms, these are counted as residences. Among the many adapted premises within the bounds of the New Town there are almost a score of trade union

Street	*Still Complete house*	*Now converted into flats*	*Still Original flats*	*Now hotel*	*Offices*	*Miscel-laneous*	TOTAL
Regent Terrace	10	11	—	5	4	4	34
Carlton Terrace	6	2	—	2	3	1	14
Royal Terrace	12	3	—	13	3	2	33
Heriot Row	17	12	3	—	11	2	45
Great King St.	9	17	13	3	17	7	66
Drummond Place	5	18	10	1	—	4	38
Moray Place	2	29	9	—	10	—	50
Royal Circus	2	9	4	6	2	2	25
Northumberland St.	20	28	8	4	8	3	71

offices, numerous trade associations such as Master Blacksmiths and Master Plumbers, Institutes like the Chartered Accountants and the Educational Institute, and the offices of Incorporations such as Tailors and Architects. The unions have shown a taste for the solid, spacious dignity of Hillside Crescent where the National Union of Mineworkers, the National Union of Tailors and Garment Workers, and the Amalgamated Society of Woodworkers are to be found. The Amalgamated Engineering Union and the Building Trade Workers are side by side in nearby Blenheim Place. Round the next corner in Picardy Place is the Plumbing Trades Union, and a little to the north is the National Union of Public Employees in Albany Street. Abercrombie Place has the offices of the National Union of Printing, Bookbinding and Paper Workers, and in the same gently curving street is the Electrical Trades Union. Further west in Randolph Place is the Scottish Painters Society, and in Walker Street the Union of Shop Distributive and Allied Workers.

In 1960 a first storey flat, either a good conversion or a corner block flat within ten minutes' walk of Princes Street, could be purchased for £3,000. Three years later this price had increased by 50 per cent and was still rising in 1964. This not only reflects the increased cost of building new houses on the outskirts, but also shows the results of recent changes in living. Travel from the suburbs to the centre of the city at rush hours is more troublesome and time-consuming; the lofty rooms of the New Town are not so difficult to heat with modern methods; and the good insulation of the old buildings makes heating costs comparable with those of the new.

"There are no stars so lovely as Edinburgh street lamps," said Stevenson; and in Heriot Row where he lived, in Charlotte Square, Rutland Square and a few favoured places a good variation of the original Stevenson-period lamp design now carries a clear white electric light. The less favoured parts of the New Town are illuminated by a colour-killing but efficient sodium light set high on inelegant concrete lamp-posts, while in a few streets gas lamps splutter to their end.

ROSE STREET

If 18th century architects purposely tried to devise a street in the New Town which would give some of the Old Town emigrants a whiff or two of the past, they certainly succeeded with Rose Street, a long narrow thoroughfare just behind and almost as long as Princes Street itself.

Narrow, cobbled, congested and noisy by day with the traffic of cars and lorries plying to and from the warehouses in its supplementary lanes, Rose Street with its old taverns, its restaurants, snack bars, chic boutiques and craftsmen's shops is one of the most picturesque streets in Georgian Edinburgh, and one of the very few on the north of Edinburgh which has acquired a legend. This is, according to that legend, the Pigalle of Edinburgh, an isle of Bohemia in a waste of commerce, a little Nineveh given over six days a week after nightfall to the worship of Bacchus, Venus and the Muse of Poetry. The legend, like most legends, exaggerates; for even in its heyday in the 1920s and 30s Rose Street was never so exotic. Then as now the flats above its busy taverns and dimly lit " wee shoppies " were inhabited, for the most part, by citizens of impeccable conventionality. They lived there for the excellent reason that they were glad to find a home anywhere in a city which has suffered from a chronic housing shortage, and they deeply resented any suggestion that they lived with orgies. Statistically, too, their indignation was justified for when one looks for facts behind the legend they are surprisingly few.

Rose Street's association with artists and literateurs is actually tenuous. True, it runs close to two of the leading Edinburgh dealers in artists' supplies, but there is no record of any artist of consequence having lived in it; and its repute as a favourite haunt of poets dates from the age of radio and is not unconnected, one suspects, with the proximity of one of its most famous taverns to the B.B.C. Edinburgh studios in Queen Street and to nearby newspaper offices. More surprising still, the street's fame as a dram-drinker's paradise goes vastly beyond the facts. At the highest recorded count " The Street of a Hundred Pubs", as it has been called, could only muster 19 taverns; and today there are only five over the eight.

Rose Street began its history on the architect's drawing boards as St. David's Lane. Later it was named Rose Street as a compliment to the " Rose of England", the name Thistle Street being allocated to the corresponding narrow street between George Street and Queen Street on the reasoning that the Thistle being the hardier growth was better fitted to stand the sterner climate to the north.

Originally the street was intended to house merchants, tradesmen and those who served the quality in the more fashionable parts of the New Town, but by the beginning of this century it had become a working class enclave. Its shops, too, were tenanted by small merchants, craftsmen and artisans who required central premises but could not afford to set up shop in the fashionable thoroughfares of George Street and Princes Street.

This phase came to an end with the last war when several of its shopkeepers went out of business; and ever since rising land values and the pressure for accommodation in the city centre have greatly changed its character. Its junk shops, most of its " Johnny-awthings", its rag and bottle store, have gone as have also most of its dairies. In their place are numbers of smart little boutiques selling hats, jewellery and antiques; and there is also a proliferation of restaurants, cafes and snack bars. The population of the street has also changed in character. It has become rather chic to have a flat in Rose Street again, and as houses become vacant they are increasingly taken over by fairly well-to-do tenants.

The street nevertheless still sheltered—in 1963—in the westerly section two plumbers, a hairdresser, a milliner, a saddler, a painter and decorator, a cutler and a watchmaker. In the next section, between Castle Street and Frederick Street, there were three milliners, another painter and decorator, an electrical engineer and a wholesale electrical supplier, a shop selling cash registers, a card and gift shop, three antique shops (one devoted to jewellery), a fishmonger, a shoemaker, a purveyor of " kitchen supplies", a sweep, a betting shop and a printing establishment. The next section, going east, housed a publisher, a ladies' hairdresser, a " Men's Hire " shop, an engraver and watchmaker, and (till very recently) a stained glass window maker. In the most easterly section, there remained a milliner and a manufacturing jeweller of repute.

That Rose Street will remain a street of houses and " wee shops " for much longer is however doubtful. The greater part of the northern frontage of the most westerly section has been occupied for a long time now by the featureless wall of a telephone exchange. And elsewhere in the street not only some of Edinburgh's largest trading firms in Princes Street but banks and other commercial institutions have established a strong foothold.

CHAPTER 4

THE PORTS, SUBURBS AND VILLAGES

LEITH

Few observers are likely to contest the assertion that, in modern times, no sizeable area of population on Scotland's eastern side has undergone more physical and social change than the ancient Port of Leith. The heart of Leith, as older residents knew it, has more or less disappeared. There is a striking absence of children. Vast cleared spaces meet the eye where formerly stood crowded tenements; elsewhere, only the aged linger on in quiet streets that once resounded to the noise and bustle of active community life.

All this would seem on the face of it a tale of depressing decay, of a continuing refugee-like procession since the war of large numbers of Leith people to the newer housing schemes and suburbs of Greater Edinburgh. Bereft of its life blood Leith appeared to be doomed. Why was it, the citizens asked, that while work was proceeding apace on the rehabilitation of the Old Town there were so many signs of neglect in Leith? Why were so many derelict tenements allowed to stand so long?

The answer lay in the peculiar circumstances of the port, which were quite different from the rest of Edinburgh. The city authorities did not deny delay, but the problem, they explained, was much more complicated than was generally appreciated. One major reason was the lack of adequate local sites for rehousing those removed from such a high proportion of old properties. Leith's derelict housing, it was stressed also, was in the main already deteriorating when Edinburgh took the port over in 1920. To add to the complexity of the problem, owners of many old properties were difficult to trace, and furthermore modern development was obstructed by many very old buildings still being used by industry and commerce. All this has posed great problems.

With the electoral register listing about 40,000 citizens in the three civic wards, it is estimated that the dispersal of population has deprived Leith of some 20,000 to 25,000 men, women and children in a decade or so. That loss, inevitably, has had serious repercussions on community life. There has been, for instance, an obvious decline in the number of the younger generation, with the accompanying implication that those who might have been expected to maintain the continuity of established customs and traditions have gone for good. With most young married couples setting up house elsewhere, Leith has in fact become, for the time being but only residentially, a place of the middle-aged and the elderly. When the hooters proclaim the end of the working day in Leith, men, boys, women and girls stream from the places of industry to crowd the buses which will take them to homes several miles away.

A look at the churches and youth organisations illuminates the picture. Over this vital 10-year period nine Church of Scotland congregations have shown a decline. Certainly two have shown small increases, but these are probably accounted for by a union of congregations and the transfer of two churches to a congregation in the outer suburbs. On the other hand the old Parish Church of South Leith lost more than 500 communicants during this period, and the decreases would doubtless have been even more spectacular but for the fact that many Leith residents scattered throughout Edinburgh and the outlying suburbs have retained membership of their old churches.

There has also been an encouraging and healthy survival of local loyalties in other spheres. The Leith Battalion of the Boys' Brigade maintains a surprisingly strong hold, so that boys who have moved elsewhere with their families still retain membership and many older boys have returned to serve as officers. Equally encouragingly, the Leith Battalion, well supported by local business men, dismisses any suggestion of amalgamation with its city counterpart. The place has still a manifest sense of local pride.

When we look at the reverse of the coin, industry presents a more encouraging picture. For although the post-war years brought periods of trade recession to Leith Docks, there have, happily, been sufficient signs of an expansion that not so long ago seemed hardly possible. This has been due in great measure to the enterprise of Leith Dock Commission, whose members have never accepted the verdict " Leith is finished " even when the decline in the coal exporting trade dealt a severe blow to the docks. Instead they took imaginative steps to counteract that loss by attracting other forms of trade. As this book recounts elsewhere, Leith is being revitalised by the modernisation of dock equipment, the reclamation of land from the sea, and by the development of both old-established and new industries. As a symbol of the vast reclamation and development project, the port's Martello Tower, surrounded by the sea since Napoleonic times, is now land-locked.

" One good thing about the Leith Dock Commission's members," writes an Edinburgh journalist with close knowledge of the subject, " is that they are not content to await developments. Leading representatives make periodic journeys overseas to press Leith's claims as a modern port. Space is taken to proclaim facts and figures at the leading trade exhibitions. And so far the results have been gratifying in the volume of inquiries about sites for new industries and facilities generally."

There is a justified note of confidence about this, as we shall see. Shipbuilding though passing through the same experiences as other British yards in a highly competitive world, continues, and the yards have also turned, more recently, to other forms of work far removed from their traditional activity. Architects and builders, well aware of the craftsmanship traditional in shipyards, now place " made to measure " orders; and so Leith supplies benches, cupboards and other furniture for schools, laboratories and factories, and air-conditioning plant for public and business buildings. It also makes or repairs boilers for industrial installations. And an increasing number of business men now sit behind " executive type " desks sent out with a gleaming polish from the Victoria Yards. But, it is stressed, despite all this, " there is no intention of turning away from the sea."

Leith was, we must remember, for centuries Scotland's traditional outlet to the Low Countries, Scandinavia and the rest of Europe. And as such traditions do not lightly die we should also visit Trinity House in the Kirkgate; for with so many old and derelict areas swept away—and with so much of the rubble being used for dock reclamation work—this ancient foundation stands proud as ever to symbolise the town's association with the sea.

TRINITY HOUSE

No one can tell exactly when The Incorporation of the Masters and Assistants of the Trinity House of Leith was founded, but research by its historian, Dr. John Mason, suggests that it was probably around 1380. The House began as a charity for the relief of indigent, aged and infirm seamen, the money being collected by the levying of " twelve pennies Scots " on every ton of merchandise loaded or unloaded by Scottish ships using the port.

In due course its members began to play an increasingly influential role in the development of trade at the port, in the instigation of safety measures at sea and in harbour, and in the promotion of all matters affecting the well-being of mariners. When occasion arose, the members also made their views known on affairs over a wider field. They frequently came into conflict with Edinburgh Town Council, for instance, as we can see from the records of quite a number of lengthy disputes, mostly arising from the city's desire to secure a share of the benefits accruing to the Leith traders.

Today the Masters and Brethren of Trinity House form a select society which zealously guards its ancient privileges. Membership is restricted to ships' captains whose applications undergo strict scrutiny and the test of the ballot box. Mates, while eligible for associate membership, cannot exercise a vote or hold office. But of course the deliberations lack the policy bite of another age, for now, although it is one of the oldest trade guilds in the United Kingdom, Trinity House functions mainly as a centre dispensing benevolence to aged deserving seamen and their widows. As such, it plays an important role in the life of the port.

This then is Leith's present position. Engineering, processing plants in great variety, paint manufacturing and a host of smaller industries undeniably support the claim by Leith Chamber of Commerce that the port plays a vital part in the economy of Greater Edinburgh, and that it will do so increasingly in the years to come—like the city's other ports, of which the nearest to Leith on the Edinburgh coastline is Newhaven.

NEWHAVEN

" The village of Newhaven has had its moments. It launched the biggest ship in the world—in 1511. For centuries its name has been synonymous with ' fish.' It has led the world of fashion."

Thus wrote an author a few years ago. What then of Newhaven now? No ships are built, and the lead to fashion given by the Newhaven fishwives after the London Exhibition in the '80s of last century has not been retained. Even the name of Newhaven has today only a faint glimmer of past glories, and means little at all to the younger generation. Yet only a few years before the second World War began, the late George Blake wrote:

> The spirit of Newhaven is ultimately concentrated in the parliament of elderly gentlemen, retired mariners and the like, which convenes daily in a shelter just inside the gates of the harbour station . . . . Every one of these old men has seen more of the world than you or I are ever likely to see.

The members of this parliament followed in the footsteps of the Society of Free Fishermen of Newhaven, which for 400 years ruled the affairs of the village; and undoubtedly the elderly gentlemen settled to their satisfaction all local problems—and those of the world as well.

But by 1962 there were only four fishing boats over 40 feet and 11 under that length operating out of Newhaven, and they employed only 48 men. This was typical of the decline in small-boat fishing not only in Scotland but throughout Europe. And of course, with those small numbers, luck played an increasing part in the fluctuating fortunes of the fishermen. For example, the total value of landings at Newhaven in 1962 was £45,454 as against £17,770 in the previous year.

But in the old days, Newhaven housewives, like their men, knew their fish; while the fame of the Peacock Inn, whose fish were always " new drawn frae the Forth," spread so far beyond the village, that the present generation of Edinburgh citizens have known difficulty in finding a table in the Inn on a Saturday night. There were also the fishwives who, once their men had landed the catch, loaded up their baskets and set off for Edinburgh to sell fresh fish to the housewives of the city. Clad in voluminous skirts and petticoats, and carrying at the outset almost one hundredweight of fish, the women's cry of " Caller herrin " or sometimes " Caller ou " (" fresh oysters ") would advertise their presence. But the musical cry is seldom heard and the number of women who carry on the old routine could be counted on the fingers of one hand.

Nowadays the true, original Newhaven woman's dress is most often seen at performances by the Newhaven Fisher-girls' Choir or its sister, the Newhaven Fisher-woman's Choir whose distinctive dresses are often heirlooms, carefully handed down from generation to generation.

Away from the streets by the sea-front, Newhaven is today just another part of Edinburgh. But in the older areas you can still see the influence of Flemish architecture; and at least one Edinburgh citizen recalls, as a boy in the 1930s, a house above the cliff where two respectable ladies proudly showed him the false-backed cupboards and secret tunnel to the foreshore devised by their smuggler ancestors.

Although the youth of this Edinburgh port and suburb now tend to turn their faces from the sea to the city, almost any discussion on Newhaven inevitably returns to fish and the fisher folk. The fishmarket is still the centre of general activity, though there is a new flour mill on the edge of the basin so that ships can berth beside it, a quick-freezing plant installed by one of the fish salesmen in 1953, and other firms with workshops.

GRANTON

Wandering through Granton, another of Edinburgh's ports and one which accommodated a fleet of minesweepers during the last war, the first impression one gets is that of a city dormitory. The green fields and quiet countryside that stretched past the busy harbour to the fringes of Newhaven in the earlier part of the century are now smothered in a welter of city housing schemes—Wardieburn, Royston Mains, East Pilton and West Pilton. But a scattering of industry still gives some local employment in the area. This includes, of course, the harbour, which is tidal and has no dock gates, and the Granton gas works. Yet even these cannot dispel the sense of peace and quiet when, turning the bend in Granton Road, one looks down on the east harbour, speckled with brightly coloured yachts and little sailing dinghies lying self-composed in the sunshine, like children's toys in a large pond.

The west harbour is a different kettle of fish. Here in 1962–3 Granton's trawlers—there were 22 motor and not a single steam trawler working out of this harbour—tied up to discharge valuable cargoes of white fish; here too lay oil tankers of as much as 18,000 tons, discharging fuel at the depots of Scottish Oils and Shell Mex Limited and of the Regent Oil Company. A few years ago the biggest import handled was esparto grass for the paper-making mills of Midlothian, but now fuel oil takes first place, and esparto, timber, box-boards, wood pulp, paper, bog ore and general merchandise follow on. Exports comprise mainly coal, coke and machinery.

Various services are provided by the harbour company which is owned principally by the Duke of Buccleuch and his son, the Earl of Dalkeith. There is a floating dock that can take trawlers and coasters up to 160 feet in length; large transit sheds for handling general cargoes; weighbridges taking 42 tons rail or road traffic; a belt coal conveyor loading at a rate of 400 tons an hour; and cranes of varying power.

In 1963 improvements were being made at the west harbour. The shoreward side was being filled in, with berths alongside. A new steel face was replacing the wooden one along the south-west half of the Middle Pier to give another berth for trawlers. At one time these ships were landing almost half a million hundredweights of fish a year at Granton. In 1962 the quantity landed was 185,000 hundredweight, valued at £656,000 but the same vessels also landed substantial quantities at Ardrossan from the Rockall grounds, and made occasional landings at Aberdeen. The Granton Ice Company's supplies allow the trawlers to box their fish at sea—which not all fishing fleets are able to do.

Granton gas holder—the largest single gas-producer in Scotland—is 275 feet high and such an eyesore that when the structure reached its diamond jubilee in 1948, the Royal Fine Art Commission was asked what should be done about it. Finally it was decided that a range of shades of blue should be used, becoming lighter towards the top; and so it remains today. The total amount of gas sold has increased each year since 1960, and in 1963 the Gas Board also installed a new computer at Granton at a considerable rental.

Some of the industries around the port are described later in this book. So it need only be said here that they are varied. They include a large firm which makes heavy and fine phosphor-bronze and brass wire, industrial gauze and heavy screening. Another industry that is still needed in Granton is net making, and there are also numerous businesses that lean on the fishing industry and shipping, with local offices. But this is hardly surprising when we remember that Granton's maritime industry is worth never less than £500,000 a year to the port, and in good years a great deal more.

The City Suburbs

It is not intended here to give a detailed picture of every outlying district in the city but rather to examine briefly some of the older suburbs and a typical new housing estate in order to complete our general picture of Edinburgh as a whole.

First let us take a look at Corstorphine, of which an interesting case study—the basis of this account—was compiled in the early 1960s by Dr. Ronald Jones of the University's Department of Geography under the title *Profile of a Suburb*.

CORSTORPHINE

Although now a suburb of Edinburgh and part of the continuous area of buildings and other urban land uses which make up the city, Corstorphine has only in recent decades lost its former physical isolation. Throughout most of its history it was an agricultural village separated from the city by open countryside, but as Edinburgh grew outwards the village was incorporated within the administrative area of the city (1920) and since then housing developments pushing towards Corstorphine from the south and recently from the north as well, have completed the process of absorption.

THE ORIGINAL VILLAGE NUCLEUS

The gently rolling plain on which the village was established is interrupted by two topographic features which have affected development. One was a long, narrow and shallow loch (now drained). About five miles from west to east this loch was divided into two sections by a tongue of land that appears to have been subject to intermittent flooding. It was near the northern end of this tongue that the village lay. The second feature was the north-south ridge of Corstorphine Hill which, slightly to the north and east of the settlement, rises to over 500 feet. Its south face falls steeply down to what was the northern shore of the loch. These barriers of hill and water determined the alignment of a major highway running westward from Edinburgh. A quarter of a mile south of this route and roughly parallel to it Corstorphine grew up as originally a single street of houses. At the eastern end stood the parish church.

For centuries farming was the mainstay of the local economy. The village was surrounded by scattered farmsteads, many of which still survive even within the built-up area of the suburb. The agricultural land, moreover, was increased by the gradual draining of the loch: reclamation measures were started in the later 17th century with the cutting of a channel, the Stank; and by about 1837 the loch had been completely drained, leaving an extensive tract of level alluvial meadows. The local farmers benefited by being so close to Edinburgh, only three miles away.

The first *Statistical Account* in the 18th century refers to three effects of the road in this context: an emphasis on growing wheat and potatoes for the city market, a reciprocal traffic in manure from Edinburgh, and the local market catering for passing travellers. Moreover, by the early 19th century market gardening had been developed to help feed the nearby city dwellers.[1] Indeed, in the later part of the century the district was referred to as " the Garden of Edinburgh."[2]

But farming has not been the sole constituent in Corstorphine's economic life. During the 18th century the village enjoyed a reputation as a fashionable summer spa for wealthy city families, with a " season " of balls, assemblies and other activities characteristic of similar contemporary resorts. The source of its attraction was a spring of " weak sulphureous water "[3] claimed to have medicinal properties. However, the spring finally became polluted—according to some accounts, as a result of digging drainage ditches while reclaiming the loch—and the pump-house itself was demolished about 1830 after some years of disuse. This decline in a once important source of prosperity seems to have been accompanied by a fall in the numbers of the village population, though it cannot be said whether there was a causal connection between the two events. In

[1] The Parish of Corstorphine, in *The Statistical Account* of Edinburghshire by Rev. David Horne, London, 1845.

[2] Ordnance Gazeteer of Scotland; F. H. Groome (ed.): London, undated (*circa* 1895).

[3] Rev. David Horne: op. cit.

1775 the parish had an estimated population of 995 and forty years later more than 1,000, but the 1801 Census recorded only 840 inhabitants.

One development in the closing decades of the 18th century anticipates by more than 100 years the path which Corstorphine was ultimately to follow when it became a dormitory suburb. This was the building of three mansions, each in extensive grounds, on the lower slopes of Corstorphine Hill a little to the east of the village. The attraction of such a position would have lain largely in the scenic qualities of the hill itself, looking across the loch towards the Pentland Hills over open countryside which only later became covered with the industrial suburbs of the growing city.

GROWTH AND DEVELOPMENT

During the 19th century the growth of the village was steady rather than spectacular. No reliable figures are available for the population of the village, as distinct from the parish, until the latter half of the period. But the Ordnance Survey maps show that by the middle of the century Corstorphine had expanded towards the north, for in addition to the line of houses along the original village street a second had appeared along the main road, and in fact the two parts of the settlement are sometimes referred to as the " low " and " high " villages respectively. Nevertheless, physical growth was not really extensive until the big development of public transport during the first quarter of the 20th century.

This started with the opening of a branch railway line in 1902 to a terminus on the eastern edge of the village. To begin with, services between Corstorphine and the Waverley Station were both regular and frequent. For at least 10 years three trains left Corstorphine for Edinburgh between 8.30 and 9.30 every morning, with others every hour during the rest of the day. Moreover, since the journey lasted only 11 minutes Corstorphine had clearly been placed within very easy commuting distance of the centre of the city. It was not long before motor bus services were also introduced, the Scottish Motor Traction Company forging the first link in 1906. Following the 1920 boundary changes the municipal tramway system was extended into Corstorphine in 1923, and the tramlines were later taken further and further along the main road until in 1937 they reached what is still the edge of the city's built-up area. In 1954 motor buses replaced tramcars along this route, whilst other municipal bus services had already linked the suburb with other parts of the city to the south.

The effect of these developments was to tie the former village more and more closely to its neighbouring city, to make it both practicable and cheap to undertake daily journeys to work from Corstorphine. Yet the response was not especially great at first: some new streets of Edwardian villas made their appearance near the station, including some on the lower slopes of the hill north of the main road, but the expansion remained limited until the middle and later 1920s. From then on, however, growth was both rapid and extensive, and it assumed a distinctive architectural form—the single-family bungalow, detached from its neighbours and set in a relatively large plot. A highly space-consuming expression of contemporary housing needs of the middle classes, the bungalow colonised large areas of land around the old village, more especially along and to the north of the main road, climbing the hillside in a series of parallel streets and spreading on to the lower ground to the west. The subsequent growth—since 1945—has done little more than to confirm these directional trends, and again bungalows are most in favour.

Easy access to transport along the main road and from Corstorphine station must largely account for such a markedly asymmetrical expansion around the original village nucleus. But other factors played their part, too. The lake-bed alluvium, for example, doubtless delayed building to west, south and east of the village; and in general terms, at least, the hill mass formed a further barrier to growth eastward. Here too the privately-held grounds of the 18th century mansions and the 19th century Convalescent Home of the city's Royal Infirmary were in the way. This land impeded growth from the city side also, and successfully prevented the direct coalescence of city and village along the main road. Today these houses still survive, though now mostly in non-residential use, and their grounds still form a belt of open land on the eastern edge of the suburb.

AMENITIES AND SERVICES

Because the district was not a good location for industry in the 19th and early 20th centuries Corstorphine developed pre-eminently as a dormitory, with appropriate economic and social services. Today, like most suburbs, it naturally possesses a large number of retail shops selling foodstuffs, household furniture and other day-to-day necessities. There is also almost every other known service in the suburb—from a Welfare Clinic and a Scout Hall to quite a number of churches in different denominations.[1]

INDUSTRY

During this long growth Corstorphine acquired some manufacturing industry including tapestry-weaving. In the inter-war period three factories were opened: two moved to Corstorphine from congested sites in older parts of Edinburgh, make metal castings and fibre board cases; the third makes bedclothes.

Since the war a printing ink factory, the Scottish Divisional Laboratory of the National Coal Board, and an English firm of football pools promoters have come in, attracted partly by the availability of land for new buildings.

[1] No fewer than 14 local organisations were listed in the Handbook to a " Know Your Neighbourhood " Exhibition sponsored by the Corstorphine Rotary Club in 1958. They included a District Association (of a more or less orthodox " community association " type), the Literary and Geographical Society, Masonic Lodges, a Women's Rural Institute and Townswomen's Guild branch, a Horticultural Society, a branch of the British Legion and three sporting clubs, for cricket, bowls and rugby. As well as these, churches have their own satellite groups, whilst juvenile organisations such as Scouting are also represented in the suburb. Moreover, the Exhibition referred to may itself be regarded as a good expression of the strength of a local community spirit, and the periodic Corstorphine Fair is perhaps another.

SOCIAL CHARACTERISTICS

Looking beyond the growth and economic aspects of the suburb, let us turn to the people who live there and their activities. Most of what follows is based upon a random sampling of households in the suburb as it was in the autumn of 1958, but excluding the Carrick Knowe and Broomhall areas into which Corstorphine merges on its southern margins.[1]

In the first place the survey confirms two points already made, namely the middle-class status of the suburb and its function as a dormitory community.

On the basis of the occupation of the head of the family the 1951 Census formulated a scale of five Social Classes, with a sixth which may be termed "Unclassified." Table I indicates the way in which the sample could be broken down into these divisions, together with a brief description of the types of occupations which would assign an individual and his family to one or other of the status groups.

TABLE I
STATUS COMPOSITION OF THE SAMPLE (PERCENTAGES OF FAMILIES IN THE SAMPLE)

		Generalised description of the occupation of the head of the family
Social Classes I and II	63	Professions, executive and commercial middle and upper middle-class occupations
Social Class III	25	Lower grades of "white collar" and upper grades of skilled manual occupations
Social Classes IV and V	2	Mostly semi-skilled and unskilled manual and non-manual occupations
Unclassified	10	No occupation stated, e.g. non-employed widows, retired persons whose former work was not stated, etc.
Total	100	

The most significant aspect of this Table is the very high figure for Classes I and II, with the corollary of low figure for Classes IV and V, as well as of Class III. Supplementing this information is the evidence of housing statistics, themselves at least a rough indication of status character. In this connection it may be noted that in 1961 about one family in 39 in Corstorphine Municipal Ward lived in houses containing at most two rooms, compared with one in four in the city as a whole; and in terms of persons instead of families, the proportions become one in 59 and one in five respectively.

In confirmation of the dormitory function the sample showed that one-half of the interviewed travelled daily to the city centre, and only one person in eight both lived and worked in Corstorphine.

[1] The interviewing in the survey was carried out by Miss M. Anderson, M.A., Miss M. Hopwood, M.A., Mr. K. Rodgers, M.A. and Miss D. Slater, M.A.

SHOPPING HABITS

In Corstorphine people tend to shop locally for day-to-day necessities and to patronise local chemists and hardware stores. In marked contrast, where durable and expensive articles such as clothing and household furniture are concerned, they shop in the heart of the city, where a far greater choice is available.

Not all the local purchases of foodstuffs, however, are made in what may be termed " fixed " shops. There are a number of mobile shops, especially greengrocers: as many as one-fifth of the families said that their supplies of fruit and vegetables were normally obtained from them, compared with approximately one in 10 in the case of groceries and one in 17 for meats. The extent of mobile shop-trading in Corstorphine is understandable: large parts of the suburb are quite far from the fixed establishments, whilst the homeward journey would be an uphill one for many shoppers, particularly those living in the northern and eastern sections.

ENTERTAINMENT

Further illustration of the divided allegiances between home and other parts of the city occurs in the patronage of commercialised entertainment. The theatre and cinema appeal to a very considerable portion of suburbanites: approximately three families out of every four in the sample contained theatre-goers, and three out of five cinema-goers, but it was apparent that the latter went more frequently than the theatre-goers. The local cinema in Corstorphine was attended by members of about two-fifths of the families concerned, though very few confined themselves to this establishment: in statistical terms centrally-located cinemas were far more important and of course it was also the centre of the city which was resorted to when visiting the professional theatre. In other words, the suburb itself cannot cater for the entertainment needs of its residents; nor can it be expected to, considering the scale on which commercial enterprises of this nature must now operate to be economically viable. And always of course there is, now, the universal entertainment of sound radio and television which have affected the cinema as a whole.

In contrast to the theatre and cinema, people depended to a considerable degree on the Corstorphine branch of the municipal library. Two thirds of the families interviewed contained persons who borrowed books from a public library and by far the greater part of these used the local branch.

CHURCHGOING

Almost 90 per cent of the people interviewed said they went to church regularly—a surprisingly high figure.

TABLE 2

Percentages of families of whom some member(s) attended church	87
Of these families, percentages attending churches were in	
(a) Corstorphine	66
(b) Central Edinburgh	15
(c) Elsewhere	17
(d) Location not specified	2
Total	100

Some travelled considerable distances, not only to the city centre but also to suburban areas, and Table 2 (above) provides a statistical breakdown in terms of the locations of the churches named by the families interviewed. For the Table the only distinctions drawn were between Corstorphine, central Edinburgh and the rest, but whilst this last category includes districts as far from the suburb as Leith, Bruntsfield and Dalry, most of the churches in this group were in fact situated in areas adjoining Corstorphine to the east and south, such as Murrayfield and Carrick Knowe.

Those who regularly worship at churches outside Corstorphine are not necessarily members of denominations without a local church. Certainly Methodists and Baptists go to chapels in the city centre; but many said they attend the High Kirk of St. Giles or St. Mary's Episcopal Cathedral, and indeed most of the 23 non-local churches in categories (b) and (c) have congregations in Corstorphine. Although no inquiry was made as to why distant churches were attended in preference to local ones of the same denomination, reasons would probably include the attractions of a particular minister or of the so-called " fashionable " churches in the city's West End, and the way people like to retain links with the district where they lived before coming to Corstorphine. Nevertheless, one of the most striking facts to appear from Table 2 is that as many as two families in three were members of congregations in Corstorphine.

EDUCATION

The suburb may be able to cater for the needs of most of its active church-attending population: the same cannot be said for its educational facilities. Four schools, all under the Edinburgh authority, are either in the suburb or near enough to it to be termed local. They furnish both primary and secondary forms of education. Yet less than two-fifths of the schoolchildren in the sample went to them. Although almost all the children in Classes 3, 4 and 5 were being educated locally, only one in four from Classes 1 and 2 was a schoolfellow of theirs—and it is these two status groups which account for approximately two-thirds of the suburban population.

The competing attraction of the city's fee-paying schools is one of the main reasons why local facilities are so ignored. Altogether, nearly three-fifths of the children in Classes 1 and 2 attended institutions such as George Watson's College (or its sister school), Melville College or Edinburgh Academy.[1]

SOCIAL RELATIONSHIPS

The survey also asked how close the contact was between neighbouring families. The social microcosm of the street, the block or even of a small group of neighbouring houses can often be important in helping the family to become integrated into the surrounding community. It can be important, too, in fostering feelings of satisfaction or the reverse with this social environment.

The families interviewed were asked to describe in their own words the contact they shared with next-door neighbours, and on the basis of their answers four grades of intimacy have been recognised (Table 3 below).

TABLE 3
CONTACTS WITH NEXT-DOOR NEIGHBOURS
(percentage of all Families in each Status Group

	Status group:			
	I & II	III	U	*All groups*
very close contacts	40	32	55	39
moderately close contact	19	21	9	19
slight contacts	33	35	36	34
very little or no contact	8	11	—	8
total	100	100	100	100

NOTE: (a) " U " is the Unclassified status group;
(b) Classes IV and V have been omitted from separate mention here because their absolute number was so small that no proper significance could be attached to the precentages applying to them in isolation. The families concerned have however been included for the computation of the " All groups " column of the Table.

Table 3 has some striking features. First is the relatively high incidence—two families in five—of extremely close relationships with neighbours. At the other extreme about one-twelfth appeared to be socially isolated; but in addition approximately one family in three had contacts of a type no more intimate than would be expressed, for example, in a nodding acquaintanceship. Viewing the status groups separately, Classes 1 and 2 combined conform statistically almost almost exactly with the figures for the sample as a whole. With Class 3, on the other hand, almost one-half enjoyed at most only a slight measure of contact with their neighbours, with a significantly lower incidence among them of the closest grade of intimacy recognised here.

THE RESIDENTS SPEAK FOR THEMSELVES

The answers to the question, " Do you like living in Corstorphine? " showed almost universal approval—only one family in 50, in fact, expressed dissatisfaction with the place. Not that Corstorphine received

[1] A private school occupies one of the large mansions on the lower slopes of Corstorphine Hill near Murrayfield. No children from the sample families were pupils of this institution.

completely unqualified support. When asked if they would prefer to live elsewhere in the city if they could, just under one-quarter named some different part of Edinburgh, usually another peripheral suburb; and a few mentioned a central or near-central area.

As regards the grounds for satisfaction with Corstorphine—and each family was asked to add the reasons for their answers—a very large variety was suggested. But broadly it was possible to discern four main groupings.

In the first place came those features which could be ascribed to the suburb's character, location and long history of detachment from the city. Thus for many people the attractions of Corstorphine lay in its "semi-rurality," in having easy access to open country, in retaining a village atmosphere despite absorption by a large city, and in being a clean and, in their opinion, a healthy place to live. Secondly, the "convenience" of Corstorphine was frequently mentioned: by many the suburb was considered an excellent shopping centre (for daily necessities, that is). Thirdly, people often talked about the "friendliness" of the district and about the variety of social activities that made it a pleasant place to live in. Finally, a small minority gave their long-standing familiarity with the area as at least one source of satisfaction.

COLINTON

Another interesting outlying district—separated from Corstorphine by agricultural land and the Sighthill industrial estate—is Colinton, once a village on the outskirts of Edinburgh and now one of the city's dormitory suburbs. But the village is still there.

In area the parish of Colinton is very much larger than the suburb of the name and comprises Colinton, Slateford, Redford, Hailes, Dreghorn, Craiglockhart, Swanston and Woodhall: the suburb itself includes only Colinton, Woodhall and Dreghorn, and it is in this suburban-village sense that the word Colinton is used in the following necessarily condensed account, written not like that of Corstorphine by a University don but by David Govan who at the time was a senior schoolboy at Daniel Stewart's College.

In 1838, when the village of Colinton lay well outside the city boundaries, the parish minister, who described it for the *New Statistical Account*, was optimistic and gloomy by turns. He thought the cultivation of the parish since the previous *Statistical Account* had been greatly improved, but there had been considerable manufacturing changes. The distillery and the skinnery had disappeared; the magnesia factory was in ruins; the noise of the work-mill no longer reminded the passenger of its existence; and the mill for beating flax was not much used. But the parish still flourished; the population had increased; and the rental had improved. The minister concluded that if a "little more of that right-hearted prudence which includes, and, through God's grace, enables man to value and steadily comply with the councils of heavenly truth, be infused into the bosom of generality of the people, they would be blessed indeed."

The industrial use of steam was then superseding water power; and this may be the reason why the mills referred to had been closed. Many, however, were still operating on the Water of Leith, some grinding grain and four making paper, while a new snuff mill was actually being erected at the time of the minister's account. A small mill-wright's business also flourished in the village. These were the mills described in *Memories and Portraits* by Robert Louis Stevenson who, shortly after the turn of the century, was a frequent visitor to his grandfather's Colinton manse. This he thought was a " place in that time like no other " since among its many beauties there was " the smell of water rising from all round, with an added tang of paper mills."

Edinburgh as a city at that time had not reached farther west than Haymarket; there was a mere straggle of houses between Bruntsfield and Morningside; and the present Colinton Road was non-existent. In fact Colinton was so well separated, both in time and distance, from Edinburgh that the village was even considered a summer holiday resort by Edinburgh families, and in addition small estates and farms were being taken over by prominent Edinburgh families.

The population of the parish in 1838 was divided among five villages, several minor hamlets, and many small knots of houses; but the population for the actual village of Colinton was 119. Although agriculture was the main employment, doubtless this figure included mill and quarry workers also. There was a school, a Post Office with two deliveries daily, and a library which had just been reopened after being closed for a number of years. Edinburgh was the nearest market town, and the nearest public transport was the Lanark Coach and a " noddy " from nearby Currie.

For the next few decades life in Colinton moved slowly along until the coming of the railway in 1875. This coincided with the building of the new bridge over the Water of Leith and over the railway, which now brought the coal which had previously come by the Union Canal. Passenger trains were introduced, and these became more frequent as the district they served increased in size. As the railway made it possible both to live in Colinton and yet do business in Edinburgh, there was a steady growth in villa houses for the well-to-do. Colonel Trotter, the last laird of Colinton House, looked at this with true feudal superiority: " The Parish is now being overrun by the new-rich from Edinburgh. Every road shows new sites being cleared for houses." Most of the building for " the new rich from Edinburgh " appears to have been in the manse glebe, although some took place on the south side of the river. Many of these houses were described by a local gentleman as " old-English looking." Shortly before this the Water of Leith was purified by the laying of a sewer for the whole length of the valley as far as Leith, and this made possible the drainage of Colinton Village and of all the new houses under construction, as well as turning the " black smelling frothy water " into " a clear stream with people fishing along its banks."

During the war years 1914–1918 little building took place in Colinton, but after the war a matter which had for long been causing concern to many people in the village came to a head. This was the threat, as they saw it, of being absorbed by the big city. Those in favour of incorporating Colinton with Edinburgh argued that since the city already supplied most of the public services such as water, sewage, gas and electricity, these would be more readily extended and more cheaply supplied if Colinton became part of the larger rating unit. The same argument was used for other suburbs, and when eventually in 1920 Edinburgh was granted a very large extension of its boundaries, Colinton became a Ward of the Capital.

At that time, although the motor-car was assuming greater importance, the railway still provided the main transport between the city and its new Ward. At rush hours the Balerno line trains were notoriously packed. A new unmanned " halt " was opened at Hailes, primarily intended to serve the new Kingsknowe Golf Course. The trams, which up till then had only run to Happy Valley, changed over from cable to electricity. As a result they were much faster, and the service was extended to Colinton Village after the road past Redford Barracks had been widened. So clearly Colinton was becoming a well-served community, to match its increasing population.

At the end of the first World War high taxation had begun to hit the more prosperous of the professional classes, while many merchants and shopkeepers had made a large profit on goods in short supply. The result was that fewer people could afford large villas of the type and size that had been built at Spylaw and Colinton after the railway came. On the other hand, more people could afford more modest houses, and the development which took place in Colinton after 1919 tended to be of smaller houses than before.

The next distinct phase of Colinton's development occurred between 1930 and the early '60s. In the first part of this period, before the second World War, only three roads were built up to the south. But Hailes House was converted into a Youth Hostel, the grounds were sold to speculative builders, and the woods on the edge of the " Dell " became a park. The housing scheme at Hailes more or less completed the infilling of Colinton's northern part. Most of the houses built at this time were small. Then came the war and building all but ceased for the next 10 years. Road transport in the latter part of this period, whether by tram or the increasing number of cars, began to draw off much of the railway's traffic, and eventually the passenger service closed down.

When building started again after the War, the remainder of the available sites were rapidly filled up, mostly by large speculative builders, although there were still a number of individually designed houses being built. As there was also an increase of traffic on the roads both the bridge and the road at the foot of Dreghorn Loan were widened. When, just after the mid-century, Edinburgh decided to scrap its tram cars, the worn-out Colinton route was one of the first to go, but in its place there was an extension and speeding up of the bus service.

Sir Patrick Abercrombie's survey and plan for the whole of Edinburgh gave the population of Colinton in 1946 as around 3,000 people. (The Ward of Colinton, much bigger than the suburb known by the same name, had a population—at the time of the 1961 Census—of 26,874.) The survey also showed that in comparison with other parts of the city, social and housing conditions in Colinton were good. The average size of a family was small; the number of rooms per house was high; and most of the houses were owner-occupied.

In the early '60s only three mills remained in use, and only one of these made the same produce as when it started. One was a wood-flour mill connected with linoleum production; the second made various qualities of paper, largely from waste cardboard; the third, which had previously built up a good name in hay foods and in porridge oats, had been taken over by the firm of Cerebos. All this has naturally added to the life of the district, and Colinton—like other Edinburgh suburbs—has therefore increased in size and population, and shopping facilities. As a place of special amenity it is also at present protected by law from unworthy depredations of the " green belt " beside it.

JUNIPER GREEN

Juniper Green is a basically 19th century village which is part of the Colinton parish and therefore within the city boundaries; but as it has no industry of any consequence, a number of its people work in the nearby Currie paper mills in the county of Midlothian, and others travel to business in the city. But with no ancient character of its own, and with nothing of historical importance to show, its significance is perhaps as a symbol of modern suburban attraction. In the words of a local resident: " It may or may not be true that the place takes its name from the juniper bushes that once flourished there, but it has no vivid personality of its own. There is still a sort of village life; the old people's association is very active; Juniper Green has its own school; and there are the usual youth organisations—Scouts and Guides. The working class inhabit the old village which is surrounded by the bungalows and semi-detached villas of the bourgeoisie. Baberton Golf Course is in the neighbourhood."

SOUTH EDINBURGH

South Edinburgh possesses a significance which contributes greatly to the understanding of Edinburgh's unique character; but to understand the peculiar relationship between the city and this suburb it is necessary to remind ourselves of the social history of the area as a whole.

The existence of Edinburgh as a city was due mainly to a triple combination of circumstances. The castle was nearly impregnable. The fertile crescent of Lothian and the Forth estuary was able to supply it with both necessities and luxuries. And finally the narrowing of the central plain by the proximity of the Pentlands, the cluster of hills upon which the city centre stands, and the many impassable lochs and marshes between them, made Edinburgh a natural gateway to and from central Scotland.

There is, however, a more subtle reason for Edinburgh's origin and continuing existence. Like Scotland itself, and also like the ancient kingdom of Lothian of which Edinburgh was the natural and functional capital, the city is composed of many divergent, even warring and incompatible elements. Yet instead of flying apart in centrifugal confusion, it maintains an indissoluble unity.

Of old, this unity was forced upon Edinburgh and Lothian by the unceasing hostility of the "Auld Enemy"; and after the union of the Scottish and English Crowns, it might well be wondered what centripetal force holds modern Edinburgh together, including its suburbs to the south. There is, however, an explanation. After the last English wars had ceased, a century and more passed before the first of its citizens took up sites in the New Town in the second half of the 18th century. Even then they did so with a certain reluctance. But as the century progressed all kinds of eccentrics, even geniuses, were concentrated for many years within its walls. They were drawn to Edinburgh for social and intellectual intercourse from all quarters of Britain and, now and then, from Europe, while every Scottish landowner of note had a town-house in the capital.

In Early Victorian Edinburgh the radicals also gained a say, and a scientific, medical, mercantile, artistic and literary aristocracy became dominant. This Edinburgh, even to less percipient inhabitants than Robert Louis Stevenson, suggested a world of Jekyll and Hyde. The classical New Town was mainly for the rich and privileged and a long entrenched aristocracy of land and law; but there, too, were the lower regions of Stockbridge, St. Bernards, Canonmills, soon to degenerate into sleazy areas comparable to the demi-monde of Rose Street and Thistle Street. The Old Town by 1830 was a noisome rookery by day and a bat-cave by night; while the deaths from malignant fever in 1837–9, a period which included Queen Victoria's Coronation, were nearly as bad as in plague-stricken Constantinople.

The escape route for many lay towards the immediate south, and it was along this road that Edinburgh, chiefly radical Edinburgh, expanded. Those Victorian pioneers whose pantechnicons breasted the pristine slopes of the Boroughmuir and the Sciennes and gazed south to the Lothian landscape saw more than a coincidence in the names Egypt, Canaan, Jordan and Eden, which ever since have distinguished parts of Morningside. The elite of the early Victorians were distinguished for optimism and particularity: in the extreme this developed into enthusiasm strangely mixed with pragmaticism. And these twin pillars of personality upheld the first phase of South Edinburgh, in that region called by Wilfred Taylor "the Bible Belt."

Churchhill is a district which overlooks the whole of Victorian South Edinburgh; and there, fittingly enough, a house was built by Dr. Chalmers, Fife-born father of the great Disruption in the Church of Scotland. How illustrative of that age is the note in his diary: "July 15 1841. Mean to build at Morningside; but let me not forget the end of the world and the coming of Christ."

Prophecy had for some generations given the end of the world as 1866; but there must have been some sceptics among the illuminati of the medical, scientific and literary worlds, for they continued to buy up feus from estates such as Falcon Hall, Braid and Plewlands. We read of many eminent men residing there, mostly now forgotten: Dr. Gregory; James Wilson, naturalist brother of " Christopher North "; Professor Syme; Meikle Kemp, ill-fated architect of the Scott Monument. Jane Welsh Carlyle failed to find sleep even in this Arcadia of 1862 and went by horse-omnibus to Edinburgh to buy laudanum. Eminent visitors came to Morningside: Froude, Blackie, Jowett, Huxley, Sellar, Noel Paton. Froude wrote, a little inaccurately, of his walks in Hermitage Glen by the Water of Braid: " Abana and Pharpar are not better than the waters of Israel and the murmur of Lothian Burn." The Lothian Burn in fact runs parallel to the Braid Burn two miles to the south.

A typical man of his age was Lt-Col. Davidson, who built a mansion in Clinton Road, Churchhill. He is remembered for his remark to Lord Rokeby at the Great Review in the Queen's Park in 1860: " My Lord, I'll tell you what makes our Scottish peasantry so stalwart; it is the porridge "—an attitude and phraseology still to be found any day in the correspondence columns of the *Scotsman* and some glossy Scottish magazines.

Nevertheless, respect is due to this disciplined if stolid army of South Edinburgh, repairing each week in satins and " stands " of Sabbath broadcloth to its respective persuasions at " Holy Corner " (Churchhill) and similar ecclesiastical meccas, and in the pleasant Sunday afternoons making pilgrimages to the large, airy, orderly and flowery cemeteries of Grange, Morningside and Newington. This society sent many of its sons and daughters to settle in New Zealand (among other regions), and to graft the names and cultures of home into places like Dunedin. Its influence has been truly world-wide. So if an Empire has been lost, this cannot be laid at Morningside's door. Moreover, the influence of its missionary zeal upon the benighted heathen has probably been greater than that of any comparable area on earth.

The opening of the suburban railway, linking up the inner periphery of South Edinburgh with the town centre and Leith, considerably accelerated the new building which Stevenson deplored. The " faddling hedonist," as an Indian critic called him, could derive little pleasure from his walk up the Braidburn valley towards Swanston under the pastoral Pentlands, until he had put the new tenements well behind him. Towards the end of the 19th century the suburban trains ran on Sundays, much to the horror of the " unco guid "; but this service, sentenced to death in 1963, was of immeasurable benefit to the young couples of those days, who for a threepenny return could go round and round the circle, doing their courting in comfort and intermittent privacy.

Morningside, it can be seen, is more than a geographical expression: it is a frame of mind, a social attitude, a form of speech. It occurs as a diluted form in Kelvinside, Glasgow and in Jesmond, Newcastle. It occurs as an endemic in the aristocratic West End of Edinburgh and in all residential areas. In fact, a study of its origin, growth and decline would interest the social anthropologist. It might even be worth someone's trouble to investigate the fact that there are 199·5 females in Morningside to every 100 males—a concentration of femininity unique in all Scotland.

One Scottish editor, writing about Edinburgh a generation ago, saw some slight resemblance between South Edinburgh especially and the " Rome of the Popes, with stately villas and great extent of walled-in garden ground." Regrettably much of this has passed away. There is still a good deal of it left in the centre of Morningside; but although this is used for children's homes or hospitals, and some of it is neglected parkland, most property of the kind has been replaced by bungalows and small flatted villas, and more recently by skyscrapers.

To look back again, the rise of South Edinburgh was mainly due to two factors—a desire for isolation and for insolation. Those who followed the pioneers found the second rather than the first: theirs was a qualified isolation, and the newer outposts of South Edinburgh have this in common with them. Like two great arms of a tidal wave, split upon the volcanic and whinny masses of the Blackfords and Braids, the new housing areas have flowed along the lower valleys of the Inch, Liberton, Gracemount and Hyvot's Bank (once Heavy Oats Bank, presumably because the oats yielded better for being on a northern slope). The western wave goes by way of Oxgangs and Hunters' Tryst to Fairmilehead.

The movement of large populations to the Midlothian border has ceased to be a matter for private enterprise only. With such an enormous city area and a relatively slow growth of total population it is now municipal policy to house the citizens in the midst of extensive rural areas. In fact, all Greater Edinburgh is a parkland with patches of habitation. These are not parks of a mere few acres. The Queen's Park occupies about a square mile on the map, and is so mountainous that this actually represents a surface area half as large again. The Braid Hills, mostly given over to golf, are equally extensive. Blackford Hill and Corstorphine Hill (nearly all woodland) are half a square mile each. There are other sequestered landscapes within South Edinburgh, a short distance only from the new housing areas, which defy the art of the builder. The city runs deep into the heart of the Pentland Hills, to the little Kirk Burn (a temple of the Stevenson followers) where the heather, knee-deep, grows by the mile and the wilderness is inhabited by blackfaced sheep, brown and mountain hares, becking grouse and carrion crows. The porphyry cliffs of Caerketton, with its acres of stone screes known as the Seven Sisters, overhang the reconstituted hamlet of Swanston. There is little likelihood that these places, all within the city boundaries, will have changed much a century hence.

Lack of social life, cost of transport, monotony of commuting are among the many points made against all suburban housing. These problems are further complicated in South Edinburgh by the terrain, which rises to over 600 feet at Fairmilehead, high for a city, though unexceptional compared with many villages not far away. The Lothian villages of Blackshiels, Howgate and Heriot are all over 800 feet above sea level, a height equal to the summit of Arthur's Seat. Nevertheless, the residents of the Fairmilehead district enjoy an uninterrupted view of the heavens and seem little the worse for their closer acquaintance with the naked elements, while magnificent vistas lie in all directions—from the Grampians, looking often like the snow-crested waves of a tumultuous sea, to the rolling greenbacks of Lammermoor. Here snow lies sometimes for weeks, long after it has melted in the city. It did so in the severe winter of 1962–3, when hundreds of skiers and sledgers disported themselves on the lower slopes of Hillend and Caerketton.

Nowadays, it is of course a difficult task to categorise a population living in such an area. The old social distinction based on annual house rent dies hard, but has little relevance today. In fact, the modern Morningsiders would surprise those who consider them " squares ": there are even some " treble-hipsters " in the parish, and it is from this area, frequently chided by the avant-garde for their philistinism, that the Festival, both Altarcloth and Fringe, draws great levies of supporters. Here the arts generally are subscribed to; people buy books here as well as borrow them; while dedicated poets and painters keep up their hearts, in company with their disciples and peers. Cacti, houseplants, budgies and angel-fish, incidentally, have largely taken over from the canaries and aspidistras. And as for the seven-pound-sirloin-on-the-bone, that went the way of all flesh after the 1914–18 war.

But here we must conclude this all too brief account of an unusually interesting part of the city. Probably the social historian of the 21st century will find no evidence that the Victorians and Edwardians of South Edinburgh belonged to the same race or civilisation as the Neo-or Duo-Elizabethans of Gracemount, Hyvot's Bank or Hunters' Tryst. They might well belong to different planets as well as centuries, so dissimilar are their modes of thought, speech and entertainment.

Even so South Edinburgh is still a little haunted by the spectre of a grim, more distant past. A hundred tales could be told, quite circumstantially, of a crude and violent age only considered romantic when it had safely passed. Two large square stones with holes to support gibbets are still to be seen in the Braid Road a short distance from Morningside Station. Here, in the year of Waterloo, thousands of people celebrated Burns Nicht and no doubt quoted " Man's inhumanity to man makes countless thousands mourn," after witnessing the public execution of two Irish highwaymen for the Braid robbery.

On a more gentle but still tragic note we may go to the Hermitage Glen and indulge our fancies in the pseudo-Gothic of the late 18th century. Here are ancient oaks and limes, craggy cliffs nodding over cataracts, the Braid Water running through a cavern measureless to man, a mock Hermits' Cave and the Hermitage of Braid itself, a building in a " grotesque style of castellated architecture " haunted by the melancholy ghost of lovely Jacky Gordon who, deserted by her husband, pined here in the early 19th century. Here also, in Braid Farm close by, the beautiful and intelligent Elizabeth Burnett of Monboddo, inspiration of Burns, died of consumption in June 1790, at the age of twenty-three.

On the Galachlaw, east of Fairmilehead, Oliver Cromwell camped in 1650, frustrated for the time in his attempts on Edinburgh, while hundreds of his men died of pestilence. Sixteen years later, on a stormy November day in 1666, a resolute band of Westland Whigs decided here to give up their expedition and march back home. Unluckily they were cut off by dragoons under Dalyell of the Binns, at Rullion Green, and lost two ministers and 50 men.

Yet if South Edinburgh can still recall these violent scenes, there is a certain appeal about the place and a beauty here and there which many will recall in years still far ahead. To give but one example, if any visitor to Edinburgh should wish for a memorable experience, let him climb to one of the many eminences within the city bounds about dusk. Not only will he see the whole city illuminated by the orange glow of sodium vapour street lamps, but all the Lothian burghs as well as the Fife towns strung along above the twinkling Forth for forty miles, outlined in orange, blue, green or white. Stranger, perhaps, than these illuminations are the great pools of darkness where the uninhabited parks and the wildernesses of Blackford, Braid and Mortonhall appear like starless patches in an expanding cosmos. In these wastelands, invested by the modern world, the bats and tawny owls still fly; badgers, hedgehogs and foxes still prowl; carrion crows croak resentfully at passing cars; and voles and wildfowl splash in the streams. They are all part of the strangely diversified life of South Edinburgh and of Edinburgh itself.

LIBERTON

Continuing our tour of the city's periphery we come to Liberton, a ward on the south-easterly side of Edinburgh, which in 1964 was engulfed in controversy over plans to build there a vast number of new Corporation houses.

Between the censuses of 1951 and 1961 the population of the Liberton ward increased by 15,467. This rise, the highest of any in Edinburgh, was due to the movement of people to the new housing schemes in the district. As a result the population in 1961 stood at 34,610, and as more housing development is planned, it is likely to rise by a few thousand more, apart from the natural increase which may be predicted from the composition of the age groups. In 1964 the most numerous age group, 10–14, had 5,029 members, and the population on the whole seemed more youthful than it is in most districts.

The post-war influx has greatly changed the character of Liberton Ward, which is a good deal less in extent than the old parish which stretched from the Braid hills almost to the sea at Musselburgh. Craigmillar is now detached for municipal purposes; the villages of Kirk Liberton, Nether Liberton, Liberton Dams and Gilmerton have been submerged by the rising tide; the estate of the Inch has been converted into a community with its churches and schools; and Liberton has become a populous suburb instead of a pastoral, landward parish of a city. It has certainly altered much since the parish minister proudly wrote in the second *Statistical Account* that " there is not in Britain a more commanding view of rich and varied scenery . . . than may be had from

Craigmillar Castle, the high grounds above Mortonhall, the ridge of Gilmerton, or the neighbourhood of Liberton Church."

Yet the commanding heights are still there, and the prospects please. Liberton Church on its eminence is a familiar landmark; it is the kind of building that used to be known as a handsome Gothic edifice, having been built in 1815 on a site occupied by its predecessors and reconstructed internally later in the century. Its pre-eminence in elevation is disputed now by the three blocks of multi-storey flats built by Edinburgh Corporation at Gracemount.

Liberton's name was traditionally explained as a corruption of Leperston but this derivation and the supposed location of a hospital for lepers there have been challenged by antiquaries, for whom the parish is a happy hunting ground, including as it does the strongly built Liberton Tower, its 17th century successor, Liberton House, and other mansions built by lairds when fortified dwellings became necessary. St. Katherine's House has become a children's home, and it is notable for its Balm Well, on which float black, oily substances; a pious legend attributed this phenomenon to drops of sacred oil deposited there by St. Catherine after her visit to the Holy Sepulchre. The noble Craigmillar Castle, though outside the bounds of Liberton Ward, was once the glory of the parish with its memories of Mary Queen of Scots.

Liberton is almost wholly a residential district. Its industries are negligible, the coal mines at Gilmerton and Straiton having ceased production. There is a depot for earth-moving machinery at Gilmerton, but no manufacturing industry. One of the largest employers in the ward is the Coal Board whose headquarters for the Lothians Area are at Greenend. At the north side of the ward the University of Edinburgh has scientific, engineering and agricultural departments in the King's Buildings complex; and research in animal diseases is carried on at Moredun Institute. Various institutes for human welfare also exist in Liberton, both Liberton Hospital and Southfield Hospital (formerly a sanitorium) being used for the care of old people and geriatric study.

In spite of the rash of post-war building Liberton is rich in open spaces, particularly in golf courses. The Braids Hill, Mortonhall, Craigmillar, and Liberton courses together provide a fair amount of recreation and greenery. Besides the Blackford Hill, on which the Royal Observatory is located, the ward is well provided with public parks, including one of 50 acres on the Inch estate and Burdiehouse Walkway (85 acres), while the housing schemes have their recreational and sports grounds.

PORTOBELLO AND JOPPA

Portobello, which the Edinburgh official guide describes as " Edinburgh's bracing seaside resort," has as fine a romantic, exotic name as any holiday place could wish. Its Spanish resonance makes Blackpool sound commonplace; and the name is certainly more euphonious than that of Joppa, also a village once in its own right and now completely absorbed by

Portobello. Portobello is reputed to owe its name to an old salt who had taken part in Admiral Vernon's bombardment of Puerto Bello in Panama in 1739 and who built himself a house near the Figgate Burn when he retired.

It was not, however, the golden sands which induced other people to follow the example of this ancient mariner. The rising village, as it was called by 18th century observers, was built to exploit the resources of the soil, the clay which could be used both for making bricks to supply Edinburgh builders and for the pottery which earned Portobello a reputation, especially for its white stoneware. Later, when the virtues of sea-bathing were discovered, Portobello became a resort for Edinburgh families, and by the beginning of the 19th century not only were hot and cold sea water baths built but the village became a fashionable centre. For in those days not only were the sands clean and the sea water pure, but the beach was enlivened by the manoeuvres of cavalry, Sir Walter Scott being one of those who trained on Portobello sands in order to repel the threatened invasion of Napoleon.

Ever since, Portobello has preserved its dual character as a seaside resort and an industrial town. Its industries may not be large, but they are tenacious. The Thistle pottery carries on the town's ceramic tradition, being itself an old-established firm and doing now a flourishing export trade. Another Portobello industry is the making of bottles. Probably however most of its inhabitants travel to work elsewhere in Edinburgh, yet Portobello remains a convenient shopping centre for a big surrounding area, including new housing schemes on its perimeter. It is still a community, in spite of its administrative absorption by the city, and a growing one. The 1961 Census showed an increase in population of 3,655. As the largest age-group, containing 2,705 members, was the important section from zero to four years, the vitality of Portobello seems assured. The total population in 1961 was 27,141.

Apart from its demographic soundness, the future of the place will be brightened if it becomes a Central Development Area (planners' jargon for a commercial centre with a big housing hinterland); and indeed Edinburgh's own planning department has been surveying Portobello to see what shopping and parking facilities it would need if it is to serve this function. Local traders also plan to brighten the streets by painting and improving shop fronts and generally carrying out a face-lift. To a great extent this is inspired by a sense of enterprise, but also it is induced by considerable local patriotism. So it can be safely assumed that as a residential suburb Portobello and Joppa, its virtual extension, will always be well populated. Some 30 years ago there was a local debate on the question, "Has Portobello a future as a watering-place?" Apparently the debaters thought it had, but time has not altogether vindicated their faith, though Portobello still has certain attractions—several excellent public parks, facilities for games such as tennis and bowls, a nine-hole golf course, a mile-long beach and a promenade two miles long, an amusement centre, periodical shows in the Town Hall, a salt-water indoor pool and an open-air swimming pool (one of the largest in Europe) and equipped with wave-making machinery. But also, by way of contrast, Portobello has a massive power station, which towers over the open-air pool, and claims that its 350 feet chimney is the highest in Scotland.

THE EDINBURGH VILLAGES

Under the tide of 19th and 20th century urban development, most of the 46 villages which, in the first half of the 18th century, were spread over the area now occupied by Edinburgh, have disappeared. There is nothing in the least remarkable about this. The same sort of thing has been happening all over the civilised world for a long time, as cities have sprung up and expanded, absorbing the rustic communities that previously stood in the fields where factories and blocks of flats have since been built. But one quite remarkable thing about the Capital of Scotland is that it has succeeded in preserving a number of its villages, right down to the present day, as semi-rural communities within the city boundaries, each with a distinctive character of its own, and each standing in the place where it stood at the time of the first and second *Statistical Accounts of Scotland* and had indeed been standing long before Sir John Sinclair produced his 18th century inventory of Scotland's habits of life.

In May 1947 the late E. J. Macrae, then City Architect of Edinburgh, submitted a report, at the request of the Lord Provost's Committee, on some of the old buildings outside the Royal Mile which were worthy of preservation. The report was entitled *The Heritage of Greater Edinburgh*, and indicated which of the old villages were still in being, and which had disappeared. Since then there has been no actual disappearance of a village; but the fate of some has hung in the balance.

As definite villages, separated from the town, most of the 46 no longer exist. Yet areas within the city, where villages once stood, still retain a village atmosphere of their own. In recent years, the removal of tramway lines and overhead wires, and the replacement of cobble-stoned streets by macadamised roads, have given a slighly countrified, if not exactly rustic appearance even to streets which for several decades had been uncompromisingly urban. For example, Stockbridge, if it no longer looks like the village it once was, certainly looks more like a county town now that it has the kind of main road which you might find in most towns. Indeed, if you pause for a few reflective moments at the corner of Hamilton Place close to the bridge over the Water of Leith on a summer evening you can feel yourself in touch with the past.

There is still the occasional angler casting an optimistic fly or a pessimistic worm over the chuckling little river, where catches of sizeable trout (though made very rare by the children who net the small fry) are by no means impossible. The sight of one or two loungers at the bridge, exchanging news or gossip as they do in country places; the line of single-storey shops along the north side of Deanhaugh Street; the little Savings Bank building crowned by its clock tower at the west end of the bridge; and the pleasant wooded left bank of the stream, stretching towards the

Dean Gardens and positively vibrating with the cheerful chatter of chaffinches—this familiar picture makes " Stockaree " (as Stockbridge has long been known to its inhabitants) a place different from the Georgian city which threatened to engulf it but never completely succeeded in doing so. Or rather, let us say that the growing city, about 130 years ago, embraced Stockbridge in its arms without spoiling its waterside tranquillity.

In the *Civic Survey and Plan for Edinburgh*, prepared by Sir Patrick Abercrombie and Mr. Derek Plumstead and published in 1949, one reads that " it was from 1920 onwards that the rural communities of Corstorphine, Cramond, Newhaven, Colinton, etc. were absorbed by expanding suburbia." With all respect for its authors, that statement needs qualification. Certainly housing developments covered large tracts of what up to that time had been green fields on the south, east, and west of the city—a process that was halted for a few years by the Second World War and vigorously renewed after it was ended. But with the possible exception of Corstorphine, where very little of the old village now remains, it is not accurate to say that the four communities named above have been " absorbed " by suburbia; they have too much of their own character, and in the case of Cramond the village is too separate from the city to justify the description.

If Cramond is absorbed, it is absorbed in itself, and in all the fascinating things which are as inseparable from the River Almond as from any other quiet river just deep enough and broad enough to make a harbour for yachts and dinghies. A miniature forest of yacht-masts—including the masts of boats admittedly belonging to many people who do not live in Cramond—gives the anchorage in the cool wooded backwater its character. In the afternoon of a week-day in summer, there is a slumbrous peace in Cramond, and almost the only sound is the companionable one of water lapping against the boats.

But villages do not survive without care, and although Cramond could truthfully be called " a beautiful unspoilt village " the Town Council's Housing Committee later condemned 26 of its outwardly picturesque cottages as unfit for human habitation ; and 20 families—about two-thirds of the population—had to be housed in other parts of the city.

This decision, announced in June 1958, inspired Miss Dorothy Craigie-Halkett, owner of Cramond House, to make an offer to buy the cottages and engage an architect to restore them at her own expense—a conspicuous example of a philanthropic attitude to village-preservation. But in January 1959, before her purchase of the 26 condemned cottages had been completed, Miss Craigie-Halkett died, However, Edinburgh Corporation took over the care of the village, and decided to spend £27,040 on its restoration and modernisation.

Cramond has been admirably re-created without destroying its charm. The white-washed cottages in Glebe Road, the steep street that runs down through the village to the Firth of Forth, and the gay window-boxes of the old Inn on the right near the foot—dating in part from 1670—make an exceedingly pleasant and promising descent to the river-front, and along

Riverside the houses are equally spick-and-span and the gardens neatly kept.

But a village is much more than a collection of houses; it is a community of human families, and in Cramond the community is undergoing the same kind of change as the houses have undergone. For one thing the houses are sparklingly new, and the rents fixed by the Corporation, which owns them, means that two-thirds of the population will necessarily be of a much higher income level than were the 20 families who had to be moved out of the condemned houses. The village thus faces a very interesting and what should be a stimulating challenge—the challenge to create a community spirit in a small population of differing economic and social backgrounds.

Of all Edinburgh's villages, Cramond is the one which has the longest history as the site of a human settlement. Its near neighbour, Davidson's Mains, is of more recent origin, but a close partnership exists between the two villages. The Davidson's Mains and Cramond Gala Association runs an annual gala at which the Gala Queen—an ephemeral but happy monarch now apparently indispensable in the lives of many small communities—is crowned for her brief bright reign. There are races, a tug-o'-war, 5-a-side football, bands, and a children's fancy-dress parade, all of which take place in the Davidson's Mains public park.

The fact that this jointly-founded association runs an annual queen-crowning gala is not altogether without significance. A village can be a village without a gala. But broadly speaking it is only a village that thinks of having a yearly open-air event of this kind. Morningside has no annual queen-crowning, nor have Fairmilehead, Trinity, Gorgie, Joppa, or any of the outer residential areas of Edinburgh which are clearly recognisable as suburbs.

In Davidson's Mains, further evidence of the community spirit, and further sustenance for it too, was produced some 30 years ago by the founding of the local dramatic society which rapidly reached a high place in the Scottish Community Drama Association's Festival. A corporate pride of this sort, springing in many cases from the enthusiasm of one hard-working leader with a vital personality and a love for the neighbourhood, may have its roots in the past. For although Davidson's Mains is mostly modern, the nucleus of the village—in the typical village street called Main Street—goes back to the centuries when it had the more amusing name of Muttonhole. The ribbon-building that brought the suburbs trailing west along both sides of Queensferry Road has threatened to absorb Davidson's Mains. But the spirit of Muttonhole has survived the threat.

This immortality of " the village ", its refusal to lose its entity as long as there are architects who can restore without destroying its features, is instanced again in Newhaven. No observant man could travel, by private car or bus, from Leith to Granton by the coast road without noticing the " village " features of Newhaven, " Our Lady's Port of Grace." As you come into Main Street and turn right into St Andrew Square and round to the harbour you are instantly in a self-contained fishing village with a strong personality—and perhaps a strong smell of fish and tar—which is quite its own.

The narrowest escape from absorption in suburbia was the one experienced by Duddingston, lying at the foot of Arthur's Seat and along the north-east verge of Duddingston Loch. Of all Edinburgh's villages, this one and the clachan of Swanston are the most rustic. In Swanston you might be in some remote Highland glen. Similarly, if you stand on the south side of Duddingston Loch and look across the reed-fringed expanse of water to the 12th century kirk and the little village with the green hill—the haunch of the *couchant* lion—rising above it, you might be in the foot-hills of the Grampians. But if you let your eye take in a little more of what lies to the right of the village and beyond it, you realise at once that you are nowhere near the Grampians.

The village of Duddingston, which up to the beginning of the '30s of this century had no municipal house nearer than a mile away, has now got houses up to within 50 yards of its north-east side: it is a monument to the inability of sentiment and seclusion to withstand a tidal wave of post-war municipal house-building made necessary by a bulge in the birth-rate.

Much talk, recorded in much print, was expended in the summer of 1953, in opposition to the Corporation's scheme to build 700 houses on the Meadowfield site, covering the eastern side of Arthur's Seat and extending down to within conversational distance of Duddingston village, which had already been closely approached by a ribbon of bungalows built along the north side of Duddingston Road in the later '30s.

The building of the Meadowfield scheme was one of the stimuli leading to the formation, in 1959, of the Society for the Preservation of Duddingston Village, founded to defend the village from any further threat to its separate existence or its rural peace. Its first Secretary was Mr. Nicholas Fairbairn, an advocate who delights to canter into arenas where some precious part of Scotland's inheritance is threatened. Lord Cameron and Sir Compton Mackenzie were among the citizens who gave the society their blessing at its foundation, and it has already engaged in a number of battles for the protection or restoration of its older buildings, such as the 17th century house where Bonnie Prince Charlie slept before the Battle of Prestonpans.

The village itself retains its charm. From the green turf that slopes gently down to the loch—for many years now a bird sanctuary—there is nothing to disturb the impression of rustic peace. The modern housing scheme is out of sight. The old kirk, where jougs still hang against the outside of the surrounding wall, marks Duddingston's link with the Middle Ages. The Sheep Heid Inn, although believed to be the oldest licensed premises in Scotland, is not quite as old as the kirk; as far as records show its oldest part dates from 1670.

But from the inn there comes at certain times of the day a characteristic sound of Duddingston—the rumble of the big skittle bowls rolling down the skittle-alley attached to the inn. It is one of the oldest skittle-alleys in Scotland, far forestalling the modern revival of the game. In the year

1888, at which time the alley had already been long in use, three Edinburgh men founded a fraternity called " The Trotters Club," which meets for play on the first Saturday of every month, except in summer-time, at the Sheep Heid; and it is perhaps true to say that the Trotters carried over into the 20th century the spirit of the convivial clubs that flourished in Edinburgh's Golden Age, and in the time when Sir Walter Scott was an elder in Duddingston Kirk.

There was another such club—the Six-Footers' Club—that met at Hunter's Tryst, on the lower slopes of the Pentlands, up to the beginning of last century; and although the little group of houses called Hunter's Tryst has been engulfed by the Oxgangs housing scheme in the last 15 years, its near neighbour, Swanston, has been not only spared by the Corporation but most admirably tidied up and rebuilt to form a model clachan tucked in among its belt of trees.

The southward spread of the suburbs was fortunately stopped half a mile away from the village, and Swanston's undisturbed intimacy with hills and sheep and larks and curlews continues today as it did when the Covenanters were meeting in the Pentlands and two centuries later when a delicate boy, Robert Louis Stevenson, was weaving his dreams in Swanston Cottage, the summer-time home of his father.

The Cottage (a two-storied villa) is a little west of the clachan, and it is the clachan that has been transformed within the last few years. Its 17th century cottages, understood to be the last surviving village of thatched cottages in the Scottish lowlands, were in a tumble-down condition when the Corporation bought them for restoration in 1954. The three-sided square of substantial stone cottages, built some years ago on the east side, stands as a separate formal group a little apart from the re-built clachan. There were ten cottages in the old clachan, and their outer walls have been retained. But the space used for ten is now allotted to seven incomparably better interiors. The cottages in the old village had no modern conveniences of any kind—no gas, electricity, running water, or sanitation. One solitary water tap served the whole village. All the cottages in the clachan—three with two bedrooms and living-room and four with one bedroom and a living-room—now have bathrooms and kitchens, electricity, and hot and cold water. Ceiling heights have been raised, and, of course, rents have been raised too; in fact, the little clachan of Swanston is for people of the same economic level as those for whom the new cottages at Cramond were designed.

And what of the other surviving villages? As Macrae pointed out in the case of Restalrig, and as we have indicated of Stockbridge, the character of a village sometimes remains even when most of the actual houses of its village days have been removed. Colinton, of course, has still much of the character of a village, and Colinton Dell is lovely; there is a vital community spirit in the heart of Colinton. Cramond Bridge retains its attractive quality; Bonnington has some fragments of its old self left, as Corstorphine has, near the fine old kirk. Bell's Mills, Slateford, Bowbridge, Liberton, and Gilmerton—all these, in differing degrees, show how difficult it is to destroy all trace of a village and with what remarkable tenacity some of Edinburgh's villages have clung to their individual characters. One of them still exists in the very heart of the West End—the Dean Village.

Strictly speaking, it should be called the Water of Leith Village. The Dean Village (and the mansion-house of Dean) stood on the site now occupied by the Dean Cemetery, and was a separate village standing at a considerably higher level than the Water of Leith Village. But it has now become a general custom to apply the name " Dean Village " to the old village still in existence in the valley on the upstream side of the Dean Bridge.

In 1958 the City Architect, Mr. Alexander Steele, laid before the Planning Committee of the Town Council proposals to restore the Dean Village at a cost of more than £100,000. The plan was modified at the time, and had not yet been put into effect when these words were written. The old Tolbooth still stands close to the ancient bridge over the stream. It was the headquarters of the Incorporation of Baxters (bakers) in the 17th century, and over the door can still be seen traces of the insignia of the Incorporation and the almost indecipherable inscription: " God bless the Baxters of Edinburgh uho bult this Hous, 1675." In the stonework of the bridge (unfortunately sometimes marked by children's chalk) there are other carvings of the Baxters—sheaves of corn and loaves of bread. On the other side of the stream stands Well Court, a high but finely designed block of houses built by Sir John Findlay in 1884 for the housing of the villagers, many of whom still live in it. Acknowledged to be one of the best examples of good Victorian architecture in Edinburgh, it gives an oddly Germanic appearance to the village as seen by anyone standing at sunset above the stream's right bank, looking down at the huddle of houses along the little river, and the small footbridge, and the irregular grouping of old buildings, with that great house over on the left bank.

The Dean Village, old and needing care, is the meeting point of *rus* and *urbs* in the heart of the New Town. Flour was being milled here and bread baked eight centuries ago. Fashionable folk from the Old Town holidayed in this little village in the time of the royal Georges, when Edinburgh was still perched on its long ridge beside the Castle. Today, the villagers are no different from men and women of similar incomes in adjacent parts of Edinburgh. Indeed, it may be said of all Edinburgh's villagers that they see the same television programmes and work in the same places as those who live in the rest of the city and its suburbs. But they are villagers none the less—villagers living inside a city boundary, holding on to a thread of separate tradition even when the thread is frayed with age.

Chapter 5

THE PEOPLE

JUDGING by statistics Edinburgh people are so tough that it would almost seem as if they have drawn vitality from their Castle rock, their hills and sea, and their ancient buildings.

Whilst forming over nine per cent of the total population of Scotland, two-thirds of Edinburgh citizens are native, and only 12 per cent of the city's total population of more than 468,000 come from outside Scotland. There has remained an overall numerical stability with the birth-rate staying lower than that of Scotland as a whole, the death-rate higher, and Edinburgh families smaller than in the rest of Scotland. Yet within the city there are more births than deaths, the birth-rate is rising, and infant mortality is declining. The Royal Burgh has also more women than men as compared with Scotland as a whole, more widows than widowers, and more emigration than immigration. Yet there is a concurrent increase in the number of families.

Unwilling to remain crammed in the city centre within the old Flodden Wall, they have expanded outward as the city has declared its professional and industrial allegiance, and now Edinburgh has a lower density of population than most other British cities. In recent years there has been a decrease of immigrants from Ireland and the crofting communities, but an increase from England and abroad has offered the Edinburgh native opportunities of a wider hospitality and growth. A number of clubs and private individuals are concerning themselves deeply with this aspect of city life, and it will be interesting to observe resultant trends over the next decades. Will Edinburgh continue to hug itself as solidly against outside penetration as in past centuries?

It has been very rightly said by T. W. Freeman in *The Conurbations of Great Britain* that our modern British civilisation is essentially and thoroughly a town one.[1] The urban character of our pattern of life is quite clearly demonstrated in Scotland where, if we judge by the figures given in the 1961 Census Reports issued by the Registrar General for Scotland, some 70.4 per cent of the population live in the cities, the large burghs and the small burghs and some 29·6 per cent in the landward areas. The figures for the 1961 Census show that 36·5 per cent live in the four counties of cities (Glasgow, Edinburgh, Aberdeen and Dundee), 16·8 per cent in the large burghs (some 20 burghs with more than 20,000 inhabitants) and 17·0 per cent in the smaller burghs. Altogether more than two-thirds of the population of Scotland live in the towns.

Edinburgh, as the capital city and the second largest in population in the country, provides a fascinating study of a modern conurbation.

[1] Manchester University Press 1959.

It amply fulfils C. B. Fawcett's definition of a conurbation as a continuously urban area occupied by a continuous series of dwellings, factories and other buildings, harbours and docks, urban parks and playing fields, etc., which are not separated from one another by rural land, though such an urban area often includes enclaves of rural land which is still in agricultural occupation.

The Royal Burgh of Edinburgh is an uncommonly pleasant city, lapped around by truly country districts and with many green spaces preserved within its bounds. Though its earliest extant charter dates from the days of Robert I or Robert the Bruce, it held its rights and privileges by royal charter from even earlier days; and for centuries it was the most populous city in Scotland—a proud position it held until ousted by Glasgow.

Since then the city, as we saw, has altered greatly, and naturally there have been great changes in the numbers and disposition of the people who have lived and who today live within the city boundaries; for as Edinburgh has expanded, so has the populace.

THE PRESENT POPULATION AND ITS CHARACTER

The population enumerated in the City of Edinburgh at the 1961 Census was 468,361. However, if one allows for Edinburgh residents that were enumerated elsewhere in Scotland and for non-residents that were enumerated in Edinburgh, this gives us a figure for Resident population of 471,004 on Census night. This represented some 9·1 per cent of the population of Scotland, and placed Edinburgh second only to Glasgow, easily the largest of the four Scottish cities. Glasgow with some 20·4 per cent of the population of Scotland concentrated within its bounds is more than twice as big as Edinburgh, which in turn is larger than both Aberdeen (185 thousands) and Dundee (183 thousands) put together.

TABLE 4

THE POPULATION OF SCOTLAND AND THE FOUR CHIEF CITIES

	Resident				Enumerated			
	1951[1]		1961		1951[1]		1961	
	Population	Per cent	Population	Per cent	Population	Per cent	Population	Per cent
Scotland	5,096,415	100	5,179,344	100	5,096,415	100	5,179,344	100
Glasgow	1,092,587	21·4	1,057,084	20·4	1,089,767	21·4	1,055,017	20·4
Edinburgh	473,866	9·3	471,004	9·1	466,943	9·2	468,361	9·0
Aberdeen	183,301	3·6	184,801	3·6	182,783	3·6	185,390	3·6
Dundee	177,385	3·5	183,339	3·5	177,340	3·5	182,978	3·5

[1] These figures have been corrected to take account of any boundary changes over the inter-census period.

Over the period Edinburgh has retained just over 9 per cent of the Scottish population. If allowance is made for the slight adjustment of the City boundaries in 1954 the enumerated population for the area corresponding to the present extent of the city would have been 473,866 at census 1951.

This gives an intercensal decrease of 2,862, representing 0·6 per cent of the 1951 population. In the corresponding period the population of Glasgow showed a decrease of 3·2 per cent, while Aberdeen and Dundee showed increases of 0·8 and 3·4 per cent respectively.

TABLE 5

INTERCENSAL CHANGES IN RESIDENT POPULATION 1951 TO 1961

	1951	1961	*% increase/ decrease*
Glasgow	1,092,587	1,057,084	—3·2
Edinburgh	473,866	471,004	—0·6
Aberdeen	183,301	184,801	+0·8
Dundee	177,385	183,339	+3·4

It is of interest to compare Edinburgh, with just less than one tenth of the population of the whole country normally resident within its bounds, with her sister cities; for we see at once how dominant Glasgow is in the Scottish economy. Her population of over one fifth of that of Scotland is not only more than twice the population of Edinburgh, but it exceeds that of Edinburgh, Aberdeen and Dundee together by over 200,000. While importance cannot be judged in terms of size alone, nevertheless such a considerable excess clearly indicates Glasgow's economic importance. That Edinburgh maintains her population as she does is a tribute not only to her professional and cultural traditions but also to that fairly substantial core of industry which forms one of the bases of her prosperity and attractiveness. It is also worth noting that of the four cities, the population of Edinburgh has remained the most stable.

It is now commonly accepted that the number of women in the population has generally exceeded that of men. At some times the excess has been greater than at others, but usually the balance has been in favour of women. There is no absolute guarantee that this tendency will continue; there are indeed some indications of a reversal of this trend for those under 21 years of age. In June 1961 (to give the relevant figures) the Registrar General for Scotland estimated that there were 902,800 males and 873,700 females under 21 in Scotland. But this change of trend will take a long time to invalidate the general greater preponderance of women in our populations. The totals for all age groups estimated in June 1961 were 2,487,200 males and 2,696,000 females. Table 6 (given below) shows the position in Edinburgh relative to the rest of Scotland.

TABLE 6

PERCENTAGE OF FEMALES IN EDINBURGH AND SCOTLAND

	Edinburgh	*Scotland*
1801	57	54
1851	55	52
1901	54	51
1951	54	52
1961	54	52

It is noteworthy that the percentage of females residing in Edinburgh has always been above the national figure, though this has not given rise to any very special feminist attitudes or movements in the city. Nor does the age structure of the population in Edinburgh differ very much from that of Scotland as a whole. In 1951, 24 per cent of males and 20 per cent of females were under 15; 66 per cent of males and 67 per cent of females 15–65; and 9 per cent of males and 13 per cent of females over 65. Edinburgh has shared in the rising numbers of old people in Scotland since the beginning of this century; but as shown later there has been a recent rise in the flow of births, and this must inevitably increase the percentage of children in the population. To understand this better let us look at the following table:

TABLE 7
CONJUGAL CONDITION OF THE EDINBURGH AND SCOTTISH POPULATIONS IN 1901 AND 1951

	Males (Per cent of all males over 15)				*Females (Per cent of all females over 15)*			
	1901		*1951*		*1901*		*1951*	
	Edin.	*Scotland*	*Edin.*	*Scotland*	*Edin.*	*Scotland*	*Edin.*	*Scotland*
Single	48	47	30	32	50	44	33	32
Married	47	48	64	62	38	44	53	56
Widowed and divorced	5	5	6	6	12	11	14	13

From this table which shows (in percentages of those over 15 years of age) the conjugal conditions of the populations of Edinburgh and Scotland in 1901 and 1951, it is clear that marriage has come more into favour in this half-century. In 1901 some 47 per cent of the male population of Edinburgh were married (which was almost exactly the national figure of 48 per cent) but only some 38 per cent of the female population (which compared unfavourably with the national figure of 44 per cent). By 1951 these percentages had risen to 64 for males in Edinburgh as against 62 for males in Scotland, and to 53 for females in Edinburgh as against 56 for females for Scotland. A very much larger proportion of the population had become married people. There may be some connection between these figures and the decrease in the number of illegitimate births. That there is a higher proportion of widows to widowers, both in Edinburgh and in Scotland generally, is due to the greater expectation of life in women.

An analysis in Table 8 (p. 98) of private households based on the number of children under 16, taken from a one per cent sample of the 1951 Census, shows that Edinburgh had more households without children than the national average and was below that average where there was one child or more. The 1961 Census figures have brought out that nearly half of the households in Edinburgh (46·6 per cent) comprise one or two persons only. In 1951 the corresponding proportion was 41·0.

TABLE 8

PRIVATE HOUSEHOLDS WITH DIFFERENT NUMBERS OF CHILDREN UNDER 16 (1951)

Number of Children	*Edinburgh*	*Glasgow*
0	61	54
1	17	21
2	13	14
3–4	7	9
5 or more	1	2

THE GROWTH OF THE POPULATION

If the population trend is a rough measure of a town's progress (or lack of it) then it can be said that Edinburgh has shown a continuous advance, though the nature and the complexity of the boundary changes mentioned earlier show how difficult it is to keep track of the population growth in earlier centuries and to give a precise account of it.

Even before 1801, the date of the first official Census, many estimates of the population were made. These have yielded some interesting figures. The first *Statistical Account* suggests that the population of Edinburgh and its immediate neighbourhood, meaning the urban population centred on Edinburgh rather than that actually inside the narrow boundary of the city, was 35,000 in 1678, 40,420 in 1722, 48,000 at least in 1753,[1] and 57,195 in 1755.[2]

When the Edinburgh minister, Dr. Alexander Webster, arranged for his famous census in 1755, from which the last figure was taken—this was one of the earliest computations for a whole nation since the days of the Roman Empire—the population of the city of Edinburgh numbered merely 31,122. But if we add the populations of the surrounding districts of the Canongate, St. Cuthbert's, South Leith and North Leith the figure rises to the 57,195 quoted above, and if we add further the populations of the parishes of Midlothian, also incorporated later within the city bounds, the figure increases to 64,679. Arnot's computation in 1755[3] gives a figure of 70,430 and the *Statistical Account* itself (1791) of 84,886. Let us look then at Table 9 (p. 99) to see what changes have taken place in the intervening years between the last 18th century tally and our own day.

In columns (3) and (5) of Table 9 the term " present area " means the area of the city at the 1961 census, which is a more suitable basis for a chronological comparison of population than the area at each census date; there have been many extensions of boundary since the census of 1801. If we reduce the data in Table 9 to 50-year periods we get the comparison as set out below the Table.

[1] *First Statistical Account*. Vol. 6, p. 560 et seq.
[2] *Scottish Population Statistics*. Introduction, J. G. Kyd, Scottish History Society, 1952.
[3] Quoted in the first *Statistical Account*.

TABLE 9
GROWTH OF POPULATION TABLE

	Scotland	Edinburgh Present area	Percentage increase	
			Scotland	Edinburgh Present area
(1)	(2)	(3)	(4)	(5)
1801	1,608,420	90,768	—	—
1811	1,805,864	112,962	12	24
1821	2,091,521	150,674	16	33
1831	2,364,386	175,407	13	16
1841	2,620,184	179,897	11	3
1851	2,888,742	208,477	10	16
1861	3,062,294	222,015	6	6
1871	3,360,018	266,081	10	20
1881	3,735,573	320,549	11	20
1891	4,025,647	360,522	8	12
1901	4,472,103	413,008	11	15
1911	4,760,904	423,464	6	3
1921	4,882,497	420,264	3	1
1931	4,842,980	439,010	1	4
1951	5,096,415	466,943	5	6
1961	5,179,344	468,361	2	0·3

	Population	*Increase*	*Per cent increase*
1801	90,768	—	—
1851	208,477	117,709	130
1901	413,008	204,531	98
1951	466,761	53,753	13

It will be seen that over the 150 years the increase of population has been just over five-fold whereas the population in Scotland has little more than trebled over the same period. It will also be seen that the rate of increase in Edinburgh has fallen greatly and was only 13 per cent in the first half of the present century compared with 16 per cent for Scotland as a whole. During this first half of this century, therefore, the population of Edinburgh has not grown as fast as that of Scotland, but over the past 150 years Edinburgh has had more than her fair share of Scottish population growth.

This is, of course, to be expected with the industrial developments and the definite urbanisation of our national life during the past 150 years. Miss Catherine P. Snodgrass, writing on population in the *Scientific Survey of South Eastern Scotland,* published for the British Association in 1951, has an interesting map showing the date of maximum population by parishes for South Eastern Scotland. This clearly indicates the drift to the towns from the rural areas from 1801 to 1931—a drift which really set in during 1841. Improvements in transport and greater ease of communication have also accelerated the growth of the urban population.

The columns showing the percentage increases are, as we should expect, illuminating. Certain decades show notable percentage increases for Edinburgh which are very much in excess of the national increase. In 1811 it is 24 per cent as against the national average increase of 12 per cent; in 1821 it is no less than 33 per cent as against 16 per cent; in 1871, 20 per cent as against 10 per cent; and in 1881, 20 per cent as against 11 per cent. The decades in the generation about the middle of the century, however, show a reversal of this trend: there is a tendency for the Edinburgh figures to be below the national figures. Thus in 1841 it is a mere 3 per cent for Edinburgh as against 11 per cent for Scotland as a whole. This same tendency has shown itself in the last half century: 3 per cent in 1911 as against 6 per cent; minus 1 per cent in 1921 as against 3 per cent. The fall in population enumerated in Edinburgh at the 1921 Census was mainly due to the fact that this Census was held in June, which is one of the holiday months.

A consideration of the broader aspects of the figures is probably even more profitable. It will be noted that, whereas the population of Scotland has grown rather more than three-fold since 1801 (317 per cent), the Edinburgh figure is more than five-fold (514 per cent). While the increases in Edinburgh's population have been materially greater than for Scotland over the whole period from 1801 the increases since 1901 are 14 per cent and 13 per cent respectively; which indicates that while the increases between the censuses do not by any means correspond, these differences have tended to smooth out in the first half of this century, and Edinburgh has now fallen slightly but not appreciably behind the national figure. In the decade 1951–61, however, the difference became still more marked; the population of Edinburgh rose by only 0·3 per cent whereas that of Scotland rose by 1·6 per cent.

ELEMENTS IN THE GROWTH OF THE POPULATION

NATURAL INCREASE

One main cause of the growth of the population is the vitality of the stock which is shown by the excess of births over deaths. The natural increase, as this is called, determines the growth; but this in turn has been considerably affected by the migration of the people both from and into the city. Tables and a graph relevant to this factor over the past 100 years are most revealing:

TABLE 10
NATURAL INCREASE AND MIGRATION

	Net increase in population (000)	*Natural increase*	*Balance due to Migration*
1861–1871	+ 29	+ 15	+ 14
1871–1881	+ 31	+ 22	+ 9
1881–1891 (1891 area)	+ 27	+ 25	+ 2
1891–1901 (1901 area)	+ 44	+ 22	+ 22
1901–1911 (1911 area)	+ 3	+ 22	— 19
1911–1921 (1921 area)	— 4	+ 11	— 15
1921–1931	+ 19	+ 18	— 1[1]
1931–1951	+ 28	+ 28	+ 10[2]

[1] Allowance for usual residence.
[2] Allowance for usual residence, war casualties and changes in the armed forces.

TABLE 11
BIRTH AND DEATH RATES PER 1000 POPULATION

	Birth Rates		*Death Rates*	
	Edinburgh	*Scotland*	*Edinburgh*	*Scotland*
1861	35·5	34·9	24·4	20·3
1871	34·1	34·5	27·0	22·2
1881	32·0	33·7	20·1	19·3
1891	28·1	31·2	21·6	20·7
1901	24·9	29·5	19·4	17·9
1911	20·7	25·6	14·8	15·1
1921	21·5	25·2	14·4	13·6
1931	16·2	19·0	12·9	13·3
1941	15·0	17·5	15·3	14·7
1951	15·7	17·7	13·9	12·9
1961	17·7	19·5	13·1	12·3

TABLE 12
BIRTH AND DEATH RATES FOR RECENT YEARS

	Birth Rates		*Death Rates*	
	Edinburgh	*Scotland*	*Edinburgh*	*Scotland*
1952	15·0	17·7	12·6	12·0
1953	15·4	17·8	12·3	11·5
1954	15·5	18·0	12·9	12·0
1955	15·2	18·0	12·9	12·0
1956	16·0	18·5	13·0	12·0
1957	16·9	19·0	12·9	11·9
1958	16·8	19·2	12·9	12·0
1959	17·4	19·1	13·3	12·1
1960	17·9	19·4	12·6	11·9
1961	17·7	19·5	13·1	12·3

The first of these last three tables (Table 10, indicating the character of population increases in the last century) shows clearly that the natural increase due to the excess of births over deaths did not by any means account for the net increase in population of the area. There is from 1861 to 1901 a positive balance of migration. In other words there were more people coming to reside within the city than were leaving it to find homes elsewhere. Edinburgh was in fact recruiting its population not only from its own stock but also from many places furth of the city, if not furth of the country. But in the period from 1901 to 1931 the picture changes and the net increase is well below the natural increase. There was clearly a considerable migration out of the city to other parts of the country, to England and overseas; and on the balance Edinburgh was losing a considerable part of its own natural stock. It is true that this tendency was slowing down in the 1921–31 decade, while the double decade from 1931 to 1951, thanks to the allowances made in the statistics for usual place of residence, war casualties and service in the armed forces, shows a return to the earlier trend. The balance of migration, which had previously been positive, had from 1901 to 1931 become negative. From 1861 to 1901 the city had made a net gain by migration of 47,000 and then from

1901 to 1931 a net loss of 35,000. It is not surprising that there should have been the slowing down, which we have already noted, in the growth of Edinburgh's population during the early years of the present century.

BIRTH RATE AND DEATH RATE

The birth rate and death rate figures (Tables 11 and 12 above) show that Edinburgh has since 1861 always had a birth rate less than that of Scotland as a whole. It may well be that, with its higher proportion of professional people and of retired people, the fertility of the population is lower. On the other hand, and again because of the numbers of retired people and the general character of the population, the death rate has been, with the exceptions of the years 1911 and 1931, always greater than that for Scotland. Only once, in 1941, does the death rate (15·3) exceed the birth rate (15). This is in contradistinction to the country as a whole where the corresponding figures are 17·5 for the birth rate and 14·7 for the death rate. It will be noticed further that for Edinburgh—after a plateau from 1861 to 1871—there is a continuous fall in the birth rate, caused by changing economic circumstances and social habits, until 1921 when the continuous downward trend is halted by the increased birth rates of the post-war years. The birth rate fell after the post 1939–45 peak to an average of 15·3 in the years 1952–5, since when there has been a gradual rise to 17·7 in 1961. The death rate, after a fair rise from 1861 to 1871, sharply declines to 1881 and then after a very slight rise continues to decline slowly until 1931. Then a fair rise actually brings the death rate above the birth rate in 1941, only to decline again since, so that the birth rate in 1951 exceeded the death rate by 1.8 per thousand. The average difference has since risen to 4.6 per thousand.

ILLEGITIMACY

The figures given in Table 13 (below) for illegitimate births per cent of all births do not put Edinburgh in a favourable light as compared with the figures for Scotland as a whole. Though Edinburgh's position is therefore not creditable, certain areas in Scotland, particularly certain rural areas, have an even less enviable position. Edinburgh has shared in the general decline in the percentage of illegitimate births, but only on three occasions do the figures for Edinburgh fall below the figures for the whole country—in 1871, 1881 and again in 1931. Otherwise Edinburgh continues to show figures in excess of the national averages. The low rate of 5·5 in 1951 decreased further to 4·7 in 1958 and 1959 but has since increased slightly, in sympathy with the national rate, to 5·7 in 1961. At present about 1 in 20 births is illegitimate as against 1 in 10 in 1861 and 1 in 14 in 1901.

TABLE 13
ILLEGITIMATE BIRTHS PER CENT OF ALL BIRTHS

	Edinburgh	*Scotland*
1861	9·9	9·3
1871	8·6	9·5
1881	8·1	8·3
1891	8·6	7·7
1901	7·0	6·3
1911	8·2	7·6
1921	7·2	7·1
1931	7·0	7·2
1951	5·5	5·1
1958	4·7	4·1
1961	5·7	4·6

TABLE 14
DENSITY OF POPULATION OF VARIOUS CITIES OF GREAT BRITAIN AT THE CENSUS OF 1951

City	*Population* (000)	*Acreage*[1] (000)	*Persons to the acre*
Edinburgh	467	32·6	14
Liverpool	789	27·3	29
Belfast	444	15·3	29
Glasgow	1,090	39·2	28
Manchester	703	27·3	26
Birmingham	1,113	51·1	22
Aberdeen	183	10·6	17
Bristol	443	26·4	17
Dundee	177	12·3	14
Sheffield	513	39·6	13
Leeds	505	38·3	13

[1] In this table acreage includes inland water.

With a population density of 14 to the acre, Edinburgh (see Table 14 above) compares very well with other cities of the British Isles. Of the four cities of Scotland, Dundee alone ranks with Edinburgh, though Aberdeen is not very far behind. Glasgow's density is twice that of Edinburgh. Only two cities shown in the table—Sheffield and Leeds—have a better record (and that by very little, only by one person per acre). All the others in varying degrees have greater population densities.

As the map based upon Table 15 shows (p. 104), the greatest population densities are to be found in the wards geographically in the central area of the city, and the lowest population densities in the wards on the city's fringes. This is the normal pattern in Britain.

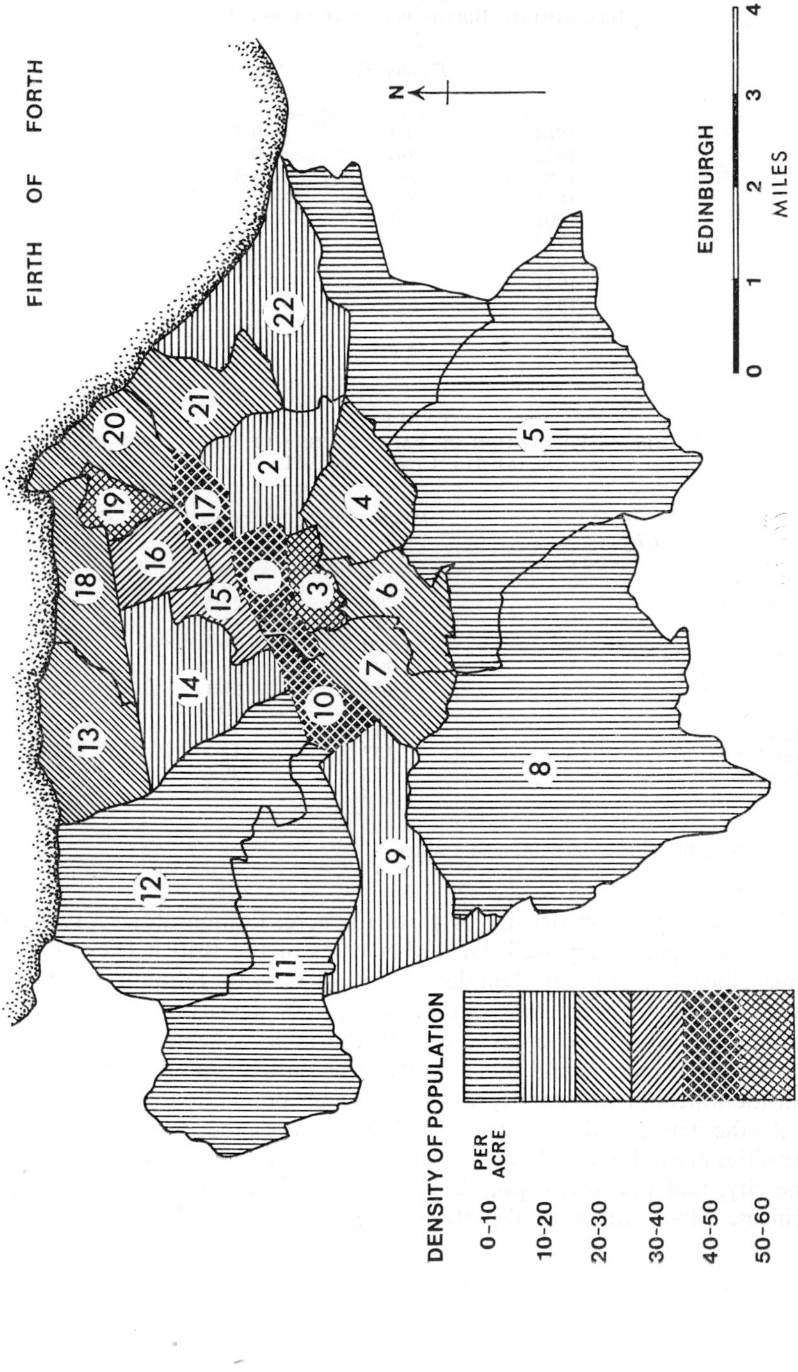
FIRTH OF FORTH
N
EDINBURGH
0 1 2 3 4
MILES
DENSITY OF POPULATION
PER ACRE
0–10
10–20
20–30
30–40
40–50
50–60
1
2
3
4
5
6
7
8
9
10
11
12
13
14
15
16
17
18
19
20
21
22

TABLE 15

POPULATION AND POPULATION DENSITY OF THE EDINBURGH WARDS AT THE CENSUS OF 1961

Ward	*Number on map*	*Population*	*Acreage (excluding inland water)*	*Persons to the acre*
Central Leith	19	17,156	295	58
Calton	17	15,389	316	49
St. Giles	1	17,687	394	45
George Square	3	16,334	317	52
Gorgie-Dalry	10	18,606	421	44
St. Andrews	15	14,495	375	39
Broughton	16	16,810	515	33
South Leith	20	18,206	623	29
Craigentinny	21	20,260	779	26
West Leith	18	16,016	648	25
Morningside	6	17,211	689	25
Pilton	13	27,840	1,066	26
Newington	4	22,958	903	25
Merchiston	7	16,066	748	22
Holyrood	2	13,949	894	16
Portobello	22	27,141	1,628	17
St. Bernards	14	25,823	1,396	19
Craigmillar	23	17,083	1,871	9
Corstorphine	11	21,543	3,480	6
Murrayfield–Cramond	12	22,489	3,334	7
Liberton	5	34,610	4,853	7
Colinton	8	26,874	6,120	4
Sighthill	9	23,815	1,629	15
Edinburgh		468,361	33,294	14

The 1961 Census, however, showed that the number of Scottish born persons has decreased since 1951 by over 5,000, while the number born outside Scotland has increased. Those born in England and Wales have increased by over 2,000 and those born outside the British Isles by over 3,000.

In more detail, we find that of the 468,361 inhabitants enumerated in 1961, 411,548 or 87·9 per cent were of Scottish origin, leaving a remnant of 56,813 or 12·1 per cent as originating furth of Scotland. The corresponding percentages for 1951 were 89·3 and 10·7. Of the 56,813 " outsiders " in 1961, 34,690 or 6·1 per cent were born in England, an increase of 4.3 per cent as compared with 1951. The numbers stated to be born in Northern Ireland (2,060) and in Wales (1,492) are slightly up on 1951, and the number stated to be born in the Irish Republic (3,108) slightly down. (In addition, 308 persons, compared with 32 persons in 1951, were recorded as being born in Ireland but did not state which part.)

Of the persons born outside the British Isles, 2,217 were visitors and 11,578 were residents. Of these residents, 5,301 were born somewhere within the Commonwealth (the Dominions, the Crown Colonies and these other lands which owe even nominal allegiance to the British Crown) and 6,277 were classified as of foreign birth. By no means all of the latter were in the true sense foreigners or aliens, for some 3,031 were citizens of the United Kingdom and Colonies and 16 were citizens of Commonwealth countries or the Irish Republic. The largest single group with citizenship of the United Kingdom and Colonies consisted of 682 who were born in Germany, most of them no doubt the children of Service families. Of the 3,122 persons classed as aliens 706 were born in the United States, 697 in Poland, 371 in Italy, 246 in Russia (a surprisingly high figure), 233 in Germany, 94 in the United Arab Republic, 94 in Norway, and 87 in France.

THE ORIGINS OF THE POPULATION

BIRTHPLACES

If we consider the birthplaces of the people who make up the population of the city, as indicated in the census returns for such selected dates as 1881, 1911 and 1951, we can construct tables which will give us the sources of the immigrants who have contributed to the growth of the population. The corresponding figures for Glasgow have been added for comparison.

TABLE 16

BIRTHPLACES OF THE POPULATIONS OF EDINBURGH AND GLASGOW FROM THE CENSUSES OF 1881, 1911 AND 1951 GIVEN AS PERCENTAGES

	Edinburgh			*Glasgow*		
	1881	*1911*	*1951*	*1881*	*1911*	*1951*
Birthplace						
Scotland	90	90	89	83	87	92
Edinburgh	54	54	64			
Glasgow				52	62	74
Crofting counties	5	4	2	4	3	2
England	5	6	7	3	4	3
Ireland	3	2	1	13	7	3
Elsewhere	2	2	3	1	2	2

It will be observed that while the proportion of Scottish-born people has remained very constant for Edinburgh at 90 per cent of her total population, the proportion for Glasgow has steadily increased throughout these years from 83 per cent in 1881 (when it was some 7 per cent below Edinburgh) to 92 per cent in 1951 (when it was some 3 per cent above Edinburgh). It is clear also that, whereas in 1881 both Edinburgh and Glasgow were drawing upon native-born people to practically the same degree, Edinburgh as the capital city drew, in 1911 and 1951, a larger percentage of its population from the more distant parts of the country than did Glasgow. This is true also of Edinburgh as compared with Dundee. We must note here that the proportion drawn from the Crofting Counties of Argyll, Caithness, Inverness, Orkney, Ross and Cromarty, Sutherland and Zetland, though never very large, began with Edinburgh drawing rather more than Glasgow; but in 1951 both cities had drawn an equal proportion from this area, itself only a portion of the whole Highland area. In 1881 this area provided enough migrants to give Edinburgh 1 in every 20 of her population. By 1911 this had fallen to 1 in every 25 and by 1951 to 1 in every 50.

It is a different story with those born in England. They were as numerous as those from the Crofting Counties in 1881, (i.e. another 1 in every 20 of Edinburgh's population in that year had been born south of the Border), but even more numerous in 1911 when the proportion of English-born had risen to 1 in 17. The more immediate neighbourhood of Edinburgh (that is, excluding the Crofting Counties) has provided some 30 per cent of her population with the Lothians, Fife and Perthshire as the city's greatest contributors.

By 1911 the picture had hardly altered from that in 1881. Edinburgh had still drawn 90 per cent of her inhabitants from Scotland and 54 per cent from within her own boundary. The percentage from the Crofting Counties, as we saw had declined a little, the percentage from England had advanced a little, and so too had the percentage from Ireland. Substantially the overall picture remained constant. Except for a few more English immigrants, Edinburgh in 1951 and again in 1961 remained as attractive, but not more attractive than before, to people from other parts.

STUDENTS FROM ABROAD

A good example of the constancy of this appeal may be seen at the University where for some years the number of overseas students has kept fairly steady at about 1,000, which in itself is an impressive figure, especially as many of the students are resident in the city for several years. A count taken in the New Year of 1963 recorded a figure of 1,060 students from abroad, and of these 617 came from Commonwealth and 443 from foreign countries. India headed the Commonwealth list with 122 students, though the U.S.A. out-passed her with 140. But if the Commonwealth countries represented in 1963 ranged from Australia and Canada to India and Pakistan and finally to Swaziland and Zanzibar, they were outmatched in number by the foreign countries which included France, Germany, Scandinavia, several " Iron Curtain " countries, Libya, the Somali Republic, Korea and most other nations.

At the start of the following session (1963–4) the total number of students had fallen a little—to 927—and of these 541 came from 35 countries of the Commonwealth, the greatest number from India, Pakistan, Nigeria, Kenya, Jamaica, Australia and Canada in that order, with single individuals representing Bermuda, Basutoland, British Honduras, Dominica, Gambia, Gibraltar and St. Kitts.

Europe sent 114 students from 18 countries. Curiously enough, more than double the number from any other European country came from Germany (34), with Iceland in second place (13); while France seemed to be breaking her traditional links with Scotland by sending only two.

Outside the Commonwealth, 16 countries from Asia provided 57 students, and 75 students came from 8 African countries. North and South America together sent 140, and of these 127 came from the United States, a country which has always enjoyed close academic links with the University.

Such figures as these are often quoted in the unending local debate as to whether Edinburgh is really a cosmopolitan city, though of this there can be little doubt judging by the city's International Festival, the big intake of tourists from spring to autumn and the sheer variety of those people who have crossed the seas to live and study within the boundaries of a city which has, in the main, been free from the colour prejudices which have disfigured community life elsewhere. For this the University, which as we shall see established a Centre of African Studies in 1963, is to a great extent responsible; and for that reason we might well take another look at the colourful influx of students which Edinburgh accepts each year from almost every corner of the globe.

For many decades before the last War the University attracted more students from overseas than any other University, and it still has more than most. To take another recent sample year, there were in the spring of 1962 no fewer than 1,200 overseas students at the University, and there were rather more the year before that when medicine alone accounted for more than 440 students from abroad, science and technological subjects almost 370, and arts subjects also some 370. There are obviously many seekers after academic truth in a colder climate than their own.

The majority of this impressive array come to Edinburgh to read for a first degree or to get training, as Mr. Julius Nyerere of Tanganyika did, in a profession or skill which may take between three and six years to complete. But some—Dr. Hastings Banda of Nyasaland for example—come for post-graduate work, particularly in the Faculty of Medicine, and these stay for shorter periods. Always too there are foreign students and some, who are not students at all, who do not wish University tuition but come as " au pair " girls or seek domestic work in order to learn English.

With such a large and varied influx, and also because many of these students have dissimilar language and cultural roots, special steps have been taken to bring them together in friendly surroundings and make their stay in the city as memorable as possible.

" It is clearly important," says an official of the British Council which plays a leading part in furthering this aim, " that while overseas students are here they should be able not only to study happily but also to enter as fully as possible into our own life, so that when they return home they will have gained both the knowledge and qualifications for which they came, and a real understanding of Britain and its people. At the same time their presence amongst us provides the opportunity of getting to know them well as individuals, and of learning from them something of the culture, history, geography, economy and not least the aspirations of their countries. By offering friendship and hospitality we can in fact help to lessen the sense of isolation which many feel as the result of separation from their families and homeland. As many of these students will return to occupy positions of responsibility in their own countries we can, by our willingness to make them feel at home here, also help to establish and maintain good relations between this country and theirs and so contribute to better international understanding."

In furtherance of these laudable ambitions the British Council receives funds from the Government. But in Edinburgh the British Council has not been allowed to work alone, for in 1959 a Committee of Welcome to Overseas Students was set up under the patronage of the Lord Provost. This Committee, of which the secretariat is provided by the British Council, comprises member-organisations that have a concern for the well-being of all overseas students, and includes the Edinburgh Christian Council for Overseas Students, the English-Speaking Union of the Commonwealth, representatives of the University and of the Students' Representative Council, the Royal Commonwealth Society, the Royal Over-Seas League, the Victoria League, Edinburgh International Club, the Y.M.C.A. and Y.W.C.A. and the denominational Chaplaincies. All this is a notable step forward.

There is a permanent centre for the activities of the British Council in Edinburgh, and this is also the Council's head office in Scotland—with administrative offices as well as student facilities for both study and entertainment on a wide and varied scale ranging from billiards and table tennis to country dancing and record playing. But long before overseas students have been introduced to these amenities, the British Council, in co-operation with the City Corporation has taken special steps to greet them on arrival; and of course the University later has its own welcoming arrangements. All this involves a great deal of organisation.

At the beginning of every University year British Council volunteers meet all overseas students on arrival either at Waverley station or at the city's airport and see them safely to their new homes. Once settled they are invited to a Reception held by the Lord Provost and the Corporation as a welcome to the city. Thereafter the British Council continues its work throughout the session.

THE OVERSEAS COMMUNITIES

THE FRENCH

Much nearer home than most of these overseas students are the people who come across the English Channel and the North Sea to Edinburgh from Britain's nearest neighbours. Here the ties are old and strong. It was not for nothing that the Franco–Scottish Alliance stayed intact for centuries, nor in vain that Scottish students, traders and mercenaries flourished in the Low Countries and those of Scandinavia, whose long boats earlier and in a different setting left both place and family names in Scotland that still persist.

Today the ties between Scotland and Scandinavia are as infrangible as ever, and Edinburgh benefits in consequence as the Scandinavian capitals do. Nor has the long affinity between France and l'Ecosse been endangered by General de Gaulle's strong attitudes during the lengthy Common Market negotiations in the early '60s. French people and many of their schoolchildren (for educational reasons) frequently visit Edinburgh, where there has long been a flourishing French Institute; and Edinburgh people, apart from cultural missions, pour into France and not least to Nice, Edinburgh's officially adopted " sister " city.

There is, of course, an old tradition behind all this, going back to the time when unruly French soldiers who settled in Edinburgh centuries ago formed colonies which may not have been altogether popular. Yet there is no doubt that since the days of Mary, Queen of Scots, French visitors to the city have fostered a firm tradition of warmth and friendliness.

This was particularly marked during the last war which found the French colony centred not in Little France, where many of Mary's courtiers lived, but around the Franco-Scottish House in Regent Terrace. This building was the joint purchase of the British Council and of the Free French Government. It was inaugurated by General de Gaulle himself on 22nd June 1942, and the Free French came to the house in hundreds, till its activities ceased with the end of the grim events which had brought it into being. Today it is the French Consulate General.

The French colony has now dwindled to its peace-time figure, with the addition of those men whose Scottish wives caused them to settle in the country, and of the French brides won by the Scots' prestige in France. (This last remark is a Frenchman's.) A few score of the Frenchmen who have settled in and around Edinburgh permanently since the war work for the most part in the local mines or on the land, or run small business concerns. According to the 1961 Census, there were then only 178 residents in Edinburgh of French birth and of these 88 had become citizens of the United Kingdom and the Colonies. The Census figure would include some of the 30 French diplomats, teachers, secretaries and others of the kind who work at the Consulate General or the French Institute, and an approximately equivalent number of students who teach in secondary schools, or at the University. These come from various French University towns, but many of them are sent by Caen and Nice, the two cities which enjoy the greatest cultural interchange with Edinburgh.

Then also there are the occasional visitors—those who come during the Festival, when you can see so many odd looking French cars, awkwardly keeping to the left-hand side of the city streets; or the members of the French rugby team; or the picturesque " Onion Johnnies" who spend half the year in Edinburgh where they can often be seen on winter days pushing bicycles heavily laden with their strings of onions. Always there is the French Institute.

" Try walking into the Institute on the opening day of an important exhibition," writes an enthusiastic Edinburgh Frenchman, " and see the numerous guests grouped before each work of art, be it French or Scottish—on the occasion, for instance, of the colourful display of arts and crafts from Nice and the Cote d'Azur with its originals by Picasso, Matisse, Dufy, Léger, Chagall . . . and with the picturesque Niçoises in national costume carrying baskets of flowers specially flown from France; or again the " France-Ecosse " exhibition which, in 1953, offered so many tangible proofs of one of the longest friendships two peoples have ever known, or the Gustave Doré Exhibition, or the annual ' Salon ' of works by young and coming Scottish artists, or that of ' Scottish Painters in France '."

The French Institute deserves a tribute here. Founded in 1946 thanks largely to the initiative of Professor John Orr, Professor of French and head of the Department of French and Romance Philology at the University, the Institute encountered in Edinburgh an atmosphere particularly congenial to its development; for already, to quote a French resident, there was " a long established tradition of culture in the city and a deep love for things French." The Franco-Scottish Society, dating back to the beginning of the century, and several other French societies had, as a matter of course, paved the way for the Institute whose ever-increasing activities outgrew the original premises so rapidly that two other adjoining houses had to be purchased in the very heart of Georgian Edinburgh, where it was possible for the Institute to preserve within its walls the elegance and discretion of a private house in appropriate surroundings.

Several nights a week the Institute holds what might be termed its " salon." On these evenings its largest drawing room on the first floor is crowded with members who have come either to hear music interpreted by excellent French musicians or to listen to some of the best known representatives from French academic, literary and artistic circles, or again to enjoy a French film or play, or to learn French songs and discuss French current affairs, and so on.

But the Institute's achievements do not rest there. Its 1,500 Edinburgh members attend one or several of the large number of weekly classes which have been organised for their benefit. Whether they wish to learn the first elements of French, polish up what they learned of the language at school, prepare for a holiday in France or widen their knowledge of French literature, art and civilisation, all seem to find something to their taste. They have, for instance, access to a library with some 16,000 French volumes and numerous collections of reviews, newspapers and magazines; and as for students from the University, they have their own classes at the Institute, specially adapted to their particular studies, while Junior members, still at school, come to put their oral knowledge of the language into practice by playing games, conversing or watching films. Finally, the youngest members of all have their own Children's Corner where they sing and play in French twice a week.

But this is by no means a one-way traffic in good-fellowship ideas. The recent " twinship " link established between Edinburgh and Nice has led to an interesting exhibition of Edinburgh's arts and crafts at Nce; and thanks to the enterprise of Scotland's largest brewers—Scotitish and Newcastle Breweries—Nice also has a Thistle Club.

THE BELGIANS

The bonds between Scotland and the Low Countries are also tinged impartially with sentimental memories of the past and friendly exchanges in the present. Going first to Belgium, France's nearest neighbour to the north, we find a constant traffic between the two countries. Beer brewed in Edinburgh finds a Belgium market, for example, and there are other exports. Always too there have been Belgians living in Edinburgh—there were 73 at the 1961 Census—and Edinburghians living in Brussels. Edinburgh is particular has been fortunate in having among her residents several notable figures including Professor Charles Sarolea.

Sarolea, son of a Belgium doctor, was a remarkable figure. Not only did he hold the chair of French Literature at the University for many years but he had some 15 languages at his tongue's end and was the owner of a private library of no fewer than 300,000 volumes in his home in Royal Terrace. He too was Belgian Consul in Edinburgh for some years.

However, there are not many Saroleas to preserve the Belgian–Scottish friendship. But there are other valuable ties such as the recent exchange between the two countries of some of their library treasures. The first was a " Treasure of Scottish Libraries " exhibition in Brussels in the late winter and spring of 1963, the second a " Treasures of Belgian Libraries " exhibition in Edinburgh a few months later.

THE DUTCH

Farther north, Holland with her own ancient Universities at which James Boswell and many other young Scottish legal students of his time studied, has for centuries maintained close ties with Edinburgh in law, religion, the arts generally and commerce. Yet there is no Dutch community as such, although, in 1961, 117 persons born in the Netherlands were resident in the city, and in the spring of 1963 some 50 Netherlands subjects were known to live there. These included two post-graduates and six undergraduates at the University; some 10 Dutch ladies either married to Edinburgh men or widows of former Netherlands residents; a few ex-members of the Netherlands armed forces and a number of merchant seamen who married Scotswomen during the war; one or two members of the Dutch Reform Church who train for missionary work at St. Colm's Church of Scotland Missionary Training College; nurses training in hospitals; a doctor who has practised in the city for many years; some nannies and au pair girls; and finally a Dutch woman who took a degree at the University and stayed on in the city as a social service worker with the Catholic Adoption Society.

One reason for the absence of any permanent Dutch body comparable with the French Institute is presumably the proximity of the Low Countries to Edinburgh and Leith, and the frequent introduction to the city of Dutch orchestras, artists, art exhibitions and films through the Edinburgh Festival. For the same reason perhaps, but also it may be because there has been insufficient business to justify a full diplomatic staff, the Netherland Government has not maintained a Consulate office and staff under a Consul General in Edinburgh since 1961. Instead, it has preferred to deal with the welfare of Netherlands subjects in the city and consular business affecting commerce or tourism by an Honorary Consul and an Honorary

"Industry, you name it and Edinburgh's got it," once said an enthusiastic councillor. *Above:* inside Ferranti's electronic laboratories. This specialised work, including many pioneer projects, has greatly expanded in the city since World War II.

Brewing (*left*) and printing (*right*) are firmly established both by years and reputation. The water is conducive to good beer, and the University, schools and book publishers have long been a mainstay of the printers.

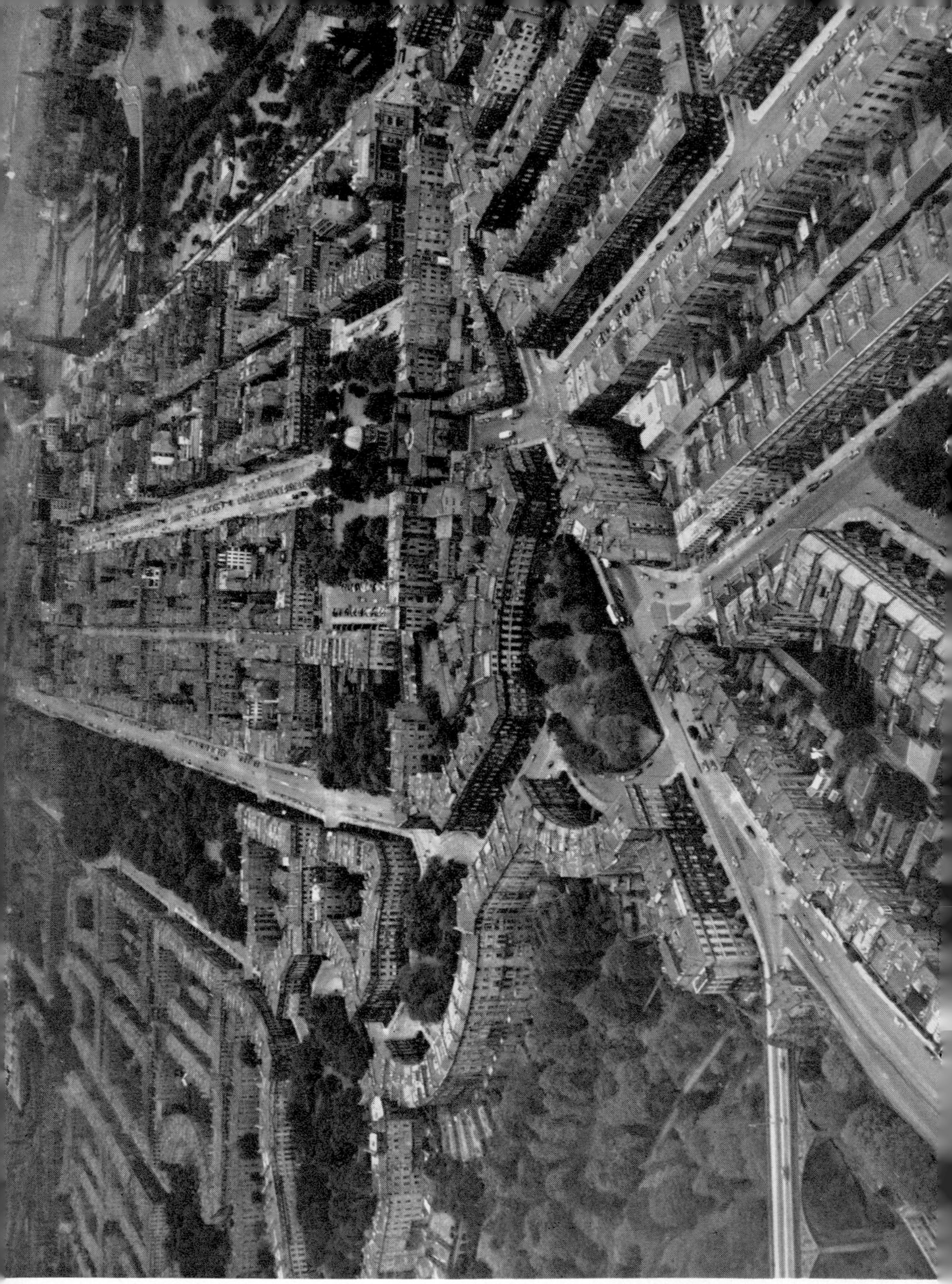

An aerial view showing the well ordered crescents and squares of the New Town, with Telford's Dean Bridge over the Water of Leith in the left hand corner. The grand scale of Princes, George and Queen Streets, the three great West-East thoroughfares, still enables them to cope with 20th century traffic 200 years later, but traffic congestion difficulties are increasing.

Vice Consul at Leith, who deal with matters affecting shipping personnel and seaborne trade between the two countries.

Cultural interests have not, however, been overlooked, for the City Corporation has arranged a Dutch language class, attended usually by about 15 young people who are either about to marry Dutch folk or have relations in Holland and therefore wish to acquire some knowledge of their kinsmen's language. This class is also attended by prospective holiday makers and businessmen with a Netherlands commercial connection; and this is important since Edinburgh's port of Leith maintains a regular cargo and passenger service to Rotterdam and Amsterdam.[1] Furthermore, an increasing two-way tourist traffic between Edinburgh and the Netherlands is sponsored and encouraged by the Netherlands National Tourist Office, The Scottish Tourist Board and, naturally by travel agents.

THE NORWEGIANS

The links between the Scandinavian countries and Scotland are particularly close—which is hardly surprising; for their histories touched each other with fire and sword and settlement more than 1,000 years ago and there is after all only a little over 200 miles of sea between Orkney and Shetland, where Norwegian names and folklore abound, and Norway itself. It is also only about 500 miles from Leith to Oslo whose relations with Edinburgh have been so warm and enduring.

" Edinburgh is beautiful, beautiful . . . . I admire Princes Street, the Gardens, the Old Town . . . and the people are so kind." So said Norway's most famous composer, Edvard Grieg, who himself was of Scottish descent. Henrik Ibsen was also believed to have had Scottish blood in his veins, and in more recent times Edinburgh has had a notable link with Norwegian visual arts, because it was here that Norway's greatest painter, Edvard Munch, showed an important group of his paintings for the first time in Great Britain. The occasion was the Society of Scottish Artists' exhibition in 1931, which resulted in Munch being made an Honorary Member of this Society. Since the war there have been other exhibitions—notably a fine collection of contemporary Norwegian paintings shown at the Royal Scottish Academy in 1950 and an outstanding exhibition, " Norwegian Art Treasures " (including some beautiful 12th century tapestries) assembled by Kunstindustrimuseet, Oslo, and held at the Royal Scottish Museum in 1958. During the Edinburgh Festival in the same year the Moltzau Collection was shown, and in 1962 another Norwegian collection belonging to Mr. Niels Onstad and his famous wife, the skating star Sonja Henie, was on view at the Royal Scottish Academy as a Festival feature. In another branch of the arts the spring of 1963 brought to the National Library of Scotland in Edinburgh a " Norway in Books and Manuscripts " exhibition, which the Library had arranged with the two-fold aim of illustrating not only the close bonds between the two countries

[1] Full particulars of this traffic are contained in the *Annual Statistics* of the Leith Dock Commission.

as seen on the printed page but also Norway's great achievements in literature, art, scholarship, law-giving and exploration. But all such exchanges are in keeping with the tradition of friendliness which has warmed the two countries' relations over the centuries.

" To Noroway, to Noroway o'er the faem," said the old Scottish ballad *Sir Patrick Spens*. During the second world war the traffic however flowed in the opposite direction, when thousands of Norwegian sailors, soldiers and airmen and also many civilians, who had escaped from occupied Norway to continue the fight for freedom over here, found a home in Edinburgh. Here they established their own hospitals entirely staffed by Norwegian doctors and nurses, and in one hospital alone, at Craiglockhart, they had beds for 150 patients.

This war-time association with Edinburgh, which they used to call their " War-time Capital," was remembered by the Norwegian Medical Services when they presented the City of Edinburgh with a silver tankard, made in Bergen in 1670, as a token of their gratitude for all the kindness and hospitality they received during the war. In the same spirit, the Norwegian Army in 1949 handed over to the 52nd Lowland Division a replica of an old chieftain sword dating back to the 6th century, which now rests among the many historic trophies in the Scottish United Services Museum at Edinburgh Castle as a symbol of the everlasting friendship between the two nations.

Norway House in Inverleith Place was started by the Norwegians at an early stage of the war, and became a centre where all could meet. It was visited during the war with acclamation by the late King Haakon and the present King Olav, then Crown-prince. But in 1946 it was discontinued although its continuance would have been of great value after the war, when so many Norwegians came to Edinburgh to study, as they still do. In the Spring of 1966 there were indeed no fewer than 115 Norwegian students studying engineering at the Heriot Watt University, 13 at Edinburgh University itself, and another two at the School of Dental Surgery. According to the 1961 Census, there were 132 Norwegian-born residents in Edinburgh at that time. Of these, 37 had become British and Commonwealth citizens.

Many of the Norwegian students and also a large number of young Norwegian girls who stay with Edinburgh families, helping in the house and learning English—the most widely spoken foreign language in Norway—find a happy meeting place at the Scandinavian Lutheran Church in Junction Street, Leith, where Swedish, Danish, Icelandic and Finnish students and seamen are also frequent visitors.

This church, started by and still run by the Norwegian Seamen's Mission, is believed to be the oldest of its kind in the world. Apparently the first religious services on board Scandinavian ships in Leith were conducted much more than a century ago by a Scottish minister named Campbell, who had taught himself to speak Norwegian. Then in 1865 a Norwegian pastor took over, first in rented premises and later in the Scandinavian Church which was built during 1868. From 1865 till 1952 there was a permanent resident Norwegian minister in Leith. But in recent years the

Port Missionary has been in charge of the day-to-day work both in the church and in the adjoining Reading Room, which some seven to eight thousand people visit annually. One of Norway's best-known authors, Gabriel Scott, whose father, pastor Holst Jensen, was a minister at this church in the 1870s, took the name Scott because he was born in Scotland and christened in the little Leith church.

There has been a Norwegian Consulate for Edinburgh and Leith since 1906,[1] and all the consuls, including the present one have been not only connected with the shipping and one time whaling firm Christian Salvesen and Company but have been members of the Salvesen family, who originally came from Mandal in Norway, and apart from maritime commerce have contributed a well-known judge to the Court of Session.

Norwegians, of course, being great explorers reach countries much farther afield than Scotland, though even so the link with Edinburgh persists. For in 1896 Fridtjof Nansen was awarded the Gold Medal of the Royal Scottish Geographical Society, and in 1950 Thor Heyerdahl was presented with the Mungo Park Medal in Edinburgh, when he lectured to that society about his adventurous Kontiki expedition.

As regards commercial relations in the past, there has been a lively trade between Scotland and Norway, but this has tended to decline in later years, and now there are only a varying number of from 40 to 70 Norwegian ships a year visiting Leith and Granton. The chief exports to Norway are coal and coke products, while Norway sends back mainly pulp, timber and pit-props, and a certain amount of Norwegian glass-ware, stainless steel cutlery, enamel jewellery, furniture, seal-skin goods and food specialities.

Yet important as all these cultural, trading and tourist exchanges are, history shows that every now and then they can be enhanced by some great symbolic recognition such as King Olav's State Visit to Edinburgh in 1962, when he was the guest of the Queen at the Palace of Holyroodhouse from the 16th to the 19th of October. As this was the first time that a foreign monarch had been on a State Visit to Scotland, it was a unique and historic occasion. People queued overnight to get a glimpse of the King's arrival, and young and old lined the streets to see the Royal procession, in itself a wonderful spectacle. There were the Household Cavalry and state coaches; school children in their thousands who had learnt to sing the Norwegian National Anthem in Norwegian; and cheering, flag-waving crowds everywhere. Even the sun greeted the King from a clear blue sky with a heart-warming welcome. At the University King Olav was given the honorary degree of LL.D.; he was made a Freeman of the City of Edinburgh by the Lord Provost, Sir John Greig Dunbar; and wherever he went the King was deeply moved by the spontaneous warmth of the remarkable reception he received throughout his visit.

At its end King Olav made a tour of the places where the Norwegians had been stationed during the war. On his last day in Edinburgh, Sunday

[1] Besides the Consulate in Leith–Edinburgh, there are 14 Norwegian Vice-consuls in Scotland and one Consul General for all Scotland, who is stationed in Glasgow.

21st October, he attended a morning service at the Scandinavian Church in Leith (redecorated for the occasion), and in the afternoon a reception for Norwegians living in Scotland. And so his State Visit ended as undoubtedly the greatest single event and the most notable landmark in the history of Scottish-Norwegian friendship.

THE SWEDES

Sweden's ties with Scotland have not quite the sentimental strength of Norway's, and the Swedish population in Edinburgh—not more than 30 in all—is smaller. Most of these appear to be Swedish women who have married professional and business men in the city. Nor is there any full-time Consulate, though there is an Honorary Consul who deals, from the Royal Swedish Consulate in the port of Leith, with trade or shipping matters: these include the signing off and on of crews for Swedish ships. None the less, the historical and trading ties between Edinburgh and Leith and the Swedish ports are noteworthy. By the time of James VI of Scotland and I of England, "Scotsmen," to quote Hume Brown, "had already given ample proof of their readiness to seek their fortunes in foreign lands. In Poland, Russia and Sweden flocks of them had settled and shown the national aptitude for making themselves at home among strangers." For this reason—and because Scotland in the 17th century sent many mercenary troops to Gothenburg from Leith—there is an obvious and appropriate historical background for the busy trading associations between Edinburgh, Leith and Gothenburg today.

There are regular shipping services between Leith and Gothenburg, Lake Vener and Stockholm, operated by Svenska Lloyd, Ahlmark and Monark Lines. In addition, tramp vessels bring to Leith cargoes of timber and woodpulp, hardboard, paper and steel products. Leith's main exports to Sweden are now whisky, steel and fireclay bricks, although at one time coal was the principal commodity exported.

Efforts are also being made in Sweden to show in Scotland a number of exhibitions depicting modern Sweden. The first of these, a 1960 exhibition of modern Swedish glass, was opened in the Royal Scottish Museum with over 200 samples from seven of Sweden's leading glass works. It was followed two years later by an impressive Scottish-Swedish Historical Exhibition. Organised by the Nordic Museum of Stockholm, this emphasised the many ties between the two countries through intermarriage; the employment in Sweden of Scottish soldiers—and sailors too—from the 16th century on; and the encouragement given in Sweden to Scottish craftsmen. Gothenburg, in whose area many Scottish names can be found to this day, was as a port the main centre for Scottish merchants—and Gothenburg firms contributed generously to the funds which made this purely cultural exhibition possible.

Yet another form of liaison between the two countries is provided by the regular visits which Swedish naval squadrons make to the Firth of Forth, and the berthing of their ships either at Leith or at the Naval Dockyard, Rosyth, by arrangement with the British Admiralty.

THE FINNS

Though very few Finnish nationals live permanently in Edinburgh, there are always a number of girls working as mother's helps in the city, and some students. What is also important for the future of Scottish–Finnish trade is the fact that the Edinburgh shipowning firm of Currie Line Limited runs a joint service with the Finland Steamship Company between Leith and Finland, and a number of other Finnish ships call each year at Leith or Granton.

THE DANES

Returning from the East of the Baltic to the North Sea is to find in Denmark one of Scotland's friendliest neighbours. Like France, Denmark has an Institute of her own in Edinburgh, an adjunct to the city which arrived in the late '50s as a pleasant reminder that the links between Edinburgh and Denmark are as close as they are old. The Danish dramatist Kaj Munk, who was the minister at a church on the West coast of Jutland, used often to talk about " my neighbour the Dean of St. Giles Cathedral," and even today the speaker of broad Scots would be able to understand phrases in the West Jutland dialect. But the historical links are many—ranging as they do from Margaret daughter of King Christian I of Denmark, who by her marriage to King James III brought Orkney and the Shetlands back to Scottish rule, and Anne, daughter of King Frederick II of Denmark, who was married to King James VI of Scotland. Cultural links between the two countries have also been numerous. Hans Andersen greatly admired the city except for the new railway tunnel which he visited in 1847. He had been told that it was not very strongly built, and he spent all his time praying for Divine Providence to protect him until he was out in the open again.

A copy of Thorvaldsen's christening font is to be found in St. Giles Cathedral. The Danish sculptor also made a bust of Sir Walter Scott, but its whereabouts are not known. More recently there have been Niels Bohr's visit to Edinburgh to deliver the Gifford Lectures, and lectures to the Royal Scottish Geographical Society by such explorers as Captain Ejnar Mikkelsen, Dr. Helge Larsen, Professor Niels Nielsen, Count Eigil Knuth, and Prince Peter of Greece and Denmark.

In acknowledgement of all these links the Danes decided in 1957 to establish their cultural office for Great Britain at Doune Terrace in Edinburgh, and from there they now cover the rest of Scotland as well as England and Wales.

The purpose of the Danish Institute, as the office is called, is to give honest, impartial information about Denmark to other nations, and to assist other nations in explaining their country's characteristics to the Danes. Among its functions are courses and classes on Danish language and literature and evenings with lectures and films on subjects Danish, concerts with Danish artists, and exhibitions showing Danish arts and crafts, painting, porcelain and other artistic products.

The Danish Institute also arranges visits to Denmark for mainly professional groups to study their own subjects there and to meet their Danish counterparts. Such groups have included lawyers, doctors, architects, art students, librarians, municipal delegations, farmers and veterinary surgeons. At the same time the Institute provides lectures and courses in Denmark on Scotland and sends groups of Danes to study in Scotland. The Institute has also published handbooks on Danish music, arts, literature, the co-operative movement, the social services and education; and in the spring of 1963 it co-operated with the Corporation's Education Committee in arranging " Denmark Days " in two Edinburgh schools.

Naturally enough, trade connections between the two countries have always been strong, not least in shipping. Sixty to seventy years ago hundreds of sailing ships came to the Scottish ports for coal. They do not come any more, but there is still a lively traffic between the port of Leith and Danish harbours. Denmark exports barley to Scotland for its whisky making, agricultural products, oyster shell for poultry grit, furniture and silver. One of Denmark's newest exports is a machine for turning the daily collection of refuse into compost, and these, during the past few years, have been extensively used by the City Corporation.

Lastly, there is the all-important world of the " inner man "; and here, romantically, the Scots–Danish affinity continues since the founder of the New Carlsberg Breweries, Carl Jacobsen, studied with a brewing firm in Edinburgh and married there a girl whose father, of Danish origin, had settled in Scotland. Carl Jacobsen's son Helge followed in his father's footsteps, for he studied in Edinburgh and eventually married the daughter of a Scottish banker. As regards Danish food, three establishments in the middle '60s were providing the famous Danish Smørrebrød (open sandwiches). These were the Denmark Room in Queen Street, the Tinder Box at the Grassmarket, and the Howgate Inn (outside the city boundaries).

The Danish community in Edinburgh, however, is not large enough now to offer these establishments extensive patronage—because—so it is said—of the difficulties which foreigners coming to Britain have in setting up business here. But 50 years ago several Danes who took up residence in Edinburgh, though they do not form a separate colony, have successfully merged into the life of the city.

First and foremost among these most respected citizens is Mr. Erik Schacke, former Royal Danish Consul-General in Edinburgh, who celebrated his 50th anniversary as a citizen of Edinburgh by donating his Regent Terrace house in 1963 to the municipality for use as a " grace and favour " home. Since then, Mr. Schacke has also handed over to the city a generous gift of Danish State bonds worth £1,500 " in gratitude for 50 happy married years in Edinburgh."

However, if only a handful of Danes are resident in Edinburgh now—according to the 1961 Census, there were 87 Danish-born residents in that year—quite a few young ones come over temporarily, mainly young girls doing a six-months' or a year's turn in private homes with the primary object of improving their English. " These visitors of ours may meet each other at the International Club," says a leading Dane in the City, " but as their main object is to meet the Scots and as the Scots are very hospitable towards them, they do not form a clique of their own. The fact, however, that the Danes coming to Edinburgh have acclimatised themselves to the extent of not feeling like foreigners shows, maybe more than anything else, the happy affinity between the two peoples."

THE ICELANDERS

Finally, from northern waters, come a few Icelanders, immigrants from a sovereign state which shares a king with the Danes and has both cultural and trading affinities not only with Denmark, her one time overlord, but with many parts of Great Britain and with Scotland in particular. Sometimes in recent years these friendly relations have been disturbed by disputes over fishing rights in the waters round Iceland. But in 1962–3 there were several Icelandic families living happily in Scotland's capital. In addition to these, at least five citizens had Icelandic wives; and there were about 15 single persons from Iceland living in the city, four of whom were at the University, two at the College of Art, and one with a private firm.

There is a Society of Icelanders in Scotland, originally formed by students at Edinburgh University which has two Icelanders among its lecturers, one in Icelandic and the other in Moral Philosophy.

The Icelandic consulate in Leith has operated since January 1941, when it was the first Icelandic consulate to be opened in Great Britain. It carries out the traditional functions of providing information about Iceland, encouraging cultural exchanges, facilitating commerce, shipping and travel—the m.s. *Gullfoss* (220 passengers) runs a weekly service between Leith, Reykjavik and Copenhagen—issuing visas, and generally looking after the interests of Icelanders in the city.

As with all these northern countries, there is a long standing bond of common interest between the Scots and the Icelanders, which shows itself in other ways. The National Library, for instance, has a splendid collection of Icelandic manuscripts and printed books, including some very rare copies; while Thomas Nelson and Sons, the famous Edinburgh publishers, have been publishing the Icelandic Sagas in Icelandic and English.

THE ITALIANS

We come now to a far bigger racial group—the Italians—of whom there are in the city some 3,500, either recent or fairly recent immigrants, or of Italian descent. Together they form one of the city's most interesting ethnical studies and one to which Professor Mario M. Rossi of the University has devoted considerable research.

To understand, he says, the social and economic aspects of this community in Edinburgh it should be remembered that the city received only a few droplets of the huge wave of Italian emigration which began after the Risorgimento in the later 19th century. This diminished after the first and second World Wars because of the immigration quotas set up by many countries where Italians had previously found employment either as permanent or seasonal workers.

More than half of this pre-World War emigration from Italy reached the Americas, and it was only a small percentage which came to Great Britain. Of the 872,598 visas secured by emigrant Italians in 1913, for instance, 313,032 were for European countries; of these only 3,884 were for Great Britain; and possibly even this amount of regularly registered immigration should be reduced since for many Italians Great Britain was no more than a convenient stepping-stone to the U.S.A. But the numbers began to grow. By the end of 1924 Great Britain had 75,118 Italians in all, and as in 1901, when there were some 24,684, half or more lived in London.

Unfortunately there seem to be no comparable statistics for Scotland. But at least we have—for 1936—a fair approximation which gave some 1,500 Italians as living in Edinburgh, 3,000 in Glasgow, 600 in Dundee and 250 in Aberdeen. Since in the smaller townships there were, and are, often one or two Italian restaurateurs and confectioners, the total number of Italians living in Scotland in 1936 may therefore be reckoned at some 6–7,000, which is slightly less than a tenth of the total for Britain as a whole. According to the 1961 Census, there were 578 Italians resident in Edinburgh in that year, of which only 201 were citizens of the United Kingdom and the Colonies.

It is safe to assume, therefore, that from the beginning Italian emigration to Great Britain, and to Edinburgh in particular, was never likely to be massive. It was always an individual occurrence, due perhaps to a successful emigrant calling in relatives, or persuasively advertising his own success among his friends as an encouragement to get them over to help him.

Because of this, Edinburgh Italians are not bound together by noticeably strong ties, nor does their common Italian origin play a great social or sentimental role in their lives. But at least something was done between the two world wars to institute a real " community " by an attempt to bring together *all* Italian settlers both socially and commercially. The oldest Italian cultural society in Edinburgh was founded in 1919. But being mainly a society of Scots interested in things Italian, it disappeared (for obvious reasons) at the beginning of World War II and was resuscitated or rather re-founded by Professor Mario M. Rossi with the help of Scottish sympathisers in post-war years.

The history of *professional* organisations is very different. We shall see later why and how, at the end of the 19th century, Italian immigrants concentrated on the catering trade and especially on the preparation and popular sale of fish and chips and ice-cream. But certainly in its earlier stages this trade seems to have been menaced by legislation in the middle '90s, which in turn gave rise to a protective association of ice-cream sellers. This association, which ranges over the main areas of Italian enterprise in Britain, is still robust and powerful; and its branch in Edinburgh is strong today.

A companion fish and chips catering association is perhaps not quite so strong. Whilst the ice-cream sellers meet regularly twenty or more times a year, the fish and chip association in the early 1960s seemed less cohesive. But at any rate both associations were mainly, though not exclusively, formed by Italians, though Italians did not associate as such. They have always the best of *personal* relations in Edinburgh, but owing to the individual character of their business they have never been nationally thrown together as Italian miners are in Belgium, Italian masons in Germany, or seasonal immigrants working on the land in France.

What is strange about this sparse, individual emigration is its revelation of definite periodical trends, so that in a certain period Italians came mostly from certain parts of Italy and were employed in certain kinds of job; in another period both their places of origin and the kinds of job they found were completely different.

As far as can be judged from family-names and the commercial documents available, the few immigrant Italians of the first half of the 19th century came mainly from Lombardy and Piedmont in Northern Italy along with a sprinkling of Tuscans selling Lucca statuettes. Nowadays 90 per cent of Italians, at least in Scotland and her capital, come from Southern Italy. Moreover, seven out of ten Italian families here come from a very small zone of Southern Italy: the small town of Cassino and the surrounding "municipality," and a short and narrow valley to the north where there are only two small villages—Atina and Picinisco.

In the fostering of Scots–Italian links music has played a notable part, for in Edinburgh, as in many parts of England, there was a sufficient love of Italian music early in the 19th century to bring in its wake a widespread wish to learn the Italian language. Many unemployed or under-employed Italians thus began to give lessons, which being inexpensive were socially not so well considered as they should have been. School teaching of the language began later, and university teaching much later still.

At this interesting period in the early part of the century there was also a steady inflow of political exiles, which had already begun after the middle of the 18th century, and a few of these arrived in Edinburgh. As they belonged mostly to the professional class there was little scope in Scotland for their original professions, such as law and teaching, and they could therefore only get a living from language lessons. In Edinburgh, however, before the arrival of a few exiles such as Giuseppe Giglioli and Agostino Ruffini, language teaching was a sideline for dancing and music teachers, laundry women and others engaged in miscellaneous callings.

Two Italians, who gave private lessons in Edinburgh, deserve to be recalled here if only because of the contrast of their life destinies. Giuseppe Martina in 1834 taught Italian: he died there in 1837, and is buried in St. Cuthbert's cemetery. Giuseppe Rampini, a Piedmontese, came to Edinburgh in 1825 and taught Italian too. Possibly he combined this profession with another; for in 1838 a firm called Rampini and Ricateau rented rooms at 45 George Street. Moreover, Rampini had issued, through Oliver and Boyd the publishers, a number of Italian grammars and classics. In 1856 he was made a consul of the Kingdom of Sardinia, and after 1863 a consul of the new Kingdom of Italy. But his sons became completely British. Once naturalized they changed their family name to Fulton; and a Robert Rampini-Fulton eventually went to India where he edited the official text for land-law in Bengal. Charles Rampini-Fulton became a judge in Jamaica, and later held several juridical appointments in Scotland.

An Italian called Lunardi having been the first " flyer " in England (1784) came to Edinburgh with his balloon—it had rudder and wings—and was the first in Scotland to succeed in many flights, his earliest taking place from the grounds of George Heriot's School. Another Italian visitor of the time was Luigi Angiolini, a careful traveller and observer who visited Great Britain between 1780 and 1790. Angiolini had this to say: " All England is full of foreigners; there are Italians, Frenchmen, Germans, etc. of every social class. Many of the first merchant houses of London and in other main towns are owned by foreigners. In Scotland, a country which now is blossoming in her handicrafts, industries and trade there are no foreigners in any walk of life. I know only three who are settled in Edinburgh and are Italians."

Two of these, Angiolini went on, were scarcely able to make a living, and the other, called Ruffini, a Piedmontese, who had introduced an ingenious type of handicraft, had doubtful prospects.

This statement, (Professor Rossi continues) seems in contrast with the considerable number of Italians we find in Edinburgh *after* the beginning of the 19th century. For Italian conductors and music-teachers were certainly already there in the 18th. There was, for instance, a fencing master called Giovanni Saverio Tremamondo from Florence, who got a certificate from the Royal Academy in 1779, after proving he had taught in Edinburgh for 16 years.

Possibly Angiolini left out of account anybody who did not have to do with trade, industry or crafts; and craftsmen and industrialists arrived here *after* his journey. As for Luigi Ruffini, he got subventions from the Board of Trustees for Manufactures, and at a certain moment (in 1793) had not only an establishment with 120 workmen in Edinburgh, all concerned with embroidery on linen, but also one in Dalkeith. Then things went wrong and further subventions were refused. But things were changing anyhow, and at the time of the Risorgimento many of the old artistic set of Italians seem to have disappeared. Many of them changed name and nationality, as Rampini did. Certainly by 1864 the numerous names of Italians which appeared in the Edinburgh Directory between 1800 and 1850 were sadly reduced.

Possibly most of these Italian merchants and craftsmen simply sold their Edinburgh businesses and returned to Italy to enjoy their savings or to open shop in a more familiar place. It would seem so from a tentative but convincing sampling of the economic destiny of a very few Italians whose names have persisted. Carlo Galli, at the beginning of the 19th century, had a shop of antiques in Blenheim Place and was associated with Felice Zappi in the making of artificial flowers, till in 1830 Zappi, having sold all his Edinburgh interests to two nephews, returned to Italy. Then there was Guiseppe Giannetti who rose from barber to perfumer, but he was associated with a gentleman bearing the un-Italian name of Pass. Giovanni Zenone, glass mirror maker and gilder, married a Mackenzie but in 1834 sold out to a new firm (Zenone, Molteni and Granzimoli) and also returned to Italy. Though more people of the same professions arrived towards 1850, this did not stop the dwindling of Edinburgh's Italian population by the early '60s, at least of those who had preserved their original name.

According to Mr. D. N. Valente and Mr. V. Crolla, there remained some Italian grocers and ship-chandlers in Leith, and these may have included a gentleman called De Pinto who acted as banker for the Italian divers and masons who between 1883 and 1890 helped to bore and set the pylons of the Forth Bridge. It looks therefore as if the existence of Italian grocers and ship-chandlers in Edinburgh between 1850 and 1880 constitutes a connecting link between the Italian immigration early in the 19th century and that which occurred towards its end.

This last wave did not probably arrive till about 1880–5. The disappearance of a market for handicrafts and the difficulty of finding employment in industry had eliminated most Italian craftsmen; and as ice-cream manufacture and fish-frying is an easy if laborious job, relatives or countrymen were always ready to come over to act as half-waiters or half-kitchen help.

The passage from craftsmen and musicians and hairdressers to ice-cream sellers and restaurateurs might seem quaint. But what was happening in London must also have happened in Edinburgh, in a smaller way. In *Life and Labour of the People in London*[1] there is a possible explanation: " The Italians are said to be extraordinarily willing and industrious, and so keen to increase their earnings that on Sunday many of them employ themselves in selling ice-cream." With the increasing restrictions in other trades, what was at first a side-line was becoming normal business.

Moreover, strange as it may seem, there is a direct line from the Italian music of the 18th century—so often played in Edinburgh—to the ice-cream selling of the late 19th century. The fame of Italian music, after all, made organ-grinders acceptable here—and barrel-organs usually had a lower drawer or hatch in which the ice-cream could be kept and from which it could be sold. At the time ice-cream was virtually unknown in Britain. It was an Italian speciality, and as many people went over to Italy for a season or more they developed a fashionable liking for Italian foods. Hence the term " Italian warehouse," used frequently by traders who had nothing to do with Italy at all.

But at this time—in the late decades of the 19th century and after the first wave of craftsmen, milliners and hairdressers had already disappeared or merged in Scottish life—there came, according to traditional stories, a new wave of caterers from Southern Italy.

[1] Vol. VIII, p. 35, edited by Ch. Booth, London, 1896.

There is real saga about these. Old Italians recall that about 1885 an Italian organ-grinder arrived in Edinburgh from Picinisco with a trained monkey. He sold the monkey and organ, and then bought gambling machines. But before the police forbade them, he sold his machines and bought a restaurant. And so a new dynasty of Italian caterers in Edinburgh was started.

There is an element of truth in this, it seems, because the first Italian caterers to arrive in Edinburgh were often humble accordionists or organ-grinders who belonged to the traditional emigrating wave of Italian musicians, and saw the possibilities of door-to-door or very simple catering. They began to call in their relatives or their fellow-villagers to help; and in this way, before the end of the 19th century, the De Marco, D'Agostino and Crolla interests had come along. The number of confectionery shops and fish restaurants, indeed, increased very steadily because it was, and still is, usual for the father, if he has no more than one shop himself, to save money to buy a shop for his sons.

But while in this way shops were spreading far and wide so that today there are some 3,000–3,500 people of Italian extraction in the city, the Italians who arrived at the turn of the present century lived in or near the Grassmarket, which according to Professor Rossi soon became known as " Little Italy." As to the location of their " business," this is governed, he explains, not only by economic but by geographical laws. First and foremost, it is well known that Italian hotels and restaurants flourish mostly in maritime towns. In Edinburgh, therefore, there has been a tendency to concentrate not only in Leith and the streets leading to Leith, but in Portobello and in Musselburgh, both coastal districts.

Another trend has been the spread-out from Edinburgh of Italian shops. This is an interesting process. The Italian immigrant usually arrives in London and only at a second stage (if ever) goes beyond it. On a smaller scale, the same seems to happen in Edinburgh. As Italians increase and new shops are opened, it is usual to establish them in towns and townships outside the city for reasons of commercial convenience; which brings us back to our earlier statistics, and to a more precise estimate of the flow of Italian immigration.

One must always keep in mind that many Italians have applied for naturalization and many have changed their name. Some names indeed *seem* Italian and are not; others can be either Scottish or Italian; and some reference books contain innaccuracies. Yet within these limits we can see from a general census of Italians in Great Britain made by Italian authorities in 1936, and from Edinburgh sources today, the broad changes which have taken place during the last quarter of a century.

There is a little difficulty here, for some of the addresses and telephone numbers recorded may be either those of the owner's shop or those of his house. In 1936 also, many people with Italian names gave as their profession " shopkeeper," possibly to avoid the terms " ice-cream " and " fish and chips." Then again many " restaurants " are in fact fish and chip shops, and many " confectioners " sell mostly ice-cream. But from 1936 till 1961–2 the fish and chip trade seems to have increased more than the ice-cream trade. Nor have new types of profession or job appeared to any considerable extent, though there are now two " guest houses " in the city which are managed by Italians, in addition to two stationers and newsagents and two billiard saloon owners who do not seem to have traded in 1936. These are indeed negligible figures if compared with the figures of the catering trade which is exercised in more than 100 shops. Reckoning only the exactly registered entries, in 1936 there were 40 confectioners and cafés compared with 47 a quarter of a century later, and 15 restaurants and " fish-restaurants " compared with 36.

A general view of comparative lists gives the impression of a remarkable steadiness. The same " fish-restaurant " in the same family will be found in the same place where it was, say, 25 years ago. But there is still only one watchmaker, and one big firm of biscuit manufacturers with an Italian origin, though to the single cabinet maker of 1936 one other has been added.

This means, broadly speaking, that even after a disruptive war like the last Italians have in the main returned to their old jobs and places. At the same time many Italian names have disappeared though certainly not so many as might have been expected after such an upheaval. New names, however, are very few but the steady trickle of the first decades of this century goes on, with families of three or four as the rule. But also there are doctors, teachers and others of remote Italian origin in the city who cannot really be considered as Italians any longer.

It might be supposed, incidentally, that immigrants occupied in the Edinburgh catering trade would remain only so long as their savings were sufficient to retire on, and then return to their native places, as seemingly the craftsmen of the early 19th century tended to do. But as it is no more usual to see " the Americans " retiring from business and returning to their place in Italy as it was in the past, so the Italian immigration of the last wave has proved more permanent than the northern immigration of the early 19th century.

The first reason for this is that life in Southern Italy, as the immigrants of the early 20th century knew it, was primitive and disheartening. To give an example, it is only in comparatively recent years that electricity and water mains reached Picinisco. But this is only part of the story, because there are also Italians from the more progressive towns of Northern Italy who are reluctant to go back. There is, for instance, a very good craftsman who arrived in Edinburgh soon after the last war. He told his friends he meant to save enough (as he did) and then go back to Italy as soon as possible. Yet he is still in the city, although he goes on buying property in Italy and swears each year he will return the next. But of course there are many such, and among them a worthy Italian who after assuring the Professor of Italian at the University that he too would go back next year, or the year after, stopped suddenly, and after a moment's reflection confessed: " But I will die behind *this* counter! "

It is not that Italians have become used to Scottish weather and ways of life or forgotten their country, but against eventual homesickness there is the compensation of easy, swift modes of travel today. On an average, Edinburgh Italians now go to Italy for a vacation of at least a month every year. It is easily arranged, is not too expensive, and in the words of one prosperous Italian: " It lifts the curtain of mist, of lack of sunshine."

On the other hand it is not commonly realised that the seemingly humble catering trades of Italians and their thrifty habits allow for good savings. The run-of-the-mill fish and chip restaurateur could in a very few years save enough to retire and return to live lazily in Italy.

But, to recall again the statement in Booth's book on London, it is just because Italians are active workers, and do not feel unhappy if they work more than is necessary for their daily needs, that they find the trade in fish and chips and ice-cream a fruitful mine. In the final analysis it is their life and work in Scotland which makes them remain. Usually they have good and remunerative positions. Italians are also " savers " far more than many Scots, and indisputably they *like* to work hard. Thus the old Neapolitan song

> . . . . lundano e' Napule
> Nun se pò sta!

(one cannot remain far from Naples) is given the lie by the higher gains of their Edinburgh trade. Because there is hard work and good money to be got in the city, few return to Naples, to Southern Italy, to Italy at large, even if they *dream* all their lives of retiring, returning, lazing in the sun.

THE SPANIARDS AND THE PORTUGUESE

The ties between Scotland and the Iberian countries are less intimate than those maintained by their Mediterranean neighbours France and Italy. But they are none the less entitled to a place in the record. According to the Spanish Consul in Leith there are about 70 to 80 resident Spaniards in his area, which reaches from the Borders up the east coast to Aberdeen; while in the 1961 Census a figure of 105 was given as the number of Spanish-born residents in Edinburgh. Of these, however, only 47 were stated to be citizens of the United Kingdom and Colonies. A fair number of those who live in Edinburgh itself have come to work as waiters and chambermaids in city hotels. But through the port of Leith Spain sends other exports to Scotland's capital, among them fruit (a lot of grapes), olive oil, olives, sherry, table wines and cork. In exchange Edinburgh's exports to Spain include electrical machinery, whisky, chemicals and paper pulp. There is also a Spanish circle which meets every other Thursday in an Edinburgh Hotel, but this is more a body for those interested in things Spanish than for Spanish nationals.

As for Portugal, in 1962 ten Portuguese citizens were registered at the Vice-Consulate at Leith, and these were mainly students, doctors and a nurse.

THE AUSTRIANS

To leave the Mediterranean countries and push north and north-east is to find the numbers of European immigrants to Edinburgh increasing—for what in the main are military and political reasons. Thus there are many Germans, Poles and Ukrainians in the city. Austrians and Hungarians by comparison are small in numbers. To take the Austrians first, in the spring of 1962 the Austrian Consul reckoned that there would be some 40 to 50 people of Austrian birth resident in Edinburgh, though the figure given in the 1961 Census was 122. But many of these were only temporarily resident as nurses in hospitals, girls working au pair to learn English, and domestic servants. Of the permanent residents a dozen or so are medical men and their wives, and women doctors. One at the time of writing is a health visitor with the Ministry of Health, and one or two are secretaries. The others are mainly Austrian women who have married Scots.

The Austrians in Edinburgh have never formed a circle or club of their own although attempts have been made once or twice to do so. The main reason for this lack of response to the pull of nationality, apart from the paucity of numbers, is that a fair proportion of Jews who managed to escape from Austria at the time of the Anschluss with Germany in 1938, although bearing no hostile feeling towards Austria, have very understandably no desire to recreate the past and in any case have their own cultural organisations. As for those with less tragic memories of their country, they seem to know one another reasonably well, and several of them are members of the German Speaking Circle which meets regularly in the city and has Austrian and Swiss members.

THE SWISS

According to the 1961 Census, 59 Swiss residents were living in the city at the time. Some of these were wives of Scotsmen, others were au pair girls. A few of the young Swiss women in the city had come expressly to Edinburgh to learn English through the medium of domestic service, and a few were students.

THE HUNGARIANS

In common with the Americans and Germans, as we shall see, the Hungarians have no corporate society of their own in the city. According to the 1961 Census there were 54 Hungarian residents in that year. They seem to suffer from a positive cleavage between two groups—the old Hungarians and the new, the latter being those who left their native country after the anti-Russian revolution in 1956.

After that uprising the University opened an English language class which catered for nearly 50 students who arrived in Edinburgh during January 1957 for tuition in English before being distributed among the Scottish universities. Most of these qualified for academic courses; 17

of them, including eight women, were enrolled as Edinburgh students; and of these four or five were still at the University in 1962.

THE GERMANS

During 1962 at any one time there were never less than 800–900 Germans in the city of Edinburgh,—in 1961, at the time of the Census, there were 934—but, as with the Americans, they did not and do not constitute any very formal community. The Consulate, originally established in Glasgow in 1953 but moved to Edinburgh in 1959, reckons that about 15 per cent of this number are former prisoners of war who have married Scottish wives and settled in the city. Domestic helps make up about 30 per cent of the total, and the remaining 55 per cent consist of au pair girls, visitors and students.

There are also in the city a number of German exchange teachers and also some lecturers at the University, but very few resident business men, as there are no German businesses in the city and direct trade between Scotland and Germany is so far not considerable.

In recent years, however, there has been a growing trade in tourism and Scotch whisky. Between 1956 and 1961 whisky exports to Germany increased eight-fold, and tourist traffic by about the same ratio. The Edinburgh Festival also often brings a sizable wave of temporary immigration from Germany in the form ot its distinguished orchestras—from Stuttgart, Hamburg and Berlin—with conductors and soloists. But the core of permanent German residents persists with a main focal point in the German speaking congregation which not only conducts regular services at No. 1 Chalmers Crescent, but is a particular rendezvous for some of the German girls working in and around the city, who, apart from worship, find it a convenient focus for social meetings.

THE GREEKS

There are sometimes quite a number of Greek students in Edinburgh—there were eight at the start of the 1963–4 University session—but these are birds of passage compared with the bevy of Greek ladies who married Edinburgh men at the end of the war. Yet despite an old friendship between two old hill countries and their two historic capitals, until 1964 there was no establishment in the Athens of the North where Greek could meet Scot. This vacuum in Edinburgh–Athens relationships has been filled by a Scottish–Hellenic Society, a development strongly encouraged by members of the University staff and by other educational leaders who had long hoped for a centre which, apart from promoting talks, art exhibitions, film shows and social activities, could give advice and help to Greeks visiting Edinburgh and to Scots contemplating a visit to Greece.

THE POLES

To many a Scotsman of a younger generation the Poles living in Edinburgh are taken for granted just as much as any British subjects from overseas, although they are foreigners who for political reasons or because they want better living conditions have come of their own free will to stay here. What the young Scots probably do not realise is that a great many of these Poles would willingly go back to their own country were it not for the simple fact that it lies under Russian domination. Furthermore, freedom-loving Poles who came to Scotland during the Second World War, to defend this country as well as to fight for their own freedom against tyranny and oppression, feel that they can do more for Poland's independence when working and living in the free world than they would be able to do in Polish villages and towns.

To go far back, there was a small Polish community in Edinburgh in the middle of the 17th century. But it was not until after Dunkirk in 1940 that there occurred the great descent of Poles upon Edinburgh, when several thousands of them arrived in Britain, and the headquarters of the Polish Army had numerous offices in the city, chiefly administrative in character. To some extent this was almost a reversal of history. For, as one of the important Scottish History Society texts show,[1] large numbers of Scots with robust trading and military sense were normally to be found in Poland from the 16th century onwards, and were apparently so hospitably welcomed that in the eye of history a long and friendly feeling between the two races seems inevitable today. After the war in 1946–7 a considerable resettlement of the Poles naturally resulted in a substantial migration to England, the Commonwealth and U.S.A. (with a small degree of repatriation to Poland). But the many Polish emigrés who remained have happily settled in to Edinburgh life.

Things were rather different after Poland's over-running by German troops from the west and Russian troops from the east in the war's early days. For the Poles were shattered temporarily as a nation. Here the University of Edinburgh can claim a worthy part. A year after the first wartime group of Poles arrived in Scotland, Edinburgh University opened a Polish School of Medicine, memorably helped by Professors Crew and Sydney Smith, and also a Veterinary School. From these hundreds of Poles graduated. The *Paderewski Memorial Hospital* at the Western General Hospital was also set up, along with flourishing social centres, a Church community and bookshops. Then came the post-war resettlement, and the decisions which so many Poles had to make as to whether they would seek their fortunes elsewhere or remain in their wartime haven.

Such decisions are always guided by many influences—family, income, personal ambition and the rest—but it says something for the cosmopolitan *mystique* of Edinburgh that in 1961 the Polish community numbered 1,118 persons of whom about 400 have been naturalised. It is known also that 250 Poles married Scotswomen, and there are some 200 children of these marriages. There are also in the City more than 150 Poles over retiral age—mainly high-ranked Polish officers. There are, for instance,

[1] *Papers Relating to the Scots in Poland*, 1576–1793, edited by A. Francis Steuart, Edinburgh, 1915.

a former Polish General of distinction, who presides over the bar in one of the city's hotels, and a Count, who once owned many acres of Polish land. He was also well-known in Poland for his support of the arts, and is now engaged as adviser to a local antique dealer.

But the range of trades, professions and employments engaged in by the members of the community is wide and varied. A considerable number of them in 1963 were watchmenders. But also, as owners of their own businesses, there were in the city seven Polish tailors, five hair-dressers, three photographers, two house-painters, three garage proprietors, two shoemakers and 20 shopkeepers. As managers a quick tally leads to three sweet shops, three wine shops, four delicatessen shops, six restaurants, 12 hotels, 15 boarding-houses, and two antique shops. In the professions, too, the community is no less strongly represented—with some 25 teachers, eight doctors, two dentists, four solicitors, two accountants, seven insurance representatives, one architect and several artists. Nor should we forget some 40 craftsmen, 26 office workers and 11 scientific workers. Most of these are men but there must also be between 150 and 200 women in these various vocations. However, the exact numbers are never too easy to compute, for many Poles became naturalized British citizens in the recent '50s and travel now with British passports. Many others have retained their own nationality, for figures supplied to the Editor of this book by the Home Office and the Scottish Office show that on 1st January, 1961 there were 571 Polish men and 162 Polish women registered in Edinburgh. Since then it has proved impossible to obtain a more up-to-date figure because ever since that date the Aliens Order, 1960 has made it obligatory for only aliens whose stay is subject to a time-limit to register with the police.

But the name of Poland does not die among these emigrés and their descendants. In Edinburgh, as in a few Scottish towns, there still exists a Scottish Polish Society which aims at increasing mutual understanding, and, at each meeting, there is a minute of silence " for the true cause of Poland." Less silent is the Polish community's social life with all its dances, film shows, tombolas, lectures and outings. This, however, is only the lighter part of its many activities.

Edinburgh Poles are organised in no fewer than 15 different societies, including such bodies as the Polish Scientific Circle " Copernicus," where for 15 years there has been a lecture every fortnight; the Polish Army Association; the Polish Ex-combatant Association which maintains contact with the British Legion; the Women's Association sending parcels with medicine, clothing and foodstuffs to Poland; the Polish Y.M.C.A.; the Polish Invalids' Association which takes care of the unfortunate war disabled; the Polish Choir " Echo " which gives about 20 concerts yearly in Edinburgh (also during the Festival); an Association of Polish Craftsmen and Workers; the Polish Charity Association which takes care of the lonely and needy aged folk; and a Social Club. There is also the Polish Roman Catholic Church, St. Anne's Chapel in Randolph Place, with an attendance at services of about 200 every Sunday, and three religious Polish Catholic organisations.

These societies—and here is the mark of a real community—together form through their delegates a Council of Polish Societies. A central body formed to co-ordinate the manifold activities of its members and to represent Polish interests in Edinburgh on general lines, the Council has many achievements to its credit. It duplicates an Edinburgh Information Bulletin in Polish—a fortnightly with a circulation of 110 copies. It organises national celebrations like Polish National Day (3rd of May) or Polish Independence Day (11th of November). It also arranges for Poles to take part in Battle of Britain commemorations, and in 1963 was busy organising the celebrations of a thousand years not only of Poland's existence as a state but as a 1000th anniversary of Christendom in Poland. Together these societies betoken a community that has settled in well in its city of adoption, but keeps its roots and traditions in the forefront of its memory.

THE UKRAINIANS

Should there be any readers of this book still doubtful of Edinburgh's cosmopolitan character a study of the city's strong Ukrainian community may come as a friendly corrective. For there were in 1963-64 some 400 Ukrainians in Edinburgh and the surrounding districts, and they are only there at all for worthy motives.

At the end of the Second World War about 25,000 Ukrainians won their way to Great Britain to escape from Russian rule. The first to reach Edinburgh were the soldiers in the Polish Army Corps who arrived in 1945–6. They had escaped from Russian camps in Siberia with the Poles, and it was in Edinburgh that the first large group founded the Association of Ukrainians in Great Britain. The headquarters later moved to London where it remained, and most of the original group stayed only a short time in the city before dispersing. But some remained and these maintained a close connection with fellow Ukrainians in the nearby Lothian and Border counties.

The second wave, which came in 1947, were soldiers in the Ukrainian formation which fought with the Germans against the Russians, most notably in East Austria. When the war ended they went through Austria, surrendered to British troops in the south, and were subsequently brought to Scotland, where they left an impressive mark on the life of the existing Scottish colony.

In 1948–9 there was a third wave of displaced persons, who came to Scotland under the European Voluntary Workers' scheme. But being entirely unknown these Ukrainians experienced many difficulties. At first, to cite one, language problems seemed insurmountable. Yet in spite of this they began to organise themselves, and in the course of a few years established in Edinburgh a whole series of organisations or their branches. There are, for instance, the Association for the Liberation of Ukraine (with its British headquarters in the city); the Association of Ukrainian Former Combatants in Great Britain (Edinburgh Branch); the Ukrainian Christian Movement (Regional Centre in Edinburgh); Ukrainian House (cultural, social and charitable centre of Ukrainians in Scotland); the Ukrainian Information Centre (with a library and materials on Ukrainian problems); and the Ukrainian Sunday School to teach the Ukrainian young generation their language, history and traditions. Finally the Ukrainians in Scotland have the Ukrainian Catholic Church in Edinburgh as their religious centre with a chapel in the Byzantine Rite.

The Ukrainians came here of course with practically no possessions, no knowledge of the language and as they had nothing like the age-old links with Scotland enjoyed by the French, the Poles the Dutch and the Scandinavians to ease their way, they had to learn to make a place for themselves. Now in Edinburgh they have three centres—all purchased, equipped and furnished entirely as a result of their own hard work. One of these is their Church and religious centre; the other is the headquarters of their social and national-cultural organisations; the third is a community house.

Through the years Ukrainians have organised a number of concerts and cultural events. A Ukrainian dancing group several times took part in the Edinburgh International Festival of Dancing, at which they were three times first prize winners. There has also been an Exhibition of Ukrainian art.

In further proof of Edinburgh's cosmopolitanism these Ukrainian organisations co-operate closely and often with Scottish societies and institutions of various kinds—with the Scottish League for European Freedom, for instance, and the 4th Edinburgh Home Guard Battalion in which a remarkable group of Ukrainians enrolled.

Space unfortunately does not permit a full description of legitimate political enterprises undertaken by the Ukrainian colony. But they certainly deserve some mention here as examples of the pertinacity with which a genuinely free-minded people can proclaim their faith. A few years after the war they had a rally to protest against the persecution of religion in Russian dominated countries (1949). Two years later they had a gathering to mark the " heroic death " as one Ukrainian called it, of the General Taras Chuprynka, Commander-in-Chief of the Ukrainian Insurgent Army, who fell in battle against Russian invaders of Ukraine in 1950. Later still they held a gathering to mark the 20th anniversary of the famine in Ukraine, which Ukrainians assert was artificially created by the Russians in 1933 to break Ukraine's resistance to their rule. Often they have tried to take action in connection with letters received from Ukrainian political prisoners in Siberian concentration camps.

So the community life of these 400 Ukranians in Edinburgh and her environments goes on. But they also work in virtually all branches of Scottish economy and industry. For although in the 1950s the number of Ukrainians in Scotland was more than 4,000, many have moved since then to England and others have emigrated to Canada and the U.S.A. But there still remained by the spring of 1963 some 1,000 Ukrainians in Scotland as a whole.

THE AMERICANS

From across the Atlantic a steady stream of Americans reaches Edinburgh year by year, but unlike most capital cities Scotland's capital does not induce in Americans the need to form a consciously cohesive group. Nor, try as one might, could one isolate an American colony in the city. A common language can be only a part of the explanation; the others may be deduced from three incidents, of which one is slightly previous to the scope of this survey, the others within it.

While Harriet Beecher Stowe, the heroine as it were of *Uncle Tom's Cabin*, was being driven about Edinburgh in 1854 by the Lord Provost, crowds everywhere cheered, clapped and stamped, and even small urchins recognised her. Their geniality, sympathy, and intelligence went to her heart, she said afterwards, and impressed on her especially the brotherhood of the two countries which had begun in the War of Independence.

Ten years later the 79th Regiment of New York—" the distinctive Scottish Regiment of the United States "—was formed and fought in the cause of negro freedom for which Edinburgh had given its heart to Mrs. Stowe.

Again, in August 1893, the same cause brought Edinburgh out to the Old Calton Burying Ground, swept by rain and a south-west wind, where a monument to Scotland's sons in the Republic's struggle was unveiled by the United States Consul, whose own idea and mission it had been. The Consul (" Both of whose names," said one of the speakers, " make the Scottish blood to tingle ") was the Hon. Wallace Bruce, and it was his daughter as Columbia, white robes billowing in the wind, who released the Stars and Stripes and the Union Jack to reveal Abraham Lincoln, a freed slave at his feet, and the legend " To Preserve the Jewel of Liberty in the Framework of Freedom," set in the shadow of David Hume's circular tower. The pipers of the Argyll and Sutherland Highlanders played " Hail Columbia," " Rule Britannia " and " Auld Lang Syne," while Wallace Bruce spoke of the bonds between them all (" each castle which sentinelled your hill-tops was a schoolhouse for our ancestors ") and of the hope, then much in men's minds, that " the nations will learn war no more, when the English language proclaims its final mission of universal brotherhood."

Americans now resident in Edinburgh actually *live* in Edinburgh as members of the community at large; and by no means do they always register at the American Consulate-General, nor is there any American club, society or school where they might stay apart. Thus their children go to Edinburgh schools and more often than not are bi-lingual, speaking with an American accent at home and an Edinburgh one outside. (The American accents on Prince's Street in the summer are taken as a matter of course; in the winter they strike the resident American ear more noticeably, and even then they sometimes turn out to be Highland or Island, a reminder of how much the American accent owes to the western parts of the British Isles.)

In these circumstances a statistical survey cannot be very exact, though the number of American-born residents in Edinburgh in 1961 was given by the Census as 1,053. There were also, in the early '60s, four businesses using the term American, three using United States, an unknown number of American businessmen associated with Scottish firms, and an American Information Service branch. But apart from the members of the Consular staff and their families, there were only three couples and five American wives of Scotsmen registered in the Anglo–American Year Book, though there were a great many more than that. Others teach in Edinburgh schools and in the University.

Of shorter-term residents there were in 1962–3 a scattering of American Air Force men and families, who prefer the life of the town to that of their base at Kirknewton outside it; a group of some 10 to 15 young Mormons on missionary duty, who, if they found this often uphill work, at least gained experience in public-speaking at Edinburgh's ancient forum, the Mound, and made some profitable business contacts; and as we saw earlier there were many undergraduate and post-graduate students at the University. The Consulate's estimate of the total was about 700.

The University students, incidentally, feeling as Wallace Bruce did that " the Scots overlook one's shortcomings if they know a man's heart is right," tend to grow beards on arrival. The majority read Divinity, others Arts, Science and Medicine, and most of them look for reasons to prolong their stay. Some take further degrees, some find jobs, and one of them, at the time of writing, ran a bookshop devoted to paperback books and recordings, near the University itself, which seems a fitting end to this brief survey of the American interest in Scotland's learned capital.

This, however, is not quite the end of our survey of overseas communities as a whole. The emergence of independent African states within the Commonwealth and the constant arrival in the United Kingdom of students, politicians, diplomats and business men from these states has led to such new and permanent organisations as the Nigerian Area Office.

THE NIGERIANS

The establishment of a Nigerian Area Office in Edinburgh during 1964 emphasised the already strong ties between the city and Nigeria. The Nigerian Government had, in fact, maintained an office in Edinburgh from 1957 onwards in order to look after the interests of Nigerian students in Scotland, north-east England and Northern Ireland. The step was timely for the number of these has been growing steadily, until the total in 1964 was nearly 2,000. Placing these students in universities and other institutions of various kinds, and looking after their welfare while studying in this country was naturally the first responsibility of the office; but over the years this work has so developed that now it also deals with non-student matters.

The new Area Office in Edinburgh has been designed not only to provide general information about Nigeria, but to stimulate investments and sustain trade and commercial links between the two countries. It will also, of course, continue to guide and assist Nigerian students training in

Scotland, to handle immigration matters, and no doubt to stage exhibitions like that of Nigerian art in the Royal Scottish Museum, a display designed to give the people of Scotland a comprehensive view of Nigerian craftsmanship, both ancient and contemporary, over 2,000 years of West African art history.

THE INDIANS AND PAKISTANIS

Lastly, we come to those from India and Pakistan, two countries with which Edinburgh has long had fruitful relations through the University. It is however quite impossible to give a precise figure for the number of Indians and Pakistanis permanently resident in the city. In 1961 the Census enumerated 354 Indians and 85 Pakistanis, but there was no information from the Census to show whether they were temporary or permanent residents or how many were students. The number of students is naturally procurable from the University itself. In 1963 there were 123 full-time and part-time Indian students in the various Faculties and 48 students from Pakistan.

POSTSCRIPT

In view of the picture we have just seen the population is patently far more cosmopolitan in the 1960s than it ever was before. In recent years there has been inter-marrying between Edinburgh people and a good many European immigrants, and naturally between the Scots and the English. The city is also influenced by the American servicemen who visit the city from their adjacent base. There is a steady influx of English business men into English industries set up within or near the city boundaries; a percolation of Irish; and a transfer of many West of Scotland miners to the Fife and Midlothian coalfields near the capital. There are other widening influences: the Edinburgh International Festival; the University with its many English professors and lecturers (and their wives) and a large inflow of students from all over the world; an impressive number of visiting tourists; and the growing urge of Edinburgh people to travel themselves. Clearly then, all these and many other factors have made even the older, now dwindling type of conservative, undemonstrative, rather aloof Edinburghians more appreciative of the world outside their ancient city, more acceptive of its influences, and perhaps also a little less condescending to those not fortunate enough to live among them. So one will find not only a considerable minority of gay, lighthearted people in Edinburgh, scholars of great knowledge and humour, lively artists and writers and people who buy their works, but a large majority of sturdy ordinary folk endowed with kindly wit, decent habits, and in view of the city's numerous jay-walkers, an obviously strong belief in the superiority of man over machines.

None the less an isolationist core remains; and it may still be true that some newcomers to Edinburgh can live in the city a year or two before being asked to someone's home. One such newcomer from an English industrial city said recently that in her opinion there was a type of Edinburgh woman, with venerable family roots in the city, who seemed to suffer from a peculiar inherited strain of snobbery which made it difficult for her to mix with outsiders.[1] If this is true, it is probably true also that these ladies are a dwindling old guard, and in Edinburgh an old guard usually takes as long to die as it takes to build up an *avant garde;* so there may be something in the remark once made by a theatrical hypnotist that Edinburgh audiences are the most difficult to hypnotise in the whole of Great Britain.

As for the young, there are some who greatly enjoy their life in the city, and others, especially in the middle and upper classes, who sometimes rage against the " stultifying boredom " of their life in Edinburgh, its narrowness, as they see it, and its " closed-shop " social tradition. But their parents are never quite sure whether this is just the young in revolt, as everywhere else, or whether it is a fairly realistic criticism of their own way of life. Whatever the answer, it is undoubted that Edinburgh society as a whole has become much more eclectic in recent years, and also (to use the word in a social and cultural rather than a biological sense) much less inbred.

[1] The Editor is indebted to Mr. George Baird, of Portobello, who has conducted much research into the city's old Street Directories, for the information that married women in Edinburgh of the upper classes often included their husbands' rank or designation in their own directory entries. Thus between 1803 and 1806 we find Mrs. Captain Skene, Mrs. Major Sands, Mrs. Colonel Irvine, Mrs. General Baillie and Mrs. Dr. Grant.

Part Two

CAPITAL CITY

CHAPTER 6

CROWN AND COURT

EDINBURGH is the capital of an ancient kingdom. Although more than two-and-a-half centuries have gone by since Scotland governed itself from the Parliament Hall, the city still has the distinctive quality that marks out a capital from a country's provincial sub-centres.

History has much to do with this. The nation's fate and experience have in large measure been acted out here—from the assassination of a royal consort to the establishment of the national church, and from the invention of the bank overdraft to the publication of the Waverley Novels. But it is not only the sentimental remembrance of things past that makes Edinburgh Scotland's capital. The city functions actively today as the centre of state and church, Court and administration, law, order and the defence of the northern realm. Both public and private bodies maintain their headquarters here; and apart from the affairs conducted in Westminster and Whitehall it is in Edinburgh that all matters of national interest are ultimately settled.[1]

All this adds richness to the life and colour of the city, and never more so than when Sovereign and Court are in residence in the Palace of Holyroodhouse, or when the Lord High Commissioner holds vice-regal court as the monarch's representative at the annual General Assembly of the Church of Scotland. To this occasion has been transferred some of the ceremony and pomp lost when the Scottish Parliament was dissolved by the Treaty of Union. To quote Dr. Charles Warr's moving account of this splendid occasion:[2]

" The northern kingdom, they tell us, is fast losing, or has already lost, its individuality. Indeed, according to a distinguished ornament of the Bar, its peculiar institutions have become completely anglicised, with the exceptions of the General Assembly and the Scottish Bench.

" Yet somehow each May, with the advent of the Lord High Commissioner, the nation seems to rise and reassert its personality. The curtain of the past is rung up and with the eye of imagination we look on the disordered stage of our changing history and see again the constitution of Church and State being hammered out over the stormy centuries. These centuries meet about us, and the ghosts of the dead ages are abroad. The duly accredited representative of the Sovereign's person has arrived and taken over the keys of the capital. The ancient halls of Holyroodhouse are opened, the cannon thunder from the Castle, the High Street and the Lawnmarket echo to the throb of drums and the skirl of pipes and the

[1] In a later chapter the City Chamberlain, Mr. Ames Imrie, describes how Edinburgh is also the centre of local government in Scotland.

[2] *The Glimmering Landscape*. Hodder and Stoughton, 1960.

tramp of soldiers' feet, the high ecclesiastics of the land have gathered, and the historic General Assembly, the dread of Cromwell and the Stewarts alike, is about to be convened." This, however, is not the only time when the old grey burgh is bejewelled with the insignia of a royal capital.

THE PALACE OF HOLYROODHOUSE

There has been a notable renaissance of the Scottish Court in modern times. This is due to the House of Windsor, who have reverted more and more to the original concept of pure kingship as the hallowed symbol of communal unity. As the United Kingdom grew up politically and Sovereigns were no longer required to be constantly at the seat of government in the south, they took advantage of modern means of travel to hold Court increasingly among their Scottish people. From 1651 until 1822 no reigning Sovereign had visited Scotland at all, but George IV, Queen Victoria and Edward VII were all fond of Scotland and each held Court on occasion at Holyroodhouse, though for various reasons they preferred not to reside there. However, when King George V and Queen Mary took up residence in the palace itself in 1911, they set a fashion for every subsequent royal visit to the Scottish capital; and the present Queen resides there with such regularity that the Court of Holyroodhouse is once again taken for granted.

At the close of the 18th century matters were very different. In the absence of the Court Holyroodhouse had come to be, as a sanctuary, the abode of debtors in danger of bankruptcy proceedings; the Order of the Thistle had no chapel in which to gather; and most ceremonial had declined to vestigial forms—but fortunately these were kept alive.

For instance, the Election of Representative Peers, though occasionally held in the City Chambers, was usually held at Holyroodhouse. On the Lord High Commissioner to the General Assembly fell the mantle of the former Commissioner to Parliament, though it was in Fortune's Tavern, or suchlike, that he held his levee, before going up the High Street to the Assembly in a sedan chair, preceded by all the heraldic state and suite which still maintained the tradition of a tribal monarchy. In those days too the Outer House judges still sat in alcoves of the Parliament Hall, and the Town Guard patrolled the City Streets, whilst the Governor of Edinburgh Castle and the Ducal Hereditary Keeper of Holyrood maintained at either end of the Royal Mile the attributes of a Scottish capital. So also civic attendance at the High Kirk—a formal matter—preserved the forms of corporate dignity. The Court of the Lord Lyon still exemplified the regal state by its proclamations, now made at the site of the Mercat Cross, which had, like the Netherbow Port, been removed; and the Lord Lyon held his court, sometimes in the Exchequer Chambers but usually in his Clerk's Office which was normally that of a prominent lawyer. From either he administered the Law of Arms, the distribution at one time of the badges and ribbons of Nova Scotia baronets and the furnishing of certificates of credence and nobility to the many Scots visiting or seeking appointments (including matrimony) at the innumerable small courts and noble houses of the Continent.

When George IV made his memorable visit to Scotland in 1822, it thus became possible to regalvanise the whole ancient machinery into action. For a few brief days the olden splendour was refurbished because the records and machinery, though rusty, were still there and in the hands of those who knew how to make them function, whilst the Treaty of Union, despite the post-Jacobite Rising legislation, still preserved most of the vital aspects of Scotland's social organisation. Even the ancient baronial jurisdictions and titles had not been in principle abrogated; and indeed as regards lairds' titles, they were protected by decisions obtained by the anglicised Law Officers of the Crown for the purpose of securing attainder of certain Jacobites.

IN THE 20TH CENTURY

When we turn from this semi-moribund condition to the mid-20th century, the picture is different, but in many respects not fundamentally so. Since 1905 the Court, even if only for brief periods, has often come to the Scottish capital, and ceremonial has been gradually resumed. The accessional ceremonies and summoning of Edinburgh Castle were resumed in 1903. Levees (now discontinued), Drawing Rooms, and, in 1937, even a full evening Court with both Heralds and State trumpeters in attendance restored regal state to Holyroodhouse. The building of the Thistle Chapel made it at last possible for the ancient Order of the Thistle—Scotland's own Order of Chivalry—to take a colourful part in the ceremonies of the capital. Finally there was the restoration of St. Giles into a single kirk to make religious ceremonial with dignity once more possible.

So too the palace has been gradually modernised to serve its proper role. King George V and especially Queen Mary took a keen personal interest in putting their palace in order. Electric light for example was put in early in their reign, and by 1931 the main work of renovation was completed. Gas roasting-ovens replaced the old open fires with their antique mechanical turn-spits in the kitchen beneath the Long Gallery. The furnishings were also much improved, and a number of Scots ladies worked tapestry covers for many of the fine chairs. The dining room china bears the royal badge of the Crowned Thistle, while the silver plate, gifted like the linen by the late Sir Alexander Grant in 1935, has the royal crest or royal arms as used in Scotland. Further modernisation of the palace has been carried out recently in the present reign.

Sir Alexander Grant's gift deserves a special mention here. He made it to mark the Silver Jubilee of King George V and Queen Mary, and imaginatively added to the silver plate and linen a certain amount of glassware, china and kitchen utensils. Only one condition was attached to the gift: it was to be " retained in all time coming " at the Palace of Holyroodhouse for the use of members of the Royal Family. To secure this Sir Alexander's gift is looked after by the Holyrood Amenity Trust at the Palace. This body was set up in 1926 and receives a proportion of the receipts when the State Apartments are opened to the public. Its purpose is laid down as the acquisition and maintenance of articles of historic, educational or aesthetic value suitable for retention within the Palace; and there are four Trustees whose appointments are all subject to the Queen's approval. One is the Hereditary Keeper of the Palace of Holyroodhouse, one a nominee of the Ministry of Public Building and Works, the third a nominee of the Lord Chamberlain and finally a nominee of the Trust itself.

If there have been changes in the fabric and the furnishings, Holyroodhouse remains the ceremonial palace of the oldest continuing dynasty in Christendom. For it must be remembered that the Queen reigns in Scotland ultimately because she is the direct descendant of Mary Queen of Scots and of the six Kings James, and earlier of Robert Bruce, Malcolm Ceann-mor and Kenneth mac Alpin. The Queen is thus the living vein of the continuing blood royal of the Picts and Scots from the very beginning of Scotland's national history. King Charles II was very conscious of this continuity when he set up his *lares et penates* in the Long Gallery of his reconstructed Palace of Holyroodhouse. He commissioned the Dutch painter, Jacob de Wet, to depict all the kings of his dynasty back to its founder in Scotland, Fergus the Great, that King of the Scots who colonised Argyll from Northern Ireland in the fifth century. It is therefore even more worthwhile recalling that the kings so spectacularly commemorated were the builders of the Scottish nation and the forefathers of our present Royal Family.

THE LORD HIGH COMMISSIONER

Besides the royal visits, the Lord High Commissioner holds Court at Holyroodhouse for ten days each May. Before the Union of 1707 Holyroodhouse had been the residence, for considerable and steadily recurrent periods, of the Lord High Commissioner to the Parliament of Scotland, and it was he who with all the state of a vice-regal court conducted ceremonial and investitures according to the olden forms, and thus gave Edinburgh the true character of a capital.

After the Union the Scots transferred most of the essentials of their Opening of Parliament ceremonial to the Opening of the General Assembly of the Kirk; and this, since Scotland was accorded no part in the ceremonial of the British Parliament, was a practical way of preserving the social structure and symbolism to which the Church of Scotland was related.

Originally the Lord High Commissioner was known by this title because of his commission to represent the King in both Council and Parliament. He was attended with all the ceremony proper to a King, and was styled " His Grace ", the old Scots form of addressing the Sovereign. The Crown was also represented by a commissioner at General Assemblies of the Church of Scotland; and thus after 1707 the historic Scottish Court ceremonial that had attended the Viceroy came to surround His Grace the

Lord High Commissioner to the General Assembly. He is still styled "Your Grace", and has precedence exactly as though he were the Sovereign, even before other members of the Royal Family.

Since 1834, the Lord High Commissioner has regularly resided at Holyroodhouse during his period of office. His principal officer is his Purse-Bearer, so called from the purse in which is carried the Royal Commission, and he is attended by a Master of the Horse and by Aides-de-Camp, while Her Grace has a Lady-in-Waiting and Maids of Honour. During his term of office, the Lord High Commissioner gives various dinners, a reception and a garden party at the palace.

THE HEREDITARY KEEPER AND THE LORD HIGH CONSTABLE

The Palace of Holyroodhouse has a Hereditary Keeper, an office held since 1646 by the Dukes of Hamilton, the first duke and his predecessors having then been for about a century heirs presumptive to the Scottish Crown in the event of the failure of the immediate Royal Family. The Keeper, who has apartments in the north range of the palace but only uses them occasionally, maintains a happy relationship with the Ministry of Public Building and works, who are responsible, as we shall see, for the maintenance of this and many other important national buildings. The adjoining Royal Park was in the hereditary keeping of another branch of the Hamiltons, the Earls of Haddington; but when they insisted on quarrying there, it was resumed by the Crown in 1843. The Dukes of Hamilton as Keepers succeeded to the special jurisdiction of the old abbots, since both the abbey girth and the royal park had been sanctuaries. To exercise this jurisdiction they appointed a skilled lawyer to act as Bailie of Holyrood, as the abbots had done, and he is still normally responsible for law and order there, although no debtors have needed to apply to the Abbey Court for sanctuary since an 1880 statute amended the civil law of imprisonment for debt.

The Duke of Hamilton still appoints the Bailie of Holyrood, an official who wears a blue velvet robe edged with white fur, and who also carries a silver baton. Assisted by the High Constables of Holyroodhouse the Bailie presides over the Abbey Court when the office-bearers are elected. Since 1914 the High Constables have worn a distinctive blue and white uniform, with traditional stag and cross badge relating to the legend and a quaint black silk top hat that has one side of the brim caught up with blackcock's tail-feathers. They also carry batons. In recent years a section of these High Constables furnished with halberds have provided the Bailie with a Guard of Honour at Holyroodhouse on important royal occasions, and so have come to fill a position somewhat analogous to that of the Yeomen Warders at similar functions in London.

Strictly speaking, the Duke of Hamilton's jurisdiction in all matters of riot or assault within the regality of Holyroodhouse ceases whenever the Sovereign is in residence, and passes instead to the Lord High Constable of Scotland. It is the Lord High Constable's Doorward Guard of Partizans that is properly the historic equivalent of the English Yeomen of the Guard. (A partizan, incidentally, is a weapon like a halberd, and not as some might suppose a Balkan guerilla sharpshooter.) The Doorward Guard is the oldest martial body in Scotland, and probably in Britain, since it functioned before the reign of Robert the Bruce, from at least the 13th century. But the High Constables of Holyroodhouse have built up their proud history and functions by the assimilation of other bodies, such as the High Constables of the Canongate. And also, by an arrangement made after the Second World War between the present Lord High Constable, the Countess of Erroll, and the then Lord Chamberlain, the Earl of Clarendon, her historic Doorward Guard is represented on ceremonial occasions by certain Holyrood High Constables who are seconded for the purpose and who wear the Lord High Constable's badge. The Lord High Constable also makes a point of giving her commission to each successive Bailie of Holyrood to be her Constable Depute there, so that jurisdiction in matters of law and order shall remain in the same competent hands whether or not the Sovereign is in residence.

The Abbey of Holy Rood (Holy Cross) was founded in 1128 by the Queen's ancestor, King David the Saint (" a sair sanct for the Croun", as King James VI remarked of his religious benefactions). In those days Scone (later Perth, nearby) was Scotland's capital; but the assassination there of King James I in 1437, coupled with the usual tendency to site a capital near the most threatened frontier, led to the centre of affairs being gradually transferred to Edinburgh. King James II was born in the Abbey of Holyrood, and was crowned, married and buried (1460) in the Abbey Kirk, of which the ruined nave alone now remains. The main Abbey buildings were attached to the south side of the Abbey Kirk, but their site is now covered bumpily by part of the palace lawn.

Even before the Reformation, King James IV had begun about 1498 to build a royal palace on the site of the Abbey guest-house, where earlier kings had lodged except when times were so rough that they had to shelter, during visits to Edinburgh, in their great Castle of the Maidens a royal mile away high up on the high rock. All that is left of his work today at Holyroodhouse is the north-west tower, the rest being demolished when the palace was rebuilt on the same site in the reign of King Charles II.

THE PALACE TODAY

The new palace takes up four sides of an arcaded courtyard. It was built from 1671 onwards by Robert Mylne, the King's Master Mason, to designs in the Palladian classic mode by that pioneer of Scottish architecture, Sir William Bruce. The north, east and south ranges form a square U, three floors in height and with dormer-windowed attics in the roof. This U is closed by the west range, of only two floors, that contains the main entrance. The U is however prolonged forward by King James IV's tower, which still gives the palace its characteristic appearance, balanced as it is by a 17th century replica in the form of the south-west tower.

James IV's Tower contained the royal bedrooms in the time of Mary

A harvest field in the city that is only three miles from its centre. Also on Blackford Hill are the Royal Observatory, a golf course, a police radio station and a television relay beacon.

Edinburgh Zoo, situated on the wooded slopes of Corstorphine Hill, is famous throughout the world. Its penguins are an especially popular attraction.

Education places the largest single burden on the rates, and recently much money has been spent on building new schools and renovating old ones. *On right:* the new school at Firrhill bears the mid-20th century architectural stamp of large areas of glass.

On left: An old-fashioned gallery classroom in Morningside School, a feature of many of the schools built around the turn of the century.

On right: Sciennes School—an ornamented stone-built school typical of many built in the city in the late 19th and early 20th centuries.

Queen of Scots, and also her supper room, into which Lord Ruthven, his black armour making his corpse-white sick-bed pallor the more ghastly, clanked one night followed by the other grim-visaged assassins of her confidential secretary Riccio. Tall Mary was not half Guise and a quarter Tudor for nothing; but Scotland was tough enough to resist centralisation, and the rooms still keep a feeling of that time. However, although the 16th century ceiling decoıation was retained, the fireplaces and floor levels were raised and the windows altered when the rest of the palace was rebuilt to Bruce's designs. Today these historic apartments on the first and second floors of James IV's Tower are no longer occupied, but are visited annually by some 200,000 members of the public who have access whenever the Sovereign or her Lord High Commissioner are not in residence.

So too, usually, are the Long Gallery and other State Rooms on the north, east and south ranges of the first floor. The Long Gallery occupies the whole *belle étage* of the north range, and makes a banqueting hall of truly historic feeling, and one redolent of Scottish high ceremonial. In this very room, Prince Charles Edward gave a colourful ball for his Jacobite chieftains after their heady victory at Prestonpans in the 1745 Rising. In the same vast room, the present Queen entertained King Olav of Norway at a splendid State Banquet in 1963, at which the then Foreign Secretary, the Earl of Home, who was soon to become Prime Minister (as Sir Alec Douglas-Home), wore the star and riband of the Thistle for the first time, and the Royal Dukes of Edinburgh and Gloucester wore the Garter as a garter round their kilt stockings.

During a Royal Visit, the Queen usually gives a great dinner here. And each year, when her Lord High Commissioner gives a similar dinner on the evening of his arrival in the capital for the Moderator of the General Assembly, the Lord Provost of Edinburgh and more than a hundred other Scottish notables, the lights of the Long Gallery shine again along the long table on a lustrous array of tiaras, velvet, tartan and the green tail-coats of the Royal Company of Archers.

Until the 1963 Act, which altered the composition of the House of Lords, the elections of the representative peers of Scotland also took place in this room on 128 of the 135 elections held between 1708 and 1959. The duration of the election meetings was uncertain: they could last anything from one to eight hours; in modern times they seldom exceeded one.[1]

" The Long Gallery," according to Sir Iain Moncreiffe, " has always housed de Wet's portraits of the Scottish kings—a collection which enhanced as it is by the general likeness in the face, seems somehow rather like a strip cartoon of Scotland's continuity. The last portrait to be added was that of King James VII (II of England), who as Duke of York and Albany resided here when he governed Scotland as Lord High Commissioner, and after whose time no Sovereign found time to visit Scotland for a century and a half. These portraits are of exceptional national interest. They form every Scotsman's family portrait gallery, representing as they do the successive heads of the whole family of Scots. For although the

[1] The detailed procedure is described in Sir James Fergusson's *The Sixteen Peers of Scotland* (*Oxford*, 1960).

Stewart portraits may be tolerable likenesses, and perhaps their later medieval predecessors were drawn to resemble their faces on coins or in illuminated MSS, it seems likely that ordinary folk from the Canongate posed for the more ancient kings. If this is true we obviously have here a fascinating iconography of the ' common man ' of Edinburgh of the 17th century, modelling for the most illustrious forefathers of his nation as a contemporary Italian shopkeeper might have modelled for a saint, and all unwitting that together these peculiarly interesting pictures would be Scotland's only series of royal state portraits."

The first floor of the east range, opening off the Long Gallery, contains half-a-dozen State Rooms, richly hung with paintings or tapestry. On the first floor of the south range is the Evening Drawing Room, opening eastwards into the Morning Drawing Room, and westwards into the Throne Room itself. In these Drawing Rooms the Queen or her Lord High Commissioner hold evening receptions, and to them they retire with their guests for conversation after the great Long Gallery dinners. In the Morning Drawing Room also, the Lord High Commissioner and his guests hear prayers by his Chaplain before breakfast. In the Evening Drawing Room, the present Lord Lyon held a Lyon Court in 1947—an occasion which, though less formal than the Lyon Court held there in 1554 by that celebrated courtier, poet and playwright, Lord Lyon Lindsay of the Mount, was nevertheless impressive in its ceremonial glory.

In the Throne Room, levees were held until the Second World War, and presentation parties continued into the early years of the present reign. Then, to recall one particular occasion, the Queen and the Duke of Edinburgh sat enthroned on a dais against the centre of the main wall. On their left sat the ladies of the Blood Royal and Household: the Duchess of Kent and Princess Alexandra, the Lord High Constable with her silver baton, the Mistress of the Robes and the Lady-in-Waiting. Behind them stood the lofty figure of the Earl of Dundee, the Hereditary Standard-Bearer of Scotland, whose forefathers carried the Lyon Rampant in battle for Wallace and for Bruce, and there too were the Colours of the Archer Guard. Other courtiers stood about the room. The Lord Chamberlain was on the Queen's right. The Bailie of Holyrood in his blue velvet robes stood at right-angles to the Throne, backed by his Guard of Honour of Holyrood High Constables in their quaint uniform. A Body Guard of the Royal Company of Archers faced Her Majesty in green uniforms and eagles' feathers, their backs to the windows that look out on the courtyard, while another line of Archers handed the debutantes' and presentors' cards to the Lord Chamberlain who announced them.

However, this particular function is held no longer. To some this is not a matter of concern. But others regard its demise with nostalgic regret. To quote Sir Iain Moncreiffe again:

> The last Presentation Party ever held in Britain by the Sovereign in person was that held by the Queen at Holyroodhouse on 3rd July, 1958. It is perhaps short-sighted that the monarchy, having by chance achieved control of one of what social anthropologists

call " the passage rites " (initiation into the community at birth and adulthood, and also marriage and funeral rites), of which all the others are undertaken among our own community by the Church, should have abandoned it instead of adapting it to meet modern requirements in a democracy. It seems particularly sad that the last occasion was lacking in high ceremony, with even the Lord Chamberlain in a morning coat instead of white knee-breeches. There was no heraldry and such little pageantry that one debutante was heard to remark when she surveyed the Throne Room: " My goodness, this *is* informal! "

It is also in the Throne Room that the Lord High Commissioner receives the keys of the City of Edinburgh in a picturesque ceremony held on the Monday evening of his arrival each May. More than a hundred distinguished guests in the varied and colourful dress that Scotland can assemble with considerable panache, stand back around the walls, bowing and curtseying as Their Graces enter behind the Lord Lyon in his red-and-gold court tabard, attended by their own Household and with the Purse-Bearer bearing the embroidered velvet purse that contains the Royal Commission. The Lord Provost of Edinburgh in his robes, attended by the other City Fathers and his halberdiers, enters simultaneously from the opposite door and with a formal speech delivers the keys, which are at once returned with suitable compliments to his safe keeping. Dinner in the Long Gallery follows, the guests going in from the Throne Room arm-in-arm and two-by-two as the Purse-Bearer calls out their names.

Beyond the Throne Room is the Great Staircase, where the Lord High Constable's token Doorward Guard stands vigilantly on great occasions. At the foot of this staircase, in 1953, the Lord Lyon King of Arms (Sir Thomas Innes of Learney) and the Lord High Constable (the Countess of Erroll) took turns of duty personally to sit in watch over the Honours of Scotland (the Crown, the Sceptre and the Sword) which lay for a few hours in the Palace instead of in the Castle. Here too hang paintings by Wilkie and Stanley Cursiter of Scotland's two most significant regal ceremonies since the Union—the Royal Visits of 1822 and 1953 (the Queen's Coronation year) on which occasions alone the Honours of Scotland were borne before the Sovereign. It is up this staircase that the Queen's guests or those of her Lord High Commissioner are conducted before dinners or receptions in the palace.

The west range on the first floor includes the Master of the Household's quarters and the green Household Dining Room, which is sometimes used by the Queen for luncheon or dinner parties. On the evening of the day in 1953 when the historic St. Giles' service was held, she gave a small dinner party in this room to which there were invited the Moderator of the Church of Scotland, the Lord High Constable, the Secretary of State, the Lord President and a few others, with their respective spouses; and this was the forerunner of the much larger dinners in the Long Gallery given by the Queen in more recent years to Scots notables.

The west drawing room, where guests staying in the palace assemble, occupies the first floor of the south-west tower. It contains the remarkable painting of King James VI mourning for his father the King Consort Henry—" commonly but irritatingly called Darnley by historians " as one authority puts it—with a background of the battle of Carberry Hill. The two upper floors of this tower (like the top floor of James IV's Tower) are taken up with bedrooms.

On the second floor of the palace, the present royal apartments look out over the quiet lawn of the palace gardens and occupy the whole of the east range. Also on this floor the north range contains not only bedrooms but the principal Private Secretary's Waiting Room, Office and Clerks' Room. The south range opposite contains bedrooms and bathrooms for the Private Secretaries, the Equerries, the Groom in Waiting and the Lord High Commissioner's guests when he is in residence. Upstairs, on the third or attic floor, are the bedrooms of the Household domestic staff—the chief chef, cellarman, pages, footmen, valets, maids and the personal police officers attached to the Queen and to Prince Philip.

It is not inside the Palace, however, but in its gardens—on the long lawns stretching among trees and shrubs from the Queen's Park over the site of the bygone Abbey and round past the remains of the Abbey Kirk that the Queen is able to entertain the largest number of her Scottish people at any one time. Royal Garden Parties are usually held in June—in 1963 it was July—while the Lord High Commissioner also gives a Garden Party every May. On such occasions guests wear morning coats or dark formal suits; those from the Highlands wear the kilt; and as a final quiet touch of pageantry, peculiarly Scots, the blue-coated Holyrood High Constables and green-clad Archers of the Body Guard wear blackcocks' tails and long eagles' feathers as a pleasant reminder of their attendance on the Queen of a realm of moorland and loch as well as of great cities.

THE ROYAL COMPANY OF ARCHERS

In preparation for these duties as the Queen's Body Guard for Scotland, when they invariably wear their picturesque uniforms, members of the Royal Company of Archers can often be seen on warm evenings from April to July practising or competing for prizes in the Palace gardens at their Field Practice. All this is not of course because the Queen is in any danger from her guests at Garden Parties, but from sheer love of archery. Nevertheless there can sometimes be real difficulty from the pressure of such large numbers of her people filled with a natural curiosity and loyal interest.

The Archers on duty are therefore posted some ten yards apart in two lines in order to form human avenues along which the Sovereign and the Consort can tour in opposite directions. But unlike the bodyguards of many political dictators the Archers face inwards towards the Queen, and not outwards to keep an anxious eye on the crowd. At intervals along these human avenues, the lines of Archers bulge out into circles of about twenty yards diameter, in which the Sovereign or her Consort can pause to meet, more easily, guests presented to them by the Lords Lieutenant in attendance from all the Scottish counties.

Royal Archer Guards are also mounted for other ceremonial occasions when the Sovereign is present—both indoors with several Archers guarding a doorway or lining a stair or anteroom, and outdoors when full Guards of Honour may be mounted with their Colours. There is nothing new in this. The Archers used to play a prominent part in the levees which ended with the Second World War, and in the presentation parties that came to an end in the present reign. In recent years they have also continued to guard the Queen in other parts of Scotland. But the great national ceremonies naturally take place in the capital.

Immensely tall Archers, made taller by their eagles' plumes, flanked the carriages of the Queen and the Honours of Scotland in the magnificent procession to St. Giles Cathedral in Coronation year. Archers also regularly mount a guard outside and line the nave inside St. Giles, the High Kirk of Edinburgh, whenever the Sovereign attends a service in the richly-carved Chapel of the Order of the Thistle. A recent occasion of the kind was in October 1962, when the Queen received King Olav of Norway as her guest at Holyroodhouse and installed him two days later as a Knight of the Thistle. Other recent Knights are an Australian Premier of Scottish ancestry, Sir Robert Menzies and that distinguished public servant Sir James Robertson, first Governor-General of independent Nigeria.

Probably the largest body of Archers to be seen on parade at one time in the Palace grounds comes together when the Sovereign receives their reddendo. This is the payment laid down by Queen Anne when she granted the Archers their royal charter, and is only rendered when asked for in terms of the Charter: eleven only have been called for since 1822. At one time it was given whenever the Sovereign arrived at Holyrood, but King George V ruled that in future it should be given only once in each reign. The reddendo is a " pair of barbed arrows " (a pair being in fact three arrows). It is presented on a velvet cushion, and the latest was asked for by the present Queen soon after her accession. As many Archers as possible were present, drawn up in two half-Companies with their officers and Colours, their own Pipe Band and that of the 1st Camerons. On bended knee, the Duke of Buccleuch as President of the Council of the Body Guard presented the Queen not with the usual " pair " of barbed arrows but with a brooch that was a miniature replica of the traditional reddendo. That evening the Queen dined at Archers' Hall with the Captain-General (her uncle Lord Elphinstone, then nearly eighty-three) and her Body Guard.

THE ARCHERS' PAST

The Archers who are no mere picturesque survival, but have increased in status and function to meet Scotland's natural emotional needs, started as a sociable club some 300 years ago to encourage and practice the sport of archery, " for many years much neglected," although the bow was still in occasional use as a weapon of war in the Highlands. Their first Captain-General, the Marquis of Atholl, was a Highlander; and " an influential body of Noblemen and Gentlemen " from all over the country joined together to form a national body of toxophilites. Since they met in the capital—then still the country's parliamentary centre—they soon also admitted some " weel-kent " burgesses to their society in the friendly Scots way.

When they were formally constituted in 1676, the Marquis of Atholl got the Privy Council to recognise them officially as " the King's Company of Archers "; and it seems possible that this was intended to imply some bodyguard function in Edinburgh akin to that of the Scottish Archers who were then still acting as picked bodyguard to the King of France.

Certainly a romantick tradition soon persisted that they were the Sovereign's bodyguard in Scotland. The idea of a royal bodyguard of picked noblemen and gentlemen was not of course new. Mary Queen of Scots had established a bodyguard of archers in 1562, though it did not outlast her short reign. Later still, 24 Gentlemen of the King's Chamber had been appointed to act as a bodyguard to protect young James VI from seizure by the Earl of Morton (1580).

The feeling that the Royal Archers had a special duty to guard their Sovereign also gained added strength from the long connection of so many of these same families with the famous Scottish Body Guard of Archers in France who protected the Kings of France for centuries from the time of Joan of Arc onwards.

The Archers' second Captain-General, the Earl of Cromartie, another Highlander, was also Secretary of State for Scotland, and as such obtained their royal charter from Queen Anne in 1704. Whatever the implications of the original Privy Council recognition as " the King's Company," the society of Scottish toxophilites was thus confirmed as the Royal Company of Archers in much the same way as a society of British geographers later became the Royal Geographical Society.

There is unfortunately insufficient room here to recount the full story of the Archers in the rest of the 18th century. But it should be noted that towards the century's end the Archer tradition was admirably crystallised by that remarkable character, William St. Clair of Rosslyn, who was Præses of the Council of the Royal Company from 1768 to 1778. He used to address new members formally on admission, telling them that the Royal Archers were not a private Company—" as some people imagine "—but the Body Guards of the King; " and if the King should ever come to Edinburgh, it is our duty to take charge of his royal person from Inchbankland Brae on the east, to Cramond Bridge on the west."

As no Sovereign, apart from the " King over the Water," had yet visited Scotland during the whole period of the Royal Company's existence, it was not until 1822 that the opportunity at last occurred to put their tradition to the test. When they learnt that King George IV was coming north, they offered " to attend on His Majesty either as his Body-Guard or in any other capacity that shall be assigned to them."

George IV, always generous towards Jacobite tradition and a determined healer of Scottish bitterness, accepted the Royal Company's offer; and so, for the first time, they functioned officially as the King's Body Guard.

During the next few years the Archers consolidated this position, acting through one of their members, the young Earl of Erroll who as Lord High Constable was constitutionally the premier military personage of Scotland as well as senior Great Officer of the Scottish Royal Household. As he was also married to King William IV's natural daughter, he was in as close contact with the Sovereign as he was with the Royal Company. In 1830 Lord Erroll wrote that " the King will give a *gold stick* to the Captain-General, and a silver stick to the next two general officers, which will put them on a footing with the Household Brigade in London ": he should perhaps rather have said with the " English royal Body Guard of Gentlemen-at-Arms."

The Royal Company next asked the Lord High Constable to secure the privilege they now claimed of being the royal Body Guard throughout all Scotland, since the Kilwinning Club of Archers were boasting themselves to be the King's Body Guard for the West of Scotland. Accordingly Lord Erroll, by command of the King, issued a declaration which settled this vital point in favour of the Royal Company. Finally, a place applied for at the Coronation for the first time and specially granted by King William IV himself enabled the Gold Stick of the Royal Company to walk in the royal procession as " the Captain of the Archer-Guard of Scotland, Duke of Buccleuch, K.T." The transition from toxophilite club to royal body-guard was at last complete.

But the Archers are still a club. They are self-governing; candidates have to be proposed and seconded and must be well-supported before being elected; they pay an entrance fee and an annual subscription; they even have an Archers' tie (red and green divided by thin golden lines.) Their eagles' feathers are graded on the family lines of a Highland clan: the Captain-General wears three feathers as a chief does; the other officers wear two feathers as chieftains do; and the ordinary members wear a single feather in the manner of a Highland gentlemen. All wear uniform and drill like soldiers. Since 1905 indeed their officers have been named in the Army List; and as a final mark of status their election as officers at a General Meeting of members has to be confirmed by the Sovereign.

AT THE BUTTS

The return of a fairly regular Royal Court to Scotland (Sir Iain Moncreiffe continues) has led not only to a marked increase in the attention to detail of the Royal Company's officers but to a marked revival in the archery talent of the shooting members. In spring and summer, by special permission of the Sovereign, they set up " a pair of butts " for their Field Practice in the gardens of Holyroodhouse. This privilege was first accorded after the second World War when their old shooting ground on the East Meadows, in use since 1798, was converted into allotments by the City Council to help the war effort. For practice they wear soft blue Balmoral bonnets and green flannel shooting jackets. Their left sleeves are sewn with leather arm-braces to protect them from the cutting slap of the bow-string when an arrow is loosed. Each Archer has a "pair of arrows" (meaning three), and these are ringed and feathered in his family colours.

Every three years a match is played against the Woodmen of Arden. This match takes place alternately at Meriden in the Forest of Arden and on the Royal Company's home ground. The Royal Company wear their green Field Uniform and eagles' feathers in Balmoral shooting bonnets which are far more comfortable than the rather stiff green Kilmarnock bonnets worn for Body Guard duty. The English Woodmen for their part wear picturesque slouch hats with the brim caught up on one side, bottle-green tail-coats, buff waistcoats and white duck trousers. In 1940, the match took place at Holyroodhouse by special leave of King George VI, who took a personal interest in archery as a sport; and indeed two of his Body Guard's finest bowmen, Brigadier Tom Grainger-Stewart and Colonel the Honourable Douglas Watson, were sent to Balmoral in August, 1946 with "the King's Graith," a present of a special set of Archer's equipment from the Royal Company.

ARCHERS' HALL

The foundation stone of this building was laid in 1776 by the Royal Company's celebrated Præses of the Council, William St. Clair of Rosslyn. His portrait in a red golfing uniform, as Captain of the Honourable Company of Edinburgh golfers, dominates the dining-room at Archers' Hall, which was rebuilt in 1899 on the same site as before at the junction of Buccleuch Street and Meadow Lane.

The entrance hall contains a set of aquatints, framed together, showing the uniforms at various periods of the Scottish Archers of the King of France's Body Guard, with whom the Royal Company have always felt so close a kinship. On the staircase hangs a glass case containing five historic bows, of which one bears the date 1650 and one is said to have been in action at Flodden (1513).

The staircase leads up to the Dining Hall, with its minstrels' gallery and magnificent chandelier. The walls are hung with portraits—mostly full-length—of famous members of the Royal Company in uniforms of different periods. The Earl of Wemyss, Captain-General at the time of the 1745 Rising and a fine marksman with the bow, wears the red tartan uniform with fantastic silver fringes that is still preserved at Wemyss Castle. But the finest painting of all, and one that is often reproduced, is that of Dr. Nathaniel Spens, President of the Council and perhaps the most famous archer of them all. Uniformed in green tartan he was painted in 1791 by the great Raeburn, who was himself a member of the Royal Company.

These portraits remind us (Sir Iain continues) that since 1779 every Duke of Buccleuch (six in all) has eventually become Captain-General of the Archers, one-third of the total number of Captains-General since the Royal Company was founded. Indeed, the present Duke of Buccleuch has been Captain-General since the death of the late Lord Stair in 1961. The Dalrymples of Stair also have given so many distinguished officers to the Body Guard that when a Dalrymple takes the chair at an Archer Mess Dinner the usual tune played for the toast of " The Chairman " is customarily superseded by their family reel-tune " Kate Dalrymple ". Today, when the Royal Company's pipers play round the table at the end of dinner, one of their pipe-banners displays that doom-laden symbol—the Dalrymple saltire charged with nine lozenges—which after the massacre of Glencoe led card-players to call the Nine of Diamonds " the curse of Scotland ".

Music is played by fiddlers in the minstrels' gallery at the end of the Dining Hall, when special tunes accompany each successive toast. The first toast of all is always " the Mark," drunk sitting down, followed immediately by the loyal toast of " The Queen," drunk standing up. Guests are invited to Mess Dinners, and the Queen herself has more than once come to them, though ladies outside the Royal Family and their suite are not normally invited. The Dining Hall is a splendid sight on such Mess Dinner nights, its great E-shaped table adorned with historic prizes each ringed with gold or silver medals inscribed with the name and often the Arms of past winners. The Musselburgh Arrow's medals, for instance, go back to 1603, which is long before the Royal Company was founded.

It is not always possible to fit in all the Archers who want to attend a Mess Dinner. Although there were 530 members before the First World War, the number of active members is now kept down to 400, and there is a non-active list of those who are " prevented from undertaking Body Guard Duty with the Royal Company, or the sport of Archery on account of advanced age, infirmity, residence abroad or other reasons." The active members include many competitors for the Royal Company's wealth of prizes. These include the Goose, the Silver Bowl, the Musselburgh Arrow, the Edinburgh Arrow, the Peebles Arrow, the Montrose Arrow, the Selkirk Arrow, the Pagoda Medal, the Butt Medal, the Spens Anniversary Medal, the Hopetoun Royal Commemoration Prize, the Dalkeith Arrow, the St. Andrew's Cross, the Biggar Jug, the Dalhousie Sword, the Treasurer's Bow, the Clout Bowl, the Papingo Medal, the Bugle Horn and the Silver Hen. The most coveted of all is the Queen's Prize, instituted by the Privy Council in 1677 and in recent years often presented to the winner by the Sovereign in person.

THE COURT OF THE LORD LYON

In reviewing all such matters as these (writes the Lord Lyon King of Arms, Sir Thomas Innes of Learney) it is important to remember the structure of Scotland's social system. Both the 25th Lord Crawford and above all Sir Walter Scott have pointed out that in this national organisation the blood of the highest nobles in the land often flows in the veins of everyday workers, and at no great distance, owing to large families and the principle of stepping down the junior members of these families to farms, professions and crafts. This, said Sir Walter, was a source of pride to both. As rank and titles and ceremonial have thus far less " class " implication in Scotland than in many other countries, peerages, baronetcies, the titles of lairds and " guidmen " and armorial bearings (in which the use of the old " strap and buckle " cap-badges has been widely continued) have been a matter of widespread pride and pleasure. This is not so in many other countries where a hard cut line has often been drawn between the aristocracy and " the rest." But in spite of the changes of science and industry the Scotland of today is still at heart, and in its special outlook, far more the Scotland of John Major[1] and Sir Walter Scott than superficially appears. This is undoubtedly because both its legal organisation and its ceremonies are so related to the national character. Today, in fact, there are far more colour and ceremonial in Scotland than there were, say, 100 or 150 years ago, and far less " change " than might have been expected; for in every direction, though some additions have appeared, the framework has been so basic and practical that the essentials of a Scottish nation have survived, and their survival has never created serious problems.

" The only problems that do arise ", says the Lord Lyon, who holds very strong views on the need to preserve Scottish institutions, " are when English officials seek to denigrate or add innovations to them, as has unhappily from time to time occurred. But at least in Edinburgh there is a special body whose duty it is to safeguard these affairs."

This is of course the Court of the Lord Lyon King of Arms, who claims it to be the oldest heraldic court in Europe and therefore in the world. It is there, he says, that the protocol and traditions which surround the formal aspects of the monarchy are zealously preserved, and there too that such matters as the matriculation of armorial bearings are officially discharged.

" Many Scots who are educated in England know far too little about the customs or history of their own land ", the Lord Lyon continues, " or what is expected of them, when they succeed to positions of importance in Scotland; but fortunately the Lyon Court is there to inform and when necessary correct them.

" The tribe-clan concept is perhaps now more strongly organised than it has been at any time since the post-Culloden proscriptive period, and has proved itself just as popular as of old, although in the Welfare State it has less chance to function practically. Nonetheless, modern forensic scientists relate much mental disharmony to " de-tribalisation "; and certainly the organisation of the patriarchal clanship or family grouping, which permeated the whole of Scotland and now centres in Edinburgh, Glasgow and Inverness, has filled a markedly important role in preserving

[1] John Major (or Mair) died in 1550. Born near Edinburgh he studied at Cambridge and Paris and later taught at the University of St. Andrews where he increased his reputation as a famous historian and theologian.

Scottish character, while the clan surname societies which embrace the most active of these tribal groups, are now showing a far more historical juristic interest in their organisation. Instead of operating mainly for social and some charitable activities, they are more and more turning their attention to economic and even business aspects of the clan family group, and to the importance of the various symbols, heraldic, territorial, and nomencular.

" More could be said of this if space permitted. But at least it is noteworthy that the use of Scottish-chieftain titles, for instance, is now more effectively maintained and applied than a century ago. On the other hand, although such influences are of great importance to the preservation of Scottish identity and the kinship and home-fondness of the Scot, there has been a tendency in recent years for some Scotsmen to do what is done in England. Thus there is a marked apprehension abroad that in the whole picture Scotland may be losing the daily social customs which form a country's identity. These things are carefully observed in most foreign countries, for on them much of the tourist attraction depends.

" In Edinburgh such matters are perhaps more keenly noticed than elsewhere in Scotland, as is only to be expected in the capital city. Nor could it be otherwise in view of the ceremonial distinctions which occur at either end of the Royal Mile—either within the bounds of Holyroodhouse or else upon and beyond the Castle Esplanade, where the Governor of the Castle is in charge, and where the Lord Provost ceases to be the Lord Lieutenant, but remains ' Right Honourable ' as a Councillor of the Sovereign.

" In Edinburgh, however, the Incorporated Trades of the capital have (unlike the flourishing ones of Glasgow and Aberdeen) sunk into insignificance, take little part in civic affairs, and have vanished from the Edinburgh Directory. Had they acquired some of the picturesque old buildings in the Royal Mile, and with due liveries organised even an annual reeption, they might have benefited civic tradition and their own funds as well as exercised some influence on City affairs."

From the above it will be seen that the present Lord Lyon King of Arms holds strong and patriotic views about the nature of his duties; which makes it all the more desirable to let him trace firstly the origins of his ancient office, and secondly to explain briefly the rights he is entitled to and the duties he must perform.

The Court of the Lord Lyon, he says, has its roots in the jurisdiction of the Royal Sennachie, a Gaelic bard, or more properly in our context, a ceremonialist and genealogist who functioned as " Inaugurator " at the enthronements of the Kings of Dalriada more than 1,000 years ago. On such occasions he had to declaim, as Chief Bard, the genealogy of each new King. This he did as guardian preserver of the Royal Pedigree and Family Records, and from this followed control of Heraldry because of its relationship to family and person identification.

The long red robe in which the Sennachie functioned at these early coronations—it was later trimmed with an ermine collar and cape—became the State robe of the Lord Lyon King of Arms as " Officer of the

Croun and also of the Kingdom." There was an old distinction between these two functions amongst the Great officers at royal Courts. Lyon however had both, and through the centuries his status and his responsibilities continued to grow, as did those of his heralds, pursuivants and other officials. " Indeed ", says the present holder of the office, " one can trace the King of Arms and the Heralds throughout the 14th and 15th centuries. It is known for instance that they had an altar in St. Catherine's Aisle in St. Michael's Kirk beside Linlithgow Palace. But it is not until the closing years of the 15th century that truly authentic records begin to survive of the Lyon Court functions; and then it is often from abroad and not from Scots records that our information comes."

A generation after Sir William Cumming of Inverallochy, who was Lord Lyon at the time of Flodden (1513)—to which part of the Lyon records go back—came the famous Sir David Lindsay of the Mount. Lindsay in turn was followed by Sir Robert Forman of Luthrie, who presided over Scotland's heraldry in the reign of Mary Queen of Scots, and left valuable records still extant, and Sir James Balfour of Denmilne, one of Scotland's most assiduous antiquaries and historians. After the Restoration and Sir Alexander Durham of Largo's tenure of office, came the Hon. Sir Alexander Erskine of Cambo, who founded the existing Lyon Register under the great and practical statute of 1672.

There is no need here to follow the Lyon lineage at length. But it ahould be noted that nearer our own time the office has grown in public estimation—notably under Lord Lyon George Burnett (1866–90) and Lord Lyon Balfour Paul (1890–1926), both of whom expanded the Lyon Register into an impressive series of volumes, and who also with the help of various artists gave Scotland a fine Armorial Register.

SITTINGS OF THE LYON COURT

In its earlier days the Lyon Court sat at Holyrood where the Heralds had rooms; its jurisdiction sometimes extended to treason; and by its awards of arms it could to a great extent determine and demonstrate succession to nobility low, medium and high.

This accumulation of power was to have important repercussions in the changes of the 20th century. But throughout the 18th and the early years of the 19th century the Lyon Office as the department entrusted with Royal ceremonial, was no less vital in preserving the customs and ceremonial of the Scottish Court. To look back for a moment, in the 16th century it was usual for a Herald and a Pursuivant to be by rota on duty at the Royal Palace, the Lord Lyon and other functionaries being only present, as required, on varying occasions. Happily today this practice still obtains, and a Herald and Pursuivant have latterly been on duty under Lyon, when either the Sovereign or a Lord High Commissioner arrives in the city.

THE COURT'S RIGHTS AND DUTIES

What then constitutes the Lyon Court in its present form; where does it sit; and what are its main rights and duties? After 1825 the Court, for which only a vaulted basement-apartment had been provided in the Register House in 1788, was housed in other rooms in the building. In these the Court not only performed its functions as of old, though the fees it collected were transferred to the Inland Revenue in 1867, but continued to operate in an ever widening field owing to the increased amount of ceremonial and the more extended use of correct heraldry. The 1867 Act, however, went further than the mere collection of fees. It ensured that the Lord Lyon in the fulfilment of his duties should be supported by three Heralds—Marchmont, Albany and Rothesay—and by three Pursuivants—Carrick, Kintyre and Unicorn—as well as by two Pursuivants Extraordinary. Collectively the Heralds and the Pursuivants are known as Her Majesty's Officers of Arms. They are members of the Scottish Royal Household and as such have many ceremonial duties to perform. They attend for instance, the Coronation, the ceremonies for which in Scotland, like other Royal progresses, are managed on the Court's orders.

To retrace our steps a little, the spreading influence of the Lyon Court in modern times, made a further expansion necessary in our own century, though like all expansions this raised difficulties. In 1906 it was decided, against the strong objections of the Deputy Clerk Register, that the Lyon Office should be moved to the centre suite in the front of the Register House; and this move obviously ended the old " miserable cellar " days.

On armorial questions the Lord Lyon's civil and penal jurisdiction has continued to be exercised, under both the old Common Law of Scotland and Acts of Parliament, by the Lyon Court in which the Lord Lyon has two hereditary Assessors—the Lord High Constable and the Earl of Angus, who of old had the first vote in Parliament and is still hereditary bearer of the Crown, the title being borne by the Duke of Hamilton.

In his book *Scots Heraldry*,[1] written when he was Carrick Pursuivant of Arms, Sir Thomas Innes of Learney, lays stress on this aspect of the Lord Lyon's powers. His penal and semi-penal (State Revenue) jurisdiction, he explains, is concerned with protecting the rights both of private individuals and of the Crown in Scottish armorial bearings and over H.M. Messengers at Arms. This is regarded as a matter of signal importance, for where persons have paid fees to the Crown in return for the exclusive right to armorial bearings, and a Scots coat of arms can only belong to one person at a time, it is only proper that these rights should be protected. The misappropriation or unauthorised display of a man's coat of arms is a " real injury " under the Common Law of Scotland. Accordingly the registered owner of a Scots coat of arms may obtain judicial interdiction in Lyon Court—or by any judge ordinary—against any person depicting his arms against his wishes or to his prejudice. The

[1] Oliver & Boyd, Edinburgh, 1934.

Crown and the public have also an interest, the former because in Scotland the fees on registration of armorial bearings and pedigrees are payable to H.M. Treasury, and the latter, for prevention of fraud through improper assumption of coats of arms—because armorial bearings are legal evidence which may be used in cases of succession and identity. Because of the Treasury's financial interest, Sir Thomas concludes, the armorial offender in Scotland is viewed with the same stern and unromantic outlook which meets any other culprit caught evading national taxation. It is often not realised that the Lyon Office is a revenue-earning Government department, as well as being not only custodian of the pageantry and romance of Scotland's medieval grandeur, but probably the oldest court of chivalry in Europe and certainly the only one surviving which is still frequently convened.

To deal with genealogical questions the Lord Lyon sits two " peremptor courts "—on 6th May and 6th November—these being the old " druidic " feasts of Beltane and Samhain. He also arranges for other courts if necessary. Usually these are held on a Monday, this being a vacant day at the Court of Session and therefore convenient for lawyers, though alas, Sir Thomas laments, too few of these make any study of Heraldry and its jurisprudence. This neglect, as he sees it, has in recent years had some effect on the Lyon Court's right and duty to keep an eye on the correct protocol of ceremonies.

" In juridical affairs the lengthy ceremony of introducing a new Lord of Session as Lord Probationer and putting him on his ' trials ' with report to the Court anent his suitability vanished in 1929; but the new judge still attends to be sworn in, attired in Court dress, before he takes his seat on the Bench. Sheriffs, however, who were formerly addressed as ' Your Honour ' have of late years become quite unwarrantably ' their Lordships,' and still more surprisingly a female Sheriff is to be styled ' Her Lordship,' whilst a Sheriff's wife seems in Scotland to be no longer styled ' The Sheriff's-Lady.' These recent incongruities will doubtless call for reconsideration by the Lord Lyon and his Court.

" During the 19th century the wives of the Lords of Session were simply styled ' Mrs.', a practice which came in about the 1780s, prior to which, if lairds' wives anyway, they were styled, for instance, ' the Lady Auchinleck.' It might well be added here that Lord Auchinleck when asked at his second marriage whether his new spouse was to be ' Mistress Boswell', tersely replied, ' I'm ower auld tae start keepin' mistresses noo.' Much later, as recently indeed as 1905, a Royal Warrant revived the older custom of recognising these ladies as ' Hon. Lady', a title which gives them a somewhat higher prefix than their former Scottish style."

PUBLIC CEREMONIAL

It would appear then that the historic functions of the Lyon Court are widely-ranging and jealously preserved. But the Court has also to deal with a great deal of public ceremonial. To quote Sir Thomas Innes again: " When proclamations have to be made, the Heralds gather in the Sheriff

Court House of the Lothians, and thence—with band and Guard of Honour on either side and preceded by the Lyon Macer and the State trumpeters—march to the Mercat Cross whence proclamations ring as of old, though now there are fewer than there were even in the 19th century. At the Mercat Cross, Lyon is received by a Royal Salute and takes his place at the end of the Heraldic procession with the Sheriff Clerk behind him as returning officer in the proclamation.

" The proclamation of a Royal Accession is the most complex of all; and the many persons present in the order gazetted by Lyon with stern orders for obeyment, gather in the Parliament Hall, whence they file in specified order to the Mercat Cross where the Royal Company of Archers are also on duty as well as the military Guard of Honour.

" With the Church the Lord Lyon has a twofold relation. He is naturally concerned with its heraldry for the Church of Scotland has its own heraldic ' emblems ' as have several of its Kirk Sessions, such as that of the Canongate; and its major clergy—the Moderator and the Dean of the Chapel Royal—have arms ensigned of elaborate ecclesiastical hats of colour and tassels related to the ascending Courts of the Kirk, In this way, many of the colourful aspects of the Church in the Scottish capital have been carried down through the past century and a half, and in some other directions too the older ecclesiastical colour of the Kirk has been reconstituted.

" At the opening of the General Assembly, the Heralds sit as of old before and below the Royal Pew in the service at St. Giles, having come up the Royal Mile in three motorcars before the Mace, which here represents ' The Honours '—Crown, Sceptre and Sword—carried before the Lord High Commissioner. Until 1926 this was a carriage procession, and went via Princes Street and the Mound. Now it goes again straight up the Royal Mile, and the Order of the procession, successor of the old Riding of the Parliament, is still as of old signed by the Lord Lyon.

" After passing to the Assembly Hall building, which replaced the Tolbooth Kirk as seat of the General Assembly, the age-old order of processions walks up the long flight of steps to the Royal seat within the Assembly Hall, where the slow entry of the Pursuivants, Heralds, Lord Lyon and Mace entering in front of the Lord High Commissioner signal His Grace's arrival, so that all have risen (and stopped coughing or shuffling their feet), and there is silence as Their Graces and the Purse Bearer enter the Royal Gallery."

THE ORDER OF THE THISTLE

As with the Order of the Garter the origin of the Order of the Thistle has often been debated, and it may, though this is unlikely, go back farther than we think. Almost certainly the Order was *founded* by James II of England and VII of Scotland in 1687, and there seems to be no evidence of any earlier foundation except the appearance of a St. Andrews badge in certain 16th century royal portraits of early Stewart kings.

Today the Chapel of the Order in St. Giles' Cathedral, with so many reminders of sovereign rule and chivalry emblazoned in its rich heraldic windows and pinnacled canopies, are fitting symbols of that look of natural pre-eminence which all ancient capital cities seem to carry. It is certainly so in Edinburgh when the Queen and her Knights of the Thistle go to their Chapel in procession, richly robed in mantles of green velvet adorned by the figure of St. Andrew and his Cross, and with the motto *Nemo me impune lacessit* inscribed on the left breast. So too it is a few hundred yards away in the Crown Room at Edinburgh Castle where the Honours of Scotland are a noble reminder that both Mary Queen of Scots and Charles II were crowned with the self-same crown there; and even earlier that the sceptre in the regalia was presented by Pope Alexander VI in 1494 to James IV, and the Sword of State and Scabbard to James IV also by Pope Julius II in 1507.

The Lord Lyon has a profound respect for this ancient Order and a part to play in its ritual. " In ceremonies affecting the Order of the Thistle, whose Chancery is now settled in Lyon Office," he says, " matters are very different from what they were in the early 19th century, for now the Knights, dressed in their mantles and insignia proceed from the Signet Library, either across Parliament Square or to and from the West door of St. Giles and pass through the Cathedral to the Thistle Chapel and either then or after the Cathedral service to the Royal Pew, the Heralds sitting in the stalls below. The dark green of the Knights' velvet mantles, and the rich green silk of those of the Officers of the Order, make a wonderful contrast with the bright tabards of the Heralds who still wear the earlier blue and white ribbon of St. Andrew before it was changed to green. At a Royal Installation Service, the Sovereign arrives usually at the West door but sometimes at the picturesque Thistle Steps beside the ante-chapel of the Thistle. It is there, on the red-carpeted pavement before the West Door, that the Sovereign is received by the Minister of St. Giles who then joins the ecclesiastical procession while she herself proceeds with the Officers of the Order to join the waiting procession of her Knights in one of the most solemn and splendid ceremonies conducted amongst the ancient buildings of the Royal Mile."

The rest of the ceremonials in which the Lord Lyon King of Arms and the Heralds play their part can only be briefly mentioned here. But like those we have just seen they all show that rites and ritual and celebrations based on a proper respect for history, and state occasions with precedents far back in Scotland's past, still stir the blood. There have been notable extensions of such occasions in recent years, and these the Lord Lyon could hail in 1964, despite the clamour of a bustling machine age, because his ancient Office and that of his Heralds had still preserved their rights and privileges. He could recall, for instance, Heralds in tabard seen walking along the " Bridges " and the High Street to official functions, crossing the " Queensferry passage " to the Bruce sexcentenary at Dunfermline, accompanying the Lord High Commissioner in his special train to Glasgow, and attending in full heraldic uniform the public funerals of Rosebery and Haig. With particular emotion, after Earl Haig's death, he could recall " the darkness of the dimly lit Cathedral, towards midnight, and the Heralds receiving in County Square the remains of the Field-Marshal, whilst the horses of the Greys surrounding the Square tossed their heads and burnished bridles in the light of the dim street lamps, and thence conveying the coffin to its appointed place beneath the great crown-tower." There have been other no less moving ceremonies.

" Lord Lyon Swinton (1927-9), who retired at the age of 70 had a short but memorable reign," says Sir Thomas Innes, " for it covered the ceremonies of opening Sir Robert Lorimer's famous Scottish National War Memorial, and ever since at the annual services commemorating the fallen soldiers of the First World War the Lord Lyon or two of the Heralds have regularly been part of the official procession. During the erection of the Memorial, it is worth noting also, several bogus county arms were razed from the walls by the Lyon Court, which under Lord Lyon Grant (1929–45) secured the matriculation in Lyon Register of almost all the burghs and counties.

" Under Lord Lyon Grant too was resumed not only the stately public swearing-in of the new Lord Lyon, and his ' blessing ' in the Thistle Chapel by the Dean of the Thistle and of the Chapel Royal, but the ceremony of installing the General Officer Commanding Scottish Command as the Governor of Edinburgh Castle. This office was revived in 1935 after more than 70 years of dormancy, and its revival brought again into existence an opportunity of associating the Lord Lyon and the Heralds with Scottish Command in ' perfecting ' the Scottish Formation Badges. It was also Lord Lyon Grant who on remembering a complaint from counsel that Lord Lyon Balfour Paul was sitting in Court one day in a lounge suit, resumed the custom of wearing in Court a crimson robe with silken tassels, and a cape of ermine worn over the tabard.

" In 1945, as the Second World War came to a close, Sir Francis Grant, who was then aged 82 resigned the Lyon Baton into the hands of King George VI; and at Holyroodhouse in July that year, his successor was, for the first time since the 17th century, invested by the Sovereign personally and given the dignity of knighthood on his appointment."

The new Lord Lyon King of Arms (Sir Thomas Innes of Learney himself) took up his new responsibilities with pride and concern. " Lyon," he writes, " had now the anxious duty of seeing to the survival of Scottish Court and family traditions in the changing times of the post-war world. For a time there was less glittering dress and ritual. But the Courts of Beltane and Samhain were held in state—with trumpeters, train-brearer and at least two Heralds in attendance—and ever since 1950 the more important decrees and judgments of Lyon Court have been reported in a Lyon Court section of the *Scots Law Times.* In the meantime there were many difficulties to be overcome.

" Years of war conditions, and the emergence of many new, or enlarged public bodies, had led to doubts and interruptions of traditional practice. But whilst many other records had been pulped or destroyed, those of Lyon Court, though ill-accommodated, had survived, and by application of both practice and principle, old threads were interwoven with the inevitable new ones, even on state occasions."

This is not the place to describe the full ceremonial which the Lord Lyon must approve for all such occasions or the various solemnities he attends such as the service in St. Giles at the opening of each annual Law Sessions in October. But there seems no doubt that he has a position which is both historically and socially important. In his own words he is deeply concerned with the Scottish laws affecting peerages, heraldic arms (whether for corporations or individuals), tenure and succession, and all the pageantry which is part of history and therefore keeps a nation mindful of its past. He is an office-bearer in many historical and literary bodies, and because he is a permanent link with Scotland's past, just as the Keeper of the Scottish Records is, he helps to retain the ties of Scotland with Scots beyond the seas—and with the rest of Britain.

CROWN APPOINTMENTS

Throughout all the ancient pomp and ritual circumstance with which the Lord Lyon has to deal, runs always the persuasive influence of the Crown; and this is no mere heart-beat in the heart itself. It is true that when the Queen holds her Court in Edinburgh, she is protected by her Body Guard, lives in her palace of Holyroodhouse, and is ministered to by her Scottish Chaplains. But also she must approve the appointments of certain Regius University professors and several other functionaries of note in the cultural and academic fields. One of these is Her Majesty's Historiographer who is very often an Edinburgh citizen, though the present holder of the office, Professor J. D. Mackie, was for many years Professor of Scottish History and Literature in the University of Glasgow. Another is the Astronomer-Royal for Scotland, who is also Regius Professor of Astronomy at the University of Edinburgh. Today the Astronomer-Royal's responsibilities are highly scientific as will be seen in a later chapter which fully describes how he carries out his duties at the Royal Observatory on a hill-top within the city boundaries, where he is not only appointed by the Crown but is himself crowned with the stars. Then too there are the Queen's Painter and Limner, the Queen's Sculptor, and her Surgeons-in-Ordinary, Physicians-in-Ordinary, Surgeon Dentist, Surgeon-Apothecary and Surgeon-Oculist.

Finally, in a more intimate if perhaps lowlier contact with the Court than say the Hereditary Standard Bearer, there are the Royal Tradesmen.

EDINBURGH ROYAL TRADESMEN

The Royal Tradesmen hold Warrants of Appointment to Her Majesty the Queen and other members of the Royal Family. They are a varied body of suppliers—boot and shoemakers, tailors and kilt makers, seedsmen and nurserymen, hothouse builders, house furnishers, purveyors of meat, milk, eggs, poultry, tea, coffee and ice cream, biscuit manufacturers, suppliers of cleaning materials, clock specialists, launderers, fruiterers and greengrocers, florists, decorators and furnishers dyers and cleaners, fine art photographers, piano and harpsichord tuners, motor engineers, booksellers, catering equipment hirers, suppliers of Scotch whisky, Scotch whisky distillers and brewers.

These Warrant Holders are all eligible for membership of the Association of Edinburgh Royal Tradesmen. This Association, which had 31 members in 1963, was formed in 1894, with the object of promoting all matters affecting the interests and privileges of the Royal tradesmen of Edinburgh. Since 1932 it has been a branch of the Royal Warrant Holders' Association, incorporated by Royal Charter (whose headquarters are in London), and all members of the Edinburgh Association are also members of the Royal Warrant Holders' Association.

Chapter 7

THE KIRK AND HER NEIGHBOURS

THE GENERAL ASSEMBLY

EDINBURGH as the capital city is the home of the Royal Court in Scotland and of the ancient Order of the Thistle. It is also the home of the head offices of the national Church, to uphold whose Presbyterial forms of church government the Monarch undertakes as the first royal oath on succeeding to the Scottish throne. In this system authority over local Congregations, Ministers and Kirk Sessions is vested in local Presbyteries, which are themselves in certain particulars under the authority of Synods and ultimately of the General Assembly as the Church's supreme court.

The fact that Edinburgh is the home of ecclesiastical officialdom and the customary venue of the meetings of the General Assembly (usually annual) does not depend on the proximity of Holyrood but flows from the Church's own decision. It is as the nation's capital that Edinburgh is the natural centre also of ecclesiastical authority and thus welcomes every year some 1,400 elected representatives of the Kirk, both ministers and elders. In itself this is a memorable event, for during " Assembly week," which usually lasts ten days, these senators of the Church enable the Church of Scotland today to play as signal a role as ever she did in the long pageant of Edinburgh's history. When the Assembly is in conclave the streets, thronged with hurrying or gossiping clergy and elders, bear witness to the changing modes. The frock coat and silk hat are no longer *de rigueur* except for ceremonial occasions, having largely yielded place to the lounge suit of decent grey. Here and there a kilted elder—or even minister—serves as reminder that Scotland is the richer by reason of her duple culture. Undiminished is the degree of ceremony with which the Queen's representative, His Grace The Lord High Commissioner, attended by Chaplain, Purse Bearer and Aides, passes from Holyrood where he holds court for ten days in the Queen's name to the High Kirk of Edinburgh, from the High Kirk to the Throne in the Assembly Hall on the Mound, and thence on visits, which he and Her Grace may undertake separately or together, to hospitals, charitable institutions and centres of learning and industry—all this in almost royal state, and often far beyond the confines of Edinburgh itself.

The fact that much of the pageantry associated with the office of Lord High Commissioner assumes a public and official form markedly denominates the Church as national and the Assembly as a Scottish occasion. This character of the Church was notably demonstrated at the special meeting of the General Assembly convened in October, 1960 (to celebrate the fourth centenary of the Scottish Reformation), since the Queen herself was present—the first monarch to be so in person since 1602, when King James VI, in an era of less happy relations between Church and Throne, bent a suspicious eye upon the doings of the churchmen. Her Majesty, who was accompanied by Prince Philip, Duke of Edinburgh had among those staying with her as guests at Holyroodhouse, the Lord High Commissioner (the Earl of Wemyss and March), the Countess of Wemyss and four members of His Grace's suite—the Lady-in-Waiting, the Chaplain, the Purse Bearer and an A.D.C. When Her Majesty took leave of the Fathers and brethren her place in the Throne Gallery was immediately occupied by the Lord High Commissioner, and when she left the Palace on the last day of her three-day visit before the Lord High Commissioner, the Lion Rampant took the place of the Royal Banner on the flagpole at Holyroodhouse.

Edinburgh, which as a traditional capital looks on official panoply with easy familiarity, is on this occasion always conscious of its profound significance. Partly this is because the pageantry of the State awakens—with trumpets and drums, troops and bodyguard of Archers—to acknowledge the nation's Church, and partly because the ceremonies and resolutions of the Assembly serve in this age of " social engineering " to keep the State mindful that her citizens have souls.

Sharp point is given to this reciprocal recognition by the fact that Church and State have not always stood on such easy terms with one another. Compare the present, signalised by so willing an accord, with the years immediately preceding the second *Statistical Account*, which led up to the Disruption of 1843. The final healing of this breach by the reunion of separated Churches is part of the recent history of Scotland—and of Edinburgh, eye-witness of the event in 1929.

Does the fact that the General Assembly meets within her bounds make the same impact upon the life of Edinburgh today as in those days of acerbated strife? Or does Edinburgh merely let

> 'her foolish heart expand
> In the lazy glow of benevolence,
> O'er the various modes of man's belief'?

Some part of the answer is supplied by the reaction to current events. Was it not as recently as 1957 that the Edinburgh citizen, concealed at breakfast behind his morning newspaper, read with startled eye a headline, as unexpected as it appeared (to him) bizarre, " Bishops for the Scottish Kirk? " followed by a report of the General Assembly's Committee on relations with the Church of England.

When questions of magnitude and grave public concern arise, the reaction within Edinburgh is conditioned by the possibility of the citizen's own attendance, if a place can be secured, in the Strangers' Gallery of the Assembly itself and even more usefully by personal contact with one or other of the 1,480 (or so) ministers and elders who, as commissioners, make up an Assembly today. When, for instance, the " Bishop's Report " appears in a journalistic abridgement, the clergyman who has the fortune to be guest of an Edinburgh family finds himself plied for details more circumstantial than gossip or the press have provided, as well as for the elucidation of the principles involved. In the streets fingers wag as points are made and parried; soon the story will be going the rounds about the University scientist of agnostic complexion, who astounded a member of the guilty committee on Inter-Church Relations by the warmth of his ire. " You've sold the Kirk to the Anglicans! " he is reported to have said; and when the churchman protested: " But what can it matter to you? I thought you were an atheist! ", the objector confounded opponent and reason alike: " Yes, I am an atheist, but I'm a Presbyterian atheist! "—a daunting logic of which, surely, only a Scot in wrath is capable.

THE CHURCH IN THE CITY

When, after the longest Ministry in St. Giles' Cathedral (the High Kirk of Edinburgh since the Reformation), the Very Rev. Dr. Charles L. Warr, K.C.V.O., Dean of the Chapel Royal, and of the Order of the Thistle preached his farewell sermon in 1962 he included these words: " One of the happiest memories that I cherish as I lay down my charge is that during the past six and thirty years I have witnessed the ecclesiastical life of Scotland become so much more gracious and mellow . . . . Never can I forget the moving and inspiring Service held here in the autumn of 1929 when the General Assemblies of the Church of Scotland and the United Free Church came together for an Act of Thanksgiving prior to the official ceremonies which ended their separation and bound them together in one. I had also the privilege of having in this pulpit the first Bishop of the Scottish Episcopal Church to preach in St. Giles' since 1689. And a few months ago I was prevented by illness from accepting an invitation to be the first Church of Scotland minister to preach in St. Mary's Episcopal Cathedral in Palmerston Place.[1] Then, within the last year, there have been a number of informal meetings between representatives of our Church and our brethren of the Roman Communion, meetings characterised by friendliness, charity and goodwill, and which brought inspiration to the hearts of all who were present at them. Such meetings could not have been held even ten years ago. Our two Churches have had no contact with each other for 400 years, and no one could for one moment expect any spectacular results from these meetings in the foreseeable future. The barriers still remain, but at least we have lowered them sufficiently to look across them into a brother's eye and to clasp a brother's hand."

According to Dr. Ronald Selby Wright, these words of Dr. Warr express what is the most outstanding feature of the general change in the religious climate in Scotland not only since the publication of the first *Statistical Account* in the 18th century but since the Reformation itself. The friendly meetings, first sponsored by the Abbot of Nunraw, between ministers and elders of the Church of Scotland with their brethren

[1] Dr. Selby Wright, Minister of the Canongate Kirk (the Kirk of Holyroodhouse) took Dr. Warr's place at this service and was thus the first Church of Scotland Minister to preach in St. Mary's Cathedral.

from the Roman Catholic Church and from the Scottish Episcopal Church, has even had the blessing of the General Assembly provided they remain " unofficial ". Frank interchange of views and " speaking the truth (as each sees it) in love " has done and will continue to do much to help the different communions to understand each other in friendship and to show the country that there is very much more in common between them than there is in difference. The differences are there and seem insurmountable, for the Church of Scotland claims to be the Catholic Church Reformed in Scotland, never a Protestant sect, and the Church established in Scotland. The Roman Catholic Church claims to be the One True Church, while those outwith its communion are now their " separated brethren ", and the Scottish Episcopal Church still claims that historically it has at least as much right to be the Catholic Church Reformed in Scotland as its Presbyterian brethren. But the important thing now is that more than ever before each recognises the good faith, the sincerity and the outstretched hand of friendship of the other.

There has also been the great change in the distribution of the population of the city itself—the migration into new housing areas of thousands of people with its vital effect and new challenge to the life of the Church, many and various and not all yet fully realised. The building of the new churches has itself been a challenge and adventure, and wherever the new communities have gone an effort has been made to have there the Church in their midst, which is often initially the only real source of community life for those uprooted from the congestion and comradeship, the noise and neighbourliness of their former lives. This movement of the people—so right and so much-needed for so long—has posed many problems for the Church and so brought to it a new and much-welcomed challenge and opportunity. The old down-town churches with their once sometimes pitifully overcrowded parishes, are now (at least until the new houses are completed or the old restored) finding themselves almost deserted villages, whereas many a minister in a new housing area is finding himself alone with a parish of more than 10,000 people. Many of these new parishioners have little or no church connection (except the usual one of baptising, marrying and burying); others are unwilling to " lift their lines " from their old church, when they have one, thus cutting themselves off both from their local church, and from their old church because of the long distance of travel. The request by ministers in the central churches to those going to the new housing areas to leave their old church and become members of the new, is often much misunderstood and sometimes resented. The decreasing numbers of communicant members in the down-town churches should indeed be even lower, since quite a number for the reasons stated above are " paper " members, just managing to keep their names on the roll by sometimes not too frequent attendances at Holy Communion, but frequent enough to have their names retained. This difficulty, however, will right itself as the large numbers of Sunday School children in the new housing areas accept the new church as their own, as families grow up and commonsense prevails, and certainly not least, as bus fares go on increasing!

Another marked change due to the distribution of the population has been the almost—and one hopes temporary—breakdown of the old Parish system. Although each minister is allotted the bounds of his parish by the Presbytery, the members of his congregation stretch often from say Pilton, Granton and Davidson's Mains on the south and west of the city to Liberton, Gracemount and Craigmillar on the east, thus making pastoral visiting—especially for those without a car—an almost impossible task.

A further, and to ministers a disturbing, result of much of the population's redistribution, is the segregation of so many congregations into income groups, professions and trades. In the past all members of the community lived within the same parish area. In the Old Town they lived often in the same house but in different flats, and certainly in the same street. In the New Town they at least lived in the same area. But as the tendency today is to move those of roughly the same income group into particular parts of the city where there is no longer an integrated congregation, by force of circumstances those in the congregations, say, of Cramond, Colinton, Murrayfield or Fairmilehead, belong largely to a different society of interests from those, say, of Pilton, Colinton Mains, Clermiston and Craigmillar. (The map of Edinburgh at the end of this book might be consulted here.)

THE CHANGE OF CUSTOMS

Along with the changes brought on by the movements of population there is the change of customs. Though the morning-coat (or its equivalent black suit) is still largely retained for Communion Sundays, gone now is the old top-hat, except for "distinguished" funerals and weddings and Holyrood Garden parties—and not even always then. And whereas, as late as the 1920s, few ministers would venture out on a Sunday morning without their "lum" hat, morning suit and umbrella (whatever the weather) it would almost be safe to say that none does so now: indeed a number wear no hat at all, and except for the distinguished occasions mentioned above, leave their umbrella at home. In much the same way the modern congregation in their light suits, blazers and bright dresses look now more as though they are worshipping the Risen Lord on His Day rather than attending a weekly funeral service. Churches too are becoming brighter (not least the new ones) both in appearance and liturgy. The effects of the Puritan influence in Scotland in the 17th century are now far less seen and a return to the principles and worship of the Reformers in their 20th century setting is now more in evidence. "Sermon tasting" may die hard, but an increasing number of people realise that a full "diet" of worship includes not only the "word truly preached" but the "sacraments rightly administered," and the orientation of most of the new churches clearly has this in mind. There is also in the Church of Scotland a return to a more liturgical form of service so that in many churches there is a more frequent opportunity for members to receive Communion, and few churches now would ignore certain days in the Christian Year. Christmas and Easter, for instance, are accepted by nearly every church, and Christmas Eve Watchnight Services are becoming a general practice. Christmas indeed is rapidly taking the place of the New Year throughout most of the churches; and services during Holy Week are becoming increasingly common, with several churches in the one district quite often combining.

The attitude towards Sunday is also changing—for better or for worse—and the rigid Sabbatarianism of the past is largely gone. Sunday, the Lord's Day, has always been regarded by the Churches of all denominations as a day of worship and of rest from daily work. But since work on Sunday now carries with it the benefit of extra pay, and since it is reckoned that less than 50 per cent attend church regularly on Sundays, the strict observance of the Sabbath has never been easy to control; and idleness has for too long been equated in too many minds with holiness.

It is said with some authority that over sixty per cent of juvenile "crime" is committed on Sunday afternoons and evenings, and—in the view of the writer—so long as the prohibition of football in the parks and other similar restrictions continue to be in force, it is scarcely to be wondered at. Whether or not Calvin or Knox—or both—played bowls on Sunday does not really matter now. What is important is that Church Elders and members can be found among those who, having worshipped God on His Day, can feel free to play golf or tennis or whatever they want; and surely it is a refreshing sign of the times to see a number of young people following the morning worship on summer Sundays by spending the rest of the day by the sea in recreation, for that too can be a re-creation. And the fact remains that morning services throughout the city are fairly well-attended; on "Communion Sundays" the churches are usually filled to capacity; and the evening service, except in certain churches usually in central districts, continues to be supported by the faithful few "twicers", the youth groups and clubs that meet "after the service," and those who for one reason or another are not able to get to church in the morning.

The number attending Sunday School and Bible Class is decreasing except in some of the new housing areas; but on the other hand religious instruction is given in many schools, and this has tended to make much of the teaching in Sunday Schools and Bible Classes a sometimes tiresome repetition of weekday lessons. There is, too, a growing tendency in the Church of Scotland for the Confirmation Class for first communicants to be almost a substitute for the Bible Class, and many are coming forward to receive their first communion at an earlier age than has for long been customary—though not at quite so young an age as those in the Roman Catholic or Episcopal Churches. (If this is thought by some to be a trend towards Episcopacy or Rome it is as well to remember that the presbyterian Divine, James Melville, was admitted at the age of twelve!).

EXTRA-MURAL RELIGION

Influences that up till well into the 20th century would never have been dreamed of have also had a very marked impact on the life of the Church. The coming of wireless and later of television has brought religion into the homes daily and opened up vast vistas never before thought possible. Now in the homes of nearly everyone in the country one can hear and see some of the greatest preachers of all denominations. Prayers, hymns, psalms, readings from the Bible and sermons enter millions of homes even though " the doors are shut ". Many today can thus receive within their own homes a comfort or challenge, instruction or edification through this miracle (as our grandfathers would have regarded it) of evangelism; and both the B.B.C. and Independent Television have done much to foster the teaching, worship and work of the Church, by entering homes which were formerly closed to religion, by bringing to the sick and aged and housebound what had previously been denied them, and by widening the horizon of the average churchman from narrow parochialism and denominationalism.

Other things too in these last years have given a wider field of support to the work of the Church. The Edinburgh newspapers have reported fully and accurately religious matters of interest and concern; and *The Scotsman* has also published each day a widely-read text and sermonette called *This Morning*.

A new development that has further helped the work of the Churches has been the appointment of industrial chaplains, who add to their own parochial and congregational duties some specific " industry " to which they have been officially appointed, usually, but not necessarily, within the area in which their church is situated. These chaplains cover all branches of industry—works, breweries, newspapers, theatres and railway stations. Then also there are, again mostly part-time, hospital chaplains and school chaplains, so that now every hospital and school within the city has a chaplain of its own. As for the Army, where there is no full-time regular Army chaplain, officiating chaplains are also appointed as well as Territorial Army chaplains whose concern is usually the unit to which they have been posted. In fact, it might be said that there is hardly a single organisation or institution within the bounds of Greater Edinburgh—except the Zoo—that hasn't got a chaplain of some sort, and though today people may not come to church in such large numbers, no one can say that the Church does not go to them.

A CLOSER LOOK

"Had a traveller in the time of the second *Statistical Account of Scotland*, more than a century ago, been able to take time by the forelock and cruise slowly above the city in a helicopter, he would have seen that the long, dark huddle of roofs stretching down from the Castle to Holyrood, flanked by the Grassmarket and the Cowgate, was the centre of a spreading population. The fashionable new town to the north and west housed in its fine squares and terraces the Victorian merchants and the lawyers. Everywhere the observer would have noticed the new churches which had followed the well-to-do population to the new town and to the rising suburbs. He would have seen, too, St. Andrew's in George Street from which in 1843 at the Disruption the long procession of ministers and elders made its way down to Tanfield Hall, there to constitute themselves 'The Church of Scotland: Free.' Already in 1845 many of the new churches of that denomination could be seen; indeed even by then they were as numerous as the parishes and *quoad sacra* parishes of the day. The Secession and Relief, too, were building to follow their people, and by 1847 the two denominations would be combined as the United Presbyterian Church. The first great movement of the population which began in the latter part of the 18th century was complete, and the second was well under way."

"Launched on his second flight, this time at the beginning of the 20th century," continues the Rev. Innes Logan, "our observer would have gazed on a much wider scene. For the second great movement of the population, as we saw, swept out to broad new suburbs and districts of well-built dwellings. These seemly and spacious suburbs in Newington, Morningside, the Grange and the rest, with their bright gardens as they extended farther out, were marked by many handsome churches. In particular his attention would have been arrested by the massive and soaring structure of the Episcopal St. Mary's Cathedral, which had risen to the west of Charlotte Square, the dome of St. George's Church in the square itself, the fine campanile of United Free St. George's nearby in Shandwick Place, and the outstanding group formed by the New College and the Assembly Hall. The New College, opened in 1850, is now the seat of the University's Divinity Faculty; behind it, beyond the court or quadrangle where stands the statue of John Knox, is the Assembly Hall. Deep shouldering into the Lawnmarket above and behind it, this fine debating chamber was built by the Free Church and is the seat of the government of the re-united Church of Scotland. Just across the road, behind the Assembly Hall, the old Church of Scotland Assembly had been housed in the Tolbooth Church. Relations were not always conspicuously cordial. Indeed, just as the members of the House of Commons refer to the House of Lords as 'another place,' so the members of the two assemblies used to speak in their debates of 'over the way'." Mr. Logan goes on to explain that on Sunday morning in those days, while the air resounded to the solemn peal of the solitary bells—there are few chimes in Edinburgh—the streets gave back the noise of many hurrying feet as top-hatted, well-dressed crowds thronged to worship. Photographs of popular preachers stood in ranks in the booksellers' windows. But the voice of the Rev. Andrew Bonar, once minister of the Canongate, still went unregarded. In the 1850s he had delivered fierce and accurate denunciations of the squalid, overcrowded and insanitary conditions in the packed lands and closes of his parish. But he had been unable to arouse the Christian community as a whole to any vital response.

In our own century, had our imaginary observer launched out on his third flight over Edinburgh, in the early 1960s, his enquiring eye would have seen something which, though apparently superficial, was significant of much. He would see small well-equipped dwellings in vast new housing schemes sprawling far and wide as a replacement for the dreadful slumdom of the past in the huddled high buildings of the Old Town.

CHURCH EXTENSION

As a result of all this the chief energy, of action and of finance, in the now united Church of Scotland, as well as in other denominations, is being directed to the provision of religious ordinances and the building of churches in the new housing areas. The amount contributed for National Church Extension by the congregations of the Church up to the close of 1960 was £1,668,000. In addition, the Extension charges repaid £390,000, making a total of more than £2 millions from congregational sources. Considerable sums were also received from donations, legacies, and grants from trusts, but another £2 millions will be required within the present decade in order that there may be a worshipping as well as a home-loving people.

These new churches are not so noticeable as those in the older suburbs. Spires and towers are fewer and farther between, since a pound note will now purchase only what five shillings did 50 years ago, and rigorous economy is therefore necessary in building and furnishing. But the work of the Church and its ministers expands even if the spires and towers contract. The modern minister has to be the centre of all the youth organisations of modern days. Cubs, Brownies, Scouts and Guides are not properly under his direction, but he must keep in touch with them, while such bodies as Girls' Guildry, The Boys' Brigade and Youth Fellowship demand his care and thought and frequent presence, as do the older Sunday School, Bible Class and youth club organisations.

As all these need to be housed, and the Woman's Guild too, a new building was devised called a Hall-Church where week-night activities could find scope, while a part called the Sanctuary was reserved and so arranged that it would contain on Sunday the Communion Table, pulpit and reading desk. In these new extension parish churches, of which some 20 in recent years have been erected in Edinburgh, it is noteworthy that a great variety of design has been employed, since to have an interesting building immediately on the scene of a new housing area makes for a large church connection. The later the church visibly arises the more difficult it is to gather the congregation. Yet even so, largely through the children who crowd the new Sunday Schools, these extension charges are full of life and enthusiasm. It is possible also to work the parochial system in them more fully, though this is very difficult in a city since city parishes are not unities and city churches are attended by worshippers from many parishes. A recent visitation of the small parish of Roseburn, for example, showed not only that the inhabitants professed connection with 46 different parishes of the Church of Scotland in Edinburgh, but that there were members and adherents of many other denominations as well.

In such conditions the Extension minister has his own great difficulties. The population is there, but he often lacks experienced helpers, especially in the Kirk Session, and these charges usually have for a time the assistance of experienced elders from an older charge as temporary or assessor elders. Out of a Scottish population of almost 5,180,000 at the 1961 Census, a million and a quarter are communicant members of the Church of Scotland. This takes no account of the adherents and the children, or of those connected with the other denominations we shall be studying.

THE SCOPE OF THE KIRK

At the time of writing—in 1963—there were, within the Presbytery of Edinburgh, 137 churches, and the Communicants' Roll was 126,899. There were 4,838 elders in the Presbytery and the Presbytery itself numbered about 400. Normally the Presbytery meets as a Court on the first Tuesday of each month, except in August when there are no meetings. There is a full-time Clerk, and membership of Presbytery includes every parish minister, and an elder appointed by each Kirk Session. There are also ministers in non-parochial appointments, including the Church's professors at New College and certain ministers engaged in the Church's full-time work as at the Church of Scotland Offices in George Street. The Presbytery itself appoints " freely-elected " elders from Kirk Sessions within the bounds to balance these.

All ministers are subject to the Presbytery and answerable to it only, and not to their Kirk Sessions. The Presbytery in turn is subject to the Synod of Lothian and Tweeddale, and ultimately to the General Assembly, the Supreme Court of the Church. Each January it elects a minister as Moderator for the year and also appoints for a term a minister as Convener of the Business Committee and an elder as Deputy-Convener. It also elects Standing Committees to deal with Business, Maintenance of the Ministry, Property, Home Mission, Foreign Missions, Evangelism, Church and City, Temperance and Morals, Youth, Probationers and Divinity Students, Records, Finance, Nomination, Stewardship and Budget, Re-adjustments, Hospital Chaplaincies, and Overseas and Ecumenical. Its Non-Standing Committees deal with Presbyterial Superintendence, Quinquennial Visitation, Bursaries, Praise, Consultative on Vacancies, and Doctrine.

To illustrate the Church's scope further, Gaelic services in Edinburgh are held in the Highland Church (Tolbooth-St. John's) as well as in the Free and Free Presbyterian Churches.

One group of Edinburgh churches known as the Edinburgh Burgh Churches is of particular historic interest because of their former relationship to the Burgh of Edinburgh. From Reformation days until the time of preparation for the Church Union of 1929, the Burgh was responsible for providing places of worship and paying stipend to the Burgh Ministers. After the Act of 1925 a sum of money was handed over to the Church of Scotland General Trustees, along with the Burgh Church buildings, and to the income from this capital is added the seat rents (or an agreed sum in lieu) from all the Burgh Churches. This sum is divided among all the Burgh Ministers and forms part of their stipend.

These Burgh Churches are the High (St. Giles'), Greyfriars, West St. Giles', Highland (Tolbooth—St. John's), St. Andrew's and St. George's, St. Stephen's, St. Mary's and Greenside. St. Andrew's and St. George's congregations were linked preparatory to union in 1962 after it was found that St. George's building could no longer be used for worship. Both Holy Trinity and Tron-Moredun are also considered as Burgh Churches, since their Ministers receive a share of the Burgh Stipend. Trinity College building ceased to be used for worship in 1959 and the congregation united with Lady Glenorchy's South to form Holy Trinity. Rather earlier the Tron congregation was transported to Moredun (1952). In addition, Canongate (Holyroodhouse), the Church of the old Burgh of Canongate, is one of the group, though it receives only half of the Burgh Stipend since it receives also an annual contribution from the Crown.

The Burgh Ministers have still certain duties to perform, including that of constituting each meeting of the Town Council with prayer. They also meet occasionally with the "Ministers of Leith and the West Kirk" (St. Cuthbert's) to present a Foundation scholarship for the "Merchant Maiden Hospital," and two or three times a year as a fraternal.

There are, then, three great movements in Edinburgh today with religious inspiration, which are shared by the rest of Scotland but are particularly centred in the capital. These are the Ecumenical movement, the Church extension enterprise, and the work among youth. (Young people also have their own annual interdenominational conference in the Assembly Hall).

Another responsibility, much more fully accepted than ever before, is the concern of the Churches for the care of the aged. The Church of Scotland has now, through its energetic Social Services Committee, not only a great number of homes and hostels for children and youth, but a remarkable establishment of Eventide Homes, based on voluntary givings, of which some are surely diverted to this praiseworthy and compelling purpose from legacies which might otherwise have properly gone to the hospitals, now State-supported.

There are also some noteworthy educational establishments. St. Colm's, which was founded in 1895 as the Women's Missionary College of the Church of Scotland, has recently had its scope greatly extended and is now the Missionary College for both men and women future missionaries and for the training also of Deaconnesses and Youth workers. The Deaconesses themselves, of whom there are some 25 at work in Edinburgh alone as these words are written, have within the last few years had their position clarified by the Assembly. The Deaconess Hospital is now State-owned. Then there is Esdaile, which was founded as the Ministers' Daughters' College in 1863.

Relations of the Churches with the British Broadcasting Corporation, the Scottish headquarters of which were for a long time in Edinburgh, are very friendly. There is a Scottish Religious Advisory Committee to which the Churches nominate and a Religious Broadcasting Organiser for Scotland who is a minister. The Church of Scotland Press Bureau at 121 George Street keeps the Church in effective touch with the Press.

Outdoor preaching in Princes Street Gardens and at the Mound and elsewhere on Sunday afternoons and evenings in summer is yet another feature of the Presbytery's evangelistic work, which stretches from the very heart of the city to its outlying districts. And here the Rev. Ian Reid of Pilton takes up the story.

THE CHURCH IN THE HOUSING ESTATES

A page or two back we noticed that the Church of Scotland early recognised the special challenge of the new housing estates. It realised that unless special steps were taken the new areas of the cities with their enormous populations would be left without any churches in or near them; and through the National Church Extension Committee (acting through the local presbyteries) the whole church has shared in the effort to meet this challenge. Before the 1939 war the Church set up nine new parishes. In Craigentinny, Granton, Craigmillar St. Aidans and Stenhouse it provided both a church seating about 800 and a hall seating about 250. At Fairmilehead it built a church, and it provided church halls at Carrick Knowe, Craigs Bank and Crewe Toll. The first two were given churches after the war, and the third was provided with a hall church at the same time.

Immediately after 1945 the problem became much more pressing. Estates were being developed at an accelerated rate, and as the cost of building was rising rapidly, the church provided firstly a temporary wooden hall, which was small though dignified, and later a hall-church seating about 400. These latter were buildings designed to be used for worship on Sundays and also for many activities during the week. But later this policy was changed, and as the result a number of churches and halls were built, though these were not quite up to the standard of those which had been built before the war. Between 1948 and 1962 hall churches were built at Colinton Mains, Southhouse, Moredun, Longstone, Drylaw and Clermiston, in addition to suites of churches and halls at Sighthill, Southfield near Portobello, Oxgangs, Gracemount and at Broomhouse, with additional buildings at Craigmillar and at the Inch.

The Church at large not only provides new buildings for these new estates but also assists with the payment of the stipend of ministers who serve in them. These in turn are helped by Deaconesses and Assistant Ministers, who are paid for by the Home Mission Committee of the Church and by the Women's Home Mission Committee. Deaconesses in the past have mainly served in down-town city parishes, but now work in the housing estates in increasing numbers. Nevertheless, the new congregations which grow up in these parishes are expected to repay a fifth of the cost of their buildings and to become responsible for the payment of their ministers as soon as possible. Much effort has therefore to be expended by these parishes in the raising of money.

The buildings themselves are of great social as well as religious importance. Many of them are in fact so much the main landmark in the housing estates that in one hundreds of taxis every year are directed to stop at the

" White Church ". But most important of all to the ministers concerned, these buildings stand as witness to the faith in their parishes; and more than ever in these sprawling estates the word " parish " has a real meaning. The Church of course has its own minister and parish. The parish is a well-defined unit consisting of a definite housing estate. People living on the estate know which is their church, and even if they do not go to church they know the particular church from which they stay away.

This relationship between Church and people is also assisted by the educational system. In the parish there is certainly one primary school, if not more; and all the children in these schools come from the parish of the same church. In fact the parish, the housing estate, and the school area coincide. Not only is the minister of the church chaplain of the schools and able to see the children regularly at school with the co-operation of the headmasters, but also the same children come as members of the school three times a year to the church for worship. Through the schools the minister is thus well known to all the children of his parish, and through them to every home.

The congregations are large in some estates and small in others, with the size of the congregation depending to a large extent on the social background of the parish. It is an unfortunate fact that the Church has largely lost the allegiance of the unskilled and semi-skilled worker and to a great extent of the skilled worker also. Its strength lies in the middle classes and amongst manual workers holding positions of responsibility. The response to the Church is therefore higher in those estates occupied by a higher proportion of skilled workers. In estates occupied by unskilled and semi-skilled workers not only is Church membership smaller, but also it includes a far lower proportion of men. Even in the estates where the Church appears to be strong, in proportion to the number who live in these estates the number who attend worship weekly is not large.

In housing estates the missionary task of the Church is therefore inescapable. It is a missionary task in a clearly defined area, in which there is only one church. The task, however, is not easy, as the congregation is small compared with the work to be done and to make matters worse there is a shortage not only of men to serve as elders but of church workers who have had the benefit of further education. Moreover, many who come to live in these parishes have had little or no contact with churches in the past. Nonetheless, all these congregations have done what they could to face this missionary task. Visitation of every household has normally been carried out when the parishes were first set up, and subsequently many parishes have organised campaigns to visit people in their estate and invite them to share in the Church's life. In the end, however, the most effective contact with those outwith Church membership has been made when parents come seeking baptism for their children or when young couples come desiring to be married in church. In these parishes there is much visitation of the sick, of the aged and of the bereaved who have had no previous church contact; and in fact the minister is often known as " My Minister " by many people personally unknown to him. But there are many he knows, and these he tries to help, when they are faced with problems, either in their homes or as they visit him in manse and vestry.

The largest Sunday Schools have been and still are those in the housing estates whose congregations have the greatest shortage of leadership. These Sunday Schools have to face the problem of teacher shortage, and in consequence the classes are much too large. In all these areas uniformed organisations for children have been well attended, though shortage of leadership has prevented them from being even more effective. These organisations do not keep many of their members after the age of 15, and mainly attract children from the more responsible homes. The churches, however, have a strong influence on a few teenagers, who are faithful and active in its life, but compared with the total in this age-group the number of those connected with the Church is very small. Most of them, it seems, have probably been at a Senior Secondary school or in the higher classes of a Junior Secondary school. So it looks as if the Church has at the moment something to say to the girl who works in an office or a shop, but little to those who work in factories. Fortunately some parishes have made a real attempt to make contact with a wider cross-section of young people, through clubs both on week nights and on Sundays.

Church life in the new estates expresses itself in much the same way as in the older parts of the city. The average age of these congregations is lower than in the city parishes, and there are greater opportunities to experiment with new patterns of congregational life, though freedom to experiment is not as great as might be thought since both men and women tend to be very conservative in their church life. One of the most significant experiments in more than one parish has been the breaking down of congregational life into smaller groups which meet monthly in the homes of members in different parts of the parish. These monthly meetings not only enable members to get to know each other in a way not possible in a larger gathering but allow members to discover together the meaning of the Christian faith. In such groups discussion also takes place as to what the congregation can do to meet the needs of the local estate. Some congregations have used literature extensively, selling a local paper both to their own members and to many others in the estate as well.

While the parish church itself houses the activities of the congregation, some congregations also use halls in the local schools, particularly for their youth organisations. The church buildings are also offered to other groups: old peoples' clubs, for example, frequently meet on church premises, and halls are used as play-centres for children through the week.

Although church membership is small compared with the total population in these areas, its influence is much greater than mere numbers would indicate. For however small it appears to be, it is in fact the biggest voluntary group in the estate, and when any public work has to be undertaken it is the main group to which the authorities can turn for assistance.

THE FREE CHURCH OF SCOTLAND

Though the main strength of the Free Church of Scotland is in the Highlands and Islands, its headquarters are in Edinburgh. Its General Assembly meets every May in the church of St. Columba in Johnston Terrace, just across the street from the meeting place of the Church of Scotland fathers and brethren. Its offices in North Bank Street occupy a fine site above the Mound, and in the same building there is the Free Church of Scotland College, where its ministers receive their theological training. Though it moved here in 1907, after the litigation with the United Free Church, the College regards itself as historically continuous with the neighbouring New College, instituted by the Free Church after the Disruption of 1843 and now a seminary of the Church of Scotland and part of the University.

The Free Church College has a Principal and four Professors, and lecturers in elocution and psalmody. There are chairs in Hebrew and Old Testament Exegesis, Greek and New Testament Exegesis, Church History, and Systematic Theology, while the Professor of Apologetics also deals with natural science, pastoral theology and missions.

Besides St. Columba's, the Free Church has two charges in Edinburgh—Buccleuch and Greyfriars in West Cross Causeway, and Elder Memorial in Hope Street, Leith. Its Edinburgh Presbytery takes in two charges in Fife and one in London, while the College professors are also members. The Free Church issues two publications from Edinburgh—*Monthly Record* and *Instructor*.

UNITED FREE CHURCH

In 1929 when the majority of the United Free Church entered into the union with the Church of Scotland, a minority remained independent, believing that " state aid or civil establishment of religion, being contrary to the spirit of Christ's teaching, is fatal to full spiritual freedom, and is opposed to the consistent testimony of our Church."

In Edinburgh, which is included in the Presbytery of the Lothians and Borders, there are seven charges of the United Free Church and one mission in different parts of the city. The combined strength of these congregations amounts to a little over 2,000; most of the churches, in addition to Sunday schools and Bible classes, engage in the usual activities for junior and senior members, such as the Boys Brigade, Girl Guides, Youth Fellowship and Women's Guild.

The U.F. Church offices are in Glasgow, where its periodicals are also published. But the ministers of the church are trained in Edinburgh at the Scottish Congregational College, which is shared with the Congregational Union. The U.F. General Assembly meets usually in Edinburgh and Glasgow in alternate years.

THE ROMAN CATHOLIC CHURCH

The shrewd observation was made a year or two ago by a broadcaster that Stornoway was less provincial than London. This was not simply perfervid regionalism and one can hardly do less than claim as much for Edinburgh where a European awareness has existed for centuries. This, writes a devout Catholic, is often ascribed to favourable trade winds and the proximity of Scandinavia and the Low Countries, but, in part the basis of such an awareness can be attributed to the establishment, growth and history of Roman Catholicism in the city. The Edinburgh Catholic is continually reminded of this influence by the now often secular remains of what was once sacred. Even within the restricted area of the High Street he finds Blackfriars Street, St. Mary's Street, the Pleasance and further out, Sciennes, which mark the sites of pre-Reformation religious communities.

The growth of the city's Roman Catholic population since 1907 has been in a diminishing ratio: and the percentage of increase in the City is even less than that of the national ratio when it was at one time so much greater. This suggests that the position of the Catholic is a much more integral one than it was a century ago, inasmuch as he is now directly affected by the institutions and modes of thinking of his non-Catholic neighbours. The large family today is as much a curiosity as it once was a commonplace, and Catholics have become conscious of social status as distinct from the days when they had fewer aspirations, or, if they had ambitions, had less chance of success. In the first half of the last century Catholics, among them many Irish immigrants, were often the holders of the most menial occupations, but since then the Catholics have absorbed the essential worth of the City. By worth is meant not the old gibe of " kippers and grand pianos " but real social and economic worth coupled with a definite sense of individual and communal good.

The phenomenon of a one time despised group emulating the best qualities in Edinburgh citizenry throughout the last four or five generations so exactly as to become more or less indistinguishable from them is very interesting. So far from this being a sheep-like and unthinking imitation it takes its rise from an intelligent and ready adaptability. Catholics now play their part in the conduct of the city's affairs; and this in itself is a notable change even in the last generation. It is not easy to determine the sociological factors which account for this change, but it might be said that emulation characterises the strength of the Catholic body and mere imitation the weakness of it.

There are, however, essential differences related to the practice of their faith among Catholics and the stand they take as a body on issues of moral principle; for however much they may err in practice they are rarely unaware of clear distinctions between right and wrong. This does not mean of course that they were or are better than their neighbours but simply that the way ahead has been clear and single for the Catholics as it often is for struggling and vigorous minorities.

A simple example of this is the building in 1896 of St. Cuthbert's

Church in Slateford Road, then a remote suburb. The incumbent, with 350 souls in his care, built this large and rather fine church in the belief that the town must move to the country. In this he was justified, for the Catholic population by the early '60s was in the region of 4,000. For other localities the most notable contemporary figures were St. Mary's Cathedral, (Leith Street, Greenside and the New Town) 5,700; St. Ninian's (Restalrig and Marionville) 4,000; Sacred Heart (Tollcross) 4,000; St. Patrick's (High Street) 3,500; St. Margaret Mary's (Pilton, a relatively new area) 3,200; and Star of the Sea (Leith) 3,150.

As Edinburgh has expanded her lungs the Catholics have been able to breathe in more senses than one, and other erstwhile suburbs have become centres of thriving Catholic communities. In 1878 when the Hierarchy was restored to Scotland there were in Edinburgh only five churches, nine clergy, one religious community and six schools. By the early '60s there were 20 churches, 66 clergy, 8 religious communities, 15 schools under the Education Committee, and three private schools. The Franciscans (the Greyfriars) returned in 1926 to somewhere near their old habitat, while in 1931 the Dominicans, (the Blackfriars) were established in George Square. Other religious communities have also been re-established in the city for longer than the present generation can remember. Together these clergy, churches and schools serve a Catholic community of some 46,000.

THE EPISCOPAL CHURCH

It was a Bishop of Aberdeen who described the city of Edinburgh as a " suburb of London ", and it may well be true that its geographical proximity to England, and the number of " incomers " from the south, provides some explanation for the comparatively prominent part which the Episcopal Church plays in this city. For of the inhabitants of Edinburgh, at least one in every 30 is a practising Episcopalian, and if all those who would claim to belong to that church were included, the proportion would probably be considerably larger. The clergy are not of course encouraged to be extravagant in their claims to numbers. They record the number of persons whom they know to have made their Communion at least once in the preceding year (the average is nearly 12 times per annum); and that is a figure about which there can be little speculation. The other number that is asked for is an estimate of the members of their church, and here in time past there has been a greater diversity of opinion as to what constitutes a member. The present usage is to disregard lapsed communicants and all adherents who do not *adhere*, and to return only the number of those who take an active part in the church's life. Even thus diminished, the number of members of the Episcopal Church in Edinburgh stands at about 16,000, while the number of communicants is approaching 10,000.

Historically, it might seem strange to find such a concentration of Episcopalians so far South in Scotland. It was Aberdeen and Angus that were the strongholds of the " gentle persuasion " in earlier days.

Yet the strength of the Episcopal Church in Edinburgh is not a new thing. The persecutions under the Penal Laws after the '15 and the '45, which caused such devastation in the north, seem to have had little effect in the Capital, and by 1756 there were 13 non-juring clergymen working in Edinburgh and Leith, not counting those who, having taken oaths to the government, served the "Qualified Chapels" to which those people went who wished to enjoy the best of both worlds. Even so, life was not altogether peaceful, but the troubles of Episcopalians in the city arose from interior disputes, rather than exterior pressure. It was King Charles I who had founded the Diocese in 1633, and long after the other Sees were electing their own Bishops, Edinburgh could not be supplied with one, unless a *congé d'élire* were forthcoming from the exiled Court. For many years the Diocese of Edinburgh, which at that time was almost co-terminous with the city, was ruled by the Synod of Presbyters, who complicated things further by claiming to be the spiritual guardians of the Archdiocese of St. Andrews, which was also reserved to the "King."

The present state of the Episcopal Church in Edinburgh dates from the early 19th century. As the city grew, so did the Church spread out. Its members increased in numbers, and many stately churches were built. St. John's had already in 1818 been fortunate in securing what must surely be one of the finest sites for a church in any city, at the west end of Princes Street, and St. Paul's had migrated from the Cowgate to York Place in the same year, although the other St. Paul's was content to remain in the obscurity of Carrubber's Close. Between 1850 and the close of the century no less than 16 new churches were built. In other cities in Scotland the Episcopal Church must be sought for in back streets, but not in Edinburgh, where they can easily be found in the main thoroughfares. Substantial buildings arose such as Christ Church, Morningside (1876), All Saints', Tollcross (1867), St. Cuthbert's, Colinton (1893), and St. Martin's, Gorgie (1887).

The greatest of all, of course, is the Cathedral Church of St. Mary in Palmerston Place, whose three spires can be seen even from the Fife coast. Begun in 1874, and finished in 1879 (apart from the Chapter House and the two west spires which were added later), it was a benefaction to the Diocese from the Misses Barbara and Mary Walker of Coates, whose old home still lies under the shadow of the church which they gave. Designed by Sir George Gilbert Scott, who died in 1878, and completed by his son J. O. Scott, the Cathedral has been described by Dr. Charles Warr as "the finest church to have been built in Scotland since the Reformation", and even those who have never been inside the building, know from its broadcast services the perfection of the musical tradition which has been built up there. It is unique, not only in Edinburgh but in the whole of Scotland, and without any doubt the greatest contribution to this achievement has been the training of generations of boy choristers in the Choir School in the Cathedral grounds.

The main problem of recent times has been the scattering of the population of the city into new suburbs, and efforts have been made to see that Episcopalians who go to live in new housing schemes will find their

Church at hand. There are always, of course, a certain number of people who for sentimental reasons prefer to return to, or even stay away from, their old church in the city, rather than to form a new loyalty; but as it is an expensive business to travel long distances to church, especially when there is a family of children, a dozen or so churches, few of them perhaps of any great architectural value, have been built since 1910 to accommodate " displaced persons."

This means that in the early '60s the city had a total of 34 Episcopal churches, served by some 45 clergymen; and this alone is an interesting aspect of the Episcopal Church's activities. There never seems to be much difficulty in finding priests who are willing to staff the churches of Edinburgh or its environs. Certainly at the moment of writing there is not a single vacancy, although only the larger churches can afford to pay their Rector more than the minimum stipend. That itself, however, is much better than it has been in time past. In the short space of 12 years it has been increased, so that a priest who would have earned £300 in 1948, receives £800 today.

Over all these churches and clergy, the Bishop of Edinburgh exercises a pastoral and fatherly oversight. He is not the potentate that he would be south of the border; and indeed during one Bishop's period of office anyone who wrote to him " The Palace, Edinburgh," was quite likely to get the letter back endorsed, " not known at the King's, Empire or Lyceum." But though he lives in a simple way in a crescent house, the Bishop is a leading citizen, and the retired occupant of the See has shown himself to be such. The Right Reverend K. C. H. Warner, D.S.O., D.D., succeeded in 1947 the well-loved Bishop Danson, who had come to the Diocese after a varied experience of missionary work at home and in Borneo. Before him, Bishop Reid had been a keen man of business, as well as a real father-in-God to his clergy and people, and Bishop Walpole (the father of Hugh Walpole, the novelist) had been a man of great spiritual gifts. To take the succession only one step farther back, the Irish scholar, John Dowden, had been Bishop from 1881 to 1910, and had made substantial contributions to the historical literature of his adopted country.

Like his predecessors, Bishop Warner made his mark in the community. He will be best remembered in the city as an ecumenical figure, who, as the phrase goes, " leaned over backward " in his anxiety to explore any way that might lead to a better understanding between the separated churches, and their ultimate re-union. He retired in 1961; and as his successor the electors, clerical and lay, chose Kenneth Moir Carey, M.A.(Oxon.), who had been a distinguished Principal of Westcott House, Cambridge, one of the leading theological colleges for the Church of England, since 1947, and who was also one of H.M. Chaplains. It is noteworthy that Bishop Carey has already shown himself to be a leader in the cause of Christian Unity since one of his first acts was to address the Presbytery of Edinburgh.

How great is the impact made by the Episcopal Church on the life of Edinburgh would be difficult to say. It has its institutions, ranging from a University chaplaincy to the Blue Door Club, which caters for those young people who find nowhere to go on a Sunday evening, a home for old people, and a lodging house for working men.

In the city, but exempt from the Bishop's jurisdiction, are also to be found two " peculiars " (in the technical sense of the word): the offices of the Representative Church Council and the Theological College both near the Cathedral. At the one the business of the whole Church is transacted; at the other, men are trained for the priesthood in all the Dioceses of Scotland.

Apart from these specific pieces of work, one would like to feel that a larger influence is exercised by the steady witness of the Episcopal Church, in commending to people outside its membership some of the good things for which it stands. The Christian seasons, for example, are no longer the monopoly of the Episcopalians and Roman Catholics. The tradition of liturgical prayer is increasingly being appreciated in churches which formerly suspected it as smacking of formalism, if not of popery. And friendship between Churches, which has at least reached the stage of " Conversations ", is perhaps closer in Edinburgh than in any other part of the northern kingdom.

OTHER DENOMINATIONS

The churches we have so far studied have long indigenous roots going far back through the centuries and at one time or other have been deeply involved by their very nature in Scottish affairs of political and ecclesiastical state. But there are many others, some with English inspiration such as the Methodists, the Baptists and Congregationalists, and some—the Christian Scientists, for example—with headquarters overseas.

THE SOCIETY OF FRIENDS

Quakerism was first preached in Edinburgh in 1653, and meetings were held for a few years in the house of William Osborne, a former officer in the Parliamentary army. The first Meeting House was acquired in 1681 in West Port. A new one was built in Peebles Wynd (Cowgate) in 1729, but in 1791 another was substituted for it in the Pleasance, on the site of a burial ground bought in 1675. This building survives, but is now the property of the Pleasance Trusts. During the 18th century the Meeting was dominated by the noted family of the Millers of Craigentinny. After that, as elsewhere, numbers declined, organisation fell away, and records were ill-kept till visitors from England effected a reorganisation in 1786.

During the 19th century membership remained small, but following on increased interest stimulated by the first World War, and thanks primarily to a well known University science lecturer named Ernest Ludlam, a second Meeting was established in the 1920s. This obtained its own premises in 1938 in the West End, and the older Meeting was subsequently merged in it (1944).

Membership of the Meeting in the early 1960s reached 174, a total which included 48 juveniles, and a number resident outwith the city. There were also a number of non-members recorded as " Attenders ", and the Sunday morning Meeting for Worship is usually attended by others, who are either local inhabitants or visitors to the city. Occasional public meetings are held, normally on Sunday evenings and at these addresses are given on Quaker thought and activities. Children's classes are held at the same time as the Sunday morning Meeting, and a Young Friends' Group, composed mainly of students, meets regularly.

For matters of business there is a " Preparative Meeting ". This is held monthly; its affairs are conducted by a " Clerk ", who combines the functions of chairman and secretary; and it is appointed annually, as are other office-bearers and committees. The Meeting is subordinate to a Monthly Meeting, which also comprises Glasgow and a few smaller Meetings. The Scottish Meetings are united in the " General Meeting ", which in the hierarchy of the Society ranks as a " Quarterly Meeting " of London Yearly Meeting, the ultimate authority for Great Britain. When this body met in Edinburgh in 1948—the first time it had ever done so in Scotland—sessions were held in the Church of Scotland Assembly Hall.

THE METHODIST CHURCH

John Wesley, the founder of Methodism, visited Edinburgh on 21 occasions, usually on horseback, the first visit being in 1751. But it was not until 1765 that a " Meeting House " was erected at the Low Calton. It was built in the octagonal shape favoured by Wesley at this time, and Wesley himself preached in it on a number of occasions. In 1814, however, the Church was demolished to make way for the Regent Bridge and what became Waverley Station. A new Church built in Nicolson Square was opened the following year; and a century later—in the centenary year—the large and commodious Epworth Halls were built alongside the Church. Sir James Falshaw, the first Englishman to become Lord Provost of Edinburgh (1874–6) was a member of the Church, and General Ulysses S. Grant, President of the United States of America, regularly attended the services during his stay in the city.

By 1880, with suburbs of villas and tenements growing fast on the west side of the city, it became clear that " The Square " could not minister to all the Methodist people in these areas, still less take an adequate part in the evangelisation of the new population. So it was that the Edinburgh Methodist Mission was born. Under the scholarly and dynamic leadership of Dr. George Jackson a start was made in temporary premises, the Albert Hall, Shandwick Place. But by 1890 the congregation had so outgrown the Albert Hall that it was necessary to take the Synod Hall seating 2,000, which was soon packed to the doors. The present premises at Tollcross were built in 1901, and there the work continues today. Since then further Methodist Churches have been built at Abbeyhill, Granton and Leith, and smaller missions in St. Clare Street and Newcraig hall (to serve the mining community there.)

The work, especially at Nicolson Square and Tollcross, has gone on satisfactorily judging by figures compiled in 1963. These showed that the total membership of Methodist Churches in Edinburgh was 1,720, and the average attendance each Sunday was 1,000 in the morning, and 650 at night.

The Methodist churches in the city number among their members many Scottish families; but they also minister to large numbers of English and Welsh people who have come to live temporarily or permanently in the capital. With the rapid growth of the University and its associated colleges the Church's work has developed rapidly among Methodist students—Scottish, English and from overseas—and the ministers of Nicolson Square and Tollcross are joint Methodist chaplains to the University.

THE BAPTIST CHURCH

Although the Baptists claim to be the largest Protestant denomination in the world, it has always been comparatively small in Scotland. In Edinburgh its 16 churches, all independent and self-governing, are organised in a consultative body known as the " Edinburgh and Lothians Association " and number 2,400 members. But the congregations, on average, are larger than the declared membership.

The origins of the Baptist Church in Edinburgh are a little obscure. We know that John Knox spoke hotly of Baptist views as " maist horribill and absurd," and that Robert Baillie published his notable book *Anabaptism* in 1647 in an attempt to prevent its establishment in Scotland. The coming of Cromwell's army to Scotland on the other hand encouraged those who held Baptist views, for many of the officers and soldiers were Baptists, including the Commanding Officer, Major-General Lilburne. The Baptist Church thus began to grow, and after a church had been established at Leith—a church active enough in 1653 to publish two pamphlets entitled *The Baptist Confession*, and *Heart Bleedings for Professors' Abominations*—Nicoll in his diary for the same year could say with truth,

> This year Anabaptists daily increst in this nation, . . . that thrice in the week on Monday, Weddinsday and Fryday, thair were some dippit at Bonnington Mill, betwixt Leith and Edinburgh, both men and women of good rank.

The withdrawal of the Protectorate Army and the restoration of the Monarchy in 1660 caused a decline in Baptist life in the city. In 1765, however, a small company of Baptists met in the historic Magdalene Chapel in the Cowgate, and subsequently baptisms took place in the Water of Leith at Canonmills. The first church building erected by Baptists was at Richmond Court in 1787. In the latter part of the 18th century considerable progress was made under the leadership of the Rev. Archibald McLean, and the Church which he founded as a " Scotch Baptist Church " is known today as Bristo Baptist Church in Queensferry Road,

The beginning of the 19th century saw a new and notable advance. Robert Haldane, who had sold a considerable part of his Airthrey estate, devoted the money amounting to over £70,000 to the promotion of evangelism throughout Scotland. He bought " The Circus ", where the burnt-out shell of the Royal Theatre stands today, and opened it as a place of worship—in 1798. Within 10 years a group of baptized believers formed themselves into a church which is known today as Charlotte Chapel in Rose Street.

THE CONGREGATIONAL CHURCH

Strangely enough the Edinburgh records of the Congregational Church claim its Scottish roots in a missionary movement which began at the end of the 18th century, principally, it is said, under the inspiration of Robert and James Haldane and John Aikman. Edinburgh's earliest Congregational church was founded in 1798.

The oldest surviving congregational church in Edinburgh is that now called Augustine-Bristo. This congregation has a continuous history back to 1802, when Aikman built a second church in North College Street for an " overflow " from the Leith Walk congregation, which had rapidly grown to massive proportions. This building has long since vanished, but the congregation now meets in Augustine-Bristo church, on George IV Bridge, which was built in 1861 and was then called Augustine church.

Today there are nine Congregational churches in Edinburgh and two in Leith. At one time or another, however, there have been 21. The total membership officially returned for Edinburgh in 1962 was 2,362 adults and 970 children: for Leith, 602 adults and 241 children. But if the oldest church is Augustine-Bristo, the largest membership in Edinburgh during 1962 was at Morningside (443 adults). At Duke Street, Leith there were 462 adult members. The latest Congregational church to be formed in Edinburgh was built in 1951 at Saughton Mains to serve a new housing estate. It is pleasant to record in conclusion that Congregational churches in the city, besides having a local District Council, which serves a wide area beyond the city, exist on the friendliest terms with neighbouring churches of other denominations, and frequent occasions are taken for united work and worship with parish churches and other Christian groups in their districts.

THE CHURCH OF CHRIST

On the last Sunday of 1839 a small group of people met in the Roman Eagle Hall in the Lawnmarket, and under the leadership of William Thompson and Philip Gray the Church of Christ thus began its witness in Edinburgh and quickly grew in numbers and strength. The earliest baptisms took place, sometimes at night, in Duddingston Loch.

In 1841 the Church moved to South Bridge Hall near the University, where it was to remain for 20 years; and a year later in Edinburgh it entertained the first Conference of the Churches in Great Britain. A second congregation which followed—in 1855—was so vigorously evangelical and grew so rapidly that in 1861 it moved to the Roxburgh Place Chapel, where the old and the new Churches united.

After this union the Church of Christ for many decades became keenly aware of the importance of Sunday School work and of the application of its faith to social problems, and the work along these lines and also in foreign mission work was not only considerably strengthened but churches were established in places outside the city. Then came a further union. For many years there had been conversations about the possibility of union between the Church of Christ and the Church of Baptized Believers; and in 1928 these bore fruit when union was effected. Five years later the Church—which in 1963 had a membership in Edinburgh of some 200 attending a Morning Communion Service and an Evening Service each Sunday, and was also running a Sunday school—moved to its present home.

THE GLASITE CHURCH

This Church, now a very small community with about 30 members and adherents, is the sole remaining one in Scotland. There is a Church in London. It meets every Sunday forenoon and afternoon for prayer and praise, and the reading of the Scriptures. In the interval between the forenoon and afternoon services the members partake of the love-feast so that mutual knowledge and friendship may be increased among brethren as members of the one household of which Christ is the Head.

The Church came into being in Edinburgh in 1734, and its first place of public worship in Chalmers Close in the High Street removed to its present meeting place in Barony Street in 1836. It arose after the deposition by the General Assembly of Mr. John Glas in 1730 from his ministry in the Church of Scotland, with the strong support of his son-in-law, Mr. Robert Sandeman.

John Glas, who opposed the binding character of the National Covenants, emphasised spiritual religion as opposed to conventional morality, and disapproved of the importance given to the Westminster Confession, or to any Catechism, as being a human document, when the Word of God should be free. He could not agree that the government of the Established Church was founded upon the Word of God, nor that the support of the Civil Power should be invoked by the Church.

THE SALVATION ARMY

The Salvation Army commenced operations in Edinburgh in 1882 within three years of having taken its present title and character, and today Edinburgh is an important divisional centre of the organisation. The Divisional Headquarters supervises 28 corps (religious centres) as far south of Edinburgh as Berwick-upon-Tweed and as far west as Stenhousemuir and Shotts, and the Social Work Division operates 12 institutions. Six of these corps in 1962–3 were situated within the city itself, each commanded by a fully commissioned Salvation Army officer, and seven of the Social Work centres are also in the capital.

The soldiers (or members) of The Salvation Army are drawn from all classes of the community, and represent that inner core of committed fighters for God—the open air meeting attenders, who take the gospel in print to the public houses and to people in their homes. In addition there are worshippers, Home League (sisterhood) members, Torchbearers (Youth Movement), " Over-Sixty " Club members, Scouts, Guides, as well as members of other Corps sections including bible classes and Sunday schools.

Every week too Salvationists visit Edinburgh public houses and with *The War Cry* and *The Young Soldier* contact many who are otherwise unreached by religion. Salvationists also hold meetings each week in the streets and by-ways of the city where Bible messages and personal testimony are given, and the strains of the band carry well-known hymns farther than the voice can reach and bring the Army's message to thousands more.

The bands which can be seen every week marching through the streets to their halls, always headed by the Salvation Army flag, have been on this important mission; but to many citizens the bands may be better known for other forms of service. Gorgie Band, for instance, plays religious music in the public parks during the summer months, and to those in Saughton Prison at Christmas time. On Christmas Eve this same band holds in the Usher Hall a carol service in which several of the leading choirs of the city participate. There are three other smaller bands in Edinburgh rendering similar services.

The work of The Salvation Army in Edinburgh also includes activities of a social or philanthropic nature designed to aid those in need of material or moral help. In three eventide homes in the city, for example, over 120 old people find care and patience, love and understanding; and in two hostels—one for men and another for women—people working away from home or even the most under-privileged may find accommodation.

At the Edinburgh Salvation Army Nursing Home, in 1963-64, there was accommodation for 25 unmarried mothers and nine private patients at any one time. The staff are all both fully trained nurses and commissioned Salvation Army officers, and so can add to the nursing care their patients need a spiritual ministry and also, although The Salvation Army is not an adoption society, advice to unmarried mothers. It also has, at Granton, a Goodwill centre where regular religious services are held and social relief of various kinds provided; and it pays continuous attention to the problems of the aged.

The Salvation Army business departments are well represented in Edinburgh. The Salvation Army Assurance Society, for instance, has both agents and officers in the city—a contact with large numbers of people which " enables them to exercise a ministry of comfort and guidance at times of sorrow and loss."

CHRISTIAN SCIENCE

Decidedly local in origin, as are all Christian Science branch churches, Edinburgh's two Christian Science churches form part of the Christian Science movement's rapid growth in the first half of this century. It is particularly apt that Edinburgh should have some part in this growth, for the ancestry of the Discoverer and Founder of Christian Science, Mary Baker Eddy, was in part Scottish through the McNeils, an old Covenanting family. Miss E. Mary Ramsay, daughter of Sir James Ramsay, was one of the founder members of First Church of Christ, Scientist, Edinburgh, and her book *Christian Science and its Discoverer* is well known, as is also *Why I am a Christian Scientist* by Thomas L. Leishman, an Edinburgh University graduate.

Historically, 1895 is significant as the year during which Christian Science Sunday services were first held in Edinburgh. By 1898 these had become regular, and a year later testimony meetings on Wednesdays and a reading room in Duke Street were added. In the same year, the members of The Mother Church engaged in this activity organised themselves as First Church of Christ, Scientist, Edinburgh, and received recognition by The Mother Church in Boston, Massachusetts.

In 1902, the first Christian Science lecture in Scotland was delivered to a large Edinburgh audience. Two years later, increase in numbers moved the church successively to premises in Queen Street and Pitt Street. By 1909, the members had decided to build their own church on a site between the Water of Leith and the Royal Botanic Garden; and the first service in the new, somewhat romanesque, edifice was duly held in July, 1911. Six months later, having achieved freedom from debt, the church was dedicated. In October, 1935, certain members of First Church, Edinburgh decided to form a second church, to be located in the West End. But owing to World War II, it was not until 1953 that Second Church was able to occupy the first portion of its new premises.

Growth was also evident in other quarters. In 1957, under special exemptions in the Nursing Homes Registration (Scotland) Act, 1938, a Christian Science nursing home, specially designated " Christian Science House ", was opened in Murrayfield; and here Christian Science nurses minister to the practical needs of Christian Science patients receiving treatment, through prayer alone, from a Christian Science practitioner. Twenty years later the Christian Science Organisation at the University began holding weekly meetings at the Chaplaincy Centre.

The Church of Christ, Scientist, never publishes membership figures, but at least it can be said that in 1966 four Christian Science practitioners were listed under *Edinburgh* in *The Christian Science Journal*, which is the official organ of The First Church of Christ, Scientist, in Boston, Massachusetts.

THE UNITARIAN CHURCH

St. Mark's Church in Castle Terrace has been, since 1835, the home of a cause which, in Scotland, began in Berwickshire and came to Edinburgh in 1776. In 1792 its members adopted the name of Universal Dissenters but later came to be known as Unitarians, and since 1835 St. Mark's has been Edinburgh's one Unitarian Church. Its membership is 200 and the average attendance 100.

Today with an Australian as minister, the Rev. Bruce Findlow, B.A., it has an increasing membership and attendance and, while trying to maintain the life of a truly family Church for its membership of all ages, it reaches out to bridge a little the gulf between the Church and the world with its liberal message, its welcome to sceptics and doubters and its participation in social work and many cultural activities including special services during the Edinburgh Festival.

THE JEWISH COMMUNITY

The emergence of a Jewish community in Edinburgh dates from the beginning of the 19th century. It was not until 1816 that the first regular synagogue was established in the city, though previously services were conducted without the aid of a clergyman. Four years later the *Edinburgh Evening Courant* reported (28th September, 1820):

> On Friday evening the Jews settled here commenced holding the feast of Tabernacles for the first time in Scotland in a temporary building near the Pleasance.

A century earlier a Jew in Edinburgh would most likely have been regarded as " an adversary of the trew religion " and would have found it difficult to obtain permission to reside and trade in the city.

One of the earliest settlers, and a leader of the original small community, was Philip Levy who established himself as a furrier about 1814. The royal appointment of his firm as " furrier to His Majesty " in 1824 is an indication that religious and social prejudices were by then steadily relaxing. At about this time too cultural barriers against Jews were being lowered. Louis Ashenheim, son of an Edinburgh jeweller, became the first Scottish Jew to graduate from a University when he graduated as a Doctor of Medicine at St. Andrews in 1839. But it was not until 1853 that his brother Charles became the first Jew to qualify as a Doctor of Medicine at the University of Edinburgh.

The Jewish population in Edinburgh did not begin to increase significantly until the persecutions in Russia in 1880 hastened a stream of immigrants to Britain. Today there are some 300 Jewish families in the city.

The synagogue in Salisbury Road—opened in 1932—is now the only Jewish place of worship in the city but until 1918 there were three congregations. Classes in Hebrew and religious instruction are held regularly in a communal hall, opposite the synagogue which also serves as a meeting place for youth groups, the old people's Friendship Club, and the Women's Zionist Society.

Among notable Jewish clergymen who ministered to the Edinburgh community in recent years have been Rabbi Dr. Salis Daiches, father of Professor David Daiches and Sheriff Lionel Daiches, and Rabbi Dr. Isaac Cohen. The present Chief Rabbi is Dr. J. Weinburg who came to Edinburgh from South Africa in May, 1961.

SPIRITUALISM

Before he died, a well-known Edinburgh journalist, J. W. Herries compiled the following account of the part played in the city by Spiritualism, a movement near his heart.

There has been (he wrote) over a long period extending back to the early days of the movement in this country, a considerable number of Edinburgh citizens interested in the theory of Spiritualism, although their number is difficult to assess. One of the newspapers has a section of its advertising space for announcement of Spiritualist meetings. There are some dozen centres at which Sunday services are held to which the public are invited. There are also a large number of smaller unattached bodies holding regular meetings which are largely confined to their own members. The Gayfield Church of the Edinburgh Association of Spiritualists holds regular Sunday services, and also carries on week-day activities, including a regular healing service. The Edinburgh Spiritualist Church, an off-shoot of the older body, holds well-attended Sunday services and week-day meetings in premises in Albany Street.

An important centre, unique except for a similar institution in London, is the Edinburgh Psychic College and Library in Heriot Row. Founded in 1932 by the late Mrs. Ethel Miller, who presented the Heriot Row property, the objects of the College are defined as " the study and investigation of Psychic phenomena and their implications and the development of the psychic powers of its members." In the early '60s it had a membership of about 200, many of whom attended the bi-weekly meetings, at which addresses were given by competent speakers and authorities and demonstrations of clairaudience and clairvoyance by leading mediums from London and other parts of the country. These meetings are open to the public.

Another group in the early '60s was meeting twice a week in the Edinburgh Psychic Studio in Queen Street, where demonstrations were being given by an Edinburgh " direct voice " woman medium who had carried on this organisation for many years. There was also in the city the White Fox Sanctuary which specialised in healing. But there seems to have been a continuing interest in Edinburgh in psychic phenomena from far back in the 19th century. In the late 1860s the Psychological Society of Edinburgh carried out an investigation. Between the two world wars in our own century a study group holding regular meetings was organised by an Episcopal clergyman in the city, and this led to the formation of the Scottish Psychical Society, with rented premises which were formally opened by Sir Arthur Conan Doyle, himself an Edinburgh graduate. This body eventually merged with the Edinburgh Psychic College in Heriot Row.

It is here, however, that we must end this survey of the various churches or crusades in the city since it is clearly impossible to study all of its numerous religious bodies in a seemingly endless list.

To take only a few more almost at random from the Edinburgh and Leith Post Office Directory is to find as great a variety as we shall discover later among Edinburgh's innumerable secular societies. There are, for instance, The Faith Mission and The Fellowship of Christian Healing; the Catholic Apostolic Church; the French Protestant Church, the Ukrainian Catholic Church, and the German Speaking Congregation in Scotland; the Original Secession Church; the Active Truth Church; the Church for the Deaf and Dumb; the Latter Day Saints; Theosophites; and a big array of missions ranging from the famous Carrubber's Close and Grassmarket Missions to the Edinburgh People's Palace Mission and the Gorgie Railway Mission.

CHAPTER 8

THE LAW OF SCOTLAND

As the capital city Edinburgh is the proper home of the Supreme Courts of Scotland. It is also appropriate that in a country with great legal and ecclesiastical traditions the Courts are housed within the Parliament House which itself lies close to the ancient High Kirk of St. Giles. Between the two buildings, and dominated by the fine lead statue of Charles II, is the Parliament Square "as foppery calls it," observed Henry Cockburn, "but which used and ought to be called the Parliament Close." Fortunately not all the fine old names have vanished; and so today the traditional legal atmosphere of this part of the Old Town is still reflected in the nearby street signs—Advocates' Close and Writers' Court—which themselves epitomise the division of the profession between those who practise the law as solicitors and those who follow it as advocates first and then maybe as judges later.

THE SUPREME COURTS OF SCOTLAND

Three differing spheres of legal authority and administration are concentrated in the city. As Scotland's capital it is the administrative centre of the country's legal system; as the principal town within the Sheriffdom of the Lothians and Peebles it is the centre of the shrieval administration; as a Royal Burgh it has a limited criminal and civil jurisdiction within its own boundaries.

The Supreme Courts of Scotland comprise the Court of Session and the High Court of Justiciary, and are housed within the Parliament House, originally built about 1640 for the pre-union Scottish Parliament but greatly reconstructed and continually extended since that date to the present day. The latest extension indeed took place in 1963 when two new courtrooms were added to make 12 in all.

The Court of Session hears civil causes only, and is composed, at the time these words are written, of 17 judges who are officially styled Senators of the College of Justice, and who also take on their appointment a courtesy title derived either from a territorial locality within the country or from their surname. Until 1948 the number of judges was limited to 13 but since that date the number has been increased by statute to permit the appointment of 18 judges in all. Of the judges two hold judicial office as Lord President of the Court of Session and Lord Justice-Clerk respectively. Before December, 1959 the appointment of all judges was *aut vitam aut culpam*, which may be interpreted broadly as for life or until no longer fitted to hold the office; and accordingly they remained on the bench until they elected to retire or died. All judges appointed after that date however must by statute retire upon attaining the age of 75 years. As for their salaries, in view of the eminence of their offices the Lord President gets £10,000, the Lord Justice-Clerk £9,750 and the other judges £8,250 each.

The Court of Session, which was set up in 1532 in the reign of King James V, is the supreme Court of Scotland in civil matters though its decisions are subject to appeal to the House of Lords. It has long since absorbed the functions of the one-time Scottish Court of Exchequer and Scottish Court of Admiralty, and also the functions in consistorial matters of the Commissary Court, which was suppressed in 1836. The Teind Court, however, still continues, though since the passing of the Church of Scotland (Property and Endowments) Act 1925 the need for it has progressively diminished. Consisting of four Inner House judges and one Lord Ordinary, known as Lords Commissioners of Teinds, it deals with the modification and locality of teinds and hears appeals from decisions of Sheriffs regarding the building of churches and manses under statute.

Certain of the Court of Session judges also sit as members of separate tribunals set up by statute. These are the Valuation Appeal Court and the Registration of Voters Appeal Court, each consisting of three members; the Election Petition Court, consisting of two members; and the Restrictive Practices Court, which has a single judge sitting as chairman with lay members.

The Court itself is divided into the Inner House composed of two Divisions of four judges each, of whom three may act as a quorum, and the Outer House of eight Lords Ordinary. The First and Second Divisions of the Inner House are of equal authority and are presided over by the Lord President and the Lord Justice-Clerk respectively, the remaining members of the Divisions being the senior judges. The Lords Ordinary in the Outer House sit alone. In cases of difficulty or importance, a Court of five or seven members, or even the whole Court, may be convened. The business of the Inner House is principally concerned in hearing appeals from decisions of the Lords Ordinary or from inferior Courts throughout the country.

Geographically the Court of Sessions has, in the main, unlimited jurisdiction over persons domiciled or resident within the country or property situated within Scotland or Scottish territorial waters; but it will also extend its jurisdiction over foreign defenders whose property is found and arrested within the Court's jurisdiction. As the supreme civil court it has exclusive jurisdiction in certain kinds of cause, principally in actions involving status, particularly divorce; but in monetary actions it will not hear causes of under £50 in value. It also has a general control over the administration of trusts, whether public or private. But in certain other causes, especially those involving matters of fact where the appropriate remedy is an award of damages, the issues between the litigants are determined not by judge alone but by a jury of twelve laymen sitting under the direction of a judge. The system of jury trial in civil cases, incidentally, has caused a good deal of controversy since the burden of manning Court of Session juries falls solely on the citizens of Edinburgh, and the aggregate of time spent on settling other people's quarrels is considerable. However, a recent official review recommended against the abolition of the civil jury.

The scope and form of the everyday work of the business of the Court at once becomes apparent to the visitor to the Parliament House. As he passes from the Parliament Hall towards the court rooms, he will observe the rows of boxes of which many legal firms and each advocate has one and in which lie their legal papers tied with legal red tape. Advocates' papers are brought from and delivered to their chambers each day during the Court terms—a service dependent upon one man, which is an unregarded but essential link in the system whereby the Courts operate. These papers are in many cases the written pleadings of litigants before the Court, since parties to an action in court are required to give fair notice to each other of the factual and legal grounds upon which they found, whether in seeking a remedy from the Court or in proffering a defence. These grounds are stated in the written pleadings which after adjustment between the parties, form the basis of inquiry before the Court.

In the courtrooms themselves, the visitor may listen in one court to witnesses giving evidence in an action for personal injury or for divorce, actions in which it is sought to resolve human problems, or in another court, he may hear more eclectic legal topics being rehearsed in debate in which evidence has no place. Here he may find one of the Divisions sitting, three or four judges dressed in the crimson Court of Session robes with the mace as the symbol of the Court's authority on the wall behind them, the Clerk of the Court sitting in the well of the courtroom below the Bench and counsel at the bar before them. Here also he may find a similarily apparelled judge sitting alone as he listens to evidence or to legal debate or perhaps a single judge sitting with a jury empanelled to adjudicate upon the evidence led before them.

THE HIGH COURT OF JUSTICIARY

As the visitor passes through the Parliament House he may enter the courtroom of the High Court of Justiciary, the supreme court in matters criminal and the scene of many notorious trials, notable among them that of Madeleine Smith, acquitted of the charge of murdering her lover by the verdict of " Not Proven ", a verdict which yet remains the subject of furious debate. The High Court is composed of the 17 judges of the Court of Session; for as they dispense justice in civil causes, so they are empowered to hear criminal trials sitting as Lords Commissioners of Justiciary, an office which they take by virtue of their appointment as Senators of the College of Justice. To signify the change of duty, the judges don their scarlet Justiciary robes and the Lord President, when sitting as president of the Court, resumes the title of Lord Justice General. Normally this Court is constituted by one judge sitting with a jury of 15 persons selected by ballot, but in cases of extreme difficulty more than one judge may be appointed. The High Court only sits in Edinburgh when hearing trials for crimes committed in Edinburgh itself and the counties of the Lothians and Peebles, though very occasionally it may for special reasons hear trials of crimes committed in other parts of the country.

Until 1926 there was no appeal from the judgment of the High Court except to the clemency of the Sovereign, but in that year a limited right of appeal was granted to a convicted person. Normally the Court of Criminal Appeal sits only in Edinburgh with three judges, but in cases of exceptional importance it may sit with a full Bench.

The original jurisdiction of the High Court extends to all crime committed within Scotland or Scottish territorial waters whether by a British subject or by a foreigner, and also to certain crimes committed by British subjects furth of Scotland—as, for instance, murder, piracy or crimes committed on British ships on the high seas. Unless expressly excluded by statute, the High Court has jurisdiction over all types of crime; but in practice it deals only with the more serious, and has exclusive jurisdiction in cases of treason, murder rape, incest, deforcement of messengers and breach of duty by magistrates.

The prosecution of crime in the High Court is, as an almost invariable rule, initiated by the Lord Advocate acting in the name of the Crown, although in very rare circumstances a private person may institute a prosecution where the crime alleged is a wrong to himself and he is so authorised by the High Court. The Lord Advocate is of course the chief law officer of the Crown in Scotland. He represents the Crown in all civil causes where the Crown is involved, and as public prosecutor it is traditional that he will only himself prosecute in High Court trials in Edinburgh. In most cases the prosecution is conducted by one of the Advocates-Depute who are selected by him from amongst members of the Faculty of Advocates. It might be added to this that probably the last occasion in which a Lord Advocate personally prosecuted outside Edinburgh was during the famous Appin murder trial at Inverary in 1752.

Thus sitting in the public gallery of the High Courtroom, the visitor will see below the scarlet robed judge on the bench, the accused person in the dock before him, and in the well of the Court a table on opposite sides of which sit prosecution and defence counsel and between them the Clerk of Justiciary or one of his two deputes acting as clerk to the Court. At one side of the court-room is the witness stand and directly opposite it the jury box in which sit the 15 laymen who are bound in terms of the jury oath they have taken before the trial began, to " truth say and no truth conceal so far as they are to pass on the assize "—in form an interesting but now anomalous historical relic of the days when jurors were themselves the witnesses presenting an accused person to the Court.

Apart from the Supreme Courts, on occasion two other Courts sit in Edinburgh, which have jurisdiction throughout the country though only with restricted functions. One of these we have already studied—the Court of the Lord Lyon King of Arms. The other Court with a special area of authority is the Scottish Land Court.

THE SCOTTISH LAND COURT

This Court was created by a statute of 1911 to take over the functions of the Crofters' Commission, which had been set up in 1886 to cope with the problems arising from over-population and consequently high competitive rents for small holdings in the crofting parishes. Subsequent legislation has considerably extended its jurisdiction, both geographically and in scope. Among the responsibilities of the Court are to determine fair rents, to revalue holdings, and to deal with the assignment of or succession to holdings. It also deals with applications for the resumption of land and the dispossession of tenants, and with questions relating to boundaries, common grazings and compensation for improvements payable to outgoing tenants.

The chairman of the Court must be an Advocate of not less than 10 years' standing, and he enjoys the same rank and tenure of office as a Judge of the Court of Session. There are also four lay members, though a maximum of six may be appointed, and one of them must be a Gaelic speaker. The administrative centre of the court is in Edinburgh, but it also sits throughout Scotland as required, individual members going " on circuit " with their own legal assessors. Decisions of individual members may be appealed to the full Court both on fact and on law, and on matters of law the decisions of the full Court are subject to appeal to the Inner House of the Court of Session.

THE SHERIFF COURT

It is probable however that the ordinary activities of most Edinburgh citizens will only bring them into contact with the various Courts which regulate and administer local matters. Chief amongst these is the Sheriff Court of the Lothians and Peebles which lies across the High Street from the Parliament House in a modern building opened in 1937.

In Edinburgh the Sheriff Court of the Lothians and Peebles has six judges: the Sheriff Principal, who is one of only two full-time Sheriffs Principal in Scotland (the other being in Glasgow) and five Sheriffs-substitute, one of whom sits also in Haddington on two days each week. All six have equal powers in both civil and criminal cases, but the Sheriff Principal is also an appeal judge from decisions of a Sheriff-substitute in civil cases, and he can appoint honorary Sheriffs-substitute who exercise the same powers and duties as a full-time professional Sheriff-substitute.

The Sheriff Court exercises a very wide civil and criminal jurisdiction within the counties of the Lothians and Peebles. In civil matters there is no pecuniary limit to the sheriff's jurisdiction and in causes under £50 in value the sheriff has what is called privative jurisdiction—that is, jurisdiction residing in one court to the exclusion of others. Otherwise he has jurisdiction in all actions apart from those which are reserved to the Court of Session. Actions by employees against employers for personal injury, for instance, can be tried before a Sheriff and jury, but other actions of damages raised in the Sheriff Court must be remitted to the Court of Session if they are to be tried by jury. Claims for sums up to £20 are dealt with in the Small Debt Court.

In civil cases, as we saw, the decision of a Sheriff-substitute can be appealed to the Sheriff Principal or, provided the value of the claim exceeds £50, to the Inner House of the Court of Session. Subject to the same monetary proviso, the decision of the Sheriff on appeal can be further appealed to the Inner House. In the Small Debt Court, however, the Sheriff is final in fact and in law, and his decision can be appealed only on grounds of oppression and malice to the High Court of Justiciary.

In criminal matters the Sheriff is empowered to try all crimes and offences committed in the Sheriffdom except those crimes, such as murder or treason, which fall within the exclusive jurisdiction of the High Court, and except also cases where the statutory penalty is more than two years' imprisonment. According to the gravity of the crime, there are two ways of bringing people before the Sheriff Court. In solemn procedure, which is the more serious, the accused person is charged on an indictment signed by the Procurator-Fiscal on the authority of the Lord Advocate, and the trial is before the Sheriff and a jury. The maximum sentence which the Sheriff can impose is two years' imprisonment, but if he considers that the circumstances warrant more severe punishment he can remit the accused to the High Court of Justiciary for sentence. In summary procedure, the less serious form, the prosecution proceeds on a complaint in the name of the Procurator-Fiscal, and the trial is heard before the Sheriff sitting alone. The maximum sentence under summary procedure is three months' imprisonment.

Sheriff Court prosecutions are normally conducted by the Procurator-Fiscal or a Depute, but in important cases the Sheriff Court Advocate-Depute may conduct the case. The administration and regulation of the business of the Court are under the direction of the Sheriff Clerk. It should also be noted here that the right of audience before the Sheriff Court is not restricted as before the Supreme Courts to the Faculty of Advocates but is extended to members of the legal profession, whether advocate or solicitor, as well as parties to an action or accused persons.

CIVIL LITIGATION

Before we go on to the city's local courts it is rewarding to glance at the increase in civil litigation in both the Court of Session and the Sheriff Court between the early 1950s and the early 1960s. Judging by the 1962 Sheriff Court returns civil litigation in Edinburgh had much more than doubled in 10 years. These returns are, of course, the only guide of local validity, since the Court of Session as the Supreme Court of Scotland draws its work from all over the country, and no statistics afford any indication of the geographical origin of its cases. But it is perhaps interesting to note the relatively very small increase in what may be termed major litigation in Scotland, as represented by the volume of Court of Session business, compared with the remarkable rise in the number of civil actions arising in the Sheriff's Ordinary Courts up and down the country.

In the decade 1953–62 the number of actions and petitions in the Court of Session, taking both the Inner House and Outer House business into account, rose barely more than 9 per cent, from a total of 7,276 in 1953 to 7,934 in 1962. This increase was due to the number of consistorial actions and of actions of damages, of which the largest proportion are actions for personal injury raised by employees against employers, which now forms the bulk of the work of the Court. The increase in consistorial actions largely followed the extension of the law of divorce following on the Divorce (Scotland) Act 1938, and has been further emphasised by the introduction of legal aid in civil cases. By contrast, civil actions in the Sheriff's Ordinary Courts throughout Scotland increased in the same period by 134·3 per cent—from 18,983 actions to a total in 1962 of 44,476. In the Sheriff Court in Edinburgh the corresponding increase was actually a little greater than the national average, working out at 136·6 per cent on the basis of 4,052 actions dealt with in 1962 as against 1,712 in 1953.

Debt, whether due or alleged, is by far the most frequent ground of action in the Sheriff's Ordinary Court. Among the other and much less bulky categories, the principal are actions for damages, those between husband and wife for separation, aliment, adherence and aliment, etc., and disputes between landlord and tenant.

The returns relating to Small Debt Court proceedings in Edinburgh Sheriff Court show almost as great an increase as those for the Ordinary Court. The burden of unwise hire-purchase commitments is probably largely responsible for the fact that Small Debt cases—that is, those involving not more than £20—numbered 13,634 in 1962 as against 6,224 in 1953, a rise of 119 per cent.

Sheriffs are concerned also with a wide range of miscellaneous and administrative business detailed in official statistics under 20-odd headings, from applications under the Dogs Act to bankruptcy proceedings, the adoption of children, the granting of special licenses for marriage and the registration of clubs for licensing purposes. The total number of applications classified as " miscellaneous and administrative business " rose in Edinburgh from 3,106 in 1953 to 5,051 in 1962, an increase of 62·6 per cent.

To look further back, comparison of the types of action in which final judgment was issued in the Court of Session over the last 60 years reveals that while there has been an increase in the number of actions raised there, there has been a marked decrease in the number of cases taken on appeal to the Inner House. This and further information on (1) the number and nature of actions ended by final judgment in the Court of Session between 1900 and 1960, (2) a comparison of the volume of civil business in the Sheriff Court, and (3) a comparison during the same period of proceedings taken in Scotland as against Edinburgh and the number of charges proved, will be found as Appendix I at the end of this book.

THE LOCAL COURTS

Minor criminal matters in the city may be taken before two local criminal courts, whose jurisdiction is limited geographically as is their powers of punishment.

The *Burgh Police Court* sits in a courtroom in the City Police headquarters in the High Street and has jurisdiction within the city boundaries over minor offences and certain statutory offences. The city magistrates take it in turn to preside, and the Burgh Prosecutor who conducts prosecutions before the Court is appointed by the Town Council. Unless specifically increased by statute, the powers of the Burgh Court do not go beyond imposing a fine of £10 or imprisonment for 60 days, and on questions of law its decisions can be appealed to the High Court of Justiciary.

Justice of the Peace Court. The Justices of the Peace of the County of Midlothian also have jurisdiction in Edinburgh and may try certain minor offences against the public peace and certain specified statutory offences committed in the city. Their powers of punishment are similar to those of the Burgh Court, and there is a similar right of appeal to the High Court. Ordinarily resident within the county these justices must be trustworthy citizens of good repute. But unless specifically authorised by statute one justice cannot act alone to constitute a court: a quorum is two justices.

There are two other areas within which affairs of moment to many citizens of Edinburgh are governed by Courts. Both Courts are essentially lay bodies but they are required to act in a quasi-judicial manner.

The *Licensing Court*, which is responsible for granting, renewing or removing liquor licences in the city, consists of all the city magistrates, and they and an equal number of Justices of the Peace for the County of the City constitute the Licensing Appeal Court. The proceedings of both Courts may be set aside by way of an action of reduction in the Court of Session. The Licensing Court also grants certificates to bookmakers and betting shops, and in these cases the appeal against grant or refusal is to the Sheriff.

The *Dean of Guild Court*. The householder who wishes to build or to alter a building within the city boundaries, will probably find himself involved with the Dean of Guild Court, which meets in its own courtroom in the city chambers and regulates and controls building construction within the city. While it has the power to impose fines, it is essentially however a civil court, and its decisions and penalties are both subject to appeal to the Inner House of the Court of Session. The Dean of Guild Court consists of 15 members, of whom five constitute a quorum, and is composed of seven members of the Town Council and seven qualified laymen, such as architects, builders and surveyors, presided over by the Lord Dean of Guild, who is also a qualified layman. The Lord Dean and the seven qualified lay members are appointed by the Town Council on the nomination of the Incorporation of the Brethren of the Guildry, and the Lord Dean himself is *ex officio* a member of the Town Council. Clearly it is an eclectic body and one which amply justifies Robert Louis Stevenson's remark " We treat law as a fine art." But equally the remark applies to the whole range of the legal system where the law is undeniably an art in the execution of which the citizen of Edinburgh may at any time be called to join whether as judge, juror, witness or litigant.

PRACTICE OF THE LAW

THE ADVOCATES

The profession of the law is divided between advocates who practice exclusively in the courts, and solicitors who perform a wide variety of legal work apart from the preparation or practice of litigation. But to the citizen or visitor the Law is symbolised by the judge and pleader rather than by the practitioner. It is from the Parliament House through the Parliament Square that on religious or state occasions the judges in long white wig and scarlet robe and the advocates in wig and black gown pass in procession to the High Kirk of St. Giles to represent the apparelled majesty of the Law of Scotland. Within the Parliament House itself is the great Parliament Hall, the home of the last Scottish Parliament, little changed today, some 70 years later, from Stevenson's description of it as " a hall with a carved roof, hung with legal portraits, adorned with legal statuary, lighted by windows of painted glass and warmed by three vast fires." The Hall still serves as the customary promenade of advocates in wig and gown as they await the summons of the Court Macers to the neighbouring courtrooms in which they will plead in civil or criminal cases. In court all counsel wear wig and gown, Queen's Counsel being distinguished by a silk gown.

Members of the Faculty of Advocates have the sole right of audience before the Supreme Courts, though a man may conduct his own case if he chooses in either civil or criminal proceedings. The head of the Faculty is the Dean, who presides at Faculty meetings and acts on its behalf. Until 1897 the Dean and the Law Officers of the Crown—the Lord Advocate and the Solicitor General—were the only people on whom the dignity of Queen's Counsel in Scotland was conferred. Nowadays it is conferred, on application, on Faculty members of some years' standing.

The rules for elevation to the Bench go further back—to the 1707 Treaty of Union between Scotland and England which provided that the qualification for appointment to the Bench of the Court of Session should be either service as an Advocate for five years or as a writer to the Signet for 10 years. In practice, the Judges of the Court of Session are appointed from among Queen's Counsel who have served as Law Officers of the Crown and have had long professional experience. Sheriffs Principal are also selected from among senior members of the Bar, and Advocates of over five years' standing are qualified by statute for appointment as Sheriffs-substitute.

Men and women entering the Faculty of Advocates—technically they are " admitted Advocate " and not, as in England, " called to the Bar "—must have received no remuneration from the profession of law in the year before their admission, and they normally spend that year as pupils to members of the Faculty. The applicant for admission first petitions the Court of Session, who remit him to the Faculty for examination. He must then satisfy the Faculty that he is qualified in general scholarship and law, pay initial Faculty dues amounting in all to about £500, and go through what is now the formality of submitting a written thesis in Latin. Thereafter on election he is admitted a member of the Faculty.

In 1923, for the first time in its history, the Faculty admitted a woman member, a Miss Margaret Kidd. Twenty-five years later Miss Kidd became a King's Counsel, as the dignity then was, being thus the first woman to " take silk " in the British Commonwealth, and in 1960 she became the first woman Sheriff in Scotland on her appointment as Sheriff Principal of Dumfries and Galloway. Another interesting precedent should be mentioned here. In March 1963 Mr. Albert Jefferson Mkandawire, who was born in Nyasaland and educated at a Church of Scotland mission school and the Universities of Cape Town and London, became the first African to be admitted to the Faculty of Advocates.

Until the introduction of legal aid in civil and criminal causes the Faculty provided free legal aid and representation for the poor.

While numbers on the roll of the Faculty have tended to fall in recent years, the number of those in practice has remained fairly constant. In 1900 there were 402 members, with an average number of nine intrants admitted annually. Towards the end of 1963 there were 287 members of whom about 110 were in active service, and the annual average of intrants had dropped to seven.

THE SOLICITORS

It is of course solicitors, many of whose offices are situated in the houses of the New Town which their forefathers built as dwelling houses, who transact the ordinary business of the law and to whom the citizen has recourse to deal with conveyancing of law, trust and executry work and all the other multifarious legal problems which will never reach the Courts at all.

In all there were, at the beginning of 1964, more than 600 practising solicitors in the city, and each one of these was a member of the Law Society of Scotland, set up by statute in 1949 to issue practising certificates to solicitors, to maintain discipline within the profession, and to make arrangements for securing that legal aid and legal advice are available in accordance with that Act. The Society has a Council of 36 elected members.

The establishment of the Law Society of Scotland has not however superseded the older legal societies, of which there are two in Edinburgh—the Society of Writers to H.M. Signet and the Society of Solicitors in the Supreme Courts.

The Society of Writers to the Signet, whose members (in 1964) carry the initials W.S. on their door-plates, is presided over by the Keeper of the Signet, who is appointed by the Crown and combines the office with that of Lord Clerk Register. The Keeper appoints a Deputy Keeper of the Signet, who acts as chairman at Society meetings. Membership of this centuries-old Society is granted on proof of legal qualification following on a term of apprenticeship with a Writer to the Signet for three years. It has a library in the County Square, adjoining Parliament House, and also a very fine hall which it bought from the Faculty of Advocates for £12,000 in 1826, and a membership which on 1st January, 1964 was 534 of whom 340 practised in the city.

The Society of Solicitors in the Supreme Courts, whose members use the initials S.S.C., received its original charter in 1797. Like the Writers to the Signet the Society also has its own library and other accommodation in a building which abuts the south side of Parliament House. Its membership on New Year's Day of 1964 was 400 of whom just over 280 practised in the city.

It is impossible to elaborate on the range and variety of the solicitor's work in Edinburgh, but one important aspect of it should be mentioned. For many years it has been a proud boast of the legal profession that from a sense of public duty it shouldered the responsibility of providing free legal aid to those unable to pay for it. While it has been relieved of this duty in civil causes by the statutory introduction of legal aid for persons of small or moderate means, it continues to provide a system of free legal aid in criminal cases by the nomination of solicitors to act as agents for the poor. It was clear however in 1963 that this system was soon to be superseded by the statutory extension of legal aid to criminal cases also. This duly happened, though not without warnings that difficulties lay ahead since, to quote the Scottish Correspondent of *The Times* (9th April, 1963), important parts of Scotland's legal machinery were overworked and creaking in cramped quarters!

This comment was directed chiefly at the Sheriff Court in Glasgow and other parts of Scotland, but the Crown Office in Edinburgh was also singled out as an instrument of the law in need of greater facilities. The Crown Office, it should be explained for readers not versed in Scottish legal matters, is the administrative heart of Scotland's legal system. It is from this office that the Lord Advocate, who broadly corresponds with the Attorney-General in England, conducts his duties as a high officer of state with powers of prosecution in the High Court and the Sheriff Court, and many other duties. Here the Lord Advocate has the assistance of the Solicitor-General for Scotland and five advocates-depute. But, as *The Times* pointed out in its serious 1963 survey of the administrative problems created by increased legal aid the establishment in the office of the Crown Agent in 1964 still amounted to fewer than a dozen people, including clerks and typists.

LAW AND ORDER

Crime, thanks to some notorious figures of the past, is as much part of the history and tradition of Edinburgh as the Porteous Riot, or the building of a wall round the city after the battle of Flodden. It was certainly not out of mere partiality that Scotland's greatest connoisseur in criminal matters, the late William Roughead, found so much of his material in the misdeeds of people in his own city.

With the possible exception of the " classical " Glasgow murders, to quote a notable example, probably no Scottish crime has exercised so abiding a fascination, on grounds of both horror and sociological interest, as the bloody trade pursued by William Burke and William Hare, and their associated females, in the squalid surroundings of Tanner's Close in Edinburgh's West Port. Burke, after his conviction, confessed that the pair and their " wives " had murdered about 16 people within a year or two in order to sell the bodies for dissection at £12 or £14 per specimen. It was a macabre extension of the practices of the " Resurrectionists " which brought a chill of fear to the heart of Edinburgh at the end of 1827; and yet Lord Cockburn, who defended Burke's reputed wife in the High Court, could recall in his *Memorials of His Own Time*: " Burke was a sensible and what might be called a respectable man; not at all ferocious in his general manner, sober, correct in all his other habits, and kind to his relations. Though not regularly married, Helen Macdougal was his wife, and when the jury came in with the verdict convicting him, but acquitting her, his remark was simply ' Well, thank God *you*'re safe.' "

Burke and Hare, through first James Bridie in *The Anatomist* and later Dylan Thomas in *The Doctor and the Devils*, have their place in dramatic literature as well as in Edinburgh criminal history. So also has the ingenious Deacon William Brodie, since he was not only the central figure of the play, *Deacon Brodie: or the Double Life*, by Stevenson and Henley, but also the reputed model of Stevenson's Jekyll and Hyde. As burgess, deacon convener of all the trades, member of the town council, and publicly respected as the holder of such offices must have been, Brodie equally enjoyed a passion for gambling, the embarrassment of two mistresses, and a consequent drain on his purse which turned him by night into the most daring burglar of his day. A profitable partnership with three less outwardly reputable operators broke up after the partial failure of their attempt to rob the General Excise Office in Tweeddale Court, off the Royal Mile, 1788. Brodie, though not betrayed, lost his nerve and made for Holland, whence he was brought back and duly executed.

Such crimes may have caught the imagination more than others, though not perhaps the murder of David Riccio in the Queen's presence, but they have their parallels. The commercialised operations in the West Port are scarcely more horrible than the murderous malignity of Nicol Muschet, who strangled his wife in the Queen's Park in 1720 after having tried unsuccessfully first to divorce her, second to poison her and finally to have her murdered by hired assassins.

The double life of the Deacon, it is worth recalling, had a modest successor in the career of " Antique " Smith, who was flourishing in the city towards the end of last century as a prolific forger of pseudo literary and historical documents. A law clerk, he branched into forgery after finding a market for some old papers which he had been asked to destroy, and for some years afterwards he haunted the second-hand bookshops, buying up large old volumes with blank fly-leaves on which he proceeded to fabricate spurious letters and poems by Burns and Scott, supposed Jacobite documents, and other manuscripts which collectors readily accepted. Less fortunate in the outcome than " Ossian " MacPherson in the 18th century he was sent to prison for 12 months in 1893.

The development of the modern capital city has all but robbed the Edinburgh crime pattern of such single-mindedness in wrongdoing. Not again, one imagines, could there be another Jessie King, the " baby farmer " of Stockbridge, whose murders of illegitimate infants passed to her for " adoption " with a few pounds as fee probably numbered more than the three brought home to her in the High Court. She earns her place in the history of Edinburgh crime not just for the stark callousness of her conduct, but also because her hanging in 1889 was the last execution of a woman in the city.

Yet the present century has produced such violence and villainy as may stand beside the monuments of the past. There was, for example, the Robertson double murder of 1954 when Robertson stabbed to death his wife and 18-year old son and gravely wounded his 16-year old daughter. And certainly few more extraordinary careers have entered criminal annals in the city than that of John Donald Merrett.

Merrett's mother, a highly intelligent woman of admirable business sense, was shot on 17th March, 1926 in the flat which she rented in Buckingham Terrace. Her son, then 17 years of age, was present in the room at the time; he claimed that his mother had shot herself over " money matters," and it was not until seven months later that he was arrested and charged with murder. Thanks to his defence by Craigie Aitchison, K.C., later Lord Justice-Clerk, he received the benefit of a " Not proven " verdict by 10 votes against five for " Guilty," but was convicted of uttering the forged cheques by which he had robbed his mother of £457 to sustain his fondness for dance hall hostesses and motor cycles.

Merrett was sentenced to 12 months' imprisonment, and on his release a friend of his mother, a Mrs. Bonner, took him into her home at Bexhill. It did not however take him long to elope with her 17-year old daughter, and little longer elapsed before the couple, under the names of Mr. and Mrs. John Chesney, were in court in Newcastle charged with obtaining goods worth £200 by false pretences. So once more Merrett went to prison.

John Donald Merrett then disappeared from the public eye. But John Chesney, adorned by an impressive beard, held a commission in the Royal Naval Volunteer Reserve during the second World War, and was stationed for a time at Scapa Flow, where colleagues remember his partiality for feminine company and his curious habit of eating raw sausage straight from the wrapping paper.

For some years after his mother's death Merrett had been a ward of the Public Trustee, and Roughead, referring to this circumstance, made the prophetic comment: " We have not heard from his ward again: but you never can tell: we may do so yet." We did so 28 years later. In 1956 a man murdered his wife and his mother-in-law and, despairing of evading police pursuit, shot himself dead in a wood in Germany. He was John Donald Merrett, alias Chesney.

BEHAVIOUR TODAY

Today, broadly speaking, the behaviour of the Edinburgh citizen in the first half of the '60s is not significantly dissimilar to that of the inhabitants of any other Scottish city. In 1962 the total of 28,625 crimes and offences reported to the police represented 60·2 per 1000 of the population as compared with an average of 78·4 per 1,000 in the four cities of Edinburgh, Glasgow, Aberdeen and Dundee taken together, and of 60·7 per 1,000 over the 10 large burghs. For about a dozen years after the end of the 1939–45 war, indeed, the city's annual tale of crimes and offences per 1,000 of population was almost consistently below the comparable figure for Scotland as a whole. Only in 1956 did the two achieve parity at a level of 40·5 per 1,000, and it was not until 1957 that the city record became slightly worse, and remained so, up to and including 1961, than the average for the whole country.

A comparison of records, without discounting the continued existence of slums, poverty and improvidence, gives some evidence of advance in social conditions and stability over the period of the city's main growth—that is, during approximately the last century. In 1854, when the Forbes Mackenzie Act came into operation, 3·18 per cent of an estimated population of 162,648 were arrested for being drunk and incapable in the street. By 1900, when the city had grown to an estimated 302,262 inhabitants, the percentage found drunk and incapable had dropped to 1·14, representing 3,448 offenders as against 5,183 in 1854. Apprehensions for the same offence in 1962 totalled 1,283 in a population of just over 468,000.

The effect of closing licensed premises at 10 p.m. instead of 11 p.m.—a change made in May, 1904—was so marked that the police superintendent of the Northern Division reported: " At present the streets are orderly by about 11 p.m., and constables are able to supervise property on their beats much earlier and without constant interruption—under the 11 o'clock closing, property could not possibly receive attention until about 1 a.m."[1]

Between 1900 and 1962 breaches of the peace made known to the police declined from 4,034 to 2,211; cases of prostitution from 534 to 97; the total number of persons proceeded against by the police from 13,080

[1] In terms of Section 4 (1) of the Licensing (Scotland) Act, 1962, the permitted hours in licensed premises and registered clubs throughout Scotland are now as follows:

Weekdays	11 a.m. to 2.30 p.m. and 5 p.m. to 10 p.m.
Sundays	12.30 p.m. to 2.30 p.m. and 6.30 p.m. to 10 p.m.

The permitted hours on Sundays are not, however, applicable to public houses.

(or 43·2 per 1,000 of population) to 10,131, or 22·2 per 1,000. (An interesting graph showing the number of crimes reported to the police between 1933 and 1962 will be found in Appendix I.)

It is tempting to ascribe so apparently favourable a situation to two principal and related characteristics of the city. One is that Edinburgh is of modest size as capital cities go, and offers therefore less scope for the cultivation of the more spectacular crimes and exotic vices which appear to flourish in proportion to numbers. The second is that, by reason of both geography and history, Edinburgh is not a heavily industrialised city. The impact of the Industrial Revolution brought no inordinate influx of immigrant labour such as occurred, for example, in Glasgow; so the population has remained notably homogeneous in make-up. It shows a relatively high proportion of the professional and the leisured and, as we saw earlier, a preponderance of women. Moreover, the nature of the city's occupations has materially mitigated the weight and consequences of unemployment both in the 1930s and since.

But social and economic conditions are not alone the begetters of lawlessness, and the net effect of these factors appears more in a reduction of the minor offences than of crime. The disparity appears clearly in a comparison of crimes and offences reported per 1,000 of population in the four cities in 1962, as quoted in the official Criminal Statistics for that year:

TABLE 17

	Estimated Population in 1000s	*Crimes and Offences known to police per 1000 of population*	
		Crimes	*Offences*
Edinburgh	475·3	30·8	29·4
Glasgow	1,049·1	38·0	54·8
Aberdeen	185·6	24·2	22·4
Dundee	183·5	26·8	48·8

While the incidence of crime in Edinburgh is not out of proportion to the population, that of offences is notably low.

The most marked increase in crime since the Second World War has been over the period 1956–62. During that time the number of crimes known to the police in Edinburgh rose from 10,956 to 14,663, or by 33·8 per cent, while in Scotland as a whole the corresponding increase was from 79,751 to a total of 117,825, a rise of 47·7 per cent. It is not surprising that although the trend has since continued, the Chief Constable, early in 1964, could allow himself a certain qualified satisfaction, as he looked back on the previous year, in the fact that the crimes and offences cited in Edinburgh had risen by only 5 per cent. But this is serious enough.

By far the major factor in the Edinburgh situation in the early 1960s has been the increase in the incidence of house-breaking, theft by opening lockfast places, and theft, particularly from motor cars. (This last crime dropped in 1963 as did the number of vehicles stolen).

The trend appears clearly in the following table of those crimes known to the police:

TABLE 18

Year	House-breaking	Theft by opening lockfast places	Theft
1956	3731	592	5643
1957	3899	595	5812
1958	3964	714	5750
1959	3631	824	5763
1960	4481	1277	6338
1961	4800	1535	6668
1962	4378	1740	6849

The aggregate increase of 3,001 in these crimes between 1956 and 1962 compares with a total increase of 3,707 in all crimes made known to the police in the city over the same period. In 1962, according to a statement by the Chief Constable in advance of the issue of that year's statistics, the increase in the number of thefts was largely in thefts from motor cars.[1]

The slight decrease in the number of thefts in 1958 as compared with the previous year, it should be noted, is more than accounted for by a change that year in statistical grouping, by which the taking of a motor car without the consent of the owner was transferred from the category of Crimes against Property without Violence (Class III) to that of Miscellaneous Offences (Class VII). A total of 507 such incidents was so transferred in 1958.

" Too many people," remarked the Chief Constable, Mr. John R. Inch, in his report for 1956, " keep large sums of money in their dwellings and business premises; too many people rely for the protection of their valuables on small flimsy safes which can easily be opened or carried away; too many people take few or no steps to secure their premises; and too many car and lorry drivers leave valuable goods in their vehicles without making any effort to protect them." The Chief Constable's view had still much point in the '60s.

However, in 1956, the year he quoted, two detective sergeants were appointed as crime prevention officers. Already an illustrated booklet on the prevention of housebreaking had been prepared by the police and distributed to occupiers of business premises. Since then the crime prevention officers have conducted a more or less continuous advisory survey of business premises, and intensified propaganda by way of posters, leaflets, talks, films, etc., has been directed to the general public and to owners of vehicles and cycles. This met with measurable success up to 1959, when the number of houses and shops broken into fell by 146 to a total of 2,070, but since then it appears to have had less effect against the carelessness of many citizens and the criminal intent of a proportion, in which the easy temptation of the prepaid gas or electricity meter has been a material factor. There were 27 per cent more meters broken into in 1961 than during the previous year.

[1] *The Glasgow Herald*, 4th January, 1963.

CRIMES AGAINST THE PERSON

Edinburgh has shared with the rest of Scotland in the deplorable recrudescence, most marked since 1956 in the most serious category of crime, that of Crimes against the Person (sub-divided under the main headings of murder, attempted murder, and culpable homicide; assault; cruel and unnatural treatment of children; sexual and unnatural crimes including rape, indecent assault, and offences against the Criminal Law Amendment Act; and bigamy). The number of such crimes made known to the police in 1962 had risen by 52·6 per cent to a total of 319 as compared with the 1956 total of 209, while in the country as a whole there was a corresponding rise of 58·3 per cent. While the 1961 figures had shown some slight improvement locally and nationally—both were 1·9 per cent below the 1960 level—it remains true that in Edinburgh the calendar of crimes of personal violence had returned after a considerable number of years to the level of 300-plus which ruled before and for some years after the first World War.

But whereas in that earlier period the main element in this class of crime was the number of assaults, particularly by husbands againts wives, since approximately the middle of the 1930s the greater proportion has been found under the heading of sexual and unnatural crimes. The total of 209 such crimes reported in 1962, though seven fewer than in 1961, was still the fourth highest in the present century; there were 286 in 1938, and 241 in 1960. In 1962 these crimes represented 65·5 per cent of all crimes against the person reported in the city. According to *Scottish Criminal Statistics* the relative positions of the four cities in this respect appear from the following table of persons proceeded against in the years 1956–62:

TABLE 19

	1956	*1967*	*1958*	*1959*	*1960*	*1961*	*1962*
Edinburgh	59	80	60	47	156	112	50
Glasgow	177	179	202	197	202	215	162
Aberdeen	41	45	46	47	46	25	30
Dundee	33	36	32	38	35	49	21

The striking increase recorded in the number of sexual and unnatural crimes between 1959 and 1960 calls for some explanation. To a large extent it may be regarded as an increase in supervision and detection rather than in commission, since the greater part of it is accounted for by intensified police action against vice and, in consequence, many more arrests on charges of homosexuality. The statistics of persons proceeded against naturally reflect the fact that every charge of homosexuality involves two persons at least.

In none of the seven years 1956–62 were there more than four reported cases altogether under the headings of murder, attempted murder and culpable homicide. But assaults multiplied from nine in 1957 to 29 in 1961 and 27 in 1962. Not proportionate, but equally disquieting, is the marked increase during the same period in cases of robbery and assault with intent to rob which, though classified as a crime against property with violence, inevitably carries an element of personal violence. Only one case was reported to the police in 1940, but there were 21 in 1950, and the incidence has since grown fourfold.

SEXUAL OFFENCES

The regrettable increase in sexual and unnatural crimes (already referred to) is parallelled by a similar rise in instances of indecent exposure. These in 1962 numbered 192, which was rather less than the preceding year's total of 222 cases—the highest of the present century. On the other hand, prostitution, in terms of statistics, has become of small consequence in the Edinburgh social pattern. The figure quoted above of 97 cases reported in 1962, as a measure of improvement in relation to the 534 offenders in 1900, undoubtedly reflects genuine gain in social conditions and standards of living.

It should not necessarily be taken, however, as implying an absolute improvement in conduct. A rising incidence of venereal disease, commented on in the M.O.H.'s annual reports contradicts any such impression. When in April, 1961, the Edinburgh Presbytery of the Church of Scotland adopted a motion aimed at reducing sexual promiscuity and consequent disease, the Rev. John Aitken was reported as saying: " Among many people sexual immorality is not regarded as dangerous or undesirable. It is regarded as a casual pleasure without regard to the consequences .... Other social factors which contribute to the spread of this disease are well known to all of us—broken homes which exist in our community; the fact that prostitution, although not extensive in Edinburgh, is still a danger; and the free-and-easy amateurs who have intercourse with casual pick-ups wherever they may be found."[1]

In fact, as in other large cities, prostitution in Edinburgh tends to be hidden indoors—in bars, dance halls and hotels—where control presents a much more difficult police problem, rather than to be found parading the streets. Nevertheless, police action against vice has been strengthened in recent years. At the beginning of 1959 the inspector in charge of licensing was given responsibility also, in co-operation with divisional superintendents, for all inquiries and action concerning vice. As a result of the greater co-ordination achieved, 90 prostitutes were arrested in 1959 and subsequently convicted. This was an increase of 42 on the previous year, and in addition, in accordance with the Scottish system which was commended in 1957 in the report of the Wolfenden Committee on Prostitution and Homosexuality, 90 women received a first caution for prostitution, 52 a second caution, and 41 a third or final caution. A further 19 women were given additional cautions in view of the lapse of time since they had last been convicted or received a third caution. Similar results were achieved in 1960, and it is a pointer to the success of the

[1] *The Scotsman*, 5th April, 1961.

campaign in other respects also that the number of indecent books declared forfeit by the court, which topped 2,000 in 1959, had fallen in the next year to just over 150.

RESET, FRAUD AND EMBEZZLEMENT

The growing dishonesty in the city which is reflected in the figures of theft quoted earlier—petty as many of the offences are, for they include shoplifting, thefts from handbags and the like—is apparent also in the other main categories, those of reset and of fraud and embezzlement, which come into the class of crimes against property without violence. Cases of reset increased by 82·0 per cent—that is from 39 to 71—between 1956 and 1962, and fraud (largely *via* hire-purchase) and embezzlement from 397 cases to 718, a rise of 80·8 per cent. In recent years there have indeed been cases where people in positions of trust in Edinburgh commercial firms have embezzled sums as large as £8,000 and even £20,000.

VANDALISM

If the social problem of vice is being contained, as seems the case, the same can hardly be said for the social problem of vandalism. Here, again in line with the general urban experience, is one of the most disturbing elements in the contemporary Edinburgh scene, and indeed early in 1963 it was the subject of a strong appeal to the citizens by the then Lord Provost, Sir John Dunbar.[1] That was at once followed by the establishment of additional police beats in the outlying " problem " areas. Much of this anti-social destructiveness is, of course, not especially serious in physical result. A good deal of it is the work of juveniles, as we shall see, but it has been costing the ratepayers a substantial amount of money. To quote the Lord Provost's appeal: " At the present rate of damage and destruction to city property such as shops, housing, schools, sports pavilions, baths, nurseries, street lighting, and Corporation vehicles, the citizens are faced with an annual bill of something like £40,000 . . . . Children must be taught to respect other people's property and learn to take a pride in the attractive appearance of their homes, their street, and their city. Destructive teenagers who roam round housing sites smashing windows, demolishing walls, and uprooting young trees must be made aware of the cost of such damage and the consequent burden on the rates."

As far back as 1957 the Chief Constable noted an increasing lack of respect for the property and rights of others as a matter giving cause for alarm. In the succeeding years countless street lamps have been smashed, fires have been started in empty premises, schools broken into and damaged, shop windows smashed, " prefab " houses vacated for area re-development have been reduced swiftly to wreckage, and in recent " vintage " exploits a public baths were set on fire in November, 1960, with damage estimated at £25,000 for complete reinstatement; two boys

[1] *The Edinburgh Evening News*, 4th February, 1963.

set a school on fire in April, 1961, causing £12,000 worth of damage; and in December, 1961, a man started a factory fire which destroyed both building and contents to a total loss of over £42,000. Juvenile vandalism was still a considerable problem in 1965-66.

Comparison with earlier years is difficult and probably misleading, since by a change of coding in 1957 all minor cases of malicious mischief to property became classed as miscellaneous offences. But the number of serious cases reported to the police—of cases, that is, ranked as crimes coming into Class IV (Malicious Injuries to Property)—rose in Edinburgh from 59 in 1957 to 86 in 1962, while the number of minor cases coming into the category of Miscellaneous Offences decreased from 668 to 549 in the same period.

By far the most heartening aspect of recent Edinburgh experience was stressed by the Chief Constable in the preliminary statement already referred to. It was that 1962 had brought a decrease of about 10 per cent in juvenile crime, a striking enough movement in contrast to city statistics of preceding years, and even more so in relation to the contrary trend in the country as a whole. The lower total was not the result of more juveniles being warned rather than proceeded against; there was in fact a corresponding drop in the number warned.

This unexpected and welcome decrease—it brought the number of juveniles (persons under 17 years of age) found guilty of crime down from 749 in 1961 to 640 in 1962—came on the heels of a period during which juvenile delinquency in Edinburgh had been growing appreciably year by year since 1956, when the comparable total was as low as 229. Malicious mischief and the various classes of theft account for all but a fraction of the yearly totals, as is obvious from the following table of the crimes most commonly committed by juveniles during the 10 years 1953–62:

TABLE 20

	Theft by House-breaking	*Theft by opening lockfast premises*	*House-breaking with intent*	*Theft*	*Malicious Mischief*
1953	104	21	22	135	23
1954	93	22	12	145	77
1955	47	16	15	145	26
1956	43	12	16	128	25
1957	66	16	9	193	7
1958	116	32	32	177	4
1959	149	44	30	282	12
1960	189	44	37	390	12
1961	217	46	57	401	7
1962	196	38	40	317	10

Source: Report of the Chief Constable, 1962.

The course of juvenile misdemeanour has fortunately not kept pace with that of crime. A system of police warnings adopted in 1945 has been well justified by its success in keeping down the numbers of those who graduate to court appearance. In the first five and a half years of its operation, 1,378 youngsters were warned, and only 135 of them appeared subsequently in court on other charges. In the years 1956–62 the number of warnings, mostly for dishonesty and petty crimes, fluctuated between a peak of 332 in 1957 and the low level of 240 in 1960, and the percentage who appeared later in court for other crimes varied from 3·1 per cent in 1956 to 8·8 per cent in 1961. In 1962 there were 243 warnings, and out of 148 of these involving acts of dishonesty and petty crime, only 10 juveniles, or 6·8 per cent, appeared later in court for other offences.

Probation as a method of dealing with juvenile offenders has been in use in Edinburgh since 1908. The present regional probation organisation covers the counties of Mid- and East Lothian and Peebles as well as the city of Edinburgh, and in 1961 it recorded 1,606 notifications in Edinburgh of the commission of offences by juveniles—1,489 boys and 117 girls. This was a gross total which included all juveniles appearing before the courts irrespective of the ultimate finding of the court, as well as offenders whose homes were outside the city and others who belonged to the city but made their court appearance elsewhere. The net delinquency in the city area, allowing for these factors, was calculated at 1421 (1,333 boys and 88 girls), giving an incidence of 2·11 per cent of the juvenile population of 67,245. This was an increase on the 1·87 per cent recorded in 1960, but hardly vitiates the claim of the Principal Probation Officer, Mr. Robert H. Edgar, that 98 per cent. of the 8–16 year-old population are relatively well behaved.[1]

DRUNKENNESS

Some reference has been made above to the altered drinking habits of the city as reflected in the respective numbers of those arrested as drunk and incapable in 1900 and 1962. Since the end of the second World War, however, drunkenness has been increasing fairly steadily, though there has proved to be no foundation as yet for predictions that the opening of hotel bars on Sunday, permitted as from October, 1962, under the Licensing (Scotland) Act of that year, would lead to a sudden upsurge of Sunday drunkenness. It was, on the whole, week-day drinking which led to proceedings being taken against 1,630 persons in 1962. The total represented a rise of 38·3 per cent in 10 years, but was still light in comparison, for example, with the annual average of 6,401 persons arrested during the 10 years 1900–09, or the annual average of 2,021 arrests in the decade 1930–9.

The serious, as distinct from the regrettable, element in the current trend is in the figures of arrests of those drunk while driving or in charge of a car. Taking the two categories of offence together, the number of persons proceeded against rose from 54 in 1953, when the offence of being drunk in charge of a car had not yet been created, to 327 in 1962—a formidable and alarming increase to put against the overall rise of 38·3 per cent in all arrests for drunkenness over the same 10-year period. Nor

[1] Report by the Principal Probation Officer relating to the Combined Probation Area of Edinburgh, East Lothian, Midlothian and Peebles, 1960 and 1961.

did this diminish the following year. According to a report by the Chief Constable in the first week of 1964 there was a 15 to 20 per cent increase during 1963 in the number of cases of drunkenness while in charge of vehicles.

Such heavy rises in a single type of road offence illustrate the change which has come upon the city and upon the responsibilities of its Police Force since the days before the first World War when each year's report of the Chief Constable recorded with due formality:

> Three horses are stationed at headquarters for the purpose of conveying prisoners from the central police chambers to the prison, and also for conveying prisoners from the district stations at stated hours throughout the day and night. . . . Bicycles are used by the police for conveying despatches and urgent messages, and a machine is kept at headquarters and at each of the divisional headquarters.

THE POLICE FORCE

The policing of the city has a history going back to post-Flodden alarm, when every fourth man was obliged to take his turn of duty as one of the night watch, but the genesis of the modern organisation came in 1805 with the first Police Bill. This divided the city into 30 wards and assigned to each a general and two commissioners appointed by the public suffrage of the householders. Active duties were under the management of a superintendent and four lieutenants, and the cost was met by assessment on houses and shops. Sixty years ago a police force of 564 men represented one effective police officer to 549 people and 19 acres of city area, at a time when there was one liquor licence to every 305 inhabitants. By 1920, with the incorporation of Leith in that year and of four outlying parishes and part of a fifth, the city had swollen to 32,402 acres, and police strength ran to one man per 42 acres. But the thirsty were less copiously catered for, there being by then one licence to every 514 citizens.

The real growth of city and police responsibility however was under way. In the last 40 years the authorised strength of the Police Force has been raised to 1,375, the actual strength at 31st December, 1962, being 1,288. New housing areas have proliferated over an extended acreage of 34,781, with approximately 517 miles of streets, and the acreage per member of the Force has been reduced to about 27. The 1962 total of licensed premises, 887, worked out at around one to each 535 inhabitants.

Modernisation of police practice may be said to have begun in 1904 with the installation of police telephone boxes at 24 points throughout the city. Finger-print identification was adopted in the following year. In the early 1930s, in an effort to maintain efficient supervision of the extending areas of new housing, a network of 141 local police boxes was inaugurated, 25 local police stations were in consequence closed, and the town council took the opportunity to lop 31 men off the authorised strength, a decision which was deplored by Chief Constable Roderick

Ross as nullifying any advantage gained by the introduction of the box system.

A direct teleprinter link with Glasgow police headquarters, established in 1934, has now become a Telex service communicating with police forces all over the United Kingdom and internationally with the Continent and North America. In 1934 also the first use was made of radio communication with police vehicles; the present radio station at Blackford Hill, opened in 1943, now houses the main transmitters and receivers for the police of the Lothians and Peebles as well as of Edinburgh, for the South-Eastern Fire Brigade, the local ambulance service, and the Edinburgh area of the Scottish Gas Board. Horses—there were still six in 1963 being used for traffic and crowd control—have their counterpart in criminal work in the team of highly trained police dogs built up since 1954, which in 1961 helped to secure 28 arrests and were responsible in 22 instances for the recovery of stolen property.

A system of policing outlying areas by mobile teams in radio-equipped vehicles was instituted by Chief Constable Inch in 1956, the year after he took over from Chief Constable Sir William Morren on the latter's retirement. It has proved an effective way of deploying limited man-power, but the continuing rapid growth both of housing schemes and of traffic has made it necessary since to superimpose beat patrolling in certain areas. A programme for the provision of five district police stations from which the mobile teams will operate has now been completed.

During 1961, because of the high incidence of crime obvious in the first three months, a special squad of detective officers was freed from routine duties to concentrate on counter-measures. This squad, working in close conjunction with officers of the Lothians and Peebles Constabulary, went into operation in April, 1961, and accounted for 230 arrests between then and the end of the year.

No brief outline of the work of the City of Edinburgh Police could be complete without reference to its "extra-mural" pursuits. Two are especially noteworthy. Since 1892 the Force has maintained what is called the Police-Aided Clothing Scheme to provide footwear and clothing for necessitous children, and up to the end of 1961 a total of almost 150,000 children had benefitted from this benevolence. The other notable activity, or rather series of activities, is comprised in the Police Welfare Association, first nurtured on the enthusiasm of Sir William Morren and his conviction that a policeman must be fit to be effective. The 15 sections of the Association cover every popular athletic and sporting interest, but from the public point of view its chief glory is undoubtedly the Pipe Band, which thousands of International Festival visitors gather to admire as it parades Princes Street each morning during the Festival. In 1961 the band had its most successful year so far, winning six first prizes, four second prizes, and one third place in Grade I contests.

Unfortunately the City police have much more serious and more incessant work to do than playing the music of the bagpipe in Princes Street often and occasionally in Edinburgh's sister city of Nice. Only too often the piper as he marches westward through the city is facing the prison where some of the human fruits of his labours may be lying in compulsory repose.

HER MAJESTY'S PRISON, EDINBURGH

The prison and training centre at Saughton, Edinburgh, is the second largest penal establishment in Scotland, the largest being Barlinnie Prison, Glasgow. Saughton has a total staff of 137 (as of 1963) and a daily population of between 400 and 500 prisoners. Barlinnie has about 1,100 inmates.

The building, completed in 1924, was begun before World War I to replace the ancient jail on Calton Hill, the site of which is now occupied by Scotland's Whitehall, St. Andrew's House. The prison consists of five separate three-storey blocks, each housing about 80 prisoners in single cells arranged in galleries around an open well, together with a chapel and worksheds. A single-storey administrative block forms the front of the prison. The grounds, including the garden and the adjacent farm lying to the west, extend to 36 acres. There is no security wall, but around the prisoners' blocks there is a perimeter fence of steel railings topped with barbed-wire. While the fence cannot be regarded as impregnable, escapes from within the prison have been few.

The categories of male prisoners accommodated at Saughton include untried and short-term prisoners; first offenders and men with one previous prison sentence who are serving sentences of less than three years; recidivists aged 28 and over with sentences of less than 12 months; corrective trainees; and prisoners, with sentences of 18 months and upwards, selected from all Scottish prisons as suitable for admission to the training centre, which is located in one of the blocks. Accommodation is also provided for juvenile adults, meaning those prisoners aged 17 to 21 who are first offenders and have sentences of three years or more to serve. There is also separate accommodation for up to about 20 women prisoners. As convicted females are usually sent to Greenock as soon as possible after sentence, women detained at Saughton are either awaiting trial or awaiting transfer to Greenock.

From time to time in recent years the accommodation has been severely taxed and some male prisoners have had to be kept three in a cell.

About half the prisoners at Saughton, mainly those who are serving short terms, are engaged on unskilled work, chiefly the making of coir mats and mail bags, but small parties are engaged on domestic duties, such as laundry work, cleaning and kitchen work, or in the market garden and on the farm. The remainder are engaged on joinery, boot and shoe repairs, and upholstery work undertaken for Scottish prisons generally and for other Government departments. Hobby classes, principally woodwork, are held on four evenings a week and all prisoners may attend voluntarily. In the autumn supervised parties of up to about 50 men go out daily at the time of the potato harvest to work on local farms.

All prisoners receive payment for work. The scale of payment ranges from 3*s*., which is paid to each prisoner on his admission, to 10*s*. a week, which is earned by prisoners who can do fairly skilled work and maintain a high level of output. Prisoners' earnings, which are of the nature of pocket money only, are spent in the prison canteen or may be saved to be taken out on release.

Prisoners receive three substantial meals per day and a light supper. The normal prison diet includes vegetables grown in the prison market garden and farms; supplementary items, such as fresh tomatoes and soft fruit, are available from time to time.

As regards dress, prisoners wear a battle-dress type of suit and are provided with weekly changes of shirts, stockings, handkerchiefs, towels and so on. Fresh underclothing is provided at least fortnightly and overalls are worn during working hours.

Two chaplains (Church of Scotland ministers), a Roman Catholic visiting priest and an Episcopalian visiting clergyman, all appointed on a part-time basis, minister to the spiritual needs of the prisoners. Attendance at the church services in the Chapel on Sundays, and bible classes and religious discussion group sessions, is voluntary. Members of an Edinburgh church pay regular evening visits to discuss with individual prisoners, mainly those serving longer sentences, the problems facing them on discharge from prison.

Extensive recreational facilities are provided at Saughton. The inmates play table tennis, billiards, darts and cards in their spare time in the evenings. They play football among themselves and from time to time a team representing the whole of the prison plays against a visiting team. For these occasions the prison team is picked by a committee of prisoners.

Television is available in the evenings for the following categories of prisoners: (1) prisoners admitted to the "Training for Freedom" Scheme, who are allowed during the last few months of sentence to go out daily to work for outside employers—these are permitted to view every evening till 10 p.m.; (2) prisoners in the Training Centre, who are allowed to watch television on Saturday and Sunday evenings from 5.30 p.m. to 9.30 p.m., as are also (3) First Offenders serving a sentence of one year or more; and (4) Recidivists, men, that is, with at least two previous sentences of imprisonment or borstal training either for crimes against person or property, or for forgery or currency offences. These, after serving 12 months of a sentence of three years or over, may view from 5.30–9.30 p.m. But the privilege is subject to good conduct and industry.

Since 1959 a Psychiatric Unit has been attached to the prison. This Unit, consisting of two psychiatrists and a psychologist assisted from time to time by other qualified persons, is under the direction of the Professor of Psychological Medicine at the University. Its primary purpose is not to prescribe or undertake treatment of prisoners who are mentally disturbed, but to carry out research projects in the criminological field as part of the work of the University's Department of Psychological Medicine. Among projects now being carried out is one to determine the ability of prisoners to learn certain responses from standard stimuli and the extent to which brain damage may be a factor in agressiveness.

The Unit does, however, assist the prison authorities. Prisoners admitted to the Training Centre are interviewed by members of the Unit to see whether there are individual factors which should be taken into account in their training. A limited number of prisoners are given a measure of psychiatric treatment. Finally, the Unit conducts seminars and discussions for members of the prison staff engaged in conducting Counselling Groups as part of the rehabilitative programme in the Training Centre.

The Training Centre, set up in 1960, accommodates about 60 prisoners in one hall of the prison. These men have been selected, after sentence, as likely to benefit from a training which will help them to secure employment on release, and to keep it. Only prisoners with a sentence long enough to allow them an uninterrupted period of training are eligible; and the minimum period of training is normally 12 months. A feature of the training scheme is that each officer has allocated to him a party of about 10 prisoners in whose progress and welfare he takes a particular interest; and they, in turn, are encouraged to go to him for help in any personal difficulty. It has been found that this close officer-prisoner relationship helps the prisoner to accept the fact, and conditions, of imprisonment and to respond better to the training given. The training includes vocational courses—for example, bricklaying, painting and decorating—and a course in light engineering. Some men are employed with trades officers on maintenance work on the prison premises. Generally, the training syllabus is designed to be as flexible as possible so that the training programme for any prisoner may be suited to his ability and needs. Emphasis is also laid on helping each prisoner educationally, which is no light task since individual needs may range from those of the near illiterate to those of a prisoner who wishes to further his professional qualifications. Talks are given by outside speakers on current affairs and on topics of general interest; each trainee must attend these lectures. There are also optional evening classes in joinery and woodwork, art, car maintenance, current affairs, together with a handyman's course; and finally prisoners may also read daily newspapers, books from the prison library, or books of an educational nature which may be sent in to them.

CHAPTER 9

SEAT OF ADMINISTRATION

THE GOVERNMENT DEPARTMENTS

As Scotland's capital Edinburgh is naturally the seat of the northern kingdom's administration. Seven Government Ministers have their offices in the city—the Secretary of State, the Minister of State, three Parliamentary Joint Under-Secretaries of State, the Lord Advocate and the Solicitor-General for Scotland.

There are two main classes of Government departments in Edinburgh—the departments of the Secretary of State for Scotland and the United Kingdom departments.

The Secretary of State's departments comprise four major ones directly concerned with powers and duties vested in him, and several minor ones for which he is responsible to Parliament. The four major departments—Agriculture and Fisheries, Education, Home and Health, and Development—are accommodated partly in St. Andrew's House, partly in large Government offices at Sighthill and Saughton in the suburbs, and partly in small offices throughout the city. The growth of administration has meant that the accommodation provided by St. Andrew's House itself has been inadequate ever since it was opened in 1939. About 1,400 are employed in St. Andrew's House and about 2,600 in the other offices of the Secretary for State throughout the city. The total number of civil servants employed in Edinburgh by the United Kingdom Departments (excluding the Post Office) was about 4300 in 1966; the grand total, including the Secretary of State's departments, is therefore about 8,300.

THE SCOTTISH OFFICE

THE DEPARTMENT OF AGRICULTURE AND FISHERIES FOR SCOTLAND

This Department has a general responsibility for, and in most cases administers, Government measures for the promotion and development of farming throughout the whole of Scotland. The functions of the Department include the administration of guaranteed prices for the major farm products; the provision of grants and subsidies and other services to agriculture; the use and improvement of land and the improvement of farm stock and crops; the application of measures for controlling plant diseases and pests and for treating infestations in stored food; the management of the agricultural properties owned by the Secretary of State; the administration with the advice of the Agricultural Research

Council of eight grant-aided research institutes in Scotland and the educational and advisory services provided by the three agricultural colleges; matters affecting animal health; the promotion of measures for safety, health and welfare of agricultural workers; the regulation of agricultural wages; and the stimulation of rural industries.

The Department is also not only responsible for the oversight and protection of the Scottish inshore, deep sea and fresh-water fisheries, but has certain functions relating to harbours, steamer services in the Highlands and Islands and other matters concerning Highland development.

THE SCOTTISH HOME AND HEALTH DEPARTMENT

The Scottish Home and Health Department is responsible for the central administration of functions relating to law and order, and of the National Health Service and associated welfare services. It is the Department concerned with the police, fire and civil ceremonial matters; law reform, legal aid and the services required by the courts, and with legislation on such subjects as marriage and divorce, shops, and licensed premises. Licensed premises in districts in which State management of the liquor trade is in operation are directly maintained by the Department. It is also concerned with criminal justice and the probation service and is directly responsible for the administration of prison and borstal institutions. The Department is responsible for the central administration of the National Health Service, comprising the hospital service, the general medical, dental pharmaceutical and ophthalmic services, and the local health authority services. Its welfare responsibilities include the supervision of local arrangements for the care of the aged and handicapped.

THE SCOTTISH DEVELOPMENT DEPARTMENT

This Department is concerned with a number of the main services affecting the physical development of Scotland, such as town and country planning, housing, roads, water supplies, electricity and with general local government matters. Included in this is the co-ordination of development plans and public authorities' land requirements; the building of new towns, the distribution of housing subsidies and the supervision of building standards; the construction of trunk roads and the distribution of grants on classified roads, and road safety (apart from the construction and use of vehicles); water supply and sewerage schemes and grants; and the administration of the Secretary of State's functions with regard to Electricity Boards in Scotland. With the exception of the last, these services are mostly administered locally by Town and County Councils, but the New Towns are the responsibility of Development Corporations.

REGIONAL DEVELOPMENT

Overall responsibility for regional economic planning rests with the First Secretary of State and Secretary of State for Economic Affairs. The Secretary of State for Scotland is, however, responsible for economic planning in Scotland and is Chairman of the Scottish Economic Planning Council, his main external source of advice and consultation on all matters affecting Scotland's economic development. These Scottish Office functions are discharged through the staff of the Permanent Under-Secretary of State and the Assistant Under-Secretaries of State. One of the Assistant Under-Secretaries also acts as the Chairman of the Scottish Economic Planning Board, comprised of officials representing the Government Departments (including the Scottish Departments) concerned with economic and physical development in Scotland.

THE SCOTTISH EDUCATION DEPARTMENT

The Scottish Education Department is responsible for supervising the administration of the Education (Scotland) Acts and for guiding the development of public education in Scotland in all its forms. The Department's functions include the supervision of the training of teachers and the issue of teachers' certificates; the regulation of teachers' salaries and the administration of the Teachers (Superannuation) (Scotland) Regulations; the control and distribution of specific Exchequer grants in aid of educational expenditure; and the award of students' allowances to those taking full-time courses at universities and colleges of education. The Department also exercises general supervision over the child care and adoption services, remand homes, and approved schools; and it is concerned with the development of the Arts in Scotland which includes responsibility for the administration of the Scottish national institutions—the National Galleries of Scotland, the Royal Scottish Museum, the National Museum of Antiquities of Scotland and the National Library of Scotland.

REGISTERS AND RECORDS

The functions and responsibilities of the Scottish Office departments we have just studied are naturally very like those of their English counterparts. But it is worth while dwelling at greater length on two departments concealed behind the handsome elevation of the Register House at the east end of Princes Street. This building was erected in 1774–89 to the design of the famous architects Robert and James Adam. The grant for this (and subsequent grants) and the whole cost of the adjacent New Register House were ultimately repaid in full out of the surplus of search fees received in the Record Office, and *not*, as many think, exclusively out of money coming from the Forfeited Estates after the '45 rising. There certainly was an initial grant of £12,000 from the Forfeited Estates funds; but this soon proved inadequate.

Today *The Register House* contains the departments of the Records of Scotland and the Registers of Scotland. It is sometimes referred to as the Old Register House to distinguish it from the adjacent New Register

House (erected 1859–63), which houses the registers of births, deaths and marriages for the whole country in the offices of their chief custodian, the Registrar General for Scotland, and also the office of the Lyon King of Arms.

THE SCOTTISH RECORD OFFICE

The Scottish Record Office, whose history can be traced back to 1282, is the oldest Government department in Scotland. It is therefore very much at home in the Register House, which is the oldest building in Europe especially designed for the preservation of national archives. Built of solid stone throughout, the Register House consists of a basement and two storeys, rectangular in shape with small storage rooms round a vast central dome contrived by Robert Adam's genius, and worthy of its purpose since his admirably functional construction and design not only give security against fire, damp and theft but enable records to be brought to the centre of the building through eight points of entry with the minimum of delay.

Eighteenth century contemporaries of the first *Statistical Account* would still recognise the Register House of today, but the steady growth of records has necessitated great extensions to the original building and those beside it during the intervening century and a half. The Historical Search Room, designed by Robert Reid as a supplement to Adam's plan, was completed in 1827. The New Register House was erected alongside the Old Register House to accommodate various classes of records created by 19th century legislation; and in 1871 a separate dome was built to the north to store Court of Session records. In 1902–4 a wing was extended to the north-east, and this now accommodates the Department of the Registers of Scotland in which current legal registers are compiled and thereafter transmitted to the Scottish Record Office for preservation. With expansion other offices which at one time were temporarily accommodated in the Old Register House have moved out.

By the 1707 Treaty of Union it was specially provided that the public records of Scotland should always continue to be kept in Scotland. Then, the records were in the charge of the Lord Clerk Register, an officer of state of high rank whose medieval predecessors can be traced back to 1282. The Lord Clerk Register remained the head of the Record Office when the earlier *Statistical Accounts* were written; but in 1806 a great Scottish scholar and archivist, Thomas Thomson, was appointed Deputy Clerk Register and immediately undertook a programme of repair, cataloguing, indexing and publication of the records, which established principles and policies still followed by the Scottish Record Office of today. In 1879 the authority as well as the functions of the Lord Clerk Register with regard to the preservation of the public records were transferred to his Deputy; and eventually in 1948 those powers and duties passed to the Keeper of the Records of Scotland who is appointed by the Secretary of State for Scotland with the approval of the Lord President of the Court of Session, and who is now the active head of the Record Office. The

Keeper of the Records is assisted by the Curator of Historical Records and other officials mentioned below.

Despite the vast achievements of Thomson and his successors, the work of the Record Office in the 19th and early 20th centuries was severely hampered by inadequacy of staff, and it is only in recent years that the department has received long-overdue increases. There are now 10 Assistant Keepers (a grade introduced in 1950), appointed by a Selection Board from graduates in history or law, 3 Research Assistants, 18 Executive and Clerical officers, and typing staff. A special bindery and manuscript repair section staffed by expert craftsmen is also attached to the department and continues the work started by Thomson. About 3,000 incoming register volumes were bound and nearly as many old bindings were repaired during 1962 (to take a recent year), and nearly 30,000 parchment and paper documents were repaired and treated with size or transparent silk. From 1954 to 1962 more than 7,000 fragile wax seals were repaired and wrapped in protective pads.

Though only the more important groups of records now in the Register House can be mentioned here,[1] it is noteworthy that modern accessions are of a bulk and variety that could hardly have been anticipated in the late 18th century, or indeed for long afterwards. The property registers alone were increasing by 1963 at a rate of more than 1000 volumes annually, and naturally modern legislation and economic conditions have stimulated an ever-increasing flow of departmental records, local records and family muniments.

Prominent among the national records are well-known state papers and diplomatic documents and also the records of the main legislative and administrative organs of the old kingdom of Scotland, notably of the Scottish Parliament, Privy Council and Exchequer. Most of the records of state closed in 1707, but the process of political devolution from the late 19th century has produced a mass of new administrative records in the Scottish Departments. Certain of these have been placed in the Register House; and as many more will be transmitted in the future.

The national records, however, are not only concerned with the affairs of the nation at large; they also contain records of private rights, which survived the Union and many of which continue in use to the present day. The most important of these relate to land and include the records of the Great Seal which are extant from the reign of Robert I; notaries' protocol books (recording mostly land transfers) from the 15th century; and the Registers of Sasines (or property registers), which have recorded, since 1617, every change in the ownership of heritable property from a large estate to a modest tenement flat. Other important records of private rights include the decreets and processes of the Court of Session and the Books of Council and Session (Register of Deeds), which for more than 400 years have been illustrating every aspect of public and private life.

[1] The various classes are described in detail in (a) M. Livingstone's *Guide to the Public Records of Scotland* (1905), (b) a supplement printed in the *Scottish Historical Review* (1947), (c) two articles by the present Keeper of the Records, Sir James Fergusson, in *Archives*, the Journal of the British Records Association, nos. 8 and 9 (Michaelmas, 1952, and Lady Day, 1953).

There are also the records of testaments (or wills) of the Commissary Courts down to 1823, and since then preserved in the Register of Deeds.

A feature of Scottish record policy in the 19th and 20th centuries has been the growing centralisation of archives formerly kept locally. In terms of the 1937 Public Records (Scotland) Act, records from 19 sheriffdoms and 25 burghs have now been transferred to the Register House; and in 1959 the older records of the Church of Scotland, including many presbytery and kirk session minutes, were placed there on loan. Since the end of last century a great collection of private charters and other documents, dating from the 12th century, has been built up in the Record Office; and, particularly since 1946, many important families from all parts of Scotland have deposited their muniments, either as outright gifts or on indefinite loan. These include such outstanding collections as those of the Marquess of Lothian, the Marquess of Ailsa, and the Earls of Dalhousie and Airlie.

With the exception of some records of government departments, which remain closed for varying periods, all the records are open for consultation by the public. Fees are charged if access is required for legal or business use; for historical research access is free on issue of a reader's permit.

Searches for legal purposes are conducted on the ground floor of the Dome, where members of the public, and especially lawyers, daily consult modern legal records. Current property registers—80 per cent of the 100,000 deeds registered each year relate to rights in land—are examined for such information as the value of a house, any burdens affecting it, the amount of a feu-duty, or the boundaries of a property. Particulars of wills and other documents are looked for in the registers of deeds, and information from valuation rolls and Court of Session decrees and processes is also regularly in demand. The bulk of searching required by legal firms, especially in connection with the transfer of heritable property, is undertaken by two firms of private searchers, each with a numerous staff; but a number of the officials and messengers of the department are occupied in making the records available to the public and searchers.

The amount of recent searching in the current records can best be indicated by a brief account of fees received in certain years during the '50s and early '60s. In 1951 these came to £2,012; but by 1959 they had risen to £3,741. In 1962 they totalled £3,922.

The steady rise in the amount of fees paid is due in some measure to an increase in the number of house purchasers and also to a slight upward revision of the 1956 dues. In addition to fees payable for access to the records, a large amount of business is done by supplying photostat " extracts " (*i.e.* authenticated copies) of the records to legal firms and the public generally; and furthermore there has been a steady rise in the number of extracts issued, judging by the rise in receipts from this source in recent years, as the following table shows:

1939	—	£770	(1,281 copies issued)
1951	—	£3,208	(5,066)
1962	—	£8,598	(10,462)

If lawyers are the largest section of the public resorting to the Register House, many historians, students and genealogists come to gather material for their studies in the Historical Search Room. Between 1947 and 1962 more than 2,000 permits were issued to new readers from Scotland and the rest of the United Kingdom, the U.S.A., Canada, Sweden, Australia, South Africa, New Zealand, Germany, Holland, Eire, Italy, France, India, Norway, Switzerland, Denmark, and Kenya; Austria, Burma, Finland, Iceland, Jamaica, Malaya, Nigeria, Nyasaland, Panama, Philippines, Portuguese East Africa, Sierra Leone, Southern Rhodesia, Spain and Tanganyika.

The wide variety of the main subjects studied (and the number of students) during the same period is worth recording: family history, 766; economic and social history, 286; local history, 260; biographical studies, 185; general and political history, 102; ecclesiastical history, 78; relations of Scotland and Scotsmen with other countries (including in alphabetical order) Australia, Canada, China, England, France, Germany, Holland, India, Ionian Islands, Italy, Natal, Persia, Sierra Leone, South, Africa, Sweden, Ulster and the United States of America, 85; geographical studies, 58; literature, philosophy, drama, painting, music, costume and crafts, 56; architecture, 49; education, 37; legal studies, 24; military and naval history, 17; place-name studies, 9; etymological and lexicographical studies, 7; paleography and diplomacy, 8; bibliography, 4; and archaeology, 4.

Sessions of readers between 1951 and 1962 also show an increase—from 2,075 in 1951 to 2,425 in 1962. During 1962, productions in the Historical Search Room numbered 7,150. Many inquiries which do not entail the issue of a permit to a new reader and a large number of postal inquiries on historical subjects are also dealt with each year.

For casual visitors a permanent exhibition of important historical documents is displayed in the Dome Gallery, where in recent years the following special annual exhibitions of manuscripts have also been held: *Montrose and the Covenanters*, *The Tobermory Galleon*, *Church and Nation*, *Scotland and Europe*, *The Appin Murder*, *The Royal Line, 1153–1953*, *The Old Scots Army*, *The Honours of Scotland*, *Raeburn and His Times*, *The Union of 1707*, *The Royal Stewarts through Eight Centuries*, *From Scottish Charter-Chests*, *The Scottish Reformation*, *Young Queen Mary, 1554–65*, *Scotland and Sweden*, and *The Queensferry Passage*.

When the Register House was built few, apart from a handful of antiquarian scholars, used the records for historical research, but a continuing series of record publications initiated by Thomson and his successors has made the texts of the older historical records available to students who may never be able to consult the originals. Publication of records, suspended during the war years, has been revived with a Treasury grant for payment of external editors. Indexes (prepared by the staff) of early registers of sasines and deeds are also published, by modern photographic methods, while photostat and microfilm copies of records can be supplied for historical research.

There is a reference library of about 10,000 volumes for use in consulting the records. This includes standard works on Scottish history, genealogy and kindred subjects, as well as most of the publications of the Scottish historical clubs and societies, and technical books on archives and paleography.

Apart from attendance on the public, the staffs of both search rooms are largely engaged in compiling catalogues, inventories, lists, indexes and other guides, which are essential if the records are to be made fully available for study. The large accessions of local records and family muniments from 1946 onwards have added materially to this work. In addition, the National Register of Archives (Scotland) is operated from the Scottish Record Office. The Register was instituted in 1946—to continue the surveying of the documents of institutions and private owners initiated by the Royal Commission on Historical Manuscripts from 1869 onwards—and it has now almost completed a survey of family muniments over the whole of Scotland. As a result of its activities a large amount of historical material has been brought to light, and full reports on the various collections are available in the Record Office. Similar surveys are planned by the Register to include other archives remaining in local or private custody.

Both as a repository for current legal records and as a storehouse for the raw materials of history, the Register House has served Scotland for nearly 200 years. In recent years, however, the total shelf space in the building (including courtyards which have been covered in to provide extra accommodation) and in the Rose Street annexe (which stores records less frequently consulted) has been insufficient, and indeed in 1959 both the Register House and the annexe were so fully occupied that it became necessary to impose a stay on the transmission of major public records and also of local authority records and family muniments. The provision in 1961 of 13 rooms in the New Register House for record storage enabled the reception of records to be resumed, but the problem of long-term accommodation remains acute. However, in 1963 a committee appointed by the Secretary of State for Scotland under the chairman-ship of the late Lord Keith of Avonholm reported on the accommodation needs of the Scottish Record Office, the Registrar-General's Office and the Lyon Office. Most of its positive recommendations were condemned by the Scottish Records Advisory Council as unworkable, but resultant discussions have gained for the Record Office a more commodious annexe than the Rose Street building. It is recognised also that further large-scale provision for the Record Office's needs will have to be made.

THE REGISTERS OF SCOTLAND

The Registers of Scotland are public registers provided for the registration of legal documents. In the main these are deeds relating to rights in lands, but they also include a wide range of deeds relating to trusts, family agreements, succession, state appointments and so on. It may be fairly claimed that Scotland was the first nation to inaugurate such a complete system of registration; and for centuries the right of the individual to record these documents in an official Register has been a feature of Scottish law and government.

Registration is not compulsory. It is a privilege which confers certain benefits depending on the purpose for which the deed is registered. These benefits are publication, preservation and execution.

Publication is desirable for deeds relating to land, as the right of the individual is proclaimed, recognised and protected; and parties proposing to acquire such rights can proceed with confidence on the testimony of the registers. When deeds are recorded for preservation the deed is retained in the Register House and an extract is issued which in law carries the full weight of the deed itself. A safe deposit is thus provided for important deeds which might be lost if left in private hands. Registration for execution is a method of obtaining enforcement of any obligations contained in a deed. If the obligant consents *in gremio* of any deed to registration for execution, he in fact consents to a judgment going out against himself in the event of his failure to implement the obligation. The writ is registered for preservation and execution, and the extract contains a warrant for diligence against the obligant without the formality of bringing an action in a Court of Law. It is possible to register a deed for all three purposes. At one time the deeds were copied by hand but they are now reproduced by photography. Each year more than 120,000 deeds are recorded in the registers, of which approximately 80 per cent relate to rights in land.

The political, economic and social changes which have played their part in the development of Scotland are reflected in these registers. This is particularly true of the General Register of Sasines, in which are recorded all transfers, bonds or other deeds relating to land. For example, when this register was first instituted in 1617 the land was in the hands of the large landowners and there were comparatively few entries in the register. Now it is estimated that there are 700,000 separate privately-owned units of property varying from large landed estates to the smallest property in individual ownership—a striking reflection of a great change which has taken place in the social structure of our country in the last century and a half.

It is beyond the scope of this account to describe fully the history and functions of the various registers and their essential position in the modern structure of the country. But it should be noted that there are 14 Registers in all, grouped under the four offices—Sasine Office, Deeds Office, Chancery Office and Horning Office—with which they are historically and administratively connected.

The General Register of Sasines, already referred to, is the responsibility of the Sasine Office.

The Deeds Office is concerned with the Register of Deeds in the Books of Council and Session (i.e. the registration of Wills, Marriage Contracts, Agreements, etc.); the Register of Protests (a Protest is a notarial statement that a Bill of Exchange has been dishonoured); and the Register of English and Irish Judgments (relating to Judgments obtained in those countries for any debt).

The Chancery Office administers the Register of Service of Heirs; the Register of the Great Seal; the Register of the Quarter Seal; the Register of the Prince's Seal; the Register of Crown Grants; the Register of Sheriff's Commissions; and the Register of the Cachet Seal.

Finally, the Horning Office is responsible for the Register of Entails which, following the abolition of the granting of Entails in 1914, is now merely concerned with registering Instruments of Disentail; and the Register of Inhibitions and Adjudications. (The effect of registering certain Deeds in this Register is to restrain an owner of heritable property from disposing of it to the prejudice of his creditors). As each of these Registers is completed annually it is transferred to the Record Office, and then becomes part of the Records of Scotland.

THE REGISTRAR GENERAL'S OFFICE

One of the most frequently visited offices in the city is the Registrar General's Office, established in 1855 after the passing of an Act which provided for the setting-up in Scotland of a compulsory system of registration of births, deaths and marriages. These events are recorded in annual duplicate registers by the local registrars of births, deaths and marriages, who are appointed and paid by the local authorities and work under the general direction of the Registrar General. The local registrar retains one copy of each register, and the other is sent for preservation to the Registrar General's Office.

This Office is lodged in the New Register House. Built in the early 1860s it consists of a lofty fireproof central repository or " Dome " surrounded by staff rooms on three floors. The Dome, if lacking some of the Adam artistry in the Old Register House Dome, is a vast and striking chamber, which is in itself of considerable interest as a piece of 19th century functional architecture. It has been used since it was built for the storage of records, and since 1962 its ground floor has been converted into what must be one of the most impressive public offices in the British Isles.

The four miles of shelving in the Dome contain about half a million volumes. These comprise more than 300,000 registers of births, deaths and marriages; records of births, deaths and marriages that have occurred abroad of persons of Scottish origin and domicile; census records; and some 4,000 parish registers of births, baptisms, deaths, burials, proclamations and marriages, kept before 1855 by the Church of Scotland. Also stored in the office are several millions of punched cards which contain registration data in convenient form for producing statistical information.

On the first floor there is an excellent Library and Search Room for the benefit of students, research workers in vital and population statistics, genealogical searchers and others who desire to do their own searching.

As many as 20,000 callers a year visit the public office in the Dome. Most of these want extracts of entries in the registers of births, deaths and marriages, but many of the inquiries relate to names and dates of personal events and family relationships. Some, particularly Commonwealth visitors in summer time, come to trace their ancestors. In addition to callers there is a heavy mail not only from Scotland but from all parts of the world. Altogether these inquiries result in about 40,000 searches a year being made by the staff.

THE PARISH REGISTERS

The old parish registers, which the Registrar General has now in his custody under statute, are the greatest treasures in the New Register House. The oldest—for the parish of Errol in Perthshire—dates from 1533—the year after a Provincial Council of the Scottish Church re-affirmed an ecclesiastical statute requiring registers to be kept in all parishes.

Canongate Parish supplies the earliest parish register for Edinburgh. It dates from 1564, and among its records of the ordinary citizens and burgesses, it contains the proclamation of banns of marriage of Queen Mary and Lord Darnley:

> The 21 of July anno Domini 1565. The quhilk day John Brand mynister presented to the Kirk ane writing written be the Justice Clark's hand desyring the Kirk of the Cannogait and mynister thairof to proclame Harie Duk of Albynye erle of Rois &c. on the one part and Marie be the grace of God Quene Souerane of this realme on the vthair part The quhilk the Kirk ordains the mynister so to do with Invocation of the name of God.

In another register recording Darnley's death, the cause of death is given almost as if in anticipation of modern legislation:

> The Kyng's grace blawen up with puder in the Kirk of Field the x of Februer 1566.

The old parish registers are much consulted by genealogists and biographers, and as they are also in regular use by the staff of the Scots Ancestry Research Society (described later) the production of the social and statistical information they contain is clearly an important and continuous task.

There are two broad classes of material available: vital statistics derived from particulars given at the registration of births, deaths and marriages; and population statistics derived from census returns. The Registrar General's clients in these two statistical fields include research workers in medicine, social science, demography and economics, mainly from the universities; local and central government departments; Parliament and the Press; and the business world.

The Registrar General also produces an Annual Report on the vital statistics of Scotland. The report is detailed: in 1962 it extended to 436 pages. But in sheer size this does not compare with his major task—the organisation and control of Censuses of Population.

THE CENSUS

The first official census was taken in 1801 and there has been one at ten-yearly intervals ever since, with the exception of 1941. The last census was taken in 1961, but because of the need for more frequent statistics for economic planning the Government have decided that an additional census on a limited basis shall be taken in 1966.

After each census the Registrar General is required to produce a detailed report containing statistical analyses of the information obtained. After the 1961 census an electronic computer was used for the first time to process the results.

With these widely used services the Registrar General's Office has become a national institution since the last *Statistical Account* was written, and no doubt it will be offering the same services, and perhaps others before another century has passed. Proof of family " events " will always be needed; and researchers and policy-makers demand increasingly a statistical basis for their work.

THE SCOTS ANCESTRY RESEARCH SOCIETY

The Scots Ancestry Research Society was established by the Rt. Hon. Thomas Johnston, C.H., in the Spring of 1945—he was then Secretary of State for Scotland—to make it easier for persons of Scottish blood to trace facts about their ancestors in the northern kingdom. Since then the Society has received some 20,000 inquiries from people of Scottish descent both at home and overseas.

A non-profit making organisation, the Society charges fees sufficient to cover its expenses. It employs a group of searchers who find their sources for the most part in the Registrar General's Office, the Scottish Record Office and the various Edinburgh libraries; and already it has given a new stimulus to interest in family history not only in Edinburgh but in many parts of Scotland, the Commonwealth and the United States.

QUEEN'S AND LORD TREASURER'S REMEMBRANCER

It is doubtful if many Edinburgh citizens are aware of the precise duties of this important Treasury representative. Some indeed may never have heard of him at all. But whatever the varying degrees of ignorance about him, all will agree that even in Scotland where picturesque designations abound few sound more resplendent than that of the Queen's and Lord Treasurer's Remembrancer.

For a proper understanding of this office we must go back once more to the 1707 Treaty of Union between England and Scotland. With the dissolution of the Scottish Parliament it became necessary to improvise fresh offices and departments to run the new system of administration for Britain as a whole. How, for example, was the Treasury to carry on and regulate the business of the Exchequer in Scotland? The first solution was to create a body called the Barons of the Exchequer with two principal officers—the Queen's Remembrancer ("Queen's" because Queen Anne was Sovereign) and the Lord Treasurer's Remembrancer. The Barons in fact formed an Exchequer Court similar to the one in England. They sat as a Treasury Board for Scotland; they acted as a Court of Law in Revenue cases but without the Common Law jurisdiction exercised by the English Court; and as such a Court they needed the services of executive officers. These were the two Remembrancers.

"The King's Remembrancer", says an official record, "was the most important officer of Exchequer under the Barons, and the best short description of his position that can be given is to say that he acted as the principal secretary of the Barons in all the varied matters in which they were concerned. The Lord Treasurer's Remembrancer was another officer of Exchequer; his principal duty was the examination and audit of the criminal accounts for all Scotland. These officers were called Remembrancers because they had to remember all things for the King's service and benefit and to take care that the whole business of the Court under their inspection was duly and regularly executed."

A change came over this scene in the 19th century when several Acts of Parliament not only transferred the whole of the Barons' *judicial* duties to certain Court of Session judges but their *ministerial* powers and duties to the Lords Commissioners of H.M. Treasury. At the same time the offices of King's Remembrancer and Lord Treasurer's Remembrancer were unified in 1837, since when the functions of the single Office have become so numerous that the staff now numbers more than 60; their salaries exceed £50,000; and their duties are wide-ranging.

To name a few, the Queen's and Lord Treasurer's Remembrancer is the Treasury representative on various Scottish boards and committees and is the Accounting Officer for the Vote for Law Charges and Courts of Law, Scotland. He is Registrar of Companies, Registrar of Limited Partnerships and Registrar of Business Names. He makes payments both from the Consolidated Fund (legal salaries, etc.) and the various Votes of Parliament administered by the Scottish departments, and generally carries out functions with regard to banking and receipt and payments of money similar to those exercised by the Paymaster General. By the Law of Scotland, he is also *ex officio* administrator of "Treasure Trove" and of estates which fall to the Crown. He is responsible for the audit of the Criminal Accounts of Procurators Fiscal and Sheriff Clerks; the expenses of Returning Officers in Scotland at general and by-elections; and the collection of the fines, penalties and forfeitures imposed in the High Court of Justiciary or in the Sheriff Courts, accruing to the Crown. But though many other duties could also be mentioned, perhaps just one will serve to illustrate the wide variety of his duties. He is the Keeper of the *Edinburgh Gazette*, which is the counterpart in Scotland of the *London Gazette* and contains items of State Intelligence, notices in Bankruptcy and other judicial advertisements.

So much then for the main duties of this busy Office. But perhaps we should take a closer look at its ways of working since these affect quite a number of other Edinburgh institutions.

The Pay Office or Accounts Branch is mainly responsible for the detailed work connected with the Scottish departments' banking business, as distinct from that of the United Kingdom departments such as the Ministry of Works and Public Buildings, whose financial arrangements are controlled by the Paymaster General. Thus every year some 700,000 payable orders drawn on the Queen's and Lord Treasurer's Remembrancer —these are equivalent to cheques—are issued by the Government departments in Edinburgh for salaries and other services. In turn these orders are collected by the Scottish banks' head offices, and presented daily to the Pay Office for settlement. After the usual examination of the orders each bank concerned receives in exchange a bearer cheque drawn on the bank at which the Exchequer account is kept.

Two accounts (says an official explanation) of this arrangement are kept in the name of the Queen's Remembrancer at one of the five Scottish banks, each of which in rotation holds the accounts for one year. These accounts are (a) the Supply Account; (b) the Drawing Account. All monies received are placed to the Supply Account, and it is operated upon solely by " write offs " or transfers to the Drawing Account. The day to day balance in these accounts is kept as low as possible; that is to say, a minimum free balance in the general pool is retained to meet immediate daily expenditure.

To meet the deficiency on any particular day, money is obtained from the Inland Revenue, Edinburgh, if that Department is able to supply it. The Inland Revenue cheque is paid into the Supply Account and the Inland Revenue receives in exchange an order on the Paymaster General payable to the Commissioners of Inland Revenue. When, as frequently happens, the Inland Revenue is unable to supply the deficiency, an order on the Paymaster General (equivalent to a cheque) in favour of the bank is simply lodged in the Supply Account. The Paymaster General is simultaneously advised in both cases as to the Vote or Votes to which the money should be charged. As an illustration of these transactions in the year 1961–2, daily receipts to meet votes and other expenditure amounted in all to about £236,000,000, of which £93,000,000 was received through the Inland Revenue, £110,000,000 through the appropriate bank, and the balance of £33,000,000 comprised departmental receipts.

Many other of the financial arrangements which the Pay Office has to manage could be listed here, if space allowed, but perhaps one or two might again serve to illustrate the variety and importance of its duties as a whole. On behalf of the Treasury it pays the salaries of Scottish Judges; the allowance paid to the High Commissioner to the General Assembly of the Church of Scotland; allowances to County Councils in respect of Highland Schools; and the annuity under the Treaty of Union to the Board of Trustees for the National Galleries of Scotland. As final examples, the Pay Office not only acts as agent of the Paymaster General in paying the pensions of some 1,500 Scottish civil service pensioners, but collects Motor Tax all over Scotland through the Scottish banks.

Next comes the Companies Branch which discharges the many duties imposed upon the Queen's and Lord Treasurer's Remembrancer by virtue of his appointment as Registrar of Companies, Registrar of Business Names and Registrar of Limited Partnerships in Scotland.

In brief, the Branch's main duties are as follows. It must maintain for public inspection all the documents required to be filed by companies in Scotland under the Companies Act of 1948. It prepares the statistical information relating to Scottish companies which the Board of Trade requires for its annual report to Parliament. It also deals with inquiries relating to the proposed names of companies about to be formed or wishing to change their names. To avoid duplication of names in Scotland and England a British index of live companies is scrutinised, and every day lists of proposed new registrations are sent to the Registrar of Companies in London before the names are registered in Edinburgh. Similarly, by arrangement with the Board of Trade, proposed names which might suggest Royal patronage or official recognition, or which contain certain words such as " Trust," are not ordinarily allowed just as proposed business names which might be held to be misleading or pretentious may be refused by the Registrar for Scotland.

The administration of the Queen's and Lord Treasurer's Remembrancer has two other wings—the Audit Branch and the classical-sounding Ultimus Haeres Branch. The main work of the Audit Branch is to audit and pay the Criminal Accounts submitted by Procurators Fiscal and Sheriff Clerks and, on behalf of the Treasury, to audit the expenses of Returning Officers at general and by-elections. It is also responsible for the local audit of fees and fines collected by Sheriff Clerks throughout Scotland, amounting to about £690,000 per annum.

The work of the Ultimus Haeres Branch is substantially that of an executor, for in Scotland the Queen's and Lord Treasurer's Remembrancer is entitled *ex officio* to administer the assets of Scottish estates which fall to the Crown. These are various, ranging as they do from moveable property belonging to Scottish intestates dying without known kin to unclaimed funds in the hands of solicitors, and " Treasure Trove."

THE INLAND REVENUE

Edinburgh plays a full part in the activities of the Revenue. Her contribution is two-fold: her citizens provide their own share of the annual offerings to the Exchequer; and as the capital she is the seat of the agencies that administer or supervise the assessment and collection of the revenue throughout Scotland.

The taxes that come under the care of the Board of Inland Revenue—the taxes on income, the stamp duties and the estate duty—are handled by different branches of the Revenue, each following the pattern that best suits its needs and taking full responsibility under the Board for the management of its day to day work. The taxes on income are mostly both assessed and collected locally; not both by one local office, for it is a Revenue rule that the receipt of the money due must be kept separate from its assessment, but by parallel networks of tax offices and collectors' offices to be found in the bigger towns of Scotland. It would be uneconomic, on the other hand, to administer the stamp duties and estate duty from a number of local offices. In all, 1,150 out of the 4,400 Inland Revenue staff employed in Scotland in 1963 served in Edinburgh; and of these, 830 worked in local offices dealing with the affairs of the people of Edinburgh and 320 in head offices concerned with Edinburgh business only as part of their national responsibilities.

The local offices reflect the character of the city. The assessment of income tax, capital gains tax and corporation tax (but not sur-tax, which is administered from one office for the whole of the United Kingdom) is the charge of the Chief Inspector's branch; and as it is fundamental to its organisation that every District Inspector takes responsibility for the assessment of all the incomes and profits coming within his district, his staff have therefore to be ready to deal with all the many different industries and professions of the area.

Two exceptions from the general rule that income tax is assessed locally are to be found in Edinburgh. The affairs of Crown servants are all handled centrally in a series of offices in different parts of the United Kingdom. The Edinburgh office deals with the assessments of all Post Office employees throughout the United Kingdom. Another office (C.I. (Claims)) deals with difficult points on repayment claims, especially claims arising from settlements of income, claims by foreign residents and repayments to charities.

In addition to the local offices, the Chief Inspector's head office in Edinburgh is the centre for three out of the five Inspecting Officers of Scotland (the others are in Glasgow). These are senior members of the tax inspectorate appointed to inspect and report on the efficiency of the local offices and generally to act as a link between the District Inspector and the Chief Inspector of Taxes. One of the Edinburgh inspecting officers also specialises in problems of peculiarly Scottish interest: for example, questions arising out of the tax liabilities of distilleries.

The other Revenue duties—the stamp duties and estate duty—are administered centrally. The Estate Duty office covers the whole of Scotland just as its sister office in London handles all the estate duty claims arising in England and Wales. Its work is to assess the estate duty payable in respect of property passing on deaths, and requires a sound knowledge of general law since claims to estate duty depend very often upon the interpretation of deeds and upon the rules of the law of property. New entrants to the office are therefore required to study for the appropriate legal examinations before they are considered as qualified.

The Scottish stamp duties are administered from the head office in Edinburgh, and that office, together with a Distributor's office in Glasgow, conducts the work of stamping documents with impressed stamps at the counters as well as by post. In these offices there is a daily stream of callers who bring their documents to the counters, wait while the duty is assessed and the documents stamped, after payment, with the appropriate stamp. The transactions charged with duty in this way cover the whole range of Scottish legal and commercial business.

THE COMPTROLLER OF STAMPS AND TAXES

All the taxes collected in Scotland, whether by local collectors or centrally, pass through one office in Edinburgh, that of the Comptroller of Stamps and Taxes, who, as well as being responsible for the stamp duties in Edinburgh, acts also as Accountant General for Scotland. He is the head of the collection service, which collects the tax assessed in local tax offices, and, as such, has under his charge the headquarters of the collection service from which the local collection offices in Scotland are controlled and supervised, including three in Edinburgh. One unit in his office takes over from local collection offices the pursuit of taxpayers whom no local pressure has persuaded to meet their obligations. Another unit is the Audit branch, which is concerned with the examination of employers' records for Pay-As-You-Earn and with the audit of repayments authorised locally by Inspectors of Taxes. The Comptroller also sees to the banking and bringing to account of the Scottish revenues, and prepares the annual Scottish Revenue Account for incorporation in the final United Kingdom Account.

The Comptroller of Stamps and Taxes, however, has wider responsibility than these executive duties. He is the senior representative in Scotland of the Board of Inland Revenue and holds an historic office. It began, if one disregards medieval forerunners, in 1799. At that date the executive administration was in the hands of local persons outside government employ, and supervision of their actions was the duty of the Commissioners for the Affairs of Taxes. In Scotland their powers of supervision must have been weakened by being shared with the Barons of the Exchequer. Parliamentary commissions of inquiry at the end of the 18th century drew attention to the faults of the system and to the very serious delays in getting the money collected from the taxpayer out of the hands of intermediaries and into the Exchequer. Scotland's record was particularly bad. The Lord Advocate gave his view that this position was due to absence of effective control and suggested the appointment of a Comptroller of Taxes to have general superintendence of that branch of the Revenue in Scotland. His advice was followed, and the office of Comptroller was established in 1799 under the aegis jointly of the Commissioners of Taxes and the Barons of the Exchequer.

Later the Barons of the Exchequer gave up their rights over the administration, and with the merger of the previously separate Board of Stamps with the Board of Taxes the office assumed much of its present form. In the middle of the century the combined post of Comptroller and Solicitor was held by a great figure in Revenue administration, Angus Fletcher, whose personality comes down vividly through the series of Annual Reports to the Board which somehow or other he had published in Edinburgh—no mere statistical returns but the personal testament of a dedicated servant of the Revenue and of a devoted Scot. With justified pride he pointed to the remarkable reforms that had taken place in the Scottish collection, which now showed a speed that put the rest of the United Kingdom to shame. He took pride in his relations with his taxpayers and referred with relish to accusations by English colleagues that he " sprinkled the public with rosewater and eau de cologne instead of blistering and burning them with the red hot iron of penalties and penal duties."

Nobody since that time has tried to fill both posts; there is a separate office of Solicitor of Inland Revenue, with the duties of advising the Commissioners on matters of Scots law and of conducting Revenue litigation in the Scottish Courts.

As the Board's chief representative in Scotland, the Comptroller is the person to whom the Scottish public brings its grievances and its problems, whether these be complaints by individual taxpayers or suggestions about the general administration put forward by professional or other representative bodies. Equally, the Comptroller is the person to whom the Commissioners of Inland Revenue look for advice on Scottish matters. He is a member of the administrative class and forms part of the small secretariat which assists the Commissioners in the general management of the Revenue organisation in the oversight of the taxes and in all matters of policy, including in particular, the preparation of the annual fiscal legislation.

THE VALUATION OFFICE

The Revenue has one remaining branch in Scotland which stands slightly apart from the others because much of its work is performed for other departments. This is the Valuation Office, which functions from a head office in Edinburgh and a number of District Valuer's Offices, one of them being situated in the city itself. The Valuation Office (with a staff of 225 in Scotland) is responsible for the valuation of heritable property for Revenue purposes—estate duty for instance—but in the course of time it has also taken on the duty of providing valuation services for government departments generally and often for local authorities and other bodies if public funds are involved. The District Valuer's Office is concerned with almost every case where property, for example, is compulsorily purchased for some public project.

H.M. CUSTOMS AND EXCISE

We need not be surprised that at the time of each of the previous *Statistical Accounts*, the Customs and Excise was active in Edinburgh, nor that by 1963—at the time of the *Third*—the total annual yielded for the Edinburgh Collection was about £105 million. What is perhaps surprising is that the modern shape of both headquarters organisation and the methods of assessment should have been so well established in the 1790s when the first *Statistical Account* was published.

ORGANISATION

At that time there were in Edinburgh, as there were in London, two Boards of Revenue Commissioners—one the Board of Customs, the other the Board of Excise. These two Boards were entirely independent of each other, for the Customs and Excise had not yet become amalgamated in either Scotland or England, although there was already one unified Revenue Board in Ireland. The Boards in Edinburgh had powers somewhat similar to those of the Boards in London except that (a) the Scottish Board had no powers over the colonial territories (which the English Board of Customs had); (b) the net yield in Scotland had to be remitted to the respective Receivers-General in England; and (c) in Edinburgh the Scottish Customs Commissioners collected the *Excise* duty on salt. On these Boards sitting in Edinburgh in the 1790s we find such noted men as Adam Smith, whose father (also Adam Smith) was Comptroller of Customs at the port of Kirkcaldy, Clerk Maxwell and Graham of Fintry who is best remembered in Scotland as a friend and patron of Robert Burns, and the recipient of various verse epistles and frequent and grateful letters. Incidentally, it is usually stated[1] that Sir John Sinclair, who instituted the first *Statistical Account*, became a Commissioner of Excise in 1811. Although he certainly entered the Excise in 1811, he never in fact became a Commissioner.

When Robert Burns was nominated late in 1787 or early in 1788 to the Excise Board in Edinburgh, it was presumably at the instance of Robert Graham of Fintry.[2] He got his " order for instruction " dated from Edinburgh on 31st March, 1788 and underwent his course of instruction, not in Edinburgh but in his native Ayrshire, under James Findlay, Excise Officer at Tarbolton. He was, upon examination, certified fit " for surveying victuallers, rectifiers, chandlers, tanners, tawers, maltsters, etc." It was not until the autumn of 1789 that he petitioned for employment in the Dumfries " collection " in the Excise " station " embracing the immediate district of his own home.

Although patronage might be an important element in promotion within the service, the selected candidate had to satisfy not only the Board but also his own immediate superiors that he was in fact fitted and competent for the higher post before any promotion was made. Furthermore, it was the practice to try the candidate in the higher post in an acting capacity before any substantive appointment was made. Thus Robert Burns, after a period of satisfactory service as a " country " officer in the district behind Dumfries, was promoted to a more responsible " town " area in Dumfries itself. It was after serving in that more responsible area that he secured—presumably by patronage—nomination for the higher post of Supervisor. He was in fact tried out as a Supervisor and presumably found satisfactory, for he was placed on the list for promotion to that post when the appropriate vacancy should occur. It is the great tragedy

[1] For example, in the *Dictionary of National Biography* and the *Encyclopaedia Britannica*.
[2] Letter to Robert Graham, January, 1788.

of his service career that he died of endocarditis after his promotion—possibly to a collectorship in Edinburgh or Leith—was already assured, but before the substantive appointment could be made.

By 1845—time of the second *Statistical Account*—the reforms associated with the names of Northcote and Trevelyan were on the eve of their introduction; which meant that entrance to the service was to be only by *open competitive* examination. As for promotion this too was to be strictly by merit, after consideration (or further examination) determined not by patronage but by seniority.

In the meantime other reforms had taken place. In 1823 an act was passed to consolidate the separate Boards of Customs and of Excise in Edinburgh and in London, and the Revenue Board in Dublin[1] The existing patents were therefore revoked on 13th September, 1823, and a Board of Customs and a Board of Excise were set up to have authority throughout the whole of the United Kingdom. In consequence therefore two Boards no longer sat in Edinburgh. In both the Customs and the Excise, however, Assistant Commissioners were appointed to reside in the city during an interim period, to attend to Scottish affairs.

A further reform was imminent. The Excise had hitherto, like the Customs, been an independent service, but in 1849 the Office of Assessed Taxes and the Stamp Office were amalgamated with the Excise, to become the Inland Revenue. This arrangement lasted only 60 years, and in 1909 the Excise was again separated from the Inland Revenue and amalgamated with H.M. Customs, to become H.M. Customs and Excise.

THE EARLY 1960s

In the early '60s the administration of the united department was still vested in a Board of Commissioners appointed by the Queen by Letters-Patent under the Great Seal. The service " in the field " was still divided into separate regions or " Collections," each under the control of a Collector, who is responsible to the Board in London for all the Department's business in his area. At the time of the earlier *Statistical Accounts* these Collections were smaller and consequently more numerous. Even until 1943 Edinburgh and Leith were separate Collections. Today there are only 35 Collections in the whole of the United Kingdom, and the Edinburgh one stretches out to include Berwickshire, Roxburghshire, Peeblesshire, the Lothians, Stirlingshire, Clackmannanshire and the southern half of Perthshire. This territory formerly included the Excise Collections of Leith, Haddington, Linlithgow, and Stirling, and the Customs Ports of Leith, Dunbar, Granton, Bo'ness, Grangemouth, Alloa and Rosyth.

The Collector's Office is today at the Custom House, Leith. This is the hub of the Collection, where captains must report the arrival of their ships and seek permission to sail again, where importers and exporters must present their documents and pay the duties on imported goods, where distillers, brewers, manufacturers of purchase tax goods and licensees of

[1] 4 Geo. IV, cap. 23.

all sorts must pay their periodical dues. The Higher Collector has two Assistant Collectors, and his office is staffed by Indoor and Clerical Officers under the supervision of Chief Clerks. Besides his responsibility for the receipt and accounting for the revenue, the Collector also controls the charging and assessing staff of " outdoor " officials. It should perhaps be mentioned here that by far the largest part of this sum comes from Edinburgh itself because of its breweries and distilleries, its manufactories of purchase tax goods, its ports and its larger population.

There are about 220 Officers of Custom and Excise employed, either singly or in small groups, in " Stations " which are spread over the Collection according to the needs of the work. In the purely Customs Stations at Leith, an Officer will be in charge of the shipping work at a particular wharf or part of a dock, examining the cargo and controlling the movement of goods. At large breweries or distilleries there will be Officers stationed on the premises; others will be in charge of a bonded warehouse or grouped in a specialised Purchase Tax Station; or a single Officer may control a General Station which could be a few streets in the commercial quarter of the city or a wide stretch of countryside embracing one or two small towns. These Officers are grouped in Districts, of which there are 15 in the Collection, each in the charge of a Surveyor. The Officers raise the duty assessment against the trader in the case of high-duty goods such as spirits (at distilleries, warehouses or at import) or imported tobacco leaf; and they verify the correctness of the merchant's self-assessments in the case of most other imports as well as at breweries or the offices of purchase tax traders. To do this efficiently, they need a sound knowledge of measuring and calculating techniques and of commercial accountancy, as well as a considerable familiarity with industrial processes and the ways of the various trades with which the Department is concerned. The modern successor of Robert Burns must still be expert in the art of gauging " vessels " of all sorts, but the range of his activities now extends to the storage tanks of a petroleum refinery where imported crude oil is refined to produce a wide range of hydrocarbon oils. Many of these are used in oil/chemical synthesis plants to produce plastics, detergents. ethyl alcohol, isopropyl alcohol and by-products—all under some degree of revenue control.

Though the range and complexity of revenue interests have grown so much, there is one great problem of the 1790s that had dwindled by the 1960s almost to vanishing-point. Throughout the 18th and early 19th centuries the Customs were engaged in a desperate struggle against smugglers. Doubtless a number of factors combined to enable the department to achieve success in this field; but, for the fact that smuggling is today so small a problem to the Board, much credit is due to the efficiency of the Waterguard Service. This preventive branch of the Customs ensures that ships, aircraft and goods are brought into the country only through the approved channels. The duties of the Preventive Officers include the boarding of ships, the patrolling of the coast, docks and sea approaches, the enforcement of quarantine regulations and the searching of ships against smuggling. These are the uniformed officers more familiar to the public when they are engaged in the examination of passengers' baggage. Grouped into Districts under Chief Preventive Officers and headed by a Waterguard Superintendent, the Waterguard branch in Edinburgh Collection numbers about 75 officials.

THE RANGE OF DUTIABLE GOODS

At the time of the first *Statistical Account*, customs and excise duties provided the bulk of the government's revenue. Since then, the direct taxes administered by the Inland Revenue have burgeoned until they now provide somewhat the greater part of the tax revenue. Nevertheless, for most of the 20th century so far, the duties of customs and excise have still yielded a fairly constant proportion of just under half the total tax revenue.

CUSTOMS DUTIES

The very complicated and confusing system of customs duties that existed shortly before the first *Statistical Account* was consolidated and considerably simplified by Pitt in 1787.[1] Even so, the duties were becoming complicated again by the 1790s, when most imported goods were liable to duty, and by 1796[2] and 1797[3], the rates on many if not most goods were complicated enough to run into twentieths of a penny. By 1845 the movement towards clearing the tariff, associated with Huskisson, Peel and Gladstone, was well on its way. In the latter half of the 19th century, the doctrines of Adam Smith had achieved their greatest effect and there remained only a few revenue duties applied equally to home-produced or imported goods. The tide began to turn in the 20th century, and the people in 1932 saw a return to a full range of protective import duties.

In the 1790s, tobacco (which could be legally imported into Leith, Greenock and Glasgow but no other Scottish ports) paid a duty of about 6*d.* the lb. compared with the current rate of about £3 10*s.* 0*d.* (this latter works out at about 3*s.* 4*d.* on a packet of 20 average-sized cigarettes); brandy paid a total (of customs plus excise) of about 8*s.* 7*d.* the gallon, compared with the current rate of about £11 15*s.* 0*d.* at proof; while beer paid a total of about 9*d.* the gallon compared with the current rate at the time of writing of about 6*s.* 6*d.* Although a number of economic and other factors tend to blur this comparison, yet broadly the figures provide a fair picture.

EXCISE DUTIES

At the time of the first *Statistical Account*, again the main articles liable to the Excise duties administered by the Board in Edinburgh were beer or malt, spirits, tobacco, glass, candles and certain other goods. There

[1] 27 Geo. III, cap. 13.
[2] 37 Geo. III, cap. 15.
[3] 37 Geo. III, cap. 110.

The High Kirk of Edinburgh, St. Giles' Cathedral, goes back to the 12th century and perhaps earlier. Here in 1637 Jenny Geddes caused a riot by flinging a stool at the head of a bishop; here many kings and queens have worshipped; and here today is still retained the strong and colourful atmosphere of Scotland throughout the centuries.

The city of Edinburgh has over the years encompassed a number of villages within its boundaries. *Above:* the lovely hamlet of Swanston, recently restored by the Corporation. The village has close associations with Robert Louis Stevenson.

On right: on the shores of the Firth of Forth is the village of Cramond where many houses have recently been restored by the Corporation.

were also duties on stage-coaches, post-horses, medicine stamps and so forth. At the time of the next (early Victorian) *Account* the range of dutiable articles was much the same (although the rates of duty had altered somewhat) with the exception of candles (repealed in 1831) and glass (repealed in 1845).

In 1786 the rates of Excise duty on distilled spirits were unified between Scotland and England at 2*s*. 7½*d*. the gallon. The total spirit duty collected in that year was £101,476 16*s*. 10*d*. in Scotland and £371,949 2*s*. 0*d*. in England. The respective populations at about this time have been estimated at about a million and a half in Scotland and about 8 millions in England, giving an apparent consumption of about 11 twentieths of a gallon per head in Scotland and 9 twentieths of a gallon per head in England; but this calculation disregards entirely the factor of removals of duty-paid spirit from one country to another. At the actual time of the first *Statistical Account*, it is not possible to make any such comparison because of differing modes of duty charge. From 1787 the duty in England was increased to 3*s*. 2*d*. the gallon; but in Scotland duty was charged as an annual licence duty at a rate calculated on the content of the still concerned, differentiated as between the Highlands and the Lowlands (£1 16*s*. 0*d*. per annum per gallon content and £1 4*s* 0*d*. respectively). This Scottish scheme was abandoned in 1814, but these complications make comparisons of output impracticable on the basis of figures from revenue yield.

In 1845 the Excise spirit duty in Scotland was 3*s*. 8*d*.—about half the rate in England of 7*s*. 10*d*. The rate in Ireland was 2*s*. 8*d*.—and in that year £1,180,852 was collected in Scotland on 6,441,011 gallons, compared with £3,554,915 in England on 9,076,381 gallons. As hinted above, it cannot be argued that this indicates an annual spirit consumption of about two and one third gallons in Scotland per person as against just over one half gallon per person in England, since removals of duty-paid spirit were much greater from Scotland to England than from England to Scotland.

THE POSITION IN 1963

In mid-19th century, over 80 per cent of the customs and excise revenue came from the duties on alcoholic liquors, tobacco and the " breakfast-table " (sugar, tea, coffee and cocoa); the most important single source of revenue being spirits. At the present time, the most important source of revenue in Edinburgh as elsewhere is tobacco, its consumption having increased eightfold in the past 100 years. A decline in the consumption of beer and spirits has reduced the proportionate yield of the duties on alcoholic liquors. The breakfast-table duties have declined steeply in importance, whilst new sources of revenue, notably hydrocarbon oils and purchase tax, have come into existence. In 1963, the Department collected some £2,668 million, of which over 90 per cent came from tobacco (£878 million), purchase tax (£571 million), alcoholic liquors (beer £254, spirits £185 and wines £26 million) and hydrocarbon oils (£545 million).

As we saw earlier the total yield in Edinburgh Collection at the time of writing is about £105 million a year. The principal items in this total are tobacco (£43 million), alcoholic liquors (whisky £20 million and beer £18 million) and hydrocarbon oils (£16 million). Again, it must be said, this does not reflect the pattern of *consumption* in the region, but rather the presence of a greater local *production* of beer and whisky and a smaller local *production* of goods chargeable with purchase tax, compared with the average for the whole kingdom.

The figure for tobacco revenue is even less susceptible to a regional elucidation, since the duty is raised, not on the number of cigarettes manufactured, but on the raw tobacco leaf when delivered from a bonded warehouse. Duty may thus be paid on leaf in Leith, London or Bristol, for example, though it will be used in a tobacco factory in some inland town in another part of the country.

Parallel with the 19th century drive towards the simplification of the customs tariff, there was a similar movement to prune excise duties. At the time of the amalgamation of the customs and the excise in 1909 all of the existing duties could be printed on a few pages. Today the *Customs and Excise Tariff* runs to 457 quarto pages and, in addition, there is a booklet of 82 octavo pages setting out the goods chargeable with purchase tax. Like the original excise duties (but unlike the modern ones), the purchase tax is levied not only on home produced goods, but also on chargeable imported goods additionally to any import duty payable. But the tax itself has some novel features.

Most excise duties are charged by reference to the quantities or the physical characteristics of the goods, e.g. the proof gallon of spirits or the quantity and specific gravity of beer. The Officer of Customs and Excise can thus impose physical checks at a convenient point in the production of the goods. Purchase tax is charged as a percentage of the value of the goods at the time of their delivery to a retailer. To control this tax, the Officer must discard his diprod and hydrometer and acquire a knowledge of accountancy. He must take into account all the permutations of trade practice in order to be satisfied that tax is charged on a fair value. Fortunately the Department has a long tradition of adaptability, and the modern Officer will visit a motor factory, a printer's firm or the head office of a chain store with the same assurance with which Robert Burns no doubt was able to survey his " chandlers, tanners, tawers, maltsters, etc."

Though it is the consumer who pays in the end, he has (with the minor exception of the baggage bench) little direct contact with the revenue official. So perhaps he will not begrudge a certain respect for a Department which operates its efficient machine on as little as 2*d.* in every £1 which it collects. Adam Smith down in the Canongate would have approved such economy.

MINISTRY OF LABOUR IN SCOTLAND

The Ministry of Labour is primarily the Department concerned with manpower. Its functions include the placing of persons in employment, the vocational training of fit and disabled persons, the resettlement of disabled persons and the Youth Employment Service (except in so far as this service is operated by local Education Authorities as it is in Edinburgh). Other functions include questions of industrial relations, payment of unemployment benefit and national insurance as agent for other Departments, the administration of the Wages Council Acts and the acceptance of passport applications on behalf of the Foreign Office.

The Controller (Scotland) is the Ministry's senior representative in Edinburgh. He has the special responsibility of ensuring that the execution in Scotland of the Ministry's policy is in accordance with Scottish conditions. The Controller and his staff are located at the Scottish Headquarters of the Ministry at Stuart House; but he also has under his direction 150 Local Offices, seven Government Training Centres and two Industrial Rehabilitation Units. The organisation in Scotland includes a Finance Officer (also located in the city) and a Superintending Inspector of Factories who work direct with Headquarters departments. About 400 staff members, of whom 180 are women, are employed by the Ministry in Edinburgh.

This is not the place to describe the far-flung ramifications of the Ministry in Scotland, but certain of its functions need explanation since they particularly apply to Edinburgh as well as to the rest of the country.

The three Employment Exchanges—at Tollcross, Portobello and Leith—provide a service to employers wanting workers, and to men and women (whether employed or unemployed) who are seeking work. Vacancies which cannot be filled locally are circulated if necessary over the whole country. In addition specialised members of the staff are available to deal with inquiries relating to the resettlement of the disabled; vocational training and training within industry for Supervisors; the Professional and Executive Register, and the Specialist Services for the placing of nurses and the resettlement of members of the Regular Forces.

An important part of the Ministry's work is carried out at the seven Government Training Centres in Scotland. These provide training for able-bodied and disabled persons in particular industries or trades where augmentation of the skilled labour force is necessary, or in order to give those who need it an oppotunity to learn a new skill or adapt an existing skill that is no longer in demand. In this work Edinburgh has a part to play. A Government Training Centre, the eighth in Scotland, is now being built in the city beside the Industrial Rehabilitation Unit at Granton, which provides courses of industrial rehabilitation for persons recovering from prolonged sickness, disabled persons and certain unemployed to enable them to undertake or retainemployment. A course of rehabilitation may take up to 12 weeks and is designed to overcome the effects of prolonged absence from work.[1]

The rest of the Ministry's work, or even then not all of it, must be

[1] Edinburgh also has a Disablement Advisory Committee with equal numbers of representative employers and workpeople, and an additional panel representing special interests and two Local Employment Committees similarly constituted.

briefly summarised. In George Street, still an eloquent reminder of Edinburgh's stately age when factories stayed far away from the New Town, is the District Factory Inspector, who is available for consultation on all matters concerning the safety, health and welfare of workers employed in factories, dock work and building and civil engineering operations. Finally, a great deal of statistical information is collated by the Department in departmental publications such as the *Ministry of Labour Gazette*.

THE MINISTRY OF PENSIONS AND NATIONAL INSURANCE

The Ministry of Pensions and National Insurance is responsible for the administration of War Pensions and Allowances, Family Allowances, National Insurance, Industrial Injuries Insurance, and related schemes. Being a United Kingdom Department (as distinct from a Scottish Department) it has its main administrative headquarters in London. But it has a Central Office for Scotland in Edinburgh, and this office has responsibility for the general control and supervision of the 107 Ministry's local offices in Scottish towns. In the remote and sparsely populated country in the North and the Western Islands of Scotland, specially appointed local government officials act as agents of the Ministry in carrying out visiting work and answering inquiries from members of the public. The Central Office in Edinburgh has a general oversight of these arrangements.

Of the 107 local offices in Scotland, to which reference has been made, four are located in Edinburgh. These are the Edinburgh War Pensions Office, the Edinburgh National Insurance Office, the Leith National Insurance Office and the National Insurance Office at Portobello. The staff in these Edinburgh offices and in the Central Office numbers about 500, of whom approximately half are women.

Of the Ministry's 224 Local Advisory Committees, 23 are in Scotland and one, the Lothians Local Advisory Committee, sits in Edinburgh. These Committees meet at intervals to advise on questions concerning the local administration of the National Insurance and the Industrial Injuries Acts. Correspondingly, on the War Pensions side of the Ministry's work, there are 155 War Pensions Committees whose functions include advising the Minister on war pensions matters within their area. Fourteen of these are in Scotland, and they include the Lothians War Pensions Committee which meets in Edinburgh.

The Ministry of National Insurance had its origins in an Act of Parliament passed in 1944 which provided, among other things, that responsibility for National Health Insurance and Contributory Pensions should pass from the Health Departments to the new Ministry. So far as Scotland is concerned, this meant a transference of duties and of staff from the then Department of Health for Scotland (centred in Edinburgh) to the new Ministry and it was mainly around this nucleus that the administration in Scotland was built, with staff recruited from the then Approved Societies as well as from local authorities and other Government departments. Then in 1953, after the amalgamation of the Ministries of Pensions and of National Insurance and the transfer of certain medical functions to the Health Departments, the Ministry of National Insurance became the Ministry of Pensions and National Insurance. Today the Ministry's total staff in Scotland is in the region of 3,000 including medical staff who advise the administration on a wide range of medical matters.

MINISTRY OF PUBLIC BUILDING AND WORKS

For many years there has been an office of the Ministry of Public Building and Works in Edinburgh, and the present organisation, in the charge of an Under-Secretary, enjoys a considerable degree of autonomy in dealing with the Ministry's Scottish affairs. Yet although the Ministry has many responsibilities which it fulfils throughout Scotland, much of it is unknown to the general public. Nonetheless, the name of the Ministry is familiar if only as a result of the blue and white signs which mark the 266 ancient monuments and historic buildings in Scotland in the Ministry's care. For these are to be found from the most northern of the Shetland Isles to the southern tip of Galloway, and from the remote western coast of Lewis to the shores of the North Sea. The preservation and protection of these popular sites is undertaken by a small staff of archaeologists, architects and craftsmen who also advise local authorities and private owners on problems arising at monuments not in the Ministry's care.

The major task of the Ministry, however, is the provision and maintenance of buildings required for the Government service in Scotland. Until 1st April, 1963, the Ministry dealt only with Civil requirements, but from this date its responsibilities were extended to the buildings and installations used by the Armed Services. These are varied ranging as they do from a hut on a West Highland pier for a Fishery Officer or a complex scientific building for a Research Station to a house on a Hebridean island for a Revenue Officer, or 500 houses for a Naval Base. But also although many buildings are thus built for the needs of Government Departments, many more are purchased or taken on lease. In almost every burgh in Scotland there is some building owned or held on lease by the Ministry.

The Ministry is also responsible for the supply of fuel to many of these buildings. Each year, nearly 37,000 tons of coal and coke and 3,500,000 gallons of oil fuel are delivered in Scotland from contracts placed by the Ministry. This fuel is, however, only one of the many items supplied to buildings through the Ministry's organisations. Furniture—ranging from office desks to laboratory benches and from display cases to coffee tables—is provided by the Ministry to offices, laboratories, museums, colleges and houses. With it go carpets, linoleum, curtains, crockery and glass from the toughest pottery to the finest bone china and crystal, brooms and pails, razor blades and soap, floor polishers and kettles. The catalogue of items is a lengthy one: all are distributed by the Ministry's own transport fleet.

ANCIENT MONUMENTS AND HISTORIC BUILDINGS

Many of Edinburgh's historic buildings are in the care of the Ministry of Public Building and Works. Best known of these is obviously Edinburgh Castle itself, for although the Castle is still an Army establishment, much of it is open regularly to the public and over 400,000 visitors pay for admission each year. The Ministry employs a permanent staff to guide and supervise these visitors and to sell the large numbers of guide books, postcards and transparencies which are required. Most visitors, it seems, are attracted to the Scottish National War Memorial, to the bonnets and plumes and kilts of the Scottish United Services Museum which records the history of the Scottish units of the British army, and to the small Chapel of St. Margaret in which christenings and weddings take place from time to time; though this is a privilege restricted to members of the Army units serving in the Castle. There seems in fact no end to the Castle's functions. Its Great Hall is frequently the scene of Government receptions. On the Castle Esplanade the well-known Edinburgh Tattoo is held each year at Festival time. And at almost any time visitors may be intrigued to see a cleaner polishing the shoes of the horse which carries the upright figure of Earl Haig in one of the Castle's most famous statues.

The task of looking after the ancient masonry, some dating back to the 11th century, is undertaken by Ministry employees and calls for much skill and knowledge. The task of maintaining the Castle includes for instance the annual clearance of loose material from the surface of the Castle Rock itself. Each year over five tons of loose rock are removed and, from time to time, large sections of rock in danger of slipping have had to be made safe by means of long steel bolts fixed to more secure parts.

The Palace of Holyroodhouse is also in the care of the Ministry and is another tourist attraction visited by nearly 250,000 visitors each year. So too, on the southern outskirts of Edinburgh, is Craigmillar Castle, an ancient keep which Mary, Queen of Scots knew well, and where she stayed. This important and impressive building was placed in the care of the Ministry in 1951, and much work has been done to preserve it. Two other historic buildings within the city boundary but a little away from the city centre, which the Ministry of Public Building and Works looks after, are the Chapel at Restalrig Church known as St. Triduana's Chapel, and the Dovecot at Corstorphine.

Many of the important buildings in the centre of the city, which should also be considered as historic buildings, are in the Ministry's care. These include the Register House, the National Gallery and the Royal Scottish Academy, the Parliament House, and the adjoining Parliament Hall. All these buildings are in use for the public service, but the Ministry is particularly careful that their architectural features are preserved. Thus in 1962 the Ministry undertook the cleaning of the Royal Scottish Academy. The satisfactory results were much appreciated and demonstrated in a striking manner the dirt which accumulates over the years as Londoners are discovering from the cleaning of St. Paul's Cathedral.

In addition to these direct responsibilities for the upkeep of the city's important historical structures, the Ministry has given financial assistance to owners of historic buildings in the city to assist with the cost of maintenance and repair.

THE POST OFFICE

The Post Office in Edinburgh has an unusually interesting story to tell. How many know, for instance, that Scotland's capital boasts the greatest telephone density in the United Kingdom outside London, or that some half a million letters are posted and collected there every weekday. Again, not many know how many street letter boxes there were in the city during 1963, or the exact number of postmen. The figures are themselves of considerable interest; but before we examine them in broad detail we should perhaps discover just how the Post Office organisation works not merely for Edinburgh itself but for Scotland at large. We should remember also that although what follows is an accurate account of Post Office activities in 1963 and most of 1964, changes have been taking place recently in the P.O.'s administration.

There are two distinct levels of Post Office organisation in the city. Firstly, there is the Post Office Headquarters for Scotland, which has the overall responsibility for administering and operating the postal and telecommunication services for the whole of Scotland. Secondly, there is the Head Post Office for Edinburgh itself: this is not only responsible for the postal and telegraph services in an area rather bigger than the city, but houses the Telephone Manager's Office, which operates the telephone service in an area stretching from the Borders to Fife. The executive offices of the Post Office for Scotland are situated within the building of the General Post Office in Waterloo Place. The Telephone Manager's Office is in Queen Street.

POST OFFICE HEADQUARTERS, SCOTLAND

Early in the 18th century and for more than a hundred years (1710–1831), Scotland had a Deputy Postmaster General who functioned under the authority of the Postmaster General of Great Britain, " to whom all matters of importance had to be referred, and whose sanction required to be given to any matter involving the outlay of money." The Deputy Postmaster Generalship was however abolished in 1831, and for the next hundred years or so limited control was vested in a Secretary of Edinburgh answerable to the Secretary to the Post Office, London. Then came a vital change.

In 1932 an independent committee of inquiry, under Lord Bridgeman, was appointed by the Postmaster General " to inquire and report as to whether any changes in the constitution, status or system of organisation of the Post Office would be in the public interest." The Committee recommended that executive control of all Post Office services should be decentralised from London to regional organisations, the head of each " Region " being given the widest possible powers. As the result of this the Scottish Region, later called Post Office Headquarters, Scotland was set up in 1936, and its chief officer, styled Director in place of Regional Director, was invested with the fullest possible powers for the day to day working of Post Office services throughout Scotland. Local control in 1963 was exercised by 73 Head Postmasters and five Telephone Managers.

To assist him the Director had a Deputy Director and five functional heads: the Postal Controller, the Telecommunications Controller, the Staff and Buildings Controller, the Chief Engineer, and the Finance Officer and Chief Accountant. These officers, along with the Head Postmaster of Glasgow and the Telephone Manager, Glasgow Area form the Post Office Board in Scotland, which meets periodically in Edinburgh under the Director's chairmanship. Each controller is in charge of a Branch of the Headquarters establishment.

POSTAL BRANCH

The Postal Branch controls postal services throughout Scotland. It organises the conveyance of letter and parcel mail between post offices in Scotland, and to those in other parts of the United Kingdom, by land (rail or road), sea and air. It plans and revises delivery and collection services in town and country, and it regularly inspects the working of the postal service in each Head Office area. To achieve this the Postal Controller is assisted by a staff of Assistant Postal Controllers whose task it is to travel throughout Scotland to inspect and check the day to day running of the service. Their special concern is to see that the staff is accurately adjusted to the needs of the work and that adequate accommodation and proper equipment are provided.

TELECOMMUNICATIONS BRANCH

The Telecommunications Branch is responsible for seeing that adequate accommodation, telephone exchange plant and operating positions, circuits, adequacy of operating staff and services are provided to meet the present needs of the community and the prospective growth of telephone subscribers' lines and traffic. It also deals with the more difficult wayleave cases—the erection of telephone or telegraph poles, or routes on private property for instance—certain claims for compensation, and demands for non-standard facilities such as private telegraph wires for newspapers. In respect of these and many other activities such as statistical returns and inspections, the Telecommunications Branch relies on the Telephone Managers and their staffs, who have initial responsibility.

As regards the telegraph services, the day-to-day running is in the hands of Head Postmasters. The Branch fixes the staffing complement, and authorises any necessary increase or rearrangement of telegraph circuits between Scottish Post Offices and other parts of the country in collaboration with other Regions and national headquarters. By means of records and personal inspection, it superintends the quality of the service given and is generally responsible for the adequacy of Scotland's telegraph arrangements as a whole. It is also responsible for the general supervision of wireless licences for television and sound radio, including measures to secure compliance with the Regulations, and refers papers to the appropriate Procurator Fiscal for prosecution in cases of evasion.

STAFF AND BUILDINGS BRANCH

The staff section of the Staff and Buildings Branch deals with many human aspects of this complex organisation—discipline for example, promotion, accident, leave and superannuation—and in all these its Controller has the assistance of an Inspector of Clerical Establishments, a Training Officer and a Chief Welfare Officer. He and his staff have also to co-operate with the Ministry of Public Building and Works on schemes for new Post Office buildings or other sites of various kinds, and for alterations to existing buildings to meet the growth of Post Office services and improved staff welfare conditions.

PUBLIC RELATIONS

A Public Relations Officer, responsible to the Director, co-ordinates Post Office public relations and publicity activities throughout Scotland.

ENGINEERING BRANCH

The Engineering Branch is responsible for all technical matters to do with the construction and maintenance of telephone, telegraph, lift, conveyor, lighting, ventilating and heating plant, postage-stamp and cancelling machines and other mechanical aids. It is also responsible for the design of large automatic telephone exchanges, for the training of engineering personnel, and for the efficient and economic running of all forms of official motor transport. This is considerable. For the Postal motor transport fleet consists of 100 vans of various sizes, ranging from the small 50 cubic foot van used for light delivery work to the 600 cubic foot articulated vehicle used for station services and the heaviest parcel deliveries. The annual mileage run by the fleet amounted in 1963-64 to 1,900,000 miles.

FINANCE BRANCH

The Finance Branch is responsible for preparing the Scottish Post Office Budget, which incorporates estimates for all receipts and payments, and for maintaining a continuous scrutiny of actual revenue and expenditure in relation to estimates. The Finance Officer exercises financial supervision and control throughout the country; and as he also acts as financial adviser to the Director and the Post Office Board in Scotland, he has not only to examine all operational proposals involving finance, but has to prepare financial and statistical data for the information of the Board generally.

But also, and this is exceptional to the normal regional arrangements of the Post Office, the Finance Officer is Chief Accountant for Scotland. He is therefore responsible for the Scottish Metropolitan Office of Account, which has been in existence for some 250 years, and is still going strong as the body responsible for the accounting work of some 2,500 offices spread throughout the country. It operates the Postmaster General's Banking Account in Scotland, the distribution of funds to and from the local offices, and the money order service. As it also audits Head Postmasters' and Telephone Managers' Offices, the Finance Branch is clearly the equivalent in Scotland to the Post Office Accountant General's Department in London, and is kept very busy.

The total staff employed at Post Office Headquarters, Scotland (administrative, technical, clerical and the rest) was about 720 in 1963-64. But as this is only part of what is a much larger army of Post Office workers let us take a closer look at the day-to-day work of the G.P.O. in Edinburgh—after a brief glance at the past.

THE GENERAL POST OFFICE

The progress of the British Post Office and its services from 1845 to 1963 was in keeping with the changes which took place in every other aspect of the nation's life. The needs and demands of the public changed; extensive technical developments took place; and the services of the Post Office underwent many changes far removed from its original function in 1660, when, with the passing of the Charles II Act, it was first established as the General Letter Office.

At the beginning of this period the Post Office provided a limited service for the conveyance of correspondence: by the end it had developed into a vast and many-sided organisation. Its primary function continued to be the provision of communications, but the range and variety of these grew wider and more diverse as the Post Office broadened its activities to include services and facilities outside the immediate field of communications, which it constantly speeded up. The conveyance of mails, for instance, passed through many stages between the days of the "post boy" on horseback and the age of the jet aeroplane. In the early days of the Post Office, mails were not collected from letter boxes or delivered at houses: they were carried from Post Office to Post Office; envelopes were not used and postage stamps were unknown. The letters were simply folded over and sealed with sealing wax, the postage to be paid being written by the postmaster across the address. Occasionally the writer would add "God preserve you" to the address; and if the letter was very urgent he would write "Haste Post Haste"—with sometimes a drawing of the gallows in case the post boy could not read.

As the railway network developed, the postal services expanded; and by the end of the 19th century a very comprehensive service had come into being. Labour was cheap and plentiful, and the service depended largely upon manual operations. At the beginning of the 20th century as many as seven postal deliveries were being made daily in the large cities, since people in all walks of life worked long hours and business extended over a long day. In Edinburgh, until 1915, when they were reduced to four, these seven deliveries a day (excepting Sunday) were at 7 a.m., 10 a.m., 11 a.m., 2.30 p.m., 4.30 p.m., 6.15 p.m., and 7.30 p.m. Train services were fast, and though passengers did not enjoy the amenities which are provided for modern travellers, the conveyance of mails from point to point was quick and reliable.

The volume of postal business naturally continued to increase throughout this period, but changes in social habits, rising costs—particularly labour costs—limitations on the use of the nation's man-power and other factors led to changes in the pattern of the Post Office services. Thus by 1963 the postal deliveries in towns had been stabilised at two per day, with a single delivery on Saturday and none on Sunday. But other forms of rapid communication were to offset this apparent decline in service.

When the electric telegraph system was invented it gave the country a means of communication suitable for urgent matters which did not call for the transmission of documents; and this system, after many stages of improvement, reached a very high level of efficiency till the later invention of the telephone drew traffic away from the telegraph system, and the volume of telegraph business declined steadily while the telephone service expanded, as it still does.

The Post Office has now established offices in all but the smallest places, primarily for the sale of stamps and the acceptance of correspondence; but with such a variety of services calling for countrywide public contact coming into operation, it was a natural development for many other activities to be added to the primary function. Thus in Edinburgh, as everywhere else, a demand for a remittance service was met by the introduction of postal order, money order and cash-on-delivery services. As facilities for small savings were needed these were provided by the Post Office Savings Bank and the National Savings services; and in addition the Post Office not only provided facilities for the purchase of Government Stock but made Local Taxation Licences available at Post Offices everywhere. During war-time too the payment of allowances to the dependants of serving men fell to the Post Office, together with much work connected with rationing, evacuation, national publicity, and many national welfare services involving the sale of contribution stamps, the payment of drafts, allowances and pensions. All of these together meant a very high level of business as the welfare services grew. And by the end of the period the Post Office had become a more intimate part of the community's life than ever before as we can see from the development of the Post Office in Edinburgh.

WATERLOO PLACE

The principal Post Office building in the city is the General Post Office at the junction of the North Bridge and Waterloo Place, where it was first established in 1821. The foundation stone of the present building was laid by the Prince Consort in 1861; and though there have been alterations and additions, the building is substantially the same as when it was built, and the public have access to it from several streets. Even more fortunate the building runs along the side of the Waverley Station and is connected to the station by lifts and a covered way, which provide direct access to the railway platforms from the Sorting Offices.

The Head Postmaster of Edinburgh whose staff in 1963 was some 2,200 is located here, together with his administrative staff and the main Postal and Telegraph operational departments which serve the Edinburgh city and district.

The public office in the General Post Office building is the principal Post Office counter in the city. It is open for business from 8 a.m. to 8 p.m. on weekdays and for a limited period and restricted range of business on Sunday. There were also 18 Branch Post Offices in 1963 in various parts of the city. These are " Crown " Post Offices, staffed by personnel employed directly by the Post Office and working in premises owned or leased by the department. In addition there are in the city 112 Sub Post Offices run by Sub Postmasters who are paid to provide service and accommodation on a scale of remuneration related to the amount of business carried on.

THE POST BAG AND THE LETTER BOX

Since the General Post Office building is the focal point in the city's postal services, the main letter and parcel sorting offices are situated there. Correspondence from the city Post Offices and street letter boxes is collected and brought in to the office for processing and despatch. The office also acts as a general forwarding office and a distribution office. As the former it receives correspondence from many offices in Scotland for treatment and inclusion in the wide range of mails made up for offices all over the United Kingdom and for many places overseas. Correspondence for India, Pakistan, Burma, Ceylon and Australia is concentrated upon Edinburgh, whence despatches are made to the full range of offices in those countries. As a redistribution office Edinburgh received correspondence from all over the United Kingdom (and some overseas countries) for the counties of Berwickshire, Clackmannanshire, East Lothian, Fife, Kinross-shire, Midlothian, Peeblesshire, Perthshire (part), Roxburghshire, Stirlingshire, Selkirkshire and West Lothian. Mails are made up for every " Post Town " in those counties.

Letter mails are despatched to 526 offices in the United Kingdom and on the average about 10,500 bags are despatched every week from the letter office. Parcel mails are made up for 286 offices, and about 16,000 bags of parcels are despatched each week. These figures are for 1963, like the others to follow.

About 450,000 letters are collected into the office each weekday, and out of this total about 250,000 come in on the evening collection. This high peak of posted traffic in the evening, and the corresponding high peak of traffic for delivery in the morning confront the postal service with not only its chief task but a considerable problem; for the very pattern of the work makes economical operation difficult and creates "unsocial" working conditions for the staff.

At the North West District, South West District and West District Offices both parcel and letter delivery work is carried on. Parcels for the rest of the city are delivered from a large office in Hopetoun Street which is devoted entirely to this work. About 7,500 parcels are delivered in the city each weekday.

In addition to the 130 Post Office counters at which correspondence can be posted there are in the city 458 street letter boxes. There are four main collections from these boxes daily, though supplementary collections are made from many of them on account of the weight of the postings.

TELEGRAMS

The Telegraph Office in the General Post Office building is the second largest in Scotland. It is in operation continuously. There are also 62 offices in the city where telegrams may be handed in, and in addition telegrams can be dictated from any telephone at any time.

All telegrams are now transmitted by teleprinter or telephone. The teleprinter network operates on a through automatic switching system. Operators dial code numbers and secure instant connection with any other teleprinter office in the United Kingdom. On connection being established an automatic signal is transmitted to indicate that conditions have been set up for the transmission of traffic. So much for the outgoing messages. Delivery of incoming telegrams in the city is effected by telephone or by hand, delivery staff being located at the General Post Office, and at offices in Leith, Strathearn Road, and West Park Place. Motor cycles and bicycles are used for this work. Lastly, in this particular field, there is the Telegraph Money Order service which gives facilities for the quick transmission of sums of money from place to place. Orders are accepted at counters in the city and are paid at 31 offices.

THE TELEPHONE MANAGER'S OFFICE

The growth of the telephone system in Edinburgh is a most interesting story, which is best understood if we see first how the local system fits into the national framework.

For Post Office administrative purposes the country is divided into the Scottish, Welsh and Northern Ireland Directorates and the English Regions. For its telecommunications functions these are sub-divided into Areas, each Area being under the control of a Telephone Manager. The number of subscribers served by the Areas differs considerably, and the Area boundaries are determined mainly by community of interest and geographical and economic conditions (e.g. situation of cable routes).

Over the whole country the system grows continuously. And here again, to understand the present situation better, we should look back to the earliest days— in Edinburgh itself, for it was here that the inventor of the telephone was born, and where, appropriately, one of the earliest British telephone exchanges came into being.

ALEXANDER GRAHAM BELL

Born on 3rd March, 1847, at 16 South Charlotte Street, Alexander Graham Bell was educated at the Royal High School and at Edinburgh University. He came of stock which had specialised for two generations in the teaching of speech and speech production, and in due course became, like his father, a teacher of elocution. In 1870, however, father and son emigrated to Canada, in an effort to improve the latter's health, and duly settled in Ontario in a house now known as the Bell Homestead and one of the Canadian Government's National Historic Sites.

The American patent was granted to Bell on his birthday in 1876; and to look far ahead before returning to the 1870s, it was in 1920 that Edinburgh honoured her famous son by making him a Freeman of the city.

19TH CENTURY GROWTH

The 1870s were a most important period in the growth of the telephone, for initially telephones were only used for point to point connection. But soon attention was directed to the means whereby any one line could be connected to any other at a switching centre; and in January, 1878 the first telephone exchange in the world was opened at New Haven, Connecticut, U.S.A. Exchanges were then established in Glasgow (March, 1879) and Edinburgh at St. Andrew's Square (October, 1879) by the Scottish Telephonic Exchange Limited. Thus Glasgow beat its rival city by a few months. But a second company—The Telephone Company Limited—opened up in Edinburgh very shortly afterwards with offices in Frederick Street. It would appear that the Telephone Company appropriately used Bell's patent only, whereas the Scottish Telephonic Company had a free hand.

Though many changes naturally occurred in the companies operating a service, it need only be recorded here that company fusion gradually occurred, notably in 1889 when the main companies operating in England and Scotland combined under the title of the National Telephone Company: this had been formed in 1881 with an increased capital of £4,000,000. The next notable date was 1896 when the trunk service was transferred to the Post Office. But by this time it was gradually becoming clear that the local services could not expand efficiently or economically under the existing conditions; and on New Year's Day, 1912, the Post Office assumed control of the entire service.

THE EDINBURGH EXCHANGE SYSTEM

The original Edinburgh switchboards, manufactured in U.S.A., were of a very simple form consisting of units accommodating the terminal equipment of 50 subscribers' lines. But by 1889 the number of subscribers in the city, including Leith, approached 700; and there may have been rather more telephones in service than subscribers. There was certainly such an increased interest in the instrument that on Christmas Day 1889—year in which a 50 line exchange was established in Granton Square—the Edinburgh *Evening Dispatch* gave its view that in many departments of business the telephone had become indispensable. Thereafter, progress was so rapid, with new exchanges coming in to serve the needs of different city areas, that at the transfer to State control in 1911 there were some 12,000 telephones in Edinburgh and Leith. Thereafter, again development proceeded apace; a total of 20,000 was reached by 1925; and on 2nd October, 1926 Edinburgh's main exchanges were converted to automatic working. This incidentally was welcomed by most telephone users as a great advance; but as with most advances there were misunderstandings. There was, for instance, the old lady, who when told by telephone how to use the dial on her instrument, said emphatically to the instructor, " Young man, if you want to twiddle this thing, come and twiddle it yourself!" During the next few years the Post Office efforts were directed towards opening automatic exchanges in the other parts of the city, and with the conversion of the Leith exchange in July, 1936 the mechanisation of the system was completed.

REMARKABLE GROWTH

The growth of telephones in the Edinburgh local area has been one of the most rapid in Great Britain. From its humble beginning with the clumsy equipment of 1879 the system grew to 40,000 telephones in 1937 and by 1958 to nearly 100,000 telephones rented by 66,000 subscribers. The record year before then for growth in Edinburgh was 1956 when 6,345 new telephones were connected.

With the city so obviously telephone-minded, there has always been a keen interest in new methods of working; and indeed as far back as 1937 it was realised by the Post Office experts and by quite a number of others that the existing system of five digit numbers would be exhausted within measurable time. In that year detailed planning for a change of system began; but this was interrupted by the second World War. Then in 1945—at the war's end—it was decided to adopt " director " working: this incorporates the use of the first three letters of the exchange name followed by a four digit number, thus giving in effect a seven digit numbering range. And that is Edinburgh's system today.

Considerable difficulties had to be faced in this operation, which by 1958 was the only transfer of the kind ever to be undertaken in the United Kingdom. The provision of accommodation to house the new equipment, for one thing, was an acute problem. In addition, there were serious limitations to the choice of exchange names, which in director working are an integral part of the automatic routing arrangements. The numerical equivalents of the first three letters of the exchange names are in effect a routing code and these could not clash with the numbering ranges in use in the prevailing non-director system. Lastly, the names chosen had to be appropriate to the district or, if this were not possible, provide a strong local connection. In the final outcome it has been possible to find names suitable for each requirement, but not always without some passing criticism. For example, when the title " Fountainbridge " was being considered for the new exchange of that name, it was suggested that in Scotland " FOU " was capable of but one interpretation.

THE TELEPHONE SERVICE IN 1963-64

As these words are written in 1963 the Edinburgh Telephone Area, with headquarters in Queen Street, covers a territory of 2,615 square miles. South of the Forth it includes a little of Lanarkshire, almost the whole of West Lothian and Midlothian, all East Lothian, most of Peebleshire, almost all Selkirkshire, most of Roxburghshire and Berwickshire and even a small portion of Northumberland. To the north it covers much of Fife and a little of Kinross-shire.

There are 164 telephone exchanges in the Area, comprising 153 automatic exchanges serving 158,000 telephones; 11 manual exchanges with 13,000 telephones; and six auto-manual switchboards for the control of trunk traffic, two in Edinburgh, (one in Rose Street and the other at Fountainbridge) and the others at Kirkcaldy, Galashiels, Bathgate and North Berwick. Edinburgh, with 22 telephones per hundred of the population, possesses the greatest telephone density outside London. It is, therefore, worth recording here that in March, 1964 the Postmaster General said in answer to a House of Commons question that 32 per cent of the private dwellings in the area served by the Edinburgh automatic system had telephones.

At July, 1963 the staff on the Telephone Manager's payroll totalled 2,450 including an engineering force of 1,296 and 402 clerical and associated grades, plus 734 operating staff and their supervisors employed in the Edinburgh Exchanges and the Penicuik Exchange. While the Telephone Manager is responsible for the provision, maintenance and operation of all telephone plant throughout the Area, the Head Postmasters other than the Head Postmaster, Edinburgh—there are 14 Head Postmasters' Districts wholly or partly in the Edinburgh Telephone Area—act as local agents of the Telephone Manager for telephone matters within their districts and exercise local control over the operating and supervisory staff employed at the various switchboards in their district. This staff totals some 320.

The Telephone Manager's main responsibility is of course the administration of the telephone service within his Area; and in this he is assisted by technical, specialist, and clerical staff under senior controlling officers who, with the Telephone Manager, constitutes a local Management

Board. But he has other duties. He is responsible for the provision and maintenance of telegraph plant, postal plant and electric light, power and heating plant in all Post Office buildings within his Area. He provides and looks after private wires and telex and teleprinter services, and also has similar responsibilities for radio and television links for both the B.B.C. and the Scottish commercial television service (S.T.V.).

HER MAJESTY'S STATIONERY OFFICE

One of the important governmental services in any country is the supply of information. In the United Kingdom, although a large amount of information is sent out by the Central Office of Information, the Scottish Information Office and the Information Sections of the various government departments, a considerable part of the burden falls on Her Majesty's Stationery Office. Thus at Government bookshops in Edinburgh the man in the street may buy a choice of printed matter, from reports of parliamentary debates to reports of Government Commissions of Inquiry, and from official statistics on housing to guides to ancient and historic monuments.

H.M. Stationery Office, Edinburgh was opened on 12th March, 1906 to provide stationery and printing services for Government Offices in Scotland, and six years later a bookshop was also opened. Before this it had been the practice for Government publications to be sold only by agents, but when the contract with the Edinburgh agent (Oliver and Boyd) lapsed in 1911 it was decided to open this, the first Government bookshop in the United Kingdom. The success of this experiment in Edinburgh led to the establishment of Government bookshops in London, Belfast, Cardiff, Manchester, Birmingham and Bristol.

The passing of social legislation in 1908 and 1911 led further to an increase in the activities of the Stationery Office (distribution of Insurance cards, etc.) and the original staff of five was increased, as it was again in 1922.

After 1922 there is little to record till 1938 when the Reorganisation of the Offices (Scotland) Act centred Scottish administration in Edinburgh, and this involved the transfer from London of staffs of the main Scottish departments and an increase in ministerial functions. The total staff in the Stationery Office, Edinburgh then was 78. But by the spring of 1966 it was 334 (including its printers); which is itself a measure of the increase in Scottish activities and of how the Stationery Office has had to keep pace with these activities as a common service department.

The increase is reflected in new buildings also. In 1950 a big new warehouse was opened on the Sighthill Industrial Estate, the first pre-stressed concrete multi-storey building, as far as is known, in Europe. In 1951 a bindery was set up to cater for the binding requirements of the National Library of Scotland. And from 1st April, 1963 the Stationery Office has had its own printing press in Scotland, through its purchase of the Edinburgh printing works of J. and J. Gray.

The Edinburgh office serves all Government departments in Scotland. Its main functions are to publish officially for Scottish departments and to sell Government publications to the public and the bookselling trade; to supply not only Government departments but (exceptionally) certain non-departmental organisations in Scotland with stationery, printing and binding, published books, periodicals, office machinery and office requisites (except furniture); and to provide centralised services of duplicating, photographic reproduction, addressing and distribution. The Scottish point of view is represented at headquarters in London by the Director at regular conferences and no decision on Scottish matters is made there without consulting him.

The main offices and the duplicating section are situated on the Sighthill Industrial Estate but there is a small duplicating section in St. Andrew's House to meet the urgent requirements of the four main Scottish Departments, whose work we studied earlier. Stationery, office requisites, printing papers, departmental forms, office machines and forms used by Returning Officers in Scotland for Parliamentary elections are all kept in the warehouse at Sighthill, and here too are the bindery and an office machinery repair shop.

The Government Bookshop in Castle Street is both retail and wholesale. A large proportion of the retail business is conducted by mail order and periodicals are sold mainly by subscription. Customers can register standing orders for all publications on particular subjects in which they are interested under several hundred subject headings.

When the bookshop was first set up it was restricted to the sale of Government publications; but it now sells publications of the United Nations and its agencies and of certain other inter-national agencies such as the European Economic Community, the International Monetary Fund, and the International Atomic Energy Agency. It also acts as agents for the publications of the Canadian, United States and Italian Governments.

The number of separate titles produced by the Stationery Office each year exceeds 6,000 and these publications are in every sense a very mixed bag. At one extreme there are single leaf Statutory Instruments sold for a few coppers and at the other expensively printed and bound volumes costing maybe 15 guineas. They include some which only sell a few hundred copies and others whose sales run into six figures, while a few sell more than a million.

Hansard is perhaps the best known of the Parliamentary series of publications. This series includes many unexciting and little-read reports and papers, but others convey the views and decisions of Government on important public issues and provide headlines for the newspapers. The non-Parliamentary series are even more diversified. They include numerous technical books on agriculture, health and welfare; science and technology; finance and trade; architecture and buildings; and education and careers. In addition the Stationery Office has published for the national museums outstanding books in the fields of the fine and applied arts, history and archaeology. In Edinburgh it acts as publisher for the

Scottish departments over a wide range of subjects, and the range keeps widening.

The book bindery at Sighthill was established to serve the National Library of Scotland's special needs in the field of general library binding and rebinding, and of special importance, the rebinding and repairing of books and manuscripts classified as " rare and valuable." The Stationery Office in Edinburgh also orders printing and binding for all Government departments in Scotland and normally places the orders with Scottish contractors under long-term contract. It stocks about 1,000 different items of paper, stationery office requisites and office machinery in the H.M.S.O. warehouse for issue to government departments, along with departmental forms for the Inland Revenue, the Procurator Fiscals and other officials. The annual tonnage despatched from the warehouse is about 3,000 tons.

THE CIVIL SERVANTS

The Civil Service in Edinburgh is part of a single national service, and entry to permanent posts is controlled by the Civil Service Commission in London. Entrants may thus come from any part of the United Kingdom. Nevertheless, in practice most of the civil servants in Edinburgh are Scots, though the proportion of non-Scots tends to rise in the higher ranks. But even in the administrative class graduates of the four Scottish Universities predominate, with Edinburgh and Glasgow (as the two largest) naturally supplying more senior civil servants than the other two. Before the last war, and even more before the 1914 war, a higher proportion came from Edinburgh than from the other Scottish Universities, but since 1945 the leading place has been taken by Glasgow.

A Civil Servant's life in the city is not unlike that of any other office worker. Such matters as hours of attendance and pay are regulated in accordance with the 1955 Report of the Royal Commission on the Civil Service. Most of the Secretary of State's staffs, like other civil servants in Edinburgh (except Post Office staff), work normal office hours, now organised in a five-day 40-42 hour week. Those in the highest grades have to spend a good deal of time in London, especially when Parliament is sitting.

As regards conditions of work, the big offices, such as St. Andrew's House itself and the outlying buildings at Saughton and Sighthill, have canteens which are largely patronised by the staff employed there. Many civil servants, however, prefer to go home for the mid-day meal since Edinburgh seems rather like the 18th century London of Hugo Meynell, who claimed that London's chief advantage was that a man was always so near his burrow.

The private interests of the civil servants of Edinburgh, as we should expect, are as diverse as those of any other body of people of similar size. They tend to form and join clubs to further these interests, either with their office colleagues or with their local neighbours. Golf, ski-ing, bird watching, gardening, Burns clubs, amateur theatricals, photography, concert going, contract bridge and canasta—all these and many other leisure pursuits are followed. Clubs of departmental colleagues are indeed so numerous and varied that they range from motoring associations and religious societies to garden guilds, football clubs and other sports. These certainly have their attractions. The central organisation for the whole of the Civil Service is the Civil Service Sports council with headquarters in London, but a local wing of this body—established in Edinburgh—has been successful in acquiring a site at Muirhouse which it has equipped with a pavilion as playing fields for various outdoor games.

An association with a much longer history has also for many years catered for the needs of civil servants in sickness. This is the East of Scotland Civil Service Nursing Association, membership of which ensures that for moderate charges excellent medical, surgical and nursing services are available at the Association's own nursing home.

As regards spiritual needs, the Edinburgh civil servants cannot be very different from the population at large. But they do have chaplains. For the large offices at St. Andrew's House, Saughton and Sighthill the minister of the established Church of Scotland within whose parish they lie acts as chaplain; and also among the staff in these offices there are undenominational Christian fellowships.

CHAPTER 10

THE DEFENCE SERVICES

A NATION'S history is preserved in the records of Scotland; and throughout that history rings the clash of armour and the stirring music of fife, bagpipe and drum. Today, although the control and composition of the defence forces have radically changed in recent years, the martial music can still be heard, and the uniforms of navy and air force blue, khaki and tartan still ornament the city streets. For the capital city is the headquarters of Scottish Command. In the waters of the Firth of Forth (whose Lord High Admiral is by ancient custom the Lord Provost of Edinburgh) the ships and men of the Royal Navy go about their business under the command of the Flag Officer, Scotland and Northern Ireland, though his office lies on the Firth's northern shore. The Royal Air Force on the other hand has its headquarters at Turnhouse, the airfield which also serves the civil transport needs of those who live in Edinburgh or visit the city by air.

THE ROYAL NAVY

Edinburgh's principal associations with the Royal Navy are threefold. Nearby, centred on Rosyth Dockyard and Port Edgar, is Scotland's main naval base with nearly 4,000 Servicemen, as these words are written, and over 7,500 civilian workers; there is also a flourishing contingent of the Royal Naval Reserve and of Sea Cadets within the city itself; and finally the senior Service takes its rightful place in ceremonials connected with the capital.

The Royal Navy's association with the Forth area began in the early days of the century, when the growth of the German High Seas Fleet caused the Government of the day to look for a site for a northern naval repair yard. The land was acquired in 1902, and after experiments to determine how to build a dockyard on the ooze of the River Forth, construction was begun a few years later. The original grandiose plans for a full-scale naval base were never realised because World War I made too many demands on men, money and material; but the main works had been completed just in time to repair the damaged battleships and battlecruisers after Jutland.

Ten years later, in an atmosphere of retrenchment and economy, the dockyard was abruptly closed down. But in another decade, the wheel of Rosyth's fortune again spun round. Once again new houses were feverishly built for additional workers, and the dockyard was brought progressively into action as the swastika threw its menacing shadow across the North Sea. By the end of World War II, Rosyth Dockyard's considerable potential was being used to the full, and every kind of warship was being refitted there. In this decade it has been further developed as the nuclear submarine refitting base for the United Kingdom.

Nowadays, most of the dockyard's civilian labour force is drawn from the immediate hinterland, but during its brief history it has provided employment for some hundreds of Edinburgh people. In 1945, the number of Edinburgh workmen travelling daily to the dockyard was 500; this figure has since dropped and finally steadied but was still over 300 in 1963. In addition, about 150 office workers engaged in professional and clerical work have their homes in Edinburgh.

In recent years, the provision of married quarters has tended to concentrate Service families in an area close to the dockyard, but it is interesting to note that at the time of writing more than 100 naval families are domiciled in official hirings in Edinburgh and, in addition a number of Service officers and men have settled permanently in the city. The city is, of course, the focus of interest for all warships attached to, or visiting, the Forth area; which is why sailors using the night accommodation facilities and other amenities of the Royal Edinburgh Institute have numbered as many as 18,000 in one year.

An account of the Royal Navy's association with Edinburgh would not be complete without reference to the minesweepers which operated so gallantly during both world wars from Leith and Granton. In peace-time, the technique of minesweeping in the Royal Navy has been kept alive by being based on Edinburgh's doorstep at Port Edgar, where both minehunting and minesweeping squadrons are concentrated. Also based on Port Edgar are the ships of the Fishery Protection Squadron.

ROYAL NAVAL RESERVE

The history of H.M.S. *Claverhouse*, the Forth Division of the Royal Naval Reserve, now centred in Granton Square, started in 1913 when a small outlying unit of the Clyde Division, R.N.V.R. was formed in Leith. By 1914 it had grown to a strength of eight officers and 100 men, most of whom served with the Royal Naval Division in the first World War.

The Reserve was reconstituted in 1921 and a year later the monitor M23 was converted to a drill ship and towed to the West Old Dock, Leith, where she was commissioned as H.M.S. *Claverhouse*. She was to serve the Reserve until she was scrapped in 1959. The establishment at Leith grew during the '20s; training facilities were increased; and at mobilisation in 1939 there were 33 officers and 400 ratings available for immediate service. Of these, five officers and 30 ratings were killed on active service.

In 1946 H.M.S. *Claverhouse* returned from her war-time duties and from then onwards the Division grew in strength. A motor minesweeper was acquired in 1949, and this was replaced by a coastal minesweeper five years later; both vessels bore the name H.M.S. *Killiecrankie*. They were also among the first craft to be manned entirely by reservists in peacetime; the latter became a member of the 101st Minesweeping Squadron. The emphasis of the training and purpose of the Reserve thereafter became the provision of minesweeper crews. The late 1950s also brought in more exercises with the Royal Navy and regular participation in N.A.T.O. exercises. It should be added here that the 101st Minesweeping Squadron later became the 10th.

A branch of the Women's Royal Navy Volunteer Reserve was formed in 1952 and added to the strength of *Claverhouse.* Later in the same decade a detachment of the Royal Marine Forces Volunteer Reserve was started. Both these sub-units have since shown a healthy rate of growth.

Today, having become in 1958 the Royal Naval Reserve, the organisation continues to train civilian volunteer officers and ratings to take their place in the Fleet in times of emergency. Men do a minimum of 80 drill hours and 14 days continuous training a year; women do somewhat less. The drills take place in the headquarters in Granton Square and the continuous training in either H.M.S. *Killiecrankie* or in ships of the Fleet and naval shore establishments. H.M.S. *Claverhouse* thus plays a quiet but active role in the city's life.

One of the two Naval aides-de-camp to the Lord High Commissioner at the General Assembly has, in recent years, been provided by the Division. H.M.S. *Killiecrankie* has had the honour of escorting H.M.Y. *Britannia* when Her Majesty the Queen visited Edinburgh, and the berthing party for the Royal Yacht was provided by the Royal Naval Reserve when *Britannia* came to Leith and Granton. *Killiecrankie* also formed part of the escort for K.N.M. *Norge* when King Olav came to Edinburgh in 1962. The strength of the Division in 1963 was 50 officers, 9 W.R.N.S. officers. 190 ratings and 45 W.R.N.S.

SEA CADETS

Edinburgh has four Sea Cadet Units, each with a following of 30 to 40 youths. The object of the organisation is to give sea training to boys between the ages of 12 and 18 years, and the high standard required in the Corps develops in its members such qualities of leadership, devotion to duty and self respect that by all the evidence they become reliable and useful members of any community. The Sea Cadet Corps as a whole is controlled by the Sea Cadet Council for the Navy League and is a voluntary youth organisation and not a pre-Service unit. Between them, however, the Units send from 12 to 15 Cadets annually to make their careers in the Royal Navy, the R.N.R., the Merchant Navy or the Fishing Fleet. Units parade at their respective headquarters once or twice a week. At their disposal are a variety of boats loaned by the Admiralty and kept at Leith. Weekend cruises and an annual summer cruise to the Continent are organised for the boys. They are encouraged to take part in every type of sporting activity, and also Cadets not only go to sea every year for training cruises in H.M. Ships but attend courses in R.N. establishments. For many boys this has undoubted attractions, and indeed many of the leading Edinburgh schools have as part of their curriculum, training in the Combined Cadet Force (Naval Section).

ROYAL NAVAL AUXILIARY SERVICE

In 1952, the Royal Naval Minewatching Service was inaugurated, and in 1962 it became the Royal Naval Auxiliary Service. This uniformed voluntary service is operated and administered by the Royal Navy. Recruits are trained to carry out duties in direct support of the Royal Navy in wartime, these duties including the spotting and fixing of parachute mines dropped from aircraft, assistance in the Naval Control of Shipping organisation, operating telephone and R/T communications and many other duties connected with the shore support of the Fleet. There is an afloat section, and in summer months training is carried out in the Firth of Forth in small vessels manned entirely by the Naval Auxiliary Service. In Edinburgh, the enrolled personnel numbers about 100.

CEREMONIAL

Naval and Naval Reserve contingents for many years have regularly taken part in Edinburgh's annual national ceremonials, but in 1959 the Royal Navy made its first appearance at the Festival of Remembrance, a function held in the Usher Hall on the evening of Remembrance Day. It was also in this year that the Royal Navy and the Royal Marines first appeared side by side in the Edinburgh Tattoo, the former as a Naval Guard performing the Ceremony of Colours and the latter in both modern and old-time drill displays. Recently, Naval bands have played in the fore-court of the Castle.

It can thus be seen that Edinburgh's close association with the Royal Navy is increased through the medium of its own citizens within the Royal Naval Reserve, the Sea Cadets and the Royal Naval Auxiliary Service. By its location, the city provides support for the adjacent main naval base at Rosyth and Port Edgar; and the sailors from these bases and the ships that visit them regard Edinburgh as a home from home, and a place of entertainment for shore leave.

THE ARMY

Most citizens are proud of the regiments connected with the town or county in which they live. As often as they can they flock to military parades and pageants or stay to watch, enthralled, a military band or even a party of soldiers passing by. Nevertheless the feeling persists, said one prominent officer recently, that soldiers are somehow different from ordinary citizens, though soldiers are citizens too, and the origins of the regiments connected with the City of Edinburgh can be traced to the bands of citizens called upon to bear arms in its defence several centuries ago.

Thus the " watch " formed by the burgesses of Edinburgh after the Battle of Flodden led to a paid and standing watch being organised because the ordinary citizens were too " weary and unfit " (as a report of the time states) to carry out their duties after a day's work. This in turn led to the formation of a permanent trained corps which later became the military Town Guard and continued in existence with scarcely a break, though with varied fortunes, until a uniformed police force appeared upon the scene.

Although soldiers were often called upon to assist the civil power in times of strife, many bodies of troops from Edinburgh and the Lowlands were formed for service in foreign countries, frequently in support of the French Kings in their wars against England. Thus the regiment now known as The Royal Scots (and formerly as The Royal Regiment) traces its origin to several bodies of Scottish troops formed for this purpose. Although The Royal Scots were not originally considered as mainly an Edinburgh regiment, they have, since 1881, been perhaps more closely connected with the city than any other, for in this year they were given the nearby barracks at Glencorse as their Depot. However, it is the King's Own Scottish Borderers which for long had the closest association with Edinburgh. Raised in the city by the Earl of Leven in 1689, it was known as The Edinburgh Regiment until 1782, when, as the result of what has been described as " a petty quarrel " with the then Provost, it was refused its former privilege of recruiting at any time in the streets of the city and ceased to be known by this name, though its regimental badge is still the Castle of Edinburgh.

A number of other old Scottish regiments have had connections with the city and are regarded with pride by the citizens. The Scots Guards have their origin in the Civil Wars of the 17th century, being first raised to help the Protestant Settlers in Ulster and later taking part in the defence of Edinburgh against Cromwell, when they suffered severe losses at Dunbar. The Royal Scots Greys, raised in 1681 as The Royal Regiment of Scotch Dragoons, provided a Sovereign's full mounted escot in Edinburgh, together with their mounted band during King George VI's State Visit in July, 1937. It is not generally known that at the restoration of Charles II, a Troop of Life Guards was raised in Edinburgh, and was known for a long time as the 4th (or Scots) Troop of Life Guards. In the museum at Edinburgh Castle can be seen the standard of the Life Guards raised in the city: this is probably one of the oldest cavalry standards in existence.

Some of the Scottish Regiments particularly connected with Edinburgh have their regimental memorials in Edinburgh. These are The Greys' in Princes Street, The Royal Scots' in Princes Street Gardens and the K.O.S.B.s' at the North Bridge.

THE TERRITORIAL ARMY

There has been a long historical connection between the city and its Volunteers since the days of Napoleon when an Edinburgh Volunteer Regiment was formed. Even before this the Artillery Volunteers of Edinburgh and Leith had erected battery sites on the Forth as defences against America's Paul Jones. In 1859 Volunteer forces were formed throughout the country, and these continued until they were converted into the Territorial Forces in 1908.

The City of Edinburgh now has Territorial Army units representing all arms of the Service. Some of these trace their descent from the earliest Volunteers. There, is for example, the Queen's Edinburgh Volunteer Rifle Brigade, with the then Lord Provost as Honorary Colonel, and whose lineal descendant, 432 Corps Engineer Regiment, R.E., still has the Lord Provost of today in the same position. The Queen's Edinburgh Volunteer Rifles were held in the greatest esteem by the citizens and are an example of how closely linked at that period this famous corps was with the life of the city. Its companies were composed of different sections of the population, there being an Advocates' company, several Artisan companies, a Civil Service company, a Bankers' company, an Accountants' company, a Merchants' company, a Freemasons' company and even a Total Abstainers' company. There were also three Highland companies raised mainly by the Highland Society of Edinburgh. The Headquarters of the Territorial Army in Edinburgh is 155 Infantry Brigade which has under command three Territorial Battalions; one of these has its own headquarters in the Edinburgh area and recruits in the city and the Lothians.

The Territorial Army later went back to a volunteer basis since the part-time training commitment of National Servicemen has not been enforced. This has had such a good effect on recruiting that the T.A. in Edinburgh by 1963-64 had a volunteer strength approaching its establishment and was building up the whole time. One or two units, particularly those of the Parachute Brigade, had reached their full strength by 1963 and even had a waiting list of men wishing to join. Recruiting also went up considerably in 1958 when the T.A. celebrated its Jubilee and was honoured by the visit of Her Majesty the Queen and the Duke of Edinburgh to take the salute at the Parade held in Queen's Park of all the Territorial Army units in Scotland. Which brings us to a friendly word for the Army Cadet Force of which one company of the Lothians Battalion is the Edinburgh Company. This Force is about 150 strong and has detachments affiliated to various T.A. units in the city. In addition one Troop is affiliated to the Royal Scots Greys and in 1959 carried out its training at Annual Camp with its parent unit in Germany. A number of Cadets go on to join either the Regular or Territorial Army.

THE REGULAR ARMY

The framework of the Regular Army in Edinburgh, in the earlier 1960s, consisted of two static headquarters, a considerable number of administrative troops and at least one major unit. Headquarters Scottish Command exercises control over all troops in Scotland and is located at Craigiehall whereas Edinburgh Area Headquarters, located in the Castle, is a subordinate formation and is responsible for the command and control of units in Edinburgh other than those Territorial Army units directly under command of 52 Lowland Division. Of the major units, one is always an infantry battalion stationed in Redford Barracks. Frequently, however, a second major unit is also stationed in these Barracks and in recent years this has been a regiment of the Royal Artillery.

The infantry battalion at Redford is the Garrison Battalion for Edinburgh and is responsible for the provision of all troops in connection with the many ceremonial events throughout the area. From this battalion is found the Guard for Holyrood House and for Balmoral, whenever the Queen is in residence, and on other occasions during a Royal visit.

Among the other ceremonial functions which recur annually, there is firstly the General Assembly of the Church of Scotland for which a Guard of Honour is provided for the Service at St. Giles Cathedral. This is a Royal Guard of Honour to the Lord High Commissioner since he represents the Sovereign. In addition, during the period that the Assembly is in session, a ceremonial guard is mounted daily at Holyroodhouse, first parading on the Castle Esplanade whence it marches to Holyrood headed by its pipes and drums or military band in full ceremonial dress. Then there is the annual service held at the Scottish National Shrine in the Castle, for which an inter-Service Guard of Honour is found by the Royal Navy, the Army and the Royal Air Force, and which is attended by their respective Commanders-in-Chief. A Guard of Honour is also provided by the resident battalion on the occasion of the Remembrance Day service.

In addition to these there are many other occasions when military assistance and the presence of troops are required. All of them involve contact, to a varying degree, with one or another of the city's civilian organisations. Thus there are few of the functions mentioned in which the Army has not to make many arrangements with the Lord Provost on behalf of the city, with the Lord Lyon King-of-Arms on questions of ceremonial, and with the British Legion for the annual Remembrance Day service. It must be remembered also that the G.O.C.-in-C., Scottish Command, is the Governor of Edinburgh Castle, an office which requires him to play a major part in many civic functions. Each new holder of this appointment is installed as Governor at an imposing ceremony whose origins go far back in history. Large numbers of the public attend this ceremony on the Castle Esplanade.

Another annual event which demands the greatest co-operation and detailed planning with the civic authorities is the Military Tattoo during the Edinburgh Festival. Held on most evenings during the Festival, this magnificent attraction must have been seen by most citizens during the 1950s and early '60s and, more than any other ceremonial function in which soldiers are engaged, it must have brought the Army before the eyes and attention of civilians, not only from the city but from all over the world.

The Territorial Army too is engaged in a number of events in the city throughout the year. During the summer months on Wednesdays and Saturdays the pipe band of one, and sometimes the massed bands of several Scottish Regiments stage the ceremony of Beating Retreat on the Castle Esplanade, a spectacle attended by large numbers of people on fine evenings. Edinburgh Castle is an official saluting station and all Royal Salutes are fired from the Half-Moon Battery. 278 Field Regiment R.A. (T.A.), Edinburgh's Territorial Gunner Regiment, which has a Saluting Battery within its organisation, has been granted the honour in perpetuity of firing all these Salutes. From the Half-Moon Battery there is also fired the one o'clock gun which can be heard in nearly all parts of Edinburgh and by which the citizens set their clocks and watches to the correct time. The gun is now fired electrically from the Royal Observatory on Blackford Hill.

WOMEN IN THE ARMY

The Women's Royal Army Corps, although small in numbers, plays an important part in the life and organisation of the Army in Edinburgh as elsewhere. The connection of the W.R.A.C. with the city may be said to date from 1917 when some Edinburgh members of Queen Mary's Auxiliary Army Corps went to France where they served as cooks, orderlies, telephonists, storewomen and as helpers in canteens. This Corps was the forerunner of the A.T.S. and its descendant, the W.R.A.C. During the second World War large numbers of Edinburgh girls served in the A.T.S. at home and overseas, many doing men's work as drivers or helping to man anti-aircraft batteries and radar stations. The A.T.S. Book of Remembrance in the War Memorial Chapel in the Castle contains the names of many Edinburgh girls who gave their lives during the war.

There are two regular units of the W.R.A.C. stationed in Edinburgh at Dreghorn Camp. The majority work either as clerks at H.Q. Scottish Command and in the District Pay Office at the Castle or as telephone operators on the several military switchboards; others are employed as cooks, drivers and orderlies. Much of their leisure time is devoted to homecraft activities and most women's sports and games are played regularly. Scottish Country Dancing is very popular and a number of Edinburgh W.R.A.C., both Regulars and Territorials, took part in the Scottish Dancing displays at the Military Tattoos in both the late '50s and the early '60s. It is of especial interest that some members of the W.R.A.C. are enlisted on a new type of engagement, the Type " R " (or Restricted), whereby they may live in their own homes but in every other respect are treated the same as those living in barracks.

In 1948 a Territorial A.T.S. Battalion was formed in Edinburgh. Today its place is taken by the H.Q., W.R.A.C., East Lowland District (T.A.) with its headquarters in the city itself and with Companies at Musselburgh, Penicuik and Dumfries. There is also a Mixed Signal Regiment (T.A.) in which the W.R.A.C. work, train and attend camp with the men of the regiment. Members of the W.R.A.C. in Edinburgh take part in most Army parades and ceremonies, and on such occasions the Regulars wear the new and smart No. 1 (Dark Green) Dress. Normally all W.R.A.C. in Edinburgh, with the exception of those serving in Signals, wear the Royal Scot tartan skirt; members of the University O.T.C. wear the tartan skirt of the Black Watch.

OFF DUTY

We have seen to what an extent the Army is involved in the life of the city; yet it is still true that the citizen regards the soldier as a man or woman whose life is not closely bound up with his own. He regards them rather, perhaps, as the theatregoer regards the actors on the stage: actors are people, certainly, like himself and they provide colour and spectacle for the audience; but the life of the actor is something apart from his own. Nevertheless the soldier does not regard himself as greatly different. He has in some respects a different bearing and outlook on life, brought about by a more disciplined and ordered existence, by training and by a pride in his regiment and service; but he is still a citizen with roughly the same pursuits and interests as civilians.

A number of aspects of his life, however, are very different from the civilian's. There is a great deal more organised sport in the Army, for the soldier must always keep physically fit; there are greater opportunities for voluntary activities in the nature of hobbies or the furtherance of academic studies, since the soldier, unless he is married, has no home to go to in the evenings and facilities for recreation or instruction must be provided to fill the gap left by the absence of home life; and finally, in addition to his pay the soldier not only receives his uniform, accommodation and food virtually free of charge but also, if he is married and living out of barracks with his family, he receives certain additional allowances to compensate him for the fact that he does not obtain free "board and lodging."

THE ROYAL AIR FORCE

Of the three fighting services the Army has the longest standing connection with Edinburgh, for although centuries have gone by since King James IV of Scotland launched the *Great Michael* from his Newhaven dockyard, the Royal Navy as we now know it came to Rosyth only in 1902, and the Royal Air Force is younger still. None the less the R.A.F. in its briefer span has played an important part in the city's life. And the citizens, too, have played an important part in the annals of the Service, for the 603 (City of Edinburgh) Squadron, one of the earliest to be equipped with Spitfire fighters in World War II, achieved a fame and reputation of its own in the Battle of Britain and the defence of His Majesty's realms at home and overseas.

The Squadron's home was at Edinburgh's Turnhouse airport, where one or two unnerving if less momentous matters have since occurred. Here on a dark and gusty night in December, 1959 a Viscount airliner arriving from London overshot the runway, swept through a fence across the A9 road and ploughed its nose into a field 15 yards short of the Gogar Burn. A similar incident had already occurred—in September, 1956 when a Lincoln bomber went just a little further and nose-dived into the rippling waters of the Gogar. No one was hurt on either occasion, but both serve to remind us that after half a century, flying can still be an exciting and eventful activity.

THE BEGINNING OF TURNHOUSE

Flying began at Turnhouse as early as 1915 when the Air Battalion of the Royal Engineers became the Royal Flying Corps, and it was realised in Westminster that several airfields would be needed throughout Great Britain for training and home defence. One was to be sited near the Scottish capital, and according to an apocryphal story still told with glee in Edinburgh, a few official gentlemen were sent north to choose it. Owing to the attractions of the city and the warmth of its hospitality the task took longer than was expected till a sharp reminder spurred the gentlemen to action. Hiring a carriage, they drove to a hill near Corstorphine to survey the landscape and pick out the flattest piece of land they could see. When their considered decision was transmitted to Whitehall, the fact that they had selected a field divided by a stream did not prevent official confirmation of their choice.

This trifling difficulty has been overcome. The Gogar has been channelled out of the airfield to make room for runways long enough to take the latest jets and allow facilities which are shared by the civil airlines, a Ferranti test unit, an Air Cadet gliding school, and the indomitable Edinburgh Flying Club.

When one thinks back to the thriving '30s and the fighting '40s, Turnhouse has become a comparatively small R.A.F. Station, with a staff in the early '60s of some 30 officers and 120 airmen. Apart from visitors, of which there are many, most of the R.A.F. flying is done by the Chipmunks of the Edinburgh University Air Squadron, the Air Training Corps, Air Experience Flight and the Pembrokes, the replacement of the faithful Ansons of No. 18 Group Communications Flight, which maintain a link between Coastal Command stations in Scotland and Northern Ireland. Gone are the vintage Farmans, the B.E.2Es, and the Avro 504s of the Flying Corps days. Gone too are the Wapities, Harts and Hinds of the pre-war Edinburgh Auxiliary Bombing Squadron, created in 1925. A solitary Spitfire remains in state to remind us of the days in 1939 and 1940 when our pilots changed over to fighters to defend our coasts and homes against the Luftwaffe and bring down on the Lammermuir Hills near Edinburgh the first enemy aircraft of the war to be destroyed over British soil.

NO. 603 (CITY OF EDINBURGH) SQUADRON

The famous No. 603 (City of Edinburgh) Squadron was finally disbanded in 1957, but its deeds have not been forgotten. The plaque beside the Memorial Spitfire, the crest in the dining-room, and the signatures scrawled on a section of the ceiling in the ante-room of the Officers' Mess, preserve the memory of those who drove the invader from the Scottish skies, roared into the Battle of Britain from their new base at Hornchurch, and flew to Malta to help to defend the island during the worst period of its blitz in 1942.

To 603 Squadron fell the honour in 1945 of escorting into Drem airfield in East Lothian the three white-painted Junkers aircraft which brought German navy, army and air force officials from Norway to discuss the surrender arrangements. The Edinburgh pilots of this, the " Queen's Squadron" , had honoured their motto: " Gin Ye Daur."

The bustle and excitement of the war years have long disappeared and the Royal Air Force has been greatly reduced in size. The auxiliary airfields of Drem and East Fortune are closed, as is the operations centre at Barnton Quarry; and more than once the same fate has threatened Turnhouse, though 19 squadrons served there at various times during the war, since there are some who would prefer to see the aerodrome's activities confined to civil flying. Some of these critics complained about the noise caused over Corstorphine by the jet engines of 603 Squadrons post-war Meteor VIIs and Vampires. The all-weather Javelin fighters allocated to No. 151 Squadron at Turnhouse in 1957, were even noisier, and as they disturbed the sleep of peaceful citizens as far afield as Dunfermline, No. 603 Squadron was disbanded, and No. 151 Squadron withdrawn.

In the absence of a fighter squadron, it has thus become increasingly difficult in the early '60s to answer the ever-recurring question: " What is R.A.F. Turnhouse doing these days?" And yet in its own way the Station carries out a multitude of tasks, none of them in itself of prime importance, but which together form a formidable list of services essential to the R.A.F. in Scotland. In the Coastal Command structure the Headquarters of 18 Group is at Pitreavie Castle, near Dunfermline. It is, therefore, convenient to have the Communications Flight stationed at the nearest airfield, which happens to be Turnhouse.

THE AIR-MINDED YOUNG

Another R.A.F. formation using the aerodrome is the Edinburgh University Air Squadron, formed in 1941. On the mild, sunny evenings of May and June many a putt is missed on Turnhouse golf course as the two-seater Chipmunk trainers skim down over the first and ninth holes to land on runway 26. The air-minded students, of whom about 20 a year are selected from over 60 applicants, attend mainly at weekends and during the vacation, since flying ground school instruction and summer camps are arranged so as not to interfere with university studies. The normal term of membership is three years, but the student is often able to fly solo after about 12 hours' instruction. If he reaches the required standard of airmanship, he can expect at the end of his second year to be awarded the Preliminary Flying Badge, his cadet " wings." Under the guidance of experienced Royal Air Force regular officers, themselves qualified flying instructors, the best members of the Squadron achieve a high enough level of flying and professional knowledge to be commissioned as pilots in the Royal Air Force Volunteer Reserve.

The ambitions of Edinburgh's youth are further nurtured by No. 12 Air Experience Flight and No. 661 Gliding School. The aim of the former is to give every Air Training Corps first-class cadet in Scotland at least half-an-hour's flying per year. The pilots, mainly ex-R.A.F. officers now living in Edinburgh or Glasgow, belong to the Royal Air Force Volunteer Reserve (Training). In 1959 a total of 2,130 Air Cadets from all over Scotland donned flying gear and were given an aerial view of Edinburgh from the back seat of one of the Flight's five Chipmunks. Volunteer instructors also train the cadets of No. 661 Gliding School. Launched from a winch, the Sedbergh and Kirby Cadet gliders circle the airfield until gracefully brought down to land by their schoolboy pilots.

It is a sign of the times that as more and more people are travelling, the air-space around our cities, like the roads, is becoming increasingly congested. Edinburgh is no exception, for the R.A.F. in recent years has shared the aerodrome with the Meteors and Canberras of a Ferranti experimental unit testing instruments and new landing aids, and with the Viscounts, Vanguards, Dakotas, Doves, Heralds and Friendships of several civil airlines. These all need help from the ground. In the first decade of its existence, Turnhouse offered as guides to the pilot a windsock, a white circle marked out on the flattest piece of grass and a few hand signals. Improvement came in 1928 with the introduction of two-way wireless telegraphy; but the control of flying was left until the last war in the hands of a junior officer chosen on a roster basis from among the pilots of the resident squadron. Nowadays, although the final responsibility for the safety of his aircraft remains with the pilot, the control tower is manned by a skilled team of professional air traffic controllers. On 1st July, 1960 a large sign " Under New Management " on the airfield reminded pilots that on that day the Ministry of Aviation had taken over the control of both civil and Royal Air Force movements in and out of the aerodrome.

TECHNICAL AND ADMINISTRATIVE SERVICES

While the prime function of any flying station is to put aircraft in the air, there are also many technical and administrative services to be provided. Aircraft must be serviced, wireless, teleprinter and telephone communications maintained. The men and women of the modern Air Force must be housed, fed, paid, educated, cared for when they are sick and conveyed by transport from place to place. The welfare of their families must be looked after, and facilities must be provided to occupy their leisure hours. It is not surprising that a fairly large percentage of the total strength of approximately 250 officers and men is occupied on one or other of these tasks, since many of the services are enjoyed not only by Turnhouse personnel, but also by many of the smaller Air Force formations in Scotland, such as the Edinburgh and Glasgow Recruiting Centres, many Air Cadet Corps units, two Movements units in Edinburgh and Glasgow—these handle the routeing of men and equipment travelling to and from Scotland and assist the United States Air Force in transporting

One of the newer suburbs on the north-west of the city, where the houses are laid out in pleasant streets of crescents and squares. Here the city sweeps down to the Firth of Forth at Cramond, with the two Forth Bridges visible in the background. This is mainly bungalow land and most of the houses here are privately owned.

Parliament Hall, in which the advocates now pace up and down, was erected in 1631-40. It was used for the sittings of the Scottish Parliament until the Union of the Parliaments in 1707.

stores for its bases at Kirknewton (near the city) and at Prestwick—and a Maritime Headquarters of the Royal Air Force Volunteer Reserve.

ROYAL AUXILIARY AIR FORCE TRAINING

No. 2 Maritime Headquarters Unit occupies a large Victorian town house in Learmonth Terrace. This building formerly housed No. 603 Fighter Control Unit whose task it was to teach the operational control of fighters to members of the Royal Auxiliary Air Force who could be called upon in an emergency. Changes in the pattern of air defence have brought about the disbandment of the Fighter Control Unit and inauguration of the new Maritime Headquarters. Here a small staff of regular officers and men spend their evenings and weekends training over 250 " Auxiliaries " in communications and in the operational control of the Shackletons of Coastal Command. Most of the trainees are ex-members of the R.A.F. who want to brush up on the skills that they learned while serving and find in the part-time work something of the comradeship of Service life. They receive the full pay of their rank for each hour spent on duty.

Some of the R.A.F. officers and men living in Edinburgh, however, do not belong to the units serving within the city, but travel daily to Royal Air Force Pitreavie Castle, near Dunfermline. Besides acting as a Group Headquarters, Pitreavie Castle in the early and middle '60s was a N.A.T.O. Maritime Headquarters with a combined staff of Royal Navy and Royal Air Force personnel. Its Rescue Co-ordination Centre controlled search and rescue operations in the North Sea and North Atlantic and also the R.A.F. Mountain Rescue Teams based at Kinloss and Leuchars. When storms lash our shores, help is often borne to ships and aircraft in distress by the Whirlwind helicopters and long-range Shackletons of Coastal Command, directed by the operations centre at Pitreavie Castle.

CONDITIONS OF SERVICE

What then of the actual servicemen who man the units in and around Edinburgh? How does their life compare with that of their predecessors in working conditions, comfort, remuneration, and leisure facilities? A recent survey in which airmen anonymously filled in questionnaire forms provided some interesting answers to these questions.

Before the war, the Royal Air Force offered a life of adventure to the care-free bachelor who worked hard, played hard, and sometimes drank hard. On engagement he earned 2*s.* a day, his pay rising to 3*s.* 3*d.* a day when he qualified as a tradesman. Nowadays the main attraction of Service life seems to be that it offers security, with sufficient pay and marriage allowance to keep a wife and family in reasonable comfort. In pre-war times marriage allowance was paid only to officers over 30 and airmen over 26 years of age. Now anyone may draw some allowance for his wife, although the full rates of £7 17*s.* 6*d.* per week for junior officers and £3 17*s.* 0*d.* for junior airmen are paid only when the officer reaches 25 and the airman 21. A married aircraftman on a long engagement can, in fact, earn over £15 a week at the age of 21. A married junior officer after about five years' service has a salary of roughly £1,450 per annum, with an additional £400 if he belongs to one of the aircrew branches.

That the general trend of younger marriages applies also to Servicemen is demonstrated by the fact that in 1963 only one officer and 23 airmen were living in single quarters. When one takes into consideration that there are always at least a dozen names on the waiting list for family accommodation, it is not surprising that "The lack of married quarters" figures most prominently in answers to the question: "What do you consider the worst feature of Turnhouse?" On camp, at the end of 1963, there were 12 officers' quarters and 21 airmen's quarters, while the married families' officer also controlled a further 58 "hirings" in Edinburgh—private houses, that is, for which the Air Ministry pays a rent, contributions being recovered from the occupant. The majority, therefore, find their own accommodation in Edinburgh, although they generally have to pay more for it than they would for official quarters or hirings.

There is little or no complaint about the accommodation provided at Turnhouse for single men "living-in." Even though many R.A.F. stations have been, or are being, rebuilt, the accommodation in the permanent barrack blocks and messes built at Turnhouse in 1939 is still recognised to be well up to standard. Officers, Senior N.C.O.s and most of the corporals have individual rooms, while aircraftmen sleep in six- or eight-bed dormitories, equipped with bedlamps, curtains, bedside mats, and individual lockers and wardrobes.

The food, too, has improved immeasurably in the last two decades. The war-time music-hall jokes about Service cooking would have little meaning for the Turnhouse airman of the 1960s who has at least four choices of meat and three of sweet at lunch-time. In pre-war times 10*d.* was set aside by the Air Force for the feeding of each man. By 1963 the daily ration entitlement for a Serviceman living-in was 3*s.* 9*d.*, and if the man was living out the sum of 6*s.* 6*d.* was credited to him. Until 1947 the choice offered at the serving counter was Hobson's. Ironically enough, the new lengthy menu was due to the period of scarcity and strict rationing when stocks of meat fell so low that they had to be augmented with sausages and tinned foods. It was found that the resulting variety was welcomed and the provision of three or four meat courses no more wasteful than the old system. The only remaining complaint is that the same cannot be done in the evenings when a much smaller number eats in the Airmen's Mess. But with a cooked breakfast, a three-course lunch, and a two-course supper inside him, the airman of today is generally as well fed as he was at home, if not better.

THE "SCOTTISH AIR FORCE"

Notwithstanding the disbandment of No. 603 Squadron in 1957, Turnhouse has preserved its character as the centre of what is sometimes called "The Scottish Air Force." In 1960, to take a recent year, of a total R.A.F. strength in Edinburgh of 311, 193 were Scotsmen, and even later, in 1963–4, some 60 per cent of R.A.F. personnel in the Edinburgh area were Scots. While the soldier in a Scottish regiment has every chance of spending half his service in Scotland, the Scottish airman, owing to the disposition of Air Force bases, generally finds himself somewhere in Lincolnshire, Norfolk, or the Home Counties. In the circumstances, it is understandable that the majority should name as the best feature of Turnhouse " nearness to Edinburgh," " comparative nearness to Glasgow," or " within weekending distance of Dundee, Perth or Aberdeen." Ninety per cent of the Scotsmen living in camp go home at the weekend. Turnhouse, is, therefore, by common admission a popular station—with Scotsmen!

SPECIAL OCCASIONS

The main annual events for the R.A.F. in Edinburgh were for many years the inspection by the Air Officer Commanding in late Spring, the " At Home " Day in September when many Stations invite the public to visit and see something of the life and work of the Service, and a service commemorating the Battle of Britain. The " At Home " Day at Turnhouse, however, has been discontinued, and the Edinburgh public must now travel further afield to R.A.F. Leuchars in Fifeshire to enjoy the annual Flying Display.

The other occasion is more solemn, for on the third Sunday in September the Royal Air Force remembers those who gave their lives in the Battle of Britain. An R.A.F. pipe band leads the parade to St. Giles' Cathedral to pay homage to the fallen. Laid up to rest in the Cathedral, the Standard bearing the battle honours of the City of Edinburgh Squadron recalls the vigilance and bravery of the pilots who defended Scotland in 1939, those who died in the smoke of the London blitz or in the sunshine of the Mediterranean, and those who returned to receive the Squadron Colours from Her Majesty The Queen at the Palace of Holyroodhouse.

CIVIL DEFENCE

Someone observed in 1964 that surely the time had come for a change in the title of The Civil Defence Corps? Prepared for the protection of the public in time of war, the Corps personnel were finding that their specialised training in rescue, first-aid and emergency feeding and shelter was being tested much sooner than anticipated. Splendid assistance was being rendered in various parts of the country during floods, gales, the collapse of buildings, and train and aircraft disasters. The Edinburgh volunteers, fortunately, have been spared these visitations, but whole-heartedly support the many who consider that, having regard to developments as a whole, the title now could well be " Civilian Emergency Corps."

Edinburgh members of the Corps, under a well-known city business man who is Civil Defence Controller, have not been conspicuously in the public eye, but, training to a high pitch of efficiency behind the scenes, they proudly claim that their headquarters building is " one of the finest in the United Kingdom." To make this possible, part of an old Victorian building called Springwell House, which older residents in the area remember as " an institution where unfortunate women and girls were trained to a better life," was demolished to permit of reconstruction and extension at a cost of over £60,000.

Among the units accommodated there are the Headquarters Section—this includes an Intelligence and Operational sub-section—a Signal sub-section and a Scientific and Reconnaissance sub-section some of whose officers have scientific degrees or other appropriate qualifications. There are also sections specialising in rescue, first-aid and welfare. The Welfare Section is staffed almost entirely by women volunteers trained to look after the homeless and arrange emergency feeding. The first-aiders are skilled in the method of resuscitation popularly known as " The Kiss of Life." Contrary to widespread belief, this is far from being a discovery of modern times. It is described in The Second Book of Kings, Chapter 4: " And he (*Elisha*) went up, and lay upon the child, and put his mouth upon his mouth and his eyes upon his eyes, and his hands upon his hands; and he stretched himself upon the child; and the flesh of the child waxed warm."

District centres, strategically situated to cover the entire city in the event of emergency, now operate in the Leith, Portobello, Stockbridge, Morningside and Canongate areas.

The training programme for Civil Defence personnel makes no undue demands upon the volunteers' leisure, the standard training course running to approximately 50 hours and being generally organised on a basis of once a week attendance from autumn to the spring. Those who pass the test and accept a three-year engagement can qualify for a bounty of £10, with a little more for officers. As for the other spheres of Civil Defence—the Warden Service, the Auxiliary Fire Service and the National Hospital Reserve—these provide plentiful opportunity for public-spirited citizens to perform useful voluntary work.

Part Three

THE PUBLIC WEAL

Chapter 11

HOW EDINBURGH IS GOVERNED

FROM as early as the 12th century, if not earlier, Edinburgh has been a royal burgh (burgus regius) holding direct as crown vassal from the King. The earliest extant charter is the one given by King Robert the Bruce in 1329. But even earlier—some time between 1143 and 1147—a charter granted by King David I to the Abbot of Holyrood referred to "Meo Burgo de Edwynesburgh"; and certainly in the roll of the Convention of Royal Burghs of Scotland, which the Treaty of Union with England preserved with the express provision that "the rights and privileges of the royal burghs in Scotland, as they now are, do remain entire after the union, notwithstanding of this treaty," Edinburgh stands in first place.

Today, eight centuries after its erection as the King's burgh, the citizens and councillors of Edinburgh are as proud as ever of their city, its long stirring history, its notable achievements and the leading role it has properly and faithfully played in the affairs of the Scottish nation. The whole civic administration is in fact coloured by the status of Edinburgh not only as the chief burgh of the Queen's realm of Scotland and the focal point of the life of the Scottish people, but as the centre of Scotland's system of local government. To Edinburgh come the members of the family of local authorities when matters of mutual concern are to be discussed. The Convention of Royal Burghs, once the third estate of the realm in the days of the Scots Parliament and still a live and useful force in public affairs, holds its meetings of commissioners and assessors in the Edinburgh City Chambers, and the Lord Provost, inheritor of the medieval Great Chamberlain whose duties we saw, is Preses of the Convention. The Association of the Counties of Cities—Edinburgh, Dundee, Aberdeen and Glasgow—also meets in the City Chambers of Edinburgh. The offices of the County Councils' Association are situated in Edinburgh. To the County Council of Midlothian, whose offices look over Parliament Square to St. Giles, the Lord Lyon King of Arms has granted a brieve of precedency of counties in Scotland, in which it is certified and made known that Midlothian is—with Edinburgh at its heart—the premier county of the realm of Scotland. Finally, on nearby Calton Hill stands the great edifice of St. Andrew's House, the office of Her Majesty's Secretary of State for Scotland and the dwelling place of the central departments of Scotland with which the City Corporation has continuous and intimate relations.

THE TOWN COUNCIL

Today in Edinburgh the Town Council consists of 71 councillors, made up of 69 members elected by the citizens, along with the Lord Dean of Guild and the Convener of Trades. The city is divided into 23 electoral wards, whose names are all drawn from the various districts, such as St. Giles, Craigmillar and Morningside. For each ward there are three councillors. Their term of office lasts for three years and they retire in rotation annually on the first Tuesday in May, when municipal elections take place in the burghs of Scotland. In the counties there are triennial elections when all councillors retire together.

The offices of Lord Dean of Guild and Convener of Trades are of historical interest. Before 1833, when the parliamentary franchise provisions of the Reform Act of 1832 were applied to burghs, the composition or " sett " of the town councils had been fixed, with only slight variation, for several centuries. The setts of the burghs were similar, due mainly to the influence in earlier times of the Court of the Burghs and in later times of the Convention of Burghs. Some authoritative body was required to exercise the powers, right and privileges granted to the burgesses by the charters which created the burghs; and the Merchant Guild came to be the constituted authority for the management of burghal affairs, with the " Statuta Gildæ " laying down rules for the appointment of aldermen, bailies and common councillors. Craftsmen however were excluded from the Merchant Guilds and consequently from the management of civic business; and this brought such trouble and disputation that the craftsmen not only began to associate in guilds also but sought the backing of authority by applying to the town council for incorporation by seal of cause. Thus in 1449 the town council granted a charter to the cordiners, and others followed. The municipal craft charters set out religious duties to be performed, such as the maintenance of an altar in St. Giles dedicated to the patron saint of the craft, as these duties had been carried out by the trades before incorporation; and indeed the Preses of the guild was called " Deacon." A central body consisting of the several deacons and called the Convenery was also established by the craft guilds under a president known (and elected) as the Deacon Convener or Convener of Trades. The craft incorporations eventually won a place in the town council, although the Merchant Guild representatives were always the more numerous, but craft members were excluded from the magistracy.

The Lord Dean of Guild, on the other hand, derives his authority from his presidency of the Dean of Guild Court. This body, which can be traced back to the 16th century, consists of the Lord Dean, appointed by the guildry of the city, and 14 other persons, of whom seven are town councillors and seven electors of the city; but five of these are architects, civil engineers, surveyors, or master builders. The Court has powers and jurisdiction not only under common law but by usage long exercised by Dean of Guild Courts in royal burghs, and is vested with statutory power to regulate building in the city by warrant. The Guildry and the Convenery of the Incorporated Trades still exist and they appoint the Lord Dean of Guild and the Convener of Trades, who are constituent members of the corporation. By a 1965 Act of Parliament, however, those elected to the offices of Dean of Guild and Deacon Convener, though constituent members of the Town Council, cannot exercise any vote at meetings of the Town Council.

The Corporation comprises the Lord Provost, Magistrates and Councillors. There are 11 magistrates, of whom the first is the Lord Provost. The other 10 are called Bailies. The town council appoints a councillor to the office of honorary treasurer, and he as chairman of the Finance Committee is charged with the statutory duty of exercising general superintendance over the council's finances. Besides the bailies, the Corporation has power to appoint any of their number who have held the office of Lord Provost or Bailie to act as Judges of Police in the Burgh Court. Eight Judges of Police have been appointed under this provision.

The Councillors are of course elected by popular suffrage at periodical municipal elections. (A full account of this together with an account of Edinburgh's part in national politics appears in the next chapter).

WIDE-RANGING DUTIES

On some town council committees, it is noteworthy, there are one or two members who are not councillors. A good example of this is the Education Committee which must by statute include members not only with experience in education but with special knowledge of the needs of the various kinds of schools; and among these must be at least two persons interested in the promotion of religious instruction. In fact the Education Committee has nine such members, of whom two are nominated by the University Court and the Educational Institute of Scotland, and seven by the churches. Again the Water Committee, which is responsible for water supply in the landward and burghal areas of Midlothian as well as the city of Edinburgh, has by local act five county members. It is also provided by local act that not less than one-third of the members of the Libraries and Museums Committee—this body was instituted in 1954 when the separate Libraries Committee was abolished—must be non-members of the Corporation.

Such duties are wide-ranging, but so of course is the full extent of the Corporation's responsibilities in fields far outwith the City Chambers. For instance, these have included, from its foundation in 1908 until 1960, the Edinburgh College of Art, whose constitution enacted that the College " shall belong to the Corporation of Edinburgh and be controlled by the Lord Provost, Magistrates and Council of the City, hereinafter called the Governors." Subject to the Governors' directions, the affairs of the College were administered by a Board of Management, under the Lord Provost's chairmanship, representing the Corporation itself and representative of the Royal Scottish Academy, the University of Edinburgh, the Heriot-Watt College, and the Edinburgh Architectural Association.

The College of Art is one of four in Scotland maintained out of Exchequer funds from the Scottish Education Department. But Edinburgh Corporation contributed an additional annual grant of £2,500 to its funds;

the Town Clerk acted as clerk and legal adviser; and the City Chamberlain was accountant and financial officer.

A change came on the first day of January, 1960, when municipal ownership came to an end and the College was given independent status and constituted as a separate incorporated body with the College functions, properties, rights and funds of the Corporation vested in the new governing board. During the term of Corporation ownership and management the College had developed steadily and extensively, gaining such stature and reputation as to merit, with the Corporation's willing asset, the dignity and benefit of its own governing body. But the link has not been broken. The Lord Provost is still *ex officio* a Governor; the Corporation appoints a further five members; and the City Chamberlain has accepted the office of Honorary Financial Officer.

Among the joint committees in which the Corporation of Edinburgh for a long time has been the major constituent member is the Forth Road Bridge Joint Board. This was established by a special act in 1947, bringing together the town councils of Edinburgh, Dunfermline and Kirkcaldy, and the county councils of Fife, Midlothian and West Lothian. In 1964 the bridge and its new approaches, which will be of immense advantage to Scotland's economy, were opened to great acclaim by Her Majesty the Queen.

The corporation is also a major constituent member of the Lothians River Purification Board, set up in 1951. It acts as Sheriff Court House Commissioners for the city and county of Midlothian. The Probation Committee covers the city of Edinburgh and the counties of East Lothian, Midlothian and Peebles. It is represented on the South-Eastern Fire Area Joint Committee embracing the seven counties of Berwick, East Lothian, Midlothian, Peebles, Roxburgh, Selkirk and West Lothian, as well as the city itself. By an agreement approved by the Secretary of State the Edinburgh Remand Home is also used as a regional home and serves the same seven counties. The meetings of the joint committees, incidentally, are held in the City Chambers in Edinburgh, and in each case the Town Clerk and City Chamberlain act as Clerk and Treasurer. They have other such duties. The City Chamberlain is responsible as honorary treasurer to Scottish Command for the business and financial management of the Festival Military Tattoo. The Town Clerk is Clerk of the Peace, Clerk to the Burgh Court and to the Licensing Court. These two Corporation officials are furthermore honorary solicitor and honorary treasurer to the Edinburgh Festival Society. The Lord Provost's Secretary acts as Clerk of the Lieutenancy.

THE LORD PROVOST'S TITLE

The Lord Provost is Lord Lieutenant of the County of the City of Edinburgh. But although he has long been entitled to the style " Right Honourable," it so happens that several years ago, in the time of Lord Provost Gumley, there was some controversy as to whether the words " Right Honourable " should be prefixed to his name or to his office, and the matter was referred to the Lyon Court, where searches were undertaken by the present Lord Lyon King of Arms. Particular regard was paid to the registration of Lord Provost Charles Lawson in 1863, when the issue was decided. An interlocutor was issued allowing the style of Rt. Hon. to be prefaced to the name, and the Lord Lyon was authorised to issue letters patent authorising the style and title to be used in this way. Lord Provost Gumley in turn presented to the Lyon Court an application to matriculate his own name and style and, no formal objection having been raised by the Scottish Office, he was matriculated in the style " The Right Honourable Sir Louis Gumley, Lord Provost of Edinburgh." In the processional list issued by the Court of the Lord Lyon for the ceremonial to be observed when Her Majesty the Queen was proclaimed at the Mercat Cross of Edinburgh on 8th February, 1952, the Lord Provost was styled " The Right Honourable James Miller, Lord Provost."[1] But there is still lack of agreement, since the Scottish Office uses a different order. The Lord Provost's style in 1964, according to the Scottish Office, was " Duncan M. Weatherstone, Esq., the Right Honourable the Lord Provost of Edinburgh." And there the matter rests in amicable difference.

CEREMONIAL

There are several ceremonies—all part of the pageantry of the capital city of Her Majesty's realm of Scotland—in which the Lord Provost, bailies and councillors take part as the representatives of the corporate community of the Queen's burgh. On these occasions the councillors are attended by the City Officer and his assistants, carrying the mace and sword. The mace of Scots silver was made by an Edinburgh goldsmith, George Robertson, in 1617; but the story of these emblems goes farther back.

In the charter granted by King James VI in 1609, when reference was made to the carrying of bundles of rods and ensigns before the magistrates as signs and tokens of their magistracy, it was ordained by His Majesty's will that in all time coming the Provost and his successors should have the privilege of bearing before them a sword sheathed in velvet; and indeed a sword was in fact presented to the city by King Charles I in 1627. By another ancient custom the halberdiers wearing their traditional liveries precede the town council in procession. In the unsettled days of the Regency early in the 16th century there were such frequent disturbances in the streets when the rival houses of Hamilton and Douglas chanced to meet, that in 1540 four men with halberds were hired to accompany the Provost as he went about his ways " within this toun this troublis tyme." Today on ceremonial occasions the town council in procession is also led by a party from the Society of High Constables of Edinburgh, made up of the Moderator and office-bearers. Each carries a baton and bears with him yet another old tradition; for the High Constables, founded in

[1] In October, 1964 Sir James Miller, as he duly became, achieved the unique honour of adding the Lord Mayoralty of the City of London to his Edinburgh Lord Provostship.

1611, are the old town guard, of which the Provost was commander, and which, until the establishment of a police force in 1805, was the town watch.

The Lord Provost's badge and chain of office in use today was first worn by Lord Provost Sir Mitchell Thomson in 1899, when the freedom of the city was conferred upon H.R.H. the Prince of Wales, later King Edward VII. It is insured for £15,000. The Lady Provost also has a chain, set with garnets and clusters of Scots pearls, presented in 1935 by the women citizens of Edinburgh. But these are not the only jewels in the city's keeping. There is, for instance, the very valuable Rosebery sapphire pendant, set with diamonds and a large drop pearl. This resplendent gift was presented to the city in November, 1956. Originally it had been bequeathed by the Countess of Rosebery, mother of the present Earl, to her daughter, Lady Sybil Grant, who in turn bequeathed it to the city for the Lady Provost's use. In making the presentation, the Earl spoke of the feeling of honour and pride his family felt about the long association between the house of Rosebery and the city of Edinburgh. As for the Lord Provost, the Bailies, the Honorary Treasurer, the Lord Dean of Guild and the Convener of Trades, all of these have chains and silver batons of office, while the common councillors have ebony batons with silver mountings. The Town Clerk and the City Chamberlain, who attend all civic ceremonies in their robes of office, also carry batons.

The Town Clerk has the city records in his care, notably the charters granted during the centuries by the sovereign overlords to the town council, and the old minutes of proceedings from which extracts, compiled by the city archivist, are published from time to time. It is the Town Clerk who is concerned in the ceremonial of the presentation of the Freedom of the City to eminent persons who, in one way or another, have rendered high service or brought honour to the city or nation. It is the highest honour in the disposal of the town council and it is bestowed only upon people of great distinction. The youngest burgess as these words are written is His Majesty King Olav V of Norway, whose State Visit to the United Kingdom in 1962—with Edinburgh providing the setting for this splendid and spectacular occasion—we have already applauded. It was the wish of the late King Haakon VII, father of the present King, that in some way like this the people of Norway should express their gratitude for the warm hospitality and true friendship with which Norwegians were received in Scotland during the dark days of the war; and certainly Edinburgh appreciated our own Queen's happy thought that the historic capital of her hereditary kingdom of Scotland—Norway's nearest neighbour over the North Sea—should be the place to greet King Olav.

In the event the Corporation played a conspicuous part in the many ceremonies and celebrations which followed the King's arrival in the port of Leith. The Lord Provost, then the Right Honourable Sir John Greig Dunbar, and the Magistrates, attended by the Town Clerk and City Chamberlain, presented an address of welcome to the King in the Throne Room of the Palace of Holyroodhouse. Thereafter for days the scenes were so magnificent that when the State Visit ended the *Scotsman* commented:

> Edinburgh has never seen such pageantry, has never been so transformed by the sense of a great occasion which captivated all the citizens. The city is the perfect setting for pageantry, but pageantry alone could not explain such a moving experience. How fitting that Her Majesty the Queen should, in the ancient capital of her Scottish realm, hold out this truly royal welcome to the King of Norway. Her personal gesture called forth a spontaneous demonstration from the Scottish people.

If the burgess roll, in which King Olav's name is now enshrined, and other records are looked after by the Town Clerk, the City Chamberlain is the custodian of the city's treasures, among which are many items of interest and value. In his care are the keys of the city, made for presentation to King Charles I on his visit to Edinburgh in 1629. An entry in the books of account for 1628–9 records " payte to Adam Lamb, Deacon of the Goldsmythe's for two keyis with the cheinze weayand XII once VII drops wecht of silver—XXXVII lbs. VIs. IIIId." There is unfortunately no trace of the earlier keys used when Mary Queen of Scots entered Edinburgh. The present keys are presented only to the Sovereign or the personal representative of the Sovereign appointed by warrant of Her Majesty.

Since her accession to the throne in 1952 the Queen, as we saw earlier, has visited the city on a number of occasions, and stayed at the Palace of Holyroodhouse. On such visits the Lord Provost, accompanied by the bailies and councillors, presents the keys to the Queen, with the words:

> We, the Lord Provost, Magistrates and Council of the City of Edinburgh, have embraced the earliest moment of approaching your royal presence and welcoming your Majesty to the capital city of your ancient and hereditary Kingdom of Scotland and of offering for your gracious acceptance the keys of Your Majesty's good town of Edinburgh.

The keys are borne by the City Chamberlain on a cushion of red velvet edged in gold braid, with embroidered thistles at the four corners.

The keys figure in another ceremony every year. Before the opening of the General Assembly of the Church of Scotland the Lord Provost presents them to the Queen's appointed representative, the Lord High Commissioner, who receives the Lord Provost and Magistrates, the Town Clerk and the City Chamberlain, in the throne room of Holyroodhouse. The ceremony is historic and impressive like all the others we read of earlier. To a fanfare from the state trumpeters the Lord High Commissioner, accompanied by his wife and attended by his purse-bearer and suite, enters the throne room at the same moment as the civic delegation, gowned in scarlet and ermine and preceded by the city officer and halberdiers, enters from the other end of the throne room. Round the walls are the Lord High Commissioner's guests, members of the noble houses of Scotland and people in places of high authority in church and state. These ladies and gentlemen are the witnesses of the ceremony of the keys, which comes to an end when the Lord High Commissioner grants the Lord Provost leave to withdraw.[1]

But there is really no end to the traditional and often charming city customs which have survived the years. At meetings of the town council, buttonhole flowers and sprays are still given to the councillors—a custom going back to the days when sweet-smelling posies were carried by gentlefolk to offset the unattractive aromas of less salubrious times. Another curious custom is that, because of permission granted by the town council shortly after the battle of Killicrankie in 1689, the King's Own Scottish Borderers may march through the city with bayonets fixed, drums beating and colours flying. The regiment may also beat up for recruits in the city. Nor is this the only warlike tradition the city observes. In the year 1665 the town council instructed " the Treasurer to provide a silver arrow to be shot for in the links ", which is why the Royal Company of Archers still holds an annual shoot for the Edinburgh Silver Arrow. In 1709 it was resolved that, upon the returning of the arrow, the council shall give to the person who " claims the same a compliment at the council's discretion." Each year the sum of £5 is paid by the town council to the Royal Company of Archers and the payment is shown separately in the accounts of the Common Good.

The arms of the city of Edinburgh, as they appear now, were recorded in the Lyon office in 1774 from a patent of 1732 as "Argent, a castle triple-towered and embattled sable, masoned of the first, and topped with three fanes gules, windows and portcullis closed of the last, situate on a rock proper—for crest an anchor wreathed about with a cable, all proper—supported on the dexter by a maid richly attired, with her hair hanging down over her shoulders, and on the sinister by a doe proper." The motto is *Nisi Dominus Frustra.*

TOWN COUNCIL MEETINGS

The proceedings of Edinburgh Corporation are regulated by standing orders approved annually by the town council. These can naturally be amended if necessary in order to facilitate the conduct of business. The standing orders deal with such things as the calling and holding of meetings, the order and conduct of business, minutes, motions, voting, appointment of committees and regulating the work they do, financial regulations and other procedural matters.

Corporation business is administered by committees appointed by the town council. Before 1959 there were several statutes which obliged local authorities to appoint committees to deal with particular services; but of these only one survives—the Children Act of 1948 which enacts that a Children Committee be appointed. In addition, the Local Government (Scotland) Act, 1947, requires local authorities to appoint committees for education and finance, and also gives them power to appoint special

[1] The scene in 1956 was painted by the Queen's Limner in Scotland, Mr. Stanley Cursiter, R.S.A.

committees for any of their other functions. The same statute provides that a local authority shall not delegate to any committee the power of raising money by rate or loan. This power is not possessed even by the Finance Committee, which occupies a central position in the affairs of local authorities because it is concerned with *all* the monetary transactions of *all* the committees.

The fixing of the city rate is of course in the hands of the town council, which is required to take into account a report prepared by the Finance Committee on the annual estimates. It is the town council which passes the resolutions to borrow money, and no money may be borrowed without the consent of the Secretary of State for Scotland. Before 1939 Scottish local authorities had power to borrow without ministerial consent if the resolution to do so was agreed by a vote of two-thirds of the members present at a meeting. This partial freedom to borrow was abrogated by order at the beginning of the war, and ever since no local authority has been allowed to borrow money without sanction from a central department conveying the consent of the Secretary of State. This wartime ruling was extended by a series of Expiring Laws Continuance Acts. In 1958 local authorities agreed to give up their former power of borrowing without central sanction, and a section to this effect is contained in the Local Government Financial Provisions Act of that year, so bringing Scottish authorities into line with those in England and Wales.

The Lord Provost's Committee is another interesting and important body. It is often referred to as the Cabinet of the town council because it deals with items of general interest, which concern the city as a whole and are not the particular business of the other standing committees: for instance selection of members to be appointed to committees; on whom should the freedom of the city be conferred; questions of major policy not delegated by statute to other committees; the administrative work of the council committees and departments; parliamentary bills, provisional orders, standing orders; maintenance of the rights and amenities of the city, grants of patronage, and so on.

By these tests alone it is quite clear that to be a good town councillor, and so play a worthy part in the city's complex administration, requires ability, knowledge, and integrity. Here there are safeguards. If a town councillor has any direct or indirect pecuniary interest in any contract or other matter which is being considered at a meeting of the town council or a committee, he must not only disclose his interest but is precluded from even taking part in any discussion and certainly from voting. A general notice in writing to the Town Clerk that he or his wife is a partner, member or employee of a company or firm, is the usual way of disclosing interest. But if it turns out that so many members are disabled that a particular item of business cannot be transacted, then the Secretary of State has power to remove the disability. Abstention from discussion and voting is not of course required when the interest is that of a ratepayer, inhabitant of the area or ordinary consumer of gas, electricity or water, or a person participating in any public service provided by the local authority.

DAY-TO-DAY ADMINISTRATION

The carrying into effect of town council decisions and the day-to-day administration of the municipal departments is undertaken by the Corporation's permanent officials. There are statutes which require local authorities to appoint certain officials—the Town Clerk and City Chamberlain, for instance, the Medical Officer of Health, Sanitary Inspector, Burgh Prosecutor, Director of Education, and the City Assessor. To all of these the town council must pay reasonable salaries, and most of them may be removed from office only on a resolution passed by not less than two-thirds of the members of the town council present at a meeting called for the purpose. Some officials however—these include the Medical Officer of Health—can only be removed from office with the sanction of the Secretary of State. Certain office-holders must also possess prescribed qualifications. The City Chamberlain, to name one, must be a professionally qualified accountant, and the Medical Officer of Health must hold a diploma in sanitary science, public health or state medicine.

The City Chamberlain and other officers prescribed by the Secretary of State are also required to provide security for the faithful execution of their offices and to account for all money and property entrusted to them. They must disclose interest in any contracts entered into by the local authority. But they are not personally liable for any act done in the execution of their duties if they acted reasonably and in the honest belief that they were required or entitled to act in that way. This protective provision does not, however, relieve the town council from any liability for acts of their officers, nor, usually, does it exempt the officers from surcharge under the audit provisions.

Although, as we saw, the town council must decide to pay reasonable salaries to its officials, the salaries and conditions of service of some local government employees are regulated by the Secretary of State; others are fixed by joint negotiating bodies representative of the local authorities as employees and of the employees' organisations. Police pay is prescribed by the Secretary of State and so also are teachers' salaries. The salaries of municipal health employees are regulated by the national joint councils for the health service. In Scotland there are separate joint industrial councils for local authority manual workers, clerical, administrative and technical staffs, probation officers and chief and senior officers; special agreements apply to craftsmen and transport employees. Since their inception the Edinburgh City Chamberlain's department has provided the secretariat for these joint councils.

In 1963 there were some 13,800 full-time and 3,400 part-time employees in the service of the town council, and most of the professions were represented among them. There were some 2,900 teachers and 1,100 police officers. Most of the part-time employees were cleaners and domestic workers. The Corporation is thus by far the largest employer in the city, and indeed is one of the largest administrative units in Scotland.

THE MUNICIPAL DEPARTMENTS

Except in the case of the Common Good, which is administered by the town council according to ancient usage and common law, local authorities possess only those powers and duties which are conferred upon them by Parliamentary statutes and statutory regulations. Transactions and dealings of the town council must rest upon enactments and the doctrine of *intra vires* must always be observed. For instance, the auditor appointed according to his statutory instruction by the Secretary of State must satisfy himself that the local authority possesses powers to execute all works for which payments are made. The greatest care must therefore be exercised by the Town Clerk, as legal adviser to the town council, to ensure that no act or dealing is *ultra vires*, and at the same time the City Chamberlain, who is defined by statute as the chief financial officer, has to see that no payment is illegal. These duties apart, the great number and complexity of the enactments which apply to local authorities place a great responsibility upon these two officials. They are at the very heart of the municipal administration, and are regarded as the principal officials of the town council, with the Town Clerk *primus inter pares*.

Edinburgh, as one of the Counties of Cities of Scotland—the others being Glasgow, Aberdeen and Dundee—is an autonomous local government area within which the town council has sole responsibility for all the local government services. In 1930 the separate local bodies for education, poor law and lunacy were abolished and their functions were transferred to town and county councils. No other local authority provides services within the city's boundaries as happens outside the cities, where the county councils administer education in both the large and small burghs, and, in the small burghs, the other major services as well.

In Edinburgh the whole civic administration is in the hands of the town council. The two central administrative departments are those of the Town Clerk, for law and procedure, and the City Chamberlain, for accounting and finance. These officials, whose ancient offices date back to the very beginnings of local government in Scotland, thus share a comprehensive responsibility for the whole field of the municipal administration. The department of the City Architect is concerned with the construction and maintenance of buildings belonging to all the departments of the Corporation, while the various municipal services are administered by the executive departments acting under the appropriate standing committee—Police, Lighting, Cleansing, Baths, Wash-houses, Parks, Recreation Grounds, Cemeteries, Libraries, Museums, Streets, Sewers, Health, Welfare, Children, Remand Home, Education, Civil Defence, Planning, Weights and Measures, Registration of Births, Deaths and Marriages, Registration of Electors, Valuation of Lands, Housing Halls, Water Supply, Transport, Markets, Slaughterhouses and so on.

Some of these departments are very large enterprises with large staffs, large budgets and a wide range of functions. Housing, for example, embraces both the construction and maintenance of Corporation dwelling houses (of which there were some 37,000 in 1963), letting, tenant exchange, rent collection, subsidies from Exchequer and rating funds, arrangements with housing associations, granting of loans to private persons to purchase and build houses, payment of grants for the improvement and modernisation of houses, upkeep of ornamental garden grounds in housing schemes, shops, garages, and other items. Among the dwelling houses erected under the Housing Acts about 15,000 were constructed between the wars, while 3,500 of the 4,000 temporary houses built as an emergency measure at the end of the war are still in use. (A full account of the city's housing schemes and problems appears in a later chapter.)

The same extensive diversity may be noted in all the larger departments, many of which have transactions and arrangements with outside bodies. The Queen's Institute of District Nursing provides the domiciliary nursing service for the Health Department. The Royal Blind Asylum co-operates with the Welfare Department. The Merchant Company schools too are included in the education administration scheme for the city. Then of course many voluntary bodies and organisations receive grants from the town council in recognition of the work they do for the citizens or of the important part they play in the affairs of the Scottish nation. Among these are the Scottish Tourist Board, Scottish Council (Development and Industry), Edinburgh Festival Society, Scottish National Orchestra, the Royal Zoological Society, Edinburgh Council of Social Service, Citizens' Advice Bureau, and the National Trust for Scotland. The field of civic interests and dealings is thus wide-ranging, and local government plays a considerable role in the public administration of the country as well as being of immense importance to the local communities. In many ways the local services are in fact part of the national scheme of things. The Edinburgh Corporation schools, for example, are part of the national system of education, the Edinburgh police force of the national police force, and the local health arrangements of the national health service.

Quite apart from the financial administration of the executive departments, the town council administers many other funds—the Common Good with funds of £450,000, the Superannuation Fund amounting to £5,500,000, and still accumulating, and some 90 trusts and mortifications with funds totalling almost £1,000,000. The largest and most interesting of these is the Trinity Hospital Fund with capital monies of £550,000, first mention of which is found in a Bull of Pope Pius II in 1460, confirming the foundation of the Collegiate Church and Hospital of the Holy Trinity by Mary of Gueldres, widow of James II of Scotland. In 1567, after the Reformation, Sir Simon Prestoun, Provost of Edinburgh, obtained from the Regent Moray a grant of the college and its lands and transferred all his rights to the town council for a hospital for the poor. Today the income is devoted to paying pensions to the needy. It is also worthy of note that over the years the fund has been augmented from time to time by legacies, and now, under a scheme approved by the Court of Session, the funds are all dealt with as one fund under the name of Trinity Hospital Fund.

Other funds include the City of Edinburgh Educational Trust, which has assets of £65,000, and the £30,000 Royal High School Endowments. Under the Lauriston Castle Trust, the Castle, contents and grounds were left in trust to the nation, and the Secretary of State duly appointed the Lord Provost, Magistrates and Councillors trustees to administer the property. Later, because of the increasing expense of maintaining the Castle and its grounds, the Corporation took power in an Order to give financial assistance from the rates to Lauriston Castle Trust. There are other smaller trusts such as the preaching of an annual sermon against cruelty to animals, and support of scripture readers in city parishes.

Here we must again remember the extraordinary range of the Corporation's functions. It not only acts as a collecting agent in the Edinburgh area for the Scottish Gas Board and the South of Scotland Electricity Board, but it arranges for vehicle and driving licence duties, to be collected on behalf of the Ministry of Transport by the City Chamberlain, as Local Taxation Officer.

FINANCIAL ADMINISTRATION

The Corporation's financial accounts, like those of all local authorities, are audited by a " fit " person appointed by the Secretary of State. The fee is fixed by agreement between the auditor and the Corporation. He is required to satisfy himself about many matters which are specified in statutory audit regulations—sufficiency and accuracy of the books and accounts, vouching of payments, bad debts, rate limitations, loan repayments, bank accounts, title deeds, securities for investments and so on. If, in his opinion, any payment is contrary to law—if for instance any sum has not been brought into account or any loss has been caused by negligence or misconduct, the auditor must report to the Secretary of State, who has power in certain circumstances to make a surcharge upon the person responsible. The accounts of the Corporation both before and after completion of the audit are deposited for inspection by any ratepayer within the city. This is advertised in the newspapers along with a notice setting out the manner in which any objections to the accounts may be lodged and heard. The abstract of the accounts and the auditor's report are then laid before a meeting of the town council and copies forwarded to the Secretary of State.

While there are innumerable financial clauses in the many enactments relating to the functions of local authorities, the main structure of local government finance is set out in the Local Government (Scotland) Act, 1947, a consolidating and amending statute which deals with transactions in land, accounts, funds and expenses, borrowing, audit, and of course rates.

LOCAL RATES

Local rates of one kind or another have been imposed in Scotland for some 350 years, since the days of an Act of the Scots Parliament which required the councils to tax and stent the inhabitants for the relief of the poor. But the pattern of the valuation and rating system which had served several generations was set by the Lands Valuation Act of 1854, and has recently been radically overhauled.

For a hundred years local rates in Scotland, levied on the annual value of heritable property, were imposed in two separate parts—on owners and occupiers—according to the incidence defined in the old statutes. But in 1957 a Government committee under the chairmanship of Lord Sorn, a Senator of the College of Justice, recommended that the divided incidence of local rates should come to an end. This was accepted, and burgh and county rates became leviable as a single rate payable by occupiers only. To compensate occupiers for their increased rating liability, their rents were reduced by the amount of the owners' rates in the previous year. Until then, owners' rates, subject to certain limitations, were recovered by the landlords in rent, and so were an element in the valuation of annual rental.

The Sorn Committee had been directed to look at the valuation system, and it, too, was revised. The old practice of taking actual *bona fide* rents as rateable value was deemed to have been rendered inequitable and untenable by the Rent Restriction Acts introduced after the first World War and the effect of holding rents below cost levels by subsidising from public funds, national and local, the houses built in great numbers by local authorities from that time. The new basis of valuation proposed by the Sorn Committee could not be brought into effect at the same time as the change in rating incidence, because some years were needed by local assessors to undertake the formidable task of revaluing all the properties in their areas. The new valuation system was introduced in 1961.

The objects were to dissociate valuation from actual rents and to promote greater uniformity in the practice and standards of valuation throughout Scotland. Dwelling houses are thus now valued on a basis defined by statute, free from rent restriction, without regard to subsidies, and assuming a balanced market with neither too many nor too few houses for the population's needs. The valuations are to be reviewed every five years.

For the year 1961–2 local authorities in Scotland raised in local rates the sum of £93,650,000 at an average rate of 19*s.* 4*d.* per £ of rateable value. In the previous year the average rate was 23*s.* 9*d.*, although rating receipts were £77,370,000. The drop in average poundage in 1961–2, notwithstanding the substantial increase in rating outlay, was due to the 50 per cent rise in aggregate rateable value under the new system. For many years and for various reasons, Exchequer grants have been paid to aid local government, and the proportion of these grants has risen steadily. Thirty years ago they were one-third of the net cost of the local government services, and this has now risen to one-half. Indeed, for some years, income from Exchequer sources has exceeded rating income, which is why the Government decided to review local government finance in the United Kingdom as a whole. The Exchequer contributions mean that the costs of local government are shared by the national Government and local authorities. Edinburgh, in fact, receives a smaller proportion of grant aid than other authorities in Scotland because of the purpose and the factors in the distribution formulae of certain grants.

In 1946–7, the first full post-war year, receipts from rates in Scotland amounted to £29,170,000 on an average poundage of 13*s*. 8*d*., but within 15 years local government revenue expenditure had more than trebled, despite the nationalisation of voluntary and municipal hospitals and local poor relief in 1948, The reasons for this include of course increases in wages and salaries and prices of materials due to inflation, extensive programmes of capital works, especially on dwelling houses and schools, and the rise in interest rates to more than 6 per cent. People talk about the financial problem of local government because local rates, which are regarded as regressive, have risen steadily and steeply; but this is only part of the greater problem of national taxation which has been taking increasing sums from the taxpayers to provide the welfare, social, defence, and other public services. At the same time there has been a far-reaching change in the distribution of income, especially after payment of tax, and the standards of living of the different classes in the community have altered correspondingly Some people have gained and others lost.

In all this local rates are an important factor, since local government simply cannot be insulated from the great changes during the post-war years in the pattern of the nation's social and economic framework. In Edinburgh the city rate per £ was 8*s*. 3*d*. in 1946–7 and 14*s*. 5*d*. in 1961–2. (It has gone up since). But the noteworthy feature here is not so much the rise in poundage, which is typical of the whole country, as the fact that the rate of 14*s*. 5*d*. was the lowest of the cities and large burghs of Scotland. Out of 24 such local authorities 13 had rates exceeding 20*s*. in the £. Edinburgh's position is the more notable since the city receives no share of the Exchequer equalisation grant which in 1962 amounted to some £18,650,000 for Scotland. In 1958 the Corporation was empowered by local act to allow discount not exceeding 2½ per centum for city rates paid before a date prescribed by the Corporation. By the end of 1962 Edinburgh was the only local authority in Scotland to have this power.

The town council is required by statute to keep an account, called the Burgh Fund, to which all receipts are credited and out of which all expenditure is met—provided, however, that unless the town council resolves otherwise the Burgh Fund shall not include the Common Good and Trust Accounts, which in Edinburgh are still kept separate. The Burgh Fund embraces the water supply and transport undertakings. There are special statutory provisions governing the levy of public and domestic water rates to finance the water supply, and there are also provisions dealing with transport which may become a charge on the city rate only in certain circumstances. A local act provides that the Corporation shall fix the fares so that the revenue may, one year with another, produce the amount of money required for providing the city's transport service. The same statute enacts that, should there be a deficiency in any year on the transport revenue account which cannot be provided for otherwise under the enactments in force, the Corporation shall fix and determine the amount of such deficiency to be met out of the city rate. This means that recourse may be had to the city rate only as a last resort. There is further provision permitting profits on transport to be credited to the city rate. Since 1951 through years of inflation and increasing expenses, fares have been increased on seven occasions and by the end of 1962 there had been no subvention from the city rate to meet increasing expenses. But if rising fares have prevented operating losses, there have been no surpluses credited to the city rate either. The procedure for the revision of fares is now contained in the Transport Charges Act of 1954, which empowers the licensing authority under the Road Traffic Acts to fix fares upon application by the town council.

The City Chamberlain is also under statutory obligation to see that all receipts and sums recoverable are carried into the Burgh Fund and that all expenditure is properly defrayed. The financial accounts and balance-sheets must be framed in the prescribed manner and show clearly certain financial provisions and balances. There are many regulations dealing with such things as bank accounts, verification of bank and cash balances, payments of accounts, issue of stock, and so on.

THE ANNUAL BUDGET

By statute the Corporation must prepare an annual budget of income and expenditure for both revenue and capital purposes of the several accounts of the council, including the Common Good and the public utility undertakings, and showing the estimated deficiency to be met by the city rate. The town council considers the budget and the report by its Finance Committee. It then approves the budget after any revision thought necessary, authorises the expenditure, and fixes the amount of the city rate. Thereafter no expenditure may be incurred unless it has been included in the approved estimates, previously authorised by the town council or, if not so authorised, incurred in an emergency. If this should happen, the expenditure must be reported forthwith to the appropriate standing committee and finance committee, and then reported by the finance committee to the town council for approval. Any expenditure on wages and salaries and other recurring annual expenditure before the estimates are approved may be authorised under standing orders or by resolution of the council.

In Edinburgh the Finance Committee has an estimates sub-committee which has a series of meetings in March of each year, in order to examine carefully and revise the provisional estimates for the coming financial year (which commences 29th May) as prepared by the City Chamberlain and the chief departmental officials. After approval by the sub-committee, the estimates go to the standing committees and Finance Committee in April and to the town council in the beginning of May. This procedure means that the expenditure contained in the provisional estimates is authorised from the beginning of the financial year. Thereafter, when the actual results of the previous financial year are known, the provisional estimates are adjusted and revised in the light of the returns, subsequent

Corporation decisions, and any changes in circumstances which have arisen in the meantime; and then, as final estimates, they are presented to the committees in July. The town council at its last meeting before the August recess approves the estimates in their final form, taking into account the report and recommendations of the Finance Committee, and the budget speech of the Honorary City Treasurer, and thereafter fixes the amount of the city rate for the year.

Throughout each year the finance department and committee exercise strict control of expenditure, and supplementary votes by the Town Council are required for all items not included in the estimates or likely to be exceeded. The greatest importance is attached to this continuous budgetary control, which extends not only to numbers and rates of pay in the departmental establishments, but also to the rents, fees and charges generally fixed by the Corporation for its various services—schools, houses, baths, wash-houses, recreations, market facilities, home helps, and so on. Recently, in order to promote greater efficiency in the running of these services, the Corporation undertook an organisation and methods investigation of its various departments and its administrative arrangements generally. This review was carried out by an official seconded from the Treasury in London, assisted by a team selected from the departments of the Town Clerk and the City Chamberlain. Responsibility for organisation and method has now been placed on the City Chamberlain, in whose department electronic accounting and data processing machines have been installed, and already several processes—pay-roll, suppliers' invoices, and interest warrants and many others have been taken over by this equipment.

The financial year 1961–2 may be taken conveniently to show the gross expenditure of the Corporation rating departments:

TABLE 21

	Revenue	*Capital*	*Total*
Police	1,659,000	£33,000	£1,692,000
Lighting	450,000	220,000	670,000
Cleansing	866,000	57,000	923,000
Baths	101,000	—	101,000
Laundries	81,000	—	81,000
Libraries	210,000	7,000	217,000
Parks	579,000	19,000	598,000
Burial Grounds	33,000	6,000	39,000
Streets	1,080,000	855,000	1,935,000
Sewers	168,000	80,000	248,000
Education	7,042,000	758,000	7,800,000
Welfare	384,000	55,000	439,000
Health	701,000	50,000	751,000
Housing	2,996,000	3,376,000	6,372,000
Planning	58,000	199,000	257,000
Children	235,000	—	235,000
Remand Home	8,000	—	8,000
Civil Defence	37,000	36,000	73,000
Miscellaneous	776,000	86,000	862,000
Water	713,000	147,000	860,000
	£18,177,000	£5,984,000	£24,161,000

The Miscellaneous Account includes many items, such as Registration of Births, Deaths and Marriages, Registration of Voters, Valuation of Lands, Halls and Museums, City Improvements, Weights and Measures Inspection, Public Clocks, contributions to joint boards and other bodies, city publicity, and accommodation bureau.

The capital expenditure for the year, amounting to £5,984,000, was met almost wholly by the raising of loans, which are repaid over periods of years fixed by statute. But certain sums, small in relation to the capital outlay, were met out of the Reserve Fund to the extent of £76,000, a sum made up of items where the loans sanction was exceeded or small special items for which no loans sanction was obtained. Sums repaid by persons who borrowed money from the Corporation for house purchase or building are applied against the capital debt of the Corporation under this heading. A sum of £126,000 received from the Exchequer for classified roads and civil defence buildings was applied against the appropriate capital expenditure.

All the loans transactions and management are consolidated in the Corporation Loans Fund. Into this are paid all the new loans raised for new capital expenditure and the repayment of maturing loans, and the annual repayments from the borrowing accounts of the Corporation. The fund advances to these accounts the sums required to meet their capital outlays. The interest on loans and expenses of management are allocated over the borrowing accounts according to the rules contained in the acts. At 28th May, 1962 the loan debt of the Corporation amounted to £61,350,000. But ten years earlier the debt was only £21,650,000. There could not be more striking witness to the rise in municipal capital expenditure during the post-war years.

At the beginning of the war the Government decreed that no moneys could be borrowed by local authorities except from the Government central lending agency, the Public Works Loan Board. Needless to say, in those stringent and arduous days local authorities spent very little capital. But in 1953 local authorities were once more allowed to borrow on the open market, and in 1955 it was further decreed that they could borrow from the Public Works Loan Board, though only when they were unable reasonably to raise loans on their own credit in the money market. This was still the position early in 1963.

These changes reflect of course the monetary and credit policy of the Government, when the nation's post-war capital investment, because of its magnitude, required measures to fit it into the available resources of the nation. Another reflection of the monetary situation is the steep rise in interest rates during these years, the Public Works Loan Board rates having risen, for long loans, from $3\frac{3}{4}$ per cent in 1954 to $6\frac{3}{4}$ per cent in September, 1957, when Bank Rate was raised from 5 per cent to 7 per cent. In 1962 the current Public Works Loan Board rate was $6\frac{5}{8}$ per cent and Bank Rate $4\frac{1}{2}$. One of the most difficult problems confronting the Corporation and other local authorities in the early '60s has been the raising of loans to meet the high level of municipal capital expenditure of which the greater part goes on housing and education. Within six years—in the late 1950s and early '60s—and with the consent of the Treasury on terms approved by the Bank of England, the Corporation has floated two stock issues, the first for £2,500,000 at 5 per cent 1968–71, and the other for £5,000,000 at 5 per cent 1975–7.

The revenue expenditure of the rating departments of £18,177,000 in 1961–2 was met from three sources. First there was the income collected for specific charges imposed for services rendered to particular persons. These included municipal house rents, fees in certain schools, water supplied for industrial purposes, services of police in the Leith Dock area, recreational facilities such as golf and tennis, the sale of processed refuse and waste paper, the use of baths and laundries, fines for late return of library books, payment for the services of home helps, letting of halls, extracts of marriage certificates, and innumerable other items. Then there were the grants from the Exchequer in aid of local services, and finally the produce of the city rate. These three sources yielded the following sums:

Specific charges	£3,313,000
Exchequer grants	6,903,000
City rate	8,467,000
	£18,683,000

There was a surplus on the account of £506,000, credited to the General Reserve Fund which in 1963 stood at £3,100,000. Of this large surplus £120,000 was from underspending by departments. The remainder came mostly from Exchequer General Grant revision, and also from the yield of the city rate in the first year of the new valuation system. In fact the Corporation did not rate in full for the total budgeted expenditure of the departments, having taken into account the difficulty of carrying out works in the conditions of high demand by all sectors of the nation's economy, private and public, for materials, labour and capital monies.

Exchequer grants which have risen steadily over the years, it should be stressed, are paid towards the costs of local government in recognition of its national importance, the part it takes in the national scheme of public services, and the fact that local rating, because of its regressive nature and incidence, cannot adequately provide all the monies required for the local services. But many people, with long experience of local government, strongly urge that the proportion of Exchequer aid be increased to reduce the rating burden. Others say that a new and more productive source of revenue such as local income tax should be devised for local authorities.

In Edinburgh public funds provided £15,370,000 in the year 1961–2, with 45 per cent of this coming from the national taxpayers and 55 per cent from the local ratepayers. As stated before, Edinburgh's share of Exchequer assistance is below the average for the country as a whole. The grants were made up as follows:

TABLE 22

General Grant	£4,773,000
Housing	807,000
Education (Meals, etc.)	527,000
Police	713,000
Civil Defence	27,000
Welfare (Blind Persons)	23,000
Health (Clean Air, etc.)	7,000
Probation	5,000
Remand Home	2,000
Miscellaneous	19,000
	£6,903,000

Before 1959 the Exchequer made a series of grants to local authorities for expenditure on particular services. These grants were calculated on the basis of a percentage of the actual expenditure incurred. The Government had carried out a review of local government finance, and the subsequent White Paper said this: " The Government do not consider it practicable to devise a satisfactory new source of local revenue, nor do they believe it right to earmark for the direct benefit of local authorities any tax which is now levied nationally." The Government proposed instead the reform of the system of Exchequer grants by the replacement of certain grants in aid of specific services by a general grant and the re-rating of industry to 50 per cent instead of 25 per cent of annual value. The purpose of this was to " give local authorities increased financial independence and to encourage electors to take a fresh interest in local government affairs."

The specific grants thus ended by an Act of 1958 were those for education (except for meals and milk), health services, fire brigades, child care, town planning (other than major redevelopment), and a number of minor grants. In 1959 General Grant became payable in respect of these relevant services. Part of the intention was to deliver local authorities from the close control over them exercised by the central departments because, in grants calculated on a percentage of outlay, every time a local authority spent money it imposed, *pari passu*, a commitment on the Exchequer.

In framing the arrangements for the working of General Grant, the Government directed " that no part should be regarded as earmarked for any particular service, that the distribution of the money be based on objective factors which cannot be influenced by decisions of individual authorities, in accordance with a formula which fairly reflects the needs of individual rating areas and does not make it possible to identify any part of a particular authority's grant as attributable to a particular service." The formula devised is based on population, to which weightings for population location and the number of children under 15 are added, so that larger grants may be given to areas whose costs are inevitably higher than elsewhere.

The Act also provides that the aggregate amount of grant for each period shall be related to expenditure on the relevant services; and it is enacted further that the aggregate amount may be increased to meet unforseen rises in the level of prices, costs or remuneration. There was an initial deduction for part of the national additional income derived from the re-rating of industry, and an addition for a consequential loss of Equalisation Grant. Such a far-reaching change in the grant system could not be accomplished without gains to some and losses to other authorities, and so a transitional period was agreed, during which in diminishing measure the gaining authorities compensated the losing authorities. It was reckoned that Edinburgh was one of the benefited authorities.

Several specific service grants remain—notably police, housing, school meals and milk, civil defence, clean air, probation, remand home, blind persons' employment, and some other minor ones. Separate classified highways grants continue, but, for the maintenance of highways, percentage grant is paid only to county councils. Cities such as Edinburgh and large burghs do not receive any maintenance grant, although they get grants for the construction and major improvement of classified highways. This is a matter of increasing concern because of the need to create highways fit for modern traffic requirements; which is why, in the early '60s, Edinburgh was improving Queensferry Road as one of the tributary roads for the Forth Bridge Road, at a cost of some £400,000 borne entirely by the ratepayers. When Queensferry Road crosses the city boundary into West Lothian County, however, it becomes eligible for a 75 per cent highways grant, an anomaly on which the Corporation has made many unsuccessful representations to the Government.

There is, as we have noted, one important Exchequer grant in which Edinburgh does not share. This is the Exchequer Equalisation Grant, which amounted for Scotland in 1961–2 to £18,650,000. It was introduced in 1948 when municipal hospitals and poor relief were taken over by the state and the former block grant under the 1929 Local Government Act was abolished. At the same time the war-time fire service was returned to local authorities by the Government. The purpose of Equalisation Grant is to ensure a minimum rating resource to all rating authorities, and it is paid only to authorities whose actual rateable value is less than a standard rateable value calculated on a determined amount per head of population. Edinburgh is above the standard.

In 1961–2 the city rates yielded £8,467,000, a total which included contributions by the Exchequer on crown properties and the payments made in respect of railways and electricity. The rate was 14*s.* 5*d.* per £, made up of city rate 13*s.* 10*d.* and domestic water rate 7*d.*, on a mean net rateable valuation of £11,750,000. The net yield of a penny rate in the city was £48,000. The city rates in the post-war period have been: 1946 and 1947, 8*s.* 3*d.*; 1948 to 1951, 8*s.* 7*d.*; 1952, 8*s.* 11*d.*; 1953, 11*s.* 3*d.*; 1954 to 1956, 12*s.* 6*d.*; 1957, 14*s.* 10*d.*; 1958, 16*s.* 5*d.*; 1959, 17*s.* 3*d.*; 1960 and 1961, 18*s.*; 1962, 14*s.* 5*d.* The drop of 3*s.* 4*d.* in the rate poundage for 1961–2 was due to the higher valuation on the new system brought in that year. The rate for 1962–3 was fixed at 14*s.* 9*d.*, a rise of 4*d.* over the previous year. In 1962–3 also there came into operation for the first time a new statutory requirement that charitable bodies be granted mandatory 50 per cent rating remission, which is equivalent to a loss of rating income of some £100,000 a year. At the end of July, 1964 the total rate, including the water rate of 8*d.*, was 17*s.* 6*d.* But another increase was soon to come. At the end of July, 1965 the Town Council approved a rise in the rates to 19*s.* 9*d.* in the £ to meet a £1,530,000 rise to £12,720,000 in rate-borne expenditure expected during the 1965–6 financial year.

TRANSPORT

Edinburgh's transport systems and general traffic are described later. It is therefore only necessary here to summarise recent developments as seen through the windows of the City Chambers.

The Transport Department, which is run so that income will match expenditure, reached an important point in its history in the late 1950s. Since 1919, when the first motor buses were purchased by the Corporation, bus services had steadily played such an increasingly large role in the city transport system that in 1952 the Corporation decided to scrap the electric tramways and operate instead a unified bus undertaking; and thus it was that the last tramcar ran on 16th November, 1956.

The abandonment of the tramways naturally meant a major reorganisation in the working of the Transport department, and the reinstating of 47 miles of roadway after the rails were lifted. In the outcome work went forward rapidly, and at the same time the Corporation took the opportunity not only to reinstate the roadways, but to improve them to meet the growing volume of motor traffic.

In 1961–2 the traffic receipts and other revenues of the undertaking amounted to £4,485,000, which was sufficient to meet the operating expenses, to redeem the remaining balance of old tramway debt, to apply a substantial sum for the replacement of buses, and to leave a surplus of £20,000. This excellent result was achieved in the face of many difficulties. For a year or two the number of passengers had fallen, partly because of the great increase in motor car ownership, partly through changing social habits, (including the stay-at-home attraction of television-viewing) and partly perhaps because of resistance to fares increases.

During the war years the department had shown profits because of the rise in traffic receipts and restrictions on the usual expenditure for renewing the permanent way and replacing buses. By 1947 the Reserve Fund had grown to £1,316,000; but by 1953 the Fund was wholly depleted as a result of rapidly rising post-war expenditure—on wages, fuel oil, permanent ways and bus purchases—having outstripped income. For a time the operating losses were met out of the accumulated war-time reserves, but when these were used up, the fares had to be revised. At the time of writing there have been seven increases in fares since 1951, all of them following wage awards to municipal passenger transport staffs. The wages of platform, traffic and maintenance staff are in fact the largest element in the costs of transport, and awards affecting pay and working conditions have a considerable effect on the financial position generally.

The Corporation has obviously acted quickly and wisely in revising the fares structure, and the department has always managed to balance its revenue account. It need only be added that this problem is not confined to the transport department, for the city rates have also to accommodate similar awards in the other municipal departments. But it can at least be said that several investigations and work studies have been carried out into the organisation and running of the city's transport in order to ensure its efficiency.

WATER SUPPLY

The workings of the Water Committee are a noteworthy example of advantageous and confident co-operation by neighbouring authorities for the discharge of an important local government function. By agreement between Edinburgh Corporation and the burghs and county of Midlothian, the Edinburgh and Midlothian Water Order 1949 made Edinburgh Corporation the water authority for the combined area, taking over the assets and liabilities of the various burgh and county undertakings. The Corporation was already giving bulk supplies to the county authorities, and it was therefore regarded as expedient and in the public interest that Edinburgh Corporation (with a Water Committee), should become the supply authority. Water is supplied to a population of about 590,000, of whom 120,000 are in the county of Midlothian.

In 1964 both industrial concerns and private consumers throughout the whole area were paying uniform charges for their water. The Act of 1949, as amended in 1961, prescribed maximum poundages for water rates in the burghs and county of Midlothian during the first fifteen years. For 1962–3 the domestic rates fixed by the Corporation were Edinburgh 8*d*., Bonnyrigg and Lasswade 10*d*., Loanhead 10*d*., Musselburgh 10*d*., Penicuik 10*d*., Dalkeith 8*d*., and Midlothian County 1*s*. 1*d*.

However, the consumption of water in the Edinburgh area and elsewhere in Scotland has been rising steadily for both domestic and industrial purposes; and consequently, in the early '60s, the question of water supply was seriously engaging the attention of the Secretary of State and other authorities, as it still does. In some places, certainly, the need is urgent. The Secretary of State has therefore directed the Advisory Committee on Water to survey the organisation of water supply and distribution in the midlands of Scotland, where there are many separate water authorities including small burghs. There have been proposals also to take water from Loch Lomond, which could supply large quantities over a wide area. In the meantime Edinburgh and the county authorities, who have been well served by the water undertaking, have gone ahead with a scheme for a new reservoir.

In 1949 the Corporation was empowered to take water into Talla Reservoir from the Fruid Water and Manzion Burn. Weirs were built on the streams and a tunnel was constructed through the hills to convey the water to Talla. By the near mid-'60s a new reservoir was being constructed in the Fruid Valley at an estimated cost of £1,500,000.

COMMON GOOD

The Common Good is the ancient patrimony of the royal burgh of Edinburgh. Until the 19th century, when the burgh's affairs came to be regulated more and more by parliamentary statutes, the municipal development and administration rested largely on the resources of the Common Good, embracing the rights, privileges and powers conferred by royal charters. The Common Good may now be regarded as a relic of these medieval days, but it still has an important place in civic administration and continues to be regulated by the principles of common law.

The Common Good is administered for purposes which, in the Town Council's judgment, are for the good of the community as a whole or in which the inhabitants may share, as distinct from serving the separate interests of any particular individual or class. By an Act of 1491 King James IV " ordinit that the Common Good of all our soverane lords borrowis within the realm be observit and kepit to the commoun gude of the toun and be spendit in commoun and necessare things of the burgh be the advise of the consule of the toun." It is used to uphold the dignity and suitable hospitality of the city, the presentation of addresses to the Sovereign in person, (a privilege granted to Edinburgh), representation at state ceremonials, granting of the freedom of the city, protection and publication of historical civic documents, promotion and defence of the rights and interests of the community, and the acquisition of land and property for the corporate benefit. Among the charter powers conferred on the town council was the holding of markets and fairs, and still to-day the accounts of the Fruit and Vegetable, Corn and Cattle Markets and Slaughterhouses are part of the Common Good. The Waverley Market is now one of the city halls.

The accounts for the Common Good for 1961–2 were as follows:

TABLE 23

Expenditure	£	£
Burdens on properties	440	
Upkeep of properties	1,270	1,710
Expenses of Management		2,000
Markets:		
Vegetable Market	620	
Cornmarket	4,180	
Cattlemarket	24,240	
Slaughterhouse	82,200	111,240
Civil Department:		
Dues to Convention of Burghs	190	
Allowances to Society of High Constables	150	
Public Monuments	520	
Time Gun	90	
City Observatory	220	
Refectory	9,680	
Incidental outlays	220	
Lord Provost's presentation allowance	220	11,290
Donations to Public Institutions		180
Public ceremonies and civic hospitality		18,440
		£144,860

Table 23 *continued*

Income	£	£
Feuduties	11,680	
Rents	1,350	
Annuity	1,000	14,030
Interest on Investments		1,910
Markets:		
Vegetable Market	2,440	
Cornmarket	4,440	
Cattlemarket	27,750	
Slaughterhouse	82,200	116,830
Civil Department:		
Burgess dues, etc.	50	
Public monuments and City Observatory	160	210
Contribution from city rate		11,880
		£144,860

In local acts of 1950 and 1958 the Corporation obtained power to meet from the city rate the expenses of public entertainment on occasions of public ceremony or rejoicing, official reception of visitors to the city, visits at home or abroad by way of official courtesy on behalf of the Corporation, and the conferment of the freedom of the city, so far as these expenses exceeded in any year the free surplus of revenue in that year from the Common Good. It will be noted that the greater part of the Common Good revenue is derived from feu duties on the old Common Good properties. The fund must, therefore, meet post-war expenses with what is largely pre-war income, and in some recent years the revenue account has been in deficit, a situation which could not be allowed to continue. The Town Clerk and City Chamberlain have taken several steps to restore financial balance and safeguard the historic and ancient patrimony of the burgh. It was decided, for instance, that the income tax paid on the income of the Common Good be charged to the Burgh Fund income tax account; which is permitted by the rules governing the unified tax liability of the Corporation, even although the Common Good is not part of the Burgh Fund. By local act the cost of councillors' robes and insignia is now charged to rating account. Many charitable donations are now paid under the relevant statutes affecting, for example, education, children, health and welfare, where the purpose of the charities enabled the donations to be charged to rating under these heads. The Corporation is also now required to fix the dues and charges of the markets and slaughterhouse so that the income will be sufficient to meet expenditure. Before this, the fees and charges for many years were confined within maximum limits set out in schedules to old Corporation orders. By these transactions and others which are contemplated, it is hoped to preserve the financial stability of the Common Good, which in 1963 held funds amounting to £450,000 at balance-sheet valuation.

MISCELLANEOUS ACCOUNTS

In addition to the main financial transactions described above the Corporation had the following intromissions in 1961–2:

TABLE 24

Funds	£
Superannuation Fund	750,000
Trusts and Mortifications	40,000
Agencies	
Local Taxation Licences	1,150,000
Scottish Gas Board—consumers' accounts	215,000
South of Scotland Electricity Board—consumers' accounts	520,000
	£2,675,000

Excluding the expenditure of the joint committees to which the Corporation contributes as a constituent member and the Festival Society which, though a separate incorporated company limited by guarantee, is closely associated with the Corporation, the aggregate expenditure of the town council for 1961–2 was £32,000,000, a figure which gives a good indication of the size of the Corporation's activities.

In 1958 the Corporation was empowered by local order to invest up to one-quarter of the superannuation fund in the stocks and shares of companies incorporated in the United Kingdom, commonly referred to nowadays as "equities." Subsequently, the Corporation invested the whole of the annual accretion to the fund on the advice of the Bank of Scotland, and for the first two years the sum invested was £850,000. Now, under the 1961 Trustees Investment Act, all trustees and local authorities may invest half their funds in equities. Under a clause in that statute the local authority associations in the United Kingdom have established the Local Authorities' Mutual Investment Trust, for the investment of local authority monies. Part of the Corporation equity investment was by means of LAMIT, as the trust is called.

One unusual and interesting fund is the British Empire Games Fund. The Corporation invited the British Empire and Commonwealth Games Federation to hold the games in Edinburgh, though it was realised that the games could not be held without the requisite facilities and financial assistance from various sources. The Corporation resolved to build, as an amenity for the city, a swimming pool of Games standard and a stadium. As it was realised also that these would be of lasting benefit to the city and beyond, they are a charge on the Corporation, which took power in a local order to create a Games Fund, to which a contribution of £15,000 was to be made annually from the rates until the total reached £150,000. More about this appears in a later chapter as do the Corporation's special interests in housing, planning and education.

OTHER POST-WAR DEVELOPMENTS

In the City Chambers, apart from politics, there is a certain pride in the post-war enterprises which the Town Council and their permanent officials have put through. Some we have already seen. Others have included the conversion of public lamps from gas to electricity, and a general improvement of the standard of lighting in streets and stairs, though not everyone likes concrete lamp standards. The cleansing department has introduced electric trucks for street sweeping, organised systems for dealing with waste food and paper and the first specialised plant in this country for the conversion of refuse into compost. Considerable progress has also been accomplished in making Edinburgh—Auld Reekie—a clean-air city, and in modernising the municipal wash-houses now called laundries.

Mobile libraries to serve the new housing areas have been introduced and a Museum of Childhood, first of its kind, has been set up in the Royal Mile. Recently the Corporation, having accepted a request from Earl Haig to take into its care the honours, decorations and other treasures of his famous father, Field Marshal Earl Haig, agreed to establish the Haig Museum in a worthy building in the Royal Mile. The school and hospital library service has been extended. A small library is maintained in the City Chambers, and there is a City Archivist; the Edinburgh Room in the central library has gained a wide reputation as a centre for research on the city's history; the Central Library has been reconstructed and modernised, while sites have been acquired for the erection of new suburban libraries; the new Scottish Central Library in the Lawnmarket is assisted by grants from the Corporation.

In the health and welfare departments there have been many developments since 1948 when the municipal hospitals were nationalised and national assistance was instituted in place of local poor relief. These are fully described in subsequent chapters but a few might be mentioned here by way of illustration: chiropody and laundry services for old people; free transport passes for blind and disabled persons and in 1965 concessionary fares to elderly persons; and co-operation with the University in a scheme for the training of child care officers.

Over the years the Corporation has given increasing attention and money to the improvement and reconstruction of roads within the city. In particular it has grasped the opportunity presented by the abandonment of 47 miles of tramways to provide signals, signs, roundabouts, one way streets, ring routes, and so on. Several bridges have been widened. An interesting development, the first in Scotland, was the laying of an electrified grid in the roadway of the steep and curving Mound, a notorious ice-trap for motorists on frosty winter days. New car parks and off-street parking places are being provided along with traffic meters.

The activities of the parks department have greatly expanded during the post-war years, especially because of the ornamental garden grounds and recreational areas provided in the new housing schemes, where several pavilions have been erected. There has been laid out the extensive ground at the Gyle, Corstorphine, venue of the Highland Show in 1956, and a scented garden for blind people in Saughton Park. During the Festival especially the department pays its usual magnificent floral tribute to the visitors, many of whom now go down also to the Granton-Cramond foreshore scheme, where a lovely stretch of open land and pleasure ground along the shore of the Firth of Forth is being preserved for the enjoyment of citizens and visitors alike. A caravan site at Muirhouse, with all the necessary amenities, has also been provided in an ideal situation among the trees, overlooking the Forth.

After the Development Plan of the city under the Town and Country Planning Acts had been approved by the Secretary of State, several schemes of major redevelopments were taken in hand—among them St. James' Square, Dumbiedykes, the Synod Hall site, and Tollcross. Others are contemplated.

The Corporation has also provided well-appointed offices for the Scottish Tourist Board at the West End in the former St. Thomas's Church, a building which was acquired and used as a kitchen and restaurant for emergency feeding purposes during the war. While this book was being compiled it was also decided to purchase Morningside Church for adaptation as an arts centre by dramatic, orchestral and other societies in the city. And in the City Chambers themselves the Dunedin committee room was recently completed, with beautiful timber panels provided by the citizens of Dunedin, New Zealand, as a tribute and token of goodwill to the citizens of Edinburgh. The Assembly Rooms and Music Hall in George Street were acquired by the Corporation at the end of the war, and have played a big part in the success of the Festival. Leith Town Hall, badly damaged by enemy air attack during the war, has been reconstructed with new facilities for stage presentation.

Civic hospitality and the provision of the many fine halls owned by the Corporation has been given to the increasing number of national and international Conferences held in the city. A publicity department too has been created, and the Corporation is now responsible for the accommodation bureau, which was started originally by the Festival Society for festival visitors but now embraces conference, holiday and other visitors to the city.

The patronage of the arts has been the subject of a great deal of comment in the post-war years, because of the diminution of private munificence in these days of high taxation (high by pre-war standards), and of far-reaching changes in the social order and distribution of wealth. Financial aid from corporate and public funds is therefore increasingly sought, in the realm of public subvention from the Government through the Arts Council and from local authorities by contributions from rates. Edinburgh, as the capital and festival city, is naturally much concerned with these things, and indeed from its beginning the Festival has been supported by annual Corporation grants to the Festival Society, including £50,000 for the 1962 financial year and £75,000 two years later. But the grants go further than the Festival. Later still Edinburgh, first local authority to do so, resolved that a comprehensive and co-ordinated policy of financial support for the arts be instituted and a sum of £75,000 be provided in the annual estimates, the sum to be devoted to the Festival Society, the Scottish National Orchestra for performances in Edinburgh, and other artistic enterprises in the city.

"THIS IS YOUR CITY"

In the light of all this the City Fathers and their permanent advisers have clearly much to their credit. As with every organised body in the world they have their critics, but every now and then even the regular, run-of-the-mill critic acknowledges a new and striking venture, such as the Edinburgh Civic Exhibition, *This is Your City*, which the Corporation staged in the Waverley Market during the autumn of 1963.

For some time the Town Council had felt strongly that some means should be found to stimulate the citizen's interest in municipal affairs, and in fact it was looking into this when it received an approach from N.A.L.G.O. (The National and Local Government Officers' Association) about the possibility of staging an exhibition in Edinburgh to show the work of local government officials in action. The Town Council felt however that it would be better to stage a more ambitious exhibition showing more precisely how the city functioned from the Town Council downwards through the committees to the departments. Two cinemas and a lecture hall were therefore incorporated in the Exhibition; more than 200 films were shown and continuous lectures and demonstrations given.

Since Edinburgh's colours are black and white, they were chosen as the basic colour motif for the impressive centre piece of the whole Exhibition, the Town Council stand. This appeared as a great hall hung with reproductions of the ornate heraldic banners of leading Scottish families. On a high black velvet dais reposed great symbols of authority—the Sword and Mace, the Lord Provost's Badge and Chain and other City jewels, and the City's silver table ornaments, rarely seen by the public. Two City halberdiers in their picturesque uniforms, dating back to the 15th century, stood on duty with their halberds at the Town Council stand, ready to answer questions; and nearby were the scarlet and ermine robes of office used by Bailies and Councillors today, and a number of beautiful hand-made heraldic banners.

But the practical note was never lost. There were photographs of the Town Council in session; push-button displays showing the names of the Councillors and their wards and the relationship of the various departments to the different committees; 448 Edinburgh school teachers at one time or another instructing some 3,000 pupils; a striking exhibit of model ships and planes illustrating the battle against infectious diseases, and an historical section showing the progress in health over the past 100 years; Edinburgh's clean air plan and smokeless zones; the necessity for dental care and the importance of correct feeding; and a chamber of horrors, where the effects of excessive cigarette smoking and food contamination—both a long concern of the Department—were emphasised.

What might be termed the " technical " departments such as the City Engineer's, the Water Department, the Lighting and Cleansing Department, Weights and Measures, and Baths and Laundries all showed the modern machinery involved in the various services they provide for the public. The City Chamberlain's Department not only exhibited electronic devices used in its calculations and other business activities, but showed some of the ceremonial duties such as the presentation of the Keys of the City to the Queen when she visits Edinburgh. Also in the " Town Council area " of the exhibition was the Town Clerk's Department, which displayed extracts from the city records, as far back as King Robert the Bruce, and explained some of the ceremonial duties which the Town Clerk has to carry out from time to time. The Libraries and Museums Stand also proved very popular because of the other interesting historical material collected from the Corporation Museums, and, in the Libraries Section, its wall " papered " with book jackets.

All in all the exhibition was a great success, not least because it was human, and explained complicated matters in simple and memorable terms. To give a few more examples: many citizens took advantage of the opportunity to learn what it feels like to drive a bus, at the Transport Department stand, where the most up-to-date gadget for instructing drivers was on view; the police and fire brigade introduced their most modern vehicles on their stands; and the public could actively participate in 999 calls, with the police giving guidance to the public on various precautions which should be taken to defeat the criminal; while the Parks Department displayed several thousand cut flowers from the Corporation nurseries, and gave popular gardening demonstrations to a large number of visitors.

AWARD FOR GOOD CITIZENSHIP

There is a pleasant, human footnote to this account of enlightened civic enterprise. While the Exhibition was being held the Lord Provost arranged a ceremony in the Waverley Market for the presentation of the first Sir William Y. Darling Award for Good Citizenship to Mrs. I. C. Bruce, chairman of the Edinburgh Association for Mental Welfare. For 16 years Mrs. Bruce as chairman of the Association had been working for the city's mentally disabled, and in particular she had been a pioneer in setting up and running the after-care service for pupils leaving special schools. Such people are not always recognised, but at least her award is proof that there is often in the City Chambers a deep appreciation of the work done by devoted welfare workers whose work we shall presently see.

CHAPTER 12

THE CITY'S POLITICS

No-one could say that the citizens of Edinburgh take a fervid interest in politics. Despite changes of emphasis the general tone of the city up to 1965 has been one of non-partisan conservatism. In 1923 four of the six Edinburgh parliamentary seats (including Leith) were held by Liberals, but from the general election of 1924 to that of 1945, the Conservatives or Unionists, to give them their historical Scottish title, held three or more of the seats. In 1945 four were won by Labour. Under the redistribution of 1948, Edinburgh obtained one extra Member of Parliament and in the general election of 1950 the Conservative position was restored, with four out of the seven constituencies returning Conservative M.P.s; and as Fig. 1 shows below there was little change in the rest of the '50s.

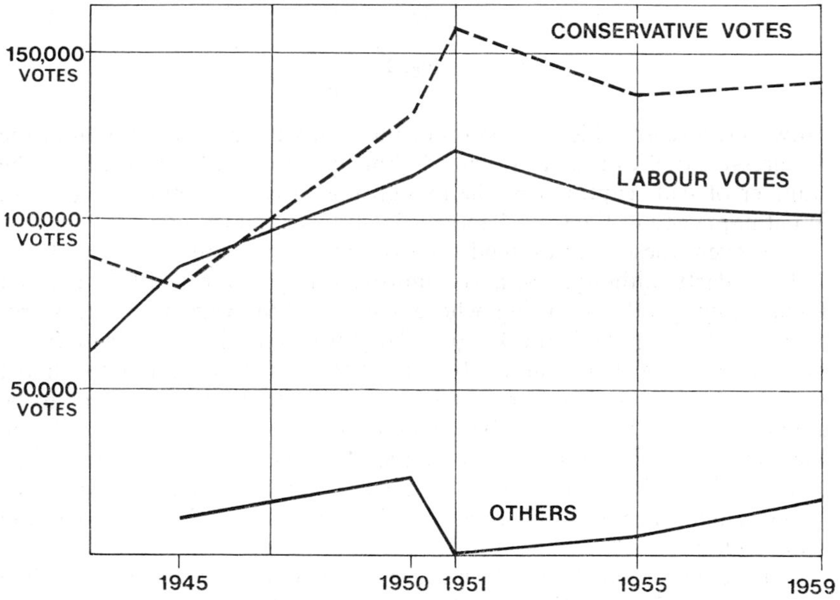

Fig. 1

This trend is clear from the total number of votes cast for the two major parties at general elections. In local elections, on the other hand, it is not possible to make a satisfactory comparison of total votes as only three of the 23 wards have been contested at each election since 1945.

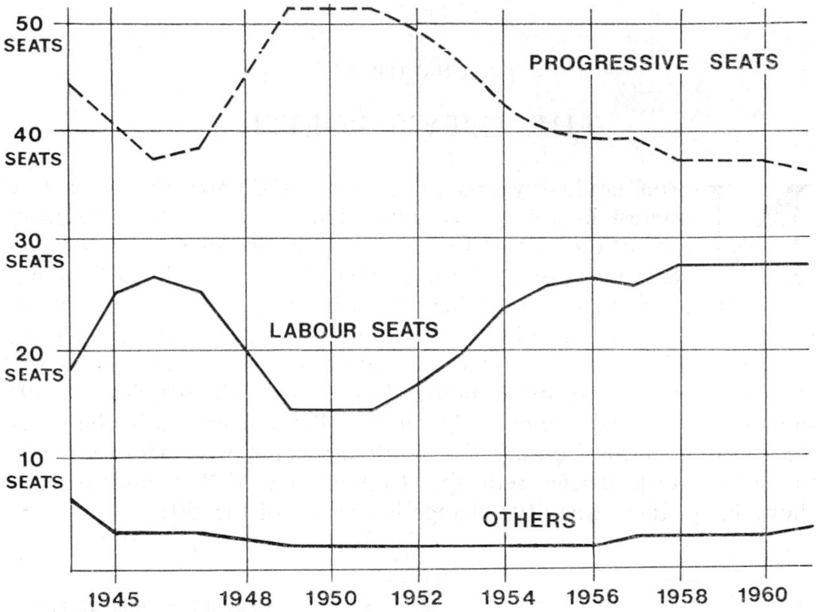

Fig. 2

However, a reasonable impression of the post-war relative strength of the Progressive (i.e. Conservative) and Labour parties can be drawn from the number of seats captured by the two groups at each election up to 1960. What happened in 1963, 1964 and 1965 will be examined later.

Yet even these figures tend to over-emphasise the strength of the Labour Party, although the party improved its position in 1962. It has a remarkably steady following whose votes seldom vary ward by ward. In the 1949–54 period, the Labour Party was suffering from a series of political and local difficulties, but by 1956 it had recovered to almost the precise position it had reached in 1947. Labour support tends to be situated in the less fashionable areas of the city such as Sighthill, the Pleasance and Craigmillar, and in the past the party has lacked outstanding individuals or bodies of sufficient weight to make its influence strongly felt. The atmosphere and outlook of the city is preponderantly middle class.

But there is no one body which expresses civic opinion, nor is it possible to point to a single institution or group of people and say that they hold the reins of power. The Lord Provost is usually a man of some influence and personal means, but as Lord Provost his function is largely honorific, and he is usually reluctant to take a public stand on any issue or to identify himself with any sectional political demand. As for the Town Councillors, probably only a small proportion of citizens turn to them naturally for guidance, and when they do it is usually over some matter directly concerning the Corporation's property or services. The number of Councillors who hold " surgeries " varies, and while those who take real interest can usually help where an individual has been unfairly treated, there are many matters in which they can take little practical action. For instance, they can do little more than explain the position to those without houses or those whose children have failed to obtain a place in a senior secondary school. As there is no institution in or around which those exercising power might gather, all that can be identified is a series of bodies or individuals who have considerable influence in certain fields.

Amongst these—since so many matters affecting the progress and well-being of an urban community come back to money—are the managers (under varying titles) of the Scottish banks whose head offices are in Edinburgh, and whose work is described elsewhere in this book. Their decisions may have relatively little effect on the economy of the country as a whole but are nevertheless of consequence in the capital city. Almost on the same level are the managers of the big insurance companies (also described later), the investment companies and four or five of the leading lawyers' offices. If the men controlling these and other smaller but still influential enterprises meet anywhere, it is probably at the clubhouses of the Muirfield, Bruntsfield or Barnton golf courses or in one or other of the clubs on or near Princes Street.

At such places, contacts will also be made with the leading members of the various professions. The Faculty of Advocates contains a number of the ablest men in the city, and as they tend to acquire widespread connections, and must always remain in Edinburgh, they are a notable ingredient in the civic establishment. Some senior medical men such as the Presidents of the Royal College of Physicians and Surgeons, and a few of the better-known ministers of the Church of Scotland—a few have private means—may mix in such circles; and clearly bodies as different as the Merchant Company, the Edinburgh Chamber of Commerce and the Royal Company of Archers may also exercise some influence in public affairs, not in their own right but because their members are drawn from among these more prominent citizens who know whom to approach if they are contemplating a major project requiring money or government sanction.

Below these senior ranks of Edinburgh society there are larger bodies with less corporate solidarity and less pull, but which can play a part and do, on occasion, take a stand on political or civic questions such as the Saltire Society and the Cockburn Association. The Church of Scotland in the shape of the Edinburgh Presbytery has concerned itself with many social and welfare questions, and has at different times pressed for more beds for tuberculosis patients, for greater attention to housing problems and the care of old people. But some think its views on licensing laws, gambling and the opening of public houses and Corporation golf courses on Sundays receive perhaps more attention at the City Chambers, since these are issues over which some councillors fear that votes may be lost. As for the Roman Catholic Church, it has naturally a special interest in its own schools and often takes a strong stand on educational issues.

The Edinburgh Chamber of Commerce is another body which states its attitudes and tries to mould civic opinion, though in the past it may have failed sometimes to exercise much influence on the authorities. Partly this is because its suggestions have tended to follow accepted lines and partly because its relations with the leading members of the Council have not always been easy. The Leith Chamber of Commerce at one time felt strongly that Edinburgh was neglecting its smaller neighbour, but mutual understanding improved after two successive chairmen of this Chamber were elected to the Town Council. Today the Chambers of Commerce have probably more influence than in the past and their views are listened to with greater respect.

On the Labour side, the Edinburgh and District Trades Council watches all matters affecting working conditions and considers general aspects of welfare such as slum clearance, services for pensioners, and technical education. It is an organisation whose roots go far back although the date of its birth is uncertain. The *Edinburgh Courant* certainly mentioned it in 1834; and there is evidence to show that it met continuously from 1849 onwards and took a lively part in the agitation for Saturday half-holidays.

The 17 trades comprising the United Trades Delegates' Association of Edinburgh and its Vicinity, as the Trades Council was called in those early days, were: the Amalgamated Engineers; United Flint Glass Makers; United Flint Glass Cutters; Edinburgh Masons; Edinburgh Joiners; United Smiths; Edinburgh and Leith Coopers; United Tailors; United Clockmakers; Edinburgh and Leith Bakers; United Brass-founders; United Plumbers; United Cabinet Makers; United Slaters; Corkcutters; and finally the Moulders and the Skinners.

The Trades Council took a leading part in 1859 in establishing a co-operative store in Edinburgh; and in May 1868 there began the long association between the Trades Council and the Royal Infirmary. This was in need of funds and the Council made a fine response. Thereafter, through the years, constant reference is made in Council records to Royal Infirmary affairs. This long association has been maintained under the National Health Service, and the Trades Council is not only represented on the Board of Management by four delegates, but one of the Council's representatives is the Vice-Chairman.

In the more militant political sphere, as the 19th century neared its end, the Council made frequent attempts to get Labour directly represented in Parliament by " men of our own order." But even in the field of local politics it was not until the annual report of 1910 that we find recorded the return of Mr. John Young as the first Labour Town Councillor (for Dalry Ward).

Since then the Edinburgh Trades Council has sustained its propaganda. Recently it has published reports on tuberculosis, housing, transport, theatres, youth employment and training, and Council house rents. It is represented on more than 20 important committees and feels it plays a significant part in city affairs. As these words are written, it has an affiliated membership of well over 52,000 in 153 branches from 64 unions.

THE POLITICAL INFLUENCE OF THE PRESS

If the Press exercises any influence in city politics, it is chiefly through the newspapers, which are printed locally. Until recently and for many years there were four of these—*The Scotsman*, the *Edinburgh Evening News*, the *Evening Dispatch* and the *Scottish Daily Mail*. It should be added here that the *Scottish Daily Express* (printed in Glasgow and possessor of the largest Scottish circulation) must obviously have some effect with its sustained campaigns on particular issues as presumably must other English-controlled newspapers which sell in Scotland, notably *The Times*, *Daily Telegraph* and *The Guardian*. By an unexpected arrangement, however, the *Evening Dispatch* in 1963 was merged with the *Edinburgh Evening News*. In its lifetime the tone of the *Evening Dispatch* had been outspokenly Conservative. The *Edinburgh Evening News* for many years—at the 1929 General Election for example—was strongly Liberal and had a special appeal to working men and women of all parties. More recently the *News*—with occasional deviations—has become broadly Conservative and is read by all sections but its appeal to lower income groups has not been lessened; and today it strives to report fairly matters of interest or concern to all political parties.

The Scotsman, a newspaper with a considerable reputation, has played a notable part in the publishing and printing life of the city since 1817. It used to be the middle-class morning paper and under the ownership of the Findlay family was strongly Unionist and a faithful reflection of the views of most of its readers. Since it was acquired by Mr. Roy (later Lord) Thomson in 1953 the editorial board has been granted considerable freedom; and on certain issues, it has not hesitated to attack either a Conservative Government or the policy of the Progressive majority on the Town Council. As a result the newspaper's position is not so clear as formerly. It maintains an overall support of Conservative principles and a strong Scottish colour, but is less markedly " Edinburgh " in its outlook. As an example of this, it was busy as a national newspaper in the early '60s, prodding the Government hard on its handling of the economic position in Scotland, and persistently calling attention to the grim facts that Scottish industrial production was lagging behind that of Great Britain as a whole; that unemployment was persistently double the United Kingdom rate; and that both factory building and the growth of new industries had not kept pace with the rest of the country.

MUNICIPAL ELECTIONS

In local politics the Labour party, and also, since the late 1950s the Liberals have put up candidates and contested the municipal elections under their own names. But the Conservatives as a party abstain and leave the field to the Edinburgh Progressive Association, which describes itself as " drawn from all walks of life, holding various political views, excepting Socialist and Communist." Among them are National Liberals who, in the post-war years, have supported Conservative governments.

After the 1962 election, the political composition of the town council was: Progressive 34; Labour 30; and Liberal 5, together with the Lord Dean of Guild and Convener of Trades. But only a few years earlier the Progressives held 40 seats and so had what might be called a comfortable majority over the Opposition parties. Since then Labour candidates have gained several seats and reduced the leeway, but the party has never been in power in the town council. At the same time a notable feature of these few years has been the growing determination of the Liberal Party, which won three seats at the 1962 election.

In the outcome this helped to create an interesting and provocative situation in the town council, in which the Progressive Party, with the additional support of the Lord Dean of Guild and Convener of Trades, held 36 seats; which meant it had a majority of only one over the 35 seats held by the Labour Party and the Liberals.

The May, 1963 election resulted in a delicate balance of party strength. Although the Progressives lost their over-all majority they were still the largest single party with 33 seats, and could count upon the support of the two non-elected members—the Lord Dean of Guild and the Convener of Trades—on most issues. But their loss of one seat to Labour, who had 31 seats, gave that party the largest number of seats in its history.

For the Liberals the election was a disappointment. Though they nominated 19 candidates, their solitary success was the retention of her seat in Newington Ward by Lady Morton. But with five members they held the balance of power, and a marked rise in the percentage poll—the highest for many years—must have been due in some measure to the emergence of the Liberals in the municipal arena.

Clearly an intricate situation had arisen, which cannot lost for long. It was in fact nearly altered at the elections in May, 1964, when although the Progressives regained Corstorphine ward from the Liberals they lost Calton to Labour; which meant that the Labour Party was only one seat behind the Progressives, and the Liberals, though they had only four seats instead of five, still held the balance of power. This power they quickly exercised. The four Liberal members helped to vote the Leader of the Labour group, Councillor Jack Kane, into the deputy chairmanship of the Town Council—the first time this honour had come Labour's way—and then, also for the first time in Edinburgh's civic history, voted a Labour woman councillor, Mrs. Anne Simpson, into the chairmanship of the Libraries and Museum Committee. Thereafter the Liberals sided broadly with the Progressives in a nicely poised balance of party power until May, 1965 when the Progressives won the Newington ward from the Liberals and thus regained virtual control of the Council. The final tally was 34 seats for the Progressives (excluding the Lord Provost); 32 for the Labour Party; and 2 for the Liberals.

RELIGIOUS POLITICS

A special feature of Edinburgh's municipal politics was the Protestant Action Party. This began in the early 1930s when there was acute unemployment and suffering in working class areas. Mr. John Cormack discovered that a few Catholic Irishmen were helping others to obtain jobs, and therefore launched a passionate campaign against "the Papist Conspiracy." At first Protestant Action turned cleverly on both sides, accusing the Labour Party of being permeated by Catholics and the Progressives of owning slum property, and by 1937 had won a dozen seats. As the war and full employment took the fire out of anti-Catholicism its leading exponent, Councillor Cormack, slowly shifted his ground, concentrating his attack on Labour and moving into a virtual alliance with the Progressives. Thus by the 1950s he was left as the sole representative of his Party. A man of fabulous stamina, the Councillor spoke for two hours every Sunday afternoon at the foot of the Mound for 30 years, and in his heyday also held an indoor meeting at 6 p.m. before speaking for a further two hours at the Mound in the late evening.

THE COUNCILLORS

The members of the town council are certainly not drawn from all sections in the city. An occupational analysis made in 1960–1 showed a total absence of bankers or the senior ranks of insurance and financial companies, and an almost equal dearth of professional men, the few lawyers (there were no advocates) coming from offices closely connected with building or shop management firms. This was the tally, and it would not be much altered in its character today:

PROGRESSIVES

Housewives	6	Dancehall proprietors	2
Manufacturing (miscellaneous)	4	Shopkeepers or managers	2
Lawyers	4	Electrical contractor	1
Builders and shopfitters	3	Plumbing contractor	1
Insurance brokers or agents	3	Chartered Accountant	1
Civil engineers	3	Property Agent	1
Retired or private means	3	Photographer	1
Quantity surveyors	2	Wig-maker	1

LABOUR

Housewives	7	Scottish Special Housing	1
Tradesmen	5	Insurance agent	1
Engineers	3	Shopkeeper	1
Co-operative employees	3	Journalist	1
Representatives	2	Workers' Educational	
Trade union officials	2	Association organiser	1

It is clear that municipal affairs tend to interest men whose daily work focusses their attention on civic questions. The businessmen among the Progressives illustrate this point, while on the Labour side, the major unions such as the miners and railwaymen take little part as compared with representatives of the shop and municipal workers, though many work in pits and on railways near if not within the city boundaries.

Some councillors point out that those in the professions and men conducting their own business may be excluded because many Council meetings are held in the mornings and therefore cut into working hours. While this undoubtedly has a deterrent effect, there are businessmen who do manage to find the time, and it is hard to see why others could not follow suit if there was a real desire to serve. At the same time it is generally agreed by many both on and off the Council that the standard of debate has declined since the war. Some businessmen have entered the Council and then left after completing their three-year term. They have complained of the numbers of meetings and left with a sense of frustration. The Council works through committees which handle the various departments such as transport and housing, and if a committee has agreed on a point their decision can be put into effect at once without reference to the full Council. As a result councillors may know very little of certain affairs unless they are members of the relevant committee; and even if they are in a position to press a matter at the committee, proposals sometimes take a long time to pass through all the official and public stages before action is taken.

In general, it is safe to say, there has been a lack of interest in local government in the post-war years. The average poll at the municipal elections dropped from a peak of 49 per cent in 1947 to 32·9 in 1961 with a slight improvement in 1962 and 1963, and the few meetings held during campaigns usually draw a handful of people and sometimes none at all.[1] The most common explanation given by Progressive Councillors for this is that Edinburgh is so well-run that the citizens have no cause to worry about politics. But the average polls in Glasgow are slightly lower and few Progressives would accept the implication that Glasgow is even more efficiently and satisfactorily governed than Edinburgh. The reasons for apathy are more complex. Local debates do raise quite important issues and some citizens of Edinburgh, albeit perhaps an active minority, are proud of their city, and are concerned to maintain its amenities and to solve its social problems. But the Council has so little discretionary power, and indeed so many of the vital decisions affecting housing, road transport, traffic congestion and many other issues are taken at a national level—that is, in the Scottish Office or the United Kingdom Departments—that many citizens tend to overlook what goes on in the City Chambers.

NATIONAL POLITICS

More interest is taken in national politics though here also the activity is on a lower key than in some of the surrounding areas or in the West of Scotland. Of the seven Edinburgh constituencies, Pentlands South and West were generally regarded as safe Conservative seats, though Pentlands was only held by 44 votes after a recount in 1966.

North Edinburgh was won by Labour in 1945, but as congested areas in Calton and Stockbridge have been cleared it has lost many working class voters to the outer housing schemes and from 1950 became steadily safer

[1] In May, 1965, the over-all percentage of voters at the municipal elections in Edinburgh was 36·5, and one of the wards—Merchiston—recorded 52·42. Holyrood on the other hand could only muster 15 per cent.

for the Conservatives till 1966 when the majority dropped to 3,035. Central Edinburgh at the same election was held for Labour by 4,015 votes; but again the character of the constituency has changed, as we saw from the earlier accounts of the Royal Mile's transfiguration. The East Division has returned a Labour member since 1935, and the majority of 312 in the 1959 election, when the Conservative candidate presented an unusually strong personal challenge, was transformed in 1966 to one of 8,809. Leith was won by the Labour Party in 1945 and at the general election of 1951 was held by only 72 votes. But the seat was kept by majorities of 3,000 in 1959 and 3,964 in 1966.

The Conservatives are by far the best organised of the parties. The headquarters for all the east of Scotland were in Edinburgh, till a reorganisation after the defeat in 1964. The constituency associations are divided into wards; each ward or area association has a committee of at least 15 devotees or as many as 30; and at meetings held monthly or more often, business is settled though social activities dominate the programme. Some constituencies have separate women's groups while others merely have a women's advisory committee. All have one or more branches of the Young Unionists, and these are represented on an executive committee in each constituency along with delegates from the ward or area associations and from the women's branch.

The average membership of the seven Conservative associations in 1963 was 3,224; all except Leith were self-financing, the average annual budget being in the region of £2,000. Less than half this money as a rule is raised from annual subscriptions of 5*s*. upwards, the rest from dances, raffles, bazaars, whist drives and coffee mornings. The objective of the organisation in every case is to keep an electoral machine in perfect readiness, and as the party does not officially contest municipal elections there are no distractions.

There is not quite the same level of professional expertise in the organisations of the other national parties, though they all have earnest supporters. Leith, for instance, has one of the two oldest Liberal organisations in Scotland (the other being in Paisley); but it is South Edinburgh which has the city's largest Liberal association, with a membership in 1963 of some 1,300, West Edinburgh running not far behind with about 1,000. The associations in the North, Central, Pentlands and East divisions have rather lower memberships. Established organisations are on a ward basis with representatives attending a monthly executive meeting for the whole constituency. There are also Young Liberal branches. The Liberals are financially self-supporting.

Though Edinburgh Liberals assert that their policy appeals equally to all age and social groups, their membership is in fact highest in " respectable " though not very well-off areas such as the late-Victorian flats in Merchiston and Marchmont or the Clerk Street and Preston Street district of Newington. In age groups, their members tend to be among the elderly who were young Liberals in the 1920s and among the under 35s, with a gap in between.

The Labour Party has a different kind of organisation. While it too has the system of constituency parties consisting of delegates from ward parties, delegates can also be sent by trade union branches and women's co-operative guilds. The constituencies in turn send representatives to the Edinburgh City Labour Party, where again the unions and co-operative guilds are represented, and it is the City party which receives and disburses the affiliation fees from the trade unions. All these organisations can send delegates to the Scottish and National Conferences of the Party, but in civic affairs it is the City party again which settles the general lines of party policy.

On the financial side the constituencies do not themselves raise all the money they use. The annual subscription—recently 6*s*.—is collected quarterly, and there are the usual jumble sales and Christmas draws. One ward which embarked on these activities systematically raised over £1,000 but the general turnover is very low. Besides these sources, each party receives one seventh of the trade union affiliation fees paid to the city party and sometimes a small grant towards municipal elections. Few of the Edinburgh constituencies have any reserves for general election purposes and do well if they can raise £200. To this Transport House adds a grant and if a candidate is sponsored by a trade union (as happened in four of the seven seats at the 1959 election) it will make a further grant.

The Communist Party and various branches of the Scottish Nationalist movement maintain a central committee in the city and have put up candidates, but their membership, their organisation and the votes they receive are alike negligible. Indeed, whatever success it attained elsewhere, Edinburgh's apathy towards the movement for a Scottish Parliament was reflected in the really rather discouraging results of the appeal for a Scottish Plebiscite Fund launched in Edinburgh in May, 1962.

This description of the city's political life may be thought by some to have placed undue emphasis on organisation and membership, since in all three national parties, the hard core of enthusiasts is small and the majority of citizens nowadays refuse to attend meetings or to pay much attention to local propaganda. When an election does come, between 74 per cent and 84 per cent of the population cast their votes according to decisions made on the basis of past habit, the views of their families or changes in their own or the nation's circumstances. It would seem to make little odds whether one party runs better jumble sales or collects more half-crowns than another. The Liberals have twice as many members as the Labour Party in North Edinburgh, but at the by-election in 1960 (when people normally cast their votes more freely than at general elections) the Labour candidate received twice as many votes as the Liberal. Another paradox is partly true also—that the wider Conservative membership is needed to pay for the elaborate professional organisation necessary to collect money from this wider membership. However, this argument cannot be carried too far when it is considered that elections do require a great deal of preparation, especially since the postal vote introduced in 1948 can give a well-organised party an edge of at least 600 votes in the average constituency. A larger membership means in fact a wider net for catching the vital few active members; and of course bright rooms and a brisk voice always ready at the end of the 'phone produce a good impression on those who might help.

Election campaigns in Edinburgh are usually quiet, though naturally enough the city is a stop on the tours of the Leader of the Opposition and of a senior Cabinet Minister or two. Nor in recent years has Edinburgh produced many outstanding candidates or members with a national reputation. One Labour and two Conservative Lords Advocate have held city seats, and a high proportion of lawyers (17 of the 68 candidatures for the two major parties between the 1945 and 1959 elections) have come forward at election time. There has also been a dearth of " characters," excepting the late Sir William Y. Darling, a Lord Provost of the city whose parliamentary career was too short to permit him to rise very far beyond his high local reputation.

At election times campaigns proceed with the usual small meetings in schoolrooms for two to three weeks before polling day. Attendances vary from 30 to 200 but there is little oratory. Indeed, in 1955 one questioner, exasperated by the (successful) candidate's failure to answer simple, direct questions, asked if he could tell the audience the time since he seemed unable to tell them anything else.

The 1966 election showed that Edinburgh can and does swing to the left with the rest of the nation. But the movements of opinion in the City are usually less than the Scottish average. Social attitudes in Edinburgh are carefully compartmented and of long standing, and it is expected that political opinions will fall into place. If one Edinburgh man wishes to place another, he picks up the accent, and once he knows school, address and occupation, all the rest can be assumed. Conservatives tend to write off certain areas while their canvassers show shock and alarm if they encounter Labour supporters in the Georgian flats of the West End. While all this may be slowly changing in the more open, less class-conscious politics of the mid-1960s, it is probably safe to say that it is changing more slowly in Edinburgh than in the other cities of Britain.

CHAPTER 13

THE PEOPLE'S HEALTH

THE PROFESSION OF MEDICINE

CHANGE in Edinburgh has always been unhurried and in the 18th century, when the first *Statistical Account* of Scotland was made, the town and its medicine retained a distinctly medieval flavour. Yet great figures like Cullen and the Monros had brought fame and many students to the Teaching School; and there was even in the city Dr. Gregory, Professor of Medicine in 1790, who not only gained immortality by his homely mixture of rhubarb and ginger but made a great reputation at the time for his strenuous view that " disease should be attacked vigorously by free blood-letting, the cold effusion, brisk purging, frequent blisters and vomits of tartar emetic."

The Royal Infirmary was established in 1714 but there was no public lunatic asylum until 1813 although a common madhouse or Bedlam existed near Bristo Street where the poet, Robert Fergusson, died so miserably in 1774. Sanitation was primitive and the notorious stenches of the High Street were so frightful that even the noses of the natives were becoming aware of them.

By 1850, however, there had fortunately been many changes. The city boundaries had been enlarged to their eternal gain by the building of the New Town; the population had risen to 170,444; and the importance of public health was recognised by the establishment of a University Chair linked with forensic medicine. The Royal Infirmary had 450 beds; 4,000 patients, including fever and smallpox cases, were treated annually; but as demands for beds and treatment continued to increase, the Board of Managers, who were looking for a fresh site, eventually chose Lauriston Place, where the present hospital was opened in 1879.

At this time the prestige of the Medical School had never been higher, with giants such as Syme, Simpson and later Lister on its teaching staff. But medicine was still an exclusively male occupation, and it was not until 30 years later that a Dispensary for women was founded at Bruntsfield largely owing to the labours of a tireless Englishwoman, Miss Jex Blake.

Medical practice too had a rigid division. Firstly there was private practice where fees were paid to family doctors and specialists, many of whom held honorary posts in the hospitals. Secondly there was the " Hospital Class " who enjoyed free treatment in the Royal Infirmary or at Dispensaries for the Poor in the Cowgate, West Richmond Street and Thistle Street. It is surprising that such an inflexible system should have continued with remarkably little change, and despite the 1911 National Health Insurance Act, until the outbreak of the last war in 1939.

NATIONAL HEALTH SERVICE

In July, 1948 when Mr. Attlee's Government gave birth to the National Health Service, some felt that its conception was unfortunate, its antenatal care inadequate and its delivery hurried. But with Mr. Ancurin Bevan as accoucheur many post-partum difficulties were overcome, and today the teenage offspring after an increasingly expensive upbringing continues to thrive in spite of manifest deficiencies.

The South-Eastern Regional Hospital Board, with offices in Drumsheugh Gardens, was made responsible for most of the hospitals in Edinburgh, Fife and the Borders, and in 1950 had an annual budget of £6 million. Ten years later this had risen to £12 million because of expanding hospital services and the decreasing value of the pound sterling. The cost of administration, also in 1960, was £439,861—a sum representing 3·6 per cent of total expenditure, which certainly reveals no extravagances and is lower than the administrative costs of many private industrial concerns. In 1963 the annual budget was £15,382,254.

All members of hospital medical staffs became employees of the Board in 1948. The honorary staff of the voluntary hospitals became Consultants, and were paid according to the amount of work they contracted to do. The old Scottish term " Clinical Tutor " gave place to Registrar, although no registers were kept, and House Physicians and Surgeons entered the somewhat uncertain grade of House Officer.

THE ROYAL INFIRMARY

The Royal Infirmary (founded in 1741) today houses the main professorial units, and is the principal centre of teaching and research in South-East Scotland. Between the two world wars considerable extensions were made within the limits of funds raised by voluntary subscriptions, including new departments for Physiotherapy, Radiology, Dermatology, Venereal Diseases, a Nurses Home, and a Maternity Pavilion to replace the old Simpson Hospital. During the past 20 years, however, and despite the labours of the Board of Management, no major works have been possible. The buildings are now black with grime and are unsuited for modern hospital needs. But fortunately plans are at last being made for extensive reconstruction, and it has been decided to erect a multi-story building on the present site, incorporating 850 beds with possibly a children's hospital of 300 beds in the vicinity.

THE HOSPITALS

The municipal hospitals—Western General, Northern General and Eastern General—together with Leith Hospital, were formed into an administrative unit, the Northern Group of Hospitals, whose history reflects many of the changes which have occurred in medicine throughout the country in the post-war years. Formerly the municipal hospitals were the poor relations of the teaching and voluntary hospitals which were high in prestige, heavy with endowments and even heavier with tradition. In Edinburgh since the late war large sums have been spent in rebuilding and redecorating the Northern Group of Hospitals, many of whose buildings bore the Dickensian stigmata of the old Poor Law Institutions. They had, however, one merit—available ground for expansion, and in this respect the Western General was particularly fortunate. The old building was modernised as far as possible; special provision was made for the teaching of students; and in 1956 the Radiotherapy Unit (costing £280,000) was opened, with 100 beds, a large Out-Patient Department and the latest apparatus for the treatment of malignant disease. The Northern General has been similarly transformed and now has modern departments for the treatment of Rheumatic, Neurological and Respiratory Diseases. The Eastern General at Seafield, possibly the bleakest of the Municipal institutions, has been vastly developed in the past 10 years. There have been new departments for Medicine and Tropical Diseases, and a large Thoracic Surgical Unit now operates where pioneer work has been done in the surgery of the heart and lungs.

The role of Leith Hospital, in the heart of the town, has inevitably altered. Formerly, as a voluntary body, it was an infirmary and dispensary for the natives of the Port of Leith, many of whom are now served by other hospitals in the group. The buildings are old and, like the Royal Infirmary, there is little room for expansion, but many local improvements have been made and each year an immense amount of excellent work is done, particularly in the treatment of surgical and medical casualties.

Founded in mid-Victorian days under the will of George Chalmers, a prosperous plumber, Chalmers Hospital is situated in Lauriston Place. It is small, having only 100 beds, and deals mainly with medical, surgical and gynaecological cases. The size of the hospital, the admirable nursing staff, and the absence of undegraduate teaching duties permit an intimate and informal atmosphere which many patients have welcomed and affectionately acknowledged.

Edinburgh has two hospitals exclusively staffed by women—Bruntsfield, founded by Dr. Jex Blake in 1886, and the Elsie Inglis Memorial Maternity established in Abbeyhill in 1925.

In 1957 the physician was due to retire and the Regional Hospital Board, acting strictly within the terms of the 1948 National Health Service Act, advertised the post and invited applications from suitably qualified male and female practitioners. At once there was an outcry, many meetings were held including a mass demonstration in the Usher Hall, the *Scotsman* columns were bombarded with letters and eventually the issue was taken to law. On 15th November, 1957 the case came up in the Court of Session before Lord Walker who judged that the Regional Board must, in the first place, advertise for a female doctor, and only if such an appointment were not practicable should a male doctor be considered. This view found widespread backing both inside and outside the profession. As one leading doctor in the city said, " Edinburgh after all is a big place and, sentiment and tradition apart, most doctors and laymen feel that there is room for one small hospital staffed by women and caring for women patients." It was in accordance with this widely held sentiment that in May, 1958 a woman doctor was appointed as Physician to the Bruntsfield and Elsie Inglis Hospitals.

It is fashionable at the moment to disparage our hospitals in comparison with those abroad, in particular Scandinavia and Switzerland; and it must be acknowledged that we are far behind those countries which have not indulged in the expensive recreation of World Wars and, in consequence, have had vast sums of money to lavish on large hospitals of modern design. A hospital, however, consists of more than bricks and mortar; the nursing and medical staffs determine the quality of its service and there is no evidence that the hospital care of the sick, taken as a whole, in Edinburgh falls short of the best continental standards.

It would perhaps be timely here to reproduce a table giving a complete list of the Edinburgh hospitals with the total bed complement and the type of case treated. The figures show the position in 1959 and the start of the '60s and is reproduced here since inquiries made in 1963 showed that the bed complement and type of case being treated in August of that year were unchanged with one exception—the Eastern General Hospital. There, as a result of powerful complaints about the inadequacy of geriatric beds in Edinburgh, the Regional Hospital Board decided to convert a number of the general medical beds at the Eastern General Hospital for the care of geriatric patients.

TABLE 25

Hospital	*No. of Beds*	*Type of Case*
Royal Infirmary	1,146	General
Simpson Memorial Maternity Pavilion	169	Maternity
Beechmount House	46	Convalescent
Convalescent House	80	Convalescent
Western General	442	General
Northern General	120	Rheumatism, Neurology and Respiratory Diseases
Eastern General	314	Medical, Tropical and Thoracic surgical
Leith	173	General
Chalmers	107	General
Royal Hospital for Sick Children	212	Paediatrics
Princess Margaret Rose[1]	170	Orthopaedics
Deaconess	96	General
Elsie Inglis Memorial Maternity	73	Maternity
Bruntsfield	81	General
Longmore	60	Long term and General
Liberton	60	Long term
City	623	Infectious diseases and Tuberculosis
Southfield	88	Tuberculosis
Royal Victoria	90	Tuberculosis
Astley Ainslie	242	Convalescent, with School of Occupational Therapy
Craig House	330	Royal Edinburgh Hospitals for Mental and Nervous Disorders
West House	694	
Jordanburn	45	

[1] In June 1965 Princess Margaret opened a lady's extension to this hospital which bears her name.

PRIVATE PRACTICE

Before the war the skill and fame of Edinburgh's physicians and surgeons attracted many private patients who were treated in the West End nursing homes; large incomes were made by eminent specialists; and surgical Rolls-Royces were regularly to be seen in the region of Drumsheugh and Moray Place. Most of these specialists held honorary appointments in the voluntary hospitals and their living depended on private practice. Today they are paid for their hospital work by the Regional Hospital Board who employed 256 consultants in 1960, 103 of them having full-time contracts. Social and economic changes have reduced the volume of private work which has not yet become negligible, as medical Bentleys can still be identified in many of the hospital car parks in the city.

NURSING

With the present day variety of ancillary services it is sometimes forgotten the the most important women in a hospital are the nurses. Edinburgh remains very well served by her nurses; some difficulties still occur, not because fewer girls are being trained, but because of changes in nursing technique and a reduction in the working week to 44 hours. There is a sufficiency of student nurses at the main teaching hospitals and there is little difficulty in finding staff nurses and ward sisters, many of whom come from other parts of the country and are anxious to live in Edinburgh. In 1963 the Regional Hospital Board employed 5,505 nurses; this figure includes students, trained staff auxiliaries and male nurses, most of the latter working in mental hospitals and special departments.

In 1956, with the aid of a Rockefeller Grant of £30,000, a Nursing Studies Unit (the first of its kind in Britain) was founded by the University in the Faculty of Arts. The Unit aims to train nurses for higher appointments, such as sister tutors and matrons. The course lasts for two years and includes subjects in the ordinary University Arts curriculum.

THE ROYAL COLLEGE OF SURGEONS OF EDINBURGH

The Royal College of Surgeons of Edinburgh is the oldest surgical chartered incorporation in Britain. It originated as the Incorporation of the Barber-Surgeons of Edinburgh whose Seal of Cause was granted in 1505. By that original charter certain duties, rights and privileges were invested in the Incorporation—to practise, to teach and to examine.

Originally surgery and anatomy were the main subjects of instruction, but in the middle of the 19th century a complete undergraduate school was founded and housed in a new building in the college grounds. It closed in 1948 because of lack of financial assistance from the State.

The main teaching and examining activities of the College have always been in relation to surgery, and to postgraduate rather than undergraduate students. At the present time a very large amount of postgraduate teaching in all subjects is carried out under the aegis of the Edinburgh Post-

Graduate Board for Medicine, a body on which the College has full representation. The great bulk of the surgical teaching is carried out by Fellows of the College.

The Fellowship of the College (or one of the sister Corporations) is essential for a surgical consultant post in the National Health Service, and is sought after and prized by surgeons from all parts of the Commonwealth and from other countries. There are well over 3,000 Fellows on the roll.

The Library of the College, containing more than 20,000 volumes, and the Museum, one of the best in the country, exist for the use of Fellows and postgraduate students, and are constantly kept up to date.

In 1954 H.R.H. Prince Philip, Duke of Edinburgh was graciously pleased to extend his patronage to the College, which in the following year suitably celebrated its 450th anniversary. In the same year the College began the publication of its own journal—*The Journal of the Royal College of Surgeons of Edinburgh.*

THE ROYAL COLLEGE OF PHYSICIANS

Since receiving the Charter from Charles II in 1681 the Royal College of Physicians has been a potent influence in Scottish medicine. At first its main concerns were licensing of practitioners, inspection of apothecaries' shops and education. For more than a century the apothecaries and pharmacists have been independent of College authority, and in 1957 only nine licentiates were appointed as part of the Triple Qualification.

It is on education, particularly for postgraduates, that much of the College resources are expended today. The examinations for Membership which is a qualification of very high professional standard had 37 candidates in 1935; this figure had increased by 1960 to 1,262, of whom 214 were successful.

Each year approximately 30 Members who have satisfied the Fellowship Committee of their professional distinction are elected as Fellows. The burden of the extensive and varied activities of the College is borne by the President, Vice-President and Council who are appointed by the Fellows from their own ranks. In 1963 there were 608 Fellows and 2,555 Members. It is noteworthy too that in recent years an increasing number of the leading Consultant Physicians in other Scottish centres have joined the Roll of Fellows so that the College has become essentially, if not nominally, a national institution.

An important extension to the College premises was made in 1955 when No. 8 Queen Street was converted to provide reading rooms and further accommodation for the ever-enlarging library which now contains 200,000 volumes and is recognised as one of the leading medical libraries in the world.

THE EDINBURGH MEDICAL SCHOOL

In 1945 the Second World War ended, and for several years afterwards the numbers wishing to begin medical studies at the University of Edinburgh were, as elsewhere, greatly increased by the return of ex-Service applicants. The trend is shown in the following table:

TABLE 26
SELECTION OF MEDICAL STUDENTS BY THE UNIVERSITY OF EDINBURGH

	Applications	*Admissions*
1938–9	521	212
1939–40	505	214
1940–41	487	206
1941–42	480	209
1942–43	492	196
1943–44	501	200
1944–45	635	197
1945–46	823	217
1946–47	1,425	207
1947–48	1,680	202
1948–49	1,466	198
1949–50	1,484	192
1950–51	1,622	190
1951–52	1,279	188
1952–53	826	176
1953–54	841	178
1945–55	849	180
1955–56	789	178
1956–57	769	146
1957–58	763	151
1958–59	884	150
1959–60	964	150
1960–61	997	150
1961–62	1,252	150
1962–63	1,529	150
1963–64	2,009	150

The largest intake of medical students in the records of Edinburgh University was in the year 1932–3, when 242 students commenced their first year studies. After 1950–1 there was a steady decline in the number of applications due largely to a reduction in the number of ex-Servicemen. There is no doubt, however, that other factors were involved. The English and Irish Universities were expanding for example, as the following table shows:

TABLE 27

Year	*England*	*Scotland*	*Ireland*	*Total*	*Scottish graduates as percentage of total*
1934	847	471	154	1,472	32
1937	1,096	593	239	1,928	31
1940	1,323	673	315	2,311	29
1945	1,268	581	428	2,277	26
1949	1,436	589	452	2,477	24
1952	1,848	673	506	3,027	22

It was argued too, by some, that after 1948 many school children and their parents were not attracted by the prospects of a career in a Health Service that had been nationalised, particularly in view of the friction about salaries that developed between successive Governments and the politicians of the medical profession. It will be seen, however, from Table 26 that in 1956 and 1957, when this friction was at its height, there were more applicants than in 1938.

In consequence of the growth of English and Irish Medical Schools, the contraction of the British Empire and Commonwealth, and the reduction in the size of the Armed Forces, it became increasingly difficult for Edinburgh graduates to obtain posts. The University therefore decided to reduce the number of medical students, and in 1956–7 only 146 were accepted for training, a fall of 32 from the previous year's figure. In the year 1956–57 the total number of medical under-graduates was 996 of whom 222 were women.

The number of medical students in Edinburgh was in fact diminished to a greater extent than these figures suggest because, following the recommendations of the Inter-Departmental Committee (Ministry of Health and Department of Health for Scotland) on medical schools (the Goodenough Committee), the extra-mural school in Edinburgh ceased training medical students in 1948. The Committee had considered that the extra-mural schools in Scotland were of a lower standard than other schools in the country, and had recommended that all four non-University schools in Britain should be absorbed by the Universities or should stop undergraduate training.

In the post-war years a very satisfactory feature of medical life in Edinburgh was the expansion of post-graduate teaching. The Edinburgh Post-Graduate Board for Medicine was very fortunate in obtaining the services of Major-General Sir Alexander G. Biggam, who had been Consulting Physician to the Army during the 1939–45 war, as Director of Studies. The Board, which had administrative offices first in the University Medical Buildings, and later at Surgeons' Hall, did not have separate hospital teaching accommodation, and made use of the undergraduate lecture theatres. At first the postgraduate medical teaching was organised by a separate Board, with three representatives each from the University, the Royal College of Physicians and the Royal College of Surgeons, and a Chairman appointed by the University with the approval of the two Royal Colleges. In October, 1953 the University assumed financial responsibility for the activities of the Board, which otherwise remained unchanged. During the year 1961–2 the number of postgraduates attending the courses was 875, a figure to be compared with the 923 medical undegraduates.

The number of the postgraduates was made up as follows, and the figures are interesting:

Internal Medicine Courses (2)	261
Surgery Courses (2)	90
Medical Sciences Course	66
Clinical Instruction in Medicine	63
Refresher Course for General Dental Practitioners	39
Refresher Course for General Medical Practitioners	66
Courses arranged in conjunction with the Education Committee of the College of General Practitioners S.E. Scotland Faculty	241

The countries of origin of those attending the courses were:

Great Britain	446	Pakistan	34
Australia	30	West Africa	2
Hong Kong	8	Canada	2
Malaya	10	Southern Rhodesia	1
New Zealand	4	Burma	10
Singapore	7	Nigeria	8
South Africa	11	U.S.A.	1
Ceylon	10	Iran	8
Egypt	44	Jordan	1
India	193	Palestine	2
Iraq	11	British E. Africa	6
Lebanon	1	Eire	1
		Malta	1

The postgraduate teaching, which consisted chiefly of lectures and of clinical instruction in the wards of the various hospitals, was carried out by teachers already responsible for undergraduate medical education. No account was taken of this extra burden when staff appointments were made, but the number of medical teachers in the Faculty of Medicine showed a large increase after 1945. In 1939 there were, in that Faculty, 18 Professors and 96 Lecturers. Many of the Lecturers and some of the Professors were part-time.

In 1962 the figures were:

Professors	23	(*New Chairs were in Dermatology, Medical Radiology, Neurological Surgery, Ophthalmology and Orthopaedic Surgery.*)
Lecturers	321	

In addition, in 1951 the Dental College in Chambers Street was incorporated into the Faculty of Medicine, and this in 1957 added one Professor and 19 Lecturers to the numbers. Similarly in 1953 the Royal (Dick) Veterinary College became part of the University, though not at first as a separate Faculty.

The welding together of University posts and clinical posts in the National Health Service, when the latter was introduced in 1948, presented many difficulties in Edinburgh, as elsewhere. Thus it came about that some consultants who were employed almost entirely in carrying out Health Service duties were included on the University pay roll as full time members of the staff, but at a lower rate of pay than if they had been full-time consultants in the National Health Service. Their concern about this difference in income was equalled only by the feelings of their colleagues of equal seniority in the Faculties of Science or Arts who received a lower salary from the University.

In 1948 the length of the undergraduate medical course was extended from five to six years, largely by an increase in the number of hours devoted to the basic sciences. Traditionally the Edinburgh Medical School had favoured systematic teaching methods, with the didactic lecture playing an important part, and these methods of teaching continued, though many members of the staff considered that the number of lectures should be reduced, and indeed after the 1939–45 war many of the English Universities allowed applicants to sit the First Year examinations without attending University classes. This meant specialisation to a greater extent at school and was not approved by those who believed in a wide general education, but in 1958 Edinburgh University had to introduce similar regulations as, naturally, some of the best pupils at school chose to attend Universities where, by sitting the First Year examinations from school, they could cut the duration of the course from six years to five. Incidentally, the Medical Buildings in Teviot Place, like the Royal Infirmary, Edinburgh, were now unsuited for modern work and plans were made for early extension.

MEDICAL CLUBS AND SOCIETIES

That doctors in Edinburgh are gregarious animals is shown by the following list of clubs and societies which continue to flourish.

The Royal Medical Society, founded in 1737, is one of the oldest medical societies in the world, and is unique in that it is the only students' society holding a Royal Charter. Its members also include recently qualified doctors. The Royal Medical Society holds meetings throughout the academic year, and at these debates are held and lectures delivered.

Aesculapian Club. This was founded by Dr. Andrew Duncan in 1773. Membership is limited to 22 Fellows of the Royal College of Surgeons and the Royal College of Physicians. They dine three or four times each year.

The Harveian Society was founded in 1782, also by the tireless Dr. Duncan. There are 200 members who dine annually, hear an oration, ceremonially eat heart and drink to the Immortal Memory of William Harvey.

The Medico—Chirurigical Society of Edinburgh was founded in the early part of the 19th century and holds scientific meetings throughout the year. Membership is open to general practitioners and consultants.

The Clinical Club was founded in 1928. The majority of its members are general practitioners in Edinburgh. They meet regularly and have lectures from their own members and distinguished visitors.

GENERAL PRACTICE

Since the formation of the National Health Service in 1948 general practitioners have been organised under the authority of the Executive Council of the City of Edinburgh. In March, 1963 there were 311 doctors on the Council's list, of whom 267 lived in Edinburgh and 44 in the adjoining county. Of the 267 doctors living in Edinburgh 103 were in single-handed practice and the remaining 164 were members of partnerships. The number of partnerships was 63 made up of 36 partnerships of two doctors, 19 of three doctors, 7 of four doctors and one of seven doctors. The number of assistants employed by doctors was six. All but 38 of the doctors on the Council's list provided maternity services as well as general medical services.

GENERAL PRACTICE TEACHING UNIT AND THE FAMILY DOCTOR CENTRE

Having glanced earlier at Livingstone House in the Cowgate, we must now look more closely at this enterprise in its important medical setting; for Livingstone House is now the headquarters of two pioneering ventures that are arousing keen interest not only throughout the United Kingdom but in many countries overseas. These are the Family Doctor Centre, operated under the auspices of the Department of Health for Scotland, and the University General Practice Teaching Unit. Made possible by generous support from the Nuffield Provincial Hospitals' Trust, the Centre, the only one of its kind in Scotland, is showing a new pattern in the doctor-patient relationship under the National Health Service. Up-to-date consulting rooms are available to any general practitioner who wishes to take his patients there for a thorough examination. There is x-ray apparatus of the latest type, a radiographer is on duty all day, and a radiologist is available for consultation. Other diagnostic services cover electrocardiography, biochemistry and bacteriology, and a laboratory technician carries out tests at the request of the doctor. There is also a trained medical social worker skilled in the evaluation of personal and human relationship problems which may be a factor in the diagnosis of the patient's illness, or which may be a complication rendering treatment more difficult than normally. The idea behind the Centre is that many problems can be resolved if, instead of the patient being sent to hospital, the family doctor has access to the latest equipment to carry out his own tests. There is evidence too that the Centre considerably reduces demands on the busy hospital services, and doctors consider that, instead of losing close contact with the patient sent to hospital, they derive more professional satisfaction by remaining, as one of them has expressed it, " completely in the picture." They appreciate also that there is a consultant adviser who gives his services on an honorary basis to help any family doctor who wishes to consult him.

The General Practice Teaching Unit, inspired by the University and sustained for a number of years by funds from the Rockefeller Foundation, is unique in Britain and has broken a lot of new ground. Begun on a voluntary basis, the scheme has proved so successful that the Unit is now an integral part of the Medical School curriculum, and every fifth year student is attached to the Unit for one academic term. With the patient's consent, and always under the supervision of the doctors, the senior student gradually takes over delegated responsibility for the patient, and, among other things, learns at first hand what illness means to the family. Each week the students and doctors assemble to review and discuss the work done during the previous week.

Also at Livingstone House are the headquarters of the South-East Scotland Faculty of the College of General Practitioners which is concerned with the post-graduate training of the family doctor to keep him abreast of recent advances, and with research into general practice.

DENTAL SURGERY

Edinburgh is the home of formal dental education in Britain. In the second half of the 18th century James Rae, a surgeon in the town, devoted much of his time to the practice of dentistry, and in 1764 was granted the use of the Surgeons' Hall to hold a class on Diseases of the Teeth. Several years later at the request of his students he enlarged the scope to include all aspects of surgery, though according to the diary of Sylas Neville, who attended one of the courses, the lectures still contained much dental information. However the separate teaching of dentistry had become incorporated in the instruction in surgery and did not reappear in Edinburgh for nearly a hundred years. But the tradition was kept alive, for Rae had two sons, William and John, both of whom practised dentistry more than surgery. William shortly after being admitted to the Incorporation of Surgeons in 1778 left Edinburgh and went to London, where four years later he gave the first course of lectures on dentistry and thereafter continued to give instruction in dentistry until his death.

Clearly then, Scots played a major part in the establishment of dental teaching in London and the Edinburgh influence is unmistakable. For in London the special character of dental surgery maintained its independence and William Rae's example was followed by others, notably Joseph Fox in Guy's Hospital. In Edinburgh, on the other hand, the special courses of dental lectures were only resumed in 1856; which brings us to the memorable work of John Smith.

Menzies Campbell in his John Smith Centenary Oration said that Smith was one of the great men of Edinburgh in the 19th century, and the Edinburgh Dental Hospital and School and the Edinburgh School of Dentistry certainly owe much to him. Having found for one thing that his dental teaching was incomplete if the students could not get practical instruction and demonstrations, Smith tried to develop clinical teaching in the Edinburgh Royal Dispensary where he was an honorary dental surgeon. As his attempt however proved unsatisfactory he determined to establish a dispensary for dental treatment and through his efforts the Edinburgh Dental Dispensary was opened at 1 Drummond Street in January, 1860 and became the forerunner of the Edinburgh Dental Hospital and School (1880). The Dental Hospital thereafter received support as a voluntary Hospital till 1948 where after the inauguration of the National Health Service the Dental Hospital became part of the Royal Infirmary Group and the Dental School part of the Faculty of Medicine of the University.

For the sake of the record it should be noted that the Dental Hospital and School has occupied premises in Chambers Street since 1894. A new wing was added in 1926, but this too proved insufficient, and in 1939 a complete reconstruction was planned. By a malign coincidence the date fixed with the contractors for the commencement of the work was 4th September, 1939, and war had broken out the previous day. In the end the new building could not be oədned until 1953.

CHANGES IN DENTAL PRACTICE

It would perhaps be an exaggeration to claim that the School and Hospital is the centre of dental life in the city for all practitioners because there is no occasion which seems to attract them all, and it is still true that a number of practitioners remain professionally isolated from their colleagues. But there are quite a number of occasions outside the School and Hospital walls where dental surgeons meet from time to time to exchange views and enjoy the fruits of recent research. There is, for instance, the strictly scientific Odonto Chirurgical Society of Scotland—now Britain's oldest dental society—and the East of Scotland Branch of the British Dental Association, which is the negotiating body for the dental profession. Both of these hold regular meetings. Other occasions of the kind are the four Scientific Dental Meetings held every year in the Royal College of Surgeons, the triennial Guy Memorial Lecture and the endowed triennial lecture given at the University in the name of its first Professor of Dental Surgery, A. C. W. Hutchinson.

The great majority of dental surgeons in Edinburgh are in general practice and take part in the National Health Service. In 1948, when the Health Service began, 150 dental practitioners were on the Local Executive Council list, since when there has been little change. By 1963 only six practitioners were known to take no part in the National Service and conduct private practice. But there are some practitioners who treat private as well as Health Service patients.

Since the last war, certain trends have become apparent in dental practices throughout the city as a whole. General dental practice is still of course an individual concern, for few dental surgeons employ an assistant and also as before the war only a few are in partnership. Then again there is no group practice nor is any woman dental surgeon the principal of a dental practice. On the other hand fewer practitioners seem to live and practice in the same house as formerly; and where this happens it is usually in the suburbs and amongst those who have been in practice for a number of years.

An obvious post-war change has been an increase in the employment of receptionists. There are in fact only one or two practices left where the dentist relies on a member of his household to open the door to patients and to answer the telephone. Since many dentists do not live in the house where they practise it has become all the more necessary to have an assistant not only to receive patients and make appointments but also, since the National Health Service requires the accurate completion of forms, to provide efficient administration. Some of the receptionists also help in the surgery; in other practices a chairside assistant (Dental Nurse) is also employed. Dental Nurses incidentally are not trained in the Edinburgh Dental Hospital as they are in some dental hospitals elsewhere; but the Education Committee of the City organises a night school class for these young girls and they are able to take the Certificate of the Dental Nurses' Society at an examination usually held in Edinburgh once a year.

Another post-war change is a reduction in the number of dental surgeons who have their own dental mechanics and run their own workshop. Consequently, there are more dental laboratories than there used to be.[1] The number of dental technicians in Edinburgh during 1962–3 was estimated at 70, and of this number 17 were employed in the Dental Hospital, two in the Sighthill Health Centre, 11 in dental laboratories and 40 in private practice. As for the 18 apprentices recorded during the same period only five were in private practice, 12 were in laboratories and there was one in the Dental Hospital.

The technicians have courses of instruction arranged by the Edinburgh Education Committee, to prepare them for the City and Guilds Intermediate and Final Certificates, and in 1962 a new class for the Advanced Certificate in Orthodontics was run for the first time. In the 1962–3 session 27 students were preparing for the Intermediate and Final Certificates.

As regards industry, which has steadily become more sensitive to the need for healthy employees, only two Edinburgh firms at the time of writing have a dental service for their employees. But most firms, large and small, allow staff time off for urgent dental treatment. At the University on the other hand there is a dental service for all students. Two full time dental surgeons are employed there and they are fully occupied treating patients throughout the year as part of the Student Health Service.

THE SCHOOL DENTAL SERVICE

The School Dental Service provides comprehensive dental treatment for school children, pre-school children and expectant and nursing mothers. In 1963 there were 18 dental officers on the establishment and a chief dental officer is in administrative charge of the whole service. This cannot be fully described here. But the annual reports of the Public Health Department which give a good picture of the treatment given, show that since the emphasis now is on filling teeth there has been a decline in the treatment by extractions and increasing appreciation by children and parents of the value of preventive dentistry and the need to save teeth where possible.[2]

The School service also includes a consultant service in Orthodontics and Oral Surgery, and provides facilities for the construction of special and complex appliances to correct irregularities in the position of teeth. In-patient treatment for school children requiring surgical operations on the teeth and mouth are available at the Northern Group of Hospitals when necessary. There were also, in 1963, three main dental clinics with seven surgeries in the city—at Lauriston Place, Links Place, and the

[1] In 1963 there were also two Dental Depots in Edinburgh for the supply of dental equipment, instruments and materials; and at least two repair shops in the city were dealing directly with the public and repairing broken dentures.

[2] As we shall see later, the view of Dr. H. E. Seiler, recently Medical Officer of Health for Edinburgh, is less optimistic than that of Professor Boyes, quoted above. Both however agree on the importance of having a fully staffed dental school service and a greater awareness on the part of parents that proper care of children's teeth should begin at home.

Sighthill Health Centre, which happens to be the first Health Centre opened in Scotland. Throughout the city there were, in the same year, 21 surgeries for the School Dental Officers. At Sighthill the Committee of Management employs and pays a dental surgeon who is apparently the only dental surgeon of the type in Scotland. He treats patients under the National Health Service. In addition at the Health Centre there are two surgeries used by the School dental officers; and also Sighthill is one of the School centres for the Consultant Service in Orthodontics and Oral Surgery.

The effect of this new concentration of effort on the children has brought an increasing awareness in the importance of dental health, and much credit must be given to the school dental service of past years that so much of fear has been removed from dental treatment. New methods and new equipment have naturally helped also, as did the Dental Health Campaign initiated by the Scottish Committee for Dental Health Education in Edinburgh and the surrounding counties in 1962. The immediate impact of this important crusade was striking, and the cleanliness of the mouths of school children improved considerably. But there are still far too many children with bad teeth and an obvious need for dental care.

CONSULTANTS

The Regional Hospital Board Consultant Service—located at the Dental Hospital—is the centre where Consultants in all divisions of dental surgery can be consulted. The other hospital where dental Consultants are available is the Royal Infirmary. All aspects of dental treatment for adults and children are undertaken at the Dental Hospital's various departments where Consultants are in charge. There are Conservation, Prosthetics, Children's, Periodontal, Oral Surgery, Orthodontic, and Diagnostic and Treatment Planning. Since there is no in-patient accommodation there is an arrangement whereby patients can be admitted to either the Royal Infirmary, The Royal Hospital for Sick Children and the Northern Group or to Bangour Hospital, West Lothian.

In the Oral Surgery Department of the Royal Infirmary, which has a 24-hour emergency service, there is a staff of two Consultants, each with an out-patient clinic once a week and three operating sessions. The Department with its 12 beds, an operating theatre and a dental surgery is the main hospital where dental post-graduates studying for a post-graduate diploma attend and where training of those wishing to specialise in Oral Surgery is undertaken. At the Dental Hospital once a week, there is an out-patient clinic for the Oral Surgery division of the Plastic and Jaw Injury Unit at Bangour. This is used as an undergraduate teaching clinic. To complete the picture it should be noted that the Consultants in the South East of Scotland Region are employed by the Regional Board or are on the honorary staff of the region by virtue of employment in the University.

TEACHING AND TRAINING

The School of Dental Surgery has an annual intake of 60 students, and only one other similar School in Britain exceeds this number. All students are accepted to read for the Bachelor's degree in dental surgery of the University. Normally it takes five years to graduate B.D.S. at Edinburgh. The majority of the students are from Edinburgh and Scotland, and of these about 25–30 per cent are from England and overseas. Women students account for 10–15 per cent of the total.

One of the greatest changes since the war has been the growth of full time teaching. Up till 1934 there was no full time teacher. But in that year a full time Dean was appointed and in 1936 came the further appointment of a full time Head of the Prosthetic Department whose teaching duties included dental mechanics and clinical prosthetics. All the other members of the staff were part time. Since the war, the introduction of the Health Service and the incorporation of the School in the University have necessitated the appointment of 20 full time and four part time members of the University staff, two full time S.H.D.O.s and two part time Consultants, one Senior Registrar, four Registrars and five House Surgeons.

Not surprisingly in the light of all this, post-graduate dental education has been developing steadily. Most of the post-graduate students are general dental practitioners attending refresher courses arranged by the Edinburgh Post-graduate Medical Board and run by the staff of the University and the Regional Hospital Board with financial assistance from the Scottish Home and Health Department. The second type of post-graduate student is preparing for a post-graduate degree or Diploma, most frequently the Fellowship in Dental Surgery of the Royal College of Surgeons.

THE OPTICIANS

At the end of 1963 there were 98 opticians in practice in the city, 88 of them ophthalmic opticians who both test sight and supply optical appliances such as spectacles and reading glasses, and the remaining 10 dispensing opticians who only provide appliances. Of the ophthalmic opticians four were women. The average age of the men was around 50 years.

The Edinburgh opticians have joined with their Border colleagues in conducting the Edinburgh and Border Local Association of Optical Practitioners, which arranges technical discussions and social events. This association is one of seven in Scotland represented on the Scottish National Committee of Ophthalmic Opticians, which acts on behalf of the profession in, for example, negotiations with the Department of Health over the National Health Service. It also keeps a close watch on all proposed legislation which might affect opticians and makes representations when it thinks these are required.

VETERINARY MEDICINE

As Edinburgh's veterinary school was founded as far back as 1823 it is the oldest in Scotland and the second to be established in Britain. It is also now an integral part of the University. The Edinburgh Veterinary School, as it was first known, came into being as the result of an arrangement between the Highland and Agricultural Society of Scotland and William Dick, a leading veterinary practitioner in the city, who had been the first Scotsman to qualify at the recently established London Veterinary School and who, on return, decided to start a similar school of his own.

Dick's efforts were quickly rewarded by the widespread fame they acquired. The first veterinary schools in many other countries such as Canada, Australia, India and the United States were founded by pupils of Dick who carried with them the aims and ideals of their instructor. Fortunately too, when William Dick died in 1866 his school was carried on by the Town Council of Edinburgh which acted as his Trustee until 1906, when it was incorporated by Act of Parliament under the name of the Royal (Dick) Veterinary College.[1] Until 1951 the College was administered by a Board of Management consisting of nominees of the Town Council, the University, the Highland and Agricultural Society and the Scottish Colleges of Agriculture along with some veterinary surgeons practising in Scotland. But in that year the College which had been affiliated to the University of Edinburgh since 1934 was embodied within the University as a section of the Faculty of Medicine with the designation Royal (Dick) School of Veterinary Studies; and there it is today at Summerhall after various extensions, reconstructions and changes of site.

After the first World War because of increases in the number of students and extension of the curriculum from three to ultimately five years extensive additions had to be made to the School in the 1930s. But these proved insufficient to meet not only the School's further growth but a complete change in emphasis from the horse to other farm species which also made it necessary to provide increased animal accommodation. To meet this need the University has recently developed a Veterinary Field Station as part of the Edinburgh Centre of Rural Economy on the Bush Estate, some five miles south of the city; and here there has been provided not only a well-equipped Large Animal Hospital but also ample accommodation and facilities for instruction and research into factors affecting the maintenance of health and the prevention and control of disease. Here too, final year and post-graduate students receive their clinical instruction in connection with farm animal species. The pre-clinical and para-clinical departments as well as the Small Animal Clinic for domestic pets remain in the city.

[1] It will be remembered that in the meantime the energy of the city's Medical Officer of Health, Dr. Littlejohn, had resulted in the appointment of its first Veterinary Officer (1904) and 10 years later, when Littlejohn was no longer on the scene, of a separate Veterinary Department. These appointments were designed to ease the solution of problems caused by slaughterhouses, animal markets and other problems such as dairy inspection.

VETERINARY STUDENTS

The Edinburgh Veterinary School accepts up to 55 students a year approximately 10 per cent being girls, and there they study for five years the various basic sciences with a bearing on problems of animal health and disease. The School also runs two post-graduate courses which are unique not only in this country but throughout the English-speaking world. These are in Veterinary State Medicine for those veterinary surgeons who decide to become Government Veterinary Officers and in Tropical Veterinary Medicine for those who intend to work in under-developed countries. These two courses attract about 30 veterinary surgeons per annum while another 20 or so post-graduate students study for higher academic degrees. Finally, the School has a professional staff of about 50 to cope with the teaching, to staff its various clinical practices and animal hospitals and to undertake fundamental research in the veterinary field.

RESEARCH

Edinburgh is well equipped with facilities for veterinary research. The Animal Diseases Research Organisation at Moredun employs about 20 full-time veterinary surgeons engaged in research into a variety of veterinary problems particularly in the field of sheep diseases. The Veterinary Investigation Officer service of the East of Scotland College of Agriculture helps with ad hoc investigational problems encountered by veterinary surgeons in practice in the course of their day to day activities. The agricultural Research Council's Poultry Research Centre at King's Buildings touches on some veterinary problems as does also its Animal Breeding Research Organisation whose headquarters are in the city; while only a few miles away at Eskgrove is the Ministry of Agriculture's Poultry Pathological Laboratory, the main centre in Scotland for investigation of those animal diseases which are the focus of official action.

In 1954 the Royal Commission on Scottish Affairs recommended that responsibility for the administration in Scotland of the Diseases of Animals Act, 1950, and other legislation dealing with animal health should be transferred to the Secretary of State. This resulted in the appointment of veterinary staff to advise the Secretary of State. There is, therefore, in Edinburgh a Deputy Chief Veterinary Officer of the Animal Health Division with a busy staff of eight veterinary officers to assist him in the city. In addition, about 12 veterinary surgeons in private practice devote most of their time to the welfare of a great many domestic pets and to the riding horses which have been increasing in number in recent years. Some of these surgeons also provide veterinary services for farms within and near the city boundaries.

PUBLIC HEALTH

THE PAST

We come now to a notable survey of the city's public health compiled for the *Third Statistical Account of Scotland* by Dr H. E. Seiler in the late '50s and revised in the early '60s shortly before his retirement in 1963 as one of Edinburgh's most energetic Medical Officers of Health. Dr. Seiler's survey is not only revealing in its presentation of many facts and figures probably unknown to most Edinburgh people, but makes salutary reading for all who wish to improve living conditions in the city as a whole. The past hundred years, he writes, have seen tremendous improvements in the health and environment of the citizens of Edinburgh, since the temporary Boards of Health set up to cope with the ravages of cholera in 1832 and 1848–9 were frustrated in their efforts by the housing and general insanitary state of the city. " The houses are the highest in the world, and the most densely peopled", said one report. " The stairs leading to the various flats have been aptly likened to upright streets, so numerous are the inhabitants that are met with on every landing."

Despite these conditions the citizens of Edinburgh slumbered on, content to leave things largely as they were until they had a rude awakening one dark November morning in 1861, when one of these tenements in the High Street " ran together with a hideous uproar and tumbled story upon story to the ground." Thirty-five people were killed and many injured, one of whom, a youth, encouraged his rescuers by calling out, " Heave awa,' lads", an incident commemorated by a sculpture of the youth's head on the arch leading into Chalmers Close, High Street.

This disaster led to so many public protests, that finally, in February, 1862, an influential deputation waited on the Town Council to urge the immediate appointment of an " officer of health." Eloquently and forcefully couched, the plea was accepted. On 30th September of the same year, Dr. Henry Duncan Littlejohn became Medical Officer of Health for the city—the first such appointment in Scotland—and for the next 46 years this remarkable man combined the duties of medical officer of health and police surgeon with outstanding success.

Faced with endemic " fever", outbreaks of cholera, smallpox, typhus and typhoid fevers, it was evident to Littlejohn that two things were needful if he was to achieve any success in improving the health of the community. The first was a complete and thorough review of the sanitary state of the city, old and new; the second, some form of notification of the prevalent infectious diseases.

Following on his appointment Littlejohn undertook the first of his projects, which resulted in his *Report on the Sanitary Condition of Edinburgh*. Published in 1865 this Report, regarded as a model of its kind, made it clear beyond argument that those districts which were densely populated and overcrowded had the highest death-rates. For example, George Square and Lauriston district had a death rate of 37·46; Abbey

36·65; Tron 34·55; Grassmarket 32·52; Canongate 31·23; and St. Giles 28·8. These districts all had population densities per inhabited acres varying from 219 to 352, and their death rates compared with a rate for the whole city, old and new, of 25·88. The Report, having also dealt comprehensively with common lodging houses, conditions of bakehouses, byres, drainage and water supply, and intra-mural burial, offered suggestions whereby the city might be improved; and all of these in due course of time were acted upon.

The immediate practical outcome, stimulated by a further epidemic of cholera in 1866, was the promotion by Lord Provost William Chambers of a City Improvement Act the following year. The attack on the slums had now begun in earnest and new streets and thoroughfares were constructed at a cost of over half a million sterling. Under successive Medical Officers of Health this policy of city improvement and expansion, of which Littlejohn was the pioneer, has been steadfastly pursued.

Two recent projects undertaken in connection with housing and sanitation were the surveys made in 1935 and 1946 to determine the degree of overcrowding and the housing needs of the city generally. In 1935, of 99,608 publicly and privately owned houses of rental of £45 or under which were reviewed, 6,740 were found to be unfit, and 2,645 of these houses were overcrowded. The number of families involved in the survey was 103,083, of which 20,244 or 19·64 per cent were overcrowded. The 1946 survey showed that there were 133,261 families resident in the 120,265 houses reviewed, which meant that 12,996 families were living in sublet apartments. Considered by the same standard as the 1935 survey, the degree of overcrowding in houses with a rental of £45 or under was 15·71 per cent, a reduction of almost 4 per cent. Revised standards introduced in 1944, however, brought the degree of overcrowding up to 32·7 per cent, and on that basis the estimated housing requirements in 1946 were 50,000 new and 12,000 reconstructed houses.

From 1923 until 1961, under the Housing (Scotland) Acts of 1919–59, some 3,723 individual unfit houses, involving 11,202 persons, were dealt with under demolition or closing orders or by acceptance of statutory declarations from the owners.

It is a far cry now from the days of "Gardyloo", the warning shout when slops were emptied into the street below from lofty tenements, but it is certainly a poor reflection on some of the citizens that in 1961 the Sanitary Department (formed in 1898) dealt with no less than 73 complaints of bread or garbage being thrown from windows.

Another long-standing problem arose from the killing of animals, and here most fortunately Littlejohn's early interest in the conditions of slaughterhouses and meat inspection led to new buildings being erected at Gorgie for the Cornmarket, Cattlemarket and Slaughterhouses. Begun before he retired in 1908, these buildings were completed in 1910. The removal of the cattlemarket from Lauriston was, *inter alia*, owing to "difficulties apt to arise with the entry and leaving of cattle and sheep when the Fire Brigade is called out on one of its numerous and sometimes hourly calls."

In 1904, as we saw, the first Veterinary Officer was appointed and in 1914 a separate Veterinary Department was set up. The Milk and Dairies (Scotland) Act did not become operative until 1925, although routine inspection of dairies in the city had been carried out since 1904, and cows showing evidence of tuberculous udder were ordered to be removed from the herd under a clause in the Edinburgh Municipal and Police (Amendment) Act, 1891. No power was given to slaughter the affected animals, however, and many of them found their way to premises elsewhere. Recent legislation has given the Veterinary Department greater and wider powers to deal with such problems.

The second of Littlejohn's projects—to obtain accurate knowledge of the incidence of infectious disease—was accomplished through the passing of the Edinburgh Municipal and Police Act, 1879, by which compulsory powers of notification were introduced into the city in respect of cholera, typhus, typhoid, diphtheria, smallpox, scarlet fever, scarlatina and measles. This was achieved several years in advance of general compulsory notification of infectious disease. But the Corporation was slow to deal with the actual treatment of infectious diseases, and after experience of using the old Canongate Poorhouse and the Old Royal Infirmary in Drummond Street as fever hospitals, the 1894 epidemic of smallpox brought with it the realisation that a new fever hospital was required and the present fever hospital at Colinton Mains was opened in 1903—a further testimony to Littlejohn's energies and foresight. By the time he retired in 1908 he had in fact seen the disappearance of cholera and typhus fever and the virtual removal of smallpox as a threat to the community. He was also deeply impressed with the potentialities of Philip's work on tuberculosis, and rejoiced when at least voluntary notification of this disease was introduced in 1903, nine years before its compulsory adoption.

Littlejohn's retirement at the age of 82 marked the end of an epoch in public health in the city. He was original in outlook and dynamic in action, but his successors have been equally individualistic in making powerful contributions to improve the city whose welfare was committed to their care. Dr. A. Maxwell Williamson (1908–23) formulated comprehensive schemes for tuberculosis (1912), maternity and child welfare (1916) and venereal disease (1919). During his term of office Leith was amalgamated with Edinburgh (1920) and port health duties were transferred also. Dr. William Robertson, Medical Office of Health for Leith and later Dr. Williamson's deputy, succeeded him (1923–30). Robertson was a leading advocate of prevention, and health slogans on lamp standards were an outward and visible sign of his approach to the citizens which was one of " taking the people with you." He organised successful health and hygiene exhibitions, and during his brief term of office Schick-testing and active immunisation of school children, the first attempt at such in the country, was undertaken on a large scale in 1924. Within a year he also introduced a system of voluntary notification of food poisoning. Dr. John Guy's period as Medical Officer of Health (1930–8) was marked by the development of the municipal hospitals scheme and the absorption of the School Medical Service into the Health Department. Guy was succeeded by Dr. William George Clark (1938–53), an able administrator and expert on housing. It was his fate to serve through World War II, and he bore the heavy responsibility of organising the city's casualty service. Fortunately Edinburgh was spared heavy bombing, the wartime civilian casualties numbering only 20 killed and 217 injured. During this period, too, the municipal and emergency hospital scheme was furthered. Dr. Clark's abiding interests were housing, tuberculosis and health education, all of which made great advances during his administration.

VITAL STATISTICS

The remarkable improvements in the public health over the past hundred or so years in Edinburgh are illustrated by the figures in the following Table, in which the rates given (with one exception) are per 1,000 of the population. The exception is the infant mortality rate, which is the rate per 1,000 live births.

TABLE 28
EDINBURGH: VITAL STATISTICS, 1863, 1913, 1953, 1958, 1961

Year	*Population*	*Birth Rate*	*Death Rate*	*Infant Mortality Rate*	*Phthisis Death Rate*	*Zymotic Death Rate*	*Population per acre*
1863	170,441 (1861 Census)	36·24	25·88	145	2·54	6·23	49·0
1913	321,645	20·07	14·39	101	1·13	0·87	28·1
1953	470,847	15·4	12·3	24	0·23	0·10	14·2
1958	467,410	16·8	12·9	25	0·06	0·03	13·9
1961	474,062*	17·7	13·1	23	0·03	0·07	13·6

* Estimate at 30th June, 1961.

These improvements are apparent in almost every aspect of health, but two disquieting statistics, the increasing death rates amongst men from coronary thrombosis and from lung cancer, have been responsible for the depressingly static death rate amongst men of middle age and older since 1920. This has contrasted strongly with the declining death rates among middle-aged women. By 1961 this levelling-off in the male death rate had begun to show an alarming tendency towards a rising mortality among these middle-aged men.

TABLE 29
DEATHS BY AGE AND SEX—EDINBURGH 1961

Cause of Death	*Sex*	*Age*					
		35–44	*45–54*	*55–64*	*65–74*	*75+*	*Over* 35
A. All Causes	Males	80	307	610	825	984	2,806
	Females	69	192	409	772	1,623	3,065
B. Arteriosclerotic and Degenerative Heart Disease	Males	22	96	214	267	313	912
	Females	2	25	84	196	532	839

TABLE 29 (*continued*)
DEATHS BY AGE AND SEX—EDINBURGH 1961

Cause of Death	Sex	Age					
		35–44	45–54	55–64	65–74	75+	Over35
C. Malignant Neoplasms	Males Females	14 23	92 80	197 126	204 171	135 160	642 560
D. Cancer of Bronchus and Lungs	Males Females	9 1	41 4	98 18	90 18	34 11	272 52
E. Bronchitis	Males Females	3 4	10 6	47 9	63 25	53 38	176 82

These figures show clearly the influence of lung cancer, arteriosclerotic heart conditions and chronic bronchitis on the differential deaths between middle-aged men and middle-aged women. In view of the excess of women in Edinburgh's population, these figures are even more disturbing than they appear at first sight, as is brought out by the following table in which the deaths are expressed as a proportion of the population at risk in each age-sex group:—

TABLE 30
EDINBURGH DEATH-RATES 1961

Cause of Death	Sex	Death-Rates per Thousand of Sex/Age Group Population					
		35–44	45–54	55–64	65–74	75+	All ages over 35
A. Arteriosclerotic and Degenerative Heart Disease	Male Female	0·73 0·06	3·11 0·69	8·70 2·56	19·93 8·67	52·34 40·00	8·69 6·07
B. Malignant Neoplasms (Cancer)	Male Female	0·46 0·69	2·98 2·22	8·01 3·84	15·23 7·57	22·58 12·03	6·12 4·05
C. Cancer of Bronchus and Lungs	Male Female	0·30 0·03	1.33 0·11	3·98 0·55	6·72 0·80	5·69 0·83	2·59 0·38
D. Bronchitis	Male Female	0·10 0·12	0·32 0·17	1·91 0·27	4·70 1·11	8·86 2·86	1·68 0·59

While it is possible that some occupational factor or factors could account for the anomalous mortality of males, it seems much more likely that smoking, so much less common among women, is the factor responsible. There can be little doubt that this is a public health problem to which the public health services must address themselves with all their energy. Equally there can be no letting-up in slum clearance and the reduction of overcrowding, for these also have a vital effect on the city's health together with the closely associated problem of hygiene.

"THE CITY CLEANED AND COUNTRY IMPROVEN"

In 1760 a hygiene tract, first written in 1735 by Robert Mein, came out with the inspiring title *The City Cleaned and Country Improven.* Mein quoted " the reproach cast upon us . . . that in a city called Edinburgh in Scotland, it rains dung from the heavens every night, and especially on Saturday nights, and Sabbath mornings, so that the people make their way through a very nasty and offensive passage to church on the Sabbath days."

Mein unfortunately did not inspire the citizens to change their ways, a century later the sanitary state of the city was still appalling. But there were signs of betterment, for in 1856, after an interval of control by the Police Commissioners, the Town Council had assumed charge and in consequence through the years the streets became cleaner, the pens and closes purged of their accumulations, and the middens replaced by communal bins called paladins—a strange euphemism to amuse the etymologist of the future.

In 1893 the first large scale destructor was opened at Powderhall. Redesigned in 1929 this was supplemented by additional plants at Russell Road in 1938 and at Seafield in 1939. An important function of these destructor plants is the salvaging of re-usable materials. This brought into the city coffers almost one and a half million pounds between 1940 and 1958, and still continues to do so.

The filling of Hailes Quarry, to hold two million tons of refuse, started in 1950, and 685,319 tons of refuse—about one million cubic yards—had been deposited by 1958. In the meantime a development of major importance took place in July, 1955 when Edinburgh Corporation became the first local authority in Great Britain to introduce composting of refuse with sewage to conserve organic materials for use as agricultural fertiliser. The pilot Dano Mechanical Composting Plant was installed to produce an average of 30–35 tons of compost per week, but a large-scale plant came into operation at Craigmillar in 1958. This plant, with a capacity of 140 tons of crude refuse per day and including as it does two Dano Bio-Stabilisers each with 310 cubic yards capacity, deals with all the domestic refuse from the south side of the city, thus serving a population of 150,000 people.

Food waste is collected in about 42,000 household pails for use as pig food, so that only about one household in four uses this method. The bulk of household food waste passes through the normal refuse system and should be invaluable for composting. Then there are the dustbins. More than 160,000 of these are emptied twice weekly from the kerbside by 49 vehicles each with three loaders and a driver. No household collection is made in Edinburgh, and visitors are often amused to see immaculate business men, with umbrella and *Scotsman* under one arm, staggering from their homes under the weight of the household refuse bin which they deposit on the kerbside before climbing aboard a passing bus.

The average weekly output per house is 26·79 lbs. varying from 21·09 lbs. in summer to 30·90 lbs. in winter. A change in household habits has thrown an enormous strain on the organisation in recent years. In 1947–8 the density of household refuse was 6·51 cwts. per cubic yard. But though in 1957–8 the density had fallen to 3·88 cwts. per cubic yard the total annual weight of refuse had increased by about 10,000 tons. The result has been a doubling of the volume of refuse that must be handled.

STREET CLEANSING

The Manager of the Lighting and Cleansing Department has reported: " The total mileage of streets cleansed by the Corporation is in the region of 490 miles. Bus tickets, broken glass and dog-fouling are the most frequent causes of unsightly streets. All are preventable by public co-operation, and all are offences under the Edinburgh Corporation Order and carry penalties up to £5." This work in the early '60s was carried out by seven mechanical sweeper collectors, 30 pedestrian-controlled electric trucks (three men each) and 79 street orderlies on the beat system.

Close washing, etc. was done by three men and a 1,400 gallon water tank is employed whole time. The emptying of 24,199 street gullies, a total of 158,258 emptyings, is done by nine machines of the compressor type.

EDINBURGH'S SEWAGE SYSTEM

" One of the characteristics of medieval towns was the absence of sanitation and the prevalence of plague." So said the Edinburgh Corporation Financial Review 1957–8. " The situation of Edinburgh, distant from running water of any volume," the Review continued, " made drainage a constant problem and prior to the 18th century it was merely a name in the town. The cholera epidemics were instrumental in stimulating the provision of sewers here as elsewhere. At the beginning of the 19th century there were three large sewers in the Old Town, one of these taking the water of the North Loch and proceeding by the north back of the Canongate; another went by the Cowgate to Holyrood Park, and a third proceeded from the district of George Square also to Holyrood Park. These three sewers delivered their contents in one united stream into a wide open ditch near the Clock Mill, the stream being known by the name of the Foul Burn, and flowing in open channels to the sea. The other districts of the city drained principally into the Water of Leith, and indeed this stream provided a ready-made open sewer not only for Edinburgh but for the whole area which it traversed.

" Acts passed in 1854, 1864 and 1889 contributed to a general improvement, and under the Act of 1889 a body of Commissioners was set up to supervise the Water of Leith, which in 1920 came under the direct control of the Corporation.

" The main sewers in Portobello were constructed about 1855 and the original outfalls on the beach at Morton Street and Pipe Street have been dispensed with and the sewage carried either to Joppa or Seafield, which also takes the Powburn Sewer constructed about 1888. This sewer, constructed from Seafield along Braid Burn and Pow Burn, with an extension to Morningside, discharges with the Craigentinny Sewer.

" The main sewers in the County of Midlothian, forming the Liberton

District Drainage Area and taken over in 1920 when the city boundaries were extended, follow the course of the Braid Burn and Niddrie Burn, and discharge into the Forth at Joppa.

" Major schemes carried out since 1920 include the provision of main sewers to cope with city expansion, the collecting together of sewers discharging by separate outfalls to the sea, providing new outfalls carried further out below the water mark, and screening plant disintegrating apparatus at these new outfalls."

CONTAMINATED SHELLFISH

Bacteriological examination of mussels from the Newhaven and Musselburgh areas has shown them to be consistently and grossly contaminated with sewage. On occasion enteric organisms have been isolated from samples and these shellfish must be considered highly dangerous. Small wonder that Sweet Molly died of the fever. Small wonder too that all along the foreshore at appropriate points from Granton to Musselburgh notices have been displayed for a number of years warning that " mussels from this foreshore are liable to infection and should not be collected as food."

Unfortunately the public health authorities in Scotland, as these words are written, have no powers to prohibit the collection of mussels from infected beds, similar to those granted under the English Public Health (Shellfish) Regulations, 1934. However, the real solution lies in the control of river pollution.

THE PROBLEM OF RIVER AND FORESHORE POLLUTION

There was, in 1959, only one small sewage treatment plant in Edinburgh—in the Liberton Ward. The great part of Edinburgh's sewage, and that of neighbouring burghs and county areas, is poured, after screening and disintegration, directly into the waters of the River Forth. Not unnaturally therefore the problem of foreshore contamination has long caused the city's Health Committee and the Medical Officer of Health grave concern, and indeed notices warning of the dangers of bathing in these polluted waters have been erected along the Cramond foreshore.

In January and February 1958 the Medical Officer of Health demonstrated bacteriological evidence of faecal contamination at the Cramond beach east of the River Almond, the beach opposite the sewer outfall at Seafield, points east and west of the Figgate Burn, the Paddling Pool, and the beach between the Paddling Pool and the Saltworks. Mussels cleansed at the Fisheries Experiment Station, Conway, Caernarvonshire, were planted in the Paddling Pool and showed evidence of marked faecal contamination.

At this time plans were in hand for the reduction of pollution around the River Almond Estuary by the extension of the main sewer through Cramond Island. This discharged some way short of Cramond Island.

Of recent years, experts and public alike have been increasingly critical of this form of sewage disposal, and it has been suggested that the standards of dilution for such highly infected sewage outflows recommended by the Royal Commission on Sewage Disposal should be re-examined in view of the possibility of virus infections persisting in tidal waters used for bathing purposes.

These fears had their legislative expression in the Rivers (Prevention of Pollution) (Scotland) Act of 1951 with its associate Firth of Forth (Prevention of Pollution) (Tidal Waters) Order, 1958, operating from 1st March, 1959. As a preliminary to this Order, the Lothians River Purification Board's River Inspector carried out, between 25th August and 19th September, 1958, a survey of the River Forth Tidal Waters from the River Almond to Gullane Point and extending out to mid channel.

The Salinity and Dissolved Oxygen Tests showed the maximum discharge of sewage between five and nine miles off shore, the " sag " in these test values moving up and down the estuary for various levels of the tide. The dissolved oxygen fell from 130 per cent in mid-channel to a level of 90 per cent in-shore, with a low level of 70 per cent around Granton Harbour. The report suggested also that, during late August and early September, when temperatures can be high and drought conditions exist, the concentration of dissolved oxygen might fall well below the 50 per cent level, and approach the level of 20–30 per cent. Where inorganic discharges form artificial barriers these result in the deposition of organic solids producing septic sludges with a resulting drop in oxygen concentration to near zero levels. Evidence of this was found in small pockets in the Leith and Portobello areas.

The distribution of coliform bacteria—indicators of sewage and organic pollution—showed the greatest concentration of bacteria in proximity to sewage outfalls and beaches. Counts ranged up to 1,000,000 coliform organisms per cubic centimetre in areas offshore from the sewage outfalls. These are disturbingly high counts, but in the case of specimens collected along the shore counts ranged from as low as 150 coliforms to 100 cubic centimetres up to 21,000,000 in an area where the waters and foreshore were described as follows:

> Samples contained considerable solids in suspension, greyish in appearance. Foreshore covered with sludge for a distance of 450 yards east of Western Boundary sewer.
>
> Samples dirty with appreciable solids in suspension. Refuse deposited on beach.
>
> Samples dirty in appearance, coarse solids (faecal matter) to be seen. Deposit of filth on beaches.

These conditions improve eastward of the Seafield Sewer but deteriorate in the vicinity of all the coastal burghs of Mid and East Lothian, with distinct evidence of pollution around Longniddry and Aberlady Bay.

It is true that a recent report of the Medical Research Council has somewhat allayed fears of danger of infection from bathing in waters into which untreated sewage is discharged, but, if only from the amenity viewpoint, the conditions shown by the River Inspector indicate a problem that Edinburgh has still to tackle.

A CITY OF CLEAN AIR

Edinburgh can boast the first smokeless zone in Scotland. This was set up at the Sighthill Industrial Estate under the provisions of the Edinburgh Corporation Order 1950, and was sensibly chosen in the south-west corner of the city in view of the prevailing south-westerly winds. The zone has now been extended by the establishment of a Smoke Control Area under the 1956 Clean Air Act in the district around Broomhouse, which has many dwelling houses.

The preliminary and laborious procedure to establish the Sighthill housing estate as a Smoke Control Area then got under way, and so by 1960–1 an area of 370 acres covering 2,321 properties, mostly dwelling houses became effectively smokeless.

Another noteworthy advance is known as The Gracemount Experiment. Since its inception in the second half of 1956 the Gracemount housing estate has been used as an experimental area in which the burning of smokeless fuel is a condition of tenancy, although the area has not been scheduled as a Smoke Control Area. The experiments there have shown that coke can be used successfully as a domestic fuel, and that there is no evidence of deleterious effects on the health of the families using them nor any detectable carbon monoxide in the room atmosphere. Within 10–15 years it is hoped the whole of Edinburgh will be a smoke control area.

INFECTIOUS DISEASE

The first function of the Public Health Department is still the control of epidemic disease. Control in Edinburgh starts at the Port of Leith—marine gateway to the city. During the period under review the six major epidemic diseases controlled by international action have practically disappeared. Plague was eliminated by flea and rat control at Leith and other ports. Cholera is now largely confined to India and Pakistan. Yellow fever, even with international air travel, is limited to endemic areas. Typhus fever, conveyed by the louse, produced millions of cases during and after the 1914–18 war, but in the second World War outbreaks were prevented by the use of D.D.T. and typhus vaccination. Relapsing fever too is controlled by insecticides. Smallpox occasionally spreads from Asia by sea and air, and is the only one of these diseases for which medical staff require to be on the alert at the port.

By the opening of the City Hospital in 1903 infectious patients could be separated from the rest of the community, and the spread of infection reduced. But the days of these isolation hospitals now appear to be numbered, as with better living standards and better nourished children and young people the common infectious diseases are so mild as no longer to be a serious problem.

Measles, of which only the first case under five years of age in a household is notified, has shown an irregular fall in incidence since 1930, when there were 7,182 notified cases, to 1,202 notifications in 1961. More startling, however, has been the diminution in deaths from measles, largely due to improved treatment with the antibiotics, the five-yearly average figures since 1932 being 42, 14, 7, 4, 2, 1.

Whilst the actual numbers of whooping-cough cases have shown the usual two-yearly rise, the number of deaths has fallen markedly from 72 in 1930 to only two in the last five years.

Scarlet fever has also shown a remarkable decline since 1930. In that year there were 1,278 cases with eight deaths, whilst in 1961 there were only 158 cases and there have been no deaths since 1945. In the post-war period there has been no return to the epidemic years which formerly occurred—to 1933, for example, when there were more than 4,500 cases, of whom 21 died.

Typhoid fever also is becoming a clinical rarity in Edinburgh. The 35 notifications in 1930 were only exceeded in 1933 and 1941 when 50 and 68 cases occurred. Since 1942 the annual number of typhoid cases has never reached double figures and only one patient has died in the period. The milder condition of paratyphoid fever still occurs with approximately 10 cases each year.

The position with regard to diphtheria is a complete transformation from the scene in 1930 when, with 1,102 cases and 71 deaths, the diphtheria wards in the City Hospital were occupied to the fullest extent, each patient remaining in hospital for many weeks. Today cases of diphtheria in the city are unexpected.

The infection which has caused most alarm of recent years is poliomyelitis, rarely seen in the city until the 1930s, when in 1936 alone as many as 46 cases were notified, a total which was only exceeded—by 28 cases in 1941—during the next 10 years. A country-wide epidemic developed however in 1947, when 151 cases were notified in Edinburgh, and each of the subsequent years produced between 30 and 70 cases until 1959, when no case occurred. Only one case occurred in 1960, and four in 1961.

Bacillary dysentry is one of the few infectious diseases to show a marked increase in prevalence during this period. Very few cases were notified in the years before 1932, when 40 cases occurred, and since then there has been a rather irregular rise in numbers, until from 1954 onwards just over 1,000 cases occurred each year.

Immunisation programmes have played a considerable part in reducing these infections, and this applies particularly to smallpox and diphtheria. Each year some 6,500 children receive primary immunisation against diphtheria, whilst primary vaccinations against smallpox number approximately 6,000. These figures refer to the numbers actually notified to the Department, but a research survey undertaken by the Health Visitors indicates that the position is, in fact, very much more favourable.

Whooping-cough immunisation has probably played a large part in the reduced incidence of that infection, and a poliomyelitis vaccination scheme, launched in 1956, may account for the absence of poliomyelitis from the city in 1959.

The way in which infectious disease had been brought under control in the city by the start of the '60s is shown by the mortality figures.

1961	
Poliomyelitis	Nil
Measles	2
Tuberculosis	15
Road accidents	70
Gas poisoning	39
Other home accidents	119
Lung cancer	325

These figures also indicate the new problems of public health in seeking to reduce accidents in the home and to take action to prevent lung cancer.

THE CONTROL OF TUBERCULOSIS

In his *Special Report on Tuberculosis in Edinburgh* (*1952*) the Medical Officer of Health, then Dr. W. G. Clark, remarked on the confusion in the minds of the public caused by conflicting statements from medical authorities. Hence the paradoxical position that while the notified incidence of the disease rose steadily from 92 per 100,000 in 1939 to 154 per 100,000 in 1952, the death rate fell from 60 deaths per 100,000 of the population immediately before the war, and 62 in 1948 to 26 deaths per 100,000 in 1952.

The Crude Death Rate and Crude Notification Rate (per 100,000) in Edinburgh during this period was as follows:

	1935–9 (*Quinquennial Average*)	*1940–4*	*1945–9*	*1950*	*1951*	*1952*
Crude Notification Rate	100	123	130	139	135	154
Crude Death Rate	61	70	59	48	33	26

The rising incidence of pulmonary tuberculosis in Edinburgh appeared to be associated with wartime conditions, having started during the war and continued steadily in the post war years from a total of 540 notifications in 1945 to 722 notifications in 1952. In February, 1953 there were 258 tuberculosis cases on the waiting lists for hospital treatment.

However, an examination of age group statistics, recounted in the 1952 Special Report, showed that incidence amongst the " peak age-group " from 15 to 20 years had been rising steadily through the 1930s, especially among young women. This rising incidence had been disguised by a falling incidence in other age groups during those years, so that the overall picture was one of declining incidence. The turning point came in 1940, as in so many countries during the war; but in Edinburgh, as for all Scotland, the incidence continued to rise alarmingly in the post-war years. The Special Report of 1952 led directly to the appointment in 1953 of a Senior Medical Officer to take charge of a much enlarged staff of health visitors engaged on tuberculosis control work, case finding, contact investigation, Mantoux testing, B.C.G. vaccination and health education.

In 1954 the first large-scale mass miniature radiography campaign was carried out in the Pilton Ward of the city. This was the first campaign of its kind in Britain, organised as a community campaign by the Pilton Health Campaign Central Committee which represented all organisations in the ward, including industry. (The development of this campaign is described later in this chapter.) Among many other campaign activities, 300 voluntary household visitors called on every house in the ward, often several times over, so that in the four week campaign 11,136 people, or almost 60 per cent of the adult population, were persuaded to come for examination. Altogether 127 unsuspected cases of pulmonary tuberculosis were brought under observation. This, in a ward with the worst or second worst record for pulmonary tuberculosis in the city, was a notable achievement of preventive medicine. When it is realised too that the usual response to mass x-ray campaigns before the Pilton Campaign had varied between 10 and 20 per cent of the adult population drawn upon, the full importance of this event becomes apparent. True, Fletcher had shown in South Wales that given many months of work it was possible to persuade or coerce over 80 per cent of a small population to come for x-ray examination. But Fletcher's methods were impossibly time-consuming for use in large urban areas, and the Pilton Campaign became the prototype for a series of short-term high-pressure urban campaigns in Edinburgh and other parts of Scotland, culminating in the great two-year National Campaign of 1957–8 in which over two million people were x-rayed. In 1958, no fewer than 308,747 Edinburgh people were x-rayed, a remarkable percentage of 84·4 of the adult population. This was the result of a campaign of publicity, community effort and voluntary household visiting on an unprecedented scale. This campaign revealed 462 cases of active pulmonary tuberculosis, and 1,439 cases of doubtful activity requiring observation. Of these, 14 active cases and 17 cases of doubtful activity came from outside Edinburgh.

The combination of really effective mass miniature radiography campaign with equally effective routine and continuous case finding and contact examination began to show results in 1960 and 1961 when only 260 and 266 cases respectively of pulmonary tuberculosis were notified in the first six months of each year. Hopes were freely expressed that this was the beginning of the end of pulmonary tuberculosis as a major public health problem in Edinburgh.

Deaths from pulmonary tuberculosis reached a peak of 314 in 1947, in which year the new antibiotic streptomycin and the drug para amino salicylic acid (P.A.S.) began to be generally used. By 1952 deaths had fallen to 125, by 1961 they had reached the record low figure of 15; and by 1964, Edinburgh had one of the lowest death rates from tuberculosis in the entire world, the main reduction being in the younger age-groups. However, in his Special Report the Medical Officer of Health has pointed out that this was, in some part, due also to a remarkable change resulting from improved case finding and contact examination in the years after the war.

TABLE 31
STAGE OF DISEASE ON NOTIFICATION FOR YEARS 1938, 1947 AND 1952

	1938	*1947*	*1952*
Number Notified	476	606	722
Stage I	86=18%	176=28%	292=40·5%
Stage II	96=20%	128=21%	174=24%
Stage III	239=50%	261=43%	148=25%

The incidence of bone, joint gland and other tuberculosis had by 1961 reached a low level largely as a result of improvements in the milk supply of the city, all milk in 1961 being either heat-treated or from tuberculin-tested herds.

VENEREAL DISEASES

Syphilis. By mid-century the public health problems imposed by venereal disease had changed greatly under the influence of the antibiotics and chemotherapeutic agents—the wonder-drugs of the 1940s and 1950s. Dr. Lees, the Physician-in-Charge (Venereal Diseases Department, Royal Infirmary), reported in 1957 that " early contagious syphilis is now a rare disease and it is difficult to find cases to demonstrate to medical students, many of whom may graduate without seeing a single case of early syphilis." During the year, only nine early cases were discovered and of these only four were Edinburgh infections. In 1960 and 1961, however, the number of cases had slightly increased to 21 and 16 respectively.

Congenital syphilis was also very rare, with no cases diagnosed amongst infants. Of 15 cases diagnosed in 1957 all but three were over 25 years of age. In 1961, of 19 cases diagnosed all were adults. Even late syphilitic disease had become comparatively uncommon, 68 cases being diagnosed in 1957 and 57 in 1961; and as Dr. Lees remarked, " it is anticipated that there will be a gradual slow reduction in the number of such cases."

Gonorrhoea. The optimism which followed introduction of the penicillin treatment of syphilis and gonorrhoea has now given way to fears that promiscuity is on the increase and with it the number of fresh gonorrhoeal infections, the majority—421 cases in 1961—amongst males. The number of cases amongst young girls is disquieting. Of 230 new cases amongst women in 1958, 163 were 18 years old or less.

Dr. Lees comments on this: " As an appreciable proportion of patients disappear as soon as their symptoms are relieved, there are many such carriers who are sexually promiscuous, and difficult to diagnose and treat. Part of the trouble was created years ago when irresponsible press articles spread the belief that ' one-shot treatment ' meant certain cure. Some medical publications, especially in America, were the start of this fiction."

Whatever the case—and the development of strains of the gonococcus resistant to penicillin may be involved—Edinburgh in the early '60s shared with the rest of the country a disturbing increase in the incidence of fresh gonorrhoeal infections.

Trichomonal Disease, warns Dr. Lees, " is not a harmless nuisance but a considerable menace—often transferred sexually," though " there are many other ways of transfer, mostly associated with defective hygiene and habits in the home. While methods of treatment are now much improved, it is still a tedious condition to cure. There is great need for renewed emphasis on cleanliness and simple hygiene in the home as very many houses and places of employment have a scandalous standard of W.C. and washing facilities."

LOCAL HEALTH AUTHORITY SERVICES

MATERNITY AND CHILD WELFARE

The considerable advances in environmental hygiene, so characteristic of the latter half of the 19th century, produced no improvement in infant and child mortality and the present century opened in Edinburgh with an infant mortality rate of 132 per 1,000 live births. Of 1,635 deaths of children under five years, 1,080 or almost two-thirds were of infants under one year. In the separate burgh of Leith a similar unsatisfactory state of affairs existed. Truly the infant then entered life under the shadow of death.

In 1961 there were 221 deaths under five years, 190 of them during the first year, and of these infant deaths 129 or 68 per cent occurred during the first week and 77 or 41 per cent in the first day. The infant mortality rate was 23. In the first quarter of 1964 the infant mortality rate was 18, compared with 29 for the first three months of 1963—a lower figure than any recorded before in Edinburgh. These comparative figures show the tremendous improvement which has taken place over the past half century; and indeed for some years now, Edinburgh has had an infant mortality rate consistently lower than that for Scotland as a whole and for Glasgow and Dundee, but a higher rate than for Aberdeen.

Gone are the deaths from rickets, malnutrition, general debility, atrophy, lack of breast milk, convulsions and such like; it is prematurity, congenital anomalies, and asphyxia-atelectasis which now constitute the main causes of infant deaths. Gone, too, are the deaths from gastroenteritis, measles, whooping cough, scarlet fever and diphtheria in the young child; accidents and respiratory diseases form the hard core at present. Indeed, infant and child deaths have now become individual matters, as the 1961 figures show. The 190 infant deaths then were 12 more than in 1960, the birth rates for the two years being almost the same, 17·7–17·9; but the 12 deaths increase was sufficient to raise the infant mortality rate from 21 to 23. Wastage of infant life from stillbirth however dropped from a rate of 40 in 1939 to 19 in 1961. Perinatal mortality, i.e. a combination of stillbirths and deaths in the first week of life, now constitutes the greatest remaining problem in the campaign for saving infant life. Care of the mother, potential and actual, has assumed paramount importance with, it may be, a part solution to be found in the field of genetics.

TABLE 32
INFANT AND NEONATAL MORTALITY AND STILLBORN RATES
EDINBURGH, 1948–61

Year	*Infant Mortality Rate per 1,000 live births*	*Neonatal Mortality Rate per 1,000 live births*	*Stillbirth Mortality Rate per 1,000 total births*
1948	34	19	29
1949	32	19	24
1950	29	18	24
1951	27	17	27
1952	29	19	27
1953	24	16	22
1954	25	19	21
1955	25	18	24
1956	24	18	23
1957	24	17	19
1958	25	17	19
1959	24	18	19
1960	21	16	19
1961	23	17	19

Leith was in the van of the infant welfare movement in Scotland, for an infants' milk depot was opened there in April, 1903. Later the burgh developed a well organised maternity and child welfare scheme which was absorbed into the Edinburgh scheme with the amalgamation of Edinburgh and Leith in 1920. Before the introduction in 1916 of proposals for Edinburgh by Dr. Maxwell Williamson, Medical Officer of Health, various services relating to the health and welfare of mothers and young children were rendered by a number of voluntary agencies. Williamson's proposals, described by Sir Leslie Mackenzie as " one of the most complete schemes and deserving of the closest study," were finally introduced in 1919 and subsequently expanded. An outlay of £4,500 was Williamson's estimate for his scheme, and this he contrasted with the £14,000 spent annually " in an effort to cure tuberculous disease." He also prophesied that this modest expenditure was likely to be attended by results " of a much more lasting and beneficient nature." His prophecy proved correct, and to-day the personnel of the maternity and child welfare service numbers about 400.

A contribution of exceptional value to public health was that of James William Ballantyne, whose advocacy of ante-natal care was finally recognised by the establishment in 1915 of an ante-natal department at the Royal Maternity Hospital in Edinburgh.

Ante-natal clinics, staffed by consultants, formed an integral part of the Corporation's service until the introduction of the National Health Service; but thereafter the 17 clinics for which the Corporation was either directly responsible or to which it had made financial grants, were absorbed into the hospital service or disappeared altogether. Two main reasons contributed to this. The first was the steadily increasing incidence, commencing in the 1930s, of institutional deliveries, the women attending, from all parts of the city, the clinics provided at the four maternity hospitals. The second was the provision by the local health authority of a domiciliary midwifery service, the midwives acting in conjunction with the general practitioners concerned. To offset the loss of these clinics and to further health teaching, mothercraft clubs were evolved.

The Corporation's present domiciliary midwifery service in the early '60s has been based on the provision of a service of 16 municipal midwives, operated from five centres. By agency arrangements with the Queen's Institute of District Nursing and the Regional Hospital Board, eight midwives are made available. In 1961, of 1,591 home confinements—these represented 19·0 per cent of the total births in the city to Edinburgh women—the municipal midwives attended 1,035 or 65 per cent; midwives from the Queen's Institute attended 143 and those from the Regional Board 402. Of the remaining domiciliary births, four were attended by private maternity nurses, six by a medical practitioner alone, and one was unattended. There have been no privately practising midwives in the city since 1948. Of analgesics administered in domiciliary deliveries, trilene is the most popular.

Edinburgh shared in the high maternal mortality rate obtaining in Scotland in the 1930s, but because of advances in obstetric care and better control of infection, a low rate has now been achieved.

TABLE 33
MATERNAL MORTALITY RATE

	Edinburgh
1932–6	5·2 per 1,000 live births (average)
1939–43	3·0 " " " "
1953	0·7 " " " "
1954	0·1 " " " "
1955	0·0 " " " "
1956	0·3 " " " "
1957	0·2 " " " "
1958	0·5 " " " "
1959	0·1 " " " "
1960	0·1 " " " "
1961	0·1 " " " "

CHILD WELFARE

Twenty-nine child welfare centres in the early '60s provided a very adequate service of advice, health supervision and health education along modern lines, and in 1961, 12,549 children under five years made 73,165 attendances. Fourteen day nurseries, open five days each week from 8 a.m.–6 p.m., and with places for 660 children, have been providing accommodation for infants and children admitted on a special priority basis. Ninety-seven per cent of the admissions belong to these priorities; the remaining 3 per cent constitute short-term stay cases. In 1961 the total attendances at the nurseries were 139,169, a figure which represents 80 per cent of possible attendances. Three residential nurseries, with 60 places, provide for the short-term overnight care of infants and children whose mothers or guardians are ill or temporarily incapacitated. Since there is a nursery nurses' training scheme in connection with these nurseries, a hostel with accommodation for 18 has been provided for girls who come for training from areas outside the city. A small number of child minders

(23 at the end of 1961) and of private nurseries (five) are registered under the Nurseries and Child Minders Regulation Act, 1948.

Welfare foods are distributed at 38 centres, but in recent years the citizens have not availed themselves fully of these foods. This decline in uptake is, however, part of a national trend.

Since 1951 an infant feeding centre has been provided each July near the beach at Portobello for the convenience of mothers with infants. Facilities are available for breast feeding, preparation of artificial feeds, and for infants' toilet.

The Voluntary Health Workers' Association, founded in 1908 and a pioneer body in the field of child welfare in the city, provides 25 toddlers' playgrounds—a unique contribution to child health measures. The children attending these playgrounds, aged three–five years, are under the general medical supervision of the medical officers of the child welfare service. In addition, a full health examination of each child is carried out annually. These annual examinations have revealed a steady improvement in the physical health of the children. In fact, by a survey conducted in 1963, Edinburgh children at five years of age were found to be three inches taller and correspondingly heavier than 30 years ago. One disquieting feature, however, is the high incidence of poor teeth.

DENTAL TREATMENT

Priority dental care for expectant and nursing mothers and pre-school children is undertaken by the school dental service at its surgeries, some of which are in the same premises as the child welfare clinics. Thus there exists a close relationship between the two services. While shortage of dental officers has been a difficulty, there still exists a general prejudice against dental treatment during pregnancy and to a lesser extent during the nursing period. Some women do, however, prefer to receive dental treatment from their own dental practitioners rather than at the clinics. The following table shows the results of dental examinations of expectant and nursing mothers at the dental clinics during the two five-year periods 1949–53 and 1954–8, which followed the introduction of the National Health Service, and for which detailed figures are available.

TABLE 34

DENTAL EXAMINATION AND TREATMENT OF EXPECTANT AND NURSING MOTHERS 1949–53 AND 1954–8

		Number of Mothers	
		1949–53	*1954–8*
1	Number inspected by dental officer	752	1,332
2	Number found to require treatment	749	1,329
3	Number accepting treatment	702	1,309
4	Number actually treated by dental officers	702	1,264

A table for the same period referable to pre-school children is shown below. The figures show that most children seen by the dental officers at the clinics require some form of dental treatment, but, of course, these children constitute but a small proportion of the population of this age group. In spite of continued efforts it has been difficult to persuade many parents of the value of regular dental inspection of their young children. Too often some decay has set in before the parents will seek help for their children, and when something has gone wrong with the youngsters' teeth there is little sign of reluctance in taking the children either to the dental clinic or the private dental practitioner.

TABLE 35
DENTAL EXAMINATION AND TREATMENT OF PRE-SCHOOL CHILDREN
1949–53 AND 1954–8

		Number of Children	
		1949–53	*1954–8*
1	Number inspected by dental officers	3,491	5,557
2	Number found to require treatment	3,153	5,512
3	Number accepting treatment	2,945	5,500
4	Number actually treated by dental officers	2,765	5,419

CHILD WELFARE

In the child welfare service, as in the school health service, more is being done in the early ascertainment of handicap, and free interchange of information takes place between the two services. It is important that this should be so, judging by the following figures which show that at the start of the '60s, among the infant and pre-school child population, almost 347 children were known to be physically and/or mentally handicapped. Of these 17 were spastics; 18 were deaf (including hard of hearing); 38 were blind (including partially sighted); 27 were epileptics. According to this tally the rest included other physical handicaps 175; mental handicap 54; and mixed physical and mental handicap 9. All of these children were under special medical supervision and treatment.

A form of physical handicap which has received special attention in the city is deafness. Screening tests for deafness in infants and young children have been carried out by the health visitors since 1956, but the original intention of screening every infant during his first year of life had to be abandoned owing to the demands on the health visitors' time for other duties. Tests are, however, carried out on all infants and young children who belong to what might be termed the " vulnerable " group, for example those with family histories of deafness, etc. Of 1,072 recently screened, three failed to pass repeated tests and required special care at the deaf children's unit at Donaldson's Hospital.

Unlike some local health authorities, Edinburgh does not provide any residential accommodation for unmarried mothers and their babies, but gives financial support to several voluntary organisations which devote their activities to this important social problem.

SCHOOL HEALTH SERVICE

The Edinburgh school health service, originally called the school medical service, was initiated in 1907 when the School Board appointed a medical officer, the first in Scotland. In the same year the Board also opened a special school for physically and mentally handicapped children making an arrangement with the Queen's Institute of District Nursing for a nurse to attend the school daily. With the introduction of the official service under the Education (Scotland) Act, 1908, two assistant medical officers and three nurses were appointed, the previous arrangement with the Queen's Institute being discontinued. In 1911, when the Merchant Company's schools were included in the scheme, a further assistant medical officer was appointed. In 1910, Leith School Board appointed a medical officer and nurse for its service.

In 1912, the Scottish Education Department allotted a special grant of £850 per annum to the Edinburgh School Board towards the treatment of children in need. To cope with this additional work, two further full-time nurses were employed, and four dentists and an oculist were appointed part-time for carrying out treatment at the Lauriston centre (opened in January, 1913). This provision anticipated the provisions of the 1913 Education (Scotland) Act, with regard to treatment of school children.

With the amalgamation of Leith and Edinburgh (1920) the combined staff comprised a chief medical officer, five assistants, and 15 full-time nurses; the part-time staff consisted of six dentists, two oculists and two aurists. In the same year the supervision of medical inspection and treatment of school children was transferred from the Scottish Education Department to the Board (later Department) of Health.

In 1930, the Corporation took over the school medical service, and, since the chief school medical officer retired at this time, the Medical Officer of Health was designated Chief School Medical Officer. Since that time the service has expanded in many directions. It has also changed its name to School Health Service, and in 1961 was responsible for the health of 65,187 children attending 146 schools under the Education Committee; of these children about 200 were in hospital classes and more than 80 were homebound and taught by visiting teachers.

To overtake the demands made on the service as stated above the full-time staff, in the early '60s, comprised in addition to the principal school medical officer who is also the medical officer of health a chief executive medical officer, eight assistant medical officers, a chief dental officer and 17 assistant dental officers, 104 health visitors, a physiotherapist, chiropodist, oral hygienist and 18 dental attendants. Part-time specialists include six oculists, four aurists, a dermatologist, an orthopaedic surgeon, an orthodontic consultant and an oral surgeon.

This considerable personnel increase reflects the greatly widened, and indeed still widening, scope of the service which, although still concerning itself with the original basic principles enunciated in the earlier days, has extended its range in many directions—in the early ascertainment of handicap, for example, in tuberculin testing and B.C.G. vaccination.

Thus the service has strengthened its position as the guardian of the school child. It must be admitted, however, that in regrettably few of the schools is the standard of accommodation available for school health work adequate, even in the new schools, where encroachments on the medical units are often made for other educational purposes. But progress continues as the following table shows.

TABLE 36
WEIGHT (LBS.) AND HEIGHT (INCHES) OF EDINBURGH SCHOOLCHILDREN

	Weight						*Height*					
	at 5 years		*at 9 years*		*at 13 years*		*at 5 years*		*at 9 years*		*at 13 years*	
Session	*Boys*	*Girls*	*Boys*	*Girls*	*Boys*	*Girls*	*Boys*	*Girls*	*Boys*	*Girls*	*Boys*	*Girls*
1907–08	40·7	39·4	56·7	54·6	79·2	80·5	41·1	39·9	48·9	48·5	56·3	56·8
1957–58	43·0	41·6	65·4	64·3	97·3	103·4	42·9	42·5	52·2	51·8	60·3	60·6

Such figures are not surprising, for the days when meals and milk were provided only for the necessitous have long gone. During the session of 1960–1, some 4,724,255 school meals were provided at a total cost of £418,419. The average cost per meal was 21·256*d.* (10·241*d.* for food and 11·015*d.* for administration). The income derived from payments for the meals was £175,195. Applications for free meals were made by 1,286 parents or guardians and 1,205 of these applications were sustained. Meals were also served during holidays. Under the milk-in-schools scheme, operated in all schools, an average of 60,483 bottles of milk were consumed daily by the pupils in the same session.

The all round improvement in the present day scholar's health is also evident in the low percentage rates, at routine inspections, of such conditions as lack of cleanliness (1·0), unsatisfactory clothing (0·08), unsatisfactory footgear (0·07), and the skin infections of ringworm and impetigo (0·2). Ringworm of the scalp, so prevalent in the earlier days that a special school was opened in 1912 for children suffering from this malady, though it ceased to function almost 20 years ago, has almost vanished.

In 1949 mass miniature radiography examination was offered to school leavers, but this was discontinued in 1959 following on the interim Report of the Committee on Radiological Hazards (1959). In 1953 tuberculin testing and B.C.G. vaccination were offered to 13-year-olds and the testing was extended to school entrants, on a limited scale, in session 1957–8. It is hoped soon to offer these facilities to all school entrants. The percentage of pupils showing a positive reaction to tuberculin-testing in 1960–1 was 13·6, a reduction in the figure of 37 when testing was introduced in 1953. This seems to be an index of the progressive shrinking of the pool of infection in the general population. The present response to the offer of B.C.G. vaccination was 92 per cent.

In 1954 the Education Authority made specially generous sick pay provisions for any teacher agreeing to submit annually to mass x-ray examination. There has been a high proportion of acceptances (97·4 per cent), indicating a praiseworthy sense of responsibility on their part. Four cases of pulmonary tuberculosis were discovered during the first such examination, and only one other case since then has been discovered.

Residential facilities by 1961 existed in special schools for the blind (one school), deaf (three schools), epileptic (two schools), physically handicapped (seven schools), mentally handicapped (six schools) and maladjusted (five schools). Of special day schools there existed those for physically handicapped (three), epileptics (three), partially sighted (one), deaf (one), partially deaf (one), mentally handicapped (six including an occupation centre), maladjusted (one), and multiple handicaps (one). Speech therapy was given by four speech therapists in small special classes by individual or group methods. For home-bound handicapped pupils, a service of visiting teachers was provided, seven being full-time and two part-time, representing a total of eight full-time teachers.

Improvements in ascertainment have been especially brought about in those categories of handicap in which hearing and vision are affected. The sweep-test by means of a portable pure-tone audiometer has been introduced for the routine audiometric screening of all children, at least three times in their school careers, the first test being carried out at five years. The work of the aural surgeons at their clinics has changed in character over the years. It would be quite erroneous now to believe that those clinics concern themselves mainly with the wholesale removal of tonsils and adenoids. Far from this being the case the surgeon is nowadays mainly concerned with the ascertainment of hearing defects and their alleviation.

Vision testing, now commencing at five years of age instead of the previous seven years, is carried out at the routine inspections. These tests reveal that a not inconsiderable number of entrants have visual defects which if left uncorrected, might be a handicap both to education and to other activities in and out of school. They also show in the older age groups the progressive rise in the incidence of visual defects and the gradual replacement of hypermetropia by myopia as the commonest visual defect. These two trends are shown in Tables 37 and 38.

TABLE 37
SHOWING RISE IN INCIDENCE OF VISUAL DEFECTS, 1957–8

Age	*Good Vision (6/6 in better eye)*	*Fair Vision (6/9 or 6/12 in better eye)*	*Bad Vision (6/18 or worse in better eye)*
5 years	92·0%	7·5%	0·5%
7 years	85·7%	12·7%	1·6%
9 years	84·6%	12·8%	2·6%
13 years	77·4%	18·3%	4·3%
16 years	82·9%	13·6%	3·5%

TABLE 38
SHOWING INCREASING INCIDENCE OF MYOPIA, 1957–8

Age	*New Referrals to opthalmalogist*	*Hypermetropia*	*Myopia*
5 years	122	44 (36%)	14 (11%)
7 years	149	83 (55%)	27 (18%)
9 years	232	87 (37%)	70 (30%)
13 years	122	20 (16%)	61 (50%)

Attendances of parents at the routine medical inspections have always been disappointing though some improvement has been seen over the years. In his 1912–13 report, the school medical officer for Edinburgh reported that the attendances of parents at the examinations were: five years, 52·9 per cent; nine years, 19·1 per cent; 13 years, 5·4 per cent. In 1961–2 the corresponding figures were 87 per cent; 62 per cent and 17 per cent.

Since the structure and activities of the Youth Employment Service have been established and expanded, co-operation between it and the school health service has been put on a sound basis and medical officers find the work of vocational guidance increasingly interesting and rewarding. Personal contact has also been secured with all the Appointed Factory Doctors in the city so that common problems can be discussed and arrangements made for exchange of information for the benefit of young people employed in industry.

SCHOOL DENTAL SERVICE

Earlier we had a glimpse of the arrangements made for children's dentistry, as seen through the eyes of Professor Boyes, writing on dentistry as a whole but with particular emphasis on its professional and educational aspects. Here Dr. Seiler lays stress on what he regards as both human and administrative weaknesses in the system as its stands.

"Until 1938," his survey continues, "school dental work was carried out by dentists on a part-time basis. But in that year, the first step was taken towards a full-time school dental service by the appointment of three school dental surgeons. Since then, the service has increased its personnel, not without difficulties, especially after the introduction of the National Health Service when entry into general dental practice was so remunerative. Even at present in the early years of the '60s, there are insufficient dentists on the staff, and in consequence routine inspections of the mouths of school children take place, not yearly, but at intervals of two or more years, and a dental officer finds himself responsible for the dental care of nearly 5,000 children. As long as this shortage persists the prevalence of dental decay will present a major health problem. The question of how to deploy successfully a limited staff leaves little time to reflect on figures, which show that in the city in 1946, with rationing still in operation, 66 per cent of pupils examined required treatment as against almost 96 per cent found to require it now. In addition to this pressing problem is the need to provide a priority dental service for expectant and nursing mothers and pre-school children.

"In 1951, two oral hygienists were appointed to the full-time staff to visit schools, community centres and other meeting places to give propaganda talks and demonstrations, and to carry out certain forms of dental treatment at the clinics. In the same year, by an arrangement with the South Eastern Regional Hospital Board, a consultant in orthodontics was appointed to attend the clinics on a sessional basis. A similar arrangement was concluded in 1954 for the services of an oral surgeon to attend to the more complex extractions and to perform minor oral surgery.

"Recent increases in the staff of full-time dental officers has been associated with an increased amount of conservation work (fillings) but with no corresponding decrease in the extraction rate. Coincident with this has been a steady rise in the total attendances at the clinics—for example, from 41,058 in 1957 to 46,059 in 1961. This increase represents, however, not more patients but only more attendances per patient, who now requires more treatment than was the case some years ago. Only too frequently children aged eight or nine require fillings in as many as four permanent teeth, and it is not uncommon to see signs of dental decay in teeth which have erupted only twelve or eighteen months before. A further significant and sombre fact is that dental decay of primary teeth among youngsters of one and two years old, seen at the clinics, is increasing.

"It is abundantly clear that the rate of dental decay is rising in proportion to the increasing consumption of sugars, sweets and biscuits. Insufficient dental care and lack of oral hygiene is evident, and much decay could be avoided by regular tooth brushing and simple methods of rinsing out the mouth after meals. Especially to blame seem to be the mid-morning snacks; and the excellent habit of drinking milk becomes a dental hazard when, by the addition of biscuit or soft starchy food, sticky particles are left within teeth crevices. 'Rinse and swallow' methods are easily taught to the youngest of school children and require no special technique, toothbrush or toothpick.

"A third method of diminishing the attack of decay may be in the adjustment of the fluoride content of local water supplies. At present the concentration is 0·15 parts per million with slight variations according to source. In the light of recent knowledge a stepping up of this concentration artificially would so protect children's teeth against decay that school dentistry might even fall within the limits of the dentists available."

HEALTH VISITING

The fall in infant mortality from the beginning of the century, when 132 out of every 1,000 infants died before their first birthday, to the rate for 1961 of 23, accompanied by the disappearance of most of the infections and the diseases of malnutrition, can be attributed in large measure to the activities of Health Visitors. These ladies were first appointed to combat the high death rate and illness amongst young children. So successful were they over the years that Section 23 of the National Health Service (Scotland) Act 1947 laid a duty on local health authorities to provide for the visiting of persons in their homes by visitors, to be called Health Visitors, for the purpose of giving advice about the care of young children, persons suffering from illness and expectant or nursing mothers, and also about the measures necessary to promote health generally and prevent the spread of infection.

Health Visitors, who are trained nurses with maternity experience and an additional qualification in medico-social work, are of inestimable value in the activities of almost all branches of the health department, although their influence and the results of their help, advice, guidance and education can never be shown by mere statistics. They are truly the spearhead of the department's medical and social activities and, as in all preventive work, it is impossible to devise a satisfactory yardstick to measure their usefulness to the community in the promotion of health and the prevention of disease.

In her primary role of health educator and social advisor the Health Visitor acts as a general duty family visitor, and her field of work includes not only the care of mothers, young children and school children—always her main preoccupation—but also the care and after-care of infectious disease, tuberculosis, disabling illness, the aged, the physically handicapped at all ages, the supervision of mentally handicapped children, mental hygiene and the after-care of mental illness. One interesting development which has made headway recently is the scheme for the ascertainment of deafness in young children by Health Visitors, who have received training in simple methods of audiometric testing.

Another important recent venture was the attendance of Health Visitors at the newly opened psychiatric clinic in Corporation clinic premises at Niddrie. This more direct association of the Health Visitor in the mental health field will be watched with keen interest, because there seems little doubt that she has an important part to play in the care, after-care and prevention of mental disease.

Apart from this routine work, the Health Visitors undertake talks to various organisations and have an important place in any health education activities. They assist in local and national research projects and give practical instruction in the duties of a Health Visitor to student nurses in general training at various hospitals in the city, to Health Visitor students, to medical students and to many visitors from abroad.

A feature of recent years has been the increased co-operation between Health Visitors and the general practitioner and hospital services, the most recent example being the invitation for H.V.s (as they are known in medical circles) to attend at the ante-natal clinic run by a group of Leith doctors. Attendance of Health Visitors regularly at all hospitals in the city where children receive treatment has proved of mutual benefit to both services, whilst the case conferences at the University general practice teaching unit, attended by Health Visitors, are another instance of advantageous co-operation.

The Health Visitor training course, which covers a 9-month period of instruction, has each year a full complement of 30 students, of whom there is seldom more than the occasional failure to obtain the Health Visitor Certificate.

There were in 1962, in addition to the Supervisor, Assistant Supervisor and the Tutor for the training course, 104 Health Visitors who, apart from their work at clinics and hospitals, undertook over 180,000 visits to give advice and guidance in a variety of circumstances. Considering their heavy duties with poliomyelitis vaccination and in connection with special investigations, it is praiseworthy that they were able to maintain their essential home visiting function at such a high level.

HEALTH SERVICES IN THE HOME

There are welcome indications nowadays of even stronger bonds between the local authority and the general practitioners in the city. The advice, guidance and assistance of the local medical committee on many health matters has been invaluable to the work of the department, while there is little doubt that there is a greater and wider realisation by family doctors in the city of the help which they obtain from their health department. The value of the district nurse, the home help and the loan of nursing equipment is readily appreciated by family doctors, particularly when caring for elderly patients in their own homes. More practitioners too are coming to rely upon the health visitors and the almoner in resolving the multiplicity of medico-social problems which so frequently hinder the clinical recovery of their patients.

HOME NURSING

The home nursing service is undertaken on behalf of the Corporation by the Queen's Institute of District Nursing with a liaison committee composed of representatives of the Institute and of the Health Committee. The services of a district nurse are provided at the request of the doctors for their patients requiring nursing treatment at home. The volume of work, particularly in the new housing sites around the perimeter of the city, has greatly increased for three main reasons. Firstly, there is the changing face of medicine with the development of antibiotic and other injection treatments, so that more than half of the nursing visits are paid for this purpose. Secondly, because of the changes in medical treatment, patients are discharged from hospital earlier than was customary a few years ago and there is greater need for skilled follow-up nursing at home. Many of the aged sick are now being nursed in their own homes and there is an increasing tendency for twice-daily visiting.

Nursing visits in Edinburgh are made between the hours of 8.30 a.m. and 1.15 p.m. and 2.30 to 6.30 daily. Morning and evening visits are paid to ill patients when necessary and a skeleton staff is on duty each evening for emergency calls and late evening visits.

In 1961 a staff of 71 trained nurses, 23 of them part-time and 31 nurses in training, paid 312,882 visits to 8,651 patients. No less than 199,523 visits were made to patients over 65 years of age. One elderly gentleman, pleased to see the nurse arrive, welcomed her with the greeting: "Oh, nurse! You're just one of these fallen angels."

HOME HELPS

In many parts of the country a home help service only came into operation after the war; but in Edinburgh a service was started on a limited scale in 1930 to relieve mothers during confinement at home. The permissive powers of the 1947 National Health Service (Scotland) Act now allow this provision for illness, confinement, mental deficiency, the elderly or the care of children.

Women with experience in domestic work are employed primarily for duties normally undertaken by the mother of the family. They are not expected to provide nursing care nor to deal with arrears of washing or cleaning. The service was designed to meet a need for a temporary period in an emergency, but old people, particularly those living alone, frequently require help of a more permanent nature.

Assistance may be requested by the family themselves, by a doctor or by some other interested person, and where the need is urgent, as is often the case with telephone requests from doctors, a home help is sent out immediately; otherwise the home is visited to assess the need and explain the service to the family. There is a scale of assessment so that by applying to the almoner the payment even for full-time help may be considerably reduced and, in fact, old age pensioners are only asked to pay 6*s*. per week, and this sum can be reclaimed by them from the National Assistance Board.

During 1961 the 288 home helps employed assisted 1,531 households. An evening and week-end service was provided for older people living alone, together with a night-sitter service for seriously ill patients. A male home help has proved his worth in the care of elderly men with chronic incapacitating disease.

The service may well need to be further expanded in order to provide adequate care for the elderly in their own homes, and although the financial return is poor this is economically sound because of the saving of hospital and institutional provision. Apart from the economic aspect, it is better for the comfort and general wellbeing of most old people to be cared for in their own homes rather than in the cold cleanliness of institutions.

THE ALMONER

The evolution of the profession of almoning has tended to connect the almoner with the solving of medico-social problems associated with the hospital patient only; and the fact that similar duties arise in general practice is sometimes forgotten. In Scotland, Edinburgh was the first authority to provide an almoning service for domiciliary patients. Not only can her assistance be invaluable to the family doctor but her work has many advantages for the family themselves. She sees the patient against his natural home background and has the constant guidance of the doctor with his intimate knowledge of his patient's medical, social and emotional needs. Moreover, she can give a continuity of service often denied the almoner whose activities are restricted to the hospital sphere. It is encouraging to find that of 531 referrals in 1961 no less than 197 came from medical practitioners, while the majority of the remaining requests were from the almoner's colleagues in the health visiting service.

REHOUSING ON HEALTH GROUNDS

In the post war housing developments throughout the country it has been recognised that certain families deserve some form of priority in rehousing for medical reasons. In some places a specific allocation of houses is earmarked for persons selected by the Medical Officer of Health, whilst other authorities allow their health department to apportion points to households for a variety of medical conditions. In Edinburgh one in nine of all houses available for letting are allocated to tuberculosis cases. Priority in respect of other medical conditions is reserved for those who may be a danger to the health of others or where rehousing is essential for the health of one of the family. For other cases where health would benefit from rehousing, points are awarded in order to reduce the period on the waiting list.

SIGHTHILL HEALTH CENTRE

The Health Centre at Sighthill, opened by the Secretary of State in May, 1953, was the first to be provided in Scotland. Built and designed by the Department of Health in consultation with Edinburgh Corporation and other interested parties, it contains six consulting suites for general practitioners, a surgery for a dentist operating under the National Health Service, a pharmacy at which National Health Service prescriptions can be dispensed, rooms for minor surgery and for dressings, a small laboratory and a physiotherapy department. It also provides headquarters for the Corporation's child welfare, school health and dental services for the area and for the local district nurses and domiciliary midwives. Health education, a psychiatric service, a sterile syringe service, an old people's health club, a toddlers' playground and provision for spastic children have developed in the Centre and emphasise its value in providing scope for a wide range of functions which would not otherwise be possible anywhere in the city. At the same time the Centre is proving successful in its initial purpose of bringing the different branches of the health service closer together and promoting co-operation in the prevention as well as the treatment of ill health.

THE MENTAL HEALTH SERVICE

Mental ill-health is one of the major present-day medico-social problems, with almost half of all hospital beds in Scotland devoted to the mentally sick and handicapped. It has been estimated that about one per cent of the population suffer from innate mental handicap and it is probable that one-third of all patients attending family doctors do so for a disorder with a mental basis. The magnitude of the problem cannot be exaggerated nor the necessity for building up an adequate service of prevention, care and after-care for the community.

To this end a Senior Medical Officer has been appointed to take charge of the Mental Health Services in the city and progress has already been achieved, particularly as regards the care and after-care of the mentally ill and handicapped. Thus the appointment of psychiatric social workers has made it possible to extend home visitation and to effect a closer liaison with other social workers in this field. Accommodation, the first of its kind in Scotland, has been provided at Willowbrae House to give short-stay residential care for mentally handicapped children under 13 years and in this way give much needed relief to parents, assist them in times of domestic difficulty or allow them a short holiday. A Day Care Centre has been established, also at Willowbrae House, where severely handicapped children, formerly house-bound or regarded as untrainable, are brought daily for simple forms of training to enable them to develop their full potential, and give their parents some relief at the same time. And furthermore, in association with the local branch of the Scottish Association of Parents of Handicapped Children, a sitter-in service has been organised on a voluntary basis for mentally handicapped children.

A satisfactory service for the mentally ill and handicapped requires, of course, the co-ordination of many diverse agencies and in particular the closest liaison and co-operation between the three branches of the health service. For this reason a small technical working party with medical representatives from the hospital, general practice and public health fields has held many meetings which have proved of value not only by giving opportunities for a frank exchange of views and ideas but also by fostering a sense of partnership in reaching forward towards a co-ordinated service in mental welfare.

One example of effective co-operation with the hospital authority is the establishment of an out-patient psychiatric clinic at Niddrie Farmhouse, staffed from Rosslynlee Mental Hospital, to provide diagnostic treatment and follow-up facilities. Health Visitors attend the clinic, and the close association of the hospital with general practitioners and public health staff provides the nucleus of a comprehensive community and after-care service for patients in the Niddrie area. There is still an acute shortage of institutional beds for the mentally handicapped, and an assessment panel reviews the waiting list from time to time to assess the relative urgency of their admission.[1] On the brighter side, Scotland's first hostel where mentally handicapped youths can learn how to return to a full and useful life in the community was opened in Leith in 1964.

HEALTH EDUCATION

The vision of Dr. W. G. Clark in particular has placed Edinburgh in the forefront of health education in Great Britain.

In his 1952 Report Dr. Clark said: " The days of the sanitary era are over . . . . Once the housing position has been remedied any marked improvement of the communal health will depend on the intelligence, knowledge and application of the individual citizen." As evidence of his faith in health education in November, 1951 he set up within the Public

[1] Subsequent developments in the field of mental illness are recounted later in this book in the chapter entitled *Caring for the Community*.

Health Department a Health Education section, under the control of a Senior Medical Officer, which was one of the earliest in Great Britain. The details of the section's day to day work are related in the pages of the Annual Reports of the Department, but some mention should be made of Edinburgh's special contribution to the development of community participation in the public health projects.

COMMUNITY PARTICIPATION

As early as 1953 a group of voluntary workers, the Pilton Working Party, had joined with the Public Health Department to promote the first mass x-ray campaign in Great Britain in which community participation, through the work of large numbers of voluntary workers, provided the impetus which previous campaigns had lacked. More than 300 voluntary workers were trained in the community problems of pulmonary tuberculosis, and in the technique of household visiting to persuade their neighbours to come for x-ray. Campaign activities of all kinds were developed by these voluntary workers and as a result, in June, 1954, 60 per cent of the adult population of the Pilton Ward were persuaded to attend the x-ray units in a four week campaign. As few x-ray campaigns prior to this had succeeded in attracting over 20 per cent of the available adult population, this was a considerable achievement, and similar success attended the efforts of thousands of voluntary workers in x-ray campaigns in Central Leith (1955) Portobello (1956) and Liberton (1956). Indeed, in the Inch district of the Liberton Ward 73 per cent of the adult population was x-rayed in about four days.

It was at this stage that the Scottish National Anti-Tuberculosis crusade opened with the great Glasgow campaign of 1957 in which almost 77 per cent of the city's adult population came forward for x-ray. Voluntary work by many thousands of household visitors, clerks and receptionists laid the foundations of this success, but there is no doubt that the work of the Glasgow Publicity Committee in developing a publicity campaign without precedent in public health history was the decisive factor in this remarkable and historic event.

The second year of the National Campaign opened with the Edinburgh x-ray campaign of 1958. The story of the remarkable publicity achievement, and of the men behind it, has been told in the Annual Report of the Medical Officer of Health for 1958, but equal credit must be given to the army of more than 8,000 voluntary workers whose enthusiasm helped to bring 308,747 people, or 84·4 per cent of the adult population to the x-ray units. The community work of these voluntary workers, based on a remarkably successful duplicate card-index of all citizens, was of massive proportions and a remarkable indication of what can be achieved by community participation in a health project which attracts the enthusiasm of public-spirited citizens. It is important to record also that a number of the ward committees decided to continue their existence and to collaborate with the Public Health Department in community health work in their wards.

THE EDINBURGH CIGARETTE CANCER CAMPAIGN, 1959

Edinburgh was the first Local Health Authority to implement the Government's instruction to bring effectively to public notice the dangers of smoking and especially cigarette smoking. A report on this campaign has already been published and its main findings are given here.

During the investigation a survey was made in Edinburgh of children's smoking habits. Four schools were studied—two Senior Secondary and two Junior Secondary and a total of 3,224 questionaires completed. Only 35 per cent of the boys said they had never smoked compared with 73 per cent of the girls. Just over 25 per cent of the boys had smoked in the past four weeks whereas only 8 per cent of the girls had done so. A detailed analysis is shown in Table 39.

TABLE 39
AMOUNT SMOKED BY BOYS OF DIFFERENT AGES WHO HAD SMOKED DURING THE FOUR WEEK PERIOD

Amount smoked	*Age in years*			
	11, 12	*13*	*14*	*15 or more*
	%	%	%	%
1– 4 cigarettes a week	73	56	40	39
5– 9 ,, ,, ,,	9	21	22	8
10–14 ,, ,, ,,	9	12	13	10
15–19 ,, ,, ,,	5	2	7	7
20–29 ,, ,, ,,	—	5	9	17
30 or more ,, ,, ,,	3	2	7	17
Not stated	1	2	2	2
Total smokers	67	91	175	72

More than 90 per cent of the children agreed that smoking was bad for their health and 60 per cent thought it could cause cancer.

The days of famous Edinburgh street characters like Coconut Tam and Saut Maggie are gone and their more modern counterparts are also fading from the scene. *Above:* the one-man band that for many years at the beginning of this century played around the city. *Above right:* the fishwife once brought fresh fish from Fisherrow and Newhaven regularly to the housewife's door. *Left:* this barrel organ pulled by a pony is still to be found twice a week in some suburban streets.

Whitehorse Close, one of the most attractive closes in the Royal Mile. It used to contain the Inn of St. Michael, and from the north side—in Calton Road—mail coaches used to leave for London. The close has just been renovated and restored by the city.

CHAPTER 14

THE PEOPLE'S HOMES

FROM 1845 TO 1958

IN the view of Professor Tom Burns and Dr. Mary Gregor, both of the University, the description of Edinburgh's housing development in the second *Statistical Account of Scotland* (1845) affords an unusually interesting comparison with the situation as it exists today. Rapid expansion had then been taking place, notably with the building of the New Town which was begun about 1770. But so rapid had been the growth that the building of houses had gone on faster than the increase of population warranted, and from 1827 till 1845 little more was done and several of the newer streets remained incomplete. Because of this over-production there was a considerable drop in house rents.

The citizens of Edinburgh evidently felt proud of their expanding city though not all its new streets were in truth beautiful. Nevertheless the writers in the 1845 survey were perhaps justified in saying that on the whole " the architectural operations and improvements in Edinburgh during the last half century rival, both in extent and beauty, those of any other city in the kingdom."

Could one, in 1958, say the same of the developments of the past 50 years? Once again there has been a great acceleration of house building, due in part to the needs of an expanding population but also to the responsibility now placed on local authorities to provide adequate housing for all who need it, regardless of their ability to pay an economic rent. These new housing schemes have spread out into the surrounding countryside, and farms, cottages and mansion houses have been engulfed in the process. The rural parishes of Liberton, Colinton, Corstorphine, Duddingston and Cramond—described separately in the 1845 survey—are now within the city boundary, though all of them still retain some unspoilt corners that recall the past. But for the most part the recent suburban development is lacking in local character or any special beauty.

The rapid spread of towns and cities and the consequent encroachment on valuable agricultural land has been much debated on a national level, and Edinburgh too is face to face with this difficulty. The city boundary was fixed in 1920, when the area of the city was nearly trebled by the incorporation of the Burgh of Leith and many out-lying areas, and was again extended in 1954. In spite of this the Town Council by 1958 seemed to have utilised nearly all its suburban housing sites. But in the same year new architectural plans for multi-storey flats in the Dumbiedykes and Leith Fort areas gave an idea of the future appearance of these districts, and not unexpectedly they gave rise to much criticism among the more conservative-minded citizens. Despite this a start was made with this type of building, and the first large block of flats was completed in Gorgie in 1952.

THE FOUR EDINBURGHS

At the beginning of 1958, there were about 150,000 houses in Edinburgh.[1] About 34,000 of these—nearly a quarter of the total—had been built by the Corporation. The rest were divided fairly evenly between those let for rent and those owned by their occupants. Almost half (about 64,000) of all these houses had been built since 1918; which means that in 40 years a belt of suburbia, two miles deep, had grown up around the built-up area of Edinburgh and Leith as it was in 1920 when the two burghs were joined. This means also that there are now four Edinburghs: the Old Town, Georgian Edinburgh, Victorian Edinburgh, and suburban Edinburgh—each not only distinctive in physical appearance and age, but containing as well something of the contrasts and the wide range of social character which make up the city.

Until recent years the Old Town had changed little since its desertion by all but the poorest families and the thousands of Irish labourers who later crowded in when railway building started. Until the last year or two, it could be said that even the successive clearances of derelict slums and their replacement by new tenements had but served to fix the social character of the area more durably. For although the clearances of the 1930s in St. Leonard's made a substantial difference for those inhabitants who now occupy the tenements built by the Corporation, even as late as 1951 the people living in the two central wards of St. Giles and Holyrood were almost wholly lower working class. Well over half the dwellings in these two wards contained only one or two rooms; 4,000 persons occupied 1,776 single rooms, and almost 2,500 were living more than three to a room. Baths were a rarity possessed by only 2,165 households out of 13,810; and almost half had no separate W.C. Since then there have been changes, and as we saw earlier many working class people have migrated to the housing estates on the city's outskirts.

The rise in living standards since 1914, which has affected housing more than any other circumstances of life, has clearly not brought uniform benefits to everybody; and unfortunately the "underprivileged," as we have learned to call them, are very often the elderly. But it is worth stressing again that the old central area of the city never wholly lapsed into the uniform depression of an industrial slum, even though Hill Square, behind Surgeon's Hall, and other islands of respectability were swamped. George Square survived as a small enclave of professional families, only to be annexed piecemeal but swiftly by the University. Ramsay Gardens, off the Lawnmarket itself, contains a handful of much sought-after flats. And with the renovation of the Canongate well under way, better-off and younger families may stay in the Old Town, and even return to it. Certainly the direct attempt to replace slums by attractive,

[1] A detailed tabular report available from the 1961 Census shows the acreage and population of each Edinburgh Ward, and the number of its private households and dwellings. This table is set out in Appendix II.

well-equipped flats looks more capable of restoring the vitality and diversity of life in the Old Town than the growing archipelago of administrative offices and University buildings.

Whatever the future may hold for the Old Town, Central Leith at any rate has become fixed as a working class industrial quarter. Vestiges of the effervescent and heterogeneous character of the old port were still, in 1958, clearly visible in the warren of streets between the Links and the Harbour. The slum clearances of the '30s, bomb damage, and the post-war housing programmes have emptied many of the wynds and streets, but reconstruction plans were in hand by the late '50s. Yet some of the old remained, and still does. The corner of the Leith Links by Charlotte Street, for example, still retained a few attractive Georgian houses, matching the style of some of the business offices in Constitution Street. Central Leith in 1958 was in fact still obstinately clinging to community life in a way the Old Town of Edinburgh had almost forgotten, though a large number of Leithers had followed the trail to the housing estates.

Comparatively few dwellings now remain in that part of the residential New Town planned by Craig 200 years ago, though the later additions, more monumental in architectural character, are still mainly residential, despite the invasion of the Melville Street quarter by professional, commercial and government offices from 1939 onwards. To the north, from Randolph Crescent through Ainslie Place, Moray Place, Heriot Row and as far as Drummond Place, the buildings still fulfil the purpose for which they were built, surprisingly little altered below the roofs and attics, which are mostly enlarged or encrusted with dormer windows. Moray Place especially, and the adjoining area, retains its old air of moneyed seclusion. Flats here, maintained and improved by successive generations of owners, change hands for four, five or six thousand pounds and more. Elsewhere in Georgian Edinburgh house purchasers are more inclined to seek " bargains " and to entertain apprehensions about whether the street is winning or losing in the constantly fluctuating contest against age, neglect, invasion by shops, offices and poorer families, and against the competition of the newer suburbs.

Georgian Edinburgh includes a good deal more than the New Town and its later extensions. Not only the warehouses of Leith, but much of Trinity and the attractive houses fronting Leith Links at its northern corner, date from the earlier 19th century, as does much of Stockbridge. But the whole northern fringe of the extended New Town, from Melville Street around to Hillside Crescent, merges into Victorian Edinburgh. Elsewhere, the transition is much more abrupt, the building slump of the second quarter of the century and the coming of the railways in the 1840s interposing a kind of interregnum in the development of the city.

The tradition of the later, heavier sections of Georgian Edinburgh was continued in the second half of the 19th century in the adjacent areas on either side of Palmerston Place and in the " little Kensington " of the terraces and crescents built on either side of Queensferry Road beyond the Dean Bridge. The massed terraces of Merchiston, Morningside and Warrender Park approach more closely the vernacular of Edinburgh tenements, but the order of preference obtaining in the Old Town, where the quality of dwellings and households rose with each storey, was now reversed; henceforward the main door flat commanded the higher price as streets became cleaner and safer, and as convenient access became more desirable with the decline in the numbers of domestic servants. By the turn of the century, the typical Edinburgh dwelling had become the tenement flat, ranging in size, solidity, and social standing from Morningside, through Merchiston and Warrender Park to Newington, and through Pilrig down to Easter Road and Dalry-Gorgie.

A new note was added, however, by Churchill, Grange and Mayfield, where suburban development in the grand manner began to challenge the social hegemony of the Moray Places. Individually designed stone-built town mansions standing in large gardens and shrubberies behind high walls, the larger south side houses expressed much of the ethos of later Victorian and Edwardian Britain. They have, perhaps significantly, fared less well than the contemporary tenement flats in the servantless 20th century. Many south side houses, and their counterparts in Trinity Leith's south side, have been converted into flats and maisonettes, though not all of them yield easily to this sort of treatment; and they house the shrunken households of the 1950s in dimmed, rather hollow splendour. Morningside as we saw has the largest proportion of elderly people of any ward in the city, a mark of its decline from the years of ascendancy, when it gave its name to an exquisitely genteel version of Lowland Scots, now itself falling into desuetude.

The nearest approach to the industrial slum familiar throughout the rest of Britain is the densely packed area between the Glasgow railway line and the canal which stretches southwest from Morrison Street through Dalry into Gorgie. Built mostly to a uniform plan of living-room (with a bed recess, and a tap and sink in the window), W.C., and bedroom, they were immense improvements on the semi-derelict dwellings of the Old Town; but the very strength of their stone construction, which one would have thought an indestructible virtue, is proving an increasing embarrassment, since housing standards are rising faster than the tenements degenerate.

The fourth Edinburgh is the creation of the years since 1918—the suburbanising trend we have already studied, which got its greatest momentum after 1951. This last carapace of buildings around the Old Town is the least idiosyncratic. The distinguishing characteristics of the tenement quarters which date from the middle of the 19th century to 1914 are essentially their solid stone construction and the device of the common stair; this is a Scottish (or North British) vernacular.

Since 1920, housing in the city has surrendered largely to the domination of Government housing standards and garden suburb development according to English patterns. Stone survived as a facing material for the more expensive private houses between the wars, but brick faced with harling became the standard building material for Corporation housing estates and for the cheaper bungalows and houses erected by speculative builders. This latter kind of house had its main design features fixed early on by the central authority. Under the Housing Act of 1923 houses for sale which conformed with Government standards of space and design received a grant of up to £70 each. In Edinburgh alone, 2,000 houses were built in the brief period before a change of Government abolished the scheme.

After the skirmishing of the early post-1918 years the stretches of raw red roofs which covered Craigleith, Greenbank and other areas, which are now the minor suburbs, heralded the main body of suburban little houses. A typical design was the semi-detached bungalow: hipped roofs; brick construction with pebble-dash facing; two bedrooms, living-room, kitchen and bathroom. The rooms were smaller than those of the middle-class tenement flats of pre-1914, the term kitchenette being used to give some countenance to the compartment in which the sink, cooker, larder and housewife were kept. The most important feature, however, which redeemed every defect of size, construction and design, was the plot of land which went with each house. The suburban garden transformed the face of urban Britain everywhere, and has now become, in the short space of two generations, the most characteristic feature of the urban landscape, as it is, in sheer area, its biggest.

Ten or twelve houses to the acre was and is the highest building density of privately owned houses. The Corporation estates represented an uneasy compromise between this norm of " open development " and the rejected tradition of tenement building. Niddrie for example was built at 24 houses to the acre, and elsewhere density rarely fell below 16. The open space in many Corporation estates was left unfenced, and by 1958 had been reduced to stretches of bare earth on which grew patches of grass and, at the back, thin copses of iron posts supporting clothes lines.

For the first half of the 1930s dwellings were being built at a cost of £2 millions a year. Rather more than a third were built by the Corporation in the large areas of uniform development which have come to dominate most of the suburban fringe: Prestonfield (662 dwellings), Restalrig and Lochend and Craigentinny (2,643), Craigmillar and Niddrie (2,593) and in the 1930s the beginnings of the mass housing developments. Thus by the late '50s Corporation housing in Pilton, with the post-war extensions into Muirhouse and Drylaw, stretched from Granton Harbour to Davidson's Mains and comprised many thousands of dwellings.

The pre-war estates at Saughton, Stenhouse and Slateford have also been expanded in similar fashion. Between the wars, Corporation housing estates and private suburban development were segregated. New housing estates grew up to the north-west and on either side of the hills of Holyrood Park; a " natural " extension of Gorgie–Dalry filled the widening wedge of land stretching outwards between the main railways and roads to the west. However, Duddingston, Liberton, Fairmilehead, Colinton, Ravelston, Corstorphine, Blackhall and Barnton were the preserves of the private builder. But after 1945 municipal housing predominated in all parts of the suburban fringe. Apart from the very big extension to the Pilton estate, and some additions to Craigmillar and Niddrie, by 1958 open land beyond Duddingston became the site of the new Corporation estates of Southfield (510 dwellings) and Milton Road (800); Liberton had become surrounded by The Inch (1,773), Moredun and Ferniehill (1,550), Gracemount, Southhouse and Hyvots Bank (2,126); Comiston, by Colinton (1,695); while Clermiston (2,198) was taking up most of the land left for development between Davidson's Mains and Corstorphine. Most of the private houses went up in the few suburban enclaves left at Fairmilehead, Colinton and beyond at Juniper Green, Corstorphine and Davidson's Mains, Barnton and Cramond. (All these places are shown in the map of Edinburgh at the end of the book.)

Suburban Edinburgh nevertheless houses as wide a range of social groups as do the older quarters. And almost deliberately, in spite of pervasive location of Corporation housing estates, the tendency persists for each category of the population to occupy a whole district to which it gives a distinct and uniform character. In the Old Town the better off lived literally on top of their social inferiors. In Georgian Edinburgh the poor were still, although more discreetly, the neighbours of the rich. Segregation began in the 19th century, but not until the 1920s did open development allow of the creation of coherent areas of development not only housing one social stratum of the City's community but separated by open space. The social distance sufficient to keep the inhabitants of Rose Street and Jamaica Street a world apart from those of Charlotte Square and Heriot Row has been replaced by physical distance. When this is abbreviated—as often in the post-war spread of Corporation housing estates—the fact has been registered by a significant fall in the prices obtainable for neighbouring house property.

Yet, although the social distinction between public and private housing is still very obvious, at least in the suburbs, the point in the social scale at which the distinction occurs has moved upwards since 1945. This is partly the effect of the very severe housing shortage of the first eight or nine years after the war, but also of the national policy of providing public housing for a much larger proportion of the population. The 1949 Housing Act deliberately deleted reference to the working class population as the beneficiaries of local authority housing schemes, and although this has not affected the obligation of local authorities to provide houses for those most in need of them, the general effect has been to expand the range of housing types. The Inch estate, completed in the early 1950s, marked a new departure by making the scheme the subject of a competition for private architects. Out of 38 schemes listed in the 1958 progress report of the Corporation Housing Committee the design of 16 was the work of private architects.

BUILDING PROBLEMS

In the early post-war years, when there was an acute shortage of building materials and labour, it was felt that those in greatest need of houses should have priority. The emphasis was accordingly placed on building by local authorities, while severe restrictions were imposed on private building for owner-occupiers.

Pre-fabricated houses were one answer to the prevailing shortages and many of these were erected in Edinburgh, about 150 of them intended to be permanent and 4,000 of a temporary character with an estimated life of 10 years. Towards the end of the '50s a start was made in replacing a few of the latter by permanent houses, and in time the districts concerned will be entirely redeveloped on a permanent basis. There was no doubt however, at the time, that the majority of the " pre-fabs " would have to remain in occupation far beyond the 10-year period, though fortunately most of them have stood up to use remarkably well. When first put up they were of great value because of the speed with which they could be made to standard patterns in central factories and erected with a minimum of time and labour on the site. Moreover they provided a compact little home with attractive interior design. Despite this the external appearance of large groups of such houses was not good and they were far from cheap. As if to compensate for their small size, their equipment was however on a lavish scale. For example, each had a gas or electric refrigerator—a luxury which Edinburgh had rather avoided in its permanent houses. Moreover they were extravagant in land use, only nine to the acre being possible, compared with about 15 per acre of permanent houses. For all these reasons, therefore, Edinburgh put up no more temporary houses after 1949 but concentrated on permanent building.

In the meantime, the growing inflationary trend in the country was causing a steady rise in the cost of both labour and materials, which has continued to the present time. Periodic increases in Exchequer subsidies helped to reduce the growing burden on the local authority, but the cost to the taxpayer and ratepayer alike was such that economies were obviously necessary if the number of new houses was not to be drastically curtailed. Accordingly from 1952 onwards the Government urged local authorities to exercise the utmost economy in design and lay-out of their houses. It was officially stressed that terraced houses and flats of three or four storeys, which are cheaper than semi-detached cottages, should when possible be used in greater numbers; that individual houses should have reduced circulation space, a compact staircase and low ceilings; and equipment such as built-in furniture, washboilers and cookers could be omitted.

In 1956 the Department of Health for Scotland made new regulations regarding the maximum overall areas of houses and the minimum areas of rooms. It was laid down that a four-apartment house for five persons must have at least 305 square feet " living space " (meaning living-room and kitchen); the principal bedroom should be 135 square feet, the second bedroom 110 square feet, and the third, for a single person, need be only 70 square feet but should have a built-in wardrobe. Ceiling height should be 7 feet 6 inches and staircases and passages at least 2 feet 11 inches in width. Rooms of this size or even a little larger can be provided within the maximum permitted house area, which varies somewhat according to the type of house being built but is around 890 square feet for a four-apartment house for five persons. These regulations represent some reduction of the standards recommended at the end of the war when the principal bedroom was supposed to be 150–160 square feet and all subsidiary bedrooms 120 square feet, while ceiling heights ranged from 8 to 9 feet, and staircases and passages were to be at least 3 feet 3 inches wide. Nevertheless in view of prevailing costs it seemed inevitable towards the end of the '50s that economies must be made.

The position of the local authority had in fact been made more difficult as a result of the Housing and Town Development (Scotland) Act of 1957, which reduced the Exchequer subsidy to £24 per annum for 60 years regardless of size of house, though it allowed an extra subsidy for flats in blocks of six or more storeys. Since 1952 the exchequer subsidy had been £39 15*s.* for a three-apartment house, £42 5*s.* for four apartments and £46 15*s.* for five apartments; so the new figure represented a severe cut and a complete departure from the previous policy of relating subsidies to prevailing costs. In Edinburgh, where the housing shortage was and still is acute, there could be no question of curtailing the building programme, but it was realised that high blocks of flats might well come into greater favour although more expensive to build since they would qualify for the larger subsidy.

The Department of Health for Scotland exercises a measure of control over local authority housing programmes. No price ceiling has been fixed for Council houses as was done for private building after the war, but designs and tenders must be submitted to the Department for approval. These tenders are then compared with average costs for similar houses in other comparable areas and if excessive can be turned down. Plans must conform to the standards laid down by the Department but the regulations leave plenty of scope for varied treatment by the city architects. The most recent housing developments reflect an obvious desire to introduce variety and colour and the results achieved are a vast improvement on the inter-war schemes such as Niddrie where the dominant impression is one of drab uniformity. Interior designs too show imagination and attention to important details such as a good supply of cupboards and a well-planned kitchen so that the restrictions on size do not lead to congestion and inconvenience.

It has already been explained that the immediate post-war housing programme of the local authority left little opportunity for the private builder, meaning either the firm wishing to erect houses for sale or the individual family employing its own architect and builder. Licences for private building had to be obtained from the local authority and were not issued unless exceptional need could be shown. Moreover even with a licence the size of house to be built and its selling price were severely restricted. In 1945 the overall area might not exceed 1,000 square feet for a two-storey house or 930 square feet for a bungalow or flat, and the selling price might not exceed £1,200 though this figure was raised to £1,300 two years later. From 1948 onwards it became possible year by year to ease the regulations a little, but building controls were not abolished until November, 1954. In the meantime it was found difficult to fix a price ceiling which should be applicable over the whole country; so in 1948 the local authorities were left to fix the selling price in relation to the cost of their own houses. This arrangement applied to licences for conversions as well as for new houses, and was obviously necessary in order to prevent profiteering in that time of acute housing shortage. Architects employed by private families in those days became expert at designing houses which kept within the permitted limits of size and cost, but which could be enlarged at some later date when the restrictions had been lifted.

By 1952 the position regarding licences for private building had become much easier, but as the cost of building showed no signs of falling a " self-help " building movement sprang up in various parts of the country and four such groups, known generally as " housing associations," approached the Edinburgh Housing Committee for permission to build their own homes. As about half the members of each group were skilled tradesmen of various kinds, a good standard of workmanship was assured and the men proposed to work on the houses in their spare time. The Town Council looked favourably on this venture and all the groups were allotted sites, three at Oxgangs and one at Barnton. Each group built 50 houses.

OVERCROWDING AND SUB-STANDARD DWELLINGS

During this period when Government, Corporation, builders, contractors, architects and the public were entangled in endless difficulties, slums and overcrowding together raised the most poignant difficulty of all. And on this we should first listen to Dr. Seiler, the city's ex-Medical Officer of Health before returning to an intimate picture of certain Edinburgh wards, compiled by Professor Burns and Dr. Gregor.

According to Dr. Seiler housing surveys in 1935 and in 1946 had shown the extent of Edinburgh's need. Of 120,265 houses surveyed in 1946 no fewer than 106,011 had rentals of £45 or less. Of these, 77,727 (64·6 per cent) were tenement homes, and 16,687 (13·9 per cent) were flatted houses in the city. Many of these provided spacious, comfortable homes of the highest quality, but too often the conditions in tenement homes were most unsatisfactory, especially in the privately owned and rented group of 61,737 houses under the £45 rental limit.

" Of this last group", Dr. Seiler continues, " 31,021 or 50 per cent were one-apartment ' single ends ' or two-apartment ' room-and-kitchen ' type dwellings. At the same time 1,558 houses had three or more families in occupation, and in extreme cases eight or nine families were found in one dwelling.

" When it is remembered that, according to the overcrowding standard in Table I of the First Schedule of the Housing (Scotland) Act of 1935, two adults, six children under 10 years and a baby living in a living-room and two bedrooms would not be classed as ' overcrowded,' it was distressing to find that 18,220 families or 15·71 per cent in these lower-rental houses were classed as ' overcrowded' .

" When the somewhat more acceptable standard recommended for ' new ' housing in the Department of Health Circular 149 of 1944 was applied to the ' existing ' houses in the city, it revealed that 43,583 families were ' overcrowded'. This standard is based on two persons of any age for each room, excluding the living-room, but it does not allow separate bedrooms for children of different sexes.

"The condition of families in sub-let accommodation was particularly distressing. Of 12,996 such families, 9,056 or about 70 per cent were living in one room, while 2,885 had two rooms.

"Of the 61,737 rented houses under £45 rental, 37,911 or 61·08 per cent had no bathroom, 11,952 or 19·36 per cent shared common water-closets, while 1,913 houses or 3·1 per cent were without sinks or shared a common sink with other houses."

Returning again to Professor Burns' and Dr. Gregor's survey we find that in 1951, a Census year for which reliable figures are obviously available, there were 134,038 houses in the city, and in these 440,986 persons lived in 471,531 rooms—more than one for each person.

The average of 93 persons per 100 rooms is not meaningless. The fact that it had fallen from 111 persons per 100 rooms in 20 years is the measure of housing progress. But in relation to anything but the entire population, the average quickly becomes misleading. In Craigmillar ward there were 155 persons to 100 rooms, against Morningside's 58. The average population per 100 rooms was highest in the wards containing the two largest pre-war Corporation estates—Craigmillar and Pilton—and this represented a rather unexpected result of the building programmes of the 1930s, which were intended to reduce overcrowding. More than a quarter of the 16,800 people living in Craigmillar ward were living more than two to a room; and in Holyrood, St. Giles and Central Leith the proportion was over a fifth. At a lower level, however, the control areas re-established their bad eminence with 1,442 persons living more than three persons to a room in St. Giles, 1,042 in Holyrood, and 1,089 in Central Leith.

With 2,500 persons in the city living more than four to a room, 2,259 persons were occupying houses of five, six, seven, eight and more rooms. The Murrayfield–Cramond district, for example, did have 21 persons living in 11 single rooms, but also 440 families with an average of four persons in each lived in houses with eight rooms and more. In Newington more than 900 families, of slightly smaller average size, lived in similar though rather older houses.

With bigger houses, naturally, went more of the conveniences regarded as essential parts of a house: a piped water supply inside, a cooking stove, a kitchen sink, water closet and fixed bath. But more than two out of every five houses lacked one or more of these "essentials," and 39 families were apparently living without any of them. The 13,000 houses added between the 1951 Census and 1958 of course altered the proportions, and some of the worst property had already gone. Nevertheless, nearly one in three households was still without a bath of its own, and some of the 14,000 households without a kitchen sink, and the 6,670 without a cooking stove in 1951 were still without them seven years later. Most of the bathless dwellings, and the other deficiencies, were concentrated in five wards: St. Giles (five out of six dwellings without a bath), Holyrood, Central Leith, St. Andrew's and Calton.

DEMAND FOR HOUSES

In spite of the enormous additions to the city since 1946, there was no sign by 1958 of over-production of new houses. It was in fact impossible to estimate the number of people waiting to purchase a house, for their names were scattered among the lists of numerous house agencies and builders; but firms that erected small or moderate-sized houses for sale could still sell them as fast as they were built, even though inflation had caused such a steady rise in prices that in 1958 the cost of a new three-apartment house or flat varied from about £1,900 to £2,700 according to district and type of construction and fittings, and the price range of a four-apartment house or flat was about £2,000 to £3,000, with correspondingly higher prices for larger ones. A six-apartment detached bungalow with a garage, for example, could cost around £4,700. Similar suburban houses of somewhat earlier date but nevertheless completely modern were likewise easily saleable and fetched a relatively high price.

Building Societies for their part reported no slackening in demand for loans for house purchase in the '40s and '50s; indeed, they did not have the capital available to meet all requests. They had perforce to take a long view of the transaction and decide whether a property was likely to maintain its value over a period of 20 or 25 years. On this basis they consistently favoured advancing money on modern houses and were less ready to grant loans on old property, especially upper flats in tenement buildings where there was risk of deterioration of the roof and consequent damage to the property.

In the poorer districts, where houses are normally rented to working class people, many landlords, anxious to rid themselves of the expense of upkeep, were trying in the '50s and early '60s to sell the houses if they became vacant. Often they were in poor repair and therefore a bad bargain to the purchaser even though one saw prices as low as £60 for one room in a tenement with a shared W.C., or £150 for a room and kitchen with shared W.C. Nevertheless, so acute has been the housing need of some of these families that they were and are still willing to buy almost anything if it is cheap enough.

HOUSING LOANS

Local authorities are empowered to lend money for house purchase under certain conditions, and Edinburgh Corporation has been very active in this field. There was a temporary cessation towards the end of the '50s due to a Government " credit squeeze " policy but by 1958 loans were once again available. One effect of the 1957 Rent Act, which in Scotland decontrolled the rents of privately-owned houses over a rateable value of £40, has been that some tenants have been threatened with eviction unless they bought their house. The Corporation has given special consideration to requests for loans from persons in this predicament. The situation does not affect people in the poorest type of property for this is still controlled under the Rent Restriction Acts. Nevertheless cases of hardship are inevitable, especially among older people living on small fixed incomes who could not consider purchasing, and it was for that reason that the Government passed amending legislation to delay eviction if all efforts to obtain alternative accommodation had failed. How these housing loans were working at the end of the '50s and the early '60s is described below by the City Chamberlain, Mr. Ames Imrie, who goes back a number of years to get a proper background:

"In 1899 town and county councils were empowered by the first Small Dwelling Acquisition Act to advance money to a resident in any house in their area to enable him to acquire the ownership of that house. The loan could not exceed 80 per cent of the market value of the house; no loan could be made where the market value exceeded £400; and there were several requirements as to the sanitary condition and state of repair of the house, title of ownership, bond and disposition in security, and so on. Now the market value of houses coming under the Small Dwellings Acquisition Acts is £5,000, having risen in a series of steps over the years; and since 1959, the loan may be as much as the market value. An important statutory provision is that the rate of interest charged to the borrower shall be a rate one quarter per cent in excess of the rate fixed at the time of the loan for loans made to local authorities by the Public Works Loan Commissioners.

"The Corporation has also lent £2,900,000 to private people for the purchase and building of houses under the Housing and Small Dwellings Acquisition Acts since the end of the war and has thereby become in effect a large building society, with total advances up to date of over £6,000,000.

"The powers contained in the Housing Acts, enacted later than the Small Dwellings Acquisition Acts, are less restrictively defined and much more extensive. Local authorities may lend money to persons subject to such conditions as may be approved by the Secretary of State for the purpose of acquiring and building houses, for converting other buildings into houses, and for altering, enlarging and improving houses. The original limitations on the valuation percentage of the loans and the market value of houses eligible for municipal lending have been repealed and now 100 per cent loans may be given on all dwelling houses, subject, of course, to valuations duly made, fitness for habitation, and so on. These housing loans may be given not only to private persons but also to companies and associations.

"The Housing Acts confer further powers on local authorities. They may, in accordance with schemes approved by the Secretary of State, guarantee a proportion of the loans given by incorporated building societies to their borrowers, and indeed guarantees can be given so that these societies may lend sums greater than they would normally have given in the absence of the guarantee. In certain instances the Secretary of State may undertake to reimburse local authorities up to one half of any loss sustained under the guarantee. A few years ago, after consultation with local authorities and building societies, formal guarantee schemes were approved by the Secretary of State and issued to all local authorities, and Edinburgh Corporation from the beginning has fully exercised these powers. Many hundreds of bulding society advances have been guaranteed by the Corporation.

" Local authorities may also assist housing associations in a number of ways and, acting under the statutory powers, the Corporation has made loans to such associations, subscribed for share capital and entered into subsidy arrangements with them. There have been dealings with such well known associations as the Thistle Foundation and the Scottish Veterans Garden City Association, which cater for ex-service men, and also with the Edinburgh Viewpoint Housing Society. A development within the last few years has been the creation of housing associations by groups of persons who have combined together to build houses for themselves by their own hands and with some assistance from skilled persons outside—the so-called self-help building groups—and with them, too, the Corporation entered into agreements both for the lending of money and, as with the other associations, for the payment of exchequer and rating housing subsidies.

" Again the Corporation, acting within its statutory powers, has made many grants to private persons for the improvement of dwelling houses and for the conversion of buildings into houses, these improvement and conversion grants being partly repaid to the Corporation by the Exchequer. There has in fact been a great drive in recent years towards the achievement of a ' property owning democracy,' as it has been called, and Edinburgh Corporation, supporting this objective, has fully exercised its powers under the Housing and Small Dwellings Acquisition Acts to get house-ownership for as many families as possible. A more recent statute—the House Purchase and Housing Act, 1959—became notable in this connection since it not only empowered local authorities to give 100 per cent loans but removed the ceiling of £5,000 market valuation, above which formerly loans could not be granted.

" There have been occasions when the Corporation has suspended the exercise of these lending powers. It did so during the war years and during the period following the raising of bank rate to the penal rate of seven per cent at the end of 1957, when restrictive monetary measures were required to meet certain conditions in the nation's economy. But it certainly looks as if no local authority has done more relatively than Edinburgh in carrying out out its ' building society ' functions. Up to May, 1962 the Corporation had advanced loans for dwelling houses amounting to over £6,000,000 of which at that time just over £4,000,000 had been repaid."

WAITING LISTS

To return to Professor Burns' and Dr. Gregor's account of the housing position at the end of the '50s, it was apparent then that there was a great shortage of privately-owned property to let, though it was impossible to estimate the numbers of would-be tenants since here, too, their names are scattered. So far as working class districts were concerned the number of vacant houses to rent was negligible. Landlords had for so long faced soaring costs for repairs and maintenance while rents remained controlled, that they preferred to sell if possible rather than re-let when a house became vacant. Clearly the demand for renting this type of property was closely linked with the waiting list for local authority houses, for if there had been enough of the latter, demand for the former would have been reduced.

To look ahead, Corporation officials were still saying in the early '60s, as they did in 1958, that their current waiting list could not give an accurate picture of the situation since it was impossible to keep it up to date, and some of the families would certainly have left the district or found other accommodation and failed to cancel their applications. Current estimates of the waiting period between lodging an application and being allotted a house were two and a half years for a newly married couple, two and a quarter years for a couple with one child, and five to six years for an old couple. Discouraging though these figures were, they compared favourably with those of a few years ago.

It should perhaps be explained that applications are accepted only from persons employed in Edinburgh, or resident in the city for at least three years (exceptions to this period being allowed for regular members of H.M. Forces and the Merchant Navy). A " points system " is in operation to ensure allocation of houses according to need. Because of the shortage no applications can be considered from people who already have a house which is not certified as over-crowded or insanitary, even though that house may be unsuitable for them on medical grounds or may be otherwise unattractive and they would dearly like to move. Their problem must be solved where possible by private arrangements for an exchange. In view of this decision, the waiting list acquires an added significance. The number of newcomers to the city who have applied for Council houses because of obtaining employment in Edinburgh certainly does not constitute a large proportion of the whole.

IN THE 1960s

From 1958 onwards there have been inevitably many changes in Edinburgh's housing plans, for as Mr. D. T. Terris points out in the following survey of the period there is of course no finality to housing. Properties can deteriorate so much that they become uninhabitable; new housing schemes spring up to accentuate the note of change in the spreading suburbs; and in fact no large centre of population in Britain is ever free from the problems and responsibilities of providing homes for the people. But more than most cities Edinburgh has to meet the especially acute difficulties caused by the external durability of centuries-old buildings in the older parts of the town.

Generation after generation buildings have stood firm to the wind and the rain, but the internal arrangements in many of the oldest houses have lost any relation to what we have come to regard as the indispensable requirements of a modern home. Sometimes occupants have even had to be hurriedly evacuated because of the danger of a collapse. And because of such slum conditions—in a few fairly well defined areas on the perimeter of the old town and in Leith—the Corporation, despite the complexity of the task, has made a considerable effort to clear up the slums and also to find quicker means of building their replacements.

SLUM CLEARANCE IN THE EARLY '60s

Estimates vary of the number of unfit houses still remaining in the city. At the worst, a figure of unfit houses approaching 10,000 presents a formidable enough problem, but inroads are steadily being made on it. Over and above such properties it has been estimated that there are more than 30,000 sub-standard houses, some of which in due course must fall into the unfit category. On the other hand many are in good districts; they are structurally sound and capable of being brought up to date.

In April, 1962 the Town Council decided to spend their largest single sum ever on re-housing—half a million pounds—for the re-development of three temporary housing areas at Southhouse, Niddrie Marischal and Muirhouse. Over 3,500 houses were then placed under contract, apart from work already proceeding satisfactorily on other schemes.

In the previous year good progress had been made in the clearance areas, and the demolition of properties in the Carnegie Street and Greenside Row districts had been completed. In the Arthur Street area 580 of the 649 families there were re-housed and a large number of properties demolished. Progress in the Kirkgate and Citadel areas of Leith was however slower, due partly to the raising of objections to the Unfitness Order.

The next significant step forward was approval of a programme for the clearance of unfit houses during the three years, 1962–4. This aimed at 3,000 houses, and approximately 800 houses not listed as unfit in terms of the Housing Acts were also included in the programme, this being regarded as unavoidable when dealing with large Comprehensive Development areas. The areas included in this programme are Salisbury Street and Brown Street, Heriot Mount, and Holyrood Road, etc. (these three areas complete the first phase of the Arthur Street Comprehensive Development Area); India Place and St. James' Square; Wilkie Place and Newhaven; Nicolson Street, Earl Grey Street and Riego Street, and High Street.

So the long process goes on. Early in 1964 it was decided to demolish a further batch of 500 homes, long regarded as some of the worst slums in the city, in the Stockbridge–India Place area, and it seems likely therefore that further skyscrapers are on the way.

There were of course those who thought this slum clearance programme insufficient, and indeed Lord Provost Sir John Greig Dunbar had occasion in March, 1961 to challenge a critic who had urged the building of 5,000 houses a year. He declared that unless essential jobs, such as the building of schools and schemes for industry and commerce, were stopped and labour directed, there was no other way in which such a volume of housing could be built in such a short time. To build 5,000 houses in Edinburgh in a year would require about 7,000 men; but nothing like this number was available, especially as schemes close to Edinburgh, such as the building work in connection with the British Motor Corporation's big new factory at Bathgate, were drawing on the city's labour force. At that date, however, the Corporation Housing Committee were not contemplating the use of prefabrication methods as seriously as they are now, and possibly the outcome of the inquiries will be an upward move in the curve of annual production figures.

CORPORATION HOUSING

Up to May, 1962, when the Corporation's capital expenditure for permanent housing was £42,732,152 the total number of Corporation houses built was 36,858, including 3,619 temporary houses which were to have an estimated life of 10 years, but have survived much longer. Since then the number of houses has increased, and by May, 1965 total capital expendit-on permanent housing had risen to £58,013,299, and the total number of houses built was 40,906.

Up to the outbreak of war in 1939 the Corporation had built 14,816 permanent houses, and the figure for the post-war period up to May, 1962, was 18,423. Of the total of 33,239 permanent houses, 410 were one-apartment houses, 3,160 two-apartment, 19,695 three-apartment, 8,840 four-apartment, and 1,134 five-apartment. Temporary houses were all of three apartments.

Provision of houses specifically for the elderly is an incidental aspect of the problem. Before the war there were only 26 houses of this kind built by the Corporation, but by the end of 1962 the figure had gone up to over 410, with more to be erected. The kind of house favoured is of the cottage type built in small communities in the middle of an existing housing scheme, where the old folks are not isolated and are able to adjust themselves to the community life around them.

Although the Corporation have been compelled by circumstances to turn attention more and more to the re-development of central sites by demolition of slum property and the erection of multi-storey blocks of flats, building upwards in this way is not the only solution to the housing problem. Once all the existing open sites have been used, building up will be necessary within the city boundary, but local authorities have power under the Housing Acts to build houses in the areas of other local authorities. So presumably a further extension of the city boundary cannot be ruled out.

Since the building of the first block of multi-storey flats at Gorgie in 1952, others have followed so fast that within 10 years two blocks went up at Slateford, one at Blackhall, two at West Pilton, one at Spey Street, Pilrig, three at Gracemount (on the southern outskirts of the city), three at Colinton, and six at Muirhouse.

" So successful is this switch from land-devouring horizontal building to the spectacularly vertical", says one authority, " that by the autumn of 1963 good progress was being made in the erection of a 23-storey project at Muirhouse (the greatest number of storeys in Edinburgh so far), and plans were approved for further developments elsewhere. These included the construction of blocks at Restalrig and Sighthill, where, because of special considerations, the height will range no higher than 16 storeys. Other big developments at the same time were in hand at Dumbiedykes and Leith Fort. These last projects are worth scrutiny if only because that at Dumbiedykes raised aesthetic and planning problems and the completion of the skyscraper at Leith Fort in 1963 had a special significance. "It was then, in the month of September," says another authority on Leith developments "that we saw the official acceptance of the 20,000th post-war house built by the Corporation. This marked a notable stage in the history of local authority housing in Edinburgh. The house was in one of the two 21-storey blocks—highest in the Scottish capital and the first major housing scheme to be completed in Leith for something like 100 years—on the site of Leith Fort. The builders and designers could also boast of new amenities: electric underfloor heating, for instance, and the equipment of each towering block with two lifts serving alternate floors. An old cannon has been mounted in the forecourt to commemorate the link with the Fort, which was begun in 1779, and served as military barracks and stores until after the second World War."

The fear that the tall buildings proposed for the Dumbiedykes–Arthur Street redevelopment scheme would seriously impair the amenity of Holyrood Park and the Palace of Holyroodhouse created a prolonged controversy between, on the one hand, the Housing Committee, and on the other, the Royal Fine Arts Commission and the Ministry of Works. That problem was satisfactorily resolved; and when the first multi-storey block, that at Dumbiedykes, was ready for occupation late in 1963 it was generally conceded (particularly by the tenants and by those citizens who were aware of the slum conditions long prevailing on the site) that an agreeable change had been effected.

Also by 1963 it had been decided that in order to give preference to low income applicants for Council houses the Corporation should amend the points scheme to give additional points to applicants with household income coming below stated weekly amounts. These amendments were scaled for childless couples, couples with one child, or two, three and four children, and so on.

THE RENT PROBLEM

Edinburgh has consistently sought to apply a greater degree of realism to the difficult problem of rents than have a number of other local authorities in Scotland, where the low amounts charged were absurdly out of relation to the changed values of money. Under pressure by the Secretary of State some of the anomalies in low rent areas have been modified; but even under the policy pursued in Edinburgh many tenants, it would seem, are not asked to pay a truly economic rent. A statement issued in May, 1962 by the Scottish Development Department showed an average standard rent per house in Edinburgh of £37 2*s.* 4*d.* compared with the average of £30 7*s.* 2*d.* for the twenty-four cities of Scotland and £30 13*s.* 4*d.* for the large burghs, after some recent revisions upward. Rebate schemes in certain of the burghs tend to obscure the real average rent charged, for although five of Scotland's cities or large burghs had standard rents a little higher than Edinburgh in May, 1962 all of them operated rebate schemes. But the fact remained that in Edinburgh the rent of Corporation houses in May, 1962 was £20 8*s.* for two apartments, £38 for three, £40 9*s.* for four and £45 11*s.* for five apartments. It was therefore the relatively low rent of two-apartment houses, purposely kept at a lower level, which brought down the average to £37 2*s.* 4*d.*

Before going any further with this we should however for a moment look at the inflationary background against which housing and other civic developments have taken place since the war.

THE POST-WAR BACKGROUND

"In the post-war years", says the City Chamberlain, "civic affairs in Edinburgh have developed in much the same way as in all local authorities throughout the land, especially in housing, education, health and welfare, notably that of children. But there have been some developments of particular interest and concern in Edinburgh. These have taken place against a background of inflation, which persisted in the earlier post-war years and which confronted local authorities, as it did private persons and enterprises, with the problem of rising costs and with difficulties in financial management and control. Not only have the city rates risen sharply, but from time to time the Corporation has had to raise the charges for many of its services to accord with the changes in money value. Rents of municipal houses, for instance, were raised in 1953, 1957, 1960 and in 1962; and of course local authorities are required by law periodically to review rents and to make any necessary changes. Again the costs of building and maintaining houses have been rising. Interest rates on current borrowing have risen from 3¾ per cent in 1951 to 6½ per cent at the present time; and so the annual revenue cost of the continuing programme of house building has risen steadily and steeply.

"The plan of rent revision applied by the Corporation has been logical in its design. The 1953 increase narrowed the gap between the rents of cheap pre-war and dear post-war houses. The 1957 increase was to create a rental system based on the rents of post-war houses to reflect broadly the variation in amenity and standards of accommodation. The 1960 increase was a general one. The 1962 increase was especially interesting and unique, because, while the existing rents were maintained, it introduced a system of rental supplements of 5*s.* per week where there were two or more earners in the household. It was suggested—in 1963—that the next periodic review might embrace consideration of a scheme of rent rebates."

This duly happened. The liability to pay in respect of the additional earners was placed upon persons who were 18 years of age and over, and who earned more than £4 per week. Special provision was made for old age pensioners and widows in order to preserve a measure of equity in the incidence of the supplementary charge. It is generally referred to as a differential rents scheme, but municipal administrators do not entirely accept this definition. They prefer to regard it as part of a differential rent scheme which could lead to a higher standard rent, with rebates for families whose usual incomes fell below the sum stated as the standard amount. It was estimated that the supplementary charge of 5*s*. would bring in about £125,000 yearly and add about £4 to the average rental figure of £37.

The working of the new rebate system, which is only for tenants earning less than £650 a year, may be seen from a report given to the Town Council's Finance Committee by the City Chamberlain's Department in early June, 1964, when the scheme came into operation. Of 17,175 claims for rebates, 2,584 had been rejected as ineligible. Most rents, it was explained, had been increased by one-third and the rebates had been claimed on the difference between the old and the new rents: a 100 per cent rebate meant that the tenant continued to pay his former rent, and those eligible for this were the tenants earning less than £575. A breakdown of the rebates granted showed that 11,781 tenants received 100 per cent rebate; 883, 75 per cent; 1,003, 60 per cent; and 924, 25 per cent.

Further changes occurred in September, 1964 when the second stage of the new rents scheme came into operation. Then, tenants in households where the combined income of the husband and wife exceeded £1,600 a year were asked to pay an economic rent. Working wives earning £4 a week or more were also in future to pay a supplementary charge of 4*s*. a week. The new rents were expected to bring in more than £240,000 a year.

Under a new scheme for houses built by local authorities after November, 1961 and approved by the Secretary of State for Scotland, local authorities have had to look carefully once again at their housing financial arrangements. In place of the uniform subsidy of £24 paid to local authorities the Government decided to introduce a dual system of payments—a lower subsidy of £12 and a higher one of £32, with some additional subsidies in particular cases.

The purpose was to give the higher subsidies to those authorities whose housing needs and financial resources required greater assistance and the lower subsidy to those whose needs were not so great. An assurance was given at the same time that the subsidy amount to be paid to Scotland as a whole would not be reduced. What the Secretary of State aimed at was to establish a new and probably more equitable way of distributing the aggregate sum on housing among the local authorities in Scotland according to their needs and circumstances.

Corporation houses have never been subject to the Rent Restriction Acts which, over the years since 1920, have affected only houses in private ownership. The Rent Act of 1957 allowed private owners to increase rents by 25 per cent or 50 per cent depending on certain conditions, and released from control houses with rents over £40 in November, 1956 and houses let under new tenancies. The next year or two are likely to see considerable changes in the general municipal rental position throughout the country. For the Housing Act of 1962 empowers the Secretary of State, where a local authority has failed to revise and charge reasonable rents, to direct the authority to charge the rents contained in a scheme prepared by him.

EXPLOITATION

Another problem which was greatly troubling the Corporation in the spring of 1964 was the exploitation by speculators of either homeless people or those living in overcrowded houses. "The real evil as we see it", said Mr. George Reid, Lord Dean of Guild, "is the exploitation of this tragic situation by a few speculators who have bought up dwelling-houses in both good and poor-class districts, and proceeded to offer a lot of single apartments with few, or no services, at exorbitant rents to unfortunate homeless people. Because of the increase in over-crowded houses the Dean of Guild Court has been compelled to take drastic action, and in addition to fines we normally order houses to be restored to single occupancy."

A large proportion of this type of sub-standard, separately-rented and lockable accommodation, was in those dwellings known as "back-to-back" houses, a form of dwelling which, according to existing by-laws and new regulations, was forbidden. "These apartments", Mr. Reid went on, "normally have no proper sanitary facilities, nor the proper cubic capacity per person, while the natural light available and the cross-ventilation provided bear no relation to the normal minimum requirements for a dwelling-house."

PRIVATE ENTERPRISE

Now let us look at the contribution made by the private builders to the provision of houses in these recent years of housing difficulties. In the period immediately after the Second World War restrictions on materials, labour and so on inevitably limited their efforts, and permission to build was difficult to get. This position continued until the early 1950s. The following figures of warrants issued by the Dean of Guild Court to private enterprise builders show the trend:

1946	156	1955	812
1947	148	1956	782
1948	185	1957	641
1949	161	1958	636
1950	105	1959	630
1951	89	1960	747
1952	182	1961	885
1953	290	1962	747
1954	431	1963	521

A voluntary agency which has done particularly good work is the Viewpoint Housing Society, a body recognised by the Inland Revenue as having charitable status. It is non-profit making and is registered under the Friendly Societies' Act of 1893. Started in 1947 with the object of providing flatlets for single women, the Society first converted a number of large houses in good residential districts. The tenants belonged to the small income group who were nevertheless in a position to pay an economic rent for their accommodation and cherished the spirit of independence. Now the Society has about 300 tenants in flats. In 1960 it also opened a residential house for older women at Ettrick Road, and this has proved very successful in providing a " home " atmosphere. Not surprisingly therefore the Corporation has shown practical sympathy in the Society's work.

THE ENDLESS PROBLEM

Before we leave this always engrossing subject of people's homes, let us take a closer look at recent developments in one sample ward of the city where the Corporation has been active in building. In the Liberton ward the population rose by just over 80 per cent between the 1951 and 1961 Censuses; and this is accounted for very largely by the 5,969 families living in Council houses as opposed to the 2,351 families who own their homes themselves.

The rate of building has been considerable. Southhouse, for instance, saw 360 permanent houses erected between 1947 and 1950, with another 269 towards the planned total of 590 during the following decade. Southfield was developed in 1946–9 and again in 1956–7, with 462 permanent houses and 98 temporary houses which are to give way to another 160 permanent ones. The Inch saw 1,773 houses built in 1950–6, Hyvots Park 950 in 1953–5 and 1960, and Gracemount 1,313 in 1956–62, while the Moredun and Ferniehill districts also contributed their quota to the grand total of 5,893 completed by 1962. As an idea of the standards of comfort and services provided here, there were in the whole of the Liberton ward, according to the 1961 Census, only 161 houses of one room, 195 without a hot water tap and 295 without a fixed bath. In Edinburgh altogether the percentage of houses with no hot water tap was 16·4 and with no bath 24·33, while the corresponding figures for Liberton were 2·17 and 3·29.

Meanwhile the basic problem of finding sufficient land for building remains unsolved. At the end of July, 1964 the Town Planning Officer, Mr. T. T. Hewitson, pointed out that there was a maximum of only 850 acres of land available for development at Wester Hailes and Alnwickhill in the Liberton area and that eventually the Corporation would have to consider housing an overspill population outside the city boundary.

CHAPTER 15

THE PROBLEMS OF PLANNING

FEW issues arouse more rancour in Edinburgh than present-day building schemes and the future planning of the city. For these and many other issues affecting the city's amenities continually exercise such bodies as the Cockburn Association and the Scottish Georgian Society which have a special interest in trying to safeguard the city's architectural graces. When the road level was lowered in Charlotte Square—long recognised as one of the most beautiful squares in Europe—the Scottish Georgian Society led by the Earl of Haddington was quick to point out that the square had been "mutilated." And in the same year (1961) the annual report of the Cockburn Association, which had vigorously protested against both the Charlotte Square operation and a proposal to turn Randolph Crescent into a big and noisy traffic way, regretted sincerely "that there should be any ill-feeling between members of the corporation and this association." The remark speaks volumes for the controversial tone of recent exchanges between these "amenity societies" and the town council. But this had been evident for some time. Nor is the persistent public discussion on whether or not the civic authorities are gradually destroying the oldest and best of the city confined to these eloquent bodies. Many other organisations have had their say, as have countless individuals writing in the local newspapers and periodicals.

As for the Corporation and its predecessors, they are often under criticism for permitting certain buildings in Princes Street, which should never have been allowed, and which the Lord Provost himself—on 30th July 1962—described as "just a shower of junk," a remark which a well-known Edinburgh writer, Mr. Moray McLaren, duly embellished in *The Scotsman* (30th August, 1960):

> Short of destruction and rebuilding there is nothing to be done. It is one of the most chaotically tasteless streets in the United Kingdom; nor is the usual excuse that the view from it is unrivalled any mitigation. It is no compliment to one's face to say that the view looking away from it is very good.

Attacks like this naturally provoke sharp protests from the civic authority, which feels there is much to be said on the other side. Bailie Ingham, for example, thought Mr. McLaren's remarks "entirely symptomatic of the attitude towards local government of an unimportant but vociferous section of the community." In itself, his own remark reflects the present-day clash between taste, sentiment, and respect for historical distinction, and the growing pressure of modern building, transport and industrial needs; which explains perhaps why the Bailie added that in certain matters affecting the city the Town Council had no powers at all.

Controversies like these are naturally symbolic of the fact that Edinburgh, despite its conservatism, is a city which is not only changing fast but must continue to do so for many years to come if certain public needs are to be satisfied. Clearly, no matter how old and picturesque their squalor, certain old slum areas have had to be or must be cleared in the interest of public health and cleanliness. The growth of industry too has meant increased demands for new, extensive buildings equipped with every modern device and general comfort. Finally, the ever-increasing density of motor traffic makes it essential to plan new roads, new one-way streets, new parking centres and new garages, and for touring motorists from a distance new hotels.

In the presence of such problems it is usually wise to forsake dogma and prejudice for calm deliberation and reappraisal of the issues involved. Reappraisal is certainly necessary, since urban circumstances now change more rapidly than ever before. A further sharp increase in the amount of transport using Princes Street, for instance, would certainly give further point to the City Engineer's proposal for a ring road round the Old and New Towns, on which no decision had been taken by 1965.

Pending any of the big decisions which must be taken in the near future, it might be timely here to let two recognised authorities explain the city's planning problem as they see it. The first authority—on the central problem—is Mr. William Kininmonth, a distinguished Edinburgh architect who is also a Royal Scottish Academician. The second is Mr. William Marr, the City Assessor.

THE CENTRAL PROBLEM

The city, which today covers an area of 54–55 square miles and takes a roughly circular form between the Forth and the Pentland Hills, has grown in a sequence of four phases which we have studied already, but perhaps they should be briefly summarised again to make the city planning problem more understandable.

The first is the medieval fortified town focussed on the Castle and clustered along the ridge leading to Holyrood. The second phase was the New Town, that remarkable series of pre-planned Georgian developments between Haymarket and the Calton Hill, bounded on the north by the Water of Leith. In contrast to the narrow streets of the Old Town, new streets were spaciously laid out and followed a geometric pattern conceived as a series of rectangles, squares, circles, crescents, octagons and ellipses which bore no relation to the earlier radial road system which gave Edinburgh access to the port of Leith and to the villages and towns of Scotland.

With the arrival of the machine age and the upsurge of a new industrial population in early Victorian times, planned expansion broke down; and during this third phase, which lasted until the second World War, the old organic road system reasserted itself and building development crept along the trunk roads to the outlying villages and into the intervening open spaces, until today practically all available building land within the city boundaries has been built over.

The fourth phase, on which we are now entering, is as yet less clearly in focus, but it coincides with the Corporation's new powers of planning control and is distinguishable by a movement back towards the centre, and by the redevelopment of slum properties, a new scale of multi-storey building and the planned reconstruction or control of the central areas.

The arrival of motor transport and the shift of emphasis to the New Town, where a geometric and self-contained road system is superimposed on the organic radial roads, lie at the root of Edinburgh's traffic and central redevelopment problems, but the issue is further confused by the natural and wholly laudable desire of the community to preserve the architectural spaciousness of the Georgian New Town with its romantic counterpart, the Old Town on the Castle Ridge. Hence the many and violent controversies which break out with monotonous regularity to bedevil the city and which in recent years have been highlighted by acrimonious disputes over Princes Street Gardens, George Square, Randolph Crescent and Charlotte Square. All of these were referred to the Secretary of State for decision.

GEORGE SQUARE

The controversy over George Square was one of the most prolonged and violent in Edinburgh's history. The square, which was built during the first half of the 18th century has seen better days; but apart from one intrusion on the north side it had retained its original form for well over 200 years and during its long history was associated with successive generations of notable citizens. Architecturally and historically it was unique in Scotland as a complete example of its period and as the immediate predecessor of Edinburgh's more famous New Town.

The dispute raged round the University's Central Redevelopment Plan, which included the destruction of the old buildings and their replacement by buildings considered to be more suitable for University purposes. It was maintained by the University that after examining all possible alternatives, the reconstruction of the Square offered the only practical solution to their problem of expansion, and they accordingly declared their intention to use the site in order to provide essential accommodation for an extended Medical School, a new Arts building and a Libyrar, retaining only the houses on the west side for smaller departments.

This plan was immediately opposed by the National Trust for Scotland, by the local amenity societies, by a majority of the University's own graduates, some of its staff, and by many influential citizens, who, while recognising the architectural and practical advantages offered by the site, held the view that the buildings could be adapted for University purposes and that the Square could and should be integrated into the University scheme as an historic and valuable architectural nucleus to a surrounding redevelopment. All were agreed that the University, in its desire to reserve sites for immediate development, regarded the Square primarily as an area to be bought up with a view to expansion, and so either minimised or failed to appreciate its historic and architectural importance.

The University's first development plan, drawn up by Sir Charles Holden in 1945, envisaged the reconstruction of George Square. It was adopted in principle and developed by his successors Mr. Basil Spence and Professor Robert Matthew (as Sir Basil and Sir Robert then were); and after considerable hesitation on the part of the Town Council, planning permission was granted in 1956.

Subsequently, however, opposition to the scheme continued to mount, and in 1959 an appeal for a public inquiry was made to the Secretary of State, who disallowed the appeal and instead called both parties to the conference table in an effort to reach an amicable solution. The working group, which comprised four members from each side, met on six occasions. They were, however, unable to reach a compromise, and it was agreed that the matter should be referred back to the Secretary of State for a decision between three possible alternatives, which were

(1) to accept the University proposals, or
(2) to amend them by adapting the houses for University purposes, or
(3) to recast the plans and prepare a new scheme.

The outcome of this unusual procedure was that the Secretary of State declined to enforce reconsideration of the University's scheme, and in a letter to the objectors he outlined his reasons. These, paraphrased in brief, were that delay would have serious consequences on the ability of the Scottish Universities to provide for those of the rising generation whose claim to a University education had been accepted as a matter of public policy; and since Edinburgh's contribution in meeting the demand for an additional 5,000 places in Scotland by 1965 seemed vital, its achievement depended on getting ahead without delay. In support of this general thesis he drew attention to the finding of the Historic Buildings Council, which had expressed the opinion that while the architecture of the square was interesting it could not be compared with Charlotte Square. He also referred to his own technical advisers, who said in effect that the buildings were dilapidated and unsuitable for reconstruction to present day standards or for teaching purposes on the scale required, and could not be converted to provide the facilities demanded by a modern University.

Faced by an opposition which now included the Secretary of State, the Historic Buildings Council, the Town Council and the University, the Preservation Societies made one last despairing effort at the public inquiry in 1960, but the cards were stacked too heavily against them and the case was closed in favour of the University.

RANDOLPH CRESCENT

No sooner was the George Square controversy concluded than another of almost equal violence appeared when the Town Council proposed to replace the gardens of Randolph Crescent in the New Town by a traffic round-about.

The case put forward by the Corporation was that traffic conditions at the junction between the Crescent and Queensferry Street were not merely deteriorating but likely to become dangerous and chaotic. The street was after all one of the two major western accesses for traffic into the central area of Edinburgh (the other, the West End of Princes Street, being already overloaded). These entrances led directly to the two main traffic arteries, Princes Street and Queen Street, and if the Randolph Crescent entry choked and became ineffective, the full weight of traffic would be transferred along Princes Street which would then develop into little more than a motorway. No alteration to buildings was contemplated, and the gardens, although early 19th century in their origin, were in fact Victorian and out of character with the architecture.

The Corporation was opposed by the local residents backed by the amenity societies, who maintained that if the gardens were replaced by a traffic round-about not only would the character of this fine Georgian crescent be destroyed but the whole of the New Town would be threatened by the entry of traffic on a large scale.

The dispute was eventually argued out at a public inquiry. The Secretary of State in his published findings agreed that traffic improvements were required at Randolph Crescent, but he was not satisfied that the proposed round-about as designed would solve the problem in an effective way. He accordingly proposed that before any irrevocable alterations were made the traffic problem in central Edinburgh should be re-examined and proposals for improvement should be included for consideration in the statutory review of the City's Development Plan which the Corporation were required to submit to him later. So, unlike George Square, the Crescent gardens were reprieved for the time being.

CENTRAL AREA REDEVELOPMENT

Before turning to consider the central area redevelopment as it is affected by the traffic problem, recognition must be made of the work accomplished by the Town Council since they were given the power to control the development of the city by statute. Starting with the Abercrombie Survey and Report on which the original Development Plan was based, comprehensive planning has gone forward steadily and schemes are now in preparation or under consideration for the redevelopment of many city areas; building controls have been re-imposed on George Street; and the whole area of the New Town and Princes Street is under careful consideration.

All this, together with a great programme of re-housing, new school and vast schemes of reconstruction by the University and the Royal Infirmary, is going forward steadily, and although it may appear superficially that many of these projects are proceeding in a haphazard way they are in fact intimately related to the programme envisaged in the Development Plan. But the central redevelopment problem, inextricably bound up with traffic and parking difficulties and with the old road systems, remains. It is, in fact, already clear that although traffic in the centre is still controllable, its steadily mounting volume, increased by the opening of the Forth Road Bridge in 1964, presents a serious threat to the city's future wellbeing.

In principle it seems reasonable that as a long term policy consideration should be given to developing an outer ring road along the southern boundary to drain off through traffic. But complementary to the outer ring, there is a more urgent necessity for an inner ring to sweep round the central areas of the Old and New Towns and gather to itself all the radial trunk roads leading to the centre. The purpose of this second highway would be to provide an easy circular route along which traffic would proceed to the nearest point of destination before entering the centre. Thus the heart of the city would be isolated from unnecessary through and cross traffic such as is at present canalised into or through the centre and along or across Princes Street.

Most of Edinburgh's traffic shuttles back and forward from the suburbs into the centre, and if the working population in the central areas is increased, as it will be, by high density building in the St. James' Square area and the Tollcross—West End—Haymarket triangle, mounting traffic will be aggravated. For this reason alone building controls must be imposed in the centre. It is also obvious that because of the contours and the existing road system the bulk of this traffic and much else besides will continue to enter Princes Street, which is already nearing its capacity as a traffic artery.

Princes Street is, in fact, the natural and at present the only central traffic route into, through and across the heart of the city; and there is little doubt that if it were redeveloped for this purpose alone and if its approach roads were remodelled it could cope with a great volume of traffic. But Princes Street is much more than a traffic way. It is not only a world-famous street in an incomparable setting but an integral part of Edinburgh's most important shopping and business precinct, enjoyed by citizens and visitors alike. It is unthinkable, therefore, that any traffic plan could be acceptable which would degrade the street from the proud position it now holds and convert it into a purely functional traffic artery slashed between the New Town and the Old.

There is, however, no alternative route other than Queen Street which could be used to drain off the potential traffic volume; and Queen Street after all is constricted by Randolph Crescent and a geometric street pattern at its western approach and has no connection southwards except across Princes Street. So the fear remains that if traffic increases as predicted, it will overtake the potential capacity of Princes Street. Its use for any other purpose will be destroyed, and Craig's New Town, which will become a traffic reservoir for the overflow, is bound to choke in its turn.

This is an alarming but by no means exaggerated picture of what may happen—as has happened elsewhere—unless steps are taken to prevent its occurrence. Professor Abercrombie clearly foresaw the inherent danger when he proposed a three-tiered Princes Street as his solution to the central traffic problem and as a means of preserving the New Town intact. But his dream of removing Waverley Station is unlikely to be realised in the immediate future; for the complexity of the tunnelled approaches, the disturbance to existing roads and properties, and the vast expense involved seem to make his solution impracticable for the time being.

It would appear, then, that there is only one alternative and practicable way of saving Princes Street and the New Town, and that is to divert the natural traffic flow, as Professor Abercrombie foresaw would be necessary. If a new road is constructed on the line of the railway in Princes Street Gardens, either above or parallel to it on the surface or below ground, and if this route is connected with the Queen Street route at either end, traffic can be diverted from the central Princes Street route by introducing one way traffic there or by closing part of the street. It will then follow the easiest course by the railway or by Queen Street; and except for vehicles which have business in the Centre, it will tend to circulate round rather than pass through or across the area between Princes Street and Queen Street.

This solution—and here readers of this book without intimate knowledge of the city may wish to consult the map at the book's end—has many advantages apart from relieving and saving Princes Street and the New Town. It is relatively economical. It provides a clear way in all directions from Waverley Station and the long distance bus terminal off St. Andrew Square. It solves the problem of finding an easy way into and out of the St. James' Square–Leith Street redevelopment other than *via* Princes Street and its East End; and if, in addition, a slip road is constructed from lower Leith Street to the eastern end of Waterloo Place, the East End of Princes Street can then be converted into a simple T junction from the North Bridge.

There may be many who will fear the logic of this solution or think it is a threat to existing amenities. But to the north, whether or not improvements are made to the western approaches into Queen Street, nothing can now prevent that street being increasingly used as a traffic route; and if there are three alternatives open to the motorist, the burden on the streets will be correspondingly lessened. To the south, even if the new road is carried above the railway instead of being concealed, it will be screened by existing trees along its route. In any case it would be less unsightly and disturbing than the great gash torn along the valley by the railway which it would replace.

THE PARKING PROBLEM

In this discussion the parking problem has been left to the last, since in the author's view its solution depends on finding the answer to the perplexing questions posed by the movement of traffic in the central areas. (These are discussed in the next chapter.) Up to date no solution has been found, although the possibilities of off-street parking in public garages and private properties and the introduction of more parking meters are being actively investigated and pursued. It seems certain, however, that sooner or later long-term parking in the central streets must be prohibited, and it is unthinkable that Edinburgh's central gardens should be utilised for parking. If this principle is enforced, owners who wish to bring their cars into the central areas will be driven to make accommodation for them in their own properties, and as this will only be practicable in a limited way, a demand for public garaging will be created. It seems not unreasonable that these garages should be sited and strictly controlled in the interest of the community as a whole, and that those who demand the privilege should pay for it. There are numerous places in the folds of the contours, in the open spaces, in the station yards, in Leith Street and in the hollow squares on either side of George Street where space for garage accommodation can be found, but these can only be used and developed after a general ban on street parking in the central areas and for some distance beyond.

On this warning note Mr. Kininmonth ends his survey. But clearly the city's future will be enhanced or disfigured not only by traffic and economic issues but by the very shape of the buildings. On this theme the City Assessor has written his comments.

"THE INFURIATE ZEAL OF THE BUILDERS"

In a mood of exasperation Robert Louis Stevenson once wrote of " the infuriate zeal of the builders." He had some hard things to say not only of the Old Town and the New Town but of the then recent villa architecture in Newington and Morningside. " Day by day", he complained, " one new villa, one new object of offence, is added to another; . . . the dismallest structures keep springing up like mushrooms."

There were many who shared Stevenson's views some 80 or 90 years ago. " And yet", he wrote, " the place establishes an interest in people's hearts; go where they will they find no city of the same distinction; go where they will they have a pride in their old home." And well they might, for if environment can be said to influence the lives and characters of city dwellers Edinburgh people can be thankful. In Stevenson's day there were, as now, buildings to which exception could be taken or upon which there could be differing yet authoritative opinions. Nevertheless there was unmistakable evidence on every hand that generations of architects and builders had aspired to a standard of design and construction that would be worthy of a city so old and distinctive. There was a sense of fitness, an awareness that some special effort was called for to harmonise the remarkable physical contour of Edinburgh with her historical background. Hence the agreement of many thoughtful lay observers that, until the first World War, those who had initiated or carried to fruition the major building works had won a large measure of success. Many experts might dispute this, and there was no doubt a lack of co-ordination which sometimes brought a crashing discord of styles, but the whole effect of the " infuriate zeal " was not displeasing. An abundance of skilled craftsmen and such excellent material as the fine but hard-working stone from the quarries at Craigleith encouraged the prolific use of stone until well into this century. And for this very reason, if the grey, not to say sooty, elevations sometimes seemed forbidding to the stranger from sunnier parts of the world, he at least felt that most of the buildings he studied somehow reflected the good strong character of the people and their climate.

Many of the developments that took place around the turn of the century (and before 1914) are shown in Appendix III which gives a list of buildings erected in Edinburgh since 1860, and seems to prove that the sponsors of not only public but commercial buildings were willing to spend large sums to secure a basic quality of design and construction as well as suitable architectural embellishments. The social and economic changes that followed the first World War had, however, a profound effect upon building trends, which we might consider here under the separate but not water-tight compartments of residential development-commercial and industrial buildings, educational and other public buildings, and finally ecclesiastical properties.

RESIDENTIAL BUILDINGS

One of the features of residential Edinburgh is the large number of substantial stone-built villas and terraces in districts like Newington and the Grange, and also in the New Town and the West End, almost all occupied by the owners. But, as elsewhere in Scotland, large numbers of houses have been built in Edinburgh for letting and a high proportion of these are of the tenement or flatted type. All house building ceased during the 1914–18 War, and at its end the demand for houses far exceeded the supply. The rest we have seen. In Edinburgh between the wars hundreds of acres of land were developed by the erection of subsidised local authority housing, and with few exceptions cost dictated that there should be a much more spartan standard of finish than in the past.

Whole new suburbs of this type were to spring up in the course of a few months, and centuries-old farm and estate names appeared for the first time on the destination boards of trams and buses taking the new suburbanites home. Those lucky enough to secure one of the new houses counted themselves fortunate, but today the new housing schemes present a monotonous, repetitive and barrack-like appearance.

Though private capital was not attracted to the building of houses for letting during this period, there was a renewed interest in the erection of houses for sale to owner-occupiers; and in this sphere also building and labour costs ensured that brick and harl became the general rule, with the occasional use of stone for sills, lintels and architraves. Less frequently the whole front of the house would be faced with stone, with the rest in brick and harl, thus providing a more up-to-date version of the "Queen Anne front and Mary Ann back"—a criticism that had been directed at some of the New Town construction. As with local authority houses, and for the same reasons, the tendency was also towards smaller rooms and lower ceilings. Another notable feature of the post-1918 designs was that a small working " kitchenette " superseded the larger kitchen with its range and scullery which has been used as the living-room in so many Scottish homes.

All of these tendencies have continued at an ever greater pace and with greater emphasis since the last War. Although some of the publicly provided housing accommodation was of the tenemental variety the rest, together with most of the private house development, has been of bungalow, cottage or terrace type with variations such as " detached," " semi-detached " or " four-in-the-bloc " construction. But in the late '50s and early '60s the Corporation and some private builders have made a determined attempt to introduce more attractive and varied elevations and a greater degree of amenity in the overall layout of the housing estates. Over a long period there has also been an increasing interest in subdividing the older villas and terrace houses into flats of more convenient size, which do not demand the same amount of domestic help as did the originals.

COMMERCIAL AND INDUSTRIAL PROPERTIES

Commercial and industrial developers, during the '20s, also had to trim their sails to the chill wind of financial expediency. By the late '30s, however, banks and insurance companies especially had recovered sufficiently to present a bolder front—hence the appearance of various Bank and Insurance company head offices in St. Andrew Square.

The new buildings of some of the insurance companies present a somewhat more severe design than some of their older and more corniced neighbours; yet on the whole most people, though not all, would say that the architectural proprieties have been observed. It is worth noting also that, while controls and restrictions discouraged the investment of private capital in dwelling-houses built for letting, the building of Lothian House in Lothian Road and Dunedin House in George Street shortly before the outbreak of World War II showed clearly that there was a good market for the letting of offices of modern design.

In the field of industry all major development since 1918 has naturally been of a functional and practical character, carried out mainly in brick and concrete and steelwork. But there are no large industrial estates of a size comparable with those found in other parts of the country, though just after the second World War some 135 acres were set aside at Sighthill for feuing to industrialists who desired either to set up new businesses in the city or to leave old premises in favour of new ones constructed more in keeping with the needs of the times. The Sighthill Estate is, in fact, now almost fully occupied by a wide variety of enterprises. Some of these are of very simple, not to say unimaginative, design; but others—a biscuit factory and a colour printing works, for example—have managed to strike an appearance of efficiency with dignity. Among other industrial developments that catch the visitor's eye are Rank's new Flour Mill at Leith docks, the new chemical fertiliser plant erected by Scottish Agricultural Industries also in the dock area, the large research laboratories belonging to Ferranti's at Crewe Toll and, perhaps catching the eye too readily, the power station at Portobello, whose large stalk abruptly severs the skyline.

ECCLESIASTICAL, EDUCATIONAL AND PUBLIC BUILDINGS

Fine churches and graceful spires have long been a feature of the city, but their number has tended to diminish in the central areas as the community has spread out to the new housing suburbs, where red brick structures with truncated belfries began to appear. Dwindling city congregations led to unions of churches and, in consequence, many fine old buildings were sold in the market and are now occupied as warehouses or showrooms.

As for the University and the schools, there cannot be many cities so handsomely endowed with notable educational buildings, most of them impressive in their different ways, for although in many respects they are obsolete internally when judged by modern standards, they and many others are notable for the vigour and variety of their external design, boldly carried out in stone and very carefully sited. It is a pity, incidentally, that the fine north elevation of Heriot's with its terrace and wide stairway towards the Grassmarket was allowed to become obscured by subsequent random development. More praiseworthy, the most important addition to the city's school buildings between the wars was probably the construction of the new George Watson's College at Myreside, with a commanding front elevation in stone and the buildings extending to the rear finished in brick and harl. In fact, the whole standard of appointment of this school, both internally and externally and its setting of spacious grounds and playing fields makes it one of the finest of all school properties.

Edinburgh University is possibly the most dispersed of the old Scottish Universities; for the David Hume Tower and another skyscraper have risen at George Square; and developments in the field of engineering, science and technology have led to the construction of new large modern teaching blocks at King's Buildings at West Mains. These together with the new Agricultural College, form an acceptable blend of functional design in the modern manner.

In the matter of large public or administrative buildings, the architects and builders have been full occupied in recent years in a very difficult effort to rise to the needs of the Edinburgh setting. The Sheriff Court House building and St. Andrew's House are instances of important development between the wars, while the new National Library in George IV Bridge is a fine example of post-war construction (though it remains to be seen how well its soft sandstone finish will stand up to the rigours of the Edinburgh climate).

All in all, if a modern Stevenson were to undertake a personal survey of man-made Edinburgh in the 1960s, he would soon find subjects upon which to sharpen his wit, as did his illustrious predecessor. The descendants of

In the grounds of the Palace of Holyroodhouse the Queen presents trophies to members of the Royal Company of Archers (The Queen's Bodyguard for Scotland).

ıe Honours of Scotland, the Scottish regalia, are taken from the Castle to St. Giles' ring a State visit to the city. The crown, carried by Sir Thomas Innes of Learney, : Lord Lyon King of Arms, is preceded by the sword of state and sceptre.

Winter holds St. Margaret's Loch in the Queen's Park fast in an icy grip. Behind on the lower slopes of Arthur's Seat is the ruin of St. Anthony's Chapel.

the " infuriate " zealots may plead expediency and a tight budget, but their most enthusiastic supporters would not deny that the building developers of the past 40 years, with a handful of exceptions, have contributed little of distinction or character to their city. It is as though modern design had suffered from the same malaise as much of our modern music; it has " nae tirl tae it." And indeed the returning traveller who takes a bird's eye view of Edinburgh from his jet plane as it circles the city is not likely to fix his attention long on the vast network of bungaloid growth below, for it is indistinguishable from those in almost any other of a hundred places he has visited.

THE ARCHITECTS AND SURVEYORS

Now that we have examined in broad detail the problems of building and planning in the city, it would seem appropriate to turn our attention to the builders and planners themselves, or more precisely to the architects and surveyors and the professional organisations to which they belong.

THE ARCHITECTS

In a city whose history is enshrined in her buildings, we must first take a backward glance to the period covered by the second *Statistical Account.* At this time there were considerable changes in architectural thought and taste in the northern kingdom. For in 1845 the three great figures of Georgian and Neo-Classic times in Edinburgh—Hamilton, Playfair and Burn—were all nearing the end of their careers and were being supplanted by architects seeking new forms of expression in various styles borrowed from other periods. This eclectic phase was by no means confined to the revival of Gothic architecture but used the forms and the ornamentation of the Venetian palaces, the great houses of Rome and Jacobean England and the turreted castles of Scotland itself.

The two representative architects of Victorian times in Edinburgh were David Bryce and David Rhind, the authors of most of the solid and stately banks and commercial offices in the centre of the city. The design of these was largely an array of Roman motifs but their architects could adopt other styles with equal enthusiasm—English Tudor at Daniel Stewart's College, and at Fettes the steep pinnacled roofs of Loire chateaux. Bryce was also the principal inventor of what came to be known as the Scottish baronial style in the large number of country houses he built throughout Scotland.

In the later 19th century the outstanding figure was Sir Robert Rowand Anderson. The breadth and originality of his Italianate interpretations are best seen in the University's Medical School (near Bryce's Royal Infirmary) with its impressive courtyards. As for his National Portrait Gallery in Queen Street many think this shows a superb blending of Florentine palazzo proportions and Gothic richness of ornament.

Another change may also be discerned about the time of the second *Statistical Account*, this time in the history of the profession.

Architects had begun to form themselves into societies. The Royal Institute of British Architects, founded in 1834, is the oldest of these, but the Edinburgh Architectural Association (1858) was the fourth in the United Kingdom and the first in Scotland. It started in a small way as a lecture club, but soon extended its activities to visiting historic buildings for intensive study. This, of course, was very much to the point in an age when new buildings were designed largely in the forms of the past, with varying degrees of permutation in the designer's mind.

From its small beginning in 1858 the Association by the turn of the century had raised its membership to 270. Today—near the eve of this book's publication—it has more than 430 members, representing about four-fifths of the qualified architects in the city itself and the surrounding region. It is also one of the 34 allied societies of its parent body, the Royal Institute of British Architects.

Training in Edinburgh is now largely concentrated in the Schools of Architecture of which there are two in the city. The larger is in the College of Art with a total of 220 students in the five yearly stages: the other, founded in 1952, is within the University. Students, as a matter of course, also pass through a period of practical training in architectural offices before qualifying.

The number of qualified and registered architects in the area of the Edinburgh Architectural Association (which includes the Lothians, some of the Border Counties and the populous part of Fife) was almost 570 in 1963; and of these the number who worked within the city itself was probably about 450. There were 67 private firms within the City (and 26 more within the Association's region). These vary considerably in size; about 20 have three or more partners; and some have a large staff of qualified men. But there are very many small firms. About half a dozen of the Edinburgh firms have practices in other parts of the United Kingdom.

A substantial number of architects are employed within public bodies such as the City Corporation, Midlothian County Council, and the Scottish Special Housing Association. This trend has accompanied the growth of social services since the second War. Much of the building required for such services is designed by these permanent staffs, but a great deal is also carried out by private firms, briefed and guided by the official architects.

After the last war local authority housing and school buildings were the main field of architectural activity, soon followed by some commercial and industrial building, churches and other buildings for the new suburbs, technical colleges of all kinds, hospital rebuilding and university expansion. All these are in progress today. Private house commissions, on the other hand, do not bulk large in architectural practice in Scotland, and speculative house building in big estates does not generally come the way of the private firms.

THE CHARTERED SURVEYORS

There is another profession who work closely with the architects and deal very often with technical problems affecting the land and property of Edinburgh citizens. These are the Chartered Surveyors.

All branches of surveying are now practised professionally under the Charter of the Royal Institution of Chartered Surveyors. Its headquarters are under the shadow of Big Ben but its Scottish home and headquarters lie naturally within the capital city.

When the layman hears the word " surveyor " he is likely to think of someone measuring land with a theodolite and chain; but while the use of these is still one of the surveyor's basic skills, the complexities and needs of the modern community in country, town and city have led to a high degree of specialisation. Thus the chartered surveyor may equally well be found in tweeds at a market or agricultural show, in old clothes in the roof space of a house, underground in miner's helmet and clothing, or immaculately dressed giving evidence in the highest courts in the land.

Historically, one of the earliest specialisations was land surveying; but except for the staff of the Ordnance Survey and those concerned with major land developments the Land Surveyor is a *rara avis* whose main natural habitat is in remoter and less highly developed countries. Also rare, but of very recent genesis, is the chartered surveyor specially trained in town planning, a much maligned but vital figure in the modern city with its choking arteries and melting green belts. More numerous are those specialising in Scottish land management—resident factors of estates, for instance—and those in general practice in the city who manage many estates outside it, advise on estate and farm management and value landed property for purchase, sale and arbitration. The Chartered Mining Surveyor in this country is engaged mainly in surveys of coal mines and coal deposits; a number are employed by the National Coal Board in Edinburgh.

But the profession's main impact on city life comes from two remaining specialisations—those of the Valuation Surveyor and the Quantity Surveyor. The valuation surveyor in private practice surveys and values property for sale and purchase, and also buys and sells property on behalf of clients. Many a burgess indeed has cause to be thankful that he employed a chartered surveyor to report on the condition of a property he thought of purchasing; and while he may have been sorry that the financial burden of running a city necessitated the services of " that awe-inspiring creature, the City Assessor", as one surveyor put it, he was at least glad that this official and his qualified staff were chartered surveyors professionally trained and impartial. Also in the public sphere are the valuers in the Inland Revenue of whom the Scottish chief has his office in the city.

Though all these varied functions have been increasing for some time, undoubtedly the profession's greatest growth has been in the last 20 or 30 years. This is accounted for particularly by what is now its largest section or specialisation, that of the Quantity Surveyor. He is sometimes styled " the accountant of the building team", and his independent professional position is widely recognised as a safeguard to the other members of the team and to the clients: he cannot become an employee of a contracting firm and still retain his professional status, and his services are often sought as an arbiter in building disputes.

Co-operation within the industry in Scotland is achieved through a Joint Standing Committee of Architects, Surveyors and Building Contractors, with headquarters and secretariat supplied by the surveyors at their Edinburgh office. Although most quantity surveyors in the city are in private practice many are employed in Government departments and by the local Councils.

To show how all this has come about, an historical note would not be out of place here. The first British association of surveyors was formed in London in 1794, and the Institution of Surveyors in 1868. It was then incorporated by Royal Charter in 1881 and a Scottish branch established in 1897. Today the ruling body is the Chartered Surveyors' Institution, formed in 1937 through the amalgamation of three separate " surveying " bodies in Scotland—the Scottish Branch of the Surveyors Institution, the Estate Factors of Scotland and the Faculty of Surveyors.

CHAPTER 16

THE PEOPLE'S TRANSPORT

BY ROAD

BEFORE looking at the various systems of transport operating in the city we ought to glance back quickly at earlier enterprises, for some are not only a picturesque part of social history but have had a direct influence on the transport services of today.

There seems to have been a form of stage coach service between Edinburgh and Leith as early as 1610. Then in 1660 a " regular " service was inaugurated between Edinburgh and London, though three or four weeks seem to have elapsed between each departure. An attempt was also made in 1678 to connect Edinburgh and Glasgow by coach, but this enterprise was soon abandoned, since the public from the outset looked upon the journey as a serious adventure and usually made their wills before departure.

Almost a century later the Edinburgh magistrates granted exclusive rights to a company to run a regular service of stage coaches in Leith Walk, with accommodation for six passengers, for a period of 21 years (1772). Next came the public omnibus of the 1850s from which the local transport of today has evolved.

In the early days of horse-bus operation—on many routes in the city—a pair of horses drew each bus and on hilly routes a third horse was traced in front. Generally these buses were appreciated by the public. But a short and noisy interlude in the evolution of the city's transport occurred in the early '70s when steam omnibuses were introduced. Although capable of carrying 50 passengers, they were unreliable and had a short life.

EARLY TRAMWAYS

In 1871 the Edinburgh Tramways Act provided for the construction of tramways in certain streets. The working of the tramways was to be by animal power only. Three years later the tramways consisted of 37 tramway cars and 300 horses. By the early '80s, when the total length of the tramways was 18 miles, the rolling stock consisted of 90 tramway cars and a few buses for use in country districts. As nothing could stop this growth, in 1893, when there were 1,100 horses at work, the Corporation exercised its right of purchase and acquired 11½ miles of the horse tramway system. The remaining mileage continued to be owned and operated by the company until 1896 and 1898, when the Corporation acquired the remaining parts of the undertaking.

CABLE TRAMWAYS

The hilly routes of Hanover Street and Frederick Street (going north from Princes Street) were unsuitable for the operation of horse tramways, but another company called The Northern Tramways Company, which was formed in 1884, saw possibilities in underground cable traction, and cable tramways were constructed by this company to serve the residents in these areas. In 1896 this undertaking also was acquired by the Corporation, which kept the slow-moving cable cars in being till electric tramways came in their stead.

All this must sound today like a most outmoded, antiquated piece of machinery. But in its time the Edinburgh cable tramway system—the " cable crawl " as it has been called—was considered to be one of the largest in the world, the total mileage of track being 36 miles. The cables were driven not from one but from three power stations and the total length of cables necessary to drive the cars on all routes was $48\frac{1}{2}$ miles.

ELECTRIC TRAMWAYS

Leith Corporation, which had acquired horse tramways in 1894, converted the system to electric traction, and the first route was opened on 18th August 1905. When Leith was amalgamated with Edinburgh in 1920 this system became part of the Edinburgh tramways.

After the expiry of The Edinburgh and District Tramways Company lease in 1919, the City Corporation took over operational control, and decided to introduce electric tramways with overhead equipment. Princes Street naturally received special consideration, and after considerable controversy it was thought wise to preserve its amenity by the erection of special centre poles: these are still in existence. Leith and Edinburgh tramway systems were connected at Pilrig, and the first portion of the converted cable tramways—namely, Pilrig to Liberton and Churchill—was officially opened on 20th June, 1922. Thereafter the development of the electric tramway system was rapid.

THE FIRST MOTOR BUSES

On 29th January, 1914 six single-deck motor buses were purchased—three Leylands and three Tilling Stevens—and these seem to have been the first buses purchased by the Corporation. They were operated by the Edinburgh and District Tramways Company, as the Corporation were not then themselves operators, and were housed at Tollcross Depot. These buses operated, however, for a very short time only as the Leyland chassis works were impressed by the War Department on the outbreak of war. Shortly afterwards the three Tilling Stevens vehicles were sold to the Scottish Motor Traction Company.

In the matter of motor bus operation the Corporation were not the first in the field. A motor bus service was initiated in Edinburgh, according to the municipal licensing records, on 19th May, 1898, by Norman D.

Macdonald, who was better known later as an advocate of improved railway services. The vehicles were small, costing an average of £350 each, and unfortunately the daring pioneers lost some £14,000. Nevertheless Scotland's capital can claim that its motor buses were in regular operation for more than a year before London took up the novel idea.

In 1905 the Scottish Motor Traction Company was formed; it began to operate on New Year's Day, 1906, and did much to open up the area surrounding the city. There was then no further development of motor buses by Edinburgh Corporation until after the first World War, when 12 buses were purchased in 1919 and used for the development of routes in areas not served by tramway cars. The first bus service was inaugurated on the east side of the city in December 1919. Since then the growth of the bus fleet has matched the expansion of the city.

BETWEEN THE WARS

Undoubtedly the first World War was responsible for the growth and improved design of the internal combustion engine, and civic authorities all over the country vied with one another in introducing motor bus services within their respective boundaries. In Edinburgh the many districts untapped by trams provided eminently suitable conditions for the new form of transport. Gradually route after route was opened up, radiating from the hub of the city to distant suburbs and indeed all points of the compass.[1] The first Corporation buses, though comfortless and noisy, offered speedier progress than the citizens had ever known.

From 1919 until the commencement of the second World War in 1939 rapid progress was made in the development of both electric tramways and motor bus services. In 1939 there were 27 electric tramway services operating over a mileage of 47¼ miles; the average distance of the services from the centre of the city was four miles; and also such considerable extensions had been made to the bus services that in 1939 there were 18 services covering 69¾ miles within the city boundaries.

Tramway cars were run from four service depots at Leith, Portobello, Tollcross and Gorgie; and motor buses were originally garaged at the lower end of Shrubhill Depot. Extensions to bus routes and the subsequent increases in the fleet, however, necessitated the acquisition of larger accommodation. Hence the Corporation's acquisition of the Industrial Hall in Annandale Street for this purpose in 1926. Originally this hall had been built for the purpose of exhibitions. When the first bus fleet was centralised there it became rather less impressively known as the Central Garage. Today its total area is approximately three acres.

THE END OF THE TRAMS

The second World War prevented any further extensions, and in fact war-time restrictions had the effect of reducing the normal service to

[1] For comparative figures of mileages, passengers, fares, etc. of Edinburgh Corporation's buses and tramways in recent years, see Appendix IV (1).

which the public had become accustomed. Normal maintenance of permanent way and vehicles also suffered, and after the war rapidly increasing costs focussed attention on future policy.

Since overhaul and modernisation of the tramway system would probably have cost £8 millions, whereas a complete conversion to buses spread over five years was estimated to cost about £2 millions, the Corporation gave considerable thought to this matter; and in the first instance it was resolved to reduce the tramcar fleet by withdrawing the vehicles that had reached the end of their usefulness. As an initial step it was planned that up to 25 per cent of the tramcar fleet should be scrapped within two or three years and replaced by buses. This duly happened. On 27th September, 1951, the Corporation accepted this scheme and four tramway services were abandoned during the 1952–3 financial year. Then came the big decision. A year later, almost to a day, the Corporation resolved " that the tramway system should be abandoned completely and replaced by motor buses." A year later still—in July, 1953—the Corporation acquired some 11 acres for use as a bus depot at Longstone.

The final exciting stage of the change-over included the conversion of routes via Bruntsfield and Morningside Station to Braids and Fairmilehead; and when this took place Edinburgh—on 16th November, 1956—paid fitting tribute to the ending of 85 years of tram operation in the city. A decorated tramcar operated over the last route during the final week; special tickets were issued on all routes; and the Corporation Transport Department's horse bus also paraded the streets. So not unnaturally there was tremendous public interest in the last run when cheering crowds estimated at 100,000 lined the entire route from Morningside Station to Shrubhill depot. A convoy of trams, including the decorated vehicle, left the Braids terminus, and when at Morningside Station the very last tram of all joined the procession with Magistrates and Town Councillors among its passengers the B.B.C. made a live broadcast of the event. One tramcar has been preserved in the Transport Department's Museum, along with the horse bus.

NIGHT BUSES

On 19th October, 1925, two All-Night Bus Services were introduced and remained in operation during the winter months only until the war. The routes of these services were (1) Foot of Leith Walk and Bruntsfield, and (2) Ardmillan and Salisbury Place. The fare was 6*d.* per person. After the war—in November, 1947—night bus services were re-introduced, but in place of the two former routes, five new routes were chosen to provide this type of service throughout the full year.

The number of passengers carried by these night buses during the financial year ending 28th May, 1961 was 207,165 compared with 243,987 the previous year; for the year ending 28th May, 1963 the total was 244,904; and the universal fare on these services was 1*s.* 6*d.* per person until 4 a.m. with ordinary fares after that time.

FARES

When Edinburgh Corporation first took over city transport on 1st July, 1919 the 1½*d.* minimum fares then in existence were reduced to 1*d.* stages, and these were retained from 1st July to 31st December, a period of six months, during which the undertaking was being operated at a loss. The fares were therefore raised on 1st January, 1920, the 1½*d.* minimum being introduced again, and the average distances of the fares at the time were as follows:

Tramways		Motor Buses	
Fares	*Distance (miles)*	*Fares*	*Distance (miles)*
1½*d.*	1·27	1½*d.*	1·11
2*d.*	2·52	2*d.*	2·19
3*d.*	4·24	3*d.*	2·91

A further increase took place in September of the same year, when the 1*d.* fare was reintroduced, but for a very much shorter distance. Further alterations took place during the next few years, due principally to the introduction and extension of the electric tramways and the rapid extension of motor bus services.

Thus on 1st September, 1939, when it was possible to give a short cheap range of fares considered to be among the lowest in the country, the average distances were:

Tramways		Motor Buses	
Fares	*Distance (miles)*	*Fares*	*Distance (miles)*
1*d.*	1·38	1*d.*	1·39
2*d.*	3·02	2*d.*	2·87
3*d.*	5·90	3*d.*	6·99

The financial position of the undertaking in the months following the outbreak of the second World War became so serious that it became necessary to increase the fares. To this end a new basis was evolved which consisted of dividing each separate route into stages of approximately ·45 of a mile and giving 2 stages for the 1*d.* fare, 3 stages for 1½*d.*, 5 stages for 2*d.* and 7 stages for 2½*d.* On the longer tramway routes the 2*d.* fare from the centre of the city to the termini was increased to 2½*d.* with a 3*d.* maximum fare on all routes. The average distances of the new fares which were introduced on 4th August, 1940 then became:

Tramways		Motor Buses	
Fares	*Distance (miles)*	*Fares*	*Distance (miles)*
1*d.*	·91	1*d.*	·92
1½*d.*	1·36	1½*d.*	1·46
2*d.*	2·25	2*d.*	1·89
2½*d.*	3·23	2½*d.*	3·24
3*d.*	6·38	3*d.*	4·99
		3½*d.*	7·86

Applications to increase fares again were considered at a public hearing in October, 1950, and new fares were ultimately introduced on 4th February, 1951, the 1½*d.* minimum fare being introduced again after 31 years. The fares and the average distances were then as follows:

TRAMWAYS		MOTOR BUSES	
Fares	*Distance (miles)*	*Fares*	*Distance (miles)*
1½*d.*	1·32	1½*d.*	1·46
2½*d.*	2·21	2½*d.*	2·38
3*d.*	6·24	3*d.*	4·71
		3½*d.*	7·95

The authority to introduce these fares came too late to be of much value in the financial year which ended in May, 1951. In the meantime the cost of wages, higher taxes on fuel, and a whole range of materials required by the undertaking increased to such an extent that a further increase in fares became inevitable.

There were thus five successive increases in fares between December, 1951 and January, 1956. A temporary increase was also introduced in November, 1956 following the Suez Canal crisis, but this was removed in April, 1957. Four further increases in fares took place however between July, 1957 and July, 1961 and a fifth in August, 1963 when the following fare structure was introduced:

No. of stages	*Fare*
Up to 2	3*d.*
3	5*d.*
4	6*d.*
5–6	8*d.*
7–11	9*d.*
Over 11	10*d.*

Season Tickets—four-weekly season ticket	50*s.*
Sunday " Run-about " (2 adults and 2 children)	3*s.*
Luggage per piece	3*d.*
Per Dog	3*d.*
Children's fare (available over all ordinary adult fare stages)	3*d.*
Scholars' fares and Scholars' Permit	5*s.*
Scholars' fare with permit	3*d.*
Average stage length	0·45 miles

Yet another increase in bus fares came into force in May, 1964. The 3*d.* fare remained unchanged, but the 5*d.* fare went up to 6*d.* and the 8*d.* fare to 9*d.* This was the thirteenth time fares had had to be raised since 1951; but as Edinburgh's public transport undertaking was currently running at a loss of £4,000 a week, the reason for the increase was plain to see. The spring of 1965 brought no respite. At the end of March, plans to increase the bus fares once again were approved by the city's Transport Committee because of the Transport Department's estimated deficit of £508,000.

EARLY MORNING RETURN FARES

During the regime of the tramways, there was a statutory requirement to provide cheap fares for " labouring classes", who were designated as artisans, mechanics and labourers. These were available not later than 8 o'clock in the morning or earlier than 5 o'clock in the evening. In practice it had been impossible to distinguish the classes of labour specified, and accordingly early morning return fares were available to all passengers travelling before 7.45 a.m.

In February, 1936 early morning return fares were introduced on buses for the first time—on the same basis and conditions—as similar fares on tramways. After periodical increases a universal early morning return fare of 6*d.* was introduced on buses and trams at the end of 1952. The Corporation, it should be noticed, was relieved by Statutory Order of the obligation to provide cheap fares for workmen in the revised fares introduced in October, 1954.

SCHOLARS' PERMITS AND SEASON TICKETS

From 1st August, 1956 the fare for scholars—as school children are grandiloquently called—travelling with a permit was fixed at the children's fare normally available to age 14. Scholars, therefore, required a permit only if they were over 14 or if it was necessary for them to transfer from one bus route to another on their way to school. In such cases the appropriate transfer point is of course specified on the permits, which are issued at a charge of 5*s.* to scholars under 18 and are restricted to scholars attending schools providing full-time secondary education.

The number of scholars' permits issued during 1962–3 was 6,556—a rise of almost 500 since 1960–1. But transport's contribution to education does not end here. Since 1933 the Transport Department has issued scholars' season tickets to the City Education Department. These season tickets, which are renewed at the commencement of the school session and again at the commencement of the spring term, entitle certain scholars to make, free of charge, one journey to school in the morning and one return journey in the afternoon. During 1962–3 just over 9,000 scholars' seasons were issued.

FREE PASSES

Free Passes are issued to blind persons and to ex-servicemen who lost a leg in either of the two World Wars. Applicants for these passes must be resident or employed in Edinburgh. In the case of the blind the pass is available every day and over all bus routes; but ex-servicemen can make use of it only between their place of business and residence while travelling to and from work. The total number of passes issued during 1962–3 was 1,364 for blind persons, and for ex-servicemen, 109.

All employees of the Transport Department are issued with free passes which are available at any time during the year of issue on all tram and bus routes while special season tickets are available to officials of other Corporation Departments at £30 each per annum. These special season tickets are limited to travel during business hours, and are available for use by any official in the Department which obtains them. Almost 460 departmental " seasons " were issued in the year 1962–3.

An arrangement is also in existence with the Police Department whereby all Regular Officers in Uniform, and Special Constables on special occasions only, are allowed to travel without payment of fare on the vehicle. For this arrangement the Police Department pays an annual sum to the Transport Department.

Following Government legislation permitting local authorities to give certain sections of the community new travel privileges the Corporation decided to introduce an Elderly Person's Travel Concession. This came into effect on 2nd May 1965 for women aged over 60 and men over 65 years of age resident in the city. The permit allows the holder to travel at off-peak times at a flat rate of 3d for any one journey on one vehicle; and in the first year of operation some 56,000 passes were issued.

PARCELS DELIVERY SERVICE

Like most municipal Passenger Transport Undertakings, a Parcels Delivery Service is operated in conjunction with the Corporation Buses. A large number of parcel ticket selling agents (principally small shopkeepers distributed throughout the city) is available for the convenience of people who have parcels for delivery. The parcels may be accepted by conductors, and are then transferred to a Central Parcel Office for sorting and delivery.

MODERNISATION OF THE TRANSPORT DEPARTMENT

Early in 1957 the whole office staff and the Lost Property Office moved to newly acquired premises in Queen Street. This move has allowed the Department to centralise its communication system. A central control room, equipped with short wave radio, has a minute by minute picture of traffic in the city 24 hours a day.

Leith Garage, which ended as a tramway depot in May, 1956, opened as a bus garage in December of that year. A year later the Corporation agreed that Gorgie depot, including the old tramway shed, should be sold and the depot be closed down within six months. The conversion of Shrubhill, another old depot, to a bus works was completed later along with other improvements including a new garage at Portobello which wisely provides a public park for cars and coaches.

While these and many other amenities were being introduced into the Corporation's bus and tramway services between the wars the bus was steadily gaining in status as a quick and practical means of reaching places outside the city boundaries, many of which were villages lacking a railway station. For this a private company was mainly responsible.

SCOTTISH MOTOR TRACTION COMPANY

Though the inauguration of the Scottish Motor Traction Company in 1905 has already been mentioned briefly, we ought to return to those early beginnings to trace in more detail the fortunes of a company which has done so much to link the surrounding country with the city.

On 1st January, 1906, the Scottish Motor Traction Company's first "bus," a Maudslay, went to the Mound to give the people of Edinburgh a unique opportunity of personally testing the new mode of travel in an exhilarating eight-mile trip from the Mound to Corstorphine and back, for the modest sum of *6d.* Of the many thousands of S.M.T. passengers who have since travelled that short journey, none can have embarked upon it with such high adventure as those who on that New Year day let the keen wind of the Forth blow away their 1905 Hogmanay headache. Next day their place was taken by more sober-sided citizens who, though assuredly considering themselves still amongst the boldest spirits, more closely resembled the season-ticket holders of today and seized upon the horseless bus to get to their offices.

The trend to bring the surrounding districts more and more within the orbit of the city was maintained steadily until the outbreak of the 1914 war when the Company was the largest of its kind in Scotland—with regular services between Edinburgh and many places outside the city.

The increasing public service rendered by this company in the pre-1914 years had not been achieved without difficulty. Judged by every modern standard the public service vehicles of these days were noisy, rough and anything but reliable. But William J. Thomson, (later Sir William), designed a bus called the Lothian, which revolutionised the company's services. It was, therefore, with vehicles of increased comfort and reliability, that the company was operating its services in the summer of 1914. Then came the War and the commandeering of the company's vehicles.

Expansion after the War was gradual but a cheap and fast American bus, obtained on hire purchase, released a flood of small concerns in the early 1920s. Many of these were well managed but as success came on routes where a growing public demand existed, an influx of still more new operators created keen competition. Operators who maintained regular services to a published time-table based on the needs of the public, and willing to provide services during the less remunerative parts of the day, were beset by competitors running only at the most remunerative times on the most remunerative routes, who were free to run a little ahead of the time-tabled services. The temporary success of such tactics was insured by the fact that more of the new operators were running a faster type of bus; and since maintenance or the lack of it had not entered their calculations they could and did operate a faster service, racing their slower competitors between stops and for a time at least operating at a high rate of profit. Many of the new operators, however, even those who had astutely chosen the most profitable routes, literally ran their businesses to death along with their vehicles. The businesses which survived were those which by experience or good common sense maintained a basically steady service backed by a well-organised maintenance system. Such firms in Scotland were mostly incorporated into the S.M.T. group of companies, as others were later. After the second War, the Scottish Motor Traction

Company and also that of the associated companies of the Scottish Bus Group were acquired by the British Transport Commission in April, 1948. A year later the group became Scottish Omnibuses Limited.

At the time of the formation of the S.M.T. 44 years earlier, the Edinburgh magistrates exercised control of stances, routes, time-tables and vehicles used. After the passing of the 1930 Road Traffic Act an agreement was entered into between the company and the Corporation for the purpose of regulating, subject to the Traffic Commissioners, the provision of road passenger transport services within the city. This agreement was replaced in 1954 by a new agreement which continues in force. Its principal provisions are (*a*) that the Edinburgh Corporation confines its operations within the city boundaries; (*b*) that Scottish Omnibuses would not operate services which are wholly within the city; (*c*) that on the company's vehicles the fares charged would be in excess of those charged by the Corporation for corresponding journeys.

The following figures give some indication of the recent growth in the number of passengers carried by the Scottish Omnibus services from Edinburgh:

Year	*Passengers Carried*	*Vehicle Miles*	*Vehicles Owned*
1957	107,000,000	33,000,000	Single deck 614 Double deck 180
1962	114,000,000	36,000,000	Single deck 546 Double deck 327

The operating cost per vehicle mile (including depreciation) rose from 24·03 pence in 1957 to 27·75 pence in 1962.

The provision of a proper bus station had been a problem for a considerable number of years. But in 1936 the Waverley Bridge stance was abandoned and permission was granted to allow buses to operate from St. Andrew Square. This arrangement continued until 1956 when the new bus station between Clyde Street and St. Andrew Square was opened.

In the early war years and immediately after, the colour scheme of the S.M.T. services varied from royal blue to various shades of khaki. But in recent years the now-familiar green and cream buses of the Scottish Omnibus service provide a pleasing picture of the road passenger services on the city streets.

A transformation has also been wrought on the erstwhile charabanc tours. Known now as Luxury Coach Tours—there is a considerable degree of comfort in the vehicles; which is one reason why the Scottish Omnibus Group is among the largest operators of road tourism in Britain, since it operates an infinite variety of routes from London, Edinburgh, the Scottish cities and most Scottish towns.

LOCAL COACH TOURS

As Edinburgh itself has always had a great attraction for the tourist also, the motor coach tours provided during the summer months include all the outstanding places of historical interest as well as those districts which, by their beautiful situation, give pleasure not only to visitors but to the citizens themselves.

These tours were discontinued during the war, but were resumed in May, 1946. A fleet of coaches is also now available for use on city tours which are in operation from May to September each year.

CABS

In 1880 the hackney carriage byelaws made it clear to passengers that the fares were to be as particularised in the table of fares; otherwise it was *6d.* for half a mile. If the fares were not mentioned in the list it was 1*s.* for any distance not exceeding $1\frac{1}{2}$ miles for one or two passengers, and a waiting charge of *6d.* for every 20 minutes. By 1910 taxi-meters had been introduced on a basis of 1*s.* for just over one mile. In the years following the second World War the sole horse-cab left operating in Edinburgh was driven up and down the Royal Mile by Mr. Tom Vallance till St. Cuthbert's Co-operative Association resurrected a few old cabs to ply for hire in the Old Town.

The first motor taxi-cab landaulette in the city was licensed on 6th July, 1907 to William Muir in Lothian Road. But about this time more taxi-cabs were appearing on the streets, under the ownership of the Provincial Taxi-cab Company; and these occupied a stance opposite the Scott Monument in Princes Street. The citizens, however, were slow to become taxi-minded, and as the Provincial Taxi-cab Company was unable to await the financial reward that accrued to its successors it closed down.

At the present time there are stances in Princes Street and Waterloo Place beside it for more than 40 cabs, and of course there are other stances in various parts of the city and at the railway stations. But the ownership of many of these vehicles has changed. On 30th December, 1954, for instance, Edinburgh's most famous taxi hirers, John Croall and Sons Limited, announced that their taxi service had been discontinued. The step was taken for economic reasons and it was stated that a taxi service was no longer an economic proposition. This firm which had been operating a taxi service in the city for nearly 50 years was the last of the big firms to withdraw its services owing to economic difficulties. Another large taxi-cab fleet was disbanded by an Edinburgh firm, and the vehicles sold to private taxi-men.

The number of taxi-cabs licensed to ply for hire in the city is about 400 at the time of writing; and a passenger may be driven any distance up to nine miles from the Mercat Cross on hailing a cab standing or plying for hire in any street. The basic fare in the mid-60s is 2*s.* 6*d.* for a distance not exceeding one mile or for waiting time not exceeding 17 minutes.

On 28th October, 1948 the Taxi Telephone Service was started: by dialling the appropriate number citizens are able to get a taxi from Waterloo Place at any time of the day or night; and this has now been followed up by Radio Cabs equipped with two-way communications between each taxi-cab and their central office. A number of private car hire firms also exist in the city.

MOTORING

How popular the motor car has become can best be appreciated by a few figures relating to Edinburgh alone. In 1927 there were registered in the city 7,399 private cars; in 1938 the number had risen to 17,245; in 1959 there was a jump to 32,850; and by 1961 the number was 42,940 and still rising. A similar rise in the number of goods vehicles also reflected the general swift development of road haulage, the annual totals rising from 1,443 in 1927 to 4,162 in 1938, with an upsurge to 9,522 after the war. By 1961 the total was 10,880.

Motor cycle registrations showed a different pattern, falling as they did from 3,769 in 1927 to 2,203 in 1938. After the war, however, there was a phenomenal rise to 6,523 in 1959 and on to 8,800 in 1961. These figures incidentally include motor scooters, for long popular on the Continent but now more and more a feature of the British road scene.

By means of traffic censuses taken at key points, these overall statistics can be translated into terms of daily vehicle density, as happened when a summary of traffic volumes in Princes Street on selected days during 1962 showed an increase as the summer season wears on. The checks were taken over a 16 hour period from 6 a.m. to 10 p.m.

TABLE 40
1962

Date	*Number*	*Average per hour*
20th February	westbound 13,500	843
	eastbound 11,600	725
14th August	westbound 15,550	927
	eastbound 13,200	825
21st August	westbound 16,900	1,056
	eastbound 14,500	906

The build-up towards the end of August is largely due to the attraction of the International Festival of Music and Drama held in the city at this time, when besides local residents there are many visitors from overseas.

THE HUMAN FACTOR

Behind these statistics lie a number of fascinating questions. What, for example, makes the Edinburgh man buy a particular type of car? How does he treat it? What use does he make of it? Could any variation in its use help to lessen the city's traffic problems? Should drivers know more about motor car engines?

As for the last question, on any day in Princes Street you can see women at the wheel—self-confident and efficient, even when the car holds an assortment of children and perhaps a dog as well. But most Edinburgh women, like their sisters elsewhere, have in general only a vague idea of what happens under the motor-car's bonnet. However, lest it be thought that every male motorist coming in and out of Edinburgh is a first-class mechanic who knows the innards of his car as well as he knows his own home, it may be well to quote the result of some local inquiries. These suggest that the average car owner does not do more than wash his car—if he has a garage attached to his house—fill the radiator, look at the dip stick to make sure there is enough oil in the sump, see that the battery is topped up and perhaps clean the plugs. Some also grease the lubrication points, but few attempt dismantling operations; that is left to the service station mechanic. Exceptions, perhaps, are some owners of fairly old second-hand cars, who cannot afford to buy anything better. They have to learn how to do things to their cars because they cannot afford high labour costs.

There are over 30 garages in Greater Edinburgh carrying the appointment of either the Automobile Association or the Royal Automobile Club or both. In addition there are many good, well-equipped garages giving excellent service to motorists which do not carry any appointment for one reason or another: there must clearly be a limit to the number of garage appointments which motoring organisations make in any one city, and Edinburgh is no exception.

In the earlier days of popular motoring there was naturally less call for service of one kind or another, for there were many fewer motorists, and most of them carried a spare tin of petrol or depended on a fuel reserve tap to get them home. But all-night fuel and service facilities do not appear to have kept pace with the great development of motoring.

Coming back to the car as a desirable, and, for some, imperative possession what kind of car do most Edinburgh people buy? The answer is that in this respect Edinburgh people are no different to those in other parts of the country, except perhaps that the final choice, out of a short leet, may be determined by the size of the boot—whether perhaps it will take a set of golf clubs lying down, since popular golfing in the city long preceded popular motoring.

Yet with motor cars one cannot fall back, as with art, on the defence: "I know what I like", since, to adapt Pascal, it is the purse rather than the heart that "has its reasons." This accounts in large measure for recent figures which show that cars of the "mini-type" up to 1,000 cc., (roughly the old 8 h.p. models), are most in demand followed by those up to 1,300 cc. (in the old 10–12 h.p. range). These smaller cars are, of course, the cheapest to buy and the least expensive to run; but often enough they are not really suitable for the requirements of families who may need, apart from anything else, more space. Hence the very considerable increase in the numbers of estate cars and mini-buses, especially for those motorists whose interests lie in camping, caravanning and the outdoor life.

THE PARKING PROBLEM

There is also abundant evidence that the parking problem in Edinburgh is becoming more and more acute, especially during the tourist season. The Edinburgh motorist, knowing his city, can usually find some place to park his car with or without the sanction of authority; and the police have the thankless task of trying to re-establish authority though, as they understand the difficulties of their errant fellow-citizens, they do their duty with a good deal of dissembled " Gemutlichkeit." But in the tourist season Princes Street, George Street and other thoroughfares become choked with traffic and the police go round in pairs to warn or to charge motorists for illegal parking.

A survey taken by the police in the early '60s showed that the peak time for parking was about 3.30 p.m. The area surveyed was from South Charlotte Street to Leith Street and half-a-mile north and south of Princes Street, and it was found that in an eight-hour period no less than 6,284 different cars were parked for half-an-hour or more in the area. There is little doubt that this figure would be considerably exceeded today.

In the matter of illegal parking the majesty of the law could perhaps be upheld more easily if there were less ambiguity in the portable kerbside signs worded " No Parking " and " No Waiting." If they differ from each other at all, it is in a Pickwickian sense. The problem of where to put the car when not in use is one facing not only the occupants of fine terraced houses and flats in Edinburgh, but people living in the suburbs, particularly in the Council housing schemes. For the great majority it is a case of having to leave the car out in the streets over-night, a practice now common throughout Great Britain.

Reasonable facilities for short-term parking at least are essential in Edinburgh where, in addition to its large commercial and professional interests, more and more visitors have to be accommodated each year.

Obviously this calls for a substantial increase in off-street parking facilities and many proposals have been put forward. The more interesting of these includes provision of a roof over the Waverley Market (at the east end of Princes Street) to take cars; re-development of the Lothian Road–Princes Street Station area; double-deck car parks in Queen Street Gardens and in Castle Terrace, and the utilisation of the lower level of East Princes Street Gardens to accommodate vehicles. This latter scheme was once even embodied in a Provisional Order, but was dropped in 1955, ostensibly in answer to the Chancellor of the Exchequer's appeal for economy but also to many local " amenity " objections.

To the Waverley Market scheme there were engineering objections, but it would be surprising if in these days of more advanced constructional techniques the difficulties could not sometime be overcome. By contrast, through not without much argument, it was agreed to go ahead with the Castle Terrace multi-story scheme. It was also agreed that this car park should be on three levels. By the time the work started in 1961 the estimated cost had however risen to £300,000 and the final cost was likely to be more, for whereas the contractors expected to find a solid rock foundation, they came across sand; and also it was decided to give the park five tiers instead of three and thus provide space for 800 cars. By September, 1964 the fear of increased cost was fulfilled when the Corporation was asked to foot a bill of about £600,000.

Whilst waiting for the completion of this parking area, motorists in the meantime were subjected to something they had hoped to avoid. The city applied for Parliamentary powers to introduce parking meters, and despite strong protests by the motoring organisations and others, the necessary authority was granted. Considering that the proposals were to instal the meters in the centre of George Square, around Charlotte Square and in St. Andrew Square, one might have expected violent opposition from the various societies who jealously guard the city's amenities, but curiously the aesthetic viewpoint was scarcely raised at the Public Inquiry which was held.

In August, 1962, therefore, Edinburgh became the first city in Scotland to have parking meters. At the same time " No Waiting " regulations were vigorously enforced in the Parking Zone by the new traffic wardens, enlisted to relieve the police of this work. But according to the motoring organisations, the meter scheme, with its fixed divisions for each car, considerably reduced the parking space available. However, by September, 1964 it appeared that the city's 500 parking meters had brought in nearly £57,000 during the first two years of operation, with a profit of £22,500 in the first 21 months. It was not surprising therefore that the Corporation should have decided to instal another 400 new meters in the Tollcross area.

TRAFFIC CONGESTION

The introduction of a parking zone may have helped in some small measure to relieve traffic congestion in Edinburgh; yet the parking of cars, if inevitable and even desirable for many reasons, is thought objectionable by many people not only on the ground of traffic congestion but also of amenity.

This problem of preserving the comparatively ancient against the onslaught of the modern is of course an eternal problem in the city as it is in other venerable places. The case of Randolph Crescent mentioned earlier, which was the subject of much heated controversy in the early '60s, is an instance. To relieve traffic congestion it was proposed to transform the crescent into a roundabout by reducing the nine-foot high gardens forming the inner part of the Crescent, thereby diminishing for the householders the pleasing suggestion of *rus in urbe*, and shifting the lowered garden area into Queensferry Street to form a roundabout. Small service roads, divided by garden strips from the main thoroughfare, were to be created as a sop to the residents who were to be further mollified by the contention that the Crescent, being thus opened up to the view, would be enhanced in appearance. But the residents were more than satisfied with their beautifully planned and lovely Georgian Crescent as it stood, and with the support of many other interested parties, they lodged strong objection to the Council proposals and won the day after a Public Inquiry.

Edinburgh's West End has also been the subject of much change and experiment; which is hardly surprising in view of its many converging streets and the density of the traffic.

An important step was taken in April, 1960 when approval was given in principle to setting up a Highway Design and Traffic Engineering Section in the City Engineer's Department. Following approval of the principle the Corporation duly granted an establishment for traffic engineers to the City Engineer's Department, and the Traffic Engineering Section is now in being. It is hoped that this will help the authorities to cope with the ever-increasing difficulties arising out of the traffic problem as a whole; for now there will be a team of specialists doing fundamental research into traffic movement and allied subjects and considering plans for the future such as large span bridges, tunnels and pedestrian subways.

If, however, we leave aside the fulfilment of plans which are dependent on Government assistance, credit must be given to the City Corporation for a great volume of less spectacular but highly essential work of advantage to motor transport. Once the conversion to buses began, instead of re-laying only the strips of road which had held the tram tracks, they had the whole surface of the roads relaid with tarmac and generally improved at the same time. It should not be forgotten too that even in the 1920s most of Edinburgh's streets had stone, cobble or granite setts; Princes Street had a surface of wood blocks; and in Shandwick Place there was an experimental section with rubber blocks which may have been all right for the diminishing number of horses or for the reduction of noise, but provided ready-made skid pans for motorists in wet weather. Not only have road surfaces improved but they are better lit for the greater safety both of motor vehicles and pedestrians.

One attempt to draw off some of the congestion in the city, and one which has proved decidedly useful to motorists is the ring route signposted by the Automobile Association in 1955. It runs from Wallyford Toll on the A1 road round by Dalkeith, Gilmerton, Captains Road, Kaimes crossroad, Fairmilehead, Oxgangs, Craiglockhart Avenue, Chesser Avenue, Sighthill and the new Broomhouse Road to Corstorphine and thence to Glasgow, Stirling and the North, thus linking east to west main traffic routes without coming into the centre of the city.

Recognising perhaps that a substitute often develops an inertia which enables it to continue to the neglect of the better thing, the A.A. never did regard their signposted directional system in the same light as a properly constructed ring road; and in fact they took care always to refer to it as a ring route. But in the absence of the real thing it certainly serves a valuable purpose and it has the further advantage that several sections of it could form the nucleus of a proper by-pass road for which there is considerable support both from the standpoint of road safety and as a time saver for commercial traffic.

TRAFFIC AND THE FIRTH OF FORTH

On the whole, a greater sense of urgency was developing in the early '60s as the shadows of the great towers of the Forth Road Bridge, completed in 1964, began to lie more heavily on Edinburgh's already congested traffic arteries. This new bridge, so long desired and attended by so many birth pains after a gestation lasting many years, has removed the handicap which the Firth of Forth had always presented to the Edinburgh motorist, and especially his acute frustration when, on returning from the north, he found that the last ferry had just left and he had no alternative but to make the long detour *via* Kincardine.

Until the outbreak of the second World War, the steam ferries *William Muir*[1] and *The Thane of Fife* were operated by the Railway Company between Granton and Burntisland. But cars could only be conveyed at suitable tides, and despite increasing numbers of vehicles nothing was done to improve facilities. The ferries, which had operated at a loss for several years, ceased during the war, and the short-lived service was abandoned after it. A private company then ran a service with tank landing craft.

There was another ferry further west at Queensferry, also operated by the Railway Company, but it was subject to tidal conditions and it cost 10*s*. each way for a four-seater car. In the early 1930s, however, under an agreement with the railways, Denny Brothers of Dumbarton put on two new boats specially constructed for car-carrying at rates of about half those formerly charged, and the response from motorists was immediate. Traffic continued to increase, improvements were carried out to the piers and by 1958 four boats were operating.

Yet welcome as these ferry improvements were, it was realised that the only real answer was a bridge or a tunnel, and in due course the decision was for a bridge. "In due course", it should be stressed here, is a relative term in this context since it took 37 years of agitation to achieve the necessary action. The Forth Road Bridge, when it opened in 1964, was in fact the longest suspension bridge in Europe. It crosses the Forth west of the existing famous rail bridge, and forms part of a direct road link between Edinburgh and the north-east coastal towns. It has also led to specially constructed link roads and multi-level interchanges which will do much to improve the pattern of travel in the East of Scotland.

THE MOTORING ORGANISATIONS

In any account of the part played by motoring in the life of Edinburgh it is necessary to say something about the impact of the motoring organisations. One cannot go much about the city without seeing evidence of their work. Admirable services are rendered by the Royal Automobile Club which has an office in Edinburgh, the Royal Scottish Automobile Club whose headquarters are in Glasgow, and the A.A. whose influence as the largest of these bodies is the most wide-spread. To borrow a French phrase from another context, the A.A. could be described as "un club sans club", for unlike the R.A.C. and the R.S.A.C. it has no club premises, and although its headquarters are in London, which might be expected to make Scottish nationalists look askance at it, no disadvantage is suffered by members of the Association because of that.

[1] An interesting account of *William Muir* is contained in the railway section of this chapter.

By a process of decentralisation the regional offices of the A.A. merge closely into, and work so harmoniously with, the host country that they are looked upon as part of it. If a thought is given to the London headquarters at all by those who apply at the Edinburgh office for information or assistance, it is as a feeder agency for the requirements of Edinburgh motorists.

It will be remembered that in its earliest form the A.A. had for its purpose the circumventing of the law as it affected motorists. The Edinburgh–Queensferry road was a favourite ground for police traps, and when one was in operation the local A.A. Patrol soon knew all about it and warned passing motorists displaying the familiar A.A. badge on the cars by a simple, negative device. The patrolman merely abstained from giving the normal salute, standing the while at attention well back in the road. The point of this was that members had been instructed to stop and find out why the salute was not given. Then they were told about the police trap.

The A.A. first spread to Edinburgh in 1913 when a small office was opened in York Place. The capital of Scotland with its natural beauty, its historic background and convenience as a touring centre, offered a great challenge to the Association who were the first motoring organisation to provide road service in Scotland. It was therefore not long before the organisation outgrew the York Place office, and moved to larger premises in Castle Street, later again to George Street and in 1953 to Melville Street.

The move to Melville Street was made the occasion of an opening ceremony when Lord Provost Sir James Miller also inaugurated another service—the despatch of the Highland Patrol, a team of specially selected men, to operate in the North-West Highlands in four-wheeled vehicles. Some years later radio communication was opened between Melville Street H.Q. and a number of Patrols on the road, to be followed by radio-controlled breakdown wagons and other innovations of advantage to members. Thereafter progress was so rapid that in 1961 a complete reconstruction of the Melville Street headquarters was undertaken to make its work even more efficient and to facilitate such services as temporary signposting for major special events. This is an expanding feature of the A.A. Road Service; and the Edinburgh headquarters erect over 3,000 of these in a year, to cover such occasions as the Royal Highland Show at Ingliston a little outside the city (300 signs), the International Rugby matches at Murrayfield (120), the Royal Garden Party at Holyrood (100) and a wide variety of events at Festival time.

ROYAL AUTOMOBILE CLUB

The Royal Automobile Club has been established in Edinburgh since 1929, and from Rutland Square it controls R.A.C. operations in the eastern counties of Scotland from the Borders to Nairn. The R.A.C. maintains a 24 hour service for breakdowns. Its other membership facilities, like those of the A.A., include weather reports and forecasts, home and foreign touring, travel service, free legal defence and advice, free technical advice, insurance benefits, road patrols, roadside telephone boxes, road service centres and road signs for important events. Again like the A.A. the patrolmen are out in all weathers and give a service which often extends far beyond helping drivers in trouble. One well known patrolman in East Lothian was known to feed horses in a field which the farmer would have had difficulty in reaching in severe winter conditions. Once too, when roads were blocked with snow, he intercepted Professor Norman Dott, the distinguished Edinburgh brain surgeon who had been called to a woman lying seriously ill. The road to her house was impassable but the patrolman conducted the Professor to the patient over familiar fields; by another irony it was some time later that the patrolman himself required the Professor's services after being badly hurt in an accident off duty.

ROAD ACCIDENTS

Not unfittingly this survey of the city's unending road problems ends with a brief survey of the rise of road accidents during the last few years. At the end of 1961 the Chief Constable announced that 51 people had been killed during the year—the highest total in the city's history. Since then the figure has continued to grow despite the efforts of the Chief Constable himself and his officers, the Edinburgh Accident Prevention Council and the city's official Accident Prevention Officer. August of 1963 was the worst month on record for road casualties inside the city, for they totalled 231 of which five were fatal and 60 serious injuries. Since then the accidents have increased.

RAILWAYS

NORTH BRITISH RAILWAY COMPANY

The original North British Railway Company was incorporated in 1844 to construct a line from Edinburgh to Berwick with a branch from Longniddry to Haddington—a total length of 62 miles. This line was opened for public traffic on 22nd June, 1846 and thus became the first railway to cross the Border although only as far as Berwick-on-Tweed. The company then bought the short Edinburgh to Dalkeith railway for a sum of £113,000.

A rapid development of the railways took place in the years around 1850, with the construction of numerous main radiating sections and branches by separately incorporated companies. Across the Forth, for instance, the Edinburgh and Northern Railway was authorised in 1845 to build a line from Burntisland to Ladybank diverging there to Newburgh and Perth and to Cupar and Ferryport-on-Craig (now known as Tayport). This line was opened throughout in 1848, and thus became the first fairly direct rail route to Dundee with ferry crossings over the Forth and Tay estuaries. There were also inaugurated on these crossings the first train ferries in the world, the most famous of which was *Leviathan* with lines of rails on deck capable of carrying some 40 railway wagons. This ship made the inaugural crossing on the Forth on 7th February, 1850 and the Tay on 28th February, 1851.

Mention of the Granton–Burntisland passage recalls the *William Muir*, originally a two-funnelled paddle steamer built by Key of Kinghorn for the Granton–Burntisland service in 1879. After the custom of the Kinghorn yard she was launched fully fitted out and with steam up, thus beginning her career like a solan goose whose loving parents pitch it off its native precipice when it is fledged. *William Muir* started paddling at once and with suitable intervals continued to do so for 58 years. But it was also in 1879 that she took to Burntisland the unfortunate travellers who were lost in the never to be forgotten Tay Bridge disaster. Usually *William Muir* plied on the Granton–Burntisland service; but she was sometimes on the Queensferry passage and spent two years as a minesweeper in the 1914–18 war. The London and North-Eastern Railway Company sold her for breaking up in 1937; but the ship's bell can be seen today in the front hall of 23 Waterloo Place.

CALEDONIAN RAILWAY COMPANY

The Caledonian Railway was incorporated on 31st July, 1845 and the Beattock to Edinburgh line was opened on 15th February 1848. In 1869 an important improvement in the services between Glasgow and Edinburgh was effected by the opening of the Clelland Mid-Calder line which gave the Caledonian Company the shortest route between the two cities (46 miles) in place of the 56-mile journey via Carstairs, which they had previously used. A year later the old station in Lothian Road, which had been in use since 1848, was replaced by a new station largely rebuilt in the '90s on the present site of Princes Street station.

Over the years the smaller lines were absorbed by the larger companies, eventually forming two big groups—London and North Eastern Railway (L.N.E.R.) and London Midland and Scottish Railway (L.M.S.). But as from 1st January 1948 the railways of Britain, nationalised under the Transport Act of 1947, became known as British Railways, and the whole industry north of the Border, including several joint lines not included in either group company, became united under the administration of the Scottish Region of British Railways.

In this post-war age, when British Railways endeavour to effect the utmost economies in operation and branch lines are being abandoned, it is of interest to note the inducements once held out by the Edinburgh and Glasgow Railway Company to attract both passengers and freight. If, for example, you built a villa costing £500 within one mile of the company's railway line and not near a town station in mid-19th century, you were entitled to free travel on the line for a period of five years.

THE FLYING SCOTSMAN

The distinction of being the first express in Great Britain to receive a title probably belongs to the train which without interruption from June, 1862 to the present day has moved out of King's Cross terminus in London at 10 o'clock every morning on its journey of 392¾ miles to Edinburgh (Waverley). Precisely when the name " Flying Scotsman " came into use is difficult to say. It has certainly been in vogue for well over half a century. But it was not until after the formation of the London and North-Eastern Railway that the title was officially adopted and began to appear on the headboards of the carriages and in timetables and other public announcements.

When it first appeared the 10.0 a.m. from King's Cross was known as a " Special Scotch Express." At York there was a halt from 2.25 to 2.55 p.m. to enable passengers to obtain lunch; and Edinburgh was reached at 8.30 p.m. after a journey lasting 10½ hours. The corresponding " up train", however, took an hour longer. With the opening up of new routes and other aids to faster running the journey in both directions had come down to 9 hours by 1876.

In November, 1887 the decision was reached to admit third-class passengers to the Flying Scotsman; and this momentous announcement helped to precipitate the " Race to Edinburgh " of the following year. Schedule times were slashed by both the east coast and west coast railway companies until in August, 1888 this famous train made the journey to Edinburgh in 7 hours 26¾ minutes, notwithstanding 26½ minutes spent at York for lunch.

As a result of agreement the following year, it was arranged that the schedule of the Flying Scotsman should not exceed 8½ (later 8¼ hours) each way. In 1900 restaurant cars were introduced for the first time.

While the schedule time agreement between east coast and west coast companies continued in force it was necessary for the rivals to find other outlets for their competitive energy. One form of their rivalry was non-stop running over great distances, which finally resulted, as from May, 1928, in the Flying Scotsman being scheduled to make the longest non-stop run in the world.

In the 1930s, when trains were being speeded up, the minimum time agreement could be maintained no longer, and various cuts were made under the summer timetable. These meant that by 1938 the non-stop journey took 7 hours. The winter journey (stops included) took 7 hours 20 minutes. When heavy loads were carried, during the second World War, however, the time was increased to 8¾ hours; but from 1962 onwards the Flying Scotsman has been doing the trip in 6 hours flat with the new 3,300 h.p. Deltic diesel locomotive. In 1966 this excellent time was further reduced to 5 hours, 50 minutes.

For some years also two other Edinburgh–London trains, the Elizabethan and the Talisman have been doing the same journey in just over six hours; and indeed, as these words were written, passengers on the Talisman were being given a foretaste of the future when British

Railways introduced eight experimental coaches between Waverley Station and King's Cross offering comforts and amenities of the kind more usually associated with luxury air travel. Air-sprung bogies and the latest insulation techniques did away with the familiar clatter of wheels, and the train cruised comfortably at more than 70 m.p.h. Each coach was lighter than those in normal service, due to glass fibre and aluminium fittings.

Two named express freight trains start from Edinburgh. These are The Galloway Piper (Slateford to Stranraer) and The Geordie (Niddrie to Sunderland).

In addition, overnight express freight train services are operated to such places as Inverness, Dundee, Aberdeen, Liverpool and London. There is no record of how the name Dog and Monkey came to be applied to the 11.50 p.m. parcels train from Edinburgh (Waverley) to York; but it may be that the name derived from the fact that the train originally conveyed horses and livestock.

SPECIALISED SERVICES

Less glamorous than these crack trains, but just as important in the lives of the citizens, are the other regular train services and various specialised services available from the city.

Special services in the summer and autumn of 1963, when this survey was well under way, included cheap day return tickets available by any train on any day from Edinburgh to selected stations. It was possible, for instance, to go to St. Andrews and back, second class, for 14*s*. 3*d*. or to Glasgow, also return, for 10*s*. 6*d*.

" Starlight Special " trains were run during the holiday season from Edinburgh to London at a reduced fare of £5 return. The outward journey had to be made by special trains on Friday night and the return on special trains on Saturday, either a week or a fortnight later. Booking, not surprisingly, had to be effected in advance, and the fare covered seat reservation in both directions.

In addition to the " Starlight Special " tickets, there were a number of other special fare facilities. A car-sleeper service became available on certain trains from Edinburgh (Waverley) to London (King's Cross). This facility provided for the conveyance of the motor car and accompanying passengers.

A " Freedom of Scotland " ticket was available for seven days' unlimited rail travel between stations in Scotland, and also by steamer services of the Caledonian Steam Packet Company Limited on the Clyde and Loch Lomond during the April–October period.

Holiday Runabout tickets from Edinburgh valid for seven consecutive days were also available in 1963 during the summer months, as were Midweek Period Excursion tickets for second class travel only, between any pair of stations in Great Britain for journeys of not less than 100 miles in each direction outward each Tuesday, Wednesday or Thursday for return on the Tuesday, Wednesday or Thursday of the following week or of the week after that. The return fare from Edinburgh to London under this concession was £5 6*s*. 6*d*. compared with the normal fare of £7 2*s*. 0*d*.[1]

RAILWAY ESTABLISHMENTS IN EDINBURGH

At the end of 1963 the railway staff employed in Edinburgh was 6,000, and they were stationed in many parts of the city.

The offices at 23 Waterloo Place housed the following members of British Railways staff: the representative of the General Manager; staff of the British Transport Commission Legal Adviser (Scotland); Medical Officer; the department of Historical Records; the District engineer and his staff; the staff of the Estate and Rating Surveyor; staff of the Public Relations and Publicity Officer; the District Commercial Manager and his staff; District Fire Inspector; staff of the Regional Accountant.

There were also five cleaning depots, and various depots for engine repair. Diesel locomotives first introduced between Edinburgh and Glasgow in 1957 were repaired at Leith Central Diesel Depot, while steam engines were repaired at the St. Margaret's, Haymarket and Dalry Road depots. With a locomotive depot such as St. Margaret's, to which more steam locomotives were allocated than at any other depot in Scotland, the provisions of the Clean Air Act have created a problem especially at week-ends when fires are kindled. A number of tests with smokeless fuel however were carried out with good results, and every endeavour made to prevent the emission of smoke as far as possible. Fortunately, as many thought, British Railways—in September, 1963—announced that the 119-year old St. Margaret's locomotive depot, which exclusively handled steam locomotives was to close down. " This", said the then Medical Officer of Health, Dr. H. E. Seiler, " is one of the best pieces of health news for years."

WAVERLEY STATION

Waverley Station, since it was rebuilt in 1893, has developed into one of the most important exchange stations in Britain, with a complete electrically-operated signalling system actuated from two signal cabins, Waverley East (with more than 200 levers) and Waverley West; these replaced seven mechanically-operated boxes.

The problems of working at Waverley Station are entirely dissimilar from those of the larger termini of comparable platform length, owing to the arrival of trains in complex formations which require splitting to form new combinations of departing trains scheduled to leave inside 20 minutes. It was to meet these special requirements that the new signalling was designed.

As a matter of interest the area of the station roof at Waverley Station

[1] Statistics showing the number of tickets issued at Edinburgh stations in the early '60s and also the amount of revenue received from both passengers and freight appear in Appendix IV (2).

is approximately 11 acres. But the suitability of the station for modern needs is now in question, and various plans for redeveloping it have been strengthened by the closure of Princes Street station and several adjacent stations in September 1965.

THE LOCAL ROUNDABOUT

In 1884 a suburban railway line was opened for passenger and goods traffic with an inner and an outer circle. The inner line ran from Waverley to Haymarket, passed through Gorgie, Morningside, Blackford and Duddingston, then used the old St. Leonard's Line for a mile and continued by the main line via Portobello to the Waverley. There was an hourly service.

This nine mile track was popular during the day of cable-car street transport, but, despite conversion to diesel trains it could not compete with electric tramways and more direct bus services. By 1962 the annual loss in running was £23,000. So together with the branch service to Rosewell the line was closed down.

AIR TRANSPORT AND THE AIRPORT

The development of air services is the outstanding feature of travel in the 20th century, and Edinburgh seems to have kept abreast of all its phases in recent years. Certainly in the days before World War II, one of the most eagerly anticipated Saturdays of the summer was the visit to Turnhouse of the various air circuses. Well patronised short flights were offered at 5*s*. and the aircraft—biplanes not far removed in design from those of the first World War—engaged in mock dog-fights and aerobatics. In addition there were delayed drops by parachutists which provided added excitement for the onlookers.

The city's aeronautical tradition is in fact quite old, for there has been an aerodrome at Turnhouse since 1915, and as recounted in the chapter on the Defence Services, it has been used ever since, first by the Royal Flying Corps and later by the R.A.F. During the last war the old grass runways were replaced by hard tarmac for almost constant use by fighter and transport aircraft.

It needed the second World War however to give Edinburgh anything like a really modern airport. For in the years before 1939 the tale was a dismal one of frustration and timidity. Davidson's Mains, Silverknowes and Gilmerton were advocated as possible sites for an Edinburgh Airport from time to time during the 1930s, but nothing came of these proposals. Then in 1935 the Corporation bought land at Gilmerton for the construction of a civic airport. But the project was abandoned and the Corporation sold the land when the site proved too small. There was also some uncertainty about the policy of the Air Ministry, which had apparently never made it clear to the Corporation exactly what facilities would be required.

In the previous year there had been what at first seemed a promising development when London Scottish and Provincial Airways Limited, a private airline, announced that they were planning a twice-daily service between London and Edinburgh with aircraft capable of travelling at 150 m.p.h. They proposed charging £5 for a single journey, with a reduction on a return ticket. Croydon was to be the London terminal and the company suggested that they might use Turnhouse, as the airport for Edinburgh. The project did not materialise.

After the war the enlarged and strengthened Turnhouse aerodrome was made the civil airport for Edinburgh and was formally opened in 1947. But the struggle did not end then. There were delays in the provision of equipment for " all the year " services—and, indeed, suspension and curtailment of the scheduled flights. But at a critical time in 1951 pressure was brought to bear by the then Lord Provost, Sir Andrew Murray, and members of the business community: this had its effect, and the services were restored and improved.

In 1952 the Ministry of Civil Aviation and the Air Ministry made a " joint users " arrangement for air traffic control at the aerodrome. To-day Edinburgh Airport is under the control of the Ministry of Aviation, the Commandant also being responsible for the aerodrome at Aberdeen.

The new terminal building at Turnhouse was opened in April, 1956 by the Minister of Transport and Civil Aviation. It cost £84,000 and was built to cope with an annual transit of 75,000 passengers. A new extension to the building was opened in May, 1957 in order to provide accommodation for passengers and public, airport and air line administration, and for customs, health and immigration control. Allowance has been made for the expansion of the customs hall to the east, the office block to the west and the concourse to the north. Upstairs, overlooking the airport, is a shelf balcony containing buffet and bar, and light meals are served.

The main airline operator at Turnhouse is British European Airways. Their town terminal was opened in May, 1947 at Princes Street Station, and in the same month services were commenced from Turnhouse to Aberdeen, Wick, Orkney, Shetland and London. In October, 1948 services were suspended for the winter period and it became necessary to travel by road to Renfrew to connect with the Glasgow to London flight; but on 1st April, 1949 direct Edinburgh to London flights were resumed by " Pionair " aircraft.

How big the growth has been may be seen from the following figures. According to *The Scotsman*'s Air Correspondent (21st April, 1962) the city's airport in 1949 handled 21,576 passengers. But in 1961 that figure had risen 12 times, and has grown ever since. To take a sample statistic from 1963, the off-season passenger total for the month of February was 22,331—a figure more than that for the whole of 1949, and 39 per cent more than the figure recorded for the same month the previous year.

Even more impressive is a table compiled in February, 1965 by the Civil Aviation Scottish Divisional Office of the Ministry of Aviation, which speaks for itself.

TABLE 41
TERMINAL PASSENGERS AT EDINBURGH (TURNHOUSE) AIRPORT

Origin/Destination	*1963–4*	*1962–3*	*1957–8*
Within Scotland	49,051	51,190	18,256
Outside Scotland	359,332	282,374	88,481
	408,383	333,564	106,737

To go back to 1950, in August " Viscount " proving flights were made by V.630 proto-type aircraft from Edinburgh to London. " Viking " aircraft were operated on the London route in 1952 when an £8 return fare was introduced; but an outstanding highlight of the B.E.A. services took place on 17th April, 1955 when the first-class flights were introduced to and from London by " Viscount " (701 series) aircraft. The first-class flight was called " The Festival " and later renamed " The Chieftain." " Viscount " 802 and 806 series aircraft appeared next on the Edinburgh–London route, while " Pionair " aircraft were employed on the services to Glasgow, Aberdeen and the North. The " Viscount " 800 series is the largest of the Viscounts; it is powered by four turbo-prop Rolls-Royce Dart engines, travels fast and carries 60 passengers. In 1961, the Vickers " Vanguard " was brought into operation on some of the Turnhouse–London services. The Vanguard, powered by four Rolls-Royce turbo-prop engines, carries 110 passengers and has a cruising speed of 425 miles per hour.

However, B.E.A. was not destined to have a monopoly of the route. A competitor appeared on the scene in the autumn of 1963, when British Eagle (formerly Cunard Eagle) introduced a daily service of jet-propelled Britannias between Edinburgh and London, Glasgow and Belfast. But in the Spring of 1965 British Eagle withdrew their services after being refused permission for more frequent fllghts. By 1966 however British United Airways were operating services between Edinburgh and Gatwick.

The Edinburgh to Dublin service opened in 1952 by " Aer Lingus " operators has also grown with the years so that extra flights have often been scheduled to cater for heavy traffic, not least when rugby supporters wish to attend the Scotland–Ireland international in Dublin. Finally, a new direct air service between Edinburgh and Belfast was inaugurated by B.K.S. Air Transport in May, 1964.

And so air transport grows. It has indeed been growing so fast that by the summer of 1966 there were almost 60 flights each week from Edinburgh to London and about 70 to other airports. These ranged from Orkney and Shetland in the far north to Jersey in the English Channel.

CHAPTER 17

FIRE AND BURIAL

HUMAN life has death as its ultimate enemy; and death in its turn has a host of allies—murder, cannibalism, treason, pestilence, earthquakes, fire and accident. As far as the records show, Edinburgh is free of cannibalism and earthquakes though unhappily not of murder, illness, accident and fire. It is therefore proposed in this chapter to look at two services in the city, which are intimately concerned with the eternal verities of life and death. One deals with fire, a terror of mankind through the ages, the other with the disposal of the dead by burial or cremation.

BURIAL

From earliest times custom dictated that responsibility for the disposal of the dead should rest with the relatives if they had the means and land wherein to bury the body. This personal responsibility met the needs of small communities and rural districts until recent times, but the growth of towns and cities has now made burial a community concern. Also the Christian Church once exercised control of the disposal of the dead and gave assistance to the poor. In later times assistance was given first by the craft guilds and then by the Friendly Societies. Today the State has taken over the responsibility, and as part of the national insurance scheme most people contribute during their lifetime towards their own funeral expenses.

The whole story of burial in Edinburgh has an interest[1] but to understand it properly we should perhaps first glance briefly at the various statutes and regulations by which burial is controlled, since there are in Scotland three types of burial grounds: parish churchyards, local authority burial grounds, and cemeteries provided by private bodies.

PARISH CHURCHYARDS

In pre-Reformation times it was the clergy's duty to provide churchyards, and it was the custom to select ground near or round the parish church. After the Reformation, it became incumbent upon the heritors (proprietors of land or houses in the parish) under the statutes of 1503, 1563, 1579 and 1597 to manage and maintain existing churchyards and provide new ones on sites designated by the Presbytery. A heritor was entitled to preference in the selection of places of burial for his family and servants, and all

[1] In addition to the text, Appendix V gives interesting figures about the disposal of the dead in the city as a whole.

parishioners were entitled to a place in the churchyard, though non-parishioners could obtain one only with the heritors' consent, which was also needed for the erection of tombstones.

LOCAL AUTHORITY BURIAL GROUNDS

The principal act empowering Scottish local authorities to provide burial grounds is the Burial Grounds (Scotland) Act, 1855, the authorities being Parochial Boards for the Management of the Poor—these later became Parish Councils in parishes of burghs outside the limits prescribed in the Lands Valuation Act, 1854, the town councils of burghs, and the magistrates of burghs of regality having parishes within such limits. Town Councils of parliamentary burghs were included under the Nuisances Removal (Scotland) Act, 1856. Under the 1855 Act burial ground authorities are empowered not only to acquire land, compulsorily if necessary, but to lay it out; and also they may purchase private cemeteries or use them by contract with the owners.

THE CITY CHURCHYARDS

In Edinburgh the oldest of the city churches is believed to be that of St. Cuthbert's or the West Kirk, as it came to be known after the Reformation. No precise date for its foundation can be given but a religious house of some kind appears to have stood on the site since the 8th century and burials must have taken place in its vicinity. Because of its frequent rebuilding there are few interior tombs in St. Cuthbert's Church, but among them is the tomb of John Napier of Merchiston immured in 1617.

No pre-Reformation tombs are to be found in the churchyard, either because of destruction by the Reforming mobs or because of the probability that memorials were frowned upon by the Roman Church; and the earliest existing tomb is dated 1606. Among those buried in the churchyard were Alexander Nasmyth, artist, architect and bridge designer (1840) and Thomas de Quincey of literary fame (1859).

Like other churchyards, St. Cuthbert's was subject to the nefarious traffic of the body-snatchers, and before the passing of the Anatomy Act, 1832 it was necessary to place heavy gratings over new graves; and to provide armed night-watchmen, who watched from guardhouses that can still be seen. Further desecration of the churchyard took place in 1841 when the Edinburgh and Glasgow Railway Company obtained powers to lay lines in a tunnel through it.

With the growth of Edinburgh further churches and monasteries were erected, most of which had burial grounds in their precincts. All were desecrated at the Reformation or ruthlessly removed by authority as land rose in value with the city's expansion.

The worst case of desecration without doubt was that of the churchyard of St. Giles. The first and most important burial ground within the city, as St. Cuthbert's was without, it had become grossly overcrowded and was closed about 1566, when Queen Mary bestowed on the city the gardens of the Grey Friars' Monastery to provide a new cemetery. The churchyard extended from the south side of the church down the steep slope to the present line of the Cowgate, and within its bounds were the residences of the clergy and, facing the Cowgate, the Chapel of the Holy Rood. On the ancient graves the erection of the Parliament Hall and Court of Session was begun in 1632, with tenements to the east, later to become the site of the Police Chambers. To the west was ultimately built the Signet Library, and as late as 1844 coffins and human remains were found during alterations.

In the churchyard lie the remains of John Knox, placed there in 1572 as a fitting resting place for the great reformer—although the churchyard had by then been closed—but only in 1868 was Knox's grave marked as such. Today its site is used as a car park. Edinburgh Presbytery at its meeting in June, 1961 agreed to a suggestion of the Ministry of Works that the tablet marking the grave should be removed, and that a plaque should instead be affixed to the wall of the High Church.

St. Giles' Church itself was for centuries the burial place of the famous, but owing to alterations and restorations there is little evidence in the shape of memorial stones. In 1879, several tons of bones were removed from beneath the floor and interred in Greyfriars Churchyard.

The Church of Holy Trinity, in the valley east of Nor' Loch (now Princes Street Gardens) was started in 1462 by Mary of Gueldres to the memory of her husband King James II (the stone being quarried from a site now covered by the Scott Monument), and Mary was interred in the choir in 1463. The Church was later known as Trinity College Kirk. It was taken down after the coming of the railway in 1848 and rebuilt in Jeffrey Street 30 years later: the Churchyard was, of course, engulfed by the railway, as was the Trinity College Hospital, also founded by Mary of Gueldres, and Paul's Work.

The burial ground of the Grey Friars of Edinburgh occupies an especial place in Scottish memory, and within its hallowed grounds were enacted scenes both brave and grim. The Order of Grey Friars made its first appearance in Scotland about 1230, and its monastery in Edinburgh was built early in the 15th century on ground said to have been granted to it by James I. At the Reformation in 1560, the buildings of the Grey Friars were attacked by the populace and left in a ruinous state, the Friars themselves fleeing to the Netherlands. The Town Council of the day, having in mind the crowded state of St. Giles' Churchyard, petitioned Queen Mary for the Friars' grounds and obtained the royal sanction in 1562. It was taken over in 1566; and in 1568, a plague year, it was first used as a cemetery. The original entrance near the Grassmarket still exists; the present gateway at Greyfriars Place was built in 1624.

In Greyfriars churchyard, where the National Covenant was signed in 1638, are buried not only Covenanters and martyrs but 41 Lord Provosts, 36 Lords of Session and Lord Advocates, and 30 Principals and Professors of Edinburgh University. In addition, there are countless merchants, nobles, poets, lawyers, painters, divines, as well as humbler figures.

In the Chapel Royal of Holyrood are the royal tombs of David II

(1371); James II (1460); Mary of Gueldres—removed from the choir of her Church of the Holy Trinity in 1848; James V (1542) and his first queen, Madeleine (1537); Lord Darnley (1567); and 10 infant princes and princesses. Also buried in Holyrood is Sir John Sinclair (1835), compiler of the first *Statistical Account of Scotland.*

Canongate until 1856 was a separate burgh possessing its own church and churchyard, which date back to 1691. It is however noteworthy that few of the aristocracy are buried in the Canongate churchyard, for before its opening, as we saw earlier, many noble families had followed the Royal Court to London. Poets, Professors and Provosts, nonetheless, share its lairs with Adam Smith (1790) and with Burns' Clarinda (1841); and since, for burial purposes, Edinburgh Castle was included first in the parish of Holyrood and later in Canongate parish, an imposing monument stands over the graves of soldiers who died in the Castle after 1692.

In the Castle itself only irregular burials have taken place, though it is known that burials took place there during times of siege even up to the 1745 Rebellion. A gold-mounted coffin was found in the Castle in 1753, and several ancient coffins in 1853. The most famous graves in Edinburgh Castle today are without doubt those of the regimental pets in the " Dog's Cemetery."

Like Canongate, Calton was a burgh in its own right until 1856. Before 1815, when Waterloo Place and Regent's Bridge were formed, Calton folk were in South Leith Parish and were usually buried in Leith, in spite of the inconvenience of the distance, although, in 1718, the burghers had obtained a piece of rocky ground for a cemetery on a spur of the main Calton hill. In 1817, after the new roadway had been cut through it, leaving a small portion to the north and the main portion to the south of Waterloo Place, a new extension of 3 acres was opened in Regent Road. This was called the New Calton burying ground. In it were re-interred remains found on the site of the road through the old cemetery, and in the 1860s more interments took place there than in any other churchyard or cemetery in the city. A large castellated watch-tower was built to house the guard, since the cemetery was laid out during the body-snatching period. One of the two monuments to Abraham Lincoln in the United Kingdom is in the New Calton.

In the Old Calton cemetery are buried a large number of shoemakers. Beside them are David Hume, philosopher and historian (1776); David Allan, painter (1796); and William Blackwood, publisher (1834). In the New Calton are Robert Stevenson, civil engineer and grandfather of Robert Louis Stevenson (1850); William Dick, professor of veterinary surgery (1866); and six Admirals.

Next in age is Buccleuch Cemetery, which has an unusual history. About 1755 when St. Cuthbert's Parish Church became overcrowded, the congestion was relieved by the erection of a Chapel of Ease on the then southern outskirts of the city on a site with an uncommon feature in Edinburgh—a windmill, used for raising water from the Borough Loch on the Meadows to a brewery nearby. Adjacent to the new church a small burial ground was established and consecrated in 1764—unusually, and somewhat surreptitiously, by an Episcopalian bishop. Unhappily, the small cemetery was desecrated by its own Kirk Session in 1901, when a large and ugly corrugated iron church hall was built over almost the entire area; and worse still the Kirk Session let the hall to a roller-skating company till speedy public protest brought this arrangement to an end. In the graveyard was buried the famous criminal, Deacon Brodie (1788).

In 1819, the Buccleuch Cemetery was so overcrowded that the St. Cuthbert's Kirk Session, a year later, opened the Newington Burying-ground. The usual watch-tower stands inside.

The remaining burial places in and about the Edinburgh churches may be dealt with briefly. Almost at the Cowgatehead is the ancient Chapel of St. Mary Magdalene, founded in 1541 and vested with the Corporation of Hammermen who after the Reformation used it as their hall. Lady Yester's Church in Infirmary Street was founded in 1644, somewhat to the east of the present building, and surrounded by a churchyard whose only remaining trace today is a walled-in enclosure and marks of an entrance on the wall in High School Wynd. The founder was buried in the old vestry in 1647; and soldiers from the battle of Prestonpans in 1745 who succumbed to their wounds in the old Infirmary opposite were buried in the churchyard. Another bountiful lady was Lady Glenorchy, who founded a chapel in the park of the Edinburgh Orphan Hospital, now covered by the Waverley Station. On her death a burial vault in the chapel was hewn out of the solid rock. At the Disruption in 1843 the minister and congregation almost in their entirety joined the Free Church and built at Greenside Lady Glenorchy's Free Church. Litigation between the Free Church and the Church of Scotland dragged on until 1856, when it was settled in favour of the latter, who built a further Lady Glenorchy's Church at Roxburgh Place, with a vault for the original founder, whose remains had meantime lain in a catacomb of St. John's Episcopal Church at the West End. This church too had its own burial ground.

THE VILLAGE CHURCHYARDS

Each of the villages in the neighbourhood of the city, and, with the spread of the city boundaries, now part of it, had its own parish churchyard.

The old parish church of Corstorphine is often likened to a miniature cathedral. The original parish church, first mentioned in a Charter of 1128, was demolished in 1646 to allow for a new aisle in the neighbouring collegiate church, which had first been built in 1404 at the desire of Sir Adam Forrester of Corstorphine Castle, who wished to have a chapel dedicated to St. John the Baptist for use as a family burial chamber. This chapel was extended by chancel, nave, porch and tower in 1429, and finally by the aisle in 1646. The founder, who died in 1405, and later members of the family are buried there. In other parts of the church lie further knights and priests; there are a number of recumbent effigies; and a mort chest stands in the outer porch of the church today. The use of mort clothes was made compulsory in Scotland as a measure to encourage the linen trade by an Act of 1686, which was rescinded in 1707.

In 1736, however, the Corstorphine Kirk Session spent £187 7*s*. (Scots) to purchase two velvet mort clothes, one large and the other small; and these were hired out at £4 and £1 10*s*. (Scots) respectively.

On the present western boundary of Edinburgh is the parish of Gogar, which possesses its own churchyard.

The churchyard of the Church of St. Cuthbert's and Hailes (in the Colinton ward) also has its mort stone. The original church was founded in 1095 and was probably destroyed during the Earl of Hereford's invasion in 1544–5. The present site dates from 1636, when a new church was built, followed by a further new church in 1771. The oldest dated stone in the churchyard is one of 1593. Also in the churchyard are the remains of James Gillespie (died 1797), snuff-maker and founder of the hospital and school bearing his name. There are five other burial grounds in the Colinton parish.

In Liberton parish, human remains in stone coffins, probably Roman, were unearthed at Morton House and on the Braid Hills. According to an 1143 Charter granted by David I, the chapel of Liberton belonged to St. Cuthbert's Parish. It has been suggested that a church was built by a Baron Malbeth on the present site about 1430 and that this was demolished in 1814. Side aisles built on at various dates for the nobility and their tenants incorporated family burial vaults. Hugh, Lord Somerville of Drum, Gilmerton and Moredun, who died in 1640, was buried in the centre of the church. The present church was built in 1815 on the old site.

Also in Liberton parish is St. Catherine's Well, the site of a very ancient chapel dedicated to St. Catherine and in which she was buried—this possessed its own burying place of which all trace has disappeared—and Mortonhall Estate, with its private burying ground and present mansion-house built in 1796. In 1635 the estate was bought by the Trotter family, and a descendant sold it to Edinburgh Corporation in 1958 for use as a cemetery and crematorium.

The ancient and now vanished village of Niddrie, which once contained three breweries and fourteen liquor houses, stood near the mansion-house of the same name; but the chapel of " Nudry Merschal " was destroyed by a mob from Edinburgh in 1688. The original burial place was on the west side of the policies, while the later site dated from 1685. In the mansion-house itself is a vault containing the tomb of William Wauchope, dating from 1587.

The parish kirk of Duddingston is mainly of 12th century origin, with a north aisle which contains the burial vault of the Thomsons of Duddingston dating from 1631. Plague victims in 1645 were buried outside the churchyard, which extends to less than half an acre and contains only about 150 lairs. Until 1800, the parish population was only about 1,000. Stone coffins have been found in Duddingston Parish, and cinerary urns were unearthed at Magdalene Bridge as late as 1881.

THE CHURCHYARDS OF LEITH

The earliest centre of religious life in the Leith district was on the outskirts at Restalrig, where a chapel had been founded by St. Rule and where St. Triduana in the 8th century was buried. A shrine was erected which still exists in the churchyard, adjacent to the successive churches built there.

The earliest burial ground in Leith itself seems to have been in the present Kirkgate area and belonged to the Church of St. Anthony's, a hospital founded in 1430, of which no trace now remains. It was damaged by English cannon in 1544 and 1560 and allowed to fall into ruin after the Reformation.

In the Kirkgate itself stands the Church of St. Mary—South Leith Church. Originally erected before 1490, it was partially destroyed in the 1560 bombardment, rebuilt and rebuilt again in 1847, a fragment only of the original plan. In pre-Reformation times each trade guild had its own altar in a chapel; in later times the trades had their own groups of pews and buried their dead first in their chapels and then in the portion of the churchyard adjacent to their sittings. At the 1847 restoration memorial tablets on the interior walls were broken up and used to pave the vestibules and stair landings. The striking features of the churchyard today are the tombstones, which are richly decorated with the heraldic devices of the guilds. Along the north wall are the iron guards which as elsewhere were erected against the resurrectionists' activities.

The North Leith Church owes its origin to the Abbey of Holyrood. The Church of St. Ninian was endowed with the rents of tenements and tolls of the users of a bridge over the Water of Leith in 1493. Apparently no churchyard was attached to this Church, for the North Leith folk buried their dead in the churchyard of St. Nicholas' Chapel and hospital which had come into being about this time.

Both St. Ninian's and St. Nicholas' fell into ruin after the Reformation, and all traces of the latter church were lost when Cromwell built his Citadel on its site in 1656. Deprived of a burial ground, the North Leithers then buried their dead in the South Leith churchyard until, eight years later, they obtained a garden extending to the Water of Leith in what is now Coburg Street. Just inside the gate is the tomb of Gladstone's grandfather Thomas, protected by slabs of stone in an altar-like shape.

Newhaven possesses a tiny churchyard which is a reminder of the days when James IV founded the New Haven of Leith wherein to build his ship "Great Michael." In the village was the chapel of St. Mary and St. James with its own burial grounds.

PRIVATE CEMETERIES

The remaining ancient burial grounds in Edinburgh pertain to different religious persuasions, the Quakers and the Jews. The tiny burial ground of the Society of Friends at 74 Pleasance is supposed to date back to 1665. A meeting-house was built in 1791 on an unused part of the ground. A Quaker is buried in an isolated grave at Craigentinny, and the grave, in accordance with his will, is 40 feet deep and surrounded by a massive memorial.

The first record of a Jewish burial in Edinburgh is found in the Town Council minutes of 6th May, 1795, when a petition was made for a burial place on the Calton Hill in a natural cave, of which nearly all trace is lost. The first Jewish cemetery in Edinburgh (and indeed in Scotland) was established in 1816 in a field of a mere one-twentyfourth of an acre in the Sciennes district at what is now called Braid Place, next to the present police station. To this burial ground in its early years Glasgow Jews brought their dead until their own sepulchre was available. When Braid Place cemetery became full, the Jews acquired first a portion of Echo Bank cemetery and later part of Piershill cemetery.

By the beginning of the 19th century the ancient churchyards of Edinburgh were more or less overcrowded, some had been extended several times, and all were in densely populated districts. Public attention began to be drawn to the evils they represented, and by the 1840s several private cemeteries had been provided in what were then the outskirts of the city but still within the boundaries fixed in 1832:

TABLE 42

Original and Present Name	*Owning Company*	*Date of Opening*	*Area (Acres)*
The Edinburgh Cemetery (Warriston Cemetery)	The Edinburgh Cemetery Company	1843	14
The Western Cemetery (Dean Cemetery)	Edinburgh Western Cemetery Company (later Dean Cemetery Trust Ltd.)	1845	17·2
The Dalry Necropolis (Dalry Cemetery)	Metropolitan Cemetery Association		
The Newington Necropolis (Echobank Cemetery)	Metropolitan Cemetery Association	1846 1846	6 8
The Edinburgh & Leith Cemetery (Rosebank Cemetery)	Edinburgh & Leith Cemetery Company	1846	13
The Southern Cemetery (Grange Cemetery)	Edinburgh Southern Cemetery Company	1847	20

Fortunately, these cemeteries were available when the city's second cholera epidemic broke out in 1849. Those who died earlier in the first series of epidemics in the '30s were buried in open fields.

Some twenty years later, Edinburgh's first Medical Officer of Health, the great Henry Littlejohn, surveyed the health and environment of the citizens, as we saw earlier. And for the first time since the extension in 1855 to Scotland of the Act, making registration of births, marriages and deaths compulsory and statistical information more adequate and available, he made it possible to ascertain precisely their mortality. He found the population's density averaged about 60 per acre, after deducting the area of the Queen's Park and other open spaces and fields. The India Place area contained 553 persons to the acre and the Tron district between the North Bridge and St. Mary's Wynd reached 646. Further studies were made of the mortality according to (1) altitude above sea level; (2) trades (52 of these were investigated); (3) cause of death (109 specified); and (4) affluence by reference to registers of parochial relief.

Littlejohn deplored the failure to close the overcrowded churchyards and burial grounds in densely populated city areas, all untidy and ill-maintained; for where graves were enclosed against the body-snatchers dirt and litter accumulated. Also, by the 1860s the private cemeteries were overlooked by buildings. On his representations, Greyfriars was closed except to possessors of private tombs; nevertheless, 73 burials took place there in 1863, of which 28 were at the lowest rate in common ground and so contrary to the Town Council's decision. It had been supposed that the introduction of the private cemeteries would have caused the practical cessation of burials in churchyards, but in fact the poorer classes continued to use the latter.

To prevent further use of the city churchyards (" intramural interment " was Littlejohn's term for it), he advocated their complete closure, and the Canongate and Old and New Calton Burial Grounds were closed soon afterwards. Overtures were next made to the authorities of St. Cuthbert's to have the common ground in the churchyard and in the extensions at Buccleuch Street and East Preston Street closed, without interference to interments in private lairs. As the church authorities did not accede to the Public Health Committee's request, the Town Council appealed to the Sheriff. They pointed out that under Section 16 (j) of the Public Health (Scotland) Act, 1867, a " nuisance " existed, i.e. " any churchyard, cemetery or place of sepulture so situated or so crowded with bodies, or otherwise so conducted as to be offensive or injurious to health." After a year-long inquiry, the Sheriff found for the Corporation, and in 1874 the burial grounds in question were closed.

The common ground in the private cemeteries having become overcrowded by the '60s and '70s, Warriston, Dean, Rosebank and Dalry cemeteries were extended, and in 1878 a new private cemetery of 18 acres at Morningside was opened by the Metropolitan Cemetery Company Limited.

Further private cemeteries were opened before the end of the century:

TABLE 43

Name	*Owning Company*	*Date of Opening*	*Area (Acres)*
New Dalry (later North Merchiston)	Edinburgh Cemetery Company	1881	
Eastern (Drum Terrace)	Edinburgh Eastern Cemetery Company	1883	
Piershill	Edinburgh & Portobello (Piershill) Cemetery Company	1887	8½
Seafield	Leith Cemetery Company	1888	
Mount Vernon	Roman Catholic Church	1895	13
Comely Bank	Edinburgh Cemetery Company	1898	

Extensions of these were made at the beginning of the present century, and two further private cemeteries were opened by the Edinburgh Cemetery Company Limited at Saughton (1919) and Corstorphine Hill (1930).

With the introduction of cremation in Edinburgh in 1929 and its immediate popularity as a means of disposal of the dead, it seemed as if earth burial might eventually die out. A study of the dividends paid by some of the private cemetery companies shows the trend. The Edinburgh Cemetery Company, operating six of Edinburgh's 15 private cemeteries, paid a dividend of 5 per cent in 1925–6, with 4 per cent in 1945–6 and 2 per cent in the years 1947–8 to 1950–1. In the next year the dividend was passed and resumed at 2 per cent in 1952–3. In 1955 the capital of the company (originally £25,000, and from 1913 £50,000) was reduced to £37,500. The dividend was passed again in 1955–6 and resumed at 2½ per cent in 1956–7.

The Metropolitan Cemetery Company, operating Morningside Cemetery, paid a dividend of 6½ per cent on its capital of £40,000 for 1941. By 1948 the dividend was 1½ per cent; during the years 1949 to 1955 3 per cent was paid; in 1956 and 1957 2 per cent, and from 1958 to 1960 the company operated at a loss. In contrast the Edinburgh Cremation Company Limited has paid a steady 6 per cent on its £10,000 of capital since its inception.

A feature of the last few years in the city has been a series of amalgamations, attempted or accomplished, between cemetery companies and "take-over" bids. Most proposals for amalgamation have suggested that improvements in joint working of cemeteries would lead to reduction in the labour costs which have helped to make cemetery maintenance so profitless.

CORPORATION CEMETERIES

Apart from the 15 churchyards taken over by the Corporation under the 1925 Act, three cemeteries have been laid out by the local authority. As previously stated, Portobello's corporation cemetery came under the management of Edinburgh Corporation in 1896, and extensions were made to this in 1931 and again in 1960. A second area was acquired at Liberton in 1926 for a municipal cemetery as an extension to the churchyard, and this was also later extended.

The latest development is at Mortonhall, where a new cemetery was laid out and opened in 1960. In common with all cemeteries, the Corporation has suffered from the rise in the expense of maintaining individual graves with cut borders and sometimes large memorial stones in addition. Such maintenance costs are mostly made up of labour costs, and to make the utmost use of mechanical means, the tendency has been to try to dissuade lair-holders from interrupting the flat surface of the graves by such ornamentation as has been common in the past.

Expenditure on municipal burial grounds started at the net amount of £152 in the financial year 1897–8—a rate of 0·016 pence per £1—with the appearance in Edinburgh Corporation's accounts of details relating to Portobello Cemetery. By 1929–30 the effects of the takeover of the city churchyards could be seen: the net expenditure was £1,568, representing a rate of 0·077 pence. Increases in expenditure over the years was matched by increases in the city's rateable valuation and the rate never varied much from 1/10th of a penny until 1947–8, when net expenditure of £6,487 produced a rate of ¼*d.* The ½*d.* rate was reached in 1956–7 with an expenditure of £17,167 and the 1960–1 expenditure of £25,441 meant a rate of $\frac{3}{4}$*d.* Revaluation of the city for 1961–2 and an estimated net expenditure of £33,190 in 1962–3 reduced the rate poundage to 0.62*d.*

CREMATION

Cremation is lawful in most countries, though it may be forbidden to members of certain religions or its use discouraged by Roman Catholics, for example, members of the Greek Orthodox Church and Jews. Although used by the Babylonians, Greeks and Romans, cremation was almost unknown in Europe for 18 centuries because of the opposition of the Christian Church. Only in the 19th century was it recognised as a sanitary method of disposal of the dead.

The first cremation in Scotland took place in Glasgow in 1895 at the crematorium provided by the Scottish Burial and Cremation Society. Edinburgh's first crematorium was opened in 1929 at Warriston.

The Leith Crematorium at Seafield was opened by the Leith Cemetery and Crematorium Company Limited in April 1939; and in 1957 a second, smaller chapel known as the Cloister Chapel was opened at Warriston. Since then cremation has continued its rapid growth as the figures show.

The number of deaths in Edinburgh annually is about 6,000—an average maintained since 1921. But to take a recent year, the number of cremations in Edinburgh and Leith in 1960 were 4,590; which proves conclusively that a majority of Edinburgh citizens favour cremation as a method of disposal of the body. Only in the Roman Catholic Cemetery at Mount Vernon is the position different. In the last year before the Warriston Crematorium opened (1928) the number of burials at Mount Vernon was 311. Subsequent figures for each 10th year were 360 for 1938, 396 for 1948, and 445 for 1958.

One welcome feature of the cremation system has been the introduction to the funeral service of the female mourner, whose attendance at funerals, once a male prerogative while ladies awaited the return of the cortege at the bereaved home, is now usual. In fact, women nowadays form a large proportion of the mourners at each of Edinburgh's crematoria.

FUNERAL UNDERTAKERS

Of the many firms offering to undertake funerals only about three are of any size. One firm, established in 1820, once maintained an establishment of over 300 horses, with 20 hearses and 100 carriages. In 1960 there were, of course, no horses; the motor hearses numbered five and motor cars 12. Another firm established in 1851 had eight horses, two hearses and four carriages, but in 1960 the same firm owned six motor hearses and 14 motor cars, with an establishment of 15 undertakers, 12 chauffeurs and 8 coffin-makers. Another firm which entered the business of funeral undertaking as recently as 1927 with one hearse and one car had three hearses and 15 cars at the end of 1961.

THE FIRE SERVICE

Edinburgh firemen make the proud claim that since they date back to 1703 they are the oldest municipal fire brigade in the world. It was that year, apparently, which saw the first recorded attempt to form a fire-fighting organisation in the city, according to a document long treasured at the Central Fire Station. Little organised procedure, however, was possible in 1703, since there was no piped water supply to fire hydrants, no firemen on constant watch, no telephone system to raise the alarm and no fast fire appliances. Instead, as all calls were on foot, there was a long delay before the alarm was given; manpower was widely dispersed; and water was obtainable only from wells and inadequate wooden mains. But the water, carried to the scene by water caddies in 300 leather buckets kept by the Town Guard, had a curious ally in large quantities of muck and horse dung. This was carried in creels.

As the 18th century wore on, there were fires from time to time in the Old Town, as indeed in other populous centres, which did great damage. Early in the next century, too, there were so many serious fires that in 1824 the Police Commissioners took fire protection over, and duly recruited and trained a body of 80 firemen under the command of a superintendent, James Braidwood, who later went to London and was killed on duty at a great fire in Tooley Street. Six insurance companies then agreed to contribute the sum of £200 each, with Police Funds adding a further £200, to purchase new appliances. The new brigade was known as the Edinburgh Fire Engine Establishment till 1870 when the title was changed to the Edinburgh Fire Brigade.

Some of the old record books give detailed items of expenditure, which show that firemen in those days were paid for services rendered and not on a weekly basis. For example:

> *10th September, 1826 at 10 p.m.* The fire began in the roof and machinery over the thrashing-mill course which were destroyed. It was prevented from extending to the barns and other offices. The Yellow Engine (the only one that played) could not be wrought with much effect on account of the great scarcity of water—water was obliged to be carried from an old quarry about a quarter of a mile distant. Bill—£14 16*s*. 0*d*.

A scrapbook in the Fire Brigade's possession which gives particulars of large fires, shows that the old Theatre Royal had fires in 1853, 1865, 1875 and 1884. Later still, in November, 1892, Jenners' shop in Princes Street suffered an " immense destruction of Property. "As one Press report put it: " When the whole building was ablaze the roar of the flames could be distinctly heard and the Waverley Hotel was lit up as at noonday . . . . As the fire began to die out the scene assumed a grand appearance. In the foreground was the Scott Monument swathed in the ruddy glare of the blazing pile, behind which there stood the spectre-like walls of the gutted warehouse, picked out on the sky like some quaint picture in a lime-light exhibition."

With this lurid scene burning in everyone's mind, plans were made for a new Central Fire Station at Lauriston Place. This was duly opened in June, 1900, and is one of Edinburgh's six stations, the newest (1961) being the one at Sighthill; the others are still on the original sites.

But how great the changes since the turn of the century! In 1900 stations were manned with hose-carts or pumps, horse-drawn. There were links between stations, better piped supplies and more men available to make an immediate response to a call. Nevertheless, progress to and at fires was a good deal slower than it is today, when to deal with a fire in the city one dials 999 on the telephone to call the brigade from its half dozen stations, all armed now with the latest pump appliances, turntable ladders, reasonably adequate water supply, alarm systems in buildings to give early warning, and the machinery to order any additional pumps required from stations beyond the city.

REORGANISATION BETWEEN THE WARS

At the end of the first World War the spread of mechanism and a general demand for higher wages and salaries had a twofold effect on Edinburgh's fire brigade. In 1920 the Edinburgh Town Council approved the raising of a Firemaster's salary from £650 a year to £800, that of a Superintendent from £375 to £470, and the pay of a 3rd Officer from £315 to £380. The fireman's rate became 70*s*. per week rising to 90*s*. Between 1920 and 1930 the fire brigade also became completely mechanised, and the work of the brigade began to take on the familiar pattern of today.

With the outbreak of the second World War the Auxiliary Fire Service was mobilised, and with this expansion a large number of auxiliary stations were opened to accommodate the greatly increased number of appliances and personnel. Although Edinburgh had no serious raids during the war, the men and their equipment were used in the fierce raids on Clydeside; and soon, as the very serious fires caused by enemy raids continued, the Government was compelled to re-consider the system of control. In May, 1941 it was announced that the fire service would be nationalised. By August the National Fire Service was formed.

This eventually caused a complete upheaval in the fire-fighting organisation. In Scotland the whole country was divided into six fire areas with a Fire Force Commander who was responsible to the Secretary of State for Scotland. Within each fire area, divisions and sub-divisions were formed with senior officers in command. At each level there was a fire control room, reporting to the level above, until the last link was made with the major control for the United Kingdom based in London.

The next steps in the evolution of Edinburgh's fire brigade as part of a national service are important to note if we are to understand its position and potentialities today. With the return of peace, the political promises of 1941 to return the fire services to local authority control had to be honoured, but many thought that the lessons learned during the years of the National Fire Service would be lost if all pre-war fire authorities, 1,400 in number, were to regain control of their small fire brigades. After long discussions with the associations representing local authorities it was agreed that larger units were desirable, and in the Fire Services Act of 1947 provision was made for the establishment of 11 Fire Areas in Scotland, instead of 288 separate fire brigades as formerly.

As the result of this, the fire service in Edinburgh today forms part of what is called the South Eastern Fire Area, and Edinburgh itself naturally provides the headquarters for an area of about 2,500 square miles, covering the city itself, the Lothians and Peebles, and the three Border counties of Berwick, Roxburgh and Selkirk. The combined population exceeds 820,000 and is served by 32 fire stations in all. The Area is administered by the South Eastern Fire Area Joint Committee, consisting of eight councillors from the city and one from each of the seven counties which make up the South East of Scotland. The Town Clerk of Edinburgh acts as Clerk; the Treasurer is the City Chamberlain; and the money required to meet the costs of the fire brigade is supplied by each of the eight authorities on a basis of an agreed proportion and with regard tc their rateable value.

Costs are arrived at by taking average annual figures. The highest costs in a fire brigade are related to salaries and wages for staff: the next block of expenditure relates to buildings and their upkeep, fire appliances and their maintenance plus running costs, equipment for men and appliances, and fire hydrants. The total cost we can see from the Final Estimates for the year commencing 16th May, 1963. These totalled £453,855 of which £382,075 went on salaries and wages, and £32,500 on an item called " Pensions etc." In addition capital expenditure on such items as new hydrants accounted for £149,400.

CONDITIONS OF SERVICE

Comparing the pay and conditions of service of firemen today with those of 1900, the picture is one of considerable change. The pay of a recruit fireman today is £700 a year, rising to £930 after seven years. His predecessor of 1900 had 22*s*. per week, which after 10 years service rose to 27*s*. Moreover, whereas the fireman of 1900 had one day off per month, the present day fireman in the South Eastern Fire Area has a 48-hour week, operating a 3-watch system of 3-day shifts of 10 hours, 3 night shifts of 14 hours with sleeping allowed, and 3 days off. In addition he has 21 days annual leave, 6 public holidays and overtime payment. This system applies to Station Officers, Sub Officers, Leading Firemen and Firemen on operational duties at fire stations. In 1964 there were about 406 of these on whole-time duties in the area, and in addition there were nearly 300 men described as " Retained " men. These hold the same rank as whole-time firemen, and are attached to stations outside Edinburgh in places where more whole-time men would be difficult to justify, or where the station is only used on a part-time basis. There are 22 such stations in the South Eastern Fire Area.

Each whole-time man is issued with standard kit on joining at a cost of £100, spends three months at the training school on full pay, and on return is fully conversant with most types of fire appliance and equipment. From the moment of joining he is covered by a large protective umbrella in matters of pay, medical benefit, pension scheme, clothing issues, and regular leave breaks, all of which have been developed to ensure his acceptance of the hazards of his job. There is an examination system for promotion, and all ranks from firemen to firemaster are filled by promotion from within the service.

HEADQUARTERS

The headquarters of the South Eastern Fire Brigade Area is situated at the Central Fire Station in Lauriston Place. At this centre are concentrated the Administration of the Brigade, the Firemaster and his Assistant Firemaster, the two Divisional Officers, each controlling 16 of the 32 fire stations in the Area—with their Assistant Divisional Officers and Instructors, the Fire Prevention Section under its Divisional Officer—this gives specialist advice on fire subjects—the Area Workshops, which repair and maintenance the 100 vehicles in the Brigade fleet, the Area Stores and the Area Fire Control. This latter is under a Sub-Officer who is the mobilising officer, and is manned by four Leading Firewomen and four Firewomen. Their job is to see that the appropriate stations send the requisite number of appliances to a fire call and to inform others concerned, such as the Police, who in turn notify Gas and Electricity Departments.

FIRE PREVENTION

Away back in 1585 (says a Fire Brigade record), a very destructive fire, with a tragic human consequence, which broke out in Peebles Wynd (now Blair Street) was caused by a baker's boy setting fire to a stack of his master's peats. At the time peat was a cheap and popular fuel, as too were heather, broom and whins, all stacked up in the wynds and closes or indoors. So once a fire got hold in such narrow confines, the result was usually calamitous. And so it was for the unfortunate boy, for according to this record, he " met with a severity of punishment highly disproportionate to his offence, being burnt quick at the cross next day."

This fire and one or two others had one good effect however. The Town Council by edict abolished the custom of heaping up fuel within the city; which brings us to the whole question of fire prevention today. That this is a vital problem can hardly be gainsaid, since the number of calls dealt with, as well as the number of lives lost in fires, increases annually. In 1962, to cite a recent year, the South Eastern Fire Brigade dealt with 5,029 calls, including 2,206 fires requiring the use of pumps. The biggest involved a loss of £450,000, and the next biggest £200,000. Six lives were lost in that year.

Since much of this damage and loss could have been prevented, the

Fire Prevention Department plays an increasing role in efforts to achieve this. Hundreds of inspections of factories and offices are carried out annually; plans are examined and discussed with architects on a variety of projects involving protective measures; talks are given to outside associations and schools, all stressing naturally such obvious dangers as leaving matches within the reach of children. Moreover, there is a growing awareness by members of the public of the free service available to them, and more than 1,000 persons in a year have sought advice at the brigade headquarters on such matters as heating appliances, treatment of fabrics, the provision of suitable fire extinguishers, and whether it is dangerous to sleep with electric blankets switched on and television sets indefinitely plugged in.

Some of these and other dangers were taken up early in 1964 by Firemaster Frank Rushbrook, who succeeded Firemaster A. B. Craig, when presenting his annual report on the work of the South Eastern Fire Brigade during 1963 and, in some detail, his building programme and staffing report.

He thought new fire stations were needed in the city's outlying districts and extra staff in the city itself. Two large fires at the same time, as had already occurred, could strain the brigade to breaking point. Deaths through fires in 1963 were 17, the same as two years before, compared with the previous highest figure of 14 in 1954. Altogether, he said, in the 2,500 square miles of the South Eastern Fire Brigade's area there had been 5,001 fires as against the previous year's 5,029. Seventeen of the 35 fires in the area, causing more than £2,000 damage, had occured in Edinburgh.

In the light of these fires it is regrettable that there should be people in the city base enough to make malicious false alarms. Most of these culprits are teenagers, young men and children; together, in 1963, they put in 294 false alarm calls compared with 206 in the previous year.

However, if this sounds gloomy, at least we can leave the Edinburgh firemen and their colleagues in the South Eastern Fire Brigade with praise for three striking innovations which came about in 1963. These were (1) a "press-button" control room, (2) an all-purpose emergency tender, (3) the inauguration of an apprenticeship scheme under which boys of 15½ years of age can don firemen's uniform. Now, as the result of the new system the control consol at the Lauriston headquarters considerably reduces the time lapse between receipt of the telephone call and the arrival of the appliance at the scene of the fire. Two-way radio contact too can be maintained with 55 tenders, and all calls passing through the central switchboard are tape-recorded. This device has many advantages, not the least of which is that it can be used to trap anyone sending a false alarm.

The pantechnicon-like emergency vehicle, which weighs eight tons and cost £10,800, carries more than 700 separate items of equipment, thus enabling the firemen to deal expeditiously with any form of emergency from a train crash or street accident to a collapsed building. It has hydraulic rescue gear which can lift 50 tons, resuscitation and first-aid apparatus including stretchers; a generator, a searchlight, and floodlighting equipment that can operate up to 900 feet away from the vehicle. It also carries oxy-acetylene and oxy-propane equipment, and radio and walkie-talkie apparatus to maintain contact with the main control centre.

The Junior Firemen Apprenticeship Scheme, the first in Scotland, as these words are written, provides for the enrolment of lads between the ages of 15½ and 16½, at wages ranging from £225 to £285 per annum for a five-day week. On enrolment as regular firemen at the age of 18, the wage rises to £700. And with this our survey must end—with the reassuring, if obvious reflection that, the stream-lined fire service of today presents a remarkable contrast to the days when the tolling of the big brass fire bell brought out a boiler on wheels, belching smoke and drawn by galloping horses.

Part Four

THE SOCIAL PATTERN

CHAPTER 18

ROOM AT THE TOP

If Edinburgh is a city of contrasts life there naturally offers a rich social variety. In the Old Town, in middle-class suburbia, and in municipal housing schemes people express different opinions on what gives life in Edinburgh its particular quality. So let us eavesdrop, first of all, on a conversation between especially articulate voices, which took place in Sir Compton Mackenzie's Edinburgh home in 1962.

Sir Compton himself had for many years lived on islands—Capri, Jethou and Barra—and then in Berkshire, without ever being long away from London. But in the early 1950s he set up house in Drummond Place, a gracious part of Edinburgh's New Town. The late Miss Anne Redpath, a Royal Scottish Academician well known as an artist far beyond Scotland's hills and shores, was one of Sir Compton's guests that night. Lord Cameron who had served as a naval officer in two wars before becoming Dean of the Faculty of Advocates, a Court of Session Judge, and Chairman of the Highland Panel was also there along with Sir David Milne, former Permanent Under-Secretary of State for Scotland, and later a Governor of the B.B.C. and Chairman of the Edinburgh College of Art, and finally two editors—the Editor of *The Scotsman*, Mr. Alastair Dunnett, and the Editor of this book, who was there to keep order. Their conversation went as follows:

EDITOR (TO ALASTAIR DUNNETT)

As a West-of-Scotlander, what do *you* think about living in Edinburgh?

ALASTAIR DUNNETT

I have been enchanted by Edinburgh ever since I came here as a school-boy, playing rugby in the afternoon and then exploring the Old Town closes at night. What a lovely—and lively—place it is! With so many interesting things going on, it's hardly surprising that I have never been in another city of this size which the natives themselves know so well. I don't mean this in any parochial sense, but Edinburgh is intimately known to its natives. Everybody seems to know every street in the place; everybody knows every district; and everybody knows at least somebody who knows everybody else. This is a remarkable thing for a city of half-a-million people.

LORD CAMERON

I should have thought that was true 20 years ago before the big expansion, when Edinburgh was still a smallish city. You could walk from end to end of it easily, and people did get to know it. But this isn't so true today with all these new housing estates, which seem like a jungle to most people, and where the inhabitants of one jungle are lost if they get into the next one.

EDITOR (TO SIR COMPTON MACKENZIE)

What impression did Edinburgh make on you when you first came here?

SIR COMPTON MACKENZIE

Well, going back to 1907, when my first play was produced here at the Lyceum Theatre—I came to Edinburgh first in 1883, but don't actually remember that—in those days, Princes Street really was, without question, the finest street in Europe. It still is potentially the finest, but practically every one of the houses has been destroyed, one after another, and replaced by chain-stores, and the whole street has changed entirely in character. It had an immense air of leisure in 1907. That, you may say, was equally true of London. But I can't remember in the whole of my life any street anywhere in the world with quite the quality that Princes Street had 50 years ago, and still has to some extent.

LORD CAMERON

There was a little sketch in a recent exhibition of J. D. Fergusson's paintings which illustrated that: a small early sketch of Princes Street on a summer evening, with a cab standing on the south side and ladies patrolling along with the obvious leisure of the century's first decade. That is Edinburgh as one remembers it 50 years ago.

SIR COMPTON MACKENZIE

To go even further back, my mother came to Edinburgh in 1868 when she was about 15, and what impressed her most then was that there was a Skye terrier sitting on nearly every door-step. Skye terriers had gone long before I knew it. I suppose today we don't even get fox terriers. What do we see in Edinburgh now?

SIR DAVID MILNE

Poodles perhaps? Toy poodles? There are quite a lot of Labradors too. I was once stopped by a very old gentleman who had a tiny little terrier on a long lead. He looked at my two Labradors and said: " Where do they all come from? Are they breeding them for the next war?"

ANNE REDPATH

That's all very well, but you don't choose a city to live in just for the kinds of dogs it has!

EDITOR

Which brings me back to my original point. Alastair Dunnett came here from the West of Scotland to live in Edinburgh and edit *The Scotsman*. I wonder what his first emotions were on becoming a resident?

ALASTAIR DUNNETT

I would say a sense of enjoyment. I know that like a Chinaman's ancestors there is inevitably a progressive deterioration in standards, and things are never what they were decades ago. But Edinburgh has one characteristic which is the best of any city I know, and that is that people enjoy the social life, deliberately enjoy it. In Glasgow they start drinking with the fervour with which they go in for religious revivals. Aberdeen drinks with a kind of well-clad, well-fed heartiness. But Edinburgh does it with social style, and in an uninhibited way which really is quite out of keeping with the classical conception of the Edinburgh approach and character. I admire that very much. I think, by the way, it is something to do with the city having been a metropolis for a long time, and consequently having a proper setting for its social occasions.

ANNE REDPATH

Also, the social occasions, I think, are more mixed than you get elsewhere. You tend to meet people doing all sorts of different jobs, which I find myself very stimulating. You go to a party, and it isn't just painters, or just writers; you meet people doing all sorts of interesting things. And this adds a great deal to the richness of life. In London many people find it much more difficult to get out of their own little boxes.

EDITOR

One reason for that, surely, is that in London people are now dispersed over such a huge area. In Glasgow, too, more people who used to live in the centre have now moved out to Largs, Bearsden, Helensburgh, Milngavie, Balfron, Stirling, or—let's whisper it!—even Edinburgh. Here everybody can get easily to each other's houses, even by walking.

SIR COMPTON MACKENZIE

In a sense, you know, London in my youth was much more like Edinburgh. Then, the London that counted was small too—Mayfair and so on. Today the whole of London is a sprawling suburb, and only a few niches remain—clubs like the Savile and a few other places where people can take refuge from the sprawl. But Edinburgh, and Dublin also to some extent, have remained small metropolises. And after all, when you know all your lawyers and your doctors, all your writers and painters, you really have a metropolis.

EDITOR (TO LORD CAMERON)

I think that of all of us here you are the one who has lived in Edinburgh the longest.

LORD CAMERON

Well, I've lived here, apart from wars, for 51 years. I came to Edinburgh as a boy of 11—in the year of King George V's coronation—and I've seen the main changes in Edinburgh life this century. From 1911 to 1914 it was still the old Victorian Edinburgh: very much the carriage and pair; all rather leisurely—like J. D. Fergusson's sketch—and comfortably off, with everybody intensely conscious of who everyone else was and how they were related. Then suddenly things changed with the first World War, with the break-up of society as it then was, and the increase of taxation. But even between the wars—I'm thinking of the legal world now—although the old formal dinner parties, the white tie and tails, practically disappeared, there was still a great deal of entertaining and a very closely knit social life. That was encouraged by the curious professional accident that the Bar, the practising Bar, had to live within half a square mile in the New Town. You lived in this particular area because the lawyers' offices were in or near there, and legal papers had to be delivered late at night, particularly in the days before typewriters, so that advocates lived near their instructors. You walked to your office, which was very good for your liver and your arteries. And at night, when you walked out of your house, if you saw a light on in Jimmy's house you just rang the bell and went in for a yarn at 11 o' clock or even at midnight. But all that changed with the second War. People couldn't get maids for one thing. Real incomes were lower. Wives couldn't stick the idea of having children going up and down stairs in tenements, or the construction of these old New Town houses, which lovely as they are, were designed to be run on a kind of slave labour. So things have broken up, and you haven't got anything like the same closely knit social life. But it is still much closer than in a town like Glasgow, where so many people don't live any longer in Glasgow itself but outside.

EDITOR

Painters, playwrights, artists of all kinds certainly seem to mix with each other here outside their own creative spheres much more often than elsewhere.

LORD CAMERON

Also our lawyers and doctors tend to mix more.

SIR DAVID MILNE

On this point it seems to me that Edinburgh's real charm is the extraordinary diversity within its essential unity. You've got the Church, the Law, both National and Local government, education, banking, insurance, commerce, industry—all very active and yet, both socially and professionally, much closer to each other than in most other towns and cities. In London, for instance, and possibly Glasgow, your friends, if you are a lawyer, tend to be mainly within the law; if you are a surgeon they tend to be in medicine. Here, socially, we're all more together.

ALASTAIR DUNNETT

My own view is that this unity—and diversity—adds greatly to the quality of life in Edinburgh. The city after all is the headquarters of so many things and has so many handpicked people who can meet and mingle on interesting levels as in fact we're doing at this very moment. I imagine, also, that the administrative devolution, which has brought top grade Civil Servants to Edinburgh, has been another large factor in fostering a varied social life. One of the things that strikes me is that so many of them opt to come here, and that other Government departments are no longer a mecca for Scottish talent. It's the same in my own profession. In journalism it's no longer inevitable for Fleet Street to take the A division and to leave the reserves here. It is indeed moving how many able people decide to create a full and permanent life for themselves in Edinburgh, and so give the city an extra cultural impetus.

SIR DAVID MILNE

This is coming on to another aspect of Edinburgh. As we agreed before, in the old days it was a quiet town where one sauntered. Edinburgh is a very busy place now, with a great deal going on, including many important industries. It's also a cosmopolitan place with more people of every colour and race in Edinburgh from the springtime until the end of September than we'd find in most places of comparable size. Partly this is due to tourism, partly to the University and partly to the Festival.

ANNE REDPATH

Yes, that's true. The Festival has made a splendid contribution. It also gives one the feeling that Edinburgh really is a capital city.

ALASTAIR DUNNETT

For myself I never lose the feeling, and never have all my life, that Edinburgh is a capital, and, even in its most run-down state, has always to my mind acted like a capital. This is in the air. The city simply cannot be compared with any English town of the same population.

EDITOR

Part of that feeling is due, would you say, to the city functions and the ceremonial? There must be more ceremonial going on in Edinburgh all the time than almost any other city in the world. The Town Council's got to be kirked in St. Giles. The Queen comes on ceremonial occasions. There's a State Entry into Scotland after the Sovereign's coronation, and then there's the Garden Party at Holyroodhouse, and a host of other things.

SIR DAVID MILNE

We can add many more—the General Assembly of the Church of Scotland, the Scots Saturday when there's a Rugby International at Murrayfield, and many international or national conferences. There are in fact innumerable occasions which are unique to Edinburgh and add tremendously to the colour and vividness of the city's life.

ANNE REDPATH

Of course, the sheer physical structure of Edinburgh helps in all this. I've been told that during the last war many soldiers from different countries chose to spend their leave in Edinburgh because it reminded them of Prague or Warsaw. What was it that reminded them—just the stone-builtness, or the Castle? It's different in Glasgow: Glasgow is just rows and rows of streets that all look exactly alike.

EDITOR

But, to the Glaswegian, each street has some element of romance, and there's always the Clyde and the Cathedral.

ALASTAIR DUNNETT

It is different, though. Glasgow is a great camp which people move into for a generation or two and then move on from. But Edinburgh is a continuity; I think all Scots feel this mysterious blossoming quality about Edinburgh. It's the bastion of one's interests and, in some sense, of one's hopes too. As I said, I've known it for 40 years on and off and it has never lost this kind of excitement for me, and I'm sure other people feel it too. That's why so many foreigners say it's the second finest city in the world—the finest being their own capital, of course.

ANNE REDPATH

Yes, they all do. Prague and Warsaw and Budapest and Paris; they're all quoted like this.

EDITOR

And of course Salzburg, which looks rather like Edinburgh, with its own Festival, and a great rock with a castle.

SIR COMPTON MACKENZIE

The nearest comparison is Athens.

LORD CAMERON (*after general agreement on Athens*)

To get back to the way we live here, I think you would agree, wouldn't you, that in our lifetime the kind of social life that we've seen and experienced has changed. It's less intense and narrow, less divided into compartments. In the past the social orbits didn't overlap. The garrison didn't touch others much except for the Garrison–Bar Cricket Match. The medical world didn't touch others except in the formal entertaining of the Colleges of Surgeons and Physicians. The University didn't mix with the Law, and the Law kept very much to itself. It was the same with Banking and Finance. But two things have happened. The physical changes and income changes as well have broken down the intensity and formality of social life altogether, and the spread of the population within the geographical limits of a comparatively small city has made the various social elements mix very much more. I entirely agree that an Edinburgh party now, instead of being all lawyers or all doctors, is a very interesting cross-section of people. I remember, before the war, you might get seven or eight advocates all together in a corner gossiping about Parliament House and golf at Muirfield. Now, if you get a party where there are advocates, ten to one you'll find there are also investment trust managers, and even despised characters such as newspaper editors! It is all still rather like old Edinburgh, when Edinburgh lived in the Canongate and the High Street, and the judge and the caddy were on the same stair.

SIR DAVID MILNE

Well, that's what I was wondering: whether in such conditions we are getting back to something like the days when Edinburgh really was a close-knit literary and artistic centre.

LORD CAMERON

I don't know, but what we are certainly getting is a much closer mingling of people in different income groups, unlike the English suburban structure where the suburb in which you live is an indication of your status and your income. Take the London suburbs: you can almost tell at which station the chap is going to get off the electric train. And there you'll go and mix with chaps who play at the same golf courses, whose wives squabble about the same dresses, whose cars are the same. But Edinburgh is getting much more like the 18th century Edinburgh, because we're living cheek by jowl.

EDITOR

However, none of these things affected Compton Mackenzie when he decided some years ago to come and live in Edinburgh. Most of us here had some birth or residential qualifications in the city at one time or another. But he chose, after a long life on islands and elsewhere, to come and live here. Monty, why did you suddenly decide that Edinburgh should be your home?

SIR COMPTON MACKENZIE

Oh, I was sentimental. I had my first real recognition here—in the year 1907. That was the first audience that gave me a welcome and said, " You're quite a chap." I said to myself all those years ago that I would end my days in Edinburgh, and I made it quite clear that I intended to do that. And if God wills—not yet, I hope,—I think I will. But long before that, Edinburgh played a very important part in my early imagination. My romantic approach to life started with Scott's *Tales of a Grandfather*. The two immortal pages which described the capture of the Castle at night I read first when I was seven, and read and re-read until I was fourteen or fifteen. And so it stands for something—this capital of the country from which my ancestors and I spring. Then also, as I said, Edinburgh audiences are always supposed to be very difficult and critical; so if they give you a warm welcome you're all the more pleased. My father always said an Edinburgh audience was the best. He put in order, as the audiences which gave him the most pleasure, when playing Sheridan or Goldsmith, Edinburgh as the first; Dublin, second; Glasgow, third. And, of course, he loved Edinburgh—that influenced my decision too—and he was the most popular actor here for some 20 years.

ALASTAIR DUNNETT

I had always thought that the reason for the practice of trying out new plays in Edinburgh was that Edinburgh was a very difficult audience, and if you could get by with Edinburgh you could get by anywhere.

SIR COMPTON MACKENZIE

Oh yes, if Edinburgh approved, well then, to hell with the rest of the world as far as he was concerned. That was very definitely true. I doubt if it's as true today. The theatrical audience today, let's face it, is not what it was, and we can't expect it to be, with the films and television. But what was true then of Edinburgh was also true of the North of England. *The School for Scandal* would play progressively longer as it went north of Nottingham. In Yorkshire it would be 10 minutes longer than in Nottingham. And by the time it reached Edinburgh or Glasgow, it would be 20 minutes longer. You could actually play 20 minutes longer—a fantastic amount of time, if you come to think of it, to *add* to a three-hour play—which meant that the audience were really enjoying it tremendously.

EDITOR

So those were the main reasons for your final decision to live in Edinburgh?

SIR COMPTON MACKENZIE

All those things accumulated. When I left Barra in 1945–6 I meant to come here. But at that time one couldn't find anywhere to live, so I got a place temporarily in Berkshire while I was waiting to come to Edinburgh—and at the right moment, I came here. I have always lived my life really in accord with providence: if I'm meant to go to a place, the place will arrive.

EDITOR

So far we've all been talking about the delights of living in Edinburgh. What about the disadvantages? I know about the weather, but . . . .

SIR COMPTON MACKENZIE

The weather? I will not have anything said against the weather! I think Edinburgh as proved over the years has got the best climate of any city in Britain. But when I tell Londoners I live in Edinburgh, they reply as if I were living in an igloo. Edinburgh in fact has far more sun than Manchester or Liverpool or any of the great cities, and less rainfall than Glasgow; but the wind is felt more here because the city is so open. There is just as much wind in London as there is here, but of course you don't feel it so much because you've got more barriers.

EDITOR

All right, we accept that the city's climate is much misunderstood. There are certainly quite a number of English and Welsh counties with more rainfall in a year than Edinburgh. But the city itself *must* have some disadvantages. My fellow author Moray McLaren has just written me a letter in which he says that Edinburgh is now nearing the depths of—well, for him—despair, because of planning gone wrong, interference with the beauties of the place, and so on. He sees the old Edinburgh of his dreams disappearing fast.

SIR COMPTON MACKENZIE

Yes, but it's very much less fast than anywhere else that I've known—in comparison, for instance, with the way that London has disappeared.

LORD CAMERON

It's also true that the pace of destruction here has been slowed down enormously by comparison with what it was up to 1931 or so. One can blame the Corporation for many things, but they've at least pulled their socks up over the rehabilitation of the High Street and the Canongate—a major operation—and they've spent a lot of money on it too, which is perhaps more surprising.

SIR COMPTON MACKENZIE

Yes, we really must give them thanks, although they do maddening things occasionally like putting up these concrete lamp posts in Drummond Place.

EDITOR

And, as many think, helping to destroy George Square?

LORD CAMERON

Well, Moray McLaren and many others are perfectly entitled to their strong feeling about that. But I must say the Square was ruined earlier when they put that school and Agricultural Department on the north side. And the east side was never very distinguished; the south side is not bad, and the west side is full of quality. But from the domestic point of view these houses have their drawbacks.

SIR COMPTON MACKENZIE

If you consider the destruction of Berkeley Square in London, it's an immensely greater crime than the destruction of George Square. When I think about the damage done by the London County Council, what happens here seems mere venial offences compared to the mortal sins committed in London.

LORD CAMERON

But then, on the other hand, you do have some appalling philistines in Edinburgh. People who ought to know better take up a low-brow higher-professional attitude to anything which may savour of cultural activity. I can think of a lot of my own profession who are scarcely interested. They give practically no support to any cultural activities, even the smallest financial support; and they are proud to stay away from anything in the way of a Festival.

SIR DAVID MILNE

On the other hand the attendances which the Scottish National Orchestra are getting for their performances in Edinburgh have been numerically higher than they are getting in Glasgow. We're certainly not devoid of appreciation.

ANNE REDPATH

Of course, it is true that there is a great deal of cultural snobbery over the Festival. Edinburgh people will go to something at the Festival when a month or two later they would not go near anything of the sort.

ALASTAIR DUNNETT

I would like to defend Edinburgh against this charge of philistinism. It's a favourite ploy of mine to take visitors to the city to see three shelters, three little summer-houses in Princes Street Gardens, just below the floral clock, where mothers sit with prams and old people sun themselves, and sometimes girls come out with packets of sandwiches and have their lunches. And if you look closely at them, you'll see that they are the strongest summer-houses that have ever been built. Their walls are about as thick as Edinburgh Castle, of beautifully dressed sandstone, and the reason for that is a remarkable one. They were built in the early weeks of the last war as bomb shelters, and they were all bricked up at the front. But these beautiful dressed sandstone ashlars—the main pillars and supports and the great concrete roofs—were designed so that at the end of the war the heavy brick bomb-proof screens could come out and glass would go in. It seems to me a wonderful example of a permanent way of looking at life—a sense of style in a capital.

EDITOR

And rightly so, Alastair, but we were trying to unearth some of the *disadvantages* of living in Edinburgh.

SIR DAVID MILNE

Well then, what about the occasional criticism that we are provincial—which I suppose, if one was trying to define it, might mean a belief that one's own affairs are more important than anything else going on outside, matched by a corresponding ignorance of what *is* going on outside.

SIR COMPTON MACKENZIE

Well, I prefer the " provinciality " of Edinburgh to the " suburbanity " of London.

SIR DAVID MILNE

I myself utterly disbelieve that the word " provinciality " applies to Edinburgh, if only for the reason that so many people who live in Edinburgh do, in fact, go far outside for all sorts of reasons—commercial, industrial, administrative, political, artistic and academic—and they all know very well what is going on. There is more travelling from Edinburgh to London and elsewhere on all these matters than the other way round. I met a Foreign Office official the other day who joined a board I'm on, and when I said I lived in Scotland he said that he knew Tashkent and all those other places well, but that he'd never been to Edinburgh. Now there *are* people in the world like that, let's face it. The provinciality of metropolitan London is far greater, I think, in the matter of space than ours; and one's hope would be, not that our travels outward should increase—heaven alone knows they are considerable enough—but that the travels from London to Edinburgh would increase; and I'm sure that will come.

ANNE REDPATH

In the painting world it has come, to a large extent, because of the Festival. Critics from England come up to cover the Festival—they've got to do it—and then they discover for the first time that something more is going on in Edinburgh than they had realised, and they continue to come.

EDITOR

But surely this is a two-way traffic. There are some Scottish painters who don't need critics to come up here to look at their work all the time, because the critics are already looking at it in London where Edinburgh painters seem to be increasingly well-known.

ANNE REDPATH

Yes, but there's still an element of surprise when people in London discover that anything really good is being done in Scotland today—quite blatant surprise.

SIR DAVID MILNE

The fact that the Scots can use paint does seem to surprise some English people.

ANNE REDPATH

Yes. Very few of the artists in the Royal Academy in London have ever been to Edinburgh, apart from those who've come up to be outside assessors for the College of Art. And many of the ones I've spoken to never come to the Festival. But some of us go to London, and therefore that does stop us having this provincial attitude which we might have: we don't believe that we're the centre of the world, which is very good for us.

SIR DAVID MILNE

Whereas London does, and sometimes with justification.

ALASTAIR DUNNETT

I think we could make a mistake and give a wrong emphasis by relating everything to London conditions and London standards. The London critics of the arts were among the last to come to the Edinburgh Festival. We had Japanese, Germans, Scandinavians, Spaniards: everybody came before the so-called recognised London critics, and many of these still come with a peculiar sense of resentment. They still—it's an extraordinary thing—get in touch with me or my secretary by telephone as if they were coming to an outpost to be met by native bearers at the station before padding off into the bush; and they want to know if someone can hire a hotel for them. And we do it for them—but I don't do this when I go to London.

EDITOR

I would like to return for a moment to the subject of painters in Edinburgh and their now considerable work.

ANNE REDPATH

Well, one can never quite explain why there are these succeeding centres of artistic activity. There used to be a tremendous interest in the Dundee area when the jute trade was at its height, and people bought pictures because there was lots of money about. It becomes a kind of competition. If one manufacturer is buying, another one does too: it becomes infectious. Then you had the Glasgow School in the early part of this century when Glasgow was *the* centre for painting in the country. They were painting pictures, they were selling pictures, and we had a lot of very fine Scottish artists who belonged to that School. At the moment—possibly I am a little prejudiced—I think the best painters are in the east of Scotland. There's no real explanation for this kind of thing except that you start with a group of people who perhaps are leaders, and this means that other painters grow up under their influence, as it were, and then you get a whole series. I don't think the present painters from the west are known at all south of the Border, whereas quite a number from the east of Scotland are. But I don't know that there's any reason to account for it.

SIR COMPTON MACKENZIE

I think it's like football teams. Glasgow Rangers are very good one year, then suddenly they fade for a time, and then they come back again and so on.

EDITOR

Would any of you think that writing in Edinburgh is as lively at the moment as painting is?

ALASTAIR DUNNETT

No, I wouldn't at all. Leaving out one or two of our established authors, there's a fair amount of a kind of urgent and self-consciously propagandist writing going on in Edinburgh. There's some very good essay writing of a journalistic kind. But there's not enough original source material; there's not enough urbanity in what we're doing. On the other hand, there's a great deal of urbanity in the recognisable native quality in our painting. The painting comes really from the root somehow, but I don't know how this is done. It's not as if we've a very great tradition historically over many centuries in painting, yet the painters in Scotland seem to be getting up to the things they can do well and which are apt to the Scottish talents and instincts, and they make an international impact. Our writers on the other hand are really searching around, I think, and sometimes in a not very appropriate way at all.

SIR DAVID MILNE

I think this lack is particularly great in the drama, which really is a field in which one would have expected the Scot in general and the Edinburgh Scot in particular to make a greater contribution. The Welsh seem to be doing it today. There are at least three quite active and good Welsh dramatists. We are not quite so well placed at the moment.

EDITOR

At any rate the city has some excellent newspaper journalists and a fine literary record. The University alone has helped to maintain a remarkable line throughout the centuries—Boswell, David Hume, Walter Scott, Cockburn, Carlyle, Stevenson, Barrie, Conan Doyle—there's a good name!—Hugh MacDiarmid and even Michael Arlen.

SIR COMPTON MACKENZIE

True enough; but today surely one of the things that should be done is to revive the *Edinburgh Review*.

LORD CAMERON

Well, there have been many attempts.

SIR COMPTON MACKENZIE

I know, but not the sort of thing I mean—it must be more like the *Edinburgh Review* of once upon a time. There was an example of what I mean the other day in *The Scotsman*—an extremely good review of Lawrence's Letters. I wrote to congratulate the paper—I didn't know who wrote it at the time—and said: "This reminds me of the old days of early reviewing."

EDITOR

But doesn't this bring us neatly into the city's newspaper life? I wonder what our views on that are.

ALASTAIR DUNNETT

Well, newspaper life is a thankless job, you know. I'm always getting backed into corners by people who want to know why I've done things and haven't done things, and so on. But there again, there's this sense of involvement, which is quite a good thing.

ANNE REDPATH

Would that not happen so much in London?

ALASTAIR DUNNETT

Not at all, for various reasons. The newspaper isn't so much an entity in London, and perhaps the people concerned are not so involved in the battle as one is here. There's not a morning paper in London which is a London institution, but, through no merit of mine, my paper *is* an Edinburgh institution.

SIR COMPTON MACKENZIE

There was a time when London did have that too, but it has entirely lost it.

EDITOR (TO ALASTAIR DUNNETT)

You must get quite a lot of people ringing you up about peculiar local problems of their own—things that are happening in the city at Cramond, say.

ALASTAIR DUNNETT

Yes I do; and I welcome it. We really have three jobs to do on the *Scotsman* instead of the usual two. We have to be not only a very local Edinburgh paper, but a kind of Scottish paper, and a national paper in the British sense as well.

EDITOR

But as an editor you must be more intimately concerned with the life of this city than any London editor can possibly be with the detailed life of London. I remember a conversation I once had with a business-man in Newfoundland. He said after a few minutes: " Would you excuse me, I've got to ring up the Prime Minister about a lamp-post." I was a little surprised; but he went on: " You're going to be here for a few weeks, so you ought to realise that if you've got a grievance here, you don't waste time going through anybody or everybody, you ring up someone in real authority." So *there*, if you know your way about, you ring up the Prime Minister just as *here* you might ring up the editor of *The Scotsman*!

ALASTAIR DUNNETT

In our little museum we have a series of letters from former Prime Ministers to Editors of *The Scotsman*. It struck me as very funny that the first time I met Harold Macmillan, after he became Prime Minister, and just after I had got my own job, he said to me " What is it you're doing? Are you actually Editor of *The Scotsman*?" I admitted the soft impeachment, and he said: " My God!" as if to say: " I've got some worries ahead of me, but here's a chap with real trouble! "

ANNE REDPATH

I don't suppose people in London pester the Editor of *The Times* or the *Daily Telegraph* about the art criticism, do they?

SIR DAVID MILNE

I'm not so sure. I think there's a good deal of pressurizing of people for one reason or another. It's very common here, you know: one gets round-robins and things like that. But this is Scotland.

ANNE REDPATH

Well, that's what I mean; it is the other side of the medal from the nice side of involvement. The very fact that you are approachable and that people can tell you off about what to do with the thing must be a nuisance at times if you are the Editor of a newspaper.

ALASTAIR DUNNETT

But that's the job. You know, there was a great deal in what Walter Scott said about having the old Parliament of Scotland. He put it into the mouth of one of his characters. She said: " You can aye peeble them in the streets."

LORD CAMERON

" We could aye peeble them wi' stanes when they werena gude bairns."

SIR DAVID MILNE

That's because Scotland is the right administrative size. In general, this goes for Government as well as for running newspapers, and for a lot of other things. When I say it is the right administrative size, I mean that it hasn't the remoteness of England, say, as an administrative unit. The contacts and the relations between the centre and the periphery in England are nothing like so close as here.

ALASTAIR DUNNETT

We were talking just now about why Edinburgh was or was not a good place to live in. In a sense, really, we're not the best kind of people to talk about that. I think a number of housewives and single women living and working in Edinburgh could give us an awfully sharp line. I was much impressed in an unexpected way by a correspondence which started in *The Scotsman* not very long ago. It started because of an article we had about loneliness; and a tremendous flood of not very happy letters came in from women particularly—widows and single women and tired women—all desperately lonely.

SIR COMPTON MACKENZIE

But don't you think that's true of every single city? I don't think Edinburgh is any worse in that regard.

ALASTAIR DUNNETT

I don't think so myself. But if there is a special warmth about the Edinburgh life, a special congeniality, why has it not spilled over into this area? We were getting letters, some of which we published, charging the churches for example with ignoring single people, with not bringing them into pastoral visitation. Mind you, a lot of the letters one gets are from eccentric people with a sense of injustice, which they carry to extreme lengths. But I would simply mention the point that we in this room are very far from being the typical kind of people who can talk from experience about some of the particular difficulties of living in Edinburgh. There is not one of us here who couldn't select any one of half-a-dozen sections of society in which to operate a social life.

SIR COMPTON MACKENZIE

Yet some of the criticism is true, Alastair. I've repeatedly heard Glasgow people say that Glasgow has a much friendlier atmosphere. I'm not talking about ourselves: I'm talking about just a simple anybody in the street. There is a feeling in Glasgow that there is a coldness of some kind in Edinburgh. It's a coldness *we* don't feel: but it may be there, let's face the fact.

ANNE REDPATH

It's quite true.

SIR COMPTON MACKENZIE

I don't think this charge could be so consistently made by Glasgow people unless they really felt there was a difference. I've heard all this for 60 years at least, and an accusation like that wouldn't last, I don't think, unless there was some foundation for it.

ANNE REDPATH

One thing I have heard criticised on many occasions in Edinburgh—I don't know whether it is particularly a feature of Edinburgh—is that at parties one tends to stand in a group of people one knows, and the poor visitors who have had invitations stand by themselves. We're not at all good at going out of our way to speak to strangers.

ALASTAIR DUNNETT

I think that's true. I think there's a more direct approach to strangers in Glasgow, an easier approach, which an Edinburgh citizen finds difficult.

SIR COMPTON MACKENZIE

He's shyer, you know. There's no doubt about that. And, if you're talking to an Edinburgh audience, you've got to get your way at the beginning. Before Mrs. Wishart can look round and see if Mrs. Ferguson is laughing, if you get them both laughing spontaneously, then nothing matters and you go right ahead. You don't have to do that with a Glasgow audience. I've watched these Edinburgh audiences here at the theatre too now and then, and I see them occasionally thinking: now am I laughing—or whatever it is—at the right place? The Edinburgh audience is definitely more self-conscious than, let's say, one in Glasgow.

EDITOR

But not most teenagers. The city's youth nowadays seem to me to be much more uninhibited than they used to be. When I was a student here, there was never any necking in the street, and couples didn't get into a close embrace in public.

ALASTAIR DUNNETT

No, I believe this is also due to the disappearance of the close more than anything else, the move into suburbia. The close was the place where Scotland absorbed its romantic courtesies. I remember a passage by Neil Munro in which he describes this at some length, and he felt a little sorry for the continental towns and for London too, which had just houses, and no closes. It has always gone on, or we wouldn't be here!

While I remember, there's another feature of Edinburgh which has fascinated me since I first read it in Henry Gray Graham,[1] and that is that every Edinburgh native has a little compass in his head. He always knows where the north-east is. Now I've never encountered this before. I do a lot of sailing and therefore I know about the compass. But the ordinary person in Edinburgh knows automatically where the north-east is, and the south-west. This fascinating Edinburgh talent, according to Henry Gray Graham, was so developed that a host seating people at a dinner party in his own house would say: "Guid Mr. So-and-so, would you kindly tak' the south-west of the table." And in my own office the other day there was a notice posted up by the Company Secretary, saying: "During the holiday season the staff address book will be found on Miss Hutton's desk, which is in the north-west corner of the main office."

LORD CAMERON

You've only got to go along the street and you'll see up on the corner "South East Circus Place" and "North West Circus Place."

SIR DAVID MILNE

I think it's a Scottish trait, and particularly an Edinburgh one. It may be something to do with our vistas—we always can see a long way—but I do believe that an Edinburgh Scot, and indeed a Scot generally, if he's in some strange place, is definitely unhappy and uneasy until he has discovered what are the points of the compass.

EDITOR

However, we were really trying to find some demerits in our city.

ANNE REDPATH

Well, we said that people aren't too friendly, as they are generally in Glasgow. And there's a touch of snobbery about the place.

LORD CAMERON

That may be so, but it is now definitely dying.

SIR COMPTON MACKENZIE

I shouldn't have thought that there was all this terrible snobbery.

LORD CAMERON

No, not now. In the last 50 years it has receded enormously.

SIR DAVID MILNE

Like our supposed shyness. We're perhaps not very good at overcoming shyness, but I do think we're improving as a whole.

SIR COMPTON MACKENZIE

I think you can say that by and large the Scots in this respect are better than the English. They're much more at home when they're abroad, for instance. The English are frightfully shy. The English coldness in railway carriages for example is really shyness. But there it is. There's always a great deal of talk about snobbery and the east

[1] An Edinburgh graduate who wrote a remarkable book, *The Social Life of Scotland in the Eighteenth Century*.

wind in Edinburgh. But I should say that the average taxi driver here, and the average railway porter, was as genial and pleasant a fellow of his kind as anywhere in Europe.

SIR DAVID MILNE

Yes, when I come off a train the taxi driver is always out of his seat quickly to open the door for me—that doesn't happen in London. Some do, but very few. The Edinburgh taxi drivers are extremely polite.

ANNE REDPATH

One gets happily involved with them, too. I take a lot of taxis, and I often sit on the folding seat just behind them so that I can pass the time of day without taking their minds off the traffic. London taxi-drivers in the main are also very friendly and helpful, but there are so many that you never really get on the jolly terms with them that you do with the Edinburgh ones.

EDITOR

Yes, I agree too. But even in Edinburgh time presses—like the need for a taxi sometimes; so on this happy note I think we must bring our talk to an end.

It is one of the joys of Edinburgh that stimulating conversation such as this can still take place in the homes of Edinburgh's authors, judges, advocates, professors, painters, medical men and leaders in industry and business, and that after the best part of two centuries the dinner party, small or large, which so often provides the occasion, is still not out of fashion in the New Town. Neither is the cocktail party nor the pleasant habit of friends visiting each other after dinner. But this of course is only one aspect of the city's varied social mosaic; there are others less agreeable; so we must now leave our room at the top for some other rooms lower down.

CHAPTER 19

PROBLEMS OF LIVING

We have just been into a notable home in the New Town, and earlier we visited the city's older suburbs and villages with their own houses of elegance and distinction. But to see the social pattern whole we must now visit other homes that are less fortunate.

THE COMMON LODGING HOUSES

Not all the traditional features of the Grassmarket–Cowgate area have been swept away during the period of slum clearance and reconstruction in the Old Town. There remain the Common Lodging Houses, and several kindred institutions which provide shelter for those without settled homes of their own. In 1963 these various establishments were all kept busy, as we shall see. But to get an accurate idea of how they are run, and who lives in them, we must first consult a realistic survey conducted by the University's Department of Social Study in 1959.

On 1st July of that year there were eight registered Common Lodging Houses in Edinburgh, seven of them in the Grassmarket, the Cowgate and the adjoining streets.[1] There was also one in Leith. These eight lodging houses were registered as providing accommodation for 1,026 men and 200 women, but there was only accommodation for 892 men and 196 women actually provided on that date. During 1958, the daily average population had been 748·5 men (84 per cent of actual capacity) and 154·1 women (79 per cent).

The charges for beds varied from a minimum of 1*s.* 9*d.* to a maximum of 3*s.* 6*d.* per night. In some of the houses, the charges included free laundry facilities, and in most of them amenities such as radio and newspapers were provided in the common room. Television was provided in five of the houses, and libraries in three. Where the traditional hotplate was provided, in four of them, the lodgers had free access to cutlery and cooking utensils (mostly frying pans and tea pots). The other four provided restaurants instead, in which a reasonable variety of dishes was available at prices similar to those of transport cafes.

In almost every house, the beds were iron bedsteads, with wire spring frames, on which there were flock, hair or coil-filled mattresses and pillows, with two or three blankets per bed. In some, sheets, pillowcases and counterpanes were provided. But the cleanliness and state of repair of the bedding varied greatly. In the better run establishments—these

[1] One of these has since been closed, and two others were technically known as " houses let in lodgings." All have been treated, in this survey, under the broad heading of " Common Lodging Houses."

provided accommodation for the majority—there were detailed arrangements for the regular cleaning, repair and replacement of bedding; and the claim was made that it was rare to find vermin in the bedding. If it were, the lodger and the bedding were sent at once to the Public Health Cleansing Station in High School Yards. Where sheets and pillow-cases were provided, sheets were usually changed fortnightly and pillow-cases weekly. But since some beds were occupied by a different person each night, it is unlikely that everyone got clean sheets.

There were three types of sleeping accommodation—single cubicles (usually more expensive), small rooms with two or three beds and larger dormitories with up to 60 beds. Usually a chair and a small locker were provided, but in some rooms there was nothing but a bed, mattress and blankets.

All registered Common Lodging Houses in the City are inspected regularly by the Sanitary Department, and must reach certain minimum standards in the provision and upkeep of washing and toilet facilities. This is in keeping with the Public Health (Scotland) Act of 1897 and subsequent amending Acts and local legislation which impose various duties on the management, particularly in relation to public health and public order. In turn, the management impose these on the lodgers in the form of rules displayed in a public part of the building. Since all bedspaces and passages must be cleaned and ventilated daily, it is normal for the lodgers to be debarred from the sleeping quarters during " working hours." In addition, it is usual to find rules against bringing alcohol (or the opposite sex) into the building, and rules aimed at imposing a basic standard of conduct and hygiene. But the vigour with which these rules were maintained in the late 1950s varied considerably and the only effective sanction available appeared to be eviction and " blacklisting." In one lodging house, the Keeper had pursued a policy of enforcing his rules so strictly that all who offended were evicted. As a result he had built up a rather more static population of " respectable " men, who appeared to value a quiet and well-ordered life. In the better run establishments, a regular full-time staff of Warders and women cleaners was employed; and in these one of the Warders' main duties was to assist the management in maintaining control and good conduct.

The National Assistance Board, it should be noted, is charged with a duty to provide free lodging to those in need, and may therefore direct " those without a settled way of life " to a Reception Centre.[1] In Edinburgh, the Salvation Army act as agents for the Board in this respect. In addition, the Salvation Army often give free lodging to others, either on their own initiative, or on the recommendation of other social agencies. Their records did not distinguish between the two types of free bed, but during 1958, they provided an average of 10·3 free places for men and 2·8 for women each night. In addition, all those (presumed to have a " settled way of life ") who were in receipt of National Assistance will have had their bed paid for by public funds. On 1st July, 1959, no fewer than 406

[1] National Assistance Act 1948, Sections 17–20.

men and 96 women were in this position, representing 55 per cent of the men and 65 per cent of the women in the Lodging Houses on that night.

An interesting census was taken of all those using the Edinburgh Lodging Houses on 1st July, 1959, and the records were then studied carefully to see how many had been at the same address 18 months previously, that is on New Year's Day of 1958. (An 18 month period was chosen to avoid counting regular seasonal migrants as static. A further check showed that some of those who were present on both dates had been away for a period in between, but no attempt was made to distinguish between the truly static and those who went away for a " holiday "). It was found that 48 per cent of the men and 58 per cent of the women were static—that is, they were present at the same address on both dates. In both sexes the older age-groups included a higher proportion of static lodgers (67 per cent of men over 65 and 72 per cent of women over 60).[1]

The census records were also marked with the Keepers' comments as to the individual's estimated age, and whether or not the lodger was thought to have worked during the previous week. Where they were thought not to have worked, the Keepers were asked whether or not the lodger was thought to be sick or disabled (whether physically or mentally). All those not so accounted for were deemed to be unemployed. Where possible, the estimates of age were checked against medical records held at the Livingstone House Dispensary and it was found that the average discrepancy was less than two years.

It was also found that 64 per cent of the men under 65 (and 16 per cent of those over 65) were thought to be doing any work, whereas only 38 per cent of the women under 60 (and 7 per cent of those over 60) were thought to be working. Of the remainder, 12 per cent of the men and 28 per cent of the women under retiring age were thought to be sick or disabled, leaving 24 per cent of the men and 34 per cent of the women able-bodied and unemployed.

The age structure of this population was as follows. Less than 8 per cent of the men were under 35; 63 per cent were between 35 and 65—in an even distribution over the age range; a further 23 per cent were between 65 and 75; and about 6 per cent were over 75.[2] As regards women, less than 8 per cent were under 35, but only 51 per cent were between 35 and 65—42 per cent of these were between 35 and 60, and of these the great majority were over 45—a further 21 per cent were between 65 and 75, and 19 per cent were over 75.

The medical records at Livingstone House Dispensary were examined at the same time, and all those giving lodging house addresses were studied to see to what extent they used the medical services. Records for 522 men and 153 women were found. The distribution between the different lodging houses was uneven, a greater proportion coming from

[1] The different ages were chosen, since they are the ages when a person first becomes eligible for an Old Age Pension.

[2] A well-known Edinburgh social worker says of these figures that the men under 35 in the lodging houses tend to be more mobile and the numbers therefore are higher than the percentage indicates.

those nearest to the Dispensary. It was also found that the records included a disproportionate number of elderly people. This may have been due to either a greater need for medical help, leading to greater readiness to register, or to the higher proportion of " static " lodgers among the elderly, so that more were present in the area long enough to consider registering with a doctor. Of the patients so registered, 59 per cent of each sex used the Dispensary during 1958. It was not however clear how far the 41 per cent who did not use the Dispensary during the year were " at risk," since they may have included a large number of " mobile " lodgers. Nor, since the introduction of the National Health Service and the abolition of the post of Parish Doctor, did there appear to be any doctor in a given area, specifically charged with the duty of attending those who are not registered with a medical practitioner. At least two of the Lodging Houses, therefore, paid a small honorarium to a doctor for the right to call upon him in an emergency. This right has seldom been exercised.

Here we must look ahead to 1963 when two prominent Edinburgh journalists with intimate knowledge of the city had another look at model lodging houses in the Grassmarket and adjoining streets.

Castle Trades Hotel, 75 Grassmarket, apparently can accommodate 300 men, and has an average of 288 lodgers nightly throughout the year. These usually book their accommodation by the week at 19*s.* 3*d.* But some transients book for the night at 3*s.*, and there are a few places at £1 2*s.* 6*d.* a week, which are not let at nightly rates. The men cook for themselves, with pots and pans supplied. Cooking is done on a hotplate. Locker and room keys are held by the lodgers on a deposit of 2*s.* 6*d.* for the locker and 2*s.* for the room key: the deposit money is returned on surrender of the key, less 6*d.* in each case. There are also baths and toilet facilities, reading room with television, dining accommodation and a store for the supply of food for cash, or in exchange for chits from the National Assistance or from the Grassmarket Mission, which frequently gives assistance to wayfarers seeking shelter.

Almost in the Grassmarket is the Greyfriars Hotel, No. 2 Cowgate. This establishment, which also has key deposits—3*s.* for the Yale key and 2*s.* 6*d.* for the locker key—accommodates about 150 men at weekly rates of £1 2*s.* 6*d.* (double room) and £1 3*s.* (single). Rooms are usually booked weekly, payment in advance.

Lodgers in the Greyfriars Hotel have meals cooked for them. But in the Victoria Hostel for Men, West Port, which accommodates up to 60 at 12*s.* 6*d.* a week or 3*s.* a night, the men cook for themselves, as in the Castle Trades Hotel, on the hotplate. There is also the Edinburgh Coffee House, Blair Street, almost opposite the Tron Kirk, which furnishes about 80 lodgers with electric light, chair, bed and chest of drawers at prices ranging from 17*s.* 6*d.* to £1 a week.

The Salvation Army provides food and shelter for both men and women, and at the time of inquiry in October, 1963 was preparing accommodation for children at its women's hostel. The men's hostel—in the Pleasance at the corner of Cowgate—accommodated 106 men at

4*s*. 6*d*. a night, or £1 11*s*. 6*d*. a week, including breakfast. The women's hostel at the corner of the Vennel and the Grassmarket had sleeping accommodation for 100 women, but this by 1963 had been reduced to 60 in order to adapt the rooms to accommodate children. The charges for women were: dormitory, 17*s*. 6*d*. a week or 3*s*. 6*d*. a night, and cubicle beds £1 1*s*. a week or 4*s*. 6*d*. a night.

Between 70 and 75 men are also given shelter by the Episcopal Church in Scotland at its Broughton Place hostel, the weekly charge being 17*s*. (dormitory) or £1 (cubicles). The men have facilities for cooking; T.V. and central heating are included among the amenities; the hostel accepts men of all demominations.

These men's hostels have a heterogeneous and constantly changing population. There is a tendency in the city to assume that they are for the " down and outs." But in fact, their residents and transients range from young labourers to old age pensioners, bachelors, widowers and men estranged from their wives and families. As Edinburgh has always had an attraction for itinerants, " worthies " and " characters," this class, which includes men of all shades of personality from sturdy independence to sheer fecklessness, is naturally represented among those who drift in and out of these hostels. Tramps, tinkers, beggars and buskers head for the area, especially as winter sets in, to mix with " winos," " jake-drinkers," and occasional " beatniks "; and these again in company with the workshy, the delinquent, the degenerate and the weak-minded, tend to gravitate to the Grassmarket and give its Bowfoot end, in particular, some of its air of picturesque squalor. Yet it would be quite wrong to assume that these typify the men who make use of lodging house accommodation.

There are many honest, hard-working people, and earnest strugglers for a decent living, among the " Grassmarket modellers." Furthermore the regulations of the establishments are designed to keep out intoxicating liquors and keep down swearing, gambling and disorderly conduct. Provision is also made for the reporting of illness or trouble, and, as we saw, the hygiene of these places is supervised by the public health authorities. But admittedly they have their shortcomings. There is no way of guaranteeing, for instance, that the men feed themselves adequately. Tea seems to be the staple diet, and it is probable that many of the residents in these hostels are living below a proper standard of subsistence.

ROOM AT THE BOTTOM

Elsewhere in the city there are still houses with rooms so damp that furniture has to be stored in a room unfit for habitation, whilst the entire family of parents and children live, sleep, eat and wash in one small room. Other homes are in the basements, consisting again of one unusable room, one windowless cupboard into which a bed can be put, but where the only tap is out in a stone corridor used by all the basement tenants. Here again all generations and sexes sleep together. In yet other houses, families live up five flights of stairs—in areas where there is no front door on to the street to guard against late-night brawlers, and the vomits of alcoholics on the stair have to be washed away on Sunday morning, as well as the removal of odours resulting from the use of the stair as a passing urinal. Moreover the stair is so dark that it presents real fear to children who have to negotiate it before they reach home.

There are still families who sleep top-to-tail in a bed, with parents and children all jumbled up. In many instances the crowding of people and furniture is so great that it is barely possible to make a passageway between furniture, and there is certainly no space in which growing children may play. This, when the house is in a traffic-filled section of the town, is particularly restrictive as careful parents fear to let their children out to the pavements. So quite a lot of Edinburgh children have been growing up in primitive conditions. These children in the slum areas have been witness to every relationship between husband and wife—the arguments, the drunken brawls, the demonstration of affection and the intimacies of illness. Forced into such close proximity, it is little wonder that tensions rise and latent neuroses flourish among many of the under-privileged citizens, or that families striving to maintain the essentials of decency have insufficient energy left over for sensitivity and gentleness, to give the children they produce a less tortuous future. Fortunately much of this very real problem is being resolved by the clearance of slums, the building of the housing estates which have taken their place, though these have their own problems, and by the welfare organisations.

THE HOUSING ESTATES

Socially the movement of people from the centre of the city to the new housing estates during the last few decades has been one of the most significant developments in Edinburgh's history. Before 1939 some of the estates were developed by private firms, and others by the Corporation. The former consisted of some houses for sale, and quite a number to rent at a figure which at the time often seemed rather high for a manual worker. As the occupants differed from each other according to the price of their houses, people of different economic status tended to separate themselves from one another. The Corporation, for the most part, provided homes for those who were overcrowded or whose homes were due to be demolished because they were classed as " slums."

During the war house building stopped; and for several years afterwards only the Corporation could build houses, with the result that a far wider range of the population moved into corporation estates than before the war. Later, when private building was allowed, there was a movement out of corporation houses into privately owned houses by those on a higher economic level. But as the cost of building continually rose, rents of houses in post-war Corporation estates were much higher than those built before 1939. Finally, the Corporation decided to raise the rents of pre-1939 houses by different amounts for different estates. Thus by 1960 different Corporation estates had houses with different rents, and not surprisingly each developed characteristics of its own. By the early '60s society in the new housing areas was stratified. But also during the same period there have been a great many signs in Corporation estates of a much higher standard of material prosperity. Whereas in 1950 few cars were seen standing in the streets, by 1960 garages were being provided in the newer estates; the streets were acting as garages in the older ones; and the process of acquiring a car had assumed such momentum that by 1963 it was estimated that one family in five in Corporation housing schemes had cars, and that very shortly the figure would be one in three. Then again, in 1950 few went abroad for their holidays. Ten years later ministers of religion and other public persons were kept busy signing passport photographs for those whose children had grown up, or for young people in their teens, who were going abroad for their summer holiday. In 1950 house floors in the poorer estates were normally covered by linoleum; by 1960 there were carpets in the living room. In 1950 again, some of the church weddings were quiet, with only the bride and bridegroom present and their two witnesses; by 1960 a wedding in church almost always meant a large number of friends present who were subsequently transported to the reception in buses hired from the Corporation's Transport Department or from one of the Co-operative Societies. All these are signs of an increasing material prosperity. Nevertheless within the more general prosperity there are considerable financial stresses in many families.

There are four groups of people who have found living very hard in the '60s. Firstly, there are retired men and women who are living on their pensions. Some draw extra pensions from their work, but this is the exception rather than the rule. A man can still retire from a firm having faithfully served it for many years, to be presented with a small gift and that is all. From then onwards he must depend on the national old age pension. It is true that this pension can be assisted by payments from the National Assistance Board, whose officers face a very difficult task, but who in most cases administer the regulations with humanity.

Secondly, there are families of manual workers earning a low wage, who, if there are a large number of children in their family, find living very difficult. Father tries to get as much overtime as he can, and mother frequently goes out to work. If she does so she is usually responsible in the kind of work that she undertakes. She may find work in the evening so that the children can be left with father after he returns from work; or she may go out to a part-time job either when the children are at school, or a relative, perhaps a neighbour, agrees to look after the children while the mother is away. The Corporation has provided fifteen day nurseries for children under school age, but places in them are in great demand.

A third category of home where there is great hardship is the one where the breadwinner is unable to work or is only fit for light work. When strength has been taken away by illness society has little material reward to offer him for the light manual work he is able to undertake.

Finally, there are some real problem families. Usually the parents are of low intelligence, often with a large number of children, and poor in physique and health. In such families the father rarely works, and year after year they live on money provided by the National Assistance Board. These families are usually very difficult to help. But a great many of them are visited by many social and other professional workers from statutory and voluntary agencies who at times offer contradictory advice, though efforts are now being made to co-ordinate their work.

The difficulty of living in these estates is increased by the fact that the rent of houses is higher than in the older parts of the city, and that considerable money has to be spent each week on the wage earner travelling to his work. The lack of competition between the few estate shops means also that prices are often higher than in shops in the centre of the city. Thus in some ways families in distress had an even harder time in 1960 than they did in 1950 as the greater prosperity of the majority tended to show up more clearly the poverty of the minority. But the internal life of the family is certainly as strong as it was 20 years ago. Wives are more likely to know what their husbands earn; and he for his part is more likely to share in household duties and to take responsibility for the upbringing of the children. More money appears to be spent on the upkeep and furnishing of the home.

COMMUNITY LIFE

There is comparatively little large scale community life on the estates. On the other hand most women have a circle of friends whom they know. On marriage there are still a considerable number of couples who live near their parents, and who therefore still share a community life within their families and amongst their friends of childhood. In many estates there is a shortage of shops and therefore innumerable vans go round selling all kinds of food. They stop as they go down the road, and give an opportunity for neighbours not only to purchase goods but also to meet one another. Women thus tend to know their immediate neighbours but not those who live on the estate as a whole. Men on the other hand know very few in the district where they live. After a day's work a great many are ready to spend the evening watching television at home.

There are few public buildings where people can meet. The most prominent buildings are the local schools, whose halls can be used at night without charge by any organisation for youth activities, and for adult activities in return for payment of a fee. A few adult groups meet in these halls at night either under the aegis of the Corporation's Education Committee to share in some organised class, or as a club; but the number of adults who share in these activities apart from further education is small. Shortly after 1946 the Corporation did try to encourage community associations in every large area. These associations normally thrived for a few years and then gradually lost their original impetus. Their success at the start was assisted by the fact that when an estate was first built they had work they could do. New estates lacked public facilities such as post offices, and community organisations could therefore press with vigour for provision of such amenities. As long as they thrived, these organisations were also able to organise picnics for the children in the summer and entertainments in the winter. But the numbers of active members gradually dwindled.

The Corporation at one time did not allow public houses to be built on its estates, but later this policy was changed. Since then roadhouses have been built in many of them, and where they have been built they are the places where the greatest number of adult residents meet. The only other significant buildings are the churches.

There are some groups which do thrive. Clubs for old people are well patronised. These are either branches of the Old People's Welfare Council or of the Old Age Pensioners' Association. They normally meet once a week, very often in a church hall, and provide the highlight in the week for the old age pensioner. Women's Guilds also meet regularly every week, being connected either with the Churches, the Co-operative movement or with the Community Associations. However, only a comparatively small number of women belong to such organisations; and of those who do, many belong to more than one.

The home—in districts like this where there is little large scale community life—is more important than it has ever been. An increasing pride is taken in its appearance and comfort. Home decorating and improvement takes up much time. Many men work late two nights a week, and women go out to work as well, so that couples are very ready to spend a night at home. In addition television means that entertainment can be shared without the trouble of a bus journey into the centre of the town.

Normally the families which move into these estates have young children, and the families continue to grow for a few years. Then inevitably the number of children drops, though with the continual movement of population families with young children are moving into the estates all the time. The Corporation has provided large open spaces in which children can play, but they prefer to play in the streets where they live rather than these open spaces perhaps only 50 yards away. Compared with the centre of the town, where there are brighter street lights and shops with exciting things to look at, the streets are dull and unexciting. There are fewer churches and public buildings per child, and therefore there are fewer clubs and youth organisations which they can attend. It is not surprising that many get into mischief. They start to grow up much younger, and some from the age of 12 attend sessions for dancing at a public dance hall in the centre of the city. As they reach their teens it is to dance halls, coffee bars and cinemas in the city centre to which they go for entertainment. A high proportion of children in the estates finish their schooling at the age of 15; and it is in fact quite hard for them to remain after that age. The majority of their friends have left school and are allowed to keep far more pocket money from their earnings than they could be given if they remained at school. Their friends also enjoy the enhanced status of wage earners, and they themselves usually realise that their own parents are making financial sacrifices to keep them at school. It is of course true that in those Corporation estates where there are higher numbers staying on for a full secondary course the pressure to leave is correspondingly less. The children who do leave school at 15 or 16 to become apprentices attend night school for several nights a week, and have therefore little spare time left on their hands.

OTHER CAUSES OF SOCIAL DISTRESS

More can be added to this ministerial view from the experience of a leading social worker who chooses housing and debt as the two main contributory causes of social distress in the city today. Unerringly, she too picks young marriages as a frequent cause of upset, and many of her findings apply not only to the housing estates but to other parts.

The earlier maturity of young people, she says, together with the high rate of employment and consequent prosperity lead naturally to earlier marriage. It is not possible for young married couples always to find rooms and to live on their own instead of with in-laws. It is extremely difficult to find unfurnished rooms and furnished rooms are costly. The arrival of children increases their difficulties. There can be great distress and hardship for young couples in these circumstances as well as for their elders, and, though housing is only one aspect of a social problem, it leads to many others.

The emotional stress of wanting a family but being afraid to have one can lead to quarrels and estrangement; living in someone else's house is rarely easy; trying to bring up children with grandparents or perhaps other people interfering leads to further conflict; and finally there is the difficulty, when a house is at last obtained, of starting a home of their own after, in some cases, many years of marriage, and of maintaining the standard of life to which the family has become accustomed.

The families who live with their in-laws or who are overcrowded in their own homes—which may consist of a single room and kitchen or a room with a bed recess—often have problems resulting directly from their overcrowded conditions. Such premises are often in poor repair, and involve sharing lavatories and carrying water. For example, in one such family where there were three children, the man on permanent nightshift had to sleep during the day. The wife was always on edge in case the children made too much noise and wakened him, while he was all too often disturbed and consequently was usually irritable and ill humoured. This situation became so serious that marital relations were strained to breaking point and the children were inevitably affected by the quarrels and tensions in the home.

Lastly, there is the housing problem of the elderly or old people. For some old people an independent life is impossible simply because they live three or four storeys up, possibly up a steep stair which often has well-worn treads. These are deterrents which can prevent an old person from shopping or joining in any social acitivities.

The obvious lessons have not been fully learned from these experiences. The creation of social problems continues and is now illustrated by the incidence of difficulties experienced by tenants living in high blocks of flats. Rents are often higher than the tenants can really afford, heating is usually wholly by electricity, play spaces for young children are few and not in the right places, shopping facilities are poor. These high flats have a large proportion of very young families living in them, and though the tenants want and like the attractive accommodation, they frequently find the attendant difficulties overwhelming.

THE PROBLEM OF DEBT

It is also unfortunate that many families fall into debt. The reasons for this seem obvious enough. When the first baby arrives in a home the mother has to face a sudden drop in income. Before her marriage she has been used to spending a considerable amount of money on herself. In the first stage of marriage there have been two incomes coming into the home. Suddenly there is only one wage at the very time when there is additional expenditure on account of the baby. Such a situation is not difficult to face if the family is established in a home before the baby arrives; but only too often a family moves into a new home with few resources behind them. Hire purchase firms provide a real service to many by enabling them to buy furniture over a period which they would be unable to do otherwise, but many people are persuaded to buy more articles than they can really afford. Salesmen selling a wide range of goods descend on the housing estates, especially just after they have been newly occupied, to persuade the tenants to buy not only durable articles but also soft goods, which may wear out before they have been fully paid up, Unless a mother is strong minded she finds it difficult to resist the pressures to buy which are put upon her. Debt mounts up, and the mother becomes more and more worried. A considerable part of soical workers' time may be taken up by helping women to organise their finances, so that debt may be cleared. This problem is not widespread, but it is assuredly a formidable factor in the life of some homes in the housing estates. Debt is often a cause of family discord and often leads to eviction or threatened eviction, or to curtailment of wages.

The habit of spending freely frequently begins without thought when boys and girls start work. Some hand over their wages to their parents and are given back, say, 10*s*. for pocket money. This arrangement appears to take place during the first year of the boy's or girl's working life. After that they give so much for their board, say from 20*s*. to 30*s*. a week, and out of the balance they buy their amusements and " clothe themselves ", as many parents express it. Some buy their clothing cash down; others join the Family Club, each paying for their own share. The habit of buying their own clothes is one which appears to have changed considerably during the last 15 years or so. Previously the mother often bought the clothing for her family, even for her sons, no matter what their age, as long as they remained at home—though of course more money was then handed over than in homes where board alone was charged. In the 1920–39 period, the custom in Edinburgh was usually to hand over the full wage and be given back a matter of shillings up till the time a man's wage was earned.

Today it is not uncommon for wage earners between the ages of 16 and 18 to have as much as £2 or more a week pocket money, after paying for their board and for their clothing. There is no difficulty in getting rid of the money. Despite television, the young spend their evenings far less frequently at home than formerly, with the result that money is required to pay for entertainment, and in instances where boys crave for further pleasures beyond their purse, this can be a factor in delinquency.

The habit of over-free spending has unfortunate results after marriage, when perhaps both husband and wife have little idea of budgeting. Discord begins when the family starts: the wife has to give up work and the husband does not want to give up any of his pocket money. Quite often a young wife has remarked of her husband, " he should never have married but remained single and enjoyed himself with his money." Later, when the young couple perhaps move into a home for the first time, a complete change of the pattern of living is frequently attempted—by hire purchase.

Rents, larger than those to which they were accustomed, are a frequent stumbling block; and this often becomes a more formidable obstacle because of lack of co-operation between husband and wife. Many men hand over part of their pay packet (having kept a share for their own entertainment), and from that part everything has to be paid. How £8, for example, is to be stretched to do the work of £12 does not seem to enter into the wage earner's head—nor does he measure his spending money with his wife's lack of it. In these families, as a rule, the man does not ask to see the rent book, and arrears are often concealed from him—with dire results later.

BETTING AND GAMBLING

When future historians turn back to investigate Edinburgh's life in mid-20th century they will doubtless note a spectacular growth of the gambling habit. Indeed with the rise of the football pools, bingo, and more recently the betting shops, its popularity places it inevitably in the sphere of favourite pastimes.

The 1960 Betting and Gambling Act was merely a legislative measure which recognised and was designed to control, as far as humanly possible, this far-reaching influence on our way of life. Generally it was recognised that since vast sums were being spent yearly on mass gambling in the United Kingdom there should be some attempt to supervise what was becoming in effect an enormously lucrative industry.

It is noteworthy too that police chiefs, more familiar than most with the social evils and distress following in the wake of the gambling mania, favoured an Act that would confine betting and gambling to channels more easily controlled than the hole-and-corner street betting and illegal gaming houses. Their contention—in Edinburgh as elsewhere—was that very large police forces would be required to make any impression upon the street gambling traffic, and that sufficient manpower could not be released without detriment to other police duties.

With the Act in force, the street bookmaker, or runner, who conducted business on the pavement, and whose activities monopolised an undue proportion of time in the courts, disappeared overnight. In his place came the betting shops with their frosted glass windows providing privacy from the curious passer-by. These multiplied so rapidly that by the autumn of 1963 Edinburgh had 191 betting shops or offices officially recognised and controlled by the Licensing Department of the City Police; and this was merely one minor aspect of the situation. Proprietors of cinemas and dance halls that were feeling the effects of rapidly changing leisure-time habits felt encouraged by the improved financial status of the masses, and were quick to seize the new oportunities provided by the law. Hence the appearance of the game of chance known as bingo in a number of well-known places of entertainment in Edinburgh, Leith and Portobello, including even the Empire Theatre.

There were soon such long queues of men and women, with women often in the majority, forming up for admission to the new Bingo Halls that the proprietors' chief problem was no longer lack of support but how to limit numbers. One bingo club in Edinburgh claimed 38,000 members. Another of the larger establishments, with playing sessions on seven nights of the week, paid out a total approaching £4,000 in prize-money and " bonuses " during one week. Bus parties from the surrounding areas helped to swell the attendances.

Another striking development in the early '60s was the opening of gaming clubs offering forms of gambling hitherto provided only in Continental casinos. Chemin de fer, roulette, faro and poker were soon attracting hundreds of devotees to these clubs, and there are also facilities for the playing of games described as " Straight dice ", " American dice " and " poker dice."

By 1964, however, the number of these clubs, for which the only kind of permission required is planning permission, and the unsavoury nature of some of them, was causing widespread concern. In the previous year or two there had been a number of incidents, and as these included assault by stabbing, suspected intimidation, arson—eight fires in two years—and other forms of violence, there could be no doubt that in some clubs an ugly element of gangsterism was at work.

As for football pools, says a social worker of great experience, a large majority of people in Edinburgh go in for football pools, including many women. Though with some people this is looked upon partly as a hobby, there seems little doubt that pools and bingo are less harmful financially than other forms of betting, since a fixed amount is usually set aside weekly for this purpose; and many women look on an afternoon bingo session as something of a social occasion.

VANDALISM

Vandalism, which we studied earlier in its legal rather than its social setting, is one of the problems presented by the younger members of society; and Scotland, in common with many other parts of Great

Britain and, indeed most other countries, suffered in the '60s from an upsurge of vandalism. The main targets in Edinburgh were schools.

The effects of all this have been far-reaching. In 1962 the damage caused by the young thugs concerned came to something like £40,000, equivalent to another penny on the rates. To make matters worse, owners of buildings where windows have been frequently smashed cannot any longer persuade insurance companies to insure them. Telephone kiosks, gas lamps, motor cars and railway trains have been persistent targets.

Towards the end of 1961 throwing of stones at trains and damage to railway property generally in the Edinburgh area had in fact become so serious that British Railways asked the education authorities to warn children how dangerous these can be. During one month, it was pointed out, stones thrown at trains in Edinburgh had not only seriously injured a guard but caused injury to three passengers, and shock to several others. These human injuries were bad enough. But there was also damage to locomotives and signal boxes which might have led to terrible disasters. On several occasions drivers and firemen narrowly escaped injury from missiles which shattered indicator panels on diesel trains and the driving windows of steam locomotives. It was hardly surprising that Dr. George Reith, the new Director of Education for Edinburgh, assured British Railways that he would do everything in his power to assist the railway authorities.

CHAPTER 20

CARING FOR THE COMMUNITY

WHEREVER there are people there are problems; and wherever there are problems, there are services and societies which try to solve or alleviate them. And so against the ever-changing background of the conditions we have just studied a great deal of valuable work is done by those concerned with social welfare. Some are chiefly engaged in work for the voluntary welfare societies and others with the statutory social services. But there are voluntary workers in both statutory and voluntary institutions, and paid workers are employed by quite a large number of voluntary organisations. The statutory social services of Edinburgh may be divided into:

THE STATUTORY SOCIAL SERVICES

(1) the Central Government services located in the city—the National Assistance Board, the Ministry of National Insurance and the Ministry of Labour;

(2) the Local Authority services—the City Social Services Department, the Child Care Department, and the social welfare activities of the Health, Education and Housing Departments.

THE RELIEF OF DESTITUTION

It might be appropriate here before looking at this far-reaching social welfare work to summarise briefly the history of the Scottish Poor Law from 1845 until its demise in 1948, so that the progress towards larger administrative units and greater humanity especially in the relief of destitition may be better understood. In the 19th century in Scotland, as in England, the Poor Law was virtually the only social service. The Scottish Poor Law of 1845 established centrally the Board of Supervision (later the Local Government Board and the Scottish Board of Health) to deal with all matters relating to the relief of the poor. The local unit of relief was the parochial board and its officer, the Inspector of Poor, had a duty to relieve the destitute young, aged and infirm till in 1894 the parochial board became the parish council. Later still, in 1929, the Local Government (Scotland) Act transferred its duties to the town and county councils.

To go back to the last century the emphasis in Scotland then was on outdoor relief; but parishes with a population of over 5,000 were authorised to build a poorhouse for " such as were aged and friendless and unable to attend to their cleanliness and comfort as well as for such poor persons who, on account of weakness of facility of mind or by reason of dissipated habits, were unable or unfit to take charge of their own affairs." Provisions were also made for vagrants. Poor persons who were refused relief had a right of appeal to the Sheriff and Board of Supervision, an advance in itself on the English Poor Law which allowed paupers no such rights. In the early years of the 1845 Poor Law they had, however, no other safeguards, and the stringent economy with which the law was at first administered deprived them of the last shreds of dignity. As for the pauper who had not achieved a residential qualification he could be removed to his parish of settlement. Wife desertion and refusal to maintain illegitimate children were criminal offences. It was also customary at the time to affix the lists of paupers to the notice board of the parish church, but the economies demanded by the first World War brought this degrading practice to an end; and by the turn of the century the treatment of paupers in any event had already become more humane, and the administration of the Poor Law was carried out with increasing understanding and sympathy until its repeal in 1948.

Outdoor relief—" needful sustentation "—was sufficient to cover bare necessities, but the Inspector of Poor had certain powers of discretion. Relief, however, was reserved only for the destitute old, young and unfit; the able-bodied unemployed had no title to assistance and in bad times were dependent on charity. Despite a ruling of the House of Lords which affirmed this, the Board of Supervision held that if an able-bodied man were really destitute he would become disabled through want of food, and the Board advised the Inspectors of the Poor that " it would probably be a safe rule of practice in such cases to afford immediate relief if the Inspector is of opinion that the Sheriff on appeal would order it." In the outcome the moralistic view that the able-bodied pauper was responsible for his own plight existed in Scotland until the depression which followed the first World War. But in the meantime the 1911 national insurance legislation gave some workers protection against short-term loss of earnings through sickness or unemployment but offered no defence against long-term unemployment or illness. While dependants were included in unemployment insurance, there was also no provision under National Health Insurance for the wife and children of the sick working man. By the Poor Law Emergency Provisions (Scotland) Act, 1921, however, the able-bodied pauper became eligible to receive assistance, if he could satisfy the Parish Council that he was destitute and unable to obtain employment. A further advance was made in 1927 when it became legal for the Parish Councils to give relief to the dependants of persons involved in a trade dispute.

By the 1931 National Economy Act, brought in at a time of acute industrial depression, local authorities were required to impose a means test on all persons who had exhausted their title to unemployment benefit. The scale of assistance was the same as the Poor Law scale for destitute able-bodied persons, and the cost of such assistance was met by the Exchequer, not by the local authority. To the unemployed man who until the depression had had reasonable security of employment, this association with the Poor Law was indeed bitter, nor did the officials applying the means test find the task a pleasant one. However, in 1934 the Unemployment Assistance Act ensured that persons between 16 and 65, who were capable of and available for work and who normally followed insurable employment became the responsibility not of the local authorities but of the Government, and received their allowances from the local office of the Unemployment Assistance Board. On the other hand those unemployed who had no insurable occupation (such as the self-employed and casual workers) continued to receive relief from the Public Assistance Committees of the local authorities until 1948. Edinburgh meanwhile—in 1943—adopted the Assistance Board scales of relief in an effort to improve the conditions of those receipients who, despite the opportunities of work created by the war, were unable to maintain themselves. The following figures show the effect, in Edinburgh, of the depressions of the '20s and '30s and the change to full employment during the second World War:

Number of able-bodied recipients on a given day in		1926 —	3,595
do	do	1930 —	1,796
do	do	1938 —	900
do	do	1941 —	638
do at 15th December		1942 —	44

Since the implementation of the National Assistance Act in 1948, no financial assistance is given by the local authority. The main functions of the Social Services Department are therefore the provision of residential accommodation for the elderly and infirm and the welfare of handicapped persons with substantial permanent disability.

FROM POORHOUSE TO PART III ACCOMMODATION

While the emphasis in the Scottish Poor Law of 1845 was on outdoor relief, some provision had to be made for poor people who were aged and friendless and for those who through " dissipated, improvident and immoral habits had forfeited the right to outdoor relief "; so in 1844 Edinburgh had a Charity Workhouse which accommodated about 600 adults and 480 children. But admission to the poorhouse was looked upon as a disgrace by the working man and his family, and memories of the bad old days still colour the attitude of many elderly towards the City's home for old people at Greenlea.

Although conditions in the Poorhouse gradually improved, as late as 1892 the diet was as follows:

Breakfast	Meal, three ounces; milk, half-pint imperial.
Dinner	Bread, six ounces; broth, one-and-a-half pints imperial.
Supper	Meal, three ounces; milk, half-pint imperial.

Substitutes for broth were pea soup (not more than three times a week); eight ounces of white fish (not more than twice a week); and for the bread and broth (not more than twice a week) one-and-a-half pounds of boiled potatoes with three-fourths of a pint of imperial skimmed milk.

While the residential treatment of the destitute and the old improved slowly but steadily during the first half of the present century, it is worth recalling again that it was not until 1948 that the Poor Law was finally buried. Under Part III of the National Assistance Act, the local authority still had a duty to provide residential accommodation for the old and infirm. And today in Edinburgh this consists of one large institution, Greenlea, (the former poorhouse) and four small homes, Firrhill, Edinholme, Craigard, Silverlea (opened in January, 1963) and a holiday home, The Abbey, North Berwick, which was opened in 1960, with accommodation for 26 men and women, to provide the old folks with short holidays outside the city. In addition, the local authority may arrange to pay for the maintenance of old people in homes run by voluntary organisations. In 1963 approximately 300 old people in 44 voluntary homes were assisted in this way.

Greenlea is a large institution in semi-rural surroundings, which with some 500 residents has more accommodation for women than men. Some residents pay the whole cost of maintenance, but as these words are written the majority contribute their retirement pensions less 13*s.* 6*d.* a week which they retain for pocket money. In place of the old open dormitories with their complete lack of privacy, so daunting to an old person accustomed to her own home, the old ladies are now in attractive one, two or three-bedded cubicles, furnished with individual dressing tables and wardrobes for their clothes and space for personal nick-nacks, and with rugs, bright curtains and counterpanes.

A praiseworthy attempt was also being made in 1963 to divide the old people into the smaller groups according to mobility, interests and personal and social habits. While the sexes are segregated, men and women may visit each other if they wish to do so. Occasionally, married couples are admitted to Greenlea, but owing to the Home Help and Meals on Wheels services given in their own homes this is becoming infrequent.

It is the intention of the Act that Part III Accommodation should be a real substitute for home life. With this aim, various facilities are provided in Greenlea—television, radio, entertainments, outings, bowling and putting, books and periodicals, a shop and a hairdresser—and to try and make their life more pleasant still, groups of old people are adopted by the Guilds of different churches, and have outings and entertainments organised for them by the Guild members.

Another significant feature of life in this Home is that those in the diversional therapy room are markedly more interested and alert than those in the other dayrooms, and more are taking part with the appointment of two occupational therapists for Greenlea and the other smaller homes. But perhaps we should remember here that as community services enable old people to remain longer at home, they are consequently frailer on admission and less able to take part in diversionary therapy; for many of the new admissions have already reached an apathy of old age which can rob the final years of any meaning. The cost of maintaining a resident in Greenlea in 1963 was £7 3*s.* 0*d.* a week.

The small homes are in marked contrast to Greenlea and at once the superiority of the small unit is evident. Firrhill has accommodation for 16 men; Edinholme takes 19 women, Craigard 22 women, and the new home, Silverlea, 54 men or women, with the number of each varying according to the need of the moment. This last home has been specially built to meet the requirements of old people in the light of present day standards, and has 21 single, 9 double and 5 three-bedded rooms, ample sitting accommodation, and a sick bay with 6 beds. These men and women, although the average age is over 78 years, nevertheless form a fitter and more active group: some who go out shopping and visit their friends are certainly more interested in each other and in daily events, and altogether they give the impression of more active enjoyment of life.

TEMPORARY ACCOMMODATION

Under the National Assistance Act the City is required to provide temporary accommodation " for persons in urgent need thereof by reason of circumstances which could not reasonably have been foreseen." This provision is intended primarily to meet emergencies caused by fire and flood, or by old buildings suddenly becoming unsafe. In addition accommodation is provided for wives and children (fathers are not admitted) in families which have become homeless for a variety of reasons, most of them not strictly unforeseen. In 1962 accommodation was provided for 40 women and 123 children in the emergency accommodation in Greenlea and plans were being made for this to be provided elsewhere. But complete families (including the father) who are in need of emergency accommodation are housed in Coillesdene, Duddingston and in the former army married quarters in Johnston Terrace. Where families have been evicted because of rent arrears they are not rehoused in Corporation housing until the arrears have been cleared.

WELFARE OF THE HANDICAPPED

The local authority has power to make arrangements for promoting the welfare of persons who are blind, deaf or dumb, and other persons who are substantially and permanently handicapped by illness, injury or congenital deformity. At present such powers are mandatory only in respect of blind persons; powers to promote the welfare of other categories of handicapped are permissive. The City carries out its duties in respect of the blind by arrangements with the Society for the Welfare and Teaching of the Blind, to which it pays a capitation fee of £7 10*s*. a year for each person on the Society's roll. At the end of May, 1962 there were 1,206 blind persons on the register. Home teachers employed by the Society teach Braille and Moon, instruct in handicrafts and help with various personal problems. In 1962 the Corporation assisted 88 persons employed in the Royal Blind Asylum. The City also pays the Royal Blind Asylum £350 per worker per year, £240 of which is recoverable from the Ministry of Labour. Special travel concessions are available for the blind (and for disabled ex-service men) at a cost, in 1962, of over £11,000.

In another field of disability a *per capita* grant of £3 is made to the Edinburgh Deaf and Dumb Society which also provides services on behalf of the Corporation to 344 persons.

The service of " Meals on Wheels " is operated by the W.V.S. Meals are prepared in Greenlea at a cost to the old people of 10*d.* for a two course meal: the balance is paid by the Social Services Department. The Corporation also provides meals for the Lunch Clubs for Old People in the city through the schools meals service.

Other duties of the Social Services Department under the National Assistance Act include registration and inspection of homes for disabled persons and old people; the protection of property of persons admitted to hospital; and the making of arrangements for burial or cremation where there is no relative to do so.

Certain charitable funds are administered by the Corporation. These include the Trinity Hospital Fund, which dates from 1450. The capital of this Fund now amounts to over half a million pounds, from which pensions are paid to over 700 old people. There are various smaller mortifications and bequests, benefiting another 170 or so old persons.

CHILD CARE SERVICE

CHILDREN WITH NO HOMES OF THEIR OWN

Under the Scottish Poor Law of 1845, a substantial number of poorhouse inmates were children. In Edinburgh, however, the majority of these children were boarded-out, although statutory authority for this was not granted by the Board of Supervision until 1934. The welfare of these children was the responsibility of the Children's Committee, composed of members of the Parish Council, until the Public Assistance Committee took it over in 1930. From then until the Children Act of 1948, this Committee cared for the young and the old. For a time between the wars infants under two years were admitted to Craigleith Poorhouse Hospital (now the Western General Hospital while older children were maintained in Crewe Road Children's Home, situated within the grounds of Craigleith Hospital. Children were also boarded out all over Scotland (particularly in Nairn, Elgin and Aberdeenshire) and a number were maintained in homes run by voluntary organisations. After the War the Corporation bought a number of large houses for conversion as children's homes. There was thus a good deal of accommodation available when the Children Act came into force (1948).

Under this Act the local authority has a duty to set up a children's committee which is responsible for the welfare of children who, for any cause whatsoever, have lost their own homes, either temporarily or permanently.

As at 30th November, 1962 as many as 1,118 children were in the care of the Children Department, 1,035 of whom were under the Children Acts of 1948 and 1958.

Of these
414 were boarded out with foster parents;
165 were in homes belonging to the Corporation;
333 were in homes run by voluntary organisations;
47 older children were in hostels, lodgings or in residential employment;
13 aged over 18 were receiving grants towards education training.

Four children from other areas were also under the supervision of the Children Department; there were 52 Child Protection cases under supervision and 19 children in the Remand Home, while 64 children were under supervision under the Adoption Act of 1958.

Illness of the parent or guardian has accounted for approximately 43 per cent of the children taken into care in the later '50s and early '60s; and over 6 per cent of the children taken into care in 1962 were homeless through the eviction of their families from houses or furnished rooms. Children needing short term care are placed in foster homes whenever possible. But when parents are unwilling that the child should be placed in a foster home, or no appropriate foster home can be found or if he is unsuitable for fostering, he remains in one of the Corporation's homes or is placed in a voluntary home. (332 Edinburgh children were in voluntary homes during the year ending 31st May, 1962).[1]

It is always difficult to staff children's homes and the high turnover among the helpers leads to lack of that continuity which is so important for the well being of children in care. Nevertheless the matrons do all in their power to make the homes friendly and attractive places. In this they are handicapped by the size of the houses: the smallest accommodates 22 children and the largest, 40. Apart from the short-stay children, the majority of the children in the Homes are those who for one reason or another are unsuitable for foster-home placement, and a number of them are retarded in school subjects, or dull and backward, or defective. These children have special coaching in the Craigentinny Annexe, where a ratio of 10 children to one teacher makes individual attention possible. It is foreseen that in the future two of the Canaan Lodge Homes will have to be moved, owing to encroachment on the grounds, and sites have already been found in new housing areas for several new homes, to take 10–15 children each.

While the Children Act makes no mention of the prevention of family breakup, Children's Officers are aware that they are often called in when the situation is irremediable. To deal with this problem Part I, section 1, of the Children and Young Persons Act 1963, legalising preventive action, is to apply to Scotland also and duly came into force in October, 1963. Under this section local authorities will be required to provide

[1] The homes established by the Corporation for children in their care were as follows in 1963: Clerwood, St. Katherine's, Redhall (Colinton) and the Canaan Lodge homes—Deanbank, The Priory, The Lodge.

The age grouping in these homes is elastic. Backward children are retained and families kept together where practicable, although difficulties arise with large families. Their facilities vary. Some might accommodate 30–40 children up to three years, others 20–30 children from three to five; and there is one which can accommodate 40 children from 8 to 15 years.

advice, guidance and assistance to families in difficulties. Although there has been no Family Service Unit working in Edinburgh at the time these words are written (nor indeed as yet in Scotland) as in some English cities, a grant was given by the Corporation to the Edinburgh Council of Social Service in 1958 to employ an experienced caseworker to give help, if necessary intensive help, to " near problem families " as they might be called, which seemed in danger of breaking up. This method of helping families was so successful that the Corporation extended the period of grant aid.

The cost of maintaining a child in a Corporation Home is approximately £11 10*s*. 6*d*. a week. The boarding-out allowance in a foster-home is the same as that paid by the other three Scottish cities—45*s*. a week. When a young person under 18 is earning and continuing to live in his foster-home, his net wages (that is, after deductions for insurance, bus fares, lunches, etc.) are supplemented, if necessary, to make the allowance to the foster-parents up to a minimum of 60*s*. a week. For a full account of the allowances sponsored by the Corporation's Children Department in a good sample year 1962, Appendix VI should be consulted.

SPECIAL SERVICES CONNECTED WITH EDUCATION

As education has extended to include more aspects of the child's life, various social services ancilliary to teaching have developed. In Edinburgh these include the School Attendance Service, the School Welfare Service in the Pilton housing estate, and the Youth Employment Service.

The percentage of school attendances is now very high, having risen from 80·69 in 1873–4 to 93.9 in 1961–2. This improvement is due to a change in the attitude of parents as well as to the improved health of the children. There are still, however, a few families where the children attend irregularly or not at all. In 1961, for instance, there were 249 such cases where parents were interviewed by the Day School Management Sub-Committee (composed of Town Councillors, Teachers and Parents) and of these 90 were prosecuted. This is a small number out of a school population of some 65,000 and it would seem that the term " School Attendance Officer " has become almost a misnomer. These officers, however, have many duties other than those relating to truancy and non-attendance. They are responsible for a house-to-house census from which an estimate of the number of children likely to enter school can be made; they advise parents to which school they should send their children; they give advice and guidance on problems of children of school age and frequently refer parents to the Edinburgh Council of Social Service, the National Assistance Board and the Royal Scottish Society for the Prevention of Cruelty to Children. A woman officer investigates requests for temporary exemption from school (generally for older girls, when the mother is ill). Special officers deal with season tickets, school meals, the employment of school children and certain aspects of admission to special schools.

The duties of the School Attendance Officer thus include a combination of administrative and welfare duties, with the emphasis on the administrative side.

In 1946 a school welfare officer was appointed by the Education Committee to help with the social problems of school children and their families in the Pilton area. This large housing estate has a population of approximately 30,000 and the welfare officer serves four Primary Schools and two Secondary Schools in the area, and where necessary, the families of children attending special schools in other parts of Edinburgh. Children attending Roman Catholic Schools are not included in this service. Most of the children are referred by teachers or headmasters, but some are brought to her notice by Health Visitors or by spontaneous application. The number of families served is normally limited to 100; children are referred because of unexplained absence, persistent lateness, apparent neglect, insufficient clothing or for similar reasons. Parents themselves approach the welfare officer about problems in the handling of their children and for advice on convalescence, holidays for delicate children, leisure activities and youth clubs.

The Edinburgh Youth Employment Service dates back to 1908, when Edinburgh was the first Scottish city to set up an Educational Information and Employment Bureau under the Scottish Education Act of that year. Until 1950 it shared with the Ministry of Labour the work of finding employment for children leaving school; and ever since it has had entire responsibility for career work for young persons up to 18 years of age. This aim of the service is to give parents, pupils and teachers up-to-date information about careers; to give school leavers advice about careers for which they are suited; to assist those who want help in finding appropriate openings; and to help employers to obtain suitable new entrants. Each year the Service helps more than 6,000 young people to find employment; and in each case a follow-up visit is made after a few months to learn if the placement has been successful. But here let the figures speak for themselves. In 1962 more than 7,000 young people registered with the Service, a rise of 27 per cent on previous years, and 2,037 boys and 1,732 girls were found jobs. In addition during 1962, over 3,000 young people who had already been in employment returned for further advice and help, while the number of interviews with parents in the same year rose to 5,163. Clearly this is a valuable service, though it could still be more fully used by the youth of the city, for great pains are always taken by the Youth Employment Officer and his staff in finding new ways of putting the school leaver into the right kind of job. In the school holidays, for instance, short courses of three or four days are organised to let boys and girls see for themselves the opportunities and conditions of work in such widely different careers as the retail trade, banking, electronics and the coal industry.

SOCIAL ASPECTS OF THE HEALTH SERVICE

THE ALMONER IN COMMUNITY WORK

Since 1943, some five years before the introduction of the National Health Service Act, Edinburgh Corporation employed three almoners who, though based on the Public Health Department, offered medical social service to patients in the three municipal general hospitals of the city.[1] In 1948 these three almoners transferred to the Regional Hospital Board as medical social workers at the Northern, Eastern and Western General Hospitals. The tradition of having an almoner attached to the Public Health Department was maintained, however, and today Edinburgh is one of the two local health authorities in Scotland to have such a service.

Cases are referred to the Public Health Almoner by family practitioners and health visitors, by her colleagues working for the Regional Hospital Board, and by other social service agencies. In any year as many as 750 cases might be referred, many of whom required minor services, information, or direction to the particular agency which would meet their need. In the outcome hundreds of such cases require more long-term and intensive service of the kind usually associated with medical social work.

COMMUNITY MENTAL HEALTH SERVICES

Under various statutes the Edinburgh Corporation in common with other local authorities has certain responsibilities in respect of persons of unsound mind and the mentally handicapped.

The underlying principle in the Health Service Act was to associate mental health care as closely as possible with the health services generally. Thus local authorities were relieved of the responsibility for providing mental hospitals and mental deficiency institutions—these were transferred to the Regional Hospital Boards—but certain statutory duties were retained and indeed some powers and duties were added.

In the mental deficiency field, not only do these duties relate to the ascertainment, certification, placing in hospitals or under guardianship, provision of reports on home conditions, and supervision of boarded-out mental defectives, but the health committee also has a duty to provide training or occupation for those mental defectives in the community who are outwith the scope of the education services. In addition, the general powers of local health authorities to make arrangements for prevention, care and after-care extend to this field and are not restricted to certified patients.

In the field of mental illness, the local health authority has the responsibility to take action to remove persons of unsound mind to hospital where there are no relatives or friends willing to take the necessary action. The general powers of prevention, care and aftercare apply in this field also.

[1] Almoners are now officially known as Medical Social Workers.

The Medical Officer of Health is now responsible, under the Health Committee of the Corporation, for developing these community mental health services.

Through the School Health Service, several of whose medical members have special knowledge and experience in the fields of mental handicap and maladjustment, the Medical Officer of Health also advises the Director of Education. In addition, the Education Department possesses its own Child Guidance Service staffed by psychologists experienced in educational work and by social workers. The Department of Psychological Medicine at the Royal Hospital for Sick Children acts in an advisory capacity when requested by the education service.

SERVICES

Mental Illness. With the coming into force of the Mental Health (Scotland) Act, 1960 increasing emphasis is now being laid on care in the community rather than institutional care, while the term " mental disorder " is being used to cover both mental illness and mental deficiency, however caused or manifested. An important development under the Act is that patients may now be admitted to mental hospitals without any formality or certification. In cases where compulsion is necessary, the new emergency procedure laid down by the Act provides for a statutory period in hospital of seven days before certification, and a high proportion of admissions turn to an informal basis after this period, as many patients quickly accept the regime of a modern mental hospital. Between 1st June and 31st December, 1962, for instance, there were 86 emergency admissions to hospitals in the Edinburgh area; of these 47 patients remained on an informal basis and 39 became formal. During the complete year, 1962, the Mental Health Officers made arrangements for compulsory admission to hospital of 191 mentally ill patients, of whom 128 were women. This compares with 265 admissions in 1957, when the high number of certifications was mainly due to the rise in the number of elderly women who became mentally ill. This may be attributed partly to the greater expectation of life of old people, with a consequently longer period of risk; but it also reflects the need for more services, both medical and social, for the elderly, which would help to prevent mental breakdown. Under the new Act more of these elderly confused patients are being admitted informally without the need, as heretofore, of certification. Out patients clinics are being opened in various parts of the city.

In November, 1961, a social club was started for hospital in-patients in Wilkie House, Guthrie Street. This experiment has been most successful and now three clubs—one for long term cases, another for ex- and out-patients, and a third for patients nearing discharge—are flourishing. The aim of these clubs is to encourage patients in happy social relationships away from the hospital atmosphere, and to offer something different from the facilities already provided by occupational and recreational therapy. This successful venture has been the result of excellent co-operation between three mental hospitals, the University and the local authority, the cost being shared between the hospitals and the Corporation. To meet the needs of patients who have succeeded in finding employment in the city but who need continuing care, a hostel for men in Northumberland Street has since been opened by the local authority.

As in other parts of the country, there has been in the Edinburgh area such a serious shortage of beds in mental deficiency hospitals that 85 defectives were awaiting institutional accommodation at the end of 1962, and 25 of these were urgent cases. There were at the same date 61 defectives living in the community under guardianship supervised by the staff of the Mental Health Service and also 170 under informal supervision. Willowbrae House, a short-stay unit for mentally handicapped children up to and including the age of twelve, was opened by the Health Committee in 1957. The aim of this unit is to provide accommodation for these children during times of domestic stress, or to give their parents a short respite from the strain of looking after them.

The local education authority must ascertain children of school age who are in need of special educational treatment and must provide the necessary facilities. Thus in Edinburgh there are five special schools which take mentally handicapped children. The roll in 1962 was 560. In addition there were 24 spastic children, also suffering from mental handicap, attending the Edinburgh Spastic Association's centre at Longstone Old School. The junior occupation centre accommodates 106 children who, though seriously retarded, are trainable. A new building designed specially to meet the special educational requirements of these children will operate in future at West Mains, to accommodate 120.

The Youth Employment Service of the Education Authority advises on the employment of mentally handicapped school leavers. The Education Committee also runs senior occupation centres for mentally handicapped adults who are not suitable for open employment. To provide more occupational recreation for girls, the University Settlement at Cameron House agreed, after a successful two months' trial in 1962, to allow the daytime use of their Youth Centre for this purpose and more than 20 girls began to attend three days per week. In 1962, however, it was decided by the Mental Health Service that plans must be made for a scheme of progressive education and training. Thus the Senior Occupation Centres at Slateford and Lauriston should be used as training and assessment centres to which all defectives would be admitted to have their capabilities measured, and those suitable for employment in a work centre or sheltered industry would then proceed to a comprehensive centre. Next a hostel, Eversley House, was equipped to take 16 male adult defectives.

The Edinburgh Voluntary Mental Welfare Association also takes an active interest in these services and works in close co-operation with the statutory authorities; and the Corporation provides office accommodation for the Association and gives it an appreciable annual grant. The Secretary of the Association has the responsibility of supervising the waiting list for the Senior Occupation Centres, and for the welfare of those attending the centres and awaiting admission.

In common with the local and national voluntary mental welfare organisations, the City Mental Health Service tries to educate the public in the principles of mental hygiene and the prevention of mental breakdown. This is done formally through lectures on such subjects as the nature of mental disorders, the opportunities for treatment, the more hopeful outlook which modern methods of treatment offer, and the management at home of mentally handicapped persons. It is also done informally, in the course of their work, by the staff of the service. An interesting and recent development is that the Mental Health Service is now providing a screening of cases thought by the police to be suffering from mental disorder, before proceeding with legal or other action. From 1st January to 31st July, 1963, 94 cases were referred, and of these about one-third were admitted direct to hospital and approximately one-quarter were charged.

THE WELFARE OF THE DISABLED

An important part of the work of the Ministry of Labour is concerned with the rehabilitation and resettlement in work of persons who have been incapacitated through injury or illness, or who have a congenital handicap. Under the Disabled Persons (Employment) Act of 1944, any person who " on account of injury, disease or congenital deformity is substantially handicapped in obtaining or keeping employment or in undertaking work on his own account . . . which would be suited to his age, experience and qualifications," is eligible for the Disabled Persons Register and can thus avail himself of the services of the disablement resettlement officer, who will give him the necessary help and guidance to find suitable employment. The disablement resettlement officer has not only a wide knowledge of the labour requirements in his area, but knows the physical and mental demands of different kinds of work. He attends Hospital Resettlement Clinics covering a wide variety of disabling conditions, where the physical condition and social background of men and women about to be discharged are carefully assessed so that employment most suited to their capacity may be found for them.

It is obligatory for employers of 20 or more workers to engage not less than 3 per cent of their staff from the Disabled Persons' Register, and certain kinds of work—at present passenger electric lift attendant and car park attendant—can only be filled by the disabled.

The number of persons on the Disabled Register in the Edinburgh–Leith–Portobello area at 16th April, 1963, was 5,004 (4,138 men, 836 women, 14 boys and 16 girls). Of these 502—429 men and 83 women—were unemployed at 8th April, 1963. It is however reassuring that 265 disabled persons (227 men, 35 women and 3 young persons) were placed in employment in the six months ending 10th July, 1963.

At least 15 Industrial Rehabilitation Units in England and Scotland provide a short period of physical and industrial toning up for men and women who are recovering from illness or injury or who for other reasons have fallen out of the labour market. One of these Units, at

Granton, serves the eastern half of Scotland as well as Edinburgh; during the year ended 31st March, 1963, 497 men and 77 women were admitted to it; and the average weekly attendance during 1962 was 70 men and 12 women. The disabilities most frequently met with at the Unit are mental illnesses (in 1962 these accounted for 20 per cent of the admissions), diseases of the heart and circulatory system and spinal injuries, injuries and diseases of the lower limbs, followed by non-tubercular respiratory diseases and organic nervous diseases. This shows a marked change from the position only 5 years earlier, when the major cause of disablement was tuberculosis, followed by disease of the digestive system.

The Unit, it should be stressed, forms a valuable bridge between hospital or convalescent home and employment; for it is here that the ex-patient undergoes a toughening up process during which he re-acquires the habits of time-keeping and concentration, and where his ears become accustomed again to the noise of machinery, while his muscles relearn old skills or adapt themselves to new ones.

When a rehabilitatee leaves the Unit he is assessed and recommended for the types of employment for which he is most suited. This recommendation will vary according to whether he is able-bodied, disabled or severely disabled, which means he is fit only for sheltered employment.

In Edinburgh sheltered employment is provided by the Lady Haig Poppy Factory, the Thistle Foundation, the Royal Blind Asylum and by other voluntary organisations. It is also provided by Remploy Limited (formerly the Disabled Persons Employment Corporation Limited) a non-dividend paying corporation which was set up in 1945 under the Disabled Persons (Employment) Act, 1944 in order to provide productive employment for severely handicapped men and women. There are 10 Remploy factories in Scotland, one of which is in Granton, adjacent to the Unit. The workers are paid at an hourly rate which has been negotiated with the appropriate Trade Union. Shorter working hours may be arranged for workers whom the medical officer considers unable to undertake a full day's work. Remploy products are sold on the open market and the Granton factory is not a charitable organisation. However, because of their vulnerability, the heavy overheads, and the need to establish factories where there are disabled people rather than where there are suitable economic conditions, Remploy factories run at a loss.

Edinburgh Corporation gives financial assistance to the Edinburgh Cripple and Invalid Children's Aid Society up to a maximum of £5,500, to provide welfare facilities for this category, including an occupational therapy centre at Simon Square where 120 persons (in 1962–3) were engaged in the workrooms on office work, tailoring, light industry and production, and pre-vocational work. Such a centre naturally brings a sense of usefulness and happiness to those so severely handicapped that they cannot reasonably be expected to earn a living even in sheltered conditions. Many disabled persons, however, are not on the Register, some because they do not need it and still others because they do not want their disability to become known. The total number of disabled persons in the city is thus unknown.

NATIONAL ASSISTANCE BOARD

With the passing of the 1948 National Assistance Act, the local authority had no longer a duty to make financial provision for persons in need, and these became instead the National Assistance Board's responsibility. Under Part II of the Act, persons in need who are not entitled to National Insurance benefit, who perhaps have exhausted their entitlement through prolonged illness or unemployment, or whose benefits are insufficient for their needs may apply for an allowance from the National Assistance Board. There are in Edinburgh four Area Offices of the Board where applicants may apply for financial help. The scale allowances in 1963 were £5 4*s*. 6*d*. a week for a married couple, £3 3*s*. 6*d*. a week for a single person who is a householder, and £2 15*s*. a week for a non-householder aged 21 or over. Non-householders between the ages of 16 and 21 have a lesser rate. Children's allowances vary from 19*s*. 6*d*. to 28*s*. according to age. To these figures are added rent allowance and discretionary additions for any special needs are considered.

In June, 1963, 16,581 persons were in receipt of National Assistance from Edinburgh offices. This figure, which includes a relatively small number from outside the city boundaries, is split up as follows:—

(1) *Those over normal working age:*			
In receipt of retirement pension—	8,301		
In receipt of non-contributory old age pension—	995		
No pension of any kind—	1,179	10,475	
(2) *Those fit and available for work*		1,686	
(3) Others (including persons totally unfit for work, widows with children, women separated from husbands, unmarried mothers and persons required at home to look after aged or sick relatives)—		4,420	
Total			16,581

Payment of assistance to persons in category (2) is conditional upon registration for work at the Employment Exchange as required, and the Board's officers endeavour to satisfy themselves that the persons are genuinely seeking work on their own behalf. A small number with prison records have difficulty in finding work, while hawkers, scrap iron and rag dealers and other casual workers who cannot earn enough to meet the high cost of living are frequently to be found on the books of the Board. It is extremely difficult for such men, particularly as they grow older, to adapt themselves to working for a master, nor are they attractive employees. Supportive case work over a long period has been found to be the most effective way of helping these individuals to self-dependence and the Board's officers do what they can from the welfare aspect. Co-operation between the Board's Visiting Officers and the Edinburgh Council of Social Service has grown steadily, a development which is in the best interests of the national assistance applicants and their families.

More visitors come to Edinburgh each year than anywhere else in Scotland. They wander in the New Town, the ancient streets and closes of the Old; they "do" the Castle and the Palace of Holyroodhouse and inspect the many fine shops. *On left:* a North American tourist photographing Holyrood is glad to slip off her shoes after the hard pavements of the Royal Mile. Was it not Damon Runyon who said of the Harvard-Yale ball game, "There are dames there that walk as if their feet hurt and the chances are they do"? *On right:* in Princes Street one can shop in slacks and climbing boots or in the latest Paris creation.

Crowds cheer H.M. The Queen and King Olav of Norway as their carriage passes down the Royal Mile during the King's State Visit in October 1962.

Reference has already been made to the high proportion of old people in receipt of national assistance. In June, 1963 there were 995 old people in receipt of non-contributory old age pension; but 213 of these had other resources and did not require national assistance. This, a dwindling group, shows a marked decrease on the number, 2,098, who drew this pension in June, 1957, since those qualifying must have reached the age of 70 not later than 29 September, 1961, whereas the number in receipt of retirement pensions has risen from 6,453 to 8,301. These non-contributory pensions payable by the Board to persons over 70 are based on means, and in 1963 the maximum rate was 46*s*. for a married couple and 28*s*. 4*d*. for a single person. Where these pensions, along with any other income, are insufficient for needs they are supplemented by national assistance. It should be added that the periodic visits of the Board's officers are a valuable service to all old people, especially as the officers who take a kindly interest in their welfare can call in other services where necessary. There are probably, however, still a few old people eligible for supplementary assistance who, through ignorance, pride or diffidence have not applied for it.

National assistance allowances at a higher rate are also paid by the Board to certain categories of handicapped persons. Blind persons by the mid-60s had the following rates: £6 9*s*. a week for a married couple where one partner is blind; £7 5*s*. a week where both are; and £4 8*s*. a week for a single blind person. Maintenance allowances for persons suffering from tuberculosis (other than chronic cases) were introduced by the Government in 1943, in order to encourage such persons to give up work and undergo treatment. The higher rate incidentally is continued for a few months after the person has been certified fit for work, but does not immediately find a job, provided of course he is registered at the Employment Exchange. And with this we put the final touch to the variegated mosaic which Edinburgh's statutory social services have become.

THE VOLUNTARY SOCIAL SERVICES

Voluntary societies carrying out social work pursue two general aims which are complementary to relieve distress—however caused—and to contribute and enable others to contribute to the well being of the community. The creative and vital societies withstand all vicissitudes and change with the times; the rest fade out and are replaced by new organisations, with different aims and run by different people.

THE PLACE OF VOLUNTARY SERVICE IN THE WELFARE STATE

The great challenge to the voluntary organisations of our times is the taking over by the State of responsibility for providing social services, and when the social legislation of 1946–8 became operative doubts were expressed as to the possible effect on voluntary organisations and on the people themselves. With the " Welfare State " appearing as a panacea for all ills, it seemed as if the voluntary societies in their traditional role of caring for the distressed members of society would die a natural death. Even worse, it seemed probable that the independence of the individual would be threatened, for his responsibilities were being taken over by the State and there would be no incentive to work. That these doubts were ill founded is now clear, but the kind of work that will be carried out by the voluntary organisations in future is still uncertain.

In practice, full employment has meant greater independence and mobility for great numbers of people, and the economic foundation provided by the State has given them greater security. At the same time, some grave problems have been more clearly revealed and others, often attributed to poverty, have been recognised as having other causes. So the voluntary organisations in Edinburgh continue to care for children, the sick and aged, the disabled and social misfits for whom there is still not sufficient statutory provision. But many old institutions have gone and others have changed. The Servants' Institution, the Soup Kitchen and the Night Asylum no longer exist, nor do Homes for Inebriates (of which there were five some 40 years ago). Organisations concerned with the welfare of women and girls, unmarried mothers, or girls away from home or without homes, have changed significantly in title, in attitude, and, for the most part, in their way of working. Previously known as the Magdalene Asylum, Rescue Home for Women, and Industrial Home for Fallen Women, the present day organisations doing welfare work with girls and women do not in their titles indicate the work they do. Claremont House offers a home before and after the birth of a baby, enabling the mother to make the best possible plans for the baby and herself. St. Margaret's House, quite different in function, provides a home for girls either without homes or with poor home backgrounds from which they go out to work.

The titles of a few organisations, however, reflect the passage of time and still emphasise the class distinctions of the days in which they were instituted: societies for the " Relief of Gentlewomen," for instance, and those for " Indigent Old Women " and " Indigent Old Men." One might also legitimately wonder if the retention of some titles indicates outmoded ideas of helping people in need: the " Destitute Sick Society ", for example, does certainly provide material aid, but its title is alien in a society with basic welfare and financial provisions. One is constantly reminded that the 19th century statements of aims of many societies were moralistic and reformatory in tone, but this tendency has, happily, given way to a more comprehensive expression of social need and the well-being of the community.

The most important developments in practice among the voluntary societies are the increasing employment of trained workers; greater opportunities for voluntary workers and a growing recognition that social welfare should include more participation by more people; closer co-operation with statutory bodies and the making of grants by local authorities to voluntary organisations either for general or specific purposes or on an agency basis; and the rapid growth of self-help organisations.

THE NATURE OF VOLUNTARY SERVICE

The tradition of giving voluntary service to their less fortunate fellows other than of the neighbourly kind seems in the past to have belonged to those members of the upper and middle classes who were prepared to give time and money—a giving prompted by conscience or a desire to serve or considered to be a duty. This picture is changing. All sorts of people are now giving time, skill and money voluntarily—the business or professional man with special skills, the housewife and mother and often grandmother, the workers in offices and factories who help in club or community organisations. They visit old people, take part in committee work as well as sharing in less attractive tasks, help in clubs of all kinds, baby homes and hostels, and raise money—always an important job in voluntary organisations.

In addition to the well-established bodies such as the Red Cross and the W.V.S., considerable scope is offered for voluntary work with the Old People's Welfare Council, Marriage Guidance Council, and societies helping the disabled. There is an increasing awareness of the need for training voluntary workers, particularly those who are to become marriage guidance counsellors, help with family casework or the handicapped, and visit the aged and housebound. Training is done through special courses and classes and volunteers are interviewed and selected.

It should be noted in passing that the Marriage Guidance Council is one of the newer voluntary organisations, and has grown to prominence through its efforts to help men and women in situations of stress and tension. Out of 1,482 interviews carried out in 1962, disharmony accounted for 28 per cent of the problems affecting the married couples who came to them. The other problems were: ill-health, legal matters, housing and family difficulties—15 per cent; husband leaving home—five per cent; wife leaving home—13 per cent; infidelity—11 per cent; physical difficulties—eight per cent; money—eight per cent; and drink—six per cent. The other six per cent involved inquiries for pre-marriage advice.

Although the Women's Voluntary Service, whose members come from all walks of life, carries out a number of welfare services, it is primarily a uniformed and emergency service, forming part of the Civil Defence Organisation and working for statutory bodies. In addition to this work, however, it provides a car service, an out-patient canteen and library service for hospitals, and clothing supplies—there is a large W.V.S. clothing store in the city dependent on gifts of clothing from the public—and it also organises holidays for children and the " spare a mile " scheme to give lifts to disabled people.

HELPING OLD PEOPLE

The services for old people are many and constantly improving, for the difficulties of old age are well known; and it is not surprising that in the past decade the greatest concentration of voluntary effort has been in this direction. The provision of homes for old people has for a long time figured largely in the work of voluntary organisations, but recently greater attention has been given to domiciliary care to help them remain in their own homes as long as possible, leading an active life so long as they are fit to do so. The need for this development can be appreciated in the light of population trends, which in Edinburgh means that out of over 50,000 old persons possibly one third live alone. In addition to the W.V.S., whose general work was described earlier and whose members supply " meals on wheels " to approximately 300 persons living alone, the organisations principally concerned with helping old people are as follows.

Firstly there is the Edinburgh and Leith Old People's Welfare Council, which organises friendly visiting, occupational classes, social clubs, lunch clubs, chiropody services and a number of homes in different parts of the city. One of the best known of the clubs is housed in premises with an historic title, Margaret Tudor House. Another very large club has Lamb's House in Leith as its centre, and here indeed history stands at the shoulders of the members. For it was in Lamb's House, residence of a 16th century merchant, that Mary Queen of Scots spent her first hour on her return to Scotland from France in 1561. Four centuries later it was another Scottish Queen, Queen Elizabeth the Queen Mother, who opened Lamb's House as an old people's centre after it had been generously restored by the late Marquess of Bute and presented by his son Lord David Crichton-Stuart to the National Trust for Scotland for use as a day club for old people. It has well over 1,000 members and is a remarkable example of voluntary effort. Another day club is being located in Gorgie. The building, Dalry House, came to the Council from the Episcopal Church of Scotland Representative Church Council, and according to figures published in 1964 Dalry House is in the middle of Dalry and Gorgie, a district where 3,200 old people, or 17 per cent of its entire population, are classified as old people. The need is obvious. Following this generous action by the Episcopal Church, the Council in October, 1964 launched a successful appeal.

The Council also provides an opportunity for happy co-operation with other bodies. For example, helpers from the long-established Edinburgh Women Citizens' Association and other bodies serve meals to the old folk in Lamb's House and Margaret Tudor House.

Another body which makes a welcome and generous contribution to easing the problems of the old is the Leith Benevolent Association which runs two homes for old people in addition to its other activities. Then there is the Red Cross, whose main activities are described later in this chapter. Members of the Red Cross help by washing old people's hair or giving them a bath or other personal services, as well as by helping in the clubs. The Churches too co-operate in friendly visiting, and many have clubs attached to them.

Such services as these make it possible for an old person to remain relatively independent and admission to a home is the last resort. Private pensions, grants and almshouses, whilst still necessary, are being over-shadowed by the newer and more practical services which give great scope for voluntary work. One of these services seems a most effective way of helping the elderly to be as independent as possible while having help at hand. Five to seven old persons, each with a private bed-sitting room, live in a house where communal meals are provided: there is a general sitting room; and a Warden who lives in the house is at hand if needed. The Edinburgh Abbeyfield Society started the first house of its kind and soon, in the early '60s, there were six—two run by the W.V.S. The houses are sponsored by local groups, often from a church congregation, and great care is taken to introduce the occupants to their neighbours in the street.

The trend of self-help is also evident in the Old Age Pensioners' Association. Here the members come together for social purposes and to safeguard and pursue their own interests by raising such matters as pensions and welfare provision with the appropriate authority.

FAMILY WELFARE

In all services there is emphasis on the maintenance of the family as a whole. The voluntary organisations who are principally concerned with the family have, in the majority of cases, a nucleus of trained caseworkers. The largest casework agency is part of the Edinburgh Council of Social Service, and the help of its seven family caseworkers is sought in every kind of difficulty concerning single people living alone, the aged, families where there are marital difficulties, the chronically sick, the physically and mentally handicapped, and in cases where a member of the family is or has been in prison, and where there are debts and housing problems. Four of its caseworkers work on housing estates, and in addition to casework take part in community activities. In all its activities the prevention of the break-up of the family is regarded as an important part of this agency's work. An average of 1,000 families are helped each year; and as these families include well over 3,000 children, the Council thus provides a large and important element of child care in the city.

The Guild of Service used to be described as being a vigilance society or as doing " rescue " work. It is now a casework agency working with single and separated parents. This is preventive work and includes making constructive plans for parents and children for the future. Such plans may include admission to children's homes, fostering or adoption.

A special organisation—well known as The Soldiers', Sailors' and Airman's Families Association—helps the families of service men, and is noticed here as an early pioneering body in this worthy field.

A Soldiers' and Sailors' Families' Association was started in Edinburgh in 1885 a few months after the formation of the Association in London. At the time there was much distress among soldiers' families because only a very few wives were on the " Married Establishment " of a unit and thus entitled, if their husbands were away on duty, to draw the separation allowance of 1*s*. per day and 3*d*. for each child. To be married " Off the Establishment " meant no quarters, no rations and no separation allowances.

The two World Wars greatly increased the work of the Association, and the Overseas Department, started during the last war, still exists. S.S.A.F.A. deals with accomodation and allowance difficulties, matrimonial and family problems and travel arrangements. In a single year during the 60s, 251 welfare enquiries were dealt with, among them such representative examples as the flying home of an airman from Singapore to see his father who died an hour later.

S.S.A.F.A. is not alone in this admirable work. There is also The Officers' Association whose purpose, in its own words, is " to aid, advise and promote the interests of ex-officers, their widows and dependents." With its headquarters in London, this Association has a Scottish H.Q. in Edinburgh and secretarial and employment offices in Glasgow. The Scottish Branch maintains a nursing home in Edinburgh for ex-officers, and on pension problems it works with the British Legion.

In a different setting many of the problems which come before these societies with naval, military and R.A.F. traditions are also dealt with by the Catholic Enquiry Office, which provides—for those of the Roman Catholic faith—casework services, children's homes, adoption, and other welfare and advisory services.

Another body concerned with families is the Edinburgh Voluntary Youth Welfare Association to which boys and girls, who are not sent to Approved School or put on probation but are in need of guidance, care or protection, may be referred from Juvenile Courts or the Corporation's Children's Department. This and other work branches of the Youth Service are dealt with later in this chapter. But here perhaps it should be stressed—from the viewpoint of the Edinburgh Council of Social Service—that as an extension of family problems, there is a continued need for more hostel accommodation for young people who may not have a home or who must live away from home because of poor conditions there or on account of their employment. This kind of accommodation is provided by the Y.W.C.A., the Y.M.C.A., the Girls Friendly Society, Ponton House, and the Scottish Wayfarers Welfare Society. The cost of living at these hostels is to some extent adjusted to the earnings of young people, just as it was 50 years ago when the Y.W.C.A. provided board and lodging to business and working girls at 9*s*. a week. Martin House is a small organisation which can take up to 24 girls or women. It gives them shelter and support, and no matter what the problem or condition no woman is turned away if a corner can be found for her.

THE VARIETY OF THE VOLUNTARY SOCIAL SERVICES

To detail all the voluntary social services in Edinburgh would be impossible, for there are over 200 organisations with charitable status as well as very many more voluntary bodies which carry on some form of social work. The work of the Royal Blind School, Dr. Barnardo's homes (who are in the forefront in meeting changing needs in child care with residential schools for maladjusted children and those with physical handicaps), the Deaf and Dumb Benevolent Societies, are well known. But in addition there are youth organisations of every kind, as we shall see, Missions, and, particularly in Leith, institutions for seafaring men.

Since 1900 there has been a Legal Dispensary in Edinburgh, which gives free legal advice to persons unable to pay for it. It is staffed by a rota of qualified lawyers. Another development of information services resulted during the war in the establishment of a Citizens' Advice Bureau. The Citizens' Advice Bureau, whilst not giving legal advice (persons requiring such advice would be referred to the Legal Dispensary), is able to provide an advisory and information service of great use to the citizen. Over 10,000 inquiries are received each year.

Apart from the ex-service organisations already noted which have a special care for ex-officers there are some praiseworthy institutions such as the famous Haig Poppy Factory, the Forces Help Society and Lord Roberts Workshop all of which assist ex-service men to find employment. Whitefoord House provides accommodation and the Scottish Veterans' Garden City Association has a number of cottages. The Thistle Foundation with its workshops and adjacent dwellings for disabled service men and their families provides the nearest thing to normal working conditions and family life possible for severely disabled men.

There are many voluntary organisations in Edinburgh principally devoted to providing grants, pensions, and other aids. These are still needed, despite the basic state provisions, for there are groups within our society who live near the poverty line because of incapacity to earn or because of age or illness. For the most part however they depend upon voluntary helpers, though some of those who are disbursing regimental funds seek the aid of a social worker in assessing the need for help.

The role of the voluntary organisation as a pioneer in social work is still a vital one, and history has many examples of a social service which began in a very small way as a voluntary organisation. The first health visitor was a voluntary worker in 1907, and for many years the Voluntary Health Workers, started by the Charity Organisation Society but quickly becoming independent, continued to work under the supervision of Local Authority Health Visitors until the Department was staffed by trained Health Visitors. The society provided play centres for the children in highly populated areas and classes in homecraft for the mothers. The first class for mentally handicapped children was started by the Charity Organisation Society (now the Edinburgh Council of Social Service): to-day there are special schools maintained by the local authority. There are, however, still gaps in even this limited field, one of which is filled by the Scottish Society for Mentally Handicapped Children, an organisation set up both to relieve the stress of parents with mentally handicapped children at home and to give the children more opportunity to develop their capacities. It has a Home to which children can be sent to give parents a respite; voluntary workers run groups to train the children as far as possible, and some children have graduated from these groups to special schools. Parents are also helped through discussion with experts towards a greater understanding of their children's needs.

Another example of co-ordination of effort was displayed when representatives from Children's Homes, Mother and Baby Homes and Casework Agencies formed the Edinburgh Children's Welfare Group in order to improve their standards, increase their knowledge and work together for a common aim. The Group now includes representatives from Local Authority Departments. Within the Group the idea of another pioneer venture was born when the Save the Children Fund started Harmony House, a school for maladjusted children.

Many voluntary organisations of course, fulfil functions which no statutory body could ever do. One example is Alcoholics Anonymous This body is a most useful association of alcoholics who help others in a way impossible for any outside person, and is literally a life line to the person who has a predisposition—inherited or acquired—to alcohol.

Although the transfer to the State of hospital services took away the chief object of traditionally charitable impulses, the administration of hospital comforts funds and samaritan funds continues. Humanitarian impulses also find an outlet in the many new organisations for the handicapped and disabled, who are assisted to find work, wage-earning if possible, and to develop their capacities for social intercourse and occupation. Simon Square Centre run by Edinburgh Cripple Children's Aid Society is a pioneer venture in Edinburgh. It offers rehabilitation and occupation for the disabled so that some people are able to begin to earn and then move out into normal employment. The Centre has stimulated great interest in the problems and possibilities of the handicapped person and illustrates practical ways of enabling them to gain independence and confidence.

The Epilepsy Association organises a club for both social and occupational purposes and also helps with personal problems, including accommodation. The Church of Scotland is planning to open a hostel for epileptics. The Muscular Dystrophy Group is particularly concerned with furthering research and is a branch of a national body. Other special groups allied to illness or disablement are the Haemophilia Society, the National Society for the Relief of Cancer, the Marie Curie Foundation and the Infantile Paralysis Fellowship. The rest we looked at earlier.

COMMUNITY CARE

Community organisations of various kinds have resulted from the rapid growth of housing estates and the new towns. The majority of these are principally interested in dealing with grievances and in social activities; but there is also the beginning of a movement of a different kind through which the community can much more effectively participate in giving service. Three examples of this trend are the Pilton Central Committee, the Sighthill Health and Welfare Association and a lunch club in Leith.

The Pilton Central Committee began with meetings of representatives of a number of local volunteer bodies. Professional people who worked in the area became interested, and from this grew two groups of people, one a representative group to which any voluntary organisation in the area could send a representative and which included members of the local authority, the other a professional group working in co-operation with the Edinburgh Council of Social Service and concerned with casework. This Central Committee is active in such things as road safety, old people's welfare, recreation and children's welfare. It has also instituted a Festival of Music, Drama and Dancing. Through the Central Committee are sifted the problems of the area and constructive ideas for the welfare of the community; irritations and complaints are aired and discussed and, if necessary, referred to an appropriate authority. This assumption of more responsibility by people in the community and their co-operation with professional and official workers seems to hold within it the seeds of effective participation by increasingly large numbers of the population.

Another development is the setting up of a Health and Welfare Association with the Sighthill Health Centre as its focal point. This Association combines the Centre staff, general practitioners, social workers, teachers, ministers, local authority and voluntary organisations in the area with representatives from the industrial estate; and together they plan and work for the good of all. A club has been formed for old people; it is hoped to establish an adventure playground for children and young people; plans at the date of writing are in hand for an occupational centre for the mentally ill.

THE FINANCIAL STRUCTURE

But how are all these voluntary societies financed? Many now receive grant aid from the local authority, but this is uneven and not necessarily related to the volume of work undertaken. In Edinburgh grants may be made for specific purposes towards the running expenses of the Citizen's Advice Bureau, for example, towards general funds, or on a *per capita* basis.

Despite such grants voluntary organisations have to find the greater proportion of the money needed to carry out their work by way of subscriptions, donations, and special efforts such as flag days and bazaars. An uncertain income is a characteristic of local voluntary organisations; it also frustrates their endeavour to meet the demands made upon them and prevents expansion and experiment.

NATIONAL ORGANISATIONS

In close relation to this vast network of voluntary welfare societies are a number of famous national organisations with headquarters in Edinburgh. Several of these we have already seen at work in the city but there are others whose work is of great importance in the welfare field.

SCOTTISH COUNCIL OF SOCIAL SERVICE

First, we must look at the Scottish Council of Social Service with its specialised committees and groups including the Scottish Women's

Group on Public Welfare, the Scottish Old People's Welfare Committee, the Committee on the Welfare of the Disabled, the Standing Conference of Voluntary Youth Organisations, and the Scottish War Memorial Committee.

The Council had an interesting start early in 1939 when Sir Hector Hetherington invited 38 people to form a body whose aim was to inaugurate a Scottish Council of Social Service. In this originating group in Edinburgh were included Sir George Laidlaw, Miss Eleanor Stewart and Sir Ernest Wedderburn (then Dr. E. M. Wedderburn). The inauguration was delayed because of the War but finally took place in June, 1943.

The Council's first Chairman was Lord Wark, and Sir John Erskine, who became Chairman of the Finance Committee and guided the Council's early development, was ultimately made President.

One of the new Council's earliest tasks was to help mobilise the resources of voluntary organisations in the war effort. In particular After-Air-Raid Welfare was an early concern, and mobile teams of workers were recruited to aid homeless people after heavy raids. Secretarial services too were provided for the Council for the Encouragement of Music and the Arts (C.E.M.A.), lineal ancestor of the Arts Council of Great Britain, and a body which did a splendid job in bringing music, painting and drama to brighten people's lives at the height of the war effort.

Since those days the Scottish Council of Social Service has grown and spread its influence far and wide. The Committee was strengthened by the addition of representatives from a number of important bodies and from the four universities. The Carnegie United Kingdom Trust made substantial grants from the start, and the Council has also enjoyed the support of the Development Commission.

THE RED CROSS

When the Red Cross Society is mentioned in conversation the generally accepted picture is of an organisation that functions mainly at times of national crisis. There is, happily, gradually increasing recognition of the fact that the Society's activities now make vital daily impact on a large section of the population.

Commemorating the centenary of this world-wide humanitarian organisation in 1963, Edinburgh members joined forces with others in the Scottish Branch to expand welfare work on a scale not contemplated in the early post-war years. The ramifications of the Welfare State notwithstanding, it has become apparent to the Society that there are vast fields of endeavour where its ministrations would be welcomed. Thus the Edinburgh members have promised their co-operation in the campaign to raise £250,000 for the benefit of worthy causes.

One aims at the establishment of holiday homes where the disabled of all ages, and the frail elderly who have been housebound for some years, may enjoy a recuperative spell in cheerful and stimulating surroundings; and indeed the Red Cross has founded a home at North Berwick for frail and aged dependents. Another aim is the provision of a second Red Cross House on the lines of that situated at Largs—a major post-war development—where the severely handicapped are trained so that they may be able to engage in useful work. The third chief aim is the expansion throughout Scotland of the welfare work that is based on the homes of the disabled and the elderly, and on the hospitals. In this sphere much has already been accomplished, if only because public spirited citizens find a sense of accomplishment in paying regular welfare visits to the disabled and the elderly whose circle of friends diminish with the passing of the years. In many cases it is readily apparent that these visits are highlights in the lives of those on the calling lists. There are also arrangements for shopping and laundry services for those who cannot easily cope with these essentials, and the regular sessions for chiropody services. Diversional therapy also operates on a considerable scale in the home and in hospital.

Another striking development in recent years is the availability of skilfully contrived pieces of apparatus, large and small, which gives the recipients a joyful mobility of movement hitherto thought impossible. Mention must be made of its work in training a vast Nursing Reserve which, while meeting pressing demands in time of peace, also ensures preparation for any future emergency.

ST. ANDREW'S AMBULANCE ASSOCIATION AND CORPS

Since the First-Aid (Standard of Training) Act came into force in July, 1961, there has been a steadily increasing number of men and women, who, instead of settling down for an evening at the fireside after work, now hurry off to first-aid classes. The Act, it is obvious, exerts an influence on social habits to an extent that was not anticipated in many quarters.

All owners of premises falling within the jurisdiction of the Factory Inspectorate, and employing 50 or more personnel, are now required to have available during business hours one individual qualified in first-aid and holding a currently valid certificate of competency. This is clearly a wise precaution. But legislation apart, many managements have seen the wisdom of seeking quite a number of volunteers from their staffs so that adequate cover can be provided during the absence of trained personnel on holiday or through sickness.

The immediate effect of the Act on the St. Andrew's Ambulance Association in Edinburgh was a sudden, heavy demand for the provision of instructors. Encouraging progress was reported within a comparatively short period after the Act was enforced, and by the end of 1963 a substantial number of factory and office staffs had passed through the training courses and gained the appropriate certificate. This certificate is valid only for a period of three years to ensure that first-aid personnel are kept up to date with advances in knowledge and technique, and their practical application, not least on public occasions.

In 1961, the Association, aware of the need to prepare youngsters for the responsibilities of adult life and at the same time provide for stability of adult membership numbers, decided to lower the age of entry to the

Junior Section of the Corps, so that boys and girls now enter as Junior Cadets from the ages of eight to eleven. A special influence in this most worthy activity has been the growing popularity of The Duke of Edinburgh's Award Scheme, which demands possession of first-aid qualifications as one of the conditions.

ROYAL SCOTTISH SOCIETY FOR THE PREVENTION OF CRUELTY TO CHILDREN

An Edinburgh Society for the Prevention of Cruelty to Children was inaugurated in December, 1884. Subsequently other societies sprang up in Scotland and in 1890 these independent, local bodies were brought together under the Scottish National Society for the Prevention of Cruelty to Children. In 1922 through incorporation by royal charter this body became the R.S.S.P.C.C. with headquarters in Edinburgh.

In its earlier days extreme poverty was usually accepted as the excuse for cruelty to children, but the experience of the society showed that laziness, drink and selfishness were the chief causes, and the principal and most common categories of cruelty included assault, neglect, infanticide, immorality, exposure, and imposing begging and vagrancy. In the 1960s the society can claim that cases of ill-treatment and assault have been considerably reduced. To take a sample year, out of 594 complaints received by the society in 1960, 497 were concerned with cases of neglect; the rest arose from ill treatment and assault, the problems of children in "immoral surroundings"; or they came under the heading of "other wrongs"—which covered, in the main, applications for admission of children to the Children's Shelter, owing to illness or other difficulties in the home.

Prosecution in the courts is regarded by the society as a last resort in the course of their work. It is their policy wherever possible to put right any wrong being done to children, and to rehabilitate broken homes so that they do not give rise to further trouble in the future.

The Edinburgh Children's Shelter is usually filled to capacity with a total of 30 to 33 children. Children are admitted at any time of the day or night, and they are of all ages: the youngest child admitted one year was a baby one day old. Children may be sheltered because they have been ill-treated, badly neglected, or because they are homeless or have no-one at home to look after them properly.

Annual expenditure by the Edinburgh branch in the early '60s was approximately £6,000 and the Children's Shelter cost a further £6,500 to run. There is a junior section of the society, the Scottish Children's League, founded in 1893, through which young people all over the country support the Children's Shelter.

And so by voluntary effort all this humane work goes on, though it is somewhat of a paradox that the society is known among its beneficiaries by the simple, if ambiguous abbreviation, "the Cruelty," and its inspectors are commonly referred to as "the Cruelty men."

TELEPHONE SAMARITAN SERVICE

The Telephone Samaritan Service, whose aim is to help those tempted to suicide or despair, started in Edinburgh on 1st June, 1959—the first branch in Britain outside London.

It was to meet the need of mentally distressed or disillusioned people that Edinburgh's Telephone Samaritans were formed to offer in the first instance a friendly listening ear and the warmth of human understanding. As a result the client finds someone who cares about the mess he (or she) is in (whether it's his own fault or not)—someone who cares whether he lives or dies and who is prepared to befriend him. Practical commonsense is applied to his problems, and where professional services or treatment are required, these are arranged for. To quote our social worker again: " The aim is to help the client to help himself; his co-operation is required all along the line."

During the year 1962–3, 720 new clients phoned to the Telephone Samaritans for help and were later interviewed. They came from all walks of life; their ages ranged from teenage to over 70; they phoned at all hours of the day and night; and each was considered as a unique personality in a unique set of circumstances. Since the organisation has naturally to be fluid enough to allow for this, the Samaritans are a correspondingly mixed bunch. Many are Christians—Roman Catholic and Protestant; others are agnostics.

KNIGHTS OF ST. JOHN OF JERUSALEM

The Knights of St. John of Jerusalem have the Queen as their Sovereign Head " in the British realm " and the Duke of Gloucester as their Grand Prior. The Scottish Chancery of this ancient order of chivalry is in Glasgow, and in various parts of Scotland it runs nursing homes, homes for convalescents or elderly persons needing rest. In Edinburgh St. John's House has taken almost 500 guests in a single year.

Clearly then the range of welfare societies in Edinburgh is far-reaching, stretching as it does from The Deaf and Dumb Benevolent Society, which in 1964 was looking after some 800 deaf people in Edinburgh and in Central and South-east Scotland as well, to the recently extended old people's home belonging to The Little Sisters of the Poor, who came to Edinburgh more than a century ago and the charitable trusts for the aged. To cite one of these as an example, the Craigcrook Mortification, founded in 1715, has for 250 years disbursed annually from 60 to 100 annuities to people over 60 years of age in reduced circumstances excepting only those " who have been servants or journeymen and have never occupied a higher station."

In a rather different setting, there are also the Friendly Societies such as the Order of Oddfellows, who were sharply affected by the introduction of the post-war National Insurance and National Health Service Acts, which created the so-called Welfare State. Older Edinburgh citizens remember well how, as Philip Stalker wrote in *The Scotsman* (14th April, 1962), they used to see them marching with their banners and their tableaux on lorries in the annual Infirmary Pageant in Edinburgh. Their names rolled off the tongue—the British Order of Ancient Free Gardeners, the Loyal Order of Ancient Shepherds, and the Ancient Order of Foresters. All these and others were Approved Societies from 1911 onwards. But the advent of the Welfare State dealt them a heavy blow, since the Government took over their insurance funds and the work they had been doing as Approved Societies. Yet although, as with voluntary welfare societies, it took some time for people to realise that unpaid social work and private generosity were still needed, many of the Friendly Societies recovered and became purely voluntary societies.

YOUTH ORGANISATIONS AND THE YOUTH SERVICE

During the last decade an excessive amount of public attention has been focussed on the adolescent population of this country. In that time the words " teenager ", " teddyboy " and " square ", along with a variety of others of the same kind, have been accepted into the language. The doings of this age-group have continued to occupy the headlines of the daily press. Their clothes, their behaviour and especially their morals have come under incessant fire and have given rise to pronouncements both informed and uninformed.

These first-generation inheritors of the Welfare State have presented an enigma to their elders who find it very difficult to come to terms with them. They are of better physique, they are maturing and marrying earlier, and they have an economic status unknown to any previous generation. Dr. Mark Abrams has calculated that the annual uncommitted spending power of Britain's unmarried teenagers around 1958–9 was £900,000,000 (a rise in real spending of 100 per cent over 1938). It is estimated that this figure will have risen by a further £500,000,000 by 1965–6 when the teenagers of the bulge have begun to earn. This money is spent by both sexes on clothes, cosmetics, motor cycles and scooters, and Espresso Bar living, but mainly on " pop " records. As well as being the overall consumers' *par excellence* in society, teenagers in the early '60s were buying records at the rate of three million per month, and this figure has risen since.

Often in sharp conflict with and indifferent to the outlook of their parents and members of the older generation, who are in their eyes " not with it ", young people in this nuclear age are seldom prepared to accept existing standards and values without question, even allowing for normal adolescent rebelliousness. Amid all their new-found affluence (which the ad-men are geared to relieving them of as quickly as possible) many teenagers, however, often seem bored, restless and rootless and sometimes violent and anti-social.

Young people in the teen years are, for the first time, conscious of being a well defined group in society. They have, for the most part, suffered from a bad press.

Public disquiet has been aroused by the fact that, although crime and delinquency figures may still be a marginal phenomenon, as against the total population figures, yet an increasingly large percentage of crimes committed are attributed to young people in the adolescent age group, particularly those between 17 years of age and 20. The fact that this is happening after a period of considerable social and educational advancement has proved upsetting to the formerly held theories which correlated crime and delinquency with bad environmental conditions due to material poverty.

It would appear in an age of rapid social and technological change that a whole new series of problems are confronting us, and that spiritual poverty and social frustration are taking the place of the material poverty of a previous age. It is little comfort to know that such problems, especially where they concern youth and delinquency, appear to be common to Western Europe, the United States, and to some Eastern countries.

All this has deep implications for the Youth Service which was brought into being in 1939 by the now famous Board of Education Circular, 1,486[1], for voluntary youth work here as elsewhere has a long and honourable history and reflects changing social and economic conditions over a long period.

THE PAST RECORD

The period from 1885 to the outbreak of the first world war saw the establishment and growth of the Y.M.C.A., the Y.W.C.A., the Boys' Brigade, the Girls' Guildry, the Boy Scouts and the Girl Guides. During that time also there were established in Edinburgh New College Settlement, the University Settlement and the Pleasance Trust, all owing their inspiration to the general influence of the Settlement movement.

Around 1916, war-time conditions brought about nationally the first tentative step at government level towards an interest in youth work. This occurred when the Home Office and the Board of Education jointly set up a Central Juvenile Organisations Committee, with a suggestion that local J.O.C.s be formed to make suggestions towards combating the then steep rise in juvenile delinquency and co-ordinating such youth organisations as were trying to provide for the leisure time activities of young people. Edinburgh established a J.O.C. in 1917. This functioned until after the second World War, during which time it helped the youth organisations and was at the same time responsible for the work of the voluntary probation officers until the present Probation Service was statutorily instituted in 1948. For 25 years it also had a Juvenile Employment Committee, and in 1937 it was instrumental in starting the Craigentinny–Lochend Social Centre, in what was at that time one of the

[1] Scottish Education Department's Circular 142 followed in the same week.

newest slum clearance areas. The J.O.C. eventually became incorporated in the Edinburgh Voluntary Youth Welfare Association.

The 20 years between the wars brought new concepts and new needs. There was in the '20s a vigorous upsurge of effort to build a better world for the young people growing up after the war, and this, together with the new social needs caused by the industrial depression of the '30s, was responsible for the growth of new youth organisations, particularly of the non-uniformed club type. There were started during this period the Edinburgh Union of Boys' Clubs and the Edinburgh Association of Girls' Clubs which in 1963 decided that it would be known in future as the Edinburgh Association of Youth Clubs because the large number of boys in the affiliated mixed clubs were embarrassed at belonging to what appeared to be a girls-only organisation. (The former as these words are written has 39 affiliated clubs, and the latter 26). To this period belong the North Merchiston Boys' Club, the Pleasance Trust Boys' Club, the Fettesian–Lorettonian Boys' Club, the Edinburgh Academy Stockbridge Boys' Club and the St. Giles Boys' Club; several of these have their own spacious and well-equipped premises.

About this time a move was made to the earliest of the housing estates, in pursuance of the city's slum clearance programme, and many of the youth organisations, uniformed and non-uniformed, and the Churches extended their work to these areas. But youth work, thus far, was almost entirely without state aid and was concerned with the under-privileged boy and girl.

Since 1939 Edinburgh has had a bewildering variety of youth groups, and adolescents have had a wide choice as to what organisations, if any, they wish to join. It seemed desirable that there should be a large number of freely chosen leisure time activities available to young people within the youth organisations. Consequently there are in the city a variety of units, both uniformed and non-uniformed. The churches of all denominations sponsor youth groups. The Edinburgh Hebrew Congregation has units for Jewish young people. There are units of the co-operative Youth Movement, the Junior Red Cross and the Scottish Youth Hostels Association. Even the Young Farmers Clubs have a unit in the city interested in farming.

Despite all this, Edinburgh, unlike some cities, has no civic youth centres. The Education Committee decided in 1939 to discharge its statutory obligations to the Youth Service through the existing voluntary organisations. The City Fathers have been reasonably generous however to the Youth Service, particularly since the setting up of the Kilbrandon Council (described later). The official attitude (unlike that of some individual Councillors) has been one of benevolent encouragement. This might well be so, since their decision did not involve them in anything like the expenditure which would have been necessary had they had to set up staff and maintain civic youth centres.

It would be no exaggeration to say that during the war and the immediate post-war years there was a boom in the Youth Service. The Scottish Education Department offered professional training for full-time leaders, as did certain University Colleges in England. Unfortunately the post-war economic blizzard, together with the need to direct available funds to school building programmes and the setting up of the new social services, brought a reversal of fortune. So stagnant had the situation become, that when the Albemarle Committee was set up in November, 1958, the Youth Service was said to be " dying on its feet." Some 15 months later this Committee presented its recommendations which were accepted almost overnight by the Minister of Education and a substantial amount of money was immediately made available to start their implementation, in order to help a generation of young people (whose numbers would, by 1964, have increased by one million over the 1958 figure) and whose standards and aspirations were vastly different from those of any previous generation.

THE KILBRANDON COUNCIL

The situation in Scotland had been one of equal urgency and the Secretary of State had already, in December, 1959, set up a Standing Consultative Council on Youth Service in Scotland under the Chairmanship of Lord Kilbrandon, to assist co-ordination both nationally and locally and to promote development. The Secretary of State then allocated an extra £10,000 for development in 1960–1, and one-and-a-half million pounds over the next four years for building projects for youth units. The Department subsequently offered an annual sum of £50,000 for three years towards capital projects, expenditure to be shared by the Department, the Local Authority and the individual unit on a 50 per cent, 25 per cent and 25 per cent basis respectively. Stress was again laid on the need to concentrate on the 14–18 age-group,[1] and already in the city highly desirable progress has been made.

The Kilbrandon Council has also given consideration to the training of both full-time and part-time leaders, and both full-time and part-time courses are now available at Moray House College of Education.

The city has recently sponsored a local Advisory Council composed of members of the Education Committee and the voluntary organisations to see that their combined resources are used to the best advantage. In a survey carried out in 1960 the Director of Education[2] reported that of the 21,500 young people in the city between the ages of 15 and 18 (27,800 by 1965), two in five were members of youth organisations, and the aim was to extend existing groups and foster new ones to cope with the teenagers of " the bulge."

State assistance with building programmes is timely, since accommodation remains, for many youth groups, a serious difficulty. Some have good premises of their own, dating from the expansion of the '30s. Canongate Boys' Club has the restored Panmure House. The University Settlement's new £15,000 Youth Centre has been opened at Prestonfield, and a number of other building projects are under way. Edinburgh Union

[1] Scottish Education Department, Circular 436, 1960.
[2] Report of Edinburgh Education Committee to the Scottish Education Department, November, 1960.

of Boys' Clubs and the old Edinburgh Association of Girls's Club (now the Edinburgh Association of Youth Clubs) have developed a fine Centre at Gracemount House (which the Education Committee has made available to them) and the Y.M.C.A. expect great results from their new Centre at Clermiston. So also does the Scottish Association of Youth Clubs from a new addition—the Edinburgh Teen-Aid Time and Talents Club (founded in 1963) which is open to all Scottish teenagers over 15 years old who had given, and would continue to give, service to others.

In the absence of any real Community Centre provision by the city, far too many groups, however, are having to meet in schools. In a school where the headmaster himself takes part in Club activities and the staff act as leaders in out-of-school hours, as at Ainslie Park and Niddrie Marischal, work of considerable value to the community can be done. The fact remains, however, that a school in the evening is not generally seen as an attractive venue by modern teenagers.

In the last two or three years there has been a veritable mushroom growth of café-type teenage centres in the city of which the pioneer efforts were the Scottish Episcopal Church's " Blue Door " and the University Settlement's " Studio 59." For the most part these centres are housed in the cellars of churches, and are imparting a veritable 18th century flavour to the city. They have attractive premises. In many instances the decor has been chosen and carried out by teenagers themselves. Of such an order are the " Greenlight Club " (Viewforth—St. Oswald's Church); the " Saints & Sinners Coffee Bar " (St. James's Mission); the " Coal Pit " (St. Giles Church); and what is perhaps the most costly undertaking, the " Cephas Teenage Rendezvous " beneath St. George's West Church. This venture in co-operation by five West End churches is boosted by an anonymous donation of £3,000. The five churches are also providing a corps of young helpers.

These experimental groups, it should be added, are all loosely structured. There is no set programme. The necessary provision is a coffee bar, modern music, and room to dance. The emphasis is on relationships rather than on activity.

HOPE FOR THE FUTURE

No-one nowadays would advocate activity for its own sake or because idleness is an invitation to the devil, but the nature of our modern society is such that it asks little of young people. Much of their work is dull and repetitive. Many of them live on housing estates, variously described as " concrete jungles " or " graveyards with lights." The only opportunity many of them have had of achieving personal effectiveness or of pursuing activities which have been personally rewarding have been through youth organisations. The Outward Bound Trust and the Duke of Edinburgh's Award Scheme have presented the idea of personal challenge and mastering a skill and have greatly enlarged the outdoor programmes of organisations. The Edinburgh Battalion of the Boys' Brigade with many Gold Awards to its credit pays testimony to this. The Scottish Council for Physical Recreation has given much help to organisations and individuals and has embarked on a new programme "Adventure on your Doorstep." Boys' Clubs own canoes which they have built and learned to sail. Cookery, beauty and poise, preparation for marriage and home-making, climbing, ski-ing and holidays abroad all help to widen the horizons of today's youth club members. Girls in the '60s are air-minded, if not space-minded. The Girls' Training Corps reported last year its biggest recruitment to the Women's Junior Air Corps. In the early 1960s officers and cadets were given flights at Scone airport and several units were granted recognition by the Air Ministry.

Consequent upon all these activities and discussions members of youth groups are made aware of the needs of others and give a considerable amount of community service. There are also a number of bodies in the city with an international fame and it is to these we must turn to complete the picture.

BOY SCOUTS

Over recent years the Boy Scouts movement in this area has experienced a decline in membership, but by 1964 there were signs of a healthy upward trend. The decrease has been concentrated in the older age group, where boys are inclined to feel "too grown-up" for continued membership. Teenagers generally, in fact, have been looking for some more exciting activity.

This challenge has now been met, and the Edinburgh Scouts' Adventure Training Scheme, the first such scheme in the movement anywhere in Britain, is now bringing in an increase in the total area membership to 8,000; and there are clear signs that this will continue. Ski-ing, pony trekking, gliding, the building of canoes to be taken on distant journeys, and similar activities directed towards adventure in the open, are getting enthusiastic support. The Adventure Training Scheme is now being expanded. Participants come from various parts of Enbland and Wales, and the promoters are kept busy examining and allocating applicants to courses. Worthy of mention too is the good work being done through the special Troops for handicapped children in hospitals and homes.

GIRL GUIDES

The Girl Guide movement in Edinburgh has some 10,000 members, a figure which has not fluctuated to any great extent over recent years. But its main problem, as with the Boy Scouts, is simply that although more adults have now come forward than in the past, the potential expansion is such that the demand for leaders cannot be satisfied.

Throughout the city the Guides make a fine contribution by brightening life for less fortunate girls, and their work among hospital patients and long-term residents of various homes is highly commended. "No-one who is aware of what is happening in the Guide movement", says one senior Guide, "need despair of the outlook of the average girl of today.

She has a sense of responsibility, and a willingness to help others that is truly impressive."

THE BOYS' BRIGADE

The Boys' Brigade is probably unique among major youth organisations in that all companies must be attached to a church, and that attendance at Bible Class on Sunday is compulsory on its members. In 1962 there were 1,904 boys on the roll, the majority being in the younger age groups, but in 1963 the total fell to 1,753. Officers have been devoting considerable research to this continuing loss of the senior boys, and discussing ways and means of holding their interest at a time when the teenage world offers so many colourful alternatives.

The situation, it is realised, can be improved if some means can be found to retain the 15-year old age-group, on the grounds that success would probably result in the boys continuing to higher rank and in due course becoming leaders for the younger lads. To this end, therefore, the Brigade in the Edinburgh and Leith area has been turning its attention to the possibilities of the Duke of Edinburgh's Award Scheme; and already the early indications have been that the Scheme is making a promising impact, and that as more boys are coached towards participation the tendency will be for them to remain members of what is the oldest of our uniformed youth organisations.

YOUNG MEN'S CHRISTIAN ASSOCIATION

Few voluntary organisations have achieved such a dramatic development over a relatively short period. The Association has purchased one of the city's old-established family hotels, and women and girls, through a Ladies' Auxiliary, are now participating in the Association's acitivities.

What is popularly known as " The Y.M." has met the challenge of the times in impressive style. The headquarters building in South St. Andrew Street is the administrative centre of a variety of activities with all the facilities of normal club life, plus many not usually provided—among them a well-appointed theatre with its own company of players, a gymnasium with steam baths, infra-red and ultra-violet lamp treatment and massage facilities, a dark room for photographic enthusiasts, and Saturday night dances. No evening is without its special attractions; and if one adds to these ski-ing, canoeing, camping and foreign travel facilities, one begins to understand the important place the Y.M.C.A. occupies in the life of the city's youth.

There is, happily, recognition of the fact that while enjoying such attractions the members must have due regard to the needs of others. Thus there is the Manor Club, which, situated in Rothesay Place, is operated as an international student hostel; the more recent acquisition, Suttie's Hotel, on the South Bridge, which accommodates Commonwealth and other students, most of them engaged in post-graduate study; and Hillside at Dunbar, a popular family holiday centre during the summer, and a conference and study centre in winter. The purchase of Suttie's Hotel was expedited by a Government grant.

The youth work done in makeshift premises in the extensive new housing scheme at Clermiston, on the west side of the city, has been expanded so that conventional club programmes will be only part of a broader pattern aiming at the strengthening of family life and mutual interests. The building of the new centre there at considerable cost has been aided by grants from the Government, the Corporation and the Carnegie United Kingdom Trust, and will provide for the training of leaders, and for experimental work of value to all interested in youth problems. Another important innovation catering mainly for young men not within the movement is the "Wider Horizons" residential courses held at Dunbar for those in their first years of employment. An increasing number of industrial firms and other organisations are supporting the venture by releasing employees for the five day courses.

YOUNG WOMEN'S CHRISTIAN ASSOCIATION

The Edinburgh branch of the Young Women's Christian Association of Great Britain, is not, strictly speaking, what it claims to be. Age matters not at all, they say at its George Street headquarters. It is the spirit, the enthusiasm that count. That is why membership of the Central Club includes not only girls, but young wives and older married women, covering, in fact, an age group ranging from eight to nearly 80! And males are by no means banned from the premises.

This generous use of the word "young" in the title, it is recognised, gives the branch a strength and a purpose it could not otherwise attain. The proof lies in widespread accomplishment touching various parts of the city where the helping hand is required. For the younger members it provides valuable links with the adult world, and opens up for older people opportunities to share in the service of youth.

At the George Street premises there are lounge facilities, a cafeteria serving morning coffee, lunches, and "teas with home-baked fare", and, among other activities, something that is deservedly popular. This is a once-a-week occasion, "The Samovar Pot", when young professional men and women meet to make new friends and talk at the coffee table.

The branch also runs hostels. These are patronised by holiday visitors and by students or young girls away from home for the first time, and also when the students are on vacation. All this, however, is subsidiary to the principal aim—the Christian and social work done in the youth clubs situated throughout the working-class districts. Most of this work is done in premises such as school halls.

The Leith–Lochend Club, for instance, has to meet in three centres, rather depressingly described by someone once as "a barren school hall, a rather bleak church hall, and a community hut, their own, but small." The hope here is that funds will be forthcoming so that continuity of activity may be secured in one convenient centre. Highly popular too are the mixed teenage clubs serving the housing schemes at Burdiehouse,

Pilton, Royston, Sighthill and in Leith, and the junior girls' clubs at Cranley School, Sighthill, Ashfield Home, Pilton, Royston, Stenhouse and Burdiehouse. The appeal of these clubs has been greatly enhanced not only by talks given by specialists on various subjects (" Poise and Personality ", " How to Entertain Your Friends ", " The Art of Conversation ", and so on), but by discussion groups, and by visits to places of interest such as the General Post Office and industrial works.

The sense of personal achievement not always found at school or at work comes to members through hiking, climbing and weekend camp outings, and here the branch's cottage at Gifford provides an ideal country centre.

CHAPTER 21

MARRIAGE AND DIVORCE

THE stresses and strains inherent in the modern social pattern increasingly find another outlet—in divorce.

The great social changes which have everywhere been apparent over the past fifty years have in many respects altered the traditional picture of marriage. Hitherto there was a predominating tendency for a husband and wife each to restrict their acitivities to certain spheres from which the other spouse was excluded. The home, the kitchen and the children were regarded generally as the responsibility of the wife, who was not supposed to bother her pretty little head about her husband's business or money affairs. A wife's role, in fact, was played out in private. It was domestic and subordinate, in contrast with the superordinate role of the husband who attended to the public side of life. Leisure time activities continued this pattern of segregation, the women busying themselves in voluntary associations, notably the church, women's guilds and charitable organisations, while the men went to their clubs, pubs or political organisations. Because of this segregation of roles and interests, emphasis in the marriage relationship was placed on the correct fulfilment of duties rather than on personal compatibilities.

MODERN PATTERNS

That is no longer the accepted pattern. Nevertheless, despite many changes in the occupational structure of society, which has been profoundly affected by two World Wars and by the increasing complexity and specialisation of occupations, and in spite of the extension of education, employment and the franchise to include women, many of the traditional attitudes still survive in Edinburgh and involve men and women in situations of conflicting role expectations.

Women are now an important source of labour, and they are often very highly trained and qualified. This has an important effect on a woman's attitude to men and to marriage. A woman who has worked alongside men, and perhaps initiated action involving men, no longer regards them as " naturally " superior, nor is she willing automatically to accept a subordinate status. New occupational opportunities also give her the possibility of a new financial independence which adds to her new independence of mind.

The first hurdle in a marriage, then, is the nature of the expectation which husband and wife have of the other's behaviour. A great number of men in Edinburgh appear still to hold strongly traditional views about the roles of husbands and of wives. Those women who share these views and adjust themselves to the segregated type of conjugal role relationship—and there are many of them—have happy married lives. Such wives are willing to see their husbands go out to spend the evening with their mates or colleagues, to leave the table to the men after dinner, to wash the dishes alone and to wheel the pram. But many women, after several years of participation in the competitive occupational world, where sex is often much less important than ability, find it difficult to adjust to such a pattern. Their ideal is the companionate type of marriage with a joint conjugal role relationship in which there is no strict division between the spheres of husband and wife, and where the husband, for example, is willing to wash the dishes or take the baby for a walk, in order that his wife will have more time to spend with him in leisure time pursuits. In this kind of marriage husband and wife want an equality of status and responsibility and a unity of interest and activity. Where this is achieved husband and wife enjoy a happy and in some ways a deeper relationship than the more traditional one.

Some women, however, are unfortunate and marry men who have a different expectation of the marriage relationship from that of their own. Marriage for these women brings a period of severe adjustment to this conflict of expectations. For some of the wives the situation is resolved by the birth of their children. Others cope with it by going out to work. If outside work for the wife accompanies a joint conjugal role relationship, then it is one more example of the co-operation between the spouses and seems to give rise to little friction. But if the husband still regards domesticity as a wife's first and often exclusive duty, and furthermore regards it as no part of his obligations to assist her in the home, then the working wife often performs two full-time roles. In such cases she may resent her husband's lack of co-operation, and a great deal of strain is imposed on the marriage relationship by the differing expectations which husband and wife bring to it. In seven cases of divorce involving Edinburgh people which were studied at first hand, the basic cause of the conflict between husband and wife, whatever the subsequent and legal grounds for divorce, seems to have been this conflict in role expectations.

STATUS OF THE DIVORCED

A great number of those who divorce do so with the intention of re-marrying. Of those who do not, the divorced man has much less of a social problem to face. He is still employed and he can enjoy his leisure in the Scotsman's traditional preserves—his club or pub with his friends. But for a divorced woman who does not re-marry the position is very different. The statistics show that most marriages are not dissolved in the first few years of marriage. Therefore, whatever the conflicts which have preceded a marital break-up, a woman has got used to her role as wife in relation not only to her husband, but in relation to the rest of the world. The most immediate problem for the *divorcée* is usually not an economic one, although this may come later, nor even so crude a social one as fear of ridicule or contempt or ostracism, although these too may emerge in time: it is the loss of social identity accompanying the loss of social role. Some women react by withdrawing from their friends and becoming suspicious of outsiders; some feel themselves to be an object of suspicion, particularly on the part of their married women friends. Women who have children and who get custody of them become over-absorbed in the children. Others plunge wildly into a round of activities in an attempt to create for themselves a new social identity. Those wives who have been married for a relatively short time or who have continued to work after marriage are often those who can adjust most easily to the new situation, for they have maintained or have access to an occupational role which will alleviate their sense of non-identity, and, like the men, they can cope with the public world from which the more domesticated wife has been isolated.

DIVORCE IN EDINBURGH

Divorce is of course by no means peculiar to the people of Edinburgh, but it is especially relevant to an account of the city because it is here that Scots congregate to terminate their marriage since all actions for divorce in Scotland are heard in the Court of Session. There have been suggestions in the past that divorce actions might well be heard in the Sheriff Courts which are spread throughout the country, and this would certainly be cheaper and more convenient for the parties concerned and the witnesses who have to attend Court to give evidence. On the other hand, it has been argued that this would be unsuitable for two main reasons. Firstly, divorce involves a change in civil status and this should be the business of the central, higher court; and secondly, the central court being situated in Edinburgh, proper legal representation can be given there by advocates and solicitors who are experienced in divorce law. Whatever the merits of the opposing arguments the fact remains that all divorces are heard in Edinburgh, and therefore every year a large number of people from the rest of Scotland come to the city in connection with divorce. They include at least one of the parties to the action and, in defended cases, often both, not to mention witnesses and relatives. This situation inevitably has certain repercussions—work for the city's legal profession, business for hotels, a strengthening of the status of Edinburgh as the administrative and judicial centre of Scotland, and finally the problem of time-consuming cases in the Court of Session.

In 1901 there were 25 cases of divorce in which both parties were residents of Edinburgh and 21 cases where one of the parties to the divorce came from the city. In 1951 the number had risen to 157 cases where both parties lived in the city and 150 where only one of the parties did so. In 1901 the rate of divorce per thousand of the total population of the city was approximately 0·1: in 1951 this had become 0·7 approximately.

To leap forward a decade, in Edinburgh during 1961 there were 162 divorces granted in which one of the parties to the case was domiciled in the city. There were 191 cases where both were residents, making a total of 353 cases involving Edinburgh citizens. In 1961 the rate of divorce per thousand of the total population of Edinburgh was a little over 0·7, a figure which may be compared with the similar rate for Scotland of approximately 0·37.

DIVORCE RATES IN SCOTLAND

This pattern of divorce in Edinburgh reflects the situation in the rest of Scotland, which also shows a remarkable increase during the first half of the century. In 1961 no fewer than 1,808 divorces were granted in Scotland, compared with 171 in 1901. In 1901 the total population of Scotland was approximately 4½ millions: by 1961 this had risen to more than five millions. Divorce rates per 10,000 of the total population would therefore be about 0·38 for 1901 and 3·68 for 1961—a tenfold increase. But though the year 1961 has been selected for the convenience of comparison, it does not indicate the considerable fluctuations in the divorce rate during the present century. A peak figure of 2,702 was reached in 1952. The figure then fell to 1,687 in 1959, and rose again in 1961. It would, however, be more useful to relate the number of marriages which are terminated by divorce to the number of those which endure, and to take into account both changes in the size of the total population and the proportion of married to unmarried by basing the rate of divorce on the number of married women in the population. In 1901 there were approximately 690,400 married females in the population. In 1961 this total had become 1,218,500. In other words, rates per 10,000 married women would be respectively 2·47 and 14·83—showing a smaller rise in rate in the sixty years between 1901 and 1961 than the crude divorce rate above. It is also usual to take into account changes in the age range of the population by introducing an age standardisation, e.g. by restricting the rate to the number of divorcées per 10,000 married women between the ages of 16 and 54. This would gives rates of 2·93 in 1901 and 19·25 in 1961.

GROUNDS FOR DIVORCE

What does this large increase mean in terms of the stability of marriage and of family life? Much public concern has been expressed on this subject and it has been claimed that the increase reflects a break-down in public morality, in the institution of marriage and of the family. Such views, although widely held, are in fact backed by little factual evidence. While it is true that both the numbers and rate of divorce have grown larger, in Edinburgh as elsewhere, there are various important factors which must be taken into account. There are the many changes in the pattern of living in the first half of the century. Conditions of employment and of payment have changed appreciably and the extension of social welfare has resulted in financial aid for those in need of it. Not less important, there has been a general change in notions of respectability. All these factors have had an undoubted effect on the way in which recourse to divorce is now regarded.

The relation of public immorality and divorce arises in many people's minds because of the nature of the legal grounds on which an action for divorce may be raised. In Scotland adultery and desertion were the sole grounds for divorce from the middle of the 16th century until the passing of the Divorce (Scotland) Act, 1938. This Act added three new grounds of divorce; namely, cruelty, incurable insanity, and sodomy and bestiality. The widening of the grounds for divorce introduced by this Act has had important effects. One of the most important is that the idea of marital offence has been separated from the idea of sin. When the only grounds for divorce were adultery and desertion a moral judgment was made on the guilty party to a divorce, but in the present day at least one ground, that is, incurable insanity implies no moral censure, and the extension of the ground of cruelty to include mental cruelty may sometimes merely infer incompatibility. Even where the ground is adultery, it is probably true to say that in a great many cases evidence of the adultery is supplied by the "guilty" party to his or her spouse and may be a formality. It would therefore appear that recourse to divorce may not be viewed simply in terms of the ostensible ground produced in court. A broken marriage has a long history of dissension before the parties ever consult their solicitors, and the legal grounds may in many cases be regarded merely as the most convenient way in which the petition is phrased for presentation to the court. What lies behind the formal ground is a relationship which has failed to live up to expectations and, perhaps, dreams. Sixty years ago the social pressures and financial circumstances, particularly as regards women, were such that partners in an unhappy relationship had to reconcile themselves to make the best of it. This is no longer the case.

The influence of the churches has also a bearing on decisions to divorce, both as regards the attitude of the churches themselves to divorce and as regards the influence of the churches on the community. In this connection the type of ceremony in which the marriage bond is forged may have some relevance. In 1960, of the 40,103 marriages registered in Scotland, 32,926 or 82·1 per cent were solemnised by a minister of religion, 7,176 or 17·89 per cent were civil marriages, and one isolated case was an irregular marriage. Officially, the Church of Scotland has always viewed divorce with more tolerance than the Church of England, and this tolerance has been increasing, so that today there is no bar in the Church of Scotland to the re-marriage in Church of either the innocent or the guilty party to a divorce. It must be stressed, however, that the attitude of ministers and members of the Church of Scotland to divorce is one of toleration and not of favour, and that the influence of the Church, as against its authority, would tend to counteract the increase in the divorce rate. This influence is much less strong today than in 1901 and this weakening of influence has undoubtedly been one factor in the increasing rate of recourse to divorce. The influence of the Roman Catholic Church and the Free Presbyterian Church is confined to certain comparatively small areas and in such areas is still a powerful deterrent.

AGE OF MARRIAGE AND DIVORCE

One aspect of the changing pattern of marriage in Scotland in the early '60s can be seen in the tendency to marry at an earlier age. In 1938 the largest percentage of males who married were between the ages of 25 and 29. In 1960 the largest percentage was in the age-group 21–24. The number of males marrying before the age of 21 also greatly increased. The highest percentage of females marrying in 1960 was in the age-group 21–24—a situation similar to that in 1938—but the number of females in the group 25–29 decreased from being almost as high as the 21–24 group in 1938 to being less than half the number of this group in 1960. Also, as in the case of males, in 1960 there was a higher percentage of females marrying under the age of 21. Moreover, they constituted just over a third of all marriages registered in that year.

However, the rising divorce rate is certainly not caused by the early age at which marriages now often take place. Figures show that in Scotland in 1961 only 1·35 per cent of those divorced in that year had been married less than two years, while in Edinburgh the figure was as low as 0·6 per cent. In Edinburgh the largest number of divorces occurred between four and seven and between ten and fourteen years after marriage. Edinburgh also showed the same high proportion of divorces after 20 years or more of marriage. In 1961 it was 18·4 per cent of the total for that year, compared with 18·47 per cent in Scotland as a whole; and it may be that a marriage that is generally unsatisfactory is endured until the children reach adulthood, when the parents at last feel free to terminate their unhappy union.

Before leaving this aspect of divorce it would be timely here to study the following table which explains how long marriages broken up by divorce in 1961 had lasted.

TABLE 44
EDINBURGH DIVORCES 1961
DURATION OF MARRIAGE

Years	*Edinburgh*	*Scotland*
Under 1 year	—	1
1 year	2	21
2 years	9	55
3 do	16	77
4 do	27	133
5 do	24	137
6 do	32	123
7 do	29	87
8 do	15	96
9 do	13	84
10-14	73	295
15-19	48	215
20 and over	65	300
Total	353[1]	1624[2]

[1] It should be noted that the Edinburgh figures include *all* divorces involving parties where either or both were resident in Edinburgh.

[2] These figures relate to persons married in Scotland. (Annual Report of Registrar-General).

NEW IDEALS OF MARRIAGE

Perhaps one of the most important factors in marriage and divorce is the new ideal of a companionate relation in marriage. Sixty years ago a husband and his wife expected to lead different lives with different interests and activities; the new relationship, which involves more contact between the parties, also imposes greater strains and provides more opportunities for disenchantment. Sixty years ago, too, marriage was indeed for better or for worse. A man or woman who had been involved in such an unsavoury business as divorce, even as the " innocent " party, sustained a severe blow to his or her reputation. Now the pervading feeling that every individual is entitled to his share of happiness extends even to marriage, and it is widely held that if the individual is unhappily involved in an unsatisfactory marriage then that individual is entitled to set the matter right. Except where children are involved and might suffer, the general feeling among younger people is that divorce in such circumstances is desirable and without shame. The former attitude still, however, lingers on amongst the older generation, particularly women who would rather continue to suffer an unhappy relationship than suffer the reputation of being divorced, even as an innocent party.

There is now, then, a new idealisation of marriage, encouraged perhaps by modern advertising and by films and stories which emphasise the importance of marrying " Mr. Right " and the subsequent " Happy ever after." Individuals set a high value on a satisfactory relationship and are less likely to endure an unsatisfactory one. From this point of view divorce may be regarded not as an attack on the value of marriage but as a move towards righting the situation. The fact that a great many divorces are the prelude to re-marriage by one or both of the divorcing parties shows that marriage itself is still highly valued.

How true is the charge that the Scottish family is breaking up? There has been no marked indication that this is so, when it is considered than in 1901, of the couples divorcing in Scotland, 41 per cent had no children and in 1951 the proportion was little different at 37 per cent. In 1961, of the 353 Edinburgh divorces, 160 involved cases where there were children under 16 years of age—that is 45·3 per cent—while in 193 cases no children under 16 years were involved, which is 54·7 per cent. Moreover, in 1901, 18·4 per cent of the divorces were of marriages of 20 years or more, and in 1961, 18·47 per cent of marriages had similarly lasted at least 20 years. It can therefore be assumed that in many of these cases any children involved were no longer of tender years. It would also seem that in the first half of this century at least there has been little progressive decay of the family as an institution in Scotland; and there seems no reason why what is true of Scotland in this respect should not be true of Edinburgh.

There are then two aspects to consider—a new form of marriage coupled with greater expectations from the marital relationship, and conditions in which access to divorce is easier. Divorce must be considered in this light rather than from the pessimistic view that there has been some kind of disastrous decline in morals, marriage and family. It is true that the divorce rate has risen, but all that this may indicate is that within a changing social context divorce is becoming an economic and social possibility of which more and more people are availing themselves. Although no figures are available, there is also an impression that a smaller proportion of couples are having recourse to judicial separation, which in the past has been largely used as an alternative to divorce and which gives judicial recognition to the break-up of a marriage without dissolving it absolutely.

CHAPTER 22

THE PURSUITS OF LEISURE

OUT OF DOORS

IN the late 18th century Edinburgh's sports and pastimes were limited to golf, curling, quoits, cockfights and angling, in all of which the various classes of society joined; but archery and fencing out-of-doors were rather the prerogative of the gentry, as were dancing assemblies and whist in halls and private houses. Since then the number and the variety of the city's public and private leisure pursuits have widened so greatly that a local sports writer truthfully says in 1963 that Edinburgh has now a " widely cultivated love of sport on a sort of ' nothing barred ' scale."

The various reasons for this are easy to find. A worldwide stirring of interest in sport has been fostered by television and radio. There has been in recent years a marked advance not only in the living standards of most wage-earners but in the time they now have for sports and pastimes and for holidays both at home and abroad. Two world wars and a great speed-up in communications have also made Edinburgh people more conscious of the outer world than ever before. Football fans, for instance, take a livelier interest than they used to do in Continental football, which some go to see, or foreign casinos which some regret later they had ever seen at all. But naturally their main sporting interests are at home where the variety of Edinburgh's life is as marked in the leisure pursuits of its people as it is in their work and social habits and their surroundings. There can surely be few cities where climbing and ski-ing take place within the city boundaries.

MOUNTAINEERING

Though this claim may sound at first surprising, it is nonetheless true that there are people in Edinburgh who enjoy climbing the many rock faces which tower up within the city boundaries, and who wonder sometimes whether any other British city can boast such internal facilities for a sport normally associated with the wilderness.

There are many Edinburgh citizens too, who belong to The Scottish Mountaineering Club. This club, long regarded as the senior in Scotland, not unnaturally has its headquarters in the capital. Founded in Glasgow in 1888, the Club's headquarters were transferred to Edinburgh in March, 1902. At one time a considerable number of the founder members lived in the city, and the Club's records show that of the total membership of 94 in the year of its foundation, 17 were Edinburgh men. The national membership in the early '60s was still counted in men—some 330 of them—and of these some 80 come from Edinburgh.

The early members included some celebrated climbers. The most famous of these was Harold Raeburn, who wrote what is still a mountain classic, *Mountaineering Art*. Raeburn made many first ascents on the great cliffs of such mountains as Ben Nevis, Buachaille Etive Mor, Creag Meagaidh and Lochnagar, and such was his reputation that he was chosen as mountaineering leader of the first Everest Expedition in 1921. In Edinburgh itself a select band of Raeburn and his contemporaries even exploited Edinburgh's own climbing potentialities by ranging so thoroughly over the Salisbury Crags that they achieved the cliff-top along its length by many routes with such names as the Cat Nick Arete, Red Slab Route and Mackay's Chimney. The last was a corner chimney climb in the Little Quarry of the Crags first ascended by an advocate who later, as Lord Mackay, became a judge of the Scottish Bench.

The habit of practising on the " hills of home " displays itself engagingly in the Club records, for these Edinburgh pioneers loved their little domestic crags and the infinitely various slopes of the Border Hills and the Pentlands. In those early days, too, they even tried the then novel sport of ski-ing; and indeed Raeburn records a days' expedition on the snowy Pentlands, which he finished—one winter evening in 1900—by ski-ing down the tram-lines from the Braids to Morningside Station.

The general growth of mountaineering, accelerated significantly since the last World War, has been reflected in the appearance of other clubs mostly composed of younger men. In 1925 the Junior Mountaineering Club of Scotland was founded largely with the aim of acting as a training club for the senior, club which sets certain essential entrance qualifications. The Edinburgh branch of this body in the early '60s had a membership of about 35, with ages ranging from 17 to 25. Both clubs are all-male, but the Scottish Mountaineering Club helped to found the Ladies Scottish Climbing Club (1908) which has some 110 members.

There are also two mixed clubs—the Edinburgh University Mountaineering Club, with about 15 members and a new foundation, the Edinburgh Mountaineering Club, which has a fluctuating membership. The latter sprang in 1955 from an original association of mountain devotees who ran what was called the " Edinburgh Mountaineering Bus ", a vehicle run regularly from Edinburgh at weekends to various climbing centres. All these clubs—except the Scottish Mountaineering Club, which the younger climbers' myth credits with senility, plutocracy and the universal ownership of motor cars—organise weekend " bus meets " almost every week. Their most popular meets are at Glen Coe, Ben Nevis and the Cairngorms.

As well as these outdoor activities, there are many " indoor meets " where lectures are given on climbing at home and abroad. The Scottish Mountaineering Club which has a splendid library and a collection of more than 4,500 lantern slides organises about a dozen of these every winter.

The total of members affiliated to mountaineering clubs in the city is

The Castle viewed from the Crown of St. Giles'. Immediately below on the left are the County Buildings and, across the High Street, the Sheriff Court. Leading up to the Castle is the Lawnmarket, at the head of which is the spire of Tolbooth St. John's.

The Castle, viewed from one of the rocky faces of Salisbury Crags in the Queen's Park, dominates the skyline above the Old Town. The tenement houses in the foreground are being pulled down and the whole area re-developed.

The golf course at Craiglockhart, one of the 20 fine courses within the city boundaries which make the city's pleasant open spaces notable.

about 250, but this figure cannot accurately reflect the actual number of active climbers of one kind or another, which may be several times as great. These modern climbers, like their forefathers, still climb in the Salisbury Crags (when authority is elsewhere) and invent new and increasingly severe routes. Some of them have also been climbing on the crags of Caerketton at the city end of the Pentland Hills; and there, to the disgust of some of their mountaineering elders, they have cleaned and "gardened" (as the climbing term goes) the little mossy virgin rock until these faces have emerged as rock routes with such names as Architects' Arete, Weeded Wall, Cave Pitch and even Prayer Mat.

SKI-ING

In recent years ski-ing has won so many followers that in Edinburgh and the East of Scotland region alone, several hundred enthusiasts are members of the Scottish Ski Club. There is also a University club with fine competitive teams which won the British Universities ski championship twice in the early '60s. Such feats as these naturally assist the spread of the sport, but its growing appeal is obvious. There has only to be a decent fall of snow around the city, and at once there is a rush to the Pentland Hills and the Braids for both the good and the no-so-good exponents to enjoy themselves. Always there are week-end treks to the Highlands where ski-ing is now firmly established as a Scottish winter sport.

ANGLING

Among the other sports which Edinburgh folk practise both inside and outside the city limits is one of the most ancient of all—angling. Moreover Edinburgh is one of the few cities with a trout stream running through it, and in past years conditions in the Water of Leith have sometimes been so good that remarkable catches of quite large fish have been recorded in this river. In 1956, for instance, the Honorary Bailiffs reported that a fish taken from the water near Woodhall Mill had been considered so worthy of preservation that a plaster cast was taken of it. The fish weighed 26 ounces, measured 15½ inches, and was believed to be approximately 5½ years old.

Five years later pollution of the Water of Leith and the disfigurement of the river bed by the dumping of rubber tyres and iron junk presented the angler with a discouraging picture aggravated by frothing scum which seemed to come from industrial plants on the river banks. By 1962, however, the emergence and steady rise in prestige and power of the River Pollution Boards gave hope for the future that in time the rivers and burns of the Lothians would be restored to their pristine state. In fact, what can be done to sustain fish life in an urban river is now being illustrated by the manner in which the Edinburgh Corporation exercises a paternal and controlled interest over the Water of Leith from source to sea. A sewer extending from Balerno to the sea follows the course of the river and draws off the noxious effluents from mills and other sources in the area. Every year, too, the Corporation stocks the river from Currie to Canonmills; official permits are issued to anglers; and the river is " policed " by voluntary bailiffs who give their services without fee.

As a further enlightened act of policy the Corporation's Water Department also provides angling facilities in the city's reservoirs, all of which are set in pleasant surroundings and offer a good day's sport. The best, and consequently the most sought after, is Gladhouse, a shallow loch for which a ballot determines the lucky applicants. To catch a two-pounder trout in this loch is not uncommon, and several fish between one and one-and-a-half pounds are caught there every week.

The adjacent reservoir loch at Rosebery is likewise noted for the quality of its trout, but though Harperrig, on the north Pentlands, is another loch with a good stock of fish, the average has gone down in recent years and pounders are much less common than they were 20 years ago. Another nearby loch is Clubbiedean, a small pleasant stretch in the hills above Colinton, but this is difficult to book as only one boat is allowed on the loch at one time. Finally there are Talla and Glencorse. Glencorse is a loch of great charm, but the water is clear and acid and the trout run at only three to the pound with an occasional half-pounder. Talla is 40 miles to the southwest of the city and is the city's largest reservoir. It lies in a deep cleft of hills, and though the angler is often baffled by local changes of wind it is well worth a visit. As there are also many other easily accessible lochs in the Pentland and Moorfoot ranges, such as Threipmuir which is privately owned, it can be fairly stated that the Edinburgh freshwater angler and the city's many angling clubs are favourably served in the matter of their favourite sport; and they also have the sea at their door.

GOLF

Still giving precedence to the city's older sports, we come happily to golf, for Edinburgh is a cradle of the game and has had golf-minded citizens for centuries. Not only that, the artisan is still as keen as that romantic figure John Patersone the shoemaker who helped his partner the Duke of York (later King James VII of Scotland and II of England) to win the first international golf match ever played. Patersone was later to become a bailie, and also he built Golfer's Land in the Canongate, a building which for centuries delighted the tourist sightseer, till in the late '50s it was scheduled for demolition, though not without a happy agreement that the stone crest, motto and anagram of John Patersone, I HATE NO PERSON, should be preserved and displayed on the front of the new dwelling-house building which took its place.

Three other worthies in an even earlier age have also been commemorated—by no less a person than Mr. P. G. Wodehouse in his enchanting book *The Clicking of Cuthbert*. The dedication reads:

TO THE
IMMORTAL MEMORY
OF
JOHN HENRIE AND PAT ROGIE
WHO
AT EDINBURGH, IN THE YEAR 1593 A.D.
WERE IMPRISONED FOR
PLAYING OF THE GOWFF ON THE LINKS OF
LEITH EVERY SABBATH THE TIME OF THE SERMONSES,

ALSO OF
ROBERT ROBERTSON
WHO GOT IT IN THE NECK IN 1604 A.D.
FOR THE SAME REASON

Today the city still boasts one of the keenest golfing communties in the country. Precise figures are not available, but the unattached players may number between 25,000 and 30,000, and to these must be added the more exactly computable number of golfers attached to private clubs who, including women, numbered approximately 15,000 in the early '60s. Clubs of various composition in works, offices, and other institutions had at the same time a total membership of some 5,000; but for statistical purposes these should be included among either the private or public course users. What is certain is that on the city's five full-length municipal courses, some 10,000 permits to play may be issued in a single year. The revenue from the Braids alone, says Mr. Frank Moran,[1] who contributes these facts and figures, shows clearly that " there's gold in them thar hills " and that the other major courses are also highly productive. As for the short-hole and putting courses, in 1958–9 (to pick a good average year in recent times) the 260,000 rounds played on them brought in £4,447.

The Corporation maintains over 700 acres of land for golf, including many short-hole and putting courses. To mention one of the most famous, Bruntsfield short-hole course, which continues a centuries-old connection with the game, was the birth place of the Royal Burgess Society and Bruntsfield Links Society (now privately quartered elsewhere); and it was deserted only when the game became " a danger to the lieges," and the Corporation acquired the Braid Hills in the 1880s. But the Bruntsfield saga lingers on. It was on these ancient links that McKellar, a famous 18th century character known as " Cock o' the Green," used to play by lamplight even when there was snow on the ground and refused to be shamed out of his addiction by the frequency of the occasions when his frustrated wife had to take his supper out to him. When the Braid Hills opened in 1890 the game was free, but the demand at once became so pressing that a fee of a penny a round was imposed. Through the years the charges have, of course been stepped up gradually, though in relation to the increased costs on every hand, the game is still comparatively cheap

[1] Mr. Moran, an outstanding golf correspondent who knows personally all the world's most famous golfers, had a signal honour paid to him in August 1963 when *The Scotsman* announced that an annual award - to be known as the Frank Moran Trophy - would henceforth be made to a Scot, or a person of Scots extraction, who had rendered notable service to the game. The first winner was the famous Tommy Armour who was born in Edinburgh, learned his golf on the Braids, and later became an American citizen.

and attracts a great many devotees ranging from salesmen to students.

The Braid Hills, it is noteworthy, have their own family circle of clubs who have always made their home there and have their own premises: Edinburgh Thistle, for example, for whom the great James Braid played in his amateur days when he was a joiner; Edinburgh Western with whom the brothers Armour began their careers; and many others, with memberships ranging from around 50 to about 100. Also on the Braids there are Corporation—sponsored events and the *Evening Dispatch* Trophy Tournament (double foursomes) which inaugurated the No. 1 course in 1890, and is one of the most popular in the country.

Of the 18 privately owned courses which girdle the city the Royal Burgess Society with more than 600 members is the senior, and has indeed claims to being the oldest in the world. Other private clubs are Bruntsfield Links Society, Dalmahoy, Baberton, Duddingston, Prestonfield, Mortonhall, Turnhouse, Kingsknowe, Lothianburn, Merchants, Liberton, Murrayfield, Ratho Park, Craigmillar Park, Swanston, Ravelston, and Torphin Hill. There can be few cities better catered for. But there is perhaps a more personal and certainly a very pleasant note on which to end this quick survey of one of Edinburgh's most ancient pastimes.

In 1963 Mr. R. D. B. M. Shade of Duddingston, a British Walker Cup player who plays his home golf in the shade of Arthur's Seat, not only won the Scottish Amateur Golf Championship but materially helped Great Britain to share the Commonwealth Amateur Golf Championship at Sydney. In the home internationals at Royal Lytham—in the same year—he won all his three single matches. He also took the Brabazon Trophy awarded to the winner of the English Amateur Stroke Play Championship, and at Turnberry in the Walker Cup he triumphed again. Within a year he had become the Lothians Amateur Champion and in the autumn of 1964, as one of a team of four, he played a vital part at Rome in Great Britain's and Ireland's historic capture of the international Eisenhower Trophy. This was a great triumph in world golf competition, for the event was the 4th World Amateur Team Championship; Great Britain and Ireland had never won it before; and Shade's score of 70 on the first day was never surpassed. To cap this quite remarkable record, in July, 1965 Shade won the Open Amateur Championship for the third successive year.

ASSOCIATION FOOTBALL

Of all outdoor pastimes, it is however Association Football which attracts the widest interest in the city and—except for an international Rugby match at Murrayfield—the biggest crowds, though these in recent years have been diminishing.[1] When either of the city's two professional clubs—Heart of Midlothian and Hibernian—are playing at home and attracting large crowds in a good season, the scene is often an inspiring and prolonged human spectacle marked by the tense waiting before the teams

Since the 1956-57 season the home League gates in Edinburgh have slumped from 714,000 to 413,000 (a figure published in March, 1965.

appear on the field; the keen club followers wearing the appropriate colours of their favourites, either maroon for the Hearts or green and white for Hibernian; a roar round the stadium when the teams appear from the pavilion in their brightly coloured shirts; the equally loud roar when the referee sets thc game going; and the thunderous applause when the home team scores a goal.

But this is the game's human side. In a commercial sense soccer is now more than ever big business, in Edinburgh no less than in any English city of similar size, and being an easy first as a box office attraction the business is conducted in a way which would seem unbelievable to its early pioneers. Instead of the old " bob a nob " days, it cost 3*s*. in 1963 to stand on the terracing, and stand seats might cost up to 6*s*. and sometimes more for specially attractive matches. Players were being paid up to £1,500 a year, with perquisites, and the stars much more.

During the mid-1950s Edinburgh's football enthusiasts had reason to acclaim their two professional teams. At the end of the last war, Hibernian, founded in 1875 by an Irish Catholic community but no longer having any religious complexion, quickly became the most accomplished soccer team in the First Division of the Scottish League, with a forward line of household names, who together scored nearly 700 goals and produced among them more than 100 international caps for Scotland. During this post-war period they won all the football honours, except the Scottish Cup which by 1964 had still eluded them. Then gradually their fortunes ebbed when what a sporting journalist might call their " star-studded side " was broken up in the modern " big business " atmosphere. In June, 1961 Hibernian Football Club collected £65,000 from the Italian club, Torino, for one of its forwards, and in the same month Arsenal paid £40,000 for another regular player.

Launched in 1874, Hibernians' nearest professional rivals, Heart of Midlothian have also many honours to their credit, and like Hibernian in the post-war years, they have paid visits to many overseas countries in Europe, and also South Africa, America and Australia. But it is still the weekly game at home that matters most, since professional football is so clearly now big business. It is also connected with another big business—that of the football pools, a form of gambling which gives the Heart of Midlothian and Hibernian Football Clubs a special significance not only for the Edinburgh plumber, say, but for the bricklayer in Heckmondwike or the fisherman in Penzance.

As for the rest of the smaller clubs in the city these are legion. Six Edinburgh amateur clubs of standing, (Murrayfield Amateurs, Civil Service Strollers, University, Spartans, City Police and Ferranti) take part in the old-established East of Scotland League, along with ten Border clubs; but the Edinburgh and District Junior League has not a single member from the capital, though Edinburgh was once a stronghold of this particular grade. By contrast many hundreds of players—in 1963 the Edinburgh Amateur Association alone had 68 clubs in six divisions—are engaged under various amateur bodies. The Juvenile clubs—from churches, welfare bodies, boys' clubs and the Boys' Brigade—provide weekly matches for thousands of youths; and in addition the city's primary and secondary schools field almost 200 teams each week.

RUGBY

Rugby football has a longer history of organised play in the city than Association, for the game is said to have been introduced into the Academy in 1851. Edinburgh Academicals (former pupils of the school) are indeed more than 100 years old; and several other clubs were formed soon afterwards. The Murrayfield ground, headquarters of the game in Scotland, is situated on the west side of the city. It attracts up to 80,000 spectators for international matches, and is the venue of two such games each season, and three when Commonwealth sides are touring the British Isles, as the famous All Blacks from New Zealand did in the 1963–4 season. The usual practice is for France and England to visit Edinburgh one year, Ireland and Wales the next; and invariably the biggest crowds gather for the English and Welsh matches. The match with Wales, most people agree, is usually the most colourful, since for days ahead thousands of Welshmen decked out in red and white favours of every kind pour into the city to sing not only in the ground itself but in the streets and pubs and wherever else they may congregate before and after the great game. In fact, an international day at Murrayfield is a great social occasion, and never more so than on the day of Scotland's encounter with the oldest " enemy " of all. The first time Scotland played England was in 1871 and ever since, these matches have been played except in wartime. It should be added that the winning side is presented with the famous Calcutta Cup, a trophy presented by the Calcutta Rugby Club and made from the melted-down rupees which remained when the club was disbanded.

Throughout the season a great deal of rugby is played in Edinburgh. No fewer than 10 city clubs take part in the " unofficial " Scottish Championship, and these run anything from three to six graded sides, as well as junior fifteens. In the Edinburgh Junior Championship there are 11 city clubs along with nine from the Lothians, and these too operate in duplicate and triplicate, as do the fee-paying schools.

Despite all this, in the middle '50s old-timers became convinced that the standard of play in the city had deteriorated. But fortunately the Scottish XV improved in the early '60s and in the 1963–4 season shared the International Championship with Wales and was the only home country side undefeated by the All Blacks. In the meantime, though the normal 15-a-side rugby game was thought by many to have deteriorated in the middle and later '50s but was obviously recovering there was, and still is, great enthusiasm in Edinburgh for the seven-a-side tournaments which follow the end of the normal season in March.

CRICKET

Though Edinburgh University has had among its students many West

Indians who were good cricketers, none has ever made quite such an impact as R. V. Webster, a brilliant fast bowler studying medicine, who deserves special mention here. Webster arrived at the University from Barbados towards the end of the '50s, and soon became the most talked-of bowler not only in Edinburgh but in Scotland as a whole. In particular his hostile pace and accuracy enabled the University in 1961 to become East League champions for the first time with 12 wins out of 12 matches played. He also played for Scotland—home of his great-great grandfather, he has claimed with pride—and in non-English county championship games for Warwickshire.

Webster's notable feats in the East League matches coincided with a distinct revival of interest in cricket, partly due to the formation of the East League itself in the middle '50s. The League consists of the University, the Former Pupils school sides, clubs from outside towns (Cupar, Stenhousemuir and Kirkcaldy) and four open clubs in the city. These last are Grange, a club formed in 1832 when several members of the Speculative Society at the University apparently became so bored with one of the debates that they walked out and decided to form a cricket club instead; Carlton, founded 30 years later by another group of angry young men who were not allowed by their Y.M.C.A. to stage a dramatic performance; and lastly Brunswick and Leith Franklin.

Another fairly recent innovation which has also helped to revitalise the game in the city is the East Association's introduction of inter-district games on Sundays. In addition, a lot of school cricket is played, but some of the Junior clubs have been finding it difficult to keep going. Fortunately the Edinburgh Public Parks Association contrives to keep interest in the Junior game alive.

LAWN TENNIS

In common with many other sports lawn tennis in the city was disorganised by the last war, but since then there has been such a great upsurge in interest and competition that by 1962 Edinburgh could boast 28 of the 39 clubs affiliated to the East of Scotland Tennis Association. Equally impressive, seven leagues for men and women were operated on a promotion and relegation basis. Some of the bigger clubs have memberships running to between 150 and 180, with the average probably between 80 and 100. And according to Ignacy Tloczynski—a former Polish Davis Cup and Wimbledon player in the '30s who became a professional coach in Edinburgh during the '50s—Scotland (and its capital) could well produce players up to Davis Cup standard in the future.

ATHLETICS

Edinburgh is reasonably well placed in the way of tracks and the pursuit of athletics. The Corporation, which showed great civic enterprise by launching the annual Edinburgh Highland Games in 1947, and thus attracting some of the world's finest athletes, provide, at the time of writing, several good cinder tracks and one at Meadowbank of international grade, which in recent years has been used by the national association for its track and field championships. In the early '60s important plans were being discussed for tbe building of a great new stadium with permanent grandstand accommodation, a sports hall and a swimming pool of Olympic standard to meet not only the rising demand in the city for up-to-date athletic facilities but to house the Empire and Commonwealth Games and other big athletic meetings in time to come.

As a city with a long athletic tradition, Edinburgh has in great measure been indebted to the University with its call on high class overseas performers as well as those from home; and in particular to the lustre shed by such great student runners as Olympic gold medallist Eric Liddell and, more recently, by athletes such as David Stevenson, who in 1963 held the United Kingdom pole vault record and was chosen to represent Great Britain at the 1964 Olympic Games at Tokyo, and Fergus Murray. Murray, a Scottish long-distance runner was able in 1964 to beat the 10-mile world record holder in a 5,000 metre race in England, take third place in an international cross country race at Brussels, win the British universities' three-mile title in a fast time, and win again for Great Britain in their match against the Benelux countries. The University has also scored many successes, including those of women students, in British and Scottish Universities Athletic Championships.

Outside the University the trend, as in other centres, is to produce higher competitive standards by the merging of clubs. Three of these, all long established, sank their separate identity in 1961 by forming the Edinburgh Athletic Club, with a membership of some 250. Only one other open club, Edinburgh Southern Harriers, formed about the beginning of the century, and with some 200 members, has been an outstanding combine in recent years. There are also, in the city, clubs composed of former pupils of the fee-paying schools. But recruitment problems have resulted in a number of these " old boys " forming a new club under the title of The Octavians. Altogether, in the early '60s, no fewer than 23 clubs and district bodies were affiliated to the Scottish Amateur Athletic Association.

The amateurs, however, have not always had it all their own way. Until the middle '50s Edinburgh housed the Powderhall New Year Handicap, a world famous annual event which from 1870 onwards attracted almost every sprinter of note in the world. So great, indeed, was the public interest in this event, long regarded as the blue riband of professional pedestrianism, that in the old days even the draw attracted a large crowd of people anxious to find out at first hand how their man or men had been drawn. Many a betting coup in those days was landed by astute gamblers who spirited their chosen runners away to secret training quarters, along with training tackle in the shape of other " peds." In those days, also, sums of £15,000 and more were landed by successful " schools ", but gradually the betting market dried up; attendances fell off especially after the second World War; and the Sprint was discontinued until 1965 when the Powderhall meeting was resurrected.

SPEEDWAY AND GREYHOUND RACING

The growth of athletics and the provisional plans for the great new Stadium at Meadowbank were seriously affecting another Edinburgh sport in the summer of 1963. For years there had been speedway racing at Old Meadowbank, home track of the Edinburgh Monarchs, who were then at their zenith. Unfortunately for the Monarchs their track lay partly on the site of the proposed new super sports centre, and the Corporation, in view of the project, refused permission for speedway racing. This decision naturally caused consternation among speedway enthusiasts, the more especially as the sport had been attracting crowds averaging 8,000, and it was reprieved.

Before this decision a suggestion had been made to the greyhound racing authorities that the Monarchs might go to Powderhall where the professional runners had once reigned almost supreme and where the dogs are now in possession. Greyhound racing has in fact become such a popular sport that every Thursday and Saturday evening the Greyhound Racing Association's meetings pull out thousands of people, most of them attracted as always by the magnetic appeal of a flutter, and some for the thrills, plus the promoting body's regard for the comfort of their patrons. They particularly like the covered accommodation round the track and the well appointed, glass-fronted restaurant in the club quarters where it is possible to have a meal while keeping an eye on the racing.

By general consent the sport is conducted under the strictest possible conditions, so that backers have the assurance of a straight run for their money. The greyhounds are quartered in the stables of the Duke of Buccleuch's former residence, Dalkeith Palace, and are brought back and forward between the kennels and the stadium for both trials and racing in large transporters, accompanied by attendants.

HOCKEY, SHINTY AND LACROSSE

Macaulay said of John Bunyan that his worst vices were " bell ringing and playing at hockey." *The Times*, (14th October, 1961) on the other hand thinks that as a game which helps to make the news, hockey is of small consequence since it attracts no rancour and remains happily uncommercialised.

This explains perhaps why never before were there so many girls playing hockey at Edinburgh schools, though for the majority the link is broken once they leave, and many take up other recreations. None the less it is computed that more than 400 players are attached to the 21 senior clubs in Edinburgh, most of them belonging to former pupil clubs, office sides and the University. Edinburgh men players play in an East District League, which in 1963 had three divisions with 8 clubs in the first, 14 and 10 in the others.

Related to hockey but a far more vigorous stick game, is shinty, a sport more or less confined to students from the Highlands and Islands, for whom there is only one pitch in the city. But the students play it robustly and the more historically-minded with, we hope, a certain respect, since shinty, like its Irish brother hurley, is so old a game that it seems to have enjoyed the patronage of King Alexander I of Scotland in the 12th century.

Lacrosse is also played in Edinburgh, but it makes a very limited appeal, being played only at a few girls' schools, and among seniors by ladies' clubs and women students.

CROQUET

There is another stick game played in Edinburgh, which has a special charm of its own and the support of some of the wittiest and most cultured people in the city. Most of the adherents of croquet are drawn from professional, legal or literary eircles; the founder and President of the Edinburgh Croquet Club is the well-known Edinburgh author, Mr. Moray McLaren; and one of its members is Sir Compton Mackenzie, who is President of the Croquet Association of Great Britain, and therefore, to quote Mr. McLaren, " the titular Pontiff of all the croquet world."

Here perhaps we might leave a fuller description of the game's past and present in the city to the Croquet Club's founder. " They say ", he writes, " that croquet is of Celtic origin and reached this island from Brittany via Ireland. Maybe, but none can deny that it was England in the late 19th century that made and fostered the scientific game we know today. In Edward VII's reign, however, croquet became popular in certain circles in the capital of Scotland, notably in the fine grounds of the then Craiglockhart Hydropathic. But the first World War and the disappearance of the Hydropathic drove the sport clean out of Edinburgh. By the 1920s no one seemed to have the time for this leisurely and spacious game.

" It was all the more unexpected then that an Edinburgh Croquet Club should have been formed after World War II, and have proved so great a success. In 1950, as a result of correspondence in *The Scotsman*, the Edinburgh Croquet Club came into existence and was fortunate enough to rent from the city authorities the splendid lawns of Lauriston Castle. Beginning modestly with 20 members and one lawn, they possessed three lawns by 1961–2 and were full to capacity with 60 members. On occasion also, visitors from the older-established clubs in the contiguous country of England have come up to give exhibition matches. In 1956 a team from New Zealand, which was visiting the United Kingdom and had crossed what R.L.S. called ' the thick of the world ', made a special journey to test the Edinburgh lawns. They defeated the Scottish team soundly, but agreed that in its fine situation at Lauriston, with the Firth just before it, the Edinburgh grounds must be ' the most beautiful in the world.'

" Granted fine weather, Scotland is an admirable country in which to enjoy this pastime. Our turf is good, and the long-drawn-out northern summer evenings give so much time for this most leisurely and reflective of games that croquet at Lauriston is often played by the ' simmer dim ' until eleven o'clock at night. Some of the matches have indeed been memorable, and none more so than the blood-match between Mr. Stephen Potter of Roehampton in England and the President. This contest, conducted before a large crowd, lasted so long as to be concluded by the amber glow of an harvest moon. But very often in the summer games last till moonlight. In the winter when croquet is out of season and claret is in, some of the sodality's annual dinners have lasted till the dawn."

BOWLS

Bowls is a pastime traditionally associated with the out-of-doors. But as it has also been an indoor game in Edinburgh for almost 60 years it might be convenient here to describe the game under cover as well as in the open air.

The opening in 1962 of a new £45,000 indoor bowling " green " in the Abbeyhill district ushered in a new era for the game. For with seven full rinks this venture brought Edinburgh into line with other centres with standard facilities for international and representative matches at any time of the year. Equally heartening, it was a splendid essay in sporting initiative, since the opening of this modern indoor bowling rink was due to the devotion of its founders and to the 800 men and 400 women bowlers who took out shares in the new company. Since then eight similar stadia have been built at a cost of over £500,000.

The real pioneers of the game however were the members of the Edinburgh Winter Bowling Association instituted almost 60 years earlier. Cellarage under the Synod Hall was gradually converted into a wonderfully popular rendezvous. Playing charges were nominal, and as many as 60,000 to 70,000 tickets were taken out each season.

The outdoor game flourishes, especially among private clubs, most of which have waiting lists. Forty-seven of these clubs in 1962–3 were affiliated to the Edinburgh and Leith Association which has often won the Scottish Counties Championship. The city also, in 1962–3, had 23 private clubs with women's sections attached to the Edinburgh Ladies' Association and 19 clubs in the Edinburgh Ladies' Public Greens Association. It need only be added that as the Edinburgh and Leith Printing Trades Association have 20 clubs in three divisions, and such bodies as the Edinburgh and Leith Factory Association make great use of the public greens, bowling in Edinburgh has clearly a strong appeal to both sexes.

ON THE ICE

Curiously allied to bowling is curling, an old sport often described in America as " lawn bowls on ice." Some authorities say the game was invented in Scotland in medieval times, and perhaps even earlier. Dutch students of the game on the other hand say that curling was played for the first time in Holland. Whatever the truth of this there seems to be no doubt that the first international legislative body for curling was founded in Edinburgh in 1838, and that four years later, after Queen Victoria had given her patronage to the game, the name of this reigning authority on curling was changed to the Royal Caledonian Club.

The game is naturally played out of doors whenever a loch freezes sufficiently hard to take the weight of perhaps many hundreds of curlers at the same time. Some of these occasions are international meetings—one took place in Perthshire in 1963—with players taking part from Canada, the United States and Sweden, and of course from Edinburgh where the game is so popular that the Midlothian Province now embraces some 30 clubs in and around the city. The clubs of Edinburgh play most of their games indoors at the Ice Rink, Haymarket, where the demand for facilities is so great that the ice is allocated each August for the entire season from September to April.

Ice hockey also boomed for a time at the Murrayfield Rink, when the Royals, largely composed of Canadians, got the game going, but according to the local sporting journalists the crowds got tired of scenes on " the pad ", and by 1963 the game was being kept alive in a modest way by team expense economies such as the recruitment of home talent and amateurs. Ordinary skating is always popular in the city whether at the Ice Rink or out of doors when weather permits.

ON THE WATER

According to Mr. Guy Christie, an authority on Edinburgh's harbours, the sport of yachting in an organised form has been enjoyed on the Firth of Forth for at least 125 years, the Royal Eastern Yacht Club having been founded in 1835. Today, he says in the middle '60s, the sport is followed as enthusiastically as ever, and within the City of Edinburgh and its immediate environs there are some half a dozen clubs actively engaged in encouraging some form of small craft sailing or another.

The sailing yachts and motor craft are not large, for several reasons; principally because the firth as a cruising ground offers no safe and snug deep-water anchorages, and also because the whole trend of yachting in the last 30 years has been towards the smaller classes.

Groups of small craft are based at Cramond, Granton, Leith and Fisherrow, and practically all the work of fitting-out and maintenance is done by the owners. Only in the necessity of a major piece of work on hull or engine are the boats slipped at one or other of the yards in the area. Laying-up for the winter is not much of a problem among the racing yacht owners however, and it is not a surprising sight to see an International Dragon class boat or a Loch Long one-design propped up on sheer-legs in an owner's garden miles from the sea.

The senior club, with a history of over 90 years, is now the Royal Forth Yacht Club. With a membership of more than 500, owning approximately 100 yachts and dinghies, there is an exhilarating feeling of life about the clubhouse which sits on an eminence above Granton harbour. In the spring of 1958 the Almond Yacht Club, which had been in existence for 61 years, folded up and 100 members transferred to the Royal Forth or the Forth Corinthian Yacht Clubs. The Forth Corinthian Y.C., founded in the year 1880, has premises in the city and sponsors a regatta and some six races during the season which each year begins on the first Saturday in May and continues until the end of September. Fixtures of the Royal Forth include the usual Saturday races for Dragon class, for handicap yachts and for dinghies; but there are, in addition, several long-distance events sponsored by the clubs—the race from Granton round the Bell Rock off Arbroath, for example, and another round the North Carr lightship off Fife Ness. There are also ladies' races, students' races and races for cadets up to 21 years of age. But the high-light of the year is Forth Week. Other active clubs include the Cramond Boat Club, which has a large class of Hornet dinghies, the Port o'Leith Motor Boat Club, and the Fisherrow Sailing Club.

Rowing boats lack the glamour of sail, and neither Edinburgh's rivers nor its canal are suitable for high-class racing such as the Thames provides. None the less jollyboat racing continues to hold its own offshore at Portobello, where the Eastern and Portobello clubs have their headquarters. The Eastern club which has a youth section was launched in 1885, and its next door neighbour five years earlier.

Rowing also takes place on the Union Canal where several clubs have the traditional racing eights, among them St. Andrews, which was established in 1857 and is the oldest Scottish club. Two other clubs operating there are Edinburgh University and University Ladies.' It is also noteworthy that two very successful and enthusiastic rowing clubs belong to George Watson's College and George Heriot's School.

And so to swimming, which has never been more popular among the young. In Edinburgh the popularity of the sport is due in no small measure to the encouragement given to youngsters at the schools which are fertile " spawning grounds " for the senior clubs, of which there are six in the city—Portobello, Warrender, Hibernian, Heart of Midlothian, Leith and 1930: the first two have ladies' sections. Other organisations fostering the sport are the Boys' Brigade, the Scouts and the Young Swimmers' Athletic Union.

Portobello is the club which boasts Ned Barnie as Scotland's greatest-ever long distance swimmer not only because he was the oldest man to swim the Channel, but because he completed the double crossing. The Portobello club can also boast Peter Heatly, originally of the Leith Club, but latterly of Portobello, who won three gold diving medals at three Empire Games (Auckland 1950, Vancouver 1954 and Cardiff 1958). But undoubtedly Edinburgh's greatest all-rounder in the water was Helen King of Warrender (and the now defunct Zenith) for she, between the wars, won every individual swimming title open to women, including diving.

IN THE AIR

There is a Flying Club in Edinburgh, and gliding, or, as an Edinburgh sporting journalist calls it, the " flighty " is also enjoyed by the 30 or so Edinburgh members of the Scottish Gliding Union, whose soaring is done from Portmoak, near Kinross. There were in 1963 seven club machines and three others were also taking part. But though these are " mechanical birds " with a growing appeal, the skies round the city can still find space for pigeon racing.

Despite prohibitions on the keeping of pigeons on Council housing schemes, there are four thriving pigeon racing clubs in Edinburgh—the Edina, Corstorphine, Edinburgh Premier and Tynecastle. Membership runs at about 150 members, and as each loft probably averages some 30 birds, the sport has clearly an enthusiastic band of supporters.

ON THE TURF

Edinburgh's race meetings under Jockey Club Rules are held on Musselburgh's famous links. The Gold Cup, competed for at the September reunion during the Scottish Autumn Circuit, is the principal award of the season's fixtures, and big crowds flock to the course not only from Edinburgh but from far and wide. In 1963, however, the future of the course seemed a little obscure, for the Stewards, among them Lord Rosebery, a notable figure in Edinburgh life and a noted supporter of racing and bloodstock breeding, were told by the Horse Racing Betting Levy Board that under a streamlining policy no more financial grants would be forthcoming in support of racing at Musselburgh. Protests against the Board's decision were naturally voiced at once by the local Town Council, bookmakers and traders; and Lord Rosebery himself put the Stewards' case with forceful eloquence. In the meantime, while this battle was raging—it ended happily in victory for Lord Rosebery and his friends—there was an ever-increasing devotion, especially among the young, to riding as an exercise, and to show jumping. Show jumping—for participants and spectators alike—is another of the sports which has won increased popular interest through television. Television apart, such equestrian shows as the Edinburgh Horse Show bring in the competitors and bring out the public.

ON THE ROAD

In motoring, the Edinburgh and District Club sponsor the Scottish Six Days, the biggest thing of its kind in the country, while the Lothians Car Club has a membership of between 200 and 300. Ferranti's too have a thriving organisation. As for the motor cycle clubs of which there are a number, these are mainly concerned with cheerful social activities with weekend runs as one of the most popular. Yet despite the appeal of the engine, pedal cycling has many followers—for time trial and road racing—and many of the younger enthusiasts have a Cycle Speedway League of their own.

In the field of competitive speed, a particularly notable success story has been written since the war—in, improbably enough, a narrow mews in the city's West End. The participants in this form of outdoor sport may be limited to a tiny handful; but their success is particularly appreciated by their fellow citizens who remember with emotion the thrill of first touching 60 m.p.h. down the Braid Road in the 1920s, who regret the passing of the superannuated Rolls-Royces which used to stand at the Princes Street taxi-ranks, and who today still use the Maybury by-pass to put their new cars through performance and road-holding tests. For Merchiston Mews is the home of Ecurie Ecosse, a motor-racing stable whose saltire-blue cars have competed at all the major European circuits as well as in North and South America.

The Ecurie was founded in 1951 with a stable of sports cars—mostly XK120 Jaguars—and one Ferrari racing-car. Shortly afterwards new C-type Jaguars were purchased, and these brought their owners international fame.

THE CORPORATION'S CONTRIBUTION

This necessarily broad survey of Edinburgh's out-of-doors pursuits might well end with a tribute to the city's administration. For many years the Corporation has not been unmindful of the " bread and butter " sports of the citizens, despite the pressure on space. In all, the Corporation by 1963 had provided more than 120 pitches for soccer, 11 for rugby, 10 for hockey, 8 for cricket, 130 hard and 4 grass tennis courts, 23 putting greens, 56 bowling greens, 10 badminton courts, 4 running tracks, and 57 pavilions; and this at a time when it was becoming increasingly difficult to solve the housing space problem.

Today the Corporation still has its eye on youth problems, and is going ahead with a new programme to provide youth and community centres with better sports facilities than they have ever had—in various parts of the city.

INDOOR PASTIMES

If obviously few outdoor sports elude Edinburgh folk, indoors they seem to find as great a number of ways of entertaining themselves. Outside their own homes, yet still indoors, they can participate in the entertainment offered by dance halls, billiard rooms, rifle ranges, squash courts, alleys, circus tents, boxing rings, and a host of other recreational resorts in the city. Inside their homes altogether apart from their own skills and hobbies they can follow on television or radio a wide range of sports and indeed almost every other form of organised diversion. One of the most popular of these is boxing.

BOXING

Between 1790 and 1799 Edinburgh had at least three visits from the celebrated London pugilist Daniel Mendoza who had an enthusiastic following. But in fact ever since barefist fighting, always harried by the law, went out, and leather-gloved boxing under the Queensberry Rules came in, the city has played a notable part in the history of the sport. Boxing booths were favourite side shows in the fair grounds on holiday occasions—at Grassmarket, Bristo, Iona Street and Tollcross. Each wave of interest in international boxing also brought its vogue of exhibition bouts to local theatres and halls, with Christmas and New Year carnivals in the Waverley Market carrying on the tradition. Three men in particular, two closely associated with these holiday carnivals, had a great deal to do with the development of boxing in Edinburgh in the present century. These were Charles Cotter, the sports outfitter Fred Lumley and promoter Nat Dresner.

Charles Cotter set up his gymnasium in Leith Street, and for more than 40 years Cotter's Boxing Academy trained boys, youth and grown men of all classes in boxing Swedish drill and exercises with dumb-bells and Indian clubs. Fred Lumley for his part became the city's most prominent sports promoter, his enterprises stretching from foot races to boxing programmes. Cotter also promoted programmes of both professional and amateur boxing, and when Fred Lumley ran the Waverley Market carnivals, the two men combined to organise boxing as one of the attractions. As for the Saturday evening programmes in the Synod Hall, almost inevitably they became known as "Cotter's Saturday Nights."

Charles Cotter, who trained on his premises members of the Edinburgh Amateur Boxing Club, Edinburgh University Boxing Club and other organisations, had among his pupils some outstanding amateurs. They included the late Sir Iain Colquhoun of Luss, who became Lord High Commissioner to the General Assembly of the Church of Scotland. As a young man, Sir Iain fought in the Scottish amateur championships as a representative of the Edinburgh club, and by the age of 26 he was an Army champion, holding the lightweight title in the service in 1913 and 1914. To Cotter's gymnasium came also the sons of the then Duke of Hamilton. The Duke's eldest son, the Marquess of Douglas and Clydesdale (the present Duke of Hamilton), became known as "The Fighting Marquess" and was Scottish amateur middleweight champion in 1924. But Charles Cotter had also professional champions under his wing, notably three men who because of their Irish names were known as The Shamrock Trio. These were Paddy Fee, Tancy Lee a winner of the Lonsdale belt outright who sensationally defeated the great Jimmy Wilde in 17 rounds at the National Sporting Club in London on Robert Burns' anniversary in 1915, and Johnny Connolly who fought Packy MacFarland, unsuccessfully, for the world lightweight championship.

Nowadays, in addition to the boxing organised by schools, youth movements, the Coal Board and the University, Edinburgh has six open amateur clubs: Melbourne, an old club in the New Town area; Leith Victoria, which began in an old Army type swimming hut at Leith Docks, and is the oldest club of all; Leith Persevere, a new club which takes its name from the motto of the port; Sparta, which sprang to fame after the last war; and Golden Gloves, a new club in the Pleasance district. Leith quickly eclipsed Edinburgh A.B.C. in the 1920s and attracted such promising boxers as Alec Ireland, who went on to win the British professional middleweight championship. Finally there is Buccleuch Amateur Boxing Club. This club is named after the Duke of Buccleuch, whose estates embrace the Granton area where the club has its headquarters, and whose honorary president is the Duke's eldest son, the Earl of Dalkeith, M.P. for North Edinburgh in the House of Commons.

Professional boxing, so far as individual prowess is concerned, has usually been worthily represented in the city—by such men as Tancy Lee, Alec Ireland, Bobby Neill, Jackie Brown and other champions—but while amateur boxing shows in clubrooms, the Music Hall, Murrayfield Ice Rink and elsewhere are fairly frequent, professional boxing programmes are now few and far between. Yet in 1923, 30,000 people saw Tommy Milligan beat Kid Lewis for the British middleweight championship in a hall which is now a Corporation bus depot. There were 15,000 spectators when Alec Ireland secured the middleweight title from Milligan in the Waverley Market in 1928. But since the last war there has been nothing quite like this, and it is now the short and swift, wholehearted amateur boxing rather than the professional which attracts most public attention.

A praiseworthy aspect of amateur boxing in Edinburgh, as elsewhere in Scotland, is the enthusiastic service rendered by officials of the Scottish Amateur Boxing Association. These men turn out as referees, judges and timekeepers at programmes organised by individual clubs, as well as the Association's own official events. Equally praiseworthy is the devoted service of vertean boxers who take an interest in the training of youth in the city—Paddy Fee's public-spirited work with the boys of the Tweedie Memorial Club, for instance, and Chad Savory's organisation of boxing tuition for the boys of Broomhouse housing estate.

WRESTLING, JUDO AND WEIGHT LIFTING

Though most wrestlers are very large men, quality rather than quantity sums up amateur wrestling. The only two clubs in the city attached to the Scottish Amateur Association are Edinburgh Milton and Leith: both have produced champions. There is also a modern variety of old time wrestling called "All-in" which had a long innings before the last war, with weekly houses of 3,000 at the Eldorado, Leith. The war knocked it out, but today it is once again popular.

Judo is another popular mat sport in which both sexes take part. Five clubs in the city, with an average membership of between 50 and 60, include the oldest of them all, the Shu-do-kai. This is headed by Scotland's national coach, Andrew Bull, Black Belt, Second Dan.

Then there is weight lifting. It would be a mistake to regard weight lifting as a matter of brawn only: there is a lot more to it than that. But not being a very spectacular pastime, it appeals mainly, as one Edinburgh sporting journalist puts it, "to the young fellow who is prepared to dedicate himself to it and perhaps win honours at it, if he wishes to go places." The sport is properly organised. In Edinburgh the Dunedin is one of the senior clubs in Scotland, and has a membership of between 30 and 40. Edinburgh University, too, are members of the Scottish Association. And to give the sport a final cachet, local, county and divisional Championships are held, the latter supplying qualifiers for the British Championships.

FENCING

The art of attack and defence with sword and rapier has more devotees in the city than many people think. In all, by 1963, there were four senior and two school clubs attached to the Edinburgh district of the Scottish Amateur Fencing Union, and the sport was making a wider appeal probably because of the encouragement given it by the Scottish Council of Physical Education. Of the senior clubs, the Scottish Fencing Club had a mixed membership of 40; separate clubs for men and women students were run by the University with about 20 in each for the 1963 autumn term; the Redford Club based at Redford Barracks for some time had been revived for the 1963–4 season with about a dozen members and with new clubrooms; while the two school clubs—at Merchiston Castle and Edinburgh Academy—had enthusiastic double figure memberships.

DARTS

In a less exalted setting, darts shares with dominoes, bridge, whist, chess and other indoor games the impetus of league competiton. In Leith especially the game is booming with no fewer than 56 teams engaged in four divisions. The Portobello League in 1963 mustered 22 clubs; Central Edinburgh 10 clubs; West Edinburgh 16; and Gilmerton 14.

RACQUET GAMES

Squash racquets is a game which seems to make an ever wider appeal. Its headquarters are in the picturesquely situated Edinburgh Sports Club, The Duke of Edinburgh has been a visitor, and it was here that the Scottish Association was formed in 1936, the year the club opened. Its 800 membership includes Mr. M. Oddy, a British captain and one of the world's best players. Academicals, Watsonians, University, University staff and King's Buildings (University scientists) are other Edinburgh clubs; and they, along with four others from outside make up a ten club League.

The number of badminton players in Edinburgh and its surrounding counties might almost be counted in battalions, since there are some 90 to 100 clubs affiliated to the East of Scotland District of the Scottish Union, each with a membership varying from perhaps a dozen to 40 or 50, and it is estimated that there are some 5,000 players in the district. Since the early 1920s Edinburgh has been represented in international matches by 20 players. Nine League divisions are carried on in the East, most of the clubs being located in Edinburgh, the rest in the Lothians.

Table tennis in the city is represented by a league with 240 registered players attached to 27 clubs. Some of these are plurally represented, so that 58 teams take part in a tournament consisting of a First Division, a Second with " A " and " B " sections, and a Third similarly constituted.

SKITTLES

Among the groups which continue to practice the game of skittles in Edinburgh probably the oldest is the Trotters Club, which meets once a month (except during the summer) in the Sheep's Heid Inn at Duddingston.

The game of skittles, it should be added, is not confined to this famous inn. It has been popularised in alleys attached to various welfare clubs, public houses and roadhouses with winter league play in three divisions of 14 clubs each.

BASKETBALL

Basketball is worth a special mention here—for two reasons. Firstly there is now a large number of players, and indeed shortage of first-class playing facilities is the only disability from which basketball suffers. Secondly, the game in Edinburgh enjoys the impetus and inspiration of a team from the adjacent United States Air Force base at Kirknewton, home of the Comets. A record number of clubs started the 1962–3 season in the Edinburgh and Leith League—20 Seniors in two divisions of ten—in addition to nine Ladies' and nine Junior clubs, (making 300 players in all). Such figures are not unimpressive, but the game has since gained further kudos in the city. In March, 1964, Edinburgh—at the Craiglockhart indoor sports hall—housed the fifth home countries international, with players of its own in the Scottish team.

RIFLE SHOOTING

It may come as a surprise to many people to learn that no fewer than 22 rifle shooting clubs in the city affiliated to the Edinburgh and Midlothian Small Bore Association have a total membership of some 450 members. The total number of marksmen in the city is however a good deal larger. In 1963 the Shoulder to Shoulder League of 48 clubs included 20 Edinburgh teams; there were 30 city clubs in a Postal League of 60 teams; the Individual League had some 200 competitors, including 90 from city clubs; and a team knock-out competition was contested by 40 teams of whom 21 were city-based. Full bore shooting takes place throughout the summer on the War Department ranges at Dreghorn.

BILLIARDS AND SNOOKER

" Billiards is on the down-grade in Scotland. You don't find nowadays big houses with their private tables; hotels no longer cater for the game to any extent, and saloons are now few and far between. If you want to play billiards you must joint a private club." These pessimistic sentiments were recently expressed to an Edinburgh newspaperman by Edinburgh's leading player, Walter Ramage of Leith, a brilliant amateur who by 1962 had won the Scottish amateur championship nine times, the Scottish Open

13 times between 1945 and 1962, and the East of Scotland championship 12 times. And undoubtedly Mr. Ramage was right. Billiards not only in Edinburgh but in most parts of the country has become a dying sport. Snooker on the other hand attracts many young players, and in both public and private club billiard rooms it is now by far the most popular game.

SOCIAL ENTERTAINMENT

By any known means of computing it is obvious that television and sound radio, described elsewhere in this book, are the country's biggest providers of entertainment and the chief means by which people entertain themselves (or their guests) at home. Yet despite the great range of interest and amusement these media offer, there are today many leisure pursuits by means of which the individual contrives his own enjoyment. Some of these, like bingo, are new. Others are as old as folklore, and have endured the passage of the centuries.

CONTRACT BRIDGE

Among the more intimate forms of self-entertainment which have been growing fast in recent years is Contract Bridge. Before the last war Edinburgh's bridge playing citizens did not show much interest in club bridge. They preferred to spend their evening having one or two or even three tables at home. The war, however, put an end to all that. Rationing made home entertaining difficult, and players perforce became more and more club-minded.

That apart, Edinburgh and the outlying districts seem to have been interested in various card games over the years. There was, and still is, a large whist playing community with a number of leagues for match playing. Then came an Auction Bridge League, and now there is a flourishing Contact Bridge League.

When this league was inaugurated there was a league division of 11 teams, and the founder members included Blackford, Carlton, Dundas, University Union and Newington Unionists. All these are still in existence. But the league has grown so fast that by 1963 there were four divisions with 10 teams in the first division, 90 in the second, 12 in the third and 11 in the fourth. Each team consisted of a minimum of eight players and the teams were affiliated, as they are now, to the Scottish Bridge Union and the Eastern District. Teams, incidentally, are drawn from all walks of life—from the railways, Post Office, Civil Service, Banks, the medical and legal professions, insurance companies, the teaching profession, accountancy, the ministry, and last but not least the housewife. There is also a flourishing Insurance League.

The first Edinburgh club founded solely for contract bridge was the Athol Club which came into being in the early 1930s. There were also various organisations such as the Edinburgh Women's Athletic Club and the University Union which had bridge sections. Then in the spring of 1936 The Melville Bridge Club was formed with 47 founder members. By 1963 this club had 335 members, and play was available seven days a week. The Carlton Bridge Club came into being in the autumn of the same year with 60 founder members: today its membership is round about 200, a figure which again reflects the growing popularity of the game. Players of both clubs, it is noteworthy, have become well known throughout the bridge world; several of Scotland's internationialsts have learnt their bridge in one or other; and both have won the various trophies open to all Scotland. By 1965 there were in the city more than 2,000 club players.

CHESS

As with bridge so too it is with chess, which for many years has also been growing in popularity. There are about 30 active chess clubs in Edinburgh, and these have been formed into a league with an annual championship. All these clubs come under the Scottish Chess Association, and, if they become strong enough, compete for the Richardson Cup which is for practical purposes the Scottish Club Championship. Edinburgh Chess Club, according to its Honorary Secretary, is undoubtedly the oldest chess club in Scotland, and probably in Great Britain, with a continuous existence. It was founded on 4th November, 1822; and not only are its rooms in Alva Street open daily for play but nearly all the greatest players of the past have visited it at one time or other.

Between 1824 and 1828 a correspondence match was played against the City of London Chess Club, and after a close contest Edinburgh won. It was in this match, incidentally, that the " Scots gambit " was invented. A little later there were famous correspondence matches between Edinburgh and Paris. Since then, Edinburgh Chess Club has always been able to muster a strong team, and by 1962 had won the Richardson Cup 19 times since that trophy was instituted in 1899.

STAMP COLLECTING

In the early 1960s philately was spreading fast in Edinburgh, which has not only a frequent and well-attended stamp auction of its own in an alley near Leith Walk, but many collectors. Edinburgh has also the Scottish Philatelic Society and the Edinburgh Philatelic Society.

DANCING

In the meantime dancing continues as one of the most delightful and popular forms of indoor social entertainment and one which sometimes, as for example in Princes Street Gardens during the summer, may happen out of doors as well. It was undoubtedly the release from wartime anxieties that in the early '20s brought the dance hall into sudden popularity. Former roller skating rinks were transformed to meet the demand, and new buildings with exotic names were erected by groups of citizens alert to the possibilities. Dancing—the acrobatic Charleston and the slightly less sprightly two-step—became not only an inexpensive pastime, but a form of big business highly remunerative to the promoters. It was possible to dance in a small hall until midnight for an admission charge of sixpence; from 10 p.m. until four in the morning in a larger hall for half-a-crown; or to patronise an establishment for the sum of 3*s.* 6*d.* where evening dress was compulsory.

With the coming of television to Scotland, attendances at city dance halls dropped almost overnight by 50 per cent. Other adverse factors have been the striking entry into big business of the record player and the long-playing record, so that many teenagers and young men and women who formerly flocked to the dance halls now spend their money on " pop " records, and gather in groups to pass an evening at home or in a club.

Also, in recent years, though there has undoubtedly been a movement towards a revival of public dancing, this, paradoxically, has been to the detriment of the traditional dance hall promoter, who has increasingly had to compete with roadhouses, hotels, and other places possessing liquor licenses some of which are owned by brewing companies. In these no charge is made for dancing, and the costs of the free entertainment and the musicians are recovered by adding a house charge to the refreshments.

Another example of the dancing public's swiftly changing preferences can be seen today in Edinburgh. The dance halls were formerly at their busiest in the winter months; now their most remunerative period is the summer—but only if the weather is seasonable. Those who do go out tend to gravitate to the no-charge dance establishments, but the surviving dance hall proprietors are beginning to find some slight encouragement in the signs of a revival of interest in what is termed " old-time dancing."

There is, however, another form of dance which is sweeping all before it as a type of recreation for those who have hitherto left the public dance hall to the teenagers and the young adults. This is Scottish country dancing. The chief credit for encouraging the country dance as a socially acceptable activity goes to a Highland lady, Mrs. Stewart of Fasnacloich, who, when Commissioner of Girl Guides in 1923, started to coach her guides in old Scottish dances such as the petronella and the eightsome in preference to the English folk dances formerly performed. With Miss Jean Milligan, Mrs. Stewart later founded The Scottish Country Dance Society.

The World War seriously interfered with the development of the organisation, but though the black-out limited activity at home, Scottish country dancing continued to flourish in the German prison camps. Here officers of the 51st Highland Division captured at St. Valery, who had themselves been enthusiastic country dancers, formed classes among their fellow prisoners. To add to their repertoire the pioneers devised *The Reel of the 51st Highland Division.* The manuscript was mailed home, and when the Queen (Queen Elizabeth the Queen Mother as she now is) heard about it, she suggested that the new dance merited official recognition; and so it was that when Volume No. 13 of *The Victory Book* appeared, *The Reel of the 51st Highland Division* was included.

The Royal family are among the most consistent supporters (and performers) of Scottish country dancing, and the Queen is the Patron of what, since 1951, has been known as The Royal Scottish Country Dance Society. Members of its Edinburgh branch have been invited to become a regular feature of royal visits to the capital city. But everywhere the Society, with almost 20,000 members and 90 branches, has been growing rapidly, with Edinburgh as one of its most enthusiastic centres. At the Edinburgh Festival, for instance, a miscellany of reels and strathspeys, songs, piping and dancing is presented every year by teams from the Edinburgh branch of the Royal Scottish Country Dance Society; invariably performances are booked out; and bookings are received beforehand from all over the world.

THE CIRCUS

The circus is another form of social entertainment which has never lost its attraction for Edinburgh people and especially the young. Almost two centuries ago circus performances took place in Broughton Street, and these continued for many years. Later there were similar shows in other parts of the city including Fountainbridge, where before the first World War the Cooke family sometimes ran three shows daily. These, however, were the last of the resident circuses, though fortunately for the city its ancient circus tradition was later kept alive by F. A. Lumley's use of the Waverley Market and the arrival at Murrayfield in recent years of such famous circuses as Billy Smart's and Bertram Mills'. At one time or another Waverley Market has of course been used for many gay and glamorous projects such as the Carnival with attractions ranging from roundabouts to a fat lady. It has even been used for a remarkable exhibition of sculptures by the great sculptor Epstein; and it regularly houses such events as the Scottish Kennel Club's Championship Show.

CHAPTER 23

SOCIETIES AND INSTITUTIONS

THE variety and number of Societies and Associations in the city are remarkable. For they range from learned bodies like the Royal Society of Edinburgh to Budgerigar, Esperanto and Highland Reel and Strathspey Societies, the Society of Chiropodists which, in one sense only, seems to go well with the Corn Trade Association of Leith, and such bodies as the Skinners and Furriers Incorporation, the Incorporation of Carters, the Incorporation of Freemen Fleshers, the Hammermen and the Royal Antediluvian Order of Buffaloes.

Among scientific bodies there are the Edinburgh Geological Society, the Botanical Society of Edinburgh, the Royal Highland and Agricultural Society of Scotland (1784), the Royal Forestry Society, a Committee for the Study of the Scottish Flora, the Scottish Ornithologists' Club and the Royal Scottish Geographical Society. In the world of industry and business there is another cluster which includes such bodies as the Edinburgh and Leith Chambers of Commerce, the Edinburgh Productivity Association, the City Business Club, the Market Gardeners Association, and the Consumers Group. And so we could go on through many walks of life—from the Scottish Rights of Way Society, the discharged Prisoners Society, the venerable Edinburgh Medical Missionary Society, the Edinburgh and Leith Society for the Relief of Deserving Foreigners in Distress, the United Nations Association, the Humanists, the Scottish Temperance Alliance and hundreds of other bodies. It is impossible to give a complete catalogue of them here.

THE MERCHANT COMPANY

The Company of Merchants of the City of Edinburgh, familiarly known as the Merchant Company, is undisputed successor of the earlier medieval merchant guilds and its position is very similar to that of the great Livery Companies in London. The Royal Charter of the Merchant Company, incorporated in 1681 by Charles II, gave its members a monopoly of trade as cloth merchants. Today it has a membership of over 600 of Edinburgh's leading bankers, merchants and manufacturers; and in all official processions the Lord Lyon King of Arms gives the Company precedence immediately after the Town Council and before Her Majesty's Judges.

The Company's main interests are now education and charitable trusts, though from time to time it brings its considerable influence to bear on public matters which affect the commercial interests of the city.

Of the charitable foundations the Merchant Maiden Hospital founded by the Company and Mary Erskine in 1694 was the first of its kind in Scotland and is now represented by The Mary Erskine School for Girls.

The other educational Hospitals were those formed by George Watson, who died in 1723, for the children of decayed merchants—these are now represented by George Watson's College and George Watson's Ladies College—and finally Daniel Stewart's College made possible by the will of Daniel Stewart who died in 1814. The Company also administers a number of bequests for old people and has a contributory fund for widows of members of the Company.

The Queen, who, together with the Duke of Edinburgh, was admitted to Honorary Membership in 1949, is now Patron of the Company. In November, 1964 the Duke agreed to accept nomination as Master of the Merchant Company in 1965 and will accordingly share in its impressive ceremonial.

Among many valued possessions is an interesting example of modern craftsmanship, the Princess Elizabeth Cup commemorating the election of the Queen, then Princess Elizabeth and the Duke of Edinburgh as Honorary Members. The Cup displays the Arms of the Princess, the Duke and the Company and is only used by the Master when drinking the Loyal Toast. But as we should expect tradition broods with grace and dignity over all the Company's ceremonies and councils. At every meeting in the handsome Merchants' Hall the Master or the Secretary opens the proceedings by reading the Company's own prayer. This was composed in 1682 by Dr. Annand, Dean of Edinburgh and Minister of St. Giles; and as the motto is *Terraque Marique*, it would be appropriate here to cite a line or two:

> The sea is Thine, and Thy hands formed
> the dry land: prosper us in our present
> undertaking with the bounties of both.

The Company has certainly prospered in the past, for the assets controlled by the Company and its trusts now amount to several million pounds.

ANCIENT FREEMASONRY

Two masonic lodges in Edinburgh have each unique distinctions. The Lodge of Edinburgh (Mary's Chapel) No. 1 has the oldest Minute of any existing Lodge in the world, since it bears the date 28th December, 1598; while Lodge Canongate Kilwinning, No. 2 which was consecrated on 20th December, 1736 claims to have the world's oldest Lodge room. As for Grand Lodge its most valuable masonic documents are the Schaw Statutes which were presented by a former Grand Master, the Earl of Eglinton and Winton, in whose family charter chests they had remained for 350 years. These Statutes were issued in 1598 by William Schaw, Master of Work to His Majesty and General Warden of the Craft for the regulation of the operative Lodges then existing in Scotland.

The Lodge Room of Canongate Kilwinning lies a few hundred yards east of the old city wall on the site of the Ancient Temple Lands of the Knights of St. John, and the chapel is aptly named St. John's Chapel. Outside, marked on the causeway, is the site of St. John's Cross, where public proclamations were read. Each year on 24th June—Midsummer's Day when the sun is at its zenith—the new Master is installed and the Lodge proceeds to celebrate the Festival of St. John the Baptist in a room which contains much of interest, notably a portrait of the first Grand Master Mason, William St. Clair of Roslin, reputed to be by Allan Ramsay, and an engraving of Boswell, who was Master of the Lodge from 1773 to 1775.

Two splendid masonic restorations have been carried out within the Royal Mile of Edinburgh since the last war. In 1954 Lodge St. David No. 36, built a beautiful Lodge room at 142 High Street, to replace a building dating back to at least 1736. The other restoration was made by the Members of the Celtic Lodge, No. 291 at Brodie's Close in the Lawnmarket, the Lodge room being consecrated in 1963 by the Grand Master Mason, Lord Bruce. This building is well worth a visit, not so much for its association with the notorious Deacon Brodie as for the ornate 17th century plaster ceiling, the open stone 16th century fire-place in the Refectory or Thistle Room, the hand carved wooden surround to the 16th century fireplace in the Master's Room, and the 14th century arch and vault which may have formed part of the Hospice of the Cambuskenneth Monks. In the Petition which was submitted to Grand Lodge in 1821 to form the Celtic Lodge we read that the petitioners were " actuated by a strong desire to promote the interests of Masonry in Scotland and from what they trust is a powerful motive in the breast of every Scotsman to promote the manufacture of the tartan of their native land and encourage the wearing of the ancient costume of their country." This tradition is still maintained in the Lodge. Many members attend the meetings wearing the kilt, and the strains of the bagpipe are heard in the Lodge.

The administrative offices of the Grand Lodge of Scotland are in the Freemasons Hall in George Street. This handsome building houses a museum and a library which contains the Morison Collection, one of the finest of all masonic book collections. Here too Grand Committee carries through a great deal of business, much of it charitable, and much of it concerned with the large total of more than 1,000 Lodges within its jurisdiction. One third of these are overseas—in countries ranging from Peru to Thailand. But this is natural enough. The Grand Lodge of Scotland prides itself that it accepts into membership of its Lodges men of good report irrespective of colour, class or creed. Certainly within Scotland itself a peer of the realm can be found in the same Lodge as the local joiner and sometimes the most august personages in the land. It was typical of Scottish masonry that when the late King George VI, as Duke of York, joined the village Lodge at Glamis, the ceremony of admission was carried through by the Master of the Lodge who was then the local postman.

Within the bounds of the City of Edinburgh there were in the early '60s 36 Lodges, half of which own their particular Lodge premises. The total membership of these Lodges is approximately 15,000. Unfortunately it is impossible to describe them all here.

In addition to the 36 Lodges in Edinburgh there are other masonic bodies—The Supreme Royal Arch Chapter, the Ancient and Accepted Scotland Rite, The Order of the Temple, and the Royal Order of Scotland.

ROTARY

The Rotary Club of Edinburgh, (1912), is one of the oldest in the movement. It is also one of the eight founder clubs of Rotary of Great Britain and Ireland, of which the first president and secretary were both Edinburgh men. After the first World War Edinburgh entertained Rotary's 12th International Convention—with some 1,500 Rotarians from America alone. The strength of the club itself is about 200; its members meet every Thursday for lunch in the North British Hotel and listen to a guest speaker. Guests from other Rotary clubs are usually present, sometimes as many as 40 or 50 including visitors from abroad.

Like other Rotary clubs in the district the Edinburgh body undertakes a great variety of community service, such as providing car lifts for spastics and for elderly people visiting Beechmount House, a convalescent home at the top of a steep brae. The club also takes a paternal interest in a home for boys from broken families. But these are only a few of the ways it furthers and co-operates in schemes to secure funds for charitable purposes. Always it maintains friendly relations with the smaller Rotary Clubs in Leith, Portobello, Corstorphine, Musselburgh, and all other clubs with similar aims and activities within or near the city. There is, for example, the City of Edinburgh Round Table, a club composed of business and professional men below the age of 40, which in 1964 made an offer to the Corporation to defray the total cost (£2,000) of a road safety training playground in Edinburgh at the east end of the city's famous open space, the Meadows.

THE BRITISH LEGION

The British Legion (Scotland) was founded in Edinburgh and has always had its headquarters in the capital, its present address at Haig House being a convenient centre of operations, as the building houses a number of other ex-servicemen's organisations with which the Legion works closely.

After the tremendous ordeal of the first World War it was realised that regimental associations could not adequately look after the welfare of the men who had returned from the front and represent their needs and views to Parliament and Government departments. Thus four main protective organisations came into existence in the early post-war years. But fortunately the view that unity was strength prevailed, and in June, 1921 the British Legion (Scotland) was founded at a meeting in the Usher Hall when the various ex-servicemen's organisations agreed to unite, with Earl Haig as their first president. A National Executive Council was the controlling body; and the country was divided into nine areas, one of which covers Edinburgh and the Lothians.

The activities of the Legion are too diverse to detail here, but they may be grouped under the headings of benevolent, social or recreational, and publicity; and outstanding success has been achieved in the field of pensions. Between 1946 and 1963 no fewer than 21,562 ex-servicemen and women had been represented at Pensions Appeal Tribunals in Scotland and no less a sum than £745,764 had been secured in pensions and arrears of pensions as a result of these appeals. The finding of jobs for unemployed ex-servicemen and women has also occupied a great deal of the time and energy of the Legion's officials who cope with all sorts of personal problems such as housing, hire purchase and many other matters.

On the social side the Legion organises competitions between the different areas in golf, bowls, curling and indoor sports, though it is in the local branches that games and entertainments are most fully developed. Burns Night suppers, dances, whist drives, children's parties and competitions in various sports all appear in the calendar of the clubs, whose functions are reported in *The Claymore*, the magazine which keeps the branches in touch. In the Edinburgh and Lothians area there are more than 40 branches, of which 11 are within the city's boundaries.

One of the most sensible things the Legion inaugurated, according to its official history, was the Women's Section, which numbers 160 branches, all very active in organising social functions and raising money for charity. But with all its benevolent work the Legion is naturally always in need of donations, and a National Appeals Organiser was appointed in 1949 to arrange sporting events, pageants, exhibitions and other fixtures calculated to draw the crowds.

THE CORPS OF COMMISSIONAIRES

This body has a noble ring to its tone and title which, chosen from the French " Commission ", denotes one who can be trusted with a message, money, or a post of duty. The Corps' original members wore frockcoats and plumed caps, and despite their wounded state the first eight veterans must have swung proudly into Westminster Abbey in 1859 to render thanks to Almighty God for the formation of their new brotherhood.

The description " brotherhood " is apt, for such it has been since Captain Edward Walter established the Corps in London, and proved that former servicemen, at that time poorly educated, could adapt themselves so reliably to civilian work that branches were later opened throughout the British Isles.

Before the Corps was founded the lot of Wellington's time-expired soldiers, living as they did on inadequate pensions and with small hopes of employment, was a sad one. But today, in Edinburgh as elsewhere, the retired professional serviceman may hold posts of responsibility secured for him by the offices of the Corps, ranging from those strictly within the meaning of " commission " to reception clerk, telephone attendant, security police, club steward, staff supervisor, and a wide range of other useful occupations. Edinburgh employed her first member of the Corps in 1882, and by 1900 was employing 73 commissionaires.

Apart from a rise to 18 in 1905 and a fall between the two wars, the number has remained steady; and in the early 1960s there were some 70 members.

THE PROTECTION OF ANIMALS

The Scottish Society for Prevention of Cruelty to Animals was founded in Edinburgh in 1839, but though national in name its sphere of action was limited by restricted local resources. This led to the formation of similar societies based upon Glasgow, Aberdeen and Dundee—a regrettable division which persists to this day, although a Central Council of the four societies helps to ensure unified action in such matters as projected legislation.

The area of the Scottish S.P.C.A. in the early 1960s comprised 25 of Scotland's 33 counties. Of 28 Inspectors stationed throughout this area, four or five were always attached to headquarters in Edinburgh, where the staff consists of a Secretary-Treasurer and Assistant Secretary (both part-time), a Field Organiser (who visits schools, lecturing and showing films) and a very small clerical staff.

The 1707 Act of Union preserved the existing legal system in Scotland; which accounts for the many Acts of Parliament applicable to England but not to Scotland, and vice versa. In the field of animal protection in Scotland the most important relic of this pre-union legislation is the authority conferred in 1667 on the Justices of each County and City to administer a form of oath *de fideli administratione* to applicants who are then known as Justice of the Peace Constables. Since 1839 all the Inspectors of the Societies for the Prevention of Cruelty to Animals in Scotland have enjoyed this authority, and J.P. Constables have the powers of a Police Constable under various Acts.

The disappearance of the draught horse from our streets and farmlands has completely transformed the work of the Inspectors. Pre-1914 ex-cavalrymen were preferred as Inspectors, but during two wars older men with farm experience were appointed and knowledge of farm-stock is now the desired qualification. Patrol by motor van, visits to markets, harbours, abattoirs, and pet-shops, and the humane destruction of stray and unwanted small animals keep the Inspectorate busy. It should perhaps be added that the provision of permanent houses, improved uniform, increased wages and superannuation benefit have all contributed to a high morale among the Inspectors, many of whom have gained awards or commendation for courageous rescues of animals from precipitous cliffs or pit-shafts.

To help the pensioner who cannot afford the cost of skilled veterinary advice for a pet, the Society has for 30 years conducted through the Inspectors a free veterinary treatment scheme. The Society also maintains cordial relations with the Police as well as the veterinary profession. Since Police Colleges were instituted the Society has been privileged to send a lecturer on the laws of animal and bird protection to each successive course of recruits.

In Edinburgh the facilities for animals are augmented by the Royal

(Dick) School of Veterinary Studies of Edinburgh University with its Out-Patient Department and the Edinburgh Dog and Cat Home, recently rebuilt on excellent lines at Seafield. The S.S.P.C.A. also has a depot in Leith and at Balerno a Rest Farm for Horses and Dog Boarding Kennels. A large motor-ambulance for horses is garaged near headquarters and attends shows and race-meetings. In an emergency it conveys sick or injured horses; and once S.S.P.C.A. Inspectors performed an excellent service with it during the disastrous floods in East Anglia when the Society co-operated with the Royal S.P.C.A. London.

Finally, the work of Humane Education calls for mention. That strange expression, Humane Education, is of American origin and defies translation into any other language. It signifies the teaching of regard for animals and birds, and is fostered by an annual essay competition in schools, for which book prizes are awarded. A poster competition is also arranged occasionally, and a Junior Division for children of 11–18 attracts thousands of recruits annually as a result of a visit and talk from the Field Organiser. The co-operation of teachers in this work is of the greatest value.

The Scottish S.P.C.A. has since 1930 taken a close interest in the international work of animal protection. In 1935 the present Secretary attended an International Congress of Animal Protection at Brussels and proposed an international journal. This he edited and published for five issues in polyglot form, till war-time caused currency difficulties and brought it to an end. In 1950 another World Congress was held in The Hague and a World Federation for Protection of Animals was founded. Since then this Federation has held Congresses in London, Zurich, Salzburg and Vienna; and it deals continually with many international animal problems—the transport of animals by road, rail, sea and in the air, for example, and the ever increasing tendency to exploit animals and birds for gain in complete disregard of possible suffering entailed. The present Secretary of the Scottish S.P.C.A., Mr. Lyndesay G. Langwill was elected President 1958–62.

The annual expenditure of the Society in the early '60s was about £35,000, of which about £25,000 is raised entirely from charitable donations, flag days, and interest on investments. No Government or other grant of any kind is received. The balance is normally more than covered by legacies and any excess of legacies is invested. The capital is about £200,000.

THE OVERSEAS APPEAL

Earlier in this book attention was paid to the large number of people from overseas who live in Edinburgh either permanently or for periods of several years. Some of them, we saw, belonged to societies like those to which many Edinburgh Poles and Ukrainians belong, or to those excellent cultural bodies, the French and Danish Institutes; and indeed the list could have been extended to include many more. Certain large and influential organisations with an overseas appeal must however be noticed more extensively, since they are social and residential and are widely used by visitors to the city from abroad.

The Royal Overseas League, whose Edinburgh and East of Scotland membership, male and female, is between four and five thousand, aims to " draw together in the bond of comradeship British Citizens throughout the world." This active branch of the league was set up in 1929 with excellent club premises in Princes Street. On a smaller scale the English Speaking Union (membership, male and female, about 800) offers services of reception and hospitality to Commonwealth and U.S. visitors. Similarly the Edinburgh branch of the Victoria League offers club facilities and accommodation to visitors such as overseas post-graduate students. Then there is the International Club which was founded in 1913 and is believed in Edinburgh to be the oldest of its kind in the kingdom. Its 250 members are of various nationalities resident in Edinburgh, and they meet once a fortnight.

Finally, a special tribute must be paid to the Commonwealth Institute Scottish Committee, a body which is doing increasingly important work in the fields of Commonwealth culture and education at a time of far-reaching change.

COMMONWEALTH INSTITUTE

The Commonwealth Institute, under its original title of Imperial Institute was founded in the Jubilee Year 1887 " to foster the interests of the British Empire," and in 1952 was re-organised as a centre for education and information about the Commonwealth, financed by the British and Commonwealth Governments. In 1956 an autonomous Scottish Committee of the Institute was set up in Edinburgh to carry on its educational activities north of the Border. These were sponsored by the Scottish Education Department, and have included one-day conferences for senior secondary schools—some 200 of these had taken place by 1964—with the Institute providing authoritative speakers to discuss Commonwealth subjects of topical interest. It also provides schools with a free Commonwealth Filmstrip Loan Service and other visual aids.

In 1961 the Institute opened its present Scottish headquarters in Rutland Square. One of its main features is a large showroom for the display and sale of teaching aids, including charts and maps and a wide range of inexpensive booklets on the Commonwealth countries, their people and products, and a very good small exhibition gallery in which works by Commonwealth artists are shown in a series of exhibitions throughout the year as well as other exhibitions of Commonwealth interest such as the Institute's annual travelling exhibitions of photographic material on Commonwealth countries. Commendably also, the Institute is building up a small Commonwealth Reference Library for use by teachers, lecturers, students, school children or anyone interested in Commonwealth affairs.

EDINBURGH PHOTOGRAPHIC SOCIETY

Photography came to Edinburgh early; for although the Edinburgh Photographic Society was not founded until 1861 there had been considerable activity among enthusiasts in the 1840s and '50s. In the '40s especially they got great impetus from a Royal Academician, D. O. Hill, who was anxious to depict in detail the memorable scenes after the disruption of the Church of Scotland in 1843. But how to secure almost 500 likenesses for the immense picture he planned? The new photographic invention of Calotype solved the problem, and large numbers of church dignitaries were photographed to make the picture both possible and accurate.

Hill's gallery of portrait photographs records many other famous men of his time; but since his day there have been great technical advances, reflected for over 80 years in the Edinburgh Photographic Society's exhibitions, which have attracted many hundreds of members not only from Scotland but also from countries as far away as China and Japan.

CLUBS AND SOCIETIES

Although quite distinct from the students' societies which meet in the University, the Speculative Society, which was founded in 1764 and is widely known as the " Spec," meets for debate on Wednesdays, between October and March, by candlelight and the glow of an open fire in its own rooms in the Old College.

Another venerable sodality is the Wagering Club, instituted in 1775 by a dozen citizens of Edinburgh who had resolved to promote friendly and social intercourse by a convivial meeting. At this meeting the members laid and engaged bets over a wide range of subjects for the following year. The early dinners were held in the taverns about the High Street, and at one held in 1784, James Boswell was present and recorded later how he " grew monstrously drunk " and did " not recollect what passed neither what wagers were made." Today the club still meets annually, and more decorously, and its officers have the duty of preparing and determining the bets, the proceeds of which, together with other fines, are devoted to charity.

Then there are the Monks of St. Giles, a society founded over a century ago with a limited membership drawn from many professions. Its members, who bear appropriate and humorous monkish names, wear robes at their monthly suppers, and entertain each other with witty rhymed contributions on matters of topical or personal interest.

For an officially Presbyterian city Edinburgh seems very liberal in her nomenclature. Besides accommodating the Monks of St. Giles she also has the All Saints Club, a dining fraternity composed of a dozen or so gentlemen drawn from literature and the arts, the University, law, medicine, the Press and business, who meet a dozen of their opposite numbers from Glasgow three times a year to drink claret with their dinner and pay homage to an absent guest from Scotland's historic past.

No less picturesque are the dining clubs associated with certain learned institutions. Some of these—the clubs associated with the medical profession for example—have already been described and others will be later. But there are certain clubs which though not strictly intellectual have real purpose. One of these is the Edinburgh Toastmasters' Club, formed in 1946 by 30 young bankers who met together in Edinburgh with the common aim of helping each other to overcome an underlying fear of public speaking. In some ways this is not a very typical Edinburgh society, for it was inspired by Toastmasters International, an American federation which has helped a great many young men and women towards freedom in self-expression. Other Toastmaster clubs in the city followed, and now there are Toast Mistresses Clubs as well.

THE SOCIAL CLUBS

The bodies we have just looked at are of course clubs for occasional meetings as distinct from the clubs with premises of their own which can be either palatial, like the New Club, or smaller and sometimes more intimate and friendly. Some of the bigger clubs in Edinburgh with day-to-day amenities are also residential, so that members from the country can have a bedroom if they wish when they come to town. But whether large or small they share certain rules of conduct, and no-one, however celebrated, can be elected without the consent of the members.

Historical pride of place among the city's residential clubs obviously goes to the New Club which was founded in 1787, and has ever since attracted a membership of wide range and influence. It also, in the 1950s, attracted members of the University Club when that deservedly famous body was merged with the New at a time when the University itself was constructing a mixed University Staff Club beside the Old College.

Also in Princes Street, and looking over to the towering crag of Edinburgh Castle are the two big political clubs—the Scottish Conservative Club and the Scottish Liberal Club.

The Conservative Club, which was founded in 1877, now has some 1,000 members, admits ladies as guests to the dining room and lounge in the evening and thereby, contrary to the trend in most clubs, keeps busy on Saturday evenings. A few doors away in the Liberal Club, junior by a couple of years, one can almost hear in the smokeroom, where a memorial library and a sculptured head of the statesman now rest, the echo of Gladstone's Midlothian campaign. So at least says an old member. But the Liberal Club also admits ladies as guests in the evenings.

The Scottish Artists' Club, founded in 1874 and reformed in 1894 into the present Scottish Arts Club, and thereby admitting members " interested in the arts though not practising them professionally," sits snugly in Rutland Square. There a painter may share a sheep's head and a bottle of claret with a doctor, at least two Senators of the College of Justice, a poet musing with a banker perhaps, a farmer, one or two professors, or maybe an architect or two.

The Trout Anglers Club was formed in 1899 and after a brief wandering settled quietly in Rutland Street with what is now claimed to be the best angling library in Scotland. The Trout Anglers have a congenial neighbour. On the other side of the street there is the Edinburgh Press Club to which tired journalists retreat for lively talk and refreshment, and where they let hot news grow cool.

One particularly interesting club is the Caledonian United Services Club which has members drawn from many vocations. It was founded in 1825 and recently the Northern Club merged with it. But clubs with Service names proliferate in the city. The Royal Scots Club, founded in 1919 as a tribute to those who fell in the first World War, has a membership of 3,300 and premises in Abercromby Place. The Royal Navy Association and Club stands trim with white flag pole in the garden at Heriothouse. The Scots Guards, the Black Watch, the Royal Engineers, Royal Artillery, Royal Gunners, the Royal Air Force and the former Home Guard each have a Club; even the Polish Ex-servicemen's Club is to be found in Great King Street; and in 1920 the Women's United Services Club was founded in the West End.

Edinburgh women have in fact quite a number of clubs and associations in the city, though obviously, since many have domestic duties to perform, they are less gregarious than men. They have, for example, two well-established clubs—the Queen's founded in 1897 (present membership 800) in Frederick Street, and the Ladies Caledonian (1909), which is elegantly accommodated in Charlotte Square. They also have the Scottish Women's Lyceum Club in Atholl Crescent. This club grew out of the Scottish First Air Corps whose members (all women) served abroad during the first World War. A social club it offers accommodation for country members visiting Edinburgh. Finally there are such well-known sororities as the Business and Professional Women's Club, the Women Citizens Association, the Edinburgh Association of University Women and two Soroptomist Clubs. One of these is in Leith. The members of these clubs are women who have reached the top of their particular profession in industry, trade or commerce, and they aim at improving the standing of women generally. Lastly, we should mention The Inner Wheel. This is designed for the wives of Rotarians; there are several clubs of the kind in Edinburgh and its suburbs; and each one does a lot of charitable work, particularly among old folk and people who are handicapped.

CHAPTER 24

DRESS, DECORATION AND FURNISHING

To complete our picture of the many social changes which have taken place in mid-20th century Edinburgh we might well turn an eye on present-day habits of dress, furnishing and decoration, for these are a very integral part of the social pattern.

During the past four decades there have been many changes. The characteristic costumes of various crafts, trades and professions have disappeared; uniformity of dress in all classes of the community has become common; and a general relaxation of many of the older conventions has modified the former varied picturesqueness of the garb of the Edinburgh citizen and his family.

WOMEN'S DRESS

Nowhere has the change been more marked than in women's dress, both formal and informal. The old " shawlie " with her tartan " screen " or shawl over her head, once to be seen throughout the Old Town and much of the New, has almost disappeared—except for a few old timers here and there. Formerly the shawl was universally worn and of varied utility, serving not only for adornment, shelter and warmth, but also as a shopping receptacle and a cradle for the " wean." Now the tartan rug and shawl in its retirement has taken on the function of chair-cover or supplementary bed-cover.

In Edinburgh today, as elsewhere, all classes tend to affect and reflect the same fashion trends in clothing and accessories, and it is often only by the quality of the material and some slight time-lag in the finer points of fashion that the " Colonel's lady and Judy O'Grady " can be distinguished at a first glance. For this the spread of the multiple shop, with its enormous output of garments modelled on the latest styles in ranges designed to suit many purses, is in large measure responsible. In fact, what the great fashion houses of London, Paris and Rome say in their " collections " is translated into " budget priced " clothes within almost a matter of days, though until comparatively recent years Edinburgh lagged almost a year behind the current phase of fashion in Paris. Moreover, the levelling up and down of incomes is inevitably reflected in the dress of the people and undoubtedly it has played a substantial part in producing the increasing uniformity in appearance and dress.

Without a doubt, too, the most consistently contemporary in dress are the girls who are executives or buyers in shops. This is particularly noticeable at about nine o'clock in the morning and again at six in the evening, when these girls are going to or from their business and a chic, though not costly, standard of dressing appears in the streets.

The circulation of the glossy magazine, with large sections devoted solely to catering for feminine tastes, has not only increased interest in dress and a desire to keep up with the general trend of fashion, but has also brought the ideas of designers and leaders of the fashion world to a greater number of people than ever before. The influence of cheaper and more extensive travel also has a bearing on the marked change that has taken place in the dress of Edinburgh women. But the limited extent of an expensive social life puts a brake on the extremes of fashion, so that there is still a certain dress sobriety and moderation in the city, whatever the occasion. In addition, the cult of tweed and wool and tartan still gives a characteristic slant to the Edinburgh scene. This is partly due to the climate, partly to a native thriftiness that prefers to spend a little more on clothes of good quality and long-lasting properties that will not date, and partly to the fact that much of the city is neither wholly urbanised nor even yet suburbanised. In addition, though many high heels do brave the east wind, the majority of " sensible shoes " being worn and seen in shop windows testifies to the number of those who are prepared to defy fashion in the interests of comfort. One other change in Edinburgh fashion is notable: the wearing of shorts for games and trousers for almost any occasion has become a commonplace. Whereas 30 years ago these garments would have earned at least hostile criticism if not pulpit anathema, now the incongruities of some Scottish female figures, when (physically) " wearing the breeks ", scarcely raises a smile.

Another expression of fashion is found in the middle and upper-middle classes, where the teenagers and young twenties deliberately dress down for parties. It is quite common for a girl who has been tidily dressed for her working day to put herself into old and faded jeans or trousers and loose " Sloppy Joe " sweater in order to go out at half past nine or ten to dance, or to a " bottle party."

As for hair fashions, the cult of the hairdresser is as strong in Edinburgh as anywhere else in Britain or the Continent, and the blown-up, bouffant styles are no different to those seen in Paris or London. The only complaints heard sometimes are that the cutters are not quite so good, and in the early '60s it looked as if hair in Edinburgh was worn rather longer than elsewhere. Oddly enough, it was exactly the same with the length of women's skirts, which have never seemed to be so short as they are in Brighton, say, or London. Perhaps this has something to do with life and love in a not always hot climate.

MEN'S DRESS

For men the tale of growing uniformity and increased informality is much the same. Even the policemen have lost their helmets, and with them something of their previous awe-inspiring dignity. The silk hat, formerly the mark of the advocate, the physician, the surgeon or the city minister, has almost disappeared, even from the heads of bank managers; and apart from fleeting appearances at weddings, Holyroodhouse Garden Parties and occasional funerals, the tall hat lies gathering dust and memories in its box. In years gone by the legal tide flowed up and down the Mound in uniform silk hat, morning coat and striped trousers, white bow tie and umbrella: now the tide ebbs and flows in a motley throng where black homburgs predominate and the morning coat is almost unknown. The professional man for the most part is no longer distinguished by his formal clothes during business hours, but by the umbrella and brief case, and sometimes the bowler hat, which generally mark the lawyer or business man. For the rest the nondescript sameness of attire no longer separates the classes from the masses or singles out the publican from the presbyter. At the weekend any clothes which come within the category of " sports clothes "—from jacket and flannel trousers to tweed suits—are the usual wear. Evening dress is no longer seen at the theatre, while the dinner jacket and black tie are sufficient tribute to formality except on occasions of extreme ceremony. For in men's clothing as well as women's the pressure of economic necessity is felt; the ready-to-wear shop replaces the bespoke tailor, and there are few men today for whom the shirtmaker is more than a purveyor of ready-made garments.

Rather more individuality is perhaps being expressed today, however, in the case of working-class and lower middle-class youths, who spend a large proportion of their wages on clothes and have become intensely fashion conscious. In the early '60s they have been particularly influenced by the Italian style, following a revival of the Edwardian style.

But it is only in the wearing of Highland dress, especially as evening dress, that the Edinburgh man can be distinguished from the inhabitant of any other large city. More and more kilts of all known (and some unknown) tartans lend touches of colour to evening gatherings otherwise respectably drab, while the wearing of the kilt by day among students, professed Scottish nationalists of varying extremes, and those who have at least one Highland grandmother adds a certain gaiety to the Edinburgh scene.

THE CHILDREN

Children's dress exhibits the same tendency to uniformity. No longer does one see children barefoot and in rags among the traffic and in the closes of the Old Town. A school cap, blazer and shorts has taken the place of those rags as well as of the Glengarry or Balmoral bonnet and kilt, and the school uniform sometimes makes it hard to distinguish whether a boy or girl attends one of the city's private schools, of which there are many, or one of the local authority schools.

DECORATION AND FURNISHING

Decoration and furnishing is an important part of the social pattern and an expression of taste and personality. It could also be said, in general terms, that the style of domestic decoration in Edinburgh is determined more by the owner's social status than by the size of his or her bank account.

To take the largest section of the community first—the middle-class with their various strata—it would appear that their motto in decoration is " Play safe ", and that safety means decorating their homes in a fashion identical with most other houses in their group.

In middle-class houses this fear of non-conformity restricts the range of colour used. The dining room is usually painted or distempered in a cream or sand colour, though very exceptionally green. The master bedroom is sometimes peach or pink, but the rest of the house is generally painted in every possible shade of beige, cream, coffee or sand, and if wallpaper is used it will be in the same colour group. A wary eye is kept open for what the neighbours might think, and the comment, " Cream is so safe—everything goes with it " comes easy on the tongue.

Another reason why the middle classes tend to " play safe " is probably because they usually employ expensive interior decorators. A room which costs a lot to decorate must last some little while to be economical. Wallpaper is usually underscaled, and is often chosen by the owner of the house as " something he will not get tired of " rather than as an original or exciting design. The fashion for plastic-covered walls has now gone from Edinburgh, but the idea has died hard, as many of the wallpapers used were slightly embossed and therefore difficult to cover.

Woodwork in the richer houses of this group is very often stripped and waxed in the passages and living rooms, and painted in the bedrooms. The lower income houses, on the other hand, are usually painted to simulate grained wood and varnished throughout, although in the bedrooms the woodwork may be occasionally painted cream or brown or to match the walls. Ceilings are cream or white or sometimes coloured; and distemper, emulsion or paint are used, depending on the householder's income. Picture rails are still common.

Curtain materials in the public rooms are often of velour in shades of rust, brown, green or maroon, and folkweaves, repps, tudoresque cottons or linens are also used. In the higher-income groups brocatelles and damasks are popular, usually in a quality incorporating rayon. Pelmets are usually plain, or shaped in what is considered to be a Georgian design, and great care is taken to match the cream, coffee or beige fringe with the cream, coffee or beige carpet.

In the master bedroom curtain materials are likely to be of brocade, damasks, rayon sateen or quilted, and will usually be lined. Sometimes there are unlined linens, cotton prints or folkweaves.

Carpets in the public rooms depend much on the family purse for quality, and are frequently patterned. Furniture, too, varies more in quality than in the taste displayed. In those families who have inherited furniture, and where status has not altered much since the last generation, there is a tendency to cling to the massive security of Edwardian and Victorian pieces, however inconvenient. But those who are furnishing for the first time show a partiality for matching suites in both public rooms and bedrooms; yet even so the taste is usually for the massive.

Genuinely working class householders seem to have no particular inhibitions about colour, and although there is a certain amount of cream, it is not so universally used as it is in the middle class homes. This group usually do their own decorating, or employ some part-time or odd-job man to help them; and since the expense of their decorating is much lower than that of higher income groups, they are more apt to go in for bright coloured paints and contemporary or unusual wallpapers, which can be changed fairly frequently.

Curtains are usually in rayon, taffetas, cretonne or cotton. Three-piece suites are popular, and are usually upholstered in uncut moquette (because of its hard-wearing properties). Small chairs are often covered with leatherette.

Furniture is mainly mass-produced and often of stained and grained imitation oak; but there is an increasing tendency to use contemporary design in light-coloured wood. As for ornaments, these are seldom purchases for themselves, but any received as gifts are invariably displayed. It could be said of the upper classes that many have developed perhaps a more cosmopolitan approach to decoration and are not hide-bound by convention. It also seems true that many such people if fortunate enough to live in old or beautiful houses tend to approach their problems with an eye sympathetic to the period in which their house was built, and also to Scottish traditions.

In such houses colour is used to its fullest extent. Ceilings are usually white, and the walls are either papered with an overscaled patterned wallpaper, or distempered in a plain colour. Their owners do not go in for rust, or colours known as " the lower end of the trade ", and are inclined to use bright red or crimson rather than maroon, much white, grey, pale yellow, blue, green, pink-red and off-beat colours. Woodwork is usually painted white (a throwback to country house days), but it may also be painted in some colour that echoes the general scheme of the room.

In materials and all soft furnishings, and also in furniture, " shine " is regarded with distaste, although sheen of silk (as opposed to shine of rayon) is generally acceptable. A great deal of glazed chintz is used, both plain and patterned, and such materials as velours, brocades, silks and silk taffetas. Pelmets are usually imaginative and elaborate in the public rooms, and swags are also widely used. Cushions which can be of many different colours in the same room, or can tone with the general colour scheme, are usually untrimmed. Carpets are for the most part plain, except for Oriental carpets in the public rooms.

Furniture in the public rooms may be antique or Victorian, with often a considerable mixture of French. Oak is very little used, probably owing to the original French influence on Scottish taste as opposed to the English. Gilt is also used extensively in furniture. Matching bedroom suites are seldom seen in these upper-class houses. Bathrooms and bathroom colours tend to be very gay, and bathrooms are frequently wallpapered and carpeted.

In lighting, standard lamps are not chosen so often, as they were and are replaced by table lamps and wall light. Very often table lamps are converted vases of oriental or other origin. A centre light is rarely installed unless it is a chandelier, but glass chandeliers are very popular. Lampshades are usually made from a plain material, unless they are in chintz, and are never patterned. Pleated silk is often used and occasionally parchment.

Paintings—even sculpture—and old china as well as modern continental bric-a-brac play a much more important part in the decoration of upper-class houses than they do in the others. Much use is also made of flowers, particularly in large mixed flower arrangements, and of branches of evergreens and winter decorations of painted dried foliage.

The contemporary style in decoration is found in all groups—top, middle or lower—but this trend in Edinburgh may partly be due to the fact that the style is better suited to small rooms with low ceilings than to the high rooms of many of the old upper-class Edinburgh houses, where much of the truncated contemporary furniture would look out of proportion. But it is also true that " contemporary " has become something of a status symbol, and whereas the best in contemporary design may be genuinely preferred by many middle and upper-class young married couples, architects, artists and writers, a degraded form of contemporary is now the popular choice of many of those who are anxious to " keep up with the Joneses."

In true contemporary design the lighting is functional with usually a crude top light, a modern standard with indirect lighting, and table lights for the convenience of the individual reader. Lamp shades are mainly of glass or metal or basket-work. Pictures are modern and ash-trays are of muddy-coloured pottery; ornaments show a wide latitude of personal taste, but are often rather self-consciously amusing or bizarre —an " *objet trouvé* " or a grotesque piece of Victoriana. Flowers are seldom employed for the purpose of decoration, but wide use is made of the new range of tropical and semi-tropical " house plants " and dried foliage is also used.

It is however in the sphere of the kitchen that contemporary design has made its greatest advance, and this applies to the houses of all sections of the community. With the decline of domestic service there is a tendency for the family—even of the upper classes—when alone, to eat in the kitchen, despite the fact that the mistress of the house, or the housewife, spends much of her time there. Accordingly, even when the rest of the house remains unchanged and out-of-fashion, a modern look is often streamlined into the kitchen with gay colour and a wide range of modern equipment.

Part Five

FINANCE AND INDUSTRY

CHAPTER 25

THE FINANCIAL STRUCTURE

Though Edinburgh is universally accepted as the financial capital of Scotland it is not a financial centre in the same sense that London is. During the 19th century and in our own, Britain for the purposes of a money market was regarded as one country, as it still is, and London was the financial capital not only of Britain but of the world. There could thus be no room for two real financial centres (or money markets) so close together in one small island. Edinburgh has a Stock Exchange floor, and accommodates the head offices of most Scottish banks, insurance companies, investment trusts and other financial institutions; but it has no money market in the sense that London has.

Of the bigger Scottish towns and cities Edinburgh is the one that has concentrated most on banking, insurance and investment trusts though its direct participation in industry at large has been growing too. Possibly the reason for this concentration lies in the establishment of the first Edinburgh banks from 1695 onwards, when Edinburgh was not only a true centre of government, but had intimate trade links with Europe through the port of Leith, and had no serious financial competition to face from Glasgow until the 1830s.

Most of the Scottish insurance companies were sited in Edinburgh during the first 20 years of the 19th century, at a time of great industrial expansion in Glasgow which, as we shall see, absorbed considerable capital and left little over for other ventures. Edinburgh on the other hand found the funds necessary for its own business expansion mainly from the city's professional classes. As for the investment trusts, which further exemplify the desire for indirect investment, these came about to give the small investor an opportunity to invest his savings, and also to obtain an interest in equities of all types.

Several things are notable about Edinburgh in this all-important sphere. The city's financial institutions operate far and wide in the United Kingdom and have in fact invested more in property south of the Border than in Scotland. This is of course inevitable since England is larger than Scotland as regards area and population, and also because Scotland is part of the United Kingdom and must integrate financially or face incalculable consequences.

Another interesting feature of Edinburgh's financial life is its position as an official headquarters and meeting place for businesses whose main producing operations are conducted not in the city itself but sometimes near and often far beyond the city boundaries. A good example is the Distillers Company at whose 1964 annual general meeting in Edinburgh, the Chairman announced a gross trading profit for the company's year of more than £36 millions. Some of the Distillers Company's products are made thousands of miles from Edinburgh, as are those of The Scottish Tea and Lands Company of Ceylon, which grows tea there in an estate fittingly called the Edinburgh Estate, and a number of other companies in Africa and elsewhere, producing tea, rubber and other commodities.

This then is the broad picture of Scotland's capital as a centre of financial operations. But as with all economic matters there is seldom any lasting agreement between the various interests involved, whether local, national or international, or even among the economists who survey them from time to time. One such is Dr. L. C. Wright of the University of Edinburgh, who towards the end of 1961 wrote what some may think is in parts a rather pessimistic account of the city's financial significance, though others may agree with Dr. Wright's findings.

Somewhat paradoxically (wrote Dr. Wright) Edinburgh can be called the financial capital of Scotland yet it does not qualify to be a true financial centre. Though it is the seat of government for Scotland, and houses many financial instititutions, it has never been a centre where risk capital could readily be raised for industrial projects. In part this has come about because Edinburgh has no money market, that is for short term obligations. Certainly the lack of such a market, with its allied foreign exchange facilities, had a strong influence on Scottish trade; for in terms of exports it meant a gradual weakening of the old trade links with Scandinavia, the Baltic, Low Countries and France, and an undue concentration on selling to England and—to a lesser extent—the Commonwealth.

Casual visitors and natives alike see little outward evidence of busy, sometimes frantic financial activity, as they might see in the city of London. Yet there can be little doubt about Edinburgh's unique position within Scotland for purely financial transactions. Four out of five Scottish banks have their head offices in the city; in the field of insurance Edinburgh stands second only to London in the amount of business done; and the Investment Trust companies continue to be a most distinctive feature of the Edinburgh scene. Completing the tale of purely financial institutions is the Edinburgh Savings Bank described later. Altogether these institutions control funds worth much more than £1,300 million. But although so much is known, it is impossible to estimate how much investment takes place each year in Edinburgh since no figures are available for direct personal investment in equities and government securities.

At this point it is useful to consider why Edinburgh out of all Scottish towns and cities has concentrated so much on banking, insurance and investment trusts to the comparative neglect of direct participation in industry. One suggestion is that the three oldest Edinburgh banks set up between 1695 and 1746 were well-established, large, and almost impregnable commercially before any banks were founded in Glasgow. However, this early supremacy did not go unchallenged. When trade began to develop with America and the British colonies, the financial centre of gravity began to move towards the West—a process stimulated by the rapid industrialisation of the Glasgow area. By the 1830s Glasgow was in a position to compete with the well-established Edinburgh banks, and four joint stock banks were set up there. In the event this was the only direct competition faced by the Edinburgh banks. English-based banks were discouraged from moving over the Border by the existence of a separate Scottish Legal Code whilst the Bank Acts of 1844–5, by forbidding the formation of new banks of issue, effectively closed the list as far as Scotland was concerned. Finally, whatever threat the Glasgow banks offered disappeared with the spectacular failure of the Western Bank in 1856 and the City of Glasgow Bank in 1879.

In the same way the siting of Scottish insurance companies in Scotland's capital seems something of an historical accident. Most of them came into existence during the first 20 years of the 19th century when Glasgow was in a phase of rapid industrial expansion, with merchants and manufacturers ploughing back profits to expand existing businesses and found new ones. Thus nearly all available capital was being actively and directly used with little to spare for purely financial ventures. In contrast Edinburgh had ample funds available for this type of investment. Much of Scotland's legal work was centred on Edinburgh, and there were many important legal firms with sizeable funds available. It is not surprising that they were more interested in government securities, insurance funds, and investment trusts than in direct participation in production. Certainly the best brains, and the best society in 19th century Edinburgh were not attracted by manufacturing, and ever since legal and professional bodies have continued to control a large part of the funds available in the city for investment.

Further evidence of this leaning towards indirect investment is provided by the investment trusts. The concept of such trusts came from Dundee, but they were enthusiastically developed in Edinburgh and have grown rapidly. Throughout they have been interested in foreign investment, and this tendency has been reinforced in the late '50s and early '60s because of continuing inflation in Britain.

In review two factors stand out about Edinburgh as a financial centre. Initially it would appear that the city's financial institutions have given greater service to the United Kingdom as a whole than they have to Scotland. The investment trusts have provided a continuous stream of invisible earnings and thus helped to a significant extent the British balance of payments. In the past Edinburgh banks and insurance companies have formed a ready market for government securities. Despite inflation and a tendency for institutions to move into equities this still holds good today. In contrast with this consistent demand for government paper, financial institutions in Edinburgh have, on the whole, been reluctant to take up bonds issued by Scottish local authorities. This is hard to explain but must reflect their estimate of the saleability and yield of Scottish bonds.

Almost as a corollary there has been a reluctance to develop the expertise and incentives for successful direct investment in industry—whether Scottish or otherwise. Moreover until very recently Edinburgh as a financial centre was resistant to change. There were too many banks (with too many branches) with policies geared to the needs of distributive trading and the professions. Now the situation is changing. There have been several bank amalgamations and much more flexible policies have been adopted to cover a wider and more industrial market for banking facilities. Insurance companies and investment trusts alike are also participating indirectly (sometimes directly) in the recent property development boom.

It is at this point (Dr. Wright concludes) that the question arises as to how far the way in which Edinburgh's financial institutions have developed is due to social conditions. Perhaps they were shaped by the New Town temperament of the 19th century, ill-attuned to industrialisation. On the other hand they grew under the perennial Scottish tradition of lower wages, lower housing standards, lower rents, and fewer opportunities for profit than prevailed in England. Whatever the social explanation the result was the same—indirect and profitable investment outwith Scotland, and frequently outwith Great Britain. That Edinburgh financiers have succeeded in doing this for so many years without major monetary loss, and with prestige well-maintained, says much for their shrewdness. It is this shrewdness, competent management, plus an unemotional, placid, near-academic approach to monetary matters which is the distinctive feature of Edinburgh as a financial centre.

Not everyone agrees with all of these views, but Dr. Wright was writing early in the 60s, and quite a lot has happened since then, as we shall see in the later, more detailed accounts of the city's financial institutions. One view of the kind of criticisms (apart from the praise) which a number of economists have mounted is that the investment trusts have backed more new industrial enterprises in recent years than they are given credit for. In particular, says one commentator, one Edinburgh investment trust was " backing commercial television at a time when other people were scared stiff." The commentator in question goes on: " The criticism one often hears that the city investment trusts do not support home industry is really not fair. They were formed in the first place to give the small investor an opportunity of taking an interest indirectly in investments which they could hardly have found on their own initiative, and as such they have been remarkably successful. Managing money through investment trusts has become in fact one of Edinburgh's most important but least publicised industries. That apart, it is not the job of the trusts to finance new ventures: their first responsibility is to their shareholders, many of whom are not resident in Scotland."

Other financial experts consulted seem agreed that many people, professedly keen to develop Scottish industry, are often reluctant to form the new financial institutions required. They therefore are pleased to see a new merchant bank[1] and a new issuing[2] house in Edinburgh. On the other hand, some of the older institutions have been backing various industrial enterprises since Dr. Wright's earlier survey. The Insurance Export Finance Company which is successful—potentially on a large

[1] National Commercial Schroders formed jointly by National Commercial Bank of Scotland and Schroders of London.

[2] An office of Scottish Industrial Finance based in Glasgow and owned by Industrial and Commercial Finance Corporation.

scale—is financed by Edinburgh insurance companies along with others in the United Kingdom. The Scottish insurance companies have also been financing the new dry dock on the Clyde. Another financial enterprise worth noticing in this setting is The Scottish Agricultural Securities Corporation whose Registered Office is in Edinburgh. The Corporation, registered in 1933, was formed to raise money by debentures for making advances on agricultural and horticultural properties up to two-thirds of the value of each property, the advances to be repayable within 60 years by equal yearly or half-yearly instalments. The whole Ordinary capital is owned by the Royal Bank of Scotland, the British Linen Bank and the National Commercial Bank. Since 1933 Scottish Agricultural Securities has lent some £7½ million secured over agricultural subjects extending to more than 632,000 acres.

BANKING

No one reading the *New* (Second) *Statistical Account of Scotland* would realise that 1845, the year of its publication, was a momentous one in the history of Scottish banking. It contains no reference to Sir Robert Peel's Act " to Regulate the Issue of Bank notes in Scotland " which was passed in that year, although it was the subject of much agitation and comment at the time. That Act ended what banking historians refer to as the " era of free banking," but it has also been responsible for the continuance until today of the private note issues which are the most distinctive feature of Scottish banking.

Edinburgh was the original home of banking in Scotland, and today it contains four out of the five head offices of the Scottish banks. To write about banking in the city solely from a local standpoint would therefore be to ignore the ramifications of the branch system which spread throughout Scotland, and the fact also that many Edinburgh bankers are employed daily not on local business but in supervising the lending and other activities of these branches, in controlling their funds, supplying them with cash and all their other requirements, and providing the specialised services they need. As Edinburgh is therefore the focal point of Scottish banking, some account of the influences playing upon the system as a whole is required if our picture is to be in perspective.

Whether future historians will regard any individual year in the mid-20th century to have been so momentous as 1845 it is difficult to say; but assuredly they will pick upon the 1950s as one of these periods of transition through which any banking system must pass from time to time in the process of adapting itself to the changing needs of the community within which it functions. Since 1950 there have been three amalgamations among Scottish banks; and the banks have made many changes in their operating methods.

The prime cause of this relatively rapid change, in a business the hall-mark of which must always be stability, is inflation. The legislators of 1845 were endeavouring to deal with the instability generated (they thought) by the unregulated issue of notes; today the increase of paper money in circulation goes almost unheeded and the efforts of the monetary authorities have been directed towards the control of credit, mainly in the form of bank lending. In 1958 the restrictions on bank lending that had operated, in one form or another, since 1939 were withdrawn, but by 1960 new measures of control were imposed. These in their turn, were removed in 1962 but returned in 1964. Whether these efforts to control the economy will be any more successful than their 19th century predecessors remains to be seen, but there can be no doubt about the effect on Scottish banking.

Until the 1930s the banks could rely on being able to lend to their customers about 50 per cent of the funds they held from depositors. The slump and the methods by which the war of 1939–45 was financed brought down the proportion lent to a very low figure and, though it rose after 1945, Government regulations saw to it that it never exceeded 30 per cent until 1958 when freedom to lend was restored. By 1965 loans were once more over 50 per cent of deposits.

Several results have flowed from these influences. The first was the alteration in the method of charging which betokened a change in emphasis on sources of income. In earlier times the borrowing customer paid in interest enough to finance most of the services which not only he but the depositor received. When lending was restricted this was no longer possible. Next, the amalgamations which have already been mentioned were designed to make possible a reduction in overhead expenses and, in time, to reduce the number of bank offices. Continuously throughout the post-war period there has also been a search for more economical methods of working. Inflation has increased vastly the number of notes and the quantities of coin to be handled and note-counting and coin-counting machines have been installed in the head offices to assist in this task. The number of cheques issued has also risen steadily and the old vast ledgers with their copper-plate headings and columns of figures have given place in many offices to machine-posted cards; the pass-book has been superseded by the loose-leaf statement and the male ledger-clerk replaced by the female " machinist." The banks have been studying and increasing the application of electronic apparatus to banking and in a few years time all cheques and other vouchers will become virtually self-accounting.

Up to 1914, the employment of women in banks was almost unknown. Some were recruited during the first war, but most of them were replaced by men after 1918 and it was not until the 1930s that they came to represent more than a tiny fraction of the total staffs. By 1963 about 850 women (37 per cent, that is, of the total clerical staff) were employed in Edinburgh by the banks. In all, the banks employ in the city about 2,400 people including a hundred or so non-clerical staff.

When we come to look at the banks individually we find that four of the names are the same as those listed in the 1845 *Statistical Account.* The other one combines two other names that were also extant then.

The table below records them, with the principle items from their balance sheets and the number of their branches as nearly as possible at the end of 1965.

TABLE 45

	£ million						
	Founded	*Capital and Reserves*	*Note Issue*	*Deposits*	*Advances*	*Total Assets*	*Branches in Edinburgh*
Bank of Scotland	1695	15·9	29·8	224·9	138·3	311	42
Royal Bank of Scotland	1727	23·4	17·0	159·4	79·8	212	34
British Linen Bank	1746	4·8	14·9	113·7	60·1	140	23
National Commercial Bank of Scotland	1810	23·2	44·7	270·2	142·9	339	48
Clydesdale Bank	1838	7·8	26·3	237·9	97·9	287	18

The bare figures, however, tell only a small part of the story. The Clydesdale Bank, for example, is the only one of these banks which does not have its head office in Edinburgh, but with 18 branches in the city it obviously cannot be excluded. Its present name is as it was in 1845, but from 1950 until 1963 it was known as Clydesdale and North of Scotland Bank. The North of Scotland Bank, with which it amalgamated, was founded in Aberdeen in 1836. The share capital in both banks was purchased by the Midland Bank in the early 1920s.

The Bank of Scotland, as the table shows, was founded in 1695, but it increased to its present size at one step in 1952 when it acquired the Union Bank of Scotland, a bank managed from Glasgow but which was itself the result of amalgamations in the 19th century of quite a number of smaller banks. The bank has no affiliations with any other institutions, and despite its age it has done some progressive things. In 1964, for instance, it opened Edinburgh's first drive-in bank, at Corstorphine, so that at times when it is often difficult to find parking space, motoring customers might be able to transact business without leaving their vehicles.

The figures of The Royal Bank of Scotland in the table do not indicate its full stature for it is the parent company in the "Three Banks Group." Between 1924 and 1939 it absorbed the Western Office of the Bank of England and Drummonds Bank, and purchased the share capital of Glyn Mills and Company and Williams Deacon's Bank. These latter continue to function separately, but the group as a whole commands resources of over £500 million.

The British Linen Bank, as its name implies, sprang from a company formed to assist the linen trade in Scotland in 1746. Its share capital was bought by Barclays Bank in 1919.

The National Commercial Bank of Scotland came into being in 1959 as the product of the latest of the three post-war mergers already referred to. Its components were The Commercial Bank of Scotland (founded in 1810) and The National Bank of Scotland (founded in 1825). The share capital of the latter had been acquired by Lloyds Bank Limited in 1918 but as a result of the merger it has only a minority holding in the combined bank. The Commercial Bank of Scotland was the first British bank to acquire—in 1954—a stake in hire-purchase finance. The growth of this form of lending has been a feature of the post-war scene, and when they were free to do so all the other British banks also acquired holdings in companies which finance the purchase of durable consumer goods such as motor cars, refrigerators and other " status symbols." What the future of all this may be no-one can tell. In the meantime the bank has made a picturesque contribution to banking history when in 1964 it opened in Edinburgh the first bank branch for women only.

Edinburgh also houses the headquarters of the Institute of Bankers in Scotland, which is responsible for conducting the professional examinations and all the other educational activities of Scottish bankers. Founded in 1875 it was the first organisation of its type in the world. Today it has a membership of 7,500.

These then are the commercial banks, but there is also, the Edinburgh Savings Bank. It was founded in 1814 and was thus one of the earliest Trustee Savings Banks to be formed. In the year 1964 it had more than 350,000 accounts, 32 branches in the city and the surrounding counties, and its funds exceeded £65 million. It employed a staff of about 180 of whom 160 (85 male and 75 female) worked within the city. The great bulk of its deposits were and are invested directly with the National Debt Commissioners, but some £23 million were in the Special Investment Department and the Trustees can exercise a certain discretion in the investment of these funds, most of which are employed in local authority mortgages. The continued development of Trustee Savings Banks when many factors might have tended to curb their activities has been one of the features of the post-war period and the Edinburgh Savings Bank, which ranks sixth in size in Great Britain, has not been behind others in the extension of its services. One example of its initiative is that it operates the largest safe-deposit vault in Scotland. It continues to grow, and, as this volume goes to press, has plans to introduce new accounts on which its customers will be able to draw cheques.

INSURANCE

In Edinburgh, as elsewhere, the idea of co-operation by groups to mitigate the effects of disasters to individuals was started by the medieval guilds and carried on by their successors, the friendly societies. One very old society, probably the oldest in Scotland and still active as a widows' fund, is the United Incorporations of St. Mary's Chapel which was founded in Edinburgh in 1475. There were, of course, other societies at the time and they were succeeded by a large number of friendly societies. In 1820, for instance, no fewer than 79 such bodies provided data for a report upon their activities at the request of the Highland Society of Scotland. In 1743 the Church of Scotland Ministers' and Scottish University Professors' Widows' Fund was established with headquarters in Edinburgh; and it is a tribute to its founders and to their enterprise, tempered by native caution, that this fund, which was amalgamated with another in 1928, is still in robust and healthy existence to-day.

The record of insurance in the modern manner starts in Edinburgh with the foundation of a fire insurance office there in 1720, which became known as the Edinburgh Friendly Insurance Office. In its early years the operations of the office were confined to the insurance of buildings in Edinburgh. But in 1767 it extended its operations throughout Scotland and undertook the insurance of goods in addition to buildings. In 1847, however, this institution was absorbed by the Sun Fire Office—the oldest insurance office in the world and senior to the Edinburgh Friendly office by only ten years. The oldest fire office, to be established in Edinburgh is the Caledonian Insurance Company which entered upon this field in 1805 and is still in business today. It had its first office at 7 Hunter Square in premises belonging to a firm of ironmongers and general merchants, and the painter Raeburn was one of the directors. The head office of the Caledonian Insurance Company is now at the corner of George Street and St. Andrew Square, where it still carries on business in all branches of insurance as an independent entity, although a few years ago its shares were acquired by the Guardian Assurance Company.

In the business of life assurance, on the other hand, Scottish institutions were relatively late in the field as compared with similar bodies in England. The first Scottish office to undertake this class of insurance was the Scottish Widows' Fund and Life Assurance Society; for the Caledonian Company did not enter upon the field of life assurance until 1833, by which year several others had started to transact the business. Life insurance was in fact discussed in a pamphlet issued in 1812, and the business was founded in Edinburgh in 1815 under the style of The Scottish Widows' Fund and Equitable Assurance Society, with a crack of the whip well worthy its high destiny, since its 25 patrons included two dukes, a marquis and an assortment of earls, barons and baronets. For some years the Scottish Widows operated in splendid isolation so far as life assurance in Scotland was concerned, but in 1823 the Edinburgh Life was established, to be followed by the North British, the Scottish Union and the Standard Life. Sir Walter Scott was the first Governor of the Scottish Union and, rather curiously from the point of view of modern practice, he was also connected with the Edinburgh Life, for according to his diary on 13th December, 1825 he attended the yearly Court of that Company and remarked that he was "one of those graceful and useless appendages, called Directors Extraordinary." Sir Walter was Governor of the Scottish Union until his death in 1832, and during his last journey to Abbotsford in July of that year he spent a night in Edinburgh at Douglas's Hotel, 35 St. Andrew Square—the present address of the Scottish Union and National. The Edinburgh Life was absorbed by an English company during the earlier part of the present century.

At the present time Edinburgh must rank as an insurance centre in Britain second only to London; and probably the most satisfactory way of giving an idea of its influence is to give short particulars of those companies which originated in Edinburgh and still have their headquarters in the city. Naturally there are in addition branch offices of many other insurance companies—Scottish, English and foreign—in Edinburgh as in every other city and considerable town in the kingdom. But it is not in respect of the volume of insurance business actually transacted by its citizens that Edinburgh may claim so high a place in the insurance industry, but rather because of the business written throughout the world by companies of Edinburgh origin, the large total of funds which they control and the premium income which they receive.

It may be remarked here that the type of office for which Scotland is especially famous is the mutual life assurance company. In these the office is owned by the policyholders and is managed—through a board of directors, of course—entirely for their benefit, and it is to them alone that the profits of the business accrue. Edinburgh is the headquarters of four of these and in addition of two proprietary life assurance companies. These latter are owned by shareholders, although now it is the practice for the regulations of the company to stipulate that a minimum proportion of the profits of the company be devoted to the interests of the policyholders and that the balance of profit only be available for payment as dividends to the shareholders. The proprietary life office is more easily started than the mutual; the shareholders are in the position of ordinary commercial adventurers; and their capital guarantees the validity of the contracts of the company, particularly during the early and inevitably precarious years. As time goes on, however, the effective guarantee provided by the shareholders' capital becomes less effective with the growth of the company; which makes it all the more interesting that two Scottish companies, which had carried on business upon a proprietary basis have changed to the mutual principle and buying out the shareholders, so that the control now rests entirely with the policyholders.

THE INSURANCE COMPANIES TODAY

Taking the existing insurance companies of Edinburgh origin in alphabetical order, we come, appropriately, first to the oldest Scottish Office—the Caledonian, c. 1805. This company transacts all types of insurance business, except industrial life assurance, and like many composite companies, it carries on a considerable business overseas. Although still maintaining its individuality as a separate company, its shares, as already stated, have been acquired by an English company.

The Century Insurance Company, with its headquarters in Charlotte Square, was established in 1885 and is now allied with the Friends' Provident and Century Life Office (an English company). In 1918 the life business of the Century was transferred to the Friends' Provident Office, and it now confines its activities to the other normal classes of insurance business. The Century introduced and still transacts continuous disability business under which the assured is paid a monthly income during total and permanent disability.

The Life Association of Scotland was founded in 1838 and is a proprietary life assurance company. It makes a special feature of children's deferred assurance policies, but issues all the normal classes of life assurance contracts.

The North British was established as early as 1809 and became the North British and Mercantile in 1862. It transacts all the main classes of insurance business, having a considerable life assurance fund and the largest fire business of any Scottish company. Its activities are not confined to the British Isles, and recently its shares were acquired by Commercial Union.

The Scottish Equitable Life Assurance Society was founded in Edinburgh in 1831 and has its principal office in St. Andrew Square. It was until recently the joint owner with the Scottish Amicable Life Assurance Society (a mutual life office with headquarters in Glasgow) of the Scottish Insurance Corporation. The Scottish Equitable transacts all classes of life assurance business and is one of the four mutual life assurance companies of Edinburgh origin.

The Scottish Insurance Corporation has its headquarters in George Street and was established in 1877. It transacts the usual classes of general insurance business and was jointly owned by two Scottish mutual life offices, as mentioned above, but recently the Yorkshire Insurance Company acquired its share capital.

The Scottish Life Assurance Company is the only other proprietary life assurance company and was instituted in 1881. In spite of all wars and disasters, it is one of a very small group of British life offices which has never failed to declare a bonus to its policyholders—and this is indeed an important achievement in view of the great social and other upheavals which have occurred since it commenced to transact business. Though one of the smaller companies, it has recently been pursuing a policy of expansion. Its principal office is in St. Andrew Square.

The Scottish Provident Institution established 1837 also has its head office in St. Andrew Square. This is another of the important Scottish mutual life companies and for long it preserved a refreshing independence of outlook in that it distributed its profits upon a " distinctive " system—although the Institution does now in fact issue policies with a normal compound bonus right of participation.

The Scottish Union was established in 1824 and became the Scottish Union and National in 1878. This company is yet another with a head office in St. Andrew Square, and transacting all the normal classes of insurance business, it has extensive connections throughout the world. It has also a picturesque specialist subsidiary—the Scottish National Key Registry, which insures against the loss or theft of keys, etc. Like the Caledonian and the North British and Mercantile, the share capital of this office has also been acquired by an English insurance company, the Norwich Union Fire Insurance Society.

The Scottish Widows' Fund and Life Assurance Society remains the oldest Scottish life assurance company. It was established in 1815 upon the mutual principle and has its head office in St. Andrew Square. One of the larger life offices in Britain, the Scottish Widows' has a proud record of service to its members and has for long ranked as one of the foremost offices in the country. Recently it has adopted the practice of transferring comparatively large sums from inner reserve to pay substantial bonuses to its members in addition to the normal distribution.

The Standard Life Assurance Company was established as a proprietary life office in 1825 and has its headquarters in George Street. In 1925 it changed to a mutual basis, so that the company is now owned by the policyholders and conducted entirely for their benefit. The Standard is the largest Scottish life office and is in fact the third largest in the United Kingdom. Enterprising and long imbued with a pioneering spirit it introduced the business of life assurance to many countries throughout the world and still transacts business in Canada, the West Indies, Uruguay and the Republic of Ireland as well as in the United Kingdom. In 1925 it went through the process of alteration from a proprietary to a mutual basis and was the first company in the world to do so.

The following table gives an idea of the size and influence of the Edinburgh insurance companies we have noticed and of their growth since shortly before the last war. In considering the expansion of the companies as shown by the table, the influence of inflation must, however, be borne in mind. A company which has not expanded since 1936 cannot be said to have stood still: its influence and impact upon the national economy has diminished.

TABLE 46

	1936		1962	
Company	*Premium Income (all classes of business)*	*Total of Assets*	*Premium Income (all classes of business)*	*Total of Assets*
	£ million	£ million	£ million	£ million
Caledonian	2·0	11·4	14·0	44·8
Century	1·1	5·6	7·6	24·5
Life Association of Scotland	·6	8·2	2·6	17·7
North British & Mercantile	6·7	63·1	42·1	154·8
Scottish Equitable	·6	11·6	4·0	35·3
Scottish Insurance Corp.	·3	1·6	2·0	3·5
Scottish Life	·7	8·6	5·3	38·4
Scottish Provident	1·5	25·1	8·9	70·1
Scottish Union & National	2·5	16·9	13·2	54·6
Scottish Widows'	2·2	34·3	20·6	186·7
Standard	2·0	28·2	47·8	370·6
Total	20·2	214·6	168·1	1,001·0

To end this review of insurance affairs in Edinburgh, it should be noted that Edinburgh is not only the headquarters of the Faculty of Actuaries in Scotland, a high proportion of whose Fellows serve insurance offices, but also has a flourishing branch of the Chartered Insurance Institute.

INVESTMENT COMPANIES

Edinburgh, in addition to being the centre of banking and insurance in Scotland, is the centre of the investment trust movement. The movement began in the early 1870s when there was a great demand for capital to develop the newer countries overseas and there were more profitable opportunities for investment abroad than at home.

Overseas investment cannot easily be conducted by individuals even to-day; it is therefore not surprising that the early pioneers should have formed joint stock companies, under skilled management, to carry on their enterprises. There are to-day in Scotland about 50 of these companies of which about one half are in Edinburgh, the remainder being in Glasgow, Dundee and Aberdeen. The funds of the Edinburgh companies at the end of 1963 were estimated to be worth over £400,000,000.

These companies—variously called Investment Companies, Investment Trusts, or Trust Companies—are all registered by statute, and each has its own board of directors. They vary greatly in size, the largest having funds valued at £40–£50 million, with between 5 and 10 thousand stockholders. The smallest has about £5 million, with perhaps less than 1,000 stockholders. Stockholders, it should be noted, come from all parts of the British Isles and also from overseas, and include insurance companies and pension funds, religious, charitable and educational bodies, and large and small private investors. The capital of the companies is usually divided into classes, preference and ordinary, in varying proportions, and additional funds are obtained by borrowing on debenture, either long term or short.

At the outset the Scottish companies invested their funds, consisting of the proprietors' capital and sums borrowed on the credit of the companies, largely in mortgages on land and in the bonds of railroads and other public utilities, mainly in North America. There was little, if any, intentional investment in what would nowadays be termed the equity of the undertaking, though often the bonds were by no means free from risk and the would-be lender from time to time found himself the owner of the land or business through foreclosure. The early companies had their ups and downs but on the whole they were reasonably, if not spectacularly, successful up to the outbreak of the first World War.

During the war owners of dollar investments were offered very attractive terms to exchange them for British Government securities. The Government sold the investments so acquired in America and used the dollar proceeds to finance the purchase of war material.

After the war the companies resumed their activities in North America, but not on quite the same scale nor in quite the same form. On the one hand the shortage of capital had become more pronounced at home than in North America; and on the other the development of joint stock company finance led to the investment companies taking an interest in the capital of industrial concerns and not merely lending money on mortgage or buying bonds. They thus shared in and benefited from the tremendous industrial development of the 1920s both in America and at home; they also shared in and suffered from the depression of the early 1930s.

They had hardly recovered from these misfortunes when the second World War broke out. This time the British Government requisitioned all dollar investments which could be readily sold and the investment companies found themselves amost entirely denuded of such securities. It was not till three years after the end of the war that they were once again allowed to invest in dollar securities.

The experience of the second World War and post-war years completed the revolution in investment theories which had been started by Keynes soon after the first World War. It was now realised that security of capital and income in terms of currency was no longer enough if the currency itself was continuously depreciating in value.

There are two accepted methods by which the ordinary investor can protect himself at least in part against this risk—first, by investing in ordinary shares as representing real values, and secondly by investing in a foreign currency which is more soundly based than one's own. For some years after the war the second method meant in practice investing in dollar securities. The Scottish Trusts thus found that the investment policies which they had been developing before the war under different circumstances were in fact ideally suited for the conditions which existed after it. The Edinburgh companies were among the leaders in extending these policies, and so to-day some companies have as much as 50 per cent of their funds invested in America and some almost 100 per cent in equities.

This policy has proved extremely profitable for the holders of the ordinary stock of the investment companies. Dividends have increased many times over since before the war and thus amply provided against the depreciation of the currency.

SCOTBITS AND SCOTSHARES

While only a few new investment companies have been floated on traditional lines in recent years, the Unit Trust movement has been very active in providing for the small investor and Edinburgh has been prominently represented in this field by " Scotbits " and " Scotshares."

The former, started in 1937 with the object of conveniently providing a sound and progressive investment spread over many quoted securities, confines its investments to Scottish bank shares, insurance companies operating in Scotland, and Scottish investment trust companies. This gives the Unit holder, who can purchase any number of units up to a maximum of 500 per day " over the counter " at all branches of the Scottish joint stock banks, a widespread interest in commerce and industry in the British Commonwealth and the U.S.A. An additional advantage has now been offered to the " Scotbits " unit holder in the shape of a monthly regular investment plan linked with life assurance.

Scotshares which came into being in the autumn of 1959 is under the same management as Scotbits. But whereas the latter confines its investments to banks, insurance and investment trusts, Scotshares spreads its interest over practically the whole of the rest of Scottish industry, including not only companies registered in Scotland but those in England and the North American continent who operate in Scotland.

The aim of Scotshares is to provide an investment giving stability of capital combined with a higher income than that to be obtained on " blue chips " together with steady but not perhaps spectacular growth. Scotbits on the other hand is an investment for eventual increase of both capital and income, but with a lower yield than the sister concern. Of both it can be said that the Unit Trust conception, of which Scotbits and Scotshares have been such successful examples, have provided an excellent opportunity of investment for the small investor, or those who wish to invest their savings safely over a large field, without the trouble and anxiety of managing the business themselves.

BUILDING SOCIETIES

The Building Society movement throughout the United Kingdom comprises about 680 separate Building Societies and is the custodian of £3,500 million of public savings—a sum almost twice that held in Post Office Savings Banks and nearly half the amount invested in all forms of National Savings. The major part of this fund of savings—about £3,140 million—is on loan to persons purchasing property, and more than 90 per cent of the money on loan is to individuals purchasing private dwelling houses for their own occupation.

The 680 Societies range from the largest of all, the Halifax with total assets now in excess of £650 million, through a number of " national Societies " with large networks of branch offices throughout the whole of Great Britain, a considerable collection of medium-sized Societies operating in limited areas, to a large number of very small Societies which confine their activities to a locality. *The Building Societies' Year Book* publishes annually the main balance sheet figures for all Societies registered under the Building Societies Acts, and the *Annual Report of the Registrar of Friendly Societies* likewise publishes extensive details of Building Society activity.

In the early '60s 10 Building Societies were registered in and had head offices in Edinburgh. They had combined total assets of some £5·8 million. Of these Societies the Dunedin, Scottish, Century and Edinburgh each had total assets of £1 million or more and the fifth, the Prudential Investment, assets of £650,000. But because these 10 Societies are registered in Edinburgh it must not be concluded that all the business they conduct is within the city. The larger ones have connections in Glasgow, the West, elsewhere in Scotland and south of the Border.

In addition to the " native Societies " there are in Edinburgh, 13 branch offices of Societies operating on a national basis, 12 English and one Scottish. The Halifax, Abbey National, Co-operative Permanent, Woolwich Equitable, Leeds Permanent, Provincial Alliance, Temperance, Huddersfield, Leek and Moorlands, Leicester Permanent, Eastbourne Mutual and Dunfermline: all these have branch offices established in the city, and they too cover areas far outwith the city boundary. Collectively these Societies form the big battalions of the Building Society Movement, as their combined assets account for nearly two-thirds of the whole. The 10 head offices and 13 branch offices do not account for all the Building Society representation in Edinburgh. Operating through Agents (generally speaking, professional firms in the city) 12 other Societies make their services available. These are the Bingley, Borough, Bradford Equitable, Bradford Permanent, Burnley, Civil Service, Cumberland, Grainger and Percy, Leeds and Holbeck, Newcastle-upon-Tyne Permanent, Northern Counties, and Universal. Together they control much more than £300 million of total assets.

The growth of the Building Society Movement has been particularly notable in the post-war years. It has coincided for obvious reasons with a spectacular growth in owner occupation. It is assessed that at the present time about 42 per cent of all dwellings in the United Kingdom are owner occupied. The percentage figure in 1951 was 31. Two main reasons account for the change: first, the accelerating programme of private enterprise house building for sale; second, the physical shrinkage by some 1·7 millions in the number of houses rented from private landlords. Because of the effects of rent control and perhaps fears of a re-imposition of those controls which have been removed, landlords prefer, when a lease is terminated, to sell property rather than re-let to another tenant.

In Scotland, the proportion of houses which are owner occupied is much less than the average for the United Kingdom. The questions asked in the compilation of the 1961 Census included several concerning the ownership of property and the answers are now known. In Glasgow the percentage of dwellings which are owner occupied was 16·25 per cent of the total. Edinburgh, on the other hand, always more owner-occupier conscious than any other city, has over 43 per cent of its dwellings owned by the occupiers—a figure slightly greater than the national average and one which accounts for the strong Building Society representation in Edinburgh, in relation to the population.

THE STOCK EXCHANGE

In the middle of last century when Britain was in the throes of a railway boom Edinburgh had its full share of the spate of flotations of the joint stock companies formed to exploit this new mode of transport. Because of this, the demand for the services of stockbrokers had expanded so rapidly that a meeting took place in the Royal Hotel, Princes Street on 16th December, 1844 to discuss a proposal "that considering the augmented number of stockbrokers and the increasing importance of the trade, it is expedient in order to facilitate the transaction of business to form a Stock Exchange in Edinburgh."

Of the seven members present at this meeting, two did not support the motion. But the others, undeterred, arranged within 11 days to rent a front room on the first floor at 71 Princes Street; and in the first few weeks there was a considerable influx of new members including the two dissentients at the original meeting. By the end of 1845 membership had increased to 27.[1] Unfortunately, the next year was a period of depression but the new Exchange stood the test and *The Scotsman* could report that " no other Exchange in the Kingdom had exhibited the same uniform stability." Despite this, it did not have things all its own way as rival bodies in the shape of the Edinburgh and Leith Stock Exchange and later the City of Edinburgh Stock Exchange made a temporary appearance.

From 1846 onwards, for 40 years, the Exchange occupied a variety of rooms all within the St. Andrew Square area; and from the records a picture can be built up of conditions on " Change " as it was called in those early days. In the Exchange room, lit by gas chandeliers, members sat round a table while the Secretary (also a member) called all the stocks in the list in turn (a " call over "). Promptly at the hour of the forenoon or afternoon meeting, the porter locked the door; and late-comers were admitted only after initialling a slip which they redeemed later on payment of a shilling fine. This was duly passed on to such charities as the fund for " Destitute Highlanders."

As time went on and the telegraph service grew more efficient, inter-city transactions grew in number, firstly with the Glasgow Exchange and latterly with the various English bodies. It was in fact the need to provide facilities for the large number of telegrams that finally decided the Exchange in 1888 to erect its own building on a nearby site at the corner of North St. David Street and Thistle Street.

The next 70 years were eventful. Marketwise, the Exchange was affected by trade cycles, commodity booms and slumps such as those in rubber, gold and oil; by major reorganisations of the companies in particular industries such as the railway mergers; and by the growth of new types of companies ranging from the early investment trusts to the investment holding concerns of the present day.

The late 1950s and early 1960s saw an upsurge of interest in the Stock Exchange and the number of investors grew steadily. The Stock Exchanges themselves played an important part in this movement and the Edinburgh Exchange joined with the other Scottish Stock Exchanges in forming a Publicity Committee and appointing a Public Relations Officer—a new departure at that time. As the Edinburgh building did not lend itself to the construction of a public gallery (as was done in some Exchanges) mock dealing sessions were held in the Market regularly during the winter months at which members of the public were able to transact dummy deals across the floor: these proved extremely popular. Many of the newcomers, it should be noted, were small investors, and the Edinburgh members went out of their way to encourage them even although in some instances the business was not very remunerative.

[1] The highest total of members in modern times was 76 in 1929.

The post-war period saw increasing mechanisation in stockbroking which was at first confined to the brokers' offices. As it was felt that the time was coming when more complicated machines would be required in the Exchange itself, a first step towards this was taken when the Exchange members decided on a new building—in a large new office block in North St. David Street.

The increasingly important part played by the Stock Exchange led to much thought being given to protection of investors through Compensation Funds and the like, and the Stock Exchange movement as a whole has been having a long hard look at this set up. The first fruits of this can be seen in the formation of the Scottish Stock Exchange. Set up in Glasgow in the New Year of 1964, the Scottish Stock Exchange embraces the Aberdeen, Dundee, Edinburgh and Glasgow Stock Exchanges, and though trading floors are retained in all these cities, a central organisation is responsible for the running of the four Exchanges.

THE ACCOUNTANTS

Edinburgh has a special place in the world of accountancy since within the city are the headquarters of the oldest existing accountancy body in the world—The Institute of Chartered Accountants of Scotland. Indeed, Scotland first invented the term " Chartered Accountant." It was also long ago—in 1854—that the Institute's first Royal Charter was granted to it under its original name The Society of Accountants in Edinburgh. This name was changed to the present one in 1951 when The Institute of Accountants and Actuaries in Glasgow (incorporated by Royal Charter in 1855) and The Society of Accountants in Aberdeen (incorporated by Royal Charter in 1867) surrendered their Charters and joined forces with their Edinburgh brethren.

The fact that Scotland thus led the way in the formation of modern professional associations of accountants shows the importance which the profession had acquired in Scotland by the middle of the 19th century and its appeal for Scotsmen; but the profession's roots lie deeper. No doubt accountants of a kind are co-eval with civilisation—and with trade and taxation. So far as Scotland is concerned, however, the beginnings of the practice of professional accountancy can be traced to late 17th century Edinburgh. At that time there were at least two accountants who acted for clients: these were Alexander Heriot and the other George Watson after whom three of Edinburgh's most famous schools are named. Equally noteworthy, it was also about this time that a teacher of book-keeping, called Robert Colinson, who had apparently been trained to business in Holland, wrote a treatise on accountancy: this was printed and published in the city. Nor was the municipal authority slow to realise the value of sound book-keeping principles. In the winter of 1705 the Town Council of Edinburgh inserted the following advertisement in the *Edinburgh Courant*:

> The Council of Edinburgh, considering how necessary the Science of Book-holding is for the advantage of Trade and Commerce, especially when the same is carried on in Co-partnery, have therefore thought it convenient to establish a publick profession of the said Science within this City, and having years of experience of the ability of John Dickson, Merchant (present book-keeping and accomptant to the Good Town of Edinburgh) do therefore nominate and authorise the said John Dickson to be Master and Professor thereof within this City . . . .

During the following century the profession continued to grow. Of one Edinburgh accountant, Charles Selkrig, it is recorded that in 1809 he was awarded what was then considered the largest fee ever earned by an accountant—some £20,000. This was for winding up the affairs of a Glasgow firm which, some years earlier, had made an immense speculation in slaves for the West Indies in premature expectation of the abolition of slavery. It is hardly surprising that by 1820 Sir Walter Scott could suggest that his young nephew could not " follow a better line than that of an accountant. It is highly respectable . . . ." In the event his nephew entered the Army and died a General.

The incorporation of The Society of Accountants in Edinburgh in 1854 posed a problem: what were the members to be designated, so as to distinguish them from other accountants? The solution was found in the words " Chartered Accountant." Purists may argue that it was the Society, rather than the member, which was " chartered." It remains true, however, that this Scottish initiative received the compliment of imitation when Institutes of Chartered Accountants were subsequently formed in England and Wales (1880), in Ontario (1883), in Ireland (1888), in other Canadian Provinces and in the Dominion, in Australia, Southern Rhodesia, India, Ceylon and—being now the only Chartered Accountants outwith the Commonwealth—in South Africa. Members of some of these bodies, like members of The Institute of Chartered Accounts of Scotland, use the designatory letters " C.A." after their names.

In Edinburgh today there are about 700 Scottish Chartered Accountants, of whom some 220 are in practice after apprenticeship with a practising member of the Institute, whose professional examinations he must pass, and classes at the University. They belong to an Institute whose 7,000 members are widely scattered throughout the world; and like their fellow members elsewhere, they make a notable contribution to the business and social life of the community in the wide variety of ways we know. For it is undoubted that since the first Edinburgh Charter of 1854 the accountancy profession has increased mightily in size, influence and prestige. In 1855 there were no more than 110 Scots Chartered Accountants. But in 1961 there were, in round figures, 7,000 members of the Scottish Institute, 34,000 of the English institute and 1,700 of the Irish Institute, making a total of some 42,700. In addition there are some 1,1000 members of the Association of Certified and Corporate Accountants, 3,250 of the Institute of Municipal Treasurers and

Accountants, and 6,900 of The Institute of Cost and Works Accountants. Nor are they all men. One can imagine the surprise of the contributors to the *New Statistical Account* in the 1840s had they been told that by 1961 there would be 156 women members of The Institute of Chartered Accountants in Scotland—46 more, that is, than the total number of qualified accountants in the United Kingdom in 1855. They might also have been surprised if they had been told that in 1963 a European Congress of Accountants would be held in Edinburgh with an exhibition in the Chartered Accountants' Hall in Queen Street called "European Accounting History."

The remarkable growth of the profession in Edinburgh as elsewhere calls for a word or two of explanation. The original accountants who set up in practice specialised in dealing with the affairs of insolvents. Soon there developed a feeling that if the accountant were brought on to the scene earlier, some frauds, and therefore some insolvencies, could be prevented: this, combined with the growth of joint stock enterprise, led to the birth of auditing as it is understood today. The next stage was the beginning of cost accounting and of more scientific methods of budgeting for the future, which involved bringing in the accountant still earlier. Parallel with this was the development of more informative methods of preparing balance sheets and, later, profit and loss accounts, and perhaps most potent of all for the growth of the profession, greater reliance on the accountant in respect of the increasingly complicated subject of taxation. Today, not least in Edinburgh, new specialisations for the accountant are emerging in such fields as management consultancy and electronic data processing.

THE ACTUARIES

Another profession which is also more than a century old, and whose Scottish headquarters are still in the city of its birth, is the actuarial profession. Scotland played a large part in setting up the Institute of Actuaries in London in 1848; and it was as a result of two reports made by Scottish members of this Institute that the Faculty of Actuaries in Scotland was established in Edinburgh in 1856 and obtained its Royal Charter of Incorporation in 1868. Today, it is a flourishing institution which celebrated its centenary in 1956 with an elaborate and successful series of functions.

An actuary is a person who—in the jargon of his profession—is engaged "mainly in transactions of a financial character involving future contingencies," and who uses the records of the past to enable him to estimate and to forecast future statistical sequences. Although originally employed almost exclusively in the service of life assurance and kindred institutions—pension funds, widows' funds, friendly societies and so on—the profession has greatly widened its scope in recent years, and nowadays its members are to be found also in the Government service and in many branches of financial and commercial activity. Few large industrial companies dare dispense, in present circumstances, with the services of a trained statistician, and actuaries have proved themselves eminently successful in this sphere, for the nature of their training is such as to turn out statisticians with a strong practical bias and a sound appreciation of finance.

The training of an actuary is long and, some consider, arduous; but normally the student is able to earn a little during his period of study and no young man of a mathematical bent, who is so unfashionable as to be prepared to work hard, need fear the examinations. It is a career that should attract such men strongly—and particularly mathematical graduates—for there is today a distinct scarcity of actuaries both at home and overseas, and the rewards are adequate both at home and overseas where many Fellows of the Faculty are to be found. The profession after all has a delightful dual character—its theoretical and mathematical side—with opportunities for original research in a variety of fields—and its business side, rich in human contacts and in scope for the exercise of originality and enterprise. Naturally enough, it is to those who are successful in the latter aspect that the largest financial prizes go; but the former is none the less rewarding to the inquiring mind.

The Faculty is not a large body: there are about 360 Fellows, of whom about one-third are engaged in Edinburgh, rather more than half the total in England or overseas, and the remainder in Glasgow or other parts of Scotland. The number of matriculated students is roughly 340.

CHAPTER 26

INCOMES AND EMPLOYMENT

INCOMES

It would seem natural to turn from these great matters of finance to the varied processes of industry and trading in the city, for all are interwoven. But first perhaps we should look at how Edinburgh's people are employed and at how they earn and spend their money, since these affect not only the financial institutions but the whole mercantile pattern.

The material well-being of Edinburgh's citizens obviously depends to a very large extent upon the incomes they earn from employment. It is convenient, therefore, to consider in the same breath, so to speak, these two important economic aspects. It is not of course suggested that other sources of income can be neglected. Income from property—whether from fixed assets such as land, buildings or machinery, or from industrial shares and government bonds—must run into tens of millions of pounds sterling; but relative to the main source, which is income from employment, even this seemingly large amount is only a small fraction of Edinburgh's livelihood.

Ideally one would like to present a kind of " Social Account " for the city in which there would be sets of Income and Expenditure statements for the main kinds of *transactor*, namely private households, enterprises and public authorities both local and central. Unfortunately, even in this day and age when statistics are thought to abound on every conceivable subject, the necessary information for such an interconnected account is not available except on a national scale. What frequently tends to happen, therefore, in practice is that a great miscellany of vaguely related figures with some sort of bearing on the subject is presented, largely on the grounds that they are not too difficult to obtain and may possibly be of interest. But just as a pile of bricks does not of itself make a house, neither does an assemblage of facts and figures tell a story; both require to be arranged according to some pre-conceived design or plan. The plan to be followed here is something of a compromise between the ideal, unattainable in practice, and the miscellany that is apt to lack co-ordination. The first aim is to attempt an estimate, under the conditions of the early 1960s, of Edinburgh's annual Income in total, with some information on its distribution; the second is to provide a statistical picture of the occupational composition of Edinburgh's working population. Lest it should be objected that any of the figures are not " correct " down to the last unit, let it be clearly stated that the word " statistical " here is being interpreted to imply the use of approximations or best estimates rather than a series of detailed figures " correct " to the last half-penny.

Although it is not possible from any existing sources to state the total incomes earned by citizens of Edinburgh, material of this kind has been published in respect of persons residing within the County of Midlothian, including Edinburgh itself. As the population of the city is approximately five-sixths of the population of the county and city combined, it is safe to assume that an aggregate figure for all incomes received in Edinburgh and Midlothian together must be somewhat greater than the true figure for Edinburgh alone. In other words, by taking the combined total of incomes, we obtain an upper limit to Edinburgh's aggregate income. According to the Inland Revenue, who have conducted a sample survey of income distribution by counties, the total net income (before tax) in Midlothian for the year 1959–60 was £167·85 millions. If the reasoning advanced above can be accepted, then the most that Edinburgh could have received net before deduction of direct tax in that fiscal year was about £160 to £165 millions, or very roughly £350 per head per annum. That it was unlikely to be much below this figure is suggested by the comparison with the average income per head in the United Kingdom as a whole. The official estimate for the latter in 1960 was close to £400. It should be remembered however that a city's wealth does not depend solely on its annual income. So it is quite conceivable that if ownership of capital could be included in the admittedly rough and ready comparison drawn above, Edinburgh would stand in quite a different relation to the rest of the country. Unfortunately, such a balance sheet is impracticable, and the issue remains in the realm of speculation.

It would be interesting to know more about the way in which Edinburgh's population has contributed to this tentatively estimated total income. Once again, the nearest official estimate we can get is for Midlothian and Edinburgh combined. Table 47 provides a classification for this area. But it should be emphasised that undue reliance should not be placed on any individual figure in it as there may be an appreciable margin of error. The figures were published in 1963.

TABLE 47

Distribution of Total Net Income (Before Tax) 1954–55 and 1959–60
Midlothian

(Numbers in thousands, Amounts in £ millions)

Range of Net Income (before tax) £ — £	*1954–5 Total Net Income (before tax)* Number	Amount	*1959–60 Total Net Income (before tax)* Number	Amount
155 — 199	18·1	3·2	5·2	0·98
200 — 249	21·1	4·8	14·0	3·15
250 — 299	21·6	5·9	16·1	4·41
300 — 349	22·7	7·4	14·3	4·65
350 — 399	24·2	9·1	14·4	5·40
400 — 449	24·9	10·6	15·4	6·53
450 — 499	20·9	9·9	14·9	7·08

contd.

TABLE 47 (Contd.)

£ £	*Number*	*Amount*	*Number*	*Amount*
500 — 599	29·2	15·9	34·1	18·69
600 — 699	17·2	11·6	29·4	19·05
700 — 799	10·8	8·1	22·1	16·53
800 — 899	5·4	4·6	15·8	13·34
900 — 999	3·6	3·4	10·6	10·02
1,000 — 1,499	7·3	8·7	19·1	22·25
1,500 — 1,999	2·8	4·8	4·9	8·40
2,000 — 2,999	2·3	5·4	3·4	8·16
3,000 — 4,999	1·5	5·6	2·1	7·93
5,000 and over	0·7	6·1	1·3	11·28
All ranges	235·1	125·1	237·1	167·85

It is possible to carry the kind of comparison shown above one stage further, by looking at the proportions of total reported incomes received by each income-group, starting with the lowest and finishing with the highest. This comparison is facilitated by the use of a simple chart, along whose base is measured proportions of all taxpayers, and along whose height is measured proportions of incomes received. Chart I provides such a picture of income distribution both for Midlothian and Edinburgh and for Lanark and Glasgow. The diagonal drawn from the bottom left corner to the top right corner represents a perfectly equal distribution of incomes. The extent to which incomes are unequally (though this does not mean inequitably) distributed is shown by the divergence of the curved dotted line from the 45° line.

Chart I shows that the division of income between recipients is slightly less equal in Midlothian and Edinburgh than it is in Lanark and Glasgow—a conclusion that one might reasonably expect. In fact the top 10 per cent of recipients obtained 31 per cent of all personal incomes in Midlothian, while the top 10 per cent in Lanarkshire obtained only 28 per cent of all incomes received in that area.

Another way of approximating to a total income figure would be to consider the average earnings in each major industry represented in Edinburgh. As information (presented below in Table 48) on the earnings distribution is not available as this is written for a recent period, this calculation relates to the year 1957. If it can be assumed that weekly earnings in each industry are the same in Edinburgh as in the rest of the country—these have since risen—then total earnings from employment in Edinburgh might have been £100–£105 millions in 1957. To obtain an estimate of total income it is necessary to add on a figure for profits and professional earnings, probably £15 millions, and for the annual value of property, nearly £10 millions. Adding these elements gives a total estimated income of £125 millions for Edinburgh's 467,000 people. This would imply a figure of £270 per head as compared with nearly £350 per head for the United Kingdom in that year, and must therefore be regarded as an under-estimate.

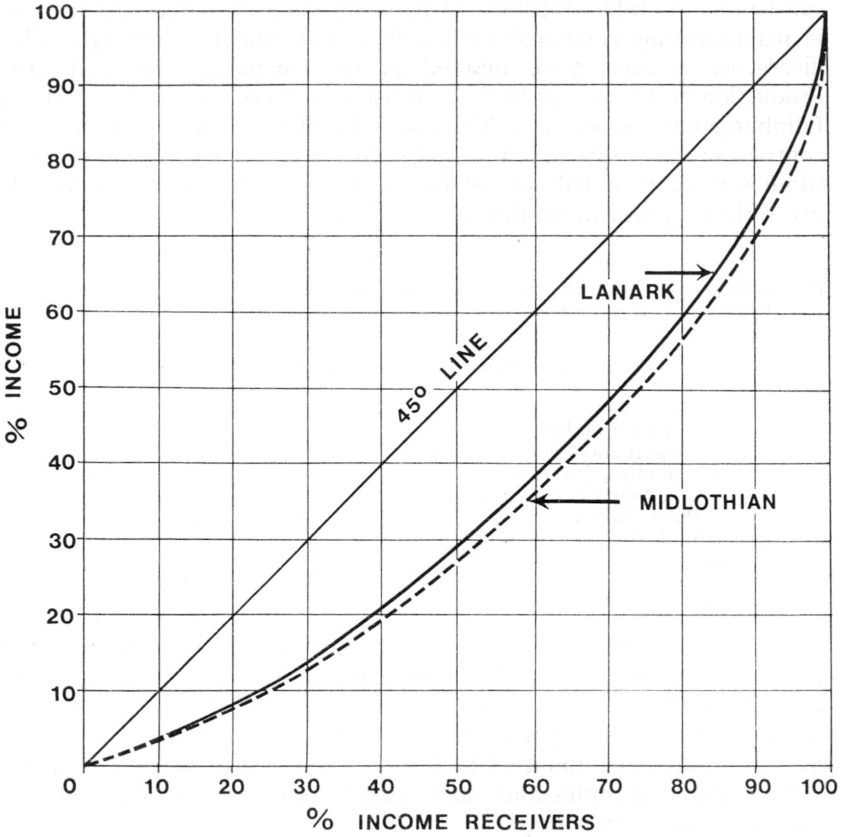

SUMMARY OF TABLES 48 AND 49[1]

	Total Employed	*Estimated Total Earnings* (£ million)
Youths and Boys	8,927	2·5
Girls	7,575	1·6
Men	112,412	68·2
Women	77,138	29·1
	206,052	£101·4 million

[1] Tables 48 and 49 are set out fully in Appendix X.

EMPLOYMENT

Looking at the jobs of Edinburgh's people nowadays one finds, not unexpectedly, that a high proportion of them are occupied in providing "services" of one kind or another rather than in turning out "goods." This is very different from the pattern for the rest of Scotland where, as can be seen in Table 50 below, 34 per cent of all employees are engaged in manufacturing compared with only 27 per cent in Edinburgh. This divergence is even more marked in the comparison for Industrial Production in which over half of all Scots workers are employed but in Edinburgh only 44 per cent. The other side of this coin is, of course, the contrast in the " service " industries group, to which Edinburgh contributes more than half of all her employees, whereas approximately two-fifths is typical in Scotland as a whole.

TABLE 50

PERCENTAGES OF INSURED EMPLOYEES IN DIFFERENT INDUSTRIAL GROUPINGS IN EDINBURGH AS COMPARED WIIH THE WHOLE OF SCOTLAND IN JUNE, 1963

Industrial Groupings	*Edinburgh* %	*Scotland* %
Manufacturing Industries	28	34
Transport and Communication	8	8
Distributive, Professional, Financial, Miscellaneous Services and Public Administration	53	40
All other	12	18
	100	000

The changes that have taken place in recent years in the proportions of wage and salary-earners in these different industries can be judged from Table 39 (i and ii). Comparing the position in 1962–3 with that in 1951 one can see how employment in, for instance, the distributive trade has risen relatively from about 14 to 16 per cent of the total " work-force " and the share of professional and scientific services has increased substantially during the period.

It might be suitably interposed here that in June, 1965 the Registrar-General for Scotland published figures based on the 1961 Census, which showed that Edinburgh (15 per cent of the population) had twice Glasgow's proportion of " upper " group men such as employers, managers and professional workers, but Glasgow (61 per cent) had the highest proportion of the " middle " group, meaning non-manual workers, foremen and supervisors, etc. In the " lower " group of semi-skilled and unskilled workers Edinburgh (26·5 per cent) had the lowest proportion in the four Scottish cities.

TABLE 51

ESTIMATED NUMBER OF EMPLOYERS IN EACH INDUSTRY SHOWN AS A PERCENTAGE OF THE TOTAL NUMBER OF EMPLOYEES IN EDINBURGH, LEITH AND PORTOBELLO EMPLOYMENT EXCHANGE AREAS AT JUNE, 1951 AND 1958

Standard Industrial Classification, 1948	*June 1951*	*June 1958*	*1951–8 Change + or −*
Agriculture, Forestry, Fishing	1·5	1·1	−0·4
Mining and quarrying	0·5	1·3	+0·8
Treatment of Non-Metalliferous Mining Products other than Coal	0·8	0·7	−0·1

Chemicals and Allied Trades	1·3	1·4	+0·1
Metal Manufacture	0·5	0·5	—
Engineering, Shipbuilding and Electrical Goods	5·2	5·8	+0·6
Vehicles	2·4	2·2	−0·2
Metal Goods not elsewhere specified	1·1	1·2	+0·1
Precision Instruments, Jewellery, etc.	0·4	0·3	−0·1
Textiles	0·9	1·0	+0·1
Leather, Leather Goods and Fur	0·2	0·1	−0·1
Clothing	1·4	1·3	−0·1
Food, Drink and Tobacco	8·4	9·2	+0·8
Manufacturers of Wood and Cork	1·5	1·5	—
Paper and Printing	5·0	5·3	+0·3
Other Manufacturing Industries	2·3	1·3	−1·0
Building and Contracting	8·7	7·5	−1·2
Gas, Electricity and Water	2·0	1·9	−0·1
Transport and Communication	9·8	9·4	−0·4
Distributive Trades	14·2	14·3	+0·1
Insurance, Banking and Finance	3·2	3·9	+0·7
National and Local Government	5·6	4·7	−0·9
Professional Services	12·8	13·7	+0·9
Miscellaneous Services	10·3	10·3	—
Ex-Service Personnel not yet allocated to any Industry	—	0·1	+0·1
Other Persons not yet allocated to any Industry	—	—	—
Grand Total	100%	100%	

TABLE 52

ESTIMATED NUMBER OF EMPLOYEES IN EACH INDUSTRY SHOWN AS A PERCENTAGE OF THE TOTAL NUMBER OF EMPLOYEES IN EDINBURGH, LEITH AND PORTOBELLO EMPLOYMENT EXCHANGE AREAS AT JUNE, 1959 AND JUNE, 1963

Standard Industrial Classification—Revised 1958	*June 1959*	*June 1963*	*1959–63 Change + or −*
Agriculture, Forestry, Fishing	1·4	1·1	−0·3
Mining and Quarrying	1·3	1·1	−0·2
Food, Drink and Tobacco	8·9	8·1	−0·8
Chemicals and Allied Industries	1·3	1·2	−0·1
Metal Manufacture	0·6	0·5	−0·1
Engineering and Electrical Goods	4·1	4·9	+0·8
Shipbuilding and Marine Engineering	1·4	0·9	−0·5
Vehicles	0·4	0·5	+0·1
Metal Goods not elsewhere specified	1·2	1·3	+0·1
Textiles	0·9	0·6	−0·3
Leather, Leather Goods and Fur	0·1	0·1	—
Clothing and Footwear	0·6	0·6	—
Bricks, Pottery, Glass, Cement, etc.	0·7	0·7	—
Timber, Furniture, etc.	1·3	1·1	−0·2
Paper, Printing and Publishing	5·2	5·4	+0·2
Other Manufacturing Industries	1·4	1·4	—
Construction	8·1	8·0	−0·1
Gas, Electricity and Water	2·0	2·0	—
Transport and Communication	8·7	7·8	−0·9
Distributive Trades	15·5	15·8	+0·3
Insurance, Banking and Finance	4·0	4·4	+0·4
Professional and Scientific Services	14·3	15·2	+0·9
Miscellaneous Services	12·1	11·7	−0·4
Public Administration and Defence	4·5	5·6	+1·1
Ex-Service Personnel not classified by Industry	—	—	—
Others Persons not classified by Industry	—	—	—
Grand Total	100%	100%	

UNEMPLOYMENT—THE GENERAL PICTURE

The number of men and women officially registered as out of work in June, 1962 is estimated to have been 3,585 (2,988 men and 597 women). Comparing this with the total number of insured employees in the same area, i.e. Edinburgh, Leith and Portobello, for that month, one finds that the proportion out of work was 1·7 per cent. The comparable unemployment rate for the whole of Scotland was then 3·3 per cent, and for Great Britain 1·8 per cent and for Northern Ireland 9·3 per cent. Nor was there considerable change by June, 1963 when the " Registered wholly Unemployed " totalled 3,424, a drop of 161 since the previous June.

UNEMPLOYMENT BY INDUSTRIAL GROUPS

Table 53 below shows which industries experienced the most and which the least unemployment in mid-1963. Building and contracting apparently had a high figure—4·15 per cent—while paper and printing and the professions in the city experienced very low rates of unemployment. It is however quite usual to find rates of unemployment above the average in the building trades, so in this respect Edinburgh is not exceptional.

TABLE 53

EMPLOYMENT AND UNEMPLOYMENT IN EDINBURGH (EDINBURGH, LEITH AND PORTOBELLO LOCAL OFFICE AREAS) AND SCOTLAND AT JUNE 1963 IN INDUSTRIAL GROUPINGS WITH MORE THAN 10,000 EMPLOYEES

Industrial groupings	EDINBURGH			SCOTLAND		
	(*a*)	(*b*)	(*c*)	(*a*)	(*b*)	(*c*)
Construction	19,270	742	4·15	189,370	13,461	7·11
Public Administration	12,995	285	2·33	122,210	4,030	3·30
Miscellaneous Services	27,027	635	2·55	179,320	7,929	4·42
Transport and Communication	17,645	386	2·30	178,690	5,623	3·15
Distributive Trades	36,539	724	2·08	300,640	11,081	3·69
Food, Drink and Tobacco	18,271	297	1·80	99,170	3,896	3·93
Engineering and Electrical Goods	12,245	106	0·99	163,880	5,332	3·25
Paper, Printing and Publishing	14,012	83	0·77	58,960	1,170	1·98
Professional and Scientific Services	34,664	166	0·53	233,370	1,986	0·85

(*a*) = *Insured employees* (*b*) = *Registered wholly unemployed*
(*c*) = *% of employees wholly unemployed*

DURATION OF UNEMPLOYMENT IN DIFFERENT AGE GROUPS

Appendix VII shows extensively how the length of time out of work varied in 1964 from one age group to another. About two-thirds of those men out of work for more than two years were between 55 and 64 years of age, whereas less than one-third of all unemployed men, whatever the duration of their unemployment were in that age group.

To go back two years, in Edinburgh in July, 1962, 569 persons (522 men and 47 women) had been out of work for more than a year; 41 per cent of these (211 men and 14 women) were over 55 years of age. In July, 1964 this last total of 225 had increased to 331.

Such figures suggest that the older the man is, the greater his chance of long-term unemployment. This is borne out by the higher proportion of younger men seen to be out of work only for a few weeks at a time, either in summer or in winter. The recent general position in the Edinburgh area is shown in the following table:

TABLE 54

UNEMPLOYMENT IN THE EDINBURGH, LEITH AND PORTOBELLO LOCAL OFFICE AREAS
NUMBERS REGISTERED AS UNEMPLOYED

	Men	*Boys*	*Women*	*Girls*	*Total*	*Temporarily stopped included in total*
10th June 1963	3,539	143	729	53	4,464	20
15th June 1964	2,520	108	495	34	3,157	4
12th April 1965	2,645	312	519	72	3,548	7

PERCENTAGE RATES OF UNEMPLOYMENT

	Edinburgh Group [1]	*Scotland*	*Great Britain*	*Northern Ireland*
10th June 1963	2·1	4·3	2·1	7·5
15th June 1964	1·4	3·2	1·4	6·5
12th April 1965	1·6	3·1	1·5	6·6

[1] This comprises Edinburgh, Leith, Portobello, Dalkeith and Loanhead local office areas.

BANKRUPTCIES

To go from the subject of unemployment to bankruptcy is a logical if not a congenial journey. It is however a necessary one, for when the economic structure of any community is under investigation, its proportion of bankruptcies to prospering concerns is usually significant. In Edinburgh over the years this interesting ratio would seem at a first glance to disclose a satisfactory measure of business acumen.

Recent figures provided by the Accountant of Court, who deals with all sequestrations coming within the province of the Court of Session, show that over a 12-month period only 21 sequestrations were registered—and this in a population which at the 1961 census totalled 468,378. Two out of that small total were joint partnerships.

Nevertheless, as the city grows and its trading concerns become more numerous, the number of those who fall by the wayside in the struggle for success continues to show a gradual increase. In 1952, for instance, there were 13 sequestrations. In the two succeeding years the total was 18, increasing by one in 1955. The year 1956 showed a drop to 16, but the figure rose to 24 in 1957; it was then two less in 1958, stood at 12 in 1959, and was up to 24 again in 1960. In 1965 is was 11.

While all kinds of business ventures have their place in the bankruptcy list, none appears to suffer more than shopkeeping. Of the 13 sequestrations in 1952, eleven concerned shopkeepers and traders; 29 of the 36 unfortunates during 1953 and 1954 were also in that class, and of the 19 in 1955, 13 were shopkeepers. Figures for more recent years (with shopkeepers and traders in brackets) are as follows: 1958—22 sequestrations (15); 1959—12 sequestrations (8); 1960—24 sequestrations (12). Considering the general trend over the post-war years it would appear therefore that approximately 50 per cent of the sequestrations registered in the office of the Accountant of Court relate to the shopkeeping and trading class. But should this be so? Does it point to rash ventures, or lack of business experience? Absence of the experience necessary in a highly competitive sphere of activity no doubt accounts for a certain proportion, but there is evidence of another influential factor.

Up to 1939 and immediately after the war it was apparent that the small shopkeepers were feeling acutely the economic pressures exercised by the three co-operative societies operating within the city boundaries. Many of the little traders had in fact to be satisfied with a very meagre existence. A change came over this scene, however, in the early '60s when the co-operative societies were themselves subjected to the competition of self-service stores. Later still, the tempo of the battle for custom has been heightened by the advent of new " keen-price " contestants—the small grocers and other traders who seemed destined for elimination by the giant concerns. Combining in co-operative groups, these private enterprise traders, buying wholesale from their own central warehouses, are bringing a new lease of life to the little shopkeepers, who now seem less despondent.

The Accountant of Courts' figures do not however tell the whole story. For every Court sequestration there are several bankruptcies which are never submitted to the expensive and rigid procedure of the Courts. In these cases, the normal procedure is for the bankrupt voluntarily to convey all his assets to a trustee who is acceptable to the creditors. He then distributes these assets amongst the creditors, sometimes carrying on that bankrupt's business if, for instance, the completion of outstanding contracts will eventually benefit the creditors. He may also liquidate the business, and of course the figures for liquidation do not appear in the Accountant of Courts' sequestration figures either. The whole picture is therefore more sombre than a first glance discloses; but there is on the other hand no reason to believe that Edinburgh business men lack acumen. Indeed, the story of the city's importance as a financial centre, suggests the reverse. And also we have to reckon with the perennial reputation of Scotsmen as prudent, not to say close, in money matters. It would certainly seem so from the National Savings figures.

SAVINGS

The traditional Scottish virtue of thrift is happily still in evidence, even although the purchasing power and the personal spending of the individual in Edinburgh have risen to unprecedented heights in what has become known as " the affluent society." The injunction to " lay something by for a rainy day " has not lost its force under the influence of the Welfare State, judging by the measure of support given by Edinburgh citizens to the National Savings Movement.

During the year ending 31st March, 1965, gross new national savings in Edinburgh amounted to almost £40,887,000—an increase of £5,310,000 over the total for the previous year. This alone was satisfactory. But even more gratifying was the fact that Edinburgh's contribution was equal to £85 17*s*. 1*d*. per head of the population, compared with a *per capita* figure for Scotland during the same year of £53 15*s*. 9*d*., and for the United Kingdom of £42 16*s*. 10*d*.

A break-down of the city's grand total savings reveals the following details:

National Savings Certificates	£1,722,799
National Development Bonds	£1,717,320
Premium Savings Bonds	£450,519
Deposits in Post Office and Trustee Savings Banks	£36,965,596
	£40,887,024

The continuing success of the National Savings Movement, judged by these figures, stems to a considerable extent from the splendid work done by the voluntary savings workers, men and women whose sheer personal effort encourages contributors, enlists new savers and stimulates where enthusiasm may seem to lag. It is really a most praiseworthy effort. For on 31st March, 1965, there were no fewer than 1,083 National Savings Groups operated by volunteers in Edinburgh, of whom 805 were at work in industry and commerce, 243 in street groups and social organisations, and 35 in schools. As Edinburgh's share of prizes at Premium Savings Bond draws in a recent year, almost £100,000 was distributed as prize money to more than 2,800 Edinburgh residents.

An increasingly vital part in the promotion of thrift is taken by the Edinburgh Savings Bank. The balance due to depositors at 20th November, 1965 reached the impressive total of £67,311,218, a figure which showed an increase for the year of £3,301,051. Total funds, including reserves, amounted to £69,015,760. Equally encouraging, there was an increase of more than 104,000 in the number of transactions; interest amounting to £1,973,371 was credited to depositors' accounts; and depositors' holdings of Government securities increased to a total holding of £9,378,961.

The original Edinburgh Bank for Savings was established in 1814, but dwindled away between 1819 and 1835, when the re-constituted Bank was born. No funds were available to furnish an office, and an advocate called Andrew Murray, junior, who been appointed Treasurer, personally advanced sufficient cash to buy the necessary equipment, to be repaid as and when the Bank had accumulated sufficient to do so. Thus on 25th April, 1836 the Bank opened its doors for business in the first flat of a house at 87 Princes Street. The first account opened was that of a working man who deposited two shillings and sixpence on behalf of his young daughter—a considerable contrast not only to the present daily transactions at the impressive offices in Hanover Street but also to its large safe deposit strong room—the first to be installed in a trustee savings bank in the United Kingdom—and also to its 23 busy branches throughout the city and the suburbs, and its 8 country offices in towns as widely separated as Haddington and West Calder.

CHAPTER 27

PRODUCTIVE INDUSTRIES

INTRODUCTION

THE variety of Edinburgh's social, administrative and cultural life is fully matched by the unusual diversity of the city's industries. For Edinburgh has avoided the economic sin of " carrying all its eggs in one basket " and has therefore not suffered in times of depression from two great a dependence on vulnerable heavy industries though these exist within the city boundaries. " None the less " says one authority, " in the days of depression, the Port of Leith suffered much like a Clydeside town, though its Siamese relationship to Edinburgh obscured, statistically at any rate, the extent of its economic woes.

" Our industrial mixed grill, offering as it does a wholesome balance of diet to the city's economy, has many tiny ingredients besides the obvious staples, such as the small concerns which are not at all impressive in figures of people employed but which contribute their indispensable quota to the general level of opportunity, as well as being ancillary, in many cases, to bigger and better known industries, and more or less part of them. There is for instance, a small adhesives factory which turns out glues, gums and pastes for all purposes, and adhesives for high-speed automatic machines as well as a white cement for manufacturer and repairs: as the ramifications of its contribution to industry include also whisky bottle labelling, joinery work and the fixing of tiles, so that it is ancillary both to the drink trade and to building and construction as well as to general engineering. A sawmill of great importance both to the trade of Leith and to the building industry, employs about 100 men and a theatrical costumier of national fame employs rather more. There is even a wigmaker with 65 employees. As for Edinburgh's large industries, we shall shortly assess their strength and importance after taking a quick look at the uncommon range of the smaller industries within the city boundaries.

By merely taking the alphabet as a first guide we can, for instance, find the manufacture of account books, badges for schools and clubs and cane furniture at the beginning, with picture frames, sealing wax and zinc at the end. In between we should find the manufacture of gelatine and glue, insecticides, jodhpurs, lantern slides, rat traps, scientific instruments, sunblinds and also, by a nice contrast, waterproof covers. Then, as it happens, the range is further widened by a number of traditionally local and famous products such as bagpipes, highland dress and herring barrels; and these along with boat-building and other industries associated with sea and river waterways make the range of Edinburgh's production wider and more colourful than most. Because of amalgamations, mergers, or plain take-overs it has also been subject to many changes in recent years so that any general survey of the city's industries made in the late '50s must inevitably need some amendment in the early and middle '60s.

During this period there have been substantial changes in some of the city's leading industries—in brewing, printing and coal for instance; and at the same time some of Edinburgh's famous old local industries have gone out of existence. Leith's long-established Roperie was rationalised into thin air. A celebrated old clay pipe and pipeclay factory became in 1962 literally a museum plece: almost as soon as it closed down, it was reconstructed as a most interesting exhibit in the Corporation's Huntly House Museum. It is however comforting in this motor-car age to find one village smith—at Kaimes—still shoeing horses inside the Edinburgh boundary, though his trade is confined largely to the horses of the Edinburgh City Police and some riding schools."

Earlier we looked at the growth of estates on the city's fringes, and the need for further building space. Fortunately a considerable amount of planning for industrial expansion has been done as a result of land reclamation schemes sponsored by the Leith Dock Commission. Additional to these and more important perhaps are the Commission's plans, approved by the Government and now started, for the introduction of deep water facilities at an estimated cost of some £6 million.

The economy of Leith is to a great extent bound up with the activity of the port. Surrounding it on all sides there is a notable variety of small and medium manufacturers; shipping lines, harbour accommodation and ship building; fertilizer and grain industries; a growing oil trade close by the port of Granton; Carlsberg importers nearby in Portobello; a large whisky establishment in Constitution Street, a sawmill and timber yard; and a factory which manufactures marquees and supplies tents and ancillary equipment. Together these are an encouraging facet of the changing life of the city of Edinburgh, particularly the new look which is coming over Leith as housing clearance and redevelopment continue.

As would be expected, such a wide variety of small and medium sized concerns caters for local industry and commerce—design consultants, for example, advertising agencies, display producers, silk-screen printers, sign-writers, label manufacturers, and the makers of stationery, to name a few out of many. There are factories which service printing firms. Ink, for instance, is supplied by A. B. Fleming and Company, well-known dye-cutters and stamp engravers with overseas interests. Then there is the large and important food-producing industry. On the catering side, there are certain specialised companies which can supply the necessaries for either a cocktail party, a banquet, or an outdoor function attended by 4,000 people. Interesting, too, is the fact that the fish and chip shops supplying the many customers throughout the city are serviced by the Chaffand Range works which manufacture fish-frying ranges. Bakery utensil manufacturing, engineering and bakery supplies and Edinburgh's own dairy produce: all these are prominent city industries.

Looking into the home itself, its decoration, flooring, fireplaces, doors, windows, wallpapers, curtain fabrics, and carpets are all manufactured in or near the city; and for their protection three Edinburgh firms supply

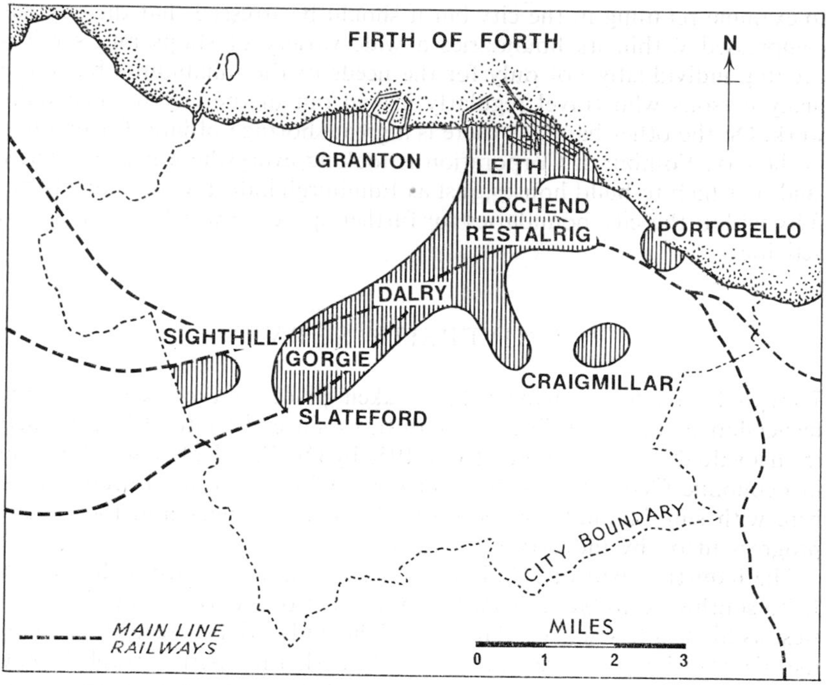

Fig. 3. Edinburgh showing area (shaded) within which most factories are situated.

fire appliances and other protection equipment. Finally, to maintain the connection with the home there are pram manufacturers for the needs of the younger couple, and carpet beating machinery for all ages.

Forthcoming plans for redevelopment, since many industries and businesses are often huddled together in congested parts of the city, mean of course much inquiry into the siting of industry, its most favourable positioning and its replacement and redirection towards other areas. Much work remains to be done on this, particularly in the siting of the smaller manufacturing industries; but the whole question—it was one of the matters discussed between the Chamber of Commerce and the Corporation in 1964—bristles with difficulties. To take one conspicuous example, a large brewery in the Holyrood area buys considerably from a wide variety of small brewery engineers and service industries clustered round it, often in small and difficult streets. Any redevelopment of this area, which has long been discussed, could drastically affect these small industries, whose sites are near their big customers and whose rents and overheads and costs are comparatively low. Again, the housing and road policies of the city affect industries supplying the public directly, as do prestige positions in advertising. In the recently rebuilt High Street, for example, prominent retailers and new businesses are flourishing. This however is not the place to examine retailing in the city but it should be stressed that the city has compressed within its boundaries a wide variety of shops and services catering individually not only for the needs of the inhabitants but those many persons who travel regularly in and out of the city to their daily work. On the other hand, as there is a great shortage of land for building in the city, Edinburgh Corporation is looking everywhere it can for new land on which to build houses, just as Edinburgh industry is looking hopefully within the city boundaries for further space on which to expand its activities.

A UNIVERSITY SURVEY

Though far-reaching changes have taken place in the techniques and ownership of certain Edinburgh industries since the late 1950s, extracts from a valuable survey conducted in 1958 by Dr. C. J. Robertson, Lecturer in Economic Geography at the University of Edinburgh, are reproduced here with suitable additions stressing both the changes and the general progress made by industry since then.[1]

The industrial belt of Edinburgh extends, (he writes) from the port of Leith southward to Queen's Park and through the centre of the city as far west as Sighthill. (Fig. 1). The axis of this industrial crescent runs along the Water of Leith, where a number of the earlier industrial establishments used the primitive waterpower, and through the old town. Brewing was being carried out at Holyrood Abbey in the 12th century and breweries later extended along the line of wells from Abbeymount westward along the Holyrood Road in the depression between Calton Hill and Arthur's Seat. The first printers in Scotland were established in Edinburgh in 1507 and before the end of the 16th century paper was being made at Dalry, while by 1770 six other small paper mills are known to have been established on the Water of Leith as well as two on smaller streams.[2] Some of these were conversions of already existing meal mills. Paper-making, however, as its scale increased, became centred on the valley of the North Esk, beyond the bounds of even present-day Edinburgh, and the small mills were abandoned. By the end of the 17th century a foundry had been established, as well as glass-works, powder and textile factories.[3] By the early 19th century ship-repairing and biscuit-making had also become established industries. Steam was substituted for water as the source of energy on some of the old sites and the industrial axis was reinforced by the building of the Union Canal in 1822 and by the development of the railways in the '40s.

The Edinburgh area lacked the raw material basis for the heavy

[1] In essence Dr. Robertson's account is the revision of a paper which appeared in the *Scottish Geographical Magazine*, Vol. 74, No. 2 (1958), pp. 65–77.

[2] Waterston, Robert, Early Paper Making near Edinburgh. *Book of the Old Edinburgh Club*, Vol. 25, 1946; idem, Further Notes on Early Paper Making near Edinburgh, ibid., Vol. 27, 1949.

[3] Malcolm, C. A. The Growth of Edinburgh: c. 1128–1800. British Association for the Advancement of Science, *Scientific Survey of South-eastern Scotland*, 1951, p.70.

industrial development characteristic of the earlier growth of production and transportation in Britain. Some expansion of engineering took place after the railways were built and shortly after the middle of the 19th century the traditional food and drink processing industries of Edinburgh were supplemented by such a forerunner of the new industrial revolution as rubber.

Greater mechanisation and transportation facilities and increasing population also encouraged and were encouraged by larger volume of production. The density of resident population increased from the late '70s in the vicinity of the railways. Industry pushed eastward into Portobello, where brick works were established, and later an outlier of the main belt was developed at Craigmillar, where brewery extension took place from 1890.

In the 20th century minor concentrations have developed on the foreshore at Granton in the north and still more recently at Sighthill in the west (See Fig. 1). While the later development of road transportation gave flexibility in industrial siting, both in supply of raw materials and in distribution of the product, the original industrial axial zone has proved to possess considerable inertia. New firms have frequently taken over already occupied sites while old firms have rebuilt or equipped on the same site to avoid the expense of taking over a new site from the foundations. This tendency has been encouraged by the existence of basic services in older areas and by the ease of travel to work to these areas from the new housing estates. In 1920–30 the main axial zone was still filling up westward in Gorgie. On the other hand the older sections of the central zone had become highly congested both in housing and traffic and this, together with the rising urban rentals in the better areas and the extension of electricity supply, accelerated the centrifugal movement of industry. One of the new areas, the Sighthill Industrial Estate, may be regarded as a further westward expansion of the main axial zone.

Gradual adoption of new sites with changing energy and transportation facilities is illustrated by the baking industry. Haulage was a difficult problem and the sites of the earlier bakeries were near the flour mills on the Water of Leith (for example, Canonmills and Bonnington) where primitive water power and local grain were used. With the use of imported grain Leith itself had an increased advantage. After a transitional dependence on the railways, the greater flexibility made possible by road transportation led to siting in the then newer housing areas (for example, Restalrig).

The city also provides some interesting examples of firms adjusting their activities to changing conditions, and new outgrowth reaching much greater proportions than the parent firm. Engineering industries, forced to be more flexible than most in order to keep abreast of technical change in industry as a whole, frequently show such developments. In Edinburgh an early example is Bruce Peebles, who began in 1866 as gas engineers; in 1898 they began the manufacture of electric motors and dynamos; and 10 years later the present firm of that name split off from the parent gas engineering firm.

EDINBURGH AS PART OF THE MID-LOWLAND INDUSTRIAL AND TRANSPORTATION NEXUS

Examination of the sources of raw materials and of the destinations of finished products of Edinburgh industries leads to the conclusion that within an area such as the Scottish Mid-Lowland, with a well-developed transportation nexus, there may be a wide choice of locations with ready accessibility to fuel, water and suitable labour. This is especially true for industries collecting their raw materials and distributing their products over an area far wider than the immediate sphere of influence of Edinburgh. The circumstances in which the rubber industry was located in Edinburgh provide an illustration. The demand for rubber products in Britain was increasing rapidly. In the first place the choice of a Scottish location was due to the accident that the Hancock patent, filed in England in 1843 and used by Charles Macintosh and Company there, had not been filed simultaneously in Scotland, where, until 1852, it was necessary to apply for separate patent rights. Goodyear had succeeded in anticipating Hancock in Scotland in 1844 and an American company seeking to manufacture rubber boots and overshoes in Britain and using the Goodyear patent was therefore able to open a factory in Scotland in 1856. It had been the original intention to locate the factory in Glasgow but the immediate availability of premises in Edinburgh at the critical time determined the eventual choice. The Edinburgh factory had readily available water, coal and female labour for the manufacture of rubber footwear, which became a leading branch, securing a substantial proportion of the British market. The manufacture of industrial belting was soon added and, after the invention of the detachable pneumatic tyre in 1890 and its application a decade later to the automobile, tyres became a major branch of production at Castle Mills. The absorption of a neighbouring vulcanite factory (founded in 1861) in 1910 added hard rubber articles to this firm's activities. Today raw materials are collected from a wide compass—raw rubber from London, synthetic rubber and sulphur from the United States, rayon from Wales and Liverpool, cotton and nylon from Lancashire, jute and flax from Dundee, carbon black from Chester, oxides and carbonates from Durham, pigments from Wilton and Manchester, china clay from Cornwall, wire for tyre beading from various firms in England, while packaging is largely supplied by Edinburgh firms.

There may be great flexibility in taking supplies from different sources according not only to mere physical availability but to prices and business connections, which may mean central buying to supply factories in different parts of the country. Thus, while Edinburgh is itself an important grain-milling centre, the movement of flour from its two largest mills is, notably in the case of the Scottish Wholesale Co-operative Society's mill, partly to tied bakeries throughout Scotland, while on the other hand one of the largest bakery firms in Edinburgh brings in flour by road from Liverpool. Much flour also comes from Glasgow, Scotland's principal milling centre, and smaller quantities from Dalkeith, Kirkcaldy and Carlisle. Again, given the possibilities of regular and speedy service, transportation differentials are outweighed by other considerations. In the brewing industry too, transportation, now mainly by road, is a relatively small factor in costs despite the fact that one of the two largest brewers has a market extending throughout Britain and the other into the North of England, while exports, now only a small part of the total though for one of the smaller firms still the greater part of its sales, go mostly through Glasgow. Similarly most of the whisky for export goes by road to Glasgow or Liverpool for shipment and whisky for export dominates the trade, about 75 per cent of the whisky blended in Leith being exported.

The presence of considerable engineering in Edinburgh is in part also accounted for by the dispersable character of the industry within a much larger area of good accessibility. It is an industry using components drawn from many sources, with varied products and many markets and calling from time to time for changing emphasis within the same firm to secure rapid adaption to technical changes. In particular the only large recent addition to Edinburgh's industry, Ferranti, is a firm using high-value components and marketing high-value products; its ratio of labour to raw material costs is also high. There are also branches that are market-bound to a particular industrial complex since they produce highly specialised machinery for a particular industry. Such a case in Edinburgh is the construction of paper-making machinery, in the first place for the paper mills of the Esk valley and neighbouring areas. Industrial linkages of this last type are however exceptional and only partial in the Edinburgh area. The stationery industry in Edinburgh is one of the few examples of close interdependence with local industries on either side, its main materials in the paper industry and its main market in the administrative and educational institutions of the capital. In the carton industry there is, of course, a partial linkage with the food industries, notably in sweets and packaged cereals.

A special instance of the transportation factor is the influence of the port of Leith. Some of the traditional " seaport industries " are in this northern sector of Edinburgh's industrial crescent. Grain-milling is the most important, depending mainly on imported wheat, and this is Leith's leading import. Of the total flour used in Edinburgh itself 70 per cent is from Canadian wheat, which is hard and so gives the light porous bread that is preferred.

A fair amount of cacao beans and fats is also brought in directly through Leith. The home-grown barley, mostly local, that the brewers use, provided it can compete with overseas supplies comes in by road. While the feed compounders get much of their grain locally, additional supplies come in through Leith and from time to time through the Clyde, whose oilseed mills have also, thanks to the large-scale operations of the port, squeezed out Leith's former oilseed-crushing industry. The compounding industry, using a wide range of raw materials—including fish meal from Aberdeen—involving little loss of weight in processing, is market-oriented and the greatly increased popularity of compound as against straight feeds means that local markets are proportionately greater.

On the other hand the fertiliser industry, like grain-milling, retains its port location by the sheer bulk of a single raw material—in this case phosphate rock from North Africa and Nauru. The largest fertiliser factory in Scotland is in operation. This is a plant for making ammonia-based fertiliser.

MECHANISATION, AMALGAMATION AND SPECIALISATION

As regards internal structure Edinburgh industries have shared in the trend toward larger units.

The stationery industry, for example, presents a picture of amalgamation and specialization, whether as a joint operation or separately. On a smaller scale an example of high specialization in the engineering industry is that of Miller and Company, originally engaged in general castings, now almost entirely concerned with the production of large chilled iron rolls, of which they are the only makers in Britain.

The baking industry, like the brewing industry (described later), has also undergone considerable reorganisation in recent years, and as in brewing, both increased mechanisation and changing consumer habits have encouraged the growth of larger units. From the weighing of the flour to the slicing and wrapping of the loaves everything is now mechanised in the large modern bakery. High costs of installation of the new ovens and machinery has meant the overshadowing of family businesses by large " plant " bakeries, some owned by syndicates with country-wide interests. Though Edinburgh has fewer of these large-scale units than most towns of its size the development of these bakeries has more than compensated in employment for the disappearance of a number of small firms.

Another fairly recent amalgamation in Edinburgh was that of two leading pharmaceutical firms in 1953. (There have been other mergers since). The city's surviving shipbuilding firm incorporated three older firms between 1924 and 1933. Several amalgamations as well as that in the rubber industry have been accompanied by control from larger organisations outside Edinburgh and some have involved also a degree of vertical integration. Within Edinburgh various units in the grain-milling industry have recently been integrated—the largest mill at Leith docks, producing flour from imported wheat, and another mill specialising on compound feeds.

FACTORS IN STABILITY

The high proportion of professional and other tertiary economic activity in Edinburgh makes the city less directly affected by any business fluctuation. But changing consumer demands, reflecting changing social conditions, naturally present problems of varying difficulty. Brewers may find it easier to switch production from draught to bottled beer than heating engineers to replace the lucrative production of hothouses once considered a social requisite for houses of a certain size. Partly because of the character of its industries Edinburgh has been relatively unaffected in the past by serious industrial disputes. New industrial development was also encouraged in the past by relatively cheap electricity.

Population, industrial or other, has not in recent decades shown much growth. A number of new factories have in recent years been built but these have as often as not meant merely the substitution of a new site for an older. Replacement of a biscuit factory in Slateford by one at Sighthill, almost complete transfer of carton manufacture from a Lochend factory to one at Sighthill are cases in point. The existing proportion of basic to non-basic industry and the development of mechanisation and automation would seem to be effective brakes on expansion beyond the half-million level regarded by the planners as a desirable limit to Edinburgh's population.

In the structure of its labour-force Edinburgh has also considerable built-in stability. While on the one hand several of its mainly male-employing industries—notably in engineering—are among the more dynamic, its large proportion of tertiary industries, notably in education, hospitals, and secretarial work, both in the civil service and in business, means much employment for women; and in several of its special industries—chocolate and sugar confectionery, manufactures of paper and board, biscuits, wholesale bottling—over half the labour is female.

Compared with Glasgow, which has half the population of Scotland within a radius of 25 miles, Edinburgh is the distributing point for an area of relatively sparse population offering little basis for economies of scale. Even its larger industrial concerns cannot take full advantage of mechanisation. In the sugar confectionery industry, for example, a wrapping machine outruns the sugar-boiling capacity; in stationery one machine could meet the demand. Industrial linkages are increasing with other branches of highly rationalised industrial groups with interests in other parts of Britain rather than with other local firms. Edinburgh is part of a transportation nexus receiving its inflow of food and raw materials —grain, flour (even part of its bread), sugar, oilcake and meal, raw rubber and steel—mainly from Glasgow and the south. Coal comes by rail for short distances from Midlothian to South Leith and to the Portobello power station. Edinburgh is itself a supply centre for general merchandise for most of South-eastern Scotland, approximately as far as a line from Eyemouth on the south-east, through Jedburgh and Hawick, and thence north-westward to Linlithgow and Grangemouth. There is also an extension of retail deliveries along the main road into south Lanarkshire, as well as into Fife and Kinross. An Edinburgh evening newspaper circulates as far north as Thornton in Fife. Beyond these boundaries the most important regular outflows in bulk include whisky and beer, tyres, cartons and stationery, books and, on special contracts, heavy electrical equipment, and other heavy engineering goods such as paper-making machinery.

To a considerable extent the city also benefits from the buffer effect of its relatively large proportion of tertiary economic activities. These service activities would appear in fact to have been throughout its history its *raison d'etre* and most of the secondary industries that have developed—the food and drink manufactures that absorb a third of the total population occupied in secondary industry, the building and contracting group that absorbs another third and even most of the remaining third, such as printing and publishing and manufactures of paper—have grown from the initial need to supply the local population, with a market extending from Edinburgh to the rest of South-eastern Scotland and, as transportation facilities improved and reputation spread, in some cases beyond.

In the course of his general survey, necessarily abbreviated here, Dr. Robertson and his assistants also made a more detailed investigation of a number of the city's leading industries. As it turned out, there were soon considerable changes in some; and so the rest of this chapter, though much of its content is happily the result of Dr. Robertson's and his assistants' work, has been expanded and brought up to date by fellow contributors. Let us start with the heavier industries.

ENGINEERING

Engineering in Edinburgh, as elsewhere, includes a wide variety of activities with fabrication of metal and a preponderance of capital equipment over consumer goods in the product as common features. As elsewhere too, the boundaries between one branch and another are frequently difficult to draw and the same firm may be engaged in several branches. Firms also frequently widen their range by producing associated tools and equipment in addition to their main products. Constructional, mechanical, marine and electrical engineering are all notably represented as well as the accessory activities of iron and steel foundries and the common activities connected with the maintenance of motor vehicles and railway services. In addition there exists a number of highly specialised branches, including the manufacture of gas meters, architectural metal work, wire and mesh manufacture.

According to the Ministry of Labour returns for 1957 there were 20,300 persons employed in engineering, of whom 85 per cent were males. Four-fifths of the total number of people employed in the industry in mid-1957 were in the 110 plants which employed more than 20 people. Roughly half of these plants had less than 50 workers, half had 50 or more, and this remained the position for some time.

To look forward to the '60s is to find in June, 1962 a Ministry of Labour record of the estimated number of employees in the area of the city's Employment Exchanges in Edinburgh, Leith and Portobello. This record broke down various industries connected with engineering as follows:

TABLE 55

Industry	*Males aged 15 and over*	*Females aged 15 and over*	*Total males and Females aged 15 and over*
Metal Manufacture	1,028	167	1,195
Engineering and Electrical Goods	9,053	2,358	11,411
Shipbuilding and Marine Engineering	2,265	118	2,383
Vehicles	992	235	1,227
Metal Goods not elsewhere specified	1,983	611	2,594

This makes a total of 18,810, but again it has to be remembered that many engineering employees live outside the city and are registered at labour exchanges beyond the city boundaries.

The largest plant, employing some 6,000 in 1964–5 is in electrical engineering (Ferranti). The other three with 1,000 or more workers are in electrical engineering (Bruce Peebles and Company Limited), shipbuilding (Henry Robb Limited) and marine engineering (Brown Brothers and Company Limited). Only two other Edinburgh plants outside the engineering industry employ 1,000 or more workers.

Wide as is the range of activities carried on by engineering firms in Edinburgh—from the heavy electrical equipment produced by Bruce Peebles and Company Limited to Ferranti's small precision material—certain general characteristics emerge that are indeed common to the industry in the country as a whole.

The engineering industry is mainly concerned with the production of capital equipment and, largely because of this, it works mainly on individual contracts. This in turn discourages specialisation, particularly in foundry work. Much of this is for bulky equipment such as papermaking machinery, hydraulic apparatus and heavy electrical machinery; and its construction requires travelling supervisory staff. The workers as we have seen are predominantly male—with the exception of the electrical branch where a considerable number of women are engaged in winding—and the majority are skilled.

The limits of specialisation by individual firms, it should be noted, are frequently blurred, not only for the reasons already mentioned but because of fluctuations in demand. An example of this was the rise in one year, 1956, of Bonnington Castings Limited to fourth or fifth place in Britain for the manufacture of steel valves. Subcontracting for components is another characteristic of the industry. In papermaking machinery, for instance, the largest firm buys big castings, chilled castings and wire from three other Edinburgh firms. Iron and steel castings are also bought from outside by the largest firm of hydraulic engineers. In shipbuilding components are taken from a very wide range of companies, and at the other end of the manufacturing processes work may be passed on to subsidiary firms for finishing. In some cases a definite association has been formed between different concerns—between Brown Brothers as makers of ship stabilizers and Denny Brothers of Dumbarton, the naval architects, for example, and between Bertrams Limited, the makers of paper mill machinery and Miller and Company Limited (now associated with British Roll Makers Limited), who produce chilled iron rolls.

In the engineering industry, components, though mainly of metal, are extremely varied and come to Edinburgh both by road and by rail. The electrical firms using large quantities of steel, copper, rubber, cotton and mica, rely largely on rail for the inflow of materials but, as in other branches, the outflow of products is largely by road. The postal service on the other hand is frequently used for the conveyance of the raw materials required for precision electrical goods. One reason for the widespread use of road transport is the large size of the products –

papermaking machinery, for example, heavy electrical plant, hydraulic machinery, iron, steel or non-ferrous castings, constructional steel, chilled iron rolls—and in general it is favoured because it reduces handling, breakages and other losses.

The markets for Edinburgh's engineering products are widely spread. Many of them go abroad directly and still more are supplied to other makers for export. About 50 per cent of the paper mill machinery goes abroad, for instance, and it is estimated that of the production of chilled iron rolls 20 per cent is exported directly and 40–50 per cent indirectly. Notable quantities of electrical equipment are also supplied to other producers for export, and altogether about half the output goes abroad.

The city's engineering industries, like many others, have had to satisfy the need in recent years for many technological changes. A well-known example is the change from riveting to welding in constructional engineering for girders, and in shipbuilding. Another arises from the increasing competition between prefabrication and casting, for this has led to greater adoption of the former by metal-founding firms. On the other hand the use of additives is enabling cast-iron to approach cast steel in specification. In a rapidly innovating industry there are continuing demands for flexibility on the part of the management and skill on the part of labour.

As Edinburgh's industries go, the engineering industry is relatively young, since most of it has grown since the middle of the 19th century. But oddly enough—or was it because of the tremendous contemporary growth of engineering in the West of Scotland?—there are two long gaps from the 1870s to the end of the century and from the end of World War I to the 1940s—when no new major engineering firms were established in the city. The following table, which shows this only too clearly, gives the dates when a number of well-known Edinburgh engineering firms were established.

TABLE 56

Bertrams Ltd., engineers and iron-founders	1821
Redpath Brown & Co. Ltd., constructional engineers	1840
James Bertram & Sons Ltd., engineers and iron-founders	1845
Alder and Mackay Ltd. (now U.G.I. (Meters) Ltd.), gas meter manufacturers	1850
Brown Brothers & Co. Ltd., general and hydraulic engineers	1861
Bruce Peebles, gas engineers (parent firm)	1866
Miller & Co. Ltd., iron-founders and engineers	1867
G. Cruickshank Ltd., bakery engineers	1868
Mackenzie & Moncur Ltd., iron-founders, heating and electrical engineers	1900
C. Henshaw and Sons Ltd., architectural metal works	1900
Bruce Peebles and Co. Ltd., electrical engineers (separated from parent firm)	1908
Henry Robb Ltd., shipbuilders and repairers	1918
Ferranti Ltd., electrical engineers (Edinburgh factory)	1943
Metal Units (Edinburgh) Ltd., engineers	1958

The largest recent addition to Edinburgh's industrial structure has been in the precision branch of the electrical industry. It came into being under the stimulus of wartime conditions, and is now not only the branch in which skilled labour bears a very high ratio in the total cost but one where the value both of the products and many of the raw materials is such that a relatively peripheral location such as South-eastern Scotland—peripheral, that is, in its relation to the main centres of population—is less disadvantageous. As for prospects of further expansion the limiting factor would seem to be labour, particularly skilled labour, which has not in the past shown high mobility. There was a notable example of this in the '50s when a persuasive attempt by one firm to recruit skilled labour rendered redundant by the closing of an Admiralty plant as near to Edinburgh as Fife proved unsuccessful.

FERRANTI LTD., *Electrical Engineers*

This is the largest industrial concern in Edinburgh. With its headquarters in Lancashire, the firm established its Edinburgh factory in 1943 and has since made a number of extensions for experimental work and apprenticeship training. It employs about 6,000 in Edinburgh, and hundreds more in Dalkeith and Dundee, and more than 250 of its employees have university degrees or equivalent qualifications. There are about 500 women employees on production and assembly, secretarial duties and even as graduates on scientific and engineering work. Four-fifths of the male manual workers are skilled. Established during the war to make gyroscopic gunsights for aircraft, it has expanded into a large research and development programme for the Government as well as in the production of all types of electronic equipment, including radar, control of aircraft missiles, specialised valves and electro-mechanical devices of great precision. Much of the work is in the design and manufacture of controls for automation.

BRUCE PEEBLES AND CO. LTD., *Electrical Engineers*

In 1866 David Bruce Peebles founded a gas engineering firm. In 1898 it took up the manufacture of dynamos and electric motors and 10 years later the firm split into Peebles and Company Limited, who continued as gas engineers, and Bruce Peebles and Company Limited, electrical engineers. Bruce Peebles now employ 1,700 in their works at East Pilton, where they manufacture heavy rotating electrical plant or generators, high-voltage power transformers and distribution transformers and rectifier equipment for railways and industry. Much of their work is for the nationalised industries, and the plant has been extended *pari passu* with the growth of hydro-electric production at home and abroad. It was not surprising that in the middle of January, 1965 London newspapers were noticing that the company's orders in hand were worth in excess of £15 million or £2 million more than at the same time the previous year.

REDPATH BROWN AND COMPANY LTD, *Constructional Engineers*

This firm, which began as a small ironmonger's shop in Edinburgh in 1802 and went on to bridge building, specialises in steel constructional work ranging from 10 tons to thousands of tons. It has branches in Glasgow, Manchester and London and carries out work all over Britain as well as abroad. A notable recent operation has been the building of the Kincardine Power Station on the Firth of Forth. It was a pioneer in prefabrication, is now a member of the Dorman Long group, and exports to 21 countries.

BERTRAMS LTD, *Engineers and Iron-Founders*

Established in 1821, this firm primarily produces papermaking machinery at Sciennes, Edinburgh for all types and qualities of paper, from the thinnest tissues to board. These are amongst the largest of any forms of machinery. A single machine may take a year or so to build. Perhaps two may be made each year on the average. One machine may cost several hundred thousand pounds. Since World War II about half the firm's output has been exported. In 1962 the export percentage was 65, and this included a complete installation for making speciality papers in Australia and a machine for Mexico to make cigarette papers. There was also a half-million sterling contract for Greece. The bigger castings are not made in the firm's own foundry but are supplied by another Edinburgh firm as also are chilled rolls and wire mesh. In addition the firm supplies pumps and cutters for the paper industry and does some trade in machinery for milk powder preparation. There is a working agreement with the firm of James Bertram and Sons Limited, founded in 1845 by a younger brother of the same family.

MILLER AND COMPANY LTD., *Iron-Founders and Engineers*

This firm, established in 1867 for general casting work, is almost entirely concerned with the production of large chilled iron goods, mainly chilled iron rolls and dual metal spun rolls. The latter are produced by casting metal to metal so that cooling is quicker and the surface made harder than in a normal casting. This is a difficult and costly method of casting but the product is thrice as hard-wearing as steel. Chilled iron rolls are used in the processing of paper, sheets, towels, soap, breakfast cereals. The firm was one of the pioneers in profit-sharing, and is now a subsidiary of British Rollmakers Limited.

MACKENZIE AND MONCUR, LTD.,
Iron Founders and Heating and Electrical Engineers

This firm, established at the beginning of the century, has two works, each employing in the late 1950s and early '60s some 180 workers, one casting in iron, semi-steel, gunmetal and aluminium and the other primarily concerned with installing heating for housing and factories.

BONNINGTON CASTINGS, LTD., *Steel-Founders*

This firm has two plants, one the only steel foundry in Edinburgh, the other engaged in finishing the castings. Electric furnaces are used and scrap is the raw material. One-third of the castings go to the oil industry, one-third for rolling stock, mostly British or Indian, and the remaining third for general purposes. This is said to be one of the most highly mechanised light casting plants in Britain. About three-quarters of the output is from moulding machines.

U.G.I. (METERS), LTD., *Gas Meter Manufacturers*

The gas meter industry presents a good example of an industry undergoing technical recession. Overall technological developments in the economy as a whole have overwhelmed successful technological change within the industry, which was established in Edinburgh by Alder and Mackay Limited as far back as 1850. Before World War II there were six firms making gas meters in the city and employing about 800 workers. Now the three surviving firms employ some 300, of whom two-thirds are with United Gas Industries, a group of which Alder and Mackay became a part. This firm has other factories, in Belfast and in New Zealand, and is one of several big groups in the industry in Britain. Half of its work force consists of skilled men, with the other half divided equally between unskilled men and unskilled women.

Meters are no longer made of cast iron and tinplate now forms the bulk of the raw material. There is also some use of plastics and more die casting in order to obtain a thin wall for the cases. Components are brought by road from England. This firm has widened its range of production by taking up subcontracts for refrigerator parts. The British market absorbs 95 per cent of the gas meter output.

UNITED WIRE WORKS LTD.

This large establishment at Granton, employing 950 workers in 1962–3, produces wire mesh and wire, particularly for the paper industry. The only other wire-weaving centre in the United Kingdom (when this survey was made) was Glasgow. The industry, which has a world-wide export trade, are large users of copper and tin. At the end of 1964 United Wire Works, were embarking on a big new expansion programme which included a new process named Unicast for the direct continuous conversion of virgin copper, tin and zinc into high quality copper alloy rods. It was said that if required this new process could produce 13 unbroken miles of copper rod weighing 22 tons. In the spring of 1965 contracts with foreign metallurgical firms were being negotiated.

SHIPBUILDING & MARINE ENGINEERING

Apart from ship-repairing work, which is shared by certain other local firms, shipbuilding in the port of Leith except for the building of small craft, rests now in the hands of one firm. This is Henry Robb Limited, a firm whose Victoria Yards are situated at West Pier, and which, with a labour force of some 700 shipyard workers, successfully carry on this important Leith industry. Established in 1918, on All Fool's Day, Robb's became the only shipbuilding firm in Edinburgh, having incorporated three older firms. The yard specialises in tugs, hopper-dredgers and intermediate cargo and passenger-cargo ships. But during the second World War it also turned out more than 40 ships-of-war for the British and Dominion Admiralties; and this tradition has been continued. In August, 1964 the firm was awarded the contract to build a large helicopter support ship for the Royal Navy. About the same time it won a £3 million contract to build five vessels for the Ellerman's Wilson Line, and decided to spend £100,000 on a new welding shop.

In the realm of marine engineering, with a particular emphasis on steering gears and stabilisers, the firm of Brown Brothers and Company

Limited, occupies a noteworthy and securely established position. Founded in 1861, and now employing about 1,000 men of whom two-thirds are skilled, the company has, in more recent times, in association with Denny Brothers of Dumbarton acquired an enhanced reputation as inventor and maker of the Denny-Brown ship stabilizer. This device has long been standard equipment in all kinds of seagoing craft, and the Admiralty as well as many shipping lines have adopted it as a measure towards greater comfort and safety. Early in January, 1965, however, Brown Brothers went a stage further by marketing a new ship stabilizer, which the designers claim is applicable to all vessels, large or small, at any operating speed and also at anchor. This new system is known as the Muirhead-Brown Controlled Tank Stabilizer. In the same specialised field the firm some years ago were made the licensees in the United Kingdom and Commonwealth for Voith-Schneider propellers, a horizontally rotating means of high manoeuvrability for harbour tugs and similar vessels. Today Brown Brothers are associated with a consortium of shipbuilding and marine engineering interests in different parts of the British Isles. They have also taken over John Greig and Sons, an Edinburgh engineering firm founded in 1810. On a grander scale the company in the early 1960s carried through a major re-organisation programme. Designed to modernise its machine shops and offices, the programme, completed in 1963, cost some £500,000. Unfortunately much of this modernisation was wiped out by a disastrous fire in the spring of 1965, and work had to be started all over again.

Other engineering and allied firms in Leith produce machinery and components of infinite variety, such as electric cranes, hoists, special valves, paper and pipe-joints; while others are concerned in the installation of space heating and oil-firing. The maritime atmosphere broods over all.

INFINITE VARIETY

Many other branches of the engineering industry flourish in Edinburgh. Some are scientific and technical industries specialising in complicated control and electrical work. Nuclear Enterprises (G.B.) Limited, for example, produce a wide variety of equipment to measure and trace radiation. Their equipment is sold throughout the world, including Harwell at home; and already numerous products such as moisture gauge meters on building sites, airfield runways and forests have been exported to Europe, the Far East and a considerable number of Iron Curtain countries. Recently also, expensive medical equipment, including human body monitors for radio isotope investigations in patients, has been manufactured for hospitals and for Universities in Germany and the United Kingdom. And so we could go on to a lengthy list of other names in this field of electrical industry—to Multitone Electric Company Limited, Airlite–Ionic Limited, and Berry's Electric Limited among others. But again a full list is clearly beyond the scope of such a survey, as it would be of the numerous small, and medium sized light engineering concerns in the city which supply local heavy engineering and building industries with equipment and tools at a time of increasing interest in pre-fabrication. It can truthfully be said that light engineering companies are showing considerable enterprise; otherwise a firm such as John Gibson and Company, which started life in Leith in the 1890s making bicycles and golf balls, would not be employing more than 200 people turning out deep freeze rooms for bakeries, butchers and fishmongers, refrigerated trucks and counters, refuse collection vehicles, alloy tower ladders, a mobile dental clinic for Fife County Council and a number of mobile banks.

THE PORT OF LEITH

Leith, one of the oldest seaports in the United Kingdom, is now the largest port on the east coast of Scotland and the second largest in Scotland. The officially recorded history of the port dates from 1329 when King Robert the Bruce granted a Charter of the Harbour and Mills of Leith to the City of Edinburgh. These mills, which occupied sites along the water course from Leith past Canonmills up to the Dean Village, were built for the grinding of grain and made use of the Water of Leith for their power.

In 1838 ownership and control of the harbour and docks was transferred to a statutory body, The Leith Dock Commission, which duly constructed the Victoria Dock. This was opened in 1853. Since then there have been built and opened for traffic the Albert Dock (1865), the Edinburgh Dock (1881) and the Imperial Dock (1904). The first two have entrances of 60 feet; the last an entrance of 70 feet. Up to 1902 the water area of Leith was 105 acres, an area increased to 308 acres in 1942 with the opening up of the Western Harbour.

The docks have been designed on the half-tide principle. The gates are opened about two to three hours before high water, and the docks are then opened to the sea until high water when the gates are closed.

TRADE OF THE PORT

In the last pre-war edition of the *Port of Leith Handbook* (1937) it was recorded that " coal is the heaviest export of Leith, as the port is the chief doorway through which it and the manufactured goods of Scotland and even some from the north of Ireland pass to the various countries bordering the North and Baltic Seas. The coalfields of the Lothians and others adjacent, all possessing abundant coal of good quality, are well served by a network of railways leading to Leith Docks for export." Coal of good quality and the railway network are still available; but since the war the coal export and import trade has been completely transformed. During the so-called " depressed " years of the 1930s, in a single year 1,500,000 tons of cargo coal and more than 400,000 tons of bunker coal were loaded at the Commissioner's hoists. During 1955 only 304,000 tons in all were shipped, while 344,000 tons were brought into the port from abroad to " keep the home fires burning." The bulk of coal exports during 1955 went to Denmark for electricity generation.

Since then further changes have taken place in the coal industry, as the following table of Leith imports and exports shows. As Leith provides the only grain elevators and warehouses in the East of Scotland, there have also been important developments in the flour industry and its ancillaries; and these too are reflected in the table which gives the 1963 figures for imports and exports going through the Port of Leith:

TABLE 57

Imports (*in tons*)		*Exports* (*in tons*)	
Grain	424,035	Flour and meal	3,428
Flour and meal	13,815	Ale and beer	4,933
Fish	17,354	Spirits, wines	26,063
Vegetables	41,483	Coal cargo	254,568
Fertiliser	274,697	Coal (bunker)	5,347
Sulphur	22,058	Iron, steel manufactures	12,010
Cement	84,749	Paper	6,337
China Clay	24,145	Oil Fuel	7,753
Iron, steel	8,624	Motor vehicles	
Wood	85,020	(including tractors)	6,469
Paper	20,266	Other	67,944
Wood Pulp	56,898		
Oil	62,593		
Other	106,657		

The quays at Leith are well served by road and rail with siding accommodation and open storage areas for the laying-down of cargoes such as timber. Several diesel-engined locomotives were recently introduced and have proved most useful in the movement of rail traffic. Power-driven capstans assist in the movement of railway traffic in and around the sheds and quays.

All the discharging berths except those in the western harbour are equipped with sheds for handling goods in transit; and most of these have smooth concrete floors suitable for the use of mechanical vehicles such as electric trolleys, fork-lift trucks and mobile cranes, all of which are employed in the moving of cargoes. At some of the sheds there are facilities for supplying vessels with electric power and light and ship-to-shore telephones.

RECENT INDUSTRIAL DEVELOPMENT

Developments since 1935 have been largely to the west—between Leith and Newhaven—in the area protected by the new west breakwater where Rank's Caledonia Flour Mills have been built on land reclaimed by the Leith Dock Commission from the Firth of Forth, with deep water berthage alongside. Additional land in that area of approximately 14 acres is available for letting to industries which will use the harbour and docks for the import of their raw material or export of their finished goods; and indeed the Scottish Co-operative Wholesale Society announced in January, 1965 that it intended to build a £2 million flour mill and grain silo at the West Dock. The wheat was to be delivered direct to the new mill and the silo would have a capacity of 33,000 tons.

Certain other industries have established themselves within the area of the harbour and docks in recent years. Firstly, there is Scottish

Agricultural Industries Limited, who have not only constructed a fertiliser factory on 18 acres of ground at the Edinburgh Dock with direct discharge of raw materials from berths in the Imperial Dock but a £100,000 grass seed plant said to be one of the best-equipped in the whole of Europe. Secondly, there is Esso Petroleum Company Limited, who have built near the north-west corner of the Imperial Dock an installation for receiving petrol and petroleum products by sea with subsequent distribution inland from the depot there.

THE GREAT DECISION

In the light of all this and the obvious need for modernising the docks, strong pressure on various Governments to give Leith Dock Commission financial support was kept up for years by the Commission itself, the Edinburgh and Leith Chambers of Commerce, the Member of Parliament for Leith, Mr James Hoy, and other interested parties. Then at last came the great day. On 17th December, 1964 the Ministry of Transport agreed to lend £6 million for the modernisation of Leith Harbour along the lines of a scheme prepared by the Dock Commission.

The scheme, which was to take three and a half years to complete, should enable the port to receive vessels up to 40,000 or 50,000 tons deadweight in all tides. A large lock about 850 feet by 110 feet by 37 feet will be constructed at the entrance to the Western harbour, thus converting the tidal area into an impounded dock. The old West Pier will be cut back and the entrance to Imperial Dock widened and deepened.

The approach channel will be dredged to provide a minimum depth of 40 feet at mean high water neap tides. Grain facilities will be improved; the East and West Old Docks will be filled in; and not only will the number of berths with 25 to 30 feet of water be increased from eight to 21 but 13 berths of more than 30 feet of water will be available.

SHIPPING AND PASSENGER SERVICES

In the meantime the port of Leith will continue to deal with the shipping and unshipping of practically every kind of import and export and offer ample and comfortable accommodation to vessels of every shape and dimension save the great passenger liners. Yet, even so, Leith can welcome these in its roadstead, when as frequently happens they call in the course of luxury cruising to send their passengers ashore on sightseeing tours round Edinburgh and tax-free shopping expeditions. Copious berthage in both west and dry docks is provided for shipping, ranging from the most modest of small fry up to vessels of quite impressive tonnage engaged in trans-oceanic business. It also provides effectively for the expert handling of every kind of inward cargo; for its safe and convenient storage, when required, pending conveyance to a home destination; and for its deposit in bond or transit shed to await release for home consumption or transference to an outward-bound ship for conveyance to a destination abroad.

The foreign traffic passing through Leith is considerable, and a high proportion of this comes from or departs to continental destinations, principally in Scandinavia, the Baltic countries, Northern France, Belgium and Holland. Germany too has had a link with the port since the summer of 1962 when the German managers of the Michigan Ocean Line operating between Hamburg and the Great Lakes extended the service to include Leith as their sole Scottish loading port. The first cargo was a consignment of whisky for Montreal, Toronto, Toledo, Detroit, Chicago, Milwaukee and Duluth. Trans-Atlantic business is also a not unimportant feature; but whaling, so long followed for the most part in the Antarctic, has now only an historical connection with the port. Formerly this whaling industry was pursued in a much more primitive fashion by sailing vessels owned, manned and fitted out here and despatched to Arctic waters around Greenland and the Davis Straits on hunting trips often extending to seven or eight months' duration. Through the years this industry was greatly developed by the important firm of Chr. Salvesen and Company, which is also agent for the Svenska Lloyd Line trading from Leith to Gothenburg and vice versa.

There are two interesting footnotes to the Salvesen saga. Having given up whaling on their own steam, Salvesen's leased their suitably named Antarctic whaling station, Leith Harbour in South Georgia, to a Japanese whaling company (Nippon Suisan Kaisha) for a term of years. They also sold the last of their whaling factory ships to the same company in 1963 but retained their catcher fleet in case some day they might go whaling again. During 1964, however, Salvesen's sold a number of whale catchers, some for scrap and others for conversion to Norwegian fishing boats; and early in 1965 it was announced that the Antarctic Leith Harbour had been leased to the Japanese whaling company for a further three years.

The second footnote is a compliment to Chr. Salvesen and Company. Having withdrawn from active participation in the whaling industry, they announced—in August, 1964—the setting up of a £50,000 Salvesen Trust fund to help ex-whalers and their dependents to start new enterprises in the Highlands and Islands. From this, Shetland in particular was to benefit because of its long association with the whaling industry.

Other steamship companies intimately connected with Leith are the Ben Line Steamers Limited, whose 26 ships (in 1965) do not operate from the port but whose headquarters are there; George Gibson and Company Limited whose ships are named after people or places in the novels of Sir Walter Scott; Shipping and Coal Company Limited; Coast Lines Limited; the Enid Shipping Company and W. N. Lindsay Limited (both with coastal services); the London and Edinburgh Shipping Company which took over the now defunct London Scottish Lines Limited, and the Currie Line Limited. For 150 years London Scottish Lines had run a service between Leith and London and for many years its regular coasting cargo-liner services on this run had been very popular with passengers. Unfortunately this traffic declined with changing times.

The origin of the Currie Line can be traced to the Forth and Clyde Shipping Company, one of many which operated from the port around the end of the 18th century. Over the years, through mergers, there arose the Leith, Hull and Hamburg Steam Packet Company. After a modest start in 1835 this company expanded rapidly and when Messrs. James Currie and Company took over the management in 1862 it was trading with most of the Baltic ports. A year later it began the Leith–Copenhagen service and in time developed other runs to Spain, Portugal and Italy. World War II disrupted the company's trade but by that time it was evident that the name of the company was inadequate in view of the wide scope of its trading; hence the change in 1940 to Currie Line.

Since the end of World War II Currie Line has like other shipping companies had to replace its older ships with larger vessels, which to-day carry timber, esparto grass, fertilisers and many other commodities. Some like the *Gothland*, an ore-carrier, and the *Highland*, which carries general cargo, are on charter to trading companies. In 1957 the Copenhagen service was withdrawn, but in 1963 the company marked the centenary of the first sailings by reintroducing a twice weekly run between Leith and the Danish capital.

One of the oldest regular lines out of Leith is run by the North of Scotland Orkney and Shetland Shipping Company Limited to Aberdeen and the Orkney and Shetland Isles. This also provides agreeable summer tours. The coasting and near-continental tramp section of the industry includes the local fleet of A. F. Henry and MacGregor Limited.

Furness Withy and Company Limited, in addition to acting as Lloyd's agents and insurance brokers, exercise the local oversight of certain Dutch and Danish shipping lines and also superintend the local interest of the Cairn Line of steamers largely dealing with Canadian traffic in grain and miscellaneous cargo transport. The firm of George A. Morrison and Company (Leith Limited), has close Swedish connections; R. Cairns and Company are intimately involved in Danish and Icelandic trading; and Charles Mauritzen Limited, serves the Faroes connections.

PILOTAGE

The pilotage in the Firth and River of Forth is under the jurisdiction of and administered by the Forth Pilotage Authority, a body set up in 1947 in terms of the Forth Pilotage Order 1947 which created a single pilotage authority in the Firth and River in place of the existing six authorities. Towage facilities at the port are provided by Leith Dock Commission, who own a fleet of tugs available for towage within the docks and the Firth of Forth.

The Leith and Granton Boatman's Association operates four motor-boats for the purpose of handling ships' ropes and assisting in moorings. Servicing of vessels in Leith Roads is also carried out by the boatmen who are available at all times.

BUILDING AND CONTRACTING

The building industry at the start of the 1960s was the largest group among the city's secondary industries. But surprisingly, at a first glance, there was a sharp decline in the numbers engaged in building in Edinburgh between 1951 and 1957, though the total for Great Britain was rising during the same period. In Edinburgh 15,543 were employed in 1951 but only 9,570 in 1957. Electrical contracting, during the same period, also dropped—from 1,568 to 1,264. Civil engineering on the other hand climbed up from 1,498 to 2,794. But looking at these subdivisions of the building and contracting industry as a whole, the Great Britain figures showed an employment increase in all three. Since then the Edinburgh figures have risen steadily so that by 1962 an official tally for the number of people employed in building and construction was almost 17,500 (including about 1,500 women), and the figure rose again in 1963.

There were various reasons for the decline in building employment during the '50s. Increased productivity, encouraged partly by greater regularity in the supply of bricks and partly by increased mechanisation was certainly one. Another is claimed to have been a reduction in house-building as the demand in the city was progressively satisfied. Thirdly, one Edinburgh firm moved from Edinburgh to Grangemouth. And lastly, a change in the compilation of the local employment statistics meant that the labour employed by Edinburgh contractors on work outside the local labour exchange area was no longer included. Equally important to note, the industry employs a considerable body of commuters from outside the city boundaries—from Musselburgh, for instance, and the East Lothian burghs—and indeed one large firm employing some 1,500 people in the late '50s and early '60s has stated that 50 per cent of its labour force were commuters.

In recent years there have been many technical and economic changes in the industry favouring the large firm. True the small jobbing builder is still representative of the industry's original dispersed character, but growth of road transportation facilities, increased mechanisation of the industry, with all that that involves in larger capital investment and capacity to do the job more speedily, and the larger scale of the jobs themselves have meant a bigger all-round organisation to carry them out efficiently. This in turn has favoured large firms operating from a central headquarters or at least a regional office. In this respect Edinburgh's position as Scotland's administrative centre undoubtedly accounts for the presence of firms employing at least a considerable office staff in the city itself and so adding to the industry's representation there. More especially this applies to the industry's civil engineering side, with its large contracts on roads, hydro-electric schemes and other public works. Another factor that has encouraged greater centralisation of the industry since World War II has been the development of prefabrication, with its effect of transferring labour from the building site to the factory.

The craft composition of the labour force on the housing side of the industry may be seen from employment data supplied by the Scottish Special Housing Association. This important body has its head office in Edinburgh. Set up in 1937 to help " distressed areas " it employs private firms of architects, engineers and quantity surveyors in addition to its

Like many other cities Edinburgh has been forced to build upwards to conserve her green belts. Here beside new blocks of multi-storey flats at Muirhouse the existing trees have been retained and the buildings are surrounded by lawns.

This modern version of the "back green" gives a fairground air to the new flats at Comiston. In place of the poles that used to protrude from Edinburgh tenements, carrying washing like so many untidy flags, the authorities now provide a fence behind which the weekly wash can be dried by wind and sun.

Skyscrapers and multi-storey flats are nothing new to Edinburgh. Here are some of the "tall lands" behind Gladstone's Land, off the Lawnmarket.

own staff, and works through either sub-contractors or direct labour as found convenient. Houses erected by it remain in its ownership unless erected for the Government or local authorities. Tenants are nominated by local authorities or bodies such as the National Coal Board, and under the Housing (Scotland) Act of 1944 and later the 1950 Act it builds wherever the Secretary of State for Scotland and the Treasury decide the need is greatest. Its labour force on 18th April, 1958 came to 1,360 men of whom only 100 worked in the city.

In April, 1964 the Scottish Special Housing Association employed a labour staff of 1,460.

RAW MATERIALS

The raw materials used in the industry are manifold. They fall into some 150 different categories, of which 30 may be regarded as main building materials. The following nine are the major materials, and their sources are in the Edinburgh district. Much of Edinburgh was built with Craigleith stone, which has stood up well to two centuries or more of northern weather. Now, however, such stone as is used is brought from Northumberland or even from Scandinavia, whence it can be obtained relatively cheaply. The largest supplier of bricks in the Edinburgh district is the National Coal Board; and the greater part of Edinburgh's supply comes from neighbouring collieries in Midlothian—Newbattle, Newtongrange, Niddrie, Ormiston, Prestongrange, Roslin and Whitehill. Tiles, as well as drainpipes and chimney pots, are made at Portobello from local clay and from fireclay brought from the Newcraighall colliery. Lime has been worked at nearby Burdiehouse for 150 years, and Gilmerton is one of the oldest sources in Scotland. Other sources of lime are at Cousland on Roman Camp Ridge and at Limekilns and Charleston in Fife just west of North Queensferry. Sand and gravel are brought from the glacial deposits at Eddleston. Timber is imported through Leith from Scandinavia. Steel comes from Motherwell, and cement from Dunbar.

MECHANIZATION

There were other changes in the ever-widening field of mechanisation stimulated not only by scarcity and the high cost of traditional materials but by rising labour costs. Mechanisation spread rapidly both on the building site and off-site. Mechanisation on the site has so far found its greatest application in the civil engineering sector; especially in road construction, in which the shifting and levelling of earth by bulldozers, excavation by mechanical navvies and the use of compressed-air machines have vastly accelerated operations. In the building sector mechanisation has so far been mainly off-site, as is the mass production of doors in a few large factories. On the actual building site something has been done to cut down the wastage due to bad weather—whether rain, snow or frost—by such means as the use of quicksetting or of frost-resistant cement.

Changing technology has also had its repercussions on the size of the firms in the industry. Building has long been notable for the large number of small family firms, partly because of its dispersion, since even small settlements required, until recently at least, the services of a jobbing builder for repairs and maintenance. Another reason is said to be the relative ease with which, again until recently, a man with little or no training could enter the industry and eventually establish his own business. In 1958 there were in Edinburgh 122 firms, of which 60 per cent had less than 20 men and another 14 per cent employed 20–50. But by 1964 one of the large combines (Wimpey's) was employing some 800 labourers and craftsmen in Edinburgh alone.

To go back again to the '50s, as elsewhere there was considerable thinning out of the numbers employed in the industry—for various reasons. Because of rising costs the small firm suffered most from quite a lot of householders building their own walls, garages and other simple constructions. Small concerns, both then and now, have also found that their big brothers compete in their usual field in order to employ their men and machinery in slack periods. The large firms, after all, have the advantage of a variety of both equipment and staff sufficient to plan and carry out an entire job expeditiously. They can more easily build up a permanent core cf experienced staff. With the expansion of motor transportation, and operating as many do on a national scale, they can also become increasingly nomadic as industrialists while retaining administrative headquarters in a city like Edinburgh, with its special advantages of easy contact with Government authorities responsible for large contracts. It is however the medium-sized firms that have been the first to be squeezed out between the relatively small number of firms employing 1,000 and more on the one hand and the small working proprietors with low overheads on the other.

One of the few firms with, until recently, a continuous family history is Colin Macandrew and Partners Limited. Colin Macandrew, a journeyman joiner, started in 1882 and ran the company almost entirely up to World War I. Among its public contracts during this remarkable phase were the Redford Barracks. His son Percy joined after World War I and took over control in 1933. The firm obtained many contracts for schools, hospitals, banks and university buildings during this fructive period, and eventually two subsidiary companies were formed to run respectively the joinery and the masonry sides of the business. In 1939, however, these two subsidiaries amalgamated to form the present firm, and a year later members of the Orchard family took over the chief administrative posts.

After World War II the firm was responsible for carrying out the first large stone contract of the post-war years, the Fountainbridge Telephone Exchange, and later the largest post-war stone contract, the National Library of Scotland. Another notable contract was for the Muirhouse estate, the first prefabrication scheme in Edinburgh. By 1964 the firm employed some 300 men, mostly stonemasons, bricklayers, joiners, blacksmiths and excavators, and it possessed the largest stone masonry department in the city.

THE FUTURE

The increasing development of the central area of Scotland has produced official comment from time to time on the capacity of the construction industry and therefore its ability to supply the area. Yet in the city itself there is an abundance of contractors varying from the small " one-man " business to some of the very large firms. And here again we meet the insoluble problem of listing everyone, but some names spring to mind.

Specialising in pre-cast concrete beams is the Scottish Construction Company, a family business, which has a large factory, spread over 14 acres, in the Sighthill Industrial Estate. It has also factories in Falkirk and Dundee, and its houses and flats are used throughout Scotland.

Throughout the city on housing estates and private land one also sees the names of Boland, who have extended their activities into Ireland; Mactaggart and Mickel; and the always prominent James Miller and Partners, who among other ventures recently completed private flats in Barnton, Queen's Park, and Morningside. Sir James Miller, who is a former Lord Provost of the City of Edinburgh, also became Lord Mayor of the City of London in 1964—the first man in the history of the United Kingdom to achieve this remarkable record.

There are many others: Arnott McLeod Limited (engaged in a number of major projects in the city boundaries); W. and J. R. Watson Contractors, (another family concern known for road building as well as the construction of large offices); A. M. Carmichael (at work on roadways including some approach roads to the new Forth Road Bridge); John Hunter and Sons, specialising in demolition to prepare the way for redevelopment of housing and office accommodation; John Henderson, Medway Building Supplies, Johnstone's and Paton Limited, G. and J. Paton, Adam Currie and Son Limited, Donald Grant Limited, Heggie and Aitchison, A. D. Kinnear and Son, Alex Stephen and Son; Tractor Shovels Limited, Scottish Plant Hirers, J. Smart and Company (a firm of building and civil engineering contractors which has three subsidiaries wholly-owned and employs the best part of 500 men on construction work for public and local authorities and commercial interests in Central Scotland), and among many others Balfour Beatty and Company who were awarded a big new civil engineering contract in 1965 for work at the new town of Livingstone.

COALMINING

Gilmerton Colliery having been closed by a fire in November, 1961, Newcraighall is now the only colliery operating within the City boundary. This colliery, sometimes referred to locally as the " Klondyke," was started in 1897. It then consisted of two inclined mines driven in the Four-Feet Seam which outcrops in the locus of the colliery.

Its former owners had considerable workings of Cannel coal, then in great demand for the manufacture of gas. But the introduction of incandescent mantles later reduced the demand for this particular type of coal since gas produced from " common " or ordinary bituminous coals could be used equally well.

When the shallow coal at Newcraighall had been worked out, it was decided in 1910 to sink a vertical shaft to exploit the seams at depth, where it was known there were very large reserves of coal. Known as No. 3 shaft, it is 811 feet deep, 16 feet in diameter and brick-lined.

From the shaft bottom a level horizon mine was driven to reach the coals. The exposure points of the coals at this horizon provided entrance to each seam in turn. A major development known as the Sea Dook, was then driven northwards towards the Firth of Forth to a point 3,000 feet beyond Fisherrow Harbour. The total distance from the shaft to the farthest working was 11,000 feet or just over two miles.

More recently a scheme of colliery concentration has been completed to improve the general efficiency of Newcraighall Colliery, which is included in the Lothians area of the Scottish Division of the National Coal Board.

It was decided early in 1962, for instance, to concentrate production on high grade house coal. Loading underground was centralised at one point, and all the coal loaded on a single shift. This had the effect of reducing the number of men servicing the coal faces, so that by 1963 the actual manpower employed was around 700.

VENTILATION AND PUMPING

Those interested in coal and collieries will no doubt like to know also that the amount of air passing through the workings each day is approximately 4,800 tons, and that large quantities of water have still to be pumped from the workings. The quantity of water pumped to the surface has been as much as 1,700 gallons per minute, or about 7½ tons per minute.

To get the coal from shaft bottom to the surface the shaft is equipped with double-decked cages, each deck accommodating two tubs in tandem. As the average weight of coal in each hutch is 12 cwts., approximately 2½ tons are raised per wind. Manually operated simultaneous decking arrangements are in use at surface and pitbottom.

Next comes the preparation of the coal for the market. To achieve this the colliery is equipped with coal screening and washing plants in order to control the quality and size of the product efficiently. The large coal is absorbed by the house coal market, smaller sizes being used for industrial purposes. As for waste, after dirt has been removed from the coal at the screening and washing plants, all waste materials are then taken by conveyors to a storage hopper on the bing top and disposed of by a Muirhill Dumper.

But here we must leave this world of engineering, shipbuilding and coal and turn to the lighter consumer industries. Some of these have been established for centuries and others in our own time. Whatever their age they again illustrate the unusual heterogenity of the city's industrial life.

BREWING AND DISTILLING

Brewing is one of Edinburgh's most important and oldest industries. It goes back at least to the 12th century, when the monks of Holyrood Abbey made the most of the excellent springs nearby to brew their own beer. In the late 18th century there came another inducement to brew in the Holyrood district (then outside the city) when Edinburgh levied an impost on ale over and above the Government's malt tax.

Before the last war the city, producing nearly all the best known Scotch ales in 23 breweries, had become the second largest brewing centre in Great Britain. The invested capital in these was then between £5 million and £6 million; and a large proportion of Edinburgh-brewed beers was sold outside Scotland.

To take a few exemplary spheres of influence, Scotch ales had always been popular in Northumberland and Durham, and Edinburgh-brewed beers had for long been exported to many overseas countries including Australia, Canada, South Africa, India and Belgium. William McEwan's and William Younger's had indeed owed quite a lot of their original success to the popularity of their beers in these overseas markets, though the setting up of local breweries and tariff barriers abroad had led, even before the first World War, to the closing of many outlets in most of them. In spite of this the technical reputation of Edinburgh brewers remained high, and Edinburgh-trained brewers were much sought after by English brewery companies.

After the last war, and more particularly in the late '50s and early '60s, there have been revolutionary changes both in production and distribution—with frequent amalgamations and take-overs. This process started before the War. In 1930 William Younger and Company (founded in 1749) united with William McEwan and Company, who started at Fountainbridge in 1856: the new combine was given the name of Scottish Brewers Limited. Younger's Abbey and Holyrood Breweries thus became united with the McEwan Fountainbridge Brewery, though the distinctive products of the two firms continued to be brewed as before in their respective breweries and marketed separately. In recent years the process of amalgamation and combination has gathered speed in conformity with the English trend, though more belatedly for reasons peculiar to the Scottish retail trade. In the event this was inevitable, for as elsewhere the city's smaller brewery companies found it difficult to maintain their independence. Some merged with English brewery companies—Usher's for example with Vaux and Associated Breweries. Watney Mann, another English company, took over Drybrough, and Charrington's United Breweries acquired a number of the smaller Scottish breweries including Murray of Duddingston and Aitchison Jeffrey, forming United Caledonian Breweries. Others were taken over by Scottish Brewers Limited.

But the English influence persisted. Archd. Campbell, Hope and King, Limited, originally founded in 1710 as Campbell and Company and the oldest brewery still brewing on its original site in the heart of Old Edinburgh, is associated with Whitbread's. The company has branches in other parts of Scotland and an interest in the wine and spirit business. Steel Coulson's and Bernard's are other old firms no longer independent. In turn of course these mergers led to the closing of quite a number of small breweries, and to the consolidation of brewing in a limited number of larger units.

Yet despite many changes there has been no diminution in the production of beer in Edinburgh. Indeed the contrary is true. For if Edinburgh-brewed beers had lost some overseas markets because of transport costs and tariff barriers, sales of Scotch ales in England, particularly in North-east England, continued to expand, and new names appeared. Carling Black Label lager, for one, is now brewed at Heriot Brewery, which belongs to United Caledonian Breweries Limited; and Harp Lager—a joint venture of Guinness, Courage, Barclay and Simonds, and Scottish and Newcastle Breweries—is now matured at William Younger's Abbey Brewery. Furthermore, in 1961 Scottish Brewers Limited (which includes Younger's) acquired the whole of the share capital of Newcastle Breweries Limited to form Scottish and Newcastle Breweries Limited, now one of the half dozen leading groups in the British brewing industry.[1]

Obviously such a far-reaching growth shows the brewing industry in Edinburgh to be vital and enterprising. At the Fountainbridge brewery of Scottish and Newcastle Breweries, for instance, not only has a large and costly programme of expansion and modernisation been carried out, but in the five years ending 1963 its output was more than doubled; and this is only one example of the expansion programme carried through by this and other companies. Generally the effect has been a concentration in fewer breweries, the use of former brewery premises for other purposes, and a much greater involvement in the retail licensed trade and in catering and hotels. This last is important since the principal Edinburgh brewery companies have been providing, at considerable expense, modern licensed premises of all kinds not only in Edinburgh and throughout Scotland but also in England.

In addition Scottish and Newcastle Breweries, and also United Caledonian Breweries, have branched out into the wine and spirit trade, by the acquisition of old established wine and spirit businesses for whose products they could provide an outlet in their many licensed premises, and whose growth they could stimulate by the infusion of new capital. Thus United Caledonian Breweries acquired the old established wine and spirit business of J. G. Thomson and Company Limited, while Scottish and Newcastle Breweries Limited acquired Charles Mackinlay and Company, and has recently acquired the premises of the historic Edinburgh Roperie and Sailcloth Company (closed by British Ropes Limited) in

[1] Within two years Colonel Charles F. J. Younger, D.S.O., a leading Scottish and Newcastle director became chairman of the Brewers Society, a United Kingdom body, and by so doing became the first member of a Scottish brewery company to attain this office.

order to provide the most modern facilities for blending and bottling Scotch whisky for both their home and overseas markets.

The distilling of whisky in Edinburgh is very important since the city is one of the big Scottish centres for the production of grain whisky, the basic component for Scotch whisky blends. It houses the North British Distillery, which is one of the largest in Europe and is owned by the independent wholesale whisky merchants. The intention of the promoters was to build a distillery to be run and financed by the trade for the trade, and thus to ensure, for blending purposes, an independent supply of grain whisky of the finest quality at the most reasonable price consistent with sound finance. That was three-quarters of a century ago, and since then, the size of the distillery has been practically doubled, and is still expanding. The Caledonian Grain Distillery, one of the group owned by the Distillers Company Limited, is also situated in Edinburgh, and its output is largely used by the blending houses within the group.

Edinburgh's port of Leith has long been very closely involved in the blending and bottling of many of the most important brands of Scotch whisky. It is plentifully provided with bonded warehouses closely adjacent to the docks. Most of these are the property of the various traders, and for a long time they have been working to full capacity in order to cope with the record world demand for Scotch whisky. To this end the bonded warehouses are furnished with the most up to date appliances for the handling of the product from the moment of its arrival from the distilleries until it appears on the market blended and bottled.

There are no malt distilleries in Edinburgh. Malt whisky, of necessity and tradition, is manufactured in the Highlands and Islands, but there is a steady traffic into the city of consignments to feed the bonded warehouses. However, because of economic pressures the blending trade is coming into fewer hands, a trend which has one advantage: it enables more ambitious schemes of expansion to be undertaken. Certainly in Leith, not only have most of the bonded warehouses been extended and improved, but some new warehouses have been constructed. One such warehouse group is owned by Mackinlay-MacPherson Limited, a company within the Scottish and Newcastle Breweries group, which has widespread ramifications, including a large and expanding export trade in Scotch whisky and branches in Edinburgh itself with a busy home distribution. The warehouse area covers 12¼ acres and has been planned to provide one of the most up-to-date blending and bottling plants in Scotland.

The Distillers Company Limited have a number of important warehouses in Leith, blending and bottling some well-known brands. But there are many other names. Hill Thomson and Company not only blend a famous whisky but operate substantial whisky warehouses within the area. Some have already been mentioned, but there are also Sandeman and Sons, Macdonald, Greenlees Limited, Macdonald and Muir Limited, Wm. Sanderson and Son Limited, the far-reaching Scottish Malt Distillers Limited, and, most recent of all, Tomatin Distillers.

With some 350 million proof gallons of Scotch whisky maturing in

Scotland by 1964, storage became still more important as did the provision of casks. Storage warehouses are therefore scattered throughout the city, and there are one or two very important cooperage undertakings such as William Lindsay and Sons which belongs to Scottish and Newcastle Breweries Limited. The other blending houses have their own cooperages in the city, where casks are not only repaired but, in some of them, manufactured.

Altogether the number of people employed in brewing and malting in the city by 1963 numbered almost 4,800; and in addition many hundreds more were employed by ancillary industries. It is however not easy to compute how many people play a part in the industry for also there are the liqueur companies—the Mackinnon family which produces Drambuie, and John Morrison and Company Glayva.

FOODSTUFFS

BREAD AND FLOUR CONFECTIONERY

The earliest Edinburgh bakeries were located with no other consideration than the immediate proximity of the consumer in the Old Town and the older part of Leith. They obtained their flour from the mills at Canonmills or Bonnington, both on the Water of Leith. But when imported wheat became predominant and horse-drawn transportation gave way to the railway it became convenient towards the end of the 19th century to locate the bakeries near railway yards. While two large bakeries—St. Cuthbert's Co-operative and that of the Rank group—have a particular link with the two large mills at the port of Leith, other Edinburgh bakeries by the end of the '50s were obtaining their flour mainly through Glasgow or Liverpool, though some supplies also came from Carlisle, Kirkcaldy and Dalkeith. Although it now draws its flour daily in large road tankers from the S.C.W.S. mill at Leith docks,[1] St. Cuthbert's Co-operative Society, which owns the largest bakery in Edinburgh, has, like one or two others, established its plant in the Fountainbridge–Dalry area. There was a further westward movement of the bakery industry in 1920–30 to Gorgie, where two of the largest biscuit factories as well as the Edinburgh and Dumfries Dairy Company's bread bakery are situated. Since then the movement has continued with the siting of two modern mechanised bakeries and a biscuit factory on the Sighthill Industrial Estate.

The size of the firm ranges from the one-man business to the large modern mechanised plant. Together they fall into four distinguishable groups. These are:

(1) The " home bakeries ", of which there were more than 70 in the late '50s and early '60s as against twice that number before the second World War. These businesses, consisting generally of one or two bakers and a shop assistant, have managed to survive only by meeting a highly

[1] At the bakery the flour reaches the storage hoppers on the top floor by suction. By 1958 the bakery had the only gas-air-oil travelling oven in Scotland and the only bread-cooling plant in Edinburgh.

localised market with the maximum freshness of product and often special lines of home-made goods to meet the taste of the neighbourhood. As this close adaptation to local requirements is also combined with minimum distribution costs and very low overheads, these " one-man businesses " have survived in the older parts of the city, but most of them limit their own output to rolls, scones, pies, and cakes, buying in bread from the wholesale bakers to meet the convenience of their customers.

(2) A slightly more ambitious type employing perhaps 10–20 employees and in the majority 10 or fewer. Such a bakery has one or two shops and supplies local cafes and grocers. But like the first group it limits its own output to products other than bread, which it, too, buys from wholesalers.

(3) The medium-sized family businesses grew from the preceding group by adding more shops and extending the market. This type has developed strongly in Edinburgh and generally associates catering with baking. In some cases it draws much of its trade from tourists and from small-scale exports. Two leading members of this group have sites in Princes Street and all have been established for over 100 years. D. S. Crawford Limited, now a part of United Biscuits Limited and the largest, had 16 shops and nine restaurants at the end of the '50s. By 1964 its annual sales had increased to more than £1,500,000. Scott-Lyon, as these words are written, belongs to the same size-group with almost a score of shops and also, in close proximity to the flour-mills in Leith, bakeries for bread, rolls, pies, cakes and shortbread. McVittie Guest claim to make the largest variety of bread in Britain, with some 40 different kinds. This large variety is said to be uneconomic in itself but is maintained for the sake of encouraging other sales. The firm of Mackie makes no bread but has many shops, in addition to its bakery and restaurant in Princes Street. There are four others in this size-group, the smallest employing 25. Two of the medium-sized firms—McDowell's and Nairn—are now associated, the former producing bread, rolls and tea-bread, the latter concentrating on flour confectionery.

(4) Edinburgh, for its size, had relatively few of the large-scale modern plants at the start of the '60s; which is not altogether surprising since private investment is sometimes inadequate to meet the heavy costs of modern installations or large-scale plants. Thus with higher costs for flour and the possibility of only a low percentage profit on bread, public companies like Smith's of Hawkhill (Restalrig) and others mentioned earlier have inevitably increased their hold on the supply of bread. Smith's for one, had become the principal wholesale bread producers in Edinburgh by the early '60s, while Martin's, a subsidiary of Associated Bakers Limited (as are Smith's) had become notable for its large production of more than 1,500 dozen morning rolls daily. In 1965 the Milanda Bread Company was advertising deliveries of its bread and cakes " to every area in the South-east of Scotland."

The modern bakery is of course mechanised throughout from the weighing of the flour to the wrapping of the loaves. Thus most of them have travelling ovens fuelled by gas. Apart from travelling ovens the Edinburgh bakeries have introduced many other innovations in recent years, such as thermostatically controlled ovens, photo-cells to give warning of breakdowns, electric detectors of foreign bodies, silicone-treated tins (to eliminate greasing at each use), humidity control, steam tray-washing machines and experiments in refrigeration to keep both dough and finished goods.

Mechanisation up to a certain point has led to an increased proportion of unskilled labour, much of it female labour for finishing and packing, but with further development the packing, too, is mechanised. All the actual baking is still carried out by men. Fermentation and the preparation of dough are regarded as critical operations and the five-year apprenticeship is strictly maintained.

By 1963 almost 2,200 people were employed in the city bakeries, and of these almost 1,500 were men.

COCOA AND SUGAR CONFECTIONERY

This industry developed as a branch of the baking industry and until quite recently the larger bakeries still employed a sugar-boiler. There are almost a score of factories making cocoa and sugar confectionery in Edinburgh, but in the early '60s only five were employing 50 or more. Among these, however, is W. and M. Duncan Limited which, with some 1,500 employees of whom two-thirds are female, is one of the largest factories in the city. The other four range from 50 to 135 employees. Duncan's, who began as a family shop in the High Street, later moved to Canonmills (1900), and now as a subsidiary of the Rowntree group, specialises in chocolates. Chocolate for export goes to Liverpool or Glasgow by rail, and this amounts to anything between 10 and 20 tons a week in winter.

The other firms concentrate on boiled sweets and Edinburgh rock. In this branch Ferguson, established for more than 130 years, is the oldest firm. Mackay Brothers started in a former stables at Fountainbridge more than 50 years ago and make toffee bars and caramels as well as boilings. A newer company, John Millar Limited also make boiled sweets, chocolates and cakes in Causewayside, while James Ross the confectioners are now manufacturing considerable amounts of rock in addition to other boiled sweets and exporting it to many countries overseas.

It is worthy of note that glucose and sugar from either of the two Greenock refineries or imported through Glasgow or Liverpool account for 80–95 per cent of the finished sweets made by these firms. Cocoa beans are imported directly to Leith. When the whole process of manufacture is completed the latest wrapping machines wrap more than 2,000 sweets a minute.

The manufacture of confectionery in the city gave employment in 1962–3 to some 2,600 people of whom almost 1,800 were women.

BISCUITS AND SHORTBREAD

Biscuit production in Edinburgh is considerable. At the time of the 1951 Census 2,700 persons were employed in the industry, but within five years this figure had risen to 3,700, and was still over 3,000 in 1962–3. This figure alone is significant, for during the five years, between the 1951 Census and 1956, while the numbers engaged in bread and flour confectionery were decreasing, those making biscuits increased so fast that biscuit-making reached second place, next to brewing and malting, among the city industries producing food or drink.

This was not altogether unexpected, for already there had been a notable expansion of the industry in Edinburgh between the wars—for several reasons apart from fame and quality. Biscuit manufacture is an industry which, if based on the larger centres, has the initial advantage of a good local market from which, since the product has a relatively high value and good conservability in comparison with other branches of baking, it can readily expand in the national market. It also benefits from a ready supply of labour, especially female labour, in the larger centres. In Edinburgh 70 per cent of the labour force in the early '60s was female.

The older firms in Edinburgh include McVitie and Price, who employed about 550 workers in 1964, and William Crawford and Sons Limited with some 700. Both belong to the United Biscuits group. The largest of the more recently established firms is the Weston Biscuit Company, a firm originating in Toronto and allied to large bread-baking interests through Allied Bakeries Limited. Its original factory was in Slateford but since 1958 a new factory, Burtons Gold Medal Biscuits Limited, has been sited on the Sighthill Industrial Estate.

Much of the attraction to these incoming firms into Edinburgh has been the city's already high reputation in the field of biscuit production. But also they have been attracted by the pool of skilled labour already in existence, for this has greatly helped them to set up and begin production speedily. Additional expansion has also been brought about by an increase in the variety of biscuits now being baked. Nor has Edinburgh lost its reputation for excellent shortbread which comes in large quantities from a number of biscuit manufacturers, notably McVitie and Price, MacVittie Guest, and Martins Limited, all producing varieties of shortbread, many packed in colourful tins depicting Scottish scenes, which are achieving a considerable success in overseas markets.

GRAIN-MILLING

Employment in grain-milling through the '50s was little more than 1,000, of whom about 85 per cent were males. Conceivably this figure might have been larger, but the increasing scale of the industry's operations has been counterbalanced by a high degree of mechanisation. The milling industry, once aligned on the Water of Leith is now located either in the older part of Leith or, like the most recently built mill, actually on the quayside; which is natural enough since Edinburgh mills rely increasingly on imported grain. For bread flour the necessary hard wheats come mostly from Canada but also from Australia and a number of other sources. With most of the flour consisting of blends of imported wheats with some home-grown, the flow of supplies has long been channelled through such ports as Leith, since it is in these ports that maximum economies in handling can be attained.

In Edinburgh two concerns—the Scottish Co-operative Wholesale Society and Joseph Rank Limited—handle three-quarters of the grain imported to Leith. The S.C.W.S. has two mills in Edinburgh, both in the port. One is Chancelot Mill, which had an output in the late '50s and early '60s of some 7,750 sacks a week (the sack flour contains 280 lb.) and employed 160 workers. The other was Junction Mill, which with some 140 workers was using wheat, oats and barley and still specialises in the production of self-raising flour for home baking, for which home-grown wheat is used when possible. This mill also produces porridge oats, oatmeal and barley meal, and markets its oat products in England as well as in the East of Scotland.

Rank's Caledonian Mills, with their own deepwater quays in Leith's Western Harbour have a weekly production of some 7,200 sacks and a labour-force of 200. In addition Rank's Edinburgh Mills market all over Scotland, mostly by road.

Other firms in Edinburgh include A. and R. Scott Limited of Colinton, a subsidiary of Cerebos Limited with 190 workers, who mill oats for "porage oats"; John Inglis and Sons Limited of Midlothian Oatmeal Mills, Leith (a Scott subsidiary which specialises now in fortified pig and poultry foods); and McGregor and Company of Quayside Mills, Leith, who mill rice and flake maize.

MISCELLANEOUS PRODUCTS

These are legion. There are Thomas Symington's coffee and Melrose's tea which is exported to many overseas countries. There is even an Edinburgh Castle tea for which Matheson, McLaren are known. A number of substantial companies supply ice to a variety of industries; others make ice cream. There is the manufacture of sauce, pickle, ketchup, cooking fat and yeast. Sausage, haggis and potato crisps are made along with salt manufacture and the brewing of vinegar. And there is also another form of human intake for which the city has long been famous. This is pharmacy.

PHARMACEUTICALS

As might be expected in a city with a famous medical tradition, Edinburgh has a variety of firms manufacturing medicines and medical appliances—from herbal remedies to surgical sutures. Gregory's Mixture is a well-known old remedy of Edinburgh origin, and the grave of its originator is easy to find in Canongate Churchyard. Dr. Anderson's Pills were made in the Lawnmarket from the time of Charles I, and the country folk of Scotland swore by them. The Physic Garden, at the East End of the North Loch basin, was, besides being a promenade for beaux, a garden of plants thought to have medicinal value.

The modern pharmaceutical industry of Edinburgh has its roots back in the early 18th century, when J. F. Macfarlan set up plant in Abbeyhill. Much later—in 1876—Duncan, Flockhart and Company established works in what is now Holyrood Road. Dr. Thomas Smith and Henry Smith also began bulk production in Canonmills near the doctor's home at Heriothill House. More recently Edinburgh's story as a centre of pharmaceutical chemical manufacture has been mainly of the amalgamation of these old firms—T. and H. Smith Limited, J. F. Macfarlan, and Duncan, Flockhart and Company—with Smith's establishing a big export business in bulk fine chemicals, Macfarlan's specialising in fine chemicals—ether, chloroform and surgical sutures—and Duncan, Flockhart and Company also becoming important in the manufacture of ether, chloroform and other indispensable aids to surgery and medical treatment.

From 1930 onwards there were far-reaching developments in the industry. Smith's established their modern research department, and by a series of mergers built up a formidable chemical and pharmacological manufacturing and distributive and dispensing group. Duncan, Flockhart became a subsidiary of Smith's in 1952, and were followed by other companies. Macfarlan's became associated in a new company—Macfarlan Smith Limited—formed in 1960 to handle the sale of the bulk product of both companies throughout the world, with overseas companies in Canada, Australia and New Zealand. In 1959 the group extended its interests in ethical pharmaceutical products by a new association with Allied Laboratories Limited of London, and in 1962 when T. and H. Smith Limited became purely wholesale chemists, the functions of the group's parent company were taken over by Edinburgh Pharmaceutical Industries Limited, which is now responsible for all research and development commercial and technical. All the manufacturing of Edinburgh Pharmaceutical Industries (now part of Glaxo-Laboratories Limited) is carried out in Edinburgh by some 320 workers among whom males predominate.

Ethicon Limited, successors in Edinburgh to T. F. Merson's business, begun in 1915 in the Pleasance, have two factories in the city—one in Fountainbridge, the other on the Sighthill Industrial Estate where they make surgical catgut, ligatures and sutures, surgical soaps and disposable examination gloves. The firm as at present constituted—it is American-owned—has been in the city since 1947, and in 1963 it employed more than 460 people with a high percentage of women (75 per cent). More recently a cobalt plant has been installed to provide greater scope and efficiency in sterilisation. It is the first plant of its kind in the world.

RUBBER

The development of the rubber industry in Edinburgh followed a general pattern. First there was the production of rubber footwear. Then came waterproofed garments, mechanical goods for the general consumer and for industry, and, with increasing predominance, tyres for bicycles and automobiles. Synthetics are a recent addition.

The origins of this industry in Scotland go far back in the 19th century, as Dr. Robertson of the University pointed out earlier. But more can be added to what is a very interesting story. The start came when Charles Macintosh discovered the use of purified naphtha as a solvent for raw rubber and duly set up a factory near Glasgow for waterproofing textiles. The next development occurred in 1839 when Charles Goodyear, at the suggestion of Nathaniel Hayward in Massachusetts, used sulphur to produce rubber of an enduring hardness. This " vulcanised " rubber at once opened up new possibilities, far beyond the production of footwear superior to the crude rubber shoes then imported into the United States from Brazil. In Britain the vulcanisation process was rediscovered by Thomas Hancock of Charles Macintosh and Company, Manchester, in 1843.

Here the story, which soon concerned Edinburgh, took an unusual turn. Hancock applied for his vulcanisation patent in England on 21st November, 1843, Goodyear on 30th January, 1844. And as it happened these applications were a significant factor in the establishment of the rubber industry in Scotland. Until 1852 separate patents of this kind were necessary for England, Scotland and Ireland. But Goodyear applied for a patent in Scotland on 12th March, 1844 and it was not until 25th June, 1844 that Hancock followed suit. There seems to have been little activity after this till J. R. Ford and Company, a New Brunswick firm using the Goodyear patent, which had failed to find suitable premises in Glasgow, discovered in autumn 1855 that a recently-built factory—the former Castle Silk Mills—was available in Edinburgh.

The advantages of this ready-made site and mill were obvious from the beginning. The factory enjoyed not only good accessibility by rail with the rest of the country but a canal connection as well with the port of Glasgow. Coal was readily available from the Midlothian pits along with water from the Union Canal, and cloth and chemicals from the North of England. The factory moreover was already producing rubber boots and shoes when in 1856 it acquired from Goodyear the sole right to manufacture " improved rubber " products in Scotland, and so became responsible for what may have been the first direct investment of United States capital in British manufacturing industry. A year later the Company, its head was Henry Lee Norris, was registered as the North British Rubber Company Limited, and in the ensuing period of prosperity American techniques were proved successful under relatively low-cost British conditions, though control of the company passed into British hands in the late 1860s.

Earlier the success of North British Rubber had led to the foundation—in 1861—of the Scottish Vulcanite Company on an adjacent site for the manufacture of hard rubber articles. A few years later William Currie and Company opened a factory for waterproofed garments, and in 1877 the Victoria India Rubber Mills were opened in Leith Walk for proofing and, after 1900, rubber boots and shoes.

Coming to our time the numbers employed in Edinburgh's rubber industry rose to a peak in 1951, though external and internal changes in the following years led to a sharp decline. Competition in this industry is severe, and apart from the Victoria India Rubber Company the other Edinburgh firms were either liquidated or absorbed by North British Rubber.

Today Castle Mills are engaged in two main branches—tyres and " general mechanicals," which include industrial products such as hose, conveyor and transmission belting and general products such as sheeting, clothing and hot-water bottles. All these are produced by new techniques which in turn have meant a personnel reduction from the high figures at the 1951 Census. Then, with 4,404 employees, of whom 75 per cent were in North British Rubber, the industry was the largest industrial employer in the city. By 1963 there were 1,355 on hourly rates (including 200 females) at Castle Mills and 430 monthly salaried staff (including 112 females); and these were engaged in an output which has become very diversified in recent years. They now make, for example, a " floating oil terminal " consisting of submergible and floating hoses, anchored to buoys, through which tankers can discharge into a series of pipes six miles off shore.

The market for tyres consists of original equipment for automobile factories in the Midlands and South of England; and domestic replacements and mileage accounts which mean the supply and maintenance for large concerns such as bus companies at a fixed rate per tyre mile.

North British has the only reclaimed rubber department in Scotland and is one of three in Britain. Supplies of worn tyres from tyre dealers, the main source of scrap rubber, were over 130 tons a week at the time of writing, while output was 100 tons of reclaim a week.

As for distribution costs these have been greatly reduced by the consolidation with Dominion Rubber Company Limited (a subsidiary of United States Rubber) in 1953. United States Rubber Company Limited owned 49 per cent of the shares in North British in 1947, when North British became its licensee and obtained technical and financial aid for the programme of modernisation at Castle Mills. In 1958 United States Rubber's holding had risen to 74 per cent, and so the company has returned to the American control with which it began, but with a new name—Uniroyal.

STATIONERY AND CARTONS

These two branches of the paper-fabricating industry in Edinburgh have considerable importance. In the late 1950s employment in both branches was about equal, with just over 1,300 in each, but these figures represent industries in very different stages of development, the much older stationery manufacture maintaining its position under rapidly changing conditions and the young carton industry in such a highly dynamic stage of growth that in the early '60s its employees had risen to almost 1,600.

THE EARLY DAYS

Much of this growth is attributable to the fact that the governmental, legal, ecclesiastical and eventually educational status of Edinburgh made it a market for the early stationers who also enjoyed a close relationship with the manufacture of paper in the valleys of the Water of Leith and the River Esk, dating as far back as 1591 when Mungo Russel was known to be producing paper at Dalry. Today the Midlothian paper mills—with a much wider market than Edinburgh itself-import large amounts of esparto and wood pulp through Leith and Granton for stationery and carton-making.

The oldest surviving Edinburgh firm of stationers, Waterson, established in 1752, was first located in the Lawnmarket. Today there is only one other survivor of the 18th century, Macniven and Cameron, a firm founded in 1770 which was later to become famous for steel pens. Several of the existing firms were founded a century later than these two, between 1858 and 1870.

The outflow from Edinburgh of stationery manufacturers in the late '50s and early '60s makes an interesting study, the more especially as quite a lot of firms were involved in supplying not only Scottish but English and overseas markets as well. These firms included Harvey's, Inveresk Envelope Company, Banks and Company, Macniven and Cameron, George Stewart, the Simpson Label Company, Gall and Inglis, Waddie and Company, George Waterson and Company, Andrew Whyte and Company, McKinnon and Hay, and Moore's Modern Methods.

INCREASED EFFICIENCY

In recent years there has been a great increase in mechanisation, integration and specialisation; and wages which account for some 30 per cent of production costs have increased too. The labour force is relatively stable, not only in numbers but in terms of actual personnel. While Edinburgh benefits from a tradition of skill in the printing and allied trades, there is little of the mobility that is found in London, where the wide choice of jobs makes labour relatively footloose; and the shortage of skilled labour, especially of printers, for whom a 5–6 year apprenticeship is required, is an incentive to mechanisation. In the late '50s and early '60s the proportion of female labour in the stationery industry has been between 65 and 70 per cent. Women and girls are mainly employed in the finishing, handstitching and calendar departments.

The commonest size of firm is in the range of 60–120 employees, with an average of about 90. But there are two smaller firms in the 20–40 range and four larger ones with about 150 or over. The largest, Waterson, has some 270 at the time of writing, but of these only 175 were on the works floor because the firm has continued the tradition of retailing as well as manufacturing.

A number of old family businesses have survived in Edinburgh mainly because they had accumulated enough capital, especially in the 19th century, to withstand the shock of wars and depressions. This reserve of capital has enabled family firms to secure loans in order to extend or modernise their businesses without having to become public companies. But some, when faced with increasing competition from larger English concerns have themselves found the solution to the problem by becoming integrated in a large public company.

The Inveresk Group, which has its headquarters in Edinburgh, includes the largest Edinburgh stationery firm in terms of factory workers, namely the Inveresk Envelope Company (Andrew Levy). It also controls most of the esparto mills. Harvey's have combined with Draeburn and with Ludgate and Company Limited, in close relationship with the firm of Banks. All are specialists; for specialisation, whether inside or outside a combine is obviously necessary in present-day conditions. Thus Simpson's now specialise in labels. Macniven and Cameron developed, at a factory in Birmingham, Duncan Cameron's invention of the turned-up steel pen, which soon replaced the rather hard sharp nibs till then in use. While the steel pen had eventually to face the competition of the fountain pen in the West, it had new worlds to conquer as literacy advanced in other parts of the world and since 1900 the firm has enjoyed an expanding trade in India and the Middle East. An earlier and classical example of enterprise in seizing new opportunities is the transition of Waterson's from the making of flambeaux to guide the bearers of sedan chairs through the streets and closes of old Edinburgh to the preparation of sealing-wax to secure the growing number of letters in the highly literate Athens of the North as well as to seal the many documents produced by its flourishing legal profession. Nor was it surprising that with the arrival of the vogue for printed stationery in the 19th century several Edinburgh stationers expanded their printing sections. Waterston's, for instance, added another highly specialised section in 1838 with the printing of banknotes including, since 1885, those of the Bank of Scotland.

CARTONS AND PACKAGING

The carton industry is a relatively recent one and became a separate and specialised branch of paper fabrication more recently still. The oldest firm in Edinburgh, Thyne's, was founded in 1870, when William Thyne set up a handmade paper-bag business at Loanhead. Later he moved to Edinburgh, and quickly widened his business to include wrapping-paper, string and lithoed labels, as well as stationery and jobbing printing. He then became interested in cartons, and in 1908 the Lochend Works were established. These were extended five years later and supplemented with another factory at Abbeyhill. The Thyne family were also owners of Scott's Porage Oats, now a part of the Cerebos organisation, and the cartons were originally developed for this product. By 1920 they had in fact become the dominant product, and in 1939 a branch factory was established in Essex to meet the demand in the South. In 1957 a second and much larger Edinburgh factory was opened at Sighthill.

Other makers include Annan's, which although established in 1875, did not enter the carton business until 1937; Hugh Stevenson, a Manchester firm, which opened a factory in 1909 and was by 1913 said to be making cartons for " virtually every shop in Princes Street "; The Reid Paper Box Company, founded in 1918, which also specialised in cartons, starting with the supply to a large chocolate firm in the same part of Edinburgh; Reeds Corrugated Cases, originally Thomson and Norris Manufacturing Company Limited, a London firm which opened its Edinburgh factory in 1934; Cardboard Converters (1949); and E. J. Smith (1955). Smith and Ritchie do a considerable amount of packaging.

The packaging trade is divided into rigid boxes and collapsible boxes, that is, cartons, and is comparable in size with the stationery industry. Indeed, eight of the 50–60 British carton manufacturers are located in Edinburgh, which is not surprising since the city is important as a distributing centre for a number of industries such as chocolate and sugar confectionery, porage oats and whisky for which cartons rather than rigid boxes are suitable packaging.

EDINBURGH WOOLLENS

Woollen manufacture, another traditional city industry, has in recent years made an important contribution to the nation's drive for exports with its women's clothing, men's tweeds and other garments. One noteworthy firm is The Munrospun Organisation, a large company with varied interests which specialises in high quality scarves, ties and socks, jerseys, pullovers and other articles. These products are widely sold overseas. Glengair Limited, a more recent firm, concentrates on the American market. Raymond Hodgson and Company Limited, manufacturing under the trade name of St. Trid's, has recently branched out from the home market and is also endeavouring to promote its products abroad. William Anderson and Company and Glenavon Woollens Limited, both producers of high quality knitwear and Highland articles as well as tartan, sell their products in both North America and Europe, especially in the Common Market countries. C. R. McRitchie, and George Harrison and Company Limited are both woollen merchants, the former supplying piece goods, lengths of high quality tweed, vicuna, worsteds etc., and the latter, well over 100 years old, supplying woollen goods and tweeds.

The woollen industry, although a prominent part in Edinburgh's economy, is not comparable in size with the Border industry. But it is thriving and employs a considerable number of people in the making of woollen garments and hosiery. The labour is largely female; and in 1962 the numbers employed came to well over 1,100. Recent developments in the industry have shown a greater realisation of the need for variety of production; which is why a number of companies have produced matching sets of ties and socks, scarves, pullovers, twinsets, and jerseys with new styles which cater more directly than before for the taste of the young. As there is also considerable concentration on improved marketing methods, the export and sales departments generally are very active.

It would be tempting here to look at many others of the lighter industries—at the firms which make bakery utensils, for instance, spades, insecticides, tin boxes, umbrellas, weighing machines, window blinds, asphalt, office equipment and lead. But this is impossible for reasons of space. We should not however end this survey without a glance at the part played in the furtherance of the city's trade and industry by the Edinburgh and Leith Chambers of Commerce and the Scottish Council (Development and Industry).

THE EDINBURGH AND LEITH CHAMBERS OF COMMERCE

The Edinburgh Chamber of Commerce, founded in 1785, is the second oldest Chamber of Commerce in Scotland, Glasgow having stolen the first march two years earlier on New Year's Day, 1783. By Christmas Day, 1964 the membership had risen to 1,550.

In the United Kingdom, where Chamber of Commerce membership is voluntary—in some countries it is compulsory—each Chamber is autonomous, levying its own subscriptions and paying its own expenses. Most of them also affiliate to the Association of British Chambers of Commerce, the Federation of Chambers of Commerce of the Commonwealth, the International Chamber of Commerce, and in Scotland (where there are 16 bodies of the kind) the Council of Scottish Chambers of Commerce.

Edinburgh and Leith have two Chambers—the Edinburgh Chamber of Commerce and Manufactures and the Leith Chamber of Commerce. There has been, however, a recent plebiscite on the question of union among the members of the Leith Chamber of Commerce, and a subsequent discussion (May, 1964) as to whether they should amalgamate with their older brother in Edinburgh's Charlotte Square. The Leith members numbered 457. Each was invited to give his view; but only 261 did so, and of these 181 were against amalgamation. The Leith Dock Commissioners on the other hand were in favour, and it may be that the issue will be revived. Before it is, let us take a brief look at the past.

Two weeks before Christmas Day, 1785, a number of leading Edinburgh business gentlemen met to consider a proposal that they should form themselves into some organisation for discussing and deciding business problems. The proposal—with a banker called David Steuart as the prime mover—was well received, and 10 days later the first meeting of what is now the Edinburgh Chamber of Commerce was held.

David Steuart's words at this opening meeting still ring convincingly:

> If ever there was a time when attention to trade and manufactures was necessary it is the present—at the end of an expensive War (the War of American Independence) with an enormous load of national debt, heavy taxes upon every article of life or convenience and the treaties of commerce with Ireland, France and America unsettled.

On 15th February, 1786, David Steuart moved a resolution that an immediate application should be made for a Royal Charter. The first application suggested that the title of the new body should be the Chamber of Commerce and Manufactures for Scotland. But this was not permitted: the phrase " at Edinburgh " was substituted; and this became the name of the organisation until 1952, when the Chamber's First Supplementary Charter authorised the use of The Edinburgh Chamber of Commerce and Manufactures as the name which had been in common use. To return to 1786, the first list of members includes printers, merchants, soap boilers, bankers and a number of other traders; and since then the dignity of the Chamber has been worthily upheld by the large number of distinguished business men attracted to its service.

As communications are the life-blood of trade, one of the first matters to which the youthful Chamber gave attention was the need for improving the light on May Island in the Firth of Forth. A Committee was formed to look into this and the following report was put before the members:

> There was only ONE man to take charge of the light. He had a family consisting of a wife and six children. Though he had a salary of £7 and 8 bolls he was obliged to go out and fish for the maintenance of his family, and if a storm happened he was obliged to take to the coast of Fife and in that case there was no person to take suitable charge in the island for weeks.

Concern about the May lighthouse[1] reflects the importance of Leith's prosperity to this part of Scotland; and in view of recent Government approval for a large scale improvement of Leith Docks it is noteworthy that as long ago as 1787 members of the Edinburgh Chamber were instructed to support any proper bill in Parliament designed to enlarge and improve the port.

Quick and efficient delivery of letters and parcels has been the subject of much Chamber discussion through the years. Indeed as early as 1790, postal matters were considered at some length, and it may have been the Edinburgh Chamber of Commerce which first advised the Postmaster-General to put the day and month of posting on all postmarks.

As many bankers took a prominent part in the establishment of the Chamber there are naturally a number of references to banking matters in these early records. In 1826, for instance, the Chamber expressed its great dismay at a Governmental decision to suppress the issue of small notes. It is probably true to say that at that time English currency was suffering from the over-issue of small banknotes. But Scotland stood in different case, and the following indignant protest was sent to Parliament:

> The only real security was the confidence of the people in the banking establishments and it proved that in spite of all that had taken place in England the people of Scotland had always maintained an unwavering faith in the systems of banking that had taken place in their country.

[1] Scotland's lighthouses are under the control of the Commissioners of Northern Lighthouses. Constituted in 1786 the Commissioners' headquarters are in Edinburgh.

Another of the Chamber of Commerce's activities comes as a pleasant shock to many people, both visitors and natives. It strikes them at one o'clock each day. In 1854 the time ball on Calton Hill commenced its famous one o'clock drop, to enable visual aid to be given to sea-faring vessels anxious to have an accurate standard for the setting of chronometers. In 1858 the directors of the Chamber recommended the firing of a gun from the Castle at one o'clock as a complementary audible signal to the Time Ball on Calton Hill, controlled by the Royal Observatory. Lengthy negotiations with various authorities followed, as a result of which the Treasury in 1861 agreed to supply the galvanic apparatus if the City would provide the wire and cannon.

When the Leith Chamber of Commerce was formed in 1840 the step was seen to follow logically on the decline and demise of the old Leith Merchant Company. This was a local body of traders primarily united for the furtherance of business interests within the port and concerned with the welfare of its members and of their dependents when the need arose.

Most probably, the Leith business men, being actuated by a natural desire to fill the vacuum created by the failure of the old Company, turned their thoughts to the formation of a more efficient type of association and chose to found a Chamber of Commerce on the lines already yielding happy results in Glasgow, Edinburgh and elsewhere. Twelve years passed, however, before the desirability of applying for incorporation was agreed and a formal petition submitted to the proper quarter. The Charter was then granted—on 2nd February, 1852—and ever since the Chamber has been consistently fortunate in having a pool of competent and devoted members.

Retracing our steps again, in 1785 it was naturally the Guilds and Merchant Companies who ruled supreme, for the business community had the firm idea that they could not prosper unless their business enterprises were supported by exclusive rights in dealing. The sale of Indian damasks and taffetas was opposed, for example, by the Merchants Company as something " destructive ", while in England people were urged to " buy woollen if you have any bowels for your country." Fortunately, when a fresh breeze was let in on business methods with the formation of such bodies as the Edinburgh and Leith Chambers of Commerce, some of the old hole and corner methods of doing business gave way to freer and wider conditions including the growth of many hundreds of Trade Associations, for whom Chambers of Commerce provide secretarial services and even house-room. Today there are a score of such Associations with offices at the Edinburgh Chamber.

Another vital concern of the Edinburgh Chamber today was first defined in the remarks of William Creech, first Secretary of the Edinburgh Chamber in the 18th century, that the Chamber had a duty " to assist the views of Parliament in so far as they may be beneficial to the country " and " to point out mistakes or partial measures that might be harmful." Creech's enjoinder is dutifully followed to this day by the Parliamentary Bills Consultative Panel whose expert views on the various Bills being considered in Parliament are regularly sent to the Association of British

Chambers of Commerce in London, where the submissions of all Chambers throughout the United Kingdom are duly collated and representations made to the appropriate Government Department.

One special subject on which the views of Chambers is sought by the Government is the Budget, and considered proposals are regularly submitted to the Chancellor, though sometimes the proposals fall on rather deaf ears. None the less it is in such ways as this that Chambers of Commerce can exert some influence on the nation's industry and commerce.

Ostensibly a Chamber of Commerce exists to provide services for its members, but in practice its doors are wide open for inquiries from all and sundry. Each month hundreds of letters are received from the United Kingdom, from the Commonwealth and from all parts of the world. Here the Statistical and Information Department has a vital role, for every day questions are received about overseas markets, sources of supplies of raw materials, the local labour situation, import and export regulations, the appointment of agents, quality control and the development of new techniques.

To complete this record we might happily note that the Edinburgh Chamber's present premises in Charlotte Square were bought in 1920, and that on 16th August, 1952 there was a splendid occasion when H.R.H. Prince Philip, Duke of Edinburgh became the first honorary member of the Chamber under the supplementary Royal Charter granted by King George VI in 1951.

THE SCOTTISH COUNCIL (DEVELOPMENT AND INDUSTRY)

In 1930, during an industrial recession when every fourth worker in Scotland was unemployed, it was suggested that a number of bodies be brought together to fight the depression. As the result of this the Scottish Development Council was formed so that chambers of commerce, local authorities and banks might come together to try and solve Scotland's economic stagnation. With very limited resources, the Development Council laid the foundations for work which the present body continues.

In 1942, the Secretary of State for Scotland created the Scottish Council on Industry to advise how to bring more defence production to Scotland. The Council was composed of the same bodies as the Development Council with the addition of the Scottish Trades Union Congress. But in 1946 the Scottish Development Council and the Scottish Council on Industry were merged to form the Scottish Council (Development and Industry). Thus, the present body has retained and developed the objectives of its two predecessors. The first objective is to work out and apply new ways of expanding Scottish production and trade; the second, to offer advice to the Secretary of State for Scotland on changes or additions to Government policy and activities needed to support Scottish industrial development.

The Council's general membership includes some 4,000 companies (many of them Edinburgh-based), the nationalised industries, and many other bodies and private individuals. Because of the breadth of its representation, and also because of its political independence, the Council can speak and act with a unique authority on issues of industry and economics affecting Scotland.

As the Council's income is subscribed voluntarily by its members, it is able to speak and act independently. Companies and local authorities are the main contributors, but membership, including private individuals, is open to all who have the interests of Scotland at heart. The Council, a company limited by guarantee without a share capital, has a staff of more than 20 executives in its three offices in Edinburgh, Glasgow and London; and these have specialist and professional knowledge in technology, commerce, economics, and publicity and exhibition work.

The Executive Committee, which decides general policy, is advised by some 30 specialist committees. Most of these operate in Scotland, but there are also active committees in London, the United States and other countries; and these committees are one of the Council's most important assets. They fulfil a two-way function: they project Scottish resources, facilities and achievements in their areas, and they illustrate their own conditions and the business opportunities which Scotland can provide.

Though most of the Council's day-to-day work is in the form of advice and help given to thousands of Scottish companies and bodies every year, major projects and policies are always being shaped. Among recent key developments in which the Council's work has played an essential part are the establishment of a new steel strip mill in Scotland, which, in its turn, has brought the motor vehicle industry to Scotland; the establishment of a new pulp and paper mill in the Highlands; the introduction by the Government of new and clearly defined grants for plant and building; special depreciation allowances to aid industrial growth in Development Districts; and the Government White Paper on Central Scotland based on new technique principles strongly advocated by the Council.

CHAPTER 28

THE DISTRIBUTIVE TRADES

SHOPS

EDINBURGH shopping centres in the early and middle '60s tell a remarkable story of social change, of rising affluence and altered values. Cheek by jowl with supermarkets and self-service stores, there are shops built 15 years ago, restaurants built 30 years ago, and in less modern shopping centres, buildings whose outward appearance has barely changed since the turn of the century.

There are in Edinburgh some 7,000[1] shops. Nearly half of these are food retailers and some 800 shops which come under the heading " Confectioner, Tobacconist and Newsagent." So it seems therefore clear that we now eat more sweets, smoke more tobacco and read more newspapers than did our forefathers, though in recent years the number of confectioners in Edinburgh has decreased. The number of licensed premises—866 in 1961—shows little change, however, from 20 to 30 years ago, despite an increase in the city's population.

CLASSIFICATION OF SHOPS

There are four classifications of retail shops in the city: (1) individual retail shops, handling one or more lines of business (this comprises about half of the total retail turnover); (2) large departmental stores with a number of departments selling different types of goods; (3) multiple shops or chain stores which handle a considerable range of merchandise; (4) co-operative societies. Furthermore, there are a number of street traders and markets of various kinds, but the amount of business they do is very small in comparison with the total retail trade of the city. In recent years there has been a new development, where a trader instead of having fixed premises for his retail business and sending out delivery vans, conducts his business from a travelling shop.

RETAIL TRENDS

The indices of weekly sales published monthly by the Board of Trade show that sales of multiple retailers and retail co-operators rose by 73 per cent and 64 per cent respectively between 1950 and 1957. The corresponding advance by independent retailers amounted to 46 per cent and by general departmental stores to 27 per cent. Between 1956 and 1957 there was a 5 per cent increase in all retail sales, which is slightly under the

[1] The 1950 Census of Distribution and other services gave a detailed and still broadly accurate account of the city's retail establishments.

average annual rate of expansion since 1950. The growth in the value of retail sales was most marked in food shops (partly reflecting the higher than average rise in food prices) and in shops selling radio and electrical goods.

By 1959, total retail sales had advanced 7 per cent over the 1957 level. Within this total, the multiple retailers continued to advance much more rapidly than the other retailers, their 1959 sales being 15 per cent greater than in 1957, compared with increases of 9 per cent for department stores, 4 per cent for independent retailers and 4 per cent for co-operative societies. The rate of increase also varied commodity-wise, the durable goods sector (furniture, radio and television, household appliances and cycles) showing the largest advance, partly as a result of the lifting of hire purchase restrictions in October, 1958. In fact, in the year 1959 sales by durable goods shops were as much as 18 per cent greater than in 1957. Clothing and footwear shops' sales showed an increase of 4 per cent between 1957 and 1959, the whole of their increase occurring in 1959, while food shops' sales advanced by 6 per cent, spread evenly over the two years. A notable feature of 1959 was the stability of retail prices; and with these showing virtually no increase on 1958 almost the whole of the increase in the value of sales (4 per cent over 1958) was attributable to a greater volume of sales.

With growing affluence among wage earners the retail trade has continued to increase, considerably; and although the six months February to July, 1963 showed a falling off in trade largely attributable to concern over the economic position in Scotland, there was subsequently a steady upsurge in trade and the Christmas, 1965 business was at record levels.

It is of course a familiar experience in most branches of retail business to find that some months are busier than others, but less easy without first making some calculation to find in which months the peaks and valleys of activity have tended on the average to occur. An attempt to solve the problem was made by Edinburgh University economists, notably Mr. Ian Stewart, at the end of the '50s. By sampling methods—involving the co-operation of a good many firms willing to state the proportion of their annual turnover done in each month of the three years 1955–7—the economists were able to prepare estimates of month-to-month changes for all retailers taken together and compare these monthly figures for Edinburgh with official figures for retail turnover, provided by the Board of Trade for the whole of Great Britain. The detailed result of this investigation is shown in Appendix VIII.

In general the calculation showed that Edinburgh retailers have tended as a whole to experience a seasonal " swing " from nearly 20 per cent below an average month's sales in January or February to around 30 per cent above an average month's turnover in December. The experiences of particular kinds of business and of individual firms may, of course, differ from this general pattern. Booksellers and licensed grocers, for example, probably have seasonal changes of greater amplitude. Clothing firms on the other hand have normally less severe seasonal fluctuations.

The comparison between the Edinburgh figures and those for the whole country seems to reveal a number of interesting features. First, there appears to a be slightly greater variability in the Edinburgh series than for the whole country, although it would be unwise to place much weight on this point. What is more significant is the tendency, in each of the three years surveyed, for the Edinburgh figures to be below the national figures in the winter and spring months and to be well above the latter in the summer and early autumn. But once again, caution is necessary in interpreting any of the comparisons for individual months, as there may be differential effects as between English and Edinburgh monthly turnover resulting from different bank and trade holidays. For example the national percentage for August may be lower than the Edinburgh figure because of the August Bank Holiday in the South, which could equally cause the July proportion for Britain to be higher than it would otherwise be. The same could apply to holidays associated with Easter, the New Year and Christmas. One way to avoid pitfalls such as these is to compare seasons, or period of months, rather than single months.

This is done, to sum up the results, in Appendix VII Table 2, which indicates the seasonal, i.e. quarterly differences between the Edinburgh and the national estimates, averaged over the three years 1955–7. The general impression remains, as one might reasonably expect, of a peak in the third or summer quarter, balanced by a trough in the winter and spring.

SELF-SERVICE

The development of self-service in retail establishments during the last 10 years or so has probably helped the multiple stores and the retail co-operative to achieve a higher rate of expansion sales. In fact, the supermarket, with its aisles of merchandise and frozen food cabinets, is one of the most potent symbols of a changing society. Nevertheless, self-service stores have developed slowly, for the Edinburgh housewife is suspicious of innovation. The first suburban self-service store was opened in 1955, and, though it has prospered since, it did little business during its first six months, and shoppers continued to queue stolidly at the slow but orthodox grocer's shop across the street. Since then self-service stores have multiplied. Housewives appreciate their convenience and their hygiene, since goods in packages are easily picked up, and are safe from dubious fingers.

Edinburgh's first American-style supermarket was opened by St. Cuthbert's Co-operative Association as part of a wide project of modernisation to celebrate their centenary year. But even here, amid the tins, the packets, the modern display, tradition had not entirely vanished: above the butcher meats a sign, bravely picked out in neon lights, announced " FLESHING."

St. Cuthbert's Co-operative Association Limited by 1962 had 47 self-service shops for groceries and provisions throughout the city, and in 1964 opened a large reconstructed shopping centre near the Old College. Multiple stores of the self-service varietv in Edinburgh are Messrs. F. W.

Woolworth and Company Limited, with a large store in Princes Street and branches at Lothian Road, Leith and Portobello, Marks and Spencer Limited, and Littlewood Limited, both with premises in Princes Street. (Incidentally, Woolworth's once famous slogan " Nothing over 6*d.*" is a modern casualty; and the title of a tailoring firm which sold men's suits for £2 10*s.* also succumbed to the post-war inflationary boom, when " The Fifty Shilling Tailors " became " F.S.T." and subsequently " John Collier "). Also, one enterprising firm has taken over an old cinema property in the High Street and is now using the premises as a supermarket for all types of merchandise.

RETAIL CO-OPERATIVE SOCIETIES

There are two large co-operative societies in Edinburgh—the St. Cuthbert's Co-operative Association Limited, (founded in 1859 with a capital of £30) and Leith Provident Co-operative Society Limited. The Portobello Co-operative Society Limited has premises only in the area of Edinburgh 15, as Portobello is now wont to be called. These are voluntary non-profit-making organisations engaged in the retail trade and controlled by the members who are also their customers. An operating surplus is returned periodically to members as a dividend—1*s.* 4*d.* in the £ in the 1963–4 trading year—and the amount distributed—just under £1 million by the St. Cuthbert's Co-op for the same period—is proportionate to the value of the member's purchases over the period. These Co-operative Societies also sell to the general public, but membership is open to anyone paying a small deposit. In addition, members may invest in their Society up to a limit of £500.

The retail societies are free to purchase where they wish or to produce their own goods, but in order to secure the advantages of large-scale production and distribution they have collectively established a wholesale society called The Scottish Co-operative Wholesale Society Limited. In a special survey carried out in 1950 it was estimated that some 10 per cent of all retail establishments in Scotland were owned by the retail co-operative societies and that the sales of the co-operatives were nearly 20 per cent of the total sales of all establishments.

CLOSING HOURS

The statutory closing hours of shops in the early '60s has been eight o'clock in the evening with nine o'clock in the evening on the late day (Saturday). The normal working hours in Edinburgh shops, however, are nine o'clock until five-thirty or six o'clock, with retailers in certain goods such as furnishings staying open late one night per week.

This, by the middle '60s, was raising other issues. In the course of an inquiry, conducted in a central area of the city with more than 1,100 retail premises, shopkeepers were asked to state their preference for a five, or five and a half or a six day trading week. But there were also the employees to consider. Their working weeks are at present a mixture of five and five and a half days, but an increasing number are now working only five days, and it looked by 1965 as if this number will increase if six day trading is permitted in the central area.

In order that shops may remain open until midnight on Christmas Day and Hogmanay, the magistrates usually grant suspension, under Section 43 (2) of the Shops Act 1950, of the general closing hours for all shops throughout the city, with the exception of licensed premises. Other requirements of the Shops Act 1950 deal with the arrangements for the health and comfort of shop workers. Such matters as ventilation, temperature, lighting, sanitary conveniences, washing facilities, meals and seats for female assistants are all regulated in detail. An Inspector appointed by a Public Health Authority may, for the purpose of his duties under the Act, enter and inspect a shop at any reasonable hour and make such inquiry as may be necessary to ascertain whether the law is being observed.

PEAK HOURS FOR SHOPPING

Saturday is the most popular shopping day. An inquiry carried out by the Edinburgh Junior Chamber of Commerce some years ago indicated that in the central area of Princes Street and the Bridges and Tollcross, as much as 40 per cent of the retail sales of the shops in that area are transacted on Saturday; and that has altered little since. The main shopping times seem to be between three and six o'clock on Saturday afternoon, and the reasons given were as follows:

(1) the influx of country and out-of-town shoppers;
(2) the prevalence of the five-day week in industry, which means that most workers have to concentrate their shopping on Saturday, coupled with the fact that Friday is still predominantly the pay-day for most weekly workers;
(3) the high percentage of married women who now work, leaving Saturday as the only free day for shopping.

HYGIENE

Whilst a great improvement has taken place in the hygienic arrangements for the distribution of food, there are still noticeable irregularities. Many premises are quite unsatisfactory for their purposes, especially shops with houses in direct communication. All the normal functions of life have to be carried on in these premises, which often consist of a one-apartment adjunct to the shop. There is also the problem of the small general shop, usually situated in back streets, where for lack of space everything is mixed together in a heterogeneous muddle. Other obvious irregularities in the distribution of food are open shop windows and doors, and the placing of packets, barrels and boxes of goods on floors and the pavement at shop doors, besides the sale of foodstuffs from barrows and stalls. Goods are often placed on counters in close proximity to customers and subject to their breathing and coughing. Exposure to infection is minimised in the better regulated shops by the provision of glass screen counters and show cases and the use of transparent paper coverings. There has also been a notable improvement in the ever-increasing usc of packets, cartons, bottles and tins; the wrapping of bread is more extensively used, and some vegetables are supplied in polythene bags. The sale of frozen foods and pre-packaged goods is also on the increase. But in general shops are not merely conforming to regulations under the constant surveillance of the health authorities, but are becoming more aware that it is always good business to provide food in the most attractive and hygienic manner.

WAYS TO PAY

For the benefit of future social historians we ought perhaps to note here the various ways in which customers pay for their purchases. Generally speaking, some form of consumer credit is now regarded as being part of normal trading, and a great many shoppers obtain their goods without tendering cash on the spot. There are various methods.

A lot of people still prefer to pay cash, and few shopkeepers refuse to accept cash for a purchase though a few operating on a " Club " arrangement are sometimes reluctant to make a cash sale if there is any possibility of persuading a customer to join the " Club." In such an arrangement the customer decides how much he or she can pay each month, and the shop allows a total credit of many times that amount. Then there is the charge account whereby purchases are payable on or before the end of a month. This method is common in large departmental stores. Hire purchase like the rest of consumer credit methods hardly needs explanation; but again—in case this method disappears in the centuries ahead—Edinburgh's social historian of 2500 A.D., may like to know that a shopper in the 1960s, through a small deposit, could secure delivery of the goods ordered and spread his payments over a period. By short-term credit, also, a purchaser can obtain goods (without deposit) and pay by instalments.

Another interesting form of credit—the pawnbroker's business—seems less prominent than it once was. One still sees the pawnbroker's sign, but in the age of the affluent society, the Welfare State and Hire Purchase, the number of licensed pawnbrokers' premises in the city has diminished considerably. In 1899 there were 53 pawnbrokers in Edinburgh. These had dwindled to 34 in 1949, and to only 12 in 1961. For probably the same reasons, the number of licensed moneylenders' offices has also declined.

STREET ASSOCIATIONS

There are six prominent Street Associations in existence in Edinburgh at present with a membership which seems to represent adequately commercial and retail interests in areas of the City. They are the George Street, West End, Royal Mile, Churchhill, Clerk Street and Princes Street

Associations. All are concerned to raise and maintain the standards of shops, offices and premises in their areas, to keep an eye on traffic conditions, and to promote Shopping Weeks and window shopping competitions. But naturally the old hands returning to the city after long absence or the new visitors wonder what has happened to some of the famous old shops in Princes Street? And indeed there have been many changes in this world-famous street in the post-war era, and the conservative Edinburgh citizen has been outspokenly critical of some of the new shop fronts and the names appearing above them.

Of the firms which were in Princes Street at the time of the second *Statistical Account* (1845) only Jenner and Company and J. W. Mackie and Sons are still carrying on business there.

The reason for the great post-war change in Princes Street was twofold. In the first place, many premises were rented, and when a succession of leases fell in after the war, businesses were faced with a notice to "buy or quit." Furthermore, many of the leases offered for renewal were at an exceedingly high rent. So the new mid-20th century picture gives the general impression that big business and capital have forced out of the Princes Street area the smaller traditional business.

Between 1947 and 1953 at least four old firms were taken over by financial concerns outside the city. John Cotton Limited, tobacconist well-known in Edinburgh since 1770 were bought in 1953 by John Duncan and Sons, an old-established Glasgow firm of retail tobacconists. Three old firms transferred to George Street. They are Alexander Lawrie and Company, mens' outfitters; Robert Grant and Sons Limited, booksellers; and Hamilton and Inches, jewellers and watchmakers. Princes Street's " wee shop " of Durie Brown, E. and J. Lennie (the oldest opticians and photographic dealers in the city), the Copenhagen Glove Depot, Gieves Limited, Darling and Company Limited, D. S. Crawford Limited, (shoes) —all long established firms—were further casualties of the post-war era, either forced out by high rents, bought over by more powerful competitors or, in company with some others in the city, willing abdicationists for other reasons.

Transfer of commercial ownership or power (or its augmentation) is not however the only sign of an east wind of change blowing through the city's main streets. There is the architectural façade and the shop windows.

Examples of the modern style of building that is changing the face of Princes Street can be seen in the new premises of C. and A. Modes, Limited, and Marks and Spencer Limited. A spectacular fire in November, 1955 completely destroyed the premises of C. and A. Modes Limited, and after a short sojourn in Frederick Street the firm returned to a newly constructed building on its Princes Street original site in the Spring of 1957. The building was the result of prolonged discussions with the Planning Committee of the Town Council, and was a compromise between the need to conform to the policy laid down for Princes Street and the modern trend of design. It has been described as a " contemporary building with clean modern lines built of natural materials with a recessed balcony on the third and fourth floors." A feature which the previous building did not have is the canopy which extends the whole length of the shop front, providing protection for passers-by and for window shoppers. The basement, ground floor and staircase have terrazzo flooring, and throughout the building fluorescent lighting gives brilliant illumination to ensure that customers can examine clothes with ease and comfort.

Recently four sites in Princes Street have been named by the Planning Committee of the Town Council as ripe for redevelopment. These are mainly office and club premises and the move merely emphasises the changing face of Princes Street in the light of retail trade trends. The existing façades are not suitable as shop fronts and such alterations would seem a natural corollary. Already the " silence room " in the Scottish Conservative Club has been sold and converted, and is now occupied by Soden's Limited and Etams.

To return to the recent changes of ownership in the retail trade, English infiltration in these recent years has been considerable, as we have already seen. In March, 1957, for example, Dolcis Limited, multiple retailers and manufacturers of shoes, took over the Princes Street premises of D. S. Crawford Limited. And as for Marks and Spencer Limited, their new sales emporium has been built on a site cleared by extensive demolition work, so that today the upper floors form part of the reconstructed Royal Hotel, while the basement and ground floors of the site form the shop. Incidentally, a striking feature of this modern shop is the ventilating and heating system. By an internal system of ducts in walls and under floors warm air is distributed from the top of the rear building down to the sales floor at a thermostatically controlled temperature. This means that warm air is distributed during cold weather and, during the summer when the heating is shut off, fresh air is supplied by the ventilating system.

And so the story goes on as the façade of Princes Street continues to alter. But what the ultimate pattern will be is not very clear, as Princes Street now is taking on the appearance of a large series of multiple shops and the old established businesses built up on personal attention are fast disappearing. There may also be some truth in the claim that George Street is now becoming the Bond Street of Edinburgh. In the 18th century George Street was planned to be the principal street in the New Town, and it is probably true to say that it has in the past few years moved steadily towards its intended pre-eminence, but as a shopping centre rather than a residential street.

THE PERSONAL TOUCH

Not far in mileage, but very far removed in spirit from the multiple stores and the quality shops of the city centre, are some of the small shops which can still be found in what, paradoxically, is the almost village atmosphere of busy, bustling districts like Stockbridge or Nicolson Street.

In these small shops husband and wife usually work together as a team, and it is their cheerfulness and courtesy, their interest, sympathy and often generosity that bring them a living as much as the commodities they sell. Often they stay open late—a great boon to a community where many housewives go out to work and have to shop in the evening. It is seldom they can take a holiday together: many have not done so in a lifetime. They are familiar with poverty, and would even cut a cabbage to suit the pocket of a customer. They keep their own accounts; they work hard; and one of their rewards lies in the loyalty of customers who still prefer " the personal touch."

How long the small retailer of this kind, or even the bigger ones will last is not altogether certain, and already concern is being expressed by many that the next 20 years will see a re-orientation of shopping facilities throughout the entire city. Present development plans covering the University area, St. James' Square and Tollcross, and the clearance of sub-standard dwellings in Leith, allied to a large scale redevelopment in that area, may shift shopping demand and increase the number of multiple stores. It is also possible that the small trader will be unable to return after any redevelopment of his old home area because of increased rents. Then too the future disposition of the retail trade is likely to be affected by the implementation of parking restrictions, and the concept of the neighbourhood centre in the housing estates which again attracts the larger type of shop, probably a part of a larger group.

There is, however, one form of shop where the personal touch continues —the hairdresser's.

HAIRDRESSING

The hairdressers are among the most forward-looking craftsmen and women in Edinburgh. This can be seen in their expertise and in the emphasis they place on the training of young people coming into the business. In the past few years there has been a notable expansion in the number of shops catering for women, many attracting the eye with brightly painted façades and girl's name artistically lettered on the signboard. It is perhaps another indication of the affluence of the 1960s that so many women can now afford to have their hair styled.

Men's saloons appear to be more conservative. Perhaps the men prefer the hairdresser's shop as a social club, where rugby and football can be thoroughly discussed. The establishments which offer manicures and similar *coups de main* can be counted on the fingers of one hand, and so proportionately to the masculine population can the men who indulge in them.

At present there are two organisations of master hairdressers in the city, the National Hairdressers Federation and the Incorporated Guild of Hairdressers, Wigmakers and Perfumers. The Edinburgh branch of the National Federation has at the time of writing 106 members and No. 7 branch of the Guild, which covers Edinburgh, the Borders and Fife, has some 53 members.

The Guild issues a General Certificate in Hairdressing, for which examinations are conducted throughout the country. These consist of a written examination of one hour, a practical lasting six hours and an oral.

The main training effort is conducted under the auspices of the Edin-

The entrance to the University's old College has been the gateway to knowledge for many throughout the years. It is also here that students pause to examine the notice boards which announce many of the social activities of the student body.

Below left: In the Science department some weird gargantuan machines have been installed for the pursuit of knowledge in the field of power.

Students listen to a lecture in the Anatomy class by their professor, one of whose predecessors was the famous Dr. Knox who became involved with the body snatchers in his efforts to promote knowledge among the medical students of his time.

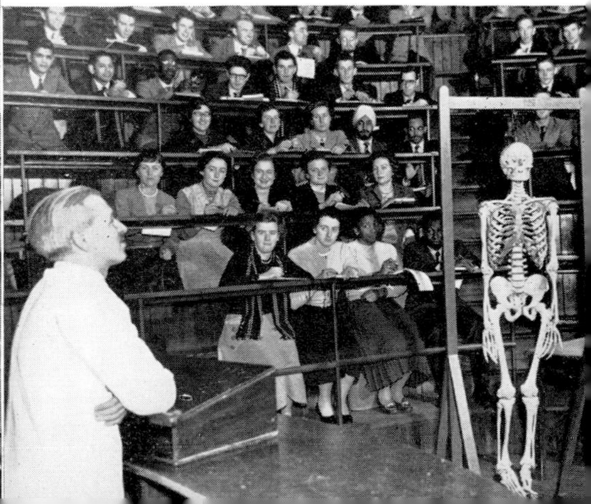

The dock area of Leith, gateway to the Seven Seas and port for cargo vessels from all parts of the world, is being expanded.

burgh Education Committee, who have established as part of the Further Education Programme a School of Hairdressing at the Regent Road Institute where students work for the certificates issued by the City and Guilds of London Institute. The two master hairdressers' organisations and the Union of Shop, Allied and Distributive Workers to which employees belong, have a joint committee which advises the Education Committee on the running of the school.

Although there is no obligation on employers to use the school for training their apprentices, some 250 students are now attending day release classes in such subjects as English and Science as well as the crafts of hairdressing and wigmaking. More than 200 go to evening school.

MARKETS

The modern decline of the market system—especially the retail markets—has coincided with the increase in the number of shops, though which is cause and which is effect would be hard to define. Both are probably the results of the population's dispersal over a wider area; for the housewife of to-day can obtain all her supplies for the family table so easily from shops near her home—even from vans at her door—that it would not be worth her while to make the journey to a central market. None the less behind the retail shops that deal with perishable goods—flesh, fish, fruit and vegetables, flowers and milk—lie the markets that supply those goods, and the markets, too, that deal in the basic commodities such as corn and cattle.

By an Act of Council (November, 1840) the Town Council defined the boundaries and hours of business for no less than 10 markets in the Burgh. These markets were (1) meal, corn and grain in the Grassmarket and the corn market building; (2) sheep, lamb and pig markets between Fountainbridge and Cowfeeder Row (now High Riggs); (3) a cattle market in the Grassmarket, West Port and King's Stables Road; (4) a horse market in the Grassmarket; (5) a straw market in Grassmarket; (6) a flesh market and meat market between North Bridge and Fishmarket Close; (7) a wholesale and retail vegetable market under North Bridge and between it and the old Physic Garden; (8) a wholesale fruit market adjoining the vegetable market; (9) a fish market in part of the vegetable market; (10) a poultry market between North Bridge and Flesh Market Close.

There was also an old market mainly for ewes at House O'Muir, on the slopes of the Pentland Hills. This continued until 1870, by which time the old droving practice had to yield to the sending of livestock by rail and the " Grit Ewe Sale " was transferred to the Meadows and later, like other livestock sales, to Lauriston Place.

None of the markets referred to in the 1840 Act of Council was newly established by it; that Act only formalised arrangements which had been in operation for centuries, but which were almost all to disappear long before another century had passed. The growth and industrialisation of parts of 19th century Edinburgh made it essential to remove the live-stock and corn markets to more suitable surroundings, though this was not effectively accomplished until 1911. As for the other markets for meat and vegetables, fruit and fish, improvement in transport facilities, changing habits and the increase in the number of retail shops all contributed to diminish their importance, so that now, except for the fish market which still operates at Newhaven, they have become mere shadows of their former selves.

The Grassmarket–Fountainbridge area had been the home of live-stock and corn markets from time immemorial. The corn market building to which the 1840 Regulations referred, stood at the western end of the Grassmarket. " An unsightly arcaded edifice, with a central belfry and clock ", it had been built in 1819, but its effective life was only 30 years. In 1849 a new corn exchange " in the Italian style " was opened on the south side of the Grassmarket; and this remained in use until 1911 when the present corn market was opened along with new cattle markets and slaughterhouses at Gorgie. The building " in Italian style " stood until 1965 and served a variety of central and local government purposes. It has now been demolished to make way for building by the Heriot-Watt University.

The Grassmarket was (and indeed to some extent still is) a centre for carriers' businesses. From here, in pre-railway days, and long into the railway era, carriers' carts set out to serve the country districts all around the city. These carts, and the general traffic, added greatly to the confusion and congestion on market-days, to such an extent that the Magistrates found it necessary to enact that " no waggon, cart, hurley, or other vehicle, other than carriers' carts . . . and carts attending the market . . . shall be allowed to stand in the Grassmarket on market-days."

In an attempt to relieve the congestion, cattle markets were built at Lauriston—only a stone's throw away—in 1844; and these were still in use in 1900 when the Central Fire Station was built on adjoining ground. The dire effect of this can be imagined, as the endeavours of drovers bringing their herds to market repeatedly conflicted with the equally laudable, and even more urgent, endeavours of firemen galloping their horse-drawn engines to the scene of a fire. And indeed it soon became obvious that something must be done. The situation was eased when the sheep sales returned, temporarily, to the Grassmarket in 1906, in which year a portion of the Lauriston Market site was given over to the Art College; and in 1911 the cattle, horse and sheep sales were removed along with the Corn market to the extensive new buildings that had been erected at Gorgie.

The markets for vegetables and fruit, meat, poultry and fish, also had a troubled history. Associated with them at first were the " shambles " or slaughter-yards, on ground inconveniently close to the North Bridge. Passers-by on the old North Bridge complained, not unjustifiably, that the sights, sounds and smells to which they were subjected from below were unseemly in the heart of a capital city, and after some ineffectual attempts to screen the shambles by closing in the open parapet of the bridge a covered slaughterhouse was built, surrounded by walls 20 feet high. In 1844, however, that building—on the site of part of Waverley Station—was acquired and demolished by the Edinburgh and Glasgow Railway Company.

There followed a period of anarchy, with no official slaughterhouses at all and the killing of animals going on in some 75 separately owned booths within the city. By 1850, however, this state of affairs had become intolerable, and slaughterhouses were built by the Corporation at Lochrin, a short distance west of Tollcross. Again they had chosen badly, for the district was rapidly becoming so much more populous and congested that almost from the first day of his appointment in 1862, Dr. Henry Littlejohn, Edinburgh's first Medical Officer of Health, agitated for the removal of the slaughter houses from this site. It was not however until 1911 (three years after his retirement) that his plea was at last listened to, and the slaughterhouses found their permanent home, along with the cattle and corn markets, at Gorgie.

The flesh market and retail poultry market were on sites (now covered by *The Scotsman* office and adjoining buildings) in the vicinity of Fleshmarket Close. Wholesale poultry, egg, butter and cheese markets were held in the streets adjoining the Tron Church, where stances were marked out to which farmers regularly brought their carts and portable stalls. A vestige of these markets lingered on until the 1930s, one farmer continuing to bring his cart to the pavement-edge not far from the Tron Church to sell his wares.

It was not long before the vegetable, fruit and fish markets were engulfed by the advancing tide of railway development as the group of terminal stations under the North Bridge grew and eventually coalesced to form the large expanse of Waverley Station. First to suffer was the fruit market, which, however, found alternative accommodation in the same area. Then in 1866 the North British Railway (New Works) Act authorised that company to acquire the whole of the " Green Market " area, on condition that the company would construct a new fruit and vegetable market on ground adjoining Princes Street and the Waverley Bridge.

Three years later the new market, covering an area of about 1¼ acres and known as Waverley Market, was completed, paved and handed over to the Corporation. It was—as the earlier premises had also been—an uncovered market, and it was not until the passing of the Edinburgh Markets and Customs Act of 1874 that the Corporation obtained powers to cover it in. The roofing was completed in 1877 at a cost of £30,000. The vegetable and fruit markets were thereafter housed within the covered area, a small adjoining building at the south-east corner being allocated as a retail market. The fish market was excluded from the new market centre and for a number of years it was held on a site at Macdowall Street, (which no longer exists), a short distance to the east of the North Bridge.

In the new market, stances were allotted to stallholders by the Market Officer, usually on the basis of a ballot organised by the stall-holders themselves. It had long been the practice, both in the old market-place and in the open Waverley Market, to use part of the space from time to time for exhibitions, menageries and other shows. This caused some inconvenience to stall-holders which was generally accepted, if not with equanimity, at least with good-natured grumbling. After the market-place was covered in it became a more attractive centre for exhibitions, and the Town Council used it more frequently for such purposes, to the growing inconvenience, though not at first the complete exclusion, of the normal stall-holders.

Flower shows and dog-shows, circuses, Wombwell's Menagerie, cycle-racing events and boxing exhibitions regularly shared the building with the market gardeners. The flower-shows, as might be expected, they accepted without demur; but the other events increasingly annoyed them. The climax came in 1882, when for three weeks the stall-holders were wholly excluded from the market to enable a great Fisheries Exhibition to be held there. During that time the market gardeners conducted their business from their carts stationed within the market area, " the market area " being defined as Princes Street, Waverley Bridge and other streets within 100 yards of the covered market.

Fortunately the weather was good, and one of the leading market gardeners, James Lindsay—whose name is still well-known in the trade in Edinburgh—urged his fellow stall-holders to accept the inconvenience with good grace in view of the national importance of the Exhibition. But the majority of his fellows thought otherwise, and 102 of them combined to bring an action against the Corporation. The action dragged its way through the Court of Session to the House of Lords where, in 1886, it was finally decided that the Corporation might restrict the space available within the market from time to time but had no power to prevent its use for market purposes entirely. This remained the position until 1933, when the Corporation's Provisional Order of that year authorised them to provide an alternative building for market purposes within 180 yards of the centre of the existing building.

Under the 1933 provision a new market building in East Market Street had almost been completed at the outbreak of War in 1939, when, along with the Waverley Market, it was requisitioned for Government purposes. The traders were once again reduced to conducting their business in the street, where the appropriate market charges were collected from them.

The new market building, covering some 20,000 square feet, with heating plant and office accommodation, was de-requisitioned after 1946, and between 1946 and 1957 twice-weekly markets were held there under the Corporation's auspices. For many years, however, the trend had been away from the market system of trading. This was a trend which had no doubt been hastened by the inconvenience of open air trading during the war years. But as long ago as 1890 several fruit and vegetable merchants had already established themselves in their own premises in Market Street, and it became increasingly the practice for market gardeners and fruit-growers to deal directly with these wholesale merchants. As a result, the numbers attending the wholesale market in the new building were small and, in the years after the war, they gradually diminished. In more recent years the average number of vehicles entering the building on market days dropped to 8, and the persons using the market to less than 50. (On some days, in the late 1950s and early '60s these figures were as low as 6 and 25.)

At the same time, the congestion of vehicles in Market Street, especially on Tuesday and Friday mornings, which remain the principal " market-days ", makes it clear that the wholesale trade in fruit and vegetables has not diminished; it has only been transferred to the premises of the wholesale merchants. As for the retail trade, it is now shared by the many greengrocers' shops. The distribution of these shops throughout the city, many of them with their attendant vans carrying goods to the housewives' doorsteps, has made it a rare occurrence for private individuals to shop in the market.

In these circumstances the Corporation proposed to discontinue the public market altogether and to dispose of the building. A nucleus of traders, however, insisted on the market's continuance, and so, after long negotiation, the building was leased to the Edinburgh and East of Scotland Wholesale Fruit Trade Association for ten years as from 1st January, 1957. By arrangement with that Association a market continues to be held there each Tuesday and Friday morning under the auspices of the Market Gardeners' Association, but it is sparsely attended.

FISH MARKET

The fish market mentioned in the 1840 Act of Council continued to be held in a corner of the fruit and vegetable market-place until it was excluded after the formation of the Waverley Market.

Even in quite early days an effort seems to have been made to preserve its cleanliness and hygiene, for as far back as 1810 the Town Council made a monthly award of 7*s.* to each of the two " Fish Women " who appeared to have best followed the Regulations in respect of cleanliness during the month, " the reward to continue for the first twelve months, when it is hoped that every individual will, of themselves, have seen the advantage of keeping the market clean without the offer of reward or infliction of fines."

After the exclusion of the " Fish Women " from the green market, they continued to hold a market in Macdowall Street, east of the North Bridge, for a number of years. This market appears in the Directory for the last time in 1895.

The " Fish Women " who traded there had no doubt obtained their supplies mainly from Newhaven, where there has been a fish market for a very long time. Until 1896 it was held on the open quayside, and according to one local resident large catches were disposed of. Writing in an Edinburgh newspaper in 1937, he said: " I remember one occasion in the summer of 1886 when some 40 boats from Anstruther, Buckhaven and Kirkcaldy, along with our Newhaven boats arrived with tremendous hauls. It was reported that 10,000 cod were landed that day."

In December, 1896 a new fish-house was opened on the quay at Newhaven. Erected by Leith Dock Commission, it has a covered area of 15,000 square feet, with offices for the fish-dealers, and cost £20,000. To this market on every week-day come catches from trawlers arriving at the nearby harbour of Granton, as well as from the diminishing number of small fishing boats that sail from Newhaven. In 1965, 19 trawlers and several seine-net fishing boats were operating from Granton and sending their catches to Newhaven. The number of small fishing boats sailing into Newhaven was about 40.

About fourteen dealers operate in the market, to which buyers come from all parts of Edinburgh and surrounding districts. Sales commence at 7.45 a.m. and continue, usually, until about 9 a.m. To take a good average recent year the total quantity of fish passing through the market in 1965 was about 18,000 tons.

FLOWER MARKET

The flowers marketed in Edinburgh come from three sources:

(1) the south of England and the Channel Isles;
(2) Scotland;
(3) the Continent.

The flowers in the first category are largely forwarded by dealers in Covent Garden, although hothouse roses and carnations are bought in bulk quantities direct from the growers in the home counties. Both market warehousemen and retailers with a large turnover will buy from agents and growers. By the beginning of June, perhaps earlier if the weather is warm, shipment of the softer kinds of flowers from Covent Garden ceases. But the hard florist's varieties—roses, carnations and gladioli—which will stand up to the overnight rail journey, continue to be sent. It is not until the chrysanthemum season starts in mid-August that large quantities of English flowers arrive again in the Edinburgh market.

Scottish growers fall into two groups—commercial market gardeners, and private estates. Very little effort is made to grow florist's varieties, and most commercial growers treat flowers as a catch crop when their houses are not being fully used for tomatoes. There is therefore usually a scarcity of choice in the Edinburgh shops during the latter half of May; and in June, when the last of the spring bulbs have ceased flowering, the Scottish hot houses have been emptied for the tomato crop, and the weather is too warm to ship garden flowers from the south.

The continental flowers are imported between November and April. There are direct shipments by Currie Line ships—from Antwerp and Rotterdam—of the more popular varieties—hothouse lilac, carnations and roses. Anemones, narcissi, foliage, etc., from the south of France, Spain and Italy are sent up by the Covent Garden dealers.

The Market Street warehousemen are by way of taking a 10 per cent commission on everything they sell, but it is believed they make a good deal more on everything brought up from Covent Garden. "Since they have to break bulk to the extent of selling single flowers." says one informant, " it is hardly surprising that they require a higher uplift." On the whole, flowers in Edinburgh are expensive, and a limited choice is offered to the public.

THE OTHER MARKETS

In addition to the public markets provided by the Corporation under the powers contained in their charters and acts, privately sponsored markets have been established within the city at various times. Such action was in defiance of the Corporation's monopoly.

Three of these private markets were opened during the 1820s. One was at Broughton; another, known as the Southern Market, was in the vicinity of Nicolson Street near the University's Old College. The third, built at Stockbridge in 1826 continued to be used, at least in a partial manner, until within the memory of some who are still alive. At Stockbridge the remains of a gateway still bears the faint legend: " Butcher meat, fruit, fish and poultry."

About 1883 a fourth private market was opened. This is the " Edinburgh Dead Meat Market " at Fountainbridge, conveniently near the old slaughterhouse at Lochrin. This market continues to be operated by the Edinburgh Meat Market Company Limited.

MILK DISTRIBUTION

Modern legislation and regulations have effected, almost within a generation, a remarkable change in the conditions under which the citizens of Edinburgh obtain their milk supplies. In 1920, the year before the extension of the City brought in several then almost rural parishes, there were 56 dairy herds within the burgh boundary, and from these a large proportion of the city's households bought their milk. A century ago there had been 170 byres within the city, with 2,000 cows, many of which were housed in dark and squalid byres in some of the most crowded districts. But by 1965, in the much greater area of the modern city, there were only 9 registered dairy herds; and since 1952 when the provisions of the Milk (Special Designations) (Specified Areas) Scotland Order were applied to the city, only the sale of " designated " milk has been permitted.

Except for the limited amounts supplied by the registered herds within the city boundaries, and a few householders in districts near its eastern and western extremities who are served by two creameries in the County, the entire population is now supplied by five large distributors to whose up-to-date and hygienic treatment and bottling plants milk is brought daily from farms in the Lothians, Lanarkshire, Berwickshire and Dumfriesshire. The grades of milk supplied are: Pasteurised, Sterilised, Premium and Standard.

On the basis of figures obtained from the distributors it has been estimated that the daily consumption of milk in the city is at least 48,000 gallons, but the amount fluctuates considerably. There is, for instance, a marked increase during school-terms when the milk-in-schools scheme is in operation.

THE AUCTIONEERS

There is another kind of market in Edinburgh. Spread throughout the city is a considerable number of auctioneering firms specialising in the sale of furniture, carpets, silver and bric-a-brac, with the odd "white elephants." The three largest firms—Dowell's, Lyon and Turnbull and the Central Auction Rooms near Tollcross—hold auctions three or four times a week and are rallying-places for dealers and purchasers of household goods, the last particularly sought by younger people. Some house auctions, by public roup, are also conducted by these firms, but most of this work is now carried out by Hillier, Parker May and Rowden.

COMMODITIES

This then is the general pattern of Edinburgh's shops and the methods by which they are run, their relationship with the public, the commodities obtainable in them, and the place of these commodities in the lives of the consumers. First in importance, and numerically by far the greatest, are the food shops.

FOOD

Edinburgh is still—as visitors from the south remark—a city of bakers' shops, mostly large concerns in and around Princes Street with neat small branches scattered thickly through the suburbs. There are also more modest places described as "Home Bakeries", but their products sometimes look stodgier and more garish than those of the big firms.

Despite the large sale of mass-produced wrapped bread, widely advertised on television, the bakers' shops are still piled high with a profusion of white, brown and currant loaves, "tea-breads" and cakes, including a vast range of wheaten loaves (fine or coarse), bran loaves, malt loaves, and loaves baked from stone-ground flour. White bread perhaps varies more in form and name than in content: there are plain loaves, cottage loaves, highpans, square pans, Vienna rolls, French sticks, crusties, twists, and even something described as a French Vienna. In addition immigrant Polish bakers now produce continental rye breads which are sold in delicatessen shops. Edinburgh's own indigenous bakers also continue to produce a bewildering variety of "tea-bread" and cakes, including morning rolls, dinner rolls, baps, dimple baps, the curiously named "Aberdeen softies", scones round and scones three-cornered, scones with currants, scones without currants, scones with soda, scones with treacle, buns of all sorts, slab cakes, iced cakes and fancy biscuits.

While the bakers continue in their traditional ways, grocers' shops are changing. The old-style family grocers continue to prosper in the suburbs, retaining their customers partly by stocking frozen foods, partly by the individual quality of their service. But in the centre of the city the traditional family grocers, handicapped by high rents, have had to change in order to survive. Indeed, the most majestic of them all, whose roasting coffee used to spice the Princes Street air, disappeared soon after the war, but others have survived by specialising in imported and exotic delicacies, fine cheeses, and the licensed trade.

The two chief developments in grocers' shops are sharply contrasted—on the one hand the self-service store or embryonic supermarket, on the other the continental grocery or delicatessen. These sprang up originally to supply the wants of foreign residents in Edinburgh; but many Edinburgh housewives, partly as the result of holidays abroad, and partly because they are encouraged by enterprising recipes in women's magazines, experiment increasingly with spaghetti bolognese or paella, and turn with pleasure from the aseptic packaged order of the self-service store to the continental grocer's intimate jumble of pastas and pickles, sausages, cheeses, and home-made pizzas.

Butchers' shops on the other hand have not changed greatly. More glass on counters, it is true, protects meat from customers, but in some places great dangling carcasses are still brushed by passing sleeves. The quality of Scotch beef and mutton is of course superlative, and housewives who move from Edinburgh to England regret the butchers more than almost any other purveyors. For one thing certain shops specialise in pork, lamb or game and poultry, though most deal generally in all kinds of meat; and one firm, which has much of the hotel and restaurant trade as well as a discriminating private clientele, regularly flies in veal and extra fillet steaks from the continent to meet the demand. Incidentally, it also flies out plane-loads of haggis every January for the Burns Suppers of Caledonian Societies in Canada and the U.S.A. As for pre-packaged meat this is now sold by the big chain stores such as Marks and Spencer and Woolworth's.

One of the changes since the war is the great rise in the use of roast chickens. Thus a number of shops selling nothing but poultry, cooked or uncooked, have been opened in various parts of the city. In many of these the birds are roasted on a spit in the shop in full view of the public.

The fishmongers, like the butchers, have changed little. The white fish is limited in variety, but it is still possible to serve at luncheon fish taken from the sea in the early hours of the morning. And there are all kinds of smoked fish—finnans, Moray Firths, Arbroath smokies, golden cutlets, smoked sole. Salmon is always expensive, but for a brief season in summer sea trout appear at reasonable prices, and a few fishmongers sell their own smoked salmon and trout. Shellfish are popular—these include mussels, cockles, prawns, crayfish, crabs, lobster, scallops—and one fishmonger has recently held an Oyster Week, supplying brown bread and butter and wedges of lemon for customers ready to eat their oysters on the spot. Occasionally in the summer mussels are sold at the kerb-side.

Fruiterers flourish in the city. The working class housewife no longer comes in only for a " forpit " of potatoes and some root vegetables for soup. She buys apples and oranges and grapes for her children if not for her husband; lettuces are no longer scorned as rabbit food, but are bought for salads, with tomatoes and cucumber and syboes; a new cheap restaurant can boldly call itself "The Salad Bowl" and prosper. Melons from Israel are cut up and sold by the piece, and gleaming pyramids of red and green peppers and purple aubergines are to be seen in the windows of the bigger greengrocers, along with occasional cumquats and uglis and ortaniques.

Small dairies, supplied by local farms, have almost disappeared, swallowed up by the big combines. Twenty-five years ago there were still many cows in Morningside and 15 years ago in Duddingston; and one could go and talk to the farmer's wife as she finished the milking and then carry away one's milk in a tin can. Now byres have been turned into garages, and the little shops still calling themselves dairies survive as tiny general stores, sometimes selling no milk at all.

Though the number of purely confectioners' shops in Edinburgh has decreased, many grocers, fruiterers and bakers now sell sweets, while the confectioners who once sold only sweets are becoming part newsagents, part tobacconists; and the traditional shops, like Ferguson's with its fine display of pink, yellow, orange and ginger Edinburgh rock, have all vanished.

One of the most lively and flourishing food shops in Edinburgh was created in 1954 by the enterprise of a department store near the University. This was not a supermarket, for until recently it has had only counter service; but it has sold bakeries, packaged butcher meat, both homespun and exotic groceries, delicatessen, sweets, biscuits in profusion, wines and spirits, and every obtainable brand of frozen food. Its cheese counter too has helped the Edinburgh public towards a greater appreciation of English and foreign cheeses, though the first consignment of Scotch Dunlop remained unpurchased on their shelves, and there is still a persistent demand for little bits of processed cheese wrapped in silver paper.

DRINKS

Wine shops are multiplying, and in Edinburgh as elsewhere more and more people drink inexpensive wines at home when they have guests or regularly experiment with the Sunday dinner bottle. The new wine shops are painted in pale, gay colours. They offer wines of respectable quality and modest cost elegantly laid out for customers to inspect, and have encouraged and educated many palates. But the old established firms still keep their traditional flavour and their knowledge, among them J. G. Thomson and Company in the historic Leith vaults, Sandemans, Cockburns, Cockburn and Campbell, and many others.

As an illustration of this swing in fashion, one small firm which caters for the cheaper end of the trade is now bottling five times as much wine as it did five years ago. This increase is attributed to tastes acquired through foreign travel and also to television viewing. When father used to go round to the pub for his beer or whisky, mother sat at home in strict sobriety; but nowadays when a whole family may be gathered round the TV screen mother often joins her spouse in a drink, asking more often than not for a glass of sweet sherry or inexpensive sweet wines such as Spanish Sauternes.

At a more sophisticated level, the demand for claret and burgundy is steadily rising, with the result that these wines are often sold and drunk before they have reached their prime. Vintage port is likewise in strong demand, especially perhaps amongst those to whom it has become a symbol of social status to offer port after dinner before moving on to brandy and cigars. Whisky of course retains its popularity, with both the modish and the true connoisseurs buying a selection of single malts. Gin sales apparently have declined, while vermouth-based aperitifs are more popular, being drunk often with ice and a splash of soda water—a custom retained after holidaying in France or Italy no doubt.

Much of the claret and burgundy is consumed at wine and cheese parties, a form of entertainment which is more economical than cocktail parties (based on heavily taxed spirits) and easier to manage, in these servantless days, than large dinner-parties. Champagne sales are also rising, not only for weddings and dances, but also because champagne cocktails, like vintage port, confer a social cachet on those who offer them. More indigent parents, on the other hand, happily settle for sparkling hock or Italian spumante instead of the traditional champagne at their daughters' weddings. Outside the home beer and whisky sales have risen, and seem unlikely to decrease. For the fact is that more liquor is consumed than formerly, even with the high price of spirits; more women and young people drink than was the case between the Wars; and a greater variety of liquor has become acceptable at all levels.

HOUSEKEEPING AND HOME MEALS

The pattern of house-keeping has obviously altered greatly since the war. Generally speaking, even low wage-earning groups are better fed, though sometimes money is not spent on the best types of food nor a balanced variety. During the 1930s, when there was considerable unemployment, many working-class families were under-nourished, though some capable and thrifty women were able to produce satisfactory meals. It was not uncommon then to hear a woman say: " We can only afford ' kitchen ' (meaning a cooked meal) once a day." But now a cooked dinner at midday and a cooked high tea followed by some form of light supper is not unusual among the working and lower-middle classes if the husband gets home at midday, though where he cannot do so the " carrying of a piece " remains the habit as in former years (unless he eats in a canteen), while his wife may either make do with a cup of tea or, if there are young children, make a pot of soup.

In the upper brackets of the middle class it is more usual, however, for wives whose husbands are at work and children at school to have a sandwich or a cheese and fruit lunch and to prepare a more elaborate evening meal (often called " dinner," when there are guests, and " supper " when the family is alone). The husband meanwhile eats a fairly substantial lunch at restaurant, canteen or pub. When there are children at home, a simple cooked lunch is prepared, with more often a fruit course instead of the former stodgy pudding.

In the old sense of the term home cooking in general is on the decline, partly no doubt because of the larger number of working wives. At all levels of society tinned or packeted soups and ready-made cakemixes are increasingly used, together with cooked meats, tinned and frozen vegetables and other frozen and pre-packed meals. Porridge, once a daily essential of diet, is on the decline, though packets of breakfast cereals quite often take its place. Jam is now less used, though the sale of marmalade has increased. Coffee, especially instant coffee, is more often drunk than formerly. Indeed, before the war coffee was seldom used by working class people, whereas today their teenage offspring spend much of their time in coffee bars. Fish and chips and ice cream are becoming extras rather than part of the main meal, and often a broiler chicken, hot from the spit, appears on the working-class table where twenty years ago there would have been fish and chips or a mutton pie. It is also noticeable that practically all families now have fresh milk, whereas 30 years ago a number had only condensed milk—not always for the sake of economy, but because they preferred it.

EATING OUT

Apart from the tourist, who inevitably eats out, those who make use of restaurants and pubs are either workers who are too far from home to eat in, or those who eat out as a form of entertainment.

There are roughly three kinds of eating place in Edinburgh. In the first category, the cheap restaurants are more varied than they used to be: there are numerous American-style snack bars and coffee bars, some old-established cafés and restaurants with a wide variety of good cheap dishes, and an increasing number of new small restaurants in districts such as Tollcross or Morrison Street, run mainly by Poles or Italians and offering a range of foreign dishes. For example, one tiny restaurant on Castle Hill offers six different kinds of pasta asciutta. Then many pubs nowadays sell soup and pies, and it is possible to eat cheaply and quite well in several of the pubs in Rose Street. Fish and chip shops also flourish, and are extending their range: one can buy (and take away in greasy brown paper) not only fish and chips, but black pudding and chips, or chicken and chips and sometimes even scampi and chips.

In the middle price-range there are the restaurants attached to department stores (mostly offering not very exciting food at moderate prices), and those attached to the big baker's shops in Princes Street or near it, which serve reasonably priced lunches and are crowded for morning coffee and afternoon tea. Menus in some of the middle-priced restaurants have burgeoned into lush American descriptions of the dishes offered (" Melting Fillet Steak fried in Butter and smothered with a rich Meat Sauce studded with Mushrooms and bright Red Peppers. Served with French Fried

Potatoes and garnished with Onion rings "): appetite sometimes cloys before the dish has actually reached the table.

Finally, there are the more expensive restaurants. Before the war the well-to-do or expense-account diner-out had little alternative to the sombre dining rooms of the big hotels, except for the Cafe Royal with its splendid mahogany, ceramic and stained glass Oyster Bar, the de Guise restaurant attached to the Caledonian Hotel, (where the Pompadour today deserves a special word of praise), and the sophisticated l'Aperitif. Since the war several more restaurants of this kind have opened; but some of the pleasantest places to eat—for atmosphere, for food and for the excellence of their wine lists, are away from the centre of the city. These include the elegant 17th century Prestonfield House, by Arthur's Seat, which has an increasing reputation for the excellence of its dishes and its wine; Cramond Inn or the Hawes Inn (where Scott's Antiquary was offered " sea-trout and caller haddocks . . . a mutton-chop and cranberry tarts, very well preserved "); or still further afield, The Open Arms at Dirleton or the Howgate Inn with its delightful soups and profusion of smorrebrod. On Sundays, however, the spirit of John Knox still broods over the city, and the unfortunate visitor's choice of eating house in its centre is limited, broadly speaking, to the bigger hotels such as the North British, the George and the Caledonian.

Since the second World War there has been a considerable increase in the habit of eating out as a form of entertainment. In fact, before then this custom was looked on by certain rather snobbish sections of the Edinburgh community with disapproval. In particular, working class people eat out more often, and there are increasing numbers of small restaurants in predominantly proletarian districts where it is still possible to obtain a wholesome three-course meal for as little as three or four shillings.

The ordinary public-house is not much frequented by women, as a feeling still persists in Edinburgh that " nice " women do not enter them. Women may take a drink at home or at a party or a friend's house—but not in a pub, if they wish to be considered respectable. At those pubs which have a restaurant and perhaps a cocktail bar, the " nice " woman may have a meal in the restaurant and even be served with a drink in the cocktail bar—but still, it appears, she must not enter the " pub " section if her reputation is to be preserved!

ADVERTISING

Closely tied to this complex world of marketing, the retail trade and consumers' habits is advertising, a necessary aid to business which in recent years has shown considerable originality. As a business in itself it also has some notable practitioners, including one who leads a respectable double life by being not only an advertising agent but a well-known fiction writer.

Like Gaul, divorce or a dry martini, he says, advertising can be divided into three parts. There are those who buy the opportunity to advertise, those who sell it, and those who handle the deal. The last are the "agents", who figure in over 90 per cent of advertising business and who, in return for the commissions and fees they receive for their participation, offer a service to the advertiser, including advice on media, writing of " copy " and preparation of artwork.

Thus in Edinburgh, of the few hundred citizens directly employed in advertising some are on the staffs of the vending organisations—newspapers and magazines in the main—some are employed by poster contractors, and a number of free-lance space salesmen handle the needs of smaller publications. These representatives total about 50 persons. If one adds the clerks and typists and book-keepers behind their efforts—employed mainly by the advertisement (not advertising) departments of the newspapers published in the city—this figure increases. It is, however, interesting that as these words are written no commercial television firm has a permanent representative in Edinburgh, far less a permanent office. This is not because Edinburgh is less immune to mass entertainment, but because commercial television apparently does not look for much of its revenue from firms carrying on business in the city.

About 30 Edinburgh firms have advertising (not advertisement) departments. These departments may vary in size from one person to a small trained coterie of three or four. Then there are the advertising agencies mainly handling the business of city firms, but also with " clients " elsewhere in Scotland, south of the Border, or abroad.

There are 13 " recognised " agencies in Edinburgh. Recognition is a necessary qualification in order that the media owners will pay commission on business placed with them. Of the 13, seven are in membership of the Institute of Practitioners in Advertising, a central organisation of British agencies devoted to professional ethics, education and efficiency. Some of the Edinburgh agencies are " man and a boy " size, and no less able for that. Others have a staff of between 40 and 50 persons, with media departments, studios, copywriting teams, marketing executives, and the other specialist individuals and departments that make a comprehensive agency. One long-established firm, Robertson and Scott Limited, has offices in Charlotte Square, and is not only the oldest practising advertising agency in Scotland but one of the oldest in the world.

It is of passing interest that the word " agent " is a misnomer in this context. Though known traditionally as advertising agents, these firms are in fact principals in the business they undertake, and there can be no " fly by night " character about an advertising agency. Many agencies over the years have also been fulfilling not only their primary function—the placing and preparation of advertisement—but have reached far into the advisory world of the business consultancy firms.

In addition to those three major sectors of advertising, there is a periphery of other assorted activities. We find in St. Andrew's House, for instance, a congenial and efficient Scottish Information Office working with the Central Office of Information in the south, and devoted to handling publicity matters of Scottish interest. There is also a notable private firm of Public Relations consultants in Young Street, which handles the publicity affairs of textile groups, counties, and individual firms. Then too we find in Edinburgh that the local, regional, or national offices of government and quasi-government departments or boards have frequently room on their establishments for advertising and publicity personnel.

There is incidentally one major commercial concern with its head office in Edinburgh, which does not allow its competing brands to deal in comparatives or superlatives. No whisky in this organisation can therefore be described as " better " far less " best "; and this is not necessarily a bad thing because the day of promoting a product by saying " Blogg's beer is best " is long outmoded. Nowadays one looks for Unique Selling Propositions (Blogg's beer comes to you in sterilised bottles; or, Blogg's beer is brewed from *processed barley*).

The advertising world of Edinburgh enjoys a corporate social life. In 1958 the Publicity Club of Edinburgh was re-instituted: an earlier club had lapsed in the 1920s. The club meets regularly and has a membership of about 130 drawn from all the sectors of advertising, including the " suppliers "—blockmakers, printers and so on.

The University of Edinburgh has also recently shown an awareness of the world of advertising, through its Department of Commerce. This opening of the academic eyes on the contemporary business scene is perhaps more belated than in, say, America, but is no less welcome. Yet the fact remains that though advertising in the city covers every activity that may result in somebody buying something, it is no more than a facet, though a significant one, of the Kind of Life We Lead. And fortunately in Edinburgh it is conducted without the rancour and without the sense of God-like decision that one finds on Madison Avenue. Even so, Scottish businessmen—who are production-minded rather than sales-minded—often neglect the talent on their doorsteps. One of the foremost exponents of advertising in the world (" The only sound at 60 miles an hour is the ticking of the clock ") was educated in Edinburgh but had to go abroad to find opportunity.

Chapter 29

THE TRAVELLER AND THE INN

THE TOURISTS

In a single year, in the early '60s, the Scottish Tourist Board has recorded some three-quarters of a million visitors to Edinburgh, a high proportion of them from foreign countries. Edinburgh stands with London, Oxford, Cambridge and Stratford-on-Avon in the order of priority drawn up by most foreign visitors to Great Britain. But it is doubtful if the Castle and the Royal Mile, or the elegance of the New Town, or the carefully chosen collections in our National Galleries by themselves are now the main or the only attractions. For although there is plenty of history past there is also history present during Edinburgh's two seasons. The first in May sees the splendid procession of the General Assembly with all its pageantry. The second marks the Queen's own summer visit to Holyroodhouse, when the Scots for a few days remember they were once a kingdom. But the real fulcrum of tourist activity, many think, is the Edinburgh Festival. It survives the keen competition of other festivals with a sharper focus; it puts in everyone's minds that once a year the best of art and artists is to be found in Edinburgh; and by some strange chemical process the aura of artistic excellence lasts throughout the whole tourist season. "A few days in Edinburgh", said one cynic, "and you acquire merit."

It is during the Festival too that the practicalities of tourism in the city are put most severely to the test. For a long time there was no permanent information centre in Edinburgh to help the visitors find room at the inn, though during the Festival the Tourist Board improvised a very successful bureau. It is the Board's proud boast that they have never failed to find accommodation for any Festival visitor who asks for help. In short, this amateur system has worked, and many visitors to Edinburgh remember best not the highlights of past Festivals but the kind hospitality they have received from private citizens. Now things have improved. A tourist information centre has been opened on Waverley Bridge with three sections—tourist information, holiday accommodation and transport and tours. There is also a City Accommodation Bureau at the offices of the Festival Society.

THE GROWTH OF TOURISM

Travellers were ill-accommodated until the New Town was developed in the late 18th and early 19th century. Since then the hotels in Edinburgh have been able to offer to the visitor accommodation suitable to his needs and at a price he can afford to pay. For this, better communications by railways and their extension to cover the whole of Britain were chiefly responsible. The railways increased the need for hotels, and people from other parts came to Edinburgh to promote commerce. Such travellers as the railways brought were wealthy rather than of modest means. Later, the rivalry of the North British and Caledonian Railways brought reductions in fares, thus making it possible for greater numbers of people to travel.

During the first World War the motor car was used to an extent few could have foreseen in the early years of this century, and between 1920 and 1939 the number of people travelling by car increased steadily. This, together with the growth of char-a-banc and motor bus traffic, brought greater numbers to visit the city. It was not, however, until after the second World War, when air travel was added to the other means of communication, that tourism became the highly organised business it is today, bringing not only ever-increasing numbers of tourists from abroad to Scotland, but also encouraging people of this country to travel more widely.

The principal factor in the success of tourism inside Scotland as in the rest of Britain was the greater financial security enjoyed by the average man and woman. Fuller employment and longer holidays with pay made it possible for greater numbers of people in this country to travel on holiday and to take holidays farther from their homes.

One result has been that the tourist season in Edinburgh—which before the second World War commenced in June and ended in September—has been extended and now runs from the middle of April to October.

ECONOMICS OF THE TOURIST INDUSTRY

Taking 1956 as a specimen year for which detailed statistics from a special inquiry are available,[1] 380,000 visitors from overseas and 1,000,000 holiday makers from other parts of Britain visited Scotland during the year, while 1,300,000 Scots spent their annual holiday there. Of this total of 2,680,000 one half visited Edinburgh.

It was estimated that these holidaymakers spent the following sums in Scotland, but this may have been an over-estimate:

Scottish holidaymakers	£20 million
Visitors from other parts of Britain	£19 million
Overseas visitors	£11·5 million
say	£50 million

It is difficult to deduce from this the amount which was spent in Edinburgh, but as tourists on the average stayed in three places during their stay in Scotland, and one half of the total visited Edinburgh, it is probably not unfair to say that at least £8 million were spent in the city. Visitors interviewed for the purposes of the survey were asked to give an

[1] A survey of the Tourist Trade in Scotland 1956, published by the British Travel and Holidays Association with the co-operation and assistance of the Scottish Tourist Board and Social Surveys (Gallup Poll) Limited.

account of their expenditure during the two days before they were interviewed; and the details of expenditure which they gave helped the inquiry to reach its grand total.

The growth of the tourist industry nationally since the 1956 survey can be gauged from some of the statistics available for 1963, when there were 710,000 overseas visitors in Scotland, and the number of holiday-makers from other parts of Britain had hugely increased. Expenditure by overseas visitors was believed to have gone up to more than £20 millions. The following table shows the trend:

TABLE 58
OVERSEAS VISITORS TO SCOTLAND

	Europe	*U.S.A.*	*Other Non-European*	*Commonwealth*	*Total*
1952	92,500	65,000	8,000	66,000	231,500
1953	103,000	74,500	8,650	74,450	260,600
1954	114,430	91,280	9,560	90,000	305,270
1955	131,250	108,000	10,750	101,250	351,250
1956	143,000	117,000	11,000	109,000	380,000
1957	160,000	120,000	12,000	113,000	405,000
1958	150,000	144,000	14,000	122,000	430,000
1959	167,000	156,000	15,000	132,000	470,000
1960	195,000	188,000	21,000	166,000	570,000
1961	217,000	188,000	23,000	192,000	620,000
1962	230.000	205.000	24,000	207,000	666,000
1963	240,000	230,000	25,000	215,000	710,000

Nevertheless, in spite of these impressive figures, the great majority of those who visit the city on holiday come from other parts of Britain.

From all of these figures it will be seen that the tourist industry is important to Edinburgh and to Scotland. The prosperity it brings to the city should not be thought to be localised in one street or even one area of the city. The presence of so many visitors makes demands on many services and for many commodities throughout the city and beyond its boundaries, bringing prosperity to businesses in many parts of the town which tourists never visit and where the people concerned would probably deny that they had anything to do with tourists at all.

THE SCOTTISH TOURIST BOARD

In Edinburgh, as elsewhere in Scotland, tourism has developed as an organised industry (although successive Governments have been slow to give it adequate positive and practical recognition) since the end of the second World War. As a means of stimulating earnings in foreign exchange the British Tourist and Holidays Board was set up in 1946 to encourage a new flow of overseas visitors. The Scottish Tourist Board, which now has offices at 2 Rutland Place, Edinburgh, was established in the same year to promote Scotland's specific interests. Its main function is to publicise the tourist and holiday attractions of the country. This it does through an active press service, specialist publications on hotels, boarding houses, etc., and recreations such as fishing or golf, through advertising, and the provision of information offices to deal directly with tourists' inquiries. The information bureau in the Board's Edinburgh office alone deals with 250,000 postal inquiries and 100,000 verbal inquiries a year. The Board has also directed publicity for the Edinburgh Festival Society since its formation.

Edinburgh Corporation is, of course, active in advertising the city, and publishes an official guide book, *Where to stay in Edinburgh*, the register of hotel and boarding house accommodation in the city, and various brochures including *Edinburgh this Month*, produced for the first time in 1959 and published from April to October inclusive. This lists the places of interest open to the public, the attractions at theatres and cinemas, sporting events, bus tours and other items likely to appeal to tourists. In 1964 the Corporation also set up two information offices in the city, one with foreign language students on the staff, and in addition published brochures on Edinburgh in German, French, Spanish and Dutch.

TOURIST TRANSPORT

Tourism obviously involves not only accommodation and entertainment but transport. Visitors to Edinburgh arrive by air, by land (using rail, motor coach and private car) and by sea—though relatively few visitors to Edinburgh now arrive at the ancient port of Leith, which in its day received kings and queens, ambassadors and the noble and mighty of many lands.

As we saw earlier, the steady increase in the number of passengers arriving and departing by air at Turnhouse in recent years certainly tells the story of an ever-growing number of people visiting Edinburgh, and although it has not been possible to separate all visitors to the city from those going to other parts of Scotland, if the Gallup Poll statement is accepted that 50 per cent of all persons touring in Scotland visit Edinburgh the intake is impressive.

Since the end of the last war, there has been a marked increase in the number of people travelling by motor coach, because they want to solve all their travel problems in one move. By booking a coach tour they ensure that they will stay at first-class hotels, that their meals will be arranged and that they will travel comfortably in specially designed motor coaches. Tipping—that constant worry of the traveller—is taken care of, and the cost of the tour as quoted by the travel agent is inclusive. It may not be a way of spending a holiday which appeals to rugged individualists, but it is undoubtedly one which appeals to a great many people who travel.

There are many companies which arrange coach tours from England to Scotland, but it is probably sufficient to quote the experience of an Edinburgh company, the nationalised Scottish Omnibuses Limited. It operates some 60 extended tours from Land's End to John o'Groats, and of the 1,500 tourists for whom beds are booked each night of the touring season approximately 100 are in Edinburgh. Among the most popular are the two, three and four day sight-seeing services between London and Edinburgh, which are particularly well patronised by overseas visitors.

Scottish Omnibuses also operates 26 whole-day tours from Edinburgh, including among others, tours to the Clyde Coast area, to Glencoe, to the Trossachs, and 26 afternoon tours of the country around the city.

THE HOTELS

Although Edinburgh has done much to encourage visitors, the city has done less to develop hotels to keep pace with their growing numbers. Of the 184 listed in Edinburgh in 1963, the two principal hotels—the Caledonian and the North British—at each end of Princes Street offer accommodation and cuisine which match high European standards. There are three or four other top-class hotels, but this is not sufficient for a capital city, and to make matters worse not a single modern hotel has been built for the past 50 years.

It is strange that the Scots have not quite realised that for many visitors the image of a country and its comforts is formed in the hotel bedroom. However, a number of the established hotels have been extensively modernised in recent years, and some have been extended to meet the demand for individual toilet accommodation. Most of the larger hotels and many of the smaller establishments also now have wash-hand basins in each bedroom and many are adapting accommodation to provide bathrooms *en suite*, which ever-increasing numbers of visitors now expect as a matter of course. In many cases it has been possible to arrange this conveniently by dividing large bedrooms built in spacious Victorian and Edwardian times to provide bathrooms.

Some idea of the effort to keep pace with the growing number of visitors, in spite of the lack of new establishments, can be obtained from the estimates of the number of persons accommodated in hotels, boarding houses and apartments in Edinburgh. In 1950 this number was 517,498; in 1955, rising annually, it was 671,437; in 1958 it was 702,169; and in 1961 the number of persons so accommodated was 822,446.

FROM STABLERS TO HOTELIERS

The inn-keepers of Edinburgh were for long known as stablers, and reference to the statutes laid down for them as shown in the Burgh Records suggests that their main care must have been the beast rather than his master. But of the inns, stablers and coaching houses of former days few remain to be identified and all those within the old city have changed from their former use.[1]

A plaque on a wall in St. Mary's Street shows the site of the White Horse Inn that flourished there between 1635 and 1868, and which was visited by Samuel Johnson in 1773 on his journey to the Hebrides. In the Grassmarket, the White Hart Inn remains as a public house today, the

[1] An excellent survey of these old inns and many of their successors in the New Town, most of them defunct, has been prepared by Mr. Douglas R. Ritchie of the City Chambers. Unfortunately for lack of space and also because in the main this volume must concentrate on present day conditions it has only been possible to use it in summarised form. (Ed.)

accommodation above having been adapted by the Corporation as dwelling houses. This inn seems to have enjoyed the patronage of poets, as a plaque records that Robert Burns stayed there on his visit to Edinburgh in 1791 when he took his farewell of Mrs. Maclehose (Clarinda of the letters), a parting which produced the beautiful poem *Ae fond kiss.* William Wordsworth and his sister stayed there some years later, though on this occasion the White Hart does not appear to have inspired any "emotion recollected in tranquillity."

If few inns of any antiquity remain in Old Edinburgh, in Leith the Old and New Ship Inns still survive on the shore, both dating from around 1680. Grant in *Old and New Edinburgh* says of them: "The Old and New Ship Inns are good examples of what these old taverns were, as they still exhibit without change their great staircases and walls of immense thickness, large but cosy rooms, panelled with moulded wainscot, and quaint stone fire-places, that, could they speak, might tell many a tale of perils in the Baltic and on the shores of Holland, France and Denmark, and of the days when Leith ships often sailed to Tangiers, and of many a deep carouse, when nearly all foreign wines came almost without duty to the Port of Leith." The Old Ship Hotel was burned down and rebuilt about 1890 and is still a hotel today.

In Newhaven the Peacock Hotel dates from the latter half of the 18th century; it is famed today for its "Fish Dinners." At Duddingston the Sheep's Heid Inn is perhaps the oldest inn in what is now part of the city.

FROM 1780 TO THE PRESENT DAY

From the early days of the New Town there have been hotels in and around Princes Street. James Dunn who was shown in the Edinburgh Directory as a stabler at the Cowgate Port in 1773–7, became a hotel-keeper in Princes Street in 1777 and remained there until 1781, opening his hotel in St. Andrew Square the following year on the site of the present National Commercial Bank's building. Also in St. Andrew Square where the Scottish Union and National Insurance Company now is, there was Douglas's (Slaney's) Hotel.

Originally built as a fashionable mansion for a leading lawyer, this was the most aristocratic hotel in the city, and the occasional abode of British and Continental royalty. Then there was the Crown Hotel, opened in the late 1770s, and still in existence today—in Torphichen Street.

A great many hotels have opened and closed in Princes Street in the 180 years since James Dunn first set up business there. Many, especially in the early days, were known by the proprietor's name and these names changed as one proprietor succeeded another. Changes in the tenor of national life also had their effect on hotel names, as when the hotel at No. 3, known in 1840 as the Turf, had by 1870 become the Gladstone, while the hotel at No. 91 was at various times in its existence known as the Buck's Head Hotel or Sorlies, Mackay's Hotel, the Imperial and the Balmoral.

At the present time there are six hotels with frontage on Princes Street. These are the North British Station Hotel, (at the east end), the Royal British, the Old Waverley, the Royal, the Palace which although its entrance is not now in Princes Street occupies upper floors looking over the Gardens to the Castle, and the Caledonian Station Hotel at the west end. It is the newest hotel in the street, having been opened in December, 1903. Adjoining Princes Street Station, as the North British Hotel adjoins Waverley, the Caledonian was built as a result of the intense rivalry between the Caledonian Railway Company and the North British Railway Company. It is difficult for those who did not live through those times to imagine the fierceness of the competition which existed between the two railway systems which are now united in British Railways and whose hotels are under the management of the Hotels Executive of the British Transport Commission.

The Royal Hotel has had the longest continuous existence in Princes Street. The exact date of its opening is not known, but it is recorded that William Ewart Gladstone as a boy in 1815 watched from its windows a salute fired from the Half-Moon Battery to celebrate the victory of Waterloo. In December, 1817 Grand Duke Nicholas, brother of the Czar of Russia, stayed there. Later King George V and Queen Mary spent part of their honeymoon there. At a later stage the hotel ballrooms became the New Picture House, which more recently was converted into a modern store by Marks and Spencer. During these alterations the property above was reconstructed to give the Royal Hotel additional accommodation.

The North British Hotel was opened as the North British Station Hotel on 15th October, 1902, with a design described as " a free rendering of the Renaissance Period in which the architects have taken every advantage of the facilities which this style presents for linking in a masterly manner, the old Scottish Architecture of the Old Town with the rather severe classical architecture of the New." Today many of the 300 bedrooms have their own bathrooms *en suite*, but although the bedrooms and toilet arrangements have been altered to take account of changes in taste, the calm, stately appearance of the public rooms of the building has changed little through the years. Many of these, including the principal dining room, have a magnificent view looking westwards along Princes Street. The opening souvenir book remarked, incidentally, that " the architect had specified that the smoking and billiard rooms should be in readily accessible, but retired situations, where they do not interfere with the comfort of the lady guests."

The Old Waverley Hotel was founded in 1848 by Robert Cranston, master tailor, Chartist and Temperance reformer. While still a tailor, Cranston opened a Teetotal Coffee House at 129 High Street near Carrubber's Close; he also edited the *North British Express*, the organ of the Chartists, after its editor was imprisoned. The year 1848 was an eventful one for Robert Cranston. Arrested after a search of the *Express* office for seditious writing he was later released for lack of evidence against him. Two days later he was arrested again and charged with preaching sedition under the guise of temperance, but was again set free. His partner in the tailoring business became alarmed by this activity and the partnership was dissolved. The Coffee House was sold and "Cranston's Temperance Hotel" opened. The Edinburgh Directory for 1854 mentions The Waverley Hotel for the first time but it was called by that name from the beginning. The name "Old Waverley" was adopted in 1876 to distinguish it from the New Waverley which Cranston opened in the premises of the Old Post Office in Waterloo Place in 1868. The New Waverley was burned down in 1935, and the building which had been purchased from the Government in 1879 was sold back and is now used again as part of the General Post Office. But many old traditions remain in this hotel. Robert Cranston's devotion to the works of Sir Walter Scott caused him to name the hotels he founded in Glasgow and London by the same name, Waverley, and in the writing room of the Old Waverley in Edinburgh stands Sir Walter's library table, while characters from the novels are shown on the tiles of the dining room grate.

Building work on the Caledonian Hotel began in 1899, and the hotel was opened on 21st December, 1903. An article on the hotel in *The Scotsman* on 12th December of that year described the architecture of the building as "flat and uninteresting." If the outward appearance of the hotel was not all that the writer could have wished, the interior however met with his entire approval. In particular he admired the Dining Hall with its 26 foot high ceiling, the height being achieved by carrying the room through the entresol floor. Fortunately a false ceiling inserted in 1935 was removed in 1958 and the room's admirable proportions were revealed. In addition to the hotel's main dining room, it has a special restaurant, with a cuisine well-known for excellent food and service.

One of Edinburgh's leading hotels is the George, which was opened at 23 George Street in 1855 by J. Stevenson or Steventon, formerly of the Bay Horse Inn in Rose Street. It continued at that address until 1890, when it is shown as being at No. 21, although this was probably only a change of entrance. Until 1948 it remained mainly a commercial hotel, but following the acquisition of the Caledonian Insurance Company's old offices at No. 19 and other property to the west, the hotel was transformed in character. The main office of the insurance company became a restaurant, and at the same time other rooms were opened for social functions.

This is far from being a complete tally of the better-known hotels in the city, for there are many others with pleasing names and service. To name just a few more, there are the Roxburgh, recently extensively modernised in Charlotte Square which apart from service thrives on being in one of the most magnificent squares in Europe; the Scotia in Great King Street where splendid paintings can be seen by the great MacTaggart; the Carlton Hotel, which claims to be the only hotel in Edinburgh with a private bath in every bedroom; the Bruntsfield Hotel with its skyline views; and the Braid Hills Hotel, high up above the main part of the city with a public golf course near its front door.

In addition the University makes available certain of its halls of residence for visitors to the Edinburgh Festival and for certain large conferences if these take place during University vacations.

Some interesting hotel statistics were provided by the 1961 Census. These show that on the day the census was taken there were 552 hotels and boarding-houses in the city, of which 253 had less than 10 rooms and 299 ten rooms or more. In the hotels and boarding-houses with 10 or more rooms there was a total population of 3,858 made up as follows: manager and staff, 661; relatives of manager and staff, 464; resident guests, 807; visitor guests, 1,926.

But are there enough hotels to welcome the increasing number of tourists, holiday makers, visiting businessmen and conferences? The hoteliers themselves seem to be satisfied that they can accommodate more visitors without an increase in the number of hotels, but as Edinburgh is an important conference city as well as a tourist centre, there are times when travel agents and others confess that it is difficult to accommodate all who wish to come with the type of accommodation they desire. Some accept a lower standard than they first requested, while others omit Edinburgh from their itinerary if they feel there is likely to be no room at the inn.

CONFERENCE CITY

Edinburgh, as a conference centre, seems to have had a special appeal for international bodies, and the steady increase in the number and size of conferences is an encouraging stimulus to the city's tourist trade.

In 1958 there was the International Congress of Mathematicians attended by 2,200 distinguished mathematicians from all over the world; and this was followed by the 1959 congress of the British Medical Association, a meeting particularly memorable because it was joined by the Canadian Medical Association, which meant a total attendance of 4,000 doctors. A year later came the World Convention of Churches of Christ, which was also attended by 4,000 delegates, many of them from the United States; the World Federation for Mental Health; and the IVth International Congress of Clinical Biochemistry. The year 1961 saw further Edinburgh examples of old Barnfield's 17th century belief that " fortune is full of fresh variety " in meetings of the International Federation of Library Associations, and the World Health Organisation Conference on " The Training of the Doctor." In 1962 the International Bar Association Conference was attended by 1,300 lawyers from a large number of countries; and also in the same year Edinburgh threw its own heraldic shield over the 550 people who attended the Sixth International Congress of Genealogy and Heraldry, followed by the International Congress of Monarchical Studies (with its picturesque appeal to history), the International Conference of Professors of English, the International Rail Transport Committee, and the International Conference of Social Scientists.

During the same period the domestic British conferences had the same many-sidedness. But space allows the mention of a few only. In 1960, a thousand members of the Institution of Gas Engineers came to the city, as did 1,000 dentists, 1,000 experts on food manufacturing, 1,000 parks experts, 750 authorities on waterworks, and many other pundits on cash registers, medical records, quarrying, gynaecology, air transport, and technical chemistry.

In 1961 this wide and learned range became even more polymathic when the city housed, in the aggregate, some thousands of conference delegates from the Liberal Party (whose Scottish headquarters are in Edinburgh), the National Union of Journalists, the Society of Furnace Builders, the National Federation of Clay Industries, the National Association of Colliery Managers, the National League of the Blind, the Scottish Clerks Association, the National Federation of Business and Professional Women's Clubs, the Institute of Medical Laboratory Technology, the British Association of Urological Surgeons, the British Cycle and Electrical Conference, the Institute of Social Welfare, the Scottish Association for Experimental Medicine, the Medical Research Society, the Psycho-Analytical Congress (1,000 here), the Institution of Fire Engineers, the Iron and Steel Conference, the Industrial Union of Architects, the Institute of Personnel Management, and the Scottish Women's Rural Institutes.

From the purely United Kingdom point of view, as distinct from its international appeal, Edinburgh as a conference venue in 1962 brought in another wide array of worthy bodies. First and foremost among them—for reasons both of local patriotism and the national purse—was the Institute of Municipal Treasurers and Accountants, whose 1962 President was Edinburgh's own City Chamberlain, Mr. Ames Imrie. And also there were the British Medical Association, the Limestone Federation, the Scottish Landowners Association, the Wholesale Grocers Association, the Association of Mining, Electrical and Mechanical Engineers, the British Paper and Board Makers Association, the Institute of Medical Laboratory Technology, the British Aluminium Conference, the Scottish Old People's Welfare Committee, the Association of Applied Biologists, the British Association of Dermatology, the Conference on Life Saving and Resuscitation.

Since 1962 this notable variety has been maintained. For again, to single out a few, Edinburgh was the venue in 1963 of the European Congress of Accountants, the 6th International Congress of Nutrition, and the United Kingdom Commercial Travellers Association Conference. In 1964 came the International Congress on Large Dams, the 17th International Congress of Actuaries, the International Botanical Congress, the International Cartographic Association, the Scottish Labour Party, the Pharmaceutical Society of Great Britain, the Association of Public Lighting Engineers, the National Federation of Business and Professional Women, the Institute of Hospital Administration, the British Association of Teachers of Dancing, and the Building Societies Association. Two other conferences in the city during 1964 deserve special mention for their international importance. One was the July meeting of the European Free Trade Association (E.F.T.A.), relations in which were soon to be strained by a new British Government's imposition of a substantial surcharge on foreign imports; the other a meeting of the Forestry Commission of the United Nations.

It is thus hardly surprising that in the summer of 1964, a year in which the city housed 34 conferences, the Corporation was seriously discussing plans for the development of a special conference centre, equipped with a hall, banking, dining and entertainment facilities, and an information office. Nor did many disagree with the late Sir Edward Appleton, then Principal and Vice-Chancellor of the University, when he said about the same time:

> " As a centre for international conferences Edinburgh possesses two further advantages. It has an ancient university in its very centre and it has what might be called a conference climate—a climate, which at the conference period, is neither too hot nor too cold, and is ideal for intellectual activity."

This is perhaps why more than 40 conferences, many of them international meetings of importance, took place during 1965.

THE CITY'S OWN TOURISTS

This survey might well end with some account of where the city's own holiday makers go at times of the year when all these visitors are pouring in. For if Edinburgh is a magnet for visitors from all over the world, Edinburghians themselves are tourists now on a quite unprecedented scale.

Leaving out of account the Scots' natural roving instinct, this is only natural (writes John R. Junor, an Edinburgh journalist who has made a special study of the subject). Heavier wage packets, the widespread adoption of the principle of holidays with pay, and longer vacation periods have together brought significant changes in the pattern of holiday planning.

In days not long gone, only a minority of the citizens ventured far afield, and most artisans and white-collar workers were content with seaside or inland places readily accessible by rail or bus. But nowadays thousands of the city's wage earners seek the sun abroad, and many little Scottish resorts traditionally dependent on the summer trade have seen it diminishing with serious repercussions on their economy.

To look back a little, older Edinburgh citizens will recall when most wage earners spent the Trades' Holidays at home, going on day picnics with their families either to the sands at Portobello, Cramond and Port Seton, or to the Blackford and Braid Hills—all within a mile or two—and the nearby slopes of the Pentlands. On those " high days " the trundling, open-top cable car was the popular mode of transport, each family usually being equipped with a little wicker basket containing the foodstuffs and a small spirit stove and kettle, or, more often, a bundle of sticks and newspapers for the picnic fire.

Fifty years or so ago Portobello was at the height of its popularity as a seaside resort, with a pier combining a restaurant and a concert hall. Pierrot groups entertained the crowds on the sands that were then almost level with the promenade. Donkeys were there to give penny rides to the children, and rowing boats could be hired in large numbers. Sea-bathing was an adventure not lightly undertaken and the majority of holidaymakers contented themselves with paddling.

Citizens able to spare a shilling or two also patronised the paddle steamers which, setting out from the West Pier at Leith, called at Aberdour, Burntisland, Portobello, North Berwick and other Forth resorts, or, on occasion, made the longer journeys up river to Stirling or round Fife Ness to Dundee. On such trips little orchestras provided music and the musicians were rewarded by passing round the hat.

Today the disintegrating remains of timber piers at North Berwick and other Forth resorts bear silent witness to these more leisurely days, when a memorable outing made no substantial inroad on the family exchequer, and men, women and children enjoyed the more simple pleasures of life. Until the early '20s weekly pocket money for the children of working-class families was invariably one penny, the spending of which demanded serious deliberation so great was the choice offered in the numerous little shops of the time. Many of these have naturally enough long disappeared, as have the " See the Forth Bridge " four-in-hand coach trips to South Queensferry—yet another highlight for those whose financial means may have made holidays at home compulsory but who nevertheless found in the galloping horses, the driver with his top hat, voluminous brass-buttoned coat and waving whip a thrilling spectacle. On race days at Musselburgh the coaches were diverted to more remunerative business, since a greater number of journeys were possible within a short period. But, while transport is much speedier in the '60s, the race meetings do not attract anything like the numbers before 1939.

For citizens rather better off than those who spent their holidays at home, a week in " digs " at the East Fife coast resorts, or in places as " remote " as Rothesay, Largs, Crieff, Pitlochry, Dunbar or Eyemouth was a fine adventure. Others more favourably situated financially—those in the professional classes, for instance—engaged houses for a month or longer at North Berwick, Peebles, Elie or Carnoustie, to mention the then most fashionable resorts. These, no doubt, heard from father and mother about the fun and excitement of earlier holidays spent even closer at hand—at Juniper Green, Balerno, West Linton or Lasswade—in days when a journey by horse cab to the railway station, complete with bulky wicker hampers, carpet bags and tin boxes, was something of an event. And, let it be noted in these days of speedy change, grandfather also probably recalled when, nearer still, Corstorphine, Liberton, Joppa, Musselburgh and Prestonpans enjoyed a considerable reputation among the citizens as summer holiday centres.

To leave Mr. Junor for the moment, another Edinburgh citizen recalls clearly the pilgrimage in June from his grandfather's house in George Street to their house on the coast at Joppa, some three miles away. The carriage, full of children, nursemaid and governess, was preceded by three drays filled with the luggage and domestic staff, while his mother and grandparents followed in the gig. This conveyance was used by grandfather for the daily journey to his office until the family returned to city life at the end of September. But these were leisurely days when customs died hard if at all.

The social impact of the motoring age on Edinburgh, which we looked at earlier, is worth a further glance. For with so many manual workers now owning cars, city families are "discovering" Scotland, England and Wales in vast numbers, and distant areas that formerly were merely names on the map are becoming quite familiar. Bus operators, too, are exerting considerable influence on the new fashions in holidaymaking, and by providing tours lasting several days, a week or longer, are attracting families previously satisfied with holidays much nearer the city. There has also been a spectacular growth in the popularity of caravan holidays, judging not only by touring activities but the renting of static vehicles on sites provided with attractive amenities and facilities, and the large post-war increase in the number of caravan construction firms and retailers. There are various reasons for this. The increased charges forced upon hotel proprietors and boarding house keepers by rising overheads and the post-war Catering and Wages Act have undoubtedly popularised caravan, car and camping holidays. With so many camping sites now available, and so many manufacturers offering luxury type tents and equipment, it looks as if this trend will continue to expand.

The financial repercussions of these changing holiday trends has naturally caused anxiety among numerous little communities which in the absence of any substantial industrial activity have long depended to a great extent on the patronage of visitors and the money they bring in. Now, with the once accepted summer holiday rush for accommodation dwindling, town councils in the Firth of Forth seaside resorts, as elsewhere in Scotland, are taking unprecedented steps to attract the volume of holiday traffic essential to their economic well-being. Most of them in fact now have their own publicity committees composed of leading citizens and information bureaux stocked with accommodation lists, pamphlets and posters and colour films, all staffed by men and women most anxious to boost the attractions of their particular resort.

North Berwick presents a particularly striking example of the changes which the post-war years have brought to the smaller resort. In its heyday, North Berwick attracted wealthy families, many from Edinburgh, who took over houses for the summer months, and others who kept hoteliers and landladies busily engaged from late spring to early autumn. Economic pressures have made most of the big house parties a thing of the past, so that nowadays this attractive town has to depend to a considerable extent on the patronage of day trippers who come by car or bus.

Similar trends are reported from other areas, though happily there are encouraging signs in various places that a new pattern is emerging. This is due, in the main, to the publicity work of the Scottish Tourist Board, with its "Come to Scotland" campaign being pushed vigorously across the Border, especially in those industrial centres where the appeal of bracing air, attractive scenery and amenities is likely to make full impact. Thus, as the Scots move out elsewhere at home and abroad, the English are moving in, and are doing so in growing numbers. The result is that some Scottish resorts that have been feeling the financial pinch are now developing links with new sources of custom. The hoteliers and landladies in Edinburgh and round about are thus becoming more attuned to the accents of Lancashire, Yorkshire and the industrial Midlands generally. However, while more and more Edinburgh citizens are exploring the out-of-the-way corners of Scotland and England, the most significant development in recent years has been the rapid expansion of their foreign travel.

Before the second World War only five travel agencies operated in Edinburgh: in 1963 there were 14, and the representatives of English and foreign firms offering holidays abroad have become much more numerous. Continental resorts that, until comparatively recently, were considered by the city's manual workers to be " millionaire class " are finding their customers to an increasing extent in the ranks of men and women drawing a weekly wage. Employees in numerous city offices, factories and workshops now operate holiday-saving schemes for trips across the Channel; so many, indeed, that travel agents work under pressure at prolonged peak periods. Significant also is the number of wage earners now participating in a new form of long-distance travel. With charter flights available direct from Turnhouse in 1963 for around £65, more and more working-class people began to make the transatlantic crossing. The sudden growth of this form of travel is amply proved by the fact that some 6,000 visas to visit the United States were issued at the American Consulate-General in Edinburgh during 1962, a total which represented an increase of 76 per cent compared with the previous year. By the same token, a few years ago one could walk into a travel agency in the early summer and book a foreign holiday without difficulty. By 1963 the number of working-class citizens seeking new scenes abroad had avalanched to such proportions that booking started in the previous December.

CHAPTER 30

THE PRINTED WORD

PRINTING

PRINTING in Edinburgh dates from the royal charter awarded by King James IV in 1507 to two burgesses of the city, Walter Chepman and Andrew Myllar. Chepman was a well-to-do merchant who had prospered as a trader in cloths and wools, and wood. Myllar was not so rich but brought to the partnership a practical knowledge of the art of printing. As he had acquired this at Rouen it was hardly surprising that the first books issued by Chepman and Myllar reflected the style and methods of printers in northern France.

After publishing Bishop Elphinstone's service book *The Aberdeen Breviary* (1509–10) these printers did little. A few books were printed during the next 30 years by other printers. By the late 1570s however an edition of the Bible had been printed and printing had become an everyday business in other parts of Scotland, apart from Edinburgh.

The industry again languished when James VI of Scotland and I of England left for London after the Union of the Crowns, but picked up again, and by the end of the century there had been a great advance in both type and engraved plates in books on law and natural history. As this growth continued, the 18th century saw the birth of several printing firms which flourish in Edinburgh today; and during the 19th and 20th centuries the printing industry as a whole became, until recent years, the city's largest industrial employer of labour.[1]

To describe the growth of printing in Edinburgh since the 18th and early 19th centuries, when literary works poured out of Edinburgh and the industry—there were 29 printers in the city in 1779—received its greatest stimulus, is far from easy. This is partly because, as now, there were printers in the city who were also publishers; there were publishers who became printers; and finally there were those, with no ambition to shoulder the risks inseparable from publishing, who were printers only. It is a tangled picture which has not materially altered through the years, except in terms of size and ownership. For if Nelson's and Oliver and Boyd were publisher-printers in the 18th century they play the same role today, as do a number of printing firms who can also boast 18th century roots and 20th century prosperity. Yet even these two leading firms have recently become associated with larger London-based groups.

All in all the printing and allied industries in Edinburgh employ between

[1] An invaluable short account of the growth of the printing trade in Edinburgh is contained in *Four Hundred and Fifty Years of Scottish Printing*, compiled by the National Library of Scotland, and printed under the authority of Her Majesty's Stationery Office by Morrison and Gibb, Limited (1958).

five and six thousand workers, and the industry can be divided roughly into six categories—general printing, book printing, map printing, newspaper and magazine publication, carton manufacture (dealt with earlier), and specialised productions. The general printing, or, as it is often called, the jobbing printing section of the industry, can be sub-divided broadly into firms who cater for different types of work. The smaller among them provide a general service to the community and print small to medium-sized runs, often in one colour. Amongst a number of the larger firms, both multi-colour letterpress work and offset lithography are carried out. This has helped to maintain Edinburgh's reputation as a printing centre. Nor can it be doubted that the progress of the bigger printing concerns in the past has been due to their attention to quality, and, in certain cases, their ability to provide typographical and design services. Those firms which have progressed in these particular fields generally supply both local and national markets and successfully compete in design and quality of workmanship in the bigger markets not only in England but overseas.

The oldest of these, and the second oldest printing establishment as such in the city is Pillans and Wilson Limited, which was founded in 1775 and is still a family business, with a considerable reputation for the excellence of its work. Of similar repute is the firm of McFarlane and Erskine Limited.

Pillans and Wilson deserve a special word of praise here. It is noteworthy, at a time when the reconstruction of the Old Town is altering some of its appearance, that the building in the Lawnmarket, in Riddell's Close, where Edinburgh's second oldest printing firm was established in 1775, not only still stands but, of even more importance, is being restored and its outside wooden staircase, of which there can be few of its kind left, preserved.

The firm, founded by James Pillans, continued as small printers, doing legal and general work, until the end of the first World War when it began to expand in the field of quality colour printing and printing for nationally known companies.

Another Edinburgh firm with a famous name, and a long tradition is T. and A. Constable whose early fortunes swung between publishing and printing for many years, but who are now regarded as printers—with an interesting start under another name.

In 1760 one David Willison set up a printing business in Craig's Close, and when his daughter in 1795 married Archibald Constable, a bookseller it was natural that the publishing side of their business should also be developed. It was indeed from Willison's office that the *Edinburgh Review* was launched in 1802, and through his friendship with Walter Scott, Constable gathered a brilliant company of authors and published not only the Waverley Novels but many other books, including the *Encyclopaedia Britannica* which was founded in Edinburgh.

In 1833 Thomas Constable, son of Archibald, took over the printing business and moved to 11 Thistle Street in the New Town. Here, in 1835, he had a fount of Greek and four presses: by 1852 with 16 presses he was printing Arabic, Hebrew, Coptic, Sanscrit, German and Music. Since 1839 he had also been Her Majesty's Printer and Publisher in Edinburgh.

Before 1853 a great proportion of the work consisted of Bible printing, but in that year Constable entered the London market and began to print books for London publishers.

In more recent times a feature of the business has been its educational work, and in common with other Edinburgh printers, extensive legal and commercial printing. There was also an acquisition in 1936, when the business of the Edinburgh Press, which printed the Tusitala and other editions of Robert Louis Stevenson, was incorporated, the name of the company continuing as T. and A. Constable Limited. To bring the record up to date, in 1964 Bracken House Publications which belongs to The Financial Times Limited, acquired the whole of the share capital of T. and A. Constable for £225,000 cash, and by so doing got itself a bigger stake in the city's printing and publishing industry for as we shall see it had already acquired control of other firms.

The products of Edinburgh's general printing firms are mainly for use within the United Kingdom, though many of them print technical literature and catalogues for firms, particularly in engineering and woollen manufacturing, which have a large volume of business with overseas countries. In this way Edinburgh printing helps the British export trade. A great deal of the output, particularly from publisher-printers, is for export markets; and although recently much has been spoken of the volume of printing being done on the Continent of Europe, particularly in Holland, for British publishing firms, the value of books exported from the United Kingdom is greatly in excess of the total figure for imports.

In the industry at large and particularly in book printing, Edinburgh's reputation for quality has been upheld and the firms engaged in this part of the industry do a considerable volume of specialist work for London publishers in educational, scientific and medical as well as in general printing. Among the well-known firms engaged in printing for publishers are William Blackwood and Sons, R. and R. Clark, T. and A. Constable, Morrison and Gibb, and Neill and Company who have the distinction of being the oldest-established printers in Edinburgh: their business was started in 1749 at Canonmills. Neill, along with the other firms mentioned, are concerned in book printing, especially for educational publishers. The largest publishing firm to print its own publications is that of Thomas Nelson and Sons Limited which was established in 1798 and at the time of writing employs between 500 and 600 people. Nelson's combined printing, binding and publishing under one roof, a distinction shared with Oliver and Boyd Limited, one of the longest-established firms of publisher-printers in the city engaged in publishing scientific, educational, literary and general work. Among the greater changes which have taken place two long established firms deserve a special mention. The printing plant of J. and J. Gray, long noted name among Edinburgh printers, now belongs to H.M. Stationery Office, while R. and R. Clark, a famous firm which printed Shaw's works amongst others was bequeathed to the University of Edinburgh in 1946, but was sold by the University to William Thyne (Holdings) Limited 16 years later.

In the early days of the expansion of Edinburgh book printing it was usual for the printer to bind the editions before delivery to the publisher; but with the advent of mechanised binding equipment, a start was made by firms specialising in binding for publishers. Apart from Nelson, Oliver and Boyd, and Morrison and Gibb, who carry out printing and binding, much of the work printed in Edinburgh is bound by Henderson and Bisset, Anderson's (Edinburgh) Limited, Hunter and Foulis Limited, and Orrock and Son Limited. Of these, the oldest is Henderson and Bisset whose distinguished work is described in a later chapter on the city's craft industries.

There are other interesting specialisations in the printing world. Because a large number of whisky-blending firms are located in the city specialisation in the production of labels for this and other industries has been encouraged, and, amongst those engaged in this particular work, produced mainly by offset lithography, are many firms already mentioned earlier. They include Waddie and Company Limited, who have recently acquired two English printing firms, Smith and Ritchie Limited, and, in the field of tag labels of all kinds an old established family business, the Simpson Label (and Stationery Manufacturing) Company Limited. In addition to label manufacture Waddie's have a world-wide reputation for die-stamping while Smith and Ritchie Limited produce labels for food manufacturing concerns, mainly located in London and Southern England. There are also W. E. Annan Limited and Alex Cowan and Sons—related to the Penicuik paper-makers—in this complex field where general printing, carton printing—a highly specialised industry encouraged by recent trends in the packaging of foodstuffs—and the myriad forms of commercial printing and stationery are intimately related. Map-making will be discussed later in our survey of the city's publishers.

The printing industry in Edinburgh, having had its beginnings with the spread of education and the proximity of the Law Courts, Banks and Insurance Companies, has, in the general sense, and with the exception of book printing, remained on a local basis, and has its own Edinburgh Master Printers' Association. Equally, it is a fact that many of the firms engaged in the industry are family businesses which have been built up by succeeding generations from small beginnings, some of them very successfully. Indeed many familiar names spring to mind in addition to those we have mentioned—C. J. Cousland, for instance, and Mackenzie and Storrie—but the list of firms such as these is too long to be enumerated here.

PUBLISHING

Edinburgh touched its literary meridian early last century when the *Edinburgh Review* and *Blackwood's Magazine* were in full vigour and when Scott and a host of lesser luminaries shone brightly. Naturally this incandescence was favourable for publishing. The ascendancy of Archibald Constable, a prince of publishers, was short, but many of the firms which took root at this period still flourish. Edinburgh's publishing houses, in fact, are nearly all venerable and well established, claiming the respect due not only to age but to the ability to survive in a highly competitive business exposed to changes in economic conditions and in reading tastes.

Thomas Nelson started to produce religious tracts just before the *Edinburgh Review* electrified the city's bourgeoisie and many outside it. W. and R. Chambers, Oliver and Boyd, Blackwood, T. and T. Clark, John Bartholomew, and W. and A. K. Johnston are all well over the century. E. and S. Livingstone celebrated its 100th anniversary in 1963. W. Green and Son, the legal publishers, were founded in 1870, while McDougall's Educational Company was born in 1878. In a few instances there has been continuity of family management as well as of the company's name. In Chambers and in Blackwood's, for example, the dynasties are carried on by great-great-grandsons of the founders, and in Bartholomew's the sixth generation is in control. Elsewhere control has passed out of the hands of the founding families, and Edinburgh publishing has felt the impact of the trend towards bigger companies. Thus Nelson's has been taken over by the Thomson Organisation; Oliver and Boyd by Bracken House Publications, itself a subsidiary of The Financial Times Limited which has also acquired Livingstone's and the printing firms of T. and A. Constable, and The Darien Press; Green's by Sweet and Maxwell.

Though the fact that men of letters were plentiful meant a genial atmosphere for Edinburgh's early publishers in their golden age, perhaps a greater impetus came from the movement for popular education. Chambers catered by issuing a cheap periodical, *Chambers' Journal* and the famous *Encyclopaedia*, which has now come under the wing of Newnes in London. Other publishers exploited and increased the demand for improving books at the lowest possible price; and Edinburgh publishing thus acquired a strongly educational bias, which it retains to this day. Fortunately, too, tradition often points the same way as economic factors Publishers, especially since the last war, have been faced by high printers' costs—not only of paper and other materials but of labour—and in such circumstances educational books, with their longer expectation of life and larger sales, suit smaller publishers who cannot compete easily in the market for fiction and short-lived books that have to be mass-produced and mass-sold in order to make a profit.

By London standards Edinburgh publishing is on a modest scale. But Nelson's, the oldest and largest of the Edinburgh houses, is a big enterprise with an international sales organisation and subsidiaries in Paris, New York and Toronto. More than 50 per cent of its output is exported to Commonwealth countries—Australia and Canada for instance—and to the United States. Nelson's has also built up a large trade with the newly independent African states, notably Nigeria, which it supplies with educational books in English and in the vernaculars. The extensive list of Nelson's may be classified under four sections—school books, books for juveniles, classics, and general. In publishing cheap editions of the classics the firm was a pioneer; and it reaps the reward of its enterprise in this field, *Nelson's Classics* still being popular in spite of much competition. The general section embraces reference books like classical and biblical atlases, theology, history, and works of scholarship in almost every subject, the medieval texts being especially worthy of note. Nelson's also serve students of Scottish history well with the standard text-books by the late Croft Dickinson and George Pryde, and the invaluable source-books by Dickinson and Professor Gordon Donaldson. The firm print nearly all their books in their own printing works at Parkside, which can turn out sumptuous volumes with colour plates as well as the more run-of-the-mill products.

As befits such an old firm, Oliver and Boyd's office in the quiet retreat of Tweeddale Court is in the heart of old Edinburgh, but the interest of the firm in educational publishing at all levels from the infant school to post-graduate studies has made its influence felt in many parts of the world. It is claimed that more children in Australia learn to read with Oliver and Boyd books than any other, and certainly the firm's reputation in mathematics, statistics, and other scientific fields has led to the use of their textbooks in universities in many countries. The Scottish connections of the firm have also produced many guide books and for upwards of a hundred years the *Edinburgh Almanac.* This was issued annually and was considered to be the *vade mecum* for all civil, political, legal and municipal affairs in Scotland. Again, in the early 1950s, the firm published the first four pilot volumes of the *Third Statistical Account of Scotland.* A more recent development has been the fine list of works of literary criticism including the now popular *Writers and Critics* series of paperbacks.

True to the spirit of its founders W. and R. Chambers still ministers to the need for accurate and quickly accessible information. Nowadays the firm is universally known for its *Twentieth Century Dictionary*—one of the best known one-volume English dictionaries and a standby of cross-word solvers. While reference books in general, such as dictionaries and gazetteers, are a strong suit in the Chambers list, their output, mainly educational, includes mathematical tables, both elementary and advanced, among them Pryde's *Seven-figure Tables* and Comrie's *Six-figure Tables*; also numerous series of school readers, geographies, histories and other books, while their stories for young readers appeal to school librarians. In their general list Chambers publish useful regional guides, histories, and books with a Scottish flavour. About 40 per cent of the firm's products go abroad, mainly to India, Pakistan and Australia.

Nowhere is the sense of Edinburgh's literary past so strong as in the salon of Blackwood's office in George Street. This handsome, domed room, surrounded by sombre panelling, presses and bookcases full of back numbers of *Blackwood's Magazine*, and hung with portraits in heavy gilt frames of Lockhart, James Hogg, Christopher North and other Blackwood celebrities, is a monument to the firm's dignity and solidity and of a heyday when the list of its authors read like a history of Victorian literature. Now, the firm has turned mainly to printing, but it still publishes a number of books every year and it keeps its famous magazine going, though the times are never easy for serious periodicals.

All Edinburgh publishers, apart from certain specialists, have a strong interest in the school market. McDougall's Educational Company deliberately concentrates on the primary and secondary schools, to which it offers a wide range of attractive books on all subjects. Its musical publications are a feature of its list, and its stationery and jotters, which sell all over the world, are a profitable side-line. Generations of school children grew familiar with McDougall's best-sellers such as *Gateways to Bookland*, and *Story and Study*, to mention two of the firm's readers which have sold by the million. Its equally notable arithmetic books were also favourites with teachers. Among the firm's present successes are the *New Vanguard* readers, its Revision Speed *Test Arithmetic*, and the *School Study Bible*, which sold nearly a million copies in two years. In pre-war days, when social history was not so fashionable, McDougall's emphasised it in the *March of History* series: today it is working on programming for teaching machines. About 15 per cent of the company's publications go to the export market, principally to West Africa and the West Indies, and its sales in England are three or four times as great as in Scotland.

Another Edinburgh firm which deserves mention for its educational works is John Cormack, for it is one of the few independent concerns in Scotland whose activities are devoted exclusively to the publication of educational text-books. Established in 1898 the firm has been mainly engaged in the production of text books for use in Scottish schools (especially primary schools), English texts, histories in which Scotland's place in the wider sphere of United Kingdom history receives a prominent place, geographies and books on mathematics. Today many of its publications are also used in schools beyond the Border.

Edinburgh shares with Glasgow the printing and publishing firm of William Hodge and Company, founded in 1872 and still an independent family business. Today, however, publishing is but a very small part of the firm's work compared with printing and shorthand writing in the courts. William Hodge and Company must have a distinguished place in any account of publishing in Edinburgh, or indeed of Scotland, because it issued from its Edinburgh office between 1905 and 1959 the 83 volumes of the world famous *Notable British Trials* series.

This famous series was begun by the late Harry Hodge, who died in 1947. Both he and his father William Hodge, who founded the firm, were court shorthand writers and it seems natural that they should have specialised in law publishing. William Hodge founded *Scottish Law Review* in 1885 and *Scottish Law Directory* in 1891. Harry's son Mr. James Hodge, the present head of the firm, extended the range of *British Trials* after World War II to include accounts of several war crimes trials, including that of the Belsen commandants, but rising costs have compelled him to discontinue the series for the time being.

Today the firm confines its publishing to *Scottish Law Review* and *Scottish Law Directory*, *Faculty Digest* (a guide to Court of Session cases) and a few standard law works, and local government books of which perhaps Dobbie's *Sheriff Court Practice* and *Sheriff Court Styles* are the best known. The market for books on Scots law is necessarily limited, and for that reason the firm has concentrated on printing and shorthand writing. Printing is also carried out in its London factory.

Today the law publishing house of W. Green and Son Limited is a monument to one of Edinburgh's most vigorous citizens of the early 20th century, Charles Edward Green. When he was 20 and in his final year as a medical student at Edinburgh University, the sudden death of his father William Green who had founded it around 1870 placed him of necessity in charge of the business.

Charles Edward Green brought to his new task the enthusiasm of a scholar and such a high capacity for business that the business flourished financially and in repute. Space permits only the barest mention of his service to law and scholarship in the publication of the *Encyclopaedia of the Laws of Scotland* (15 volumes); *Encyclopaedia of the Laws of England* (15 volumes); the *Scots Digest* (reported cases from 1800 to 1914 with supplements to keep it up to date); and *Scots Statutes Revised* (1424–1918). In addition to these he produced an *Encyclopaedia of Accounting* and those standard textbooks by such authorities as Gloag and Henderson, which have been used by successive generations of students in the Faculty of Law. He started also the *Scots Law Times*, which reports leading cases in the Session and Justiciary, and the *Juridical Review*, devoted to theoretical studies of law with frequent excursions into literature and history.

Despite the call of law publishing Green never however abandoned his interest in healing: he published an *Encyclopaedia of Medicine* and himself wrote a treatise on cancer; and as another of his interests was farming he also brought out an *Encyclopaedia of Agriculture*. By cruel chance he died prematurely at the age of 54 in 1920; but the firm continues as a member of the Sweet and Maxwell Group, and in the middle 1960s had on hand a project which would have delighted his heart. This was a complete 20-volume revision by leading authorities on the whole law of Scotland under the auspices of the Scottish Universities Law Institute. Another fact must be recorded about the firm. Soon after the first World War Green's acquired the business of Bell and Bradfute, established in 1734 and who were publishers of *Stair's Institutions*, *Erskine's Institutes*, *Hume's Commentaries on Criminal Law* and other great legal works of the 17th, 18th and early 19th centuries.

Founded in 1821 the family business of T. and T. Clark is extremely busy as a publisher of theological and scholarly works. In the 19th century the house of Clark earned a high reputation throughout the English speaking world for numerous translations of Continental and particularly German theologians. This reputation is being maintained today by the production of a magnum opus, the translation in five volumes of Dr. Karl Barth's *Church Dogmatics* under the general editorship of the Rev. Professor T. F. Torrance and the Rev. Professor G. W. Bromiley. As for the firm's many standard works, these include such works as *Dictionary of the Bible* (Hastings), *A Grammar of New Testament Greek* (Moulton), *A Concordance to the Greek New Testament* (Moulton), and *A Companion to the Bible* (Manson). Also on the Clark list is an *Encyclopaedia of Religion and Ethics.*

Suitably for a city with a world famous school of medicine, Edinburgh has a medical publishing firm of international repute. This is E. and S. Livingstone, founded in 1863 as a bookshop by Edward Livingstone. Two years later he was joined by his brother Stuart and the firm was given the name under which it still trades. The firm developed alongside the University Medical Faculty and the move by the Livingstone brothers into medical publishing was both natural and courageous. In the past 100 years E. and S. Livingstone has published many standard medical dental and nursing books. Today its catalogue lists some 400 works; it publishes medical journals; and many of its publications have been translated into Chinese, Danish, Dutch, French, German, Greek, Italian, Japanese, Polish, Portuguese, Spanish, Swedish, Turkish and Yugoslavian.

The city's geographical and map publishers are also widely known. Of these the principal are W. and A. K. Johnston and G. W. Bacon (both now associates of Morrison and Gibb, the printers) and John Bartholomew. The Johnston and Bacon group issues school atlases and road maps, history, geography and children's reference books for school use and a series of books on Highland clans and regiments, among which is the standard work, *Clans, Septs and Regiments of the Scottish Highlands.*

At Bartholomew's the sixth generation of the family is now in control. First of the dynasty was George Bartholomew (1784–1871) who began work as a map engraver in the city in 1797, but the business takes its title from his son, John Bartholomew (senior), who died in 1861. Including Mr. John C. Bartholomew, one of the present directors, there have been five men of that name at the head of the firm; and two of them, John George (1860–1920) and John (1890–1962) were honoured with the degree of LL.D from the University. Together the family have made significant contributions to map making. They have not only produced the well-known series of *Half Inch Maps*, the *Edinburgh Atlas of Modern Geography* and *The Times Atlas of the World*, to mention but a few, but as far back as 1878 they pioneered layer colouring as a means of portraying relief in maps, the system which is now almost universally used. Besides producing its own publications the firm also supplies many other publishers and organisations at home and abroad with maps. In all, the present directors, who have almost entirely re-equipped their printing works with the latest machinery since the war, estimate that about one third of the firm's output is exported either directly as Bartholomew maps or atlases etc., or as part of works published by others. Production since the war has trebled although the numbers employed have declined.

Other publishers with their own special niche in Edinburgh include Gall and Inglis, who specialise in ready reckoners and aids to calculation; Albyn Press who have produced cookery and other books with a strong Scottish flavour; Malcolm Macdonald, who has done no small service to present day Scots literature by issuing poetry and reviews; and the Edinburgh University Press, whose works, many of them written by University staff, maintain a high standard of scholarship.

In its present form, the University Press came into existence quietly in 1946 and published its first book two years later. Until that time, although the Scottish Universities had always encouraged learned printing, they had never attempted to establish Presses in the manner of Oxford or Cambridge. Yet it was as early as 1596, only 13 years after the foundation of the college, that Edinburgh University published its first book, the *Theses Philosophicae* of that year. The printer of the book was Henry Charteris, the King's Printer. The custom of printing first the class theses and then the degree theses continued, and it was round this nucleus that there slowly formed the office of Academiae Typographus, a title first used by James Lindsay in 1645.

Of those who followed him as University Printer over the next 200 years, perhaps the most notable was Thomas Ruddiman, who applied for the office in 1728. Ruddiman was the famous keeper of the Advocates' Library, editor of Buchanan, author of the *Rudiments* on which Scotland's Latinity was to be thereafter based, and publisher of Ramsay's *Poems* and *The Gentle Shepherd.* He sought the business title of Academiae Typographus in order to challenge the long-established foreign market in text books; and this he successfully did.

In 1859 the Senatus Academicus appointed Thomas Constable to the honorary office of Printer. But in 1881, when Constable died, the University for the first time conferred the title on a firm in place of an individual. Thereafter, until the present University Press was established as a publishing organisation, Messrs. T. and A. Constable used the imprint " University Press, Edinburgh."

Today the Edinburgh University Press is owned and controlled by the University Court of the University of Edinburgh, and is directed by a Committee appointed by the University Court and composed mainly of professors and lecturers from the various Faculties. It is a scholarly publishing house, producing specialist monographs and textbooks by members of the University and of other universities throughout the Commonwealth. These it distributes and sells throughout the world, with a particularly strong market in the United States, where there seems to be a " strong academic belief (as a member of the University Press puts it) that the central disciplines of the University of Edinburgh show great philosophical and theological strength."

THE PRESS

NEWSPAPERS

Edinburgh has played an interesting part in Scotland's newspaper history. In the troubled middle years of the 17th century it gave birth to the first Scottish newspaper, though this was only a reprint of the *Diurnall Occurrances* which began to publish news of Parliamentary proceedings after the abolition of the Star Chamber in 1641. *Mercurius Scoticus,* Scotland's second newspaper, was issued not in Edinburgh but in Leith (1651). It gave extracts from English newspapers and was primarily intended for the English garrison in the port. There was then a lull till 1660 when there appeared the *Mercurius Caledonius*. This journal had a very short life—only 10 issues in all—but at least it had the honour of being the northern kingdom's first indigenous newspaper, and it paved the way for the *Edinburgh Gazette* (1680), the Edinburgh *Evening Courant* (1718), the *Caledonian Mercury* (1720) and their 18th and 19th century successors. Today three newspapers appear in Edinburgh every day except Sunday. They are *The Scotsman*, the *Edinburgh Evening News and Dispatch*, and the *Scottish Daily Mail*.

The Scotsman

The Scotsman, founded in 1817 and widely recognised as one of Britain's best quality newspapers, can claim a readership and influence far beyond the confines of the city in which it is printed. It is not only bought and taken away by many of the large army of overseas visitors to Edinburgh and elsewhere in Scotland, but in London's railway stations it can be bought on certain holidays—Christmas Day for instance—when English newspapers cease publication. It wins, as it did in 1963, such accolades as the Honour Medal presented annually to distinguished newspapers by the University of Missouri, and the top award for the Best Designed Newspaper of the Year, in the Annual Award for Newspaper Design competition organised by *Printing World*. These were notable recognitions; but probably they were outshone in the autumn of 1964 when a panel of 26 United States professors of journalism selected *The Scotsman* as one of Britain's top three newspapers and also placed it among the world's top 20. Also within recent years, *The Scotsman* has sponsored a travelling exhibition of Scottish products, which toured the Continent, and a " This Scotland Exhibition " to coincide with the Edinburgh Festival. In 1961 it installed what was then claimed to be the fastest teletype setter in the world—14 lines per minute—mainly to give its readers the latest and fullest information on the London Stock Exchange.

It is however neither enterprise of this kind nor effective layouts and attractive type which alone give distinction to a newspaper. Apart from well-presented news and excellent feature articles, *The Scotsman* has faithful readers because of its literary, music and art criticism, its leading articles and not least its correspondence columns in which famous as well as lesser-known figures conduct keen controversies.

The newspaper itself, at the time when many journals of repute were amalgamating with others or quietly folding up, has had financial security because of its association with the Thomson Organisation Limited. This powerful group, with its headquarters in London, apparently had its origins in a Toronto barber's shop, since the barber's son Roy (now Lord Thomson of Fleet) was to become the owner of a great many North American newspapers before buying *The Scotsman*, taking up residence for a time in Edinburgh, and securing the contract to run the commercial Scottish Television service. As it turned out, the association between S.T.V. and *The Scotsman* was to prove beneficial and convenient to both.

Scottish Television, which would otherwise have had to set up an enormously costly news service, got its news direct from *The Scotsman* and duly paid for it. *The Scotsman* on the other hand got valuable publicity from Scottish Television.

The rest of Lord Thomson's empire quickly followed. He took over Kemsley Newspapers, a group which included not only the *Sunday Times* but provincial newspapers such as the *Aberdeen Press and Journal*, and after its 1963 merger with Lord Thomson's *Evening Dispatch*, the *Edinburgh Evening News*. This last was an unusual transaction, because the *Evening News*, which did not belong to Lord Thomson, was making a profit while his own *Evening Dispatch* had been losing money for a number of years and showed little sign of recovery.

The Edinburgh Evening News and Dispatch

Let us look first at the *Evening News*. Founded in 1873 it was owned by Provincial Newspapers Limited, and by 1963 was publishing four editions daily and circulating not only in Edinburgh and the Lothians, but in the Border counties, Stirling, Clackmannan and Fife. It had helped to build up its position by printing a lot of local news and articles of local interest, and it carried an unusual number of small advertisements, including classified advertising on its front page. The *News* was in fact one of the last newspapers to follow this rather old-fashioned practice which the *Dispatch* had already abandoned by going over to tabloid form. The *News* had also firmly entrenched itself with the unusually high proportion of 80–90 per cent letter box deliveries by newsagents to regular subscribers. Also, by 1963, it had built up a circulation of about 155,000 compared with the *Evening Dispatch*'s 51,000 or so.

To understand this notable disparity in circulation we must take a brief glance at the *Dispatch*'s history. First published in the New Year of 1886 as a sister paper to *The Scotsman*, it shared the same premises and technical resources, but was always manned by a separate staff. Strongly Conservative it had readers in all walks of life, but always it appealed particularly to the business and professional community. Originally rather like the *Evening News*, though aimed at a more well-to-do class of reader, the *Dispatch*, when it became a tabloid newspaper, lost much of its old distinctive character without being able to dislodge its competitor the *Evening News* as an evening paper of particular appeal to the lower income groups. Now and then it scored successes in its losing battle with the *News*. In 1961, for example, it was highly commended for its design by a special committee of experts on newspaper and printing techniques; the trophies it donated to almost every sport were also much esteemed; and its old ultra-Conservatism ended in its having no real political attachments at all. Yet none of this supposedly wide appeal was sufficient to prevent the *Dispatch* from making a continuous and substantial loss from 1957 onwards—a fact made clear in the evidence given to the Royal Commission on the Press by representatives of the Thomson newspaper group in September, 1962.

At this point the Thomson interests suggested an arrangement whereby Provincial Newspapers Limited, predominantly an English newspaper group, should sell them the *Edinburgh Evening News* (which had just spent vast sums on new plant and was promoting an annual Ideal Homes Exhibition) so that the *News* and the *Dispatch* might be suitably merged. In return Provincial Newspapers would take over the Thomson-owned *Sheffield Telegraph*. And so it happened. In 1963 the exchange was made, and the *Evening News* became *The Edinburgh Evening News and Dispatch*. Since then the merged newspaper has combined most of the features of both papers, with news on the front page, and by the summer of 1964 had a circulation of some 176,000 of which about 90,000 were sold in Edinburgh itself and the remainder in the neighbouring counties.

The effect of this important deal was threefold. Firstly, it meant that London and Glasgow were to be the only cities in the whole of Great Britain with more than one evening newspaper. Secondly, it gave the *Evening News* a less old-fashioned look, for hitherto not only had several of its inside pages been covered with advertisements but its front page as well; which meant that both world events and momentous happenings at home could only be described on an inside page. Obviously the new lay-out was more acceptable to the majority of readers. The third effect of the merger was much less happy.

At the time the newspapers published and printed in the city employed just over 2,000 people in Edinburgh itself. Of these the majority belonged to *The Scotsman*, the *Evening Dispatch*, the *Weekly Scotsman* (a magazine-newspaper popular among expatriates in England and elsewhere) and the *Evening News*. Many others were employed by the *Sottish Daily Mail* which, unlike the Glasgow-produced *Scottish Daily Express*, has been printed in Edinburgh since 1946—and is a widely circulated daily newspaper. This Scottish edition of the *Daily Mail* belongs to Associated Newspapers; it has the second Viscount Rothermere as its chief proprietor; and it gives employment to a goodly number of people. But the number of those employed by the newspapers as a whole was reduced by several hundreds owing to redundancy caused by the *News–Dispatch* merger. From this redundancy, however, there at least quickly appeared the first Edinburgh news agency, an organisation called United News Services run by four former *News* reporters, who were busily collecting news for Press, radio and television as this book went to the printers.

Among the daily newspapers competition is as severe in Edinburgh as in the rest of Scotland. The English *Times*, *Daily Telegraph* and *The Guardian* have their devotees. But inevitably their Scottish, and therefore their Edinburgh circulations, depend to a great extent on the success which attends the efforts of the newspapers printed on the spot. The Edinburgh-printed newspapers certainly are far from having it their own way in Edinburgh itself, where both the *Scottish Daily Express* and the *Daily Record*, printed in Glasgow, have substantial Edinburgh sales, and in common with the *Glasgow Herald* keep editorial, advertising and circulation branches in the city.

Newsprint and paper for the Edinburgh newspapers comes from

Finland, Sweden and Canada by way of Leith, although a certain amount is manufactured locally at mills in the Lothians and the West of Scotland. Printing ink is purchased locally.

PERIODICALS

Edinburgh as a city has always been remarkably rich in magazines. Although now somewhat declined from the palmy days when such diverse figures as Madame de Stael and Napoleon looked forward pleasurably to the next edition of the *Edinburgh Review*, ambitious and interesting magazines covering literature and Scottish life and industry are still being published here.

The ancestor of the modern magazine is the *Edinburgh Review*. Founded in the autumn of 1802 by a group of intelligent and lively young Whigs, including Francis Jeffrey, Brougham, Sydney Smith and Francis Horner, it struck a new note in its independence and in the princely sums paid to its contributors. Before this, literary magazines had been produced by publishers to puff their own wares, and the *Edinburgh Review*'s remarkable success and influence is attested by the speed with which the Tory party brought out a rival, the *Quarterly*. Nowadays Jeffrey is chiefly remembered outside Edinburgh for his attack on Wordsworth, and Byron's *English Bards and Scotch Reviewers*. What is too often forgotten is that for 20 years he was editor and chief contributor to a journal of wide-ranging interests and strongly held opinions expressed with a lucidity and vigour which opened a new exciting chapter in journalism. Other journals followed. In 1832 the Edinburgh publisher William Chambers, who had already (in 1821–2) published a fortnightly called *The Kaleidoscope*, issued the first weekly sheet of what became the famous *Chambers' Journal*, a periodical destined to last for a century and a quarter. Later still came *The Scots Observer* with Barrie and Kipling among its contributors.

Although the *Edinburgh Review* and *Chambers' Journal* are no more, one survivor from the period is still with us—*Blackwood's Magazine*, a monthly which inappositely appeared for the first time on April Fool's Day, 1817, and is still published from the same office in George Street. *Blackwood's* nowadays contains articles and fiction, much of it dealing with faraway places, and written in the main by non-professional writers; but in addition to the great triumvirate of its early days—John Gibson Lockhart, James Hogg and John Wilson (Christopher North)—it has in its time published George Eliot, John Galt, Susan Ferrier, Mrs. Oliphant, Alfred Noyes, Bernard Fergusson, the early Hugh MacDiarmid and many other writers of note. Several novels by Ian Hay and John Buchan also first appeared serially in " Maga," as *Blackwood's* was familiarly called, and these included *The First Hundred Thousand* and *The Thirty-Nine Steps*. It is still under the direction of a Blackwood—five generations since the founder and now the seventh Blackwood.

In the early 1960s—almost a century and a half after *Maga*'s foundation —one of the most enterprising magazines appearing in Edinburgh was the *New Saltire*, published by the Saltire Society. Although it existed to encourage all aspects of Scottish life it was politically open-minded, and its wide range of subjects for the general reader included new poems and stories, articles on various aspects of the Scottish economy, reviews, pictures, photographs and competitions. It had many ups and downs but was nonetheless still looking forward to a long life when according to *The Scotsman*'s Literary Editor, writing in his newspaper on 27th April, 1964: " The legend says you can have only one phoenix in the world at a time. The *New Saltire* has just suffered one of its cyclical immolations . . . ."

There has always been an insistent poetic voice speaking in Edinburgh. In recent years it has found an outlet in several journals: the *New Saltire*, which encouraged new poetry; *Lines*, Alan Riddell's poetry magazine founded in Edinburgh in the early '50s; and, more recently, in *Poor Old Tired Horse*, published by Jessie McGuffie at the Wild Hawthorn Press. This latest effort has been appearing at irregular intervals, and is *avant garde* and controversial in appearance, content, and illustrations. The editor believes strongly in the new poetry, and publishes many contributions from overseas, as well as the work of native poets. Her fierce championship of the superiority of the modern has made the magazine well known; it has also stimulated many arguments which suggest the flytings of earlier times.

Then there is the " glossy " monthly magazine, *Edinburgh Tatler*, which belongs to The Illustrated County Group Limited. Though it has an Edinburgh office, this paper is printed in Nottingham.

INDUSTRY AND FINANCE

Scotland, founded in 1947, and appearing monthly, is the organ of the Scottish Council (Development and Industry). This is a non-political body which exists to stimulate Scottish trade and industry, and its magazine is therefore mainly for those concerned in production, although many of its articles on the Scottish economy can be profitably read by the general public. It gives information on new developments in industry, management, export and anything that can be of use to the Scottish industrialist. It also gives free space to any industry wishing to make it known that it is not using its plant to capacity, and generally fosters business.

The Three Banks Review is an unusually interesting periodical partly because of its contents and partly because it is sponsored by the Royal Bank of Scotland, which is the only Scottish bank to control two English banks—Glyn Mills and Company and William Deacon's Bank Limited. Hence the periodical's title; hence too the wide variety of its articles which in 1963 ranged from early banking in Dundee and Association Football finance in Britain to economic development in the Sudan.

Also concerned with trade and industry are the Edinburgh Chamber of Commerce *Journal*, which circulates among the Chamber's members and is therefore intimately concerned with every commercial development in the city itself; and the *Accountant's Magazine* published in Edinburgh by the Institute of Chartered Accountants of Scotland.

Scotland's Magazine, a fine publication which incorporates the old *S.M.T. Magazine* and *Scottish Country Life*, is published by Scottish Omnibuses Limited and is mainly concerned with rural Scotland. It contains articles and stories about the countryside, and various topics of general interest; it also publishes photographs of a very high standard, and comes out monthly.

PROFESSIONAL PERIODICALS

The Scots Law Times, published once a week while court is in session and once a month during vacation, publishes articles on various aspects of the law, not confining itself exclusively to Scotland, and also reports cases of special legal interest. It should also be mentioned here that Nelson's publish *Common Market Law Reports*, while as we have already seen there are also the *Scottish Law Review* and the *Juridical Review*, published by Green's.

As the Educational Institute of Scotland has its headquarters in Edinburgh, it publishes from there the *Scottish Educational Journal*, a weekly with articles on educational subjects and those of professional interest to teachers.

Other professional journals with an Edinburgh connection are the *Scottish Geographical Magazine*, published three times a year by the Royal Scottish Geographical Society, but printed outside the city (at Perth); the *Edinburgh Journal of Science and Technology* (sponsored by the Royal Scottish Society of Arts); and the *Scottish Historical Review*, published by Nelson's twice a year with the Scottish History Society behind it. Published principally for historians, the *Review* prints papers on Scottish affairs and history, much of it early history, and also articles and reviews.

The philosophers and psychologists have several journals printed in Edinburgh, including the quarterly *British Journal for Philosophy and Science*, and *Mind*. Both are issued by Nelson's which also publishes *The Political Quarterly*. Oliver and Boyd are responsible for the *Philosophical Journal*, a new publication announced in 1964 with the sub-title, " Transactions of the Royal Philosophical Society of Glasgow."

There are also of course various official medical journals to widen still further this astonishing range of periodicals published and printed in the city. There are, for example, the University's *Synapse*; *Paraplegia* which T. and T. Clark publish for the International Medical Society of Paraplegia along with the *British Journal of Oral Surgery*; and *The Journal of the Royal College of Surgeons of Edinburgh*.

THE RELIGIOUS OUTPUT

Life and Work is a monthly magazine published by the Church of Scotland, as is the *British Weekly*, a journal once famous in London and now so established in Edinburgh's Queen Street that it even has its own coffee room there. *Life and Work* although it is taken up mostly by reports of the Church's work also contains some general reading for the family, book reviews and articles on world affairs, national affairs, and aspects of Scottish history. It circulates all over Scotland, and had a sale in 1963–4 of no fewer than 214,000 copies every month. The Episcopalian *Scottish Journal of Theology* is a scholarly periodical published in the city by Oliver and Boyd. Nelson's for their part publish *Scripture* for the Catholic Biblical Association and *Catholic Documents* for the Pontifical Court. T. and T. Clark publish monthly *The Expository Times*.[1]

THE SCHOOLS

Edinburgh is famous for both its University and its schools, and most of them publish their own magazines. The oldest established school magazine is the *Merchistonian*, of Merchiston Castle School, which appears three times a year, and was founded in 1872. The *Fettesian*, from Fettes College, was founded in 1878 and also appears three times a year, as does the *Edinburgh Academy Chronicle*, founded in 1893. To name two more almost as samples, for there are many other school publications, the year 1904 saw the foundation of the Royal High School magazine, *Schola Regia*, and also the *Watsonian* from George Watson's Boys' College; both appear twice a year.

THE UNIVERSITY

Several periodical publications are associated with the University of Edinburgh. The University *Gazette*, not to be confused with *Her Majesty's Edinburgh Gazette*, which like the *London Gazette* comes out regularly with notices of official appointments, proclamations and so on, is an official University publication containing lists of appointments, grants and so forth which is circulated to members of the staff. The *University of Edinburgh Journal*, published for the Graduates Association by Oliver and Boyd, appears at irregular intervals and is intended for members of the University, past and present. It contains reports on the work and life of the University and reproduces addresses delivered by distinguished visitors either to the University at large or to specialist academic audiences. There is also *Scottish Studies*.

Student magazines, which necessarily have a quick succession of editors, are more exposed to the winds of fortune than most. *The Student*, which goes back to 1895, and was for most of its history more of a magazine than a news medium, was being produced in the early 1960s as a weekly newspaper, with about three pages of news and various feature articles on and around the University, of general and particular interest. *Gambit*, also officially sponsored by the Students' Representative Council, was intended to be a platform for student writing, but when this was not forthcoming in the necessary quantity, it widened its scope to give an introduction to modern prose and poetry writers outside the University. There is also *Cleft*, which according to *The Scotman*'s

[1] One or two other religious magazines were mentioned earlier in this volume.

Literary Editor is " a schismatic magazine, similar in kind to *Gambit*, but further out in style." There are also a new magazine called *Perspective* which aims at a general range of reader; *Forum*, the Edinburgh University independent Conservative review; and *Synapse*, which in 1962 won a trophy presented by the *Glasgow Herald* for the best student medical magazine in the United Kingdom.

Edinburgh Gazette

Finally there is the *Edinburgh Gazette* which is published by authority twice weekly—on Tuesdays and Fridays. Carrying judicial advertisements and information about bankruptcies, sequestrations, company liquidations and reductions of capital along with other official notices, the *Gazette* can claim to be the oldest indigenous newspaper in Scotland, for it first appeared in 1699 with, among its contents, diplomatic and public intelligence, public advertisements and miscellaneous notices voluntarily inserted by private bodies. In the 18th century it passed for a time into private hands but was still issued " by authority " until the Bankruptcy Act of 1793 put it under the control of the Supreme Court, which in turn by an Act of Sederunt in the same year ordained that until further order it was to appear on Tuesday and Fridays. This the *Edinburgh Gazette* has done ever since. It is now issued from the Exchequer Office.

BOOKSELLING

Edinburgh has long been one of the leading bookselling cities within the British Isles, and still is today. It houses the headquarters of John Menzies, who are the second largest book distributing and bookselling business in Britain. It has in James Thin one of the three main University bookshops, and in Dunn and Wilson it has one of the leading specialist library suppliers of children's books. The strength of bookselling in the city, however, does not spring from the giants alone but derives more broadly from the total number of booksellers, many of whom are specialists in one particular facet of the trade. Although membership of the Booksellers Association of Great Britain and Ireland is not compulsory there are 35 members in the city, and there are in addition many small shops which sell books. They fall mainly into two geographical areas—the more general shops in the Princes Street and George Street area, and the University and educational shops in the Old Town.

In the first group fall the three main Menzies shops, one at each end of Princes Street, and just off it, in Castle Street, the third, Douglas and Foulis, where David Douglas made his name in Victorian times both as a bookseller and as a publisher of Scottish books. In Rose Street, between Princes Street and George Street, Menzies have their headquarters from which they supply not only all their own shops and stalls in the South, East and North of Scotland, but also the book trade generally. This is not an easy task, for today there are approximately 300,000 books in print, and as about 26,000 new titles are added each year, it is obviously impossible for any bookseller to stock more than a fraction of all the available titles. The wholesaler has in consequence an important function to fulfil by enabling a bookseller to get for his customers those books which he has not got in stock. In the last 15 years Menzies have notably expanded with the acquisition of two companies in London, one in Leeds and one in Belfast.

Books are sold in Princes Street additionally, despite its very high overheads, by the two department stores, Jenners and Binns, and by Boots the Chemists. In George Street are four shops, The Edinburgh Bookshop, The Church of Scotland Bookshop, Alexander Brunton's, and the Grail Book and Art Centre, one of the three Catholic bookshops. The Edinburgh Bookshop stems from the merger of two old bookshops, Robert Grant's, which was founded in 1804, and William Brown's, which dates from 1877. The Church of Scotland Bookshop is the main Presbyterian Bookshop, and Brunton's is a favourite haunt for book collectors and book hunters. Other members of the trade in the New Town area are Charles Burns, who specialises in evangelical publications and who also has a shop opposite St. Giles' Cathedral, The Catholic Truth Society of Scotland, The Georgian Bookshop, The National Bible Society of Scotland, which distributes the Bible all over Scotland and through certain missionary fields in various parts of the world, and The Society for the Promotion of Christian Knowledge, which has a primarily Episcopalian business.

In the University group comes James Thin, one of the great bookshops of the country. They celebrated their centenary in 1948, and in their second century have shown youthful vigour by opening new shops to follow the expansion of the University and the opening of the new Napier Technical College. Thin's mailing list is one of the most extensive in the book trade, and they have customers all over the world. Nearby Baxendine's have a fine school and text book business, and they too have opened a new shop nearer the new University buildings in George Square. A little farther west Robert Maxwell has bought the two businesses of Cairns Brothers and H. D. Bryce, and near them is Donald Ferrier, the leading specialist medical bookseller, whose medical library also provides an invaluable service. The Paperback, though restricted in its stock by its name, shows how wide is the range nowadays of such material. Clustered near the Central Public Library in George IV Bridge are three other specialist shops. John Grant is celebrated as an antiquarian bookshop which issues many interesting catalogues, and also for its range of Scottish books and old prints. Bauermeister, who is noted for his stock of foreign and art books, has just opened a new and very much larger shop, whilst, A. Harkins and Brothers is the third Catholic bookshop. This Old Town group is completed by book departments, operated by John Menzies, in the two stores, Patrick Thomson's and J. and R. Allan's.

Farther afield there are in Morningside Andrew Tait and Lennox, and, at Churchhill, Neil Melrose, the newest recruit to bookselling in the city. Bruntsfield has Crerar's and the antiquarian shop of Robert Aitken, and Corstorphine the St. John's Library and Bookshop.

There are two other aspects of bookselling which should be mentioned. The first is school book contracting, and this is the only form of bookselling in which McDougall's Educational Company Limited and R. M. Cameron and Sons engage. The second is libraries, and here public libraries are pre-eminent today. Edinburgh is particularly fortunate, for not only is the service available extremely good, but by its deliberate policy of supporting the local bookshops the Edinburgh Public Library has strengthened them materially, thus enabling them to offer a better service to the public. Douglas and Foulis run the biggest library service outside London, and in addition there are libraries at the Edinburgh Bookshop, R. M. Williamson's Libraries, The Viewforth Library, D. I. Scott's Everyone's Library and The St. John's Library.

CHAPTER 31

THE CRAFT INDUSTRIES

THE state of a community's traditional crafts is a sure touchstone of the state of its culture. While the current debate on the " two cultures " remains undecided it may be questioned whether this is still a viable doctrine. In an age of intensive mechanisation and legislative control of labour it is inevitable that the status and quality of the crafts should deteriorate. Anyone concerned with the history of the Edinburgh crafts must be struck not only by the recent decline in the aesthetic quality of the examples which have survived in official and private collections, but also by the meagre information available about the craftsmen in public records. Anonymity has, of course, always been a notable characteristic of the craftsman's way of life, yet even today, despite the revival of interest in the arts and the growth of publicity, it is the exception rather than the rule to hear the name of a craftsman mentioned when new work is unveiled.

Apart from this tradition of anonymity, it is evident that with the advent of mass production the crafts have ceased to occupy the place in the mind of the community which they formerly held; indeed, from the start of the machine age their life was threatened. Many craftsmen continued working against the tide until well into the 20th century. But two world wars not only interrupted the work of the artist craftsmen for disastrously long periods, but accelerated the decline of the crafts in other ways. Craftsmanship depends after all upon the transmission of skills and funded experience from master to apprentice. But many potential craftsmen, after four or five years of war service, were no longer willing to continue their apprenticeship; while others had acquired new skills which were more lucrative in the changed economy of the post-war years. Scientific warfare, on the other hand, added new techniques to the craftsman's competence, but it did not enlarge the ranks of the dedicated who find in craftsmanship not only a living but a way of life.

In this generation the process of decay has been all too patent. Today it is doubtful if there are in the entire community of the city half a dozen craftsmen who can earn enough to live on without other employment. Likewise the number of apprentices engaged in the fine crafts, such as silver and glass, and working with a master craftsman, cannot exceed two or three. Personal pride in good workmanship, which is the mark of the true craftsman, is little in evidence—or, at all events, much less in evidence than it was. Few workmen today make things from start to finish. Assembling pre-fabricated machine-made parts—the chief occupation of the majority—does little to promote the latent moral responsibility and aesthetic pride in every skilled workman. The prevailing attitude is that there is " no future " in the fine crafts; that the handmade article is all but an anachronism in an age of automation and machine technology. Personal pride in good workmanship would seem to be contrary to the social ideology and spirit of the age.

Besides these impalpable factors behind the decay of the crafts, economics has played a critical role in shaping the course of events. The mass production of " consumer goods " (as they are termed nowadays) has reached astronomical dimensions. Both skilled and semi-skilled labour are in greater demand than ever before. Wages and conditions of work have improved beyond all recognition. Many young men of aptitude are thus more attracted by the prospect of high wages in a motor car factory, say, than by the freedom and creative opportunities of the studio-workshop. Indeed, the whole notion and practice of apprenticeship have radically changed; and the present system bears little relationship to the traditional arrangement between master craftsmen and the young tyro. Apprenticeship training is now largely regulated by the trade unions in place of the old craft guilds.

The need for evening study, which every ambitious apprentice took for granted a generation ago, is no longer popular. Personal ambition and the spur of personal responsibility have manifestly lost favour. " Day release " courses, which allow the apprentice to learn during the employer's time (and often at his expense) have for many replaced the " night classes." Changing social habits and behaviour have further militated against the practice of the traditional crafts. Television alone has adversely affected the study and practice of the crafts which now attract few apprentices. Indeed, it is doubtful whether there is a single self-employed master-craftsman in the city with an apprentice in his shop to carry on his trade. The Art colleges in consequence are virtually the only places capable of keeping alive and transmitting the skills and expertise upon which the traditional crafts depend. The college studio, however, cannot simulate completely the intimate and versatile atmosphere of the master's workshop. But at least the college student is given an all-round training, not only in the craft skills and techniques but also in design. The teachers themselves are practising craftsmen who bring into the academic atmosphere a healthy sense of the practical world. This service is vital to the continuity and well-being of the Scottish crafts; for there is little doubt that without it the crafts would eventually disappear from our ken and with them the funded experience of centuries. But it must be said that, of the college-trained craftsmen, few are able to set up workshops of their own; the majority become secondary school teachers and a few continue to practise their craft as a sideline. The colleges thus not only teach; they are the repositories of traditions which have survived the test of history.

SCOTTISH CRAFT CENTRE

The concern with which the position and state of the crafts was viewed at the end of the second World War is evidenced by the founding of the Scottish Craft Centre in 1949. This body was set up to promote the traditional crafts by establishing a sales organisation for the smaller craftsmen and creating a focal point for everything pertaining to the preservation of our craft heritage. Situated in Edinburgh, the Centre is administered by a council of 20 drawn from many fields, including working craftsmen. Standards of design and workmanship are maintained by a panel of assessors, which advises the council both on the admission of new members and on the quality of the work exhibited for sale. At the time of the foundation of the Centre another body, Workshops and Studios Foundation (Scotland) Limited, which had been planned a little earlier to assist craftsmen to find suitable working premises, was in the process of organisation. This body agreed to merge with the Centre, whose scope was correspondingly enlarged. For the first three years the Centre depended entirely on its own financial resources, but after long negotiations the Board of Trade, recognising the Centre's importance, agreed to make a grant-in-aid so that its activities might be consolidated and extended. This was obviously a right decision, for valuable work has been done by the Centre to promote and develop all that is best in Scottish craftsmanship. Since its foundation some 175 craftsmen by the early '60s had been admitted to membership; they covered a wide range of expertise from fine knitting to silversmithing; and many of them were drawing a substantial part of their income from work sold by the Centre.

The following figures indicate the progress of the organisation and the importance of the work it has accomplished during its most formative period. In 1951 some £1,500 was paid to craftsmen for work sold by the Centre; in 1956 the figure was over £6,000; in 1960 it exceeded £8,000. In all, nearly £100,000 has been paid to craftsmen by the Centre since its foundation. And the principal aim remains essentially what it was at the beginning: " to increase the quality and quantity of the best type of handcrafts . . . which should at one and the same time benefit the craftsman by giving him economic security, and benefit the consumer by assuring him of a high standard of design and workmanship in the thing he buys, whether for ornament or use."

The Edinburgh crafts today comprise a varied group besides the traditional fine crafts such as silver and glass. Some, like the crafts of the pewterer, virtually died out towards the middle of the 19th century; others, like die-stamping, which in Edinburgh was linked with the rise of the sealing-wax industry for which the city is still famous, is less in evidence than it was, as a result of changes both in legal procedure and business practice. A craft to which our Victorian great-grandmothers were much addicted was the making of pictorial designs from pressed and dried flowers. This has recently been revived in Edinburgh by Miss Biddy Russell, who has a studio in the city where she creates flowerpieces for interior decoration as in many Danish and Italian houses. Other crafts seem to persist as part of wider traditions. Gun-making is a highly skilled craft industry which requires a sensitive appreciation of line, balance and engineering precision. Fine engraving of " the action " was a distinguishing feature of the " Edinburgh gun ", contributing much to its reputation, beauty and individuality. The embellishments were carried out by expert engravers of whom there were many at the beginning of the century. The last surviving exponent of this craft employed in Edinburgh is James Anderson, who still works for J. Dickson and Son, a firm established in 1820. Anderson learned his craft from his father who worked for Dickson for many years until he retired. Another old-established Edinburgh craft is that of medal-making. This craft has been chiefly associated with the name of Alexander Kirkwood and Son. Founded in 1826, this firm has executed many famous commissions, including the City of London's seventh centenary medal, the Matrix of the Great Seal of Scotland, the Stall Plate for the Duke of Edinburgh at St. George's Chapel, Windsor, and 112 bronze and silver medals for the centenary of the Bombay–Burmah Trading Corporation in 1963.

SILVERSMITHING

Among the fine crafts pride of place must be given to silversmithing. The richness and high quality of the output of the 18th century craftsmen such as William Aytoun are widely acclaimed. In the 19th century, although technical skill is not lacking, we look in vain for the continuation of this high achievement. The Industrial Revolution had already done irreparable harm to the crafts; and as the century advanced fewer and fewer craftsmen could earn a living from the pursuit of their trade because of the rising flood of mass production and the material attractions of industrial employment. It is notable, for instance, that, whereas the Royal Scottish Museum possesses more than 20 examples of 18th century work, some of it of the first rank, it does not possess a single comparable example from the 19th century and only a few from the 20th. Even the contemporary records, as Jackson points out in his *English Goldsmiths and their Marks*,[1] are scant and unreliable. The " work-books " of the Assay Office, on the other hand, record some 30 odd names of Edinburgh craftsmen, although only a few are known to have executed work of their own design. Perhaps John Pears Hutton, an example of whose work is in the collection at Huntly House Museum in the Canongate, is the most important. John Crichton may also have produced some work of his own designing. But the evidence all along is poor and often conflicting.

It is not our purpose here to assess the aesthetic merits of the output of this period; but it may be said that while technically the work is often remarkable there is little evidence of originality of design among the examples preserved in public collections. Design tends to be ornate and florid, though often exquisitely wrought; the shapes are uninspired, debased and fussy—all signs of a degenerating culture. Taking the 19th century as a whole the available evidence indicates that in the decade from 1843 to 1853 there were three self-employed silversmiths at work in Edinburgh and two firms employing silversmiths; from 1853 to 1860 there were four silversmiths and one firm; and from 1861 to 1870 there were eight silversmiths and five firms. The period from 1871 to 1880

[1] C. J. Jackson, Macmillan and Company Limited, 1905 edition.

appears to have been a peak period with 10 self-employed silversmiths and three firms. Thereafter the number falls to two between 1881 and 1890, and rises again to six between 1891 and 1903, with no less than nine firms trading in silver, most of it no doubt in the form of jewellery or reproductions of earlier examples. It is also worth noting that among the working jewellers at the turn of the century there appear to have been two chasers.

At the start of the 20th century there was virtually no high-quality original work being done. Most of the craftsmen and firms were doing reproduction and repair work, a state of affairs which has continued with little change until the present time. Of the leading firms employing skilled craftsmen Henry Tatton and Son had three men in 1891; after the first World War they had none; but in 1935, when the firm was entrusted with the production of the " Holyrood Silver," they were able to employ four craftsmen for a number of years while the work was being executed. Since then all special work has been subcontracted, most of it being done south of the Border. Another leading firm, Hamilton and Inches, formerly of Princes Street, established their own workshop in 1906, employing two silversmiths, one finisher, one burnisher and one apprentice. This was the position until the outbreak of the first World War. Between 1925 and 1935 they employed three silversmiths, a finisher and an apprentice. In the early 1960s they were employing five silversmiths, one finisher and one apprentice, who were mainly occupied in making reproductions and carrying out repairs. In 1935, however, the firm's foreman silversmith, Edward Hamilton, executed the new mace for the University of St. Andrews from the design of C. d'O. Pilkington Jackson, the Edinburgh sculptor-craftsman. This is regarded as one of the most important examples of the silversmithing craft carried out this century.

Today there are in Edinburgh three self-employed silversmiths: William Kirk, Elizabeth Kirkwood and Charles Creswick, all of whom have carried out distinguished original work in the best traditions of the craft. The Chalice presented to the Canongate Kirk, a work of great beauty and skill, was designed and executed by Kirk in 1959. Another important work is the " Everest Trophy," which was designed by Ernest Dinkel of Edinburgh College of Art and executed by Charles Creswick. It is also noteworthy that Ernest Dinkel's design for the Royal Hunt cup in 1960 was chosen by Her Majesty the Queen.

A new phase in the history of the craft began when Ian Davidson was appointed to the Silversmithing Department of the College of Art in 1961. Since then not only has the teaching been greatly extended but the academic status of the craft has been enhanced. More students are taking Silversmithing and Jewellery as main subjects, and through the introduction of new techniques are acquiring a wider range of skills than has hitherto been possible. The old hand-skills are being maintained while the industrial aspect of the craft is being developed. Ian Davidson is himself a first-class craftsman-designer with extensive knowledge of both silversmithing and jewellery. Recent examples of his work are to be found in private, official and church collections throughout the country. Besides his ecclesiastical silver, such as the Processional Cross and Ambry for St. Martin's Church, Bradford, he designed and made the Presidential Badge for the Royal College of Surgeons of Edinburgh and the "Frank Moran Trophy" for *The Scotsman*. As consultant-designer to Hamilton and Inches, he has played a formative part in shaping modern taste in domestic silverware.

ENAMELLING AND JEWELLERY

Closely linked with silversmithing are the ancient crafts of enamelling and jewellery. Very little is known about the practice of enamelling in Edinburgh before the beginning of the present century. About this time a certain Meta N. Brown gave elementary lessons in the technique of the craft in the "Dean Studio", Belford Road. Here Elizabeth Kirkwood, the last practising enameller in Edinburgh today, received her first lessons and was introduced to the secrets of producing the translucent effects for which she is justly reputed. Simultaneously the versatile artist Mrs. Phoebe Traquair, having studied the craft in Italy, was practising enamelling in the city. Elizabeth Kirkwood joined a class run by Mrs. Traquair and subsequently purchased a small furnace of her own, supplementing practical experiment with extensive reading. Very soon she was exhibiting at Craft exhibitions in London and at the Royal Academy and the Royal Scottish Academy. Among her more important commissions of this early period is the large Processional Cross in translucent enamel now in St. Mary's Cathedral. Extending her skill she began to do champlevé work, and in the next few years executed the gold and enamel badges for the Order of the Thistle, the heraldic shields for the mace for the School of Medicine, St. Andrew's University, and many other memorials in enamel for St. Giles Cathedral and other churches and institutions. Her first stall-plate for the Knights of the Thistle was made in 1915. Elizabeth Kirkwood still uses eighteen carat gold for ceremonial badges, such as those recently made for the President of the Institute of Bankers and the President of the Town Clerks of Scotland.

The craft of silversmithing is closely linked with another ancient craft—the craft of jewellery. Many silversmiths in the past have engaged in both. But in recent times, partly because of the high cost of precious metals and partly because of the mass production of cheap jewellery, few craftsmen work in this specialised field. Individual commissions can still be carried out by most silversmiths; but Charles and Nora Creswick have been leaders in this field for many years, and are known for their work in the traditional Celtic style with its interlacing patterns.

GLASS ENGRAVING

If silversmithing takes pride of place among the Edinburgh crafts, glass engraving comes very close in point of importance and excellence of achievement.

The history of the glass industry in Edinburgh goes back to the 17th century. In the particular field of engraving, with which we are mainly concerned here, the story is of somewhat later date.[1] Originally the local centre of the industry was at Leith, but with the purchase of the Caledonian Glass Works in the Canongate in 1810 by William Ford, the Leith industry gradually diminished. William Ford died in 1819, when a new company was formed with John Ford, a nephew of William, as a director. This company was dissolved in 1835, but John Ford continued the firm under the name of Holyrood Flint Glass Works, and four years later he became sole proprietor. A glass, presumably made to mark the founding of the firm, is in the Ford Ranken Collection at Huntly House.

The firm expanded rapidly, and in 1837 John Ford was appointed Flint Glass Manufacturer to Queen Victoria. A large epergne dating from this time is also in the possession of Huntly House. This specimen was exhibited at the Edinburgh Exhibition in 1886; and in 1911, during George V's first official visit to the city, the epergne was placed on the Royal Table at the State Dinner at Holyroodhouse.

Every kind of table ornament, crystal and glass, was manufactured and cut under John Ford's supervision. In 1842 the list included sugar bowls, chemical bottles, cruets, confection jars, custard cups, wine glasses, decanters, root glasses, goblets and tumblers. There was a special line of goblets and tumblers, containing a coin inserted into the base, which became very popular about the time of Queen Victoria's jubilee. Another innovation was the production of paper weights and bottles with inserted cameos of the famous, such as Shakespeare, Byron, Walter Scott and Wellington. Not the least interesting as curiosities were the goblets and christening mugs engraved with views of Balmoral Castle made for the Queen. In token of her appreciation of these services the firm was permitted to take the title of the Royal Holyrood Glass Works in 1898. Two hundred men were steadily employed by the firm about the middle of the century.

When John Ford died in 1865 the firm became John Ford and Company with William Ford (John Ford's son) and Francis Ranken as partners. The Ranken family were also glass makers; and, by the marriage in the next generation of William Ranken to William Ford's daughter, the two families were united. The business continued to flourish and showed original work abroad and at the Edinburgh Exhibition in 1886. One of the most notable commissions was the wedding gift in 1896 from the City of Edinburgh to the Duke and Duchess of York (later King George V and Queen Mary), consisting of 256 pieces of table-ware engraved with coats of arms and national emblems. In 1904 the factory closed down. But the business was continued on a retail basis by William Ranken. Ranken's son, who succeeded his father in 1924, died in 1959 and the trade name of Ford came to an end.

The Edinburgh and Leith Flint Glass Company has been in existence for a little over a century. Founded originally by J. Thomas in 1846, it was

[1] The contributor of this chapter on Edinburgh's crafts is greatly indebted to Mr. George Young, Superintendent of City Museums, for his valuable assistance in the preparation of this particular section.

taken over by Alexander D. Jenkinson and Company in 1847, and shortly afterwards the company opened new premises at Abbeyhill. Their main production was cut table glass and plain straw stem glassware. About 1923, the owners sold the glass works to the Webb Crystal Glass Company and the production continued as before. The Edinburgh Crystal Glass Company was first registered in 1955, the original name of Edinburgh and Leith Flint Glass Works being retained. The Company now operates under the aegis of Crown Investments Limited, London, of which Webb Crystal Glass Company is a subsidiary.

Among the more important recent commissions is the Commemorative Goblet produced to celebrate the opening of the Forth Road Bridge. The Company has also produced a number of Coronation pieces and many presentation sets for Royal and other notable occasions.

As in other branches of art, notably textiles and painting, the Scots owed much to the influence of the Low Countries; for it is fairly certain that the early engravers learned much from Flemish craftsmen. But with the rising demand for engraved table glass many skilled craftsmen came to this country, setting up small independent workshops for the practice of the craft. Among these, one of the most notable was an emigrant Bohemian called Millar or Müller. Millar, whose workshop was initially staffed by fellow countrymen, played a very important part in the history of the glass engraving of the period. Although closely associated with the Holyrood Glass Works (for whom Millar and his son, J. H. B. Millar, executed many important designs) he carried on an extensive business of his own, exhibiting under his own name at both the London Exhibition of 1862 and the Paris Exhibition of 1867. His firm and incisive style established standards which have rarely been surpassed in the history of Scottish glass engraving. Figure subjects (mostly Greek and Roman), flowers, trees, birds and animals were his favourite themes, and it is probable that the fern pattern, associated with Holyrood glass, originated in his workshop. There was also John Smith, an engraver of some distinction, who worked in Leith for some 20 years or more after the middle of the century. Smith appears to have specialised in heraldic design and in the engraving of tableware for noble families.

Many hundreds were employed in the industry at the middle of the century, but, although the number of engravers must have been considerable, few were distinguished in the finer aspects of the craft. Large quantities of glass of all kinds were produced throughout the 19th century. There was no lack of skill and ingenuity (indeed the skill is often very high), but the cult of ornateness displaced restraint and sensibility for the medium, without which engraving becomes a mere ornamental technique.

It is not known exactly how many engravers were working in Edinburgh during the last years of the century, but there is evidence that quite a number were employed both in the glass works or in small separate workshops in close touch with the works. In the early years of the present century, however, this activity dwindled as the Victorian taste for thin-walled, elaborately engraved table-ware gave way to a predilection for heavier cut crystal glasses. One engraver only was employed by the

Edinburgh and Leith Flint Glass Company, his production being restricted more or less to the conventional motif of thistle and fern.

The wars of 1914 and 1939 brought engraving virtually to a halt. But with the founding of a new Department of Glass Design in the College of Art in 1946 a new chapter in the history and practice of the craft was begun through the fine example and enthusiasm of Helen Monro. The department, which started with a single copper lathe, is fully equipped to teach a comprehensive range of glass processes including cutting, engraving and sandblasting, as applied to domestic hollow-ware and also to flat glass. Recently the installation of a small experimental furnace for glass melting and experiment in the production of coloured glass has extended the range of teaching. A liaison with the College of Further Education at Stourbridge, where facilities for glass blowing are available, enables students to become familiar with the techniques of blowing and to see their own shapes executed. The course is flexible and stresses the imaginative creative qualities latent in the craft of copper wheel engraving. Craftsmen engravers have thus now reverted to the practice of working independently of the glass works, utilising glass from various sources, both British and foreign. Already the department has gained international recognition as one of the most important centres of the craft in the United Kingdom. Among those who have trained in the College, several have already acquired distinction in their craft: Marjorie Finlay, John Lawrie, Ronald Renton, Val Rossi, Jean Dickinson and Jean Murray, all of whom are practising in the city. Another craftsman who has achieved distinction is Alison Geissler, who received her early training in the College. Among Alison Geissler's most important pieces are the set of engraved glasses, each decorated with one of the Queen's Beasts, which were presented to Her Majesty by the High Constables on the occasion of Her Majesty's coronation visit to the city. Another fine example is the large plate commissioned by the Royal Scottish Museum to mark the Museum's centenary.

In 1956 Helen Monro set up her own workshop at Juniper Green (the " Juniper Workshop ") where she has executed a number of important commissions. Perhaps the most notable are the engraved book-ends presented to Lord Halifax at the opening of the new buildings of the British Glass Industry Research Association in 1959; the goblet engraved for the Guild of St. Margaret as a wedding present for H.R.H. Princess Margaret in 1962; and the silver bowl with engraved crystal medallions presented by members of the Threlfall family to Gonville and Caius College, Cambridge in 1961. But before founding her studio at Juniper Green she had already executed the goblet presented to Mr. Alexander Laurie by the Sir Walter Scott Club on his retirement in 1953 from the office of Treasurer. The goblet, about 10 inches high, was specially made by the Whitefriars Glass Factory. It is designed on sturdy and simple lines appropriate to the early 19th century when Scott was active. A medallion (after the Chantrey Bust) containing a profile of Sir Walter is surmounted by a scroll and crossed plumes and flanked by laurel branches; beneath, a ribbon bears the motto " Them that guide the purse rule the house"; the ribbon entwines a leather purse in the ring of which is inserted a spray of thrift. The whole is beautifully drawn and exquisitely engraved by copper wheel and is one of the artist's finest pieces.

POTTERY

Earthenware potting, one of the oldest crafts in human history, was practised in Scotland as a peasant industry up to the middle of the 18th century. About then a large number of potteries began to be founded for large-scale production; and by the end of the 19th century some "eighty operated in Scotland on a commercial basis, many of them substantial employers of labour."[1] In the Edinburgh area there were some 16 potteries, mostly in the Portobello and Prestonpans region, where suitable clay was available nearby. There was a steady demand for the ware produced by these potteries and many surviving examples have found honoured places in public and private collections. The chief products were ornamental earthenware jugs, etc., small decorative figures such as fishwives, soldiers, sailors and shepherds, cows and horses and "bocages" which were sold as mantelpiece ornaments. Among the celebrated special pieces were the Florentine Lions made by Thomas Rathbone and Company. From the beginning of the 19th century ornamental plaques had been popular; and these sometimes commemorated historic events such as Queen Victoria's first visit to Scotland in 1842. The Rathbone production ceased about mid-century and the works were taken over by Dr. W. A. Gray under the name of Midlothian Stoneware Potteries. Other potteries were simultaneously in operation, and of these the most important was Milne Cornwall and Company, founded in 1830 by Hugh and Arthur Cornwall. This company made traditional stoneware carrying decorative motifs depicting hunting and other sporting subjects, of which there are several interesting examples at Huntly House Museum and the Royal Scottish Museum.

By 1867, however, Portobello clays were exhausted. A. W. Buchan then took over the Milne Cornwall plant and began producing Portobello faience ware, but this was soon dropped because of competition from the south. The firm's principal output consisted of whisky flagons and hot water and beer bottles. At the end of the second World War, however, the firm began to explore the market for new lines. The sale of large whisky jars was a thing of the past; stoneware hot water bottles were likewise replaced by rubber bottles and electric blankets. Eventually a chemist was engaged to experiment with new coloured glazes; in 1947 the firm began to produce "art ware" such as jugs, vases, beer mugs, casseroles and plates; and in 1953 the production of "ovenproof" ware became a prominent feature of its output. Today A. W. Buchan is the most important commercial pottery in the area, and its "Thistle Pottery" is widely known.

[1] G. Bernard Hughes in "Pottery from Portobello," *Country Life* (Scottish Supplement, August, 1958).

Many examples of Buchan's modern productions have been selected for display in the industrial design centres in Glasgow and London. The company also won an award for a Scottish souvenir in a competition arranged by the Scottish Tourist Board and the Council of Industrial Design in 1947, and had stalls in the Glasgow Trade Fair and at the British Industries Fair in London. In addition, their products have been selected for various exhibitions overseas and their markets extend to almost every part of the world.

Changes in the processes of production have included modernisation of plant. In particular the old brick kilns, fired with coal and controlled by rule-of-thumb temperature measurements, have been given up. Kilns are now electrically operated and are automatically controlled. Cleaner and more accurate firing has eliminated many faulty products, and the whole process of manufacture now requires much less arduous labour. The labour force of approximately 50 people has also changed in composition. Skilled throwers, who make the flagons and various other items, are still employed, but a considerable quantity of ware is made by the casting process. Elsewhere in the factory a decorating department of 15 or more decorators is now in existence; the women, who did the glazing by hand dipping, have been replaced by a few workers operating in spraying booths. The once arduous task of filling and supplying the brick ovens required a team of workers; today it only takes two men to fill trucks at hand-level and push them on rails into and out of the kilns. So the factory employs about the same number of people as it did 12 years ago.

In addition to the commercial potteries in Edinburgh, thanks to the influence of the Department of Pottery at the College of Art, there are half a dozen or more private potteries doing high-quality individual work in red clay with variously coloured glazes. Notable among these is the "Castle Wynd" pottery, founded after the war by James Crawford, a former student of the College of Art, but now transferred to Gifford in East Lothian. The small decorative animals, among other items, produced by this pottery are well-designed and finished and find a ready sale in the export market. The other free-lance artist potters who have made names for themselves include the late R. W. Hay, Alexander Wolfenden (one-time lecturer at the College) and J. F. Coull. And also there is Miss K. Horsman, herself an imaginative artist and skilled technician who runs the Department of Pottery at the College of Art. Miss Horsman has done much to raise pottery to its present high standard in the city, not only at a professional level but among a large number of very keen amateurs, such as Lady Milne, who feel the primordial appeal of this ancient craft.

BOOKBINDING

In a city renowned for its printing and book production (described earlier) the craft of bookbinding has had a continuous history since the Reformation. Indeed, Edinburgh has been recognised as the chief centre of the craft in Scotland. But after the golden age of Scottish bookbinding in the 18th century the aesthetic quality of the decoration declined, although the volume of work done was considerable. In all essentials bookbinding is basically a handcraft; for " casing " (the commercial binding) is not binding but a mere protection attached to the text and is relatively temporary. With the expansion of machine production the numbers of hand-craftsmen dwindled, despite the fact that the demand for special bindings continued to keep many of the older craftsmen active until well into the present century.

Before today's massive output of books began there were some 20 to 40 binderies in Edinburgh, many of them one-man businesses employing only a few craftsmen.[1] Perhaps the last of these was the bindery conducted by William Geddes, whose premises were situated in North Bank Street and latterly, until the early days of the second World War, in the Lawnmarket. Another bindery owned by J. Rosenbluth in the High Street (afterwards Rosenbluth, Riddle and Company, trading as the St. Giles Bookbinding Company) continued until 1939 when it was taken over by Henderson and Bisset. There was also Thomas Wood and Sons Limited until 1946.

From then onwards the making of fine bindings was in the hands of Orrock and Sons and Henderson and Bisset, who are still the leading bookbinders in the city. Oliver and Boyd and Nelson's, although primarily engaged in printing and publishing, have continuously employed a few hand-binders to carry out special commissions. In addition, there have been a few free-lance professional binders, working independently and executing work for private patrons.

The firm of Henderson and Bisset, believed to be the oldest bookbinders in Scotland, was established in 1823. The founder, James Henderson, was born in 1796 in Fife. James was given a " college " education and became the pupil apprentice of a leading London bookbinder between 1810 and 1830.[2] When he had finished his apprenticeship he set up his own bindery in Edinburgh and not only quickly established a leading place among his contemporaries by the restrained excellence of his designs, but was appointed Bookbinder to Queen Victoria in 1839. James Henderson died in 1851 and was succeeded by his son, George. This George took another George called Cormack as his partner and the high quality of their work earned them a renewed appointment from Queen Victoria in 1889. George Henderson was succeeded by Miss Mary Henderson, who later assumed Campbell White as business partner. On her death in 1911 Campbell White became sole partner; and since his death in 1930 the business has been carried on by his sons.

In 1939 the " edition bindery " of St. Giles Bookbinding Company was acquired and, while this part of the business became the more important in size and output, the two partners decided to maintain the old craft-binding of Henderson and Bisset as a separate department. In recent years, however, the struggle to maintain this interest in hand-binding has

[1] Campbell White gives the figure of 44 for Edinburgh bookbinding firms in 1833. See *A Century of Bookbinding in Edinburgh*; Proceedings, Royal Scottish Society of Arts (April, 1941).

[2] This was Charles Lewis.

been made more difficult by the lack of apprentices willing to undergo the long and arduous training which the craft requires. Moreover, agreement between the Employers' Association and the appropriate Trade Unions limits the number of apprentices who may be employed; which means that as the number of journeymen qualified in hand-binding becomes fewer each year, the recruitment of apprentices is similarly reduced. Here we can let the figures speak for themselves. The number of employees in the hand-binding department before World War II was about 12 to 15 men, including apprentices; on 30th June, 1962 there were five men-of whom one was about to retire at the age of 70—and one apprentice.

Orrock and Son began under the name of Orrock and Romanes during the early part of the 19th century.[1] The firm carried out hand-binding for private and professional libraries in Edinburgh and other parts of the country and exhibited at the Edinburgh International Exhibition of 1886. Subsequently, under the name of Orrock and Son, the firm moved to larger premises in Victoria Street where the trade side of the business was developed. Hand-binding, however, remained a separate department, carrying out work for Royalty and for University libraries.

Oliver and Boyd's part in the history of 19th century bookbinding is a little obscure; but in any event bookbinding was only incidental to the firm's main business as printers and publishers, though it has been invited from time to time to prepare presentation bindings for Royal and other occasions.

The same is true of Thomas Nelson and Sons. From an early date Nelson's employed a few craftsmen binders, but hand-binding has not played a very large part in the history of the firm. Apart from the binding of legal books (often executed in leather) and an occasional presentation volume, the firm is primarily engaged in printing and publishing. In the winter of 1962–3 Oliver and Boyd employed four craft-binders, Nelson's four. But in addition to the craftsmen employed in commercial firms, others were employed by Register House, H.M. Stationery Office and the University. Yet the fact remains that at the same period the total number of hand-craftsmen employed in the city did not exceed 30.

Of the individual craftsmen in this field who have been most influential in the matters of style and craftsmanship during the past century, Otto Schultze of Frederick Street, who set up a bindery in Edinburgh in the 1880s, is perhaps the most outstanding. About this time, Cobden–Sanderson and some others fostered an important revival in the art of hand-binding in Britain. "An interesting feature of this revival of artistic bindings was the establishment in Edinburgh of the new bindery under the control of Mr. Otto Schultze. Schultze gained a considerable reputation for his artistic bindings, and many of his designs were carried out by David Thomson, a member of his staff, who had learnt his craft at Henderson and Bisset. Unfortunately the war of 1914–18 saw the end of this enterprise . . ."[2] David Thomson is reputed to have been an

[1] The earliest record of the firm is dated 1822.

[2] See Campbell White's *A Century of Bookbinding in Edinburgh* in the *Journal of the Royal Society of Arts*, April, 1941.

" outstanding decorator of books " during the early years of the century and at one time worked for Douglas Cockerell.

Taken as a whole the 19th century saw a general decline in the aesthetic character of bookbinding. With the increasing mechanisation of book production in the 20th century, and the decline in private patronage among book collectors, the best traditions of the craft are now maintained by a very few firms and a small number of private craftsmen. Notable among contemporary binders is Arthur W. Currie, the first full-time trade instructor in bookbinding at the old Heriot-Watt College. When with Oliver and Boyd, Currie was associated with the production of special bindings for Royal and other occasions. He has also designed and executed several " signed bindings ", including the visitors' book for the Museum of Modern Art, New York. Other works of this craftsman are in the possession of the Colorado College, the University of Montreal, and the Huntingdon Library and Art Gallery.

A re-awakening of interest in the craft of hand-bookbinding has clearly taken place during the past 12 years or so, and it is now extremely difficult to meet the present demand for hand-bound work owing to the lack of skilled labour. Strenuous efforts have been made to obtain special permission from the Unions to train more apprentices in this field, but these efforts have been unsuccessful. It would appear, certainly at the time of writing, that unless the Trade Unions are willing to make special arrangements to allow firms to train boys in hand-bookbinding, the craft as a commercial enterprise will die out and will thereafter be practised only in a limited way by the " artist " binder.

CALLIGRAPHY

Not unrelated to the making and binding of books, the craft of calligraphy was practised in Edinburgh from the 1850s to the early 1900s mainly by engravers using debased examples of late " copperplate " lettering and letters. During this period the ground was gradually being prepared for the revival of lettering inspired by William Morris and his disciple, Edward Johnston. Johnston's influence as a teacher was far-reaching; and his reintroduction of the " broad " pen raised calligraphy to a new level. Johnston's influence and teaching began to be apparent in Edinburgh about 1908 and was much in evidence among those who had learned the craft at the College of Art, notably Irene Wellington and Nora Paterson, both of whom taught and practised in the city. Following this tradition Tom Gourdie and George Thomson, both students of Nora Paterson, have been active in the Italic handwriting movement which got new impetus about 1945.

In recent years a reappraisal of calligraphy has been taking place, less stress being given to the craft aspect of the subject which Johnston and his followers initiated. The main contemporary influence in Edinburgh derives from the Continental school of calligrapher-letterers, Van Salden and Zapf in particular, both of whom were pupils and associates of Rudolf Koch. The relation of calligraphy to the wider field of design, especially in the sphere of the fine crafts and publicity, is now firmly established, and a number of craftsmen specialising in lettering of distinctive creative character have settled in the city. Notable among this group are Stuart Barrie, John Martin, Roy Benzie and Andrew Chisholm. Stuart Barrie, who was trained at the College of Art under Nora Paterson, followed her as teacher of calligraphy at the College. A prolific craftsman, he has carried out many important commissions including the Book of The Scottish Window for Guildford Cathedral. Several ex-members of the College are professional members of the Society of Scribes and Illuminators (founded in 1921).

TAPESTRY-WEAVING

Though hand-loom weaving had virtually ceased in Edinburgh by 1840, weaving was continued in the more specialised form of tapestry with the founding, towards the end of the 19th century, of The Dovecot Tapestry Studio at Corstorphine by the then (third) Marquis of Bute. Bute had known William Morris and had discussed with him the possibility of founding a new workshop. It was his son, however, who actually started the Tapestry Company and who brought the last of the Morris weavers to Edinburgh after the master's death to work and train young craftsmen. In 1911 these representatives of the Morris tradition, John Glassbrook and Gordon Berry, began to train Scottish apprentices " on the upright looms " which Morris had preferred to the horizontal type used in France.[1] One of the original apprentices, Ronald Cruickshank, who rose to eminence in the company, has spent a considerable time in recent years training tapestry weavers in the U.S.A.; the other, Richard Gordon, is now the company's master-weaver.

From 1912 until 1940, save for the period of the first World War, the company was under the fourth Marquis of Bute's own supervision. A series of vast tapestries, depicting incidents in Scottish history and domestic life, was produced for the Marquis's house at Mount Stuart in Bute. Finely woven with a range of hundreds of colours, these tapestries were executed from cartoons made by Skeoch Cumming, a painter of historical subjects. The first panel was a direct copy of the artist's painting. A very fine warp of 24–27 to the inch was necessary; the wool colours were selected from the Gobelin palette to match the colours of the original; and this required some three hundred wools of closely related tones.

In 1946, after the second World War, the studio was reopened and the Edinburgh Tapestry Company was formed. Four members of the Bute family took control—Lady Jean Bertie, Lord Colum, Lord David and Lord Robert Crichton-Stuart—and these inspired a new policy, with Ronald Cruickshank in charge of the work. Although still regarded as a non-profit making concern they began to produce smaller tapestries designed by leading artists, which were offered for sale. A less fine weave was used and the palette was restricted to about 30 colours. In 1954 the

[1] See Preface to the Catalogue of the Jubilee Exhibition of the Dovecot Studio, published by the Scottish Committee of the Arts Council.

Bute family agreed to transfer the main responsibility for the running of the company to a new Board of Directors, under the joint direction of John Noble of Ardkinglas and Harry Jefferson Barnes. Under this new Board the Studio carried out commissions for tapestries designed for special purposes and locations. During the last few years the company has devoted itself almost entirely to the execution of commissions. Among these the tapestry made for the English Electric Company has been described as " the finest textile to have been produced in this country for many centuries." Another notable production of special local interest is the tapestry designed by the late John Maxwell, R.S.A., for the Scottish Committee of the Arts Council. In 1962 the company celebrated its jubilee, which was marked by an exhibition in Edinburgh mounted under the patronage of the Scottish Committee of the Arts Council.

Besides the craftsmen engaged at the Dovecot factory there are others in the city working independently. Of these the best known is Sax Shaw. Shaw at one time worked for the Dovecot Studio under Ronald Cruickshank and became its chief designer and master craftsman in 1954. He now works in his own studio, where his output is confined to tapestries of domestic scale, spontaneously worked from small sketches, with particular regard to the nature and qualities of his medium. Archie Brennan, another tapestry artist, was trained at the Dovecot under Cruickshank and at Edinburgh College of Art, where he teaches now.

It should be added to this account that on leaving the studio at Corstorphine Ronald Cruickshank set up The Golden Targe Studio in the city; and there he wove a number of experimental designs of his own—notably " The Phoenix ", now in Phoenix, Arizona—and designs by others such as a large decorative panel by Dom Robert for the P. and O. liner *Iberia*, and a lyrical " Fools of Summer " by Cecil Collins for a villa in Fiesole. He has kept in touch with Jean Lurçat, the Director of the Aubusson studio in France, and has woven for him a number of variations on Lurçat's designs. He has also experimented with the weaving of synthetic materials such as rayon and terylene. Recent Dovecot Studio works can be seen in the Edinburgh Crematorium, the Rolls Royce offices in Glasgow, St. Thomas' Church (New York), Martin's Bank (London), and the new London headquarters of the Clydesdale Bank.

CRAFTS IN ARCHITECTURE

WROUGHT-IRON, WOOD-CARVING & FURNISHING

The crafts revival which began about the beginning of the century, and which reached its peak in the '20s, deserves particular mention not only because of the high quality of the work it produced but because it was inspired largely by one man—the architect, Robert (later Sir Robert) Lorimer. Fired by the ideals of Ruskin and Morris, Lorimer, who regarded the architect as the key-stone of the artistic structure, believed that under modern conditions the architect must have a definite say in the design of every decorative feature incorporated in a building. A craftsman himself, he knew how to guide and enthuse those who worked for him in the new buildings and the restorations of old buildings for which he became responsible. Under his forceful but sympathetic influence the crafts burst into life and continued to flourish under his kindly dominion. Today his name is indissolubly linked with the Scottish National War Memorial which, in a sense, is the epitome of all that is best and most worthy in the crafts of the present century.

It was Lorimer's rule to discuss with the craftsman every detail of the work in hand, suggesting how improvements and modifications might be effected. Thus there is a Lorimerian flavour in most of the craftwork carried out under his supervision. In the craft of wrought-iron, which suddenly began to flourish during his time, Lorimer was fortunate in his choice of a partner. For Thomas Hadden, although a working blacksmith, possessed an intuitive gift for the creative side of his craft. Before Hadden's time there was a faltering wrought-iron tradition in Edinburgh deriving from the robust work of the 18th century smiths; but under Lorimer's influence and enthusiasm the craft suddenly took on a new life. Thomas Hadden had been trained first in a country shop at Howgate. When he came to Edinburgh, after finishing his apprenticeship, he found work with James Milne and Son at Abbeyhill. Here a tradition of decorative wrought-iron existed thanks to the inspiration of a Belgian craftsman employed by the firm at the time. After a period in London Haddon came back to Edinburgh; and soon an invitation from Lorimer initiated a life-long friendship and collaboration.

Lorimer had many commissions at this time and employed Hadden continuously throughout his working life as a craftsman. Typical of the work of this happy partnership are the magnificent screens in the Thistle Chapel at St. Giles, Cathedral which were completed in 1911. Hadden was then employing between 25 and 30 craftsmen in his own workshop at East Silvermills. Other leading architects in Edinburgh also employed him whenever they were fortunate enough to secure his services. The 1914–18 war, however, brought all craftwork to a halt until after the Armistice Lorimer began the restoration of Dunrobin Castle for the Duke of Sutherland. Here eight craftsmen from Hadden's were employed for many months. Gradually new work began to be commissioned, and by the '30s the firm had again about 30 craftsmen fully employed. Besides the magnificent screens and casket for the Scottish National War Memorial Hadden executed the massive Gothic screen which Lorimer designed for Carlisle Cathedral (1934–35) and the large entrance gates for Pittencrieff Park, Dunfermline, designed by Jamieson and Arnott of Edinburgh.

Unfortunately by the middle '30s there were signs of a recession in the volume of work being commissioned. This was due partly to the adverse effects of the financial crisis in the early '30s, and partly to the change of taste and design occasioned by the growth of the modern spirit in architecture and the arts generally (" There were more straight bars and fewer motifs "); costs too were rising and church work was less in evidence. Nevertheless, the firm of Hadden's has executed many commissions since the end of the second World War and maintained high standards of craftsmanship. Among these particular mention must be made of the Glasgow University Quincentenary Gates (1952) designed by the architect Graham Henderson, the Memorial Gates for the Royal High School at " Jock's Lodge ", designed by Gordon and Dey, and the tercentenary Memorial Gates at George Heriot's School, designed by Everston Henderson.

Another workshop with a fine record of craftsmanship in wrought-iron is that of Thomas Bogie and Son. Thomas Bogie, the founder of the firm, began business in 1920 when he took over a small blacksmith's shop in Circus Lane. A craftsman himself, he had a natural sense of design which quickly won for him a reputation among architects of standing like Reginald Fairlie, R.S.A. From 1920 until the outbreak of the second World War Thomas Bogie and his son, Robert, carried out a large number of commissions directly for Fairlie and in collaboration with him in churches and other buildings throughout Scotland. Among these perhaps the most important are the Canopy and High Altar in St. Mary's R.C. Church at Fort William, executed in 1934, and the ironwork, including the light fittings, grilles, gates and railings at St. Salvator's College Chapel, St. Andrews, between 1933 and 1936. Robert Bogie, the founder's son, designed and executed the gates at Eilean Donan Castle in 1939 and also, in 1954, the gates at the east entrance of the Royal Botanic Garden. Besides carrying out architectural and ecclesiastical work the firm has all along specialised in smaller work such as balcony and stair rails, grilles and fire irons.

A large amount of Lorimer's work, in both his original buildings and his many restorations, demanded the craft of the woodcarver. As with wrought-iron there was a continuous, if not a very distinguished woodcarving tradition throughout the 19th century, which industrialisation did not wholly destroy, but the first World War nearly did. For then the woodcarver's services were hardly required, and after the war changes of fashion, trade slumps, and increasing mechanisation wrought havoc with the craft. Fortunately a few of the older craftsmen, who possessed both skill and determination as well as the artist's sense of vocation, continued to produce work of considerable quality.

Lorimer, again fortunate in his friendships, was also able to enlist the expertise of the brothers, W. and A. Clow, who had a workshop in Ramsay Lane. These two brothers had a rare sense of their trade and the true craftsman's selfless dedication to its finest traditions. Devoted servants of Lorimer, they found " that no architect gave them such scope and they set themselves to study and develop his ideas. The stalls of the Thistle Chapel and the great organ cases at Marchmont, Lattingtown and Dunblane illustrate how perfectly these fine craftsmen came to understand his mind."[1] Working almost exclusively for him, the Clow brothers did much to maintain and perhaps improve the traditions which in the great creative periods had inspired every craftsman serving the " Mother of the Arts."

[1] *The Work of Sir Robert Lorimer* by Christopher Hussey, *Country Life*, 1931, p.105.

Thomas Good, whose high-ceilinged workshop was situated just off Castle Hill, was another worthy craftsman of the period. Good, himself a designer in the Gothic style, employed as chief assistant an equally distinguished carver, John Sime. Together they created a tradition of their own, which possesses all the forthrightness and vigour of the Scottish character. Although Good may have worked for Lorimer he was employed mostly by other architects such as Reginald Fairlie, executing commissions as far distant as Pittsburg; but a great deal of his work was for Scottish churches and patrons. Perhaps his best work in Scotland is at St. Magnus Cathedral, Kirkwall, and the University Chapel, St. Andrews.

In contrast to the highly individual workshop of Thomas Good there were the firms of Scott Morton and Whytock and Reid, both of whom have employed skilled craftsmen carvers in varying numbers for many years. Scott Morton did a great deal of work for Lorimer, carrying on the tradition of church decoration and furnishing which Lorimer revived: while Whytock and Reid, who also worked in close collaboration with Lorimer, have continued the same tradition mostly in the domestic sphere of furniture and interior woodwork, felicitously adapting it in recent years to the modern idiom. Both firms have earned renown for the excellence of their work, not only in this country but in other parts of the world.

Among Scott Morton's most notable work are the Screen at Dunblane Cathedral, the Guildry Stalls at St. John's Church, Perth, and the Queen's Stall at Stowe School Chapel, all designed by Lorimer. At Stowe school there is also the magnificent panelling and Shrine of the War Memorial designed by John Matthew (Lorimer's partner) in association with the firm's own designer, David Ramsay. Here the necessary blending of Renaissance and Gothic has been triumphantly and sensitively accomplished. All the woodwork furnishings and fittings of the Reid Memorial Church, designed by Leslie Grahame Thomson, R.S.A., (now Leslie Grahame MacDougall) were also executed by the Mortons; and in 1950 they carried out the carving of the screens, reredos and furniture for the War Memorial Chapel at Bagshot, designed by John Matthew. This memorial is distinguished not only for the magnificent carving but for the ingenuity and sensitivity with which the many symbols and motifs associated with the Colonies were so effectively blended with the native style. In more recent times Scott Morton executed the carving of the reredos and elders' seating in the chancel of St. Michael's, Linlithgow (1956), and the large wood screen for Trinity Chapel, Glenalmond, designed by Sir Basil Spence.

Most of the work executed by Whytock and Reid consisted of interior woodwork fittings and furniture for various large houses and country mansions then being built or renovated by the architect. The fittings of the house of Marchmont in Berwickshire and many other Scottish mansions are testimonies to the superb craftsmanship and taste which imbued everything for which they were responsible. But of course they worked in gracious days for patrons who valued the traditional qualities of the great craftsmen. Today the private aristocratic patron has been largely replaced by the large corporations, the banks, insurance companies and mammoth business concerns, whose prestige in an affluent society finds dignified symbolic expression in palatial buildings, such as the Head Office of the National Bank of Scotland, St. Andrew Square, the furnishings and interior fittings of which were executed by Whytock and Reid under the firm's designer-director, J. Connel Pringle. Here refinement and ancient dignity proceed hand-in-hand with solid, confident craftsmanship of a high order.

In their heyday these two firms employed between them some 20 to 30 carver-craftsmen. By the early '30s they were employing four, and only one apprentice. It may very well be, therefore, that the present group of craftsmen will be among the last in Edinburgh to practise this ancient craft.

EMBROIDERY

Of the minor but no less important crafts revived by Lorimer perhaps embroidery deserves more than a word. Already towards the end of the century in Scotland the Arts and Crafts movement had stimulated a new interest in the craft. Lorimer's enthusiasm gave it a new pace and purpose. Foremost in the revival Mrs. Phoebe Traquair was executing large figure panels in the Morris tradition for domestic and ecclesiastical purposes. The craft, however, got a fresh impetus when Louisa Chart was appointed to take charge of the teaching of the craft at the College of Art. Louisa Chart's wide knowledge and expert skill inspired a new generation of embroiderers by directing attention to the treasures of the past and to the decorative possibilities of the craft. Encouraging imaginative experiment and the highest standards of technical excellence, she created a fresh interest among her students, which soon accomplished a revolution in the teaching of the subject in the secondary schools.

Another source of stimulation was the Needlework Development Scheme started in 1934. Through the circulation of embroideries from many countries a wide knowledge of styles was disseminated which fertilised the native tradition and opened up the way towards new experiments and techniques. Since the second World War, however, due to fundamental changes in social habits and in the arts and architecture, the craft has virtually been moribund. In the past 20 years only an occasional student in the College of Art has made a serious study of the subject; and, whether because there are few teachers of the subject available or because the craft itself now makes no appeal to older children, there appears to be little interest in it in the secondary schools today. On the other hand, the founding of a flourishing branch of The Embroiderers' Guild in the city may foreshadow a new revival.

MOSAICS

It has already been noted that the revolutionary aesthetic inspiring modern architecture has contributed in some measure to the decline during the past quarter of a century and more of a number of the traditional crafts. On the other hand, the new architecture has given a fillip to certain ancient crafts which were in danger of passing into desuetude. Among these the most notable is probably the craft of mosaic which the modern style of architecture to some extent has inspired. The many large buildings now being constructed, such as schools and hospitals, have provided the mosaicist with inviting floor and wall surfaces for the exercise of his skill. In the forefront of this revival stands J. Kingsley Cook, head of the School of Design and Crafts at the College of Art. Already this artist craftsman has designed and executed a number of important commissions in Edinburgh and elsewhere in Scotland. The mural mosaics for the College of Agriculture at West Mains, extending in all to some 400 square feet, are notable alike for their boldness of design and their technical construction. Using natural stone and other materials and employing a special method of setting, a high degree of flexibility and freedom has been attained, enabling the artist to produce a wider range of aesthetic effects than was hitherto possible and in a much shorter time. Other notable examples include the relief mosaic in ordinary brick for the Knox Academy, Haddington; the large wall mosaic for the Church of St. Teresa, Dumfries, set direct on the wall in marble and Venetian tesserae; and the altarpiece for the Church of St. Francis Xavier, Falkirk. Under Kingsley Cook's inspiration interest among students, architects and others is growing; and in view of the vast public building programme still to be carried out it looks as if the craft of mosaic is acquiring a new impetus.

FOOTNOTE ON THE FUTURE

Until the advent of the " Modern " age the craftsman was a man of many parts, a man who could " turn his hand to anything " and leave his mark on whatever he made. This versatility has all but disappeared: only one representative of the ancient tradition of the widely skilled craftsman remains in the city—C. d'O. Pilkington Jackson. In the broad range of his talents and his intimate understanding of materials Pilkington Jackson, who is chiefly known as a sculptor, has an unrivalled reputation as a designer in silver, metal, stone, plaster and wood and may be the last in the lineage of the many-sided craftsmen of the Renaissance.[1] For the fact remains that the clamour for improved standards of industrial design, so much in evidence today, has provided new scope for the craftsman's skill and ingenuity. Many craftsmen are turning their attention to the making of prototypes for industry whilst simultaneously practising their special craft. But what kind of influence this may have on the future of the fine handcrafts in an increasingly industrial and scientific economy is at this stage hard to predict.

[1] It should be noted here that not every craft in Edinburgh has been noted in this chapter. In the usual meaning of the terms there is often very little difference between some arts and some crafts, and often, as with stained glass, the work of the creative artist and the craftsman is often intertwined; or they are one and the same person. In another chapter of this book, sculpture, bronze founding, stained glass and lithography are dealt with by another contributor.

Chapter 32

AGRICULTURE

We come now to agriculture, an industry which, inside the city itself, encircles and is sometimes intertwined with the many commercial and industrial activities we have been looking at. It is however doubtful if the average citizen has the slightest dea of the large stake Edinburgh has in agriculture and its ancillary activities.

The first and most immediate part of the industry is the physical amount of farming or farming commerce carried on within the city boundaries—the actual number of farms and the business done in the auction marts, the animals passing through the slaughter houses and the trade done in such institutions as the Corn Market.

Secondly, there is the large share which Edinburgh, as Scotland's capital, has in the administration of Scottish farming. Not only does it house the Department of Agriculture for Scotland and all its main branches, but some years ago the Department took over the administration of the former Animal Health Division of the Ministry of Agriculture in London, which had been a United Kingdom administrative organisation until this devolution took place. Now the Department administers animal health so far as general legislation goes—the eradication scheme for bovine tuberculosis, for example—but there is one exception. The operative control of an outbreak of foot and mouth disease still rests with the Ministry, and is on a U.K. basis for the simple reason that the virus, which knows no legislative borders, is also the hottest and fastest travelling virus known in human or veterinary medicine.

Thirdly, Edinburgh is also the home of most of the large organisations which serve the industry in a variety of unofficial but nevertheless important ways. In Edinburgh, for instance, are the headquarters of the National Farmers Union of Scotland and the offices of the Royal Highland and Agriculture Society of Scotland, one of whose founder members was Sir John Sinclair, originator of the first *Statistical Account*.

The fourth part which Edinburgh plays in this wide agricultural sphere is concerned with commerce. Because of Leith, Edinburgh is a big centre in the sale and distribution of such essentials as fertilisers and feeding stuffs. Being also the biggest brewing centre in Scotland, with its own distilleries as well, the city is a big consuming centre for the grains from the rich hinterland of the Lothians and other neighbouring counties north as well as south of the Forth. By the same token it is a big centre for milling and the compounding of feeding stuffs and fertilisers.

Last of all, but by no means its least contribution to agriculture, Edinburgh is concerned with agricultural education over a wide field.

THE FARMLANDS

Edinburgh's physical share in the notable amount of farming inside the boundaries in recent years may be seen from two tables showing at a glance the extent of the farmlands within the burgh boundary in 1947 (Table 59) and again in 1957 (Table 60). Since then the acreage has continued to decline.

TABLE 59

AREA OF AGRICULTURAL LAND AND NUMBER OF AGRICULTURAL HOLDINGS OVER 1 ACRE IN THE PARISHES IN EDINBURGH AS AT 4TH JUNE, 1947

Parish	*Arable Acres*	*Permanent Grass Acres*	*Total Crops and Grass Acres*	*Rough Grazings Acres*	*Total Agric. Holdings Over 1 Acre*
Colinton	1,080¾	717¾	1,798½	727½	46
Corstorphine	1,436½	338¾	1,775¼	19	31
Cramond	1,697¼	543½	2,240¾	2½	36
Edinburgh	571½	453¾	1,025¼	763½	37
Leith	—	—	—	—	—
Liberton	2,796¾	687½	3,484¼	97¼	64
Total	7,582¾	2,741¼	10,324	1,609¾	214

Considering the size of the city these figures are impressive. Table 60, however, tells a rather different story, as no doubt will a comparable Table for 1967.

TABLE 60

ACREAGE OF AGRICULTURAL LAND AND NUMBER OF AGRICULTURAL HOLDINGS OVER 1 ACRE IN THE PARISHES IN EDINBURGH AS AT 4TH JUNE, 1957

Parish	*Arable Acres*	*Permanent Grass Acres*	*Total Crops and Grass Acres*	*Rough Grazings Acres*	*Total Agric. Holdings Over 1 Acre*
Colinton	740¾	504¾	1,245½	719½	35
Corstorphine	1,137¾	183½	1,321¼	3	19
Cramond	601	208½	809½	2½	11
Edinburgh	133	273¼	406¼	757¾	25
Leith	—	—	—	—	—
Liberton	2,321	601½	2,922½	9	48
Total	4,933½	1,771½	6,705	1,491¾	138

It will be seen at once from these tables that in 10 years there was a considerable drop in the city's farmland acreage, due to the acquisition of farmland for urban development—housing and playing fields, for instance. It should however be made clear that some of the holdings including in these tables may have part of their lands actually outwith the city boundaries, though this is a small qualification, and that the "rough grazings" in column 5 include "mountain and heathland" units which in Edinburgh are mainly grazing lots on golf courses. (Such units are excluded from the number of holdings in column 6). Another way of looking at the farming inside the city boundary is through the rating of holdings or other allied " subjects." The above tables give the number of " agricultural holdings " over one acre; but in fact the rating authorities have many more on their list because there are many small gardens and " miscellaneous subjects " which come under the general heading of " agricultural subjects." The gross annual value and also the actual rateable value of agricultural holdings in the late '50s (after making the appropriate derating allowances) may be seen from the following table:

TABLE 61
1957

	Number	*Gross Annual Value*	*Rateable Annual Value*
Farms	52	£19,634 10*s.*	£2,450
Market gardens	120	7,585 17*s.*	1,033
Piggeries	37	3,478 3*s.*	438
Small holdings	17	875 0*s.*	108
Miscellaneous subjects	746	7,966 9*s.*	810
Total	972	£39,539 19*s.*	£4,839

It will be seen that the De-rating Act applies to these subjects and it should also be mentioned that " the miscellaneous subjects " contain areas which are not perhaps real farming subjects but gardens, allotments and parklands or other subjects which enjoy the benefits of agricultural de-rating.

The next table gives the 1960–1 figures and there it will be seen that the trend of decrease in market gardens continues. Incidentally, 1960–1 is the last year for which this type of statistic will be available as under the new rating legislation which came into force at Whit Sunday 1961 agricultural buildings other than dwelling houses would not merely be exempt from rating but would not be entered in the Valuation Roll. So, as a matter of interest, details are also given in Table 62 of the 1962–3 Valuation Roll in respect of the city's agricultural houses.

TABLE 62
VALUATION ROLL 1960–1

	Number	*Gross Annual Value*	*Rateable Value*
Farms	54	£19,223 13*s.*	£2,412
Market gardens	77	5,882 10*s.*	739
Piggeries	32	3,263 7*s.*	411
Small holdings	17	875 0*s.*	108
Miscellaneous	708	7,990 7*s.*	983
Total	888	£37,234 17*s.*	£4,653

VALUATION ROLL 1962–3

	Number	*Gross Annual Value*	*Rateable Value*
Agricultural houses	320	£15,773	£12,197

ORGANIC WASTE

While dealing with Edinburgh's farmlands it would be appropriate here to mention that Edinburgh has given a lead to other corporations in the United Kingdom and indeed to many countries in Europe by introducing recently a method of turning municipal organic waste into a highly valuable humus for use on farm land. This plant, the first of its kind in Britain, was started as a pilot experiment a year or two ago and has succeeded so well that a huge quarry at Craigleith, within the city boundary, will house a much bigger version of the same plant. This is an engineering approach to organic composting and reduces the production of compost from many weeks to a few days. Town sewage, organic waste and some chemical waste—which would otherwise cost ratepayers money for their disposal—are turned into a product which is in great demand by farmers. It is *not* a fertiliser, but is a valuable humus product which improves the land. Quite apart also from saving money and bringing income from otherwise waste and offensive material, always expensive to dispose of in that huge dumps were used or massive incinerators necessary, the process helps to solve a severe space problem by reducing the amount of land used for dumping refuse. It also helps gardeners as well as farmers.

DAIRIES

So far as actual farming enterprises go, perhaps the biggest and most impressive social change is the reduction in the number of dairies. A century or more ago there were hundreds of dairies in and around Edinburgh. They were known as " town dairies " and never had more than a few cows, some serving only a street or two with the milk. Housing and health regulations were the chief reasons for the disappearance of the town dairies, but the growth of efficient farming, which gave the bigger farmer with more grass an advantage, was another factor; and also, of course, improved transportation made it possible to bring in milk from quite distant areas more naturally suited to milk production.

The campaign against bovine tuberculosis started in the 1930s, when strict regulations to control the size, type and equipment of buildings for housing cows and water supplies administered the final blow to the small town dairy. Today all of Scotland's cattle (beef and dairy) are in T.T. (tuberculin tested) herds.

The decline in recent decades of the number of dairies in the city is shown in the following table:

TABLE 63

Year	*1927*	*1937*	*1947*	*1956*	*1961*
Number of dairies	97	54	31	17	12
Number of cows (estimated)	3,732	1,461	1,110	600	400

PIGGERIES

Another form of intensive farming carried on within the city is piggeries and the veterinary officer in 1962 had 90 piggeries listed. In the earlier list of farm subjects assessed as such only 37 piggeries were mentioned, but some of the other holdings on that list—farms, market gardens and miscellaneous subjects—might have added piggery enterprises and would not therefore be assessed as separate piggeries. One piggery in Corstorphine at the time of writing has about 2,000 pigs. In all some 58 premises are licensed to handle and feed swill to their animals, with periodical inspections by the local authority. In 1961–2 there was a big reduction in the number of pig keepers who feed swill, the change being due to the cheap price of meal feed resulting from cheaper cereals, to the saving in transport and to the fact that the carcase fat of meal-fed pigs is of much better quality.

Most of the city piggeries are commercial enterprises producing pigs for pork or bacon; but Edinburgh has a national name in the pedigree pig world, and within its boundaries are pedigree herds which have won fame in the show rings and in the sale rings with their breeding stock. There are four noted herds breeding the Large White breed of pig in the city—the Gyle, Brunstane, Brunstane Mill and Gogar Mains. There is one Wessex breeder at Gogar and an Essex breed enthusiast at Braehead, Barnton. At many sales these herds get well over 100 guineas or more for their pigs, the highest price being 600 guineas paid for a pig bred by Mr. W. H. Gray of the Gyle a few years ago. This famous herd was wiped out by swine fever but has been built up again.

HORSES

The horse population of the city has suffered the drastic decimation that has overcome the farm horse with the advance of the tractor; but it was estimated in 1962–3 that there might be about 90 horses in the city, 65 used by St. Cuthbert's Co-operative Association; seven by Younger's Abbey and Holyrood Breweries; three by the Leith Provident; six by the Police Department; 10 " miscellaneous " and an unknown quantity in the local riding stables.

AGRICULTURAL MARKETS

Another important sub-division of physical agriculture within the city is its function as a selling centre for farm stock. There are four firms engaged in this enterprise, two with extensive premises of their own—Messrs. Oliver and Son, and Messrs. John Swan and Sons—and two which use the Corporation premises: these are Wm. Bosomworth and Sons Limited and the Berwick Auction Mart Company.

All these premises are situated at Gorgie, the Corporation marts being alongside the Corporation's Slaughterhouse. Also in the same place is the Corn Exchange where the merchants meet every Wednesday and do business, buying grains and selling feedstuffs, fertilisers, seeds etc. The big petrol companies too have stands in the market since the sale of fuels and oils are big items in the business done by modern mechanised farmers.

The following table gives recent totals of all animals passing in recent years through the fat markets at Gorgie (animals, that is, sold for slaughter for food as opposed to store animals sold for fattening).

TABLE 64

	1927	*1937*	*1947*[1] *Grading Centre Ministry of Food*	*1956*	*1957*	*1961*
Cattle	46,504	50,916	6,552	20,844	20,914	23,818
Calves	6,279	5,838	1,702	2,859	3,108	3,356
Sheep	227,461	256,202	27,358	159,766	176,722	241,653
Pigs	19,034	32,602	10,526	24,816	23,618	20,179

[1] These figures occurred during a period of rationing.

It will be seen from this that the number of sheep has been returning to pre-war figures, though the numbers are very much less than pre-1939. The reasons for this and other decreases are as follows:

(1) During Ministry of Food control, farmers sent their fatstock to the nearest grading centre and, as a result, some of the pre-war small markets became popular and have remained so.
(2) Before 1939, fat cattle in large numbers were sent from Northumberland and Cumberland to Edinburgh. Now, with full employment in the industrial Midlands of England, the cattle are being sent there from markets further south.
(3) Cost of transport may also play some part.

Under the Regulation of Movement of Swine Order 1954 (which requires the licensing of all pigs from markets) 79,791 store and pedigree pigs were licensed in 1961 in addition to the 20,179 fat pigs shown above. This necessitated the issue of over 5,000 licensces, and the checking of these throws a large amount of work on the Diseases of Animals Inspectors.

The number of freshly imported Irish cattle passing through the market or consigned directly from the ports to the slaughterhouse in recent years is shown in the following table:

TABLE 65

	Market	*Direct to Slaughterhouse*	*Total*
1934	20,212	649	20,861
1953	14,275	5,403	19,678
1955	12,240	4,892	17,132
1956	11,607	4,500	16,107
1961	12,499	3,951	16,450

As for the numbers passing through the slaughterhouse these are set out here in Table 66, a particularly interesting one since it shows that the total of 346,511 animals for 1961 was a record for any one year.

TABLE 66

	1927	*1937*	*1947 Ministry of Food Control*	*1957*	*1961*
Cattle	33,287	36,273	23,822	39,118	43,649
Calves	4,936	3,702	7,508	5,740	5,145
Sheep	158,995	136,417	116,390	192,030	252,041
Pigs	16,660	21,045	6,893	43,257	45,676
	213,878	191,437	154,613	280,145	346,511

Large numbers of store cattle—reared either in Ireland or on the hill or upland farms of Scotland, and bought by lowland farmers for fattening and for the essential by-product of fertility which they give to the richer lands—are also sold at Gorgie, the biggest single sale of this type being All Hallow Fair which goes on for three days during the second week of November. This is a very ancient cattle fair, and in 1407 its date was moved to November to avoid its clashing with holy days. Its location was in several parts of the city over the centuries; but now at the great live-stock selling centre of Gorgie it has its natural home, and for the period of the sale Gorgie has become the home of a very large invading force of Irish cattle dealers from the Republic, for nearly all the cattle sold at All Hallow Fair are Irish stores At the 1961 Fair, for instance, some 4,000 Irish cattle worth nearly a quarter of a million pounds sterling were sold in three days.

Here are some recent records—there being no old ones—of the numbers exposed at Hallow Fair in recent years: 1948—3,899; 1951—3,682; 1954—3,218; 1957—4,252; 1961—3,237. Many cattle, incidentally, are also sold by direct deals between the man in Ireland and the buyer but many more Lothian farmers, the chief buyers of these cattle, prefer to buy their stores at auction.

A careful watch is naturally kept for signs of any animal disease before and during these transactions, as the following statistics show.

TABLE 67

Incidence of Tubercule in Cattle

	1937		*1947*		*1956*		*1961*	
Oxen	5·96	11·66%	10·57	18·02%	3·99	4·53%	0·37	0·38%
Bulls	28·48		17·15		7·29		—	
Cows	44·53		35·39		8·15		0·65	
Heifers	6·5		8·96		9·60		0·39	

The percentage of cattle infected with tape-worm (Cysticerous bovis) in 1961 was 0·45 per cent lower than in previous years. This was due to the reduction in infestation in home-reared cattle. As regards the incidence of liver fluke, figures are available. In 1955, 16 per cent of ox livers and 3 per cent of sheep livers were condemned because of the effects of liver fluke. In 1956 the comparable figures were 21 per cent of ox livers and 2·8 per cent of sheep livers, and in 1961 21·8 per cent of cattle livers and

3 per cent of sheep livers. The parasite irritates the bile ducts and causes the formation of scar tissue which spreads throughout the liver substance and renders the organ too tough to consume.

Apart from the fat stock and the store stock sold live, these figures show that many animals go direct to the slaughterhouse as it is possible for a farmer to sell his fattened stock either through the auction ring or privately to a butcher who will slaughter it, or to the Fatstock Marketing Corporation (widely known as F.M.C.) which pays the farmer on a dead weight and grade business. This Corporation was started by the farmers of the United Kingdom when meat rationing ended in 1954, and as it offers an alternative method of marketing it also helps to put a bottom in the market. Edinburgh is an important centre of the Corporation's operations.

Yet another type of stock sold in the Edinburgh markets is pedigree stock for breeding; but apart from pigs and Hereford cattle, Edinburgh is not a very important pedigree stock selling centre. In pedigree pigs it is easily the biggest centre for sales in Scotland and is one of the biggest in the United Kingdom. One firm, Messrs. Oliver and Son, have the main share of this trade and not only conduct the pedigree sales in Edinburgh but actually on the farms for breeders in many parts of Scotland and Northern England. Messrs. Swan do not hold many pedigree sales in Edinburgh—they share with other firms a special sale of Down sheep held in the different marts each year—but in their St. Boswell's mart they hold a large and very fast developing sale of pedigree Aberdeen-Angus bulls, used for cross-breeding purposes to produce the commercial cattle which, when fattened, will find their way to the Edinburgh markets or to the slaughterhouse. Messrs. Bosomworth hold the annual sales of Hereford cattle, an " invading breed " which became more popular in Scotland since the war, again for cross-breeding purposes, to produce commercial fat stock. At the 1962 spring sale the Hereford bulls sold for an average price of £261 and a top price of 750 guineas.

Before passing from the physical farming carried on within the city mention must be made of the grazings in Holyrood Park, formerly known as the King's or Queen's Park. The extent of the grazing area is 590 acres; the average number of sheep on it is 500; and a startling fact is that these sheep may graze up to the top of Arthur's Seat which is higher than the highest point in the original land used in the Great Glen Cattle Ranch at Fort William.

AGRICULTURAL SOCIETIES

The oldest of the organisations with headquarters in Edinburgh is the Royal Highland and Agricultural Society of Scotland, founded in 1784. The Society got its " Royal " prefix in 1948, when it held its first post-war show at Inverness and was visited then by King George VI.

Its first show in 1822 was held in a one-acre site off the Canongate. Then the gate drawings came to £52 1*s*. In 1935 there was a show in the city which covered 86 acres (excluding car parks), and had 156,226 paid admissions. The 1955 show cost a total of £119,979 to stage, of which the showyard erection alone amounted to £69,561. The profit was £2,834. However, rocketing costs and the problems involved in finding suitable sites in the show's eight " show divisions " in Scotland turned some members to the idea of a permanent site in or near Edinburgh. In 1958 the Society bought a permanent site at Ingliston on the western outskirts of the city; by 1962 it had spent close on £250,000 on its purchase and development; and there the shows are now held.

The Society has completed its first documentary film—on the Clydesdale horse. The decision to make this film was taken because of the decline in the number of horses on Scottish farms, due to mechanisation, and it was thought essential to have a film record showing the part the horse played at a time when farming was established as the country's major industry. The Society will have a master copy of the film in its library and copies will be available for showing in this country and abroad. The film was made by an Edinburgh company.

Another organisation which has its headquarters in Edinburgh is the National Farmers' Union of Scotland. Its membership is about 25,000 and as there are estimated to be just over 30,000 " full-time " farms in Scotland the Union is not far from 100 per cent representation.

Also in Edinburgh are the offices of the Scottish Federation of Young Farmers' Clubs whose membership is about 8,300 in its 164 clubs. Recently this youth movement of the countryside decided on an innovation in forming Young Farmers' Clubs in cities, and Edinburgh is now one of the cities where young people interested in the country or country ways have a club. One of the most interesting activities of the Association is its participation in the International Farm Youth Exchange Scheme under which young farmers from the Commonwealth and other countries, including the United States of America, spend three months in Scotland, staying for a short time on different types of farms, while young Scots farm boys and girls are in Canada, America and Australia. Edinburgh is the " channel " through which these comings and goings are organised.

Other organisations with headquarters in the city are the Scottish Agricultural Machinery Organisation, which looks after the interests of the machinery distributors; the Scottish Centre of the Institution of British Agricultural Engineers; the Scottish Agricultural Organisation Society, a Government-aided body which encourages the development of agricultural co-operatives and other schemes, ranging from the Central Farmers in Fife (with an annual turnover of something like £1,000,000) to a co-operative scheme for marketing eggs for crofters in the Lochboisdale area of South Uist.

EDUCATION AND RESEARCH

Agricultural education is one of the most important contributions which Edinburgh makes to the industry, and because of a great visionary scheme evolved just after the last war, the city now has a unique part to play. Briefly, the University's Agricultural Department gives degrees which are respected throughout the industry. An ordinary degree takes four years, an honours degree five years, plus post-graduate diplomas in rural science for the degree of Master of Science with a normal course of two years for ordinary graduates and one year for honours graduates. Finally there are Ph.D. courses with a normal minimum of two years.

The Edinburgh and East of Scotland College of Agriculture gives diploma courses in agriculture and in agriculture and dairying combined: these take three years. There are also courses in horticulture. The provision of instruction to post-graduate degree and diploma students is shared between the University and the College, which also provides courses in Chemistry for students studying Forestry at the University, and a course in Bacteriology for students taking a degree in pure Science. In 1962–3 the number of students enrolled was well over 200.

In 1962–3 also there were 18 staff members in the University Department of Agriculture. There were at the same time 185 members of the staff of the College working in or administered from Edinburgh in the College's south region, but there were also 37 in its north region, administered from Perth. Apart from education the College undertakes a large amount of advisory work in its area—from Angus and East Perthshire down to the Eastern Borders.

These facts indicate that there is both a University department *and* the College, which is true; but as it has turned out, College and Department are completely integrated under one head. Professor Stephen J. Watson, of the Chair of Agriculture and Rural Economy in the University, is also Principal of the College, and since 1959 the two bodies have operated from one building and under one title—The Edinburgh School of Agriculture.

The school, which cost £709,000 to build and equip, is situated on land feued from the University adjacent to its science departments at West Mains Road. It was officially opened by H.R.H. the Duke of Edinburgh, who is Chancellor of the University, on 12th October, 1960. And without doubt it is this closeness of co-operation—so close, it has been said, that it is difficult sometimes to know where the dividing line between the two is—which has contributed to Edinburgh's unique place in British agricultural education. But there is more to add to this story.

In 1948 a great plan came into being to create the Edinburgh Centre of Rural Economy. This was achieved by the purchase of estates just outside the city boundary and an experimental farm within it, plus a hill area in the Pentlands leased from the War Office.

This great farm educational and research estate of 3,000 acres—all in one piece—stretches downwards from the top of the Pentland Hills through a complete range and variety of soils to the rich valley of the Esk; and it gives an unrivalled variety of land as well as plenty of space for research. Hence the fairly recent move of the Scottish Society for Research in Plant Breeding from Corstorphine and the commodious research institute on the estate. Other research stations have been planned. So close together in the same area will be a complete range—from pure research, through higher education in agriculture, through diploma and certificate courses, to short part-time courses on special subjects, which may be either " refreshers " for graduates or for the training of farm workers.

This great estate has on it a variety of farms embracing dairying, arable, hill sheep in the Pentlands; and it is also, apart from research, a practical training ground for Edinburgh School of Agriculture students. As a striking photograph in *The Scotsman* showed recently (17th September, 1964), beside the main School building are the new home of the Animal Breeding Research Organisation, the Poultry Research Centre, the Engineering and Chemistry Departments, the Institute of Animal Genetics, the Film and the Bio-Physic Units and the Veterinary Science Centre. It is an admirable and impressive concentration.

On an entirely different plane, Edinburgh saw the beginning of what is believed to be the first scheme of its kind in the world—" The Scottish Joint Apprenticeship Scheme for Agriculture and Horticulture," which was launched after meetings held in the city in 1948 and 1949.

One of the most interesting features of the scheme—for which several hundred boys have applied—is that some 70 per cent of the apprentices have come from towns. Another more recent apprenticeship scheme, again the first in the U.K., enables agricultural engineering apprentices from Edinburgh to sit the London City and Guilds examination in this trade. It was born out of a voluntary scheme run by the Scottish Agricultural Machinery Association, an organisation of dealers in farm machinery and implements which has its headquarters in Edinburgh. But after the Education Department and the Ministry of Labour were brought in, the scheme was put on an official footing and now, under a special release programme, these boys come from all over Scotland to do their training in the Ramsay Technical Institute, Edinburgh, where their full time training is supplemented in the months they are actually working with the firms to whom they are indentured.

Being a big book publishing centre, it is not surprising that Edinburgh also produces important works on farming. The standard textbook at most British farm educational centres and University Agricultural Departments is *Agriculture; The Science and Practice of British Farming*, by Sir James A. Scott Watson, formerly Professor of Agriculture in Edinburgh, and the late Mr. James A. More. This book, published by Oliver and Boyd, is to agricultural students what *Gray's Anatomy* is to medical students. It came out first in 1924, and in 1962 the 11th edition appeared after revision by Sir James and other writers and contributors. Noteworthy also is an agricultural series published by another Edinburgh publishing firm, Thomas Nelson and Sons, which ranges from books on sheep and dairy farming to a history of Scottish agriculture.

RESEARCH CENTRES

Within the city boundary are several very important agricultural research centres. They include the Animal Breeding Research Organisation of the Agricultural Research Council; the Hill Farming Research Organisation; the Animal Diseases Research Association; the Plant Registration Station of the Department of Agriculture for Scotland's Scientific Services Station; the Poultry Research Centre; and the Livestock Records Bureau, which deals with analysis of milk records in Scottish dairy herds.

This list impressive though it is for one city, does not by any means exhaust the extent of agricultural research carried out within the city boundary. The University and the College have within them research and trial units. The University has, for example, the Institute of Animal Genetics, the leading institute of its kind in Britain, and this Institute houses the Commonwealth Bureau of Animal Genetics, a world-wide clearing house for information on this subject. The College also run such things as local centres in the National fruit trials and the trials held by the National Institute of Agricultural Botany. The headquarters of the latter are in Cambridge, but these bodies try out varieties and species of plants in varying environments, and Edinburgh is one.

THE INDUSTRY'S RAW MATERIALS

The final category in which Edinburgh has a very big stake in agriculture or its allied industries is in the commercial firms which supply the industry with its seeds, feeding stuffs, fertilisers and machinery and so on. The Leith Corn Trade Association with more than 70 members are mainly importers of grain and other cereals for sale as seeds or feeding stuffs and there is a Scottish Compound Feedingstuffs Association, also with headquarters in Edinburgh which looks after the compounders—the firms which provide ready made compound feeding stuffs for all types of stock.

Easily the biggest single example of these numerous enterprises is the huge plant built by Scottish Agricultural Industries Limited for the production of a new fertiliser—their Complete Concentrated Fertiliser better known as C.C.F. This proprietary product—like the compound feeding stuffs produced by the feed firms—saves the farmer mixing his own. Twelve acres of land were reclaimed from the shores of the Forth for this vast plant and by its opening date—17th March, 1958—it represented an outlay of £3,000,000. This firm also has its own research laboratory, opened in 1954 at Leith, for work on the development of fertilisers and allied problems. In 1962 another well-known firm, Messrs. Fisons, opened a big storage and handlery plant. But these are only two outstanding examples of how farming's allied firms have staked their claim in Scotland through Edinburgh and helped to give the city even firmer links with the country around it. In conclusion it should be noted that several other big firms such as British Oil and Cake Mills buy much of their raw material from local farmers and use it in making compound feeds; and there are many other firms, some including old-established family businesses, who trade from Edinburgh in machinery and other farming requisites.

Part Six

EDUCATION

CHAPTER 33

THE ROAD TO LEARNING

EDINBURGH has long been famous as one of the world's leading educational centres. Its ancient university, accustomed to welcome twice as many foreign students as the United Kingdom average, is at one end of the scale; at the other are the infant and primary schools for the city's own children. Between these extremes lies a wide range of institutions of every kind—public and private schools, technical and vocational colleges—which together cater outstandingly for the educational needs of Edinburgh citizens of all ages. It is of course true that other cities of comparable size can boast many of the facilities available in Edinburgh; but, as we shall see, there can be few which offer such a diversity or such a consistently high level throughout.

Domestically, the city provides many occupations in the lighter and more specialised industries, in all kinds of commerce, in the professions of law, medicine, teaching, banking, accounting, insurance, architecture, surveying and the rest. Civil servants abound there also; and the very preponderance of clerical workers of all kinds along with the high proportion of professional people in general have an important impact on the education provided. It looks in fact as if most parents in Edinburgh go out of their way to seek high standards of education for their children and are keenly interested in their educational progress.

RICHNESS AND DIVERSITY

It has indeed been said by many authorities that a child born in Edinburgh has a better chance of gaining a first class education than he would anywhere else; and in particular there has been praise for the Scottish day school's virtues, which combine the influence of home and school, and so give many middle class parents an advantage over their counterparts across the border. For advantage this certainly is. Edinburgh has many fee-paying and non-fee-paying secondary schools, either under independent management or under municipal control, all of which are capable of giving an education of quality right up to the stage of entry to higher technical college or University. Most of the municipal schools provide for both boys and girls in marked contrast to the independent schools where mixed classes exist only at the nursery or lower elementary stages.

Provision in the city for children handicapped in mind or in body is also noteworthy, both in the special day schools of the municipality and in the great residential schools for the blind and for the deaf which are striving to improve the quality of their teaching by the installation of modern equipment of all kinds.

TECHNICAL TRAINING

Edinburgh is fortunate too in having a group of central institutions which provide higher technical education and training in a wide range of subjects such as engineering, art, design and architecture, agriculture, veterinary medicine, domestic science and nautical matters. Some of these are closely related to the University; and furthermore with the foundations laid in the further education courses of the city authority these establishments form an asset of supreme value at a time of technological challenge.

One thing is common throughout the whole range of this educational largesse, and that is the need for an adequate supply of well-educated and professionally trained teachers. This is met by the University and by the Moray House College of Education, which not only trains one-third of the teachers of Scotland, but lets women non-graduates continue their general education along with professional training. In recent years the College has established a department for the further education and training of teachers from overseas and also training courses for leaders in youth organisations and community centres. Developments in educational thought and practice are of course kept constantly under review, and not only accommodation but other facilities are being expanded to help meet the urgent need for more teachers in every branch of education. And so it is with extra-mural studies for adults, an interesting feature of Edinburgh's education we shall come to later.

PIONEERS

One striking aspect deserves a tribute here—the long line of Edinburgh's sons who became outstanding educationalists. To them the city, Scotland and the world at large owe much in the advancement of education. To mention but a few, there have been Simon Somerville Laurie, a famous Professor of Education at Edinburgh, who for more than 50 years laboured for education in one sphere or another in the 19th century; Alexander Darroch, his pupil and successor, who was unequalled in Scotland in his day as an administrator and as a pioneer of new ideas for the better training of teachers; and Viscount Haldane, a statesman of original and enlightened ideas, who helped to frame the laws under which the Scottish system of education has developed in modern times. Yet if these distinguished sons of Edinburgh have been aptly described as the makers of Scottish education, there have been many others since—some publicly honoured and others largely unrecognised, like the progressive educationalists in the early School Boards and on the Education Committee of the municipality and the governing bodies of the great endowed schools. The modern classroom is a testimony to their work.

IN THE CLASSROOMS

If the teachers in local authority schools, who finished their professional careers 30 or 40 years ago, could return to the present educational scene, they would notice a great difference between the old solid stone three or four storied buildings in the central areas of the town, where they taught, and the new structures in the suburbs. The old high-set windows, drab colourings, smut-laden air, and the too close proximity of other tall buildings, have been exchanged for class-rooms with great stretches of glass in their walls, unobstructed views and bright delicate decoration; the restricted concrete playgrounds have been replaced by grass meadows and playing fields; and well-known artists have been producing murals, statuary and engraved panels, so that the artistic as well as the utilitarian aspect of the buildings shall be given prominence.

Gone therefore are the partitioned rooms opening from central halls, the iron staircases, the heavy fixed furniture of uniform size, the inadequate and often inconveniently placed cloakrooms, and the outside lavatories. Desks and chairs are now made from light materials, easily moved and stackable, and graded in size to suit the individual child. Storage space is adequate, and there is provision for the display of visual aids and of the children's own creative efforts. Cloakrooms are adjacent to classrooms and toilets are no longer situated at the other side of the playground. Old buildings still remain in commission, but in almost all of them some effort has been made to modernise conditions.

These material differences are naturally more obvious than the important changes which have taken place in methods and attitudes; for these require a deeper examination which would probably end in an admission by most inquirers that it was in the younger classes of the Primary schools that the greatest transformation had taken place.

Pioneers among infant teachers have for some time accepted the need of introducing a more active type of programme, but have been frustrated by the lack of suitable physical conditions. The situations in which they found themselves restricted the free investigation by children of their environment, and made free movement difficult. Fortunately the new buildings allowed them to put their ideas into practice; and an ever increasing number of these teachers have been adopting a freer and less circumscribed curriculum, in which the children are encouraged to become active participants in their own education, instead of passive receivers of presented knowledge. Their natural interests are thus developed and used to further their progress in mastering the basic subjects. Effort is still required of them of course, but it is an effort much more regulated to their capabilities, and one in which they see a purpose leading to a desirable end. Acceptance of individual differences in personality, mental ability and physical growth is usual, and the grouping of a class into units composed of children of similar aptitudes has become the rule rather than exception.

Throughout the Primary schools, though the three Rs still hold the most prominent place in the time-table, and though examinations are still frequent and their results considered important, at least as an instrument of *teaching* assessment, there are evidences of a widening of the field of study. More stress is laid on children's participation in all forms of creative activity—the practice of the plastic and dramatic arts, for instance, the writing of original verses, the playing of orchestral instruments, and the study of modern dance. They are also encouraged to extend their aesthetic appreciation and power of oral expression, and through daily discussions on a wide variety of topics—sporting, political or social—to develop their ability to state a case and uphold an argument.

Physical Education though not always receiving its just time allocation, is becoming more and more valued as a means of helping the maladjusted pupil to become stable and controlled. Here again an imposed regimentation is disappearing in favour of a more imaginative approach. The child examines his own physical reactions to his environment, and discovers with pleasure the varied movements of which his body is capable. He thus learns to use his muscular power to the greatest advantage, and this he achieves in an easy rhythmical progression in which many of his senses unite.

Time-tabling is no longer such a precise dividing up of the school day into isolated lessons as it used to be. It is now regarded rather as a guide or as a reminder of the dates on which the visiting specialist is due, and the teacher is thus allowed to extend the duration of any lesson in order to take the fullest advantage of the interest or enthusiasm shown by the pupils at any particular time, and the grouping of subjects are re-arranged accordingly.

This new method of teaching, which can only be very briefly described here, has been greatly assisted by a notable improvement in the production of textbooks and books of reference suitable for inclusion in class libraries so that children will know how to set about collecting specific knowledge. This is so important that the library has become a common-place part of class equipment.

Nature study lessons are no longer confined within the four walls of the classroom. Visits to farms, sea-shores, woods, the Royal Botanic Garden, the city's museums and the Zoo where the living flora or fauna can be examined are regarded as matters of course, and crocodiles of children can be observed almost any day moving through the city to one centre of interest or another.

Thus gradually for the retired inquiring teacher from the past of 30 years ago, a picture would emerge of a serious attempt being made to stretch to their fullest capacity all the powers of the child, without either overburdening or deadening his spirit, so that he or she may become an independent self-reliant personality able to sum up situations and judge them for himself. The inquirer would also notice at once a change in the relationship between teacher and pupil, and a different approach to the whole question of discipline. Corporal punishment has disappeared from the Infant departments and is used sparingly in the upper sections of most Primary schools. Teachers are less autocratic in their attitude. They meet the children on common ground, show interest on all aspects of their lives; and so today, more than ever before, teachers and pupils take part together in a wide range of extra-mural activities.

Our old-time teacher, however, might not be as impressed as one might expect at the end of his inspection. With truth he could assert that most of these " modern " methods have been tried before, and indeed some can be traced back to long before his own time. Rod measurement first comes into the picture in 1806 with the introduction of the Tillich bricks; projects were used by Maria Edgeworth's French governess; Madam Montessori laid great stress on the benefit to the child of that flash of insight in which he discovers the solution to his problem; and well over 30 years ago in Edinburgh itself at least one private and one Corporation school were being run on individual or group lines.

So much then for modern methods in the classrooms. But also by way of prelude to our survey of the city's educational institutions it might be profitable here to glance at some of the boys themselves and discover their view of the turbulent world about them.

ADOLESCENT ATTITUDES

Basically these boys must differ little from the adolescent of their teachers' generation or of generations before; but bearing in mind the recent rapid changes in the pattern of living, it is perhaps surprising that there are not more young people intolerant of adult attitudes, which obviously adapt less readily to change and cling too long to cherished memories of " the good old days."

One constant attitude in youth is in ever looking forward. But the developments of science and technology during the last 50 years have been so revolutionary that the outlook of the youth of today must be greatly changed. Concepts of time and distance are radically altered. Millions travel by plane at great speeds. Radio is in nearly every home, and the more revealing and hypnotic power of television makes an even stronger claim on leisure time. In school the teenager enjoys additions to an ever-widening range of educational aids—from technicolour sound films to B.B.C. Schools programmes which condense into a few minutes the efforts of many experts. For those who like being in two places at once, there is the tape recorder; and so a boy may now play for his rugby XV in the evening and next morning hear the lecture he should have attended earlier; or he can listen to Bach in his bath instead of being at the actual performance. On holiday he may enjoy all the experience of easy travel abroad, or elect to interchange with the Lycée Henri IV and spend spring-time in Paris—or elsewhere. In sport there are ever increasing facilities. And in the most serious setting of all, atomic and nuclear discoveries and the resultant wide range of scientific research and technological application present an exciting new horizon.

It is revealing, according to the schoolmaster of many years' experience who writes these words, to find so many young men interested in so varied a range of pursuits and extra-mural activities. One wonders, he asks, whether they concentrate less than people did one or two generations ago: have they in fact a kind of grasshopper mind jumping from this to that, with a superficial knowledge about a great deal and a profound attachment to little or nothing? It is interesting to discover that in one particular school attached to the Merchant Company every boy finds time to read part at least of a daily newspaper; that 65 per cent watch television most nights and the same percentage listen to B.B.C. sound broadcasts—which means that some boys do both and must therefore exercise a degree of preference or discrimination. Some 50 per cent go to the cinema once a week on the average, and half that percentage go dancing once a month. This includes those who prefer Scottish Country dancing to modern ballroom dancing or recent fashions like " rock an' roll " and " skiffle." Few are regular theatre-goers: even an average of quarter-yearly visits produces only 7 per cent. A higher proportion—around 12 per cent—attend orchestral concerts, while important art exhibitions attract a slightly greater number.

In after-school activities, games and the Combined Cadet Force take priority over other pursuits: 37 per cent play rugby, 5 per cent hockey, 45 per cent golf, 22 per cent skate, while badminton and squash are played by 11 per cent. In the summer 25 per cent play cricket, but twice that number prefer tennis. A surprising number, about 20 per cent, are active members of sailing and boating clubs; 10 per cent take part in organised athletics. The Corps claims the greatest number, for no fewer than 60 per cent of the boys are members. While these percentages represent those taking an active part in the major games played, many of course attend as spectators. And of these—in the fee-paying schools most support rugby—the percentage is 48, but 30 per cent prefer to watch soccer, while lesser numbers watch horse-racing and motor-sport. A large number are members of the Boy Scout movement. But also, says our authority, there are the Literary Society, the Dramatic Club, the Edinburgh Schools Citizenship Association, the Scripture Union, the Radio Club, the Scottish Schoolboys Club, the Scottish Youth Hostels Association, School choirs and orchestras: each of these attracts around 10 per cent of adolescents after school hours, and they are by no means all the clubs and societies that attract their attention.

Another adolescent activity new to this generation is foreign travel. In holiday time, especially in summer, many go abroad with their parents; and a great many others travel to the Continent in parties organised by the schools or the Schools Holiday Associations. More than 50 per cent of the boys in one of these schools have left these island shores at one time or other, and half have travelled by air. Ski parties go to Switzerland at Christmas and receive coaching in winter sports. And, surprisingly, as many as 50 per cent have said they would, if given the opportunity, go overseas to take up a career rather than remain in their home country. This view often changes when the potential emigrant leaves school.

The wearing of school uniform during the week tends to be more strictly enforced than in former times, and this has spread to an ever-increasing number of schools. The kilt is rarely seen as a day dress, due probably to the high cost of this form of clothing; but many boys possess kilts and wear them on Sundays and special occasions, or, less sensibly, when touring abroad. The " teddy-boy " cult of drapes and drainpipe trousers appears to be limited to a narrow section of lower social and lower mental groupings, and such styles are never seen caricaturing the excellent physique of the youth covered in this analysis. Yet it must be admitted that they are perhaps no less odd than were "Oxford Bags" in 1926, which were as stupidly wide as the present styles are stupidly narrow. "Crew cuts" and other oddities of hair styling are similarly restricted in most Edinburgh schools. But the duffel coat—designed for seamen in the war—has become a popular addition to the young man's wardrobe, and on Saturdays on Princes Street he feels quite a beau in this sporting navy rig.

Many complain that the youth of today is spoon-fed, and admittedly every facility is laid in their way to be active in mind and in body; but proof of initiative is to be found in the fact that 30 per cent of young people go out and take holiday jobs—often heavy manual ones like lumbering or navvying—to earn money for travel or to buy some particularly desired possession. One youth recently became a builder's labourer on a factory extension so that he might be able to visit Sweden to study contemporary architecture; and this is only one example of a realistic adolescent attitude.

If manners maketh man, the majority of our youth is well on the road to manhood, although there are still too many who lack the elements of common courtesy. Although the popular press tends to play up the shocking behaviour of the few, most schoolmasters believe that the average boy of today tends towards a better pattern of behaviour and a healthier relationship with his seniors, in which, even if he is a little more outspoken, he is open and natural. He respects good and firm discipline and enjoys good humour.

In the appreciation of art and architecture it is stimulating to find the interest and often the enthusiasm displayed by schoolboys and the degree of application given to such study. In painting they are less readily attracted to the historical aspects, and prefer the Impressionists and Colourists to the earlier masters. Enthusiasm is more often displayed in the creative field, and especially when opportunity is given to produce large-scale abstract compositions.

There is also evidence in schools today of a ready acceptance of services and facilities provided by the welfare state and enriched by corporate bodies; and the enthusiasm and generosity of individual bequests is taken much for granted, without, quite often, any attempt being made to express appreciation or thanks. But this maybe is the sad side of this report. It often looks as if the old Scottish characteristic of independence is on the ebb; and yet as one looks at the youth of today, if they seem to have a less happy sense of heritage and affection for the things of the past that have enriched their lives, they have also a new and often original awareness of the fast-changing patterns of modern life.

Chapter 34

THE UNIVERSITY

Youngest of the four ancient Scottish Universities but none the less older than many venerable Oxford and Cambridge Colleges, Edinburgh draws the majority of its students from Scotland itself and the rest of the British Isles. But as we saw earlier it has seldom less than 1,000 students from abroad, and often several hundred more.

In the University itself the present century has seen great changes. Some of these would seem to flow in a natural course from the ancient watershed of its past and others from the startling scientific developments of our modern age, which have also helped to create several new Scottish Universities in the last few years.

In our own century the changes have been greater and have come faster than before. Thus today there is much more bustle and ferment in the University than there was, say, in October, 1910 when a recent Minister of St. Giles' Cathedral, also a Dean of the Thistle and of the Chapel Royal in Scotland, arrived at the University as a student. "You could not help feeling, 48 years ago ", Dr. Warr wrote in his book *The Glimmering Landscape*[1], " that you were enveloped in a care-free atmosphere of *dolce far niente*. The tempo of administration, teaching and learning was calm and unhurried. The University, with half the number of professors, lecturers and students that it has now, bore little or no resemblance to the vast complex and vital academic centre it has since become. The octogenarian professor Malcolm Taylor could, without any over-exertion, combine the office of Secretary to the University Court with the Chair of Ecclesiastical History. Sir Ludovic Grant, Professor of Public and International Law, enjoyed as if it were a minor recreation the Secretaryship of the Senatus. After all, the habits of the former Principal, Sir William Muir, who reigned from 1885 to 1903, had shown what the pace of University life was like only a decade before. Every morning he rode on horseback to the Old Quadrangle from Deanpark House, his mansion on the Queensferry Road. On his arrival, which occurred punctually at noon, a University servitor advanced to hold his horse's head. The Principal dismounted and entered his room. At half-past twelve he emerged, mounted his horse, and rode away. The long day's work was done! "

Today the pace is very different as we shall see from the account of the University's past and present, written by the Secretary to the University, Charles Stewart.

[1] Hodder and Stoughton, London 1960.

FROM 1583 TO 1845

Robert Rollock, the University's first Regent, opened the College—an adaptation of the Kirk o' Field buildings—with an attendance of over 80 students in October, 1583. The original course of study lasted for four years. All teaching was in Latin, with instruction for "non-matriculated" students deficient in that tongue, and for many years the scope of the College was confined to the fields of Arts and Divinity. Looking in vain for an early foundation of a Faculty of Law, the inquirer reads only of an abortive attempt (between 1590 and 1594) which withered under the disapproval of established Advocates who took the view (still not without its modern application) that "there is as muckle law in Edinburgh as there is silver to pay for it." So the first chair in public Law had to wait until 1707. A Professor of Medicine, however, had been appointed in 1685; but it was not until the first quarter of the succeeding century that the University offered a regular course of medical education. It was also in the 18th century, that in order to provide for a steadily increasing number of professors and students, and partly perhaps, in emulation of some of the fine building already going on in Edinburgh, the Old College (though then it was the "New") was designed by Robert Adam. Work on the actual building commenced in 1789. The financial stresses of the wars with France delayed its completion for many years, but, with the help of an annual Parliamentary grant from 1815 onwards, the building was completed in 1827, though without a dome, according to a modified design by William Playfair. The dome was added in 1887.

In the year 1844–5, (time of the second *Statistical Account*), the University of Edinburgh had 32 Professors, 1,056 matriculated students, and a library of about 100,000 volumes. It had no independent status as a corporation. Eight of its Chairs were in the patronage of the Crown, but the appointment of Professors, and indeed the whole business of the University, including even the regulation of the courses of study, lay in the hands of the Town Council. But not without protest; as early as 1703 the Regents were advancing claims to self-government—claims which were sternly (and be it admitted, with legality) rebutted by the Town. For more than a hundred years public and violent discussion was avoided, while the Professors (since 1708 no longer Regents but specialist teachers of clearly defined subjects) became generally recognised under the collective designation of the Senatus Academicus, and the University steadily increased in size and in prestige. At the beginning of the 19th century the smouldering embers of controversy (as is their wont in this city) burst into magnificent flame. In 1815 and 1816 difficulties about the payment of the Librarian were evaded rather than settled, and in 1821 a dispute about the posts of Librarian and Secretary was amicably solved—ending, it would appear, in a victory for the Senatus, whose status in respect of the appointment of their Secretary was, for the first time, formally recognised by the Town. This success may have given the Senate a false sense of the strength of their position, since in 1824, mainly on a question of changes in the medical curriculum they were again ready to take issue with the Town. Their grievances were later exacerbated by a not entirely necessary show of power on the part of the Town Council in its demand for the submission of the Matriculation Fund accounts, and in other matters of lesser import. The Senate sent a petition to the Home Secretary of the day, and decided soon afterwards (somewhat wrong-headedly, as it now appears) to challenge at law the right of the Town to dominate the University. The consequence of the petition was a Royal Commission (on all Scottish Universities) whose findings proved to be so unpopular in Scotland (though many of them were adopted in 1858) that the Government allowed them to stand unimplemented. The legal result, however, was that the Second Division of the Court of Session found in favour of the Town. This was in 1829; yet within 20 years the Senate dauntlessly gave battle again to the City on the same point of principle. After the case had pursued its laborious and costly way through both Divisions of the Court of Session and eventually, the House of Lords, the University of Edinburgh found itself in 1854 much poorer, though possibly wiser, and still a subordinate of the Town Council.

CONSTITUTIONAL DEVELOPMENTS 1845-1964

The night is always darkest before the dawn. Partly as a result of the necessity for reforms in consequence of the disruption of the Church of Scotland, and partly, no doubt, because some of the arguments employed in the course of the "Thirty Years War" had not fallen upon deaf ears, the famous Lord Justice General, "Chancellor" Inglis, introduced in Parliament a Bill to make provision for the better Government and Discipline of the Universities of Scotland, which became law in 1858. The Act was founded largely on the work of the long dormant Royal Commission of 1826-30. So far as the University of Edinburgh was concerned, the overriding fact was that the Act of 1858 established its complete independence. This Act gave to the University, for the first time in its history, a constitution at once reasonably clear and effective, which, subject to the modifications introduced by the Universities (Scotland) Acts of 1889 and 1922, still provides the working basis of the University's government and administration. To describe the system briefly, the chief governing body—a body corporate, with perpetual succession and a Common Seal—is the University Court, the composition of which reflects the various interests in the life of the University community. Four of its 14 members are elected by the Senatus, and four by the General Council of Graduates. The Lord Provost of Edinburgh and an Assessor appointed by the Corporation stand for the Town's continuing interest in its College, and the other places are filled by the Rector, the Rector's Assessor, the Principal, and an Assessor appointed by the Chancellor. The Chancellor, titular head of the University, is elected by the General Council of Graduates. Since 1952 this office has been held by His Royal Highness The Prince Philip, Duke of Edinburgh, who will go down in history as the only Chancellor who has in person carried out the arduous task of capping not merely those receiving honorary degrees, but all the very numerous graduands present at the same ceremonial. (6th July, 1956). The Rector is elected triennially by the matriculated students of the University. He, or in his absence the Principal, has the duty of presiding at meetings of the Court, As a general rule, the Principal is in the Chair.

Subject to the general review of the Court, the Senatus Academicus regulates the teaching and discipline of the University. This body consists of the Principal, all the Professors, and certain Readers and Lecturers nominated by Faculties to the number of not more than one-fourth of those otherwise entitled to membership. Much of the detailed supervision of educational matters falls to the separate Faculties which act as Committees of Senate. In order of seniority (from the date of their formal institution) the Faculties of the University, till 1963, were Divinity, Law, Medicine, Arts, Science, and Music. In that year, however, the Faculty of Social Sciences, though still closely related to its parent Faculty of Arts, set out on its separate existence. The number of Faculties did not long remain at seven. A separate Faculty of Veterinary Medicine came within the year and this will certainly not be the last group of studies to attain full maturity within the academic community.

Formal University legislation is carried out by the Court through the medium of Ordinances, which require to be communicated to the Senate, the General Council, and to the Courts of the other Scottish Universities before submission to the Universities Committee of the Privy Council. When these Ordinances have received the approval of Her Majesty in Council they have the force of law.

Apart from these formal acts of legislation, the making and implementation of University policy is mainly carried out by Committees, either of the Court or of the Senate. The Library Committee is answerable to both Court and Senate. Chief among the standing committees of the Court are Finance, Development, Major Buildings, and Works, whose names speak for themselves. On the Senate side, perhaps the most important are the Educational Policy Committee, and the Principal and Deans Committee, which in addition to other duties, acts as a court of first instance in questions of student discipline. In recent years, there has been evolved a system of closer consultation between the Court and the Educational Policy Committee, particularly in regard to the annual allocations of income to individual Faculties.

A noteworthy development of the last decade has been the steadily increasing part played in the government of the University by members of the teaching staff other than Professors. Over the last few years, at the time of writing, the number of non-professorial members of the Senatus has increased from six to nineteen. Until very recently, this was the maximum permissible under the relevant Ordinance—one-quarter of the total number of Professors, including the Principal; but the number of Professors has undergone a significant and sudden increase in 1963 and 1964, and was expected to mount at a comparable rate in 1965, so that the number of non-professorial members of Senate will very soon be at least twenty-five. At the present moment (February, 1964) the number of Chairs in the University has just exceeded the total of 100. The University

Court, for its part, in appointing its numerous *ad hoc* Committees, has made a practice of drawing in increasing measure upon the experience and judgement of Readers and Lecturers. In view of the change in composition of the staff of the University revealed in the statistical tables set out below, this development is scarcely surprising.

By an Ordinance (Edinburgh No. 112) which came into force in the academic year 1961–2, the University created the new grade (for Scotland) of Assistant Lecturer. The great majority of those teachers who were previously known as Assistants are now included in this category.

Since then, the University has been turning its attention more and more closely to reform " from within " of its own Constitution. At the same time it has been taking part in a joint constitutional conference of the four Scottish Universities—an operation which, it is fair to say, was originally suggested by Edinburgh, and one from which the University of Edinburgh may reasonably hope for increased autonomy, and greater flexibility of constitutional processes.

THE SOCIAL CHANGES 1845-1964

Perhaps the most important change in this period of the University's history was not so much constitutional as social. In 1889, by one of the clauses of the Universities (Scotland) Act of that year, provision was made for passing Ordinances to permit of the admission of women to graduation, and to provide for their instruction. The ground had been broken for this tremendous change by the Association for the Higher Education of Women whose efforts, beginning in Edinburgh in 1867, had wrung from the University authorities a " Certificate in Arts," and by the (vain) struggle of Miss Sophia Jex-Blake and her friends to graduate in Medicine. After 1889, however, although the relevant Ordinance was not passed till 1892, the whole field of University education was open to both sexes.

Almost equally important was the contemporaneous growth of student self-government—in which Edinburgh can undoubtedly claim to have led the way for all the British Universities. In 1884, Robert Fitzroy Bell, fresh from experience of the Studenten Ausschuss in Strasbourg, persuaded his contemporaries who were Presidents and Secretaries of Student Societies to form themselves into a Students' Representative Council. The success of the organisation, and the part it played in the Tercentenary Celebration of the University won it official recognition in the 1889 Act. Since then, the Council has continued to play an important part in University affairs, representing the interests of the student body, providing a recognised means of communication between the students and the University authorities, and promoting social life and academic unity amongst the students. The most striking tribute to the success of the Council is that Edinburgh's example has since been followed, in one form or another, by every University in the country. It was the efforts of the Students' Representative Council, in the main, which resulted in the establishment, in 1887, of the University Union.

Apart from the initiative and energy of its founder and his friends,

The Upper Hall of the Signet Library in Parliament Square.

A meeting of the Town Council in progress at the City Chambers in the High Street.

the institution of the Students' Representative Council must largely be regarded as a consequence of the vitality of those student societies and clubs which in this University have long abounded. There are, for instance, the Associated Societies (Dialectic, Scots Law, Diagnostic, and Philomathic) which, like the Speculative (founded in 1764, but not confined to students) have their own inalienable privileges and the exclusive use of rooms within the Old College. The Royal Medical Society is the oldest of its kind in the Kingdom. And to these could be added a list of 50 or 60 others, some new, some of respectable antiquity, covering almost every aspect of student spare-time life, from music to mountaineering. The *Students' Handbook* of the day is indispensable to a complete understanding of the University.

The beginning of the 20th century was marked for all the Scottish Universities by the princely donation by Andrew Carnegie of the sum of ten million dollars, to be administered for their benefit by the Carnegie Trust for the Universities of Scotland. Much of the income of this fund has in the past been applied in assisting students who might not otherwise have had the financial resources to attend the University; the changed social conditions of the present day, when nearly every student accepted by a University is entitled, provided that his family's income is below a certain level, to maintenance and payment of fees from Government funds, have greatly reduced the proportion of the Trust's income which is applied in this way; but over the past 50 years, at any rate, it is true to say that many a student of Edinburgh has to thank the Carnegie Trust for his or her University education.

Currently, however, the Trustees spend very much more of their endowment income on direct grants to the Universities and on postgraduate education and research than on assistance to undergraduates. The beneficiaries include both distinguished young graduates fresh from their final examinations and spare-time scholars devoting their leisure to the pursuit of knowledge, as well as many members of the staff of the University for whom research is a professional obligation. Substantial amounts were, and are, available from the same source for building. Without this aid, the contribution of Edinburgh to the world of learning would have been substantially less in quality and quantity.

Two World Wars within a quarter-century left many a mark on this as on all our Universities. The evidence is to be found elsewhere than in the long, proud list of names on a wall of the Old College Quadrangle. Sharply rising costs and the urgent need of the nation for more and more trained men and women have brought to the University more and more students whose fees represent year by year a smaller fraction of what their education costs. The consequence has been a steadily growing dependence of the University upon financial assistance from the Government. In 1893–4, the grant received by the University from the Government amounted to £25,920. In 1930–1 this sum had risen to £105,800. In 1959–60 it slightly exceeded £2¼ millions, and the University was dependent upon public funds for more than 75 per cent of its income. The situation has been only slightly affected by a recent substantial increase in students' fees, which account for 12 per cent of total income. In the year 1963–4 the University's Parliamentary Grants reached the staggering, though by no means excessive figure of £3,305,000, which was 80 per cent of a total income of £4,725,035. In 1964-65 this had increased to £5,481,365.

In such a situation it would be surprising if the cry of Ichabod had not been raised. Thanks to the institution in 1919 of the University Grants Committee, however, the glory has not departed, and Edinburgh, with its sister institutions, has preserved its autonomy, and can, and does, direct its own destinies. The Grants Committee, a Standing Committee of H.M. Treasury, is composed almost entirely of "university" men, in touch and in sympathy with the academic world. The sums made available by Parliament are administered in a spirit that combines justice with a liberal outlook and the Universities consult with the Grants Committee in mutual confidence, regarding them not as paymasters but as friends. The price of freedom, of course, is constant vigilance, and the unremitting exercise of care and responsibility by those in charge of University expenditure. The Universities may from time to time wish that they still possessed their own representatives in the House (a privilege lost under the Labour Government of 1945) but even without this they would not lack their champions—the best of which by far are moderation and good sense in the conduct of their own affairs.

Even the far-reaching recommendations of the Robbins Committee on Higher Education leave unchanged the essential functions and responsibilities of the University Grants Committee. The effect of the accompanying change in Ministerial responsibilities must await the assessment of experience.

In Edinburgh, though the funds at the disposal of the University, whether from public or private sources, have always had as their most important product the knowledge, skill, and character of the graduates, the evidence of both public and private support is tangible and impressive.

The most recent of the University's appeals to its graduates and friends was launched in 1959 and this brought in many hundreds of thousands of pounds; and the appeal, which was given a new stimulus in 1964, continues. Why in the first place such an appeal was necessary at all and why the University's programme of capital expenditure needs support on a much enhanced scale, whether from public or private sources, is best considered, as we shall see later, in relation to the extent of its buildings as they exist at present, and of the plans for their extension and development.

ACADEMIC DEVELOPMENTS 1845-1964

There were many important academic developments in this period, but this account can do no more than select those changes and innovations which are essential to a moderately comprehensive record of the state of the University as it is today.

The Faculty of Divinity. To deal with the Faculties in order of seniority, Divinity, after 1806 when ecclesiastical tests were removed, could on longer expect to see a Minister of the Church of Scotland in the office of Principal of the University. In other respects, however, it has good reasons for pride. Having survived the effects of the Disruption (which benefited the University as a whole by emancipating its lay Professors from religious tests) the Faculty gained greatly by the Church Reunion in 1929. It was enlarged by the addition to its then existing Chairs of the Chairs in New College, and although the total number of Chairs has within the past decade suffered a (possibly temporary) reduction, the actual teaching strength of the Faculty has increased. Its post-graduate school draws students in considerable numbers from all quarters of the globe, particularly perhaps from the New World. It is interesting to note that the test of allegiance to the Church of Scotland as an essential condition of appointment to a Chair has now been abolished. The Faculty has also recently revised its curriculum, and a new Ordinance will provide for a Licentiate in Divinity, and make the degree of Bachelor of Divinity a first degree, eliminating the necessity for previous graduation in Arts.

The Faculty of Law. In this type of innovation, Divinity was forestalled, only by a few years, by its sister Faculty of Law. From October, 1961, the old degree of Bachelor of Law ceased to exist, subject, of course, to the appropriate safeguards of the interests of students in the transitional period. At the same time a new degree of Bachelor of Laws was instituted —no longer a second degree requiring a previous degree in Arts. The new degree involves full-time study—three years for the Ordinary Degree and four years for the degree with Honours, with appropriate modifications for students who choose to combine the degree with that of Master of Arts. Provision is made for the possibility of spending a year at another of the Scottish Universities or at other Universities recognised for this purpose.

The Faculty maintains its close associations with the law courts and with professional societies, but has of late begun to show a rapidly increasing enthusiasm for the more academic aspects of its works. Without losing any of its interest in the Law of Scotland, it has developed a wholly admirable tendency to concern itself with questions of comparative law and to extend its perspectives of study beyond the strictest limits of purely professional training.

The Faculty of Medicine. Its contribution to the University's history has already been described. But certain important administrative changes must not be overlooked here. Perhaps the most significant feature of the period as a whole is the rapid development and increasing reliance upon clinical teaching as distinct from formal lectures: to this must be added a steadily increasing interest, particularly in recent years, in laboratory work and in medical science in general. Within this century, the scope of post-graduate medical study has grown significantly, with the addition of Diplomas in Radiodiagnosis, Radiotherapy, Psychological Medicine, Public Health, Medical Statistics, Tropical Medicine, and Medical Services Administration.

Since 1948, the University has taken over the teaching duties of the School of Medicine of the Royal Colleges, and now carries the sole responsibility for undergraduate medical training in Edinburgh. Since

1953, the Edinburgh Post-graduate Board of Medicine (though still including representatives of the Royal Colleges) has become directly responsible to the University Court. The advent of the National Health Service in 1948 provided the Faculty and the University with many problems, and involved, and still involves, much friendly negotiation with the South-Eastern Regional Hospital Board, and with its Boards of Management. But the association grows closer as more and more University departments are provided with quarters within hospitals, and both sides of this invaluable public service can now look forward with some confidence to the rebuilding of the Royal Infirmary and to the rehabilitation and development of the Western General Hospital as an important centre of clinical teaching.

Space must be found here for what can be no more than a special mention of the General Practice Teaching Unit and its related James Mackenzie Chair (instituted in 1963) of General Practice in relation to Medicine: and this account would also be incomplete without some record of the beginning (in 1963) of the Pfizer Foundation (founded by the generous action of Messrs Pfizer Limited) soon, we hope, to be the centre of academic conferences and symposia of great distinction and of international composition. Work has begun on an extension to the facilities of the Post-Graduate Board—which at last provides an appropriate use of the funds collected as long ago as 1913 to provide a memorial to Lord Lister. And in 1963 also the University accepted the municifient benefaction (and the grave responsibility) of a quarter of a million pounds from the Distillers Company Limited for research into congenital abnormalities.

In the midst of all its duties and pre-occupations the Faculty has found, or made, the time for a radical and comprehensive revision of its curriculum. One of the many consequences of this impressive piece of planning will be that most of the students who enter for a medical degree will from 1964 onwards have the opportunity to take the degree of Bachelor of (Medical) Science within the same course of study. (Dental Surgery and Veterinary Medicine are dealt with elsewhere.)

The Faculty of Arts. In this Faculty, still the largest in number of students, the beginning of a great change came with the Arts Ordinance of 1892, which, apart from setting up a uniform Preliminary Examination, instituted the first of a series of reforms which have progressively extended the area of choice of subjects for the Ordinary Degree of Master of Arts, and, perhaps with less conscious intent, limited and intensified the curricula for Honours Degrees—a sacrifice of breadth to depth which has found both critics and defenders.

For the sequel, though not, it is to be hoped, the conclusion, the observer must shift his gaze from 1892 to 1960, when a reconsideration of the regulations for the Ordinary Degree produced what is believed to be a more rational and purposeful arrangement of alternative courses, offering the student a somewhat wider choice than in the past, together with an increased degree of specialisation. It is now no longer necessary to include both a language and a science subject, though one or the other is essential. Two related double courses supply the basis for each of the eight types of degree, which, by reference to their basic double course, can broadly be described as Classical Languages, Modern Languages, English studies, Mathematics and Natural Sciences, History, Human Sciences, Philosophy, and Mathematics—which last allows for a combination of Mathematics with a second double course in Language or Literature, or appropriately, with Music.

The ramifications of the Arts degree have reduced this account into an attempt, impossible in this context, to expound the University Calendar: but the digression may be allowed to stand as an illustration of the vastness of the field covered by the Faculty of Arts and its still closely allied Faculty of Social Sciences.

The Faculty of Social Sciencies. This Faculty attained separate status in 1963; it continues, of course, to present students for the degree of Master of Arts, but it bears the responsibility (to mention only first degrees) for those of Bachelor of Commerce and Bachelor of Architecture. It also presents candidates for the important second degree of Bachelor of Education. The Chairs in this Faculty, as at present constituted, are Economic Science, Education, Accounting, Organisation of Industry and Commerce, Psychology, Geography, Architecture (founded in 1948), Economic History (1956) and Politics (1963). This galaxy is being increased by Architectural Science, Urban Design and Regional Planning, Social Anthropology, Sociology, and another Chair in Economics.

Expansion and diversification is by no means confined to the new Faculty. Within its parent Faculty of Arts, the Chairs in History, beginning with Modern History in 1893, are now four in number, with Scottish History added in 1901, Medieval in 1954, and Commonwealth and American History in 1963. The Watson Gordon Chair of Fine Art was established in 1879, that of Celtic (Language, Literature, History, and Antiquities) in 1882, and the Sir William Fraser Chair of Ancient History and Palaeography in 1901. If great names have to be selected, the Chair of Rhetoric and English Literature can point to that of Saintsbury, who occupied the Chair from 1895 to 1915. English (now with three Chairs) and French (with two) present the literary and linguistic aspects of the field under separate auspices. Recent additions in the field of Modern Languages are Italian, Russian, and Spanish. All three subjects, though of course previously taught in the University, recently attained the dignity of Chairs. Phonetics, for long an important subject in its own right, and at the same time a department busy in the service of others, and frequented by visitors from all parts of the globe, became the first " personal " Chair—that is to say a Chair not necessarily continuing beyond the tenure of the individual first appointed—in 1963. A Chair of General Linguistics is soon to follow.

In the field of Philosophy, of particular importance in a Scottish University, a third Chair was added in 1964.

The Faculty of Science, as a separate Faculty, was not established until 1893, but the Chairs of Natural History (Zoology), Chemistry, Natural Philosophy (Physics), Astronomy, Agriculture, Engineering, and Geology had long been established within the Faculty of Arts, and the University could pride itself upon Lyon Playfair, P. G. Tait, and Archibald Geikie. It is of interest to note that the abortive Chair of Technology, whose short existence began in 1855 and terminated in 1859, was eventually succeeded, one hundred years after its foundation, by a Chair of Chemical Technology—a joint appointment by the University and the Heriot-Watt College. The title of this Chair has recently been changed to Chemical Engineering and is likely, in the near future, to become a wholly " University " Chair, consequent on the translation of the Heriot-Watt College (with the goodwill and ready support of the University) to the new level of a technological institution of University status. The University will then have Chairs in the four " classical " fields of Engineering—Mechanical, Civil, Electrical, and Chemical.

The growing strength of the Faculty was increased in 1919 by the Chair of Forestry—now with the significant title of Forestry and Natural Resources—and in the same year by a second Chair of Zoology, which remained vacant for many years after the death of its first occupant, but is now filled. Animal Genetics, now a centre of growing influence in the world of research, was added in 1928, and a second chair of (Organic) Chemistry in 1947. An appointment has only just been made to a third Chair of Physics, and a Chair of Biology is contemplated within the immediate future. A new appointment has also been made to a Chair of Mathematics, in addition to the Chair already existing within the Faculty of Arts.

Like Law, Medicine, and Arts, Science has recently introduced important changes and adjustments in its courses of study and degrees. Particular mention should perhaps be made of the new degree of Master of Science to which a parallel is to be found in the even more recent Arts degree of Master of Letters.

The Faculty of Music was established in the same year (1893) as the Faculty of Science, though the Chair upon which it is based was founded by the Trustees of General Reid in 1839. This Faculty has exercised on the University, and indeed upon the City, a beneficial influence quite disproportionate to its size. The Reid Orchestra, in reconstituted form, is one of the amenities of life in Edinburgh, and the Chair has been graced by such men as Frederick Niecks and Donald Francis Tovey. In recent years, the University has provided practice rooms, which are used by many more students than those who are actually within the Faculty. The University's expansion and the implementation of its central Comprehensive Development project have raised critical accommodation difficulties for the Faculty, but there is no doubt that ingenuity and determination can produce solutions. Aided by the generosity of Mr. Raymond Russell, the University has acquired the charming and historic Saint Cecilia's Hall, once a centre for the musical world of 18th century Edinburgh, where it hopes to house Mr. Raymond Russell's unique collection of 18th century keyboard instruments, and classical concerts which will once more stir the echoes of the Cowgate.

All the larger Faculties have proliferated into Diplomas in a bewildering variety of studies—Applied Linguistics, History of Art, Islamic Studies,

Phonetics, Geography, Regional Planning, Education, Management Studies, Public Administration, Biophysics, Electronics and Radio—but it is possible to list only a representative selection.

To take a more general view, the most striking feature of this period has been the increase in volume (and expense) of research as opposed (though it is not opposed) to teaching. It is not that the University has in any way shirked its teaching responsibilities: its teaching interests have widened, its methods have improved, and it is at last beginning to pay closer attention to the more individual needs of students. But it is at the same time true to say that the University is more fully alive than ever before to its tremendous tasks and responsibilities in the research sphere. It is not merely a question of increased numbers of higher degrees, of M.Sc.'s and Ph.D.'s, many of which can fairly be described as " guided " if not a " closely supervised " research. It is a fact that the University as a whole devotes to research of one kind or another a larger proportion of its time and resources than it has done in the past. The benefits of these labours, of course, are daily realised, not merely in the printed work which may eventually result, but also in the interest and inspiration inevitably passed on by the active research worker, particularly where he is also a teacher, to the students with whome he comes into contact. If only the sinews of this particular war could be strengthened by a more liberal provision of the necessary funds!

In this connection, grateful mention must be made of the substantial support, through research units, departments, or individuals, provided by such government organisations as the Department of Scientific and Industrial Research, the Medical Research Council, and the Agricultural Research Council. Similar support is derived from many of the more progressive businesses and industries. It is to be hoped that it is not ungracious to remark that to describe the support as substantial is not to describe it as adequate. For the sake not merely of the University but also of the whole country it is most earnestly hoped that government organisations, limited companies, trusts, and all those who have funds at their disposal will recognise the value of the efforts of the University, and will do everything in their power to see that the scholars and scientists of this country have material resources in keeping with the potential of their work.

More and more frequently, research is seen to be a matter of team-work, with its ultimate fulfilment achieved through co-operative projects. Instances of this are to be found all over the University—in the newly instituted Computer Unit which makes use of large-scale computers as far distant as Manchester and Harwell, in the Centre of African Studies, uniting many of the older fields of economic, historical, and linguistic study in a common project, and in the work of the Committee on Co-operation in the Social Sciences. The School of Scottish Studies and the Linguistic Survey of Scotland are also worthy of special mention since both enterprises are striking examples of the growth of a scholarly, as distinct from sentimental interest in certain aspects of the history and general culture of the Scottish nation.

Fundamental and basic to the entire academic process are not only the University Library, fully described elsewhere in this book and soon to be enlarged, but the separate Central Medical Library in the Medical School, and some 75 departmental and class libraries serving various parts of the University.

BUILDINGS AND DEVELOPMENT

This is perhaps the appropriate point to introduce a brief statement of additions, by new building or by purchase, to the University's property since 1845, and, more important, an exposition of its building plans for the future.

The list of additions is impressive: in the early part of the period, the purchase of the site of the Royal Infirmary at High School Yards, for the Natural Philosophy and other departments; the New Medical Buildings in Teviot Place—which have followed the Old College by surrendering their pristine title to the new extension in George Square; the magnificent McEwan Hall; the Usher Institute of Public Health in Warrender Park Road; and the extensive development (built between 1920 and 1931) known as The King's Buildings at West Mains, where most of the Science Departments are established. Farther afield at Bush and Dryden, some seven miles to the south, lie the farms and buildings of the Edinburgh Centre of Rural Economy, where Agriculture, Veterinary, and Forestry students undergo their practical training.

At one time this account was to record the fact that Cowan House and Masson Hall provide Halls of Residence in George Square for men and women students respectively. By 1964, however, both Halls had moved, in order to make room for the new Library. Masson Hall will eventually be housed in an entirely rehabilitated building in South Lauder Road, while Cowan House is to find quarters in the interesting and historic Mylne's Court, near to New College, to form an integral part of the University's scheme for developing much of its life within the oldest part of the City of Edinburgh. On the magnificent site at Salisbury Green, the University already possesses separate Halls for men and women; and in 1965 it was announced that six more halls of residence were to be built, which would provide accommodation for more than 1,000 students. For both site and buildings (and for many another gift of funds and property) the University will always be indebted to Sir Donald Pollock, its Rector from 1939 to 1945. To the older Halls on this site, Holland House (150 men students) was added in 1960. To it has been added its " twin " Hall, Fraser House, and an immediate start will also be made on a central Refectory, with study-bedroom units to house, when complete, at least one thousand students.

Perhaps the most significant contribution to the problem of student residence is the development (of which Edinburgh can claim to be a pioneer) of Student Houses, in which relatively small groups of students live and make their own meals, with senior members of the University sharing the life of a small community. The system has many attractions for the older and more independent-minded Scottish student, and has allowed Edinburgh to provide some hundreds of badly-needed student places which cost much less than the study-bedroom of Halls of Residence, and are greatly in demand. Over the next few years it is hoped to provide many hundreds more.

This list of sites and buildings is by no means exhaustive and serves only to indicate the present physical extent of the University. The incorporation in the University of the Edinburgh Dental School and of the Royal (Dick) School of Veterinary Studies has further increased its territorial, as well as its academic area. A most important addition is the new School of Agriculture at The King's Buildings, shared by the University of Edinburgh and East of Scotland College of Agriculture. Four-fifths of the cost of this building was borne by the Department of Agriculture for Scotland. On the same site stands the new extension to the Department of Engineering, opened in 1960.

Chambers Street, next to the Old College, has been left to the last since it is here that some of the most interesting developments have taken place. Minto House was acquired in 1926, and for many years (too many) housed the Departments of Modern Languages, now transferred, with most of the other departments in the Faculty of Arts, to the David Hume Tower. In 1954 the University, in the same street, erected its first major building since the war—Adam House, on the site of the family house of the famous architects. This is a multi-purpose building, mainly used as an examination school. It includes a small theatre, a most valuable addition to the amenities of the University and of the City. A year or two later, again in Chambers Street, came the new Students' Refectory and the Staff Club, separate institutions sharing a common kitchen. The Staff Club, of which wives of members of staff may become associate members, has exercised a most beneficent influence in the integration of an inevitably dispersed academic community.

From the Old College, the centre of University government, and the adjoining Staff Club, the centre of its social life, it is natural to pass on to an outline of the University's Development Plan. Plans for the central area, including George Square, with the object of providing for expansion as well as integration, had occupied the University's attention for at least a quarter of a century prior to 1958–60 when the future of this famous Square became, for brief periods, a cause cèlebre of the day. It would be inappropriate in this context to traverse the details of the controversy, but it is necessary to state that the University succeeded, first in convincing the Town Council (the Planning Authority) of the soundness of the George Square Plan, and later (1960) in defending the legality of its actions, and its right, within the law, to build as it proposed.

This success has set the University free, provided always that the necessary funds are forthcoming, to proceed with its Development Plan, which for the central area is based on the three fixed points of the Old College, the Medical School (in contiguity to the Royal Infirmary) and the new University Library in George Square. In 1962 the first part of the extension to the Medical School, on the north side of the Square, was officially opened, and work on the opposite corner had begun.

The University has been fortunate in the expert help and guidance it has received from Sir Basil Spence, Sir Robert Matthew (its own Professor of Architecture) and from its Planning Consultant, Mr. Percy Johnson-Marshall. The central development can now be seen to be fairly started with the 14 storeys of the David Hume Tower dominating the south-eastern corner of the Square, and with its associated lecture-rooms providing the centre of a complex of buildings which will eventually house all, or practically all, the teachers and students of the Faculty of Arts. This complex will stretch along the south side of the square to the new Library, southwards into a rebuilt Buccleuch Place and northwards towards the First Year Science Building, on which work began in 1963, to provide a vital link between the Faculties of Arts and Science. The Women's Union is about to be moved from George Square to the old Mathematical Institute in Chambers Street. Its quarters there, though relatively palatial, are only semi-permanent. The Women's Union will give place to a much needed expansion of the Staff Club, and move to permanent quarters in the new Student Centre on the Island Site (bounded by Bristo Street, Marshall Street, Potterrow and Lothian Street).

All this building is part of a carefully phased and planned project for " the University within the City." Mr. Johnson-Marshall's proposals for a Comprehensive Development Area have been welcomed by the University and, accepted in principle by the City of Edinburgh, so that in years to come a new " New Town " or rather a rejuvenated University town, with its appropriate shops and restaurants, with its relatively secluded quadrangles, and with provision for pedestrian and vehicular traffic at different levels, will add much to the pleasure and charm of thie city. In this wonderful, but not over-ambitious scheme, the Town, the University and commercial developers are co-operating with good sense and goodwill, " to achieve ", in the words of the Principal, " a harmonious integration between the University and the city in which it is set."

The development of The King's Buildings could not, and has not been neglected. A new building for Botany has been transferred from Inverleith and brought into close relationship to its sister departments; Forestry and Natural Resources, making room for a further extension of the Medical School, is also to move to The King's Buildings from George Square. A Science Library, and extension to the refectory facilities of the Common Room, and most important, a new and large building for Mathematics and Physics, will all be built at the West Mains site within the next few years. If funds suffice, provision will be made on the same site for residential accommodation.

There are many " outliers " to the central scheme, some of no small importance, and many additions and explanations would be required in a full exposition of the University's plans. Here it is intended only to indicate their nature. Like all good plans, they are flexible, and susceptible of alteration and adaptation to meet changing circumstances. Readers of this Account will be able to judge, within the next ten years, of the success of their execution. That success, to a large extent, depends upon the provision by Her Majesty's Government of adequate and timeous capital grants for building. If the University is to accept (as it is very willing to do) additional numbers of students on the scale envisaged by the Robbins Committee, these funds will have to be forthcoming in much more generous measure than, so far, has been evident. The proceeds of the Appeal will undoubtedly be necessary, but at the very best, they can do no more than allow the University a few buildings or parts of buildings (residences perhaps), which are regarded, by us in Edinburgh, as essential, even if they do not qualify for Government grant.

The following statistics (with a few comparative figures from earlier periods) may serve to illustrate succeeding observations on the extent and scope of the University today:

FACTS AND FIGURES

(1) COMPARATIVE FIGURES: MATRICULATED STUDENTS

Year	*Divinity*	*Law*	*Medicine*	*Arts*	*Science*	*Music*	*Total*
1790–1							1,193
1844–5							1,056
1883–4	108	505	1,763	998			3,374
1931–2	142	274	1,312	1,875	680	44	4,327*

* In this year (1931–2), 649 students came from outside the United Kingdom compared with 1,317 in 1962–3.

MATRICULATED STUDENTS 1962–3

Faculty	Full-time			Part-time			*Totals*
	Men	*Women*	*Total*	*Men*	*Women*	*Total*	
Arts	1,305	1,450	2,755	226	102	328	3,083
Divinity	108	6	114	98	8	106	220
Law	216	43	259	21	1	22	281
Medicine	1,262	310	1,572	414	40	454	2,026
Music	22	17	39	4	1	5	44
Science	1,627	344	1,971	149	9	158	2,129
Totals	4,540	2,170	6,710	912	161	1,073	7,783

(2) TEACHING STAFF

	Professors	*Readers*	*Senior Lecturers*	*Lecturers*	*Assistants, Assistant Lecturers, and Demonstrators*	*Total*
1620	7*					7
1708	15					15
1844–5	32					32
1883–4	39			3	26	68
1931–2	59	9	4	144	99	315
1962–3	88	43	124	359	144	728

* Including Principal.

These figures are in themselves noteworthy. But between 1962 and 1964 great changes were taking place. Social Sciences, detached from the Arts, had become a Faculty as had Veterinary Medicine. So the figures for 1963–4 have a different look:

MATRICULATED STUDENTS FOR 1963–4

Note. Full-time students are those studying for a Degree, Diploma or Certificate. Part-time students are part-time Ph.D. students and non-graduating students. During this year 113 non-matriculated students were also admitted to certain classes.

Faculty	Full-time			Part-time			Totals
	Men	*Women*	*Totals*	*Men*	*Women*	*Totals*	
Arts	797	1,158	1,955	57	67	124	2,079
Social Sciences	540	375	915	150	17	167	1,082
Divinity	99	4	103	81	9	90	193
Law	237	45	282	27	4	31	313
Medicine	987	258	1,245	400	36	436	1,681
Veterinary Medicine	276	29	305	6	—	6	311
Music	21	17	38	2	3	5	43
Science	1,715	370	2,085	158	7	165	2,250
Totals	4,672	2,256	6,928	881	143	1,024	7,952

The teaching staff for 1963–4 had also increased—to 745 full-time and 121 part-time Professors, Readers, Senior Lecturers, Lecturers and Assistants; a total which does not include demonstrators and clinical teaching staff.

(3) INCOME AND EXPENDITURE

Changes in the value of money and incomplete records render it difficult to assess with any accuracy the income of the University prior to 1858. Sir Alexander Grant (*Story of the University of Edinburgh*) states that in that year the total income did not exceed £8,000. On the same authority, the income of the University for the year 1881–2 amounted to £34,163. It is to be remembered, of course, that prior to the Act of 1889, Professors collected their own class fees.

In the year 1963–4, the University's income from all sources was estimated at £4,100,000. Student Fees accounted for 11·7 per cent of this figure, and Parliamentary Grants for more than 80 per cent. On the expenditure side, some 70 per cent was applied to directly educational expenditure, 17 per cent to the maintenance of premises, 6 per cent to administration, and the remainder to the provision of student facilities, pensions, hospitality, and small miscellaneous items. The University, it should be added, enjoys an income from its own endowments of some £90,000 per annum.

THE SCOPE OF THE UNIVERSITY

These figures, in comparison with those of former days, serve to represent the scale of the University in 1963–4. It is doubtful if they can properly represent its true scope—the number, the complexity, and the far-reaching nature of its various enterprises. How tempting, for example, when writing of the Faculty of Medicine, to describe at length the imaginative experiment in medical teaching and international co-operation which is being conducted at Baroda, in the State of Gujarat in India. The University, with the assistance and financial support of the World Health Organisation, provides from its own staff a group of medical teachers to work with, and to advise their Indian colleagues, over a period of six years. How much could have been written also on the phenomenal growth in scale and reputation of Edinburgh's Department of Astronomy and of the International Seismological Centre—a joint venture of the University and of the Royal Observatory. The Department of Astronomy, it must be added, received in 1963 a grant of £100,000 from the National Science Foundation of America, for the purpose of extending its seismic studies, which owe so much to the development of magnetic tape recording and electronic computation.

On a more modest scale—but with substantial support from friends of the University—the Committee on European Community Studies has attempted, with some success, by lectures, by discussion, and by building up the necessary documentary material, to focus the attention of lawyers, economists, and business men on the operations of the Common Market, and on this country's future legal and trade connections with the other countries of Europe.

But these are only a few examples of the less obvious work of the University. Those who are privileged to serve it steadfastly believe that it is no less conscious today than in the past of its primary aim—the extension of the boundaries of knowledge. For the full attainment of this aim, however, in the specialised and highly competitive atmosphere which pervades even the groves of Academe, many activities outside the classroom or laboratory are necessary. Farms, Plantations, Field Centres, Dispensaries, Medical and Veterinary Practices are all essential to the practical teaching of the appropriate subjects. These, and the activities of biological, geological, linguistic, geographical, social and many other workers in the field demand heavy maintenance of transport and equipment. Through its Extra-Mural Department, the University, over a wide area, carries interest and enlightenment to those who are not privileged to seek them as matriculated students. Common Rooms, Refectories, and Halls of Residence provide another set of problems, and not in term-time alone. Over the years, the University has acquired a world-wide reputation as a centre for conferences of learned societies and professional associations, which hold their meetings on the largest scale. It is a reputation for which the City of Edinburgh itself, with its natural beauty, its historic interest, and International Festival of Music and Drama, is largely responsible; but, wherever the credit lies, those conferences have to be accommodated and entertained. The University would not have it otherwise, but the cost to it, in time and maintenance, is by no means negligible.

The picture of varied activities would not be complete without a word on the University Press, with a rapidly lengthening list of distinguished and attractive publications to its credit, with increasing financial stability, and best of all, with a mounting scholarly reputation, not confined to this country, nor indeed to Europe. The University Press and more mundane, but essential organs of external and internal communication such as the *Gazette*, the *Calendar*, the *Introductions to the Faculties*, many another pamphlet, *The Student*, and other publications of like origin, diversify the scene and add the activities of a publisher, not to teaching and research alone, but also to all the normal business, financial, legal, and factorial, of any large property and investment-owning concern.

THE ACADEMIC SCENE

This lengthy list of varied and varying activities, like the figures which precede it, serves only as a background to the one main and dominant activity—the academic life of teaching and learning. If it does anything else, it is to suggest that this life is not so academic (in the popular literary sense) as might be imagined. It is a hard, busy life where men have to stand up to the sternest criticism.

The essential University is a community of students. Until his death in 1965, the late Principal, Sir Edward Appleton, himself a Nobel prize-winner, was the first to recognise the value of every scholar, novice or senior, and the first to show, by example as well as by precept, that what matters most of all is enthusiasm and application, and the genuine zeal for knowledge, old or new.[1]

In this sense, everyone in the University can be a student, whether he is 17 years of age or 70, and not forgetting the still, on occasion, top-hatted servitor whose years of service have made him not only a student, but an excellent judge of men. The youngest of us, still searching for a degree, are probably not so different from their ancestors, say in the days of Walter Scott. There are the same friendships, the same enthusiasms, and the same affections—though Scott, I fear, might have been a little shocked to behold how uninhibitedly they are expressed. Even the present-day senior members of the University are still not entirely unembarrassed by the hand-in-hand or even more intimate public attitudes of the Corydons and Phyllises of the Old College Quadrangle. The Old College, by the way, is not deserted, nor merely a place of offices—though offices also have their place. It is still well and truly occupied, over-occupied, perhaps, by the historians, of whom there are many, and by the lawyers, whose name is legion—and both groups are increasing at an encouraging (and also alarming) rate. But students of today, though their numbers constitute a problem, are no less intelligent, no less athletic, and no less ready to try—though theirs is not the easiest of worlds to grow up in, what with bombs and rumours of bombs, a steady tendency on the part of the University authorities to pack more and more into the curriculum, and a public opinion which has at last realised that Universities cost money and that the citizen has to pay.

Scottish Universities, of course, have at no time been the preserve of the wealthy, and today the gates are open to everyone—provided always he has attained an entrance qualification—or almost everyone, to be strictly accurate, since the heavily taxed professional man may still have income enough to disqualify him from any significant public bounty,

[1] The new Principal is Professor Michael Swann.

and burdens enough to make impossible the additional sacrifices demanded by a University education for his children. Perhaps this last social injustice will be set right in the post-Robbins era.

There are other problems. We think much—or perhaps we have ceased to think so much—of the " right " size of the University, (what is the right length of a piece of string?) of the need for more scientists, of the shortage of teachers, of rates of failure, of entrance qualifications, of new Universities, of new teaching methods, of changes of outlook, of reform. The inter-university (Scottish) Conference on constitutional reform has already been mentioned, as well as the University of Edinburgh's own Committee (of somewhat longer standing) on constitution, procedure, and organisation. It cannot be long before both these investigations begin to bear fruit.

THE STUDENTS

According to a fairly recent Senior President of the Students' Representative Council, Mr. David Steel who is now a Member of Parliament, the " Freshers " arriving at Edinburgh University for their first session are pretty well catered for. Over the week-end before the session opens, most of them attend a Freshers' Conference where they are officially welcomed in the magnificent Upper Library Hall by the Principal and the Rector of the University. Thereafter for a couple of days they attend talks and lectures in the Pollock Hall given by members of the University staff, student leaders and Edinburgh notables such as Sir Compton Mackenzie. The fresher is thus given a comprehensive picture of University life at the start of his or her student career, and though some of the advice given may be contradictory, most of it is useful. As more than 1,000 students now participate in these conferences their large scale organisation is one of the S.R.C.'s most important official duties—" To promote social life and academic unity among students."

To address this vast gathering of freshers packed into the Pollock Hall is to many a delightful experience, for they are a most pliable audience not yet imbued with that corporate and critical spirit which a student audience normally and sometimes excessively possesses. The freshers also have guided tours of the University; they attend what is usually the most hilarious debate of the year in the Union; and at least two dances are organised for them. Oddly enough the Freshers' Conference is perhaps the first and last gathering of real academic unity which the student will experience, for thereafter the " separated brethren " of the Sciences tend to lead their own lives out at The King's Buildings, a mile or two away from the Old College and other undergraduate centres. This academic division is undoubtedly an unfortunate feature of life at the University today but it is partially offset by the increasing provision of halls of residence; and in fact the student has never had such a wide choice of accommodation. The motherly Edinburgh landlady is no longer as familiar a figure as in decades gone by, although a few certainly still exist who line their sitting room walls with graduation photographs of their successful lodgers, and who rule their charges with an iron rod or rather with one of flexible and friendly alloy. I recall visiting a friend on the evening of his graduation day (*says Mr. Steel*). His landlady had organised a huge supper. Present were his parents, fellow lodgers and the landlady's neighbours. The graduate presided over the proceedings still wearing gown and hood, and dominating the table was a large iced-cake decorated with the University crest.

THE STUDENT AT HOME

The University is attempting to provide sufficient accommodation in new halls of residence to allow every student to spend at least one year in such a community. But undoubtedly the most striking development in student accommodation has been the success of an experiment begun a few years ago when the University offered a limited number of places in two self-contained flats. These consisted of single bed-sitters, each flat also housing one member of the academic staff as Warden. This form is now adopted as policy, and the University has been quick off the mark in obtaining suitable houses for conversion to accommodate anything from six to 30 students. This gives the student the benefits of independence—he can cook and eat what he wants and when he wants but it is likely to lead to a reduction in the number of student flats in the town. Some of these flats, rented jointly by three or four students, are well run and entirely satisfactory. Others are often inhabited by men whose sense of cleanliness and tidiness is not very marked and whose domestic arrangements and resultant diet are sometimes astonishingly primitive and inadequate. The new University houses and flatlets are therefore to be welcomed as providing another range of accommodation from which to choose.

THE COST OF LIVING

Perhaps the biggest change in student life over the past few decades has been the relative affluence of today's student compared with his forebears who came to Edinburgh with their bag of meal and a parental " allowance ", frequently obtained by considerable sacrifice on the part of the student's family. Nowadays education is accepted as a national investment, and the nation pays. Indeed within the last three or four years the system of student grants has been streamlined and improved under the control of the Scottish Education Department. The amount of grant received by an individual is easily calculated on a formula, which takes account of the fees, cost of accommodation, travel incurred, parental income and other factors. Every student regardless of parental income is entitled to a minimum of £50 which sometimes covers University fees. The maximum grant given is now over £400 per annum. The result of this system is that no qualified person may be prevented from entering a University course through lack of finance.

Unfortunately, in the view of many, the Anderson Committee's recommendation that grants should be awarded regardless of parental income is one of the many views of expert committees set up by Parliament which

Parliament has chosen to ignore. This has produced one rather odd consequence, and here perhaps we should quote our contributor exactly: "The sons and daughters of all but the wealthier homes are independent while the richer parent is still free to dictate to his children and can prevent them from going to University if he wishes. This rarely happens, but it remains an anomaly that the higher income citizens who pay most income tax are the only ones nowadays who also have to pay for the University education of their children." To this Mr. Steel adds: "There is a tendency among ill-informed sections of the community to deplore the financial security of today's student. In fact the state grants only pay for the necessities of life, and if students are seen driving motor scooters or cars or quaffing beer in the city's public houses, then these luxuries are being provided either by indulgent parents or by the vacation earnings of the students. Indeed probably more students take vacation jobs these days than in former times when money was scarcer. The Students' Representative Council runs an employment exchange which finds about 1,000 jobs for students each summer. At Christmas many act as temporary postmen. The summer vacation jobs are incredibly varied and range from hotel domestic service to lucrative hard labouring. There are also duller jobs such as selling ice-cream from a van, and interesting ones like acting as a guide to some historic place such as the Palace of Holyroodhouse.

"Some academics are critical of those who spend their vacations earning money instead of studying. But this is a narrow viewpoint and, provided a sense of proportion is maintained, vacation jobs are surely a valuable part of the student's wider education. The student, after all, is a relatively privileged member of society and in a minority position. It is good that he should have a taste of how other people earn their daily bread."

THE STUDENT'S SOCIAL LIFE

How does the newly-arrived student make contact with others once the organised cosiness of the Freshers' Conference is over? In Edinburgh this is essentially a matter for the individual. While one student—simply by attending lectures, going to the inaugural meetings of a few of the 180 or so University societies and drinking coffee in one of the Students' Common Rooms—may have made a large circle of acquaintances in a short time, another, following exactly the same routine, may speak to no-one. There have been a few girls so paralysed by shyness that they later confessed to having spoken to only one other student during the whole of their first term.

The University societies may be divided into two groups—the "giants" and the "others." The "giants" comprise the Unions and the Athletic Clubs—both separated into masculine and feminine subdivisions. The "others" are self-explanatory: all sporting clubs fall under their general supervision. The accommodation and facilities offered are of a high standard, the one glaring deficiency at present being the lack of a University swimming pool.

Membership of the Men's and Women's Unions is open to all students.

But while the Women's Union provides a useful service and a focal point for women students most of its members would agree that it is the Men's Union, which has a fine debating hall, that traditionally provides a hub for much of the University's social life. It is there that many of the main social events are held, including the Rectorial and Graduation Balls, and the Saturday night dances which are a regular social occasion. The Union is run by a Committee of Management elected from its members and until recently was entirely independent of the University itself.

The " other " societies consist of departmental, religious, racial, regional, political and debating Societies. Some of these—the Dialectic Society and the Diagnostic, for example—are exclusive and the rules of procedure are strict. The debates are fairly esoteric, and the more realistic debates take place in the Union Debating Hall.

Apart from the formal societies there are other communal activities which vary in participation from the many to the few. The most popular is of course the annual charities week which apart from its public image of fancy dress, decorated lorries and outrageous publicity stunts produces nowadays something like £20,000 each year for deserving charities.

LINKS WITH OVERSEAS

Edinburgh nowadays is fortunate in having an unusually large percentage of overseas students in its community. They have their own national societies within the University, but as individuals contribute greatly to a broader outlook and more international spirit among Edinburgh students than is perhaps found in certain other universities. Political societies flourish and fade independently of the nation's current political temperature, but generally party politics are not so strenuous as in many other academic centres. Political demonstrations, however, are well supported and at the time of Suez there was quite a turbulence in the Old Quad. Normally, stormy scenes in the Old Quad are reserved for the traditional triennial election of the University Rector by the student body; and despite his usual distinction beyond the University precincts the Rector is of course a transitory figure.[1]

Travel abroad is arranged cheaply through the Scottish Union of Students, and most undergraduates like to take advantage of the available concessions during their vacations. S.U.S. also arrange, in co-operation with the British Council, at least three group exchanges each year with the Soviet Union. These exchanges are very popular and a place on one of them has usually to be secured by selection at an interview. The participants pay only about 50 per cent (£45) of the actual cost of a three-week visit to Russia. Other student exchanges for one or two participants only are maintained between Edinburgh University and such continental universities as Warsaw, Berlin and Helsinki.

[1] The least transitory Rector in the long history of the Rectorship was the incumbent of the office as this book neared publication. James Robertson-Justice by name, and a well-known actor by profession, Mr. (or rather Dr. Justice since he is a Doctor of Laws of Edinburgh and a Doctor of Philosophy of Bonn) was elected Rector by the students for 1957–60. By being re-elected in 1964 he became the first Rector to be elected for a second term.

Chapter 35

THE INDEPENDENT SCHOOLS

THE FEE-PAYING DAY SCHOOLS

THE independent schools have their own governing bodies, and some of these—the Merchant Company and George Heriot's Trust for example—have their own resources supplemented by a grant from Government funds. In all, these bodies control almost 40 schools, varying greatly in size and nature.

The secondary schools prepare pupils for a wide variety of examinations including those for the Scottish Certificate of Education, for the General Certificate of Education in England, and for university and college entrance both inside and outside Scotland. But as many of the pupils attending these independent and direct grant schools are Edinburgh children, the local authority is consequently relieved of the need to make provision for them. Some idea of the part played by independent schools will be evident from the fact that the total number of pupils of all ages in schools under the management of the Education Committee in 1961–2 was 65,750: at the same date the number of pupils in fee-paying schools in the Edinburgh education area was 13,793, or roughly 20 per cent of the total.

This high proportion differs from the pattern over the country as a whole, since 96 per cent of Scottish children receive their education in local authority schools. But the difference is largely explained by the existence in Edinburgh of the five great, independent, endowed schools of the Merchant Company and of Heriot's Trust which, about 1870–80, a time of increasing demand for fee-paying schools, changed their character to serve, in the main, middle-class families.

Edinburgh is singularly fortunate in having so many excellent schools for her young people. Parents from the south who come to make their homes in Edinburgh—and in these days many are transferred to an Edinburgh office or factory—often wonder if they will find a suitable school in the city for their children. They are naturally relieved to discover that ample provision has in fact been made for the kind of school in which they may wish their children to be educated: any boy or girl clearly capable of taking a Scottish Certificate of Education on the higher grade will, at the age of 11 or 12, be able to gain a place in an Edinburgh fee-paying school, each one of which has its own special character. Admission at 12 is in fact easier to obtain in these schools than at the age of five or six, since more places are available. It is also true that too many five-year olds are annually enrolled for too many schools; which is why one of the oddest features of Edinburgh life in the spring is the sight of parents trailing their five year olds from school to school for " testing."

To the English parent who has accepted as normal the need for a change of school at 11 plus or 13 plus it seems strange that a school should take pupils at the age of five and keep them until they are 18. But the strangeness turns to relief, and the relief to gratitude, when it is realised that change of school is not part of the natural order of things in Edinburgh, and that the whole course of schooling from age five to age 18 can take place in one school and so be planned as a unit. Educationally such an arrangement has advantages. Schooling is seen as a single process: teachers of the young man or woman of 17 or 18 know from their colleagues in the junior school the difficulties that young people have in learning; and teachers of little boys and girls learn what will be expected from their pupils at a later stage.

These Edinburgh fee-paying schools with two exceptions are not co-educational—in this they differ from the normal Scottish school. They are broadly alike in the courses they offer, in the high standard of efficiency, in the staffs they have attracted, in the multiplicity of activities they provide outside the classroom, and in their endeavours to ensure that in those activities as much as possible is done by the pupils themselves. They differ in spirit, some emphasising one aspect of the educational process, others another; and they also differ in their origin, in the fees they charge and in the constitution of their governing bodies.

But there is another tie that binds these schools together. As we shall see, many of them have changed their names with their changing histories; yet in Edinburgh, ever tenacious of its traditions, they are still called by familiar names which would mean little to the stranger or the consulter of educational directories. " The 'Stution ", " Queen Street " and " George Square " conceal, to all but Edinburgh people, the identities of Melville College, the Mary Erskine School for Girls, and George Watson's Ladies' College, while the alumni of other establishments are proudly (or disparagingly) referred to as " Accies ", " Herioters " and " Sonians."

All these schools have different backgrounds. Some were charitable foundations; and of these the oldest is George Heriot's, founded by the Court Jeweller to James VI, " for the publick weile and ornemenent of the burgh of Edinburgh, for the honour and dew regaird whilk I have and bear to my native soyle and mother citie of Edinburgh and in imitatione of the publick pious and religious work foundat within the citie of London called Chrystis Hospital thair." Few benefactors have remained for so long an inspiration to so many. What George Heriot did for Edinburgh boys, Mary Erskine attempted to do for Edinburgh girls, and today her school, which was founded in 1694, claims to be the oldest girls' school in the country. The examples of these two inspired George Watson, whose " hospital " was opened in 1738, and Daniel Stewart, whose " hospital " was opened in 1855. The Edinburgh Academy on the other hand was founded by Sir Walter Scott and some of his friends in 1824 because they were at the time dissatisfied with the High School.

Characteristically enough on utilitarian grounds, the Victorians questioned the value of so many charity schools, established as they were for a relatively small part of the population under conditions very different from those of Victorian Scotland. The Merchant Company gave the lead in 1870 by transforming their " hospitals " for a small number of boarding pupils into day schools for a much larger number. Some criticism of the decision was made at the time; but the testimony of Dr. George Ogilvie, one of the greatest of Scottish headmasters, is convincing. Headmaster of Stewart's under the old system, he was transferred to Watson's to inaugurate the new regime, and said of his experience in Stewart's: " With sixty foundationers and two assistants I expected to procure high educational results and strove earnestly to accomplish this end, but fell far short of my expectations: and came to the conclusion that the system was radically wrong, that physically, morally and intellectually, it was depressing and unwholesome."

The opening of these schools was like the opening of a great and hitherto closed door to many Edinburgh boys and girls (George Watson's Ladies' College was founded in 1871), for they were given the opportunity of a higher education, which up to then had been denied them. What the Merchant Company did in 1870, the Heriot Trust did in 1886 when they re-established George Heriot's School as it is known today, and gave it a bias on the scientific and technical side which it is still fortunate to have. In these schools, too, the pupils have come from homes which differ widely in their financial resources, the son of the widowed waitress sitting side by side with the son of the merchant paying surtax perhaps on one of the higher scales, or the sons of the missionary, tea-planter or colonial administrator. Schools with boarding-houses, such as Watson's and the Academy, offer a great deal to such parents: rather than send their boys to a possibly minor English public school, they can, at roughly the same cost, give them the double advantage of boarding-school discipline and fellowship together with the characteristic traditions of these notable foundations.

Edinburgh Academy, which has always tended to look south and recruit its staff mainly from Oxford and Cambridge, and its rectors from Oxford and Rugby, is alone among the boys' schools in being entirely independent of government grant, and its fees (£156 in 1963) are therefore higher than those of the others. For the same reason the fees at St. George's and St. Denis' schools for girls are relatively high (£93 and £105 respectively).[1]

The four Merchant Company schools (The Mary Erskine School for Girls, George Watson's College, George Watson's Ladies College and Daniel Stewart's College) all get a grant from the Scottish Education Department and have fees up to £78 per annum. Melville College, the smallest of this type of school in the city, is also now a direct grant school. The Royal High School for Boys (£21) and James Gillespie's School for Girls (£15) on the other hand enjoy the advantages (and some think suffer the disadvantages) of being managed by the Corporation. All these

[1] All these and subsequently mentioned fees were those in being during 1963. There were some slight changes while this account was nearing publication. In 1966 the fees at all the Merchant Company Schools ranged from £78 to £99 a session. But some 110 Foundationers received free education or a monetary allowance for maintenance. In addition a considerable number are educated at restricted fees.

schools, grant-aided and independent alike, are subject to inspection by the Scottish Education Department.

In all kinds of ways the fee-paying schools have been pioneers. They have been the makers of manners and the setters of standards; and it has long been the endeavour of other schools not only in Edinburgh but in other parts of Scotland to emulate their example. After the passing of the great Education (Scotland) Act of 1918 several of the masters in Merchant Company schools became Directors of Education for Scottish counties and because of their special experience established standards of efficiency hitherto unknown in most country districts.

In their classrooms the fee-paying day schools have maintained a very high level of work, a level surpassed by perhaps only a few of the English public and grammar schools. On the playing fields their example has established rugby and cricket as popular games for boys in many schools. Rugby football was first played in Scotland on the Edinburgh Academy ground in Raeburn Place. Similarly, the Academy pioneered Scottish school cricket.

The value of the Academy's example in securing a playing-field is attested by the Royal Commission on Education in 1868. Within recent years some of the more important Burgh schools, following this lead, have provided fields as sports grounds for their pupils at a convenient distance from the school.

But sport is not the only extra-curricular activity. Almost all of the schools have orchestras, some of which attain a remarkably high standard of playing. All run literary and debating societies where young Edinburgh, sometimes with considerable passion and eloquence, comes to its hopeful conclusions about the great problems which have perplexed and still continue to perplex the older generation. All have dramatic societies, while some have produced operas, both serious and comic. The boys' schools have units of the Combined Cadet Force which offer a valuable training and indeed, occasionally, the possibility of trips under service discipline to distant parts. As for the girls' schools some have Girl Guide companies; all of them interest their pupils in games and in charitable work.

One indication of the success of these schools is the number of clubs which exist to keep their old pupils in touch with their old school and foster their loyalty. These clubs are to be found all over the world. Each has its annual dinner, at which the ritual varies; but the chief toast is always the toast of The School.

THE MERCHANT COMPANY SCHOOLS

The four schools administered by the Merchant Company have a high reputation far beyond the borders of Scotland and since as a group they form one of the mainstays of Edinburgh's educational structure, we should look at them more closely.

GEORGE WATSON'S COLLEGE

The average boy entering Watson's today probably resembles closely enough his predecessors of over two centuries ago; and unless he is one of about 110 boarders accommodated in three boarding houses, he will live at home. But at the outset the chances against his getting in to Watson's were three to one, there being so many other applications for the places available. If his father is a member of the Merchant Company he will naturally have obtained some degree of priority, but even then, like all the others, he will have to undergo an entrance test.

Selection procedure at the age of four, however, is notoriously unreliable, and he will not in fact be joining an aristocracy of academic brilliance. Yet he and his contemporaries will prove to have a wide range of ability and intelligence. For Watson's is far more comprehensive than, say, an English grammar school whose entrants can be more reliably selected at the age of 11. The great majority of boys remain at school until 17 at least and are able to obtain passes on the Higher Grade for the Scottish Certificate of Education. Of the 165 boys who left in 1962, for instance, on the completion of their courses, 95 went on to University or professional training. An increasing number of boys elect to remain at school for another year after qualifying for University entrance in order to work for bursary examinations. Recently several pupils have been awarded scholarships at Colleges in Oxford and a number have obtained places at Cambridge. At the time of writing, the School has some 1,500 boys in Preparatory, Junior and Senior Departments; and their hours are from 9 a.m. until 3.25 p.m. from Monday to Friday, divided into seven 40-minute periods of instruction organised in a six-day time-table.

After third year various alternative courses are offered in preparation for the Higher and Ordinary Grades of the Scottish Certificate of Education. Although there are now twice as many members of the staff teaching scientific and technical subjects as those teaching Classics, the School's strong Classical tradition is upheld by the fact that some of the most able boys consistently choose to follow Classical and Language courses.

Games are provided in great variety. The Cadet Force, is divided into Army, Navy and Air Force sections. The oldest school society is the Literary Club whose records go back to 1879. There is also the School Orchestra and Choir, together with at least 12 other clubs and groups in which boys can pursue common interests and practise the art of self-government. These range from birdwatching to chess and film-making. There are two school magazines and, in the summer term, a weekly news-sheet to produce, while every year the Art Department stages an exhibition of painting and drawing, sculpture, pottery and textiles created by the young artists in the school.

On leaving school, two out of three former pupils join the Watsonian Club, which has 38 branches at home and abroad. The Club which is a great source of strength to the School has provided many amenities for the college over the years. The branch in North America, for example, largely provided the funds for an annual scholarship for a Watson's boy at Hamilton College, New York State, while the Ceylon Club provided a loud speaker system for the Myreside grandstand. It is also to the Former Pupils that the school owes the furnishing and equipping of its library. Even more generously by 1963 not only had former pupils subscribed over £100,000 in six months towards the building of a separate Music School, VIth Form laboratories and tutorial rooms, but by the spring of 1964 this development fund was nearing £200,000, and the Earl of Harewood had opened the new music school, a remarkable building with a hyperbolic paraboloid roof specially designed to help acoustical conditions.

DANIEL STEWART'S COLLEGE

Also managed by the Merchant Company Education Board and strongly supported by its former pupils Daniel Stewart's College is situated in ample grounds on the Queensferry Road within a few minutes of the West End. It has about 950 pupils of whom 500 are in the junior school (ages 5-plus to 12) and 450 in the senior school (ages 12 to 18). Its youngest pupils, who normally are taught by the same teacher for three years, have their lessons in rooms ideally situated (with a garden on either side) and admirably planned. At that stage most of the instruction is given to the boys individually or in groups. Class teaching is the normal method of instruction in the upper part of the junior school where a start is made to the study of science and of foreign languages, and where, in recent years, pioneer work has been done in the teaching of handwriting.

In the senior school for the first two years all boys study the same subjects, except that the intellectually able may have Latin instead of technical subjects. At the end of the second year, at the age of 14, boys are given the opportunity of dropping some of the subjects in which they have little interest. About three-quarters of the boys, however, elect to continue the study of science. Whatever they choose, most boys wish to remain until they have gained at least one or two passes on the higher grade in the Scottish Certificate of Education examination; and very few leave before they are 17.

A well equipped technical department, with forge, casting equipment, and lathes, and a new science block in the modern idiom, with six classrooms, give the future scientist or engineer ample opportunity for the development of his interests.

Those artistically inclined may find in pottery and printing opportunity for the exercise and development of their talents. Nearly all boys learn French: small groups of boys take Greek or German or Russian; and some of the less able linguistically attempt Spanish. Indeed so great is the variety of courses taken now, that the old Scottish custom of having an annual dux boy has been abandoned.

Most of the senior school work is done in the main building, an impressive Victorian structure. On the upper floor is the Chapel which has played an important part in the lives of many boys and in which each morning the Headmaster or the School Chaplain conducts a service. In the past 35 years one in six of its duxes, after taking his " first " in university studies, has become a minister of the Church of Scotland.

The Combined Cadet Force has an Army and an R.A.F. section; and at Easter a party of boys and officers goes off for arduous training in the highlands. The school orchestra has its strings, its wood and its brass. There are debating and dramatic societies as well as clubs for playing chess and studying radio and learning about motor cars. At the 16-acre school grounds at Inverleith both rugby and cricket are played. Other games are golf—one of the boys was British golf champion in 1959—and tennis—one of the boys was Scottish junior champion in 1963. A post-war feature has been an increased interest in athletics, all of the school athletic records having been broken in recent years.

THE MARY ERSKINE SCHOOL FOR GIRLS

Of the two Merchant Company girls' schools, the Merchant Maiden Hospital, now the Mary Erskine School for Girls, is the older. It was founded in 1694 " by the Company of Merchants and Mary Erskine." One of the earliest foundations for female education in Britain, it was laid down that the children were not only to " be taught and brought up in vertue," but instructed " to Read, Work Stockings, Lace, Coloured and White Seam, Washing and Dressing of Linnens, Dressing of Meat, Cleaning of Houses, and all other ordinary Household Thrift: also Writing, Arithmetick and the Common Parts of Vocal Musick." By the middle of the 19th century the curriculum had become less domestic: French and German were taught, as well as Drawing, Dancing and " Pianoforte."

In 1870 the Merchant Maiden Hospital with its 70-odd resident pupils gave place to a day-school called the Educational Institution for Young Ladies (a name later changed to the Edinburgh Ladies' College). There were 1,200 girls, 300 applicants having been rejected. The " Governess " was replaced by a Headmaster who was assisted by an authoritative Lady Superintendent and a staff of 77, the 26 men of that number being responsible for the senior work of the school, The Lady Superintendent was responsible among other things for " deportment " and the " chaperoning " of the school. This office declined with the appointment of a Headmistress in 1914, and gradually a staff which had become predominnately male became entirely female. At present there is one master—to teach music.

The curriculum in the latter half of the 19th century was not so very different from the modern curriculum. But there has certainly been a change of emphasis, especially with regard to Mathematics and Science. Provision is made for girls to learn various musical instruments, and in consequence the school orchestra now plays an important part in school life. Hockey sticks, tennis racquets and golf clubs have replaced croquet mallets, skipping ropes and swings, which were advocated in 1869.

The school, which became " The Mary Erskine School for Girls " in 1944, is now one of the foremost fee-paying day-schools in Scotland.

Of the 960-odd pupils, about 200 are presented each year for the Scottish Certificate of Education and 20–30 girls annually proceed to a University.

In 1944 the School celebrated its 250th Jubilee when the Princess Royal was the Guest of Honour. *The Merchant Maiden*, one of the first girls' school magazines, celebrated its Jubilee in 1958.

Inadequate accommodation has been the school's main problem in the last ten years. But it is on the threshold of a great era in its history, for it will soon be accommodated in a modern building—designed by Mr. William Kininmonth, R.S.A. and incorporating Edinburgh's historic Ravelston House—which will do justice not merely to its great tradition, but to its pioneering spirit as well.

GEORGE WATSON'S LADIES' COLLEGE

George Watson's Ladies' College is the most recent in date of the Edinburgh Merchant Company Schools. The college was opened in 1871 in its present buildings in George Square, the last great square to be built before fashionable Edinburgh moved across to the New Town. As numbers increased, the school building became an amalgam of several old houses with strong links with the past, notably with Viscount Melville and Admiral Duncan of Camperdown, both of whom lived at No. 5, the present address of the school. Although the college has been pleasantly modernised many features of the original structure are preserved, notably the "Admiral's Kitchen."

The school by 1962–3 had outgrown the George Square building; and of the total school roll of 960, only 650 of the pupils, the Senior School and the last two years of the Primary School, were housed there. The Nursery Class and the first five years of the Primary School occupy delightful buildings—with spacious gardens and playing fields—in St. Alban's Road.

Educationally the present situation is the outcome of a combination of inherited school tradition and changes brought about by the social and economic pressures of the post-war years. On the one hand certain basic attitudes of personality are cultivated from the pupils' earliest years—the importance of good manners and taste for example; the value of charity in the widest sense of the word; and an acceptance of the importance of the individual, gifted or not. On the other hand a sound academic tradition has existed since the inception of the school, and now that women have become important in the industrial and commercial life of the country, academic qualifications have assumed even greater significance. Each year 80–90 pupils are awarded the Scottish Leaving Certificate and pupils from Form VI appear high in the University Bursary Award list.

The changing shape and attitudes of society have their impact on the school: an immense change in the numbers in Form VI from under 10 in 1945 to 60 in 1962–3; an earlier specialisation in Form III to meet the new "O" level Certificate; an increased emphasis on scientific courses; a comparative decline in such subjects as do not fit women for careers in the modern world. Apart from English, five languages—French, German,

Russian, Latin and Greek—are now taught, and there is good accommodation in four laboratories where instruction in Physics, Chemistry and Biology is given.

The long and fine tradition in Art and Music is also maintained; excursions to art galleries, historical buildings and concerts are frequent. Art is practised in three studios, and Music (though pupils are no longer instructed in instrumental playing as part of their curriculum), in highly successful school choirs and a large orchestra which plays each morning for Assembly. For Cookery, Housewifery, Needlework and Embroidery there are well-equipped rooms and in these subjects all pupils follow courses until Form III Senior, while older pupils may specialise for the Scottish Leaving Certificate (Higher), as is the case with Commercial subjects.

The physical welfare of the pupils is provided for by a staff of three gymnastic teachers. As part of the curriculum, each girl attends one class in gymnastics and one in modern dancing each week as well as attending on one afternoon a week the playing fields at Liberton. The games played there are hockey, netball, golf and tennis, while athletics is becoming increasingly popular.

THE OTHER BOYS' SCHOOLS

THE EDINBURGH ACADEMY

The Edinburgh Academy was opened on 1st October, 1824. The chief inspiration for its foundation came from Lord Cockburn and Leonard Horner, who believed that the decline of classical education in Scotland could be arrested only by the creation of a new school on an improved model. The cost was met by public subscription. To meet the needs of the New Town, the school was built in a field to the north of Edinburgh, a field extensive enough for the games of those days; so the need for exercise was not overlooked.

Sir Walter Scott, who presided at the opening, insisted that the teaching of English should have an important place in the curriculum. The Directors expressly provided not only for the " unequivocal supremacy " of the Rector over the other members of the staff, but for classes smaller than was then normal (the maximum was to be 100). They also made it compulsory for boys to attend all classes. Under its first Rector the Academy set up new standards for a classical education; a Seventh Class was established for boys whose parents considered 14 to be too tender an age for embarking on University life; and boys were attracted to the Academy from all over Scotland and farther afield.

Thirty years after its foundation a Modern side was established and a new playing-field acquired This was intended for the playing of cricket, but in the following year (1855) migrants from Durham School to the Academy introduced Rugby Football into Scotland, and Raeburn Place later became the scene of Rugby Internationals. Athletics soon followed, and in 1858 the annual " Academy Games " were instituted. In 1888, after a period of decline, the appointment of a new Rector inaugurated an era of far-reaching reforms. These included a restriction of classes to a maximum of 30, the making of football and cricket compulsory throughout the school, the institution of ephors (the Academy equivalent of prefects), the raising of the leaving age, the diversifying of the life of the school by, for example, the encouragement of music, the acquisition of additional playing-fields, the erection of two boarding houses, the establishment of a Science Department, and the institution of a school magazine. But while making more effective provision for boarders the Rector aimed at making " the Academy all that was best in Home School education." The day school, he held, owed its peculiar strength to the fact that it combined the life of the home with the life of the school.

Today the Academy retains its special characteristics. It is an Independent School, receiving no grant from State or Local Authority and depending for its survival on the generosity of Academicals and the willingness of parents to pay its comparatively heavy fees. The Upper School, still on the original site, contains about 620 boys. About a quarter of the older boys are boarders and they play a peculiarly important part in the life of the School. Games remain compulsory, for those who are physically fit, as is the Combined Cadet Force, the descendant of the Officers' Training Corps founded by an Academical, Lord Haldane. In the Sixth and Seventh Classes about 160 boys work for the Higher Grade of the Scottish Certificate of Education and for the Advanced Level of the G.C.E. and University Scholarships, and the School figures prominently in the lists of open awards at Oxford and Cambridge, in Classics and Modern Subjects, Mathematics and Science.

Since 1945 the Preparatory School has moved elsewhere, and this has made it possible to carry out an extensive scheme of reconstruction for the Upper School. In particular, with help from the Industrial Fund for the Advancement of Science in Schools, the Science Department now has facilities of a high order, with two lecture theatres, five Chemistry or General Science laboratories, two Physics laboratories and two Biology laboratories, all recently modernised or constructed and equipped. A Mathematics laboratory, new Geography and Music Rooms, and four Modern Language classrooms have also been provided, and further developments are on the way.

GEORGE HERIOT'S SCHOOL

Founded as George Heriot's Hospital after the pattern of Christ's Hospital in London in 1628 (when the first sod was turned) George Heriot's School has occupied its original site immediately south of the Castle for almost three and a half centuries. That site once lay outside the city boundary, and parts of the Flodden and Telfer walls today mark the western limits of the school grounds.

From 1659, when the first boys entered the school, until 1886 the records show that 180 boys were maintained and educated on the Foundation within the original building. But in 1886 Heriot's became a day school, educating boys from the age of seven up to university entrance. In that same year, being unable to secure advanced training for their boys in what would now be called applied science and technology, the Governors founded the Heriot-Watt College, whose past and present are described later. By the end of the century the school roll had reached 1,000. In 1965 it stood at slightly over 1,500.

Boys are nowadays first admitted to the school at age five, and for the next two years attend in the forenoon only. The subjects in the Preparatory department are reading, counting, writing, drawing and elementary nature study: gymnastics, taken by male specialist teachers, consist of simple exercises involved in group and team games.

In the Junior School, the curriculum embraces English (including composition), history, geography, arithmetic, nature study, art drawing, class singing, gymnastics, swimming (the school has its own pool) and organised games.

In the Senior School the broad general curriculum followed in the first years is narrowed at later stages to meet the emerging needs and capacities of individual boys; vocational guidance is offered to all boys and there is a full-time careers master. Subjects professed to Certificate standard are English, history, geography, mathematics, applied mathematics, physics, chemistry, biology, botany, zoology (there are separate and special laboratories for each branch of science and engineering, and the School has its own botanical garden), technical subjects (woodwork, metalwork, technical drawing, mechanics), art drawing, commerce, economics, music, Latin, Greek, French, German, Spanish, Italian and Russian. In addition all boys must take part in class music lessons; physical education is compulsory except for boys medically excused; religious instruction is given at all stages unless parents seek exemption for a boy on conscientious grounds. The school has a full-time chaplain.

Organised games have a large part in the life of the school; and every week most boys in the Junior and Senior School will be found at the spacious playing fields at Goldenacre. During the first three years in the Senior School boys have a choice in winter and spring of rowing or badminton, and in summer of tennis or golf. Each season the school has fixtures for 36 rugby fifteens.

Much emphasis is laid on corporate activities. Not only is there a strong contingent of the Combined Cadet Force and a popular Wolf Cub pack and Scout Troop, but opportunity for group activity can be found in the Literary and Dramatic Society and in the choral, radio, chess, music, natural history camera, sub-aqua, cycling, judo, and model railway clubs. The division of the school into Houses provides the basis of inter-house competitions in sport, swimming, music and drama. A school orchestra plays a large part in the concert given each year in the Usher Hall.

Exchange visits to schools in foreign countries send large numbers of Heriot boys to the continent each year. There is a yearly exchange of some 30 boys with the Lycée of Sens in France; of 30 others with the Humboldt Gymnasium in Cologne; a biennial exchange of about 20 with the Instituto Maeztu in Madrid; a party of 35 visits the Tyrol at

Easter; and three Easter tours have been made in recent years to Rome.

In 1963, when the 400th anniversary of the birth of its founder George Heriot was celebrated, ambitious plans were announced for a £120,000 extension to the school buildings, which would have pleased that goldsmith and great benefactor mightily could he have attended the splendid commemoration of his name, and seen how his charitable purpose is maintained in the substantial number of foundationships, bursaries and scholarships still available under the Trust.

MELVILLE COLLEGE

Melville College was founded in 1832 to meet the needs of the New Town which was too far from the High School, then situated at Kirk o' Field. It was at first known as the Edinburgh Institution in George Street. After successive moves it came in 1920 to Melville Street, hence its name.

Primarily the aim of the College was to prepare a boy to become a merchant, an artist or an engineer rather than a member of the learned professions which were well catered for elsewhere. Twenty years later its principles were stated to be " to open the classes for the branches of a liberal education and to leave the selection of those branches to the friends of the pupil." By this and a judicious mixture of Scottish and English examinations Melville College forestalled some of the recommendations of the 1959 Report of the Working Party on the Curriculum of the Senior Secondary School.

In the early years the Institution was not a cheap school: half a guinea per quarter—a much larger sum than 10*s.* 6*d.* is today—was charged for each subject on the curriculum. In our own time the comparative prosperity of the post-war years and a government grant have brought the fees within the reach of many who would previously have been unable to contemplate them. Nevertheless, not all classes have been equally lucky in the social redistribution of wealth, and many boys from professional homes who before the war might have gone to more expensive boarding schools now go to Melville. There is another attraction. The present trend in industry towards " take-overs " and amalgamation has led to a great increase in managerial and staff transfers; and since Melville College, unlike the Merchant Company schools, has no entry priorities to fulfil, entry for those coming to Edinburgh from other parts of the country is not so difficult. In 1956 the school Governors, recognising the need for a more powerful Senior School, acquired additional property and the school was able to increase the roll from 375 to 500 boys. The necessary loan to make this possible was granted by Edinburgh Corporation, who have always viewed the school's problems with sympathy, for even with its increased numbers, Melville is still less than half the size of most of the other Edinburgh independent day schools. In 1959 the school ceased to draw a grant from Edinburgh Corporation and was added to the Scottish Education Department's Direct Grant List. The school life today, as distinct from that of its early days, is rich in activities outside the classroom, in physical education, school societies and expeditions; and a large number of former members of the school hold positions of importance in law, medicine, the services, as well as in industry and commerce.

There are also, it should be noted here, those fee-paying day-schools which, like the Royal High and James Gillespie's (both for boys and girls) are administered by the Corporation. These we shall look at more closely within the context of the local authority's provision for the education of Edinburgh's children.

BOARDING SCHOOLS FOR BOYS

From the predominantly day schools we come to the well-known boarding-schools modelled largely on the Arnoldean English public-school system. It is certainly true to say that their inspiration is alien to the main stream of Scottish educational tradition, as this is represented either by the co-educational high schools which predominate throughout the country, or by such schools as the Edinburgh Academy or George Watson's College, but the boys who attend them are conscious of having been educated in Scotland. They play rugby and cricket with Academicals, Watsonians and the rest, shoot at Bisley with them, camp with them on Combined Cadet Force manoeuvres and engage together in sailing races.

Some children, of course, go out of Edinburgh to be educated at independent boarding schools elsewhere; but the number is small and probably does not exceed two or three hundred. In contrast the number coming in must be in the region of 2,000, and, amongst the boys, the majority go to the three great Public Schools (in the English sense of the designation)—Fettes, Loretto and Merchiston. Loretto, which is situated just outside the city boundaries at Musselburgh has a preparatory school of its own; the other two educate boys from the age of 13 to 18 only. Day boys are rarely accepted at any of them.

These schools are represented on the Headmasters' Conference. While it is generally considered that they belong to the English Public School tradition, though all of them are small by English standards, it is nevertheless true that their outstanding reputation has been gained through the capacity of Scottish youth to derive the very best from this particular kind of schooling. A greater measure of ambition and enterprise, plenty of energy and a greater readiness to accept the " hard life," make Scottish boys excellent material for Public School methods of training; and it might be added that, in these days, the relative absence of snobbery in Scotland is an extra advantage. Consequently there is great demand for places at these schools, not only from north of the border, but also from England—particularly the north—from overseas and, in lesser degree, from Ireland. It should also be mentioned that there is a strong connection through Scottish parents who have gone to work in England or abroad, and who are anxious to send their sons " home " for their schooling. Figures vary from year to year and from school to school, but it is probably a fair estimate that 60 per cent of the pupils come from Scotland, 15 per cent are English, 15 per cent are Anglo-Scots and 10 per cent come from overseas. Fettes has the highest percentage of the last three groups, and Merchiston has the highest from Scotland.

It is interesting that these schools should afford such classic examples of two out of the three main ways in which English public schools have developed. Merchiston and Loretto advanced slowly from the status of small private schools; Fettes, launched through a large endowment, was provided with buildings and grounds on a considerable scale before the first boy was admitted. There is no example in Scotland of an independent public school emerging from an ancient grammar school foundation.

LORETTO SCHOOL

Loretto School began in 1825 when the Reverend Dr. Thomas Langhorne, who had for some time taken pupils for private tuition, moved into Loretto House, Musselburgh. There he developed what was really a preparatory school, with anything up to 50 boys, few of whom were over the age of 14. Dr. Langhorne was succeeded by his son, but numbers fell until 1862 when Loretto was taken over by Hely-Hutchinson Almond, who reigned there till 1903. Several schools during this period owed their survival and development to a great schoolmaster, with Merchiston as an outstanding example. But in Almond, Loretto gained not only a great builder of their own fortunes but also a man who by his original ideas and pioneer methods was to become a national figure. Almond's great creed was that a healthy mental and moral atmosphere could only be generated in a life which was healthy on the physical side, and to ensure this he gave great prominence to games, the open air life, comfortable clothing and everything which might today be termed " school hygiene."

There is considerable evidence that Almond influenced the Public School system throughout Great Britain and New Zealand; and there can be no question whatever that he built up a great institution at Loretto. It became known as a place where boys grew strong and healthy and where they developed a quite exceptional esprit de corps. Indeed the Headmaster insisted on a family atmosphere, which survives to this day in the organisation of the school. For many years it was accepted that the total number of senior boys must not exceed 200 and various measures were taken to prevent sectional divisions through the establishment of a conventional House system. Today Loretto is a Public school for some 240 boys over the age of 13 and it runs a preparatory school of its own where there are usually 55 " Nippers".

MERCHISTON CASTLE

The history of Merchiston Castle begins in 1833 when Mr. Charles Chalmers, who had previously had a small school in Park Place, moved with about 30 pupils to the old Merchiston Tower. This was the family home of the Napiers amongst whom was numbered the inventor of logarithms: today the old tower is preserved as the central feature of the new technical college.

Looking from East Princes Street Gardens, the spires and towers of the Old Town are silhouëtted in the morning sunshine.

Early morning anglers at Duddingston Loch, the bird sanctuary on the south side of Arthur's Seat.

Chalmers had a successful headmastership from 1833 to 1850 during which time he built up a reputation as a man who could not only teach, but who could also look after his boarders with a touch of inspiration. As the school was on the outskirts of Edinburgh, it flourished mainly on the admission of Edinburgh boys and those from the immediate neighbourhood. In 1863, however, there was appointed as headmaster John Johnston Rogerson who, though not destined to become a national figure like Almond, soon gained the reputation of being a leader or "Chief" (as he was known) of quite outstanding merit. He remained the inspiration of the School from 1863–98; and during this time Merchiston developed from the position of a popular private school to that of a public boarding school of considerable importance.

If Merchiston was well established by the time that Rogerson retired, the opportunities for expansion around the Castle were limited as were the school's financial resources. Nevertheless the Governors made the brave decision to build a new school on an estate at Colinton with modern equipment and spacious playing fields. The boys moved to Colinton in 1930.

Today Merchiston Castle, which is administered by a Board of Governors partly elected by Merchistonians and partly nominated by the University of Edinburgh and other bodies, is a school of relatively small size—about 290 boys in all—and the preparatory department has been given up.

FETTES COLLEGE

The Fettes Endowment was provided by the late Sir William Fettes, Bt., of Comely Bank and Redcastle, who was twice Lord Provost of Edinburgh and died in 1836. The Trustees decided in 1863 that the most valuable way of using the considerable sums at their disposal would be to build and equip a boarding school for boys, some foundationers and some fee-paying. The architect was David Bryce, R.S.A., who also designed the British Linen Bank in St. Andrew Square and St. George's Church in Shandwick Place. For the detail Bryce drew largely from French chateaux, and he certainly produced a remarkable building. The 200-acre site was on the founder's Comely Bank estate less than two miles from Princes Street, and the School was opened in 1870 with 70 boys of whom the majority were Foundationers. So quickly did it achieve success that 10 years later there were over 200 boys of whom 150 were fee payers. Today the total is about 450.

Fettes began with a great headmaster, Dr. A. W. Potts, who was strongly influenced by what might be called the "Arnold of Rugby" tradition. He was himself a fine classical scholar and a keen sportsman, who expected the highest standards in morals, work and games, and soon the school achieved a high reputation, notably in classics and rugby football.

In the post-war years it benefited by re-organisation and the broadening of the curriculum under Donald Crichton-Miller as headmaster. A new

Assembly Hall, Music and Art rooms have been built and thanks to the generosity of Old Fettesians a new dining hall as well. There is also no longer such a strong classical bias; nor is recreation confined to the more conventional games. But traces remain of the original Rugby connection, and it must be said that in general Fettes is nearer the conventional pattern of English Public Schools than Loretto or Merchiston.

But of course, the austerities of 50 years ago have been modified; food is generally very good; there is ample hot water; and there is no longer an hour's school before breakfast. But outside activities, both voluntary and compulsory, have also multiplied; examinations are more demanding; and the assistance of domestic servants is greatly reduced. A small boy plunged for the first time into Public School life may find that he is expected to put in a 14-hour day during which he may have to clean his prefect's shoes as well as his own; play rugby football; rehearse his part in a House play; clean his rifle; clear away the supper; and satisfy the practice requirements of his music master. Yet he still has the usual amount of class work and preparation, the latter done during specified hours under the supervision of a prefect. Furthermore there are entirely voluntary activities such as woodwork and the cult of the model aeroplane for which he is eager to find time. As he grows older he may be relieved of some of the chores, but in return he is expected to help with the supervision and instruction of younger boys, particularly in games and the Cadet Force.

The masters have clear advantages in their small classes (an average of 25 boys, perhaps, as opposed to about 35 in the State-aided schools) and in the opportunities they have for extending their teaching in various ways during the evenings and on half holidays. Masters are indeed on duty all day, and often on Sundays as well. Amongst them must be found experts—or enthusiasts, if they are not precisely experts—in every kind of game, in hobbies of all sorts and in a variety of educational pursuits for which there is no room on the time-table. The staff ratio is therefore considerably higher than in day schools—possibly one master to 14 boys instead of one to 20 or more.

Owing to rising costs and slightly different methods of charging for "extras" it is difficult to say exactly how much it costs to be educated at these establishments. But the sum can not, at the time of writing, be much less than £460 per annum including extras. This figure compares favourably with the charges at most of the well-known English Public Schools, and it is probably true that more numerous and more valuable scholarships are available than in the south. Certainly the question of cost does not seem to have affected the demand for places, since waiting lists at these three schools are well filled for many years to come.

CARGILFIELD

There is one important preparatory school in Edinburgh—Cargilfield School which was founded in 1873 by the Rev. Charles Darnell. Originally situated in Trinity, the school in 1899 was moved to new specially designed quarters in Barnton Park. It stands in its own grounds of about 20 acres, near Cramond, and with two golf courses to the east and south, it cannot be shut in by other buildings.

In order to ensure the permanence of the school, a company called Cargilfield School Limited was incorporated in 1919, the capital having been subscribed by Old Boys and parents; and in 1947 a new company with the same name, limited by guarantee, having no share capital and not carried on for profit, was incorporated to take over the assets of the original company.

The control of the school is in the hands of a distinguished board of governors, one of whom is nominated by the Faculty of Advocates, one by the Governors of Fettes College and one by the Governors of Rugby School.

There are usually about 120 boys, all of whom are boarders. The teaching staff consists of the Headmaster, ten assistant masters and one mistress; and the administrative staff includes the Housekeeper, Matron, two Assistant Matrons and a fully qualified Nurse, all under the supervision of the Headmaster's wife.

The School is preparatory for all Public Schools. The ordinary standard subjects required by the Public Schools for entrance and scholarship examinations are taught in accordance with the recommendations of the Headmasters' Joint Conference and include Latin, mathematics, French, English, history, geography and elementary science, and (in the three top forms) Greek. In every subject boys are arranged in classes small enough to secure individual attention.

Cargilfield boys have won many scholarships at Public Schools. They are encouraged to aim at scholarship standard, but there is no "cramming" and boys who are likely to be up to this standard do not do any extra work.

Everything possible is done to encourage the playing of musical instruments and singing. In addition to masters on the staff who are responsible for the music, there are visiting teachers for piano, 'cello, violin, clarinet and chanter. Cricket and tennis are played in the summer term, rugby football in winter and association football and hockey in Spring. There are also a fives court and an indoor swimming bath. There is a voluntary class for those who wish to learn dancing, and there is a voluntary Scout troop. A well-stocked library provides literature for the boys; and there is a Library-Chapel, designed by E. Auldjo Jamieson, in memory of 126 Old Boys who fell in the 1914–18 War.

On Sunday mornings boys attend services at Cramond Kirk and the Episcopal Church at Davidson's Mains, and in the evening there is a special School Service in the Library-Chapel conducted by the Headmaster and attended by the household. On weekdays prayers are read every morning and in the evening there is a short Service in the Chapel.

GILLSLAND PARK SCHOOL

Of the smaller independent day schools for boys, Gillsland Park School seems to have a character of its own. It is run on preparatory school lines and has accommodation for about 150 boys from five to 13 years of age. Latin and French are taught from age nine and the senior classes learn algebra, geometry and science. There are the usual organised games; and boys coming to the school from distant places may live in " Nedlands " School Children's Residence (an independent establishment). Boys are prepared for the entrance examinations to the secondary day schools, such as George Watson's College and for the Common Entrance Examination to the Public Schools. And also there is a well-equipped Nursery School on the premises for boys and girls aged three to five years.

SCHOOLS FOR GIRLS

For girls there are fewer places in the Edinburgh fee-paying schools than there are for boys. St. George's, by the foresight of its governors, has ample grounds but, though it intends to expand, at present it has only 400 pupils. The other well-known independent schools for girls—St. Denis, Lansdowne House, St. Margaret's, St. Hilary's—all began as proprietary schools and, through the generosity of former owners, are now non-profit-making schools performing a very useful function in offering boarding facilities. Cranley continues to this day to prosper under private ownership, as do several others mentioned later in this survey. Some of these—and schools like Craigmount and St. Trinians which were till recent years part of the Edinburgh scene—take a few boys in the early preparatory classes.

ST. GEORGE'S SCHOOL FOR GIRLS

St. George's is a non-denominational day school for girls of ages from five to 18, with two school boarding houses adjoining the grounds. The school is governed by an independent Council and has been registered by the Secretary of State for Scotland on the Register of Independent Schools. It is inspected by the Scottish Education Department, but not aided by grants or rates. The school in 1965 had a staff of 28 full-time and 13 part-time mistresses, at salaries on the Scottish scale. The pupils number 450, divided into a Preparatory Department of 80, a Junior School of 120 and a Secondary Department of 250. The present school building, on a commanding site on the Murrayfield ridge, mainly dates from 1914 and is surrounded by its own playing fields.

The founders of the school were a small group of remarkable Edinburgh ladies set on securing higher education for women. Before women were admitted to Arts degree courses, they organised, with the help of friendly professors, classes of University standard where—as a school authority reminds us—" Sally Mair sat throned on the boot-bench declaiming ' Cogito, ergo sum '." When Edinburgh University required women to sit the Local Examinations these same ladies found that they were very weak in certain elementary subjects. " S.M." therefore wrote a letter to

The Scotsman inviting any ladies who required coaching to get in touch with her. They joined classes which were held in the Parish Hall of St. George's Church, Charlotte Square. In 1886 they started St. George's Training College for Secondary School Teachers and brought in Miss Mary R. Walker from the Maria Gray College in London. Two years later they went on to open St. George's School for Girls in Melville Street, to make available a sound general education for girls from the age of seven up to University entrance. Miss Houldsworth, Chairman of the Committee, quiet and neat, provided sagacious guidance and business sense; Miss Sally Mair, later Dame Sarah Siddons Mair, provided the drama and the grand style; Miss Mary Walker, shy, dignified, gracious and very able, was one of the great first headmistresses.

In 1888 the school opened with 60 pupils. The new development was not essentially alien to Edinburgh tradition, always noted for strong-minded ladies rather than clinging tendrils. Yet there was never a tone of militancy or mannishness about St. George's, nor, on the other hand, of introspective nervous strain. There was instead a sober idealism: the knightly motto, chosen in the '90s—" Truth and Honour, Freedom and Courtesy "—was felt to be appropriate. The early founders, much influenced by the Froebel ideals of the Maria Gray Training College, decided to have no prizes or competitive placing of individuals.

In the Melville Street period the emphasis of the curriculum was on intellectual training—the gap most felt at that time in women's education. In 1912 and 1914 the school matured into its present general shape, and a fine new building on the Murrayfield site gave enlarged opportunities for music, art, science and games.

After the second World War—which meant the evacuation of the school, the end of the Training College, military occupation of the buildings, and the eventual trickle back to Edinburgh—the school re-established itself and is still prospering. At the time of the Jubilee in 1938 there were about 250 pupils: now there are some 450, and in 1962 the Council decided to enlarge the school still further. True to its lengthy pioneering tradition it has not only introduced courses in the History of Science for non-scientists and in Classical background for non-Latinists, but lets the Upper VI study a course on the changing social environment.

ST. DENIS SCHOOL FOR GIRLS

St. Denis School for girls was founded in 1855 by Miss Jane Simson in a house in Great King Street. In 1858 the school, known quite simply as " Miss Simson's School ", moved to 6 Royal Circus.

In the course of the next 50 years the school had several changes of address, passed through the hands of three headmistresses and was known successively as " Miss Simson's School ", Miss Saunders's School ", and " Miss Mack's School."

In 1908 it was taken over by Miss Bourdass who had recently been on the staff of " La Maison d'Education des Jeunes Filles de la Legion d' Honneur " at Saint Denis on the outskirts of Paris. This famous French school was founded by Napoleon in 1806, on the day after the battle of Austerlitz, " pour les filles de mes braves." It was therefore Miss Bourdass who gave the Edinburgh school the name " St. Denis ", and its French motto, " Loyauté sans Reproche ", which catches an echo of the knight " sans peur et sans reproche," Bayard, whose statue stands in the grounds of its French counterpart.

To this day the staff and pupils of St. Denis, Edinburgh, are intensely proud of their Franco-Scottish connections and regard the school as a living example of the Auld Alliance. Thus a representative of the staff of Saint Denis, Paris, attended the centenary celebrations in Edinburgh in 1958; and each year a double prize is awarded, part to the Dux in French in St. Denis, Edinburgh, and part to the Dux in English in St. Denis, Paris.

From 1908 onwards sports, mainly hockey, tennis and swimming, began to be more important in school life, and emphasis began to be placed on study for examinations leading to careers for women. Inspection by the Scottish Education Department was applied for and soon the school was recognised as " efficient ", so that pupils could be presented for the Scottish Leaving Certificate Examinations.

Although the first World War brought many difficulties, St. Denis School moved to larger premises in Chester Street during April, 1915; and in April, 1932 it moved again to Ettrick Road, where the beautiful gardens afforded excellent facilities for children to play out-of-doors. At the same time St. Denis ceased to be a private or proprietary school, and became an independent school under the ownership of a private company and administered by a Council of Governors. During the second World War the school was evacuated to Drumlanrig Castle. In the post-war years it was obvious that considerable expansion both of the premises and of the scope of work must take place, and this has duly materialised. The school has doubled its roll, increased the number of its academic courses, and opened two newly built and well equipped laboratories to meet the increasing demands for courses in Science.

OTHER GIRLS' SCHOOLS

The city has many other independent day schools for girls, each with its own distinctive personality and attractions, but all conforming in the main to the same ideals and aims, and catering for the needs of broadly the same kinds of people.

The girls at these schools come mostly from well-to-do professional or business families. There is a traditional emphasis on the early study of French and later of other modern languages, while music, dancing, gymnastics and games are also given considerable weight. Religion too is often emphasised; and naturally the cultivation of character and manners is carefully fostered. But at the same time these schools increasingly give especial attention to girls who show a real desire for academic work and wish to prepare for the universities. Many of them have in recent years built new science laboratories for biology, physics and chemistry teaching:

in earlier decades they were sometimes content to stray little beyond the limits of " nature study."

As we should expect these schools vary considerably in size. Some—like St. Margaret's in the Newington district—have around 400 pupils on their roll: St. Margaret's has an age-range of 5–18 years and a small Nursery Department where boys, as well as girls, are accepted below the age of five. Others are comparatively small. Again, some cater principally for day-girls—Lansdowne House with some 280–290 pupils is an example—while others, like St. Hilary's, have 50 to 60 boarders and 250 or so day pupils. Esdaile School, formerly known as " The Ministers' Daughters' College ", was founded in 1863 for the particular benefit of the daughters of Church of Scotland ministers and Scottish university professors. Lansdowne House, which includes fencing among its sports, has especial links with the Scottish Episcopal Church. Cranley is notable for its music, its course in Russian, and VIth form reading wide enough to include Greek drama in translation and modern writing in French and English. St. Serf's (an old established school which has always prided itself on the diversity of its curriculum) like some others derives perhaps more from educational and social ideals than inherited religious tradition. But probably the individual character of each of these schools is to be detected rather by those who know them intimately than by casual observers: they are, as an Edinburgh educational expert once observed, like a band of sisters in a large and engaging family.

P.N.E.U. AND RUDOLF STEINER

Queen Margaret's P.N.E.U. School falls into another category together with the Rudolf Steiner School. Both are guided in their policies by the strongly held educational ideas of their founders, and are Edinburgh examples of a number of schools of those persuasions in various parts of the country. The former school—its initials stand for Parents' National Education Union, a movement founded in 1888—takes boys of five or six years age only, but girls from 14 to 17; while the latter—the only Scottish example of some 60 in various countries and six in the United Kingdom—is co-educational and has some 300 day pupils.

INDEPENDENT CO-EDUCATIONAL FEE-PAYING SCHOOLS

JOHN WATSON'S SCHOOL

The main school of this kind in Edinburgh is John Watson's School, a quite old charitable foundation, which has expanded and developed since the war and is now a direct grant school. It is situated in a pleasant district of Edinburgh, on the north-western outskirts of the city, and has a park of its own.

John Watson, from whom the school derives its name, was an Edinburgh Writer to the Signet, who died in 1762. He left the sum of £1,300 " in the sight of the Magistrates of Edinburgh to apply to such pious and charitable purposes as they shall think proper "; and within 16 years the two trustees, by whom this estate was administered, had increased the sum to nearly £5,000. The W.S. Society then became the Trustees, and under their skilful guidance the capital had by 1822 risen to £110,000.

After much deliberation it was decided to build a school for the education and maintenance of necessitous fatherless children between the ages of seven and 14 years. William Burn, a leading city architect who later designed the Edinburgh Academy, was commissioned to draw up plans for the school, which, when completed was of an elegant yet simple Grecian design, the building, with its Doric portico, corresponding in point of beauty with the nature of its surroundings. The school was then opened—in 1828—and for more than a century, including the happy years spent during the last war at Marchmont House in Berwickshire, has proved of inestimable benefit to children of professional and business men, whose widows have been left in straitened circumstances.

Admission to the school as Foundationers is obtained on the recommendation of a Commissioner of the Society of Writers to the Signet, and up to 1964, 2,028 boys and 840 girls had passed through the school as Foundationers, very many of whom have attained high positions in all walks of life.

In July, 1934 the Education Endowments Commission, after a thorough investigation into the nature and purposes of the school, drew up a scheme under which it was also opened to fee-paying pupils (boys and girls). In the last six years a " top and bottom " have been added to the school, and it is now possible for a child to enter at five years, complete a full education, and leave at 18 with a Scottish Certificate of Education.

The Endowment still remains vested in the Keeper and Commissioners of the Signet, Trustees of John Watson's Fund, who exercise a general supervision and control over the Endowment. The management of the school is in the hands of the Board of Directors appointed by the Governors, partly from their own number, partly from the City Education Committee, the Edinburgh Merchant Company, and the Former Pupils who are one of their old school's greatest assets since they contribute generously to school activities.

THE GRANGE HOME SCHOOL

Another interesting co-educational fee-paying establishment, with an international flavour, is the Grange Home School, a Registered Independent School in its own grounds which accommodates 30 boarders and approximately 90 day children from three to 11 years (boys to eight or nine years, and girls from three to 11). There are six classes: Nursery Group three to five years; two Kindergarten Classes five to seven; and three Junior classes seven to eleven. The children are taught by trained teachers and visiting staff take classes in music, painting, singing and dancing.

The school's chief aim is to provide a real home and a comprehensive primary education for those children whose parents reside abroad. Coloured children are welcomed both as boarders and day children; and these have recently included Ghanaians, Nigerians, Indians and Chinese.

THE BLIND AND THE DEAF

The Corporation as education authority makes provision for the schooling of the mentally and the physically handicapped; but in the city there are two schools, each with its own Board of Governors, one of which teaches the blind, the other the deaf. The Royal Blind School and Donaldson's School for the Deaf were originally established by private enterprise and charity, but now receive Government grants. Both have done pioneer work and are famed far beyond Edinburgh itself.

THE ROYAL BLIND SCHOOL

The Royal Blind School exists to meet the educational needs of those Scottish children who read with their fingers. It provides primary and comprehensive secondary education for them from the age of five until they enter on their chosen training for employment or their professional education.

As the School must needs be a boarding school, it is surely right that a child should be established as a member of his family before he must make the adjustment involved in being away from home for much of the year. As an essential part of such adjustment a child must be kept in the closest possible touch with his family by letter, by week-ends at home as frequently as age and distance permit, and by the attendance of his family at school entertainments and at Scout or Guide Camps. For those boys and girls approaching school-leaving age there is a period of living in the Boys', or the Girls', Hostel with consequent increase in privilege and personal independence. In the Opportunity Unit, at Muirburn Lodge, the child who has one or more further handicaps beyond his blindness finds himself a member of a smaller group, receiving even more individual attention to help him to give of his best; but this special group, by sharing in all possible out-of-school activities, is in touch with and a part of general school life.

In early 1963 the number of pupils was about 150; but if present trends continue the numbers may fall to 125 by 1970. Blind children are a small group, perhaps one in four to five thousand school children; so that only one school is required in Scotland. Classes are small, because pupils may join the school at any age of onset of handicap and, of course, they vary in ability and aptitude. This calls for a teaching staff of some 20 members covering the whole educational range and a house staff of similar size.

The school is governed by the Education Executive Committee of the Royal Blind Asylum and School. One half of this Committee are members of the Board of the Royal Blind Asylum and School; the other half are representatives of Scottish local authorities and other bodies concerned in the education and welfare of blind persons.

Historically, the Royal Blind Asylum and School is the result of the union of two organisations. The older, the Blind Asylum, was from 1793 concerned in the employment of blind people and from 1795 in methodically instructing young persons by almost purely oral methods; while the Edinburgh School for Blind Children was set up in 1835 to teach blind people to read using the special alphabet devised by its founder, James Gall. Then came the union—in 1876—a signal event marked by the school's entering into occupation of its building at Craigmillar Park where it is today.

By this time experience of a variety of embossed alphabets, culminating with that of Braille, had demonstrated that this system could, unlike all its predecessors, be easily written and as easily read by those persons who were no longer thirled to the idea that an embossed alphabet must be derived from Roman type. The new school, whose opening was marked by one of those exhibitions of military and masonic pomp that characterised the period, was originally a boarding school for some 50 children situated in the then rural suburb of West Craigmillar.

From almost the beginning selected pupils were trained in music and 30 years afterwards the association with Edinburgh University, which has continued unbroken to the present day, began. During the present century schools in Glasgow, Aberdeen and Inverness were closed and the roll of pupils steadily grew. In 1936 the Scottish Education Department recognised the ability of the blind child to profit by secondary education, and from that date the school assumed its present function of providing for blind children of all ages the type of education best suited to their needs. For the last 30 years the school has rarely been without one or more former pupils proceeding to graduation at Edinburgh University and twice as many have entered physiotherapy or other professional training. Today an increasing number of girls enter some type of clerical employment such as shorthand typing and telephone switchboard operating and a growing proportion of boys find a place in ordinary industry. However, so long as Scotland is dependent on the heavier industries for employment a majority of boys and a number of girls will seek employment in one or other of the crafts practised in the four large workshops for the blind in the cities of Scotland. It is an object of sober pride to those responsible for the conduct of the school that well over 90 per cent of pupils are placed in employment where as fully contributing and independent citizens they are carrying out the aspirations of those who founded the parent bodies so long ago in order to bring light into darkness.

It should be added here that the annual report of the Royal Blind Asylum and School, issued in Edinburgh during November, 1963, said that during the financial year it covered, the Scottish Braille Press had produced 157,643 magazines and pamphlets, 11,872 Braille volumes and 2,386 sheets of music and manuscript transcriptions—a most creditable achievement.

DONALDSON'S SCHOOL FOR THE DEAF

This school emerged, in 1938, from the amalgamation of two older schools in Edinburgh—the Royal Institution for the Education of Deaf and Dumb children situated in Henderson Row (founded 1810) and Donaldson's Hospital, situated at West Coates (founded 1850). The governing body constituted under the provisions of the Donaldson Trust Scheme comprises a number of life governors together with representatives elected by the Town Council of Edinburgh, the Church of Scotland, the Educational Institute of Scotland, the Scottish Association for the Deaf, Edinburgh University and the Association of County Councils.

This school provides full-time education for some 190–200 deaf children from the age of three to 16. In addition, a clinic started in 1954 offers a guidance service for very young deaf children. Pupils are accepted from any part of Scotland on application from local authorities and attend as day or as boarding pupils. Fees are charged, present figures being £190 per annum for boarding pupils and £105 per annum for day pupils. Scottish Education Department grants in respect of the children are paid to the school and not to local authorities.

The young children aged three to seven are taught at Henderson Row and then transfer to West Coates where they remain until they are 16. At both premises a major programme of internal reconstruction and the building of new classrooms was completed in 1961.

Classes in the school are small, averaging some 10 pupils per class. The staff of 24 full-time teachers includes a teacher of Art and a teacher of Technical Subjects. In addition, a full-time psychologist is employed and a number of part-time specialist teachers. Courses in Homecraft are provided for senior girls at the Edinburgh College of Domestic Science.

The curriculum approximates to that in a normal school but, as deafness acts as a barrier to normal linguistic development, progress in academic, as distinct from practical, subjects is at a slower pace than for hearing children. The school does not offer senior secondary courses, but pupils of high ability are considered, at the age of 12, for entry to two schools in England which provide such courses for deaf children.

At the age of 16 the children leave school and, with few exceptions, seek employment. In bygone days the deaf were thought to be fit for only a very restricted range of humble occupations. Nowadays pupils enter a wide variety of careers and show quite clearly that deaf people can make a worthy contribution to the life of the community.

CHAPTER 36

THE LOCAL AUTHORITY SCHOOLS

It now seems certain that Edinburgh's first educational establishment was that of the Abbey of Holyrood in the 12th century, and that in Leith school lessons were also given by monks in the preceptory of St. Anthony. Then came " vulgar " schools for the teaching of reading and writing—there were at least six of these according to the Town Council records for 1590—and " sang " schools, instituted no doubt for the training of choir boys.

THE ROYAL HIGH SCHOOL

The Royal High School traditionally dates back to King David I and the seminary attached to the Abbey of Holyrood (1128), and it remained within the patronage of the Abbey till after the Reformation. In 1531, Town Council records refer to the " High " School, then under its administration, and destined to have a new school building in 1578 in the garden of Blackfriars Monastery: the pediment of this remains incorporated in the present school building. Towards the end of the century King James VI of Scotland granted the school the royal favour, " Schola Regia Edinburgensis." Today the school colours, black and white, are the heraldic colours of Edinburgh, and the triple castellated tower of the school badge part of the city arms.

To the present building, designed by Hamilton on the Calton Hill in 1829, came 30 years later H.R.H. the Prince of Wales to study under the Rector, Dr. Schmitz. In 1903, as King Edward VII he renewed his acquaintance during a royal visit to Edinburgh, as other members of the Royal Family, with their special link, have done from time to time.

" One of the most interesting things about us," says a school authority, " is the roll of our former pupils. All our distinguished sons are too numerous to recount. But we can cite Sir Walter Scott, the poet Drummond of Hawthornden, George Borrow, James Boswell, Alexander Graham Bell the inventor of the telephone, three Lord High Chancellors of England, Archbishops of York and Canterbury, many Lord Provosts of Edinburgh and Moderators of the General Assembly of the Church of Scotland, Naismith the inventor of the steam-hammer, the Adams brothers and, let us whisper, Angus Buchanan who scored the first-ever rugby try for Scotland against England."

OTHER OLD SCHOOLS

Another old foundation, Leith Grammar School, came under the Kirk Session at the Reformation. It struggled on through many vicissitudes until in 1848 it passed to the Municipal Council. Today the ultimate outcome of this process of change is seen in the present Leith Academy which provides for its pupils a sound grounding in the basic secondary subjects and at the same time offers to those who can profit by it the chance of continuing their studies to university level. A succession of distinguished Rectors shaped the character of the school in the first half of the 20th century—men who stood fast by sound old Scottish principles rather than birling obediently to every wind of fashionable educational doctrine. Nevertheless there has been a steady growth in facilities for the study of scientific, commercial and technical subjects to an advanced level. A significant feature of this period has been not only the growth of clubs and societies—literary and debating, photographic and musical—but the mark made by Leith Academicals in war and in peace, in their professions and in sport. It is also noteworthy that the school's crest includes a black galley, two masted and with sails furled and red pennants flying signifying its connection through the centuries with the life and work of the sea port of Leith.

Another establishment with an interesting lineage is James Gillespie's High School for Girls.

James Gillespie, a prosperous Edinburgh tobacco and snuff merchant, left the greater part of his fortune for the erection and endowment of a hospital for aged men and women, and for a free school for boys. The hospital and school were built on the same site, and the school opened in 1803 with 65 boys and one master, whose salary was £65 per annum, and who served in this capacity for forty years. The school moved into new buildings on the same site in 1870, still an " elementary " school but with girls attending now as well as boys. Fees were then introduced, and the new system proved so popular that 1,000 boys and girls were enrolled. The Merchant Company of Edinburgh in turn took over the Gillespie Trust Fund, and the school flourished for the next 26 years mainly as a preparatory school for the Company's secondary schools. Then in 1904 the school developed into James Gillespie's Primary and Higher Grade School. In 1908, however, when expansion was necessary, the Gillespie Trust, accepted earlier by the Merchant Company, did not have sufficient means for this expense, and the school was handed over to the Edinburgh School Board. Subsequently—in 1914—the school moved into the present building on Bruntsfield Links previously occupied by Boroughmuir School. It amalgamated with Warrender Park School and younger children from the infant and junior departments attended; but it did not become a full secondary school until 1928 when it was so recognised by the Scottish Education Department. In 1929, Warrender Park School became James Gillespie's School for Boys, and it had no longer any connection with the girls' school, which as " James Gillespie's High School for Girls " became so big and successful that by 1963 it had a roll of 1,300 girls—500 in the primary department and 800 in the secondary department. Girls stay on in large numbers to complete six years in the secondary department and then proceed to Universities, Teacher Training Colleges, technical apprenticeships, nursing, Civil Service, and other training courses.

THE RISE OF THE SCHOOL BOARDS

In the 17th and 18th centuries, as we saw, great hospitals were established under private benefactions for the maintenance and education of poor and fatherless boys and girls, which led ultimately to an important group of modern secondary schools. But except in the High or Grammar School very little beyond the bare rudiments was taught and those mainly to boys: girls, at that time, were trained at home except for those sent to nunneries. The main preoccupation for girls seemed to be industrial training, and for them the higher branches of education were apparently considered unnecessary and even undesirable. Only after the extension of the franchise in 1867 did universal compulsory schooling seem to be a matter of national concern, and one which could no longer be left largely to voluntary effort. In 1872 the administration of education was transferred from the Church to the people acting through popularly elected School Boards.

Soon after the turn of the century in Scotland, when there was a rapidly increasing demand for " Higher Grade " education, the Edinburgh School Board founded Boroughmuir School (1904). Beginning with 600 post-primary pupils in a handsome, up-to-date building on Bruntsfield Links, the numbers were doubled within a few years. To accommodate the increasing roll the present school in Viewforth was opened in 1914.

With a roll that has fluctuated around 1,500, this large school has reflected the developing provision for secondary education during this century. It was one of the first free secondary schools, and is co-educational. The increasing tendency of pupils to continue at school to the completion of the Fifth or Sixth Year has resulted in a drastic reduction of First Year admissions; but the number of candidates presented for the Scottish Certificate of Education is probably the largest in the country—over 700 in a recent session. These developments have been accompanied by a widening of the school's curriculum and activities to embrace full provision in all departments—literary, scientific, artistic, technical and commercial—and by notable achievements in games and athletics.

About the same time similar provision emerged on the other side of the city in the shape of Broughton Higher Grade School. From 1909 until 1923 the school enjoyed a stable curriculum and during this period it placed more than 130 names on the open Bursary List at the University of Edinburgh and secured every major scholarship there in the faculties of arts, science, law and medicine. It provided four Professors at Cambridge, McGill (Canada), Northern Ireland and Liverpool and a fifth, both Professor and Principal, at Melbourne University, Australia. There has emerged also, it claims with some pride, five editors of important newspapers, half a dozen novelists, a major Scottish poet, Hugh MacDiarmid who also went to a Border school, and a Judge of the Court of Session, Lord Guthrie. In short the extension of secondary education " to the children of the industrial classes " has reaped a rich harvest, and will no doubt continue to do so; for the curriculum of the school, which keeps a steady roll of 850–900 pupils, today offers, in addition to the older, basic subjects, a wide choice in modern languages, biology, technical and commercial subjects.

In the early days both Boroughmuir and Broughton made a unique contribution to the academic training of intending teachers through provision for pupil teachers ranging up to 20 years of age or over, who attended in two shifts (morning and afternoon) on release from their Primary schools where they received practical training in the classrooms. In 1906 these arrangements gave place to the Junior Student system which was in force until 1925 when the training of teachers was undertaken solely by the Provincial Training Colleges.

Trinity Academy is about the same vintage, the first pupils being admitted in 1893. The furnishings included what was then the latest and the best voice tubes and electric bells—from headmaster's room to the classrooms—and also gas lighting and pitch pine dual desks at 14*s*. 3*d*. each. The cost of erection was £18,850, and the salary of the headmaster was £400 and that of the science master, £160.

Increases in the roll were met by temporary extensions which, alas, remained far beyond their allotted span until 1960 when the long awaited new building was able to provide modern classrooms, laboratories, technical department, gymnasia, library, music room and assembly hall. At present the Primary Department houses 540 children with a staff of 15 teachers and the Secondary Department, 800 pupils and 50 of a staff. Though now an Edinburgh school with pupils drawn from all parts of an expanding town, Trinity Academy still cherishes a local pride and thinks of itself as primarily a Leith School. It has no badge, no written motto: its distinctive monogram, it feels, is blazon enough, and its unwritten legend can be read in those ideals of service to the community which it strives to inculcate in succeeding generations.

At the other end of the coastal strip lies Portobello, proud of its Burgh Public School which at its opening in 1876 had 290 pupils. By 1881, however, this roll had grown to 700, with classes containing from 62 to 138 children. Then gradually this grave overcrowding was reduced by poor attendance and epidemics. It is interesting, incidentally, to discover that attendance was always low on Musselburgh Race Day for no other reason than the inability of the younger children to cross the High Street safely because of the horse drawn traffic!

Education was not of course free in those days and fees ranged from 1½*d*. per week for infants to 7*d*. in Standard Seven. By 1901 the higher grade department was established and, with retrogressions caused by lack of accommodation and changes in policy, it so expanded that today this school provides comprehensively for the secondary education of children in this district right up to the 6th year. As the building has however proved inadequate for modern requirements, a new school to accommodate more than 1,550 pupils was opened in 1964, and this has proved to be the most modern school building in Edinburgh—with a swimming pool, an eight-storey class room block with lifts each capable of transporting 30 pupils at a time, and with class rooms, laboratories and workshops all equipped with the latest type of equipment.

ROMAN CATHOLIC SCHOOLS

The Roman Catholic Church authorities took advantage of an option under the 1918 Education Act to transfer their schools to the local Education Authority, with safeguards in regard to religious education. The two main establishments so transferred were Holy Cross Academy, opened in 1907, and St. Thomas of Aquin's Secondary School, founded by the Sisters of Mercy in 1905.

Pressure on Holy Cross Academy was severe during the 1920s but since then improvements have been effected from time to time. At last however a new Primary Department for 560 pupils has come about and also extensions to the present Secondary School, designed to provide adequately for 750 pupils. The Academy has taken full advantage of current study and experiment in teaching methods and curriculum content in the primary schools of the city including science, mathematics and modern languages. Visual aids, school broadcasts and televised lessons are regular features especially in Science, Geography, History, appreciation of Art, Music and Literature, and Current Affairs. There is a school orchestra, and tape recorders are used not only for musical training but also to correct faulty vowel sounds. The school library holds 7,000 volumes.

The school building of St. Thomas of Aquin's began in two or three 19th century houses in Chalmers Street, but since then extensive reconstruction has resulted in up to date class rooms, laboratories, homecraft rooms, assembly halls and the other necessary adjuncts of a modern secondary school such as a gymnasium, dining hall, music room, and a library with several thousand volumes. An outstanding feature of the school is the number of works executed by modern Scottish artists: these include carved stone panels, murals, sculpture groups, plaques and pictures.

The Catholic population in Edinburgh has been increasing, and as the need for a new secondary school is apparent the Education Committee have planned such an establishment for the west of the city to be known as St. Andrew's. In the meantime the nucleus of this school is being housed in temporary premises. Approval of the Corporation's plan for a new Roman Catholic primary school and two non-Catholic schools of the same kind was made known by the Secretary of State for Scotland in the spring of 1964.

IN THE HOUSING ESTATES

In the great new housing estates, modern, well equipped secondary schools have also arisen, and these are already building up their own traditions and history of achievement; so that in time the names of Liberton, Gracemount, Firrhill, Forrester and Craigroyston should live in the memories of thousands of Edinburgh children as warmly as the names of the older and renowned schools remain in the affection of earlier generations. More about this comes later in this chapter.

THE CITY'S NEEDS

One measure of the task of educational provision is the total child population of the city. A tally made in the 1962–3 session showed that in schools under the municipal authority (the " public " schools as they are called in Scotland) there were 64,959 children. These were enrolled in establishments from nursery school stage to senior secondary, and another 13,800 children were catered for in schools under other management.

The following table gives some idea of the structure of the public school system of the city:[1]

TABLE 68

	Number (As at August 1962)	*Roll*
Nursery Schools and Classes	25	1,261
Primary Schools	85	41,064
Secondary Schools (5 with Primary Departments)	24	21,544
Special Schools and classes for handicapped children including classes in hospitals and children taught at home	15	1,090

Included in the above are schools for Roman Catholic and for Episcopalian children, opened in accordance with the 1918 Act which ensured full and equal share of secular provision together with the continuance of religious rights.

The Education (Scotland) Act of 1946, while it consolidated and strengthened trends which were then evident in regard to normally endowed children, was a charter for those who were handicapped. The Act introduced the concept of special educational treatment for any child deprived of normal mental or bodily faculties; and it recognised for the first time as coming within this ambit those children who are socially maladjusted or emotionally disturbed. This gave an impetus to the development of special day schools for handicapped children and the tuition at home of children unable to attend school. It also led to the establishment of a child guidance service for the psychological study of associated problems, and the provision of advice to teachers and parents and of treatment in conjunction with the national health service and other agencies. In 1960 a day school for children with moderate maladjustments was established.

There is nowadays an encouraging new outlook in regard to the education of handicapped children. The general aim is to get as near to the education of a normal child as is possible; and to this end teachers of handicapped children are specially trained and classes are smaller. The basic essentials of an ordinary child's education are given, but at a slower pace and with much more practical and creative work; and indeed the standard of art and craft often astonishes visitors. The visible evidence of improvement and the growing confidence of their children is a comfort to parents and improves relations between home and school. Nearly all

[1] A full list of schools under the management of Edinburgh Corporation Education Committee is to be found in the *Edinburgh and Leith Post-Office Directory*.

the children manage to get jobs and the fact that they are accepted by society gives a boost to their self-respect.

The percentage of attendance of children at city schools has risen from nearly 81 in 1872 to about 94 per cent in the early '60s. The proportion of children staying on voluntarily beyond the statutory leaving age of 15 has also been rising steadily. While many social, economic and health factors contribute to these desirable trends, they are in the main a measure of the increasing attractiveness of modern schooling and of the satisfaction which it brings to children and their parents.

HOW EDUCATION IS ADMINISTERED

The disappearance of the old School Board became inevitable as the provision of education became more complex and costs rose, and the task clearly had to be placed on broader shoulders. Thus in 1918 control was vested in Education Authorities specially elected for the purpose, but in 1929 administration passed to the local authority which took as its province all services for the area including education. In recognition of its importance, however, Parliament ordained that education in the four city and 31 county areas of Scotland should be administered by statutory Education Committees of special composition. So in the city of Edinburgh today, educational affairs are controlled by a Committee of 20 elected members of the town council and 9 members representing various interests—the University Court, the Educational Institute of Scotland, and the various churches.

The Committee is advised by a Director of Education while an administrative staff carries out the executive work arising from policy decisions. The Committee and its officials do not work in isolation. Consultation has grown, and today there are recognised channels through which the views of headmasters and teachers, and of parents, employers and other trade representatives, can be made known.

It is the task of the Education Committee, which draws upon the help of other civic departments particularly in matters affecting law, finance, school buildings and child health, to secure the climate in which the education of children can thrive. This involves not only well-designed and equipped school buildings and well chosen staffs, but also sympathy, mutual confidence, and effective supervision and guidance throughout the great design.

The magnitude of this role and the variety of persons required to minister to the schools can be judged by the following staff figures (1963):

TABLE 69

Section	*Men*	*Women*	*Total*
Day School teachers and other professional staff	863	1,820	2,683
Teachers in day Institutes	132	52	184
School clerical Assistants	—	153	153
Janitors and cleaners and school meals staffs	229	1,893	2,122
Administrative staff	72	64	136
	1,296	3,982	5,278

There is also a notable trend towards providing certain facilities for neighbouring counties in the south-east region, particularly in regard to handicapped children, psychological services and technical education and training, which the more sparsely populated areas find increasingly difficult to sustain on their own financial resources.

THE NEW FABRIC

There is no better indication of social progress than the housing of the people. Since the war the Corporation have rehoused almost a fifth of the city's families. So in the great new housing estates on the outskirts of Edinburgh one finds, besides good well-lit roads, efficient transport, open spaces, shops and churches, also new schools where children can be cared for from tender age and educated for their life work.

The Education Committee have carried out a formidable programme to meet the upward surge of population, complicated as it is by the unevenness of the birth-rate since the end of the second World War. A " wave " or " bulge " of thousands of additional children passing through the primary schools dislocated class organisation and demanded temporary expedients. There is evidence too that instead of falling to pre-war levels the birth-rate is again rising.

Since the war the Education Committee, by 1963, had not only erected 26 primary schools, seven secondary schools, two nursery schools and one special school but had arranged for major adaptations at 22 primary and seven secondary schools along with 135 temporary class room units. These new schools have naturally demanded careful thought and consultation between educationists and architects and builders. They are places of good design as well as of utility. Light and airy, they are congenial in size, design and decoration to the young and growing child. They are attractively equipped and are provided with spacious surrounding for play, in vivid contrast to the all too many schools in the older parts of the city with their general lack of amenities.

In view of the Corporation's decision on housing policy, particularly to replace pre-fabricated houses by permanent houses and to re-develop the older areas, the Education Committee in the early '60s reviewed the needs for primary, secondary and special school accommodation over the whole city for the next 20 years.

" Where old schools cannot be economically and satisfactorily adapted they are to be replaced ", said a leading authority at the time, " so that the long term programme of new schools, shall consist of 39 primary, seven secondary and six special schools. In most cases new sites will be necessary."

Notable among the new secondary schools are one in Barnton to replace the Royal High School buildings (for regrettably its historically interesting site at Calton Hill is too small for expansion), and a new James Gillespie's Primary and Secondary establishment within the walled enclosure of the former Warrender estate close by its present location.

THE SCHOOLS IN ACTION

The scheme of education for the city is an unpretentious looking document. Nevertheless it is a social contract guaranteeing to parents that adequate provision will be made for their children. The translation of this into practice constitutes the work of the schools, which is worth studying from the youngest stage to those on the brink of higher education of one kind or another.

The Nursery School is so much the natural extension of the home for instilling good habits and promoting good health, for the early detection of crippling conditions and for the beginning of social training and formal education that one day it may be the first stage in the education of every child. In the meantime, because of more pressing tasks, provision has been made for a bare five per cent of the age groups affected, (from two to five years). Sites for something like 40 new nursery schools have, however, been reserved.

The Primary School is where children from five to about 12 years of age acquire the tools of communication and learning, and where other needs of growing children are met. It is here therefore that pace and rhythm are adjusted to the changing phases of child life. The fundamental importance of good physical and emotional health is recognised in the establishment of child guidance in clinic and school with its preventive work and adjustment of learning disabilities. Edinburgh indeed has been in the van in providing tutorial classes in primary schools, where difficulties can be smoothed out before the children are returned to the ordinary stream; or, if more deep seated causes are detected, appropriate treatment can be given in co-operation with other agencies with which the child guidance service is in touch. During 1961–2 no fewer than 2,500 children in primary schools were helped in this way. As a measure of the general work in guidance there were also during that session, 6,800 diagnostic and treatment interviews.

The most significant developments in recent years have been the increase in group methods of teaching; the adoption in practically all the primary schools of the Cuisenaire method of teaching arithmetic, which is concerned more with number concept than with the rapid acquisition of computational accuracy, and the experimental introduction of Science with simple apparatus. Boys and girls can now learn that Science is not something remote but an activity through which they can discover the world in which they live and one in which they can participate with enjoyment and a sense of achievement. Experiments have also been started in the primary schools to determine the age at which the study of modern languages, particularly on a conversational basis, can begin.

Transfer to Secondary Schools. When children reach the last year of the primary course class-work is assessed, verbal reasoning tests applied and the teachers' opinions sought, so as to guide parents as to the kind of secondary studies best suited to their children's abilities and needs. In 1962–3, the number of children dealt with between 11 and 13 years old was 5,633, the average age at transfer being 12 years 4 months.

Secondary Courses. Secondary education is a stage in the education of every child. A variety of courses is provided for children with different capabilities; for the kind of education suited to the intellectually gifted is quite uncongenial to the more practically minded who form the bulk of the school population. So there have evolved two streams of three-year and five-year courses which differ in character and aim. Some people fear that the one type of course is inferior to the other, and demand comprehensive schools to which all children of a neighbourhood shall go after the primary stage. Many experiments are afoot therefore to try to meet public feeling without endangering the purpose and success of senior secondary schools in dealing with the able minority upon whose full development a great deal depends.

In Edinburgh a variation of the comprehensive system is being tried out in certain segments of the city. Common secondary school education is provided until age 14 and pupils of proved academic bent are transferred thereafter to senior secondary schools. The experiment promises well: the presence of an academic stream in junior secondary schools has stimulated teaching and has raised the tone of these schools. Developments are also afoot to bring the three year junior secondary courses into closer accord with the world outside the school.

The changing pattern of our international relationships has brought a sense of urgency to the need to raise our standard of skill in the use of modern languages, particularly in spoken communication. So today there are experiments in the use of audio-visual aids, consisting of native speakers recorded on magnetic tape synchronised with illustrative film strips. The resulting achievement in vocabulary and patterns of speech has been remarkable. For the older secondary pupils and adults language laboratories have been installed, which allow guided individual approach to the mastery of spoken language; and furthermore there is a newcomer in the field of modern languages in day schools. This is Russian which is now being offered in all senior secondary schools as staff becomes available.

In the secondary school the effect of modern scientific advance is no less marked. The extension of the frontiers of the sciences takes place with incredible speed; and every year brings a host not only of new techniques but of new concepts. The implications of this for the science curriculum are far-reaching. Nowhere are these more important than in the Scottish Certificate of Education courses which lead to further education in technical colleges and universities. As a consequence changes are being made in the requirements for the Certificate, to allow new forms of syllabus geared to contemporary thought in physics and chemistry to be introduced. The new syllabi are to be available as alternatives to the existing ones. The response of the teachers to the new proposals is so favourable that it looks as if the new syllabus in physics, the first to be discussed, will in fact supplant the present one. There seems little doubt that these developments are but the beginnings of considerable change in the content of science curricula.

Examinations. In 1962 the Scottish Leaving Certificate was replaced by the Scottish Certificate of Education and a new ordinary grade introduced. This allows a pupil, after four year's secondary study, to gain a certificate of value for entry to a variety of employments and to the intermediate stages of technical and commercial education.

The countrywide increase in the numbers present for the Scottish Certificate Examinations is not merely parallelled but surpassed in Edinburgh. This trend is likely to continue since, in 1963, there were 1,842 candidates in the fourth year for the Ordinary Grade and 1,413 candidates who will have completed at least five years of the secondary course.

Not only are Higher Grade papers being retained but a new Advanced Grade is being introduced. Some are beginning to think that for the academic pupil there is a growing danger of too much concentration on examinations, for as yet sixth form work is not strongly established in the sense of being a period for consolidation, the development of personal interests and preparation of the individual in methods of study.

THE WIDER OUTLOOK

Schooling has been criticised in the past for concerning itself too much with the formal side of education. There is now a full realisation that education must cover the present needs of young people in the formative period of their lives. Nothing shows better this wider concept than the development in the city schools of such creative subjects as the following:

Music. Visiting specialist teachers are laying sound foundations in primary schools in choral work and more pupils are taking Music in the leaving certificate examination. The last few years have seen the formation of brass bands as an extra-curricular interest. Active music-making with violin, viola and 'cello has been introduced as part of the school work in 26 primary schools to the enrichment of their cultural life; and as these pupils move into secondary schools the standard should rise and allow the establishment of school orchestras.

Art and Craft. A generation ago the aim in school was to train children to represent objects pictorially as their teachers taught them. Today, children are encouraged to create and express their own experience and to draw and paint their mental images in their own way. A closer association is developing between the teaching of art and crafts. This extends the child's sensibility to beauty of form and gives satisfaction in the use of a wider range of materials in sculpture, modelling, pottery and weaving. And all this in turn should make him realise the relation of good design to everyday life.

Technical Subjects. There has been a rapid expansion in technical subjects in secondary schools during the last two decades. Boys are now leaving school with a considerable measure of skill in the use of wood, metals and plastics and in technical drawing in three dimensions. In these ways the day school is preparing for further studies leading to the National Certificate in technology and in craft. Courses have been arranged for teachers to help to keep them abreast of changes in industry.

Home-Craft. The teaching of sewing, cookery and laundry has been transformed in the last 30 years because of changes in the way people live and the many modern gadgets in their homes. Originally these subjects were thought of as something only for girls intending to enter domestic service. But war conditions obliged many women to master the necessary arts for running their homes themselves; and this gave an impetus to the teaching of housewifery and mothercraft in schools. As soon as the basic knowledge is mastered the assignment method is introduced so as to give girls experience in planning their own work. It may be necessary to change the needlework curriculum because attractive factory-made garments are making home-dressmaking uneconomical. Instruction must keep abreast of new products and appliances as they appear on the market. The growing habit of combining marriage with a job implies the sharing of household work by husband and wife: an experimental course in home-craft for boys is proving its worth.

Physical Education. The outstanding change in physical education in primary schools has been a freer method of teaching which allows individuals to work at their own natural rhythm without the formalism of group instruction. Inevitably this has made for more informality in secondary schools also, particularly for girls.

Organised games and athletics now play a much greater part than formerly, and performance and enjoyment have gained from expert coaching. Swimming has always been fostered in Edinburgh schools, as we can see from a recent good average year—1960—when attendances for instruction numbered 159,859, and 7,400 certificates of proficiency were awarded. Set dances too are included in the syllabus, along with a scheme of creative movement based on various themes.

New Tools. Changes in emphasis have seen the introduction of various kinds of modern aids—new tools to enliven and enrich the old job of teaching, like films, tape recorders, micro-projectors, radio and television. There is also an experimental approach to programmed learning by using machines and programmed texts, to say nothing of organised use of the rich storehouses of teaching material in museums and galleries. History, nature study, science and the arts are covered, with visits and lecture-demonstrations for 15,000 pupils annually and school clubs and societies which provide valuable supplemental educational experience.

Schools are in fact reaching out beyond their gates for inspiration through educational journeys at home and abroad. Children are given a valuable social experience of living communally in the National Camps, attended by about 2,000 children from 40 or so schools each year, at Glenmore Lodge—nature's classroom in the Cairngorm mountains—at the National Recreation Centre at Inverclyde and at the Moray Sea School. In these places they often discover unsuspected strengths in themselves and develop qualities of initiative, courage and resourcefulness. Edinburgh children also eagerly take part in a venture reserved before the war for the pupils of the fee-paying schools—school cruises in the *Dunera* and *Devonia*, ships which combine in their voyages schooling and the enrichment of foreign travel.

The Place of The Teacher. However important the environment the most vital factor is of course the quality of the teaching staff. Scarcity of teachers is a national threat to efficiency and to new educational developments. Despite the difficulties, however, school staffs in city schools have risen steadily since 1938 and the pupil-teacher ratio has improved, though the rapid turnover of staff in secondary schools is perturbing. On the brighter side, the number of married women teachers returning to service after their family responsibilities are eased is noticeably rising. There exists between Education Committee and school staffs machinery for consultation upon conditions of service, and upon professional matters of organisation, curriculum and equipment of schools.

THE HEALTH OF THE SCHOOL CHILD

A headmaster remarked recently that half of his forenoon was taken up by school doctors, the X-ray unit, child guidance staff and youth employment officers, and by making arrangements for children to attend aurist and dentist: he was impressed by the variety of services, medical and educational, which assisted in the upbringing of children.

The school of today is indeed a social as well as an educational instrument. Because of confidence between teacher and child the spectacular improvements in social conditions and in the health and welfare of the community have been facilitated by the influence exercised and the examples set in the classroom. Their effect on family life is enormous but little recognised.

Nowhere is this more striking than in regard to health. The 1872 Education Act did nothing to ensure that children should be in a fit condition to receive education. An investigation into the health of school children in Edinburgh and Aberdeen, which revealed a staggering amount of disease and defect, was largely responsible for medical inspection becoming part of the national system of education in 1908. Five years later School Boards were empowered to provide medical treatment just as they already had to provide food and clothing in cases of necessity. Improvements in housing and other social ameliorations, and the steady rise in the standard of living, have virtually revolutionised the situation.

Ringworm, for which Edinburgh had to keep a complete school in 1912 for segregating child sufferers, had by 1938 disappeared. At medical inspections in 1912, 35 per cent of girls had nits in their hair; in 1960 the percentage was 2·2.

There has been as striking a change in serious illness. Chronic middle-ear disease, for instance, which claimed 15 per thousand in 1912, dropped in the same period to four per thousand. There has, indeed, been a fall in all types of serious defect with the exception of poliomyelitis and congenital deformities. Here the number of sufferers has been maintained because more premature children are born alive and kept alive, and the incidence of such defects is particularly heavy in the premature. Children found to suffer from bad nutrition numbered 20 per 10,000 in 1912, and in 1960 one per 10,000. A comparison of heights and weights between 1907 and 1960 is particularly illuminating:

	Heights		*Weights*	
	1907	*1960*	*1907*	*1960*
13 year old *boys*	56·3 ins.	60·5 ins.	79·2 lbs.	99·8 lbs.
12 year old *girls*	56·8 ins.	60·17 ins.	80·5 lbs.	103·4 lbs.

Some of the credit for improvement in nutrition must be given to school meals: a bottle of the best grade of milk is given free of charge to every child daily, and a meal to all who desire it at the bare cost of the ingredients. Only scarcity of kitchens and dining rooms has prevented the daily meal from becoming a part of the educative process, provided in the same way as books and all the other equipment of a child's education. A small boy when asked what he liked best in school replied " the dinners ", and there are certainly plenty of them; for each year more than 12 million bottles of milk and nearly five million lunches are distributed in Edinburgh schools, a catering business in itself and a revolution in social conscience and wisdom.

The school health service has not been content to deal with the discovery and the remedying of defects. It has become the foremost agency in preventive medicine. Vaccination against infectious disease began in the schools in 1924. The figures for diphtheria bear testimony to the worth of these precautions:

	% children vaccinated	*Number of cases of diphtheria*	*Number of deaths*
1934 (earliest year giving figures)	10%	544	27
1960	88%	1	0

The search for unsuspected pulmonary tuberculosis has been strenthened by the introduction of a simple skin test which picks out children who have been in contact with the disease. They are then examined by the mobile X-ray units which visit the schools. Among 9,257 children thus tested in 1960 fifteen cases of the disease were found.

Vaccination against poliomyleitis was made available in 1956 to younger children in primary schools and to all school age groups in 1959. By 1960, 79 per cent of the school population had been vaccinated. As for defects in children's teeth these still give ground for concern.

EDUCATION FOR WORK AND LEISURE

At the turn of the century technical skills were largely learned in the factory, workshops and office. The art and craft of a task were all that mattered; and there was little study of any principles underlying the process. Since then standardisation and the growth of machine methods have brought education into partnership with industry in the training of skilled workers.

Some two-thirds of our children leave school before their 16th birthday; and to take 1960 again as a good average year 35 per cent entered apprenticeships and learnerships. As increased numbers of craftsmen and technicians are called for, the " bulge " offers a challenge and an opportunity to make the most of our human material.

Apprenticeships normally begin at 16 years of age. In Edinburgh the transitional year after leaving day school can be spent in pre-apprenticeship courses for the engineering and building trades and the catering industry. Stress is laid not only on training boys as better craftsmen but on their preparation as young citizens. Preliminary nursing courses and courses for nursery staff are available for girls in the largest college of its kind in Great Britain. Intensive day Commercial Courses are meeting a keen demand.

In this country vocational training of young workers on one day a week is not yet compulsory, but since the late '50s the number of young people released voluntarily for this purpose has increased in Edinburgh from some 150 to more than 3,500. This is, however, only one-fifth of those who could benefit if all employers were equally enlightened and co-operative.

Further education is therefore mainly carried on in the evening schools. Some 50 years ago there were 10,000 evening students in the city: in 1960–1 there were more than 23,000, who put in more than one and a quarter million hours of attendance over a range of 407 separate subjects including art, commerce, technology, literature, languages, music, drama, physical education, the domestic arts and so on. Such a choice is offered that it includes subjects which some might consider too frivolous for a public service. For instance, there is fly-tying; but this may perhaps claim respectability through the writings of Isaak Walton, and golf might likewise come under the cloak of a cultural pursuit because of the devotion of James IV and other Stuart kings to the royal and ancient game. The work in further education, it should be noted here, is considerably helped by an Advisory Council which has functioned since 1909.

There was necessarily much improvisation in accommodation during and between the two world wars. The Education Committee accordingly decided to replace their stop-gap measures by building several large modern colleges. The first is the Napier Technical College (described in a later chapter). The next is a College for advanced studies in Commerce, and lastly it was decided to build the first of four district technical colleges on a site at Crewe Toll: these will feed not only the more advanced central establishments but will also meet the more general needs of boys and girls as the part time education of young workers increases.

In 1958 the Youth Employment Service celebrated its jubilee, for it was in January, 1908, the former School Board instituted an information and employment department, probably the first in the country. Two years later the Board of Trade opened its first labour exchange in Edinburgh; and from then onwards a joint scheme for juveniles operated until 1950 when the Education Committee assumed responsibility for the service. The main purposes are to give vocational guidance to boys and girls seeking employment on leaving school, to advise on further studies, and to keep in touch with the young people until they reach 18 years of age. The service is linked with careers masters and mistresses in secondary schools. For the year ended 30th September, 1962, 6,481 boys and girls were interviewed at school and at the central office. The Committee is much concerned at the lack of suitable craft apprenticeships for the increasing number of boys leaving school. It is evident that much wider considerations lie ahead in regard to methods of training skilled workers as technological advances change industry fundamentally.

Closer co-operation between employers, trade unions and education committees is essential for action on a broad front. Apprenticeship training is still too much regarded from the standpoint of the length of time to be served rather than from that of the techniques to be learned or the quality of craftsmanship to be attained.

WHAT IT COSTS

More than one-third of every pound taken from the pockets of the ratepayers in the city goes to run the educational service. Over a recent span of 25 years the gross expenditure of the Education Committee has risen from £1,106,000 to £7,458,000 in 1962–3. The main items were as follows:

	1938–9	*1962–3*
Day School teachers' salaries	£574,000	£3,313,000
Books, apparatus and stationery in day schools	12,000	208,000
School meals	18,000	651,000
Further education including technical and leisure time provision	56,300	470,300

Most striking of all has been the increase in bursaries and grants for young people to take advantage of opportunities of higher education without hardship to themselves or their parents; this absorbed a mere £7,678 in 1939–40 but showed a phenomenal rise to £316,769 two decades later. The bulk of this assistance had gone in the past to the lower income groups, but recent changes in the scale of parental contributions favoured middle-class families who, at the present scale of taxation, are finding it increasingly difficult to support more than one member of the family through college or university.

The scale of grant from national sources towards local educational expenditure advanced in like degree from £494,781 in 1938–9 to £3,459,328 in 1958–9. In the following year the basis of grant aid changed from specific grants for different local services to a general grant fixed for a period of two or three years and based on such factors as total population, children of school age, etc.: the application of this new grant is a matter for each local authority. It is therefore no longer possible to say exactly what is received by way of aid towards the gross cost of the educational service.

Formidable as all these figures appear they are modest indeed when spread over the number of children they benefit, and they are fruitful almost beyond calculation as a national investment. Nevertheless, the burden of sustaining and developing the public services is increasing alarmingly. Even the largest local authorities are well nigh crushed by the weight of their building programmes for houses and schools and the running costs of such an expanding service as education.

THE WAY AHEAD

Education is not a visionary speculation but an important public service. It cannot fail to take note of the society which it serves and the changes and trends within it.

A long road has been traversed between the Education Act of 1872 and the Act of 1946. The first was designed to ensure a degree of literacy—the three Rs—among the masses; but the emphasis of the second was on three As—on education for every child according to his age, aptitude and ability. As for the future, the rapidity of technological advance and scientific discovery is probably the touchstone to the changes in the aims and content of schooling which lie immediately ahead for Education has been overtaken by an expansion of knowledge that demands a drastic change in outlook. No longer can the education of children mean the imparting of a static body of facts: rather must it become the training and equipping of minds to achieve flexibility, adaptability and an openness to new ideas and new developments. In particular the approach to the teaching of science and of mathematics will require to be changed radically. There will have to be the utmost flexibility of school time-tables; the present almost rigid demarcation of subjects must disappear; and it will be vital to come to terms with examinations to prevent them from imposing their pattern upon teacher and child.

To achieve all this every part of the educational system must become acquainted with the aims and methods of every other part. In particular the day school must find a bridge across the present gulf between it and the technical college and other places of higher learning, as well as finding a partnership with the work-a-day world so as to give knowledge and training to the whole mass of young people with a continuity and a directness of aim and purpose that seemed to many woefully absent in the early 1960s. The vocational element must be made educationally respectable and fruitful.

It is against this background of a reformed and revitalised educational system that the whole range of modern aids must be assessed, each taking its place and being deployed by the teacher to make his work more productive. The aim must be to communicate ideas and give the satisfaction of discovery and personal achievement.

Closed circuit television will of course render obsolete much existing practice, and mechanical devices will more and more relieve the teacher of the drudgery of repetitive work and the routine testing of acquired knowledge and information, thus leaving time for that contact of mind which is of the true nature of education and which alone can ensure the ascendancy of the human spirit over the machine. As for the library this will become the power-house of every school; not just a repository for books but for materials of every kind, written or visual or recorded in sound, upon which young people can draw for stimulation, guidance and the extension of their experience into realms of which we at present have little conception.

CHAPTER 37

TECHNICAL AND VOCATIONAL TEACHING

WE have traced the road which Edinburgh's young people follow from primary to secondary education and thence, if they are gifted academically, to the university. But these last are a small proportion of the total. Many others go from school into a trade apprenticeship—in which case they may attend day-release or evening classes—or else take some other form of higher technical or vocational training. Again, there are many who return after an interval of years to take evening classes run by the Corporation, the Workers' Educational Association, or the University's Department of Extra-Mural Studies. So let us now look at the wide range of further education available in the city's various colleges and institutions—from those which train teachers, engineers, brewers, and textile designers, say, to those which train the typists who serve them.

THE HERIOT-WATT UNIVERSITY

THE SCHOOL OF ARTS

The intellectual renaissance which swept Europe and America in the late 18th and early 19th centuries brought many changes in the educational pattern. It seems natural therefore that in 1821 a School of Arts and Mechanics' Institute—the first of its kind and destined to become a university a century and a half later—should have been founded in Edinburgh with the express purpose of holding evening classes in the principles of science in order to educate young artisans unable to attend full-time courses.

The first humble premises occupied by the School of Arts were in Niddry Street, but after a time the school was moved to a building rented in Adam Square at the corner of the South Bridge. Leonard Horner, F.R.S., a native and citizen of Edinburgh for many years, is recognised as its founder. He was also one of the founders of Edinburgh Academy and became Principal of University College, London in 1836.

That the first classes established in the Edinburgh School of Arts were in Chemistry and Mechanical or Natural Philosophy, followed soon by Mathematics and later Mechanical Drawing, is a sign of singular understanding by the promoters; for these fundamental subjects have been, and continue to be, the basic subjects on which have been built the courses of study in day and evening classes. The organisation of a library at the very commencement of the project, also showed remarkable foresight. But the whole venture was so commendable that it was quickly emulated elsewhere—in Glasgow, for instance, Manchester, Aberdeen, Dundee, Bristol, and many other cities.

THE WATT INSTITUTION AND SCHOOL OF ARTS

In 1824 a group of influential citizens led by Henry Cockburn, later Lord Cockburn, decided to erect as a memorial to the great James Watt, an " architectural edifice " for the accommodation of the School of Arts. The Directors of the school themselves contributed generously to the fund raised for this purpose, but even by 1851 the money was insufficient for a new building. So instead the funds were used to purchase the premises then occupied and also to erect a monument to James Watt in the square outside the school. At the same time the name of the institution was changed to " The Watt Institution and School of Art."

In 1871 the old building in Adam Square was pulled down and arrangements were made for the transfer of the school—during the winter of 1873–4—to its present situation in Chambers Street.

As the years passed by additional classes had been added to the curriculum—English Language and Literature (1837), arithmetic and French (1843), physiology (1863), German (1866), botany (1870), geology (1872), Latin (1874), Greek (1875), biology, freehand drawing, theory of music, history and economic science (1877). Even Sanskrit and Hindustani were on the programme in 1866.

THE HERIOT-WATT COLLEGE

With the continued need for the expansion of technical education, the Governors were forced in time to seek help from the large Educational Trusts in the city. This led in 1885 to an amalgamation of the endowments of the Watt Institution with that of George Heriot's Hospital, and the management was transferred to the Governors of George Heriot's Trust. In this scheme provision was made for the maintenance, improvement and extension of the Watt Institution as a College providing technical and general education for the industrial classes of both sexes. Hereafter the institution was called The Heriot-Watt College.

With commendable zeal the new Governors set about expanding the development of evening classes in art, trade, technical and commercial subjects and also founded a Day Technical College for students wishing to obtain a sound technical training on University lines. The premises in Chambers Street were enlarged to provide suitable laboratories, classrooms and workshops. A Principal and Professors of Mechanical Engineering, Chemistry, Physics and Electrical Engineering were appointed.

In 1902 there was another great step forward when the Scottish Education Department granted the rank of *Central Institution* to the College under the Scottish Continuation Class Code of 1901. By this decree certain established colleges " which had already an outstanding record of success, were well staffed and well equipped for a considerable variety of work and were situated at the natural centres of population" were "allowed to proceed on lines of their own in the hope that they would develop into institutions worthy to rank, not in numbers of students but in quality and advancement of work, with the best of their kind in any other country."

At this time also the long association of the College with the University in the training of engineers and chemists began under an agreement giving recognition to courses conducted in the College. Simultaneously the Governors decided that the College Diploma, gained after three or four years' full-time study in the various technological departments, should carry the title of Associateship of the Heriot-Watt College. Since that date this award has gained wide recognition until today it is regarded by the various professional institutions, by the Scottish Education Department, the Department of Scientific and Industrial Research, the Ministry of Labour and National Service as of University Degree standard.

A Department of Mining, established in 1913, became a joint Department with the University in 1928 by the endowment of the Hood Chair of Mining, and new buildings were erected in the Grassmarket with suitable laboratories, lecture rooms, and drawing offices. A Mine Rescue Station was also established in 1915 and here much pioneer research was conducted into safety in mines. Technical Mycology was added to the curriculum in 1905 to provide for the training of brewers. In 1921, Pharmacy day classes were commenced under the auspices of the Chemistry Department, and in 1925 the Royal Dispensary School of Pharmacy was amalgamated with the College Courses.

By the late '20s the continued expansion of technological education and the cost involved therein became too heavy a burden for the Governors of the Heriot's Trust to bear simultaneously with the upkeep of George Heriot's School, and an independent Board of Governors for the College was instituted by the promotion of the George Heriot's Trust Order Confirmation Act (1927). Since then the Board of Governors has had 31 members representing the Corporation of the City and its Education Committee, George Heriot's Trust, the University, the Royal Society of Edinburgh, the Chamber of Commerce and Manufacturers, industry (both employers and trade unions), and the County Education Committees.

RECENT PROGRESS

In the last few years the Heriot-Watt College has made notable strides. In 1933 an Order in Council by King George V approved its affiliation with the University. It was also in the '30s that the College buildings were extended, as they were again in the '50s, when the last extension of the Chambers Street premises was opened by H.R.H. the Duke of Edinburgh (1958). But all through the '50s and '60s the incessant growth was maintained not only through the acquisition of the old Corn Exchange in the Grassmarket but through the introduction of new professorial chairs and courses, a College Fellowship, special developments in the departments of Pharmacy, Printing and Brewing and Applied Biochemistry, and the establishment jointly with Edinburgh University of the new Department of Chemical Technology and Chemical Engineering. There have been many other additions to the curriculum ranging from gas and electrical engineering to mining and applied mathematics; and a Sirius computer has been installed in the mathematical department. The College evening classes too have continued to attract large numbers of students. These courses are conducted over the same technical fields as day classes. But in addition there is a very wide range of commercial subjects including banking, insurance, stock exchange practice, shipping, cost and works accountancy, law, management studies, and general educational subjects such as languages.

To cope with all this, the full-time teaching staff which fifty years ago totalled 30, with 53 part-time teachers, had risen in 1961 to 90 and 183. In addition 111 technicians and other workers were employed. By 1962 there were 13 departments, with nine professorial heads of whom two held their chairs jointly in the college and the University.

Industry is naturally keen to recruit Heriot-Watt products. This is partly because of the teaching standards, and partly because of the valuable new research—often but not always sponsored by industrial concerns—carried out by members of the college, on subjects as wide-ranging as metal fatigue, gas chromotography, psychrophilic yeasts and coal spores. As an index of the interest shown by leading firms, in a single year personnel officers visited the College from 43 different organisations, each of them—for example, Esso, Joseph Lucas, Ferranti, the Distillers' Company, I.C.I., and the United Kingdom Atomic Energy Authority, to pick a few at random—well-known as load-bearing pillars in the structure of Britain's economic and industrial life.

Technology is, in the long historical view, one of the indices of culture. And if the index seems to be standing higher and higher in Edinburgh, much credit must go to " the Heriot-Watt ", as it is usually called in the city. However, this is far from being the end of the story. In 1964 it was announced that the Government had approved the granting of university status to the College—a momentous step which quickly followed the decision to transform Glasgow's Royal College of Science and Technology into the University of Strathclyde. A year later the Heriot-Watt University was in being with an ex-Premier, Sir Alec Douglas-Home as the first Chancellor.

NAPIER TECHNICAL COLLEGE

Inevitably there will be close relations between the new University, the ancient University of Edinburgh, and the ambitious Napier Technical College, biggest of its kind in Scotland, which was completed in the spring of 1964 and officially taken over by Edinburgh Corporation. If, as seems likely, the Heriot-Watt University moves outside the city boundaries to get the space a university needs, Napier College, which by excellent judgment enshrines the venerable Merchiston Castle Tower and thus keeps Napier's memory alive as the inventor of logarithms, will take over most of the part-time Heriot-Watt students.[1] Napier College too is likely to have a rewarding future. Successfully opened before this reference to it is published, its many-storeyed buildings are designed to accommodate 100 workshops, 24 laboratories, 34 classrooms, 16 drawing offices, a dining hall, gymnasium, library, hall, and all the usual administrative offices. Not least among its special concentrations are to be electronics courses run by the Electrical Engineering Department, highly specialised courses in every form of printing and photography—run by a Department of Photography and Printing—and much work in the field of chemistry and physics.

MORAY HOUSE COLLEGE OF EDUCATION

The 17th century house now used as a College of Education was originally the home of the second Earl of Home and later of the fourth Earl of Moray. Moray House ceased to be used by the Moray family in the 18th century; and in 1846 the house—distinguished by an obelisked gate and a balcony overhanging the Canongate—and its grounds were purchased by the Free Church for use as a college for teachers and a school.

But the history of the college goes further back—to a Hogmanay riot in 1811. The new year had a boisterous reception with " atrocious scenes of riot and bloodshed " at the Tron. Moved by such an affray the Presbyterian ministers of Edinburgh resolved to be more active in the business of popular education, and established in 1813 a sessional school, destined to grow into a training college. Their action reflected the Kirk's deep concern for the cause of education throughout Scotland in the opening decades of the 19th century. The General Assembly established Assembly schools to supplement existing parish schools, especially in poorer areas; and by 1826 it was decided that teachers intending to serve in the Assembly schools should attend for teaching practice and observation at the Edinburgh sessional school. A training department was officially added in 1835 and the institution came to be known as a Normal Seminary.

At the Disruption in 1843 the great majority of students and their superintendent favoured the Free Church and, for their accommodation, Moray House was acquired. From then until 1907 there were two training colleges for Protestant teachers in Edinburgh; but at that date, anticipating the union of the Churches, the two were combined as the Edinburgh Provincial Committee for the Training of Teachers. Four years later the main college building was opened with room for 750 students. But it was not until 1959 that certain important changes in administration helped to change the name of the college from Moray House Training College to Moray House College of Education.

The College trains one-third of the teachers in Scotland. As in other Scottish colleges many categories of teachers are trained in one institution; and in this respect Scotland has evolved a pattern not commonly found elsewhere.

[1] At the end of January, 1964 the Heriot-Watt College had an academic staff of 110 teaching 830 full-time students, 147 part-time staff and 2,356 part-time students.

Women students, after completing a full secondary course, are admitted to training—this lasts three years—and thus qualify as teachers in primary schools. No men are admitted to this course. Graduates follow courses extending to one year and prepare themselves, according to their university qualifications, to teach in senior secondary schools, junior secondary schools and primary schools. Men who have completed apprenticeships in appropriate trades and have undertaken related studies are trained as teachers of technical subjects in a two year course. Training for approximately one session is given to men and women who hold diplomas in art, music, domestic subjects, commercial subjects, agriculture, horticulture and similar matters. In recent years women following the three year course as primary teachers have numbered approximately 800: some 280 are admitted each year. About 320 graduates are enrolled, of whom 120 have honours degrees. There are about 250 students amongst the technical teachers and holders of diplomas. In 1960 the college accepted responsibility for training youth leaders.

Moray House College has now become the main centre in the United Kingdom outside London for the further education and training of teachers from overseas. When the Commonwealth Bursary scheme was instituted in 1960, more Commonwealth bursars came to Moray House than to any other educational institution in the United Kingdom.

The largest group of overseas students is concerned with the teaching of English as a second language. A further group studies education in tropical areas. In 1960 a course was instituted for training the staff of overseas training colleges. In these courses almost 100 overseas students are enrolled, and they come from many countries, the majority being Africans from territories within the Commonwealth. The College also conducts examinations for entrance to secondary education for Mauritius and the Cayman Islands.

The regulations made by Parliament restricting university representation on the governing body have now been amended and the University has four members of the Senate on the governing body. The University of Edinburgh and Moray House have also collaborated in establishing the new degree of B.Ed. The course, which begins in October 1966 will be taught mainly by College lecturers recognised for this purpose by the University. It extends to four years and provides concurrent academic and professional studies designed to train teachers for service in primary schools and in the early stages of secondary schools. The Principal of the College was inducted to the Senate of the University in 1965.

At Moray House developments in educational thought and practice are kept continually under review, and the courses undergo scrutiny and reform in order that teachers may be prepared for the new tasks that are laid upon the educational system. Each year about 4,000 teachers attend refresher courses conducted by the College either in the College itself or in various centres throughout the country, mainly in Southern and Central Scotland and Northern England.

Work of this nature is especially important when considerable changes are occurring, as at present, in primary, secondary and further education in Scotland. The growth in the educational system has indeed made such increasing demands on teachers that in December, 1963 the total enrolment in the College was 1,753. This total included 96 overseas students and 59 in the specialist courses for youth leaders, infant mistresses and teachers of handicapped children. Unfortunately the numbers of teachers trained in Scotland have not increased proportionately with the growth in educational demand and in consequence many pupils are taught by uncertificated teachers. This situation poses a crucial question: will sufficient entrants to the colleges be found in future if entrance qualifications are maintained and, if not, how serious will the effects on Scottish education be if standards of recruitment are lowered? It is no answer to the question to insist on high entrance qualifications at the price of having a large force of uncertificated teachers. Part of the answer is to be found in ensuring adequate status, remuneration and conditions of service for teachers. A further part of the answer is to be found in the ability of the college to offer courses that are attractive, effective and responsive to new ideas in educational thought and practice.

In the meantime the College has been extending its buildings, most notably by an extension, Dalhousie Land, which the Moderator of the General Assembly opened in 1963. It has also instituted an extensive programme of research into historical investigations such as the excavation of the Roman Fort at Cramond, programmed learning, linguistics and the teaching of English, and social and psychological conditions associated with child cruelty and neglect.

EXTRA-MURAL EDUCATION

With the dawn of the 19th century and the spread of the industrial revolution adult education became a reality in the city. As we saw earlier, the Edinburgh School of Arts, founded in 1821, was the first mechanics institution in the country, and later became the Heriot-Watt College. Four years later the Edinburgh Mechanics Subscription Library was founded. By the middle of the century this had the largest circulation in the United Kingdom; and it existed until 1893 when the rise of the Edinburgh Public Library system reduced its usefulness.

If during this long period of valuable service the mechanics institutions were created specially for the artisan, societies like the one which became the Edinburgh Philosophical Institute (1832–1950) satisfied the needs of other citizens. Several of these existed during the century and flourished alongside the scientific and other societies which catered for specialised groups. Among the latter were the Literary Society of Edinburgh (founded in 1802), Wernerian Natural History Society (1808), Caledonian Horticultural Society (1809), Royal Society of Arts (1821–41), Botanical Society (1836), Royal Scottish Academy (1838), Edinburgh Ladies Educational Association (1867) as a result of which women were admitted to the University, Edinburgh Literary Institute (1872), Royal Scottish Geographical Society (1884), Scottish History Society (1886), and the Bibliographical Society (1890). It is an impressive list and one which shows the gathering momentum of an ever-increasing thirst for knowledge beyond the University classrooms. Thus by 1888 when the University Extension Movement begun by Professor James Stuart of Cambridge came to Edinburgh, lecture programmes were arranged not only in the city but at places as far away as Montrose, Stirling and Perth.

A year earlier Professor Patrick Geddes had located in Edinburgh the first summer school to be held in Europe, and one which was to be the model and pioneer summer school for the country as a whole. Today the Scottish Universities combine in a summer school held in Edinburgh while numerous groups and associations hold schools, seminars and conferences each summer both at home and abroad.

In all these ways, then, the movement continued in the 19th century, nor was it abated in our own. In 1912 a meeting was held in the Free Gardeners Hall to start a branch of the Workers' Educational Association, which had been so successful in England. The Edinburgh branch, with the support of a number of University professors and the school boards of Edinburgh and Leith, was quickly successful. The first classes of the W.E.A., as it became known everywhere, enrolled 160 students and the movement gathered steady momentum. By 1926 the Edinburgh branch was one of the largest in the kingdom.

In that year, however, because of a national proposal to link the W.E.A. more closely to the Trades Union Congress, the Edinburgh branch seceded on the grounds that this proposal would introduce sectarianism into the movement, and formed the Edinburgh Workers' Educational Association. The new association was recognised both by the University and the Corporation, and grew so steadily that by 1962–3 some 3,960 students were enrolled in 116 classses under the joint auspices of the three bodies. In 1965 The E.W.E.A. was dissolved and became The Edinburgh University Extra-Mural Association. Under a new agreement with Edinburgh Corporation Education Committee the Edinburgh University Extra-Mural Association is responsible for academic subjects, the W.E.A. will devote more of its resources to the shop floor in industry, and the Education Committee will deal directly with the remainder.

Retracing our steps, in 1942 the national W.E.A. movement re-established an Edinburgh and District branch which now carries on a number of classes side by side with the E.W.E.A.; and this new branch in the 1962–3 session had 1,051 students in classes mostly concerned with language instruction.

Languages in the meantime were being taught by another adult education body. This was Kirk o'Field College opened in 1933, as a venture of faith, by the Chancellor of the University as an extension of the University Settlement. The first students numbered 578 of whom half were unemployed persons; and ever since Kirk o'Field College has continued to serve the adult educational needs in the city although the immediate neighbourhood of the College has lost its population and the reason for its formation has long since gone. In the 1962–3 session there were 431 students in 18 classes many of whom were studying languages in tutorial classes of three years' duration.

To go back further still, in 1928 the University in association with the education authorities of the South-east of Scotland formed a regional Joint Advisory Committee on Adult Education which also included representatives of voluntary bodies in the field of adult education like the E.W.E.A. and the Women's Rural Institutes. When the University made grants to assist in developing adult education in the area it created in 1931 an Extra-Mural Committee to administer these. The result has been beneficial. But from the start the University has interpreted adult education in a wide and liberal fashion and thus enabled many classes of general cultural value to be held as well as those on specific academic subjects.

The University of Edinburgh appointed its first director of extra-mural studies in 1949 and the Extra-Mural Committee was reconstituted to take over the functions of the Joint Advisory Committee. The director became the organiser of the classes. The University, in general, engaged the tutors, while the costs of tutors' fees were paid by the Edinburgh Education Committee. At the same time the University provided the accommodation, and such bodies as the E.W.E.A. and W.E.A. assisted with the recruitment of students. The expected expansion followed quickly and soon the department had to increase its staff to cope with a rise from some 1,500 student enrolments in the city in 1949–50 to more than 5,500 in 1962–3. Fifty years earlier (1912–13) the number of adult education classes in the city was four and the number of students enrolled 160. This striking advance has not been accomplished without a struggle. Trade depression, economic cuts, general elections and an often indifferent population have often made the task exceedingly hard. When also fees were increased there was a fall in enrolments for a year, but new maxima were generally reached in the following session. Fees charged to students in Edinburgh only amount to one shilling per evening. A course of 20 lectures in 1962–3 cost £1 and one of ten lectures 10*s*.

There seems almost to have been fashions in the subjects studied in adult education. Forty or fifty years ago the principal subjects were history, philosophy, economics and English literature. By 1963 these subjects had become more specialised. History therefore now deals with local affairs, archaeology, foreign countries and international affairs; while economics deals with the problems of trade groups, and the effects on modern society of new inventions and developments. Scientific subjects were introduced first in 1919. By 1962–3 classes were being held in astronomy, geology, natural history, botany, bacteriology, nutrition, atomic physics, chemistry, horticulture, agriculture and ornithology. In 1919 appreciation of the arts was introduced; and ever since classes have been regularly held in the history of art, music of different kinds or periods, architecture, the spoken word, art of the theatre, modern design and appreciation of antiques.

In Edinburgh adult education classes are held over three terms each of ten weeks' duration. In the third or summer term opportunity is taken by most of the classes to undertake field work either following up the winter studies or in preparation for the following winter. This is especially true of classes of a scientific kind. The Zoology class for example meets in the

Royal Zoological Park to study the animals. In the summer of 1961 the archaeology class excavated and recorded an Iron Age site which was about to be destroyed by quarry workings.

In recent years many societies have linked their activities with the University's extra-mural department. Among these are the Natural History Society, the Georgian Group, the Jewish community, the Scottish Tourist Board, the Y.M.C.A., and the Townswomen's Guild movement many of whose social study classes are conducted by University tutors.

During this period of growth, however, it has become increasingly difficult to separate vocational and non-vocational subjects. Classes have been arranged for local and central government bodies, and various ministries have asked for special courses for their executives and others. The Ministry of National Assistance, for example, has held a class for several years on human relations, and the Scottish Home Department has provided classes in child care directed at those employed in voluntary and state controlled children's homes. Police officers, prison officers and school attendance officers too have had courses arranged for them. And to illustrate the range further, by 1962 the adult education programmes included not only courses for persons in management at various levels but classes for professional lawyers in specialised aspects of law covered by new legislation.

Another illuminating series are the three public Town and Gown lectures presided over by the Lord Provost. Inaugurated in 1951 these lectures are given in the City Chambers and are nearly always over-subscribed since they give the citizens a chance to hear distinguished professors of the University and at the same time give the professors an opportunity to address a wider public than in the University classroom.

The Extra-Mural Department of the University is also concerned with adult education in the Forces. One of its staff is a staff-tutor-organiser for this purpose. Lectures are given to units; classes are organised for service examinations; candidates are prepared for staff college examinations; officers are briefed to conduct discussions with their men; tutorial education and directed reading are provided for individuals and smaller groups.

An adult student, it should be explained, is defined as anyone over 18 years of age but the average age of students attending adult classes is considerably higher. Younger persons are generally pursuing courses leading to diplomas or certificates of a vocational nature. Having obtained these they are often found making homes and bringing up young families, but when the families grow up many return seeking cultural development. This in itself is very important for although the serious student of 1966 has much more leisure for reading and private research than his fellow of 1910, say, he has much more to distract him in the entertainment world.

Mansbridge devised his Workers' Educational Association for industrial workers but they have never attended classes in large numbers, and only about four or five per cent enrol in Edinburgh. It has sometimes been suggested that the technique of an hour's lecture followed by a period of discussion is beyond such an audience. Whether or no the vast majority of students come from the first three classes of the Registrar General's classification of social class. Many are graduates, and in recent years the Edinburgh classes have enrolled a peer and several knights. But how to win the masses is still one of the unsolved problems of the educationist in general and of the adult educationist in particular.

In recent years Edinburgh has broken with tradition in organising morning and afternoon classes. It was felt not only that the elderly who might be deterred by dark winter nights would enrol but that changes in social life whereby husbands and children obtain canteen mid-day meals would release many housewives for study. This duly happened. In three years the numbers attending these day classes has risen to 500, but further expansion will have to await the provision of additional accommodation.

SPECIALIST TRAINING

There are of course many other ways beyond those we have seen in which the younger generation can equip themselves for a career. There are colleges for commercial training which offer courses in shorthand-typing, book-keeping, and the languages of foreign commerce; there are tutorial colleges or "crammers" which prepare their pupils for entry to the university or elsewhere; and there is also a college which specialises in the training of young men for the merchant marine.

One must not forget, either, the schemes for training nurses, both in the Royal Infirmary and in the other city hospitals; while a pre-nursing college is housed in the agreeable neo-classical building of the old Dean Orphanage. Schooling in the Orphanage was given up some years ago; and the orphans now live in a large house nearby and attend a local primary school.

LEITH NAUTICAL COLLEGE

Established in 1855 after the Merchant Shipping Act of the previous year, Leith Nautical College was originally administered by a representative committee of shipowners and merchants of the town. To these have been added representatives of the Edinburgh and local county councils. During its history the College occupied various premises until 1903 when it became established in Leith's Commercial Street. In 1927 a new wing was added to accommodate the Marine Engineering School, and four years later there was a further extension for the School of Radio Telegraphy and Electrical subjects. Further additions to the curriculum were made in 1944 for deck ratings in the Training Ship *Dolphin* in the West Old Dock. And ever since new courses and equipment have followed steadily—courses for catering ratings (1946); a modern well-equipped galley in the *Dolphin* for training ships' cooks (1949); and a new two-year course for engine room ratings (1960).

The College now comes under the supervision of the Scottish Education

Department, and has been granted full recognition as a Nautical Marine engineering and cookery school and by the Post Office as a R.T. school.

EDINBURGH COLLEGE OF DOMESTIC SCIENCE

If budding sea-cooks can learn their trade on board the T.S. *Dolphin* in Leith Docks, their sisters can also learn to cook in one of the dignified terraces of Edinburgh's New Town. To say of a woman that she is " Atholl Crescent trained " is usually in Scotland to place her domestic virtues beyond common questioning, though there is often talk of " cordons bleus " and " cordons rouges " elsewhere. However, for many the phrase " Atholl Crescent " conjures up a vision of melting meringues, crisply laundered bed-linen, and—to adapt an old Scots proverb—a highly practical view of how many house-keeping beans make four.

The College owes its origin largely to the energy and foresight of a lady called Miss Christian Guthrie Wright. Convinced that instruction in cookery and the domestic arts was both needed and desired in Edinburgh, Miss Wright started the Edinburgh School of Cookery in 1875, with one teacher and classes in a single hired room. The classes proved so popular that more commodious premises had to be found, and two years later the School moved into Shandwick Place.

As the cookery classes in Edinburgh had proved so successful, it was decided to offer courses in other parts of Scotland; and the work done outside Edinburgh became an important and popular branch of the School's activities. The teachers travelled about with their utensils and oil-stoves, teaching in halls and school-rooms. These classes, although the charge for attendance at a demonstration was only a penny or two, were a success; and thus began the useful extra-mural work still carried out by the College, as the old School is now styled, throughout Scotland today.

In 1891 the School moved to a house in Atholl Crescent; and in 1908 it was recognised by the Scottish Education Department as a Central Institution for the purposes of education. Today its premises consist of 12 houses in the Crescent, and there are over 500 full-time students engaged in studies far beyond the concept of its founder. Some students may prepare themselves as teachers in any branch of homecraft, and for this purpose three- and four-year training courses are available. To meet the growing need for professional trainees in hospitals, industrial concerns, colleges and schools, the College prepares students for the Diploma in Institutional and Catering Management and the Certificate in Institutional Housekeeping and Catering of the Institutional Management Association. There is also a shorter course of four terms to which a student may add a one-term course in large-scale cookery.

TRAINING OF HOTEL STAFFS

In recent years, with more affluence in society, more tourists, more festivals of music and drama and a growing appreciation of the merits of good food the hotel trade has become of considerable importance as a social as well as an economic factor in the life of the country; which makes it all the more desirable to make hotel catering as efficient as possible.

It is generally admitted that skilled workers in any trade or vocation should acquire their skills not merely by watching other men do the job, but should be trained in technical schools and colleges while undergoing an apprenticeship. Unfortunately catering came into this field later than the more traditional trades of the country. But now it is generally agreed that a properly organised scheme of training will benefit not only the boys and girls who enter this trade (and their employers) but also the general public who will enjoy an overall improvement in the preparation and service of food and drink.

Some time ago Edinburgh Corporation organised a pre-apprenticeship catering course lasting one year in which instruction is given in basic cookery and other skills required of hotel workers. Attendance at this full-time course counts as part of an apprenticeship. Having taken it the student then enters employment in the catering trade, and during his first two years is released for one day each week to attend the Catering Trade Basic Training Course whose syllabus is laid down by the City and Guilds of London Institute. The subjects studied are Theory and Practice of Cookery, Kitchen Practice and Hygiene. Calculations for Caterers, Catering Commodities, Counter Service and Waiting and Services: about half of the time is devoted to practical cookery and service, the remainder to theory. There is also a parallel evening course for students unable to attend by day.

Although its main emphasis is on cookery, this course is for all sections of the catering industry. But to meet the needs of those students who wish to make cookery their career, a new two-year course, Preliminary Trade Cookery (City and Guilds of London Institute, Course 153) was introduced in 1959.

TUTORIAL COLLEGES

Edinburgh has a number of privately owned tutorial colleges which perform a useful function. That of the Misses Dugdale is perhaps the smallest, being concerned mainly with giving secretarial training to girls from middle class and upper class homes. Skerry's, which is the largest, covers a wide range of courses and offers its help alike to the young person ambitious to join the civil service, the school pupil who wants to supplement the tuition available at his school, and the university student anxious about his degree examinations. Basil Paterson's is smaller than Skerry's, but has earned the gratitude of a number of young people at school and university for the coaching it has given to get them over the examination hurdles.

DUGDALE'S SECRETARIAL SCHOOL

The aim of this school is to give its 95 students, who must be at least 16 years of age and of good education, a thorough training that will fit them for a variety of posts. The classes are never large, so that individual attention to the girls can be given by an efficient and experienced staff.

Students are advised not merely to study shorthand and typing, but to enter for the full course of training. This comprises shorthand, typing and at least one extra subject each term. There are classes in English, book-keeping, journalism, librarianship and languages; but although a student may vary her extra subjects from term to term, one term's book-keeping is compulsory. Girls taking the full course are also given tuition in business correspondence and training in office routine and secretarial duties.

SKERRY'S COLLEGE

Although organised on a broad basis in Scotland and England, Skerry's College had its origin in Edinburgh where it was founded in 1878. The original purpose was to provide tuition for Civil Service candidates; but it was not long before activities were extended to prepare candidates for University and other preliminary examinations and for secretarial and office training. Later, branches of the College were opened in Glasgow, Aberdeen, Newcastle and Liverpool.

Skerry's, which also pioneered correspondence tuition, was apparently the first college in Great Britain to offer "tutorials through the post" for examinations.

BASIL PATERSON AND AINSLIE

This well-known independent tutorial college, co-educational and non-residential, is sited in the New Town and occupies about 40 rooms in all, including laboratories and library.

It gives instruction in all school and many university subjects; it has a commercial department covering shorthand, typing and secretarial practice; and it teaches English as a second language to foreign students.

Most of the instruction is given in small sets of about four students, each one receiving individual attention and working independently of the others. It also arranges private tuition—one student with the tutor—and for secretarial practice and overseas English it runs small classes.

In a single year it usually enrols about a thousand students for day and evening classes. Many are full-time, some are still at school, and about 10 per cent come from overseas. The greater part of the work is concerned with the preparation of candidates for school-leaving and university entrance examinations.

Part Seven

THE ARTS AND HUMANITIES

PRELUDE

Despite the modern urge in an increasingly materialistic world for better machines, higher speeds, more nuclear energy and even journeys to the moon it is still true that age-long tradition and an inherited sense of art and culture still help to mould men's minds for the better much more than certain scientists (and some politicians) think. It should however be added quickly that many scientists—and the University of Edinburgh has helped to produce a goodly number—are men and women with an interest in learning far beyond their own laboratories and their test tubes. Equally it is true that the city's leading scholars in the classical tradition have always hailed the scientific discoveries of their fellow scholars in medicine, say, or geology because they were all part of a wider progress of culture and mental comfort. But not every seat of learning is so enlightened. In April, 1964 Professor E. R. Dodds, a former Regius Professor of Greek at Oxford, complained that out of seven newly founded universities only three proposed to make any present provision for teaching the classical languages, despite the fact that Latin was the key to an understanding of European literature. *The Times* in a forceful leading article (9th April, 1964) thought this " shameful " and " wrong that those wishing to do Latin and Greek should be sent empty away from any seat of learning."

Edinburgh escapes this charge. As we shall see, it has always been a literary city. It has great and better libraries than most other parts of Great Britain and fine art galleries. For many centuries it has housed famous writers, philosophers, theologians, and statesmen of intellectual calibre such as Haldane. And so today though science has won increased recognition at the University in an age of astonishing scientific advance the arts and humanities continue to flourish.

We looked at the University earlier, but here we might well give it a final backward glance if only to reassure ourselves that the ancient classic studies still hold their own in the broad field of culture we are about to enter. According to Professor Arthur Beattie, an ex-Dean of the Faculty of Arts, there were between 20 and 30 students reading for Classical honours in the University in the decade following the first World War. Nowadays, despite the fact that neither Greek nor Latin is any longer a compulsory subject for the M.A. degree, and although in consequence the number of pupils in Scottish schools who take these subjects has diminished, the number of Honours students in the University has occasionally risen as high as 35 and is normally more than 25.

It is noticeable too that whereas before and after the first World War many classical graduates from Edinburgh entered the Home or Indian Civil Service, or else embarked on careers in Divinity or Law, their successors at the present time enter a greater variety of professions. The Church, Law and Civil Service still attract a number of them but many also find their way into the management side of industry and commerce. In the past, Classical graduates often pursued an academic career but nearly all who did so transferred to other faculties or to other branches of study. In recent years a fair number have taken up university teaching in Classics. About a dozen graduates of the last 15 years hold posts of this kind in universities either in the United Kingdom or in the Commonwealth.

The outlook for Classical studies, contrary to general opinion, is now more promising than it was in the inter-war period. The students who interest themselves in Greek and Latin now do so of their own free choice and not merely because these subjects are considered to be an essential part of a long-standing tradition. Moreover, the method and content of Classical study are developing in the same ways as in other sections of the Faculty of Arts. A great deal of time used to be spent on purely linguistic work and in particular on training students to write Greek and Latin as far as possible in the style of the great authors of antiquity. At the present time much more attention is given to reading and interpreting ancient literature and to the study of Greek and Roman civilization.

The impact of archaeological discoveries and of new techniques in historical and literary research have also re-vitalised the teaching of Classics. In keeping with this trend it is now the general rule that a student should visit Greece and Italy during his course of study and gain first-hand experience of historic places and of living conditions in these countries; until quite recently, it was rare for any but dedicated scholars to visit these countries. Classical studies may have lost something of their traditional rigour but in compensation they are becoming of more immediate interest to people of the 20th century. It may be expected that the tendencies now apparent will continue to develop and that in the work of the Faculty of Arts, which is the study of Western civilisation from its origins to the present day, classical scholars will as before play an integral part. Nothing could be more heartening to those in the city who encourage the arts and humanities in a classic environment where they have flourished for centuries.

CHAPTER 38

THE EDINBURGH FESTIVAL

The glory of a capital city depends both on its material prosperity and its cultural interests:
Sir John Falconer, Lord Provost of Edinburgh, 1944–7.

THE first Edinburgh International Festival of Music and Drama, which opened on Sunday the 24th of August, 1947, was also the first major post-war festival of the arts in Europe. It rapidly established itself, and within ten years was attracting over 90,000 visitors to the city during the three weeks of its passage. The Edinburgh Festival was, from the start, unique both in its setting and in the number and variety of artistic events of the highest standard which it offered. Nor has its general pattern since then significantly altered.

In the sphere of music there are usually nightly concerts in the Usher Hall (mainly orchestral but also choral, chamber music and some solo recitals); opera in the King's Theatre; and morning concerts in the Freemason's Hall by soloists or chamber-music groups.

Drama is represented at the Royal Lyceum Theatre by three plays, each running for one week; at the Assembly Hall of the Church of Scotland by plays presented on the open stage; and more recently at the Gateway Theatre and the Church Hill Theatre.

As for art, in the Royal Scottish Academy there have been, since 1949, major exhibitions of pictures including important exhibitions of the works of Rembrandt, Degas, Renoir, Gauguin, Cezanne and Braque. There is also an International Film Festival which in 1962 became an official part of the Festival itself.

The Music Hall and Assembly Rooms become for the three weeks a Festival Club. A Tattoo is staged by Scottish Command on the Castle esplanade before a nightly audience of 7,000. The pipes and drums of the Edinburgh City Police march every morning along Princes Street.

And then there is the Fringe. This consists of performances and exhibitions which are not officially sponsored by the Edinburgh Festival Society but which take place during the Festival. There are frequently more than 20 plays and as many exhibitions on the Fringe, materialising somehow from a planless void. To house them halls, churches, galleries, courtyards and clubs throughout the city sprout stages and auditoria, loud speakers and lights; and every hall which can be made to resemble some sort of theatre is likely to be booked up by a Fringe company months before the Festival starts. Notable among early comers was the Theatre Workshop Company of Joan Littlewood.

Though the Fringe has remained amorphous and quite outside the official Festival, there is now a Fringe Society which provides some degree of co-ordination as far as booking halls, selling tickets and publicity are concerned. The essential spirit of the Fringe, however, has been preserved, and companies, often undergraduates, still steal into the city like thieves in the night, set up their stages, paint their scenery, often sleep in the same hall, and perform their plays. Many now well-known actors and directors have also appeared—in courtyards, churches and halls or directed plays with brilliant improvisation under makeshift Fringe conditions. Plays and late-night revues have always been the keystone of the Fringe, although there are also exhibitions and concerts. While the Festival Society resolutely refuses officially to acknowledge its existence, the Fringe and the Festival nevertheless live in a happy symbiosis and the Festival would be poorer without it.

That the Festival has become the major event of the Edinburgh year, with an atmosphere of its own, is now accepted. It is not simply that the city is full of visitors, for the visitors are about in their thousands from May until October. Nor is it that Princes Street is gay with flowers and illuminated decorations, varying from banners and flags through onion-shaped and lollipop-shaped lanterns to baroque electric rose bushes of painted metal. It is an atmosphere in which everyone walks with a certain lightness of step, and once a taxi-driver refused a fare from T. S. Eliot.

When it is over brightness falls from the air. The Festival usually ends with fireworks and when they have gone out it seems that the winter has begun. For although Edinburgh is reasonably well supplied with concerts and plays for the rest of the year the Festival is the city's great annual jamboree of the arts.

It is not possible to calculate in monetary terms the value of the enterprise to the city. Various figures, ranging from £1 million to £3 million, have been given for the additional trade brought to the city in the three weeks of the Festival alone. But whatever the figure, at least 30,000 visitors from outside Britain come each year to the Festival; so the contribution in foreign currency must be substantial. More important still in terms of artistic prestige, the Festival has clearly brought a new renown to Edinburgh. But how did all this happen? How did Edinburgh in the middle of the 20th century come to be a world centre of music and the arts?

THE BEGINNING

In 1944 the remarkable opera centre of Glyndebourne, which John Christie and his wife had created in Sussex, was in a state of suspended animation. Its General Manager, Rudolf Bing, was engaged upon other work during the war, and it seemed unlikely that opera at Glyndebourne could restart for several years.

Mr. Bing and the Christies in the meantime had been discussing the possibility of starting a festival of music and the arts in Britain. They knew that the pre-war festival centres of Salzburg, Munich and Bayreuth would not be able to operate for some considerable time, though with the impending end of the war it seemed certain that people anxious to rediscover the glories of European culture would inevitably have their travel restricted. It was clear, too, that the sooner international artists were able to move about again, the better it would be for everyone. The problem was to find the ideal site.

Christie himself said that the idea of Edinburgh as a festival site first struck his wife (Audrey Mildmay) when she was on tour with the Glyndebourne Opera in Edinburgh in 1940. However, various other cities were being considered—among them Cambridge, Chester and Canterbury—when towards the end of 1944 in London Rudolf Bing met Harvey Wood, who was then Director of the British Council in Scotland. Mr. Wood suggested to Mr. Bing that Edinburgh had the requisite background, attractive surroundings and, most importantly, an adequacy of theatres, concert halls and hotels to accommodate such a festival as was being planned. He invited Mr. Bing to visit Edinburgh in order to meet a number of influential and sympathetic Edinburgh citizens; and as it turned out they were all so enthusiastic that immediate arrangements were made for Mr. Bing to see the Lord Provost, Sir John Falconer, and to put the proposal for a festival before the city authorities.

The project was a formidable one, particularly in the conditions of the time. But by the middle of 1945 Sir John Falconer had become convinced of its value and of its feasibility. Money was voted to allow Rudolf Bing, working from Glyndebourne, to explore the possibilities and attempt to draw together a provisional programme. This he did, and The Edinburgh Festival Society Limited was duly registered under the Companies Act on 18th November, 1946.

THE FIRST FESTIVAL

It is not possible here to detail the difficulties overcome by the first Festival committee under Sir John Falconer's chairmanship not only in bringing into being the first Edinburgh Festival so soon after the end of the war, but in conceiving a Festival unique in the world.

It was certain, however, that the first Festival would incur a financial loss. An early estimate was that if, as seemed reasonable, 80 per cent of the available seats were filled, the loss would be in the region of £35,000. It was hoped by some that it might be less; others feared that some unforeseen calamity might make it more. But the great plan went ahead. A sum of around £20,000 was quickly raised in donations from well-wishers. The Arts Council of Great Britain gave a further £20,000 and a similar sum was contributed by the Edinburgh Corporation. It was on this reserve fund of about £62,000 that the Festival started. The first year deficit was about £21,000.

In future years the reserve fund continued to receive donations, though not for 10 years as large as the initial contributions from the Town Council and the Arts Council. In 1955, nevertheless, the fund had risen to £75,000 but thereafter it fell severely and stood in 1957 at only £27,000. The cost of bringing artists to Edinburgh, the costs of administration, and the cost of every part of the Festival meanwhile was rising acutely.

Over the years a number of appeals have been made by successive

Lord Provosts in the hope of increasing the sums raised from private donations. In March, 1961 a Festival Guild was inaugurated to form a world-wide link between people interested in the Festival and what it stands for. Within a few months the membership had reached 2,500, half of the members living in Edinburgh, and its early meetings and functions have continued to command support.

While money was being found to launch the first Festival, Rudolf Bing began to prepare a programme of concerts and drama. At first little interest was shown in the project and major orchestras and dramatic companies felt unable to tie themselves down, even provisionally, for a time so far ahead and for a new Festival about which they knew nothing. There were also in 1945 and 1946 enormous difficulties, geographical and diplomatic, in arranging to bring artists to Edinburgh from other countries. In March, 1946, however, Dr. Bruno Walter accepted an invitation to come and conduct the Vienna Philharmonic Orchestra at the first Festival in 1947, and this had the effect of catalysing future negotiations. The highest standard had been set, and other artists suddenly became anxious to appear as well.

The Programme Committee under the chairmanship of Mr. Harvey Wood finally arrived at a programme which was duly presented, as follows. The Glyndebourne Opera performed *The Marriage of Figaro* and Verdi's *Macbeth.* Concerts were given by the Vienna Philharmonic Orchestra under Bruno Walter, including what was to become one of the Festival's first jewels—Mahler's *Das Lied von der Erde*, with Kathleen Ferrier singing the contralto part—l'Orchestre des Concerts Colonne under Paul Paray, the Hallé Orchestra under Barbirolli, the Liverpool Philharmonic Orchestra under Sargent, and the Scottish National and B.B.C. Scottish Orchestras under Walter Susskind and Ian Whyte. Three concerts of Piano Trios by Schubert and Piano Quartets by Brahms were given by a specially formed quartet consisting of Artur Schnabel, Joseph Szigeti, William Primrose and Pierre Fournier. These artists also appeared as soloists with the orchestras. Other soloists were Michelangeli, Casadesus, Peter Pears and Cyril Smith. Recitals were given by Elizabeth Schumann and Bruno Walter, Todd Duncan, Roy Henderson and Szigeti and Schnabel. Morning concerts were also given by the Jacques Orchestra, the Czech Nonet, the Menges and Calvet Quartets, the Robert Masters Piano Quartet, the Carter String Trio with Leon Goossens and by the Glasgow Orpheus Choir. There were two concerts of Scottish songs, one of Gaelic and one of Lowland songs.

The works performed in these concerts were for the most part accepted masterpieces from the standard repertoire. Standard of performance rather than originality of programme was to be the magnet to draw people to Edinburgh. Drama was represented by the Old Vic company in *The Taming of the Shrew* and, with Alec Guinness, in *Richard II*: and by Louis Jouvet and his company in *L'Ecole des Femmes* by Molière and *Ondine* by Giraudoux. The Sadler's Wells Ballet with Margot Fonteyn performed Tchaikovsky's *The Sleeping Beauty*. So by any standards it was an encouraging start.

The first Festival opened in the fourth week of a month of unbroken sunshine. The weather continued hot and clear until well into the second week, and when it changed it changed gently. Moray McLaren in his book *The Capital of Scotland* has well caught the mood of those early days:

> Evening after evening the long twilight illuminated the north west, not only in the customary colours of sunset, but in saffron and pale green, as if the midsummer nights were lengthening into autumn. Our capital qualities of space, light, colour and air can seldom have displayed themselves so triumphantly, so appropriately. And on three occasions the Minister of Fuel in England sent to us over the telephone permission to illuminate our own castle after nightfall! "Is it always like this?" visitors from the claustrophobia of newly released Europe would ask us. "Always," we would reply casually and dreamily. "Yes, always." Then we would ask them about music.

On the day before the Festival opened, Sir John Falconer, who had early become convinced of its spiritual and social value, and whose championship of it from the key position of the Lord Provost's chair had brought it to fruition, spoke at a Civic Reception. "We grasp a new motif of life", he said, "This lovely city, so dear to Scottish hearts all over the world, held in such warm affection by men and women in every country of the globe, awakens to a new future . . . . The conception of the development of Edinburgh into a permanent and recognised world centre, with the necessary buildings and accommodation, with schools of music and drama, and overall cultivating the necessary spirit of universal friendship, and stirred above all with devotion to the graces, is one which should certainly stir the imagination and arouse enthusiasm."

The Festival was visited by Her Majesty the Queen (now Queen Elizabeth the Queen Mother) and by Princess Margaret. From the beginning it was a success, 180,000 tickets in all being sold for the various performances. Notably successful were the morning concerts which, somewhat hesitantly put on as an experiment, drew long queues to the Freemasons' Hall.

The Festival began with a Service of Praise and Thanksgiving in St. Giles. Rumour had it that Mr. Bing had unthinkingly proposed a High Mass there; but perhaps the origin of the Service might be left to the then Minister of St. Giles', Dr. Charles Warr, who wrote about this in his book *The Glimmering Landscape*:

"In 1946, while the preparations for the first Festival were in hand, Mr. Bing came to see me. He said that both he and Sir John felt strongly that it would be out of keeping with the traditions of Scotland if the Festival were not to open with a religious service. Could this be done in St. Giles' and a service produced which, while in no way departing from the generally accepted worship of the Church of Scotland, might be of a character in which members of other denominations could feel at home? I was delighted with the idea, and eventually produced an Order of Service which fully satisfied Sir John and Mr. Bing." So when the following

August came round, the First International Festival was opened by a great and impressive act of worship in St. Giles', and at the request of successive Lord Provosts it has remained unaltered ever since.

FROM STRENGTH TO STRENGTH

The first Artistic Director of the Festival was naturally Rudolf Bing himself with Mr. Ian Hunter, who succeeded him in 1950, as his Assistant. The Festival Society was run by a Council consisting of 36 members, of whom 17 were members of Edinburgh Town Council, and with the Lord Provost (Sir John Falconer) as Chairman. An Executive Committee, also under the chairmanship of the Lord Provost, consisted of Councillor (later Sir Andrew) Murray, Mr. Harvey Wood, Councillor W. P. Earsman, Councillor (later Sir Ian) Johnson-Gilbert, a later Lord Provost, and the Countess of Rosebery. Mr. John Reid was Secretary to the Society and later became the Festival's Administrative Director. Mr. Robert Ponsonby succeeded Mr. Ian Hunter as Artistic Director in 1956 and was succeeded by the Earl of Harewood in 1961.

During the years of growth the Festival authorities have arranged and received a great deal of publicity for their venture. Each year a Festival Press Bureau is set up in the basement of the Freemason's Hall, and indeed the growing importance of the Festival as an international event may be traced in the hundreds of visiting critics and journalists who attend it. The B.B.C., too, naturally regards the Festival as a major event of the broadcasting year, and concerts and other performances are relayed annually to most countries in Europe. Many events, including the Tattoo, are also televised at the time and others recorded for later transmission overseas.

Later in this chapter we shall see in greater detail how the Festival flourished in the early 60s, and especially in 1963 which turned out to be a rather controversial year. But of course there has been criticism. Some critics have denounced the conservatism of its programmes and the deficiency of indigenous Scottish material in them, though the Festival Society has generally maintained that the Festival's aim is to provide the best possible performances of the best works. In 1961, however, Lord Harewood successfully introduced overall planning into the musical programmes with a panorama of the works of Schoenberg and a liberal ration of the music of Liszt. In 1962 most of the major works of Shostakovich were performed and many of those of Debussy.

In the history of the Festival there have been other high-water marks. In opera Glyndebourne's *La Forza del Destino*, *Ariadne auf Naxos* under Sir Thomas Beecham, *Falstaff*, and the wonderful ebullient *La Cenerentola* will be particularly remembered. The Hamburg State Opera presented a noble *Fidelio* and a lively *Mastersingers*. Madame Callas sang in Bellini's *La Sonnambula* with the Piccolo Scala from Milan.

The Azuma Kabuki Dancers provided probably the most exotic spectacle the Festival has seen, except perhaps the march of the Janissaries in the Tattoo. The Diaghilev year was a notable one in ballet, with the exotic Diaghilev exhibition and the revival, among other ballets, of *The Firebird* with Margot Fonteyn. Jerome Robbins in his *Ballets U.S.A.* brought something new and exciting to the Festival in 1959.

In the theatre, O'Neill's *Long Day's Journey into Night*, Sir Tyrone Guthrie's open-stage production of the 400 year old Scots classic *The Three Estates*, Barrault's *Hamlet* and Edwige Feuillère's *La Dame aux Camélias* were exceptional. Of new plays few have been remarkable, but three plays by T. S. Eliot, Charles Morgan's *The River Line*, Bridie's *The Queen's Comedy* and Thornton Wilder's *A Life in the Sun* had Edinburgh premières.

Musical performances have been numerous and many of them memorable, with each Festival having its own small miracles. There has, moreover, been an unexpected tendency for certain artists to gain new stature at the Festival, and to be taken in a particular way to the hearts of Festival audiences. Such was notably the case with Kathleen Ferrier, with Rosalyn Tureck when she played the Bach Goldberg Variations, with Isaac Stern, Cantelli, Rostropovich and Antonio, the Spanish dancer. Bruno Walter, Schnabel and Beecham dominated the Festival when they were there, but the artists mentioned seemed to become in a special way a part of the Festival and of its history.

The Festival of 1961 was voted by many old Festival hands as one of the best since 1947. Lord Harewood, directing his first Edinburgh Festival, seemed to cast a new glamour over the scene, and his gambles paid off. The Schoenberg-filled morning concerts were as popular as if they had been devoted to music by Mozart and Beethoven; the Epstein Exhibition, showing over 200 pieces by the recently deceased sculptor and brilliantly mounted in a transformed Waverley Market by Mr. Richard Buckle, drew 100,000 people and was the talk of Europe as well as of Edinburgh; while Britten's *A Midsummer Night's Dream* was packed for all its five performances. The Festival excitement spread also to the fringes of the Fringe, with late-night revues and folksy cabarets booming as never before. Then a year later there came another great development when the 1962 Festival successfully breached the Iron Curtain with Shostakovich and a handful of the most celebrated Russian musicians who were warmly applauded at all their concerts.

THE 1963 FESTIVAL

Halfway through October, 1963, the Edinburgh Festival Society received an open letter from a group of personalities prominent in the arts and literature including Sir Laurence Olivier, Victor Gollancz and Kenneth Tynan. The letter complained of an " insidious campaign of denigration " waged against the Festival, and went on to speak of its " being under attack from certain persons, institutions, organisations and newspapers." The attacks fell under two main headings. One perennial school of thought had it that the choice of programmes was too esoteric and therefore of limited interest to the majority of its potential patrons and ipso facto financially unjustified. In short, the Festival was too highbrow and too expensive. The other criticism was more confused, for it assumed that moral and artistic issues could be discussed in the same terms. A letter from an Edinburgh town councillor to *The Guardian* suggested that the comparatively sparse attendances at the opening nights of Britten's *The Rape of Lucretia* indicated a general local distaste for such a subject. That comment was greeted with supercilious or ribald laughter, not least in Scotland, but the councillor was not so far off the mark if one recalls the shocked reactions provoked in some quarters by Ben Jonson's *Bartholomew Fair* many Festivals ago.

Matters came to a head with the Drama Conference in the McEwan Hall, promoted by the publisher John Calder. Its merits will be assessed later, but in general it soon became apparent that there was a gulf between some of the speakers and many in the audience. Moreover, the momentary appearance of a naked girl, wheeled on a trolley across the organ gallery, in a surrealist " happening ", though it caused no particular emotion among those actually present, led to considerable indignation among those who were not. Accordingly the Festival was now charged with being not only too highbrow and too expensive but also morally degrading. For two or three weeks afterwards, the correspondence columns of *The Scotsman* resounded with furious exchanges of opinion; the whole thing was inflated out of all proportion by press, radio and corridor gossip, to the extent that the public picture of the Festival bore little relation to the experience of those who chronicled its daily progress.

This controversy also tended to obscure the wider issues at stake in the year of the 17th Festival. For, in the last resort, the future career of the Festival was going to depend less on the choice of isolated plays, symphonies or " happenings " than on the size of subsidies, the provision of a proper opera house and on a much wider public recognition of the facts of Festival life.

Cosmopolitan and comprehensive as always, the 1963 Festival programmes comprised music, drama, ballet, the visual arts and films—with the addition of the Tattoo, which in that year saw the debut on the Esplanade of camels hired from Chipperfield's Circus. The Fringe, more extensive than ever with about 40 different activities, gained the reputation of being less Bohemian in its outward manifestations than formerly but also, perhaps. slightly less distinguished.

In principle, it was the music of Berlioz and Bartok which was especially emphasised. But with some exceptions, the larger scale choral works, operas and songs of Berlioz were left over for 1964, and the opportunity was taken to introduce a number of the less familiar orchestral pieces, notably the *Tristia*. More spectacular were the performances of his *Damnation of Faust* by Covent Garden forces under Georg Solti, and of *Lélio*, that strange hybrid autobiographical sequel to the *Fantastic Symphony*. Bartok's works enjoyed a fuller survey. In addition to most of his major orchestral works, including the three piano concertos played by John Ogdon and the violin concerto by Menuhin, the six quartets were shared out between the Tatrai and the Amadeus Quartets, while the Budapest Opera and Ballet brought to Edinburgh their triple bill of

Bartok's *Duke Bluebeard's Castle*, *The Wooden Prince* and *The Miraculous Mandarin.* Eloquent expositions of his songs and piano music were to be heard in the Freemasons' and Leith Town Halls.

Britten and Mahler also emerged as key figures of the musical programme. The attention paid to Britten (a composer somewhat neglected by earlier Festivals) could be construed as the Festival's commemoration of his 50th birthday. The English Opera Group visited Edinburgh with *The Rape of Lucretia* and *The Beggar's Opera,* the second of which had not hitherto been played in Britten's arrangement in Scotland; and John Pritchard, with the chorus and orchestra of Covent Garden, was responsible for the *Spring Symphony.* Mahler's interests were forwarded on three successive evenings, when the B.B.C. Symphony Orchestra and the Concertgebouw (the only foreign orchestra to be invited to Edinburgh) presented the Adagio from the Tenth Symphony, the Sixth and the First Symphonies.

Unfortunately, none of the new or newish works (whether commissioned or not) by Ton de Leeuw (*Mouvements Retrogades*), by Stravinsky (*Eight Instrumental Miniatures*), by Henze (Fifth Symphony) and Tippett (*Concerto for Orchestra*) caused any particular stir, a negative reaction which provided some spare ammunition for critics of Lord Harewood's forward-looking policies. However, at the other extreme, of old music, Julian Bream whether in partnership with Peter Pears and an ensemble of viols, or with a mixed consort gave two enchanting concerts devoted to Dowland and other Tudor and Jacobean composers.

But dominating the Festival's catalogue of non-orchestral music and overlapping the dance and the visual arts was India. With Dr. Narayana Menon as compere, a team of superb instrumentalists and one singer, Subbulakshmi, introduced Edinburgh to the complexities, formal and improvisatory, of their traditional arts. It was the most extensive manifestation of this nature ever attempted outside their own continent. In addition to revealing their own techniques and ways of thought, these Indian visitors sought to define the possible relationships between Eastern and Western idioms; and to that end some joint recitals were given, with Julian Bream on his guitar and Larry Adler with his harmonica as Western champions in exercises of communal extemporisation. In that general setting, there should also be a word of praise for the admirably arranged exhibition of Indian arts in the Royal Scottish Museum and of the dance recital by Balarasvati.

Without Tebaldi as originally advertised, and with a repertory of three operas, of which two were virtually unknown in Britain, the popular success of the Naples San Carlo company was problematic. In the event, it did very well because of its gusto and its sheer delight in the act of singing. Even if the production of Verdi's *Louisa Miller* led to little critical reappraisal of its modest virtues, the Neapolitan version of Cilea's pastel-shaded *Adrian Lecouvreur* was warmly welcomed, not least on account of the dramatic artistry of Magda Olivero in the title role, and Donizetti's *Don Pasquale* was a sell-out.

The ballet side of the Festival was dominated by Martha Graham.

Hieratic and hermetic and appearing to stand traditional conventions on their heads, her repertory of two triple bill programmes and a whole evening of *Clytemnestra* was, in the words of one observer, " strong meat." For the unprepared spectator, her obsessive symbolism and angular choreography led to total acceptance or total rejection.

Drama has always been the Achilles heel of the Festival, less through any lack of interest on the part of successive directors than from the practical problems of its promotion. But 1963 saw a determined effort to redress this situation. The Chichester Festival company could hardly go wrong with *St. Joan* in the Assembly Hall, but *The Shaven Cheek* by the Australian playwright Ray Lawler was disappointingly drab after the effectiveness of his earlier *Summer of the Seventeenth Doll. The Rabbit Race* by Martin Walser, translated by Ronald Duncan, was an honest attempt to deal with one of the besetting German psychological problems spotlit by wartime conditions; much more controversial was Ionesco's death-haunted *Exit the King* with Sir Alec Guinness in the lead. It was one of those pieces that split critical as well as public opinion down the middle. Ibsen, for too long absent from the Festival, was represented by that rarity *Little Eyeolf*, while at the Gateway Theatre Roddy Macmillan's genre piece *All in good faith* spoke up robustly for the Scottish Theatre.

Scotland indeed made a more impressive showing than usual in 1963. In addition to the Gateway play, there were admirable exhibitions of Scottish art, past and present, including one devoted to Allan Ramsay and his contemporaries and a retrospective survey of John Maxwell. There were also concerts, ceilidhs, recitals of voice and verse, and numerous small scale activities on the Fringe.

In the field of international art, the major display in the Royal Scottish Academy was devoted to a very comprehensive collection of the work of Soutine and Modigliani assembled from many quarters. If there was nothing as spectacular as the earlier Epstein or Diaghilev exhibitions, taken as a whole the standard of Festival art was very distinguished.

Finally there was the Drama Conference, mentioned earlier, which took place during the Festival's third week. About 50 more or less prominent personalities associated with the theatre from both sides of the Atlantic busied themselves with such topics as " The differences and sympathies between the Theatre and the Cinema", " The conflict between the Theatre of Committal and the Theatre of the Absurd", or " Who makes today's theatre—the playwright, the director or the actor". With Kenneth Tynan as overlord of the proceedings, and with a number of fiery and argumentative speakers available, the proceedings were rarely dull—though sometimes inconclusive. But, as Tynan said, probably the most fruitful encounters and discussions took place out of public earshot. Given the easy articulateness of those taking part in the Conference, the debates tended to be more fully reported than much else in the Festival. And when there was a row, or somebody said a rude word, it stole the headlines in a way denied to a sumptuous performance by Menuhin or Stern or any of the other great artists gathered in the city.

What then of the future? The Edinburgh Festival of 1963 was held under the shadow of looming crisis: a financial situation, on the one hand, which in the next year or two would be circumscribed not by a level of profitability or non-profitability, but by a fixed-ceiling level of expenditure; and on the other by a cultural situation with a background of criticism in certain quarters of the standards which Lord Harewood had been striving to attain—the new, the adventurous and the exploratory. Certainly, said many critics in 1964, there were powerful arguments that the State should grant far more money than the £20,000 which the Festival was then receiving at present from the Scottish Committee of the Arts Council of Great Britain. There was also in existence an Appeal Committee of the Festival Society which, it was hoped, would raise more money from private industry which the same critics thought should contribute more in view of their gains from the big influx of visitors at Festival time. " But ", said one prominent visitor during the 1964 Festival, " Edinburgh must be prepared to accept the ultimate responsibility for financing the Festival if outside support fails. It is, after all, Edinburgh's own Festival."

Things are never quite so easy as this in any city with costly housing and transport problems, and therefore increasing rates which have to be borne by citizens who, as this book goes to Press, were being asked to shoulder increased taxes as well.

So what the outcome will be is a little uncertain—for various reasons. When the accounts for the 1963 Festival were published in April, 1964 they showed a loss of almost £122,000. The bulk of this heavy deficit was fortunately reduced by contributions—£50,000 from the Corporation, £20,000 from the Scottish Committee of the Arts Council, £18,660 from private donors and £10,000 from the Scottish Command's Military Tattoo—but a net deficit of more than £23,000 remained. In June, 1964, however, Lord Provost Duncan Weatherstone announced that the Edinburgh Corporation would double its annual grant to the Arts and give henceforth £150,000. Of this £75,000 would go to the Festival, subject to an independent professional review of the Festival Society's administration. The rest would go to the Scottish National Orchestra Society, the Scottish Opera Society and other cultural bodies.

In the meantime the Earl of Harewood resigned. He had been responsible for the artistic direction of four Festivals, and since the early spring of 1960 had introduced many inspiring ideas. As he said in his letter of resignation (dated 5th November, 1964), he had found his four-and-a-half years stimulating and exciting. In reply the Lord Provost, on behalf of the Corporation, said that the Corporation had always enjoyed the friendliest co-operation with Lord Harewood and had valued his ability, commonsense, reasonableness and strength of purpose.

In the meantime the Festival goes on under a new director. In April, 1965 it was announced that Mr. Peter Diamand, general manager of the Holland Festival, had become the Edinburgh Festival's full-time Director; soon it was apparent that apart from the friendly reception given to Mr. Diamand's appointment he was starting his work in a sudden glow of financial sunshine. For on June the 3rd it was announced that by cutting costs the 1964 Festival had made a profit of nearly £40,000. Needless to say this had a heartening effect on everyone connected with the arts in the city, and not least the Corporation which in July approved a scheme for the Lyceum Theatre–Castle Terrace area[1] comprising two new theatres—one especially designed to accommodate grand opera—a conference hall and a hotel which should help to ease the pressure on accommodation during the Festival and naturally in the tourist season as well.

[1] An account of the preliminaries to this decision is given in Chapter 40.

CHAPTER 39

MUSIC AND THE BALLET

EDINBURGH is a city of paradox and contrast. The fair and the foul, ardour and lethargy, gentility and earthiness have grown used to one another's company over the centuries, and the arts are no exception. Here is a capital city that had the energy and vision to promote an International Festival; yet it has no professional orchestra of its own, nor an opera house, still less an opera company, nor even a conservatoire of music—amenities which many less populous and less prestige-laden continental cities take for granted.

The view is sometimes advanced in Metropolitan quarters, and more regrettably by residents or near residents that for 49 weeks of the year Edinburgh lies in a state of cultural coma. But this is based on ignorance. It is not, for instance, generally realised that between October and April there is an average of five concerts a week taking place in the city. Their nature and calibre will be investigated later, and no one would pretend that Festival standards obtain all the time, but the fact remains that during the winter months at least there is a constant discharge of crotchets and quavers into the Edinburgh air. From mid-June until early October, excepting during the Festival, there is however something of a close season for concert hall music.

Whether Edinburgh can properly account itself a musical city in its own right apart from the Festival is a more complex question. If in terms of urban status, it is legitimate to compare the city with, say, Munich, it is almost certain that an assessor of such matters would rank the capital of Scotland well below the capital of Bavaria. But the comparison would be unfair because of the divergent histories of the two cities. Furthermore it is sometimes assumed that because of its primacy as a city, Edinburgh, *de jure* and *ex officio*, ought to be music-minded. But there are no particular reasons why this should be so. Music has flourished here in a modest way over the centuries especially in the 16th and 18th centuries, but among the exercises of the heart and mind, it has been held in less esteem than metaphysics and literature. In those great days when the city bore the title of "The Athens of the North", a nice taste in music was by no means an essential ingredient in the equipment of the educated Edinburgh citizen.

Although this generalisation may be over-bold, the impression persists that the most active support for music comes from the middle classes. But certain events have uncovered some revealing public attitudes. During the 1958 Festival the Menuhin–Cassado–Kentner Trio gave an extra morning concert in the Embassy Cinema, Pilton for which the charge was a shilling a head. It was a tremendous success, and about 2,000 people were turned away including, inevitably, many local residents with less time on their hands than the Festival visitors. Two local comments, reported in the press, were worth noting: " This music is not for the likes of us " and secondly, " We have proved that appreciation of good music is not confined to the so-called highbrows." The implications of both points of view need no exposition. For varying reasons, they may be deplored, but they are not to be overlooked in a conspectus of this kind. It is also relevant to mention the experience of the Scottish National Orchestra. Trying some years ago to reach a wider audience than that which customarily attends the Friday night concerts in the Usher Hall it arranged periodic " Industrial Concerts " a little lighter in flavour than average, with very favourable block booking terms for factories, works and firms. The response was adequate but not overwhelming. Yet sociologists might register with interest the fact that the title of those concerts was subsequently and successfully changed to " Mid-week Concerts".

Who then goes to concerts in the city? Although each series, and type of programme, is bound to attract a particular clientele, there is a voracious minority of *aficionados* whose presence may be relied upon at most events. In addition there is the main " floating " audience whose numbers can vary in sometimes unpredictable ways. What may be counted on always is a predominance of women over men; and of those women the greater number seem to be in the middle or senior age groups. They constitute the foundation of support without which many of the concert promoting organisations would soon founder. Equally, a large proportion of these organisations, groups and societies are themselves run by women.

To what extent that " petticoat influence ", either at the distributing or the receiving end, conditions the prevailing musical atmosphere is hard to say. But at any rate, the character of musical life in Edinburgh is on the whole conservative, with the German classics firmly entrenched in popular affection. The period of composition between roughly 1720 and 1920 is repeatedly traversed—though less often explored—to the detriment of the old and even the not-so-new. Were the alert, local music lover to be deprived of the consolation of radio and gramophone, he would find the staple diet of programmes both limited and limiting. Yet it has been for some years a principle in the Lunch Hour concerts in the National Gallery of Scotland that one modern work should be included in each programme. Thus although Edinburgh's concert season is busy it is also restricted in range, and a little remote from the facts of musical life as understood in many continental cities of equivalent size. Those who have the initiative to expand public taste rarely possess the means, and to a much lesser extent, those with the means rarely possess the initiative.

Even the Festival cannot be said to have effected a major change in listening habits. It has accustomed the Edinbourgeoisie to the highest standards of performance and with its relatively large resources provided many unforgettable experiences in every medium; but it too has learnt to its cost that the unfamiliar is cautiously welcomed, unless introduced with the greatest tact and under the most imposing auspices.

At this stage it is necessary to remind readers that so amorphous a quantity as public taste can to a certain extent be swayed. It is something for the formation of which various categories of people are responsible. There are the casual, essentially passive concert goers for whom music is an occasional joy or relaxation. There are those who themselves play or sing, either at home or in public with other amateurs (in choirs or orchestras). This group may include ex-professional musicians. And thirdly there are those who make their living from it. Into that category should also go those who promote performances—though there are no Edinburgh impresarios in the London meaning of the term. It is naturally this third group which is the most influential, including as it does the University Faculty of Music. Indeed the Reid Professor, Professor Sidney Newman, who succeeded Sir Donald Tovey in 1941, takes by virtue of his office and by his personal qualities a place at the top of the local musical hierarchy.

That hierarchy is made up of musicians whose main source of income derives from teaching, whether in schools and colleges, or privately. Some of them have connections outside Edinburgh; the Royal Scottish Academy of Music in Glasgow, for instance, has several prominent Edinburgh artists on its staff. But whereas there are sufficient instructors in stringed and keyboard instruments in the city there is an obvious shortage of teachers of wind and brass instruments, and not many teachers of singing. With regard to composition, its technique can be learnt in Edinburgh, and the city in the early and middle '60s had a few composers in residence. Dr. Hans Gal and Dr. Kenneth Leighton have long since achieved, or are achieving international recognition, but both are Edinburgh citizens by adoption. In that respect they differ from such figures as the late Dr. W. B. Moonie, Robert Crawford, David Gwilt (who is on the staff at Winchester) or Isobel Dunlop. Thea Musgrave, by far the most distinguished of the Edinburgh born composers, lives in London, which, with its wider opportunities, contacts (and competition) exerts a continuous attraction on the more ambitious of the native executant and creative artists. The example of the well known 'cellist Joan Dickson may however be cited as an exception to this trend.

THE ORCHESTRA

Although Edinburgh does not run to a full-time orchestra of its own, it has a part share in the Scottish National Orchestra. The Corporation and the Edinburgh Concerts Society are represented on the board of directors, whose chairman is Sir David Milne. Financially, the city subsidises the S.N.O. to the tune of £16,000. In return the S.N.O. provides a weekly concert in the Usher Hall during the winter, and occasional ones during the summer. It has also played an increasingly important part in recent Edinburgh Festival programmes.

The Usher Hall, for the hire of which a charge of £75 is made per concert, holds 2,700, and the average attendance at S.N.O. evenings represents 84 per cent capacity, which is relatively more than was the case in Glasgow's late lamented St. Andrews Hall. The price range is from 4*s.* 6*d.* to 10*s.* 6*d.* with attractive reductions for seasonal and block bookings. The cheapest places, in the Upper Tier, are usually well filled, especially with the younger generation who will brave the cramped squeakiness of the seats for the sake of economy and of hearing better than anyone else in the hall. Unfortunately it has not been found practicable to provide refreshments in the Usher Hall. In the theatres, the audience may shamelessly mix Anouilh and alcohol; Beethoven in Edinburgh must be taken neat.

The Scottish National Orchestra has significantly enhanced its reputation under its present conductor, Alexander Gibson, and is now about 90 strong. Although a tendency towards caution in the choice of programmes reflects box-office considerations, new or unfamiliar works are systematically introduced. For Edinburgh music lovers Friday is the traditional S.N.O. night. But it is also the evening most favoured for social gatherings, dances and functions of all sorts.

On alternate Thursdays during the winter and spring terms of the academic year, the University Reid Orchestra under Professor Newman gives concerts in the Reid School of music, which holds about 400. These are well patronised, though it should be recorded that a charge is made for the programme book but not for admission. For larger, more elaborately scored works the resident instrumentalists have to be augmented from outside, but much of the standard repertory is within the orchestra's capacities. Although its personnel is largely professional, it is not made up of primarily orchestral musicians in the sense of the S.N.O. or B.B.C. Scottish Orchestras. The standard of performance is accomplished, and the playing is marked by its zest. Since box-office considerations are of lesser account in this case, the programmes can afford to be more enterprising than those of the S.N.O. but the standard classics are well in evidence, in particular for the benefit of the music students of the University who are required to attend rehearsals.

There are of course other orchestral groups operating in the city. The Edinburgh String Ensemble consists of about a dozen players conducted by Eric Roberts, a former B.B.C. Scottish Orchestra violinist, with a repertory that stresses the early 18th century but also makes a point of introducing 20th century scores to its audience, including those of Scottish provenance. (Mr. Roberts in the early '60s was running a series of " Connoisseur concerts " on Sunday nights during the winter, alternating between chamber music and string ensemble music, the former category sometimes provided by visiting artists from London or farther afield.) The Edinburgh Chamber Orchestra, formerly conducted by Dr. Hans Gal, is a larger and less professional body covering rather the same field. A recent entry into the field is the St. Cecilia Orchestra, conducted by Miles Baster, better known as the leader of the Edinburgh Quartet. The better local players, incidentally, are often to be found in several local organisations, whether the latter are named or anonymous. Finally, the Edinburgh Youth Orchestra and the Edinburgh Corporation School Orchestra, both of recent foundation, have won their spurs.

CHAMBER MUSIC

Chamber music, which is here taken to include all kinds of small scale music-making, is apt to be the least popular branch of the art save when promoted by a handful of world famous artists. None the less it finds a surprisingly large number of outlets in Edinburgh.

The weekly Lunch Hour recitals in the National Gallery of Scotland on Wednesdays, held between October and April, had by 1963 been organised for over a decade and a half by Miss Tertia Liebenthal. The use of the Gallery by courtesy of the Trustees, the loan of a grand piano, an Arts Council grant and a waiting list of artists anxious to take part in these concerts at almost nominal fees makes this valuable enterprise possible at a charge of only a half a crown a head. Sporadically a Peter Pears will appear (as indeed he did to celebrate the series' 400th concert) and treble the average size of the audience—this is about 100—but for the most part the artists are up and coming rather than established stars. They originate from all parts of the world—from South America, Canada, Europe, London and from Scotland itself: the standard of performance is in general high and the choice of programmes discerning.

One of the most distinguished series of recitals used to be held in the Freemasons' Hall, at which on Monday nights artists or ensembles of international, Festival calibre played or sang to audiences drawn from a wide area, particularly from the Borders. Unfortunately, some years ago, attendance started to dwindle and it became impracticable to carry on this venture. Its place has latterly been taken by the New Town Concerts.

Alternating with the orchestral concerts in the University Reid School of Music are fortnightly chamber recitals, provided either by visiting ensembles, by members of the Faculty or by the Edinburgh Quartet. These evenings, whose artistic value is almost invariably excellent, tend to be less well attended than those devoted to orchestral music. The Edinburgh Quartet is maintained by the University. Its basic allegiance is to the Music Faculty, but its members are free to engage in teaching and solo work and to take joint engagements elsewhere as far as their immediate academic duties allow. This quartet-in-residence, the membership of which has changed over the years, quickly established itself as a major asset in the city's musical life. The availability of four expert string players has been a boon not only to the Reid Orchestra but to sundry other bodies.

In marked contrast to the Freemasons Hall Recitals are the Nelson Hall concerts, dedicated to the proposition that the man in the street can enjoy good music if it is put over without pretentiousness and without admission fees. In three out of the four public libraries founded by the publisher Thomas Nelson (now administered by the Edinburgh Corporation Library Committee) about five concerts are held between October and May on Tuesday evenings. Run on a very small budget, they are patronised by an unusually mixed variety of listeners, including old people who creep in for the warmth, and when they have had enough, creep out again. Devised by the late Dr. Douglas Dickson, a prominent and distinguished Edinburgh amateur musician, they are nowadays carried on by his daughter, Miss Joan Dickson, and for the most part are given by local musicians.

As it happens, Tuesday night is also chamber music night at the French Institute. The visiting artists, comparable in standing with those who appear at the Lunch Hour recitals, are for the most part French, with programmes to match. The audience is fairly specialised, and has a smaller percentage of the hard core of music lovers whom one sees elsewhere, their place being taken by members of the French Institute circles with a general interest in all Gallic artistic manifestations. The amenities of the Institute's elegant salon are sometimes offered to local groups apart from those who appear there under French auspices. Rather the same category of audience is to be found at the occasional Tuesday evening recitals and lecture-recitals organised by the Italian-Scottish Society.

The organ, the " king of instruments", is not neglected, and besides the sundry recitals given in various churches and in St. Giles, the big organ in the McEwan Hall (a Hope-Jones refurbished by Willis in 1953) is used for celebrity recitals by such great names as Germani, Demessieux, Flor Peeters and prominent English executants. Attendance varies considerably from under 200 to more than 800, as with so many other local musical activities, the economics of the series are precariously balanced.

It will have been observed that Edinburgh's musical life is maintained by a variety of organisations, which also includes the Edinburgh Wind Quintet and the Bernicia Ensemble, but a feature that needs comment is the comparative absence of artists who give concerts in Edinburgh of their own volition. (The regular visits of the ever-popular Vienna Boys Choir are an exception). Yet this is not surprising. When, for instance, the Leipzig Gewandhaus orchestra gave a concert here some years ago in April, the Usher Hall was barely half full. Other groups have had similar experiences. But although that sort of reaction seems odd in a Festival centre, the truth is that for a city of its size, Edinburgh has already as many concerts as its audiences can absorb.

Choral music is dominated by the Edinburgh Royal Choral Union. Founded a little over a century ago, and conducted by Herrick Bunney, Master of Music at the High Kirk of St. Giles, it is about 250 strong. Though not the equal in reliability and richness of tone of the great Yorkshire choral societies, nor of a virtuoso body like the Philharmonia chorus, it is a thoroughly serviceable choir whose efficiency and repertory have gained immeasurably from the galvanising enthusiasm of its conductor, and it has long since won its spurs in the Festival lists. Apart from its traditional *Messiah* on New Year's Day (a social as much as a musical event) it gives two main concerts a year with the S.N.O. in the Usher Hall. But the problems that face it are those of any large choral society—the recruitment of younger singers and, in particular, the lack of tenors. The Edinburgh Churches Choir is smaller and until recent years more restricted in its repertory, but its conductor in the early '60s, Walter Wilkinson, is a man of lively ideas who has done much to raise its standard of performance. Still smaller is the Edinburgh Bach Society, run for many years by Dr. Mary Grierson, but now directed by James Sloggie. Although it lives up to its title, the Society opens its programmes to music by other composers, old and new. (A prominent feature of its activities under Dr. Grierson was the annual performance of the St. Matthew Passion with a chorale choir of a thousand school-children).

Student voices *en masse* can be heard at the interesting choral concerts of the Edinburgh University Musical Society Choir, which under its conductor Professor Sidney Newman tackles large scale and difficult works with considerable success. Also nominally connected with the University—although its members are not necessarily still at their studies—are the Edinburgh University Singers. This is a small, elite group, founded by the Rev. Ian Pitt-Watson shortly after the war and latterly carried on by Herrick Bunney. Though its quality fluctuates with the talent available, its prestige is very high, and the Singers have appeared in London as well as during the Festival. A recent development is its first rate Easter-tide performance of the Bach St. Matthew and St. John Passions, sung in German, and with more or less authentically proportioned forces. Finally, there is the Festival Chorus, trained by Arthur Oldham, over one third of which is recruited from Edinburgh. It won international praise in its debut in Mahler's 8th Symphony at the 1965 Festival.

OPERA

For opera Edinburgh is dependent on the Festival, upon the visits of the Sadler's Wells touring companies and, since 1963, on the newly founded Scottish Opera which in 1964 presented three full-scale operas in the city—*Faust*, *Don Giovanni* and *Otello*.

Sadler's Wells tends to leave its more enterprising productions at home; which leads some local opera lovers to claim that they do not really get value for money, however polished the performance of *Bohème* or *Rigoletto* that are provided. On the other hand, the experience of Sadler's Wells is that Edinburgh, out of Festival time, does not support performances of the less popular works. Until such time as the city builds a proper opera house—agitation for which boils up more furiously at each successive Festival—the King's Theatre has to serve as an opera house. Suitable for modest scale performances, it is notoriously cramped for anything involving some degree of spaciousness. This affects visiting international companies in August and September more than Sadler's Wells.

Amateur operatics are sustained by the Edinburgh Opera Company, Edinburgh Grand Opera, and Opera da Camera, and light opera is promoted by the Bohemians, the Southern Light Opera Company and the Gilbert and Sullivan Society.

CHURCH MUSIC

As regards church music, the two main sources are St. Giles, where there is a mixed choir, and St. Mary's Episcopal Cathedral, where the choir and the ordering of the sung services are after the Anglican pattern. The sweetness of the boys' tone at St. Mary's is deservedly famous and was one of the specialities of a well known former organist, Dr. Robert Head. (The present organist is Dennis Townhill, who instigates a number of variegated musical activities in the cathedral additional to the regular services). As regards the other churches, it is evident that increasing attention is being paid to music in the Church of Scotland, and besides St. Giles, there are praiseworthy choirs at the Greyfriars and Canongate churches. Meanwhile at the St. Mary's Catholic Cathedral, the director of music, Arthur Oldham, who is himself a composer, is making special efforts to revive old Scots pre-Reformation music.

THE UNIVERSITY

Mention has already been made of the concert promoting activities of the University's Faculty of Music, but its main function is the education of students in the higher disciplines of their art, leading to the degree of Bachelor of Music. At a later stage, doctorates are awarded either for research, for composition or for performance. The prestige of the Edinburgh degree, the quality of the staff and the valuable scholarships attract students from many quarters. Many go into teaching, but a number become instrumentalists like Alastair Graham and Audrey Innes (piano), Susan Landale (organ), conductors like Roderick Brydon of Sadler's Wells, or composers like Thea Musgrave.

Apart from Professor Newman, past and present members of the staff include the late Dr. Mary Grierson, Dr. Hans Gal, Dr. Hans Redlich, Dr. John Clapham, Dr. John Fairbairn, Dr. Kenneth Leighton and Dr. Peter Williams. The musical amenities of the University were signally advanced when it became known that Mr. Raymond Russell had donated to Edinburgh his priceless collection of old keyboard instruments.

THE SCHOOLS

As is to be expected, music plays its part in Edinburgh's other and varied educational establishments, whether at a teacher training college like Moray House, or in the Merchant Company, State or boarding schools. Obviously no generalisation is possible here, for in each case the musical climate of a school depends so much on the drive and personality of the man in charge and also on the degree of support which he has from his headmaster. It can be said however that music is being taken far more seriously at all levels of education than was the case formerly, the amenities being in several cases of the first order: the new Music School at George Watson's is a case in point.

SOCIETIES AND CLUBS

Mention must be made here also of the concerts and activities sponsored by the Saltire Society either at its headquarters in Gladstone's Land or elsewhere. Latterly they have considerably diminished, but early in the

1950s excellent, specialised programmes were devised under the aegis of Hans Oppenheim and Miss Isobel Dunlop. In furtherance of these enterprises was the establishment of a professional vocal quartet, the Saltire Singers. This was a first class group, much admired abroad, which made recordings for the Deutsche Grammophon Gesellschaft and Columbia companies. At home support was more fitful, and eventually the Singers moved to London. But among other Saltire schemes which have commendably continued are the creation of the Stevenson Trust (through the munificence of the Dunlop family) which awards scholarships to talented young artists, and commissions works from promising composers.

In order to foster local interest in the Scottish National Orchestra, an Edinburgh supporters club was founded some years ago; and this meets on Monday nights for lectures, recitals and discussions, most of which have a direct or indirect bearing on the S.N.O.'s work. The Edinburgh Gramophone Society is a more select organisation and its members often have a very detailed and critical knowledge of music in the context of their own particular interest.

For sociability plus live performance, however, the best answer is undoubtedly provided by the Saturday evening meetings of the Edinburgh Society of Musicians. With a pleasantly old fashioned and informal atmosphere about the proceedings and both a chairman and tankards of beer in evidence, this entertaining body meets in a large, upstairs room in Thistle Street, reached by a winding and windy stair; and many of the great figures of the musical world have given " unofficial " performances there, listened to with respect by an audience which is apt to include more ordinary mélomanes than professionals.

THE YOUNG

There is a school of thought which denies the virtue of competitive festivals, but it would be received with ill grace in Edinburgh and its surrounding districts. Although the Edinburgh Competitive Festival is anything but affluent, in terms of prestige, it ranks very high in the British Isles. It gives a great deal of innocent pleasure—and qualms—to many young people who have no thought of making music their career, and more positively it serves a useful purpose in accustoming would-be professionals to the trials to come. A number of well-known local instrumentalists and singers have graduated from this " testing school." But the Festival is as much a social as a purely musical event. It is a yearly gathering of friendly rivals, be they competitors, teachers or anxious parents; which brings us inevitably to one of the phenomena of Edinburgh, the annual concert given by the pupils of the Misses Waddell who have trained generations of young Edinburgh string instrumentalists. It is a moving experience to hear these children play and to wonder what will happen to them thereafter. Some go on with violin or 'cello, win their Caird Scholarships and embark on successful professional careers; others fall by the wayside; and others again replenish the stock of good amateurs without whom the smaller orchestras could not survive.

And so from the very young—the ten year old gravely playing his or her half size 'cello—we return to the Edinburgh Festival, where the giants of the musical world meet in Edinburgh for three weeks every year. There is a link between them. On the one hand is the aspiration; on the other the realisation. And also there are other forms of artistic expression where music, of one kind or another, is an inevitable partner. There is, for instance, ballet dancing—a great and beautiful art—and the stirring spectacles and sounds of the pipers and the drummers.

THE PIPERS

Almost every visitor will readily agree that one has only to be in Edinburgh during the Festival to appreciate the tremendous attraction which the massed pipers and drummers have on their march along Princes Street to mark the opening and closing of a world famous event. In between times the daily march of the eye-fetching Edinburgh City Police Band is also responsible for the boulevard being lined deep with spectators. Apart altogether from the handsome stature of the bandsmen, they are first class performers, winning the World and Scottish Championships of 1963. In addition to the many Territorial Army bands attached to infantry and other units, as well as the Royal Naval Volunteer Reserve and the University Officers Training Corps, Edinburgh has in addition to the City Police, the Special Constabulary, Edinburgh City Transport, the S.M.T. and Colinton and Currie Pipe Bands. Then there are the School Cadets and Boys' Brigade units in which youngsters get basic training. The senior bands have their summer engagements in the Gardens and parks of the city, and elsewhere they have competition appearances, for which they practice assiduously. As each band probably numbers between 18 and 20 pipers and drummers, Edinburgh could put on a parade of " a Hundred Pipers " at any time without much difficulty.

It may be invidious to pick out one from among many distinguished Edinburgh pipers but it is appropriate to mention John Burgess who must be accounted a virtuoso. Finally there is the Scottish Command School of Piping at the Castle, for long ruled over by the famous Pipe Major Willie Ross and now run by Pipe Major John MacLennan. There are usually about a dozen advanced students in the School—all budding pipe majors—representing Canada, the Gurkha Regiments, Ireland, India, Pakistan and even Transjordania as well as Scotland.

THE BALLET

Scotland has a rich tradition of dancing. This is not really surprising since for the Scots with their natural vivacity and traditional neatness of footwork it is as natural to dance as to eat and drink. There is however a curious similarity between the Scottish dance and the Classical ballet technique, as practised today, which obviously goes back to the French cultural invasion of Mary Queen of Scots and her retinue in the 16th century. When Mary and her French courtiers introduced to Scotland many of their favourite dances—the galliard, the tordion, the courrante, la volta and others, naturally some of the steps and the balletic style crept into Scottish national dances. That heritage is commemorated in Miss Marjory Middleton's ballet, *Pavan for Mary* with music by Leighton Lucas and costumes and decor by Valerie Prentis. Owing to inadequate financial backing, only its first act had been mounted by the summer of 1963, but it had a great artistic success when presented at Edinburgh's Lyceum Theatre.

In the last 30 years Classical ballet has also come into its own in Scotland. This is mainly due to the pioneering energy and enthusiasm of Miss Marjory Middleton, founder and principal of Edinburgh's Scottish Ballet School, which began life as the Shandwick School of Dancing. Yet although there was little Classical ballet taught in Edinburgh when Miss Middleton began her teaching in 1935, a certain foundation had been laid by a ballet instructor called Donald G. Maclennan who though he had started to teach there during 1899, divided his time between Edinburgh (in the winter months), and London for the rest of the year. In London Donald Maclennan's remarkable knowledge of Highland dancing so won the esteem of Dame Adeline Genée and her uncle Alexander Genée that when the Association of Operatic Dancing (now the Royal Academy of Dancing) was formed in 1923 Donald Maclennan was asked to join the committee, and pure Classical ballet was seriously taught in Edinburgh thereafter. Its subsequent progress was rapid. In 1930 the Operatic Dancing Association held its first dancing examinations in the city. Later Miss Middleton's own Scottish Ballet School not only began to train dancers who have since become famous but introduced a new syllabus called Ballet in Education, which achieved immediate fame. This was commissioned by the Royal Academy of Dancing in conformity with her own strong feeling that the disciplined art of ballet should be a necessity for children rather than a luxury. Since then there has been another syllabus, *Ballet in Further Education*, especially designed for the amateur dancer and equally suitable for either the teenager, who has studied ballet before, or for the adult who is a beginner.

In these ways, ballet has continued to spread in Scotland—with Edinburgh as a vital focal point. It is highly significant that Scotland now has its own bi-annual professional examinations, and that as many as almost 80 candidates have been examined in a recent year. The children's examinations, held three times a year, may result in an annual total of some 1,400 for Scotland. So clearly the ballet cult is progressing satisfactorily. At intervals, the public has also had an opportunity of seeing the Scottish Ballet School's work when the Gateway Theatre is taken over for a short season; and on those occasions there is usually some representation of Miss Middleton's gifts as a choreographer.

It is significant too that Scotland has produced many notable dancers in recent years with Alexander Bennett as the most outstanding. He trained at the Scottish Ballet School, and subsequently made his debut with the Edinburgh Ballet Club, which started in 1943 and has proved a wonderful training ground for young dancers. Alexander Bennett became Madame Rambert's leading male dancer, and afterwards became a first soloist in the Royal Ballet. Kenneth Bannerman also trained in Scotland at the school, and has been Madame Rambert's leading male dancer in the early '60s. William Wilson of Edinburgh is a soloist in the Royal Ballet, and other pupils of the Scottish Ballet School who have achieved international recognition include Maureen Bruce, Stella Claire, Irene Claire, (all original members of the Edinburgh Ballet Club), and many other successful in the commercial theatre. It is a splendid result, achieved only after hard endeavour and not unaccompanied by various difficulties. " For example ", Miss Middleton has put on record, " there seems to be a lack of cohesion in Edinburgh artistic life which is frustrating. One would think that a gallant little company like the Edinburgh Ballet Theatre would get more help from the musicians of the city. For many years the club has had to *import* musicians from England to play for its performances. It is a sad thing when one must call for help." But the growing interest in ballet continues. For apart from the stimulus provided by Edinburgh's own Ballet Club, interest in this composite art form has been increased by the visits of many companies of international fame to the Edinburgh Festival; and it is certainly the hope of all who work in this sphere in the city that one day Scotland will have its own National Ballet Company.

Chapter 40

THE THEATRE

By mid-20th century the theatre in Edinburgh, as elsewhere, had experienced a change. It was no longer the theatre of 30 years before. The character of its audience had altered, and with it the plays presented. Except at rare times going to the theatre was no longer a social occasion. In the old days stalls and circle had been resplendent with evening dress, but with the passing of each year " shirt fronts and sables " were of rarer occurrence.

The new audience sought the theatre for its entertainment value, as they might seek the cinema; they liked to see themselves and their own small problems reflected in its mirror, and they did not care if it was the distorted mirror of farce or sentimental comedy which reflected them. They wanted to laugh. The consequence was that the most popular plays were farces, comedies and thrillers, and they were naturally all the more popular if presented by star actors and actresses or by those who had made a popular reputation in films or on radio or television.

Occasionally, a play more important than the average one would slip through and often prove highly popular. Such were *Twelfth Night*, in an Old Vic production, with Peggy Ashcroft as Viola; *The Rivals* with John Clements, Kay Hammond and Athene Seyler; John Gielgud's production of *Lady Windermere's Fan*, with Isabel Jeans and décor by Cecil Beaton; *The Eagle Has Two Heads* with Eileen Herlie and James Donald, both Scottish players, in the leading parts of Queen and Poet. Yet there was always the feeling that if a real classic were presented, backed more often than not by the Committee for the Encouragement of Music and the Arts (C.E.M.A.), which grew into the Arts Council, it was rather by accident or artificial encouragement than by the desire of the public. Of course, many such plays were presented in Edinburgh in the course of trial runs and often opened there, but their appearance in the city seemed always more fortuitous than deliberate.

Then, astonishingly and to most people quite out of the blue, there came the first Edinburgh International Festival of Music and Drama in 1947. This memorable event, however, brought some early difficulties for play producers and the play-going visitors and public.

With two of the city's principal theatres usually denied to drama—during the Festival the King's became the temporary home of opera and the Empire the temporary home of ballet—the playwright's art was, in the three weeks the Festival lasted, less in evidence at first than the more ardent theatregoer wished. Even so the drama fared better than might have been imagined, for Scottish playwriting and acting had now developed to an extent that made a Festival in which it was not represented incomplete. The hour supplied the man. This was Tyrone Guthrie, whose great reputation as a producer had been built upon his early experience in Glasgow with the Scottish National Players.

For his first Festival production Guthrie was given a short leet of three plays from which to choose, one of them Sir David Lyndesay's 16th century morality, *The Three Estates*, which had languished in obscurity for centuries, unread by all but scholars, but which in fact had already been suggested for possible production by *The Scotsman*'s drama critic. Against all probability Guthrie chose *The Three Estates*, a play in pawkie rhyme which had helped to create the Reformation in Scotland. But where could such a play—with its mass appeal, written for a theatre entirely different from our own and with its picture-frame stage—be presented? Again, against all probability, Guthrie found the place in the Assembly Hall of the Church of Scotland—a church which had admonished John Home for writing *Douglas*, a play revived at a later Festival with Dame Sybil Thorndike and her husband, Lewis Casson, in the cast.

Not only had Guthrie found an additional stage for Festival purposes, but this " open stage " became a feature of each successive Festival, though not every subsequent production on it suggested that the Festival Council had quite realised the exact nature of Guthrie's discovery. *The Three Estates*, after a slow opening booking, leaped into favour, for Guthrie produced it with panache in a version by Robert Kemp. It was the forerunner of productions in Stratford, Ontario, on a similar type of stage, and this theatre in turn decided the form of the new theatre planned for Chichester where Guthrie was again consulted.

Restricted as the official count of Festival drama was, the restriction did not prevent a wide variety of plays being acted. For not only did English, Canadian, French, German and Italian companies present on the official stages plays by Shakespeare, Sophocles, Molière, Racine, Marivaux, Goethe, Goldoni, Giraudoux, Pirandello, Anouilh and others, but an unofficial festival of drama (popularly known as " The Fringe " which we glanced at earlier) grew up beside the official one and easily surpassed it in size and sometimes rivalled it in merit, as, for instance, when Lennox Robinson brought a company of Irish players, including Siobhan McKenna, to the Lauriston Hall. Just as wits had been racked in a search for Scottish drama worthy of being officially presented, so they were also racked by the host of in-comers who wished to find halls in which to exhibit the wares they peddled. At one time or another the Universities of Oxford, Edinburgh, Durham, Dublin and Aberdeen all entered student teams, and by 1956 well-known professional actors and actresses had begun to appear on *The Fringe*. These included Donald Wolfit, Robert Speaight, Catherine Lacey and Sonia Dresdel. Among others Mr. Brian Bailey, later Director of the Belgrade Theatre in Coventry, brought for many years a fine professional company with new plays.

Among the other groups whose productions were of real value were the London Club Theatre Group, the Gateway Theatre (ultimately given official status) and the Edinburgh District of the Scottish Community Drama Association, while the productions of religious drama in St. Giles' Cathedral by the Church Touring Group (an amateur organisation associated with the Gateway) became for a time Festival events. Among their productions was Byron's *Cain.*

If the Edinburgh Festival not only astonished the world but, through the abilities of its early artistic directors, Rudolf Bing, Ian Hunter and Robert Ponsonby, seemed almost effortlessly to attain international celebrity, quite a large section of the Edinburgh public—and a section in some ways characteristically " Edinburgh "—refused to be astonished or elated by the phenomenon, which to them remained a little suspect and artificial. Indeed, it was almost a standing joke that after the captains and the kings had departed some quite low-brow entertainment or sentimental comedy would come into its own.

Perhaps one reason for this was that first-class entertainment was a great deal harder to come by in the ordinary way than it had been 30 years before, when there was, as yet, no dearth of touring companies presenting London successes, and the last of the old actor-managers, Sir Frank Benson and Sir John Martin Harvey, were still on the roads and making fairly regular visits to the Scottish capital, the one offering a repertory of Shakespearean plays and the other his famous melodramas —*The Only Way*, *The Breed of the Treshams* or *The Burgomaster of Stilemond.* Even when they no longer came, their places were taken for a time by others. Both Henry Baynton, a popular and frequent visitor to Edinburgh in the 1920s, and Donald Wolfit, who came later, excelled in the rapid presentation of Shakespeare's comedy and tragedy. Long before his death however (1951) Baynton had ceased to tour, and in 1947 Wolfit's decision to abandon Shakespeare deprived Edinburgh of almost all contact with the poet's plays, except for amateur or Festival productions of them or occasional visits of the Old Vic Company.

As a result of the decline in touring and competition from the cinema and radio drama, and also after March, 1952, from television, the theatre for long stretches of the year lived from hand to mouth. It was no uncommon experience in Edinburgh for contracts to be signed at the eleventh hour and for poorer productions to be staged than would, under happier circumstances, have been selected. It was therefore not to be wondered at that those responsible for the theatre industry in the city welcomed the invention of the summer show in which popular " comics " like Harry Gordon and Dave Willis alternated with " song scenas " and dancing. The first of these entertainments to be introduced to Edinburgh (1935) ran for six weeks, the fourth (1939) for 28 weeks. After that the length of the runs varied considerably.

The summer show soon established itself as an annual feature. It attracted much the same type of patron as the pantomime attracted in the winter season. Its home was the King's Theatre, which, after alterations completed in December, 1951, was slightly reduced in seating capacity but could still accommodate 1,495 theatregoers in area, circle and upper circle, as well as 48 purchasers of box seats.

A large portion of the annual programme of the King's was also filled by regular events such as visits from the Carl Rosa and D'Oyly Carte Opera companies and presentations by amateur light opera companies.

The result was that " serious " playgoing became less and less in evidence at the King's, and tended to be concentrated in the Royal Lyceum Theatre (capacity 1,680 seats), opened by Sir Henry Irving on 10th September, 1883.

For certain periods of the year a resident repertory company was introduced to the Lyceum Theatre. The practice began as early as the summer of 1929, when the Masque Theatre, an offshoot of the Oxford University Dramatic Society, gave its first performance there. If the Masque Theatre, popular at first, lost its popularity, it did so because its standards were high, and since its disappearance from the Edinburgh scene in the summer of 1932, none of the many repertory companies to succeed it gave an equal satisfaction to the intelligent playgoer. Chief among these were the Brandon Thomas Company, which began operations in 1933, and the Wilson Barrett Company, which first appeared in Edinburgh at the Empire Theatre in 1939 and throughout its many seasons at the Lyceum maintained a fine standard of production.

In March, 1938 Messrs. Howard and Wyndham, proprietors of the two principal Edinburgh theatres, had taken for the first time the unusual step of forming their own company, the Howard and Wyndham Players. The company, which included players of the calibre of Sonia Dresdel, filled in the gap between the Brandon Thomas and the Wilson Barrett Seasons. " Bill " Barrett, a grandson of the Victorian actor, was a noted figure in Edinburgh for 16 years, and his decision in 1955 to disband his companies and retire from the stage first awakened the Edinburgh public to the seriousness of the theatre situation in its midst. During his long stay in Edinburgh, when for most of the time he was also responsible for repertory productions at the King's Theatre, Glasgow and His Majesty's Theatre, Aberdeen, he had relied upon such West End plays as suited his all-round and constantly changing companies, as soon as those plays were released for repertory production, with a leavening of stage classics in a decreasing measure.

After the dispersal of Barrett's company, Henry Sherek experimented with a season of 12 plays which were also staged in Glasgow. Responding to what was believed to be a popular demand for Scottish plays, Sherek included in his season comedies by Alexander Reid, Robert Kemp and Donald Mackenzie as well as the première of *A Man Named Judas* by Ronald Duncan. The Sherek Season was, however, short-lived and was succeeded by the productions of the Curzon Players, the second repertory organisation sponsored by Messrs. Howard and Wyndham in 27 years. These in due course gave place to the Whatmore Productions.

It must not be assumed that resident repertory at the Lyceum Theatre left no time for the visits of London companies. They continued to appear there, mainly during the spring and early autumn, and many plays were produced in the Lyceum Theatre before they were seen in London. Some never got so far.

In Edinburgh, as in other centres, the post-war mood of relaxation was favourable to comedy (Noel Coward was for long popular) and audiences showed appreciation of the type of social play which mirrored middle-class everyday life. The " whodunit " thriller, in which the audience was invited to play the part of detective, had also numerous followers, as had the American mid-century " musical " in its noisiest incarnation. Indeed this lighter type of show business induced so many country dwellers to travel to the city with block bookings for bus and theatre that many young people had their first sight of the stage. They might, on occasions, have been caught leaning goggle-eyed over boxes—a contrast to the more sober spirit of the regular Edinburgh theatregoers, who maintained the reputation for non-emotional behaviour they have for so long possessed.

The chief Edinburgh home of " variety " was the Empire Theatre in Nicolson Street (seating capacity 2,300), though occasionally a straight play or a musical play was staged there. During the Festival the size of the Empire's stage and auditorium made it the obvious though by no means ideal choice for ballet, but before the Festival of 1963 it succumbed to the bingo craze. Lesser homes of light entertainment which survive include the Palladium Theatre in Fountainbridge (capacity 895), built on the site of the old Cooke's Circus. Here the staple entertainment is variety, though there have been periods, especially during Festivals, when plays and late night shows have taken its place. In the '30s Millicent Ward presented in the Palladium a repertory which included some of the classics of the stage, and for a time in the mid-'50s Sonia Dresdel was the leading player in a season of repertory plays staged there by the Fraser Neal Company. In Leith the Gaiety Theatre in the Kirkgate (capacity 1521) was chiefly known for melodrama and pantomime.

Theatres which have vanished during the first half of the century include the Theatre Royal (capacity 1,500), burnt down, like more than one of its predecessors on the same site, in 1946. In December, 1950 it was announced that what remained of the theatre and its site had been purchased by the Roman Catholic Church for £10,000, with a view to the development of the adjacent cathedral precincts. The Royal had been noted for pantomime and variety, and here Florrie Ford, Tommy Lorne, Harry Gordon and Dave Willis made numerous appearances. The Alhambra (capacity 1,423), once a Leith music hall and also a home of melodrama and second class opera, became a picture house. The Grand, in Stockbridge, where musical shows and pantomime were once presented (it was formerly the Tivoli Theatre), and where Gertie Gitana sang *Nellie Dean* and Florrie Ford *Down at the Old Bull and Bush*, suffered the same fate before becoming a bingo hall which now flourishes under the name of the Grand Mecca Casino. As for the Pavillion in Grove Street, where a stock company once acted melodrama, and the Operetta House in Chambers Street, these no longer exist though the latter is now the site of Adam House, which contains the charming but miniature University Theatre (seating capacity 180, expandable to 210 without its removable apron stage). The extinction of the short-lived Princes Theatre, constructed in 1954 within the New Gallery in Shandwick Place for the Edinburgh Play Club, in which the leading spirits were Christine Orr and Robin Stark, meant the loss of an intimate theatre too small to be a financial success, even had it been better patronised than it was.

The Princes Theatre venture was a professional one. In earlier years Miss Orr had been one of the pioneers of amateur drama in Scotland, having founded The Makars, now Edinburgh's senior amateur dramatic group. Under changed leadership, the group continues to be one of the most worthwhile amateur organisations in Scotland. Both at the Little Theatre (built as an integral part of the University Settlement) and at, the Gateway Theatre, as well as elsewhere, it has staged notable plays sometimes in a notable way.

Other groups, particularly the Davidson's Mains Dramatic Club, the People's Theatre, Edinburgh University Dramatic Society, and, later, the Edinburgh Graduate Theatre Group, Theatre One, and the Jason Players were served by some of the best amateur talent in the city. Most of these clubs competed and sometimes took high place in the annual Festival of the Scottish Community Drama Association, and through their efforts, often disproportionate to the duration of the " runs ", playgoers were at least given an opportunity of seeing many plays they might otherwise have missed.

It might have been expected that this amateur movement would have reflected the growing interest in Scottish drama, but as it turned out, while Scottish plays were staged by the amateurs, and among them an occasional original one, the amateur groups appeared to show no stronger bias towards the native drama than towards any other. Indeed it may have been rather less, since quite a number of groups persisted in staging West End comedies which they were ill-calculated to interpret.

About the mid-'50s, however, the Gateway Theatre demonstrated that there was a considerable public for Scottish plays. This theatre, unique among world theatres in having been sponsored by a church—the Church of Scotland—staged a succession of Scottish plays, many for the first time. Before this the theatre had passed through a number of phases from the time when the block of buildings in Elm Row, which housed it and other activities as well, was presented anonymously to the Church. Part of the building had already had a miscellaneous history as a place of entertainment. It was an early home of cinema, a skating rink, a variety theatre and the scene of more than one short-lived attempt to establish a repertory company—the last made by a brother of Dame Clara Butt. The O'Mara Opera Company had appeared here, and De Valera had delivered an address within its walls. Just before the building was placed in the hands of the Church it had reverted to films. After some reconstruction, it was opened in October, 1946 as a combined theatre and cinema by the then Secretary of State for Scotland, Joseph Westwood, with a seating capacity of 476, later increased in the middle '50s to 542.

In the early days the theatre did not seek a fully professional status for its actors, but later a professional company was engaged, with Noël Iliff as producer. Another phase followed, in 1952, when productions were staged by players directly engaged by the theatre. In 1953 a non-profit-making company, under the chairmanship of Robert Kemp, took over and instituted a fortnightly repertory season.

The venture secured the support of the Scottish Committee of the

Arts Council, and though the capacity of the theatre was barely large enough for much of a profit to be made even under the most favourable circumstances, it was attended by a fair measure of success. The adroit and devoted front-of-house management of Miss Saidie R. Aitkin, who encouraged 'bus parties from Women's Guilds as one of her many ways of helping the theatre, counted for much, and the Church's Home Board through the Gateway director, the Rev. George Candlish, took a broad view of the theatre's function.

After a season or two the Edinburgh Gateway Company established a standard of acting—particularly in Scottish comedy—which led to its inclusion in the official Festival programme. Players like Lennox Milne (Mrs. Moray McLaren), James Gibson and Tom Fleming excelled in the new plays by Scottish authors for which the theatre began to provide an outlet. Gibson, who had been a member of the Scottish National Players under Tyrone Guthrie and other producers, had that Scottish pawkiness which appealed to Gateway audiences, and Miss Milne impersonated a succession of sharp-witted, blunt-spoken females which made her name almost synonymous with that of the Gateway. In particular she achieved a personal tour-de-force in Robert Kemp's *The Heart is Highland*, in which she virtually played all the 13 parts. The play was one of those taken on tour by the company, and performances of it were also given by Miss Milne in Canada.

Robert Kemp has been the most prolific of the Gateway dramatists. Among his early successes, apart from his famous adaptation of *The Three Estates* (1948), was his *Let Wives Tak' Tent*, produced at the Gateway Theatre in the same year. This, founded on *L'Ecole des Femmes*, was a charming transposition of Molière's French rhymed couplets into " an idiomatic Scottish prose " which had something of the flavour of sit period setting. It was revived at the 1961 Festival. Later on, Robert Kemp was to turn *L'Avare* into a Lallans play under the title of *The Laird o' Grippy*, with John Laurie as a guest artist.[1]

Kemp's resource seemed inexhaustible and only equalled by his endeavour. *The Man Among the Roses* (1956) was an ambitious attempt to do for the Border ballad of *Tamlane* what Alexander Reid, in *The Lass wi' the Muckle Mou'*, had done for *Thomas the Rhymer*, but though it had a beauty of speech in its woodland scene, the play was not a success. Neither was *Festival Fanfare*, a revised version of *Seven Bottles for the Maestro.* But *The Other Dear Charmer*, a study of Burns's relations with Clarinda, in which Burns's portrait is drawn without sentiment but with an appreciation of its spiritual aspect, was Kemp at the top of his form.

Not all his plays have been on Scottish subjects. *Conspirators* (1955), based on a story by Walter Duranty, has its setting in a frontier town of a satellite country. It was described by the playwright as " a plea for the proper observance of the Habeas Corpus Act."

[1] Laurie had already appeared at the Gateway in *The Scientific Singers* (1948), also by Kemp, which was revived nearly eight years later in an altered form as *A Nest of Singing Birds.* Unpromising as its theme is—the attempt of an Aberdeen professor to reform Church psalmody—the play is one of Kemp's truest Scottish comedies.

Of the other Edinburgh writers whose plays have been seen at the Gateway Alexander Reid, whose *Lass wi' the Muckle Mou'* has been presented on many stages, is among those whose dramatic instinct is sure. *The Wax Doll* (1956) has faith-healing as its subject, and its first production owed much to the creation of the extrovert showman, "Professor" Sardou, by Roddy McMillan.

The late R. J. B. Sellar, who turned to drama only in his middle years, was for some time a popular Gateway playwright. His plays included adaptations of Scott, Stevenson and Galt, as well as original work like *Arise, Sir Hector*! in which he satirised, against a background of modern history, the career of a Scottish tycoon. His best play is the early *Brief Glory*, an unfavourable study of Prince Charles Edward Stewart.

Other Edinburgh writers whom the Gateway has encouraged include Albert Mackie, whose three-act plays on Edinburgh life, though popular, never achieved the level of *Gentle Like a Dove*, his colourful one-act play on the wartime anti-Italian riots in the capital; Moray McLaren, who, in *Muckle Ado* (1957), developed a turn for farce on the theme of the Stone of Destiny; and Ian R. Hamilton, a busy advocate from the west of Scotland.

In 1960 after some seven years in office Robert Kemp resigned from the chairmanship of the Gateway company and was succeeded by John B. Rankin, during whose short tenure of office the Home Board used its veto in the case of the proposed production of the *Lysistrata* of Aristophanes in a version by Dudley Pitts. The sequel was Mr. Rankin's resignation and the appointment of Moultrie Kelsall, a former member of the Scottish National Theatre Company and a well-known actor.

It was maintained that dual control adversely affected the success of the Gateway, and the Church was for long reluctant to emphasise its existence to passers-by. But the theatre's difficulties were also difficulties shared by the theatre at large and keenly felt in Edinburgh. There was a period in 1961 when the only form of theatrical entertainment in the city was the summer show at the King's Theatre. The dearth of plays occasioned inquietude among the theatre's devotees, who began to ask themselves what was the remedy. The announcement that the Lyceum Theatre—a period house—had been sold to Mr. Meyer Oppenheim, for £100,000 would have caused greater gloom had it not been stated that its demolition would be followed by the erection of a more modern theatre or opera house on the Synod Hall site.

The Earl of Harewood had been appointed Artistic Director of the Edinburgh International Festival, and it was rumoured that one of his requirements was an opera house able to accommodate opera in a way impossible in the King's Theatre. It was therefore felt likely that the type of building to replace the Lyceum Theatre would be an adaptable one in which could be staged intimate drama as well as opera. Negotiations had been entered into between Mr. Oppenheim, chairman of Argyle Securities Limited, and the Corporation for the re-development of the whole Lyceum–Synod Hall site, but the position was for long obscure, and it remained so after a statement by Lord Provost Greig Dunbar that the

Lyceum Theatre could become Scotland's National Theatre, if the Corporation wished to develop it for the purpose.

The advantage of Scotland possessing a National Theatre had for long been debated, and in the Abercrombie Plan (for the re-development of Edinburgh) a site for such a theatre had been tentatively marked on a spot close to the now burned out Theatre Royal. As far back as 1948 the then Chancellor of the Exchequer, Sir Stafford Cripps, had also made what appeared to be a conditional offer of assistance for a National Theatre in Scotland. The offer was dependent upon the Scottish people subscribing a quota of the cost. Though demands for such a theatre have come since then not only from individuals but from corporative groups—Dundee Town Council even went so far as to offer a site—and though the project was considered by the civil authorities of Edinburgh and the Festival Society, no definite step has yet been taken towards the building of a National Theatre in Scotland.

To return to the Lyceum Theatre, in June, 1963 a definite statement was made by Lord Provost Duncan Weatherstone, who had succeeded Lord Provost Dunbar, that an agreement on terms had been reached between the Corporation and Mr. Oppenheim for the re-development of the Lyceum Theatre–Castle Terrace sites under which a new theatre and office block would be erected. The hope was expressed that the new theatre would be built by May, 1966. The Castle Terrace site was to be leased to Mr. Oppenheim for 99 years at a premium of £300,000. He would then build a civic theatre which he would sell to the Corporation for about £700,000. The Lord Provost's Committee was to decide the type of theatre required, though the scheme would provide more than a theatre and result in the establishment of an art and cultural centre.

Later, the Lyceum issue became more complicated like most issues affecting building, streets and cultural aims in all such areas ripe for far-reaching planning schemes; and the Oppenheim scheme was abandoned. But at least, by the spring of 1964, there seemed no doubt that the Lyceum Theatre or any future theatre to be built on the Castle Terrace site would be operating as a civic enterprise on a non-profit-earning basis. The hope was also expressed by Lord Provost Duncan Weatherstone on 12th March, 1964, that this civic theatre should have a first-class resident company; and a year later still came the official announcements which we saw in the earlier Festival chapter.

In the meantime there had been certain stirrings in less ambitious sectors of the city's theatre life. In 1962 the Corporation bought Morningside Church for £6,000 in order to provide a 400-seat theatre primarily for amateur groups, and as an art centre. During 1965 work was proceeding on the conversion of the church into a theatre which should have the further advantage of providing an extra theatre during the Festival. In a rather different setting—also in 1962—the Traverse Theatre Club sprang into existence in the Lawnmarket. Its aim is to present the kind of play generally dubbed *avant garde*, and in the club's theatre it ranges widely most nights from translated foreign plays to very "advanced" productions by British writers.

In 1964–5 the Traverse was still going strong. But by early 1966 when it had an overdraft of nearly £4,000, it was seen to be in danger. The increased state grants for the arts, announced on the eve of the March General Election, saved it from collapse. But a change had come over the Gateway scene. In March, 1965 it was announced that the Gateway Company, in its familiar guise, was to be wound up after 12 years of sustained and often distinguished repertory; and that in future its owners, the Church of Scotland, would use the theatre for occasional theatrical productions by professional companies and for its own Kirk Drama Federation activities. There would also be showings of special films and conferences in the theatre on anything that seemed to affect both the Church and the Arts.

The Edinburgh Civic Theatre meanwhile had come into being with Tom Fleming as its director, some old members of the Gateway Company among the players, and an international programme which opened with Carlo Goldoni's *The Servant o' Twa Maisters* in a Scots translation by Victor Carin. In the opening months, unfortunately, audiences were sometimes thin, and thc director must have been relieved when the Royal Lyceum Theatre Company of Edinburgh, acting under the Edinburgh Civic Theatre Trust Limited, received a State Grant of £35,000 for the financial year commencing in April 1966.

Chapter 41

THE WORLD OF ART

SET on the south side of Princes Street between the New Town and the Old the National Gallery of Scotland and the Royal Scottish Academy buildings represent the solid and respectable position of Art in the capital. With proper state and courtesy the Lord Provost and Magistrates attend the opening of the Annual Exhibition of the Royal Scottish Academy; and in solemn procession, robed in decorative vestments, with chain of office and other symbols of the Royal Burgh's dignity, they also honour the opening of the exhibition of the Society of Scottish Artists. But some artists, not unnaturally, think that perhaps a little more of the city's money should be spent on the purchase of works of art; or so it seemed both before and soon after the last War. In recent years however the Corporation has shown increasing respect for the skill of Scottish artists, and a number of works by contemporary painters now hang in the City Chambers. This is due chiefly to two generous gifts to the Corporation in the 1960s.

The first of these came from Miss Jean F. Watson of Edinburgh, who in July, 1961 presented a substantial cheque to Lord Provost Greig Dunbar " for the foundation and development of a municipal art gallery " as a memorial to her parents. Within a few months a Corporation-appointed committee including leading artists had made the first purchases—a sculpture by Epstein, to commemorate the exhibition of his works at the 1961 Edinburgh Festival, and a portrait by the notable " Scottish Colourist ", J. D. Fergusson. Others have been added since. The second gift consisted of no less than 300 paintings and pieces of sculpture collected by the Scottish Modern Arts Association whose work and devotion to art are described later in this chapter.

THE ROYAL SCOTTISH ACADEMY

" You are looking very distinguished ", said the gentleman in the frock coat and top hat to his friend resplendent in wine-coloured robes, red velvet Rembrandt-styled hat, black hose and silver-buckled shoes. " I am the President of a very distinguished Society ", replied Sir William Hutchison, then President of the Royal Scottish Academy, to the frock-coated Sir Gerald Kelly, President of the Royal Academy, London. The occasion was the Coronation of Her Majesty The Queen in 1953.

The Royal Scottish Academy, as the original Scottish Academy became, was founded in 1826, and the following year its first exhibition was held at 24 Waterloo Place. Later, as we shall see, it got its present imposing home at the Mound.

There were no women in the early membership except for one honorary member elected in 1829 and a second in 1854. The roll of honorary members includes James Whistler (1902); Rodin (1907); Degas (1911); Ivan Mestrovic (1919); and Georges Braque (1956).

In 1963 there were 30 members (Royal Scottish Academicians, that is) made up of 20 painters, five architects and five sculptors, of whom three of the painters and one sculptor were women. There were also 29 associates or A.R.S.A.s; these were made up of 16 painters, six architects, seven sculptors: three were women.

A frequent feature of the annual exhibition has been the inclusion of invited works by leading contemporary artists of other countries. This has served to keep the public and the Academicians cognisant of developments elsewhere, and made it possible for Scottish exhibits to be measured against others of importance. Three other factors have assisted in the acceptance of a more catholic outlook than is usually associated with academies: the tradition that the Scottish student should travel and should study in Europe; the close link between members of the Academy and the schools of art; and the fact that, in the small community of artists sustained in Scotland, one group cannot be ignorant of nor ignore others.

The artists' own approach to the Royal Scottish Academy—the kind of pictures they send in and how many—may be seen from an interesting analysis made of the 1961 exhibition. Of the 1,539 works submitted, 860 inspired a courteous, " The President and Council desire to intimate that they have been unable to give one of your works submitted a place in the Exhibition ", while 679 prompted a simple invitation to the artist to visit the Galleries on a certain day " to varnish or retouch." Very few, if any, varnish or retouch on that day, but many go to see where each work is hung. Of the works accepted, 178 were contributed by members and associates, and only three were invited works. The oil paintings numbered 363. Of these 126 were landscapes or seascapes, 74 were still-life studies, 43 portraits, 34 houses or street scenes, 38 of a non-figurative nature, 26 figure paintings (including two nudes), six animal studies and 16 unclassified.

Such a catalogue does not of course reveal that many are painted in the current manner with heavy impasto and expressionist brushwork. Some have patiently built up, scraped, dried and repainted surfaces, while others have laid on paint with such generosity and bravura that the passionate expression so made may prove to be, in the material sense, far from permanent and indeed fleeting. The Academy cannot however assume the responsibility of an artists' guild and ensure a high standard of craftsmanship.

The sculptures, according to this analysis, may be described as 30 figures in varying degrees of naturalism, expressionism or abstraction, 17 portraits, seven non-figurative, six animals and one mermaid. The materials used in these exhibits included stone, wood, bronze, wire, welded and gilded brass, concrete and fibre glass, and plastic material on iron. Of the 54 architectural exhibits, 26 could be described as contemporary, 14 as traditional and four restorations: the remaining exhibits were water-colours and drawings.

Most of the exhibitors were resident in Scotland, but 53 were resident in England. No less than 31,355 people paid for admission; 1,080 purchased season tickets; and the 182 works sold were valued at £7,263.[1]

For the period of the second Edinburgh International Festival the Academy organised an important loan exhibition of the works of Bonnard and Vuillard. This was such a success (with an attendance of 23,605) that it probably inspired subsequent exhibitions of 19th century French paintings. These were arranged in collaboration with the Festival Society.

In 1959 William MacTaggart, grandson of the famous Scottish impressionist, was elected President. Now *Sir* William, MacTaggart maintains the family tradition in making a personal contribution to painting by being one of the best known expressionist painters in Scotland.

It is the President's opinion that the robustness of the Academy is both well-founded and growing. This, he believes, is due to the artists, the public demand which makes the artists' response effective in society, and the increasingly favourable comments of the national Press on its annual exhibition.

THE ROYAL SCOTTISH SOCIETY OF PAINTERS IN WATER-COLOUR

In order to " encourage and develop the Art of painting in water-colours and the appreciation of this art " this Society was founded in Glasgow in 1878 by 24 artists, of whom a dozen were members of the Royal Scottish Academy (eleven R.S.A.s and one A.R.S.A.). Its first exhibition was held in 1879, and in 1888 Queen Victoria bestowed upon it the title " Royal."

The first rule of the Society states, " An Annual General Assembly of the Society shall be held alternately in Edinburgh and Glasgow . . ." and until 1945 exhibitions followed the pattern of the assemblies and were held alternately in the west and the east. Since that date the annual exhibitions have been held in Edinburgh during a five or six weeks' period from January to March. Other exhibitions have been held in Perth, Dundee, Aberdeen and London.

Non-members, incidentally, may submit work to the annual exhibition, and many do so. About half the 400 exhibits in the annual show are derived from landscape, and in recent years all the work has tended to become less representational and more decorative, or imaginative.

THE SOCIETY OF SCOTTISH ARTISTS

As the Royal Scottish Academy did not satisfy the needs of all the younger artists, in 1891 a dozen, discontented with the treatment they had received, met in the Albert Hotel and formed a Society. The constitution they adopted defined their objects as being " to foster a taste for Art by instituting an Annual Exhibition of different Schools and to facilitate the intercourse of those connected with and interested in Art."

At first the young Society was heavily opposed by the Academy and bitter struggles ensued, but these have now been so far forgotten that the

[1] This last figure compares with that of 1926, when out of 827 exhibits 51 were sold for £1,304.

Academy almost regards the S.S.A. as a training-ground for recruits to Associateship.

From the beginning men and women artists were admitted on equal terms and a strong lay membership has supported and reinforced the professional membership. Painting and sculpture were at first the only works considered, till in 1913 design and crafts (or " Applied Art " as it was then termed) were included and, in 1929, architecture. An invited or loan section in several of the annual exhibitions has also added greatly to the importance of the Society. The first major group of Edvard Munch's work to be shown in this country, for example, was in the Society's 1931 exhibition.

Although efforts have been made to encourage artists in the west of Scotland to join the Society of Scottish Artists, these have never been very successful. In part this is due to a healthy difference of opinions on art, and in part the expense of transporting works from one centre to another. Nevertheless membership is spread throughout Scotland and there are a few members resident in England.

In spite of a present total membership of about 400—half lay and half professional members—the fortunes of the Society are never very secure. The very purpose of its existence after all is no longer wholly valid, for the R.S.A. has become so catholic in its taste that the younger movements in painting and sculpture are well represented in its exhibitions. That there is room and need of both societies is not of course in doubt, but how the younger one can retain its identity in new purposes poses a question for the future.

THE SCOTTISH SOCIETY OF WOMEN ARTISTS

The Scottish Society of Women Artists was founded in 1924 by the initiative of William McDougall, father of Miss Lily McDougall, one of the most independent and personal of women painters. The objects of the Society, which came about because women at the time had some difficulty in getting their pictures accepted for exhibition, were clearly stated to be " the promotion of interest in Art and in the works of Women Artists generally, and the fostering of this interest by such means as the holding of Exhibitions and other functions periodically."

The first President, Miss Anna Dixon, held office for 17 years, perhaps by virtue of the fact that she is said never to have made a speech in council or in public. Mrs. Jean Hunter Cowan, who was President for seven years, was the first Scotswoman to fly—in 1911—and was a musician until her hearing was impaired by flying high in an unpressurised plane. Giving up music, she took up painting and modelling in clay, and soon won a place among the women artists, who recognised her several abilities by electing her President of the Society. Having ably assisted in bringing it to a state of importance and prosperity she found her way, at ground level, from Morocco to Uganda via the Congo and the Mountains of the Moon, leaving the Society's affairs in the capable hands of Mrs. Lily Cottrell, and others.

There are two honorary and some 160 ordinary professional members whose membership was gained by election; and there are about 200 lay members, of whom about a dozen are men. As this is quite an impressive total, the question arises as to what these women artists paint. Their most popular themes seem to be landscape, still-life and portrait; but while few show any leanings towards pure abstraction, surrealism, expressionism or tachisme, occasional gestures of sympathy with these movements are made.

THE NATIONAL GALLERIES OF SCOTLAND

In 1781 the earth excavated from the building sites of the New Town was, by order of the Town Council, dumped in an orderly manner to form an enlargement of " Geordie Boyd's Mud Brig " and eventually became the Mound which, crossing a valley, still joins the New Town with the old Castle hill. Of the two buildings which grace this mound, the more northerly was built as the Royal Institute in 1823 and became the exhibition rooms and offices of the Royal Scottish Academy in 1911. The more southerly, completed in 1859 as premises for both the Royal Scottish Academy and the National Gallery, was in 1910 made over wholly to the housing of the National Collection and was re-opened in 1912.

The control of the Galleries was first entrusted to the Board of Manufacturers whose maintenance funds came from an annuity granted to Scotland by the Treaty of Union and the Revenue of Scotland Act of 1718. No regular grant for the purchase of works of art was available however until 1906 when that Board's duties were taken over by a Board of Trustees, appointed by the Secretary of State for Scotland. The annuity of £2,000, together with a grant, then became available for the purchase of works of art and the costs of maintenance were transferred to the Parliamentary Estimates (National Galleries of Scotland Act, 1906). In 1958 the combined grant-in-aid for the National Gallery and the Portrait Gallery was increased to £15,000. It should be added that the three National Galleries of Scotland—for there is now in Edinburgh a Scottish Gallery of Modern Art as well—share the same Board of Trustees and the same Director (Mr. David Baxandall at the time of this survey) but each has its own day-to-day administrative heads. Mr. Baxandall is Director of the National Gallery of Scotland, Mr. R. E. Hutchison Keeper of the National Portrait Gallery, and Mr. Douglas Hall Keeper of the Gallery of Modern Art.

THE NATIONAL GALLERY OF SCOTLAND

During the last 100 years, but especially since 1906, so many important additions have been made to the National Gallery of Scotland by gifts, bequests and purchases that the collection is recognised now as one of the finest of the smaller collections in Europe. Among the additions made in the last half-century are: " An Altar-piece with Wings " by Bernardo

Daddi; " The Court of Apollo " by Perugino; " Hendrickje Stoffels " by Rembrandt; " Christ in the House of Martha and Mary " by Vermeer (an outstanding gift made in his memory by the two sons of W. A. Coats); " Three Legends of Saint Nicholas " by Gerard David; a portrait by Bernard van Orley; the study for the head of " Saint Ambrose " and the " Feast of Herod " by Rubens; " Saint Jerome " and " The Saviour " by El Greco; and " An Old Woman Cooking Eggs " by Velasquez. This last picture was purchased for the sum of £57,000 in 1955, with assistance from the Treasury as well as from the National Art Collections Fund. The French School has been enriched at a cost of £47,000 by the magnificent " Landscape with Apollo, the Muses and River God " by Claude, dated 1652, and also by the portrait of " Diego Martelli " by Degas; " The Vision after The Sermon " by Gauguin; a late landscape by Monet, " Poplars on the Epte "; and an early river scene by Pissarro, " The Marne at Chennevières." Van Gogh is represented by one of his last works, " Les Oliviers."

But these are only a few of the treasures. In other parts of the gallery there are paintings by Tiepolo, Veronese, Van Dyck, Zurbaran, Ruisdael, Bassano, Watteau, Boucher, and many other famous painters; and recently a whole new group of French paintings through a gift which any other gallery might legitimately envy. This splendid acquisition happened in February, 1960 when Mr. Alexander Maitland, Q.C., a member of the Board of Trustees, presented to the National Gallery in memory of his wife, a collection of 21 French paintings which are of such importance that this section of the Gallery is now one of very great distinction. Two Gauguins, his most important " Martinique Landscape " and the monumental " Three Tahitians "; three oil paintings, two of the ballet and one head study, and one pastel nude by Degas; and an early and a middle period Van Gogh alone make the representations of these artists eloquent of their several developments. But also there are three works by Courbet, a small Renoir and a sketch by Seurat, a Sisley and a late Cézanne, " Mount Sainte Victoire ", a work by Bonnard, two by Vuillard, a Modigliani, a Roualt, and a small Picasso to carry the records into the present century. The whole gift can be seen to unite with and extend most happily the former collection, and each item of the gift reveals the foresight and taste of collectors of unusual discernment.

To the English School has been added a large upright landscape, " The Vale of Dedham ", which the artist John Constable described as " perhaps my best ", and a landscape of charm by Gainsborough has been brought near the famous and beautiful portrait by the same artist, " The Honourable Mrs. Graham ", which was bequeathed to the Gallery in 1859 on condition that it should never leave Scotland. Reynold's group portrait " The Ladies Waldegrave " has also been added to this school.

The Scottish section has been strengthened with several portraits by Sir Henry Raeburn, who remains high in the affection and admiration of visitors for such contrasting paintings as the charming Mrs. Scott-Moncrieff and the bold Colonel Alastair Macdonell of Glengarry, and examples from different periods of both Allan Ramsay and Sir David

Wilkie, while William McTaggart's impressionist style is illustrated by "The Emigrant Ship", and a large storm piece. In particular, during recent years, the works of Allan Ramsay have attracted much attention, notably the lovely portrait of his second wife.

An expressionist painting, the work of the Czechoslovakian Kokoschka was given by the Government of Czechoslovakia in 1942 in recognition of "sympathy and assistance." This was the only painting the artist was able to bring with him out of Germany at the outbreak of World War II.

Although it claims only an obscure place, one may be surprised at the presence of a painting of a pet dog called "Callum." The label however reveals that it was bequeathed in 1919, together with a sum of over £55,000 by Mr. James Cowan Smith. This bequest has made possible many of the purchases which are now the pride of the collection.

The water-colour section was greatly enlarged in 1901 by Mr. Henry Vaughan of London who bequeathed 38 water-colours and drawings by Turner. A condition of the bequest is that these works should be shown only during the month of January; so presumably the donor intended that the delicate tints should not be subject to the brighter sunlight of the other months.

The interest and value of the permanent collection at the National Gallery is at present, and has been since 1945, greatly enhanced by the courtesy and generosity of the Earl of Ellesmere, who has lent some 30 paintings from the famous Bridgewater House Collection. Of this selection the large "Diana and Actaeon" and the "Diana and Calisto" are two of four Titians; the "Bridgewater" Madonna is one of the four Raphaels; and of four Rembrandts the most memorable is a self-portrait, painted when he was about fifty. A soft light on his wrinkled face discovers his quiet searching of himself and of life. Seven sacraments of life are represented in the paintings of Poussin in this collection.

Her Majesty The Queen has continued the gracious loan, first made by King George V, of two votive panels by Hugo van der Goes. Among other loans of importance made to the Galleries from time to time are works from the collection of the Earl of Crawford and Balcarres, Chairman of the Board of Trustees. And certainly in this of all accounts it would be ungracious not to acknowledge the kindness of the Rt. Hon. Viscount Thurso who has for so long placed on loan the portrait by Sir Henry Raeburn of Sir John Sinclair, Bart., whose energy and persistence brought *The* (First) *Statistical Account of Scotland* into being in the 18th century.

Because of lack of space, the National Gallery's prints and drawings, of which there are about 7,000, are stored, almost in secret, in a house at Ainslie Place. The best that can be done under the present circumstances is a series of exhibitions in one of the smaller rooms at the Mound, which many artists and art-lovers in the city think is a poor way to treat such a rich harvest, but one which seems inevitable until some suitable accommodation can be provided.

In the meantime visitors from many parts of the world continue to patronise the National Gallery. Earlier we looked at an analysis of the number of works and the total attendance at the Royal Scottish Academy in 1961. So we should perhaps look at the attendance figures for the National Gallery in the same year. The total was 187,734—a figure which may be compared with the attendance at the loan exhibition of 36 paintings by Rembrandt, arranged as part of the Edinburgh Festival in 1950. On that occasion, which lasted no more than three weeks, 119,197 people visited the Gallery.

The Gallery's busiest times occur on bright Saturday and Sunday afternoons when a sudden shower of rain causes the audiences of the public orators at the Mound to become visitors to the National Gallery. These remain the busiest days when the weather is constant, and in winter the lunch hour concerts increase the attendances on Wednesdays. Marked increases can be observed on the days of important sporting events such as international rugby or football matches, and naturally during the Edinburgh Festival.

THE NATIONAL PORTRAIT GALLERY

" In all my historical investigations ", wrote Carlyle, " it has been, and always is, one of the primary wants to procure a bodily likeness of the person enquired after, a good portrait if such exists, failing that, even an indifferent if sincere one." A year after Carlyle's death the National Portrait Gallery of Scotland was founded on the initiative of Mr. J. R. Findlay of *The Scotsman.* He gave half the endowment fund and met the cost of the building which was opened seven years later in 1889. The portraits still share the building, in Queen Street, with the Museum of Antiquities (described in a later chapter).

The collection is composed of works transferred from the National Gallery, such as Ramsay's portrait of David Hume and Naysmith's of Robert Burns; works donated or bequeathed—a portrait by an unknown artist of Charles Edward Stuart, for instance, and Count Nerli's portrait of Robert Louis Stevenson—and works purchased, among them such notable paintings as Raeburn's Sir Walter Scott and Peter Oudry's Mary Queen of Scots. A few copies of important portraits have been commissioned. But there is still much to be done either by bequest or benefaction, gift or grant, to make the National Portrait Gallery of Scotland a truly great representation of the country's famous figures. For the time being, we can at any rate see portraits of David Hume, Lord Brougham, Thomas Carlyle, Dugald Stewart the moral philosopher, Jeffrey, J. M. Barrie, James Maxton, Sir Alexander Fleming (of penicillin fame) and other notable Scotsmen.

The entry of each of the honoured dead to these select archives is scrutinised by the Director and the Keeper of the Portrait Gallery, then by a panel of four historians and two members of the Board of Trustees. But the initial qualification required of each aspirant is that a portrait of suitable quality should come on the market when sufficient funds are available to the Gallery, or should be offered by a generous donor. A number of distinguished deceased Scots have so far failed to qualify in this first round, among them James Clerk Maxwell, Graham Bell and

Thomas Telford. For the inquiring scholar, however, the gaps are bridged with the help of an extensive reference library of engravings, of photographs of portraits and of photographs, of the persons inquired after. This is augmented by a reference file of reproductions of costume pieces and by a bibliography of Scottish painters. In all perhaps 50 inquiries, entailing varying amounts of research, may be received in a month, and the most frequent subjects are the Stuarts. In the meantime the gaps are filled from time to time. To give a recent example, towards the end of 1964 the Gallery purchased a portrait of Robert Moffat, the famous missionary (and father-in-law of David Livingstone).

The collections have been conserved and enlarged under the care of a number of curators and directors, but the task of cleaning and re-touching has only been undertaken in the Galleries since the appointment in 1946 of a Keeper who is himself a skilled technician. The holder of that office, H. R. H. Woolford, has carried out routine maintenance in both the National and the National Portrait galleries, and in particular has restored to freshness several paintings of especial note, such as " The Honourable Mrs. Graham," " The Vale of Dedham," Zurbaran's " The Immaculate Conception," " The Finding of Moses " by Tiepolo, and the recent acquisitions by Velasquez and Claude.

SCOTTISH NATIONAL GALLERY OF MODERN ART

That a central gallery, other than the Royal Scottish Academy, is necessary for the display of temporary exhibitions and a permanent collection of modern art was demonstrated clearly by Stanley Cursiter who was Director of the National Galleries from 1930 to 1948. When the National Collections were removed to country houses for greater safety during the war he organised more than 50 temporary exhibitions in the vacated galleries at the Mound. Among the subjects were the works of Scottish artists, the arts of our several allies, the industries of Edinburgh and Leith, wartime housing, ballet design, film decor, and a dozen exhibitions of child art. The public interest was such that in one year, 1944, no less than 233,000 visited these exhibitions. This total is more than three times that of admissions on the last normal pre-war year.

The Board of Trustees in their annual reports to the Secretary of State for Scotland repeatedly drew attention to the need for a Gallery of Modern Art. On 9th March, 1951, the Secretary of State for Scotland stated in Parliament that with the Ministry of Works he had " agreed that ultimately a Gallery of Modern Art for which plans will be prepared as opportunity offers should be built on the site of York Buildings in Queen Street and that a new Museum of Antiquities will be provided on a site still to be determined." In 1956 a site for that museum was named adjoining the Royal Scottish Museum in Chambers Street. But the need for a gallery in a nearer future than this long-term plan envisaged remained, and on 10th August, 1960 temporary premises were provided at Inverleith House in the midst of the Royal Botanic Garden. With little delay the building was adapted to the needs of a gallery with marked success by the Ministry of Works, and garden space for the display of sculpture was also provided.

The gallery comes under the control of the same Trustees and Director as the other National Galleries in Scotland, and the appointment of an assistant keeper to be responsible for its immediate control was made in 1961. An initial annual purchase grant of £7,500 was made by the Treasury; but in 1964 this was increased to £20,000—with markedly beneficial results for the gallery.

The opening ceremony was enlivened with the good humour of the Chairman, the Earl of Crawford and Balcarres, enriched with a well-balanced lecture by Sir Kenneth Clark, then Chairman of the Arts Council, and honoured by the extraordinary hats, shaped like beehives or large inverted nests of birds, worn by several ladies.

The first exhibitions were necessarily of loan works, but a few works had been donated by the time the Gallery opened. For example, a decorative painting by Duffresne, " The Rape of Europa " was gifted by Mr. and Mrs. A. F. Reid, and works by Edward Wadsworth and Graham Sutherland by Mr. and Mrs. Henry Macdonnell. Almost the whole of the first year's grant-in-aid was set aside for the purchase of a large and important piece of sculpture by Henry Moore, " Reclining Figure." Other purchases have included a bronze " Winged Figures " by Lyn Chadwick, a painting by Matthew Smith, a water-colour by John Maxwell and 15 lithographs. A start has also been made with exhibitions such as that of Paul Klee, which was opened in the summer of 1962 and attracted many of the visitors to that year's Festival. Since then the gallery has made great progress with the addition of works by foreign artists and such distinguished home painters as Graham Sutherland, Sickert, Sir William Nicholson, S. J. Peploe, and Joan Eardley.

THE SCOTTISH MODERN ARTS ASSOCIATION

Since its foundation in 1907 the Scottish Modern Arts Association had purchased more than 300 works and had lent or donated these to various galleries, and to schools, hospitals and clubs. In the very early 1960s it also lent two fine Scottish works to the Gallery of Modern Art, but as the establishment of the gallery had, in large measure, fulfilled the purpose for which the Association existed, and its membership had declined, the members decided—in 1961—to take preliminary steps to disband the Association and decide on the future of its fine collection.

For the city the decision could not have been bettered, since in 1963, when the Association gifted the entire collection to the Corporation, it was realised at once that this generous gift, following so swiftly on Miss Jean Watson's benefaction, would enable Edinburgh to have a really fine municipal art collection of its own. Among the well-known artists represented by important paintings are Fergusson, Cadell, Leslie Hunter and S. J. Peploe, William McTaggart, Sir D. Y. Cameron, Stanley Cursiter, Joan Eardley, W. G. Gillies and Anne Redpath. The sculptors include Pittendreigh MacGillivray, Reid Dick and Alexander Carrick.

THE EDINBURGH COLLEGE OF ART

Although the College of Art can trace its antecedents to the " Trustees Academy " which began in 1760, its present form is traceable only to 1907. Later still—in 1960—its constitution was altered by Royal Assent to make one single *ad hoc* body responsible for both the government and the management of the College. On the Board are representatives of the Town Council, the Royal Scottish Academy, the University Court, Edinburgh Chamber of Commerce, Edinburgh Architectural Association, the Governors of the Heriot Watt College, the Merchant Company, the Scottish Committee of the Council of Industrial Design, and Edinburgh and District Trades Council.

There are five schools within the College: Architecture, Town and Country Planning, Drawing and Painting, Design and Crafts, and Sculpture. Each of these offers a recognised diploma course and post-diploma study. One Fellowship may be bestowed each year upon a student from any one of the schools. And in conjunction with the University a course leading to the degree of M.A. (Hons.) in Fine Art, and one to M.A. in Architecture[1] were instituted in 1945 and 1949 respectively.

It has been a tradition that the instructors should be practising artists. The Principal and Head of each School has a studio for his personal use within the College, and until recent times teaching posts were all essentially part-time. The application of the terms of the 1946 Staff Salary Scales, however, reduced the time which many of the staff enjoyed for creative work of their own. Yet the prestige of the staff is high. Most of the leading artists, in any field of plastic art in Scotland, are associated with one of the four central institutions, and Edinburgh has attracted to its staff a worthy share of ability. The College, at the time of writing, employs some 36 architects, painters, designers, sculptors and planners as full-time teachers, and also employs as many part-time. The present Principal, a Scotsman, strangely enough, for the first time in the history of the College, is the distinguished painter William Gillies.

The number of students is considerable, and apparently does not suffer many fluctuations. In one recent year the full-time students numbered about 600, and the others over 780; which makes an impressive total of almost 1,400. Of these more than 900 were normally resident in Edinburgh; while almost 370 came from the rest of Scotland, about 60 from England, more than a dozen from Northern Ireland and Eire, and over 30 from other lands ranging from Greece to the U.S.A.

By the will of the late Andrew Grant of Pitcorthie the College was endowed with a very substantial sum of money; and since 1931 the income derived from this has made available about £14,000 annually for use as intermediate, post-diploma, and travelling scholarships, bursaries and fellowships. The travelling scholarships which take students to art centres in both the New World and the Old have, by common consent, been quite invaluable.

[1] The degree course is now transferred wholly to the University of Edinburgh.

ARCHITECTURE AND PLANNING

The air terminal buildings at Turnhouse and Renfrew, and a number of University and hospital buildings, are among the few recent opportunities that have offered local scope for the talents of former College students. But outside Scotland the most talked-of works by former students include the Royal Festival Hall, London, by Sir Robert Matthew (and colleagues) who is now Professor of Architecture in Edinburgh; Coventry Cathedral by Sir Basil Spence; and still under construction, as these words are written, the giant memorial by the late Joseph Gleave to Christopher Columbus, which is being erected in the Dominican Republic for the 21 republics of the Americas.

Several of the former students of the Town and Country Planning School are now employed by the Department of Health for Scotland which influences in many ways the broader aspects in planning.

DRAWING AND PAINTING

Sir William MacTaggart, William Gillies, the late John Maxwell whose pictures were much sought in England as well as in Scotland, and Robin Philipson, (much influenced at one time by Kokoschka, and himself represented widely in English collections, though he lives in Edinburgh), all of whom serve or have served on the College staff, are among the former Drawing and Painting Students who have won recognition both at home and abroad. The late Anne Redpath who had many distinctions bestowed upon her and whose work is to be seen in public and private collections in Wellington, Adelaide, Paris, Vancouver, London and many other places, had, as a painter and a member of the College board, influenced greatly the work of the students. She was a very Scottish character, who sported occasionally a French accent derived from long stays in France. She could also wear what someone once called " an air of kindly defiance "; always she talked wittily and wisely in self depreciation or in praise of others; and she painted with a personal vision which translated the objects of still life or landscape into beautifully textured oil painting or luminous water-colours. At the time of her death—in 1965—Anne Redpath's paintings were eagerly sought by private collectors of taste and distinction in many countries.

Of those who have moved south and regularly claim space in the galleries of London and New York, the best known are Charles McCall and two non-figurative painters, William Gear and Alan Davie. But the list of teachers or students connected with the College who have won far-reaching recognition is quite impressive, for in addition to those we have seen it includes Sir William Hutchison, Stanley Cursiter and many others.

DESIGN AND CRAFTS

Until recently the School of Design and Crafts was most noted for its stained glass section, with William Wilson, R.S.A. as its most distinguished former student. Today typography, glass engraving and industrial design are assuming a greater importance.

SCULPTURE

The best sculpture in Edinburgh is to be found in old graveyards such as Greyfriars and St. Cuthbert's; there is also a sprouting of 19th century street furniture. No sculpture has been commissioned by the Corporation for the adornment of its thoroughfares or gardens for many years, but Miss Watson's recent gift to the city made possible the purchase of an important work by Epstein and a commissioned work by Shilsky for the Corporation's own collection. It will be remembered that an important figure piece by Henry Moore was the first acquisition by the Scottish Gallery of Modern Art. In 1960 the Education Committee sanctioned a commission, suggested by an architect, for some sculpture at the main entrance to the new Gracemount School.

The National Galleries have comparatively few pieces of sculpture on show, perhaps through lack of space; and of these the most interesting are three wax models (attributed to Michelangelo) of the Madonna, and the two Medicis of the New Sacristy, Florence. But fortunately the contemporary work being purchased for the Gallery of Modern Art will help to fill a gap in the city's art treasures. Fortunately, too, there have been and are some notable sculptors in Edinburgh. For although the School of Sculpture at the College of Art is small it has numbered among its students Hew Lorimer and Thomas Whalen.

Today in the city three sculptors maintain themselves wholly by the produce of their studios, and they are dependent to a considerable extent on architects for commissions. Tom Whalen, R.S.A. works in wood, metal, stone and plaster. A good example of his work is an eight-foot high bronze figure " The Sower " for the enrichment of Kirkcaldy's municipal buildings. Across the Dean Valley from Mr. Whalen's studio James H. Clark, A.R.S.A., in the early '60s, modelled six portraits in clay for casting in bronze, on their way to a building in Malaya. C.D'O. Pilkington Jackson who recently finished a mace for the city of Singapore, and whose work is discussed elsewhere in this book (in the chapter on crafts), has also modelled a triumphant equestrian Robert the Bruce of heroic size to mark the site of Bannockburn.

Of the 19th century work the most dramatic is that of John Knox, the most romantic the little dog Greyfriars Bobby, the most heroic the Duke of Wellington who is challenged from Parliament Square by Charles II and from the Castle Esplanade by Earl Haig, Wallace and Bruce. Fighting men and great regiments are commemorated at vantage points in streets and gardens and on bridges, Gladstone graces a crescent and Melville meets the winds on his high pillar in St. Andrew Square. Forbes of Culloden is to be found in legal company, Robert Louis Stevenson in the High Kirk of St. Giles, David Livingstone in East Princes Street Gardens and the poet Allan Ramsay in the western gardens.

Here however it can only be concluded, in the words of Douglas Percy Bliss, a sensitive critic, and head of the Glasgow School of Art for fruitful years, that in Edinburgh the sculptors have had "a thin time", since public monuments have tended to be "eminently moral and therefore uninteresting."[1] "Edinburgh", Dr. Bliss continues, "has raised monuments to soldiers, to writers, to monarchs, statesmen and divines, and it has raised war memorials, one of them—in the Castle—world famous. It gave to Sir Walter Scott a monument which is better known than any other commemorating a man of letters, be he Shakespeare, Dante, Homer or Virgil. The Scott Monument may be a Victorian folly, but it is brave and unforgettable, an act of faith, a tribute of adoration.

"Being a Protestant city, Edinburgh has avoided Madonnas and Saints: and it has given no opportunity to the sculptor to indulge in his favourite subject, the naked human figure. The most remarkable omission is that of poetic or fancy subjects. Portraits are numerous and not unwelcome . . . . But one does sigh for the non-utilitarian, the piece of sculpture which exists only for its own sake."

The truth is that the future of sculpture is never quite certain; and even the tombstone makers' future is threatened by the establishment of crematoria, which dispense with tombstones, and by restrictions on size.

The largest of the monumental sculptors and granite merchants in the city is a firm in Piershill, which apart from normal commercial work prepares large or small blocks of stone for sculptors. One member of the firm is a carver who can carry out in stone what is designed in plaster. Unfortunately, apprentices with ambitions beyond the carving of letters are hard to find.

BRONZE FOUNDERS

In 1852 the sculptor, Sir John Steell, cast his statue of the Duke of Wellington in an iron foundry in Leith; thereafter no bronze founding took place in the city for 50 years or more. Then Charles Creswick came to Edinburgh in 1912 to assist in the casting, silvering and enamelling of an altar for the Marquis of Bute's private chapel at Mount Stuart, Bute.

After the interruption of World War I the firm of MacDonald and Creswick was established at Harrison Road, and in the 1920s, when much work was being done for the Scottish National Shrine in the Castle, three founders and one apprentice were employed there; but as these words are written even this small staff has dwindled.

In 1923 the firm was joined by George Mancini whose father Frederico Mancini had left Rome for London about 1895 to cast a great equestrian statue of Lord Roberts for India. Before settling in Edinburgh George had trained in his father's and other workshops.

Seven years later Mancini started his own foundry in Eyre Terrace and in 1933 he moved to Fountainbridge where he has remained. There he has cast bronze figures from a few inches to more than 12 feet high and his work has been sent to India, Australia, South Africa, Canada and the

[1] *The Scotsman,* 1st August, 1959.

The finale of one of the Edinburgh International Festival Tattoo productions staged by Scottish Command on the Castle Esplanade. This annual production is one of the most popular events of the Festival.

The buildings on and around the Calton Hill viewed from under one of the arches of the North Bridge. On the right is St. Andrew's House, the main government offices in Scotland; to its left is part of the old Calton Jail. Behind St. Andrew's House is the Nelson Monument on the top of which may be seen the 'mast' down which a ball slides to show that it is 1 p.m. This is synchronised with the firing of the 'One O'Clock Gun' from the Half-Moon Battery in the castle.

U.S.A. as well as to many parts of the British Isles. An example is the figure of Wallace which overlooks the drawbridge of Edinburgh Castle.

In these small foundries the work—all done by the craftsman himself—ranges from mould making, furnace building, metal melting and casting to chasing and colouring. Little has changed since the days of Benvenuto Cellini. It is therefore the more to be regretted that Mancini has never had an apprentice, more especially as, unlike most founders, he is able to cast from plasticine models with a precision that almost reproduces the modellers' finger prints.

STAINED GLASS ARTISTS AND STUDIOS

The only pre-Reformation stained glass in Edinburgh is the re-assembled shattered pieces to be seen in some windows of the Palace of Holyroodhouse and four heraldic panels in the Magdalene Chapel. The four panels are probably of French origin and are dated 1541. There is no evidence of stained glass windows having been made here prior to the 19th century when a number of undistinguished commercial and private studios were established.

The first artist to be noted here was James Ballantyne who established his studio in the 1850s. He was then known as the author of some poems, published in 1844, under the titles *The Miller of Deanhaugh* and *The Gaberlunzie's Wallet*, and his windows may be seen in St. Giles. Unfortunately those he made for the old House of Lords, which in the fashion of his time had more of the character of oil painting than of stained glass, were destroyed in the blitz of the 1939–45 war. Much of the actual glass used was imported from Munich; indeed in the middle of the 19th century whole windows were imported from Germany to Scottish as well as to English churches. Two succeeding generations, Alexander Ballantyne and James Ballantyne, flourished after him; and by the time his grandson, James, was in charge the studio was exporting windows to Canada, Bermuda, South Africa and other parts of the world.

Douglas Strachan, a portrait and mural painter in Aberdeen, began working in stained glass with some success and moved to Edinburgh about 1912. He brought a refreshing realisation of the natural qualities of the medium and his work did much to gain for the city recognition as a centre for glass. While many of his windows are in and around London, his best known are probably the " Peace " window at The Hague, and the series of windows in the Scottish War Memorial on the Castle Rock. A very individual artist and a strong personality, he worked with few assistants and unfortunately trained no apprentice.

From 1927 when he had become established on the staff of the College of Art until his death in 1946, Herbert Hendrie exercised a considerable influence and developed a large glass studio in the College. His biggest works are the transept windows of Liverpool Cathedral.

Among other stained glass artists working in the city until a few years ago was John Duncan, R.S.A., a painter of subjects inspired by Celtic mythology. But of the several firms and individual studios that produced windows in the 1920s and 1930s only three firms and one studio remain. A studio has been maintained by William Wilson, R.S.A. since 1938. Wilson trained in Ballantyne's studio and then, as a Fellow of the Edinburgh College of Art, studied profoundly the work of the Middle Ages. By study he rediscovered for himself the inherent qualities of his medium, but his work is neither coldly academic nor flushed with the heat of passing fashion. It is distinguished by a freshness, dignified by a knowledge of the symbols of his subject-matter and their decorative values, and enriched by his personal enthusiasm for the colours and shapes of glass.

He was elected to the rank of Royal Scottish Academician primarily because of his achievement as an etcher and engraver. Later he became noted also as a painter in water-colour.

In his studio, which overlooks the Dean Valley and where he has employed several craftsmen, he designs cartoons, cuts the glass which is made in Sunderland, paints it, fires it in a kiln, assembles portions up to 15 feet high, leads it and cements it. Incidentally, the lead which was obtained in Edinburgh until the last war is now obtained ready milled from England.

Wilson's most distinguished works are to be found in The Royal High School, Edinburgh; Brechin Cathedral, Angus; Canterbury and Liverpool Cathedrals; The Dutch Church, London; the Knox Church, Ottawa; and Holy Trinity Church, Princeton, New York.

LITHOGRAPHY

The process of lithography was discovered by Aloys Senefelder in 1796. One of his apprentices in Munich, Frederick Schenck, moved to Scotland and more than 100 years ago, in partnership with W. H. Macfarlane, established a lithographic printing workshop in St. James' Square, Edinburgh.[1] In the same premises the press was continued, under the direction of Mr. Johnston Douglas, with the business name of Harley Brothers, and for several years the firm built up a splendid reputation for the printing of artists' lithographs.

Because the work is done with chalk and/or ink directly on stone (or rather stones, for one is required for each colour and four are normally used), the artist did the actual drawing at St. James' Square. The colours were mixed by the artist and matched in ink by a craftsman. That the stones are heavy may be judged by those required for the six prints of Michael Ayrton's " Greek Suite ", each made with four colours, which in all weighed not less than three-and-a-half tons.

John Piper, whose prints are in highest demand, was the first of the well-known artists to appreciate the facilities offered by Harley Brothers and his lead was followed by Ayrton, MacTaggart, Philipson, Anne

[1] Schenck was awarded a gold medal and 20 sovereigns by Edinburgh's Royal Society of Arts for his invention of a lithographic test-bench. As the Secretary of the Society pointed out in a letter to *The Scotsman* (11th May, 1960), he was also awarded a silver medal, value six sovereigns, for a work on the progress of lithography in Scotland and a display of his methods early in 1848.

Redpath, Earl Haig and several of the younger Scottish artists, as well as some in England, and one from Poland—Aleksander Zyw—who has long made Edinburgh his home and therefore the source of the exhibitions of his work arranged in various European cities.

ART DEALERS

The firm of Bruce and McDonald, founded in 1840, became Doig, McKechnie and Davies in 1857. As well as dealing in works of art they carried on a large business making ceiling decorations and cornices, setting fireplaces of Adam's design and fitting the decorations of ships.

In 1895 a grandson of Doig named Benjamin Wheatley, joined the firm which became Doig, Wilson and Wheatley at 90 George Street. Before the first World War a staff of 50 were employed there, but this was sadly reduced during the war. R. J. Wheatley, who succeeded to the business, deserves especial credit for helping to re-establish the reputations of Allan Ramsay and the Naysmiths. With the exception of a number of photographs, whose negatives are now lodged with the National Gallery, the records of the pictures and fine prints which passed through their hands were either pulped as salvage during the last war or destroyed when the firm closed in 1958.

Aitken Dott's were established as Carvers and Gilders, Artists' Colourmen and Fine Art Dealers in South St. David Street in 1842; and ever since the nature of their business has changed more in degree than in character. There are now fewer works of old masters bought or sold in Edinburgh, as higher prices are obtained in London, and the number of frames carved and gilded may be judged by comparing the number of craftsmen employed with that of former years. In 1900 no less than nine gilders and three ornamenters were employed; 60 years later one man and one apprentice were sufficient.

Trade in artists' materials, including books, has increased as the number of amateur and semi-professional artists has increased. At the firm's present address in Castle Street about eight exhibitions are held each year. While the size of the contemporary house is reflected in the demand for fewer large and more small paintings, oil colours remain more popular than water-colours, landscape is the most popular subject, with still-life a second choice; and if one may judge by sales in these galleries, the most popular painters recently have been an Edinburgh quartet—William Gillies, Anne Redpath, William MacTaggart and Robin Philipson.

Most of the old records of the business were pulped for salvage during the last war, but there was a considerable trade in Raeburns and Ramsays, and some interesting records of sales of the first McTaggart's and S. J. Peploe's work exist. There is, for example, a record of a client buying five small paintings by Peploe for £52 10*s*. Each one of these paintings would now command far more than that total sum.

John Mathieson supplies artists with frames and materials and has a small gallery in his shop in Frederick Street.

GALLERIES AND EXHIBITIONS

Premises that exhibit and sell pictures have increased in number in the last few years. In George Street a second flat room, with one graceful north window, formerly rented as a studio by a sculptress, Miss Daphne Dyce-Sharp was made available by her on modest terms to young artists for exhibitions when she left for Canada and matrimony. This, the '57 Gallery, is maintained by an association of some 200 members, who in 1966 were negotiating for new ground floor premises in the same area.

Another new gallery which gave encouragement to more than local artists when it opened in 1962 was a venture sponsored by Douglas and Foulis (the Menzies controlled booksellers) who thought imaginatively, that some paintings might well be added to the books they already had on their first floor in Castle Street. A couple of years later three ladies opened in George Street a graceful suite of rooms, The Crestine Gallery, and although their exhibitions are mainly of Scottish works they have introduced others of importance such as Meninsky's. At the same time a neat little pair of rooms were opened, under a cafe, in the west end to become the William St. Gallery.

With less emphasis on the commercial and more on the cultural side handsome galleries for local and for visiting exhibitions are provided at the Commonwealth Institute, the English Speaking Union, the French Institute and the Danish Institute.

On a more domestic scale the Saltire Society offers its 17th century rooms in the Lawnmarket for occasional exhibitions. For a good many years the Gateway Theatre sponsored and held in its cafe a series of exhibitions of the works of artists, professional and semi-professional, from many parts of Scotland. The Traverse theatre has also sponsored exhibitions in its premises in the Lawnmarket.

ART SOCIETIES

The Royal Mile has been the birth place of no less than three societies of clubs or amateur artists who work on their own, train under professional art teachers and hold their own exhibitions. The first and highest in the sense of being nearest to the castle rock is the Edinburgh Sketch Club which was provoked into existence by a letter published in the *Edinburgh Evening News* in July, 1936. In fair weather and foul some of the members, whose total is about 70, meet on Saturdays, Sundays and holidays to paint in the city or farther afield; and also they meet to discuss their work or paint portraits on two evenings a week. It is a kindly club—with a high incidence of matrimonial engagement among its members. In close kinship to the Sketching Club but at the other end of the Royal Mile the Holyrood Art Club began on similar lines. Although its meeting place has been moved its aims remain the same and its numbers are as many as 100.

The third society is the Arts Centre, originally a Church of Scotland foundation. Today it has a larger membership with activities that include music, lectures, art classes and exhibitions. This modest Centre is democratically run by means of several committees whose official recognition by the Corporation is the granting of a place in the annual procession to St. Giles at the opening of each Festival.

FESTIVAL EXHIBITIONS

Each Festival produces an extraordinary number of exhibitions. At one Festival there were as many as 40, and while these included embroidery, pottery, vintage cars and model railways, about half were concerned with drawing and painting in one form or another. Every available room that even remotely resembled a gallery was draped with hand woven materials, set with silver work, pottery, dolls or musical instruments, or hung with paintings by professionals or amateurs. Even the walls of the long stairway which joins the North Bridge with Market Street near *The Scotsman* offices are hung with paintings by young ambitious artists.

EXTRA-MURAL ARTISTS

The truly extra-mural artists are men of simple ambition who confine themselves to chalk work on a fairly large scale. Their subject-matter follows a tradition of its own. It is influenced little by art fashions and yet often it is topical. Portraits of popular persons and comments on matters of immediate moment are frequently to be seen alongside landscapes of a romantic nature and an occasional still-life. Although one cannot say these men ever formed a distinct school, there was perhaps 30 years ago about a dozen working on the same lines in the city. Change in social conditions has brought about their reduction in numbers, and as some would think strangely enough, the remaining few cling to the University area. There in dry weather beside the passing feet of students and shoppers they draw upon the flagstones, and as pavement artists claim a living from passers-by.

CHAPTER 42

LITERATURE

EDINBURGH has always been a literary city. Tradition has it that the earliest Welsh poem was composed on the shores of the Firth of Forth by the bard Aneirin, and certainly from medieval times onward the city has harboured an impressive array of poets and prose-writers, historians and critics, philosophers and scientists, all of high distinction in the world of letters. Some were born in the city, while others came to it from elsewhere. Many were educated at the University or became professors there; and it was, after all, the University which not only established the first Chair of English Literature in the world, but filled it with such notable incumbents as George Saintsbury and Herbert Grierson.

One day someone will write the literary history of Edinburgh in full. Here, if we are to trace any connection between the present and the past, we can only hurry over the impressive roll call from the poets who decorated, brightly as a French Book of Hours, the 15th century court, to Drummond of Hawthornden (whom Ben Jonson visited in 1608 after walking from London) and so on to the leading Scottish poet of our own age, Hugh MacDiarmid, who also studied at the University some 300 years later.

From Drummond's day to the end of the 17th century there was nothing really memorable save what William Watson, a literary critic and Editor of *The Scotsman*'s *Weekend Magazine*, calls the " agreeable epistles " of Samuel Rutherford, and notable poems by the great Montrose who knew the city well and perished in it. But at least a very strange character had been added to the list of writers who studied at the University. This was John Toland.

Born a Roman Catholic, this Irishman took his M.A. at Edinburgh in 1690. He then went on to Leyden and to Oxford where he wrote *Christianity not Mysterious*, a book which, though professedly Protestant and orthodox—he had abandoned Roman Catholicism—deeply shook the theological world by its barely concealed free-thinking argument. It also shook the House of Commons, which ordered the book to be burned by the common hangman. Soon in debt for his wigs and lodging, Toland was helped by various booksellers, later secured the patronage of certain German courts, and was " admitted to her philosophical conversations " by the Queen of Prussia. Thereafter he became little more than a Continental literary adventurer until his return to England where he died after composing a boastful epitaph—in Latin—which extolled both his independence and his mastery of many languages.

While Toland was gathering strength in his University days a little boy called Allan Ramsay had just been born at Leadhills in Lanarkshire.

The father of the great painter of the same name, he won fame for his *Gentle Shepherd* (1725), but also, to quote Mr. Watson again, he was significant in Edinburgh's literary history for another reason:

> He stands as one of our significant literary men, adding to the lyrical merits of his poetry the distinction of having animated in Edinburgh a more considerable sense of the artistic pleasures, and by his collecting of quantities of Scottish verse and balladry turning the minds of his countrymen to the native exercise of these arts.

"The native exercise of these arts" was soon considerable, for the whole of Lowland Scotland during the 18th century seemed to be breaking into song. There were James Thomson of *The Seasons*, Lady Nairne and Mrs. Cockburn, Robert Fergusson and many others including, greatest of all, Robert Burns, who lived in Edinburgh for a time. While they sang, as Walter Scott and James Hogg did after them, Edinburgh also became an intellectual capital, with a galaxy of historians, philosophers and economists shedding what Gibbon called "a strong ray of philosophic light" over the whole of Europe. Then there was Boswell, whose great literary achievement should be honoured for ever by his two home Universities, Edinburgh and Glasgow, and a number of visitors from overseas of whom two might be singled out for special mention.

One of these was Oliver Goldsmith, who in the autumn of 1752 came to Edinburgh for medical studies after a lively time at Trinity College, Dublin. The other visitor from overseas lived in that very different world where politics and literature touch wings. Benjamin Constant de Rebecque, likely to be remembered more for his association with Madame de Charrière and Madame de Stael than with Napoleon or Goethe, and whose novel *Adolphe* may well be read when his political treatises are forgotten, arrived at Edinburgh in 1783 to study Greek and History. He was then 15 years of age.

At a small Bavarian University he had already run up pretty big gambling debts, paid much attention to the ladies at the court of the Margraf of Anspach-Bayreuth, tried unsuccessfully to seduce "a girl of shady reputation"—as he described her—and remembered no doubt his earlier childish infatuation for a little English girl at Brussels, whom, he assured his grandmother, he "infinitely preferred to Cicero and Seneca." Accordingly his father took him to Edinburgh and duly enrolled him at the University. During the first year of his 18 month stay—"the most agreeable year of my whole life" he said later—Constant lived with a professor and for the last six months with "an excellent family." At the time, as we know, high seriousness was the key-note of the University, and it was in great measure because of the habits of hard work acquired there that Constant was able to apply himself to serious study later in his life.

Of his time at Edinburgh Constant himself wrote: "I enjoyed myself immensely, I studied sufficiently and I behaved in such a way that everyone spoke highly of me. Unfortunately a little Italian, from whom I was taking music lessons, introduced me to a faro bank which was run by his brother. I played; I lost; I made debts to right and left, with the result that my sojourn in Edinburgh was marred." But not altogether. As Sir Harold Nicolson has pointed out[1] Constant's 18 months at the University remained of durable value to him. He had acquired the precious habit of solitary study. He had learnt to speak English with fluency, although with a Franco–Scottish accent. He had made many friends who, in spite of his conduct, remained loyal to him for many years. And above all he had achieved a real understanding of British institutions, of the true meaning of constitutional monarchy, and of what was meant by liberal democracy.

Returning to the home products (and to William Watson's appreciation), at the centre of this glittering period stood one of Edinburgh's first writers of good English, as opposed to good Scots. This was David Hume, before whose impetus the Scottish school of philosophy gained the force and originality that attracted scholars to Edinburgh from all over the world. Sharing with Hume in this contribution to the intellectual dynamism of the 18th century were William Robertson, whose famous *History of Scotland* was published in 1759; Adam Smith, most famous for his *Wealth of Nations*; Hugh Blair, whose lectures on Rhetoric and Belles-Lettres were published in 1783; and Lord Hailes.

Now too, Edinburgh could pride herself that she nourished for a time a more purely literary genius in Tobias Smollett, one of the founders of the novel. But by every token Edinburgh in the late 18th century could more than hold a candle to London in the way of literary prestige. Among its townsmen flourished not only John Home the dramatist but also his biographer Henry Mackenzie, who epitomises the change from one era to the next. For Mackenzie was born in 1745 in Libberton's Wynd in the Old Town, and had his last house in Heriot Row in the New Town, with a view on to the civilised landscaping of Queen Street Gardens, ground which he had shot over as a boy. It was Mackenzie, author of *The Man of Feeling*, whose warm review of Burns' poetry in the *Lounger* assisted Dr. Blacklock in securing support and patronage for the poet. Among the other notable figures of the time were the famous moral philosopher Dugald Stewart, and the poet Robert Fergusson, who when only 24 years old died demented in 1775, four years after the birth of Walter Scott.

Scott's reputation zigzags like a snipe between the ranks of the faithful on the one hand and the puritanically modernist conventicle on the other. It is as a symbol, as one of the architects of the Romantic revolution, however, that Scott's real significance is seen by critics of a sober complexion. As an author he had a special towering genius, and his influence is still felt in Edinburgh, as in many countries for his powerful contribution to the historical novel and the whole rich floodwaters of European Romanticism.

Beside this distinguished Tory we must set his Whiggish friends of *The Edinburgh Review*, the mordant Francis Jeffrey, Sydney Smith the

[1] *Benjamin Constant*: Harold Nicolson, Constable, London, 1949.

wit, Henry Cockburn, author of a fascinating book, *Memorials of His Time*, and Thomas Carlyle, who wrote for the *Review* after meeting Jeffrey, lived pleasantly in the half-rurality of Comely Bank, and was much visited there by Thomas de Quincey.

Among the novelists of the day who were contributors to the *Review* or *Blackwood's Magazine* and also in other ways part of the Edinburgh scene were John Galt, whose reputation could stand reviving; Scott's biographer and son-in-law John Gibson Lockhart; and the normally verse-devoted James Hogg, prosaically remarkable for his *Confessions of a Justified Sinner*. The women writers of this remarkable time included Susan Ferrier, Anne Grant, Mrs. Johnstone, and Mrs. Brunton (whose writings however failed to entertain Jane Austen). But despite them all the century was running on into a lesser period, relieved by the social observation of Dean Ramsay and the more self-conscious efforts in the same vein by Robert Chambers, co-publisher with William of their famous magazine. Dr. John Brown, of course, was much loved and esteemed; and both Catherine Sinclair and the much more considerable Mrs. Oliphant deserve our notice too.[1]

In the far less glittering age that followed the passing of Sir Walter Scott and his famous Edinburgh contemporaries there were few if any writers of genius in the city, though a literary flame was kept alive mainly by the city's famous periodical literature; by some of its professors such as Aytoun and the poetical Secretary of the University, Alexander Smith; by a good many divines, of whom probably Dr. Chalmers was the most prolific; vicariously, by the work of many distinguished figures such as Thomas Carlyle who had been educated at the University before going elsewhere; and finally in addition to the philosophers, the professors and the hymn writers, by a vast number of lesser figures who lacked real genius but for whom writing was their craft as well as their livelihood.

A NEW RESURGENCE

As the Victorian era drew to its close there came a resurgence of literary creativeness in Edinburgh and one considerably overdue, since England by contrast with Scotland had been enjoying the flowering of a remarkable, unbroken lineage of poets and prosewriters right through the 19th century.

But now at last a new dawn was breaking on Scotland's capital. The latter part of the century was illuminated by the lively genius of Robert Louis Stevenson, whose short but brilliant career made a mark all the more notable for being aimed straight, as it were, at all men of goodwill and free from the smallest taint of pedantry. A peerless story-teller, a volatile executor of narrative, and an enthusiastic admirer of the picturesque, he had in him also a store of that sympathetic imagination that sometimes rears into fantasy, and recalls the cheerful truth-stretching of the yet undeceiving child. There is a mass of subsequent writing that

[1] Though he played no part in this period, Samuel Smiles, author of many books, was born near Edinburgh in 1812 and also deserves notice here as a doctor, editor and author of many books including *Self Help* which was translated into a score of languages.

stems from him, some of it distinguished but none superior to the work of the originator; and still more directly there is, in addition to those who admire him as a literary talent, a band of people who relish the flavour and respect the force of his gay and gallant personality. The more particular ability of Arthur Quiller-Couch whose *Dead Man's Rock* was clearly influenced by *Treasure Island* can also be traced to the Edinburgh of this time,[1] together with the detective talent of Arthur Conan Doyle which finds part of its source in the forensic atmosphere in which the city, where he was a medical student, had so long been wrapped. At this point too we become aware of James Barrie, who flourished mildly in Edinburgh for a while before his later fame in London, and of the fact that Kenneth Grahame, famed for his *The Wind in the Willows* and *The Golden Age*, graced the city with, at any rate, his birth.

Before going on to discuss the 20th century writers with more or less permanent roots in the city, we must recall many other writers of note who lived and worked in Edinburgh for a time or were educated there. These include R. M. Ballantyne, one of the most famous writers of boys' books; William Archer, a leader writer on the *Edinburgh Evening News* while still a student, and in the '80s and '90s not only one of the most famous of all dramatic critics in London but also the author of many books and plays; Archer's newspaper colleague J. M. Robertson who won high reputation for his literary criticism and, most notably, for his book *Modern Humanists*, which according to the late Professor Laski contained some of the best work done in Great Britain since Matthew Arnold; and F. S. Oliver, another contemporary distinguished man of letters. Then there were two poets: Henley, who lived and wrote in the city for more than two years in the middle '70s, and John Davidson, the tragic, impoverished poet-composer of *Ballads and Songs*, *Fleet Street Eclogues* and many other works, who also in the '70s had studied at the University. S. R. Crockett, too, who studied at the University at this time later became a minister and later still the full-time author of romantic novels—notably *The Raiders* and *The Lilac Sun Bonnet*. Nor must we omit Henry Gray Graham, an Edinburgh graduate and historian whose name through the years has gained increasing lustre for his scholarly and highly readable *Social Life of Scotland in the Eighteenth Century*.

THE TWENTIETH CENTURY

And so (Mr. Watson continues) we have turned into the present century and find ourselves looking with some astonishment at the quantity of names calling for attention with various degrees of force. We can attach to ourselves our adoptive resident Sir Compton Mackenzie, whose ebullient talent flowered profusely with his early and piquantly active novels, where encounter and event match thought and speculation in the speed and variety of their passage. This was the special eloquence of a youthful voice unmuffled by the rising walls of convention that generally

[1] In 1898 Quiller-Couch completed Stevenson's *St. Ives*.

accompany a man's growth; but his powers have remained curiously undamaged by time, and the early volumes of his autobiography have recalled and sometimes matched the efflorescence of the younger imagination.

We have no-one to match Mackenzie living in Edinburgh at this moment, but there have been competitive talents which departed to flourish elsewhere, and there are those resident here whose reputation continues to grow. Rebecca West, who was educated at George Watson's Ladies' College, and Hugh Walpole, whose father was Episcopalian Bishop of Edinburgh, made their names elsewhere; Bruce Marshall and Muriel Spark (a striking and ascending talent), who went to school in the city, live now away from it, although both have written Edinburgh into their books. Surprisingly too, there was Michael Arlen (of *The Green Hat*) who after the first World War emulated Charles Darwin long before him by studying botany at the University but wrote rather different kinds of books to those of his illustrious predecessor. Much earlier than Arlen, the University saw Algernon Blackwood, whose many books, some brilliantly eerie, appeared from 1906 onwards until the '50s. In this contemporary setting we must also include that "stormy daughter of Edinburgh," Dr. Marie Stopes, who was not only a distinguished scientific writer before her famous books on birth control but an interesting poet. But she again, like Algernon Blackwood, Annie S. Swan and so many others, could only claim a certain degree of inspiration from having been educated in the city.

We have had, however, Winifred Duke, an historical novelist of style and imagination; the agile fiction of Christine Orr; the travel-writing of Burn-Murdoch; and the stirring stories of Alasdair Alpin MacGregor, as well as the literary excursions of W. Forbes Gray and the antiquarianism of John Geddie. Truly the list seems endless. There is the Edinburgh-born D. E. Stevenson whose own family is directly related to Robert Louis, and who created an enduring character, *Mrs. Tim*; Neil Paterson who played football for the University before writing *The China Run* and other successful novels; and that well-known son of an Edinburgh doctor, John Connell, a serious writer with much to his credit including his biography of W. E. Henley, which won the James Tait Black Memorial Prize (an award within the patronage of the Professor of Rhetoric and English literature at the University,) and more recently his books on Field-Marshal Auchinleck and Lord Wavell. Lord Kinross, too, was born in the city but wrote most of his books south of the Border.

Edinburgh has also had, since 1900, her fair share of semi-literary "book-making"; but both before and since then she has enjoyed the steadying and compensating presence at the University of some outstanding talents. Blair's chair was soon filled by some notable professors, including Aytoun, Masson and George Saintsbury, whose genial style and generous range prepared the academic and literary public for a standard of commentary and insight from the school of English literature at Edinburgh that has not since been disappointed. Grierson's great and original mind, his profound and scholarly interpretation of the Metaphysical poets, and his lively and imaginative exploration of the qualities of literary genius, made him a major figure who gave a renewing impulse to literary criticism. Another great occupant of the chair was Dover Wilson, the ever-active and distinguished Shakespearean scholar. He was succeeded in 1945 by Professor W. L. Renwick, the authority on Spenser whose reputation has been reinforced by a recent volume on the early Romantics in the *Oxford History of English Literature*, while John Butt, the late incumbent, was the undisputed voice on Pope. John Oliver, who worked under Grierson, was another scholar both admired and loved; Arthur Melville Clark both before and after his appointment as Reader in English Literature at the University has also produced scholarly works, notably on Thomas Heywood; and Edinburgh of course can lay its claim to David Nichol Smith. Similar achievements can be recorded for the Professors of Fine Art and of Archeology. The present incumbent of the Chair of Fine Art, David Talbot Rice, has written many works on various aspects of art and particularly Byzantine art on which he is a leading authority, while his predecessor Sir Herbert Read has been a most prolific writer on subjects stretching from painting to poetry and politics. Stuart Piggott is yet another holder of a chair—that of Archaeology—who has made a number of contributions to the literature of his subject, and to other branches of literature as well. Also in the field of art scholarship, Alastair Smart, the author of a book on Allan Ramsay and later of *A Study in Florentine Painting of the Early Fourteenth Century* is to be recalled—this time from the College of Art.

It would however be excessive here to congratulate the city and the university on owning each of the intellects, on whatever subjects, who write and have written in their field, some of them graduates of the university in which they now teach. But we must mention, amongst recently deceased University historians, Richard Pares and W. Croft Dickinson. Dickinson's historical volumes testified not only to his own powers but to the general momentum of historical scholarship in Scotland, always an ineluctable part of the Scottish literary character and mode of thought, and the academic background behind it.

Before Pares there was Professor Williams, a noted authority on the Earl of Chatham and the Whig supremacy, who was a contemporary of Berriedale Keith, noted for his great knowledge of the constitutions which made up the British Empire. Today in Edinburgh there is a goodly crop of other historians with valuable books to their credit: Professor Gordon Donaldson, Professor of Scottish History; Ian Finlay on the history of Scottish crafts; that interesting though not professional social historian, A. R. B. Haldane (*The Drove Roads of Scotland*) and, among many others, Sir James Fergusson of Kilkerran, who is Keeper of the Scottish Records. Apart from his own more personal contributions such as *The Curragh Incident* and *The White Hind* Sir James, in company with other Edinburgh writers and scholars including Dr. William Beattie, Chief Librarian of the National Library of Scotland, helped forward the Yale Editions of *The Private Papers of James Boswell* by serving on the Advisory Committee appointed to assist Professor Frederick A. Pottle of Yale University and his colleagues. Hence in great measure stem not only the accuracy of the Scottish vernacular, literary and legal phrases used, but also the footnotes with their crisp and clear explanations of names and events mentioned only briefly by Boswell in his *Journal.*

This account of scholarship is however only part of that story, for there are also the poets amongst the professors. These include Sir Alexander Gray (whose work is appraised later in this chapter), Stuart Piggott and Wreford Watson—the first an economic historian, the second an archaeologist and the third a geographer who won the Queen's Gold Medal for poetry.

The divinity school, like the philosophy and literary departments, also has a quota of scholars whose books have often reached a wider public than the specialists in their own fields. Then too there have been many famous scientific writers from the University—Sir Archibald Geikie and his younger brother James, Sir David Brewster and that versatile graduate John Francis Campbell of Islay, who besides writing on geology was responsible for collecting the oral tales of the West Highlands in the Gaelic he had spoken as a boy with his father's servants.

" Leaving once more the academic field to look at other writers in our midst ", Mr. Watson asserts, " we first discover the names of Robert Kemp and Moray McLaren. Kemp, a protégé of Bridie and a native of Orkney, settled in Edinburgh in 1943 after refining his play-writing technique in the south. He set the Edinburgh Festival on its dramatic feet with his modern adaptation of Lyndesay's *Thrie Estatis.* Since then he has developed his own personal talent, in both the novel and the drama, for expressing with acute satirical sense the pretentious cultural and social excesses of the bourgeoisie. Moray McLaren on the other hand has established around his personality a literary structure composed of the traditional elements of biographical writing, the nostalgic and reminiscential recognition of an earlier day, and an unusual capacity for matching the pace of his time.

" In Marion Lochhead one sees the continuing tradition, for which Edinburgh is famous, of the historical-sociological theme that runs through Scott and Stevenson, and within that focus she has enlarged upon more aspects of Scottish life than certain other talents, contemporary with her own, who seem to have lost their way.

" Hannah Aitken, Jean Matheson, George Scott-Moncrieff (whose own delightful book on Edinburgh has sold for many years) and Neil McCallum are others whose reputation is now confirmed, while Mary Kelly and Mary Stewart are high among the British writers specialising in books of excitement and suspense. A talent that emerged with a flourish in that powerful evocation of Renaissance Scotland, *The Game of Kings*, is Dorothy Dunnett, and the most promising writer for sheer intellectual brilliance is probably David Caute. Finally we must add the names of Elizabeth Holland and Joan Lingard, very different from each other, but each having a singular and personal tone that distinguishes their writing and holds great promise.

" Yet it must be said that from the high days of the 18th and early 19th centuries the literary progress of Edinburgh mirrors what many have seen as the increasing provinciality of the city. At the beginning of our own century this had an inevitably deadening effect; but the modern development of communication and the tendency for the people of our whole island to receive the message of contemporary thought and changing artistic currents through a small handful of influential journals and a number of television and radio programmes, have taken much of the meaning out of " provincialism." Edinburgh may not again produce a literary " school ", unless it be in the purely academic sense; but this is not today an affair for regret. What would be depressing would be to see the city continuing an over-produced line of traditional literary ware, and failing to match the collapse of the barriers between cultures and branches of thought that characterises our age. We are, in fact, establishing our proper place in this changing world, harbouring young writers whose promise is modern and indifferent to local accidents, but maintaining that passion for reading that has been one of our long-standing, if quaint, vanities. In Edinburgh, for some years, the words of Scotland have in fact been the impetus behind two gallant ventures—the Scottish National Dictionary and the Dictionary of the Older Scottish Tongue, which deals with the language before 1700. Both dictionaries—in many volumes—are being compiled at the University, and both need additional funds to expedite what is a long and arduous undertaking, albeit a labour of love."

EDINBURGH'S POETS

Looking at the last half-century we see that the period was dominated by a literary re-birth which was styled, perhaps prematurely and rather grandiloquently but not altogether inaptly, the Scottish Renaissance. This re-birth occurred at the end of the first World War and was allied to the growing national feeling which had begun to permeate the country during the Boer War; and primarily it was a re-birth of poetry.

The new poetry, writes the eminent Edinburgh critic, Charles Graves, was inspired partly by a reaction against the often insipid Victorian versifiers who had followed in the wake of Burns, and partly by a feeling for Scotland's past achievement. Its chief promoters were Christopher Murray Grieve (Hugh MacDiarmid), who was born at Langholm in August, 1892 and studied at the University of Edinburgh, and Lewis Spence (1874–1955), a free-lance journalist from Broughty Ferry with a taste for anthropology and occultism, who supported his family mainly by writing books on the beliefs of ancient Mexico and the theory of the lost continent of Atlantis. In his early days he was a sub-editor on *The Scotsman* and afterwards a member of the staff of *The British Weekly*, under W. Robertson Nicoll.

Spence's early poems, *Le Roi d' Ys* (1910) and *Songs Satanic and Celestial* (1913) reveal a number of influences, among them those of Swinburne and the poets of the 'Nineties; but in the poem, *Andrew Fletcher of Saltoun*, the national note was already challengingly sounded. With the publication of *The Plumes of Time* (1926) Spence's style was formed, and in this collection a statelier Scots, consciously imitative of the tongue of the Auld Makars, was used in some of the poems as a protest against the debased doric or " gutter Scots " (as Spence called it) of the vernacular versifiers. The form of Spence's poetry was traditional, but the beauty and finish of many of the poems in *The Plumes of Time* and *Collected Poems* (1953) should keep their memory green. There was, of course, no future in Auld Scots (except for a stray word) and Spence wrote his two or three poems in this medium more as a challenge to writers in what he considered to be a decaying tongue than as an example to be followed.

MacDiarmid, the more original poet of the two, saw at once the limitations of the strict art form. After a brief lyric outburst which resulted in some of his finest poems—in *Sangshaw* (1925) and *Penny Wheep* (1926)—he used a more colloquial style in *A Drunk Man Looks at the Thistle* (1926) and *To Circumjack Cencrastus* (1930). Though later he wrote poetry of much power, especially in *First Hymn to Lenin* (1931), it was these first four books which established his reputation as the greatest Scottish poet since Burns.

MacDiarmid claimed that Scottish poetry, far from being the hole-and-corner affair it had become, should be able to stand on an equal footing with the poetry of Europe. He moved like a natural force among Scottish literary circles, expounding his ideas. He had the faculty, too, of inspiring the younger generation, among them another poet of considerable attainment. This was Albert D. Mackie (b. 1904), also an Edinburgh University student. Mackie, a journalist in Edinburgh and Jamaica and afterwards editor of the Edinburgh *Evening Dispatch*, developed a simple style in *Sing a Sang o Scotland*, a long poem in quatrains in praise of his native land, with a glossary of over 500 words, symptomatic of the general thirst for a Scots more saturated with survivals than any previous writing in the vernacular. But he could use a subtler artistry when he cared, as in poems like *The Young Man and the Young Nun*.

Closer to MacDiarmid in sympathy and of a generation younger than Mackie's, yet another University student, Sydney Goodsir Smith (b. 1915), also made use of a " synthetic " Scots which became a highly individual instrument in his hands. He is a kind of Scottish Catullus, singing lyrically of love's bitterness but, like Catullus, also delighting in satire. To the 1960 Edinburgh Festival he contributed *The Wallace*—a play written for the open stage of the Assembly Hall.

Douglas Young's incarceration in Saughton Jail on a political issue hardly entitles him to a mention among Edinburgh poets, though various engagements bring him so frequently to the city, as they do such other leading literary figures as Eric Linklater, that he is as much part of the Edinburgh literary scene as Nigel Tranter the novelist is, though he too lives outside the city boundaries. Classical influences are strong with Douglas Young who has translated into Lallans *The Frogs* and *The Birds* of Aristophanes, both of which have been " fringe " events at Edinburgh Festivals, and into English the *Hippolytus* of Euripides, performed by students at St. Andrews in May, 1963. Under the title of *The Burdies* the former was announced for performance at the 1966 Edinburgh Festival.

In recent years Robert Garioch Sutherland (b. 1909) has busied himself with the translation into Scots of the Latin plays of George Buchanan. *Jephthah and the Baptist* appeared in 1960. But he has also written much original verse of an amusing and satirical nature. 17 *Poems for 6d.*, which he published with Sorley Maclean in 1940, caught the attention of those on the look-out for new Scottish verse, and it was followed by *Chuckies on the Cairn* (1949) and *The Masque of Edinburgh* (1954). Sorley Maclean (b. 1911) is a Raasay-born poet, who graduated with Honours in English at Edinburgh University. His remarkable verse in Gaelic and English has the authentic accents, concentrated and realistic, of native Celtic poetry. In the poetry of George Mackay Brown (b. at Stromness, Orkney, 1927) a miniature epic note is to be heard. Brown studied at Newbattle and proceeded to Edinburgh University to read English Literature. His first volume, *Loaves and Fishes*, appeared in 1959. With the publication of *The Year of the Whale* (1965) he attained a leading place among Scottish poets of the period.

Two poets who stood aloof from the " Lallans " or vernacular revival were the late Edwin Muir (1887–1959) and Norman MacCaig (b. 1910). Muir had lived in Glasgow, St. Andrews and Edinburgh and then, as British Council representative, in Prague and Rome before going as Warden to Newbattle Abbey College, an educational foundation for working men just outside the city boundaries. An Orcadian by birth, the doric was not his natural tongue, and after trying his hand at it in some early ballads he soon abandoned it. His acquaintance with Rilke and Holderlin helped to form his outlook, and he began to emerge as an integrated poet in the early '30s. His keenly speculative and reflective mind,

> Knocking at dead men's gates
> To ask the living way. . . .

led him to regard appearance in a symbolic aspect. His dream-like poetry has intensity of feeling, and his sense of form and colour are highly developed.

Norman MacCaig, who has been gaining a considerable reputation in England, was first heard of in association with the movement called The New Apocalypse, with which two other Scottish poets, G. S. Fraser and J. F. Hendry, were connected. But soon he rid himself of the excessive imagery he used in *Far Cry*. His later verse is simpler, has no ulterior motives, and relying upon accuracy of observation and imaginative expression, aims at revealing the beauty of the natural and the spiritual worlds. It has a quiet dignity but occasionally a cryptic utterance which demands unusual concentration from the reader.

Scotland has frequently produced women poets who have survived in popular estimation by one or two poems, and in the period under notice two may be noted here who are in the Scottish vernacular tradition, with an occasional recourse to English and a freer style. They are Bessie J. MacArthur who, in *From Daer Water* (1962), collected work from three earlier publications and some later writing, and Agnes Hall, whose poems have a warmth of feeling for human experience and at times a spirit which links them with balladry. Traditional, too, is the varied verse of David Cleghorn Thomson which ranges from *vers de société*, often of a light and sometimes flippant nature, to the ironic and satiric, and more occasionally reveals a heart-felt personal emotion.

Alice Vandockum Stuart, born in Burma and educated at St. Hilda's School, Edinburgh, and Somerville College, Oxford, is a poet of high purpose, deep feeling and a controlled and honest technique who has gradually rid herself of a tendency towards certain conventional expressions evident in her first collection. Her latest volumes are *The Dark Tarn and Other Poems* (1953) and *The Door Between* (1963).

An indication of the changing temper of Scottish poetry in the last 50 years may be had by comparing the Rev. W. H. Hamilton's anthology *Holyrood*, Grieve's *Northern Numbers*, Maurice Lindsay's *Modern Scottish Poetry* and Norman MacCaig's *Honour'd Shade*.[1] The climate becomes sterner with the years; the psychological and political factors which had influenced English verse in the '30s begin to intrude without jeopardising the national spirit; and finally, in *Honour'd Shade*, there is little which may be mistaken for English poetry.

Many of those who first sounded the new note in Scotland were neither natives nor at the time citizens of Edinburgh. Among those who were may be included Alexander Gray (b. 1882), Professor of Political Economy first in Aberdeen and afterwards in Edinburgh University; Helen Cruickshank, like Gray of Angus descent, and William Soutar (1898–1943), whose remarkable development, as he lay bed-fast in Perth, had hardly begun when he was an undergraduate in Scotland's capital. The Elgin-born Andrew Young (b. 1885) who studied at New College, Edinburgh, and left Scotland and its Church ultimately to become a country parson in England and a Canon of Chichester Cathedral, belongs to the English rather than the Scottish tradition. Miss Cruickshank (b. 1886), who for many years was an untiring secretary of the Scottish Centre of PEN, was late in appearing before the public with a volume. *Up the Noran Water* (1934) contains " Shy Geordie ", a poem likely to live long in anthologies of Scots verse, though there are others as good—if not better—in her *Sea Buckthorn* (1954).

The verse of the Edinburgh architect, William Ogilvie, who contributed to the Porpoise Press " broadsheets " which, with other more substantial verse publications under the same imprint, were a feature of the earlier part of the last half century, has never been collected. It is in both Scots and English. The lovely lament, *There's nane o' my ain to care* was included by Walter de la Mare in one of his anthologies.

Here we must leave the varied Edinburgh literary scene, both past and present, as it has been portrayed for us by literary journalists accustomed to work in the daily hurly-burly of newspapers and magazines, book-reviewing and theatre going, and personal dealings with authors and publishers. Another view is presented by an academic critic—Dr. Kitchin—who, accustomed to estimating reputations with detachment in the

[1] Published by the Scottish Committee of the Arts Council.

larger perspective of history, may perhaps see the picture as future generations are likely to. This only time can tell—but his view is reproduced here even at the risk of some repetition.

A UNIVERSITY VIEW

Edinburgh (Dr. Kitchin says) is eminently a case where proper handling can make the past and present thrive on each other. Nevertheless, if a critic had the past too much in mind his standards of good writing might make it difficult for him to give due place to the present. This should be resisted, for though nobody thinks of our literary output today as anything but a dwindling inheritance from our Augustan age, a great deal of versatile talent can be discerned.

In the early '60s it would perhaps be true to say that writers count for less than cultural institutions—the English Association (though it still looks back nostalgically to the Edwardian era of its founding), the Franco–Scottish Society, the Scottish–Italian Circle, and so forth. More particularly thanks are due to the British Council for having given Edwin Muir the opportunity to organise the various National Houses during the war and so bring distinguished writers to Edinburgh. The French Institute also has institutionalised the work of the old French House in such a way as to provide a cultural centre for Edinburgh. The University, too, has come prominently into the picture by setting up its own Press and by founding the School of Scottish Studies. And there is also the Saltire Society with its manifold activities. Although these institutions foster culture rather than creative writing, it is a general rule that creative writing demands a cultural background, and that is what Scotland as a whole has sometimes lacked.[1]

Looking to the immediate past and considering not only Edinburgh-born but Edinburgh-based writers, Sir Herbert Grierson might be regarded as the link with the " heroic " past; that is, he has the dimensions which attract attention far outwith Scotland. His great work on Donne has greatly stimulated English poetry, and if it is objected that that is critical rather than creative work, his *Sir Walter Scott*, *Bart* with which he crowned his edition of the Scott letters, ranks with John Buchan's life of Scott as inspired rewriting of the story with more truth (but not more genius) than Lockhart thought fit to dispense.

Grierson's younger colleague at the University, Sir Alexander Gray, by a diversity of talent and great social gifts, is a reminder also of the age of writers of large dimensions. It would seem that his various works on the ballad, Scots, German and Danish, are likely to eclipse his fame as a poet; but we have only to take down one of his little verse collections to recognise a master of the " couthie " tradition of Scots which goes to the heart in a way that " Lallan " poetry seldom does.

To come to the other poets, these would include Edwin Muir and, at

[1] In the spring of 1965 it was announced that a collection of new poetry emanating from Scotland or written by Scots was to be published annually for three years by the Edinburgh University Press with the financial support of the Scottish Committee of the Arts Council.

a stretch, Andrew Young, who though resident in England, was bred up and educated at Edinburgh. Muir wandered far, but it is probable that he regarded Edinburgh as his home ground or place-of-return. He is the only recent Scottish writer (with the possible exception of Hugh MacDiarmid) to enjoy international standing both as critic and poet. He is that Scottish *rara avis*, a metaphysical poet, and one as fine in his way as the famed metaphysical poets of the 17th century.

Hostile to the tradition in which those two poets write are the " Lallan " poets who are rather ambitiously referred to as the " Scottish Renaissance." That Hugh MacDiarmid and his closely knit group of followers—Sidney Goodsir Smith, Douglas Young, A. D. Mackie, Robert Sutherland, Tom Scott and others—have rescued the vernacular muse from the sentimentality and flat rhyming of previous Scots poetry stretching back to Dunbar (Burns they hardly admit as an exception) is undeniable; and MacDiarmid has claims to be considered a major poet despite the cactus growth of wilful obstruction he places in our way.

With Edinburgh University honouring him by an LL.D., and journals like *Encounter* giving him pride of place, we may say all is forgiven him. Sidney Smith, poet of *The Eildon Tree* and several books of erotic lyrics, raised expectations which could only be satisfied by a work of major importance, which however, by the early '60s had not yet appeared. Norman McCaig's *Divided Bird* (in English) marks him as a poet of some distinction. A. D. Mackie keeps more to the vulgar tradition and is witty. A later recruit, Tom Scott's *An Ode Til New Jerusalem* looks like being either the last flare-up of the school or a promise of renewal. (*Dr. Kitchin wrote this some years ago.*) Hamish Henderson's affiliations are with the " Lallan " poets but his long poem on the North African campaign is epical and in English. If Sidney Smith is our Scottish Catullus, Henderson might be dubbed our Scottish Lucan. But we must not throw about those august titles irresponsibly.

One might say that the rest is journalism if it were not for the impressive figure of Sir Compton Mackenzie, who presides over the literary scene in the city. Sir Compton is vulnerable, no doubt. His high and serious moments are often succeeded by moods in which the spirit of sheer fun sometimes lands him in the ditch. But we suspect that he knows very well what he is doing when he indulges in Highland or other " romps," and one must not be ungrateful for sheer fun.

Round Sir Compton gyrate men of proven loyalty but lesser talent. Journalism, either of the B.B.C. variety or the daily press, has enormously increased the opportunities for writers with the necessary wit or even without it. The circle of such writers is narrow and there is inbreeding due to the preference of editors and the B.B.C. for men of local reputation. Wilfred Taylor of *The Scotsman's Log* is for one irreplaceable.

The trouble with the novelists is that they, or the public, seem to be looking for a new *House with the Green Shutters* or a Grassic Gibbon, which would mean the perpetuation of the sordid Scotland so painfully displayed in the half-dozen novels adapted in recent years for the B.B.C. Either that or we have the romantic adventure with subdued local colour of which Maurice Walsh was the chief practitioner—now succeeded by Nigel Tranter, a near-resident of Edinburgh, who complains or explains that London publishers insist on subdued colour. Then there is Janet A. Smith who explores romantic Scotland with, however, more respect for and interest in history than others. Other and estimable practitioners of the novel are Winifred Duke, John Connell and George Scott-Moncrieff, though the last two have concentrated more on other literary forms in recent years.

Of biography and autobiography there is singularly little. Journalism was written up some years ago in *I Came I Saw* by that genial and versatile writer the late J. W. Herries. Edwin Muir's autobiography, first published as *The Story and the Fable*, is now a classic. Another Edinburgh product, David Daiches, has added to his prodigious output of critical works by publishing the story of his early years in Edinburgh (*Two Worlds*) in which critical acumen gives place to nostalgic piety.

I have said nothing (ends Dr. Kitchin) of other recently dead writers like Lewis Spence—learned as an anthropologist, witty as a journalist and original begetter of " Lallans " (so he ruefully claimed)—or of more fleeting eminences like Sir Robert Bruce Lockhart and—dare we claim? —Lord Beveridge. For a year or two after the war these and many others resided in the city, and for a time recalled the spacious days of literary Edinburgh.

CHAPTER 43

THE LIBRARIES AND MUSEUMS

THE LIBRARIES

THE richness and variety of its libraries have long been notable features of Edinburgh, and rightly so. According to the *ASLIB Directory* (1957) there are no fewer than 68 libraries in the city, and no other city or town in Great Britain, with the exception of London, Oxford and Cambridge, has anything like as many. To make the total even more impressive the many departments and branches of the municipal public libraries count merely as one. And even so the ASLIB list is far from complete.

Some of these libraries can trace their descent from the troubled but formative years of the 16th and 17th centuries. The 18th, when the city ranked high among the main intellectual centres of Europe, saw a considerable addition to their number, wealth and variety, while in the 19th century there was an unprecedented expansion of new kinds of libraries, many of a specialised character. Probably the most noteworthy of these is the Edinburgh Central Library, since its opening in 1890 signalled the beginning of a city-wide public library system of enormous importance in the development and moulding of the reading habits of the general body of citizens. Today the expansion and diversification continues, for the first six decades of the present century have seen the establishment of many more libraries, and the vigorous growth of certain of the older ones.

The oldest Edinburgh library with a continuous history is that of the University. This was founded late in the 16th century, and its record therefore could possibly be challenged only by the Royal College of Surgeons, were it not for this body's chequered fortunes in the past. The intellectual stirrings of the late 17th century, the dawn in Scotland as elsewhere of a more humanistic and scientific age, gave birth to three new libraries which have survived: that of the Royal Botanic Garden (1670), the Royal College of Physicians (1681) and, also in the 1680s, the Advocates' Library which soon became, *de facto*, a national library of Scotland. Later still the century of Hume and Adam Smith saw the foundation of the Signet Library together with at least six others more specialised: legal, scientific, medical, antiquarian and agricultural.

At the present day the concentration of so many libraries within a quarter of a mile or so of the junction of George IV Bridge and the Royal Mile is indeed remarkable. They include the National Library of Scotland, three law libraries (those of the Advocates, the Writers to the Signet, and the Society of Solicitors in the Supreme Courts of Scotland), Edinburgh University Library, the city's Central Library, the Scottish Central Library, the New College (theological) Library and others besides. The proximity of these to each other has led to a high degree of interrelationship, resulting in greater efficiency, the sharing of common experience, the avoidance of much needless duplication in purchasing and in services, and in greater convenience to readers, who can be easily referred from one to another of these rich storehouses of knowledge.

THE EDINBURGH PUBLIC LIBRARIES

The enormous growth of public libraries administered by local authorities has been a remarkable feature of British life since Victorian days, and during the last 75 years Edinburgh has shared to the full in this development. No other large British city approaches the city's average of over 13 book issues per annum for each man, woman and child of the population, a record which it holds in spite of the fact that it spends far less per head than the average on its libraries, its total expenditure in 1960–1, for example, being over £7,000 less than Bristol, and over £105,000 less than Sheffield, to mention only two towns of comparable population. Edinburgh is also well ahead in the proportion of non-fiction books borrowed. Of 6,307,024 books issued to readers between June, 1964 and May, 1965 nearly 12 per cent were juvenile, over 30 per cent were fiction, and the remaining 58 per cent were other books borrowed by adults. Works of history and travel, literary works, general works, technology, Scottish books, fine arts, science and sociology—to name in descending order of popularity the classes from which there were from nearly 600,000 to more than 100,000 issues—were those most frequently sought after. Much has been said of the diminution of the reading habit in the age of television, but the Edinburgh statistics do not suggest that this is serious. Initially a fall away was noticeable but only in the field of lighter recreational reading, and that mainly in the issues of this type of book from mobile libraries in new housing development areas. Later, however, the trend was not so marked, and the book is again regaining lost ground as the television set loses the appeal of novelty.

The history of the present-day public library system, administered for the Corporation through the Libraries and Museums Committee, can be traced back to 1886 when Mr. Andrew Carnegie offered £25,000 (which he later raised to £50,000) to finance the erection of a library building in the city. The building, designed by Sir George Washington Browne, in the French Renaissance style, is situated on George IV Bridge; and from the beginning with 80,000 volumes it contained reference, lending and juvenile departments, and a newsroom. The first librarian, Dr. Hew Morrison, was appointed in 1887 and he held office until 1922.

Seven branch libraries in different parts of the city followed in fairly rapid succession up to the outbreak of the first World War. In the case of four of these branches, the Libraries Committee had co-operated with the trustees of Thomas Nelson, the publisher, who had left funds to establish recreation halls in which classical concerts are still held in the poorer districts of the city; and Nelson Halls were built in close association with the new libraries.

After the expansion of the city's boundaries in 1920 and under the direction of the new librarian, Mr. E. A. Savage (1922–1942), the conversion of the bulk of the holdings of the libraries to open access was soon undertaken. More children's rooms were provided, and soon a new scheme of suburban and deposited libraries was started to supply books in outlying areas not only through the schools to pupils but also to adults. Since 1949 adults in the new housing areas have also been receiving their books from mobile libraries; schools in these areas are supplied with books for their pupils; and the service has been extended to cover youth clubs, adult education and other centres including H.M. Prison at Saughton.

Closer collaboration between the Libraries Committee and the Education Committee resulted in the establishment of secondary school libraries at Bellevue School in 1929 and at Leith Academy in 1930. These are full-time undertakings in which trained librarians co-operate with the teaching staff; library periods feature in the school time-table; pupils are given guidance in the use of books; and steadily this valuable service is being expanded to other secondary schools. It should also be remembered here that the long existing independent libraries of some of Edinburgh's boarding schools and older secondary schools, such as the Royal High School, contain notable collections of books old and new.

The extension of the city limits in 1920, as we saw earlier, made the burgh of Leith—where an adequate library was badly needed—a part of Edinburgh. To meet the need a new branch was opened in 1932, and it shared greatly in the rapid growth of the Edinburgh libraries until it was badly damaged by a land-mine in 1941. Makeshift arrangements and a curtailed service had to suffice until the opening, in 1955, of the present modern, spacious and attractive building. The Leith branch again consists of a lending library with children's section, a reference library and a newsroom, and has regained its place, as one of the busiest of the city's branch libraries.

Corstorphine, which was also absorbed in 1920, had possessed its own village library before its incorporation in Edinburgh, but since 1936 the well-built stone library facing the ancient parish church across a spacious green lawn has added to the attractiveness of the scene. Internally, until recent extensions it consisted of a single large room with a book stock of over 23,000 volumes, a newspaper bay and a delightful children's corner, but a room far too small to meet the needs of a rapidly growing community with a wide range of reading interests. Now, however, the building has been enlarged and the stock increased to more than 33,000 books. In Colinton, in 1934, a smaller suburban library was formed in a converted house from which the partition walls were removed. Its popularity can be gauged from the fact that from its meagre stock of a little over 10,000 books, there were over 156,000 issues in 1964-65, compared with over 400,000 at Corstorphine.

Despite the city's rapid expansion, the building of new branch libraries has proceeded less rapidly since the second World War than it did after the first. Scarcities, restrictions and mounting costs are, of course, the main reasons; which makes the rebuilding of the Leith branch an important achievement. At Blackhall also, in 1948, a library was opened in a temporary structure to serve that area together with Davidson's Mains, a structure which had to serve until the opening of the new permanent building in 1966. In October, 1963 a new library building, a great advance on the old, was opened at Portobello.

Going back to the early post-war years, a new method of bringing library services to the outer suburbs was begun in 1949. This was a mobile library in a large van. In 1952 a second van was added, and these vehicles, painted in black and white, and each carrying some 2,400 volumes, became a familiar sight in Edinburgh streets. A third was added in the winter of 1963–4. With regular times and pre-arranged stopping places, they cater both for adults and children. The popularity of the mobile libraries is left in no doubt by the fact that there have been as many as 188,000 book issues in a single year.

A library scheme for the hospitals of the city was instituted in 1946, and had grown so rapidly by the '60s that more than 48,000 book issues were being made by two full-time librarians aided by volunteers. Trolleys convey the books to the bedsides, but also in several hospitals there are comfortable library rooms where patients able to walk can escape the atmosphere of the ward and read in different surroundings.

Some recent developments have taken place in the oldest of the city's branches, that of Dundee Street. The district is densely populated and contains a large number of children living among somewhat gaunt surroundings. The present library building, opened in 1940, although closely hemmed in, has, with its tall clean lines and surfaces and its extensive use of glass, a spaciousness which is much needed. In January, 1959 a separate junior department was opened on the ground floor, where during school holidays a story hour is held each week. In addition, a collection of picture story books for children who are too young to read may be borrowed by parents, and the enthusiastic response is seen in the fact that there were 3,000 issues of these books during the first six months.

Special needs of other districts are also catered for. Books on the sea and seafaring activities, together with text-books and other reading material, are to be found at Leith, where they are especially appreciated by students of the Nautical College and many others among that maritime community. Books on foundry work and printing are prominent features at McDonald Road, and on rubber technology and brewing at Dundee Street. The favourite topics of general reading still vary a good deal according to the residential nature of the district, but this differentiation is becoming noticeably less marked of recent years as a result of all the influences which tend nowadays to produce a more uniform outlook and taste.

The important Central Library on George IV Bridge has kept pace with the growth of branch and mobile libraries, and properties adjoining the original building have had to be taken over. As early as 1930 the part of the main building which housed the Central Home Reading Library had become too small for the purpose; it was therefore decided to put into effect a policy, already accepted on its own merits, of setting up subject departments. Among these was the Edinburgh Room, housing eventually before its 1961 transfer to more commodious space beside the Scottish Library, some 25,000 books and 21,000 prints, other illustrations, slides, negatives and films and gramophone records, which together comprise a wealth of material on every aspect of Edinburgh life both past and present. The collection includes all the directories of the city, large collections of plans and newspapers and works of many authors who were either born in or were closely associated with Edinburgh, or have written about it. This research material is of course for use in the Library itself, and in recent years anything from 29,000 to 33,000 items have been consulted annually.

An important project is the photographic survey of Edinburgh which in the early 1960s was being undertaken by the Library with the co-operation of the Edinburgh Photographic Society. It provides a fine record of a city rich in architectural features of historic interest, and is of particular value and urgency in a period of change and reconstruction.

A great advance was made with the opening in May, 1961, of the spacious new Scottish Library, alongside which the contents of the Edinburgh room were transferred and indeed expanded, for it houses over 60,000 books and over 27,000 other items such as prints. Scottish literature, history and topography come within its scope and the collecting of Scottish topographical prints and drawings and slides is an important part of its function.

The popularity of the Fine Art Library, where there are over 24,000 books and 38,000 illustrations, is indicated by the 141,000 issues during the year 1964–5. As in the case of all the special libraries, other than the Edinburgh Room, most of the contents can be borrowed, and the use made of coloured prints, transparencies and other reproductions by students, teachers and lecturers, is extensive and ever-increasing. The exhibition of material in this collection creates much interest and serves to make known the wealth of its resources. The Music Library, opened in 1934, has grown to 39,000 volumes and in a single year there have been over 76,000 issues. Scottish music is constantly sought after, and the collection is strong in this field; but the resources are by no means confined to it, since they range from medieval service books on vellum to ballet and its stage presentation, concert programmes, the scores of great composers and music periodicals.

Together with the Edinburgh Room, the Department of Economics and Commerce was the first specialised section to open, in 1932. It has served the public well, but in 1959 it was decided to merge it again with the Central Reference and Home Reading Libraries. Experience had shown that it would be an advantage for books on the economic aspects of such things as road and rail transport, for instance, to be in proximity to books dealing with the technical aspects of these subjects, and the return of the books on economics and commerce to the main lending and reference department led to a considerable increase in use.

The Central Reference Library, with its 159,000 volumes, of which about 16,000 are on open access, covers many subjects which are not the concern of the special libraries. It is particularly strong in literature and history, medicine, science, religion and archaeology, and is well equipped with bibliographical material. There were over 118,000 consultations of various items in the year 1964–5 and the habitués of this well-frequented room represent a fairly wide cross-section of the Edinburgh public. But a good deal wider is the clientèle of the large Central Home Reading Library, although a falling away was seen in 1959 following the opening of a Central Fiction Library in a near-by room. The issues from the Central Fiction Library during its first year of separate existence reached 494,512 volumes and over half-a-million in 1960–1, with a fall however to 431,623 in 1964–5. Those from the Central Home Reading Library, even after the transfer of novels in English, fell only from 785,000 to 409,783, and reached over 447,232 in 1964–5.

Of the other public rooms in the Central Library, there remains to be mentioned the Inquiry Office with its much-used reference books, world-wide directories, Edinburgh voters' and valuation rolls, and its attractive and much appreciated array of colourful guides to holiday resorts; the Newsroom (removed in 1965 to the apse of the former Trinity College Church); and the attractive Junior Library of some 15,000 books and other illustrative material of which use was made during the year 1964-5 to the extent of over 106,000 issues, mainly for home reading.

The total income of the municipal public libraries of Edinburgh amounted in 1964-5 to more than £288,000 of which over £261,000 came from the rates. This means an average annual contribution of 12*s.* 2*d.* from each inhabitant, the library rate being 5.21*d.* in the £1. Salaries and wages accounted for almost £129,000, the purchase of books, periodicals and other reading material for more than £52,000, binding and repairs for over £17,000. The staff of central, branch, mobile and other libraries and services totals more than 250.

SUBSCRIPTION LIBRARIES

The rapid expansion of the municipal public libraries has by no means put an end to the commercial circulating libraries, which have thrived in Edinburgh since the first one was opened in the Luckenbooths by Allan Ramsay in 1726. They are usually associated, as Ramsay's was, with a bookselling business and like his, a few others, and particularly those of Robert Grant and Son and of Douglas and Foulis have been long-lived and characteristic institutions in the city. Ramsay's library retained its identity for over a century, although in the hands of various owners, such as Sibbald after 1780 and later Mackay. Known as the Edinburgh Circulating Library in its latter days it contained over 30,000 volumes, and was frequented by the young Walter Scott who made eager use of it. In 1832 it went under the hammer, but much of its contents can be traced as part of the stock of the rapidly increasing circulating libraries of Edinburgh around the middle of the century. The Directory for 1848 records about a dozen of these libraries and by the '90s there were twice as many.

The subscription library of Robert Grant and Son, founded about 1840, is still flourishing, although removed in 1957 from Princes Street, where it began, to George Street when the firm merged with another to form the Edinburgh Bookshop. The type of book in demand has changed with the times. No longer are there rows of shelves laden with the classics, collected correspondence and large biographies published over a lengthy period of years. As in the other circulating libraries of the city today, the supply is of recently published books of fairly general appeal. But the increase in the price of books and the growth of public libraries is making this position more difficult.

The largest commercial circulating library in the city is Douglas and Foulis. The bookselling firm of Edmonston and Douglas, later Douglas and Foulis, was formed in 1847, and David Douglas (1823–1916) became not only a prosperous bookseller but a publisher of many important books on Scottish history. In 1863 this firm introduced, under the direction of Thomas Foulis, the " Select English and Foreign Library and Reading Club " which lent books for a subscription of a guinea or more; and since 1877 this library has been situated in Castle Street in varying forms. Early in 1957, however, the firm was taken over by John Menzies and Company, who already owned a circulating library at the West End Bookshop, but under its old name the Douglas and Foulis Library continues to function under its old rooftree, with a stock of nearly 30,000 books. There is only a slight preponderance in the demand for fiction, books on travel and biography being among the other favourites. The patrons of this busy library form a fairly wide cross-section of the city's populace. The Boots' Library, opened in 1911, was recently closed.

There are still several other libraries associated with booksellers' shops; and in recent decades the growth of commercial libraries of light recreational reading, catering for mass taste, and usually run on a non-subscription basis, is no less marked in Edinburgh than elsewhere. It is equally true, says the librarian of a subscription library in Edinburgh who has served in several other British towns, that Edinburgh readers are often more precise as to which books they want, and more insistent on getting them than people elsewhere.

THE LEARNED LIBRARIES

THE UNIVERSITY LIBRARY

Among learned libraries of general scope in Edinburgh pride of place on grounds of seniority goes to that of the University. It began with some 300 volumes, mainly theological, which were bequeathed to the Town Council in 1580 by Clement Litel, advocate, in order to found " ane common librarie " for the use of men " beiring functioun in the ministrie." These books were housed in the manse of St. Giles until soon after the Town's College, now the University, was founded in 1583. Other early acquisitions include the collection of 700 volumes given by the poet, Drummond of Hawthornden, among them many works of English and

European literature. Litel's and Drummond's books are still the proud possessions of Edinburgh University Library, available for consultation though well guarded with other treasures by the metal grids of the Strong Room. The Library enjoyed the right, from 1710 onwards, of claiming under the Copyright Act of the previous year every publication registered at Stationers' Hall, and the exercise of this privilege led to great enrichment in the field of English and Scottish books. The right to claim was later commuted for a Treasury grant of £575 a year. By 1965 the Library held nearly 900,000 volumes, more than 165,000 pamphlets, some 89,000 unbound periodical parts, over 8,200 volumes of manuscripts, and over 29,000 letters and pieces.

Notable among this library's monetary bequests have been that of General John Reid from which an annual sum was set apart in 1846 for book-purchase, and that of Cathcart White in the early '40s of the present century. A considerable amount is drawn from other sources, including the Carnegie Trust, but most of the revenue comes today from general University funds. The annual expenditure on books and periodicals, including binding, together with stationery and equipment, is now approaching £80,000 and salaries amount to about £100,000. The grant was nearly £70,000 in 1964-5, and there were also endowments of £79,000.

The scope of the Library is as wide as the needs of the University faculties; and indeed some 100 faculty and departmental libraries have been set up. Prominent among these are the Reid Musical Library of some 35,000 volumes and scores, and the Central Medical Library of about 58,000 books and pamphlets and 30,000 unbound periodical parts.

A recent development has been the establishment of the Law Library (1960), formed by amalgamating the class libraries in law and the general library's holdings of legal books. The stock amounts to some 16,000 books. The Centre of African Studies, established in 1962, has the beginnings of its own library, and this is certain to expand greatly.

The proliferation of separate libraries brings with it its own problems and a new policy has now been approved whereby in future the broad structure of the University library will consist of a main library and a number of sectional libraries.

Until 1827 Edinburgh University Library was housed in what had by then become a very inadequate building, now pulled down, which stood to the east of the quadrangle. Robert Adam's plan for the new University had to be greatly modified, by Playfair, when work was resumed after Waterloo, and the magnificent interior of the Upper Library Hall, the last part to be built, was largely Playfair's. This finely proportioned hall, with its majestic pillars and curved ceiling of great splendour and beauty has been described as the finest interior in Edinburgh. During the last 130 years there has been much expansion into various parts of the old and the New University Buildings but construction began in 1965 of a new library building on a more adequate scale to meet present-day needs.

Among the many notable special collections are the Cameron and the MacKinnon on Celtic subjects, part of the library of Andrew Fletcher of Saltoun reflective of the wide European interests of this Scottish patriot, a wealth of early almanacs and herbals, the Blöndal Icelandic collections, and others ranging from oriental studies to Reformation tracts, science, medicine and law—and modern Greek. There are over 8,000 Western and Oriental manuscripts and charters, including those collected by David Laing, who had supervised the 1827 move into the present building and in 1879 left his own very fine manuscript collection to the library he had so illustriously served. Seven years earlier about a thousand printed volumes, mainly of Shakespearean interest had been presented by J. O. Halliwell-Phillips out of a much bigger collection; and as some of these were rare, Edinburgh suddenly became far richer than ever before in material for the historical study of English drama. But as one Edinburgh litterateur puts it, the benign ghost of Mr. Halliwell-Phillips was to haunt the University for almost a century and pay a final tribute in 1964. Halliwell-Phillips, erudite collector, built up four scholarly collections in all. Two went to Washington, one was his gift to Edinburgh University; there remained his fourth collection—in the possession of the Penzance Library until 1964 when it came up for sale at Sotheby's. With the help of the University Court, those two admirable institutions the Friends of Edinburgh University Library and the Friends of the National Libraries, and an anonymous private benefactor, the University Library in 1964 was able to purchase this large collection of 17th-century plays for £21,000. It was a memorable acquisition, for the plays not only composed a big part of the original Halliwell-Phillips Collection, including works of the period by Ben Jonson, Beaumont and Fletcher, Wycherley and other playwrights of the period, but some were playhouse copies with contemporary stage directions added in manuscript. Furthermore, since this Collection with only a little overlapping, is complementary to the splendid Bute collection of plays bought by the National Library of Scotland in 1956, Edinburgh has now become one of the three principal European centres for research in Elizabethan drama, the other two being the British Museum and the Bodleian.

The staff of Edinburgh University Library number about 120, of whom a high proportion are graduates. Some have undergone professional training before appointment; others are trained in the library afterwards. With the growth of the University increasing use is made of the library which has seating accommodation in its general and departmental sections for more than 3,000 persons. But many students also use the reading-rooms of the Edinburgh Central Library; and on Wednesdays and Saturdays in particular these are often overcrowded.

In the year ending September, 1965 the number of books borrowed from the University's General Library alone was 52,000; those borrowed from the Central Medical Library were 22,000; and the corresponding figure was 5,200 for the Reid Music Library. There were also 33,000 borrowings from 14 class and departmental libraries. These figures, incidentally, do not include consultations in the library itself where the main use of the books is made.

The absorption of other libraries, such as that of the Royal Dick Veterinary College and the Edinburgh Dental Hospital, has been a trend of recent years. In 1931 all the separate departmental libraries of the Medical School, except the Physiology Library, combined to form the Central Medical Library, which is housed in the New Buildings of the University. It is intended primarily to house modern books and periodicals required for medical and scientific work, the older medical books being retained in the General Library.

Three major building schemes were at the planning stage in 1963. These were a new main University Library, a science library and the reconstruction of the Central Medical Library. But before we leave it the University Library deserves a tribute on other counts. It has naturally kept pace with several kinds of modern developments in photographic processes and the treasures of other libraries are frequently brought to Edinburgh in photostat, microfilm or microcard form to facilitate research by members of the University staff, while the Library's photographic department also prepares slides and film strips for various teaching departments. The availability of the Library's resources has also been facilitated by allowing open access to most of the shelves, by extending the privilege of home borrowing to graduates of all the Scottish universities and by allowing the public, on application, to consult books on the premises during the usual hours of opening.

THE NATIONAL LIBRARY OF SCOTLAND

Scotland can claim to have, in one, the oldest and the youngest of the four national libraries of the four nations of the British Isles; for the Advocates' Library, formally opened in 1689, soon became *de facto* a national library, although the National Library of Scotland, which was its offspring, did not exist under that name before 1925. The former was set up at the instigation of Sir George Mackenzie of Rosehaugh, the King's Advocate, who insisted in his opening speech that, in addition to law-books, place had to be found for History, Criticism and Rhetoric—" The Handmaidens of Jurisprudence." The first catalogue (1692) reveals that this policy was followed from the beginning, but the granting in 1709 of the copyright privilege, whereby the bulk of British publications could be claimed, ensured that the founder's wishes would be fulfilled in ample measure.

The tradition of a library for the nation was fostered by the liberal policy of offering facilities for study to scholars and men of letters, by the influence of men of distinction associated with the Advocates' Library, by the broad European interest of its purchasing policy, and by success in acquiring much material of the highest importance for the study of Scottish history and literature. Lord Hailes, Boswell, Sir Walter Scott and Robert Louis Stevenson were all associated with this library both as advocates and as literary men, while among the Keepers were Thomas Ruddiman and, above all, David Hume (from 1752 to 1757) who did much to enrich the library in the fields of French literature and learning. The purchase, as early as 1698, of the historical collections of Sir James Balfour of Denmilne, was a fine beginning to the acquiring of a rich store of Scottish manuscripts, built up for more than two centuries by the

Advocates, and bountifully transferred as a gift to the nation in 1925. Long before then, however, Boswell's " old magazine of antiquities ", had become a great abode of study frequented by the lawyer in pursuit of his vocation, the scholar pouring over the cultural heritage of the ages, and the man of letters, such as Boswell himself, seeking consolation in the permanence of books and papers on that rainy day when David Hume was borne to his rest.

The regular display of treasures accumulated by the Advocates, until 1956 in the Laigh Parliament Hall and since then in the new Exhibition Hall of the National Library, has been one of the main links with the public. And here is history indeed. The last letter of Mary Queen of Scots, the earliest contemporary Scottish royal portraits (on an early charter), the diary of Andrew Melville with his reference to the " twa Kingdoms ", signatures on the Solemn League and Covenant, writings in the hand of Knox, Hume, Burns, Scott and Stevenson—these come readiest to many minds when the library is thought of. Other outstanding treasures are the blood-stained Edinburgh Codex (one of the earliest complete manuscripts of the Old Testament in Hebrew), a 10th-century Martial, a fine illuminated manuscript of St. Augustine's *De Civitate Dei*, and several delightful Books of Hours. With printed books the same two-fold policy of acquiring the fruits of Scottish and world culture brought in the splendid copy of the Gutenberg Bible and the Chepman and Myllar prints—the only known copies of the earliest recorded products of the press in Scotland (1508), printed in the Cowgate (then the Southgate) almost within a stone's throw of where they are now proudly shown. The Thorkelin (Scandinavian) and Astorga (Hispanic) collections, bought early in the 19th century by the Advocates, the latter on the recommendation of J. G. Lockhart, give the National Library a special standing in these fields of study.

The housing of the Advocates' Library had presented problems from the beginning when, in 1682, rooms were secured in a corner of Parliament Close. Things came to a head in 1700 when the Close was devastated by fire; but the south end of the Laigh Parliament Hall was obtained and in 1790, when the Records of Scotland were transferred to the newly erected Register House, the whole of the Laigh Hall was given over to the library. Thereafter throughout the 19th century there was a piecemeal policy of thrusting out into adjacent premises including prison cells under the Courts of Justice. By the middle of the century the library was a strain on the resources of the Faculty of Advocates, and as early as 1839 the first attempt was made to obtain a government grant-in-aid. In 1874 Thomas Carlyle lent his pen to the still unavailing efforts to the same end: " My clear testimony ", he wrote of the library, " is that essentially it belongs to Scotland at large . . . and that it fairly deserves all reasonable help and support from whatever calls itself a Government in that country."

In 1919 a Committee of Faculty was set up to review matters, with special reference to the project of instituting a National Library; and in February, 1921 the Faculty approved the Committee's scheme whereby they should " subject to the provision by the Treasury, or from other sources, of the necessary funds " transfer to the nation as a free gift the books and manuscripts other than those whose subject was law. In 1923 the Scottish National Library Endowment Trust was formed and the public invited to contribute. First came £1,000 (later raised to £5,000) from the 5th Lord Rosebery, the interest on which is still used for the purchase of manuscripts. The decisive gift, however, was that of £100,000 by Mr. (later Sir) Alexander Grant. The Government then moved, and in 1925 Parliament passed the National Library of Scotland Act. The Faculty handed over about 750,000 books, together with priceless manuscript collections. The printed books that it retained in order to continue fulfilling its function as a working legal library amounted to about 45,000. The Advocates' Library continues to exist along these lines. Both libraries are now housed in adjacent premises, and the books of each can be read in the reading-room of the other. The copyright privilege has been transferred to the National Library, but law-books thus acquired are immediately transferred to the Advocates.

An economic depression, a second World War and years of post-war scarcities and stringencies were to intervene before the National Library was to have a building of its own. A Building Fund had, however, long been in being, and Sir Alexander Grant had enriched it with a second gift of £100,000. The New Library was opened by Her Majesty The Queen in 1956, on the site of the demolished Sheriff Court House. Externally the most impressive feature of the new building is the west façade, rising high above George IV Bridge, the main central elevation windowless in its upper part so as to muffle street noises in the Reading Room with its seating for about a hundred persons, and bearing in relief seven elongated sculptured figures (the work of Hew Lorimer) representing various branches of learning and the arts. Massive though the façade may be, the lie of the land conceals the true size of the building, which rises from the steep slope of the Cowgate valley and which at its southern end reaches down through nine floors, mainly of stackage.

The part of the interior best known to the public is the L-shaped Exhibition Hall, to the right of the main entrance from George IV Bridge. A wide staircase, doubling back on itself in two flights leads to the Catalogue Hall, beyond which is the Reading Room, occupying the whole length of the main block and flanked to the north and south by four smaller rooms of domestic scale which house some of the special collections. The building was designed by Dr. Reginald Fairlie whose plan was approved in 1936. The new Map Room, completed in 1958 to Mr. Stewart Sim's more modern design, is situated to the north of the main building. It contains three sound-proofed booths where readers may type or enter into consultation with one another over maps or books, a service which is increasingly called for.

Recent years have seen rapid advance in several ways, and not least in the general awareness of the library's existence, its holdings and the services it provides. The number of readers is constantly increasing and they come from ever widening walks of life; such exhibitions as the English Bible Exhibition (1961) are well attended; more and more clubs

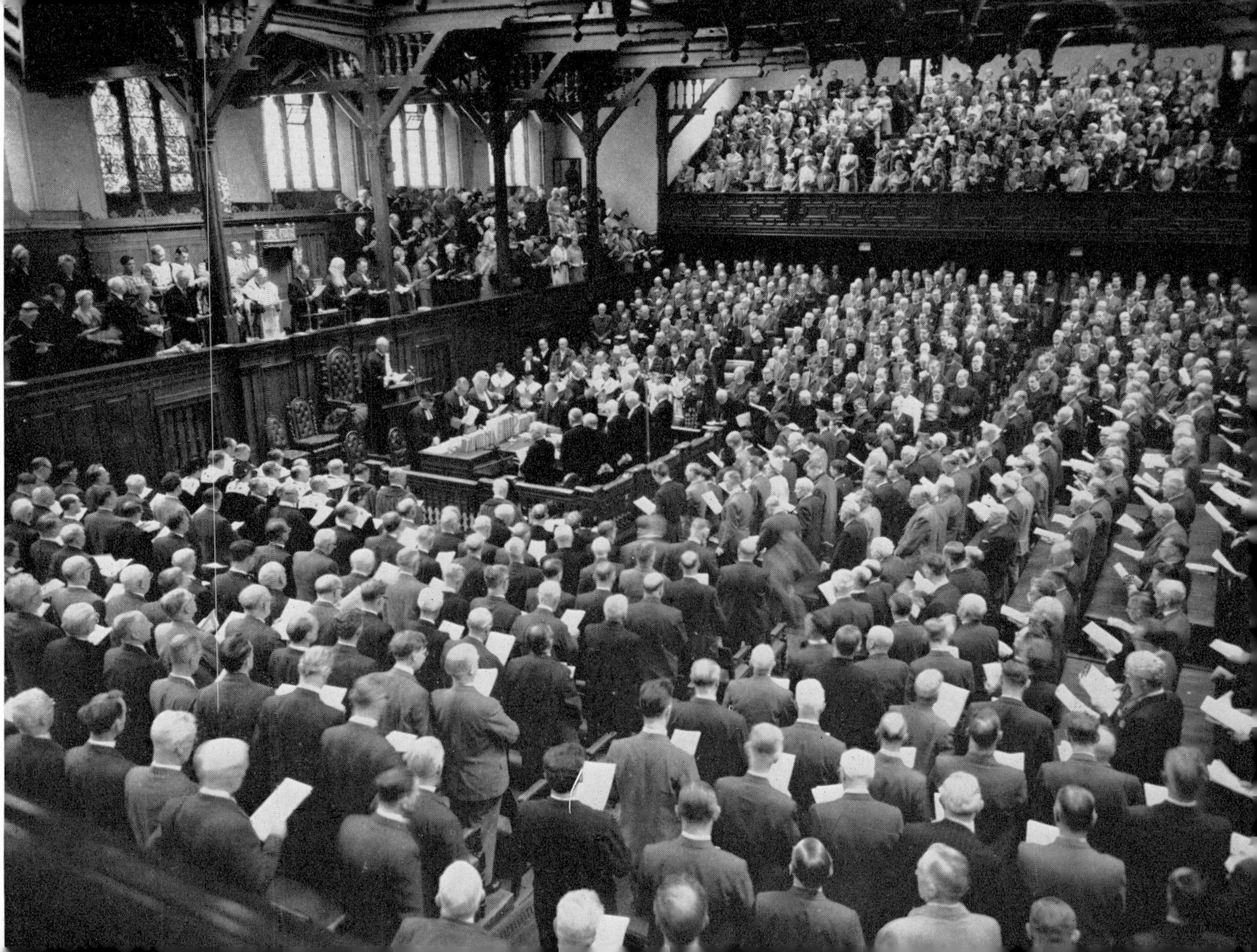

The opening ceremony of a session of the General Assembly of the Church of Scotland in the Assembly Hall at the Mound. Her Majesty's representative, the High Commissioner, sits in the Gallery above the Moderator.

A try for Scotland about to be scored at Murrayfield during an international rugby match between Scotland and Wales—an occasion made the more exciting by the invasion of thousands of singing Welsh supporters.

A tussle for the ball during a local derby at Easter Road between the Hibernian and Heart of Midlothian football clubs.

and societies pay corporate visits to the Library; and the frequent organised parties of school-children are a means of sowing the seed at an early age in the minds of Edinburgh's future citizens. Lectures and recitals given in the Board Room usually at Festival time are increasingly well attended. Among other Exhibitions during the last decade have been Treasures of the Advocates' Library, Four Hundred Years of Scottish Printing, and, by far the best attended of all, Dead Sea Scrolls (1966).

Rapid advance during recent years can also be seen in the great increase of staff, in the number of readers and visitors, and in the acquisition of notable collections by purchase and donation. In 1959 the annual grant from the Treasury for the purchase of books and manuscripts was increased more than sevenfold—to £7,500, and in 1963 to £9,000—but these figures were quite inadequate, although in fairness it should be said that special grants have, in addition, been made to meet special demands, such as the purchase of the Iona Psalter (1960) and a large collection of printed books from the Signet Library. The position over the lean years, before 1959, would have been desperate but for other funds held by the Trustees, notably the income from the sum of nearly £80,000 bequeathed in 1926 by Mr. and Mrs. W. R. Reid, of Lauriston Castle. Fortunately, the Earl of Crawford and Balcarres, presiding over the 1964 annual meeting of the Trustees, was able to take some satisfaction in the Government's decision to increase the grant from £9,000 to £25,000. The recent large bequest of money by the late Professor T. Graham Brown is another substantial addition to the purchase funds.

The range and extent of collections acquired, either outright or on deposit, since 1925 are remarkable. Manuscripts, include the archives of the publishing house of Blackwood (a rich cross-section of English and Scottish literary activity in the 19th century), papers of a number of important Scottish families and of notable Scotsmen such as the first Earl Haig, letters of Sir Walter Scott, Thomas and Jane Welsh Carlyle, and the papers of leading figures in public affairs including Lord Haldane and the 5th Lord Rosebery.

Turning to printed works, the books and pamphlets given by the 5th Lord Rosebery have greatly enhanced the resources on Scottish history. Other special collections are rich in chap-books (Lauriston Castle)—the poor man's reading matter in former times—in liturgies and psalmody (Dowden and Cowan), early Scottish books (F. S. Ferguson), Scottish music (Glen and Inglis), Berlioz (Cecil Hopkinson), and the inter-relationships of French and English literature (D. Nichol Smith)—and there are many others. The purchase of the Bute collection of English plays (1956) gave the library an entirely new status in the field of English drama, and the extensive buying of Signet Library books (1960) means that these fruits of the labour and vision of several great librarians of the past have not been lost to Edinburgh.

The Governing Body of the National Library is the Board of Trustees, composed of representatives of the Crown, the Faculty of Advocates, the Scottish Universities and Scottish local authorities, together with *ex-officio* and co-opted members. It meets annually and its Standing Committee four times a year. In 1965 the staff, who are in the Government service, numbered a little over 130. They consisted of the Librarian, the Keepers of Manuscripts and of Printed Books, five Deputy Keepers, 13 Assistant Keepers, 24 research assistants (mostly cataloguers), together with executive officers, clerical and typing staff, cataloguing assistants, a photographer, an office-keeper, library assistants, paper-keepers, attendants, messengers, a telephone switchboard operator, porters, cleaners, and night-watchmen. Cataloguers are usually graduates with Arts degrees, proficiency in languages being a useful qualification. At all levels the Library undertakes its own professional training of new members of staff.

The maintenance of the building is the responsibility of the Ministry of Public Buildings and Works, and Her Majesty's Stationery Office undertakes the binding and repair of books and manuscripts, some at its own bindery at Sighthill, and others by contract with private firms.

It is estimated that the total number of printed books and pamphlets in the Library now exceeds two million, and there are over 10,000 volumes of manuscript. Nearly 3,000 current periodicals are received and about 160 newspapers, the latter mainly Scottish. The intake of printed items in 1964 amounted to 117,010 items of which 92,433 were received under the Copyright Act. Books received as gifts in the same year amounted to 8,948, and the number bought (mostly foreign or antiquarian) were 6,460. The music publications acquired were 3,004, and 5,220 maps were received. Among recent developments have been strenuous efforts to amalgamate catalogues, to build up special bibliographies that will make readily available the Library's ever-increasing holdings, the improvement of photographic facilities and the extension of evening hours of opening.

THE LAW LIBRARIES

THE ADVOCATES' LIBRARY

It would not be true to say that Jurisprudence was deserted by her " handmaidens " when the National Library of Scotland rose proudly from the Advocates' Library in its ancient form. The " handmaidens " did not wander far, and are always on call. There is complete interavailability; for the books of the National Library and the law-books and manuscripts retained by the Advocates may be consulted as readily in the Reading-Room of the one as of the other.

The legal manuscripts retained by the Advocates number about 350. They include a magnificent illuminated 14th-century manuscript of the civil law, from Bologna. The main interest of the collection, however, is in the field of Scots law. The " Practicks " of Balfour and Hope are summaries of court decisions compiled for the guidance of advocates and judges, and the *Regiam Majestatem* gives an idea of the Scots–Norman laws followed in the King's courts in Scotland and which lie at the base of the Law of Scotland as later formulated.

The collection of printed law-books journals, periodicals and papers retained in 1925 was estimated at about 45,000 volumes. This total has been considerably augmented since by the 200,000 published legal items which have been acquired by copyright, as stipulated in the National Library of Scotland Act, many of which are separate volumes, and others being papers and issues of periodicals to be bound into volumes. The Advocates' Library is rich in modern holdings, but it also possesses legal incunabula of note, and an important historical collection of some 5,000 legal works, chiefly civilian and canonist, covering the period from 1500 to about 1750, many of which are part of the original library founded in 1682. Much recent work has been done in bringing these books together, and they have been augmented by the addition of the late Lord Macmillan's law library. The Pilgrim Trust has also honoured the memory of Lord Macmillan by repairing and rebinding more than 1,200 books in the historical collection. This collection is quite unique in Scotland, and provides scholars with the materials on which the development of Scots Law from the early 16th century is based. It is particularly rich in expositions of Roman Law by Continental jurists, thus throwing much light on this important factor in a formative period of the Law of Scotland.

Other important collections received since 1925 have augmented the holdings on civil, canon, and Scots law. These included 48 volumes which belonged to James Graham of Airth, Judge of the High Court of Admiralty of Scotland (1702–46), 41 volumes from the library of Lord Corehouse (1826–39), and 20 volumes from that of W. S. Dickson, who was Keeper of the Advocates' Library in 1925, and afterwards first Librarian of the National Library.

The chief administrative officer, the Keeper, is an advocate, and is served by a professional librarian who devotes his full time to the Library.

THE SIGNET LIBRARY

The largest of the seven libraries or so, which were founded in Edinburgh in the 18th century, is that of the Writers to H.M. Signet, the oldest society of solicitors in Scotland, whose origins are even earlier than the 15th century. At one time by far the widest of the seven in its interest, it is now in process of retrenchment; for with the opening of the 1960s it shed a wide range of general books, and the new policy is to confine it very largely to law books and books on Scotland and Scottish activities.

The Signet Library can be traced back to 1722 when the Society resolved to purchase Scots Law books and statutes. The decision to form a general library was made in 1778, and progress from that date was rapid. Funds for book purchase were obtained from intrant fees, fines and levies on festivities, and by much voluntary support on the part of members and their friends. It was also fortunate in its librarians. The first, Macvey Napier, was appointed in 1805, and notable among his successors was David Laing, appointed in 1837. Napier was editor of the *Edinburgh Review*, and he supervised the publication of the 7th edition of the *Encyclopaedia Britannica*. Laing, librarian of the Signet for 41 years, published about 80 works on the literature, history and antiquities of Scotland, and was secretary, throughout its period of existence, of the Bannatyne Club which took upon itself the publication of much material bearing on the Scottish past. In recent years a later librarian, Dr. Charles Malcolm, earned the gratitude and affection of countless authors, especially historians, for making their researches so much easier than they might have been.

By 1800 noteworthy Italian, French, and other collections of antiquities and ecclesiastical history had been acquired. During the 19th century further great wealth was accumulated, largely of natural history (including Audubon's *Birds of America*), art, archaeology, a fine Polish collection, British topography and local history, Scottish history, world travel and exploration, reference books of all kinds in great number, British and foreign early printed books including 250 incunabula, prints (including a good deal of Piranesi), and much cartographical material.

The Library was confined within very restricted premises in Writers' Court until the completion, in 1815, of the commodious and elegant buildings adjoining Parliament Hall, which cost the Society £10,800. The magnificent Upper Library Hall was purchased from the Faculty of Advocates in 1826 for £12,000. Dibdin's enthusiasm for the " absolutely palatial air " of the " Paradise of Bokes " was by no means excessive when he described it as fit for " grandees with fur cloaks " and as " spacious, ornamental, commodious, and replenished thickly with goodly and gorgeous tomes." By the end of the 19th century no Scottish library could vie with the Signet except the Advocates' and the University libraries; and there is no gainsaying the claim made in 1890 in a volume of the Society's history, that " no other professional community, whether legal, medical, or ecclesiastical—no scientific academy or society in the whole of the United Kingdom, can point to a collection of equal dimensions formed by similar means."

The number of books prior to the recent curtailment exceeded 163,000, including a thousand volumes of pamphlets. Recent sales and disposals have diminished this total by nearly 40,000.

Use is made of the Signet Library mainly by members of the Society, although accredited enquirers are admitted on application, and many historians have been deeply in the Library's debt. The books most in demand, at least of recent years, have been those relating to law, with Scottish family history and travel as the other kinds most called for or about which enquiries have been most often made.

THE SSC LIBRARY

This library belongs to the Society of Solicitors in the Supreme Courts of Scotland. The Society was formed in 1784, and has now accumulated more than 30,000 volumes, old and new, mainly on law, but also including books on other topics such as general literature and history. Housed in the Society's premises by Parliament Square, poised high over the Cowgate, the library is intended primarily for the use of members, but its books may be loaned to other libraries and institutions; and application can be made, by accredited enquirers, to the Keeper for permission to consult them in the Library itself. So all in all, between this and Edinburgh's other legal libraries including the Juridical and that established recently as a separate branch of the University Library, there seems little excuse for anyone in Edinburgh to plead ignorance of what Shakespeare called the ' nice sharp quillets of the law.'

THEOLOGICAL LIBRARIES

NEW COLLEGE LIBRARY

After the Disruption of 1843 New College was established for the training of ministers of the seceding body, the Free Church of Scotland. But since 1929 it has served the Church of Scotland and houses the Divinity Faculty of the University. The Library, one of the most remarkable in Edinburgh, contains more than 160,000 volumes, some 22,000 pamphlets and over 320 sets of periodicals. It is the richest theological collection in Scotland and is now officially part of the University Library.

By the 1930s the problem of housing such an array had become very difficult, but in 1935 the High Church moved to Blackford, and the buildings thus made available beside the College were adapted at a cost of over £23,000. The high-roofed main body of the church is now the Library Hall and reading-room, and thas hree stackage floors below.

Manuscripts range from medieval redactions of Church Fathers and Schoolmen to a plentitude of sermons and other writings by ministers —from Covenanting times to the voluminous papers of Thomas Chalmers, and later those of Dr. John White. There is also a wealth of oriental manuscripts, now deposited for custody in the University Library, and more than 100 incunabula and many printed books of the 16th and 17th centuries, including not only the expected theological works but also historical and rare scientific books. The hymnological collection alone runs to more than 3,000 volumes. Oriental and Gaelic books are numerous, the latter now including those bequeathed by the late Rev. Roderick McLeod. But secular works abound. To give but one example, half the library of Adam Smith, the economist, is also to be found here, along with works by Luther and his German contemporaries in the pamphlet collection, which is very rich although the bulk of it springs from the unceasing religious controversies of the 17th and 18th centuries.

OTHER CHURCH OF SCOTLAND LIBRARIES

The Library of the General Assembly of the Church of Scotland, to give its full title, was formerly housed in the Tolbooth—St. John's Church, but recently, by decision of the General Assembly, it was divided into two main parts. The Manuscript Records of the Church were taken to Register House, and the other section, some 10,000 printed books, to New College. These deal mainly with the history of the Church of Scotland, and include an almost complete set of Acts and Records of the General Assembly, together with other official publications, works of controversy from the 16th century onwards, and very many histories of individual parishes and congregations.

The Church of Scotland Lending Library is maintained by the Church at 121 George Street, and strives to keep up-to-date its collection of books on Bible Study, the history, doctrine, and all aspects of the work and worship of the Church at home and in the mission fields. It has been of great use to ministers, teachers of religious instruction, and others whose interests lie in the Church and its activities. It holds nearly 6,000 books and about a dozen current periodicals.

EPISCOPAL LIBRARIES

The Edinburgh libraries of the Scottish Episcopal Church bear all the marks of the scholarship and perseverance of a number of distinguished learned churchmen who laboured long to assemble them, and many of the books have the added interest of their erudite annotations. At Coates Hall, which is the theological college of the Scottish Episcopal Church, there are some 16,000 books, of which about 5,000 form the Bishop Jolly Library and 4,000 the Forbes Library. The remainder is the General Library, a collection built up since 1846 to aid in the pursuit of theological study ; it is particularly strong in Scottish Church history, and in liturgical works. There are also important manuscripts, and among these, jealously guarded in the ' Episcopal Safe ', are the documents relating to a famous link between Scotland and America, the Consecration in Scotland of Samuel Seabury, the first bishop of the American Protestant Episcopal Church.

Alexander Jolly (1756–1838), Bishop of Moray, and George Hay Forbes of Burntisland were great collectors of religious books. Their libraries came to Coates Hall, but 2,000 of Bishop Jolly's books have been deposited in the National Library of Scotland where they are more conveniently placed for the use of scholars and where they can be studied in conjunction with much related material. Some 875 volumes from the 4,000 which constitute the Bishop Dowden Memorial Library in the Chapter house of the Episcopal Cathedral Church of St. Mary, have been deposited in the National Library for the same reasons. Many books in this fine liturgical collection bear the annotations of Bishop Dowden himself, a liturgist, who was the brother of Edward Dowden, the Shakespearean scholar.

CONGREGATIONAL

The Scottish Congregational Library is part of the College, founded in 1811, and situated in Hope Terrace. In addition to being a working theological library it has specialised in publications bearing on the history of Congregationalism in Scotland, and also on missionary enterprise, particularly the London Missionary Society. The Forrester Collection of over 2,000 volumes, presented by Dr. D. M. Forrester, to the United Free Church, is also housed in the same building. Pamphlets of the 17th and 18th centuries are a feature of this collection.

ROMAN CATHOLIC

The Dominican Library, long housed in George Square, consists of over 12,000 books, mainly but by no means exclusively theological, biblical, historical and classical, together with French and English manuscripts of literary interest dating from the 1890s and the early 20th century. The classical section is especially strong, and the known works of all Greek and Roman authors up to A.D. 600 are here to be found. The books include many of the 16th and all subsequent centuries, and are the products of a wide range of western and central European presses.

The nucleus was formed from the libraries of Canon John Gray and Mark André Raffalovich, augmented with large donations by R. A. G. Burn, sometime lecturer at Glasgow University; much of the correspondence of the founders, Canon Gray and Raffalovich, is preserved here. Incidentally, applications from *bona fide* scholars to use the reading-room are made to the Dominican Father who acts as Librarian, and considerable use of it is made by Roman Catholic students at the University.

It should be noted here also that Columba House, Drummond Place, now contains the Scottish Catholic Archives, to which are added considerable collections of Scottish historical printed works. Much material once belonging to the Scots College, Paris, is to be found here as well, and among the many pre-Reformation items are Ratisbon manuscripts. There is also an immense collection of letters of Scottish Roman Catholic interest from the 16th century onwards and a number of notable 16th-century printed books; which proves again how fortunate Edinburgh is to house such a vast range of books and records in so many libraries and reading rooms.

MEDICAL LIBRARIES

ROYAL COLLEGE OF SURGEONS OF EDINBURGH

The library has had a chequered history. The College can trace its origins back to 1505, but its Royal Charter and present title are as late as 1778. Long before then, however, the Incorporation of Barber-Surgeons had instituted a library and a museum to aid in the teaching of anatomy to its apprentices. In 1696 the new Hall at Surgeons' Square was occupied, and provision made for the housing of books. Many presentations soon followed, the most notable being the 200 volumes given 13 years later by Thomas Kincaid. In 1764 the library and museum were transferred to the University and the surgeons given the use of the University library for an annual payment of £5 by the Incorporation. Difficulties arose, however, and although the £5 continued to be paid until 1887 the surgeons had begun to collect a new library more than 50 years before that date. In 1845 about a thousand books were presented by the family of Dr. John Abercrombie, and this was the beginning of the steady growth which still continues. The library contains lecture notes by Lister and a good selection of older books. It is mainly, however, a modern working library of surgical interest, extending to about 25,000 volumes, and over 400 sets of periodicals of which well over 170 are taken currently. There is a full-time professional librarian. Admission is granted to Fellows, Members of the College, postgraduate students and to accredited enquirers.

ROYAL COLLEGE OF PHYSICIANS OF EDINBURGH

The College received its first charter, from Charles II, in 1681, and the library was founded in the same year, when Sir Robert Sibbald presented the first 100 volumes, mainly books on medicine and related topics. Early benefactors included Sir Isaac Newton and Sir Hans Sloane, and some of the manuscripts acquired early had belonged to Napier of Merchiston, the discoverer of logarithms. Two of the three known copies of the first edition of the *Edinburgh Pharmacopoeia* (1699) are in this library.

The 18th century saw great expansion and development, notably the acquisition of the library of John Drummond, President of the College (1722–7), a move to more commodious premises in 1704 and again in 1781, and the appearance of the first and second printed catalogues (1767 and 1793). Both these catalogues testify to the active pursuance of the policy referred to in a letter by William Cullen where he stated that the College was determined to acquire all the important works within its field of interest. The library moved to its present elegant rooms at 9 Queen Street in 1846, but the rate of growth has necessitated expansion on several occasions, from 1864 onward, of the space allotted to it. The present stock of what is one of the three largest medical libraries in Great Britain runs to about 200,000 volumes and pamphlets, including 20 incunabula, and over 400 volumes of manuscripts mostly of the 18th century. The periodicals are a feature of prime importance, ranging from the set of the *Philosophical Transactions* received in the foundation year (1681) to the 450 currently received from British, Continental and American sources. The history and practice of medicine are well represented in this very fine library. It is rich in the notebooks and correspondence of notable medical scholars and physicians from the founder, Sir Robert Sibbald, to those of Archibald Pitcairne and Sir Robert Pringle, and the 29 volumes of the consultation letters of William Cullen from which much can be learned of the practice of medicine in the 18th century. This library is open to the public; there are lending facilities to other libraries; and there is a full-time professional librarian.

ROYAL MEDICAL SOCIETY

As befits the oldest medical society in Great Britain, the Royal Medical Society's library was in being as early as 1753; by 1778 there were 1,500 well-chosen books, and this necessitated the acquiring of a Hall (opened in 1776); by 1837 it contained 12,000 books. Meanwhile—in 1820—stringent rules had been laid down: a fine of sixpence was imposed on the librarian for each book that remained uncatalogued for a week; two shillings were charged for speaking when another member was reading; removing a book three miles from Edinburgh cost half a guinea. Books were chosen for purchase by ballot by a committee of seven. Catalogues were printed on several occasions, that of 1835 being of considerable note for it is one of the earliest classified catalogues of a medical library in existence.

In 1852 the Society moved to premises at 7 Melbourne Place where it remained until recently. At that time it possessed 14,000 books; but in recent years it has not attempted to keep pace with the enormous output of medical literature, so that the chief importance of this library today lies in the light it throws on the growth of medical science from the 16th century. Not least among its illuminating contents in this respect are the Society's own records from 1737 onward, and the collection of medical dissertations from 1751. There has been much reorganisation of recent years. Thousands of volumes of non-medical books have been disposed of; rehousing, repairing, binding and cataloguing have been undertaken. The present holdings consist of 240 volumes of dissertations and 230 of theses, 70 record books, about 8,000 volumes ranging from the 16th to the early 20th century, some 500 current textbooks and more than 3,500 journals.

CENTRAL MEDICAL LIBRARY

Finally there is the Central Medical Library which is part of the Edinburgh University Library, as we saw, and is housed in the New Buildings of the University.

SCIENTIFIC LIBRARIES

These are numerous and extremely varied, and the increase in their number and strength during the present century is very rapid. They range from an old established general library of science, that of the Royal Society of Edinburgh, to many specialised libraries, old and new, some academic in interest and others linked to great industrial concerns like the technological libraries of Ferranti and Bruce Peebles. The scope of this chapter allows only for a detailed treatment of a very few of these libraries, and it would be vain to try to include even a brief mention of all of them.

THE ROYAL SOCIETY OF EDINBURGH

When this body was founded in 1783 its Royal Charter covered a wide range of interest including the natural sciences, medicine, archaeology, linguistic studies and literature. But in the 19th century the literary activity of the Society languished and it became more and more, in the modern meaning of the term, a *scientific* body. The fine library of 200,000 volumes reflects this bias.

Among the manuscripts housed in the spacious and stately Georgian buildings in George Street, which the Royal Society has occupied since 1906, are 13 volumes of the manuscripts of David Hume, the philosopher. But the Library's main strength consists of the publications of learned institutions from all parts of the world with whom about 600 exchanges are made annually. The collection of scientific periodical literature is considered to be among the most complete in the British Commonwealth. Of the 2,500 periodicals of which there are sets, 2,000 are currently taken. The Library is intended primarily for use by the Fellows, but is open to sponsored members of the public, and loans are made to other institutions at the discretion of the Librarian.

ROYAL OBSERVATORY

The founder of the Royal Observatory Library was the distinguished astronomer, Ludovic Lindsay, 26th Earl of Crawford and 9th Earl of Balcarres (1847–1913). He presented to the nation in 1888 his magnificent collection of instruments and books, which had been brought together at Dun Echt, on the understanding that they would be properly housed. But in time the present buildings on Blackford Hill were erected as the Old Royal Observatory on Calton Hill was found too small. Today the library has over 35,000 books, of which the 11,000 presented by the founder form, together with valuable manuscripts, the Crawford Collection. The nucleus of this foundation collection came from the library of Charles Babbage, a mathematician and inventor of the calculating machine, but rare books had been gathered from all parts of the world to enrich the Crawford collection, and some were from the family library at Haigh Hall. As is evident from the scholarly catalogue (Edinburgh: H.M.S.O., 1890) the library is exceedingly rich in the early editions of the world's great astronomers, and Comet literature is one of its notable features. Astronomy's related subjects, particularly physics and mathematics, are well represented and, less to be expected, so is life insurance.

On turning to the two-thirds of the Royal Observatory Library which do not form part of the Crawford Collection, it is soon seen that the modern library has been energetically built up. Exchanges are effected with 400 other institutions, and there are files of 1,000 periodicals. A professional librarian is now in charge.

ROYAL BOTANIC GARDEN

The Garden has a history dating back to 1670. Today it possesses nearly 30,000 volumes and about 40,000 pamphlets; together with a great deal of illustrative matter including 30,000 negatives and 3,500 coloured slides. The library of the Botany Department of Edinburgh University has been amalgamated with that of the Garden, and that of the Botanical Society of Edinburgh is also housed with it. Over 300 periodicals are currently taken and held; the library is open to the public; and there are lending facilities to other libraries.

HERIOT-WATT UNIVERSITY

The Heriot-Watt College achieved University status in February 1966. The library contains nearly 20,000 volumes, more than 2,000 pamphlets and has a regular intake of nearly 350 periodicals, bearing on science and technology. There are lending facilities to other libraries, to staff and students, and the reading-room is open to the public for reference.

Heriot-Watt College held for years the very fine Edward Clark collection, on printing, consisting of some 2,000 volumes including 55 incunabula, but it has been transferred to Napier College. To it has recently been added the Bernard Newdigate Collection on typography.

SPECIALISED SCIENCE LIBRARIES

A notable feature of 20th-century development in Edinburgh has been the establishment and growth of an ever increasing number of specialised science libraries. Some of these specialised libraries, it is noteworthy, have their main strength in books, others in pamphlets and they vary a good deal in their holdings of periodicals. The Scottish Marine Biological Association Library has over 4,000 volumes, well over 3,000 pamphlets and reprints and about 100 current periodicals, whilst the Poultry Research Centre (founded 1947) has about 530 volumes, and almost 4,250 pamphlets and 60 current periodicals.

The now combined library of the Commonwealth Bureau of Animal Breeding and Genetics (1929) and of the Animal Breeding Research Organisation (1947), housed in the University King's Buildings, contains over 3,200 books, 15,000 pamphlets (including reprints), 290 current periodicals, and over 3,000 annual reports. Although physically combined, two separate purchase funds are drawn upon. The Animal Diseases Research Association (1920) has nearly 1,000 volumes and about 80 sets of periodicals, and the Fair Isle Bird Observatory Trust and Scottish Ornithologists' Club (1948) over 1,000 volumes and about 1,500 pamphlets.

There are also a number of important libraries attached to manufacturing and industrial concerns in the city, especially those that undertake research work of a scientific and technological nature. It is usual for these to participate in inter-library lending schemes. Among the most notable of the firms with libraries of this kind are Messrs. T. Smith Limited, manufacturers of pharmaceuticals, Ferranti Limited (electronics) and Bruce Peebles and Company Limited (engineering).

MISCELLANEOUS LIBRARIES

AGRICULTURE AND FORESTRY

Libraries in Edinburgh which deal specially with agriculture and forestry are as follows:

(1) The Royal Highland and Agricultural Society of Scotland, founded in 1784, which now possesses over 6,000 volumes and 1,200 pamphlets,

and takes about a score of current periodicals; (2) The Royal Scottish Forestry Society (1884), with some 800 volumes and nearly a hundred sets of periodicals, about a quarter of them current; (3) The Scottish Association of Young Farmers Clubs (1938) with well over 7,000 volumes, 2,000 pamphlets and about 20 current periodicals; (4) The Edinburgh School of Agriculture Library. This last was established in 1945 and includes the former libraries of the Department of Agriculture of the University and the Edinburgh and East of Scotland College of Agriculture. The holdings exceed 7,000 volumes, 15,000 pamphlets, and an intake of about 400 periodicals. A good deal of indexing of publications is done, and a certain amount of translation work.

GEOGRAPHY

The Royal Scottish Geographical Society, founded in 1884, has a well known library of rich resources, which is open to the public, and lends to other libraries through the usual channels. The collection of early maps of Scotland is noteworthy, as may be seen from the printed catalogue (1936). The library contains 30,000 volumes and pamphlets, and over 50,000 maps. More than 200 periodicals are received, and there is a large and growing number of slides and film strips.

PROFESSIONAL AND ADMINISTRATIVE

Several professional organizations and societies have their headquarters in Edinburgh, and some of these have interesting and valuable collections covering the appropriate field of interest, ranging from rare early works to current literature. Among these are the Faculty of Actuaries, the Institute of Chartered Accountants of Scotland, with its mathematical rarities, and the Pharmaceutical Society.

All aspects of Government activity are covered by the St. Andrews House Library which serves the various departments of the Secretary of State for Scotland. Its holdings are about 40,000 volumes and double that number of pamphlets. Nearly 1,000 periodicals are currently taken. There is also the library of the Ministry of Works.

EDUCATIONAL

The Moray House College of Education, established in 1907, has about 39,000 volumes inclusive of pamphlets, 200 current periodicals and great quantities of other illustrative matter. These are mainly for the use of staff and students, but other accredited enquirers are admitted. The library of the Educational Institute of Scotland (1847) contains about 5,000 volumes. Other more specialised educational institutions, such as the Edinburgh College of Art, to name one of several, are well equipped with libraries of their own.

ANTIQUITIES AND GENEALOGY

The Society of Antiquaries of Scotland, founded in 1781, presented their library to the nation in 1851, but they retain responsibility for its care and management. It is also the library of the National Museum of Antiquities of Scotland. Open to the public, its scope covers European pre-history and wide aspects of Scottish history and culture, including family history and topography. There are over 20,000 volumes, 5,000 pamphlets, 633 manuscripts, ordnance maps of Scotland, over 5,000 slides, more than 600 sets of periodicals, and over 5,000 photoplates.

The library of the Royal Scottish Museum contains about 30,000 volumes, together with ordnance survey maps, several thousands of slides, over 200 brass rubbings, and more than 350 sets of periodicals. Its scope bears relation to that of the Museum, and it is primarily intended for research by the staff in the execution of their duties.

MILITARY

The Scottish United Services Museum was founded in 1939, and is housed in Edinburgh Castle. The library of nearly 6,000 volumes and also maps, illustrative matter, manuscripts, archives (including thousands of documents) and periodicals, contains a complete collection of Scottish regimental histories and most of the histories of English, Welsh and Irish regiments. The public is admitted.

The Queen's Bodyguard for Scotland, widely known as The Royal Company of Archers, also has a library of considerable interest.

FOREIGN

The library of the French Institute was founded in 1949, and by 1966 contained some 20,500 books. The Institute's membership is about 2,000 and much use is made of the wide range of books supplied, particularly French fiction, the works of the main authors, drama, books relating to the theatre, art books and tourist literature. Most of the books are contemporary and supplied by the French Government. There is a full-time librarian.

The Danish Institute has a library of some 6,000 volumes in Danish and English of which about two-thirds are Danish. These include works of Danish literature and books on all aspects of Denmark's life, and they are available for direct loan by interested individuals or through other libraries.

DRAMA

The popularity of amateur dramatics has created a demand for borrowing facilities of individual copies of plays and also for sets to cover the needs of a whole cast. There are several sources in the city where this need is met, and the demand is brisk. Among libraries which cater for it are (1) that of the Scottish Community Drama Association, now in South Bridge School, which receives a specimen copy, sent by the publishers, of almost every full-length play published, and has also technical books on production; (2) the Kirk Drama Federation which keeps a small collection of plays for the use of members at the Gateway Theatre; (3) the collection at the Edinburgh Bookshop, which holds the agency for Central Scotland for plays published by French. Specimen copies are held of five to six hundred plays which can be consulted by drama societies.

THE SCOTTISH CENTRAL LIBRARY

The Scottish Central Library has, in jest, been called the Library with no books and no readers. This remark has point, but is not entirely accurate. In fact, although no one comes to this restored " land " of Old Edinburgh to read, there is a collection of over 40,000 volumes; and certainly the words " Rax Me That Buik " on the brightly painted coat of arms beside the entrance indicate the library's function. Originally uttered by the Rev. Dr. John Erskine in the General Assembly, in 1796, they are here given a new significance. The last three or four decades have seen throughout Britain a rapid advance in inter-relating the work of libraries, and the Scottish Central Library is a major link in the strong chain which has been forged. Its prime function is to facilitate the movement of books from one Scottish library to another according to need. Its reach, however, is much further, for it brings books from very far afield to Scottish homes and reciprocates by placing Scotland's resources at the disposal of many enquirers living across the border and even further afield.

The library began its existence in 1921, and was first called the Scottish Central Library for Students, but until 1953 it was housed at the headquarters of the Carnegie U.K. Trust, in Dunfermline. In 1939 there began the compilation of the Scottish Union Catalogue, an attempt to build up a consolidated record of the holdings of libraries all over Scotland. This catalogue now has entries for over 465,000 different books from more than 90 libraries of various kinds. There is a full-time staff of five concerned solely with the maintenance of this great book-finding instrument.

An advisory committee was set up in 1947 by the Carnegie UK Trustees to enquire into the library's future. The new Constitution, framed on the lines they recommended, came into effect in 1952 and, in the following years, the new headquarters—one of Edinburgh's oldest buildings—was opened by the Duke of Edinburgh. The Carnegie Trustees had spent £70,000 on the reconditioning, a fine contribution to the restoration of the Royal Mile. The two main sources of revenue are the Scottish local authorities and the Treasury. In the financial year 1965–6, the combined contributions of the local authorities came to £8,000, and the Treasury gave pound for pound.

The work of building up the Union Catalogue, which enables books to be located with a view to inter-lending between libraries, is immense. During 1962–3 more than 140,000 entries were received from Scottish libraries, and on checking it was found that 17,700 were for books new to the catalogue. The various locations of the others were all noted.

Some idea of the rapid advance made recently can be got from the fact that in 1954–5 the new accessions of various libraries notified to the Central Library were only about 19,000. Notices of withdrawals are also received, and even of *proposed* withdrawals for thus a library can be warned against withdrawing what may prove to be the only recorded copy of that particular book in any Scottish library.

It is also the function of the Scottish Central Library to provide bibliographical information. In pursuit of this aim it has issued a catalogue of newspaper holdings held in Scottish libraries (1956) and a catalogue of the Scottish Family Histories (1960) that they hold. A scheme is well in hand to produce bibliographies of many Scottish authors of the early part of the present century. There has been rapid growth of the photography department, where microfilms and other reproductions of scarce, out-of-print books are made. During the last four or five years assistance has been given to Scottish libraries in working the National Inter-Regional Subject Coverage Scheme, whereby various libraries undertake to build up their holdings within special fields allotted to them.

Lists are circulated to discover where there are copies of wanted books, and in a recent year 87 out of 186 books sought were thus found. During the same period nearly 21,000 books were borrowed through the instrumentality of the Scottish Central Library. The stock of 40,000 is held partly for reference by the staff, and partly to supplement the resources of other libraries for lending purposes.

Here this remarkable but far from complete story of Edinburgh's libraries must end with a final reflection that there can be few stretches in the world—there are certainly none in Scotland—whose density of books to the acre can compare with that in the Old Town only a quarter of a mile or so away from the meeting-point of the Royal Mile and the George IV Bridge. Eleven libraries, situated so closely together, contain between them more than 3,700,000 books; and of these the vast majority are in the National Library, the University Library, or the Edinburgh Central Library. One may ask how many books there are in libraries within the whole city which a citizen of Edinburgh, or indeed a visitor, might consult either as a right, or by permission and with little formality in case of need. Whatever the grand total may be, it would certainly be an understatement to place it below 4,750,000.

THE MUSEUMS

The variety of museums in the United Kingdom is very wide. Quite apart from the range of materials with which they deal—from minerals, rocks, plants and animals to man himself and all the arts, crafts and techniques which he has invented—museums also differ in the way they are administered and the kind of public they cater for. Edinburgh has every kind—from national institutions to private collections, some with histories stretching back for more than a century, others of recent foundation. And as tastes in collecting, display and even museum architecture have changed during this period, it can be said that the Edinburgh museums are themselves a museum of museum fashions.

THE OLDEST MUSEUM

The oldest museum in Edinburgh, still extant, is that of the Royal College of Surgeons, which was founded in the early 16th century. The early collections were housed partly in apartments in the west end of the old Surgeons' Hall, off what is now Drummond Street, and partly in a house in the adjacent Surgeons' Square. In 1807 nine members of the College were appointed curators of the museum, signifying its increasing importance. The first conservator was Dr. Robert Knox, the anatomist associated with Burke and Hare. A new site in Nicholson Street was purchased in 1828, and four years later a new Surgeons' Hall, with an imposing Ionic façade, was built and opened. In it, accommodation was provided for the rapidly growing museum, founded on the famous anatomical collections of Dr. John Barclay and Mr. Charles Bell, later added to by the Macintosh obstetrical collection, the purchase of which was financed by the members of the College paying for their traditionally free biennial breakfast. Today the museum, although its 15,000 exhibits in the field of surgical pathology are mainly directed to meeting professional needs in both general teaching and more specialised research, is open to the public upon application.

THE NATIONAL MUSEUM OF ANTIQUITIES OF SCOTLAND

The second oldest museum is the National Museum of Antiquities of Scotland, founded in 1780 as an integral part of the Society of Antiquaries of Scotland by the eccentric 11th Earl of Buchan. In 1826, after some years of wandering, the Museum was moved into part of what is now the Royal Scottish Academy building and, being able to show its treasures there to greater advantage, attracted many more. The collections, though containing the finest Scottish material available, also included foreign archaeological and ethnological specimens and even natural history objects. But in 1829 the natural history material was transferred to the Royal Society and later passed to the Royal Scottish Museum.

In November, 1851, the Society's collections and all subsequent additions were made over to the Government, on condition that proper accommodation was provided for their public exhibition and the Society's meetings, and that their charge and management were to remain with the Society. The collections were vested in the Board of Manufacturers, later the Board of Trustees. Thus the Museum of the Society of Antiquaries of Scotland was reopened in premises on the Mound in 1859, and more than 67,000 people visited it in the first ten months.

Around 1872 the word National was added to the title; about 1890 the reference to the Society was omitted; and in 1891 the collections and library were moved to a new building in Queen Street, provided by (Sir) John R. Findlay, of *The Scotsman*, to house both the museum and the National Portrait Gallery of Scotland. Like the National Gallery of Scotland and the National Portrait Gallery of Scotland, the National Museum of Antiquities of Scotland was then administered by the Board of Trustees for the National Galleries of Scotland, and was, for administrative purposes, attached to the Scottish Home Department. Following the findings of a Departmental Committee in 1952, however, the museum was given a new constitution and now enjoys a Board of Trustees of its own.

Emphasis was specially laid from 1870 onwards on the importance of collecting Scottish material and a start given to planned excavations yielding specimens upon which the systematic study of early Scottish history could be based. Since 1852 the detailed accounts of these excavations and their results have been recorded in the *Proceedings of the Society of Antiquaries of Scotland.*

The museum's right to Treasure Trove—this was established in 1808, but in effect the museum has had the first refusal of all Treasure Trove since 1859—has secured many outstanding exhibits. The two largest and most important accessions received in this way are undoubtedly the Orkney Skaill Hoard of Viking Silver (brooches etc.) in 1959, and the Iona Hoard of Anglo-Saxon Coins in 1951. The St Ninian's Isle treasure, unearthed in 1958 by an Aberdeen archaeological team, has also been placed in the museum, despite spirited claims put forward on behalf of the museum at Lerwick, Shetland.

In the Victorian Gothic Queen Street building the main floor of the museum attracts the general visitor with its assemblage of more readily comprehended and appreciated bygones and antiques, not unlike many of the objects with which he is daily familiar: these range from the silver jewellery of Highland dress to the stern reality of " The Maiden ", a decapitating machine employed between 1564 and 1710. The first floor provides a detailed survey of Scotland from the Stone Age through the Bronze Age to the Iron Age and the time of the Vikings, and the top floor portrays Roman Scotland, houses the library and administrative offices, and provides a meeting place for the Society of Antiquaries of Scotland.

As Queen Street is some little way off the main stream of city traffic, a branch museum, the Museum Gallery, was opened in Shandwick Place in 1956. An old showroom has been cleverly converted to provide a main display hall with a balcony above, supplied with modern fittings and decoration, while behind the scenes are extensive stores and work rooms. The exhibits are, in the main, fine pieces from medieval to recent times, leading to costume of the 1930s.

The next major project to be undertaken is the institution of an open air Scottish National Folk Museum to illustrate the way of life of the people, especially before the Industrial Revolution, when rural and small town life was largely self-supporting and often highly individualist. Typical old Scottish buildings will be secured, re-erected against appropriate backgrounds and furnished with domestic pieces, utensils and equipment, while outbuildings will house carts and implements, to the collection of which a good start has been made. As a first step, plans were announced in 1963 for the establishment of an agricultural museum.

In the meantime the National Museum of Antiquities keeps its interest. As many as 140,000 people have visited the main museum, and 23,000 the Museum Gallery in a single year.

THE ROYAL SCOTTISH MUSEUM

The University of Edinburgh was founded in 1583, but naturally enough it did not seem to need in its earlier days a museum in our modern sense of the word. But later on as science subjects became taught, the need for specimens to illustrate lectures and practical classes arose, and departmental museums were the natural result. In 1812 there was initiated one of the most famous of these, that of the Department of Natural History which, while serving the needs of teaching staff and students, was at stated times open to the general public. Its collections were zoological and geological; but, as time passed, a certain amount of ethnographical material, probably often brought home by the naturalists and explorers who contributed the scientific collections, swelled the displays and added to the congestion in the Old College buildings.

The middle years of the 19th century saw an upsurge of interest in general industry, not only from the raw materials through processes to end-products but in industrial design. This culminated in the Great Exhibition of 1851, in which the Prince Consort played so notable a part. In Edinburgh, as elsewhere, there was a strong movement in favour of the founding of an industrial museum; and in 1854 the Treasury awarded a sum of £7,000 for the purchase of a site and other initial expenses in connection with the new Industrial Museum of Scotland. This lay immediately to the west of the University, where there was an open space and, beyond it, two old buildings. Together these formed the first home of the new collections illustrating industrial art. The museum was to deal with the industrial art of the world as a whole, to accommodate a reference library and to include an analytical laboratory and a lecture hall.

In 1855, by a vote of the Town Council who were then the Patrons of the University, the Natural History Museum of the Old College was added to the new museum, and in October, 1861, on one of his last public appearances, the Prince Consort laid the foundation stone. The first museum exhibitions were staged in the two old buildings in 1862, where for the first two years the attendance averaged 64,000 a year, throwing light both on the educational needs of the people and on contemporary leisure opportunities. In 1864, with the fusion of the two parts of the museum, its title was changed to the Edinburgh Museum of Science and Art; and by 1866, attendance at the museum was 274,031, university students gaining admission by the stone bridge connecting the two institutions; which seemed to everyone an unusually happy symbol. Then in 1875 the Crystal Palace Main Hall was opened, and for a number of years thereafter the museum offered a restaurant and a bar as additional attractions, and admissions (for which payment was made) quickly rose to almost 460,000 a year. With the erection and opening of the west wing in 1890, the building presented a well-balanced front to Chambers Street.

In the early days of the museum, the keepers of the departments of Natural History and Technology were also holders of university chairs in their respective subjects; but by the opening years of the present century the staffing was beginning to take its present shape, with full-time keepers in charge of the three departments of Art, Natural History and Technology. Then came a big change. In 1901 the museum was transferred from the Board of Education to the Scottish Education Department, and admission fees were abolished. Three years later, it celebrated its Jubilee, and its name was changed to the Royal Scottish Museum.

During those 50 years, it had naturally accumulated extensive collections by gift, by purchase and by loan, but such material, being limited by the likes and dislikes of private collectors, or the availability of objects to purchase or borrow, made it difficult to achieve the systematic, comparative or chronological series desired in an educational institution. The museum therefore embarked upon a new policy to meet those needs; and as the result the keepers of the departments of Art and Natural History conducted research and collecting expeditions in regions as far apart as Egypt and St. Kilda, while the keeper of the department of Technology systematically recorded progress in science and engineering by the introduction of new material and novel inventions.

Some of the searches have been very rewarding. After a successful bid at Sotheby's saleroom, for instance, there has recently been brought back to Scotland a large and exciting clock watch which has a peculiar association with the Scottish capital. The inscription—HIERONYMUS HAMILTHON SCOTUS ME FECIT 1595—engraved on the backplate, suggests that it is the earliest watch to be made by a Scotsman, pre-dating David Ramsay by a decade or so; and it now takes a permanent place in the museum where it was shown for many years in the splendid loan collection of horological instruments belonging to the late Sir John Ritchie Findlay.

Returning to our chronology, as time went on the collections grew and museum activities expanded. For example, an Advisory Committee was founded in 1912 to link schoolmasters, inspectors and the museum staff in encouraging the Edinburgh School Board of the time to organise school class visits. During the same period various aids to comfort and efficiency were introduced, not least in the field of lighting. In its early days the museum was lit by gas jets. But in 1906 arc lamps were installed; in 1911 these were replaced by filament lamps; and in 1960 the fluorescent lighting of the building was completed.

Other important steps forward in the great period of expansion before the First World War included the completion in 1914, of a new administrative block with laboratories, and the addition of a large block of exhibition halls to the south-east of the old building. This was opened almost as a thank-offering for peace, it would seem, at the end of the First World War. In the meantime while these halls were being constructed the architects found *in situ*, among some broken-down town property at the rear, a part of the Flodden Wall of 1513, and duly incorporated it in the building.

After the First World War there was a re-arrangement of collections in the new block, and all seemed set for further developments till the need for economy in the great slump severely curtailed the museum's internal activity. Despite this it played a notable part in encouraging local museums throughout Scotland to reorganise their often miscellaneous and badly arranged collections so as to be of more service to schools, and sent its senior officers on tour to give advice where needed.

As the period of financial stringency passed, the museum entered upon its next stage with the erection of a new hall with two balconies in the south-west corner of the building—the ground floor to accommodate the collection of ship models—and attendances again rose. Indeed 1937, which brought in 654,791 visitors, was a record year for museum attendances, the great attraction being the impressive exhibition of Coronation Robes. For this there was an entrance charge which yielded handsome support to the King George V Memorial Trust in aid of the provision of playing fields in Scotland.

At a later date the Gallery of Oriental Art was opened above the Shipping Hall, but that was to be the last forward step for a good number of years, since with the beginning of World War II the museum was not only closed to the public but all the more movable and more valuable specimens were packed into boxes and removed to four houses and castles in the relative security of the depths of the country.

By early 1946, all the collections had returned to the building, and their detailed overhaul and rearrangement brought back peace-time routines and services to the museum. Soon, too, there were new and exciting projects—a new lecture hall and cinematograph theatre, with three smaller temporary exhibition halls to the side of it; and a reference library for the use of the staff and of research students and specialists working on the collections, To the rear is the printer's shop, where labels, notices and handbills are prepared. Behind the scenes, the most modern equipment is available for treating and constructing exhibition and study material. Since the war, such aids to museum projects have included a range of high grade machine tools for building scale models accurate to one thousandth of an inch, a fumigation chamber for exterminating insect pests and fungoid growth, a deep-freeze chamber for preserving zoological raw material and an insectiary for breeding insects for investigation and display.

Another post-war development has been the staging of temporary exhibitions, dealing with special aspects of the museum's collections or with kindred subjects, thus bringing to the notice of the Edinburgh public a very varied group of arts and crafts, studies and hobbies, occupations and expeditions. In the last 18 years there have been 120 such exhibitions, each occupying a hall on the ground floor, remaining open from one to three months, and attracting about a thousand visitors a day. Some of these, like the " Byzantine Art Exhibition ", were arranged in co-operation with the Edinburgh Festival Society. Other displays have been topical—progress on the building of the Forth Road Bridge, for instance, the work of the Calder Hall nuclear power station, the generation of electrical power from nuclear sources, and an exhibition seismograph which proved a great attraction.

But so is the museum as a whole. The total number of visitors for 1962 was 317,070, of whom an average of 1,120 came each Sunday afternoon between the hours of 2 p.m. and 5 p.m. In the winter months this figure may be anything around 2,000. It must be admitted, however, that many well-behaved teenagers are attracted to the museum that afternoon of the week not by the exhibits alone but by shelter, warmth and company.

THE SCOTTISH UNITED SERVICES MUSEUM

The third national museum in Edinburgh is the Scottish United Services Museum in the Crown Square of Edinburgh Castle. This museum originated in 1930 as the Scottish Naval and Military Museum in connection with the Scottish National War Memorial. For many years previously there had been a display of early Scottish arms as a decorative treatment of the Banqueting Hall, along the south side of the square; and the new developments extended to other floors. Relics of Scottish regiments, of Scottish soldiers and sailors, and of Scottish engagements and exploits were accumulated, and the history of Scottish regiments and their uniforms, arms and equipment illustrated. When, after World War II, the collections returned from storage, the museum began a new chapter, being taken over in 1948 by the Ministry of Public Buildings and Works (the body responsible for the Castle), administered by an Advisory Committee, staffed by whole-time officers and given its new title, the Scottish United Services Museum. From being a show-place for military relics it has developed into a historical centre with a large reference library, dealing with all three services, an important print collection and an extensive series of photographs of uniforms and equipment. Among subjects of special interest are regimental badges, headdresses and uniforms ranging from the 17th century to modern times, and the historic exhibits in the Jacobite Room. On an average, some 280,000 people inspect the museum annually.

CIVIC AND OTHER MUSEUMS

As Edinburgh, being the capital city, was appropriately provided with national museums and art galleries, the City Fathers found their responsibilities in these fields lightened. But there was still work for them to undertake in providing museums to illustrate non-national subjects, such as the history of the city and its personalities, and other special collections.

The Corporation Museum was at first housed in the City Chambers, and displayed articles of local interest and history such as the National Covenant, letters written by Mary, Queen of Scots, and relics of Robert Burns and Walter Scott. Part of the collection was later placed on exhibition in Lady Stair's House in the Lawnmarket, which, originally built in 1622, had been restored and presented to the city by the Earl of Rosebery in 1907 and opened as a museum in 1913. It now houses a valuable collection of Burns and Scott relics together with periodical exhibitions of topical appeal.

In 1932 the main general collection, which had grown with the passage of time, was transferred to Huntly House, a reconstructed 16th century dwelling-house in the Canongate, once the home of the Incorporation of Hammermen. The largest room accommodates temporary exhibitions but all the others are devoted to the history of Edinburgh, its arts and crafts, its citizens' organisations and their personalia—charters, maps, prints and pictures, furniture, uniforms and costumes, regalia, and domestic and trade equipment.

The old Tolbooth in the Canongate, erected in 1591, had a varied history until it was restored by the Corporation and opened to the public as a museum in 1954. It houses the fine Telfer Dunbar collection of Highland costumes and tartans, detailed models of old Edinburgh and the Canongate and various exhibits associated with Canongate history.

Lauriston Castle, between Granton and Cramond, was left to the nation in 1926 and is administered by the Edinburgh Corporation as trustees. Set in attractive gardens overlooking a wide view of the Forth, the house is open to visitors, who may inspect the furnishings, both antique and reproduction, installed by the late owners, and the collections of Blue John pieces and of wool mosaics.

A late recruit to the city's specialist institutions is the Museum of Childhood. This fascinating museum commenced with the gift of two costume dolls, which deserve to be specially commemorated here as symbols of what can so often be done by private initiative and imagination.

As a member of Edinburgh Town Council, Councillor (as he then was) Patrick Murray was attending a meeting of the Libraries and Museums Committee when someone mentioned that a woman possessing two rare antique dolls had sent them to England because there was no appropriate place for them in Scotland. That, remarked the Councillor, was a great pity. There should be some place where the intriguing subject of childhood could be studied objectively. In that case, asked one member, " why don't you start a museum of your own? " At the time this casual remark raised a smile or two, but it stimulated an idea that had been in Councillor Murray's mind for some time. Here, he thought, was the opportunity. He would attempt the collection of every possible item associated with the years of childhood; old toys of every description; school books, home readers, schoolboy and schoolgirl magazines; the traditional medicines for childhood ailments; the hundred and one things forming the daily background of early years. It would be a museum about children designed and presented for the edification and entertainment of adults—an authentic " look-back " to the years that had gone.

Soon gifts of every kind poured in to give the museum a start, and in due course the Museum of Childhood opened in 1955 in Lady Stair's House (off Lawnmarket), where most of the civic museums have made their debut. But as only a fraction of the stock—from all parts of the United Kingdom and later from Europe and North America—could be displayed in the accommodation available, the Town Council authorised expenditure on the reconstruction of an old mansion house in Hyndford's Close in the High Street. Two years later the new, enlarged museum was opened to the public and immediately caught the imagination of citizens and visitors. Indeed by 1963 it was reported that despite the spaciousness of the accommodation, so many rare and valuable articles had been received that many of outstanding interest could not be displayed. It is also gratifying that gifts for the museum still come in not only from individuals in many countries, but often through the cultural and educational departments of foreign governments.

In July, 1961, there was a new " arrival "—le mot juste—on the Corporation Museum scene. This was the Transport Museum in East London Street, which houses some 20 vehicles illustrating the progress of civic transport. It is administered by the Transport Committee and is open at stated times and for conducted parties.

A purely private museum project in Edinburgh until recently was the Robert Louis Stevenson Memorial House at 8 Howard Place, in which the author was born in 1850. It was bought in 1920 by the Robert Louis Stevenson Club, who administered it and who opened it to the public in 1926. The exhibits included portraits, photographs, personalia and souvenirs, letters and manuscripts, which were displayed in the rooms on the first floor. Much of the collection is the property of Edinburgh Corporation, to whom the Guthrie collection of some 300 items has been returned on the closure of the museum in 1963. There was widespread agreement that this collection should be exhibited, with the Burns and Scott material, in Lady Stair's house on more or less permanent loan.

And so our survey ends—but with a final reference to the museums in various departments of the University—those of the pure and applied sciences, that is, such as geology, natural history and engineering. These collections are essentially designed for use by students but some of them may be inspected at convenient hours by outside visitors.

CHAPTER 44

GUARDIANS OF TASTE AND LEARNING

EDINBURGH contains a number of societies and organisations which either on a local or a national scale concern themselves with cultural activities, the sciences and the arts. Very often they bridge the gaps between other institutions. Thus there are amenity societies, historical and antiquarian societies and so forth, whose members and office-bearers have their own professional commitments in such institutions as the University, the museums or the architectural associations. And also there are scientific and technical societies whose members are again members of the staff of the University, the Royal Scottish Museum and the technical colleges, or, in certain instances, act as a focal point for scientists in all parts of the country.

THE ROYAL SOCIETY OF EDINBURGH

This renowned body was founded in 1783 on the initiative of Principal William Robertson of the University and incorporated by a Royal Charter of George III. Principal Robertson's original scheme called for " the establishment of a New Society on a more extended plan and after the model of some of the foreign academies which have for their object the cultivation of every branch of science, erudition and taste." Today its members include some of the most famous scientists and scholars of our age, while a glance over past membership lists falls upon many great names, including Goethe and Benjamin Franklin and many world-famous figures who are honorary fellows today. The Society meets regularly to receive and discuss learned scientific communications, and can elect no more than 25 fellows a year.

Royal Society members have also a long tradition of social conviviality, rivalled only perhaps by the Society of Antiquaries of Scotland. Both bodies have their own dining-clubs, and of the Royal Society's club Sir Walter Scott wrote in 1820: " It is a very good institution; we pay two guineas only for six dinners in the year, present or absent . . . this perforce of a good dinner to be paid whether you partake or not, brings out many a philosopher who might not otherwise have attended." He also wrote that he " listened (on one occasion) without understanding a single word, to two scientific papers, one about the tail of a comet and the other about a chucky-stane."

More than a century junior to the Royal Society of London, the Royal Society of Edinburgh was modelled to some extent on the Berlin Academy. The Duke of Buccleuch of the time was the first (titular) president and the first secretary was John Robinson, Professor of Natural Philosophy at Edinburgh, who had fought with Wolfe at Quebec. Originally, the membership was divided into two sections—physical and literary. But the literary side soon ceased to have a separate existence, although Sir Walter Scott was the first and last literary president—at the time, incidentally, when a famous scientist, Charles Darwin was a student at the University.

It also appears from the records that Robert Louis Stevenson, as a very young man, read a scientific paper to the members. But obviously much more important and earlier contributors of scientific papers were Sir David Brewster, James Clerk Maxwell and Lord Kelvin, who was president of the society for 21 years.

It need only be added that the society has a number of prizes and medals in its award for communications and publications, and receives a direct Treasury grant.

THE ROYAL SCOTTISH SOCIETY OF ARTS

Another body concerned with scientific matters, and especially the applied sciences, is the Royal Scottish Society of Arts, which offers facilities of a kind that no one interested in scientific development can afford to neglect, whether he be layman or professional member of a learned body.

Founded in 1821 and granted a Royal Charter in 1841 in recognition of the valuable part it had played in stimulating technical progress, the society provides the only forum in Scotland for the discussion and publication of contemporary scientific and technical development over the whole field covered in detail by specialist institutions.

Twenty volumes of transactions lining the society's book-shelves testify to the devotion of generations of office-bearers and detail a host of original ideas which are to-day a commonplace in our lives. Among the famous names of its members are Thomas Telford the builder of roads and bridges, Robert Stevenson the lighthouse builder, Michael Faraday the scientist and Bruce Peebles the engineer.

During 140 years the society obviously has witnessed enormous changes. In the early years of the 19th century when industry, transport and navigation were adopting the steam engine, opportunities for the inventive mind were available to everybody and not only those with specialised training. Today original invention depends more and more on the highly-trained specialist, and it is increasingly difficult for any one individual to keep abreast of even the main lines of advance in the ever-widening field of technical and scientific development. Thus the society, superseded in some of its activities by the more specialist bodies, still provides invaluable services. This it does principally by a series of discourses, published in the *Edinburgh Journal of Science and Technology* (issued to all members), slide and film presentations and practical demonstrations in the fine old hall of the Royal Medical Society in Melbourne Place. There is also a programme of summer visits to centres of industry and other places of technical interest, where the speed of modern development and the rapidly changing order of things industrial may be studied—all for a moderate annual subscription of £1.

THE ROYAL OBSERVATORY

The Royal Observatory, Edinburgh, was built on Calton Hill by the Astronomical Institution in the year 1818. A Regius Chair of Astronomy, first held by Robert Blair, had existed in the University of Edinburgh since 1786, and in 1834 the Professorship and the Directorship of the Observatory, with its new title " Astronomer Royal for Scotland " were combined, and the post offered to Thomas Henderson, a distinguished astronomer born in Dundee. In his 10 years at Edinburgh Henderson became known throughout the astronomical world for his publication of the distance of the star Alpha Centauri from observations he had made at the Cape of Good Hope, one of the very first determinations of the distance of a star. In 1846 Henderson was followed in office by Charles Piazzi Smyth, a most colourful personality in the scientific world of the 19th century. His interests ranged over a wide field, but he is best remembered for his work in optics and photography, and particularly for his introduction of the miniature and stereo cameras.

Ralph Copeland, who followed Piazzi Smyth, succeeded in transferring the Observatory from its unfavourable position in the centre of the city to its present site on Blackford Hill in 1896. The move and the building of a much enlarged establishment was greatly assisted by the 26th Earl of Crawford who endowed the new institution both with instruments from his private observatory and manuscripts from his library (described earlier).

Copeland's successor, Sir Frank Dyson—" one of the greatest of the makers of modern astronomy " according to the late Sir Arthur Eddington—spent only five years (1905–10) in Edinburgh, but his work in positional astronomy was kept up by his successor, Ralph Allen Sampson. During Sampson's 28 years of office the Observatory gained prominence by researches into the use of free pendulum clocks for precision time-keeping, and by pioneering studies of the distribution of energy in the spectra of the stars. For this Sampson installed a 36-inch reflector, which, in a modernised form, still serves as the Observatory's primary telescope. Sampson's investigations of stellar spectra were perfected under W. M. H. Greaves, who took office in 1938 and spent 15 years in it until his death on Blackford Hill. Despite the difficult conditions of war and post-war years, Greaves was able to produce a large volume of fundamental work and to extend the scope of observations by installing a 16/24-inch Schmidt telescope.

The 36-inch reflector has been modernised by the addition of a powerful stellar spectrograph, and the Schmidt telescope is now equipped with two 16-inch objective prisms of ultra-violet transparent glass. A third telescope, a twin 16-inch reflector of the most advanced design was installed on Blackford Hill in 1962, and a second Schmidt telescope has been planned for the new Italian outstation of the Observatory at Monte Porzio. The now obsolete 8-inch Transit Circle has been dismantled, and the site used to build workshops and stores. Between them and the main observatory building a new laboratory and office block was completed in 1963.

Two years earlier an observing outstation was acquired on a site near Earlyburn in Peeblesshire, 18 miles away from Blackford Hill, where the paths of artificial satellites are tracked and photographed with a kine-theodolite.

The work of the Observatory is at present concerned with four fields: astrophysics, astronomical instrumentation, space research and seismology. For some time the Observatory has specialised in the introduction of automatic methods of observation, measurement and computation into astronomy. Astronomical research has been concentrated on three problems: the constitution of individual stars; the distribution in space of stars and interstellar matter; and the question of the structure of our galaxy. The constitution of individual stars is studied spectroscopically by measuring the intensities of absorption features in their spectra. The aim is to detect small differences in chemical composition between stars which, according to modern theories, may be the result of differences in age and place of star formation. Measurements of the highest possible accuracy are essential, and past experience has shown that if carried out by conventional methods, such work involves an overwhelming amount of slow and tedious reduction and computation. This then is a field in which modern technology is able to produce improvements of fundamental importance. Work is now proceeding whereby the raw data of observation are converted into a form which can be understood and processed by electronic computers with a minimum of human intervention.

A similar problem occurs in the measurement and reduction of photographs with the Schmidt telescope for studies of stellar distribution. A single photographic plate taken with the Edinburgh Schmidt may show images of more than 10,000 stars all of which could be measured for brightness and position. If the wealth of information contained in photographs of this type is to be made use of, the introduction of fast automatic methods of measurement and computation becomes essential. In Edinburgh a measuring machine has been developed recently which is semi-automatic; the observational data are punched on computer tape, and the necessary calculations are carried out speedily on " Atlas " or other fast electronic computers. A completely automatic engine for the measurement of both brightness and position of stars on photographic plates has been designed and has been constructed by Ferranti's at Dalkeith. This machine—" Galaxy "—will be able to deal with 1,000 stars per hour and, in this way, make it possible to tackle even the most complex problems of stellar astronomy. The automation of measurement is carried one step further in the case of the new twin 16-inch reflector which works completely automatically and records its observation of stellar brightness directly " in computer language".

Work has also been started on the design and use of instruments for observations from rockets and satellites. Present plans concentrate on the study of the far ultra-violet radiation of the sun and stars which is normally absorbed by the Earth's atmosphere. The first Edinburgh experiments were rocket-borne from Woomera and Sardinia in 1965.

The Observatory's work in the field of automation and data processing has attracted to Blackford Hill a new major centre of seismology which specialises in the design of modern seismological instrumentation. The Observatory seismologists have already started studying Scottish earth tremors by new methods. This activity has led to the setting up in Edinburgh of an International Seismological Research Centre which collects and studies seismic records from stations distributed all over the world.

The Royal Observatory, Edinburgh, which has a staff of some 30 scientists supported by a similar number of technicians, clerical and other workers, is unique among British observatories in that it combines a Government Research Establishment and a University Department of Astronomy. Both undergraduate and graduate students of astronomy receive their training at the Observatory, and a similar arrangement is being planned for the training of seismologists. University courses in astronomy and astrophysics have been expanded in the hope that in due course the Royal Observatory will play its part not only in advancing astronomical knowledge, but also in providing a new generation of astronomers.

THE ASTRONOMICAL SOCIETY OF EDINBURGH

Moving from the Royal Observatory on Blackford to the City Observatory on the Calton Hill, is to find within its largest dome keen members of the Astronomical Society of Edinburgh meeting on winter evenings to enjoy lectures and discussions on the wonders of the universe.

The Society was inaugurated in 1924 and since 1937 has made its headquarters at the City Observatory—once the Royal Observatory in Scotland—where it affords facilities to the public to study astronomy and to examine celestial bodies through the McEwan telescope when favourable meteorological conditions permit. Some 4,000 visitors take advantage of this service annually including groups of senior school children from many miles around. The Society itself has a membership of about 130 and includes a number of study groups. Some of these specialise in regular observation of particular celestial objects—sun, moon, planets, variable stars, globular clusters and nebulae, etc.—while others maintain the observatory instruments or design and construct cameras for astronomical photography. In recent years this group has found interest in observing and photographing artificial earth satellites. Recently, also, the Director of the Observatory, Mr. Norman G. Matthew, F.R.A.S., F.R.S.E., finding a strong desire for astronomical knowledge amongst the young, formed the fellowship of Junior Astronomers. A subsidiary of the Society, the fellowship is designed to sustain and foster a desire for knowledge of the night sky amongst boys and girls of school age.

The Society owes much to the encouragement given by one of its founder members, the late J. H. Lorimer who, by a legacy, provided the means of inviting astronomers of international repute to visit Edinburgh and deliver public lectures on astronomical subjects of popular interest. From the same funds, the Society is enabled to honour those outstanding in their efforts towards a wider appreciation of knowledge of the science of astronomy by awarding the Lorimer gold medal.

THE SOCIETY OF ANTIQUARIES OF SCOTLAND

Thanks to David Steuart Erskine (1742–1829), Earl of Buchan and both the most celebrated and most eccentric of his line, the Society of Antiquaries of Scotland was founded in 1780 and received a Royal Charter in the same year (1783) as the Royal Society of Edinburgh. This was not, however, achieved without strong opposition, for Buchan's plan to start the Society included among other things a grandiose scheme for a "Caledonian Temple of Fame" in which by a prolonged ballot over the years the names of Scotsmen both living and dead would be enshrined for the enlightenment of posterity. All this and many of the Earl's other notions caused both the University and the Advocates' Library to protest against his petition to George III for a royal charter of incorporation. Their protest was, however, in vain since the eccentric earl was not without influence on his eccentric king. Nor was he without a certain wisdom. True he raised a temple and a vast monument on his Dryburgh estate in memory of James Thomson the poet and of William Wallace, who by defeating the English in 1297 seemed to merit some commemoration on the anniversary of his victory five centuries later. But he also built a wire suspension bridge across the Tweed, which proved extremely useful for more than 30 years.

"In its earlier days", says a Society report, "it not only functioned as a learned society but also maintained a museum, till in the 19th century so ambitious a programme proved to be beyond its resources, and in 1851 it made over its collections to the nation, to form the nucleus of what is now the National Museum of Antiquities of Scotland. Collaboration with the Museum has not unnaturally always remained close, and an official connection is kept through the Society's right to appoint representatives to the National Museum's Board of Trustees. Today the Society which contains just over 1,000 fellows, elected by ballot, is governed by a president and council, with the necessary officers and with its same old purpose to study the antiquities and history of Scotland."

It functions by holding winter meetings for the reading of papers, by publishing annual *Proceedings*—these are internationally recognised as the main organ of Scottish archaeology—by making grants for excavation and by allotting prizes under two small trusts. It also administers the valuable Rhind Lectureship, and appoints a lecturer annually.

SCOTTISH COMMITTEE OF THE ARTS COUNCIL

In August, 1946, the Arts Council of Great Britain was formally constituted in order to develop, in the stately words of the Royal Charter, "a greater knowledge, understanding and practice of the fine arts exclusively, and in particular to increase the accessibility of the fine arts to the public throughout Our Realm. . . ." But already it was at work in

Scotland. Dr. Mavor (James Bridie) presided over the first meeting of the Scottish Committee in September, 1945, and by June, 1947, it became an autonomous body. Members of the Committee, who all give their services voluntarily, are appointed by the Secretary of State as individuals and not as representatives of art organisations. Its headquarters are in Edinburgh, and it has local voluntary organisers throughout the country.

The Scottish Committee encourages the arts, partly by subsidising the Edinburgh International Festival, the Scottish National Orchestra and the repertory theatres, and partly by its support for the direct provision of concerts, drama, the visual arts and puppet shows. Art exhibitions mounted by the committee included displays of leaded glass, tapestries and contemporary British sculpture. Local concert societies received help, and musical tours by chamber music groups were made from Stranraer to Shetland. Tours of " Opera to All ", which presented popular operas, were greatly appreciated, according to the 1962–3 report; and the newly-formed Scottish Opera Society made a highly successful start with performances of professional standard in Glasgow and Edinburgh. Two or three drama companies usually go on circuit in the Highlands and islands each year; and verse speakers, with the committee's help, give recitals in remote towns and villages as well as the cities.

ROYAL FINE ART COMMISSION FOR SCOTLAND

The Royal Warrant which brought the Royal Fine Art Commission for Scotland into being was dated 22nd August, 1927, but this was superseded by a new Royal Warrant dated 8th May, 1953, which, briefly summarised, empowered the Commission (1) to report on questions of public amenity or artistic importance in Scotland, which might be referred to them by Departments of State and to advise public or quasi-public bodies when asked to do so; (2) to call the attention of all these bodies to any new project or development which might affect amenities at large; and (3) to make a thorough inquiry and report on all such questions.

The Commission which has its headquarters in the city at 22 Melville Street consists of a Chairman and nine members drawn from a wide cross-section of the arts and professions including painting, sculpture, architecture and engineering. The Chairman is usually a layman and the artists and professional members are balanced by other lay-members representing both urban and rural interests. The Commission has a full-time secretary.

For the most part the Commission concerns itself with visual amenity in towns and in the countryside, but often other aspects of amenity, in the widest sense of that term, come to its notice. " And then ", says the secretary, " we venture to make recommendations concerning these matters. Over the past four years the Commission has been concerned with airports, bridge designs, industrial and civic buildings, churches, monuments and memorials, electric power schemes, electric transmission lines, roads, street furniture, street lighting, the preservation of landscape, tourist amenities, hotels and motels, tall masts and chimneys."

Closely associated with the ideals of this Commission are a number of local amenity societies and national bodies concerned in the broadest way with cultural values.

THE AMENITY SOCIETIES

For a long time the Cockburn Association has kept a watching brief on the amenities of the city and the preservation of its natural and artificial beauties. In recent years, especially, the Association has spoken its mind on unimaginative traffic plans, the University's destruction of George Square, butcher-like tree-lopping, the alteration of the Charlotte Square roadway, ugly concrete street-lamps, townscape views, and many other subjects which have roused high emotion and sometimes intemperate language.

Another such body is the Scottish Georgian Society, whose architectural preoccupations are enshrined in its very name. The Society whose current president is the Earl of Haddington has its headquarters in Saxe-Coburg Place, one of the latest developments in the New Town. It arranges a winter lecture and summer excursions to such historic places as St. Andrews, Dumfries House (Robert Adam's first mid-18th century country house), Kilkerran, and to Newton-on-Ayr Old Church and Town House. Thc Society also makes a practice of publicly deploring retrograde plans that would harm interesting buildings, and commending organisations and individuals who follow an enlightened policy in such matters.

THE SALTIRE SOCIETY

On a wider national scale there is the Edinburgh Branch of the Saltire Society, founded at a meeting held at Glasgow University in 1936. It is strictly non-political and has branches not only in Edinburgh, Glasgow, Aberdeen, Dundee, Kirkcaldy, Kelso and Helensburgh but in London, Cambridge and Newcastle. Among the founders were Professor Dewar Gibb of Glasgow, Robert Hurd the Edinburgh architect, Mrs. Alison Shepherd, the Rt. Hon. Thomas Johnston, J. D. Fergusson the painter, Edwin Muir the poet, Sir Frank Mears the architect and Agnes Muir Mackenzie, historian. The headquarters—at Gladstone's Land in the Lawnmarket—are in one of the oldest surviving houses in the Royal Mile.

The activities of the Saltire Society have covered many aspects of Scottish culture and life, from conferences on current problems and a series of art and craft exhibitions to housing and community awards.

The housing award in particular has achieved a status of great value to architects and planners, and is much sought after by local authorities. The Scottish Crafts Centre evolved out of a series of small Saltire exhibitions of arts and crafts. Contributions aimed at the solution of educational problems have included a report on broadcasting in Scotland for the Pilkington Committee, *Scotland in the Schools*, and *Scottish Books* as a bibliography for teachers. Other publications on the Society's list have included a wide range of classics, poetry, chapbooks, and a valuable series on crafts.

THE NATIONAL TRUST OF SCOTLAND

The National Trust for Scotland was founded in 1931 to help preserve places of historic interest or natural beauty. It is a voluntary body supported by subscriptions, donations and legacies, and the increasing public interest in its aims can surely be measured by the growth of membership; for the total has risen from 1,000 in 1945 to 7,000 in 1955, 17,500 in 1960, and more than 28,000 in 1963. By 1965 it was nearly 30,000.

The Trust fulfils its function by acquiring and caring for properties, by working as far as possible in consultation with the Scottish Office, the Ministry of Public Building and Works, and the local authorities in Scotland, and by striving to inform public opinion of the need for conserving architecture and landscape of genuine merit. In this task it is particularly fortunate to have the patronage of the most loved and respected of all Scotswomen, Queen Elizabeth the Queen Mother, and distinguished sponsors of taste and learning—the Earl of Wemyss and March as chairman, and among its vice-presidents the Earl of Crawford and Balcarres, whose encouragement of the arts in Scotland has long had Scotland in his debt, and Major Michael Crichton Stuart of Falkland, whose family has made such notable contributions to the restoration of the Royal Mile and the encouragement of tapestry weaving as a well-known Edinburgh craft.

The Trust is also associated with great houses—Culzean Castle, for example, Brodick Castle, Crathes Castle and Falkland Palace—large tracts of mountainous territory including Glencoe, Goatfell and Glen Rosa, Ben Lawers, Kintail, and such remote islands as St. Kilda and Fair Isle. It also restores and converts to modern uses the "little houses" of the ancient royal burghs—an enterprise in which local authorities have begun to follow the Trust's example. In Edinburgh it has greatly assisted the restoration of the Royal Mile and the preservation of certain unique features in the 17th century fabric of Prestonfield House.

Some of the principles which the Trust seeks to establish for the protection of buildings and landscape have been given statutory authority and also, following the publication of a circular to local authorities by the Scottish Development Department, positive action is now being taken to secure orderly development of the tourist trade—a process to which the Trust, which receives half a million visitors a year on its properties, can make a singular contribution.

THE OUTLOOK TOWER

This institution is uniquely engaged in the cultural texture of Scottish life. Situated close to the Castle Esplanade and properly looking across the city and the Firth of Forth to Fife and the Highlands, the Outlook Tower was founded in the former town-mansion of the Laird o' Cockpen as a "training centre for citizens" in 1892. Its active life has dwindled somewhat in the intervening years, more particularly since the death of its pioneering founder Sir Patrick Geddes, whose influence still lives on in the Tennessee Valley Authority in the U.S.A. as it does in India, Palestine, France and Cyprus where his ideas on social ecology have affected potently the planning and healthy development of local communities. The Camera Obscura in the Tower is open to the public for a small payment throughout the summer, and makes with its pastel-coloured synoptic vision of the city an excellent introduction to further sightseeing trips.

The inside of this unusual building is best seen on the way downstairs. In the founder's time the Edinburgh Room was a museum of town-planning with maps, charts, sketches and models. These have given place to mural sketches round a quiet rest room since there are no longer so many lively meetings and discussions as in the old days, now that television and films compete for the interests of the citizens. The educational side of the Outlook Tower's approach, however, is still to be found—in the Scotland Room where a large floor map is supplemented with illustrations, photographs and historical friezes. According to one of the Outlook Tower records, this floor-map is correctly oriented, so the view from the tower is extended north and west with a composite picture of the Gaelic and Viking traditions of the Highlands and the Hebridean Isles from which today's hydro-electric projects, forestry, fishing, peat utilisation, seaweed chemicals extraction, whisky distillation, weaving, spinning, mechanised farming and the rapidly changing crofting communities have all developed. Some of the lower rooms in the Outlook Tower are in use for making stained glass windows and for pottery, and in one, the " laigh hall " or lowest room, visitors are sometimes glad to find a coffee shop.

While living in this house, Sir Patrick Geddes established two self-governing student hostels, believed to be the first of their kind in Europe. He also established the first children's playgrounds where arts and crafts were taught, and he took a hand in starting the city's lovely zoological park. " While we are catching up on our future ", the record ends, " we shall always be overtaking Sir Patrick Geddes' past."

HISTORICAL AND LITERARY SOCIETIES

Inevitably in a city with such a notable literary tradition (and such a liking for societies with a purpose) there are a number of bodies which exist to encourage literature in its various forms. The English Association, the Verse-Speaking Association, the Edinburgh Bibliographical Society (under the wing of the National Library of Scotland), and the Scottish Text Society are amongst the chief of these. Then there are such bodies as the societies founded to commemorate a great literary figure—there are 11 Burns Clubs in and around Edinburgh, a Carlyle Society, the Edinburgh Sir Walter Scott Club (founded 1894) and the Edinburgh Robert Louis Stevenson Club (1920). These last two, commemorating two of Edinburgh's greatest literary sons, provide annually essay prizes for Edinburgh schools, and hold each year a luncheon or dinner at which distinguished presidents for the year are invited to speak.

The Scottish Text Society was founded in 1882 to edit and print texts illustrative of the Scottish language and literature; and it continues to flourish. In 1963, for example, the membership was 245 compared with 185 ten years before. True, the number of private members had fallen off, but this loss was balanced by an increase in corporate membership including American Universities.

A recent volume to be issued was Vol. III of the *Works of Allan Ramsay*. This completed the reprinting of his poetry but two more volumes have still to come, one of prose and the other of editorial material. The works of Gavin Douglas have also been issued, together with reprints by photo offset process of earlier and out of print Society publications.

The literary societies have their counterparts in the field of historical study. There are, in Edinburgh, several well-known societies devoted either to the history of the city itself or that of Scotland. These bodies have delved for many years into particular aspects of the past, and have a fine array of historical works to their credit. The Scottish History Society in particular can boast a remarkable series of publications ranging from accounts of Scottish activities many centuries ago in Poland and elsewhere to burgh records and absorbing private journals.

Another body with an imposing number of volumes behind it is the Old Edinburgh Club, which according to one of its leaders, Dr. Douglas Guthrie, might have been called the Auld Reekie Club. But, said Dr. Guthrie at the Club's annual meeting in 1958, Edinburgh did not get its nickname, "Auld Reekie ", from the pall of smoke which sometimes hung over it but from the foul odour of the streets in early times. The club therefore decided *not* to call itself the Auld Reekie Club, but chose instead the present title. In 1965 the Club published its 32nd volume on Edinburgh history.

Yet another body with books to its credit is the legal Stair Society which has produced important works on the historical background of Scots Law. The Stair Society has suffered one disadvantage in recent years. Its many lawyer members are often so busy in practice that they find it difficult to be punctual contributors to the Society's publications, and this as every editor knows can be a not inconsiderable delaying factor.

So one could go on. There are quite a lot of other societies in Edinburgh with historical interests—the Scottish Genealogical Society, for instance, the Scottish Ecclesiological Society, the Scottish Church History Society and the Scottish Record Society, all of which act in their special way as learned guardians of the nation's past.

CHAPTER 45

FILMS, RADIO AND TELEVISION

THE CINEMA

FILM-GOING in Edinburgh over the period 1929–66 may be seen as an almost perfectly-balanced curve. At one end is the modified appeal which the silent cinema held for the citizens. This was the cinema seen at its best in the work of Chaplin and Douglas Fairbanks, Greta Garbo and Emil Jannings, the Swedish and the German directors, and at its most popular in the films of Mary Pickford, Rudolph Valentino, Harold Lloyd and Tom Mix. The end of the silent period, when the introduction of sound was still a highly controversial issue, brought to Edinburgh some of its finest products, including Fritz Lang's *Metropolis* and Carl Dreyer's monumental *Passion of Joan of Arc*.

But the cold visual perfection of Dreyer's work seen at the Palace Cinema in Princes Street (now part of Woolworth's store), could not compete with the warmth of Al Jolson's voice singing " Mammy " in *The Singing Fool* at the New Picture House, farther west in Princes Street (and later to be absorbed in another large store). The queues which formed outside the picture house then, and wherever else sound films were introduced, led to cinema building all over the city.

During the '30s the curve of cinema-going in the city climbed steadily. The Caley Picture House was rebuilt to hold twice as many patrons. The Playhouse, with 3,300 seats the largest in the city, was built in Leith Walk. The New Victoria in South Clerk Street, the Rutland tucked out of sight beyond Rutland Square, and the Capitol in Leith each added 2,000 seats to the city's steadily growing capacity. Later the development moved towards the suburbs with such cinemas as the Dominion at Churchill, the Astoria in Corstorphine and the Carlton at Piershill. Last of the large new cinemas was the Regal, seating 2,750 and forming part of Lothian House, erected on the long-disused canal basin site at Port Hopetoun.

Meanwhile some of the smaller cinemas were disappearing—the tiny Operetta House opposite the Royal Scottish Museum in Chambers Street, for example, and the old Cinema House in Nicholson Street, now the headquarters of the Salvation Army. But these disappearances, nostalgically regretted though they may have been, did not affect the increasing scale of film-going. The maximum number of cinemas open in the city was 36 in 1939. They had a total seating capacity of approximately 45,000, so assuming an average of two performances a day, they could have accommodated the entire population of the city in a week.

For many people in the '30s, a weekly visit to the cinema was normal. The sound film had opened up a new phase of experience, brought the cinemagoer into an artificially intimate relationship with a new range of personalities. These were the days of George Arliss and Ronald Colman, of Clark Gable and Carole Lombard, of Bette Davis and Joan Crawford (long before they emerged from retirement in *Whatever Happened to Baby Jane?*). In Britain and in Hollywood the stage was raided, both for such simple pleasures as the Aldwych farces with Tom Walls and Ralph Lynn and for more demanding works such as Lillian Hellman's *These Three. The Broadway Melody* began a long series of musical films which were among the most popular to be shown in Edinburgh cinemas.

In Edinburgh, little affected by enemy raiding, the outbreak of war marked no break in the rising curve of film-going. With few other forms of entertainment available the cinemas prospered. Cinema-going reached its peak in the immediate post-war period. But with the appearance of television in Scotland in 1952 the decline in film-going, already apparent in London, was accentuated. Television had brought the screen—the little screen—into the home; and it was no longer necessary to leave the fireside or to journey into town to go to the movies.

By the summer of 1963 there were 23 cinemas open in Edinburgh, one or two of them combining films with bingo sessions. The New Picture House and the Palace had disappeared from Princes Street and the Monseigneur News Theatre, formerly the Princes Cinema, was closed.[1] What had originally been the Rutland and was latterly known as the Gaumont had been destroyed by fire. The former St. Andrew Square Cinema, with its quaint frontage recalling its former existence as a veterinary college, had been demolished after partial destruction by fire, the site forming part of the bus station. The Lyceum Cinema, latterly used for bingo, had also been badly damaged by fire, reopened, and again partially damaged by fire. Leith's largest cinema, the Capitol, was wholly devoted to bingo while the nearby Alhambra, with a long and richly varied record in entertainment, had been standing empty for years.

Cinema-going had contracted and changed in character. More than ever it had become the pastime of young people. While their parents were content to watch television or go to the theatre or the concert hall, the teenagers in the family still found the cinema, with its shared participation in romance or adventure, a powerful magnet.

Inevitably the films seen by these predominantly teenage audiences reflected and catered for their interests and attitudes. Among the most popular films were *Saturday Night and Sunday Morning* with its down-to-earth qualities, *A Kind of Loving* carrying into the cinema the new frankness of the theatre, and *Summer Holiday* with its gay and persuasive escape into a world of colour and perpetual sunshine. Sustaining the appeal of the cinema in a more massive way were the vast spectacles, on ever larger and wider screens—*Lawrence of Arabia; Cleopatra; The Sound of Music*. The largest screen of all, Cinerama, arrived in Scotland in September, 1963.

This is one aspect—the film as a popular entertainment—of the cinema story in Edinburgh. There is, however, another, involving a smaller

[1] In 1965 it reopened as the Jacey Cinema, showing the more exotic films from the Continent.

section of the public, yet of deep and far-reaching influence. Edinburgh was a stronghold of the film society movement which flourished in Britain during the '30s and provided the main outlet for the documentary idea, growing lustily alongside it. The Edinburgh Film Guild was founded in 1929 and was to become, for a time, the largest in the world. From this power house of enthusiasm for the developing art of the film there emerged *Cinema Quarterly*, one of the first journals to take film aesthetic seriously. It was in its pages that the leaders of the documentary movement—John Grierson, Basil Wright, Paul Rotha, Arthur Elton—first expressed their ideas.

It was the Edinburgh Film Guild also which, when the Edinburgh Festival was launched in 1947, simultaneously established in Edinburgh the International Festival of Documentary Films. The choice of the documentary idea was natural enough. Here if anywhere lay Scotland's distinctive contribution to the cinema—the search for truth, the respect for authenticity, the preference for fact over fiction. For a film society to launch a festival, with no financial aid from city or government, was a brave gesture; but with little more than enthusiasm to sustain it, the Edinburgh Film Festival has survived for 20 years on a basis of voluntary effort and has a longer record than any other film festival in the world with the single exception of Venice.

Over the years the film festival has inevitably changed in character. It was never wholly a festival of short films—a mistaken impression widely held—and even in the first year the programme included such major works as Rosselini's *Paisa* and Rouquier's *Farrebique*. The basic concern with the creative treatment of reality—in films of any length—persisted and honest projections of a country's life were always preferred choices for the Edinburgh programmes. The leading film-producing countries were given the opportunity of presenting their work in national programmes and among those to take consistently distinctive advantage of this were the Netherlands, Poland and Czechoslovakia.

In 1962–63 the film festival was formally integrated with the Edinburgh International Festival. At the same time the programme policy was re-aligned to take account of the closer association with the parent event. The aim was to reflect the links between the cinema and the older arts: in the first years, literature and drama. The policy brought some notable films to the festival, including *Electra* from Greece, *Long Day's Journey Into Night* from the United States and *The Given Word* from Brazil. At the same time the festival maintained its interest in the documentary idea on which it was founded.

A recurring criticism of the Edinburgh Festival is that it has resulted in no independent achievement in the arts on display each year in the capital. It is true that there is as yet no national cinema in Scotland in the sense that other comparatively small countries like Sweden and the Netherlands have national cinemas. But a beginning has been made. John Grierson, the Scottish founder of the British Documentary Movement, chose Scotland as the location of the key films he produced—*Drifters*, *Night Mail*, *North Sea*—and he played a leading part in the work of the first Films of Scotland Committee which, in 1938–39, produced a memorable group of films including *The Face of Scotland*, *They Made the Land*, and *Wealth of a Nation*.

Dr. Grierson again lent his experience and imagination to the second Films of Scotland Committee when it was revived, with headquarters in Edinburgh, in 1955. The remit given to the body by the Secretary of State was to promote the production and distribution of Scottish films of national interest. Accompanying the remit was no remittance and the Committee had to find financial help where it could. So successful was it in finding sponsors for broadly based Scottish films that by 1966 the total was nearing 70. They included one film, *Seawards the Great Ships* (script by Grierson, direction by a young American, Hilary Harris) which had become a classic throughout the world and had earned the distinction of an Oscar in Hollywood.

The value of the Films of Scotland effort lay not only in the service it offered to anyone who wished to have a film made in Scotland but also in the stability it provided for the film producing groups. Any country which is going to build up a national cinema must have some continuity of sponsorship if the emerging talents are not to disappear at once to communities where the rewards are richer. This is the beginning which has been made and the support and stimulus flow from the offices at Film House in Edinburgh, headquarters of the Edinburgh Film Guild and the Film Festival.

There are other aspects of the cinema story in Edinburgh which must be mentioned. The capital has its specialised cinema, the Cameo, where foreign-language films are regularly shown and the most ambitious and advanced work in film-making is screened for a general public. It is the creation of J. K. Stafford Poole, son of the showman John R. Poole, whose name is inseparably associated with the Myriorama spectacles staged annually at the Synod Hall. Jack Dunbar, Arthur and Willie Albin, Louis Dickson, Robert and John McLaughlin and the Maguire family are among the other exhibitors long associated with film-going in Edinburgh, who deserve commendation here.

In addition to the Edinburgh Film Guild, still one of the largest film societies in Britain, there are several other groups of film enthusiasts in Edinburgh. The Edinburgh Cine Society has for many years guided and assisted ambitious young film-makers. The Scientific Film Society has held the interest of a large membership devoted to the use of film in various specialised fields. The leading film unit in the city is Campbell Harper Films, producers of scores of films, from *Caller Herrin* to *The Fibre Web* and in 1965 of a film in colour on the Edinburgh Festival for Films of Scotland.

One recollection may sum up what Edinburgh has come to stand for in the world of the cinema. Robert Flaherty, the father of the documentary, chose Edinburgh as the setting for the world premiere of his most successful film, *Louisiana Story*. In the following year the Grand Old Man himself attended the festival's opening performance. In the chair was Norman Wilson, leading spirit of so many of the progressive film developments in Edinburgh. Flaherty was introduced by Sir Stephen Tallents and Dr. John Grierson, both old friends and close associates with him in building up the documentary movement. Their speeches set the stage for him.

When the fine old man, with his head of flowing white hair, rose to address the audience, the applause went on and on. Edinburgh was showing its informed appreciation, not only of *Louisiana Story* but also of all the films Flaherty had made since *Nanook of the North.* At last Flaherty was allowed to speak. But what could he say that would not be an anti-climax? With a characteristic sweeping movement of his arm and a bowing of his head he said: " Thank you, thank you, thank you." Applause broke out again. We Scots do not readily show our emotions but there were many damp eyes in the great audience that night.

TELEVISION AND RADIO

THE BBC

Anyone who walks from the corner of North St. David Street westward along Queen Street, will find it easy to reach Hanover Street without noticing that he has passed Broadcasting House, Edinburgh. The B.B.C.'s premises in Scotland's capital—Nos. 4, 5 and 6 Queen Street, with the legend " Scottish Broadcasting House " above the door of No. 5—are part of the Georgian New Town, unobtrusively merged in a terrace much older than broadcasting.

The B.B.C. began operations in Edinburgh on May Day, 1924. Four years later it housed itself in what had been the old Queen Street Hall—this hall became the Corporation's No. 1 Edinburgh studio—and for a while this was the largest studio used by the B.B.C. in the United Kingdom. Today it remains a fine music studio. Broadcasting House, Edinburgh meanwhile has added two other sound radio studios, recording facilities, control room and transmission equipment, and offices for its production, studio and engineering staff. As the occasion requires, the No. 1 studio can also become a temporary television studio and as such gives useful service at the time of the Edinburgh International Festivals. There is also a small television studio for news, current affairs, religious and sporting programmes. This simple studio will give place to a larger studio with multi-camera and telecine equipment so that a wide range of television programmes can be envisaged from Queen Street. Unlike the B.B.C., Scottish Television Limited (commercial television, that is) do not maintain office and studio accommodation and staff in Edinburgh. Their operations, certainly in 1963 and early 1964, were handled by visits from Outside Broadcast or Film Units.

Television as a public service came to Scotland on 4th March, 1952, and when the B.B.C.'s Kirk o'Shotts transmitter opened, the occasion was ceremonially marked in the No. 1 studio at 5 Queen Street. Since then the B.B.C. television audience in Scotland has grown so fast that it now far outnumbers the audience for sound radio.

Much of the administrative and production television work is centred on Glasgow, but much is done in Edinburgh. The B.B.C.'s Scottish school broadcasting production staff, for example, have their headquarters in Edinburgh. They are concerned mostly with school programmes in the Scottish Home Service, but they are branching out into television with educational programmes and series which were being managed if not yet transmitted from Edinburgh in 1963 and early 1964 when these words were being written. Edinburgh houses also B.B.C. producers specialising ('ambidextrously' in both sound and television) in agriculture and gardening, natural history, Scottish music, the arts and traditions of Scotland, and magazine and general programmes whose material is drawn from all walks of life.

To leave the matter like that would miss, however, a fundamental point in the relationship of the B.B.C. with the people of Edinburgh. For " the B.B.C. " in Queen Street is really an organic part of two Edinburghs: Edinburgh the city and royal burgh, and Edinburgh the Scottish capital. There is thus a natural and constant traffic, both ways, between the B.B.C. on the one hand and, on the other, the City Corporation in the High Street, the Church of Scotland in its George Street offices and its places of worship, the Law, the Administration and the Government in Parliament House and St. Andrew's House, the University in all its scattered faculties, the Royal Scottish Academy, the Festival Office and other cultural organisations, the Merchant Company of Edinburgh, the Chamber of Commerce and many other social and industrial organisations. It is of course easy to describe the anatomy of organic relationships (and even easy to appreciate the " export " impact of broadcast Edinburgh events—Royal occasions, the General Assembly of the Church of Scotland, the International Festival, the Royal Highland Show at Ingliston, the great national religious occasions in St. Giles Cathedral, Rugby football internationals and so on—when they reach the outside world). Such an occasion was the brilliant State visit to Edinburgh of King Olav when the city's geography and 18th century town planning brought a new dimension to a State visit. Fifteen cameras and four television Outside Broadcast Mobile Control Rooms presented an Edinburgh bedecked with the national flags of Britain, Scotland and Norway, and the heraldic banners of the ancient Scottish families in the golden autumnal sunshine. An added dimension was achieved by mounting a camera in Edinburgh Castle high over the city: with this camera it was possible to sweep the whole processional route. This concentration of material and manpower was accomplished by assembling resources from many parts of the United Kingdom. The impact of all this is clearly easy to measure. Much more difficult is the task of assessing the effect or the impact of one organ—the B.B.C. in Edinburgh—on the whole body politic and personal of the city itself.

Only one statistic is conclusive. This is the Post Office record of broadcast receiving licences. To take a good sample year, on 31 May, 1961, there were in Edinburgh 130,137 joint licences (television and sound radio) and 46,880 licences to receive sound radio broadcasts only. Considering that the population of Edinburgh, according to the latest Census return, was 468,378, this meant that there was one "joint" licence for just over every three people (man, woman and child), and one sound receiving licence of any kind for roughly every two-and-three-quarter people. Even the "television" licence proportion must be near saturation point, allowing for the average number of persons living in each household. At the time of writing the full figures for 1963 were not yet available, but it was known they would show a substantial increase.

That being said, there is still no dependable way of judging the effect of the B.B.C.'s programmes on Edinburgh itself. The B.B.C.'s Audience Research Department establishes, by daily sampling, the numbers of people in the United Kingdom looking at or listening to the programmes, and a general idea of the acceptance of the programmes among the viewers and listeners. It breaks the totals down into figures for Scotland, Wales, Northern Ireland and the English Regions, but not regularly into figures for individual cities.

However, in the full generation during which there has been B.B.C broadcasting in Edinburgh, there has certainly developed a taste for music of all sorts, for drama, story-telling, entertainment of a more or less sophisticated kind. And among minorities there has grown an attention to the affairs of the world at large, to the things of the spirit (even among non-churchgoers), to the Gaelic traditions of Scotland—broadcast Gaelic song recitals are often listened to by twice as many Scots as there are Gaelic speakers in the land—and to Scottish traditions. Indeed, where the interests of Scotland tend to be ignored there tend to be protests. Where the interests are nurtured (in current affairs, religious, sporting and other outdoor entertainment, broadcasts, and so on) there is applause. While the B.B.C. has been televising "The White Heather Club" as a series during the early '60s, the programme has regularly drawn an audience of one in three of the entire population of Scotland. Large numbers listen regularly to the Scottish Home Service Scottish News and to broadcast Scottish dance music. When the B.B.C. in Scotland drops the U.K. network to televise a programme about current Scottish affairs, the Scottish audience is proportionately larger than the various English audiences at the same time.

INDEPENDENT TELEVISION

Independent television came to Scotland on 31st August, 1957. At 6.30 p.m. on that date, Scottish Television Limited (S.T.V.) presented their first programme, *This is Scotland.* It was seen on the Independent Television Network and also, of course, in the central lowland area of Scotland, which includes the city of Edinburgh.

I.T.V. programmes are provided by independent companies which are responsible for building, equipping and staffing their own studios. Mr. Roy H. Thomson (as Lord Thomson then was), Chairman of Edinburgh's *Scotsman* Publications Limited, headed the group to whom the contract for Central Scotland was awarded by the Independent Television

Authority (I.T.A.). The group purchased the Theatre Royal, Glasgow, transformed it into a modern and compact television centre, and the programmes produced there are transmitted through the I.T.A.'s transmitter station at Black Hill, between Edinburgh and Glasgow.

The potential audience in S.T.V.'s service area in the summer of 1963 was about 4,000,000; and of these 466,000 lived in Edinburgh, where there were 141,250 television sets, 125,000 of them capable of receiving I.T.V. programmes. This means that approximately 430,000 of Edinburgh's population can, if they wish, watch I.T.V. programmes in their homes. It also looks, says S.T.V., as if an average of some 150,000 people view I.T.V. in Edinburgh during the peak evening hours throughout the year, and that for particular programmes the number can be 200,000 or more.[1]

Because the I.T.A.'s transmitter stations are linked, by lines supplied by the Post Office, the programme companies can exchange programmes on a network basis. Thus, programmes selected from the output of the other 14 programme companies operating at present can be viewed in Edinburgh. There is nothing to indicate that the kind of programmes popular with Edinburgh S.T.V. viewers differ greatly from those which are popular in other parts of the country. To take at random a list of favourites for the week ending 28th July, 1963, is to find, for example, quite a number of programmes popular in all parts of Great Britain, such as *Bus Stop* (film series—crime and adventure), *Emergency Ward* 10 (hospital serial), and another serial *Coronation Street.*

Letters about programmes, received from Edinburgh viewers, are no more or less frequent than letters from viewers elsewhere. They conform to the general pattern, most letters being in the nature of enquiries with a sentence or two inserted giving the writer's subjective reaction to programmes. For example, the mention of a certain illness, in a number of unrelated programmes over a period of time, once provoked an allegation that sufferers from the illness were being exploited. Again, a merchant seaman, quick to spot an error in the gold braid of an officer's uniform, lost no time in pointing out the slip. Controversial programmes, on the other hand, can stimulate a flood of telephone calls: the majority of these come from within the Glasgow " local call " area.

In addition to programmes which may be classed as entertainment, S.T.V. present a variety of serious programmes, and themselves produce locally programmes of both types. Thus they have their own family programmes and a magazine offering comment on news and current affairs, both of which, on occasion, draw material from Edinburgh sources. The Law Society of Scotland and the Faculty of Advocates, for instance, have co-operated with S.T.V. in the production of a series

[1] It should perhaps be interposed here that the B.B.C. and the Independent Television Authority often differ on the size of their respective viewing audiences. There are basic differences in the methods on which the two bodies rely for their estimates of audience size. B.B.C. Audience Research ask a large representative national sample of people about their listening and viewing yesterday. S.T.V., like other programme contractors, get their estimates from Television Audience Measurement who " meter " the sets in a sample of homes. It would appear that neither method is normally operated on a large enough basis to supply reliable programme audience estimates for individual towns or cities. (Ed.)

designed to illustrate the good sense of taking legal advice on problems which, only too often, land the layman in difficulties if he tries to deal with them unaided by a lawyer. There are also many religious programmes including a nightly epilogue broadcast from the Glasgow studios, with Edinburgh ministers playing their part at the end of the day, and another programme entitled *The People's Kirk*.

Then there is education, which is increasingly exercising the minds of everyone concerned with or interested in the influence of television. In 1963, 57 Edinburgh schools were registered for the purpose of receiving I.T.V. Schools programmes.

As for the arts, during the annual Edinburgh Festival it has been S.T.V.'s practice to produce programmes daily (Monday to Friday) with the emphasis on festival personalities and events; and notice is taken also of the concurrent film festival. Grants have also been made to the festival, film festival prizes, and to the Edinburgh Gateway Theatre indirectly through the Scottish Repertory Theatre Trust. This body was founded on an original grant of £5,000 from S.T.V., and the Gateway Theatre profited from the grant along with the repertory theatres in Glasgow, Perth and Dundee. But it is impossible here, as with the B.B.C., to describe the operations of S.T.V. at any length. Occasions like the visit to Edinburgh of the then Supreme Allied Commander in Europe (General Norstad), are naturally covered;[1] and also the outside broadcasts include such colourful events as a Territorial Army Review, the Installation of the Rector at the University, the Royal Highland Show, the Edinburgh Horse Show and numerous sporting events. News coverage of such events and other happenings in Edinburgh is of course a normal feature of S.T.V.'s Scottish News twice-daily programmes and, should there be an Edinburgh occasion demanding a wider audience, S.T.V. cover it for the Independent Television News bulletins from London.

[1] The B.B.C. enjoys an exclusive contract for the famous Tattoo on the Castle Esplanade during the Festival. S.T.V. for its part gets access to the event for film coverage limited to news bulletins. (Ed.)

Part Eight

NATURE

Chapter 46

THE EDINBURGH WEATHER

In no other city has the weather been so well observed and recorded as in Edinburgh.[1] An unknown medical man "resident in the vicinity of the present (1898) Royal Exchange" made the earliest reliable observations of pressure, temperature, rainfall, wind and weather during every year from 1731 to 1736. From 1764 onwards, a series of observers then provided a continuous weather record until 1855, year of the foundation of the Scottish Meteorological Society, which thereafter carefully organised observations not only in Edinburgh but over the whole country and even as far afield as the Faroes, Iceland and Brazil. The familiar white-painted box with louvred sides, now used all over the world to ensure that the thermometers placed inside it record true air temperature unaffected by direct radiation from the sun, was designed in Edinburgh for use by the observers of the Scottish Meteorological Society. The inventor was the lighthouse engineer, Thomas Stevenson, father of R.L.S.; the box is known universally as the Stevenson Screen.

The secretary and presiding genius of this society from 1860 until his death in 1907 was the renowned Dr. Alexander Buchan, F.R.S., who achieved international fame by his distinguished work in meteorology, and whose portrait can be seen above the library fireplace in Edinburgh's Meteorological Office.[2] The first sequence of weather charts in the world, in the now familiar form showing isobars, was prepared under his supervision in 1867 in the rooms of the society at 10 St. Andrew Square. Oddly enough—it certainly would have seemed very odd to Buchan himself had he lived to see the day—his name has become a household word in Western Europe as the originator of "Buchan's Spells", a series of cold and warm periods recurring at about the same time each year.[3] Buchan derived the dates of his spells from an examination of observed temperatures over 10 years at five stations in Scotland. Since the existence of these spells seemed to be confirmed by the results of a previous examination by Professor Forbes of 40 years of observations of Edinburgh temperature, these so-called "periodic anomalies" came to be accepted as a permanent feature of the climate of the city.[4] In the 1920s, the

[1] The Meteorology of Edinburgh by R. C. Mossman. Transactions of the Royal Society of Edinburgh, Vol. 38 (1896), 39 (1897), and 40 (1902).

[2] The Meteorological Office collects weather reports from all over Scotland. Among the reporters are a great many experienced amateurs who are enthusiastic enough to provide their own equipment such as rain gauges, and who send in a constant flow of reports from both near and remote districts.

[3] *Interruptions in the regular rise and fall of temperatures in the course of the year* by A. Buchan. Journal of the Scottish Meteorological Society, Vol. 2, No. 13.

[4] *The Climate of Edinburgh* by Professor J. D. Forbes. Transactions of the Royal Society of Edinburgh, Vol. 22, (1861).

weather correspondent of a London daily newspaper pointed out in his column that a current period of bitterly cold weather coincided with one of Buchan's cold spells and quoted the dates of the six cold spells (7th–14th February, 11th–14th April, 9th–14th May, 29th June–4th July, 6th–11th August and 6th–13th November) and three warm spells (12th–15th July, 12th–15th August and 3rd–14th December). Several coincidences, apparently verifying the accuracy of Buchan's predictions, whetted public interest and for some time it became common practice for newspapers to give their readers a few days warning of the imminence of the spells. Buchan was in effect pitted against the official forecasters of the Meteorological Office, and naturally the latter were quick to investigate the reliability of these predictions. Careful examination of the temperature records of Kew Observatory led to the conclusion that " On the whole it seems improbable that there exists in our climate an abiding tendency for any part of the year to be either abnormally warm or abnormally cold for the season. . . . While Buchan's cold spells were probably true for Scotland in the 1860s, they are certainly not true for London in the twentieth century." Later a thorough statistical examination was made of the long series of temperature records for Edinburgh itself and it was concluded that " recurrences on the days of Buchan's spells are found not to depart to a significant degree from chance expectation." Though statistically they are shown not to exist, the Buchan spells have nevertheless become firmly established in the weather lore not only of Britain but apparently also of parts of Western Europe.

What the Edinburgh weather observations do establish beyond doubt is that there has been no significant change in the climate of the city at least over the period of two centuries covered by the instrumental records. The accompanying climatic summaries (Tables A, B, C, D in Appendix IX) of weather observations at the Royal Observatory, Blackford Hill, have been kindly supplied by the Superintendent of the Meteorological Office, Edinburgh. At a less exposed and less elevated place, extreme maximum temperatures are likely to be a few degrees higher, and extreme minimum temperatures considerably lower; figures for other meteorological elements should be correspondingly modified.

Between October and March it is on the average no colder in Edinburgh than in London and south-east England; it is not until the late spring that the effect of the difference in latitude of five degrees begins to appear. The summer months in Edinburgh are appreciably cooler than in the south of England but there is the compensation that uncomfortable spells of very hot weather rarely occur; it is seldom too hot to work in the city. While mean monthly temperatures in, for example, South Wales (Swansea and Cardiff, say) exceed those in Edinburgh by a few degrees, Glasgow is not significantly warmer than Edinburgh in any month of the year.

What is likely to cause surprise is the fact that during the period from October to March, Edinburgh, even with its shorter days, enjoys more hours of bright sunshine than London, the excess for the six months being sometimes more than 50 hours. This is a measure of the comparative freedom of the city from fog and serious smoke pollution during the winter months. Virulent fogs, both " pea-soupers " and the kind that turns day into night by forming a black, sooty canopy low overhead, are almost unknown. The city belies her name " Auld Reekie ", for the average rate of deposition of solids from the atmosphere even in the Old Town with its concentration of breweries is less than in other cities of comparable size. It is surely the many vantage points and open spaces that permit its smoke to be observed more readily than in less hilly and more built-up towns. Over the whole year, Edinburgh enjoys on the average over 150 hours more bright sunshine than Glasgow.

Mean rainfall is but little in excess of that of London and is about two-thirds of that recorded at Glasgow and in South Wales. Snow is observed to fall on the average on about 18 days in the year at Blackford Hill and on 22 days at the same height above sea level at Hampstead.

These comparisons with conditions in other parts of the country should do much to dispel the notion, widely held south of the border, that Scotland generally and our " east-windy, west-endy " city in particular are subject to climatic rigours of a severity unknown in the south of England. Our own R.L.S. has fostered this misconception in his essay, *Edinburgh: Picturesque Notes:*

" Edinburgh pays cruelly for her high seat in one of the vilest climates under heaven. She is liable to be beaten upon by all the winds that blow, to be drenched with rain, to be buried in cold sea fogs out of the east and powdered with the snow as it comes flying southward from the highland hills. The weather is raw and boisterous in winter, shifty and ungenial in summer, and a downright meteorological purgatory in the spring. . . . For all who love shelter and the blessings of the sun, who hate dark weather and perpetual tilting against squalls, there could scarcely be found a more unhomely and harassing place of residence."

While his fellow citizens would hardly take this fiery diatribe seriously, they would be forced to concede that it contains some germs of truth. The averages of temperature, sunshine and rainfall obscure occasional rigours. For example, a damp easterly, blowing off the North Sea on exposed Edinburgh in winter with a force a point or two greater than in London, is felt much more acutely by the human frame, though temperatures may be the same in the two cities.

The topography of the surrounding country, and indeed also of the city itself, exerts a considerable influence on Edinburgh's climate. The Southern Uplands and the Lammermuir and Pentland Hills reduce the force of winds from between southwest and southeast, and the more distant Grampians provide some shelter from northwesterlies and northerlies. By contrast, the estuaries of the Clyde and Forth and the belt of low lying land around and joining them, permit the prevailing winds between west and south-west to sweep in from the Atlantic almost as freely as do the north-easterlies and easterlies from the North Sea. This channelling effect of the Clyde–Forth gap on air flow in the west–east and east–west directions is quite marked. It is unfortunate that this also is the direction of the principal, and most exposed, street in the city. North-easterlies and easterlies, bitterly cold in the spring, are concentrated by funnelling through the gap between the Calton Hill and Arthur's Seat and sweep relentlessly over the North Bridge and along Princes Street; the westerlies blow on the average even more strongly in the opposite direction. On approaching the North Bridge in stormy weather, the citizen instinctively clutches his hat for he knows from experience the violence of the vortex that swirls upwards at one or other end of the bridge, according to the direction of the wind; the unwary visitor stands to see his headgear sail upwards, eventually to alight on the glass roof of the Waverley Station, there to remain tantalizingly visible but apparently irretrievable. (A porter will be sent to recover it, if the stationmaster is informed of the loss.) Westerly gales sweep under the glass roof into the station itself and blast their way out up the Waverley Steps with such force that a permanent protective barrier has had to be erected at the kerbside opposite the top of the steps to prevent passers-by from being blown among the traffic. Gales occur most frequently between December and February, *not* at the equinoxes as is popularly believed. Perhaps the worst recorded gale was that on the afternoon of 24th January, 1868, when 16 chimney stacks in various parts of the city and the gable of a church in Morningside collapsed and a hearse and cabs were blown over in the streets; the wind approached hurricane force, and four people were killed. The form and shape of most of the older buildings in the city are well adapted to withstand the worst rigours of our weather. Not only are the solid, grey walls of Craigleith stone so impenetrable to driving rain that they barely show traces of the weathering of centuries but the slated roofs are steeply pitched to shed rain and wet snow.

Rapid changes in wind direction with associated changes in temperature are frequent, especially in the winter and spring. The coldest weather then comes with winds from around a north-easterly direction bringing arctic air from the region of N. Scandinavia and Spitzbergen accompanied by squally snow showers in the early months of the year. Kingsley's "jovial wind of winter" does *not* turn Edinburgh children out to play; if they give any thought to its meaning, they recite his ode of welcome to this zephyr with their tongues in their cheeks and with involuntary shivers. At this time, south-easterlies are only slightly less unpleasant than the north-easterlies. The air they bring usually originates over the cold continent and is therefore slightly heated during its passage over the North Sea, whose temperature in winter remains above 40°F., but it nevertheless arrives raw and bitter. As the continent heats up in the spring, it becomes the source of air that is warmer than the North Sea. The air in the easterlies is now cooled and dampened during its passage over the North Sea and fog is likely to form before it reaches the Scottish coast.

The cold and wet sea fog—the haar—that blows in with spring easterlies is unquestionably the most unpleasant feature of the climate of the east coast of Scotland. The haar is brought in over Edinburgh when the wind direction is between north-east and east. It may invade only the lower coastal parts of the city from Joppa to Granton, so that on ascending towards Princes Street one may suddenly emerge from dank gloom into bright sunshine; much more frequently, it blows over the city in a pall of very low cloud that reaches the ground and so appears as fog over the higher parts of the city from Liberton to Fairmilehead and Colinton. When the wind is south-easterly, Edinburgh is protected by the Lammermuirs and escapes the blight, which can then be observed to envelop the Fife coast in an apparently solid white mass. Haar may occur at any time between mid-March and September but is at its worst between May and July. At this time of the year, however, the sun may cause it to disperse for a few hours near midday, though it often closes in again later in the afternoon and thickens by night. The most striking and accurate description of sea fog and haar in literature may be found in *The Silverado Squatters*; it is hardly surprising that it should come from the pen of an author born and brought up in Edinburgh. The Californian sea fog, from which R.L.S. fled up the mountainside to escape the raw and dank air that kept him coughing, was no different from the haar that had driven him from Edinburgh. A certain correspondence between the unpleasant weather described in this paragraph and the strictures in the quotation from R.L.S. may be observed and, in particular, the remark "a meteorological purgatory in the spring" may be recalled. In fact, the distribution of pressure over Western Europe that causes easterly winds to blow over the British Isles has a habit of establishing itself in the late winter and early spring. However, translation from the sufferings of purgatory to a happier, more comfortable, state may occur at any time, even in mid-winter or in the worst rigours of spring, when easterlies may be replaced by south-westerlies bringing warm air from the Atlantic, perhaps from as far south as the Azores; it is not then uncommon for maximum temperatures on successive days to differ by more than 15°F. The citizen may at these times be led, like R.L.S., to malign our weather, yet is it not possible that the winds are hardly so ill as to blow him no good and that their capricious changes may provide for him a not inconsiderable mental, as well as physical, stimulus? But perhaps he can hardly be expected to appreciate this possibility when a snell and blustery north-easterly whistles through the closes; the reactions of Christopher North's shepherd are perhaps rare. "Well, do you ken, sir, that I never saw in a' my born days what I could wi' a safe conscience hae ca'd bad weather? The warst has aye some redeeming quality about it that enabled me to thole it without yaumerin'."

In spring, the mean temperature in the city passes 42°F., the temperature above which growth of vegetation becomes noticeable only a fortnight later than in London, but the rise in temperature in April is usually slow; and the lawn mower is seldom brought into use until the latter part of the month. The highest temperatures in summer and early autumn usually accompany light southerly winds that bring air heated by a long path over land. Sultry days with oppressive heat are rare; the sea breeze sets in to temper the heat on quiet sunny days. The average temperature of the North Sea in summer is about 55°F. so that winds from the east continue to feel quite cool, often preventing the temperature from reaching 60°F. The lowest temperatures in summer occur in strong westerly to north-westerly winds bringing air that has originated over Greenland, whose extensive icy mountains remain icy, winter and summer alike.

It is an indication of the variability of the weather that the highest temperature of the year has occurred as early as 11th May and as late as 25th September, while the coldest day of the winter has fallen as early as 7th November and as late as 29th March, an interval of about 20 weeks in each case.

The heaviest falls of rain or snow in the city occur in easterly winds associated with the movement of a depression over England and the adjacent North Sea. It was a situation of this kind that caused the disastrous floods in south-east Scotland on 12th–13th August, 1948, when extensive damage was done to crops and to road and rail bridges. The rainfall in Edinburgh during that August was 9·40 inches, the highest that had fallen in any month since September, 1785. The greatest recorded fall in one day, 4·20 inches, occurred on 9th December, 1787, and caused such flooding in Leith Harbour that the water was as high at low tide as at ordinary high tide; some lives were lost and ships in the harbour were damaged. But such cataclysms are rare; the average rainfall at Edinburgh is only moderate and is usually well distributed over the year. During the first nine months of 1959, however, only 9½ inches of rain fell in Edinburgh; this was by far the lowest rainfall ever recorded for this period of nine months since records began to be kept two centuries ago. There was a serious shortage of water and supplies were cut off at night periodically in different parts of the city in order to conserve supplies. The water engineers predicted that even if normal rainfall ensued during the winter, the reservoirs would still remain at a dangerously low level in the spring. However, meteorological balance was soon restored; the year ended with a total rainfall of 18·04 inches; and abundance of rain and snow in the early weeks of 1960 had the reservoirs overflowing by the end of February.

Snow has never been reported to fall within the city itself during the four months June to September. The first snow of the winter has fallen as early as 1st October and as late as 31st January; the earliest date on which the last snow has fallen is 17th January and the latest 30th May. One of the most severe periods of snow recorded in Edinburgh occurred during January and February of 1795, when on 12th February " snow lay deep in the streets of Edinburgh and three hundred soldiers and labourers were employed by the Magistrates to clear the roads to the coal hills."

The winter of 1962–63 produced comparable rigours. Snowstorms, interspersed with milder spells in November and early December, heralded the onset on Christmas Eve of a spell of Arctic weather that was to last for 10 weeks. Fierce blizzards alternated with quiet periods of bright sunshine by day and severe frost at night. The measures of 1795 were repeated in modern fashion, and over 200 men were employed by the City Engineer's Department in continuously clearing snow and spreading over 300 tons of salt on the road each day. They certainly did not have to " dig to the coal hills "; but in late January stocks held by coal merchants and at power stations and gas supply centres became seriously low.

Reductions in electric mains voltage had to be imposed, though these in Edinburgh never exceeded 5 per cent. In other parts of the country, supplies both of electricity and gas were severely reduced. During one weekend, processions of coal trains distributed stocks from the mines over all the country in what the Coal Board described as " the biggest extraordinary coal lift in the Board's history."

At times, too, deep drifts prevented milk deliveries from the farms to the dairies and the Scottish Milk Marketing Board had to make emergency arrangements to supply the city with milk from Aberdeenshire and Carlisle. Roads out of Edinburgh were repeatedly blocked, and shopkeepers in the city reported a sharp fall in bus ness which they attributed to the enforced absence of visitors to the citiy from the surrounding country. Only a handful of revellers assembled at the Tron Kirk to bring in the New Year, and the City Police reported an unusually small number of arrests at Hogmanay. Hungry pigeons clamouring for food swarmed round those few who ventured into deep snow in Princes Street Gardens. Neither of the two senior association football clubs, Hearts and Hibernians, was able to play a game on their snow-covered and frost-bound grounds at Tynecastle and Easter Road between 15th December and 6th March, an unprecedented interruption that caused officials of the Football League to examine the question of establishing a close season in mid-winter and extending play into the summer. By contrast, the foresight of the Scottish Rugby Union in installing underground electric heating at their ground at Murrayfield made possible the playing of international games with Wales and Ireland on excellent green turf, while the land all around was hard frozen and snow covered. On one Saturday in late February, three rugby matches took place at Murrayfield one after the other. In East Lothian, not far from the city, exposed cottages were completely covered in snow drifts, their existence being revealed only by the ubiquitous television aerial attached to the chimney and projecting through the snow; the cottagers emerged by tunnelling upwards from the door. In quiet periods between the storms, the sun raised the temperature above freezing point by day and the surface of hard packed snow on the roads melted, only to freeze again at night and to provide hazards for pedestrians and motor cars. Householders and shopkeepers found it well nigh impossible to fulfil their obligation to keep the pavement and gutters in front of their premises clear of snow; no sooner was the snow cleared than another sharp fall had been trampled in by passers-by. In such conditions accidents were frequent and doctors were kept busy attending to bruised and broken limbs at a time of year when normally influenza and pneumonia were their main concern; the incidence of these bronchial diseases was abnormally low. Oddly enough, the number of motor accidents during the worst of the weather was surprisingly small, probably because conditions were so bad that many, particularly the less experienced drivers, left their cars at home and used public transport. On one occasion, however, morning bus services were seriously disrupted by the enforced withdrawal of 50 buses for repairs after damage sustained on the icy roads. Building workers marched in procession to the City Chambers to protest against being paid off because of the weather conditions and received the sympathy of the Lord Provost and Town Council, who were critical of the building industry for failing to prevent work coming to a standstill on building sites in severe weather. Builders were asked to investigate the possibility of using special techniques for the pouring of concrete and huge polythene sheets to protect building sites from storms. The builders contended that when abnormally low temperatures continued unabated for long periods, nothing could be done to prevent the cold penetrating into all materials and making them unworkable.

The abnormally protracted period of cold in January and February of 1963 accompanied winds from directions between northerly and south-easterly through east, associated with high pressure to the north and east of the British Isles. The mean temperature for Edinburgh of the winter months December to February was 34·1°F., the lowest since 1879. In the spring of 1963, ice extended far across the Norwegian Sea from Greenland towards Norway, where open water extended for no more than 100 miles off the north and north-west coasts, a situation unparalleled since about 1820. There was exceptionally deep snow and frozen water surfaces over almost the whole of Europe north of the Alps and the temperature of the North Sea was about 6°F. below normal. It was cold comfort to be told by the climatologists at the height of these rigours of the winter of 1962–3, that winters like this must be expected to become common in the coming decades and that local authorities should consider seriously whether their present arrangements, snow clearing equipment and the like, that had been sufficient to cope with the relatively snowless winters since 1930 (apart from 1941 and 1947) were now adequate. Records had shown that there have been 40 years with mild winters since 1897, but these have not been typical of the winters during previous centuries since 1550. Nearly half a century of mild winters has led to shoddy practices in plumbing and, since plumbing for the majority, as opposed to plumbing for the better-off, has come in with the extensive building of " council houses " during this period, burst pipes on outside walls and in exposed places in this severe winter of 1962–3 kept water officers and waste inspectors working night and day. At this time, too, there was disquiet about the city's water supply, for there had been only between one-half and three-quarters of the normal winter precipitation, a fact that most who had endured the successive snowstorms, particularly those whose cottages had been completely buried in snow, found difficult to accept. However, by 4th March deep Atlantic depressions had nibbled sufficiently into the continental anticyclone to cause a replacement of the bitter easterlies by a balmy south-westerly air flow from the Azores. Temperature rose by 25°F., suburban dwellers saw their lawns for the first time for nearly three months, golf courses that had been skiing grounds reverted to their normal function, footballers played overtime to reduce the backlog of unplayed league and cup matches, and the warnings of the climatologists that had been so disturbing were promptly forgotten.

Thunderstorms occur infrequently and only rarely outside the summer months. That there are only two deaths recorded in thunderstorms in

Edinburgh over a period of at least two centuries indicates that the storms are not often severe. The *Caledonian Mercury* gives a graphic account of a great storm on 13th August, 1744.

"From 10 in the forenoon till near 3 afternoon there were a great many and most terrible peals of thunder with lightning which broke upon the Castle in several places, damaged the roof of the great lodging over the Half-moon, also the carved stone thistle that stood above one of the large windows. Three soldiers in one room were hurt and several others beat off their legs. James Campbell, gunner, suffered most and lies dangerously ill; the blow he received has left a fair impression of a star on his shoulder bone. A house or two in the Grassmarket was also damaged, the windows of a house at Fountainbridge were quite demolished, the walls of the church of Liberton rent, etc. Though the oldest people living do not remember to have seen a storm so dreadful, yet we hear that it did not extend above a very few miles from this city." It was this storm that provided the cloud-burst on Arthur's Seat and the ensuing torrent that tore up the Channel under the Lion's Head known as the 'Guttit Haddie.' The hailstones measured 5 inches round and entirely threshed the standing corn.

Though it is easy to discover in the long and well kept records of Edinburgh weather accounts of extreme events of the kind quoted here, it is important to stress that such events are few. The weather of Edinburgh is certainly erratic but not more so than in other parts of these islands. It does not compare unfavourably with that of, say, Copenhagen in the same latitude. The temperature may fail to reach 50°F. on a June day yet may exceed 60°F. in December, but extremes of heat or cold, or indeed of any weather factor, are rare. Haars may blight the spring and early summer, but seriously no more than once in several years. Successions of grey days with low cloud are not uncommon, but as the records of average sunshine show they are amply compensated for by sequences of bright sunny days. Who does not recall occasions of exceptional visibility in the clear air brought down over the Highlands by a north-westerly on the evening of a long summer day, providing vistas of quite extraordinary beauty over the Forth to distant mountains or out to the Pentlands? Even Stevenson was led to qualify his strictures in *Picturesque Notes*: "But there are bright and temperate days, with soft air coming from the inland hills, military music sounding bravely from the hollow of the gardens, the flags waving in Princes Street, when I have seen the town through a sort of glory."

CHAPTER 47

THE LIVING WORLD

IT has been said of the City of Edinburgh, in time past, that within its boundaries one could fish a salmon, shoot a grouse or hunt a deer. Grouse and roe deer are there still, and also, after a prolonged absence due to industrial pollution, salmon must again be venturing into the River Almond since a grilse was recently caught there, while another was fished from the sea at Granton. This is some indication of the surprising wealth of interest which Edinburgh offers its own naturalists, and its many visitors with a kindred interest.

Most of Edinburgh's inhabitants have little idea of the variety of wild life around them. Yet they share their city with foxes and badgers; snow buntings from the Arctic drift over the Queen's Park on a winter day; and in August, 1964, a hoopoe was sighted in the West End; sponges grow on city rocks; sea anemones and soft corals expand in the tide within the same boundaries that enclose the pavements and offices of the New Town. To this an exile from the city adds: "When staying at a club in Princes Street on my Edinburgh visits I frequently hear owls hooting in Princes Street Gardens. In one sharp winter a friend of mine has seen both hares and foxes in city streets, and I have often thought that Edinburgh must be one of the few cities of its size where you can see sheep grazing from a main street."

Much of Edinburgh's richness is due to the unusual range of habitats which are available to plants and animals. What other city could offer within its boundaries moorland and crags, fields and woodland, marshes and reedbed, lochs and streams, sandy and muddy sea-shores, reefs and an offshore island?

In its earliest beginnings Edinburgh was hewn out of the great forest of oak trees, bog and moorland which covered most of southern Scotland. Remains of some of its earlier denizens have been excavated within the boundaries—wolf and reindeer bones from a rock fissure above Dreghorn, the skull of a seventeen-pointer stag from the Meadows, and others; these and the subsequent fate of the forest were well described by Professor James Ritchie in his *Animal Life in Scotland.* At first the town was a cluster of houses sheltering under the protection of the castle. As it expanded trees were cut down around it and woodland was replaced by moor. This opened the land for grazing, gave easier access to peats, discouraged wolves which attacked the stock, and reduced the danger to travellers from outlaws who used the forest as a refuge. Where woodland was preserved it was for hunting—a wood of great oaks persisted in Holyrood Park even in the 17th century. Agriculture, as it improved, introduced new forms of vegetation and cover. The marshes of the Nor' Loch (Princes Street Gardens) and the Borough Loch (the Meadows) were drained. The city boundaries expanded to include not only cultivated land but rocky hills, wooded parks and valleys, moorland and sea-shore. The most heavily built-up area came to represent something akin to a desert, but parks and gardens, providing varied forms of shelter, remained as oases even at its heart. Thus, although the original life of the forest was all but lost, it was replaced by plants and animals suited to the less extensive but more varied habitats which we enjoy at the present time. A greater variety of smaller forms flourish under these conditions as they could not otherwise have done.

The pattern of life which has evolved is far from static. The balance between man and the plants and animals among which he lives is always a delicate one and especially sensitive to the increasing complexities of urban life. Records show that within the last 50 years there have been many changes in the fauna and flora, and the next 50 may produce many more. Not all of these changes are due to human interference but where this has occurred its results have sometimes been unexpected. Urban natural history can thus have a special interest and importance.

Such an environment could scarcely fail to capture the interest of sensitive and observant citizens; and in fact societies devoted to the study of living things have long flourished in the city. Many of the earlier observations of local natural history were made by members of the Wernerian Natural History Society and published in their *Memoirs*, but in 1858 its membership was joined with that of the Royal Physical Society of Edinburgh (primarily zoological and geological in its interests) and the Botanical Society of Edinburgh. Both of these societies still flourish, the former being mainly concerned with aspects of experimental biology. The Edinburgh Natural History Society, formed in 1923 by the amalgamation of the Edinburgh Field Naturalist and Microscopical Society and the Scottish Natural History Society, is also very active and has recently taken part in surveys of local fauna and flora. The Royal Zoological Society of Scotland and the Scottish Ornithologists' Club are referred to below. All these and other societies have provided meeting grounds for naturalists in recent years. In addition extra-mural classes on natural history topics organised by the University are well supported. The Royal Scottish Museum maintains splendid public exhibits as well as its reference collections of study material and an unfailingly helpful staff. The Royal Botanic Garden and the Scottish National Zoological Park contain displays of living plants and animals which are world famous.

There is also associated with the city an impressive list of distinguished naturalists, many of them members of the University. A remarkable number of its graduates earned distinction in the 19th century as explorers, often describing for the first time the natural features of new and unfamiliar territories. Some of its students made outstanding contributions to science. For a brief period one such student was Charles Darwin, who came to Edinburgh at the age of 16 to study medicine. Medical classes did not appeal to him but during rambles in or near the city his interests in natural history flourished. Among many others the " scholar-naturalist " Sir D'Arcy Thompson, Professor of Natural History at Dundee and

St. Andrews for over 60 years, described with affection childhood explorations on the seashore of Edinburgh from which grew his later interests in the life of the sea.

One of the city's most important contributions to natural science has, indeed, been in marine biology; hence the extended reference later in this chapter to some of the men, associated with Edinburgh, who laid the foundations of the science.

The study of bird migration is another which owes much to Edinburgh naturalists. A pioneer in this field was Dr. W. Eagle Clarke, who, while assistant and later keeper of Natural History at the Royal Scottish Museum (between 1888 and 1921), made extensive studies of bird movements around the British coasts. More recently the charting of bird migration was furthered by the establishment of bird observatories on the Isle of May and Fair Isle, both of them places where Eagle Clarke had worked. In fact this enterprise originated in Edinburgh in 1929 when six Edinburgh Academy schoolboys met in a house in Inverleith to form themselves into a bird-watching club. From the Inverleith Field Club, as the new body called itself, grew the Midlothian Ornithological Club which in turn gave rise to the Scottish Ornithologists' Club and the two observatories, a tribute to what can be achieved by youthful enthusiasm. The Scottish Ornithologists' Club has gone from strength to strength. In 1959 it acquired premises in Regent Terrace which are now the Scottish Centre for Ornithology and Bird Protection. The Centre contains the Club's offices and library and also the Scottish headquarters of the Royal Society for the Protection of Birds—a valuable combination.

In face of all this activity one might assume that the natural history of Edinburgh is now fully known, but this is not so. Even for some of the more familiar groups, recent reliable records are not to be found and much that is known is seemingly unrecorded. For less conspicuous animals the dearth of records is acute. In 1906 Mr. William Evans gave in his presidential address to the Royal Physical Society of Edinburgh a valuable review of the state of knowledge of the local fauna at that time, and referred to much work carried out in the previous century; he specifically indicated many gaps in our knowledge which will certainly have widened with the changes of the last 60 years, but little has been done to fill them. Naturalists, both amateur and professional, seem increasingly disinclined to tackle the complexities of identification involved in the study of smaller animals. For city naturalists there is also a growing temptation to escape from the city into attractive countryside where observations can be made in congenial quiet. The city which has inspired so many naturalists has thus been neglected more than one might suppose.

It is a surprise to many naturalists to learn what an amount of exploration may still be done within range of a Corporation bus. Probably many small animals as yet unrecorded are awaiting anyone who cares to take the trouble to search for and identify them. It is still even possible to find a completely new species within the city boundaries as, for example, the Duddingston midge. Nowadays the mere collection of lists and records does not satisfy the true naturalist, but it is still an essential step to the more exciting problems of distribution, ecology and behaviour.

A word of explanation might be timely here. The account which follows this introduction is necessarily illustrative rather than comprehensive. It commences with an account of the geology of Edinburgh by which all of the city's life is inevitably affected. Then follows a description of the main features of its vegetation. Among the animals most space has been given to the more familiar groups. There is then an account of the city's important part in the study of marine biology. The chapter closes with a description of the achievements of the Royal Zoological Society in its Zoological Park.[1]

GEOLOGY

Geology has held an important position among the natural sciences in Edinburgh for many years. Dr. James Hutton (1726–97), the "father" of the science, was a citizen of Edinburgh and a founder member of the Royal Society of Edinburgh. The Scottish capital became the platform of the plutonian–neptunian controversy, the views of the former school being supported by disciples of Hutton such as Sir James Hall (1761–1832) and Professor John Playfair (1748–1819), and those of the neptunian theory by Professor Robert Jameson (1774–1854). Jameson assembled a valuable collection of minerals and fossils which, during his lifetime, was displayed in the Natural History Museum of the University. This collection was later transferred to what is now the Royal Scottish Museum, which has developed geological collections since its inception in 1854. In the same year the Geological Survey started in Scotland with its headquarters in Edinburgh. Although the subject was taught in various departments of the university, it was not, however, until 1871 that the Murchison Chair of Geology was founded. The Edinburgh Geological Society was founded in 1834 by Alexander Rose (1781–1860), a lecturer in geology and mineralogy and a mineral dealer in the city.

Rocks found within the Edinburgh city boundary belong to the Old Red Sandstone and Carboniferous systems.[2] But also there are Lower Old Red Sandstone rocks from the Pentland Hills, a north-eastwards pitching anticline or arched structure, which extend into the city outcropping in the Braid Hills and Blackford Hill. Within the city, Lower Old Red Sandstone rocks are predominantly lavas—basalts, andesites and rhyolites—with beds of volcanic ash and subsidiary sediments. Around the nose of the Pentland Anticline, Upper Old Red Sandstone sediments occur as fine conglomerates, sandstones, cornstones and marls. Carboniferous rocks underlie the rest of the city and, except for the

[1] It should be noted that as many plants and animals have no English name precise enough for accurate reference, all plants and invertebrate animals, for the sake of the record, are given their scientific names. In this country the English names of most vertebrates are, however, well established, and for the sake of non-scientific readers scientific names have been omitted from the sections dealing with these animals.

[2] For a detailed description of the rocks and lists of fossils of the Edinburgh district see *The Geology of the Neighbourhood of Edinburgh*, 3rd Edition, H.M. Stationery Office, 1962. An excursions guide to the city and its environs is provided in *Edinburgh Geology*, Oliver & Boyd, 1960.

volcanic lavas and ashes of Arthur's Seat and the Calton Hill, are almost entirely sedimentary. With the exception of the eastern suburbs, the Carboniferous rocks of Edinburgh are cementstones, sandstones and shales of the Calciferous Sandstone Measures which have been gently folded into a series of troughs and ridges. The most notable structure is the Wardie syncline which is succeeded to the west by the Granton Dome and to the east by the expression in Carboniferous sediments of the Pentland Anticline. The calciferous Sandstone Measures, together with the Old Red Sandstone, are cut off to the east by the Pentland Fault, a north-easterly trending reversed fault which passes between Liberton and Stenhouse and reaches the sea at Portobello. Strata bearing limestones and coals occur to the east of the Pentland Fault and form the western limb of the Midlothian coal basin with a steep dip to the east.

Igneous bodies intruded into the Carboniferous sediments are an important feature of Edinburgh geology. Volcanic necks, such as the Castle Rock and those of Arthur's Seat, are almost certainly connected with the Lower Carboniferous volcanic episode marked by the lavas of Calton Hill and Arthur's Seat. A large number of intrusive sills of Carboniferous and Permo-Carboniferous age are found in the Edinburgh district, the most important within the city being the teschenite sill of Salisbury Crags, the basalt of St. Leonards Craig and Heriot Mount, the essexite of Lochend, and the dolerite and picrite of Corstorphine Hill. The volcanic and intrusive igneous rocks stand out as characteristic hills and crags, many of the sills forming spectacular dip and scarp features.

During the glacial period ice, having its origin in the Loch Lomond area of the Highlands, flowed across the district from west to east as indicated by erratics, striae and the directions of drumlins and crag and tail features. The latter are well developed, the Castle Rock and the High Street being a classic example. Morainic tails have also been developed on the eastern sides of most of the city crags such as Corstorphine Hill, Blackford Hill, Arthur's Seat and the Calton Hill. The ice finally retreated northwards leaving on the higher ground incised channels caused by the flow of meltwater. Two meltwater channels may be traced within the city, one from the valley of the Water of Leith at Colinton by way of the alluvial flat at Redford and the Braid Burn valley to Craigmillar; the other flowed through the Craiglockhart valley to Morningside Station. In other parts of the city spreads of sand and gravel mark the retreat of the ice. Post-glacial lakes were formed, not all of which have survived as lakes to the present day. They have been called Gogar Loch, Corstorphine Loch, Craigcrook Loch, Borough Loch (the Meadows), Holyrood Loch, Lochend Loch and Duddingston Loch. There are records of shell marl up to 20 feet in thickness being found in a number of these old loch sites. Because their pre-glacial valleys had become blocked with boulder clay, the River Almond and the Water of Leith have cut new sections of their courses. The picturesque gorges of Colinton Dell and the Dean on the Water of Leith, and the valley of the Almond between Carlowrie and the sea represent post-glacial cuts by these rivers. A raised beach at 100 feet O.D. of late glacial age is developed but is not a continuous feature. Laminated clay associated with the beach was formerly worked at Portobello brick works. The clay at Portobello is 100 feet in thickness and the uppermost portion is probably associated with the 25 foot raised beach which is well developed as a low terrace of loosely cemented sand and gravel bordering the present coastline. Intermediate raised beaches at 75 feet and 50 feet form impersistent and poorly developed terraces but may be seen at Leith and west of Granton.

The rocks of Edinburgh have been wrought commercially for a number of products. Sandstone was formerly quarried widely for building purposes; quarries in the Granton Sandstones included Craigleith, Granton land and sea quarries, Blackhall, Craigcrook, and Ravelston, and in the Hailes Sandstone the Hailes and Redhall quarries. Some of the very siliceous sandstones such as the Craigleith, Ravelston and Barnton Park stones were used for making wheels for glass-cutting. The Upper Old Red Sandstone has also been quarried for building stone notably at Craigmillar. Igneous rocks are quarried in the neighbourhood for roadstones and concrete aggregate and formerly for curb-stones and setts. Within the city this type of working is now discontinued but in the Lower Old Red Sandstone basaltic lavas there were important quarries at Blackford Hill and Mortonhall. The whinstone sills were worked on a large scale at Corstorphine Hill and Barnton and even the teschenite of the Salisbury Crags was quarried until the workings were stopped as prejudicial to the scenic splendour of the crags, an early example of nature conservation for which public opinion was largely responsible. Lime was once obtained from workings in the cementstones overlying the sill of the Salisbury Crags but more important workings were in the non-marine limestone at Burdiehouse and Straiton and in the limestones of the Carboniferous Limestone Series such as those at Gilmerton. Coals of the Limestone Coal Group are or have been worked within the city at the New Craighall, Niddrie and Gilmerton pits where the western limb of the Midlothian Coal Basin falls within the city boundary. Fireclays associated with the coals have also been worked in a number of places such as New Craighall pit. A blackband ironstone in the Lower Limestone Group was formerly worked at Gilmerton, and it is recorded that the clay-band ironstone nodules in the Wardie Shales at Trinity, famous for their fine fish fauna, were once used by the Carron Ironworks. Aquifers from which water is obtained by bores are provided by the sandstones of the Old Red Sandstone and the Oil Shale groups. Hard water, used mostly for brewing, is obtained from marly beds in the Cementstone Group.

FLORA AND VEGETATION

Vegetation depends to a great extent on the geology of the area and its climate. Edinburgh's climate, as already noted, is generally dry, sunny and equable enough to allow the successful growth of a wide range of plant species in relation to the local soil conditions.

The first comprehensive account of the native plants of Edinburgh and its environs was R. K. Greville's *Flora Edinensis* published in 1824. This important work, amounting to 478 pages, describes all the species then recorded for the area and gives notes of abiding interest regarding the habitats and local distribution of these species, thus shedding light on the vicissitudes of the flora in relation to changes in the environment. No work comparable in scope and thoroughness to that of Greville has subsequently appeared, but a very useful list of plants found in the vicinity of Edinburgh entitled *Flora of Edinburgh* was published by J. H. Balfour and J. Sadler in 1863 and again, as a second edition, in 1871. This list includes 1,008 species and 78 varieties of flowering plants, 43 species and varieties of ferns and their allies, and 520 species and varieties of mosses, liverworts, lichens and stoneworts; but many of the plants recorded were found well outside the boundaries of the city and some occurred as escapes from gardens. Then, in 1894, C. O. Sonntag produced *A Pocket Flora of Edinburgh and the Surrounding District* which, although it embraced only flowering plants and ferns, gave concise key descriptions for all the species mentioned, with references to localities. A similar work to that of Sonntag, and incorporating much material in his book, was published in 1927 as *The Field Club Flora of the Lothians* by the Botanical Committee of the Edinburgh Natural History Society under the editorship of Isa H. Martin. A fuller edition, with descriptions, keys and ecological lists was issued in 1934, and this comprises the latest account of the flowering plants and ferns—native or naturalised—in the area, with references to the many alien species introduced by the agencies of commerce and industry.

In 1900 Robert Smith's *Botanical Survey of Scotland—*1. *Edinburgh District* appeared in *The Scottish Geographical Magazine* (Vol. XVI, p. 395). This important paper of 31 pages, with a coloured map of vegetation zones, was the first work along ecological lines dealing with any region in Scotland, and as a work of reference for the Edinburgh area it has not been superseded.

Since the land within the city boundary, some 50 square miles in all, ranges in elevation from sea level at the Firth of Forth to 1,617 feet at the summit of Allermuir Hill on the Pentlands, the vegetation includes maritime lowland and sub-montane plant communities. The basic igneous rocks more or less exposed as prominent well-known eminences—for example, Arthur's Seat, Salisbury Crags, the Castle Rock, Blackford Hill, Craiglockhart Hill and the Braid Hills—are of special interest because of their considerable lime content and local association with bands of limestone: thus on disintegration, they tend to support a flora distinctive from that of neighbouring habitats comparatively poor in lime.

The flora of Edinburgh and its suburbs includes over 500 species of native flowering plants and ferns, most of these being widespread in South-east Scotland, particularly in the Lothians. In addition, many alien species occur in waste places, ballast heaps, plantations, etc., while a greater number have been purposely introduced and cultivated by man. Rather more than half of the city's total area is occupied by open spaces, some 60 per cent (in area) of these being used for various agricultural purposes, about 11 per cent for golf courses and over 9 per cent for public open spaces.

The seashore area by the Firth of Forth has been modified by the construction of docks and other works and, except for small parts of the coast, chiefly near Cramond, the conspicuous plants are mainly casual species of waste land, including aliens established from seeds in dockyard refuse. Among the plants on Cramond Island are sea campion *Silene maritima*, English stonecrop *Sedum anglicum*, sea pink *Armeria maritima*, henbane *Hyoscyamus niger*, and buck's-horn plantain *Plantago coronopus*.

Although the oak woods which stood near the Old Town, particularly in Holyrood Park, have long since disappeared, there are within the present city considerable areas of woodland especially in the districts of Cramond, Corstorphine, Craiglockhart, Colinton and Fairmilehead; and some of the trees have reached a considerable age, being up to 250–300 years old. These woods, which are mainly plantations, usually consist of a mixture of deciduous trees, frequently sycamore *Acer pseudoplatanus*, wych elm *Ulmus glabra*, oak chiefly *Quercus robur*, ash *Fraxinus excelsior*, beech *Fagus sylvatica* and lime *Tilia x europaea*. Often associated with these are smaller trees or shrubs such as birch *Betula pendula* and *B. pubescens*, holly *Ilex aquifolium*, hawthorn *Crataegus monogyna* and elder *Sambucus nigra*. Especially in the more open woods and copses there are many attractive species of herbs, as recorded in *The Field-Club Flora of the Lothians* (1934). Sycamores are very common and usually of vigorous growth wherever they are established, and at Corstorphine there is the distinctive Corstorphine sycamore *Acer pseudoplatanus corstorphinense*, the young leaves of which are bright yellow.

On the slopes of the Pentlands above the village of Swanston there are strips of woodland containing chiefly sycamore, beech, oak and Scots pine *Pinus sylvestris*, and in the same area, up to an altitude of about 1,200 feet, there are, locally, scattered junipers *Juniperus communis*—doubtless remnants of more widespread juniper cover in the past.

The public open spaces (parks, etc.) which occupy more than 1,600 acres within the city, include such well-wooded areas as the Hermitage of Braid, but several consist chiefly of pastures, crags and heathland, such as Holyrood Park (which includes Arthur's Seat and Salisbury Crags), Blackford Hill, and Hillend Park on the north-east slopes of the Pentlands. On the hilly pastures of these open spaces (usually well grazed by sheep) gorse *Ulex europaeus*, bent-grass *Agrostis spp.*, sheep's fescue *Festuca ovina*, wavy-hair grass *Deschampsia flexuosa*, and mat-grass *Nardus stricta*, are generally conspicuous, with patches of bracken *Pteridium aquilinum* dominant locally, especially on the Pentlands, where also ling *Calluna vulgaris*, blaeberry *Vaccinium myrtillus* and crowberry *Empetrum nigrum* are frequent at higher elevations. The crags of basic igneous rock have for long been known to support in places a flora of special interest which has been somewhat depleted except, fortunately, on rather inaccessible rocks. Among the more local species which persist on the crags are the following: forked spleenwort *Asplenium septentrionale*, maidenhair spleenwort *Asplenium trichomanes*, hairy rock-cress *Arabis hirsuta*, dyer's rocket *Reseda luteola*, rockrose *Helianthemum chamaecistus*, German catchfly *Lychnis viscaria*, maiden pink *Dianthus deltoides*, spring sandwort *Minuartia verna*, dropwort *Filipendula vulgaris*, spring cinquefoil *Potentilla tabernaemontani*, blackthorn *Prunus spinosa* and wild basil *Clinopodium vulgare*. Wallflower *Cheiranthus cheiri* is particularly prominent on parts of the Castle Rock.

Plants occurring at the ruined Castle of Craigmillar include pellitory-of-the-wall *Parietaria diffusa*, wallflower *Cheiranthus cheiri*, evergreen alkanet *Pentaglottis sempervirens*, Good King Henry *Chenopodium bonus-henricus*, alexanders *Smyrnium olusatrum* and French sorrel *Rumex scutatus*, the last three species mentioned being introduced herbs which have probably persisted at the Castle since the mid-16th century when the building was a residence of Mary, Queen of Scots.

One of the most important areas of botanical interest in Edinburgh is the Duddingston Loch Bird Sanctuary with its various zones of vegetation. A very conspicuous reed swamp, with the common reed *Phragmites communis* dominant, occupies some twelve acres at the western end of the loch and a large part of its southern shore, with smaller extensions at the east end where there is a marsh of some three and a half acres. Behind the reed swamp, on the southern side, there is an area, originally of damp meadow land, now largely occupied by trees and shrubs, mainly introduced. The northern shore of the loch rises more steeply and has generally an open margin or only comparatively narrow belts of reeds and sedges. Within the sanctuary as a whole there are about 150 species of native flowering plants and a few dozen introduced species, the latter being chiefly trees and shrubs planted for shelter. The water plants present include hornwort *Ceratophyllum demersum*, mare's tail *Hippuris vulgaris*, horned pondweed *Zannichellia palustris* and fringed water-lily *Nymphoides peltata*. Plants of the reed swamp include water plantain *Alisma plantago-aquatica*, bogbean *Menyanthus trifoliata*, yellow iris *Iris pseudacorus*, great pond sedge *Carex riparia*, great reed-grass *Glyceria maxima*, branched bur-reed *Sparganum ramosum* and great reedmace *Typha latifolia*, while among the species in the marshland are bog stitchwort *Stellaria alsine*, ragged robin *Lychnis flos-cuculi*, marsh cinquefoil *Potentilla palustris*, marsh ragwort *Senecio aquaticus*, tufted water forget-me-not *Myosotis caespitosa*, marsh speedwell *Veronica scutellata*, marsh foxtail *Alopecurus geniculatus*, marsh horsetail *Equisetum palustre* and great spearwort *Ranunculus lingua*.

In the past the chief dangers to the flora of the city and its environs were the overcrowding of buildings, the careless disposal of waste, and the destruction of woodland. Nowadays these depletions are to some extent offset by the increased planting of trees and laying out of gardens; and indeed in 1963 Edinburgh Corporation appointed a forestry graduate to make a complete survey of the city's trees—roughly estimated at half-a-million—as a start to a long-term plan of care and replacement of Edinburgh's woodlands. Apart from the effects of building operations, the vegetation and flora of the remaining open spaces have suffered in places from intensive sheep grazing and fires, while indiscriminate plant collectors have at times seriously reduced the numbers of locally scarce or rare plants.

During recent years reasoned conservation of our plant life has been promoted and developed by education, careful planning and legislation. In Edinburgh the plants, native and introduced, which are cherished in the various public parks and gardens are protected by bye-laws and there is increasing appreciation of the wild flora within and around the city. This is much encouraged by the activities of the Botanical Society of Edinburgh (founded 1836) and other natural history societies.

THE ROYAL BOTANIC GARDEN

The Royal Botanic Garden (under the Ministry of Public Building and Works) occupies some 62 acres at Inverleith, in the northern part of the city. This famous garden, which originated as a physic garden established in Edinburgh in 1670, is of outstanding botanical and horticultural interest and has in cultivation about 35,000 species of British and foreign plants. Among its most important features are the rock garden, one of the finest in the world, the arboretum, with its splendid collection of trees and shrubs (particularly rhododendrons), the woodland and peat gardens, the plant houses, and the herbarium, containing over 2,000,000 specimens. The garden has been effectively planned to provide attractive vistas in relation to its undulating site, while the pond, near the East Gate, is a fine example of the informal landscape treatment of water as a habitat for plant and animal life. From a vantage point on the slope south of Inverleith House, a very impressive view is obtained over the main wooded area of the garden to the chief landmarks of the city, with Arthur's Seat and the Pentland Hills in the background.

THE CITY'S MAMMALS

Animals depend on plants for their food and shelter and as the vegetation of the city has changed so has its fauna. Of all animals the mammals are perhaps those which come most directly into competition with man and his domestic stock. Nevertheless more of them survive within the city than many people suspect.

In the extensive rural areas of Edinburgh moles are abundant. So too are common and pygmy shrews; these two species, especially the former, are caught by cats in surburban areas still bounded by fields. The water shrew occurs on some stretches of the Braid Burn. It can on occasion wander an appreciable distance from the stream, having been caught, for example, in the garden of a house in Pentland Terrace; another was caught on the Mortonhall estate near an old walled garden where the only nearby water was a mere trickle. Hedgehogs are common on the outskirts and in the summer evenings are sometimes seen wandering in suburban streets such as Mayfield Road and Dalrymple Crescent. In the Royal Botanic Garden there are several hedgehogs in the woodland areas.

The Royal Botanic Garden has colonies of bats, probably mostly pipistrelles, and this species also occurs in the Hermitage of Braid, Lauriston Castle, Liberton, and elsewhere in the city. In 1956 a long-eared bat was found in a Liberton garage.

Foxes are quite common all around the outskirts of the built-up area. They have been seen on Blackford Hill, Corstorphine Hill, Granton-Cramond, Silverknowes Golf Course and Barnton, to mention only a few. In autumn 1963 one was found drowned in the waterworks at Fairmilehead. Farmers have naturally suffered from their raids on poultry, sometimes in broad daylight, and many enclosures in the Zoological Park require to be specially fox-proofed. Occasionally meets of fox-hounds take place inside the city boundary. A fox is sometimes seen in the Royal Botanic Garden and may be the same animal which in 1960 was frequenting the grounds of Fettes College. In order to go from one of these places to the other, it would have to traverse at least two streets. A stoat has also been seen in the Garden, and the species is common on the city's outskirts in such areas as Blackford Hill, the Hermitage of Braid and Davidson's Mains Park. Weasels, less frequently seen, also occur.

Although the polecat has long been extinct in the area hybrid polecat—ferrets have been seen in a number of widely separated areas and one was killed in Colinton in 1954. Another newcomer to the scene is the American mink, and numerous escapes from mink farms seem to be establishing themselves in the wild, despite an intensive eradication campaign. So far, two examples have been noted in Edinburgh, one killed by a car in 1957 and one trapped at Duddingston Loch in 1964.

Badgers are resident on the west side of Corstorphine Hill and are occasionally picked out at night by motor car headlights. Otters have occasionally been seen on the Water of Leith. This is not surprising as they are great travellers and occur as near as Penicuik, where they are found on the River North Esk. The common seal occurs in the Firth of Forth, off the Edinburgh foreshore, and the grey seal may also be an occasional visitor since it recommenced breeding on the Isle of May in 1956.

Rabbits, whose numbers were greatly reduced by the myxomatosis epidemic in the '50s, are gradually returning. They are found in outlying parks and in the Royal Botanic Garden. The brown hare too lives on the outskirts of the built-up area and in the outlying parks. One was seen in the Meadows about 1955, and in the circular flower bed in front of the University Zoology Department in West Mains Road a female hare with three leverets was found in the summer of 1958; another frequented allotments in the Blackford area, reaching them by going along the streets from its headquarters on Blackford Hill, always by the same route. The Blue Hare which occurs on the Pentlands is much less common elsewhere in the city. One was seen, however, on the Braid Hills before the late war.

Of the small rodents, the bank vole occurs here and there in suitable places. There is, for example, a colony near the walled garden at Mortonhall. Water voles are common; there are colonies of them along the Braid Burn in its Blackford Glen and Liberton stretches. The short-tailed field vole and the long-tailed field mouse occur in fields up to the edge of built-up areas. Both species, especially the field mouse, are often caught by cats. Field mice also occur in the Royal Botanic Garden and in the narrow strip of woodland which lies alongside the south of the railway line near St. Margaret's Well in West Princes Street Gardens. Some also live in the rank herbage on the steep slope to the west of the Castle.

The black rat is found mainly in the Leith dock area where its numbers may be augmented by rats from incoming vessels. During the last war, black rats also became established in the Haymarket area. From there they spread mostly in an easterly and southerly direction, and premises in many streets became infested. After the war, rodent control considerably limited this outbreak. In 1951, out of 296 complaints of rodent infestation 40–50 per cent were found to be due to black rats. By 1956, of 61 rodent infestations only 10–12 per cent were black rats. The Dock Commission staff undertake rat destruction in the dock area of Leith. In 1956, 20,000 rodine baits were laid in addition to continuous baiting and trapping using "Warfarin." Of 111 vessels examined for rats in 1956, de-ratting exemption certificates were issued to 104, indicating that few or no rats were present. After rat destruction measures had been applied to the seven infested vessels, 187 dead rats were recovered. None of those examined was found to be infected with plague. By 1958 the black rats in the city were considered to be held in check and reduced in numbers, although infestations are still liable to occur in the areas near Leith docks. The brown rat in Edinburgh, as elsewhere, establishes itself wherever it gets the chance and where food is plentiful.

One unusual and unpleasant consequence of the presence of rats was recorded in the city in 1959. Heavy infestation of rats on stream banks can cause contamination of the water with a spirochaete *Leptospira icterohaemorrhagia* causing Weil's disease (spirocheatal jaundice) in man. Naturally, it is especially dangerous when the water level is low and the stream relatively stagnant. During these conditions in the drought of 1959 a man washing his lorry with water from the Niddry Burn became infected through a cut on his hand and contracted the disease.

The red squirrel is a scarce animal in Edinburgh, though it occurs sparingly in Midlothian in places only two miles south of the city boundary. One was seen soon after the last war in Ravelston Park. Grey squirrels are common in the grounds of the Zoological Park at Corstorphine. They are found also on Corstorphine Hill, at Davidson's Mains, Lauriston Castle Park, the Hermitage of Braid and in the Newington area, despite housing density.

Roe deer live unobtrusively in woodlands on the Pentlands and in other places. They have been seen in the parkland near Mortonhall House, and in the spring of 1957 one was seen crossing a road on Corstorphine Hill. They have even strayed on to Blackford Hill. Recently one was drowned in the water works at Liberton.

There are no recent records of stranding of whales on the Edinburgh foreshore. However, in August, 1958 the Press reported that two whales, vaguely identified as being of the " grey-black variety," were seen about 30 yards off Portobello Promenade.

THE BIRDS OF EDINBURGH

If Edinburgh's mammals are apt to be elusive many of the birds are much less so, and no part of the city's natural fauna attracts more attention. City bird-watchers are well-served—both by the local branch of the Scottish Ornithologists' Club, which attracts over 150 members to its monthly meetings and which for eight years published a regular local magazine (the first of its kind in Britain), and by the city itself, where a wide variety of habitats have a corresponding appeal to a wide variety of birds. In all about 200 species have been recorded as occurring within the city boundaries, but an account of this kind can only take note of the more interesting regular features.

Even in the busy city centre some interesting birds remain. Carrion crows nest on St. George's Church in Charlotte Square; a mistle thrush sings every spring from a flag-staff in George Street; swifts haunt several of the central churches and house martins nest in Walker Street. In May and June, 1955 fulmars were prospecting the Castle Rock and one was even seen to alight there for a few minutes. In the preceding year there had been several other records of fulmars, including three from as far inland as Colinton, but apart from occasional stragglers no attempts have been made in succeeding years to follow up these bold pioneering bids. Kestrels and tawny owls are firmly established even in the centre of the city, and in 1956 a pair of magpies attempted to nest in a tree in Drummond Place. The status of this species in Edinburgh is typical of its patchy distribution throughout Scotland as a whole. It is common in the western and southern suburbs, but almost completely absent from the east side of the city and the neighbouring county of East Lothian.

The central public gardens are too much frequented and too devoid of ground cover to hold many birds, but willow warblers may be heard singing from Princes Street and a spell of severe weather in winter is almost certain to bring some redwings into Charlotte Square, St. Andrew Square and Queen Street Gardens. Snow buntings have even been seen in Princes Street Gardens under these conditions, and in 1958 a mallard elected to nest there and succeeded in hatching 12 ducklings.

Outside the city centre the built-up area is largely suburban in character and the familiar garden birds are the dominant species. But Edinburgh is particularly fortunate in its public parks, each with a character of its own, and these form island sites for several interesting species. The Royal Botanic Garden, for example, by its very nature offers a wide variety of habitats. Among the species breeding there (within a mile of the city centre) are magpie, redpoll, linnet, yellowhammer and spotted flycatcher, and even such retiring birds as hawfinch, woodcock and stockdove have been recorded breeding there this century. The hawfinch may in fact breed there regularly. A turtle dove spent some time in the gardens in May, 1957 and might well have bred if it had been able to attract a mate. This was also one of the three localities within Edinburgh at which collared doves, now widespread, first made their appearance in 1960-1. This is an

Asiatic species which during the present century has achieved a dramatic extension of range across almost the whole length of Europe. A most delightful feature of these gardens is the remarkable tameness of the birds, many of which have learnt to feed from the hand.

Queen's Park, by contrast, consists largely of the rugged massif of Arthur's Seat whose grass and gorse-covered slopes provide breeding sites for wheatears, skylarks, meadow pipits, linnets and up to a half a dozen pairs of kestrels. Stonechats also used to nest here but, as in so many other places, they disappeared after the extremely severe winter of 1946–7 and there has only been one subsequent breeding record. Snow buntings are often to be found on the high ground in winter.

The Queen's Park holds three lochs of which by far the biggest and most important is Duddingston, created a bird sanctuary in 1925. This is the headquarters of the pochard in South-East Scotland. Breeding was first recorded in 1926 and about 15 pairs now nest within the park, mostly in extensive reed-beds at Duddingston but also apparently at Dunsapie Loch, which superficially appears quite unsuitable. Duddingston is equally important as a wintering resort for this species and over 3,000 were counted on these lochs in the 1961–2 winter. Other notable breeding species at Duddingston are sedge warbler, green woodpecker (1959), teal (1955 and 1959) tufted duck (since 1953, though it also used to breed in the 1920s), great crested grebe (since 1937, with a maximum of three pairs in 1959), little grebe (but not since 1960) and water rail (1951). This last species is a common winter-visitor amongst the reeds, where there is also a remarkable winter roost of yellowhammers, reed buntings and corn buntings, up to 300 of the last-named species having been counted coming in at dusk. The sanctuary has attracted a number of rarities over the years, notably bitterns which have been recorded on four occasions since 1947. The other lochs in the Queen's Park are much smaller and devoid of cover, but mention must be made of the little flock of wild wigeon that comes in every winter to Dunsapie and quickly learns to join the resident mallard in the scramble for scraps thrown down by passers-by. In hard weather these wigeon often go down to the Figgate Pond or Lochend Loch to find more shelter. Lochend Loch lies only a mile from the sea and in winter used to be frequented by scaup, often in fair numbers, until recently the Loch was largely filled in. Gadwall have been occurring on these lochs with increasing frequency and now rank as regular winter-visitors.

Of the other parks one may mention especially the Hermitage of Braid—a well-wooded valley where regular feeding has made many of the birds remarkably tame. The valley holds a rich variety of woodland birds, including green woodpeckers which first bred here in 1956. This is a species which is only now beginning to expand northwards from the Tweed Valley, and the first record within the city boundaries came from the Blackford Hill on 31st August, 1951. There is also good woodland on Corstorphine Hill where redstarts, tree pipits and wood warblers may still be found, and the Zoological Park nearby looks like adding an interesting newcomer to the Edinburgh fauna in the shape of the night heron. Birds of this species (of the Canadian race) have been allowed to nest in the Park in a free-winged state, and individuals have been recorded from different parts of Edinburgh on a good many occasions, although so far there has been no known attempt at breeding outside the Park.

The Water of Leith forms a natural park along certain sections of its course, notably between Murrayfield and Stockbridge where the breeding birds include linnet, yellowhammer, grey wagtail, mute swan, mallard and moorhen. Until about 1948 this stretch of river also held what was probably the last pair of kingfishers left in Midlothian. Near the mouth of the river is a mute swan " centre ", and over 150 may be counted from the Bernard Street bridge in winter, with sometimes a whooper swan in their midst. In all about 11 pairs of mute swans breed annually within the city boundaries—on the Water of Leith and the Union Canal and in the parks. As recently as 1954 two pairs of lapwing nested within a mile of the West End on the north side of Queensferry Road opposite Stewart's College.

Despite building extensions, there is still a broad strip of agricultural land round the south and west sides of the city. In addition to many of the birds already mentioned, this supports good numbers of tree sparrows, corn buntings and lapwing, and the flat, low-lying fields to the west of Corstorphine hold large flocks of golden plover and lapwing in the winter. There used to be a small marsh in this area and two, or possibly three, pairs of yellow wagtails were found breeding there in 1951, but the ground was subsequently levelled for building purposes and there have been no subsequent records. The few earlier breeding records for this species all came from the Craigentinny–Portobello area which has now been completely built-up. Corncrakes are not infrequently heard in the fields round Edinburgh but there have been no breeding records for many years. The constant encroachment of town into country has inevitably had some effect on the rook population, but a census of rookeries in 1956 showed that there were still about 2,600 nests within the city boundaries. Mention might also be made of the crows, many of which (especially in the Colinton–Pentlands area) show varying degrees of hooded plumage. At Colinton Dell and at Dreghorn there are fine woods of mature trees with good undergrowth, and chiffchaff, wood warbler, garden warbler and blackcap have all been heard singing here recently, while a pair of kingfishers bred in Colinton Dell until the early 1940s. Bullfinch, redpoll, goldfinch and long-tailed tit are other species which are relatively common in this area, and in recent years there have been wintering records of blackcap and chiffchaff.

In the extreme south the city takes in a section of the Pentland Hills, the boundary running along the summits of Caerketton and Allermuir (1,617 ft.) and then projecting southwards to include the whole of Capelaw and Bonally Reservoir. This enables Edinburgh to claim dipper, curlew, common sandpiper, redshank and red grouse as breeding species.

Edinburgh's 10 miles of coastline, almost all of which is built-up, has little appeal for the coastal-nesting species. Cramond Island, however, (which is accessible on foot at low tide) also lies within the city boundary and amongst its breeding birds may be mentioned rock pipit, shelduck, eider and ringed plover. Kittiwakes nested in Granton Harbour in 1933 but this attempt at breeding was not repeated, although these birds may be found in numbers both at Granton and at Leith outside the breeding season.

It is really in the winter that the Forth Estuary comes into its own as a resort for all kinds of sea-birds, especially after stormy weather. The extensive mussel beds opposite Leith form one of the main wintering grounds in Britain for scaup, and more than 10,000 have been counted there at times. Examples of recent counts of other regular winter-visitors to this coast are: 660 great crested grebes in February, 1964; 400 red-breasted merganser in October, 1957; and 1,000 scoter in April, 1958. Numbers of long-tailed duck and eider are much smaller, but the latter species has increased considerably during the past few years. The largest concentration of goldeneye in Britain is probably to be found by the sewer outfall at Seafield, where up to 2,500 have been counted at a time, and the large population of pochard (normally an exclusively fresh-water species) wintering on the Queen's Park lochs habitually flight down at dusk to feed off this stretch of coast. During hard weather large numbers of pochard and tufted duck may be seen on the sea during the day. Twenty or more cormorants may be counted resting on the pylons in the sea, gulls may be counted in thousands outside the breeding season, and during the summer both common and sandwich terns can usually be seen flying past. Skuas (mostly arctic) regularly appear each autumn, and at low tide the muddy shore at Seafield often holds surprising numbers of waders. Up to 110 bar-tailed godwit, 300 knot and 400 dunlin have been counted on different occasions, with smaller numbers of the other common species, and hard weather will often drive down large numbers of golden plover and lapwing. Another attractive feature is the presence of small wintering parties of turnstone and purple sandpiper on the harbour breakwaters. The waste ground round the railway sidings holds an enormous flock of greenfinches which may number up to 500 birds.

In this short account it is impossible to deal with the wide variety of birds that have appeared in Edinburgh on migration, their arrival usually coinciding with a spell of easterly wind and poor visibility. But there are certain passage movements which are sufficiently regular and obvious to deserve mention. Geese (usually pink-feet but sometimes grey lag) are often to be seen over the city in winter, but there is a particularly heavy movement every October when they are making their way from Loch Leven (the first big gathering ground in this country after the flight from Iceland) to their traditional wintering grounds in the Moorfoot and Pentland Hills and farther south. Less spectacular but just as regular is the diurnal movement of skylarks and meadow pipits over the town each spring and autumn. Curiously enough the direction followed at both seasons is the same—south-west—presumably because the spring migrants are locally-breeding birds, heading up to the inland moors from the coast. The arrival of the wintering thrushes from Scandinavia (redwing and fieldfare) in October mostly takes place by night, but their call-notes suggest that large numbers must pass low over the town at this season. Edinburgh also lies at the beginning of a well-marked wader migration route across country to the Solway. These birds (most frequently oyster-catcher and curlew) are also largely nocturnal migrants, and their call-notes may often be heard over the city on calm nights in August–October. Sometimes these migrants are unexpectedly grounded in the city centre, like the jacksnipe flushed from a gutter in Albany Street in October, 1956, or the golden plover that spent a week in Charlotte Square Gardens in September–October, 1958.

The appearance of Edinburgh may have changed greatly during the last century or so, but it does not necessarily follow that the change has resulted in an impoverishment of the city's bird fauna. The birds of agricultural land may have been forced to recede in front of the constant suburban development, but their place has been taken by the typical garden species, and the parks continue to provide refuges for a variety of birds that must be unrivalled in any other city of comparable size in this country.

REPTILES, AMPHIBIANS AND FRESHWATER FISHES

The only reptile reported from the city in recent years is the common lizard. This occurs in the rockery near the south boundary fence of the Royal Botanic Garden and also on the Pentlands (there is a record within the city boundary for May, 1960). Slow-worms which used to live on Blackford Hill have evidently disappeared.

The smooth newt breeds in the Upper Elf Loch (or Dead Man's Pool) near the highest point of the Braid Hills. The palmate newt may also occur in Edinburgh but has not been recorded so far; it breeds in a pond on the Bush Estate in Midlothian. The crested newt was found in the Upper Elf Loch prior to the second World War. The common frog spawns in several ponds including a pool in the Royal Botanic Garden. Toads spawn in the Lower Elf Loch. These two species of animals are not often seen outside the spawning season.

Trout *Salmo trutta* occur in Bonaly Reservoir near Capelaw Hill to the south of the city and occasionally in the Water Department's Reservoir at Alnwickhill Road. They also live in the Braid Burn and the Gogar Burn. The Water of Leith is annually stocked with trout which are purchased from the Howietoun and Northern Fisheries Company Limited of Stirling. For example, on 9th April, 1958, 200 three year old and 1,600 two year old fish were released. In 1959 the fish hatchery was asked to supply 500 three year old trout and the balance in two year old fish up to a total value of £200. Restocking took place on 8th April and fish were released at Currie, Juniper Green, Stenhouse Bridge, Murrayfield Bridge, Coltbridge Terrace, Dean Village and St. Bernard's Well. Fishing is free but a permit has to be obtained from the Town Clerk. In 1959 549 permits were examined; over the past few years an average of 700 have been issued annually. A trout obtained from the Water of Leith on 18th August, 1935 measured 15½ inches in length, weighed 26 ounces and was 5½ years old.

Reference has already been made to the re-appearance of salmon in the Almond. But sea-trout too have returned and are now quite often caught near its mouth, a tribute to the success of river purification.

Three-spined sticklebacks *Gasterosteus aculeatus* are found in all the streams, in the canal and in many of the ponds including Inverleith Pond and the Lower Elf Loch, Braid Hills. Minnows *Phoxinus phoxinus* occur in the Gogar Burn, Water of Leith and the Canal but they are less common and less widely distributed than the stickleback. Loach or " beardies " *Nemacheilus barbatula* are very common in the Gogar Burn and in the Water of Leith. Perch *Perca fluviatilis* are found in Duddingston Loch, ponds at Craiglockhart and in Dunsapie Loch. Pike *Esox lucius* are abundant in Duddingston Loch and also occur in Dunsapie. At Duddingston they are known to take the young of some species of water birds. In 1926 the loch was drag-netted five times in one day and 41 pike weighing up to 3 lbs. were taken. The following year 55 larger pike were netted; two were three feet long with a girth of 16 inches. Twenty-two pike netted in 1928 ranged in weight from 2–4 lbs. each. Roach *Rutilus rutilus* were also caught in nets at Duddingston, and this fish also lives in the canal. Eels *Anguilla anguilla* also occur and have been seen in the pond in Figgate Burn Park, Portobello.

THE CITY'S INSECTS

Among the smaller animals insects, by their overwhelming numbers, attract much the greatest attention. Since many of them are also attractive in appearance and are conveniently preserved they have made more appeal to the amateur naturalist than most other small creatures.

In the great expansion of entomological studies that took place during the 19th century Edinburgh collectors were well to the fore. Comprehensive lists of beetles by Duncan (1831) and Wilson and Duncan (1834), and of butterflies and moths by Lowe and Logan (1852), are of great value and show that by 1860 the Edinburgh area had been studied more intensively than other parts of Scotland. Edinburgh, indeed, is the only Scottish locality quoted by Stainton in his *Manual of British Butterflies and Moths* (1857–9). Since this time relatively more attention has been directed to the rest of Scotland, particularly to some highland areas, and interest in the Edinburgh district has correspondingly decreased. Much interest in the fauna of the area was revived during the early part of this century by William Evans, whose presidential address to the Royal Physical Society of Edinburgh in 1906 (published in 1909 under the title *Our present knowledge of the Fauna of the Forth area*) provides a valuable key to the entomological literature of the area, but in the last 30 years very few lists of any insect order have been published for any part of the Lothians.

This state of affairs results from three main causes: increasing urbanisation and more intensive methods of agriculture have driven collectors to look farther afield for favourable localities; secondly, improved methods of transport have made it easier for them to do so; and thirdly, there has been a marked decrease in the number of resident collectors. The last factor is partly a consequence of a widespread reaction amongst entomologists, amateur and professional, against collecting as an end in itself, perhaps coupled with a mistaken belief that our fauna is sufficiently well-known. For few, if any, parts of Scotland have yet been adequately studied, and consequently studies on faunal changes—so important in this country where many species reach the limit of their range—are extremely scarce. There are welcome signs of a post-war reversal of this trend: in particular, the establishment of national and other Nature Reserves should encourage collectors to provide data which in time will prove valuable. Edinburgh as we have seen is fortunate in possession of one such reserve, the Duddingston Loch Bird Sanctuary for which useful lists of some insect orders are also in existence.

Of the several types of terrain included by the Edinburgh city boundaries none have remained unaffected by the increasing demands of the human population and none are very prolific in insect species. The hill areas look promising at a distance, but disappoint at close quarters, and are not now known to support any species of special interest. Just outside the city boundary, however, a local speciality still maintained a precarious existence on the few remaining junipers at least as recently as 1952—this is the Edinburgh pug moth *Eupithecia helveticaria*, now recognised as a subspecies of the more widespread highland *E. intricata*. A previously unknown Hyponomeutid moth was found by Lowe and Logan in an unspecified part of the Pentland Hills and described by Stainton in 1849 as *Zelleria fascia pennella*, but has not been seen here for over a century: elsewhere it is only known to occur in central Europe. The heavy grazing and burning, already referred to, have doubtless been responsible for the gradual elimination of many hill species, and the disappearance of some species from Arthur's Seat must be attributed to this cause. The most notable of these was the Scottish subspecies *artaxerxes* of the brown argus butterfly *Aricia agestis*, for which Arthur's Seat was the type locality—it was last taken here in 1868, and appears still to be on the retreat in other parts of Scotland. More likely to be benefited by heavy grazing is the dung-beetle *Aphodius paykulli*, for which Arthur's Seat has long been a well-known locality: it is still there, but is now known to occur as abundantly elsewhere. Gorse has not been much affected and the gorse-feeding species are particularly well represented on Blackford Hill. Some of the steeper rocky slopes must be quite unaffected by grazing and probably support many interesting species, but it is only the wanderer from these areas that will fall into the hands of the average collector.

Adjoining Arthur's Seat, Duddingston Loch supports a good variety of aquatic insects. From its margins Kettle and Lawson collected and described as recently as 1955 a strikingly distinct new midge, *Culicoides duddingstoni*. A moth which is very local in its distribution and much sought after by collectors is here very common: this is the butterbur moth *Hydraecia petasitis*, whose larva feeds in the roots of the butterbur *Petasites officinalis*. Another local moth, *Eucosma turbidana*, attached to the same foodplant, is not to be found here but in Blackford Glen, where the butterbur grows in a drier situation. Even around Duddingston Loch many species have evidently disappeared in the last 100 years, and there is a remarkable dearth of species in the reed-bed and the surrounding wood. Birds will account for some of the deficiencies, but the woodland species are probably also reduced by flooding.

In the woodland areas of Edinburgh the ground flora is generally much trampled and it is therefore the tree-feeding insects that have been most successful in maintaining a population. More interesting, perhaps, are those species which thrive in gardens throughout the city. A list of 165 beetle species collected in a Morningside garden during 1943 and 1944 was published (*Entomologist's Monthly Magazine* 81: 112–3) by Mr. D. K. Kevan in 1945: most noteworthy among these was the weevil *Otiorrhynchus porcatus*, at one time considered a rare species, but since Mr. Kevan's discovery found to occur commonly in Edinburgh gardens. A well-known garden moth, the golden plusia *Polychrisia moneta*, the larva of which feeds on *Delphinium* and *Aconitum*, is well established in Edinburgh but was almost unknown in the British Isles before 1890, since when it has spread very rapidly: it probably first reached Scotland about 1930, and eight years later was recorded as widely distributed in the south of Scotland. Some moth species occur in gardens in enormous numbers, but these are generally small species which do little damage to the plants on which their larvae feed—such are *Gracillaria syringella* on privet, and *Leucoptera laburnella* on Laburnum. Edinburgh gardens, compared with those in the south of England, are in fact relatively free from serious insect pests.

The true city-dwellers, those species which depend entirely on man and his activities, range from parasites to scavengers and to feeders on stored products. Many occur only sporadically and perhaps cannot maintain populations here without occasional reinforcements. Such species are continually being carried round the world by shipping and other forms of transport, but the use of modern insecticides now usually prevents their importation in numbers. The bark beetle, *Ips typographus*, a serious pest of spruce on the continent, was imported into Leith in quantity in unbarked spruce from Germany just after the second World War (see *Entomologist's Monthly Magazine* 82: 241), but luckily failed to establish itself in any Scottish forests. Other completely exotic insects appear in Leith from time to time, but few have any chance of establishing themselves.

The parts of Edinburgh that are often the most productive for the collector of insects are small areas of temporary waste land. Many interesting species are to be found at present among the disused shale and limestone workings in the Straiton area. Those include the sallow hornet clearwing moth *Sphecia bembeciformis*, a handsome species which is rarely seen at large in the adult state unless sought in its particular haunts.

Entomological research in Edinburgh is now being carried out at the following establishments: University of Edinburgh (Zoology, Agriculture, Forestry and Natural Resources and Genetics departments); the Royal Scottish Museum, in which are housed some of the valuable early collections formed by Edinburgh entomologists; Edinburgh and East of Scotland College of Agriculture; and at the Department of Agriculture for Scotland Scientific Services, East Craigs. In 1961 the Edinburgh Entomological Club was revived under the presidency of Dr. C. B. Williams, F.R.S., as a discussion group chiefly for professional entomologists, meeting in the Royal Scottish Museum.

LIFE IN FRESHWATERS

Of the many other kinds of small animals which live in the city, there is space to review only those which are associated with two special modes of life—in freshwater and in the sea.

Freshwaters within the city boundary comprise streams, a small river, a length of canal, natural and artificial lochs and ponds, reservoirs, flooded disused quarries and filter beds. Two of the streams, the Braid Burn and Niddrie Burn, lie wholly within the boundary. The Lenny Burn (called in its upper reaches the Gogar Burn) lies partly within the city before it joins the River Almond. This river forms the northwestern boundary of the city after receiving the Lenny Burn. The Water of Leith and its tributary the Murray Burn rise outside the city, but another tributary, the Stank, is artificial and entirely within the city. The two largest natural bodies of still water in the city are Lochend Loch and Duddingston Loch. There are artificial ponds in several of the parks and some quarry ponds particularly in the north of the city. From Sighthill to Fountainbridge the city is traversed by the terminal stretch of the Union Canal.

The calcium content of some of these waters has been estimated and is rather high. For example, the Union Canal at Craiglockhart has given values of 98 and 105 parts per million of calcium. The Braid Burn at Torduff has given 47·2, at Portobello 77 (samples taken on 10th November, 1959); and other values for this stream range from 28 to 120. The Water of Leith at Canonmills was 53; Duddingston Loch gave values of 44, 72, 78 and Dunsapie Loch 30. Others give values of the same order of magnitude. Partly because of this high calcium content the city's freshwaters support some of the richest freshwater faunas in Scotland. Reference has already been made to the city's fish fauna.

Amongst invertebrates the green hydra *Chlorohydra viridissima* occurs in the Lower Elf Loch and Deadman's Pool (Upper Elf Loch), Braid Hills. Other species of *Hydra* are common in static waters especially perhaps in Duddingston Loch and an inlet into the storage reservoir at Alnwickhill Water Works. The freshwater sponge, *Spongilla*, occurs in the canal and Duddingston Loch. Polyzoans are sometimes common in Blackford Pond and St. Margaret's Loch.

Several species of higher invertebrates have been chosen for special mention. The common freshwater shrimp *Gammarus pulex pulex* is found in many of the fast flowing streams; it also occurs in Bonaly Reservoir, Dunsapie and St Margaret's Lochs and in Alnwickhill Reservoir. It does not occur in the canal nor apparently in the Water of Leith, at any rate from Colinton downstream, which may be due to some degree of pollution. The rarer *Gammarus lacustris* (first recorded for Scotland from Sutherland) occurs in Duddingston and Lochend Lochs, where apparently it is the only species of *Gammarus* present, and also, though sparingly, in Blackford Pond. This species of shrimp is considered to have entered the country soon after the Ice Age and to suffer in competition with the commoner *G. pulex* which was a later arrival. It is unusual for *G. lacustris* to occur in small and artificial bodies of water. A similar history is apparently true for the two species of *Asellus* (the Water Hog-Louse), *A. aquaticus* and *A. meridianus*. *A. aquaticus* is very common in the Canal, the Braid Burn, the Water of Leith, Gogar Burn and other places. *A. meridianus* is the only species present in Blackford Pond, Duddingston, Dunsapie, St Margaret's and Lochend Lochs.

Of the eight species of freshwater leech so far noticed, three—*Glossiphonia complanata*, *Helobdella stagnalis* and *Erpobdella octoculata*—occur almost everywhere. The duck or glass leech, *Theromyzon tessulatum*, is nearly as common but is absent from fast streams; it is sometimes the commonest leech in Dunsapie Loch. *Glossiphonia heteroclita* occurs in Duddingston Loch and Figgate Pond. The leech *Dina lineata* was only added to the British List in 1952, although it is now known to be not uncommon in Scotland; it also occurs in Figgate Pond. The so-called horse leech *Haemopsis sanguisuga* occurs in the canal. In February, 1959, a large leech *Trocheta bykowski* was found in the Braid Burn at Redford House, Colinton. Later in the same month three specimens were found on one piece of submerged wood in the same burn at Peffermill. Leeches of this species were first collected in Britain at Belfast and in Lake Windermere in 1957. Since then it has been found in Staffordshire and Berkshire, but the Braid Burn is so far the only known locality in Scotland. This leech which was originally described from Poland is apparently extending its range. The three lochs in Holyrood Park, the Canal, Figgate Pond and the Water of Leith at Canonmills all have a rich leech fauna.

Amongst molluscs the swan-mussel *Anodonta anatina* occurs, though sparingly, in the canal; its dead shells are often seen at Dunsapie Loch. *Lymnaea stagnalis* is a snail which has apparently appeared in the area in recent years and is now much commoner and spreading its range. In the later 1940s it was found, though rarely, in the canal at Craiglockhart. It is now very common there and also occurs in Dunsapie and Lochend Lochs, the Royal Botanic Garden pond, the Murray Burn, the Water of Leith and the Stank. More recently a young specimen was found in Duddingston and spawn was collected in St Margaret's Loch. *Bithynia tentaculata* occurs only in the canal where, however, it is extremely abundant. A small operculate snail *Potamopyrgus jenkinsi* was first noticed in the canal about 1934. For several years it was very common. In 1948, however, perhaps because of pollution, many snails in the canal were wiped out, and although other species of snails recovered, *P. jenkinsi* has not so far returned. This is surprising, as it occurs in a considerable length of the Water of Leith and also in Blackford Pond.

Amongst these various bodies of freshwater perhaps the canal and the

Stank provide the best conditions for aquatic life in general. Especially is this true of the canal with its rich vegetation of several species of submerged plants. Here such animals as leeches and snails grow to a larger size than elsewhere. As already mentioned the Braid Burn increases its calcium content by 30 parts per million between Torduff and Portobello. This increase, aided perhaps by an increased organic content of the water, certainly improves living conditions for snails. As a result specimens of the common snail *Lymnaea peregra* at Torduff are generally smaller than those at Portobello. In contrast to these rich localities Bonaly Reservoir in the Pentlands has a comparatively sparse fauna.

Unfortunately, as in most cities, the fauna of some of the streams is affected by pollution. The Braid Burn, for example, becomes somewhat polluted not far from its source. Above Redford House septic tank effluents enter the stream and it is obviously affected. The stretch through the Hermitage and Blackford Glen appears clean but the stream is again heavily polluted in the Prestonfield-Craigmillar stretch, where snails and *Gammarus* may be scarce or absent. On the other hand *Asellus* becomes more numerous. By the time it has reached Portobello, the Braid Burn (now called the Figgate Burn) has once again improved; snails reappear, and so does *Gammarus*, though it is not now abundant.

The Water of Leith like the Braid Burn rises in the Pentland Hills. It is already contaminated with organic matter when it crosses the city boundary at Juniper Green. As far as Canonmills, however, measurable pollution does not increase. Contamination is obviously not sufficient to kill fish but *Gammarus* which occurs near the bridge over the Water of Leith at Balerno does not occur at Colinton and points below.

The River Almond though still suffering pollution upstream has a varied fauna of leeches, snails and planarians in rapid stretches near Turnhouse. Like the Water of Leith this river is under the surveillance of the Lothians River Purification Board and conditions are improving.

LIFE OF THE SEA-SHORE

The city of Edinburgh meets the sea along some 10 miles of varied shore. At its western boundary the River Almond enters the firth between soft mud-banks populated by typical estuarine animals, including oligochæte worms, the rag-worm *Nereis diversicolor*, the amphipod *Corophium* and the shell-fish *Hydrobia ulvae*. Between there and the Brunstane Burn, its eastern boundary, lie beaches of sand combined with mud in various degrees and broken by outcrops of sandstone and shale, boulder stretches and mussel beds. This range of habitats attracts a correspondingly varied flora and fauna representing, perhaps, the city's closest approach to a state of wild nature.

Few among the crowds of holiday-makers on Portobello or Joppa beaches can be aware of the teeming life beneath their feet at low tide. Casts of the lugworm *Arenicola marina* and scattered tubes of the sand-mason worm *Lanice conchilega* are usually the only visible evidence of a fauna comprising many typical sandy shore species, including the tellins *Tellina tenuis* and *fabula*, the wedge shell *Donax vittatus*, the cockle *Cardium edule*, and others. In muddier places, especially towards Cramond, *Tellina* is replaced by its close relative *Macoma baltica*. The razor-shell *Ensis siliqua* and the trough shells *Mactra corallina* (especially at Seafield) and *Spisula solida* are among other bivalve shellfish which may be found.

The rocks, ranging in character from the exposed boulders of Cramond Island to the muddy reefs at Granton, carry animals too numerous to detail. Among them barnacles are usually prominent, and they now include the Australasian species *Elminius modestus* which reached the coast of southern England some time before 1945, presumably on the hulls of ships, and has since spread round our shores. It was first recorded in the city in 1960 but had probably reached the Forth at least two years earlier.

East of Granton Harbour the Wardie shales provide a habitat for rock-boring molluscs and these occur also in large numbers in the belts of shale exposed at Joppa. The oval piddock *Zirfaea crispata* is the most conspicuous but *Barnea candida* and *Hiatella striata* are also there. Their empty burrows provide shelter for many other animals; and these, particularly at Joppa, include the cave-dwelling anemone *Sagartia troglodytes*, which is perhaps the commonest anemone on the Edinburgh shore and exhibits a fine range of colour variants for which the locality is well known.

In spite of the variety of their fauna the coastal waters are not unaffected by the city at their back. Hector Boece in the 16th century (quoted by Ritchie) described them (in Bellenden's translation) as ' richt plenteus of coclis, osteris, muschellis, selch, pollock, merswine and quhalis, with gret plente of quhit fische.' Save for the mussels the same could scarcely be written to-day, and the oyster, alas, is gone. Oyster shells, seemingly indestructible, are still plentiful and recall the flourishing fisheries described (though not without some foreboding) in the previous Statistical Accounts. But on inspection they prove to be long worn by the tide and riddled with burrows of the shell-boring sponge *Clione celata* and the worm *Polydora ciliata*. The final decline of the fishery commenced in the middle of the 19th century, and about 1920 it was abandoned. A survey of the oyster-beds was made in 1896 by Fulton, and in 233 ten-minute dredge hauls he obtained only 317 live oysters. In 1957 a Scottish Marine Biological Association research vessel which made 65 hauls over the same ground found no live oysters and only one pair of valves suggesting a recently dead specimen. Causes of the general decline of oysters are complex, but here there is little doubt that it was due to the effects of over-fishing on a species nearing the limits of its range; so human influence on their habitat may have hastened the end.

Human activities have entailed direct alteration of the physical form of the shore, and pollution of the water by sewage and industrial effluents. One practice which gravely altered some parts of the shore, the dumping of cinders and other rubbish, has fortunately been discontinued and the Corporation has done much to restore the affected stretch west of Granton.

Other physical alterations such as docks and harbour works are necessarily more permanent; the parts which are covered by the sea provide surfaces for the establishment of animals similar to those of nearby rocks though generally less numerous and varied. Leith Docks, for example, support flourishing colonies of tunicates such as *Ciona intestinalis* and *Ascidiella scabra* as well as bryozoans, sponges and other sessile organisms. Where wood is submerged a small crustacean, the gribble *Limnoria lignorum*, is a serious pest, and the steady growth of mussels *Mytilus edulis* necessitates regular clearing.

Mussels interfere with the working of another man-made feature of the shore, the Electricity Generating Station at Portobello. Here sea water is used as a cooling agent in the condensers; it is drawn from the firth some 600 feet beyond low water mark through a series of inlet tunnels, passed through the condensers and discharged. Between March and October this water carries among its many small organisms great numbers of larval mussels originating from the neighbouring beds. These floating, unshelled larvæ settle on the inner surfaces of the tunnels and condenser tubes where, if undisturbed, they develop into young shellfish. Their food supply is constantly renewed by the continuous current of water which, with the somewhat higher temperature beyond the condensers, provides better living conditions than obtain outside the pipes; growth is therefore rapid. If allowed to continue unchecked their steady increase in size and numbers soon restricts the flow of water through the system; blockage of the small condenser pipes by large mussels can also result in corrosion where decaying organic matter accumulates at the obstruction.

When the Portobello Power Station was built methods of preventing mussel growth were investigated by Dr James Ritchie of the Royal Scottish Museum (later Professor of Natural History in the University), and his solution of the problem has since proved valuable in many places besides Portobello. Like so many scientific discoveries this one was partly accidental. Some experiments on the effects of chemicals on larval development were conducted in an outside shed during a spell of very hot weather, and it became clear that the larvæ were adversely affected by the heat. Since heat is available at power stations Dr Ritchie followed this observation with experiments of which the present method of control was the result. Each tunnel is now back-flushed with water raised to a temperature of about 100°F. over a period of 24 hours, during which time the young mussels are killed. Back-flushing is repeated at seven-week intervals during the breeding season (March-October) to ensure that young mussels are never allowed to grow too large or become too firmly attached.

Recently some of the older generating sets in the station were replaced and a chlorination system introduced into the new condensers and the discharge tunnel. This has little effect on organisms in the water but the chlorine is absorbed into surface slime on the walls, killing off young mussels. In the intake tunnels the hot water treatment is still continued. The total cost of controlling mussels varies, but it has been calculated that the approximate cost of mussel-killing in one intake tunnel alone in 1963 was about £600.

The effects of these human modifications to the available habitats of the shore are, perhaps, easier to assess than the effects of pollution, a problem of urban life which has already been noted in fresh-water habitats. Between Cramond and Joppa seven sewers discharge comminuted but otherwise crude sewage into the sea. This results in a rather high proportion of suspended particles in the water, deposited on the shore as sludge especially near the sewer outfalls. Organic matter of which the sewage is largely composed is subject to bacterial decay which makes unusual demands on dissolved oxygen in the water, and this has been shown to drop on occasion far below saturation. The salinity is also lowered. All of the city's shore is affected in this way, although it is most obvious near the larger sewers.

Industrial discharges intensify the effects of sewage where they occur, for example by adding poisons to the water which reduce the rate of organic decay. The much diminished fauna of some of the reefs west of Granton Harbour, together with the increased proportion of mud, may be ascribed to such influences.

How pollution has affected the life of the shore is not yet fully known. Animals and plants which require clear, well-oxygenated water are unlikely to survive and many which were recorded as present during the last century have no doubt disappeared for this reason. On the other hand these conditions favour animals adapted for muddy habitats, which can utilise the suspended particles and their bacteria as food. For example, many of the rocks in muddy regions, especially west of Granton and at Seafield, are covered with a close muddy felt in which live enormous numbers of little tube-building worms especially *Fabricia sabella*.

Thus while some shore animals are evidently tolerant of a very wide range of conditions it seems that one effect of pollution is to create a situation favouring the more general distribution of certain species which on unpolluted shores are characteristic of muddier regions. This is in line with its effects on fresh-water faunas and a similar gradation of animals may be detected with increasing degrees of pollution.

One animal which clearly thrives on a moderate degree of sewage pollution is the mussel, which feeds by filtering suspended particles from the water, discarding excess filtrate by a copious supply of mucus and thus adding to the silt around it. The mussel constitutes the main public health risk arising from pollution, Wherever crude sewage is discharged it carries with it vast numbers of bacteria of human intestinal origin, mostly harmless but including inevitably a small proportion of food-poisoning and other pathogenic organisms. These form a part of the filtrate on which the mussel feeds. While pathogenic organisms widely dispersed in the water are not a serious risk to man, even when bathing, they become a genuine danger when concentrated in the bodies of mussels which may be eaten insufficiently cooked. Food poisoning organisms are in fact present in a large proportion of these mussels. The public health authorities have displayed warning notices along the shore but it is doubtful if they are sufficient to prevent the collection of mussels for food by the ignorant or unscrupulous. The same findings might be expected to apply to cockles.

Fish and a few edible crabs are the only other animals taken from the shore for food, and fortunately they are less likely to transmit infection. Fishing from harbours and breakwaters is a popular pastime especially for the young. Rod or line may be used according to the circumstances of the fisherman and small fish, mussels or other shore animals serve as bait. " Chugging " is the method of using ' murderers ', a group of large hooks tied together and jerked up quickly. Several kinds of fish are caught, including sprats (probably the commonest), whiting, saithe, flounder and mackerel, but only the last-named seems generally to be regarded as worth eating—except by the cat.

It is all too clear that the natural history of Edinburgh's coast-line, however interesting it may be, has suffered from its contact with a large human population. After a period of ill-usage, however, it is becoming recognised as an amenity. A recent extension of the powers of River Purification Boards to include tidal waters should alleviate the effects of pollution, and it might not be too much to hope for a slow return to the conditions of last century.

A hundred years ago the flora and fauna of the firth were much richer than they are to-day. They were described by a group of distinguished naturalists whose researches extending to other waters gave Edinburgh a unique place in the development of the science of marine biology, a place which indeed it maintains. By these studies of plants and animals in the sea the city has made a substantial contribution to natural science and to all who depend on the sea for their livelihood.

MARINE BIOLOGY

The study of life in the sea is not a new science, the first recorded observations being those of Aristotle, who described and named one hundred and eighty species, two-thirds of them fishes, from the Aegean Sea, and who also speculated on the saltness of the sea. After Aristotle, however, there appear to have been few original enquirers for many centuries. From about 1500 to 1750 many scientists and explorers made observations on the physical and chemical characteristics of the seas, and some studied marine animals and plants. During the period from about 1750 to 1850 much more was done to extend our knowledge of life in the seas, following the introduction of improved techniques and the more frequent inclusion of naturalists in the staffs of expeditions of exploration. Yet much was still in doubt and, encouraged perhaps by the work of Edward Forbes (Regius Professor of Natural History at Edinburgh in 1854) in the Mediterranean, Michael Sars in Norway, and Wyville Thomson (Regius Professor at Edinburgh 1870-81) in the Faroe-Shetland area of the Atlantic, representations were made to the Royal Society in 1871 urging the need for a large scale study of the oceans. Thus was initiated an expedition charged with " investigating the physical, chemical and biological conditions of the great ocean basins." The work was carried out by *H.M.S. Challenger* during the years 1872-6, with a full scientific staff headed by Wyville Thomson. The Reports of this expedition, published from the *Challenger* Office at 32 Queen Street, Edinburgh, to-day form a valuable and major part of the foundations of modern oceanography. The untimely death, in 1882, of Sir Charles Wyville Thomson was an irreparable loss, but one of the scientists of the expedition, John Murray, undertook the task of completing the Reports.

Murray (later Sir John Murray), while still busy at the *Challenger* Office, found time to institute the small Scottish Marine Station at the margin of a submerged quarry at Granton, Edinburgh, with a barge, the *Ark*, as a laboratory, and a small yacht, the *Medusa*, for collecting. Work continued in Granton for some time, directed especially towards fishery problems, and in 1885, a branch of the Granton Station was established at Millport in the Firth of Clyde. The *Ark* was transferred to Millport and functioned as a laboratory until a storm in 1900 resulted in her total destruction. Fortunately a permanent building had been established in 1897, and after some early difficulties the Millport Station gave rise, in 1914, to the Scottish Marine Biological Association.

Work at the Granton Station appears to have come to an end after 1887, by which year the staff had dispersed. Murray became increasingly preoccupied with the work of the *Challenger* Office and other commitments, culminating, in 1899, with the inaugural meeting of the International Commission for the Exploration of the Sea, at which he was the chief British delegate. An attempt by W. S. Bruce, leader of the *Scotia* expedition, to maintain oceanography in Edinburgh did not succeed, as the laboratory he opened in 1906 was closed in 1920.

There was then no oceanographic laboratory in Edinburgh until 1937, when a branch laboratory of the Department of Zoology and Oceanography of the University College of Hull was established at Sandport Street in Leith. The objective was to extend into the northern North Sea investigations on marine plankton which were already being carried out at Hull for the southern North Sea. This work was planned and directed from Hull by Professor A. C. Hardy, now Sir Alister Hardy, F.R.S. After an interruption from 1939 to 1945, due to World War II, the work was resumed under Dr C. E. Lucas at Hull and Edinburgh, and the sampling was extended well out into the Atlantic. In 1948 Dr Lucas became Director of Fisheries Research to the Scottish Home Department and, in 1950, the administration of the work was transferred from Hull to the Scottish Marine Biological Association. The Hull staff moved to Edinburgh and, in October, 1952, the new Edinburgh Oceanographic Laboratory of the Association was inaugurated at 78 Craighall Road, less than two miles from the site of the original Granton Marine Station set up by Sir John Murray. The cycle was therefore completed since the Granton Station had given rise to the Millport Laboratory from which the Scottish Marine Biological Association was born.

The work of the Edinburgh Oceanographic Laboratory is financed by grants from the Treasury, on the recommendation of the Natural Environment Research Council, and by the Office of Naval Research, Department of the United States Navy. The general objective is an ecological study of marine plankton, but the ultimate aim is the application of knowledge about the plankton to a better understanding of the causes of fluctuations in commercial fisheries. Such fluctuations may result from natural mortality, from the depredations of the fishing fleets, or from changes in the physical, chemical or biological environment. The drifting animals and plants of the plankton are the most important part of the biological environment of such fish as herring and mackerel which feed directly on them, but because plankton is near the beginning of the chain organic production in the sea, all fish are to some extent affected by fluctuations in its distribution and abundance.

Research at the Oceanographic Laboratory is divided between two teams of biologists under the direction of Mr R. S. Glover who succeeded Mr K. M. Rae in 1957; both teams use automatic plankton samplers which were designed by Sir Alister Hardy for use from commercial vessels at sea. The use of such equipment provides much more regular sampling over a far wider area than could be covered if the work were carried out from research ships alone.

One team uses the Continuous Plankton Recorder for a general study of plankton over a very wide area of the North Atlantic and North Sea. The Recorder is towed by freighters, passenger ships and Ocean Weather Ships of nine nations, and U.S. coastguard cutters as they steam about their normal business. The plankton is filtered on to a continuously moving band of silk so that it is possible to chart the distribution and abundance of each organism along the ships' tracks. Recorders are towed regularly on twenty-three routes, providing samples from an area which extends from the North Sea, northwards to the Arctic Ocean, westwards to Iceland and Greenland and from there to the Newfoundland Banks and the Gulf of Maine, throughout the north-eastern Atlantic southwards to the Bay of Biscay, and along the English Channel. In 1965 Plankton Recorders were towed for a total of about 106,000 miles. The collections thus obtained form the basis for the construction of monthly synoptic charts of the distribution and composition of the Plankton.

The other team uses the Plankton Indicator for a detailed study of the planktonic environment of the herring in the summer drift-net fishery off the north-east coast of Scotland. The Indicator is a smaller instrument designed for use by fishing vessels as they steam to and from the fishing grounds; the plankton is collected on a small flat disc of silk which is returned to the Edinburgh Laboratory for analysis. Fishermen working from Fraserburgh and Lerwick collect samples on each night of the summer fishing season, providing a picture of the planktonic background to the fishery.

The Recorder and Indicator collections have been used to add to knowledge of the bio-geography of plankton communities and to study variations in the plankton in relation to the environment and the fisheries. It has been possible to trace water movements around the British Isles, and to compare the conditions obtaining in different years, from which valuable information on variations in the Atlantic inflow has already emerged. There appears to be a close connection between the success or failure of the summer herring fishery off north-east Scotland and the inflow of Atlantic water into the North Sea; it is possible that the plankton might be used as an indication of the changes in Atlantic inflow, leading, with the three months warning which it could provide, to a technique for forecasting fluctuations in the herring fisheries off the Scottish east coast.

All this work has been planned and executed in collaboration with other marine laboratories and, in particular, with the Marine Laboratory, at Aberdeen, of the Department of Agriculture and Fisheries for Scotland. The results of the board survey of the planktonic environment are made available to other laboratories who may be in need of the information. In addition to the main objectives of the two teams, individual biologists have made contributions to knowledge of the taxonomy and life histories of plankton organisms, to studies of fluctuations in the abundance of larval fish, to work on the vertical distribution of plankton, and to methods of sampling plankton at high speeds. Special studies have been made of the planktonic stages of bottom living echinoderms and lamellibranchs, and an unexpected product of the herring research programme has been a clarification of the effects on catches of the aggregation and dispersal of fishing vessels.

The work carried out in Edinburgh has been described in the usual scientific publications, but most of the papers have appeared in the laboratory's own journal, *The Bulletins of Marine Ecology*, which is a continuation of the earlier series, *The Hull Bulletins of Marine Ecology*. Many major advances in instrumentation, techniques and data handling are being developed and incorporated in the work of the laboratory.

THE ROYAL ZOOLOGICAL SOCIETY OF SCOTLAND AND ITS PARK

Professional scientists have received inspiration from the natural richness of Edinburgh. It is highly important that the general public should likewise be educated and inspired, for in their hands lies continuance of its wealth. The Royal Zoological Society is one body which attempts to achieve this, with great effect.

The Zoological Society of Scotland was formally constituted at a Meeting in Edinburgh City Chambers on 18th March, 1909. It was incorporated by Royal Charter in 1913, and granted the privilege of adding the prefix ' Royal ' to its name by King George VI in April, 1948.

A Supplementary Charter granted by our present Queen in 1958 defines the aims of the Society as " to promote, facilitate and encourage the study of zoology, animal physiology, pathology, dietetics and kindred subjects and to foster and develop among the people an interest in and knowledge of animal life; to investigate the habits, migrations, and life histories of animals occurring in Scotland and in Scottish seas, and to disseminate knowledge thereof; to effect the preservation of wild animal life in Scotland, and to promote legislation therefor; and if deemed necessary to oppose legislation tending to have adverse influence thereon; to establish, equip, carry on and develop the Royal Zoological Society of Scotland's Park at Edinburgh (later changed to The Scottish National Zoological Park), and zoological parks or gardens and living zoological collections at such places in Scotland as the Society shall determine."

The site eventually selected and acquired in 1913 for the Society's Zoological Park was Corstorphine Hill House and its grounds, then on the western outskirts of Edinburgh. To-day, although surrounded by residential areas, its 75 acres constitute The Scottish National Zoological Park, one of the most attractive in Europe, situated on the southern slope of Corstorphine Hill from the highest point of which, 500 feet above sea-level, the visitor enjoys magnificent views of Edinburgh to the east, the River Forth and the Fife coast to the north, the expansive strath of the Forth and Clyde to the west, and the undulating range of the Pentlands to the south.

In laying out this ground for the reception of animals it was decided to adopt as far as possible the barless enclosures introduced so successfully by Carl Hagenbeck of Hamburg, the Society being the first in Britain to adopt this method of displaying animals to greatest advantage in natural settings of grassland, woodland, rock and water.

Operations began in April, 1913 with a view to the new Zoological Park being opened to Fellows of the Society on 15th July, and, a week later, to the public. Several animals were acquired by purchase, gift and loan, including a polar bear, two brown bears, a pair of lions and a small herd of reindeer, but one inmate had already arrived in October, 1912. It was a young gannet picked up by the police at West Pier, Leith, and this stray from the Bass Rock resulted in *Sula bassana* appearing on the Society's seal and documents as its emblem. With such a small collection of animals, however, it is doubtful whether the Park would have been opened that year but for the generous offer of Mr H. G. Tyrwhitt-Drake, later Sir Garrard Tyrwhitt-Drake, to loan his private collection for three months from Maidstone. This enabled the Park to be opened to Fellows and public on the dates arranged, and by the following summer the Society had acquired its own comprehensive collection of world animals. The importance of Sir Garrard's loan was not fully realised till the outbreak of war in 1914; for if the Park had not opened its gates with a year in which to become established before the years of world conflict, it is doubtful whether the embryo zoo could have weathered the storm.

The period between the wars saw many major improvements introduced. The widening of the Edinburgh–Glasgow road necessitated rebuilding the frontage of the Park ground, with a new lodge and entrance gates, the latter incorporating the falcon-topped stone pillars from the old mansion of Falconhall. Another important addition at this period was the Carnegie Aquarium, built from the proceeds of a grant made by the Carnegie United Kingdom Trust to the design of A. M. Paterson, A.R.S.A., of Glasgow. The Aquarium occupied two years and was opened on 6th July, 1927 by the Earl of Elgin, Chairman of the Carnegie Trust.

During the second World War the Park suffered more severely than during the 1914–18 years. Several of the more dangerous animals had to be killed as a precaution against air-raids, customary foodstuffs became unobtainable, and renovation of houses and enclosures was halted due to lack of materials and labour. Once again, however, it survived, under the dauntless direction of Mr T. H. Gillespie who had been a prime mover in the Park's conception, the Society's Secretary since 1909, and its Director-Secretary from 1913 till his retiral in 1950.

The Scottish National Zoological Park today contains many interests which are unique, and at least one that is world-famous . . . its colony of Antarctic penguins. Ever since Lord Salvesen interested himself in the formation of the Society and became its first President, the firm of Christian Salvesen and Company of Leith has generously presented consignments of penguins, year after year, sparing neither trouble nor expense in bringing large numbers of birds north from South Georgia when its whaling ships returned from Antarctic expeditions. Resulting from this generous interest the Society's Park contains the largest captive colony of Antarctic penguins in the world, and that this colony thrives in the Edinburgh climate has been proved by the annual breeding successes with such species as kings, gentoos, macaronis and even the more difficult little ringed penguin. In 1919 the first king penguin to be bred in captivity was successfully hatched and reared by its parents in the Park, and annually since then visitors have been able to observe incubating penguins and chicks in various stages of growth and moult. When old enough to be hand-fed these chicks are sent to other Zoological Societies in Britain, on the Continent and in America, the demand for Antarctic penguins hatched and reared to hand-feeding in the temperate climate of Edinburgh always exceeding the supply.

Almost as widely known as the colony itself, and even more keenly appreciated by many visitors, is the unique Penguin Parade which is held daily during the summer months. Originating accidentally, it was discovered that these normally sedentary birds enjoy a walk outside their enclosure, and at the afternoon parade hour there is always a company of from 15 to 20 penguins waiting for their perambulation which is taken through the Park oblivious to the press of visitors and clicking of cameras.

Another of the Park's unique exhibits is its free-flying colony of night herons, a further example of a happy accident. In 1936 three pairs of the American sub-species of night heron escaped from their aviary adjoining the Sea-lion Enclosure. Attempts to recapture them were unsuccessful, but the birds remained in the vicinity, perching in the trees and descending for fish thrown to them at the sea-lion's feeding time. The sexes of the night heron are identical in appearance, but the Society had fortunately received both male and female birds, and in their new-found freedom the sextet remained in a vicinity where food was plentiful, nesting the following spring in the tree overhanging the sea-lion's pool. Since then they have bred successfully every year, and the colony which now numbers some fifty birds has extended its nesting range to the trees adjoining the Elephant Seal Enclosure, the Park's market garden, and the Fellows' House where, from the library and lounge windows of the first floor, the parent birds of this interesting species can be observed tending their young. Birds of the colony are frequently reported being seen at the Water of Leith in central Edinburgh, at the Gogar Burn in West Lothian, and as far afield as Kirkcaldy, Stirling, the upper reaches of the River Tweed and Carlisle. But it would appear that natural sources of food are inadequate in these areas as no attempt at nesting or colonising has been observed outside the Zoological Park.

One of its principal objects being " to foster and develop among the people an interest in and knowledge of animal life ", the Society has originated a scheme of labelling for its animal enclosures consisting of glass-fronted cases containing columns of printed cards giving comprehensive information on distribution, description, habits, breeding, related species in the Park, etc., and where more than one species inhabits an enclosure identification is simplified by the inclusion of reliably coloured cut-outs of each. These unique information boards, replacing the usual small labels bearing only the popular name, scientific name and habitat of a species, have been welcomed by interested visitors and teachers with classes, enabling them to utilise the Park as an open-air Book of Natural History illustrated with living pictures. A similar but faintly illuminated system of labelling is being installed in the darkened halls of the Carnegie Aquarium.

With this belief in the educational value of its Park the Society gave serious thought to the formation of a corner devoted to children's interests, and in 1957 it was decided to depart from the normal Pets' Corner or Children's Zoo and to pioneer again with an entirely new scheme, a complete farm in miniature. This, it was felt, would give young visitors additional instructional interest without restricting their natural desire to handle and fondle animals. Furthermore, the buildings of the farm, with its attractive Afrikaans architecture, had been made possible by a bequest from the late Thomas Ritchie of Joppa, Midlothian, in memory of his brothers who had farmed in Southern Rhodesia. The Children's Farm is therefore a complete steading in miniature, with farmhouse, stabling and harness-room, cowhouse, piggery, goat-house, sheep-pen, cart-shed, and a corn-stack where white mice and rats can be seen here and there between the stalks. In the centre of the yard there is a grassy plot forming an enclosure for ducklings, chickens, rabbits and guinea pigs, with a duck-pond and a dovecot housing fantails. As everything is reduced to the scale of Shetland ponies representing Clydesdale cart-horses the farm's stock is composed of young or miniature animals: calves, lambs, piglets, dwarf goats, bantams and Shetland ponies. The implements are also undersized but exact to scale and perfect in detail; plough and harrows, horse-rake, swathe-turner and carts being as carefully modelled as the collars, hames, bridles and saddles of the working harness. Indeed, the day is perhaps not far distant when the Children's Farm will be the only place where one will be able to see (in miniature) a cart-horse in complete harness. Adjoining the farmyard are fields where young visitors can try their hand at ploughing and harrowing, hay-raking or loading, carting and unloading miniature sacks of grain between the yard and the farm's grain store; and in the yard itself there are " horses " to be groomed and harnessed, together with all the other tending and animal feeding of a well-run farm. The Children's Farm was opened on 25th March, 1958 by Lady Primrose, daughter-in-law of Lord Rosebery, the Society's President.

Unfortunately it is impossible to chronicle all the Zoological Society's activities though these are of unfailing interest and attract a never-ending audience. There are many who will remember the arrival of a young elephant seal from South Georgia, generously presented to the Society by Christian Salvesen and Company. At the time this seal created considerable interest among visitors not only because it was the only one in the country but because of its great size for an infant and the ease with which it could swallow 80 half-pound fish at a meal and remain underwater for 10 minutes at a stretch.

In 1959, the Society's Jubilee Year, Lady Whitson of Edinburgh made it possible to fence a considerable area of mixed woodland as an enclosure for Scottish roe deer, the collection at that time comprising a buck and three does. Two years later, in the early summer, one of the does gave birth to a single fawn, and the following week another increased the wood's population with twins. From then began a period of particularly interesting observations in the family life of Scotland's indigenous and smallest deer. For although the European roe deer has been bred in zoological parks on the Continent this is believed to be the first captive breeding of the Scottish sub-species, a happy proof of what can be achieved when animals are maintained in natural surroundings such as those—to give them their full and resonant title—of the Scottish National Zoological Park at Edinburgh.

END PIECE

Clearly in a short account such as this it would be impossible to give a detailed survey of the natural history of even a small part of Edinburgh. Equally it is impossible to do justice to all the work being done in the city by both professional and amateur biologists to advance our knowledge of the living world. Omission from the foregoing pages of such interesting animals as rotifers, millipedes, land molluscs and mites does not mean that the animals are lacking or that they have been totally ignored. A student of spiders, for example, might be greatly encouraged by Dr A. B. Roy's recent study of the spiders inhabiting a very small area of Pentland grassland not far from the city boundary, from which he identified 37 species, several not previously recorded in the region, and provided a useful comparison with studies made elsewhere. (*The Scottish Naturalist* Vol. 70, 1961).

Then too there is a city habitat to which we have scarcely referred—the houses themselves, especially the older ones. Here, often unsuspected, is a fauna of small animals living on organic debris, together with more familiar but less acceptable household pests. Some are largely restricted to domestic habitats and their origins and distribution make a worthwhile study. Likewise there is much to be done on the distribution of algae, mosses and lichens on city walls, or the soil animals of city flower-beds. Interests in these organisms converge with the work of applied biologists in agriculture, horticulture, or pest-control, and help to clarify our understanding of the interaction between man and his habitat. For despite their concentration of human activity cities have much to offer the discerning naturalist; and in this, as in so many other things, the riches of Edinburgh, as the foregoing pages must have shown, are unending.

APPENDIX I

COURT OF SESSION

Number and Nature of Actions ended by Final Judgment

	1900		*1920*		*1938*		*1950*		*1960*	
	Inner House	*Outer House*	*I.H.*	*O.H.*	*I.H.*	*O.H.*	*I.H.*	*O.H.*	*I.H.*	*O.H.*
Ordinary										
Debts	68	451	22	161	17	78	6	160	7	232
Succession	45	54	31	15	21	15	14	24	8	12
Heritable Estate	32	154	6	21	13	13	7	12	1	4
Landlord & Tenant	4	21	3	3	3	3	4	2	2	—
Damages	112	155	73	202	50	346	60	408	77	874
Copyright, Trade-marks & Patents	—	23	—	2	—	—	—	—	—	—
Other	50	142	15	98	29	32	52	93	74	60
Admiralty & Commercial	3	25	7	13	4	10	3	5	—	2
Consistorial	7	212	9	767	5	839	15	2,246	11	1,886
Petitions		362		80	65	497	216	449	189	460
Adminstrative & Miscellaneous	200	653	304	480	360		291			477

	1900	*1920*	*1938*	*1950*	*1960*
Teind Court	34	28	37	42	16
Valuation Appeal Court	6	9	36	9	16
Registration Appeal Court	—	—	—	—	5
Electoral Petition Court	—	—	—	—	—

SHERIFF COURT, EDINBURGH

Comparison of Volume of Civil Business

Actions Disposed of by Judgment	*1900*	*1920*	*1938*	*1950*	*1960*
Ordinary Court (excluding appeals)	943	595	674	1,305	3,925
Small Debt Court	6,506	3,340	5,626	4,462	14,192
Miscellaneous No. of Applications	2,767	5,155	3,260	2,825	4,190

continued on p. 1005

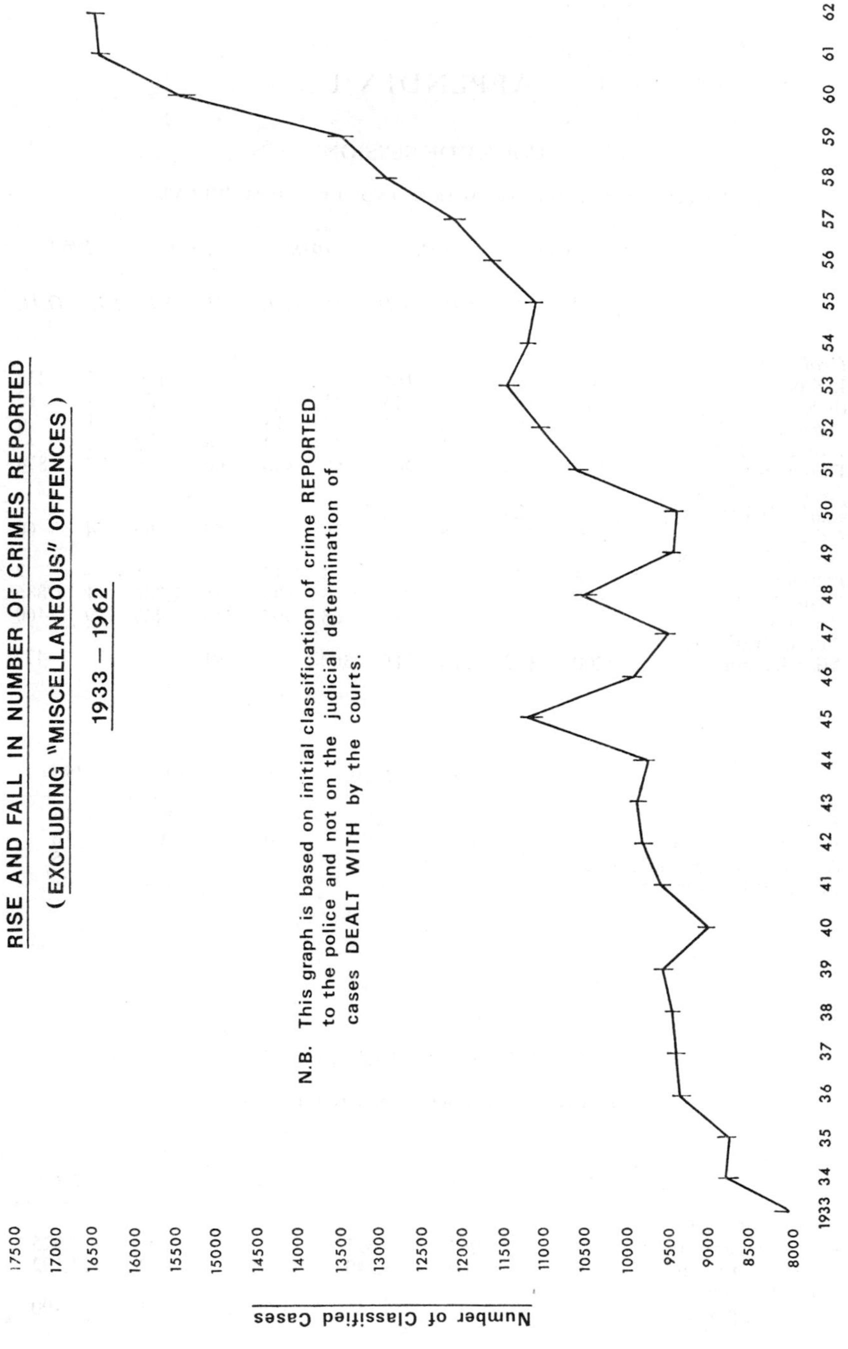
RISE AND FALL IN NUMBER OF CRIMES REPORTED
(EXCLUDING "MISCELLANEOUS" OFFENCES)
1933 – 1962
N.B. This graph is based on initial classification of crime REPORTED to the police and not on the judicial determination of cases DEALT WITH by the courts.
Number of Classified Cases
17500
17000
16500
16000
15500
15000
14500
14000
13500
13000
12500
12000
11500
11000
10500
10000
9500
9000
8500
8000
1933 34 35 36 37 38 39 40 41 42 43 44 45 46 47 48 49 50 51 52 53 54 55 56 57 58 59 60 61 62

APPENDIX I (*cont'd*)

CRIMES AND OFFENCES

Comparison of Proceedings Taken in Scotland as against Edinburgh and Number of Charges Proved

	1900	*1920*	*1950*	*1960*
Total No. of Persons proceeded against by Police in Scotland	179,821	143,075	109,054	177,336
,, in Edinburgh	13,080	11,283	6,334	11,188
No. per thousand of population in Edinburgh	47·8	23·1	13·0	23·7
Charges Proved	11,812	8,950	5,676	10,478
Population in Edinburgh (in thousands)	272,000	420,000	486,000	471,000

Comparison of Types of Offence Tried in Edinburgh

	1900	*1920*	*1950*	*1960*
Crimes against the Person	62	257	110	206
Crimes against Property with Violence	56	178	441	782
Crimes against Property without Violence	1,099	881	958	1,527
Malicious Injury to Property	279	180	90	22
Forgery and Coinage Crimes	2	3	5	9
Other Crimes	17	38	84	47
Offences	11,565	9,746	4,706	8,595

APPENDIX II

EDINBURGH AT THE 1961 CENSUS

Acreage, Population, Private Households and Dwellings

Notes: (1) Acreage figures have been supplied by the Ordnance Survey Department and relate to land area only, exclusive of inland water, tidal water and foreshore. (2) * indicates an area with boundary change since 1951. The 1951 population figures relate to the area as altered. (3) Households temporarily absent on Census night and their dwellings and rooms are included in columns h, k and l but not in column j. The density figures in columns m and n are based on the population present on Census night as shown in column j, and on the number of rooms occupied by that population.

Area	Acreage	Population					Private households and dwellings, 1961					
		1951	1961									
		Persons	Persons	Males	Females	Persons per acre	Private households	Population in private households	Structurally separate dwellings occupied	Rooms occupied	Persons per room	% of persons at more than 1½ per room
a	*b*	*c*	*d*	*e*	*f*	*g*	*h*	*j*	*k*	*l*	*m*	*n*
*Edinburgh County of City	*33,294*	*46,943*	*468,361*	*216,881*	*251,480*	*14·1*	*156,259*	*446,039*	*151,808*	*541,631*	*0·85*	*18·6*
City Wards:												
1 St. Giles	394	23,864	17,687	8,650	9,037	44·9	6,268	15,702	6,056	15,929	1·01	29·5
2 Holyrood	894	19,959	13,949	6,521	7,428	15·6	5,250	13,323	5,139	13,078	1·04	29·3
3 George Square	317	18,929	16,334	7,010	9,324	51·5	5,597	13,487	5,026	18,990	0·73	11·9
4 Newington	903	21,856	22,958	9,881	13,077	25·4	7,839	20,647	7,444	32,269	0·66	9·1
* 5 Liberton	4,853	19,143	34,610	16,678	17,932	7·1	9,119	34,033	9,077	35,102	0·98	22·5
6 Morningside	689	17,696	17,211	6,660	10,551	25·0	6,594	15,880	6,346	29,726	0·56	4·0
7 Merchiston	748	17,197	16,066	6,856	9,210	21·5	5,750	14,187	5,529	21,515	0·68	9·7
* 8 Colinton	6,120	18,606	26,874	12,865	14,009	4·4	7,711	24,598	7,683	31,160	0·81	12·1
* 9 Sighthill	1,629	25,314	23,815	11,854	11,961	14·6	6,854	23,366	6,813	22,485	1·05	21·5
10 Gorgie-Dalry	421	22,001	18,606	8,520	10,086	44·2	7,476	18,594	7,382	19,611	0·97	21·9

APPENDIX II (*Cont'd*)

a	*b*	*c*	*d*	*e*	*f*	*g*	*h*	*j*	*k*	*l*	*m*	*n*
*11 Corstorphine	3,480	17,404	21,543	10,040	11,503	6·2	7,324	20,648	7,293	28,278	0·75	7·6
12 Murrayfield-Cramond	3,334	13,012	22,489	10,362	12,127	6·7	7,298	22,255	7,245	32,385	0·71	7·3
13 Pilton	1,066	28,350	27,840	13,793	14,047	26·1	7,367	27,570	7,317	24,692	1·13	29·9
14 St. Bernard's	1,396	19,791	25,823	11,413	14,410	18·5	8,615	23,867	8,184	32,480	0·77	16·1
15 St. Andrew's	375	13,034	14,495	6,476	8,019	38·7	5,712	13,034	5,205	17,853	0·78	20·9
16 Broughton	515	19,276	16,810	7,553	9,257	32·6	6,426	16,132	5,974	21,376	0·78	13·4
17 Calton	316	19,530	15,389	7,118	8,271	48·7	6,046	14,781	5,774	17,084	0·89	20·8
18 West Leith	648	18,529	16,016	7,276	8,740	24·7	5,756	15,479	5,648	21,831	0·73	12·9
19 Central Leith	295	22,310	17,156	8,252	8,904	58·2	6,412	16,732	6,285	16,636	1·03	29·8
20 South Leith	623	21,633	18,206	8,461	9,745	29·2	6,874	17,877	6,714	20,278	0·90	20·4
21 Craigentinny	779	24,153	20,260	9,480	10,780	26·0	6,959	19,902	6,920	22,385	0·91	18·1
22 Portobello	1,628	23,486	27,141	12,718	14,423	16·7	8,570	26,888	8,363	33,093	0·83	15·1
*23 Craigmillar	1,871	16,870	17,083	8,444	8,639	9·1	4,442	17,057	4,391	13,395	1·29	43·7

APPENDIX III

BUILDING PROJECTS SINCE 1860

PUBLIC BUILDINGS

1896 Royal Observatory, Blackford Hill (extensions 1930 & 1963)
1898 Present North Bridge erected
1900 Central Fire Station, Lauriston Place
1902 Merchant Company Hall, Hanover Street (reconstruction)
1903 City Infectious Diseases Hospital, Greenbank Drive
1905 Midlothian County Buildings, George IV Bridge
1906 King's Theatre, Leven Street
1910 Gorgie Corn and Cattle Markets, Newmarket Road
1910 Zoological Park, Corstorphine Road
Aquarium added 1927
1911 Empire Theatre, Nicolson Street. (Opened as Empire Palace Theatre 1892. Rebuilt after 1911 fire and after internal reconstruction in 1928, opened as Empire)
1912 Haymarket Ice Rink
1914 Usher Hall, Lothian Road
1914 Portobello Town Hall
1916 Redford Barracks (completed)
1922 Labour Exchange, Tollcross
1923 Portobello Power Station and Offices, High Street, Portobello opened. Extended 1926 and 1930
1923 Royal Blind Asylum Workshops, Gillespie Crescent. (Formerly James Gillespie's High School)
1924 Seed Testing Station, East Craigs, Maybury Road
1925 Scottish Rugby Union Football Ground. (Roseburn, opened)
1925 HM Prison, Saughton. (Calton Prison demolished)
1925 Elsie Inglis Maternity Hospital, Spring Gardens
1927 Scottish National War Memorial and Shrine, Edinburgh Castle
1929 Warriston Crematorium, Warriston Road
1932 Princess Margaret Rose Hospital, Fairmilehead
1932 Leith Town Hall and Library, Ferry Road Opened. (Hall re-instated 1957)
1934 Extensions to City Chambers, High Street. (East Wing 1934, Cockburn Street 1937)
1935 Granton-Cramond Sea Promenade started. Completed 1947
1935 Ross Bandstand, Princes Street
1936 Portobello Swimming Pool, High Street, Portobello opened
1936 Lothian House, Lothian Road
1937 Sheriff Court House, Lawnmarket
1937 St Andrew's House, Regent Road founded
1937 Lighting and Cleansing Department Disposal Plant (Russell Road)
1939 Lighting and Cleansing Department Disposal Works, Seafield
1939 Murrayfield Ice Rink, Roseburn
1939 Dreghorn Barracks started
1939 Seafield Crematorium, Seafield Place
1940 Nurses' Home, Salisbury Road
1945 Sighthill Industrial Estate and Government Offices
1951 The Thistle Foundation (Housing and Medical Centre for disabled servicemen, Craigmillar)
1952 Health Centre, Sighthill
1953 Scottish Central Library, Lawnmarket
1953 Restoration of Canongate commenced
1953 Telephone Exchange, Fountainbridge (first used 1953)
1955 Western General Hospital, Crewe Road South. (Cancer Research Radiotherapy Wing 1955, Neurological Unit 1959)

1955 Northern General Hospital, Ferry Road (new Rheumatic Diseases Research Unit)
1955 National Coal Board Laboratory, Glasgow Road
1956 Turnhouse Airport Administrative Block, Kirkliston Road
1956 National Library of Scotland, George IV Bridge
1957 National Union of Seamen Offices, "Maritime House", Shore, Leith
1958 Telephone Exchange, and N.W. District Sorting Office, Comely Bank
1958 National Coal Board Offices, Green Park, Gilmerton Road (reconstructed)
1959 Stuart House, Semple Street
1960 Meldrum House, Drumsheugh Gardens
1962 Royal Botanic Garden, Inverleith Row (Herbarium)

Museums in the Royal Mile acquired by the City

1907 Lady Stair's House
1932 Huntly House (restored)
1938 Scottish Craft Centre, Acheson House (reconstructed)
1959 Museum of Childhood, Hyndford's Close (reconstructed)

EDUCATIONAL BUILDINGS

1897 McEwan Hall, Teviot Row
1899 Cargilfield School, Gamekeeper's Road
1902 The Usher Institute, Warrender Park Road
1903 Leith Nautical College, Commercial Street erected (additions 1927 and 1931)
1906 Ramsay Technical Institute, Portobello Road (erected as a factory; taken over as a school 1924)
1907 The College of Art, Lauriston Place (founded)
1913 (dates back to 1848) Moray House Training College, Holyrood Road erected (extension 1956)
1916 Royal Dick Veterinary College, Summerhall
1927 Moredun Institute, (Animal Diseases Research Association) Gilmerton Road (extensions 1962)
1930 Merchiston Castle School, Colinton Road
1931 George Watson's College, Colinton Road
1931 Leith Academy, Duke Street
1934 and 1959 Heriot-Watt College Extensions, Chambers Street

University Extensions

1924 King's Buildings, West Mains Road opened. (Extended 1929; School of Agriculture 1959)
1927 Minto House, Chambers Street
1928 Mining Department, Grassmarket
1955 Adam House and Examination Halls, Chambers Street
1958 New College of Engineering, King's Buildings, West Main Road
1959 Staff Club, refectory and common room for students, Chambers Street
1960 University Halls of Residence, Salisbury Green, Dalkeith Road
1961 Extension to School of Medicine, Meadow Walk
1963 Arts Block, Windmill Lane
1964 David Hume Tower, George Square

Current and Future Building Projects

University Extensions, George Square
Napier College, Colinton Road

CHURCHES AND WELFARE BUILDINGS

1901 The Archers' Hall, Buccleuch Street (modernised)
1911 The Thistle Chapel, St Giles' Cathedral, High Street
1911 Church of Scotland Offices, George Street
1928 St Patrick's R. C. Church, Cowgate (new front constructed)

1930 Jewish Synagogue, Salisbury Road
1932 Pleasance Trust & Little Theatre, Pleasance
1933 Reid Memorial Church, Blackford Avenue
1933 Portobello U. F. Church, Moira Terrace
1936 Old Sailors' Ark, Canongate
1947 Restoration of Canongate Kirk, Canongate (interior restored)
1952 Reconstruction of Blackie House, Lawnmarket

(*In recent years there have also been Church Extension schemes in new housing areas, and various churches have been sold for commercial use.*)

COMMERCIAL PROPERTIES

1890 Edinburgh Stock Exchange, North St David Street
1892 Caledonian Station, Lothian Road
1893 Present Waverley Station, Waverley Bridge
1897 Prudential Insurance Building, St Andrew Square
1898 Royal Insurance Building, George Street
1900 Patrick Thomson's, North Bridge
1902 North British Hotel, Princes Street
1903 Caledonian Hotel, Lothian Road
1904 *Scotsman* Offices, North Bridge
1904 Extensions to Leith Docks (Imperial Dock 1904)
" " 1933-39
" " 1949-54 (including Grain) Elevator—Caledonia Flour Mills, etc
1906 North British & Mercantile Insurance Company Building, Princes Street
1938 Caledonian Insurance Building, St Andrews Square
1940 Edinburgh Savings Bank, Hanover Street
1942 National Bank of Scotland, St Andrew Square (extension 1963)
1958 C. & A. Modes, Princes Street
1958 Marks & Spencer and Royal Hotel, Princes Street
1959 London & Lancashire Insurance Building, St Andrew Square
1959 Sun Insurance Building, George Street
1962 Scottish Life Assurance, St Andrew Square (reconstruction)
1962 Scottish Widows' Fund, St Andrew Square (reconstruction)
1963 Jenners, Princes Street (extension)
1963 Automobile Association, Melville Street
1963 Goldbergs Ltd, High Riggs
1963 Scottish & Newcastle Breweries Ltd, Holyrood Road (reconstruction)
1963 Woodlawn Investments Ltd, North St Andrew Street

INDUSTRIAL SUBJECTS

Year	*Description*	*Situation*	*Proprietor*
1860-61	Works	Parkside Works, Dalkeith Road	Thos. Nelson & Sons Ltd
1874-75	Works	Rosebank Iron Works Broughton Road	Brown Bros
1879-80	Workshop and warehouse	Bernard Terrace	C. & J. Brown
1882-83	Works	Easter Road 7	Andrew Whyte & Son Ltd
1888-89	Factory	33 Sciennes	Bertrams Ltd
1894-95	Works	146 Fountainbridge	Mackay Bros
1897-98	Distillery	Wheatfield Road	North British Distillery Company Ltd
1900-01	Works	64-72 Albion Road	Redpath Brown & Co
1901-02	Workshop	67-77 Dundee Street	John H. Thom & Co
1902-03	Works	Warriston Road	Geo. Waterston
1907-08	Factory	172 Easter Road	John Cotton Ltd

Year	Description	Situation	Proprietor
1908-09	Works	Blandfield Chemical Works, Wheatfield Road 11	T. & H. Smith
1909-10	Factory	78 Albion Road	Jas. Dunbar Ltd
1921-22	Dye Works	Inglis Green	A. & J. McNab
1930-31	Works	Hopetoun Street	T. & A. Constable
1935-36	Factory	McDonald Road	Hunter & Fowlis Ltd
1939-40	Factory	McDonald Road	Inveresk Envelope Company
1944-45	Factory	Crew Road North	Ferranti Ltd
1951-52	Factory	Bankhead Avenue	Ethicon Ltd
1957-58	Works	Bankhead Drive	William Thyne Ltd
1958-59	Factory	Bankhead Crossway Square	Golden Wonder Crisp Company
1958-59	Extension	Edinburgh Dock	Scottish Agricultural Industries Ltd
1959-60	Factory	Bankhead Drive	Burtons Gold Medal
1961-62	Extensions	Salamander Street	Scottish Agricultural Industries Ltd
1961-62	Extensions	Imperial Dock	Fisons Fertilisers Ltd

APPENDIX IV

EDINBURGH CORPORATION TRANSPORT

	1929	*1939*	*1961*
Mileage of routes	51	70	123
Mileage run	3,166,526	7,595,310	25,776,535
Passengers carried	25,946,507	60,306,416	209,755,409
Average fare paid per passenger	1·454d	1·395d	4·657d
Average working expenses per bus mile	11·92d	9·75d	34·684d
Number of buses and coaches	111	215	706

TRAMWAYS

Mileage of track, single	1½	1¾	—
Mileage of track, double	41	45½	—
Mileage run	10,622,777	13,730,387	—
Passengers carried	130,284,383	145,972,840	—
Average fare paid per passenger	1·283d	1·308d	—
Average working expenses per car mile	11·03d	10·43d	—
Number of cars	357	360	—

RAILWAYS

Tickets	*1952*	*1961*	*1962*
Number of tickets issued at Edinburgh Stations.	2,516,149	2,405,460	1,931,587
Revenue from Edinburgh Stations	£1,306,804	£1,931,321	£1,904,718
Number of Season Tickets issued	107,137	81,846	66,666

Tonnage

Total tonnage, forwarded and received within City area:	*Tons*	*Tons*	*Tons*
(a) Goods	988,519	784,436	745,468
(b) Coal Class	1,408,506	1,152,498	1,004,205
(c) Other minerals	278,339	269,478	166,807
(d) Livestock	26,184	10,314	6,690
Total	2,701,548	2,216,726	1,923,170
Revenue from freight (a) (c) and (d)	£1,673,013	£1,968,038	not available

APPENDIX V

CHARGE FOR FUNERALS MADE BY CEMETERIES

In the 1840s

	Funeral by Hearse and Coaches				*Funeral by Hearse, Company walking*				
Cemetery	*Hearse and 4 horses*	*Hearse and 2 horses*	*Hearse and 1 horse*	*Child's Funeral with coach*	*Hearse and 2 horses*	*Hearse and 1 horse*	*On shoulders*	*On spokes*	*Use of mortcloth*
Dalry	£5 8s 0d	£2 8s 0d	£1 10s 0d	16s 6d	£2 0s 0d	£1 1s 0d	£2 4s 6d	7s 0d	6s to 2s
Grange	£5 7s 6d	£2 10s 0d	£1 10s 6d	17s 0d	£2 3s 6d	£1 7s 6d	£1 17s 0d	9s 6d	£1 to 2s 6d
Newington	£6 18s 0d	£3 13s 6d	£0 14s 6d	—	—	—	£2 4s 6d	7s 0d	—
Rosebank	£5 8s 0d	£2 8s 0d	£1 6s 6d	16s 6d	£1 18s 0d	£1 0s 0d	£2 4s 6d	10s 0d	£1 to 3s 0d
Warriston	£5 8s 0d	£2 8s 0d	£1 10s 0d	16s 6d	£2 0s 0d	£1 0s 0d	£2 4s 6d	10s 6d	£1 to 3s 0d

In 1963

Cemetery	*Funeral by Motor Hearse Interment Dues*	*Child's Funeral by Car*	*Interment of Cremation Casket*
Grange	£15 0s 0d	£8 0s 0d	£8 0s 0d
Mount Vernon	£10 0s 0d	£7 0s 0d	—
Piershill	£12 0s 0d	£2 15s 0d to £3 0s 0d	£2 10s 0d
Seafield	£12 0s 0d	£2 15s 0d to £3 5s 0d	£2 10s 0d
Rosebank	£12 12s 0d	£3 0s 0d to £6 0s 0d	—

APPENDIX V (*cont'd*)

COST OF LAIRS

In the 1840s

Cemetery	*Charge for one space*	*Vaults for Interment*	*Catacombs*
Dalry	£1 11s 6d to £7 7s—	—	From £10 10s—for vault to hold one coffin, to £36 for four.
Dean	£2 to £12	£15 per grave	—
Grange	£2 to £12	—	—
Newington	£1 11s 6d to £4 13s 4d	—	From £5 10s—for vault to hold one coffin, to £90 for eighteen
Rosebank	From £1 10s—	—	—
Warriston	£2 16s 8d to £6 13s 4d	£90 to hold 10/15 coffins	From £7 to hold one coffn, to £120 for eighteen

COST OF LAIRS

In 1963

Cemetery	*Cost of one lair*
Dean	£12 0s 0d to £ 50
Grange	£16 0s 0d to £100
Mount Vernon	£ 9 5s 0d to £ 20
Piershill	£ 8 8s 0d to £ 21
Rosebank	£10 0s 0d to £ 28
Seafield	£10 10s 0d to £ 20
Corporation	£ 6 0s 0d to £ 15

CREMATION CHARGES

In 1963

Crematorium	*Adult*	*Child*	*Private Niche*
Edinburgh	£10 and £12	£1 to £2 10s 0d	From £6 6s 0d
Leith	£11	1 year £1	£3 3s 0d

APPENDIX VI

THE EDINBURGH CORPORATION CHILDREN DEPARTMENT

ALLOWANCES, JUNE 1962

With Foster-parents

Children of school age and under—45s per week with discretion in exceptional cases.
Pocket money as follows:

2 to 4 years	1s 0d per week
5 to 9 ,,	1s 6d ,, ,,
10 to 12 ,,	2s 6d ,, ,,
13 to 15 ,,	4s 0d ,, ,,

Young persons taking senior secondary education—60s per week. Pocket money at the discretion of the children's Officer.

Young persons in employment—Nett earnings supplemented to allow 60s per week for board with discretion in exceptional cases.
Pocket money, in addition, as follows:

At 15 years of age	10s 0d per week
,, 16 ,, ,, ,,	12s 6d ,, ,,
,, 17 ,, ,, ,,	15s 0d ,, ,,

In Hostels and Lodgings

Requisite rates from £4—£6 less sums contributed from wages in hostels and from £3 to £4 5s less sums contributed from wages for lodgings.

Clothing Allowances

Up to 7 years of age	£20 per annum
8 to 12 years	£30 ,, ,,
13 years and over	£40 ,, ,,

APPENDIX VII

Analysis of Wholly Unemployed persons (including Non-Claimants) according to age and duration of unemployment in the Edinburgh, Leith and Portobello Area at 13 July 1964

Duration	*Males*									*Females*								
	Under 18 years	*18-19*	*20-24*	*25-39*	*40-49*	*50-54*	*55-64*	*65 and over*	*Total*	*Under 18 years*	*18-19*	*20-24*	*25-39*	*40-49*	*50-54*	*55-59*	*60 and over*	*Total*
Less than 1 week	80	43	63	98	44	16	24	—	368	39	15	12	21	14	7	4	2	114
1 week and up to 2	103	11	28	61	27	10	27	—	267	48	9	5	15	6	2	1	2	88
2 ,, ,, 4	16	15	41	86	52	19	44	2	275	13	8	11	14	13	6	6	1	72
4 ,, ,, 6	10	6	27	57	29	21	39	1	190	1	2	4	7	4	6	5	1	30
6 ,, ,, 8	5	8	18	42	35	9	31	3	151	—	2	5	1	6	2	5	2	23
8 ,, ,, 13	4	10	20	67	31	18	68	1	219	1	3	5	11	11	6	11	1	49
13 ,, ,, 26	7	7	22	87	54	32	109	11	329	—	1	11	9	13	9	19	3	65
26 ,, ,, 39	2	5	8	69	42	35	92	4	257	1	2	1	2	6	5	9	—	26
39 ,, ,, 52	—	2	6	29	30	21	78	3	169	—	—	—	3	5	2	7	—	17
Over 52 weeks	—	1	8	67	84	81	319	12	572	—	—	—	5	18	9	29	1	62
Total	227	108	241	663	428	262	831	37	2797	103	42	54	88	96	54	96	13	546

APPENDIX VII (*cont'd*)

ANALYSIS OF WHOLLY UNEMPLOYED PERSONS (INCLUDING NON-CLAIMANTS) ACCORDING TO AGE AND DURATION OF UNEMPLOYMENT IN THE EDINBURGH, LEITH AND PORTOBELLO AREA AT 13 JULY 1964

11 JANUARY 1965

Duration	*Males*									*Females*								
	Under 18 years	*18-19*	*20-24*	*25-39*	*40-49*	*50-54*	*55-64*	*65 and over*	*Total*	*Under 18 years*	*18-19*	*20-24*	*25-39*	*40-49*	*50-54*	*55-59*	*60 and over*	*Total*
Less than 1 week	55	41	91	122	57	28	42	—	436	43	36	46	46	15	11	8	5	210
1 week and up to 2	10	16	29	49	29	20	29	5	187	6	6	12	14	7	1	4	1	51
2 ,, ,, 4	33	28	45	149	50	22	57	1	385	9	8	15	24	15	8	8	—	87
4 ,, ,, 6	10	24	36	98	53	21	46	1	289	1	9	8	14	15	7	8	1	63
6 ,, ,, 8	6	13	23	62	29	18	39	1	191	2	3	8	11	10	10	7	1	52
8 ,, ,, 13	7	30	46	128	55	34	89	6	395	1	3	17	11	11	8	20	—	71
13 ,, ,, 26	3	21	29	113	74	37	164	10	451	—	3	6	7	14	8	16	—	54
26 ,, ,, 39	—	2	8	60	27	17	86	5	205	1	—	—	2	6	3	4	1	17
39 ,, ,, 52	—	4	3	30	21	15	58	3	134	—	—	1	1	1	3	6	1	13
Over 52 weeks	—	2	5	65	89	71	323	15	570	1	—	—	5	16	5	21	1	49
Total	124	181	315	876	484	283	933	47	3,243	64	68	113	135	110	64	102	11	667

July 1964/January 1965 figures have been added to give changing seasonal pattern of unemployment.

APPENDIX VIII

SEASONAL VARIATION IN RETAIL TURNOVER

PERCENTAGE OF ANNUAL TURNOVER IN EACH MONTH 1955-1957, DONE BY ALL RETAIL BUSINESSES IN EDINBURGH COMPARED WITH ALL RETAIL BUSINESSES IN GREAT BRITAIN

	1955		*1956*		*1957*	
Month	*Edinburgh*	*G.B.*	*Edinburgh*	*G.B.*	*Edinburgh*	*G.B.*
January	7·3	7·7	6·9	7·5	7·7	7·8
February	6·9	7·3	7·4	7·4	7·0	7·5
March	7·9	7·7	7·7	8·0	7·5	7·8
April	7·4	8·0	7·4	7·8	7·9	8·0
May	8·0	8·3	8·1	8·3	8·0	8·2
June	8·4	8·0	8·5	8·1	8·0	8·3
July	8·7	8·6	8·8	8·3	8·6	8·4
August	8·5	7·6	8·8	7·9	8·7	7·9
September	8·6	8·1	8·4	8·1	8·4	8·1
October	8·7	8·8	9·0	8·6	8·8	8·4
November	8·8	9·0	9·1	9·1	8·9	8·9
December	10·8	10·9	9·9	10·9	10.5	10·7
TOTAL	100·0	100·0	100·0	100·0	100·0	100·0

QUARTERLY DIFFERENCES BETWEEN TURNOVER PERCENTAGES FOR EDINBURGH AND GREAT BRITAIN, 1955-57.

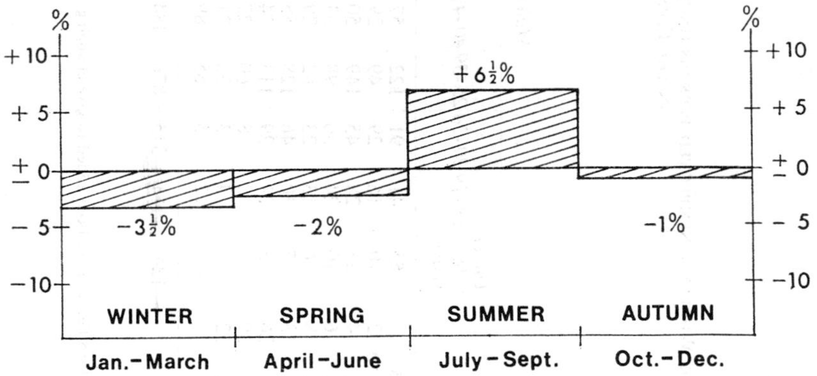

Note. The figures represent the percentages by which the Edinburgh quarterly retail proportions of annual sales fall below (—) or exceed (+) the national quarterly proportions.

APPENDIX IX

TABLE A

CLIMATOLOGICAL TABLE FOR EDINBURGH (BLACKFORD HILL) 57°00′N. 3°24′W. 441 feet.

Month	TEMPERATURE				RAINFALL	BRIGHT SUNSHINE		AVERAGE NUMBER OF DAYS OF					
	Average daily		*Absolute*		*Average monthly fall*	*Average monthly total*	*Daily mean*	*Snow or Sleet*	*Snow lying at 9 a.m.*	*Gales*	*Thunder*	*Fog*[1] *at 9 a.m. (Visibility less than 1,100 yards)*
	Max.	*Min.*	*Max.*	*Min.*								
	(degrees Fahrenheit)				*(inches)*	*(hours)*	*(hours)*					
January	43	35	57	17	2·45	52	1·69	4·3	4·9	3·1	0·2	6·1
February	43	35	57	15	1·68	76	2·68	4·3	3·2	1·9	0·1	4·4
March	47	36	68	21	1·60	114	3·69	3·4	2·2	0·7	0·1	4·6
April	50	39	72	25	1·62	139	4·62	1·7	0·2	0·7	0·3	0·7
May	55	43	76	30	2·21	172	5·55	0·3	0·1	0·2	0·7	1·1
June	62	48	83	37	1·88	196	6·52	—	—	0·4	1·0	0·6
July	65	52	83	42	3·03	161	5·20	—	—	—	1·9	0·8
August	64	52	82	40	3·15	143	4·62	—	—	0·2	1·0	1·2
September	60	48	79	33	2·55	127	4·24	—	—	0·5	0·7	1·4
October	53	44	71	28	2·83	100	3·21	0·2	—	1·2	0·2	2·8
November	47	39	67	24	2·42	62	2·08	0·8	0·1	1·3	0·1	4·3
December	44	36	58	20	2·11	43	1·40	3·1	2·1	2·2	0·1	4·4
Year	53	42	83	15	27·53	1,385	3·79	18·1	12·8	12·4	6·4	32·4
No. of years	30	30	30	30	35	30	30	30	30	30	30	21
	(1921-1950)		(1921-1950)		(1916-1950)	(1921-1950)	(1921-1950)	(1921-1950)		(1921-1950)		(1939-1959)

[1]Average number of days of fog (period 1939-1959) relate to observations made at the Royal Botanic Gardens, Edinburgh.

TABLE B

EDINBURGH—(BLACKFORD HILL)—MIDLOTHIAN (1921-1950)

Month	MONTHLY MEANS OF DAILY VALUES															EXTREMES FOR MONTH					
	Mean Maximum					*Mean Minimum*					*Mid=½ (Max.+Min.)*					*Maximum*			*Minimum*		
	Average	*Highest*		*Lowest*		*Average*	*Highest*		*Lowest*		*Average*	*Highest*		*Lowest*		*Average*	*Highest*		*Average*	*Lowest*	
	°F	°F	year	°F	year	°F	°F	year	°F	year	°F	°F	year	°F	year	°F	°F	year	°F	°F	year
Jan.	42·7	48·2	1932	35·5	1941	34·6	39·3	1932	28·6	1941	38·7	43·7	1932	32·1	1941	52	57	1932	25	17	1940, 1941
Feb.	43·2	49·2	1945	32·3	1947	34·5	39·0	1945	25·9	1947	38·8	44·1	1945	29·1	1947	52	57	1945	26	15	1929, 1947
Mar.	46·6	52·7	1938	38·3	1947	36·1	42·6	1938	30·1	1947	41·3	47·7	1938	34·2	1947	58	68	1945	27	21	1947
Apr.	50·4	55·1	1943	46·0	1941	38·6	42·3	1943	34·3	1922	44·5	48·7	1943	40·4	1922	61	72	1946	31	25	1950
May	55·4	59·3	1940	51·6	1923	42·9	45·2	1940	39·4	1923	49·1	52·3	1940	45·5	1923	68	76	1922, 1939	34	30	1927
June	61·8	68·6	1940	57·0	1927	48·1	51·6	1940	44·3	1927	54·9	60·1	1940	50·7	1927	74	83	1939	41	37	1927, 1935
July	64·9	69·3	1934	60·7	1922	52·1	55·0	1933	48·1	1922	58·5	61·9	1933, 1934	54·4	1922	76	83	1933, 1943	46	42	1928
Aug.	63·6	68·1	1947	59·5	1922	51·6	54·3	1947	48·4	1922	57·6	61·2	1947	54·0	1922	73	82	1930	45	40	1931
Sept.	59·8	63·3	1949	57·0	1922	48·4	52·2	1949	44·7	1925	54·1	57·7	1949	51·0	1925	70	79	1926	40	33	1943
Oct.	53·2	58·4	1921	49·1	1926	43·6	47·4	1921	39·2	1926	48·4	52·9	1921	44·1	1926	63	71	1921	33	28	1926, 1931
Nov.	47·0	50·7	1948	42·0	1923	38·5	41·9	1931, 1938	33·7	1923	42·8	46·3	1938	37·9	1923	57	67	1946	29	24	1947
Dec.	43·9	48·9	1924	36·8	1950	36·2	41·7	1934	30·5	1950	40·1	44·7	1924	33·7	1950	53	58	1948	27	20	1947, 1950
	ANNUAL MEANS OF DAILY VALUES															EXTREMES FOR YEAR					
Year	52·7	54·7	1949	51·2	1922	42·1	43·5	1945	40·6	1922	47·4	49·1	1949	45·9	1922	78	83	4.7.33, 4.6.39, 5.6.39, 31.7.43	22	15	16.2.29, 23.2.47

NOTES ON ENTRIES IN TABLE B

(a) *Columns headed "Mean Maximum"*
(i) The column headed "average" gives the mean *daily* maximum temperature for the named month, i.e. the highest daily temperature reached on average in the average month. (ii) The columns headed "Highest" and "Lowest" give the highest and lowest values of the mean *daily* maximum temperature and the years of their occurrence, i.e. the years in which the days of the named month were hottest and coldest.

(b) *Columns headed "Mean Minimum"*
(i) The column headed "Average" gives the mean *daily* minimum temperature for the named month, i.e. the lowest daily temperature reached on average in the average month. (ii) The columns headed "Highest" and "Lowest" give the highest and lowest values of the mean *daily* minimum temperature and the years of their occurrence, i.e. the months in which the nights were hottest and coldest.

(c) *Columns headed Mid=½ (Max. + Min.)*
(i) The column headed "Average" gives the average mean *daily* temperature for the named month, i.e. the average daily temperature to be expected on a day in an average month. (ii) The columns headed "Highest" and "Lowest" give the highest and lowest values of "mid" or mean temperature and the years of their occurrence, i.e. the years in which the named months were hottest and coldest on the whole.

(d) *Columns headed "Extremes for Month"*
(i) The columns headed "Average" give the average *monthly* maximum and minimum temperatures, i.e. the highest and lowest temperatures reached in the average year at some time or other during the month in question. (ii) The columns headed "Highest" and "Lowest" give the highest and lowest temperatures on record for the named month and the years of their occurrence.

TABLE C

WETTEST AND DRIEST MONTHS AND YEAR DURING 35-YEAR PERIOD 1916-1950 AT EDINBURGH (BLACKFORD HILL)

WETTEST	*Jan.*	*Feb.*	*Mar.*	*Apr.*	*May*	*June*	*July*	*Aug.*	*Sept.*	*Oct.*	*Nov.*	*Dec.*	*Year*
Inches	5·27	3·53	3·75	4·07	4·46	5·18	8·26	9·40	7·91	6·38	5·13	4·80	39·00
Year of occurrence	1948	1925	1947	1934	1924	1928	1940	1948	1927	1935	1944	1932	1916
DRIEST	*Jan.*	*Feb.*	*Mar.*	*Apr.*	*May*	*June*	*July*	*Aug.*	*Sep.*	*Oct.*	*Nov.*	*Dec.*	*Year*
Inches	·77	·09	·20	·15	·66	·35	·62	·19	·35	·86	·24	·63	21·12
Year of occurrence	1940	1934	1929	1938	1919	1921	1935	1947	1929	1946	1937	1926	1917

Greatest amount of rainfall recorded at Blackford Hill, Edinburgh in a day during 35-year period 1916-1950=3·00 inches on 17th August 1920.

TABLE D

SUNNIEST AND DULLEST MONTHS AND YEAR DURING 30-YEAR PERIOD 1921-1950 AT EDINBURGH (BLACKFORD HILL)

SUNNIEST	*Jan.*	*Feb.*	*Mar.*	*Apr.*	*May*	*June*	*July*	*Aug.*	*Sept.*	*Oct.*	*Nov.*	*Dec.*	*Year*
Hours	79	108	176	220	226	278	224	225	169	139	99	65	1617
Year(s) of occurrence	1932 1933	1946 1949	1929	1942	1946 1949	1940	1935	1947	1934	1931	1947	1929	1949
DULLEST	*Jan.*	*Feb.*	*Mar.*	*Apr.*	*May*	*June*	*July*	*Aug.*	*Sept.*	*Oct.*	*Nov.*	*Dec.*	*Year*
Hours	23	41	58	85	108	126	99	99	73	60	35	17	1147
Year of occurrence	1942	1940	1928	1941	1933	1947	1931	1942	1936	1940	1946	1927	1944

APPENDIX X

TABLE 48: YOUTHS' BOYS' AND GIRLS' ESTIMATED EARNINGS IN EDINBURGH IN 1957

Industry Group	*Youths and Boys (Under 21 years) Number Employed*	*Average or Estimated Average Weekly Earnings (in shillings)*	*Estimated Total Weekly Earnings(s)*	*Girls 18 years Number Employed*	*Average or Estimated Average Weekly Earnings(s)*	*Estimated Total Weekly Earnings(s)*
Agriculture, Forestry, Fisheries	249	105·0	26,145	54	84·4	4,554
Mining and Quarrying	199	125·2	24,907	—	—	—
Treatment of non-metalliferous mining products other than coal	73	118·2	8,624	—	—	—
Chemical and Allied Trades	6	109·9	659	49	84·8	4,148
Metal Manufactures	258	119·10	30,924	24	84·0	2,016
Engineering, Shipbuilding and Allied Trades	198	99·11	19,782	191	86·2	16,459
Vehicles	632	95·5	60,305	97	87·7	8,495
Metal Goods (not elsewhere specified)	104	103·3	10,738	28	81·8	2,287
Precision Instruments	30	98·7	2,957	34	82·4	2,799
Textiles	24	104·11	2,517	110	93·2	10,249
Leather, leather goods and fur	28	102·8	2,875	4	76·10	307
Clothing	74	100·5	7,431	206	81·8	16,822
Food, Drink and Tobacco	280	99·1	27,952	257	80·4	20,645
Manufacturers of Wood and Cork	297	102·0	30,294	145	81·0	11,745
Paper and Printing	57	104·0	5,928	685	79·0	54,115
Other Manufacturing Industry	108	108·3	11,691	9	81·7	734
Building and Contracting	1,301	115·4	150,044	26	83·11	2,181
Gas, Electricity and Water	54	107·11	5,827	—	83·11	—
Transport and Communications	1,065	110·4	117,501	125	83·11	10,490
Distributive Trades	1,266	105·0	132,930	2,682	83·11	225,073
Insurance, Banking and Finance	302	105·0	31,710	672	83·11	56,394
Public Administration and Defence	1,289	104·1	135,126	416	74·0	30,784
Professional Services	708	105·0	74,340	853	83·11	71,584
Miscellaneous Services	325	105·0	34,125	908	83·11	76,199
Total	8,927		955,332	7,575		628,080
			£2,483,863 =£2·5 million/annum			£1,633,008 =£1·6 million

APPENDIX X (*cont'd*)

TABLE 49: MENS' AND WOMENS' ESTIMATED EARNINGS IN 1957

Industry Group	*Employed Men 21 years and over*	*Average or Estimated Average Weekly Earnings(s)*	*Estimated Total Weekly Earnings(s)*	*Employed Women 18 years and over*	*Average or Estimated Average Weekly Earnings(s)*	*Estimated Total Weekly Earnings(s)*
Agriculture, Forestry, Fisheries	1,895	241·6	457,640	470	126·3	59,340
Mining and Quarrying	1,763	233·6	411,660	367	124·6	45,690
Treatment of non-metalliferous mining products other than coal	1,430	244·7	349,750	248	118·11	29,492
Chemical and Allied Trades	1,890	249·9	472,030	802	124·6	99,849
Metal Manufactures	932	271·3	252,810	120	131·0	15,720
Engineering, Shipbuilding and Electrical Goods	8,276	253·5	209,730	1,502	134·6	202,019
Vehicles	3,070	258·11	794,880	709	140·10	99,849
Metal Goods (not elsewhere specified)	1,746	249·5	435,490	644	123·1	79,747
Precision Instruments	474	243·0	115,180	340	128·7	43,717
Textiles	580	225·9	130,940	1,340	126·7	169,617
Leather, Leather Goods and Fur	198	219·6	43,460	57	119·5	6,807
Clothing	657	217·4	142,790	1,785	123·10	221,037
Food, Drink and Tobacco	10,694	221·10	2,372,790	8,156	118·3	964,447
Manufactures of Wood and Cork	2,302	224·11	517,770	542	128·1	69,826
Paper and Printing	6,277	275·1	1,731,390	4,200	131·2	550,914
Other Manufacturing Industry	1,881	246·11	464,460	727	121·4	88,207
Building and Contracting	13,556	238·9	3,236,090	1,040	112·0	116,48
Gas, Electricity and Water	3,450	228·10	789,460	405	129·10	52,581
Transport and Communications	17,021	227·10	3,877,890	2,477	168·1	418,192
Distributive Trades	11,550	241·6	2,789,320	13,816	126·3	1,744,270
Insurance, Banking and Finance	3,746	270·0	1,011,420	2,857	140·0	399,980
Public Administration and Defence	5,111	186·11	951,259	2,854	140·0	399,560
Professional Services	8,336	400·0	3,334,000	18,000	200·0	3,600,000
Miscellaneous Services	5,577	241·6	1,346,850	13,680	126·3	1,727,100
Total	112,412		26,239,050	77,138		11,204,441
			£13,119,524/week or £68,221,530/year = £68·2 million/annum			£5,602,229/week or £29,131,544 = £29·1 million/annum

INDEX

L

T

U